The Child as Musician
A handbook of musical development

Gary E. McPherson is the Ormond Professor and Director of the Melbourne Conservatorium of Music at the University of Melbourne, Australia. He has served as National President of the Australian Society for Music Education and President of the International Society for Music Education. His research interests are broad and his approach interdisciplinary. His most important research examines the acquisition and development of musical competence, and motivation to engage and participate in music from novice to expert levels. With a particular interest in the acquisition of visual, aural, and creative performance skills, he has attempted to understand more precisely how music students become sufficiently motivated and self-regulated to achieve at the highest level.

The Child as Musician
A handbook of musical development

SECOND EDITION

Edited by

Gary E. McPherson

OXFORD
UNIVERSITY PRESS

OXFORD

UNIVERSITY PRESS

Great Clarendon Street, Oxford, OX2 6DP,
United Kingdom

Oxford University Press is a department of the University of Oxford.
It furthers the University's objective of excellence in research, scholarship,
and education by publishing worldwide. Oxford is a registered trade mark of
Oxford University Press in the UK and in certain other countries

© Oxford University Press 2016

The moral rights of the authors have been asserted

First Edition published in 2006
Second Edition published in 2016
First published in paperback 2017

Published in the United States of America by Oxford University Press
198 Madison Avenue, New York, NY 10016, United States of America

British Library Cataloguing in Publication Data

Data available

Library of Congress Cataloging in Publication Data

Data available

ISBN 978–0–19–874444–3 (Hbk.)
ISBN 978–0–19–881715–4 (Pbk.)

Acknowledgments

The first draft of each chapter was independently reviewed by the editor and three additional reviewers who included a selection of other authors from the book and where relevant, anonymous external reviewers.

I take this opportunity to thank the various representatives of Oxford University Press. I am especially grateful to the OUP Senior Commissioning Editor Martin Baum and his assistant Charlotte Green for answering all of my questions and steering me in the right direction whenever I had a problem. Their enthusiasm for producing this second edition of *The Child as Musician* is appreciated.

Throughout the process of compiling this second edition, I have been fortunate to have worked with Solange Glasser as my editorial assistant. Her sharp intellect, superb eye for detail, and generous nature have made the processing of collecting, reviewing, editing, and formatting each of the chapters so much easier. Solange deserves very special praise for a job well done.

I extend my heartfelt thanks to each of the authors for agreeing to be involved. I am extremely grateful to them for putting up with the endless correspondence and the many suggestions from the reviewers. They deserve praise for their commitment to the project and the quality of their work.

Now that all of the authors can see their chapters in the context of the whole book, I hope that they will agree that our journey together has been worthwhile. I hope also, that our readers enjoy the fruits of our labor.

Gary E. McPherson
June 2015

Contents

List of Contributors

Daniel Abrahams studied music education at Temple University and completed a master of instrumental conducting degree at the University of Nebraska at Omaha. He holds a Ph.D. in music education from Oakland University in Rochester, Michigan. He is Assistant Professor of Music Education at Indiana University of Pennsylvania, and has presented research at numerous, state, national, and international conferences. He has contributed several book chapters in edited publications. His research interests include the acquisition of learner agency and the use of reciprocal teaching in classroom music and ensembles. His dissertation research examined how pedagogy fosters personal and musical agency among beginning instrumental conductors.

Frank Abrahams is Professor of Music Education at Westminster Choir College of Rider University in Princeton, New Jersey. A native of Philadelphia, he holds degrees from Temple University and New England Conservatory. He has pioneered the development of a critical pedagogy for music education and has presented research papers and taught classes in the United States, China, Brazil, Taiwan, Hungary, Israel, Italy, and the UK. He is the curriculum facilitator for the Society for Music Teacher Education. He is senior editor of *Visions of research in music education* and has been a member of the editorial board of the *Music Educators Journal*. With Paul Head, he is co-author of *Case studies in music education* (GIA Publications), *Teaching music through performance in middle school choir* (GIA Publications), and the *Oxford handbook of choral pedagogy* (Oxford University Press). With Ryan John, he is co-author of *Planning instruction in music* (GIA Publications).

Andrew R. Brown is an educator, researcher, musician, author, and programmer. He holds a Ph.D. in music and is Professor of Digital Arts at Griffith University in Brisbane, Australia. His academic expertise is in technologies that support creativity and learning, the creation of computational music and art, and the philosophy of technology. His creative activities focus on real-time audio-visual works using generative processes and live coding performance. He has performed live coding and interactive music in many parts of the world and his digital art works have been shown in galleries across Australia, the United States, and China. He is the author of *Music technology and education: Amplifying musicality*, co-author of *Making music with computers: Creative programming in Python*, and editor of *Sound musicianship: Understanding the crafts of music*.

Pamela Burnard is Professor of Music Education (Creativities and Culture) at the University of Cambridge in the UK. Her research interests include diverse creativities, digital technologies, intercultural arts, across education sectors, industries, and communities. Her books include *Musical creativities in practice* (OUP), *Creativities in higher music education* (Routledge), *Bourdieu and the sociology of music, music education and research* (Ashgate), *Music education with digital technologies* (Continuum), *Teaching music creatively* (Routledge), and *Reflective practices in the arts* (Springer). She is Co-convenor of the British Educational Research Association (BERA) *Creativity in Education* SIG and Convenor of the *Creativities in Intercultural Arts Network*.

Patricia Shehan Campbell is Donald E. Peterson Professor of Music at the University of Washington, where she teaches courses at the interface of education and ethnomusicology. She is the author of *Lessons from the world* (1991), *Music in cultural context* (1996), *Songs in their heads* (1998, 2010), *Teaching music globally* (2004), *Music and teacher* (2008), co-author of *Music in childhood* (2013, fourth edition), and co-editor of the Global Music Series and the *Oxford handbook on children's musical cultures* (2013). Her training includes Dalcroze Eurhythmics, piano and vocal performance, and specialized study in Bulgarian choral song, Indian (Karnatic) vocal repertoire, and Thai mahori. Campbell was designated the MENC Senior Researcher in Music Education in 2002, and in 2012 received the Taiji Prize (shared with Ravi Shankar and Bruno Nettl) for the preservation of traditional music. She is chair of the Advisory Board of Smithsonian Folkways and has served as and president of The College Music Society.

Kathleen A. Corrigall holds a Bachelor of Arts (Honors) degree in psychology from the University of British Columbia and a Ph.D. in experimental psychology from McMaster University. She completed a postdoctoral fellowship at the University of Toronto, and is currently an Assistant Professor in the Department of Psychology at MacEwan University. She has received research scholarships at both the doctoral and postdoctoral levels by the Natural Sciences and Engineering Research Council of Canada as well as the Social Sciences and Humanities Research Council of Canada. Her research interests center on the development of music perception and cognition in early and middle childhood, with a focus on knowledge acquired through enculturation. She also studies associations between music training and nonmusical abilities and traits, including cognitive skills, personality, and social and emotional competence.

Gordon Cox studied at the Royal Academy of Music, London, and then at Memorial University of Newfoundland for an MA in Folklore, and at the University of Reading where he gained the Ph.D. for a study in the history of music education. He is currently the Chair of the History Standing Committee of the International Society for Music Education (ISME). Prior to his retirement, he worked for over 20 years in the School of Education, University of Reading. He is a past-editor of the *British Journal of Music Education*. His research is primarily in the history of music education, and his latest book in this area is *The origins and foundations of music education* (2010), co-edited with Robin Stevens. More recently (2011), his study *The musical salvationist: The world of Richard Slater 1854–1939 "Father of Salvation Army music"* has been published by Boydell Press.

Jane W. Davidson studied in music, dance, and education in the UK, before undertaking a master of music performance studies at Université Laval in Canada and City University London, and a Ph.D. at City University London. She is currently Professor of Creative and Performing Arts and Head of Research at the Faculty of the Victorian College of the Arts and the Melbourne Conservatorium of Music. She is also Deputy Director of the Australian Research Council's Centre of Excellence for the History of Emotions. She is former Editor of Psychology of Music (1997–2001) and has served as President of the Musicological Society of Australia and been Vice President of the European Society for the Cognitive Sciences of Music. Her research interests are broadly in the area of musical performance studies, embracing development through to reflective performance practice.

Sharon G. Davis holds a doctorate of philosophy in music education from Oakland University in Rochester, Michigan. She is Assistant Professor of Music and Director of Music Education at Lebanon Valley College in Annville, Pennsylvania, USA. She has had diverse teaching experiences in elementary and secondary general music, choral and instrumental music in the United States, and in international schools in Germany, Switzerland, and Singapore. She has published in the *International Journal of Education and the Arts, Research Studies in Music Education*, and the *International Journal of Music Education*. Her contributions to edited books include *Learning, teaching and musical identity: Voices from across cultures*, Lucy Green (Ed.), The *Oxford handbook of music education*, Gary McPherson and Graham Welch (Ed.) and *Musicianship: Composing in band and orchestra* (Clint Randles and David Stringham (Eds.). Her research interests include music education in relation to informal learning, popular music, identity, and the aesthetic experiences of children.

Franziska Degé studied psychology at the Justus-Liebig-University Giessen. She also received her Ph.D. from the Justus-Liebig-University Giessen. She is an Assistant Professor of Developmental Psychology at the Justus-Liebig-University Giessen. She is currently part of the executive council of the German Society for Music Psychology. Her research focuses on the effect of music lessons on cognitive development. One important aspect of her work concerns the influence of music training on precursors of reading in preschool children. In particular, she investigates the effect of music training on phonological awareness and attempts to reveal underlying mechanisms of that relationship. She is also interested in the association between music as well as joint music-making and prosocial behavior in infants.

David J. Elliott studied at the University of Toronto before completing a doctorate in music education at Case Western University. He is Professor of Music and Music Education at New York University. From 1977 to 2002 he was Professor of Music Education at the University of Toronto. He has held visiting professorships at Indiana University, the University of North Texas, Northwestern University, the University of Limerick, and the Puerto Rico Conservatory of Music. His research interests include philosophy of music and music education, community music, jazz, music composition, and multicultural music education. He is the author of *Music matters: A new philosophy of music education* (Oxford, 1995), co-author of *Music matters: A philosophy of music education*, 2nd ed. (Oxford, 2015), editor of *Praxial music education: Reflections and dialogues* (Oxford, 2005/9), and co-editor of *Community music today* (Rowman & Littlefield, 2013). He is an award-winning composer/arranger with works published by Boosey & Hawkes.

Paul Evans studied music education at the University of New South Wales before completing his Ph.D. at the University of Illinois at Urbana-Champaign. He is a lecturer in the School of Education at UNSW Australia, where he lectures in educational psychology, music psychology, and motivation in educational settings, at both undergraduate and postgraduate levels, and supervises postdoctoral research in music education and motivation in educational settings. His research interests cover an array of topics broadly related to motivation in educational settings, with an emphasis on music learning: motivation from childhood through to young adulthood, self-determination theory, the quality of interactions between students, their teachers, and their parents, and self-regulated learning.

Robert Faulkner graduated from the Royal Academy of Music, London, and went on to study music education at the University of Reading, before completing a master of arts in music psychology and Ph.D. from The University of Sheffield. With extensive experience at every level of education from kindergarten through tertiary and adult education in the UK, Iceland, and Australia, he has worked as teacher, lecturer, consultant, and researcher. Until 2013, he was Associate

Professor in Music and Early Childhood Education at The University of Western Australia, where he presently holds an adjunct research position. He has been Deputy Chair of the Icelandic Music Examinations Board and served on the national executive of the Musicological Society of Australia. His research interests focus broadly on music education and psychology, with a special interest in music practices in Iceland. Presently, he is Director of Music at Methodist Ladies' College in Perth, Western Australia.

Susan Hallam MBE studied the violin at the Royal Academy of Music prior to becoming Principal 2nd violin in the BBC Midland Light Orchestra and Deputy Leader of Orchestra da Camera. She studied for her B.A. in Psychology externally with London University and her M.Sc. in the Psychology of Education and her Ph.D. at the Institute of Education, University College London. She is currently Professor of Education and Music Psychology at the Institute of Education, University College London. She is past editor of *Psychology of Music, Psychology of Education Review*, and *Learning Matters*. She has been Chair of the Education Section of the British Psychological three times and is an Academician of the Learned Societies for the Social Sciences. Her research interests in music psychology and education are broad and include the development of expertise, practice, performance, motivation, the wider benefits of music, and music education in the primary school.

David J. Hargreaves studied psychology at Durham University, and is Professor of Education and Froebel Research Fellow at Roehampton University, having previously held posts at the Universities of Leicester and Durham, and the Open University. His books in psychology, education, and the arts have been translated into 15 languages. He has appeared on BBC TV and radio as a jazz pianist, and is organist on the East Cambridgeshire Methodist church circuit in the UK.

Lee Higgins is the Director of the International Centre for Community Music based at York St John University, UK, and an Associate Professor of Music Education at the Boston University School of Music. As a community musician he has worked across the education sector as well as within health settings, prison and probation service, youth and community, and orchestra outreach. As a presenter and guest speaker, he has worked on four continents in university, school, and NGO settings. He is the senior editor for the *International Journal of Community Music* and was author of *Community music: In theory and in practice* (2012, Oxford University Press).

Donald A. Hodges earned degrees in music education from the University of Kansas (B.M.E.) and the University of Texas (M.M. and Ph.D.). He served as Covington Distinguished Professor of Music Education (2003–13), and is currently Professor of Music Education and Director of the Music Research Institute at the University of North Carolina at Greensboro. Research projects include brain-imaging studies of pianists, conductors, singers, and music listeners. His biographical sketch is in the *New Grove dictionary of American music*. A current vita and copies of many of his papers can be accessed at <http://sites.google.com/site/donaldahodges/>.

Judith Jellison is the Mary D. Bold Regents Professor of Music and University Distinguished Teaching Professor in Music and Human Learning at the University of Texas at Austin. A devoted advocate for children's quality music experiences, her career began as a choral and instrumental public school music teacher in classrooms with widely diverse populations of children and as a music therapist in hospital settings. These early experiences shaped her philosophy of inclusive education, guiding her later work in higher education, first as founder and Director of Music

Therapy at the University of Minnesota and now as a Distinguished Teacher of Music and Human Learning at the University of Texas. An active contributor to professional organizations in music education and music therapy, she is the recipient of the Senior Researcher Award from the National Association for Music Education and the Publication Award from the American Music Therapy Association.

Alexandra Kertz-Welzel studied music education, Germanics, philosophy, and piano and harpsichord performance at Saarland University and the University of Music in Saarbruecken, Germany, before completing a Ph.D. in Musicology at Saarland University. She is Professor and Department Chair of Music Education at Ludwig Maximilian University in Munich, Germany, and was Lecturer of Music Education and Philosophy of Music Education at the University of Music in Saarbruecken and Visiting Scholar and Guest Lecturer of Music Education at the University of Washington in Seattle, Washington, United States. Her research interests are comparative music education, music education policy, community music, philosophy of music education, and children's musical cultures. Her book, *Every child for music: Musikpaedagogik und Musikunterricht in den USA* (2006), is the first comprehensive German study describing music education in the United States since the 1960s. Along with David G. Hebert, she is co-editor of the book *Patriotism and nationalism in music education* (2012).

Hsu-Chan Kuo (郭旭展) obtained his Ph.D. in Education from the Faculty of Education, University of Cambridge, UK. He is a research fellow of the Center for Creativity and Innovation Studies at National Chengchi University (NCCU) in Taiwan. His research interests and publications focus on creativity and imagination education, policy/program evaluation, positive psychology, social justice, and counseling and guidance. He has been involved in several governmental educational research projects, including evaluating the effects of creative learning programs, investigating the international trends of creativity education, and developing creative learning curriculum and teaching materials.

Kathryn Marsh holds an honors degree in music, a diploma of education, and a doctorate of philosophy in ethnomusicology from the University of Sydney, where she is Associate Professor and former Chair of Music Education at the Sydney Conservatorium of Music. She is editor of *Research Studies in Music Education* and a member of the editorial boards of *Psychology of Music* and the *International Journal of Play*. She has written numerous scholarly and professional publications, including *The musical playground: Global tradition and change in children's songs and games*, winner of the Katharine Briggs Award (Folklore Society) and Opie Award (American Folklore Society). Her cross-cultural research in Australia, Europe, the UK, the United States, and Korea is documented in a named collection in the British Library. Areas of research interest include children's musical play, children's creativity, primary music education, cultural diversity in music education, and the role of music in the lives of refugee children.

Katrina S. McFerran Ph.D. R.M.T. is Head of Music Therapy at The University of Melbourne and Co-director of the National Music Therapy Research Unit. She is author of the books *Adolescents, Music and Music Therapy* (Jessica Kingsley Publishers) and *Creating Music Cultures in the Schools* (Barcelona Publishers), and has authored over 50 articles in peer-reviewed journals. She is co-editor in Chief of the open-access online journal *VOICES: A World Forum for Music Therapy*, and a former editor of the *Australian Journal of Music Therapy*. Katrina's research career has been focused on the healthy and unhealthy ways that young people engage with music both through music therapy and in other musical contexts. Her research has particularly focused on youth mental health in schools, hospitals, and pediatric palliative care.

Gary E. McPherson studied music education at the Sydney Conservatorium of Music, before completing a master of music education at Indiana University, a doctorate of philosophy at the University of Sydney, and a Licentiate and Fellowship in trumpet performance through Trinity College, London. He is the Ormond Professor and Director of the Melbourne ·Conservatorium of Music at the University of Melbourne, and previously held a position as the Marilyn Pflederer Zimmerman Endowed Chair in Music Education at the University of Illinois at Urbana Champaign. He has served as National President of the Australian Society for Music Education and President of the International Society for Music Education. His research interests are broad and his approach interdisciplinary. His most important research examines the acquisition and development of musical competence, and motivation to engage and participate in music from novice to expert levels. With a particular interest in the acquisition of visual, aural, and creative performance skills, he has attempted to understand more precisely how music students become sufficiently motivated and self-regulated to achieve at the highest level.

Janet Mills, now deceased, studied music and mathematics at the University of York, trained as a teacher at the University of Leeds, and held a doctorate from the University of Oxford. Following posts as head of music in secondary schools, she was a teacher educator at Westminster College, Oxford and the University of Exeter, and then HM Inspector of Schools and Ofsted's Specialist Adviser for Music for ten years. She worked as teacher, researcher, adviser, and inspector in over 800 primary, special, and secondary schools, and also in the community. She is author of *Music in the primary school* (CUP) and *Music in the school* (OUP), and many articles on music education and education in research journals, books, and magazines. At the time of writing her contribution for the first edition, she was a Research Fellow at the Royal College of Music, London, where she taught and ran several music education research projects.

Adrian C. North is interested in the social and applied psychology of music. His research concerns musical taste, and the relationship between this and consumer behavior, well-being, and lifestyle. He is currently Head of the School of Psychology and Speech Pathology and Professor of Psychology at Curtin University, Western Australia.

Adam Ockelford studied at the Royal Academy of Music in London, before embarking on a career that has embraced performing, composing, teaching, researching, writing, consultancy, and management. His Ph.D. drew together thinking from music theory and music psychology, in investigating how music intuitively makes sense to us all. Today, his research interests are in music psychology, education, theory, and aesthetics—particularly special educational needs and the development of exceptional abilities; learning, memory and creativity; and the cognition of musical structure and the construction of musical meaning. He has over 100 publications to his name, including 20 books. He is Secretary of the Society for Education, Music, and Psychology Research ("SEMPRE"), Chair of Soundabout, an Oxfordshire-based charity in the UK that supports music provision for children and young people with complex needs, and founder of The AMBER Trust, a charity that supports visually impaired children in their pursuit of music.

Susan A. O'Neill has an interdisciplinary background, with graduate degrees from England in three disciplines: music performance studies (M.A., City University), psychology (Ph.D., Keele

University), and education (M.A., Open University). She is Professor in Arts Education at Simon Fraser University and Director of MODAL Research Group (Multimodal Opportunities, Diversity and Artistic Learning) and Research for Youth, Music and Education (RYME). She has held visiting fellowships at the University of Michigan, USA (2001–3), the University of Melbourne (2012), and Trinity College Dublin (2015). Her international collaborative projects explore young people's musical and artistic engagement in ways that contribute to expansive learning opportunities, positive values, self-identities, motivation, well-being, learning relationships, and cultural understandings. She has published widely in the fields of music psychology and music education, including contributions in 15 books published by Oxford University Press. As a flautist, she performs with her husband, pianist Yaroslav Senyshyn, and records with Albany Records, New York.

Margaret S. Osborne studied psychology at Macquarie University, Sydney, before completing a Ph.D. at The University of Sydney, contributing substantially to knowledge of the phenomenology and treatment of music performance anxiety in adolescents. She is a consulting Registered Psychologist, Occupational Rehabilitation Counselor, Postdoctoral Research Fellow in Music Psychology at The University of Melbourne, and immediate past President of the Australian Society for Performing Arts Healthcare. She undertakes research evaluating the effectiveness of performance psychology programs to help musicians manage performance anxiety and enhance their performance potential, as well as the empirical evaluation of factors that impact on engagement in music learning and subsequent academic and non-academic outcomes. As a result of her academic and professional practice, she is passionate about integrating cognitive, behavioral, and neuroscientific research to formulate best-practice methods to build mental and physical health and resilience, and maximize performance potential.

Stephanie E. Pitts studied music at the University of York, then moved to the University of Sheffield to undertake a PhD on the history of music education, while also completing secondary school teacher training with the Open University. She is now Professor of Music Education at the University of Sheffield, and has served as co-editor of the *British Journal of Music Education* and is on the editorial board of Participations. She is the author of *Valuing Musical Participation* (Ashgate, 2005), *Chances and Choices: Exploring the Impact of Music Education* (OUP, 2012) and, with Eric Clarke and Nicola Dibben, *Music and Mind in Everyday Life* (OUP, 2010). Her ongoing research concerns the experiences of lapsed and partial arts participants, and she has recently edited (with Karen Burland) a new book on audiences, *Coughing and Clapping* (Ashgate, 2014). Her teaching and research interests include musical participation, arts audiences, and lifelong learning.

Richard Parncutt is a music psychologist with qualifications in music and physics from the University of Melbourne and an interdisciplinary Ph.D. in psychology, music and physics from the University of New England, Australia. Since 1998 he has been Professor of Systematic Musicology at the University of Graz, Austria. He has served as a board member for all the leading music psychology journals, and as founding academic editor of the *Journal of Interdisciplinary Music Studies*, and (co-)founder of three conference series: Conference on Interdisciplinary Musicology, Conference on Applied Interculturality Research, and International Conference of Students of Systematic Musicology. His research involves music theory, psychoacoustics, sound and music computing, music information retrieval, music sociology, music philosophy, music history, ethnomusicology, music education, interculturality, and interdisciplinarity. His publications address musical structure (pitch, consonance, harmony, tonality, tension, rhythm, meter, accent), music performance (psychology, piano, applications), the origins of tonality and of music, and musicological interdisciplinarity.

Chris Philpott studied music education at Middlesex Polytechnic (London) and the University of London, Institute of Education. He taught music and performing arts in secondary schools in England, moving into higher education as a lecturer in music education at Canterbury Christ Church University before becoming Dean of Education at the University of Greenwich, London. He is currently Deputy Pro Vice-Chancellor at the University of Greenwich, where he also holds a Readership in Music Education, and has particular responsibility for teacher education and outreach with schools and colleges. He has written widely in the field of music education and teacher education in England, where his texts are used in teacher training programs. He has a particular interest in the relationship between the nature of music and how music teachers learn how to teach.

Costanza Preti studied at the UCL Institute of Education, University of London, where she completed a masters in music education, a masters in research methods, and a PhD. She is currently a Postdoctoral Researcher at the Centre for Research into the Arts as Wellbeing at the University of Winchester and a Research Associate at the International Music Education Research Centre (iMerc), UCL Institute of Education, University of London. Her doctoral research has been funded by the UK Economic and Social Research Council (ESRC) and has been awarded a Wingate scholarship. She has been reviews editor for Psychology of name of a journal (Sage). Her primary research is in music and health, and includes a major study examining the impact of live music programs in pediatric hospitals in Italy and the UK.

Glenn E. Schellenberg is a Professor of Psychology at the University of Toronto Mississauga. He holds degrees in psychology and linguistics from the University of Toronto (B.Sc.), and in psychology, cognitive studies, and statistics from Cornell University (Ph.D.). His research focuses on reciprocal influences between music and cognition—how psychological predispositions influence musical structures and how exposure to music affects cognitive abilities. Two provocative findings from his laboratory indicate that: 1) the so-called Mozart effect is a consequence of the listener's mood and arousal level, and 2) music lessons are associated with small but general enhancements in IQ. In 2002 he received the Premier's Research Excellence Award from the Canadian province of Ontario. Throughout his childhood and adolescence, he took piano lessons. He subsequently played in many rock bands and composed music for film and television, including a feature-length musical and the theme song for a children's television program.

Emery Schubert completed his doctoral studies in music and holds undergraduate majors in psychology with honors in music. He is currently an Associate Professor in Music at the University of New South Wales, Australia and holds an Australian Research Council Future Fellowship until 2016. He has published over 100 peer-reviewed papers, and has both contributed to Oxford University Press volumes "Emotion in music" (2001 and 2010) edited by Patrik Juslin and John Sloboda, and co-edited a volume on "Expressiveness in music performance," also published by Oxford University Press. He is a foundation member of the Australian Music and Psychology Society (AMPS), serving as Secretary (until 2007) and President (2008–9). He is a founder of the International Conference on Music Communication Science (ICoMCS) and served on the editorial board for nearly all the major music psychology journals. His research specializes in the continuous response and the psychology of emotion and aesthetics in music.

Marissa Silverman studied English literature at New York University before completing a master of fine arts in music at State University of New York (Purchase), a master of teaching at Pace University, and a doctorate of music performance at New York University. She is Associate

Professor and Coordinator of Undergraduate Music Education at the John J. Cali School of Music, Montclair State University, New Jersey. A Fulbright scholar, her research interests include philosophy of music and music education, urban music education, interdisciplinary methods of education, and music education and identity. She has published in *Action, Criticism, and Theory for Music Education, The International Journal of Music Education, Music Education Research, Research Studies in Music Education*, and *The International Journal of Community Music*. She is co-author of *Music matters: A philosophy of music education*, 2nd ed. (Oxford, 2015) and co-editor of *Community music today* (Rowman & Littlefield, 2013).

Mark Tarrant is a social psychologist with expertise in group processes and intergroup relations. He is a member of the Psychology Applied to Health Group in the University of Exeter Medical School and currently leads a program of research looking at the relationship between group membership, social identity, and health.

Sandra E. Trehub studied economics and philosophy before obtaining her master's and doctoral degrees in experimental psychology at McGill University in 1973. Since that time, she has been a faculty member in the Department of Psychology at the University of Toronto, where she is currently Professor Emeritus. Although most of her research is conducted in laboratory contexts, she has travelled extensively to observe cross-cultural differences in musical interactions with infants. Among her scholarly honors are the Kurt Koffka Medal from Giessen University (Germany, 2012) and the 2013 Achievement Award from the Society for Music Perception and Cognition. Her research focuses primarily on infants' and young children's perception of pitch and rhythmic patterns in music, the nature of maternal singing and its consequences for infant attention and emotional regulation, and the perception of music and speech prosody in deaf children with cochlear implants.

Peter R. Webster is Professor Emeritus of Music Education at the Bienen School of Music, Northwestern University and a Scholar-in-Residence at the Thornton School of Music at the University of Southern California in Los Angeles, where he currently resides. He has taught on the music education faculties of Northwestern and Case Western Reserve universities for 40 years. He has taught in the public schools of Maine, Massachusetts, and New York. His teaching responsibilities at the University of Southern California include courses in philosophy of music education, graduate research, music technology, assessment, and creative thinking in music. He is co-author of *Experiencing music technology* (Cengage, Boston, USA) and co-editor of the *MENC Oxford research handbook on music learning* (Oxford University Press, New York). He was chosen as the 2014 Senior Researcher in Music Education for the Society for Research in Music Education, USA.

Graham F. Welch holds the Institute of Education, University College London Established Chair of Music Education (since 2001). He is a past President of the International Society for Music Education (ISME) (2008 to 2014), elected Chair of the internationally based Society for Education, Music and Psychology Research (SEMPRE), and past Co-Chair of the ISME Research Commission of ISME. He holds Visiting Professorships at universities in the UK and overseas, and he is also a member of the UK Arts and Humanities Research Council (AHRC) Review College for Music. Internationally, he has acted as a specialist external consultant on aspects of children's singing and vocal development for UK and Italian Government agencies, as well as for specialist research centers in the United States, Australia, and Sweden. Publications number over 300. He has been appointed to Chair for the new Paul Hamlyn Foundation Expert Commission on music education in the UK from 2015.

Jackie Wiggins holds two degrees in music education from Queens College of the City University of New York and a doctorate in music education from the University of Illinois at Urbana-Champaign. She is Distinguished Professor of Music Education and Chair of the Department of Music, Theatre, and Dance at Oakland University, Michigan. Internationally known for her work in constructivist music education, children's musical creative process, and the nature of musical understanding, she is a prolific author and active presenter. Her professional work includes about 50 publications, over 200 presentations, and invited keynotes on four continents. Oxford University Press recently published a third edition of her seminal book on teaching music with a social constructivist vision of learning, *Teaching for musical understanding* (2015).

Aaron Williamon holds a B.A. in music and B.Sc. in psychology from the University of South Carolina and a Ph.D. in music psychology from Royal Holloway, University of London. He joined the faculty of the Royal College of Music in 2000, first as Research Fellow, then Senior Research Fellow, and was appointed Professor of Performance Science in 2010. He is the founder of the International Symposium on Performance Science and the specialty chief editor of performance science in the journal *Frontiers in Psychology*. His research focuses on skilled performance and applied scientific initiatives that inform music learning and teaching. In particular, he is interested in developing and testing novel methods and technology that can enhance the training of advanced musicians.

Paul Woodford is a graduate of Northwestern University (Ph.D.) and Professor of Music Education at the University of Western Ontario, Canada. He is past Co-Chair of the executive committee of the International Society for the Philosophy of Music Education (2005–7) and a member of the advisory boards of the *Bulletin of the Council for Research in Music Education*, the *British Journal of Music Education*, and the *Philosophy of Music Education Review*. His interests in philosophical, historical, sociological, and political issues affecting the profession have led to many publications, including his 2005 book, *Democracy and music education* (Indiana University Press), which emphasizes the importance of music teachers introducing children and undergraduates to fundamental political principles and to the most contentious issues of the day so that they are better prepared to participate in political life. He is co-editor of the 2015 Oxford Handbook of Social Justice in Music Education.

Susan Young recently retired as senior lecturer in early childhood studies and music education at the University of Exeter, England. She is a Senior Research Fellow at the University of Roehampton, London and an Associate of the Centre for Research in Early Childhood, Birmingham. She initially trained as a pianist at the Royal College of Music, London, winning the prize for the most outstanding academic student. She spent her early career teaching music in secondary and primary schools and in a range of early years settings before gaining a Ph.D. in music education from the University of Surrey. She has published widely in professional and academic journals on the topics of early childhood music education, musical play, and technology in music education, and is frequently invited to present at conferences, both nationally and internationally. She has written several books, including *Music with the under fours* and *Music 3–5*.

Introduction

The contributions in this book celebrate the richness and diversity of the many different ways in which children can engage in and interact with music. It presents theory—both cutting edge and classic—in an accessible way for readers by surveying research concerned with the development and acquisition of musical skills. The intended focus is on musical development from conception to late adolescence, although the bulk of the coverage concentrates on the period when children are able to begin formal music instruction (from around age 3) until the final year of formal schooling (around age 18).

As with the first edition of the book, there are a number of elements that distinguish this second edition from others in the literature. First, chapter authors have focused their attention and interpretation on citations that apply to and have relevance for the age groups studied. This means that the majority of references deal with actual studies of the types of children being depicted in the chapter, rather than attempts to extrapolate information from studies with adults. Second, I wanted to ensure that authors synthesized the available literature from the UK, North America, and Europe (as well as other regions such as Australia and Asia). The volume therefore attempts to bring together the main research traditions in a way that would maximize its appeal worldwide.

Third, the book is broad in its scope, but is not intended to be comprehensive. Even before contacting the authors, I realized that no survey of the magnitude provided here could ever hope to cover every dimension of musical development in a single volume. I especially became aware of deficiencies in various parts of the literature, and of the need to focus the authors' efforts on the main threads that help to explain how children develop musically. I am particularly aware that many more studies deserve to be undertaken that address children's musical development, especially in informal and non-Western contexts. I have tried to address these important aspects by including special chapters devoted to these topics, but I acknowledge also, that there is still much to learn from how children in various non-Western cultures interact with music, and how this might be different from musical engagement in Western cultures. Finally, the intention of the book is to provide an overview of the biological, environmental, social, cultural, and historical factors that have shaped the acquisition of musical skills, understandings, and attitudes. To achieve this aim the chapters draw on research from a variety of disciplines, including music, psychology, education, sociology, philosophy, and medicine.

There is obviously no single or unanimous voice that can be used to explain musical development, but rather a rainbow of ideas and opinions. Consequently, in the early stages when I was considering the content, I was keen to ensure that the volume would include authors who study musical development from a range of theoretical perspectives and research traditions. During the editorial process, I therefore allowed authors to retain their own personal voice to explain from whichever paradigm they may work within the aspect of musical development that they had been assigned. The result is that readers are able to enjoy a range of approaches to the 35 chapters that reflect the differing paradigms from which the 42 authors work and the wealth of experience they have brought to the project.

In the general field of educational psychology there are a number of publications that survey the issues surrounding child and adolescent development. Some of the more innovative present research and theories, and their educational implications, in a style that stresses the fundamental interplay among the biological, environmental, social, and cultural influences at each stage of a child's development. Until now, no similar overview has existed for child and adolescent development in the field of music. *The child as musician* attempts to address this imbalance, while complementing the now extensive range of music psychology publications available in the Oxford University Press catalogue.

As can be seen from the title, this volume acts as a "handbook" on musical development. But the use of the term "development" is used with caution because there are many conceptions of how musical development might take place, just as there are for other disciplines and areas of human potential. What I hope this volume will help achieve, however, is to highlight the diversity in current literature dealing with how we think about and conceptualize children's musical development. Each of the authors has searched for a better and more effective way to explain in their own words and according to their own perspective the remarkable ways in which children engage with music.

The book is intended for a range of different groups of readers. The development of national curricula and national standards in various countries during the 1980s and 1990s demonstrated that music educators internationally are becoming increasingly interested in developmental issues related to children's engagement with music, and are keen to explore the practical applications of the various strands of research that impact on their day-to-day work. For this reason, the main group of readers will be music educators, especially those with a specific interest or expertise in music psychology and research. Another major target group consists of music psychologists and educational researchers who I hope will also welcome the publication of an authoritative account of the development and acquisition of musical skills and understandings, and use this as the theoretical basis for subsequent work in the area.

The 35 chapters are organized according to five loosely constructed sections—*Development, Engagement, Differences, Skills*, and *Contexts*—even though I realize that some of the contributions could have easily been included in another section of the book. The first section (*Development*) deals with fundamental issues of development; two chapters on the critical months and years from conception to the end of infancy, and five dealing with how the musical brain develops, the nature of musicality, music cognition, musical agency, and the potential impact of autism on musical development. Section two (*Engagement*) scrutinizes claims about whether exposure to music is associated with nonmusical abilities. This is followed by six chapters on musical literacy, music as language, engaging in a sound musicianship, mechanisms and processes in the development of emotion perception, felt experiences in popular musics, and changing musical preferences during childhood and adolescence. Completing the section are two chapters dealing with the child as music critic and popular music and identity.

Section three (*Differences*) focuses on those issues that explain and identify individual differences. One of the most obvious, yet also one of the most multifaceted, concerns how motivation for experiencing and studying music changes throughout childhood. Information on this topic is followed by a chapter that provides a framework for defining giftedness and talent in music, plus three chapters dealing with inclusive music classrooms, well-being during illness, and adolescent uses of music. Each of the chapters in this section is written from a very different perspective. Together, they provide a powerful explanation of the importance and value of music in the lives of all children.

Six chapters cover *Skills* that can develop as a result of exposure to music. Chapters dealing with the acquisition of vocal and instrumental skills in addition to performance confidence are complemented by chapters focusing on the use of computers and technology plus informal activities associated with musical play.

The final section of the book discusses five musical *Contexts*. The first of these surveys four historically different formal music education settings. It aims to provide readers with information that will assist them make comparisons between how children learned and developed their musical capacities in the past with current opportunities. An additional six chapters focus on children as musical apprentices, global practices, transcultural childhoods, non-formal music experiences, transformative music engagement, and musical identity. This section and the book conclude with a contribution on fostering lifelong engagement in music.

As a young university student about 30 years ago, I have a vivid memory of asking one of my lecturers, "How do you keep up with research on children's musical development?" Her reply was something like, "Gary, I don't have any problems because there is only a small stream of research being published." This statement could not be made today—in fact, the explosion of ideas and literature generated in the last three decades years has revolutionized the ways in which we study, define, and debate the many issues surrounding children's engagement with music. With this as our basis, the current volume attempts to provide an informed summary of where we are up to with our thinking, while at the same time identifying many of the challenges that lie ahead in our quest to better understand children's musical development. My sincere hope is that readers will find the information illuminating and that it will encourage them to think more deeply about the many different ways in which music can affect children's lives and the quality of life in communities throughout the world. I also hope that the information provided here will help those who need to defend music education so that they are able to articulate even more precisely why all children deserve to have access to music throughout their childhood.

Section 1

Development

Chapter 1

Prenatal development

Richard Parncutt

Prenatal development: Introduction

Infants have a wide range of skills that can be described as musical (see Trehub & Degé, Chapter 2). What is the origin of those skills? This chapter considers the possibility that the fetus becomes familiar with the internal sound patterns of the mother's body and associates these patterns with her physical and emotional state. The chapter covers musically relevant aspects of the fetal environment and musically relevant fetal/infant abilities and behaviors. It asks how we can evaluate and reconcile conflicting research findings on *prenatal musicality*, meaning any musically relevant perception, cognition, or behavior.

The fetal sound environment

The most important sounds to which the human fetus is regularly exposed are its mother's voice, her heartbeat, her movements (including footsteps), her breathing, and her digestion (stomach growling or borborygmi—the rumbling sounds caused by gas moving through the intestines) (Lecanuet, 1996). Less important, but often still audible, are sounds produced by the fetus itself (heartbeat, movement) and sounds from outside the mother's body.

The internal sounds of the mother's body may reach the fetal ears by different paths. For example, maternal heartbeat sounds may be transmitted via the umbilical artery, the uterine artery, or uteroplacental blood flow. The loudness or audibility of internal sounds may be different in different parts of the amniotic cavity, so what the fetus perceives depends on its physical orientation.

All the sounds to which the fetus is exposed, regardless of whether they originate inside or outside the mother's body, are *muffled*. The high frequencies are attenuated by the amniotic fluid and body of the mother, which act as a *low-pass filter* (Armitage, Baldwin, & Vince, 1980; Richards et al., 1992). Sounds below about 300 Hz may not be attenuated at all, while higher frequencies are increasingly attenuated; frequencies beyond about 2 kHz are generally inaudible (Abrams et al., 1998). Sounds in the range 100–1,000 Hz may even be amplified (Richards et al., 1992).

Audible sounds from outside the mother's body include the voices of other people, sounds in the environment, and music. These sounds are attenuated considerably (estimates range from 10 to 30 dB) by comparison with internal sounds, as they pass through the mother's body. This makes them more susceptible to masking (drowning out) by internal sounds (Peters et al., 1993; Querleu et al., 1984).

Uterine muffling does not affect the ups and downs in pitch (prosody or intonation), the timing of phonemes (rhythm), variations in loudness (accentuation), or variations in pitch register (including the difference between male and female voices) (Smith et al., 2003). As all but a few lower partials are inaudible, the timbre of the mother's speech, which determines the identity of individual vowels and consonants, is strongly affected; it is nevertheless possible for adult listeners and even the fetus itself to distinguish between different phonemes (vowels and consonants) in uterine recordings of the mother's voice (DeCasper et al., 1994). The complete preservation of pitch information may explain newborns' adult-like sensitivity to musical intervals as investigated by Stefanics et al. (2009).

For the infant, motherese (baby talk)—the way mothers or carers communicate with their infants—triggers associations with the mother's voice as it sounded in utero (Moon, Cooper, & Fifer, 1993). Motherese also involves multimodal exaggeration of speech, including pitch, loudness, rhythm, and facial expressions. From an evolutionary viewpoint, infants in ancient hunter-gatherer societies depended primarily on their mother (and perhaps other women) for their survival: nutrition, hygiene, protection from danger. That can explain why infants are strongly motivated to seek the proximity of attentive carers and bond with them, which in turn frees infants to playfully learn language and social skills such as turn-taking.

Musically relevant fetal abilities and behaviors

Postnatal musicality involves not only hearing, but also movement, balance (essential for dance), and emotion. All of these depend on neurocognition, and all have roots in the prenatal period (Hepper, 1992). The fetus has no reflective consciousness, and it is unlikely that it distinguishes between music and other patterns of sound and movement. Instead, it may learn to associate maternal sound/movement patterns with the mother (mother schema) (Parncutt, 2009).

The prenatal brain

Before birth, different brain regions develop at different rates; sensory organs initially develop independently of the brain regions to which they will later be connected. Connections between periphery sense organs and the central nervous system start to mature in about the twenty-fifth week,[1] after which sensory learning can begin (Oerter & Montada, 1995; see also Hodges, Chapter 3). From this point, brain development is influenced by external sensory stimulation (Panicker, Wadhwa, & Roy, 2002).

Prenatal hearing

The most important organ for hearing is the cochlea in the inner ear.[2] Here, vibrations are converted to neural impulses, and different frequencies are separated. Studies both behavioral (Hepper & Shahidullah, 1994) and physiological (Pujol, Lavigne-Rebillard, & Uziel, 1991; Rubel & Ryals, 1983) have demonstrated that the fetal auditory system begins to process sounds at about 20 weeks gestational age, before it is anatomically mature.[3] The range of frequencies to which the cochlea responds initially lies between 200 and 1,000 Hz (Hepper & Shahidullah, 1994; Rubel & Ryals, 1983). As the frequency response of the cochlea gradually broadens, so too does its ability to separate simultaneous frequencies (frequency discrimination), to separate rapid sequences of sounds as in ordinary speech (temporal discrimination), and to perceive very quiet sounds (auditory threshold). At birth, these abilities approach adult levels (Ptok & Ptok, 1996), but sensitivity to quiet sounds improves for several years after birth (Trehub et al., 1988). Numerous empirical studies are consistent with this general picture (reviews: Busnel & Granier-Deferre, 1983; Lecanuet, 1996).

An important, survival-promoting function of postnatal hearing is the *localization* of sound sources (Blauert, 1997). Different cues indicate the direction from which a sound arrives in the left–right dimension (interaural time and intensity differences), the up–down dimension (spectral envelope variations due to reflections from the irregular shape of the pinna), and the front–back dimension (acoustic shadow cast by the pinna). The distance of the sound source is estimated on the basis of known relationships between loudness and distance for specific sound sources in specific situations. All these cues depend on frequency. Although babies can localize in the left–right dimension at birth (Furst et al., 2004; Morrongiello et al., 1994), they could hardly have had prenatal practice at this task. First, the fetal head does not cast an acoustic shadow at the relatively low frequencies that are available in the uterus. Second, interaural time differences, which are important for sound localization by adults at low frequencies (Wightman & Kistler, 1992), are an order of magnitude smaller for the fetus than for an adult due to the smaller size of the fetal head and the faster speed of sound in fluid. Thus, anecdotal reports of the fetus turning its head toward a sound (e.g., Bitnour, 2000) are implausible.

Prenatal balance and orientation

Music generally implies movement (Godoy & Leman, 2010) and is associated with dance in all known cultures (Blacking, 1979). A prenatal origin of this association is possible since the cochlea (organ of hearing) and vestibule (organ of balance) are anatomically and physiologically united (Todd & Cody, 2000) and develop prenatally in parallel (Lai & Chan, 2002).

The vestibular system enables adults to perceive and monitor orientation (up vs. down) and acceleration. The vestibular sense or *proprioception* begins to function before the fetus first shows a *righting reflex* at 25 weeks (Hooker, 1952) and may play a part in bringing the fetus into a head-down (cephalic) position before birth (Hepper, 1992). Like all other senses, the vestibular sense needs stimulation to develop normally. Animal experiments (e.g., Ronca & Alberts, 2000) have demonstrated that prenatal proprioceptive abilities are not only present but also trained before birth, consistent with the existence of fetal cognitive representations of orientation and acceleration.

Prenatal responses to sound

Fetal hearing can be investigated by checking whether fetal heart rate and movements consistently change after repeated exposure to a sound. Heart-rate accelerations or decelerations in response to sound begin at about 20 weeks (Lecanuet, 1996) and occur in most human fetuses from about 26 weeks (Abrams, 1995). Spontaneous fetal movements begin at 6–9 weeks, but are not felt by the mother until about 20 weeks (Hooker, 1952; Oerter & Montada, 1995). Motor responses to loud, broad-band noises begin at about 24 weeks (Lecanuet, 1996); responses to pure tones begin a few weeks later. Motor responses to sound become consistent at 28–32 weeks (Birnholz & Benacerraf, 1983; Kisilevsky, Muir, & Low, 1992). Motor and heart-rate responses to music are more frequent at 38 than at 32 weeks (Wilkin, 1995/6). Responses have greater amplitude (e.g., greater heartbeat acceleration or deceleration) and are more likely when the fetus is awake, and depend on levels of alertness within sleep/wake states. While the fetus may perceive something and not react to it (Hepper, 1992), no consistent auditory brainstem responses (auditory evoked potentials) have been observed before 25–30 weeks (Lecanuet, 1996).

The literature about sound levels of external/internal stimuli and internal background noise as perceived by the fetus is contradictory, suggesting misunderstandings of relevant physics and underestimation of the difficulty of the measurement task. Gerhardt, Abrams, and Oliver (1990) calibrated and surgically implanted hydrophones in the intact amnion of pregnant ewes and measured absolute and relative sound levels in different frequency ranges. They concluded that "the fetus is developing in an environment that is rich with internal and external sounds" (abstract). Prenatal psychoacoustics is an area that is ripe for further investigation.

Prenatal emotional communication

Does prenatal emotion exist? Psychologists study the behavioral, physiological, and experiential aspects of emotion, and the relationships among them (Strongman, 2003). As experiential aspects of fetal emotion are absent or inaccessible, fetal emotion can only be investigated by tracking changes in physiological and behavioral states (Van den Bergh, 1992). These may primarily reflect arousal; the existence of prenatal emotional valence is additionally suggested by the combination of arousal and valence in the earliest infant behaviors and vocalizations (positive/negative facial expressions for low arousal, fussing/crying and exploratory behaviors for higher arousal; Fox & Calkins, 1993; Gibson, 1988) and their neural foundations. "In adults and infants, the experimental arousal of positive, approach-related emotions is associated with selective activation of the left frontal region, while arousal of negative, withdrawal-related emotions is associated with selective activation of the right frontal region" (Davidson, 1992, abstract).

Communication is a meaningful exchange of information between living creatures, and animal communication is any transfer of information that affects the behavior of other animals (Bradbury & Vehrencamp, 2011). Like perceptual learning (Gibson, 1969), communication can happen in the complete absence of attention, task relevance, human-like deliberate planning, or reflective awareness (Watanabe, Náñez, & Sasaki, 2001). Yet we can only use the word "communication" if there is successful transmission of information in both directions. If there is maternal–fetal communication, the signal can only be encoded in sound, movement, and biochemical information; it cannot involve the indexical content of language, or visual images, and the signals can only become "meaningful" by association (see following sections).

The idea of emotional communication between mother and fetus may underlie the emotional implications of musical sound and movement patterns as explored by Juslin and Persson (2002). The evidence is both biochemical and behavioral. Biochemical evidence involves many hormones that are actively exchanged between mother and fetus. Behavioral evidence includes the sophisticated emotional and musical communicative abilities and sensitivities of infants, suggesting that they had prenatal practice.

Young infants communicate emotion through crying, babbling, facial expressions, and bodily gestures (Trevarthen, 1985; Zeifman, 2001). Infant behaviors inform the mother or other carer about the infant's physical and emotional state (which are largely inseparable) and hence its current needs. The nature and origins of these processes may involve their contribution to infant survival in prehistoric human and prehuman societies (evolutionary psychology). The primary evolutionary purpose of infant–adult communication is presumably to motivate carers to help infants survive into childhood.

Physiological emotional communication

If the fetus perceives or shares maternal states by hormonal transfer across the placenta and blood–brain barrier, it may associate changes in pitch–time–movement patterns with associated changes in hormonal concentration patterns; a possible mechanism is classical conditioning (Mastropieri & Turkewitz, 1999). Hormones implicated in transplacental transfer include epinephrine, cortisol, and maternal thyroid hormones (e.g., Loubière et al., 2012). Prenatal hormonal interactions have the potential to explain strong emotion in music, even though the fetus does not "experience" anything in the adult sense. Hormonal processes that develop prenatally are the physiological foundation of later emotional experience.

Physiological emotional communication may be said to occur when emotionally implicated biochemicals pass between the mother and the fetus via the placenta. Biochemicals that act as messengers within the body are either hormones or neurotransmitters. A hormone is produced in one organ and transported by the blood to another organ whose function it influences. Hormones are associated with emotions such as anger, fear, sex, love, stress, or exertion; these emotions also depend strongly on the social and physical context (Buchanan, Eccles, & Becker, 1992).

All hormones and neurotransmitters have multiple physiological functions, which can have multiple psychological repercussions. If hormones enable emotional physiological communication between mother and fetus, the emotional message is generally redundant and often ambiguous. The same is true in music performance (Juslin & Persson, 2002).

The fetus is anatomically connected to the mother, but physiologically to some extent independent of her. It shares some, but not all, of its mother's physiological states. For example, the maternal and fetal heartbeat correlate from about 32 weeks (DiPietro et al., 2004). The placenta is a filter that primarily passes nutrients and oxygen in one direction and wastes and carbon dioxide in the other. It partly filters out bacteria, viruses, toxins, drugs, and chemicals including alcohol, nicotine, and cocaine. Fetal steroids are highly lipophilic and so easily cross the placenta (Welberg & Seckl, 2001). Biochemicals that pass through the placenta are a possible avenue for mother–fetus communication.

Changes in maternal physical and emotional state (such as stress or relaxation) affect fetal behaviors such as heart rate, heart-rate variability, body movements, and breathing movements (Van den Bergh, 1992, cites numerous studies). These effects are presumably biochemically mediated. For example, maternal anger can be communicated to the fetus via high cortisol and adrenaline and low dopamine and serotonin levels (Field et al., 2002).

Stress is associated with activation of the hypothalamic–pituitary–adrenal (HPA) axis and the sympathetic nervous (or sympatho-adrenomedullar) system (SA) (Van den Bergh, 1992). Stressors produce responses in a variety of endocrine systems and involve hormones such as cortisol, adrenaline (epinephrine), noradrenaline (norepinephrine), prolactin, thyroxine, insulin, and testosterone (Mason, 1975) as well as the corticotrophin-releasing hormone (CRH) and adrenocorticotrophic hormone (ACTH) (Mulder et al., 2002). Levels of neuropeptides such as CRH in the amygdala, hypothalamus, and pituitary gland are associated with emotionality, anxiety, and stress (Brown & Gray, 1988; Davis, 1992). Corticosteroids, a class of steroid hormones, are involved in stress and immune responses and associated with fear and anxiety (Korte, 2001). Stress and fear affect levels of glucocorticoids, of which cortisol is the most important (Welberg & Seckl, 2001). Such processes allow maternal stress to be perceived or shared by the fetus.

In humans and other mammals, maternal emotion and stress affect both the *physiology* (neurochemistry, endocrine function) and the *psychology* (emotion, cognition) of the offspring (Buitelaar et al., 2003; Maret, 1997; Weinstock, 1997). Against a background of steadily increasing blood concentrations of CRH, ACTH, and cortisol throughout pregnancy, information about maternal stress can reach the fetus as a temporary reduction in blood flow, transfer of maternal hormones across the placenta, or release of placental CRH; CRH enters fetal circulation via the umbilical vein, whereas cortisol enters via the umbilical arteries (Mulder et al., 2002). Prenatal exposure to glucocorticoids such as cortisol affects fetal development (Coe et al., 2003), produces hypertension and other medical and behavioral problems in later life (Seckl, 2001), affects the development of internal organs including the ear (Canlon et al., 2003), and plays a part in the etiology of schizophrenia (Koenig, Kirkpatrick, & Lee, 2002). The intrauterine hormonal environment affects development of the fetal hippocampus and amygdala, and hence programming of the HPA axis (Matthews, 2002). The neuroendocrine system acts as a link between prenatal biochemical, neurodevelopmental variables such as plasma levels of ACTH and cortisol, and elements of the maternal psychosocial environment such as stress, social support, and personality (Wadhwa et al., 1996). Maternal prenatal stress and associated placental levels of adrenocortico-trophin, endorphins, and CRH can lead to premature (preterm) delivery, adverse neurodevelopment, and chronic degenerative diseases and psychopathologies in adulthood (Huizink, Mulder, & Buitelaar, 2004; Wadhwa et al., 2002).

Research on postnatal emotional development offers additional evidence for prenatal emotional communication. Elevated prenatal cortisol levels caused by excessive maternal stress can cause temperamental, behavioral, emotional, motor, and cognitive problems in infants (DeWeerth, van Hees, & Buitelaar, 2003). Infants of "emotionally disturbed women" are "typically described as restless, irritable, poor sleepers, and prone to gastrointestinal difficulties"; and "mothers under severe emotional stress tend to have hyperactive fetuses" (Van den Bergh, 1992, pp. 159 and 160, citing various studies). Children of women treated with the glucocorticoid receptor agonist dexamethasone (DEX), which readily passes the placenta (Welberg & Seckl, 2001), are shyer, more avoidant, and more emotional (Trautman et al., 1995). The effect of prenatal stress on cognitive development and temperament of infants is stronger when it occurs later in the pregnancy (Buitelaar et al., 2003).

Biochemical emotional communication between mother and fetus is not always associated with stress. Estrogen and testosterone levels can influence the probability of hyperactivity and social and emotional problems (Williams, Greenhalgh, & Manning, 2003). Oxytocin is not only used to induce labor (Loghis et al., 1999)—it is also associated with singing (Grape et al., 2003), social contact, and sexuality (Keverne & Curley, 2004), and has therefore been implicated in aspects of mother–infant bonding such as breastfeeding and lullabies. Melatonin helps the circadian rhythms of fetus and mother to synchronize (Reppert & Weaver, 1988).

The word "communication" implies that information travels in both directions. The feto-placental unit produces human chorionic gonadotropin, progesterone, human placental lactogen, oxytocin, and vasopressin, which manipulate both fetal and maternal physiology (Kota et al., 2013). The fetus of a stressed mother produces hormones that influence placental blood supply (Pincus-Knackstedt et al., 2006). Before the onset of labor in rhesus monkeys, an increase in fetal plasma androgen concentration leads to increases in maternal plasma estrogen, oxytocin, and amnion fibronectin (Mecenas et al., 1996). In sheep, fetal cortisol levels trigger maternal endocrine changes leading to labor (Wu et al., 2001). In humans, cortisol levels change with onset of labor depending on the mode of delivery—whether normal/spontaneous, instrumental, or Caesarean (Mears et al., 2004).

The claims I have made in this section about the emotional correlates of biochemicals should be treated with caution. Each hormone has multiple physiological and psychological functions. The link between biochemicals and emotions is indirect (Korte, 2001). Changes in biochemical levels may be due to circadian variations and developments during pregnancy rather than emotion (Walsh, Ducsay, & Novy, 1984).

Behavioral emotional communication

Behavioral emotional communication between mother and fetus may be said to occur when the fetus picks up patterns of sound and movement from within the mother's body that carry information about maternal emotional state. The most clearly audible sound sources are the voice, breathing, heartbeat, digestion, and walking. In each case, the sound or movement pattern depends strongly on the mother's physical and emotional state (e.g., heart rate: Ekman, Levenson, & Friesen, 1983; respiratory changes: Averill, 1969; uterine contractions: Moawad, 1973). Mastropieri and Turkewitz (1999) explain:

> For example, changes in voice intonation associated with an emotional state such as anger may be accompanied by increased respiration, causing a different pattern of diaphragmatic movements, as well as increased muscular tension and an increase in heart rate. Additionally, those physiological changes involved in the production of speech and which contribute to vocal intonation may also be detectable to the fetus, particularly because autonomic changes immediately precede and influence changes in voice intonation (Scherer, 1986). Temporal relationships between distinctive prosodic acoustic stimulation and distinctive responses associated with maternal physiological changes would provide an opportunity for associative learning (via classical conditioning) in utero. This form of learning would serve as a basis for the perception of and a differential response to different vocal expressions of emotion after birth. (p. 205)

In the ecological approach to perception (Gibson, 1966), perception involves active interaction with environmental objects. Since this ability is so fundamental, we might expect the fetus to start developing it soon after it becomes physiologically possible. In the case of sound, that involves not only processing incoming information, but also interpreting it, and constructing auditory images of possible sound sources (McAdams, 1984). This process is essentially the same in human and non-human animals (Hulse, 2002). If the fetus constructed an image or a schema of its mother based on the combined information that it receives via hearing, movement, and biochemical fluctuations, that schema would promote its postnatal survival and lay the foundation for the development of other perceptual schemata (Parncutt, 2009). The mother schema is analogous to the infant schema of Lorenz (1943); it is consistent with the active two-way nature of maternal–fetal and maternal–infant communication (Murray & Trevarthen, 1986). Almost by definition, bonding (attachment) is not possible without both the mother schema and the infant schema. The mother schema continues to develop after birth, as infants spontaneously link sensory inputs from different modalities (Trehub et al., 2013).

Evolutionary psychology provides complementary insights. In traditional hunter-gatherer societies, and even today in developing countries with poor medical facilities, fetal survival is threatened by premature delivery, regardless of whether the mother survives the birth. The fetus is therefore under "evolutionary pressure" to prepare for premature delivery. Prehistoric infants often died from natural causes or infanticide. A baby's chance of survival was better if it was sensitive to, and actively perceived, the changing physical and emotional states of its mother (or other caretaker) (cf. de Rosnay et al., 2006; Tronick, 1989). In a dangerous situation, a baby should not make demands on its mother that are unlikely to be met. The fetus could prepare for this challenge by monitoring its mother's physical and emotional state, taking advantage of the link between biochemical correlates of emotion and emotionally informative sound and movement patterns.

Behavioral psychology provides further clues. Prenatal sources of information about the mother's state may be associated with each other by classical conditioning (Parncutt, 1993, 1997, 2009). Presumably all animals are capable of classical conditioning; the existence of fetal classical conditioning was demonstrated by Spelt (1948) and discussed by Hepper (1992). Changes in maternal sound and movement patterns in response to an external event are faster than associated biochemical changes, so they are also predictive of those biochemical changes. Once the different responses have been linked by association, the faster sound and movement responses can act as an early warning system. Such a process requires no reflective consciousness; it is barely comparable with the conscious process of a 5-year-old trying to infer emotions from prosody or music (Dalla Bella et al., 2001).

Fetal physiology is plastic: it responds to environmental factors, preparing the fetus to respond optimally to environmental conditions outside of the uterus (Welberg & Seckl, 2001). The fetuses of anxious women tend to be more active (Van den Bergh et al., 1989). Prenatal stress increases the likelihood of premature delivery, low birth weight, and small head circumference (Dunkel-Schetter, 1998). The fetus can evidently go into a state akin to shock, shutting down all developmental processes to maximize its chances of survival in a potentially hostile external environment; mothers who survive fetal death are also usually in shock (Rogers et al., 1999). All these phenomena increase the chance of surviving premature birth due to maternal crisis, including accident or illness.

Fetal sensitivity to the emotional state of the mother is integral to pre- and postnatal bonding. Live maternal speech and singing have physiological benefits for preterm infants (Filippa et al., 2013) and psychological benefits for mothers (Cevasco, 2008). The same applies to maternal heartbeat sounds and maternal vocalizations that have been acoustically filtered to replicate prenatal conditions (Doheny et al., 2012; Zimmerman et al., 2013). They presumably indicate both the presence and the caring attention of the mother—indicators of postnatal safety that are conducive to happiness and playful exploration (Sorce & Emde, 1981). Infant behavior is influenced by maternal facial and vocal expression (Campos, Thein, & Owen, 2003) and infants as young as 3 months can detect (or at least discriminate) depression in their mothers (Weinberg & Tronick, 1998). Presumably on this basis, infants are sensitive to emotional implications of pitch contours in both speech (Mastropieri & Turkewitz, 1999) and music (Trehub & Nakata, 2001–2). Such sensitivities could be prenatally learned (Parncutt, 1993, 1997, 2009), genetically predetermined (Masataka, 1998; Trehub, 2003), or both. To the extent that all such sensitivities involve both arousal and valence, the word "emotion" is appropriate.

Again, caution is warranted. There is no conclusive evidence for the psychological or physiological reality of prenatal emotion. All that we know for sure is that infants can differentiate between emotional stimuli. Some of the conclusions about the emotional sensitivities of infants in this section may be adult projections.

Auditory learning and memory

Without auditory learning and memory, there could be no prenatal psychological or musical development. How do learning and memory develop prenatally? Learning is acquisition of knowledge or skill based on experience or training. Memory is storage of information in a form that allows coding and decoding (retrieval). In the absence of language, the existence of learning and memory can be investigated by observing behavior. Since the fetus has no language, prenatal memory is procedural (implicit) rather than declarative (explicit): it is not memory in the everyday sense of remembering a phone number or what happened yesterday, which presupposes adult, linguistically mediated consciousness. Rather than "prenatal auditory memory" it may be more accurate to speak of "transnatal retention of auditory experience" (Arabin, 2002, p. 428). That experience is without reflective consciousness.

The only studies that have convincingly demonstrated fetal memory have involved many stimulus repetitions (details follow). For that reason, fetal memories are presumably fundamentally *statistical*, based on frequency of exposure (Saffran, 2002); prenatal events that happen more often produce more fetal brain activity (Partanen et al., 2013a). Fetal memories are also *implicit* (Roediger, 1990)—a kind of priming based on past experience. The creation of fetal memories requires neither conscious (reflective) experience of the original stimulus nor a conscious process of recollection.

Implicit, statistical fetal memory enables associations to be formed between stimuli that frequently occur in close temporal proximity. Fetal memories clearly cannot be *declarative* (*explicit*) or *semantic* (*conceptual*) in the everyday adult sense, as the fetus has no language. There is no direct, convincing evidence of fetal *episodic* (*autobiographical*) memory, or fetal memory for individual events.

Experiments on prenatal auditory learning can be divided into two categories: those where both exposure and behavioral demonstration of learning are prenatal, and those in which exposure is prenatal and behavioral demonstration is postnatal (transnatal memory). Regarding prenatal–prenatal memory, numerous studies have confirmed that the fetus can habituate (get used and stop responding) to a repeated stimulus (e.g., Leader et al., 1982; Peiper, 1925; van Heteren et al., 2000). The same applies to premature infants (Cassidy & Standley, 1995). Experiments on habituation do not necessarily demonstrate learning, because the subject may also stop responding for reasons of perceptual or motor fatigue; but given that prenatal learning occurs in many animals, it is not surprising that it occurs in humans (Hepper, 1992, 1996).

Regarding transnatal memory, newborns' sensitivity to heartbeat sounds is presumably due to prenatal exposure to the sound of the mother's cardiovascular system (Dettermann, 1978; Salk, 1962). Hepper (1991) also demonstrated transnatal learning: babies who had heard a specific piece of music regularly before birth (the theme from the TV soap opera *Neighbours*), but not between birth and the experiment, responded with heightened alertness, lower heart rate, and fewer movements. Granier-Deferre et al. (2011) observed a clear cardiac reaction four weeks after birth following six weeks' exposure to a prenatally presented melodic stimulus. Partanen et al. (2013b) showed that repeated prenatal exposure to a melody (*Twinkle, Twinkle, Little Star*) can induce neural representations that are maintained for several months after birth. In a comparable postnatal–postnatal study, 7-month-old infants presented with the same music daily for two weeks remembered it for a further two weeks (Saffran, Loman, & Robertson, 2000).

Statistical learning is the ability of humans to respond to transitional probabilities: the probability of event B occurring given that event A has just happened, where both events may be complex, such as words composed of phonemes, or phrases which are composed of words. In the case of speech, we must also consider characteristic variations in pitch and loudness. Statistical learning has been demonstrated in non-human primates (Hauser, Newport, & Aslin, 2001). The probability that the human fetus is capable of statistical learning when exposed to maternal speech is high, especially considering the repeatedly demonstrated sensitivity of newborns to features of their mother's speech.

The neurophysiological basis of learning is Hebb's postulate that "cells that fire together, wire together." The strength of a memory trace for a given pattern depends on the number of repetitions. On this basis, we expect that postnatal memory for prenatal sounds will last longer when those sounds are heard more clearly and more often. The sound of the mother's voice as perceived by the fetus, and sounds associated with her movements and digestion, fall into this category. We might expect even stronger memory traces for sounds that are heard almost constantly before birth, such as the mother's heartbeat and breathing.

Evaluating research on prenatal musicality

The terms "prenatal musicality" and "prenatal music psychology" refer to any prenatal perceptual, cognitive, motoric, or emotional skill or behavior that may be relevant for later musical development. The fetus is presumably unable to distinguish what adults call "music" from other stimuli (even adults find this difficult, and there is no widely stable or accepted definition of music in musicology; Parncutt, 2010). If any sound pattern has a special status for the fetus and can be discriminated or categorized, the most likely candidate is the mother's voice. Perhaps all internal sounds of the mother's body are grouped by the fetus into a mother schema.

Research relevant to prenatal musicality is a minefield of poorly defined terms, inappropriately motivated research, poor communication between research groups with different backgrounds and underlying assumptions, and tenuous connections between research results and practical applications (including applications in music education). Popular sources are not always reliable. The value and applicability of literature can depend strongly on researchers' motives. Searching the internet can be a problem, because much of the easily accessible literature is politically motivated (e.g., the pro-life, anti-abortion movement).

Consider the following example. Several sources (Karmiloff & Karmiloff-Smith, undated; Whitwell, undated; Wilkin, 1995/6) report that the fetus moves in time to music ("dances"). I could find no plausible empirical evidence for this claim, which seems to be a misinterpretation or exaggeration of the fetus's tendency to change its pattern of movements depending on the kind of stimulation it receives—regardless of whether adults hear that stimulation as music. Any repeated movement can be regarded as rhythmic, but synchronization to music is another matter. Children cannot entrain, that is, they cannot synchronize their movements to a beat until their second (Moog, 1963) or even fourth postnatal year (McAuley et al., 2006).

Scientific-conservative vs. romantic-progressive research

Gooch (1972, cited in Boyce-Tillman, 2004) classified human cultures into two types, according to the way in which they construct knowledge: "Type A" systems focus on products, objectivity, impersonal logic, detachment, and discrete categories of knowledge based on proof and scientific evidence; "Type B" systems favor being, subjectivity, emotion, magic, involvement, association, belief, spirituality, and non-causal knowledge, and are suppressed in modern Western culture. The literature on prenatal psychology may be similarly divided into two categories, which I call *scientific-conservative* and *romantic-progressive*.

Scientific-conservative literature relies on carefully controlled experiments, and is represented by respected medical journals such as the *Journal of Obstetrics and Gynecology* and the numerous journals associated with the American Psychological Association. While these traditions exemplify high academic standards and successful quality control mechanisms, they downplay apparently successful paramedical approaches that are difficult to investigate empirically or reconcile with a Western, materialist approach, and they may not have eliminated their patriarchal and sexist tendencies (e.g., Bickel, Croft, & Marshall, 1996; Woodward, 1999; Yedidia & Bickel, 2001). The association between fetal psychology and women's bodies and issues may explain why, until a few decades ago, the scientific and medical mainstream showed remarkably little interest in fetal psychology. Questions about corporality (the dependence of human psychology on the human body) and everyday verbal discourse (qualitative analysis of interview transcripts) are stereotypically female and may be intuitively avoided in male-dominated research. Scientific-conservative and patriarchal thinking is also strong within cognitive psychology, which traditionally treats the brain as a computer separate from the human body and the physical/social environment, and tends to regard quantitative research methods (statistical analysis of numerical data) as inherently superior.

Romantic-progressive researchers tend to the other extreme. United in their opposition to groups as diverse as conservative scientists, the political right wing, and feminists (Verny, 1999), they address scientifically problematic topics such as the interaction between emotional and physical health, paramedical healing, and spirituality. Their flagship journal is the *Journal of Prenatal and Perinatal Psychology and Health.*

Romantic-progressive claims may nevertheless be valid and important. Regarding "prenatal and birth themes and symbols in dance, movement, art, dreams, language, myth, ritual, play, and psychotherapy," Menzam (2002, abstract) wrote: "Although we cannot prove that specific movement patterns re-enact prenatal and birth events, we can conclude that prenatal and birth themes appear to present everywhere in our lives." Nor is there always a clear distinction between romantic-progressive and scientific-conservative research. For example, the scientific-conservative Hepper (1992) adopted a progressive stance when he pointed out the danger of underestimating fetal abilities: "a fetus may sense a stimulus, but exhibit no response" (p. 133).

Some romantic-progressive researchers wildly exaggerate fetal abilities. For example, Cheek (1986) found evidence for out-of-body prenatal memories in memories accessed through hypnotic regression. The call for papers of the 16th International Congress of the International Society for Prenatal and Perinatal Psychology and Medicine (ISPPM, held in Heidelberg in 2005) begins as follows: "Research in the field of prenatal psychology has extended our life-history back to conception and beyond—right back to our parents' thoughts and plans for a child of their own." The theme of the 12th International ISPPM, held in London in 1998, was *Conscious Birth: The Experience of a Lifetime*, and the website explained:

> The dawning awareness that the human baby is normally conscious at birth lays the foundation for a paradigm shift with immense consequences. The Congress will review the now irrefutable tide of evidence for prenatal and perinatal consciousness, examine its impact on the dynamics of the human condition, survey the history of the emergence of the new paradigm and the reaction it has met and explore the implications for a range of fields.

Chamberlain (1993) drew on anecdotal evidence from psychotherapy to support claims of "fetal intelligence" and "thinking before birth." Sallenbach (1993) even wondered when the "intelligent" prenate has "the capacity to formulate hypotheses" (p. 77). These authors failed to distinguish between intelligence and the more elementary abilities to learn and react. Intelligence is normally understood to involve both the possession of knowledge and the ability to use it efficiently and adaptively in real and unexpected situations (Sternberg, 1985). It is misleading to apply this term to the fetus.

The gap between radicals and conservatives in prenatal psychology may stem from the strong emotions that babies evoke in adults—combined with the mystery and fascination of a largely inaccessible experimental subject (the fetus) and epistemological differences between evidence-based and intuitive or philosophical approaches. Adults are strongly motivated to meet babies' needs by caring for and playing with them, which has clear survival value (Bjorklund, Yunger, & Pellegrini, 2002). To what extent should researchers in pre- and perinatal psychology be objective about these feelings? Parenting behaviors are incompatible with the airs of self-importance traditionally cultivated by university professors to maintain the respect of their students and of the general public, who may not be in a position to evaluate their research and intellectual competence. The parental instincts of music educators can motivate them to devote their lives to child musicality, but at the same time cloud their judgment when confronted with scientific questions. It is a classic example of the tension between objectivity and subjectivity, or facts and values, in scientific research (Lassman & Speirs, 1994).

This chapter aims to steer a middle course between "Type A" scientific-conservative and "Type B" romantic-progressive extremes, but with a bias toward "Type A." I acknowledge both the explanatory power of "Type A" systems and the descriptive relevance of "Type B" systems for musical experience and meaning. Like a scientific-conservative, I avoid claims that contradict the best empirical literature. Like a romantic-progressive, I consider promising theories and scenarios for which little or no empirical evidence yet exists on either side. I support my claims with available empirical literature, abstract logic, evolutionary arguments, and everyday experience. I acknowledge, and attempt to combine, the different (tacit) philosophies and criteria of "truth" that characterize the sciences and the humanities: empiricism, rationalism, intersubjectivity, and pragmatism.

Music and consciousness

Romantic-progressives may project adult or postnatal concepts onto the fetus. The words "music" and "consciousness" are good examples. Both have different implied definitions that may not be clearly stated. "Primary intersubjectivity" (Trevarthen, 1979) is a romantic-progressive term that lacks a clear operational definition. These differences need to be resolved so that people with different approaches can communicate and collaborate.

Music

What does a fetus perceive, when it perceives *music*? Clearly, not what an adult perceives. First, the fetus has no language or reflective awareness. Second, music perception always depends on previous musical experience. If music is an integral feature of human culture, then it can hardly be relevant to the fetus, which—romantic-progressive objections to the contrary—has not yet been initiated into that culture. That initiation involves a gradual, mainly postnatal process of musical and linguistic enculturation (Soley & Hannon, 2010).

To understand fetal responses to music, we may consider music perception by non-human animals, which—like the fetus—do not contribute actively or directly to human culture and therefore, presumably, do not experience music as "music." Cows, for example, may produce more milk when exposed to slow music and less when exposed to fast music, simply because a slow beat reduces arousal and a faster beat increases it (North & MacKenzie, 2001). Similarly, the human fetus may prefer musical tempos close to the resting heart rate of the mother, without perceiving music as "music" (Whitwell, undated).

Consciousness

Romantic-progressive researchers who are also psychotherapists, psychoanalysts, or hypnotists such as Cheek (1986) suggest that the fetus has a kind of consciousness (or awareness). A term such as "sentient prenate" (Chamberlain, 1994) may be appropriate, the word sentient referring merely to perception. But the parallel claim that "unborn children are sensitive and aware" (abstract) is misleading, as is the claim that "consciousness may not be dependent on the central nervous system, or even on the body" (Wade, 1998, abstract). A scientific-conservative approach regards the anecdotal experience of therapists and clients in psychoanalysis, psychotherapy, and hypnosis as unreliable, because the factors that influence it cannot be separated and controlled.

The confusion about consciousness in the literature on prenatal psychology is unsurprising considering the continuing confusion in the general philosophical, psychological, and neuroscientific literature on consciousness (e.g., Baier, 1999). This confusion appears to stem from unstated variations in both the (operational) definition of consciousness and underlying philosophical assumptions: for example, is consciousness associated with the brain or the body, or with being or doing (Noë, 2009)? To understand consciousness, we must separately consider its various aspects: reflection, wakefulness, attention, preference, working memory, and cognitive representations.

Reflection (or reflective consciousness) distinguishes humans from non-humans. Humans *realize* that they are attending to or doing something, do things deliberately (*intentionality*), know that they know things (*metacognition*), and know that others have different knowledge, opinions, or experiences (*theory of mind*) (Garfield, Peterson, & Perry, 2001; Noble & Davidson, 1996; Szendre, 1996). We cannot conclusively disprove that fetal reflection exists, because if the fetus had a private world of reflection, adults would have no access to it. The only known way to access the reflection of another being or group is through language. However, current knowledge about the role of language in the ontogenesis of reflection makes the existence of fetal reflection seem very unlikely. Phylogenetically, the gradual prehistoric emergence of human speech and language presumably ran parallel to the gradual emergence of reflection and associated characteristically human behaviors (Corballis, 2004). Ontogenetically, babies acquire language, reflection, and a concept of self gradually as they interact imitatively and socially with caretakers; the process begins actively around the age of 1 and continues for at least ten years (Asendorpf, 2002; Decety & Chaminade, 2003; Flavell et al., 1999; Papoušek & Papoušek, 1995; Slobodchikov & Tsukerman, 1992). Both fetuses and babies dream in REM sleep (Roffwarg, Muzio, & Dement, 1966), but that is no evidence for reflection, since REM sleep also occurs in other animals.

The concept of *fetal wakefulness* is relatively unproblematic. Fetuses—like newborns—are more likely to react to and process sound when they are awake—but they are more often asleep than awake. An infant's eye, body, and respiratory movements allow five behavioral states to be identified—two sleep states (non-REM and REM) and three states of wakefulness (Prechtl, 1974). At 36 weeks gestational age, four of these five neonate states can be identified from fetal heart rate and its variability: quiet sleep, active or REM sleep, quiet wakefulness, and active wakefulness; and the amount of time the fetus spends per day in each state gradually changes as it develops (Nijhuis et al., 1982). It is also possible to determine sleep/wake states from prenatal body movements using ultrasound (Arabin & Riedewald, 1992). Sleep-state differentiation begins somewhere between 14 weeks (Oerter & Montada, 1995) and 28 weeks (Awoust & Levi, 1983; Selton, Andre, & Hascoet, 2000). The circadian rhythms of the fetus are synchronized to those of the mother: the fetus tends to be most awake and active when the mother sleeps (Reppert & Weaver, 1988).

What of fetal *attention?* Attention is not the same as reflection, but it is involved in the selection and maintenance of conscious contents (Baars, 1997). The word "listening" (as opposed to merely hearing) implies attention, which may be psychologically defined as a state of heightened wakefulness or vigilance in response to a stimulus, coupled with selective perception of that stimulus. The fetus cannot turn toward an external sound source, because it has no means of determining its direction (see the previous section which discusses *sound localization*). A change in fetal behavioral state in response to a stimulus does not necessarily imply attention, either. However, many studies have shown that the fetus *habituates* to a repeated stimulus (Lecanuet, 1996). If habituation is defined as a discontinuation of attention, then it is evidence for the existence of attention, but not of reflection.

Preferences for sound patterns begin early. Infants prefer happy to sad sound patterns, and speech to singing (Corbeil, Trehub, & Peretz, 2013); they tend to prefer sounds that indicate maternal presence and attention. Moreover, newborns prefer the sound of their mother's voice when the high frequencies have been filtered out so that it more closely resembles the muffled sound of the mother's voice *in utero*, presumably due to prenatal exposure (Fifer & Moon, 1988; Querleu et al., 1984). Babies can show preferences for different sounds by sucking in different ways on a pacifier (DeCasper & Fifer, 1980). On that basis, the fetus would presumably show preferences, given an appropriate experimental paradigm such as a brain scan (Weiskopf et al., 2003) or a procedure based on behavioral reactions (movements, heart rate). It is normal for non-human animals to show preferences, such as for different foods; again, that is no evidence for reflection.

According to Baddeley's (1986) concept of working memory, stimuli must be processed in working memory before they can be memorized, implying that the fetus has working memory. If working memory is "an essential contributor to the neural basis of consciousness" (Osaka, 2003), the fetus may be conscious in this sense. But a scientific approach should preferably distinguish concepts such as consciousness, attention, perception, and working memory (Baars, 1997).

In a cognitive approach, perception involves the construction of *cognitive representations* of environmental objects, usually by comparing sensory inputs in different sense modalities. The concept of prenatal bonding (e.g., Sallenbach, 1993) implies that the fetus forms a cognitive representation of the mother: it combines auditory, movement, biochemical, and other signals that it picks up from the mother so as to construct her as a unified object. Oberhoff (2005) has suggested that this cognitive representation has two essential qualities that might enable a later connection to music: it is *big* and *moving*, just as music is considered to have virtual spatial properties that are associated with bodily motion and independent of the physical spatial locations of musical instruments (Eitan & Granot, 2004). Again, this is no evidence for fetal reflection, as it is normal for non-human animals to form cognitive representations of environmental objects.

Summarizing this section, fetal "consciousness" is probably limited to *wakefulness, attention, perception*, and *preference*. These capabilities are shared by non-human animals (as well as non-human fetuses), suggesting that prenatal human development is not essentially different (and therefore no more wonderful) than prenatal development in other animals. Neither the fetus nor the baby is capable of *reflection*. The expression "prenatal experience" (as used, for example, by Hepper, 1992 and Lecanuet, 1996) implies reflection and should be avoided.

Animistic projection

The Freudian concept of *projection*—a defense mechanism by which feelings or impulses are attributed to another person (Baumeister, Dale, & Sommer, 1998)—has been considered an important element of religion (Beit-Hallahmi & Argyle, 1975). It may be human nature to attribute mental processes, including one's inner life and reflective consciousness of sensations and emotions, to other beings or objects such as pets (Archer, 1997). Animistic projection plays a role in the origin of art (Wulf, 1947) and religion (Roheim, 1932), and the theory of mind. As animistic projection involves the assumption or attribution of human characteristics, it may be regarded as a form of *anthropomorphism* (also called *anthropomorphization* or *personification*), which is an important issue in fields as diverse as veterinary science, ethology (animal behavior), animal welfare, evolutionary biology, anthropology, primatology, psychology, history, philosophy, and literary criticism (Mitchell, Miles, & Thompson, 1997). In the sciences, human qualities may be projected onto animals such as dolphins (Hafemann, 1987), while in areas addressed by the humanities (religion, myths, fairy tales, children's literature), reflection and intentionality may be projected onto living and non-living objects, non-human animals, and gods. The psychological function of animistic projection may be to overcome the loneliness that accompanies the discovery of self, which in turn accompanies the onset of reflection (Davis & Franzoi, 1986).

Animistic projection onto the fetus begins when a mother starts to feel her fetus move at about 20 weeks, and gets the impression that it is kicking on purpose, or trying to communicate (Gloger-Tippelt, 1988). Later, adults project reflection onto a baby or child during infant–adult vocal play (otherwise known as *motherese*: Papoušek & Papoušek, 1995; see also Trehub & Degé, Chapter 2); that is, they speak and behave as if the baby or child can reflect.

Children appear to learn both reflection and animistic projection by imitating the behavior of their carers. Animistic projection is taught directly when adults project reflection onto animals or other objects during infant–child interactions. Such behaviors help the baby or child to gradually discover that others have different minds, and to conclude that they have their own (Garfield, Peterson, & Perry, 2001). The child then projects its reflective consciousness onto objects and animals, when such assignment is plausible and meaningful (Szendre, 1996).

Animistic projection can explain why many romantic-progressive researchers accept the idea of prenatal reflection. It can also explain the belief that the womb is a safe and happy place, in which the fetus experiences well-being and perfection (Montagu, 1962; Whitwell, undated; I committed the same logical error in Parncutt, 1993, 1997). But even if the fetus could reflect, it could only be "happy" if it could compare its present state with a previous, less ideal, "sadder" state. Sounds associated with prenatal "experience" are not, therefore, necessarily associated with positive emotions. To imagine things from the perspective of the fetus, it is necessary to leave all aspects of the adult world behind, including associations between positive emotion and abundance, and between negative emotion and work or responsibility.

"Prenatal music education"

Those who believe that music education should begin before birth may point to the following arguments:

- *Fetal abilities.* During the third trimester, the fetus is mature enough to survive birth. It can hear, process, and remember musical patterns of sound, and associate them with emotions. Moreover, sound is the most complex (and therefore interesting) prenatally available stimulus: as soon as the baby is born, the amount of competing information that it can potentially extract from the other senses (primarily vision) increases dramatically, while the simultaneous increase in available acoustic information is relatively small. This point can explain the contrast between newborns' striking perceptual musical abilities and the relatively slow rate at which infants learn specific musical structures such as tonality (Krumhansl & Keil, 1982, cited in Trehub, 2003).

- *Parental motivation.* The parents' desire for a child increases steadily during pregnancy and reaches a peak just before the birth (Gloger-Tippelt, 1988). During the last ten weeks, expectant mothers actively imagine the appearance and behavior of their baby and what it will be like to care for it. During that time, the parents (and especially the mother) are highly motivated to participate in activities that will promote the health and well-being of their child.

Is this not a perfect window of opportunity to get the child started on musical development? Should parents take advantage of this period to give their child a head start in musical education? The answer would be "yes" if it could be demonstrated that prenatally stimulated babies or children had superior musical abilities. And a number of studies seem to have shown that prenatal sensory-motor stimulation—beyond the wealth of sounds and other stimulation normally available in the mother's body—can contribute not only to musical development, but also to general sensory-motor, language, emotional, social, and even physical development (Chen et al., 1994; Manrique et al., 1993; Panthuraamphorn, 1993).

Unfortunately, all such studies are methodologically problematic. To my knowledge, no researcher has yet succeeded in clearly separating prenatal from postnatal effects on musical development. For example, Lafuente et al. (1997) attempted to "advance the intellectual and physical development of the fetus by means of musical stimuli" (abstract). Fetuses between 28 and 40 weeks were regularly exposed to violin sounds, and their postnatal development was monitored. The authors claimed that the babies in the experimental group were "superior in gross and fine motor activities, linguistic development, some aspects of body–sensory co-ordination and certain cognitive behaviours." If that were true, it would be a sensation. Why might violin sounds have such specific effects, while the sound of the mother's voice and the multitude of other sounds to which the fetus is exposed do not? More plausibly, Tafuri and Villa (2002) suggested that prenatally musically educated babies produce musical vocalizations (babbling) earlier, more frequently, and with musically higher quality than control. But in both cases it was not possible to control or eliminate postnatal effects on musical development.

We thus have no convincing evidence that prenatal fetal acoustic, tactile, or movement stimulation influences intelligence, creativity, or later development. Hepper (1992) wrote: "My own studies indicate that there may be some benefits resulting from prenatal stimulation, but this appears to be not the result of stimulation per se, but rather the results of increasing the interest of the mother in her pregnancy, which has 'knock-on' effects for development after birth" (p. 149).

If prenatal exposure to music indeed gives the fetus a head start in the development of musical abilities, what kind of music should the mother listen to? Should the mother *like* the music, encouraging the fetus to associate it with positive emotions that might later motivate it to become actively involved in music? Or should the mother choose music whose emotion she feels strongly, regardless of whether those feelings are positive or negative, given that memories associated with strong emotions are more salient and last longer (Kulas, Conger, & Smolin, 2003; Phelps, 2004)? Again, confounds make this question hard to test empirically, and it is not (yet) possible to investigate fetal preferences. A further problem is the holistic, amodal nature of fetal and infant perception (Sallenbach, 1993). Neither the fetus nor the infant distinguishes between music and speech; infant–adult vocal play is a combination of speech and music, suggesting that children do not begin to separate the two until their second year. Similarly, the idea of talking to the fetus to encourage prenatal bonding (e.g., Sallenbach, 1993) can only work in one direction: the mother may get the impression of bonding (Bitnour, 2000), but the fetus has no "idea" that speech is normally directed toward people, and has no way of "knowing" whether speech is directed toward it or someone else.

In summary, empirical studies have not yet demonstrated the success of prenatal music education. The best musicians tend to be those who work the hardest, and the ones who work the hardest are the ones who are most motivated to work and most persistent when the going gets tough (O'Neill & McPherson, 2002). There is no known way of promoting the prenatal development of these attributes.

Contraindications

The problem is not only that the benefits of prenatal music education cannot be verified. Attempts to educate the fetus by regularly playing music or other sounds through a loudspeaker strapped to the mother's abdomen could be also dangerous—or at least negatively affect development—in the following ways.

Hearing damage. The fetus is not evolutionarily prepared to hear sound more loudly than the mother does, as it may do when a loudspeaker is strapped to its mother's abdomen. In this situation, the mother may not be in a position to adjust the loudness to an appropriate level. Children of mothers who were working in noisy environments such as factories while pregnant, which is now illegal in some countries (Brezinka, Lechner, & Stephan, 1997), may be more likely to develop high-frequency hearing loss (Lalande, Hetu, & Lambert, 1986; Pierson, 1996).

Stress. Prenatal noise can have other long-term effects. For example, airplane noise can lead to a reduction in newborn body weight and height at age 3 years (Kawada, 2004). Noise-induced stress may impair the development of the fetal immune system (Sobrian et al., 1997).

Sleep. An abdominal loudspeaker could disturb the wake/sleep cycle of the fetus (Nijhuis et al., 1982) and disrupt the timing of brain development (Fifer, reported in Bitnour, 2000). The same applies to fetal massage or games. The fetus is more often asleep than awake, and sleep is important for physiological development. Interrupted sleep may be regarded as a kind of prenatal stress. No one would place a blaring loudspeaker next to a sleeping baby (DiPietro, reported in Bitnour, 2000).

Bonding. From the viewpoint of the fetus, bonding with the mother involves perceiving her in all sense modalities. An abdominal loudspeaker could disrupt and confuse the development of a cognitive representation of the mother, inhibiting bonding.

Researchers do not yet know enough about the developing fetal brain and auditory system to be sure about the possible positive or negative effects of deliberate prenatal auditory stimulation. Its consequences are hard to predict. Until things become clearer, it may be better to avoid such procedures altogether.

Ethics

Is it *ethical* to try to educate the fetus? Clearly, it cannot hurt if the fetus gets a head start on musical skill acquisition that will later help it to compete with musical peers. But there are also serious problems.

Parentification. Parents who feel inadequate about themselves may try to compensate by encouraging their children to make up for their own failures—such as their (perceived) lack of musical talent. This is an example of *co-dependence*, which involves shame-proneness, low self-esteem, and *parentification* (Wells et al., 1999). Children are "parentified" when they are expected to take on the role of caretaker to their siblings or even to their own parents (Chase, 1999). Parents should avoid projecting their wishes onto their child, who has (or will develop) its own wishes, and instead focus on creating a loving environment in which the child can develop in its own, individual way.

Pressure. If too much emphasis is placed on achievement and "hothousing" in early childhood, the child may achieve less rather than more, miss out on valuable childhood experiences, and develop psychological problems (Hyson et al., 1991). Placing unreasonable expectations on the fetus may set up a negative and lasting dynamic between parents and children. Modern children are under enough pressure (Elkind, 1981) without it starting before birth (DiPietro, reported in Bitnour, 2000).

Priorities. We cannot foresee the contribution a fetus will later make to society. Music is one of countless positive alternatives, but surely not the most important. The world is threatened by poverty, war, and climate change. Because tomorrow's adults will have to solve these problems, they are a challenge to education in general. Peer and teacher–student interactions are important for social development (Kim & Stevens, 1987). Parents can contribute by nurturing their children's natural altruism (Hurlbut, 2002), promoting situations that encourage them to think clearly, independently, and critically, and nurturing their natural abilities and tendencies. "Our ultimate objective, of course, is to help create not a musical genius but a person well integrated in his [*sic.*] physical, emotional, intellectual and spiritual self" (Whitwell, undated).

Author note

I am grateful to Sandra Trehub for detailed criticism and Peter Sedlmayr for advice on issues of biology and endocrinology. For discussions and suggestions about the previous (2006) version of this chapter I thank Ellen Dissanayake, Michaela Gosch, Donald Hodges, Thomas Hutsteiner, Annekatrin Kessler, Gunter Kreutz, Carol Krumhansl, Peter Liebmann-Holzmann, Gary McPherson, William Noble, Bernd Oberhoff, Glenn Schellenberg, Günter Schulter, Kazue Semba, Caroline Traube, and Sandra Trehub. The original research was supported in part by NSERC Grant #228175–00 and VRQ Grant 2201–202 to Daniel J. Levitin.

Reflective questions

1 What does the fetus perceive when the mother walks? Why is this musically relevant?
2 In what sense might the fetus be "conscious"? In what sense is this word misleading?
3 Why might the fetus associate specific patterns of sound with specific emotions?
4 How might prenatal hearing and proprioception have promoted the survival of infants in ancient hunter-gatherer societies?
5 What are the advantages and disadvantages of "prenatal music education"?

Notes

1 The age of the fetus is referred to throughout this chapter in the conventional way as gestational age, or age since last menstruation. This is two weeks greater than conceptual age. For example, normal birth at 40 weeks gestational age corresponds to 38 weeks since conception. The term *embryo* applies during the first 8–12 weeks of gestation, while gross body structures and internal organs are developing; the term *fetus* applies from the third month (Oerter & Montada, 1995).

2 Vibration can also be perceived through the skin or by bone conduction to the inner ear (Gerhardt et al., 1996), but experimental attempts to demonstrate this in animal fetuses (e.g., Parkes et al., 1991) have been unsuccessful. The mucus that fills the fetal middle ear throughout the prenatal period does not prevent it from functioning (Keith, 1975), but it may cause some attenuation (Abrams, Gerhardt, & Peters, 1995).

3 Anatomical maturity involves several developmental stages. At about 10 weeks, hair cells begin to appear on the basilar membrane; at about 20 weeks, the efferent innervation of the outer hair cells begins; and at about 24–28 weeks, the cochlear receptors and auditory synapses mature (Pujol, Lavigne-Rebillard, & Uziel, 1991). The organ and tunnel of Corti are present in all turns of the cochlea at about 26 weeks (Altmann, 1950). The auditory pathway (from cochlear nerve to inferior colliculus) undergoes myelination between weeks 26 and 28, which improves the speed and synchronization of auditory impulses (Morre, Perazzo, & Braun, 1995).

Key sources

DeCasper, A. J., & Fifer, W. (1980). Of human bonding: Newborns prefer their mothers' voices. *Science*, **208**, 1174–1176.

DiPietro, J. A., Irizarry, R. A., Costigan, K. A., & Gurewitsch, E. D. (2004). The psychophysiology of the maternal–fetal relationship. *Psychophysiology*, **41**, 510–520.

Hepper, P. G. (1992). Fetal psychology: An embryonic science. In J. G. Nijhuis (Ed.), *Fetal behaviour* (pp. 129–156). Oxford: Oxford University Press.

Lecanuet, J.-P. (1996). Prenatal auditory experience. In I. Deliège & J. Sloboda (Eds.), *Musical beginnings* (pp. 3–34). Oxford: Oxford University Press.

Parncutt, R. (2009). Prenatal and infant conditioning, the mother schema, and the origins of music and religion. *Musicae Scientiae*, Special Issue on Music and Evolution (Ed. O. Vitouch & O. Ladinig), 119–150.

Reference list

Abrams, R. M. (1995). Some aspects of the fetal sound environment. In I. Deliège & J. Sloboda (Eds.), *Perception and cognition of music* (pp. 83–101). Hove, Sussex, England: Psychology Press.

Abrams, R. M., Gerhardt, K. J., & Peters, A. J. M. (1995). Transmission of sound and vibration to the fetus. In J. P. Lecanuet et al. (Eds.), *Fetal development: A psychobiological perspective* (pp. 315–330). London: Lawrence Erlbaum Associates.

Abrams, R. M., Griffiths, S. K., Huang, X., Sain, J., Langford, G., & Gerhardt, K. K. (1998). Fetal music perception: The role of sound transmission. *Music Perception*, 15, 307–317.

Altmann, E. (1950). Normal development of the ear and its 2 mechanics. *Archives in Otolaryngology*, 52, 725–730.

Arabin, B. (2002). Opinion: Music during pregnancy. *Ultrasound in Obstetrics and Gynecology*, 20, 425–430.

Arabin, B., & Riedewald, S. (1992). An attempt to quantify characteristics of behavioural states. *American Journal of Perinatology*, 9, 115–119.

Archer, J. (1997). Why do people love their pets? *Evolution and Human Behaviour*, 18(4), 237–259.

Armitage, S. E., Baldwin, B. A., & Vince, M. A. (1980). The fetal sound environment of sheep. *Science*, 208, 1173–1174.

Asendorpf, J. B. (2002). Self-awareness, other-awareness, and secondary representation. In W. Prinz & A. N. Meltzoff (Eds.), *The imitative mind: Development, evolution, and brain bases* (pp. 63–73). New York: Cambridge University Press.

Averill, J. R. (1969). Autonomic response patterns in sadness and mirth. *Psychophysiology*, 5, 399–414.

Awoust, J., & Levi, S. (1983). Neurological maturation of the human fetus. *Ultrasound in Medicine and Biology*, 2(Supplement), 583–587.

Baars, B. J. (1997). Some essential differences between consciousness and attention, perception, and working memory. *Consciousness and Cognition*, 6, 363–371.

Baddeley, A. (1986). *Working memory*. Oxford: Clarendon.

Baier, W. R. (Ed.) (1999). *Bewusstsein*. Graz: Leykam.

Baumeister, R. F., Dale, K., & Sommer, K. L. (1998). Freudian defense mechanisms and empirical findings in modern social psychology: Reaction formation, projection, displacement, undoing, isolation, sublimation, and denial. *Journal of Personality*, 66, 1081–1124.

Beit-Hallahmi, B., & Argyle, M. (1975). God as a father-projection: The theory and the evidence. *British Journal of Medical Psychology*, 48, 71–75.

Bickel, J., Croft, K., & Marshall, R. (1996). *Enhancing the environment for women in academic medicine*. Washington, D.C.: Association of American Medical Colleges.

Birnholz, J., & Benacerraf, B. (1983). The development of human fetal hearing. *Science*, 222, 516–518.

Bitnour, M. B. (2000). What's it like in the womb? *WebMD Feature Archive*, <http://my.webmd.com/content/article/11/3608_285.htm>.

Bjorklund, D. F., Yunger, J. L., & Pellegrini, A. D. (2002). The evolution of parenting and evolutionary approaches to childrearing. In M. Bornstein (ed.), *Handbook of parenting*, Vol. 2: *Biology and ecology of parenting* (2nd ed., pp. 3–30). Mahwah, NJ: Lawrence Erlbaum Associates.

Blacking, J. (Ed.) (1979). *The performing arts: Music and dance*. The Hague: Mouton.

Blauert, J. (1997). *Spatial hearing: The psychophysics of human sound localization*. Cambridge, MA: MIT Press.

Boyce-Tillman, J. (2004). Towards an ecology of music education. *Philosophy of Music Education Review*, 12, 102–125.

Bradbury, J. W., & Vehrencamp, S. L. (2011). *Principles of animal communication* (2nd ed.). Sunderland, MA: Sinauer.

Brezinka, C., Lechner, T., & Stephan, K. (1997). Der fetus und der lärm (The fetus and noise). *Gynäkologisch-geburtshilfliche Rundschau*, 37(3), 119–129.

Brown, M. R., & Gray, T. S. (1988). Peptide injections into the amygdala of conscious rats: Effects on blood pressure, heart rate, and plasma catecholamines. *Regulatory Peptides*, 21, 95–106.

Buchanan, C. M., Eccles, J. S., & Becker, J. B. (1992). Are adolescents the victims of raging hormones? Evidence for activational effects of hormones on moods and behavior at adolescence. *Psychological Bulletin*, 111(1), 62–107.

Buitelaar, J. K., Huizink, A. C., Mulder, E. J., Robles de Medina, P. G., & Visser, G. H. A. (2003). Prenatal stress and cognitive development and temperament in infants. *Neurobiology of Aging*, 24(Supplement 1), S53–S60.

Busnel, M. C., & Granier-Deferre, C. (1983). And what of fetal audition? In A. Oliveito & M. Zappella (Eds.), *The behavior of human infants* (pp. 93–126). New York: Plenum.

Campos, J. J., Thein, S., & Owen, D. (2003). A Darwinian legacy to understanding human infancy. *Annals of the New York Academy of Sciences*, 1000, 110–134.

Canlon, B., Erichsen, S., Nemlander, E., Chen, M., Hossain, A., Celsi, G., & Ceccatelli, S. (2003). Alterations in the intrauterine environment by glucocorticoids modifies the developmental programme of the auditory system. *European Journal of Neuroscience*, 17, 2035–2041.

Cassidy, J. W., & Standley, J. M. (1995). The effect of music listening on physiological responses of premature infants in the NICU. *Journal of Music Therapy*, 32, 208–227.

Cevasco, A. M. (2008). The effects of mothers' singing on full-term and preterm infants and maternal emotional responses. *Journal of Music Therapy*, 45(3), 273–306.

Chamberlain, D. B. (1993). Prenatal intelligence. In T. Blum (Ed.), *Prenatal perception, learning, and bonding*. Hong Kong: Leonardo.

Chamberlain, D. B. (1994). The sentient prenate: What every parent should know. *Journal of Prenatal and Perinatal Psychology and Health*, 9(1), 9–31.

Chase, N. D. (1999). *Burdened children. Theory, research, and treatment of parentification*. Thousand Oaks, CA: Sage.

Cheek, D. B. (1986). Prenatal and perinatal imprints: Apparent prenatal consciousness as revealed by hypnosis. *Pre- and Perinatal Psychology Journal*, 2(2), 97–110.

Chen, D. G., Huang, Y. F., Zhang, J. Y., & Qi, G. P. (1994). Influence of prenatal music- and touch-enrichment on the IQ, development and behaviour of infants. *Chinese Journal of Psychology*, 8, 148–151.

Coe, C. L., Kramer, M., Cvéh, B., Gould, E., Reeves, A. J., Kirschbaum, C., & Fuchs, E. (2003). Prenatal stress diminishes neurogenesis in the dentate gyrus of juvenile rhesus monkeys. *Biological Psychiatry*, 54, 1025–1034.

Corballis, M. C. (2004). The origins of modernity: Was autonomous speech the critical factor? *Psychological Review*, 111, 543–552.

Corbeil, M., Trehub, S. E., & Peretz, I. (2013). Speech versus singing: Infants choose happier sounds. *Frontiers in Psychology*, 4, 372.

Dalla Bella, S., Peretz, I., Rousseau, L., & Gosselin, N. (2001). A developmental study of the affective value of tempo and mode in music. *Cognition*, 80(3), B1–B10.

Davidson, R. J. (1992). Emotion and affective style: Hemispheric substrates. *Psychological Science*, 3(1), 39–43.

Davis, M. (1992). The role of the amygdala in fear and anxiety. *Annual Review of Neuroscience*, 15, 353–375.

Davis, M. H., & Franzoi, S. L. (1986). Adolescent loneliness, self-disclosure, and private self-consciousness: A longitudinal investigation. *Journal of Personality and Social Psychology, 51*(3), 595–608.

DeCasper, A. J., & Fifer, W. (1980). Of human bonding: Newborns prefer their mothers' voices. *Science, 208*, 1174–1176.

DeCasper, A. J., Lecanuet, J. P., Maugais, R., Granier-Deferre, C., & Busnel, M. C. (1994). Fetal reactions to recurrent maternal speech. *Infant Behaviour and Development, 17*, 159–164.

Decety, J., & Chaminade, T. (2003). When the self represents the other: A new cognitive neuroscience view on psychological identification. *Consciousness and Cognition, 12*, 577–596.

de Rosnay, M., Cooper, P. J., Tsigaras, N., & Murray, L. (2006). Transmission of social anxiety from mother to infant: An experimental study using a social referencing paradigm. *Behaviour Research and Therapy, 44*(8), 1165–1175.

Dettermann, D. K. (1978). The effect of heartbeat on neonatal crying. *Infant Behavior and Development, 1*, 36–48.

DeWeerth, C., van Hees, Y., & Buitelaar, J. K. (2003). Prenatal maternal cortisol levels and infant behavior during the first 5 months. *Early Human Development, 74*, 139–151.

DiPietro, J. A., Irizarry, R. A., Costigan, K. A., & Gurewitsch, E. D. (2004). The psychophysiology of the maternal–fetal relationship. *Psychophysiology, 41*, 510–520.

Doheny, L., Hurwitz, S., Insoft, R., Ringer, S., & Lahav, A. (2012). Exposure to biological maternal sounds improves cardiorespiratory regulation in extremely preterm infants. *Journal of Maternal– Fetal and Neonatal Medicine, 25*(9), 1591–1594.

Dunkel-Schetter, C. (1998). Maternal stress and preterm delivery. *Prenatal and Neonatal Medicine, 3*, 39–42.

Eitan, Z., & Granot, R. Y. (2004). Musical parameters and spatio-kinetic imagery. In S. D. Lipscomb, R. Ashley, R. O. Gjerdingen, and P. Webster (Eds.), *Proceedings of the 8th international conference on music perception and cognition* (pp. 57–63). Adelaide, Australia: Causal Productions.

Ekman, P., Levenson, R. W., & Friesen, W. V. (1983). Autonomic nervous system activity distinguishes between different emotions. *Science, 221*, 1208–1210.

Elkind, D. (1981). *The hurried child*. Reading, MA: Addison-Wesley.

Field, T. M., Diego, M., Hernandez-Reif, M. A., Salman, F., Schanberg, S., Kuhn, C., Yando, R., & Bendell, D. (2002). Prenatal anger effects on the fetus and neonate. *Journal of Obstetrics and Gynaecology, 22*, 260–266.

Fifer, W. P., & Moon, C. (1988). Auditory experience in the fetus. In W. P. Smotherman & S. R. Robinson (Eds.), *Behaviour of the fetus* (pp. 175–188). Telford, England: Caldwell.

Filippa, M., Devouche, E., Arioni, C., Imberty, M., & Gratier, M. (2013). Live maternal speech and singing have beneficial effects on hospitalized preterm infants. *Acta Paediatrica, 102*(10), 1017–1020.

Flavell, J. H., Green, F. L., Flavell, E. R., & Lin, N. T. (1999). Development of children's knowledge about unconsciousness. *Child Development, 70*(2), 396–412.

Fox, N. A., & Calkins, S. D. (1993). Multiple-measure approaches to the study of infant emotion. In M. Lewis & J. Haviland (Eds.), *Handbook of emotions* (pp. 167–184). New York: Guilford Press.

Furst, M., Bresloff, I., Levine, R. A., Merlob, P. L., & Attias, J. J. (2004). Interaural time coincidence detectors are present at birth: Evidence from binaural interaction. *Hearing Research, 187*(1–2), 63–72.

Garfield, J. L., Peterson, C. C., & Perry, T. (2001). Social cognition, language acquisition, and the development of the theory of mind. *Mind and Language, 16*, 494–541.

Gerhardt, K. J., Abrams, R. M., & Oliver, C. C. (1990). Sound environment of the fetal sheep. *American Journal of Obstetrics and Gynecology, 162*, 282–287.

Gerhardt, K. J., Huang, X., Arrington, K. E., Meixner, K., Abrams, R. M., & Antonelli, P. J. (1996). Fetal sheep in utero hear through bone conduction. *American Journal of Otolaryngology, 17*, 374–379.

Gibson, E. J. (1969). *Principles of perceptual learning and development*. East Norwalk, CT: Appleton-Century-Crofts.

Gibson, E. J. (1988). Exploratory behavior in the development of perceiving, acting, and the acquiring of knowledge. *Annual Review of Psychology, 39*(1), 1–42.

Gibson, J. J. (1966). *The senses considered as perceptual systems*. Oxford, UK: Houghton Mifflin.

Gloger-Tippelt, G. (1988). Die Entwicklung des Konzeptes "eigenes Kind" im Verlauf des Übergangs zur Elternschaft. In E. Brähler and A. Meyer (Eds.), *Partnerschaft, sexualität und fruchtbarkeit. Beiträge aus forschung und praxis*. Berlin: Springer.

Godoy, R. I., & Leman, M. (Eds.) (2010). *Musical gestures: Sound, movement, and meaning*. New York: Routledge.

Gooch, S. (1972). *Total man: Towards an evolutionary theory of personality*. London: Allen Lane, Penguin.

Granier-Deferre, C., Bassereau, S., Ribeiro, A., Jacquet, A. Y., & DeCasper, A. J. (2011). A melodic contour repeatedly experienced by human near-term fetuses elicits a profound cardiac reaction one month after birth. *PLoS One, 6*(2), e17304.

Grape, C., Sandgren, M., Hansson, L. O., Ericson, M., & Theorell, T. (2003). Does singing promote well-being? An empirical study of professional and amateur singers during a singing lesson. *Integrative Physiological and Behavioral Science, 38*, 65–74.

Hafemann, M. (1987). Delphine—totem-tiere des New Age? (Dolphins: totem animals of the New Age?) *Psychologie Heute, 14*(8), 28–33.

Hauser, M. D., Newport, E. L., & Aslin, R. N. (2001). Segmentation of the speech stream in a non-human primate: Statistical learning in cotton-top tamarins. *Cognition, 78*(3), B53–B64.

Hepper, P. G. (1991). An examination of fetal learning before and after birth. *Irish Journal of Psychology, 12*, 95–107.

Hepper, P. G. (1992). Fetal psychology: An embryonic science. In J. G. Nijhuis (Ed.), *Fetal behaviour* (pp. 129–156). Oxford: Oxford University Press.

Hepper, P. G. (1996). Fetal memory: Does it exist? What does it do? *Acta Paediatrica, 416*(Supplement), 16–20.

Hepper, P. G., & Shahidullah, B. S. (1994). Development of fetal hearing. *Archives of Disease in Childhood, 71*, F81–F87.

Hooker, D. (1952). *The prenatal origin of behaviour*. Lawrence, KS: University of Kansas Press.

Huizink, A., Mulder, E., and Buitelaar, J. (2004). Prenatal stress and risk for psychopathology: Specific effects or induction of general susceptibility? *Psychological Bulletin, 130*, 115–142.

Hulse, S. H. (2002). Auditory scene analysis in animal communication. *Advances in the Study of Behavior, 31*, 163–200.

Hurlbut, W. B. (2002). Empathy, evolution, and altruism. In S. G. Post, L. G. Underwood, J. P. Schloss, & W. B. Hurlbut (Eds.), *Altruism and altruistic love: Science, philosophy, & religion in dialogue* (pp. 309–327). London: Oxford University Press.

Hyson, M. C., Hirsh-Pasek, K., Rescorla, L., Cone, J., & Martell-Boinske, L. (1991). Ingredients of parental "pressure" in early childhood. *Journal of Applied Developmental Psychology, 12*, 347–365.

Juslin, P. N., & Persson, R. S. (2002). Emotional communication. In R. Parncutt & G. E. McPherson (Eds.), *Science and psychology of music performance* (pp. 219–236). New York: Oxford University Press.

Karmiloff, K., & Karmiloff-Smith, A. (undated). Hören: *Das Leben Ihres ungeborenen Babys* (The life of your unborn baby). Germany: Pampers. See also <http://www.pampers.com>.

Kawada, T. (2004). The effect of noise on the health of children. *Journal of Nippon Medical School, 71*, 5–10.

Keith, R. W. (1975). Middle ear function in neonates. *Archives of Otolaryngology, 101*, 376–379.

Keverne, E. B., & Curley, J. P. (2004). Vasopressin, oxytocin and social behaviour. *Current Opinion in Neurobiology, 14*, 777–783.

Kim, Y. O., & Stevens, J. H. (1987). The socialization of prosocial behavior in children. *Childhood Education*, **63**, 200–206.

Kisilevsky, B. S., Muir, D. W., & Low, J. A. (1992). Maturation of human fetal responses to vibroacoustic stimulation. *Child Development*, **63**(6), 1497–1508.

Koenig, J. I., Kirkpatrick, B., & Lee, P. (2002). Glucocorticoid hormones and early brain development in schizophrenia. *Neuropsychopharmacology*, **27**(2), 309–318.

Korte, S. M. (2001). Corticosteroids in relation to fear, anxiety, and psychopathology. *Neuroscience and Behavioral Reviews*, **25**, 117–142.

Kota, S. K., Gayatri, K., Jammula, S., Meher, L. K., Kota, S. K., Krishna, S. V. S., & Modi, K. D. (2013). Fetal endocrinology. *Indian Journal of Endocrinology and Metabolism*, **17**(4), 568.

Krumhansl, C. L., & Keil, F. C. (1982). Acquisition of the hierarchy of tonal functions in music. *Memory and Cognition*, **10**, 243–251.

Kulas, J. F., Conger, J. C., & Smolin, J. M. (2003). The effects of emotion on memory: An investigation of attentional bias. *Journal of Anxiety Disorders*, **17**(1), 103–113.

Lafuente, M. J., Grifol, R., Segerra, J., Soriano, J., Gorba, M. A., & Montesinos, A. (1997). Effects of the Firstart method of prenatal stimulation on psychomotor development. The first six months. *Pre- and Perinatal Psychology Journal*, **11**, 151–162.

Lai, C. H., & Chan, Y. S. (2002). Development of the vestibular system. *Neuroembryology*, **1**, 61–71.

Lalande, N. M., Hetu, R., & Lambert, J. (1986). Is occupational noise exposure during pregnancy a risk factor of damage to the auditory system of the fetus? *American Journal of Industrial Medicine*, **10**, 427–435.

Lassman, P., & Speirs, R. (1994). *Weber: Political Writings*. Cambridge: Cambridge University Press.

Leader, L. R., Baillie, P., Martin, B., & Vermeulen, E. (1982). Fetal habituation in high-risk pregnancies. *BJOG: An International Journal of Obstetrics & Gynaecology*, **89**(6), 441–446.

Lecanuet, J.-P. (1996). Prenatal auditory experience. In I. Deliège & J. Sloboda (Eds.), *Musical beginnings* (pp. 3–34). Oxford: Oxford University Press.

Loghis, E., Salamalekis, N., Vitoratos, N., Panayotopoulos, D., & Kassanos, C. (1999). Umbilical cord blood gas analysis in augmented labour. *Journal of Obstetrics and Gynaecology*, **19**, 38–40.

Lorenz, K. (1943). Die angeborenen Formen möglicher Erfahrung. *Zeitschrift für Tierpsychologie*, **5**, 235–409.

Loubière, L. S., Vasilopoulou, E., Glazier, J. D., Taylor, P. M., Franklyn, J. A., Kilby, M. D., & Chan, S. Y. (2012). Expression and function of thyroid hormone transporters in the microvillous plasma membrane of human term placental syncytiotrophoblast. *Endocrinology*, **153**(12), 6126–6135.

Manrique, B., Contasi, M., Alvarado, M. A., Zypman, M., Palma, N., Ierrobino, M. T., Ramirez, I., & Carini, D. (1993). Nurturing parents to stimulate their children from prenatal stage to three years of age. In T. Blum (Ed.), *Prenatal perception, learning, and bonding* (pp. 153–186). Berlin, Germany: Leonardo.

Maret, S. (1997). *The prenatal person: Frank Lake's maternal–fetal distress syndrome*. New York: University Press of America.

Masataka, N. (1998). Perception of motherese in Japanese sign language by 6-month-old hearing infants. *Developmental Psychology*, **34**, 241–246.

Mason, J. W. (1975). A historical view of the stress field. *Journal of Human Stress*, **1**, 6–12.

Mastropieri, D., & Turkewitz, G. (1999). Prenatal experience and neonatal responsiveness to vocal expressions of emotion. *Developmental Psychobiology*, **35**, 204–214.

Matthews, S. G. (2002). Early programming of the hypothalamo–pituitary–adrenal axis. *Trends in Endocrinology and Metabolism*, **13**, 373–380.

McAdams, S. (1984). The auditory image: A metaphor for musical and psychological research on auditory organization. *Advances in Psychology*, **19**, 289–323.

McAuley, J. D., Jones, M. R., Holub, S., Johnston, H. M., & Miller, N. S. (2006). The time of our lives: Life span development of timing and event tracking. *Journal of Experimental Psychology: General,* **135**(3), 348.

Mears, K., McAuliffe, F., Grimes, H., & Morrison, J. J. (2004). Fetal cortisol in relation to labour, intrapartum events, and mode of delivery. *Journal of Obstetrics and Gynaecology,* **24**(2), 129–132.

Mecenas, C. A., Giussani, D. A., Owiny, J. R., Jenkins, S. L., Wu, W. X., Honnebier, B. O., Lockwood, C. J., Kong, L., Guller, S., & Nathanielsz, P. W. (1996). Production of premature delivery in pregnant rhesus monkeys by androstenedione infusion. *Nature Medicine,* **2**(4), 443–448.

Menzam, C. (2002). Dancing our birth: Prenatal and birth themes and symbols in dance, movement, art, dreams, language, myth, ritual, play, and psychotherapy. *Dissertation Abstracts International, Section B: Sciences & Engineering,* **63**(1-B), 567.

Mitchell, R., Miles, L., & Thompson, N. (Eds.) (1997). *Anthropomorphism, anecdotes, and animals.* New York: SUNY Press.

Moawad, A. H. (1973). The sympathetic nervous system and the uterus. In J. B. Josimivich (Ed.), *Problems of human reproduction,* Vol. 1: *Uterine contractions—side effects of steroidal contraceptives* (pp. 65–82). New York: Wiley.

Montagu, A. (1962). *Prenatal influences.* Springfield, IL: Charles Thomas.

Moog, H. (1963). *Beginn und erste entwicklung des musikerlebens im kindesalter. Eine empirischpsychologische untersuchung.* Köln: Wasmund.

Moon, C., Cooper, R. P., & Fifer, W. P. (1993). Two-day-olds prefer their native language. *Infant Behaviour and Development,* **16**, 495–500.

Morre, J. K., Perazzo, L. M., & Braun, A. (1995). Time-course of axonal myelination in the human brainstem auditory pathway. *Hearing Research,* **87**, 21–31.

Morrongiello, B. A., Fenwick, K. D., Hillier, L., & Chance, G. (1994). Sound localization in newborn human infants. *Developmental Psychobiology,* **27**(8), 519–538.

Mulder, E. J. H., Robles deMedina, P. G., Huizink, A. C., Van den Bergh, B. R. H., Buitelaar, J. K., & Visser, G. H. A. (2002). Prenatal maternal stress: Effects on pregnancy and the (unborn) child. *Early Human Development,* **70**, 3–14.

Murray, L., & Trevarthen, C. (1986). The infant's role in mother–infant communications. *Journal of Child Language,* **13**(1), 15–29.

Nijhuis, J. G., Prechtl, H. F. R., Martin Jr., C. B., & Bots, R. S. G. M. (1982). Are there behavioural states in the human fetus? *Early Human Development,* **6**, 177–195.

Noble, W., & Davidson, I. (1996). *Human evolution, language, and mind: A psychological and archaeological inquiry.* Cambridge: Cambridge University Press.

Noë, A. (2009). *Out of our heads: Why you are not your brain, and other lessons from the biology of consciousness.* New York: Macmillan.

North, A., & MacKenzie, L. (2001). "Moosic Study" reveals way of increasing milk yields. Leicester, England: Press and Publications Office, University of Leicester. <http://www.le.ac.uk/press/press/moosicstudy.html>.

Oberhoff, B. (2005). Das Fötale in der Musik. Musik als "Das Große Bewegende" und "Die Göttliche Stimme." In B. Oberhoff (Ed.), *Die seelischen Wurzeln der Musik. Psychoanalytische Erkundungen* (pp. 41–63). Gießen: Psychosozial-Verlag.

Oerter, R., & Montada, L. (1995). *Entwicklungspsychologie* (Developmental psychology) (3rd ed.). Weinheim, Germany: Psychologie Verlags Union.

O'Neill, S. A., & McPherson, G. E. (2002). Motivation. In R. Parncutt & G. E. McPherson (Eds.), *Science and psychology of music performance* (pp. 31–46). New York: Oxford University Press.

Osaka, N. (2003). Working memory-based consciousness: An individual difference approach. In N. Osaka (Ed.), *Neural basis of consciousness* (pp. 27–44). Amsterdam, Netherlands: John Benjamins Publishing Company.

Panicker, H., Wadhwa, S., & Roy, T. S. (2002). Effect of prenatal sound stimulation on medio-rostral neostriatum/hyperstriatum ventrale region of chick forebrain: A morphometric and immunohisto-chemical study. *Journal of Chemical Neuroanatomy*, **24**, 127–135.

Panthuraamphorn, C. (1993). Prenatal infant stimulation program. In T. Blum (Ed.), *Prenatal perception, learning, and bonding* (pp. 187–220). Berlin, Germany: Leonardo.

Papoušek, H., & Papoušek, M. (1995). Intuitive parenting. In M. H. Bornstein (Ed.), *Handbook of parenting*, Vol. 2: *Biology and ecology of parenting* (pp. 117–135). Mahwah, NJ: Lawrence Erlbaum Associates.

Parkes, M. J., Moore, P. J., Moore, D. R., Fisk, N. M., & Hanson, M. A. (1991). Behavioral changes in fetal sheep caused by vibroacoustic stimulation: The effects of cochlear ablation. *American Journal of Obstetrics and Gynecology*, **164**, 1336–1343.

Parncutt, R. (1993). Prenatal experience and the origins of music. In T. Blum (Ed.), *Prenatal perception, learning, and bonding* (pp. 253–277). Berlin: Leonardo.

Parncutt, R. (1997). Pränatale Erfahrung und die Ursprünge der Musik. In L. Janus & S. Haibach (Eds.), *Seelisches Erleben vor und während der Geburt* (pp. 225–240). Neu-Isenburg, Germany: LinguaMed.

Parncutt, R. (2009). Prenatal and infant conditioning, the mother schema, and the origins of music and religion. *Musicae Scientiae*, Special issue on Music and Evolution (Ed. O. Vitouch & O. Ladinig), 119–150.

Parncutt, R. (2010). The origins of music: Comparative evaluation of competing theories (talk). International Conference on Music Perception and Cognition (ICMPC11, Seattle, USA, 23–27 August).

Partanen, E., Kujala, T., Näätänen, R., Liitola, A., Sambeth, A., & Huotilainen, M. (2013a). Learning-induced neural plasticity of speech processing before birth. *Proceedings of the National Academy of Sciences*, **110**(37), 15145–15150.

Partanen, E., Kujala, T., Tervaniemi, M., & Huotilainen, M. (2013b). Prenatal music exposure induces long-term neural effects. *PLoS One*, **8**(10), e78946.

Peiper, A. (1925). Sinnesempfindungen des Kinds vor seiner Geburt. *Monatsschrift für Kinderheilkunde*, **29**, 237–241.

Peters, A. J. M., Abrams, R. M., Gerhardt, K. J., & Griffiths, S. K. (1993). Transmission of airborne sound from 50–20,000 Hz into the abdomen of sheep. *Journal of Low Frequency Noise and Vibration*, **12**, 16–24.

Phelps, E. A. (2004). Human emotion and memory: Interactions of the amygdala and hippocampal complex. *Current Opinion in Neurobiology*, **14**(2), 198–202.

Pierson, L. L. (1996). Hazards of noise exposure on fetal hearing. *Seminars in Perinatology*, **20**, 21–29.

Pincus-Knackstedt, M. K., Joachim, R. A., Blois, S. M., Douglas, A. J., Orsal, A. S., Klapp, B. F., Wahn, U., Hamelmann, E., & Arck, P. C. (2006). Prenatal stress enhances susceptibility of murine adult off-spring toward airway inflammation. *Journal of Immunology*, **177**(12), 8484–8492.

Prechtl, H. F. R. (1974). The behavioural states of the newborn infant (a review). *Brain Research*, **76**, 185–212.

Ptok, M., & Ptok, A. (1996). Die Entwicklung des Hörens. *Sprache Stimme Gehör*, **20**, 1–5.

Pujol, R., Lavigne-Rebillard, M., & Uziel, A. (1991). Development of the human cochlea. *Acta Otolaryngologica (Stockholm)*, **482**, 7–12.

Querleu, C., Lefebvre, C., Titran, M., Renard, X., Morillion, M., & Crepin, G. (1984). Réactivité du nouveau né de moins de deux heures de vie à la voix maternelle. *Journal de Gynecologie, Obstetrique et Biologie de la Reproduction*, **13**, 125–134.

Reppert, S. M., & Weaver, D. R. (1988). Maternal transduction of light–dark information for the fetus. In W. P. Smotherman and S. R. Robinson (Eds.), *Behaviour of the fetus* (pp. 119–139). Telford, England: Caldwell.

Richards, D. S., Frentzen, B., Gerhardt, K. J., McCann, M. E., & Abrams, R. M. (1992). Sound levels in the human uterus. *Obstetrics & Gynecology*, **80**, 186–190.

Roediger, H. L. (1990). Implicit memory: Retention without remembering. *American Psychologist*, 45(9), 1043.

Roffwarg, H. A., Muzio, J. N., & Dement, W. C. (1966). Ontogenetic development of the human sleep–dream cycle. *Science*, 152, 604–619.

Rogers, F. B., Rozycki, G. S., Osler, T. M., Shackford, S. R., Jalbert, J., Kirton, O., Scalea, T. et al. (1999). A multi-institutional study of factors associated with fetal death in injured pregnant patients. *Archives of Surgery*, 134, 1274–1277.

Roheim, G. (1932). Animism and religion. *Psychoanalytic Quarterly*, 1, 59–112.

Ronca, A. E., & Alberts, J. R. (2000). Effects of prenatal spaceflight on vestibular responses in neonatal rats. *Journal of Applied Physiology*, 89(6), 2318–2324.

Rubel, E. W., & Ryals, B. M. (1983). Development of the place principle: Acoustic trauma. *Science*, 219, 512–514.

Saffran, J. R. (2002). Constraints on statistical language learning. *Journal of Memory and Language*, 47(1), 172–196.

Saffran, J. R., Loman, M. M., & Robertson, R. R. W. (2000). Infant memory for musical experiences. *Cognition*, 77, B15–B23.

Salk, L. (1962). Mother's heartbeat as an imprinting stimulus. *Transactions of the New York Academy of Sciences*, 24, 121–124.

Sallenbach, W. B. (1993). The intelligent prenate: Paradigms in prenatal learning and bonding. In T. Blum (Ed.), *Prenatal perception, learning, and bonding* (pp. 61–106). Berlin, Germany: Leonardo.

Scherer, K. R. (1986). Vocal expression: Review. *Psychology Bulletin*, 9, 143–165.

Seckl, J. R. (2001). Glucocorticoid programming of the fetus; adult phenotypes and molecular mechanisms. *Molecular and Cellular Endocrinology*, 185, 61–71.

Selton, D., Andre, M., & Hascoet, J. M. (2000). Normal EEG in very premature infants: Reference criteria. *Clinical Neurophysiology*, 111(12), 2116–2124.

Slobodchikov, V. I., & Tsukerman, G. A. (1992). The genesis of reflective consciousness at early school age. *Journal of Russian and East European Psychology*, 30(1), 6–27.

Smith, S. L., Gerhardt, K. J., Griffiths, S. K., Huang, X., & Abrams, R. M. (2003). Intelligibility of sentences recorded from the uterus of a pregnant ewe and from the fetal inner ear. *Audiology & Neurotology*, 8, 347–353.

Sobrian, S. K., Vaughn, V. T., Ashe, W. K., Markovic, B., Djuric, V., & Jankovic, B. D. (1997). Gestational exposure to loud noise alters the development and postnatal responsiveness of humoral and cellular components of the immune system in offspring. *Environmental Research*, 73, 227–241.

Soley, G., & Hannon, E. E. (2010). Infants prefer the musical meter of their own culture: A cross-cultural comparison. *Developmental Psychology*, 46(1), 286.

Sorce, J. F., & Emde, R. N. (1981). Mother's presence is not enough: Effect of emotional availability on infant exploration. *Developmental Psychology*, 17(6), 737–745.

Spelt, D. K. (1948). The conditioning of the human fetus *in utero*. *Journal of Experimental Psychology*, 38, 338–346.

Stefanics, G., Háden, G. P., Sziller, I., Balázs, L., Beke, A., & Winkler, I. (2009). Newborn infants process pitch intervals. *Clinical Neurophysiology*, 120(2), 304–308.

Sternberg, R. J. (1985). *Beyond IQ: A triarchic theory of human intelligence*. Cambridge: Cambridge University Press.

Strongman, K. T. (2003). *The psychology of emotion: From everyday life to theory* (5th ed.). Chichester, West Sussex: Wiley.

Szendre, E. N. (1996). Children's assignment of intentionality to people, animals, plants, and objects: Challenges to theory of mind and animism. *Dissertation Abstracts International, Section B: Sciences and Engineering*, 57(3-B), 2184.

Tafuri, J., & Villa, D. (2002). Musical elements in the vocalisations of infants aged 2–8 months. *British Journal of Music Education, 19*, 73–88.

Todd, N. P., & Cody, F. (2000). Vestibular responses to loud dance music: A physiological basis for the "rock and roll threshold"? *Journal of the Acoustical Society of America, 107*, 496–500.

Trautman P. D., Meyer-Bahlburg, H. F., Postelnek, J., & New, M. I. (1995). Effects of early prenatal dexamethasone on the cognitive and behavioral development of young children: Results of a pilot study. *Psychoneuroendocrinology, 20*, 439–449.

Trehub, S. E. (2003). The developmental origins of musicality. *Nature Neuroscience, 6*, 669–673.

Trehub, S. E., & Nakata, T. (2001–2). Emotion and music in infancy. *Musicae Scientiae* (special issue), 37–61.

Trehub, S. E., Plantinga, J., Brcic, J., & Nowicki, M. (2013). Cross-modal signatures in maternal speech and singing. *Frontiers in Psychology, 4*, 811.

Trehub, S. E., Schneider, B. A., Morrongiello, B. A., & Thorpe, L. A. (1988). Auditory sensitivity in school-age children. *Journal of Experimental Child Psychology, 46*(2), 273–285.

Trevarthen, C. (1979). Communication and cooperation in early infancy: A description of primary intersubjectivity. In M. Bullowa (Ed.), *Before speech: The beginning of interpersonal communication* (pp. 321–347). Cambridge: Cambridge University Press.

Trevarthen, C. (1985). Facial expressions of emotion in mother–infant interaction. *Human Neurobiology, 4*, 21–32.

Tronick, E. Z. (1989). Emotions and emotional communication in infants. *American Psychologist, 44*(2), 112.

Van den Bergh, B. R. H. (1992). Maternal emotions during pregnancy and fetal and neonatal behaviour. In J. G. Nijhuis (Ed.), *Fetal behaviour* (pp. 157–208). Oxford: Oxford University Press.

Van den Bergh, B. R. H., Mulder, E. J. H., Visser, G. H. A., Poelmann-Weesjes, G., Bekedam, D. J., & Prechtl, H. F. R. (1989). The effect of (induced) maternal emotions on fetal behavior: A controlled study. *Early Human Development, 19*, 9–19.

van Heteren, C. F., Boekkooi, P. F., Jongsma, H. W., & Nijhuis, J. G. (2000). Fetal learning and memory. *Lancet, 356*(9236), 1169–1170.

Verny, T. R. (1999). Finding our voice. *Journal of Prenatal and Perinatal Psychology and Health, 13*, 191–200.

Wade, J. (1998). Two voices from the womb: Evidence from a physically transcendent and a cellular source of fetal consciousness. *Journal of Prenatal and Perinatal Psychology and Health, 13*, 123–148.

Wadhwa, P. D., Dunkel-Schetter, C., Chicz DeMet, A., Porto, M., & Sandman, C. A. (1996). Prenatal psychosocial factors and the neuroendocrine axis in human pregnancy. *Psychosomatic Medicine, 58*, 432–446.

Wadhwa, P. D., Glynn, L., Hobel, C. J., Garite, T., Porto, M., ChiczDeMet, A., Wiglesworth, A. K., & Sandman, C. A. (2002). Behavioural perinatology: Biobehavioural processes in human fetal development. *Regulatory Peptides, 108*(2–3), 149–157.

Walsh, S. W., Ducsay, C. A., & Novy, M. J. (1984). Circadian hormonal interactions among the mother, fetus, and amniotic fluid. *American Journal of Obstetrics and Gynecology, 150*, 745–753.

Watanabe, T., Náñez, J. E., & Sasaki, Y. (2001). Perceptual learning without perception. *Nature, 413*(6858), 844–848.

Weinberg, M. K., & Tronick, E. Z. (1998). Emotional characteristics of infants associated with maternal depression and anxiety. *Pediatrics, 102*(5)(Supplement), 1298–1304.

Weinstock, M. (1997). Does prenatal stress impair coping and regulation of hypothalamic–pituitary–adrenal axis? *Neuroscience and Biobehavioral Reviews, 21*, 1–10.

Weiskopf, N., Veit, R., Erb, M., Mathiak, K., Grodd, W., Goebel, R., & Birbaumer, N. (2003). Physiological self-regulation of regional brain activity using real-time functional magnetic resonance imaging (fMRI): Methodology and exemplary data. *NeuroImage, 19*, 577–586.

Welberg, L. A. M., & Seckl, J. R. (2001). Prenatal stress, glucocorticoids, and the programming of the brain. *Journal of Neuroendocrinology*, **13**, 113–128.

Wells, M., Glickauf Hughes, C., & Jones, R. (1999). Codependency: A grass roots construct's relationship to shame-proneness, low self-esteem, and childhood parentification. *American Journal of Family Therapy*, **27**, 63–71.

Whitwell, G. E. (undated). The importance of prenatal sound and music. <https://birthpsychology.com/free-article/importance-prenatal-sound-and-music>. Read on 31.5.2004.

Wightman, F. L., and Kistler, D. J. (1992). The dominant role of low-frequency interaural time differences in sound localization. *Journal of the Acoustical Society of America*, **91**(3), 1648–1661.

Wilkin, P. E. (1995/6). A comparison of fetal and newborn responses to music and sound stimuli with and without daily exposure to a specific piece of music. *Bulletin of the Council of Research in Music Education*, **127**, 163–169.

Williams, J. H. G., Greenhalgh, K. D., & Manning, J. T. (2003). Second to fourth finger ratio and possible precursors of developmental psychopathology in preschool children. *Early Human Development*, **72**, 57–65.

Woodward, C. A. (1999). Medical students' attitudes toward women: Are medical schools microcosms of society? *Canadian Medical Association Journal*, **160**, 347–348.

Wu, W. X., Ma, X. H., Unno, N., & Nathanielsz, P. W. (2001). In vivo evidence for stimulation of placental, myometrial, and endometrial prostaglandin G/H synthase 2 by fetal cortisol replacement after fetal adrenalectomy. *Endocrinology*, **142**(9), 3857–3864.

Wulf, M. (1947). L'mahuta shel haomanut (About the nature of art). *Ofakim*, **4**(3), 2–9.

Yedidia, M. J., & Bickel, J. (2001). Why aren't there more women leaders in academic medicine? The views of clinical department chairs. *Academic Medicine*, **76**, 453–465.

Zeifman, D. M. (2001). An ethological analysis of human infant crying: Answering Tinbergen's four questions. *Developmental Psychobiology*, **39**, 265–285.

Zimmerman, E., Keunen, K., Norton, M., & Lahav, A. (2013). Weight gain velocity in very low-birthweight infants: Effects of exposure to biological maternal sounds. *American Journal of Perinatology*, **30**, 863–870.

Chapter 2

Reflections on infants as musical connoisseurs

Sandra E. Trehub and Franziska Degé

Reflections on infants as musical connoisseurs: Introduction

The term *connoisseur* is generally reserved for experts in matters of taste, especially with reference to the expressive or culinary arts. In the case of music, a connoisseur might be a discerning listener in a narrow or literal sense—having keen perceptual skills—or in a broader, more important sense—distinguishing musical compositions and performances of high quality from those of lesser quality. The latter sense necessitates extensive knowledge of the musical conventions of a particular culture, such knowledge being beyond the reach of inexperienced listeners. How, then, might infants qualify as musical connoisseurs? In our view, their precocious music listening skills, excellent memory for music, highly musical environment, and intense interest in expressive musical performances compensate for their obvious ignorance of musical conventions. In the pages that follow, we summarize scientific evidence in these domains and explore the implications of that evidence.

Methods for assessing the fine-tuning of infant ears

How do researchers establish which aspects of music are perceptible, memorable, and even pleasurable for infant listeners? Infants cannot report what they hear, nor can they follow instructions. Unlike dogs, whose raised earflaps indicate attentive listening, infants generally provide no obvious clues to their perception of auditory events unless those events are very loud or have sudden onset. To circumvent infants' response limitations, researchers develop specialized procedures for discerning what infants hear while minimizing the potential biases of adult observers. With the conditioned head-turning procedure, depicted schematically in Figure 2.1, 6- to 10-month-old infants watch a live puppet show directly in front of them while a repeating musical pattern (e.g., a sequence of five to ten notes) plays in the background from a loudspeaker off to one side (e.g., Trehub, Thorpe, & Morrongiello, 1987). Infants become engrossed in the puppet show, seemingly oblivious to the background music, but their response to subtle changes in the music indicates otherwise. The occurrence of a melodic or rhythmic change typically leads infants to turn spontaneously toward the loudspeaker, presumably to explore the source of the salient sound event. Without an interesting object or event at that locus, infants would not continue responding to the same auditory change. To encourage infants to continue responding, they are rewarded with interesting visual events when they turn promptly to a change. If they turn at other times, there is no consequence or reward. Initially, infants turn as an automatic consequence of their sound localization ability. Once they learn the links between turning at the right time (i.e., immediately after a sound change) and the visual rewards, they maximize the available "entertainment" by

Fig. 2.1 Layout of test room for conditioned head-turn procedure. Infant sits on parent's lap (left side of figure) facing the experimenter (right side of figure), who entertains the infant with puppets. If infants turn to the loudspeaker immediately after a sound change, they receive a visual reward at that locus.

watching the puppet show except when opportunities arise for visual rewards (i.e., after relevant changes in the music). Most 6- to 10-month-old infants learn the rules of this game within a few minutes, at which time they proceed to the test phase, which features trials with musical changes and those without changes. A higher incidence of turning on trials with changes than on those with no changes indicates that infants detect the change under consideration.

With the head-turn preference procedure (e.g., Trainor, 1996), depicted schematically in Figure 2.2, there is no necessity for rule learning. Infants' attention is simply attracted to their left or right side, often by a flashing light at that location. Looking in that direction results in the presentation of one musical pattern (e.g., a melody) until infants look away. Their attention is then attracted to the opposite side, which results in the presentation of a contrasting musical pattern (e.g., a different or altered melody) until infants look away. The procedure continues, with infant listening times to each musical pattern accumulated over successive trials. If infants learn anything in this context, it is that they control the onset and offset of music by their looking behavior. Longer cumulative listening to one pattern, as revealed by relative looking times, reveals differentiation of the patterns. Comparable listening to both patterns is difficult to interpret because it may reflect comparable interest rather than failure to differentiate the patterns.

Many scholars regard differential listening to contrasting musical samples as an index of infants' preferences. For example, longer listening to one of two contrasting performances is presumed to reflect greater preference or liking for that performance (e.g., Masataka, 2006; Trainor & Heinmiller, 1998). It is presumptuous, however, to consider infants' longer listening in such situations to reflect aesthetic preferences that are comparable to adults' explicit judgments of pleasantness (Trehub, 2012). One of two stimuli may evoke greater attention or interest because of its familiarity, novelty, or complexity without implicating aesthetic preferences (Plantinga & Trehub, 2014). In any case, the preference procedure is useful in revealing infants' differentiation of one

Fig. 2.2 Layout of test room for preference procedure. Infant sits on parent's lap, with loudspeakers ahead on either side.

musical pattern from another, especially for infants too young to learn the rules of the conditioned head-turn procedure (e.g., Masataka, 1999, 2006; Plantinga & Trainor, 2009).

Precocious listening skills: Pitch patterns

The use of these techniques has revealed a great deal about infants' listening skills. For example, infants can detect pitch differences of a semitone or less, even when such differences are embedded in a melody (e.g., Trainor & Trehub, 1992; Trehub, Schellenberg, & Kamenetsky, 1999). In essence, infants are sensitive to the smallest meaningful pitch distinctions in music. Although smaller (i.e., microtonal) variations are present in Indian and Arab-Persian music, these variations are considered relevant to intonation rather than pitch structure (Burns, 1999). Music listening is primarily about pitch relations rather than pitch resolution, especially the relations that underlie the functional equivalence of transposed melodies. For example, knowing the tune of *Happy Birthday* means recognizing it regardless of its pitch level. After limited exposure to a melody (e.g., a few repetitions), infants consider transpositions of that melody—all pitches changed, but pitch relations preserved—as equivalent to the original (Trehub, Thorpe, & Morrongiello, 1987). By contrast, they perceive a melody altered by a single note as novel if it changes the melodic contour or pattern of directional changes in pitch (Trehub, Thorpe, & Morrongiello, 1985).

Infants' ability to perceive relational aspects of pitch does not mean that they ignore absolute pitch cues. In some situations, they focus on absolute rather than relative pitch cues (Saffran, 2003; Saffran & Griepentrog, 2001) and in others, on relative pitch cues (Plantinga & Trainor, 2005; Trehub, 2003a). The specific stimuli and task demands influence infants' inclination to attend to absolute or relational cues (Saffran et al., 2005), which is also the case for adults. Although adults typically focus on relative pitch cues in music, which enables them to recognize or reproduce familiar tunes at different pitch levels, they show surprisingly good memory for the pitch level of their favorite pop recordings (Levitin, 1994) and the theme music from their favorite television programs (Schellenberg & Trehub, 2003).

For infant listeners, pitch contour (i.e., successive directional changes in pitch direction) is the most salient feature of a melody, as it is for maternal speech (Fernald, 1991). Even when the melodies to be compared are separated by several seconds, infants notice differences in contour (Chang & Trehub, 1977a). Under certain conditions, they also detect subtle interval changes, most notably when the melodies are consonant (i.e., containing sequential intervals that Western adults consider pleasant-sounding) rather than dissonant (i.e., containing intervals that Western adults consider unpleasant-sounding). For example, infants respond to a single semitone change in the context of melodies based on the major triad (e.g., C-E-G-E-C to C-E-G#-E-C), but not those based on the augmented triad (e.g., C-E-G#-E-C to C-E-G-E-C) (Trainor & Trehub, 1993). They also respond to a semitone change in the context of a repeating perfect fifth sequence (e.g., C-G-C-G-C-G), but not in the context of a repeating tritone (e.g., C-F#-C-F#-C-F#) (Schellenberg & Trehub, 1996). Although processing advantages for consonant *harmonic* (simultaneous) intervals could arise from the manner in which frequencies are represented in our auditory system, such explanations cannot account for the aforementioned advantages for consonant *melodic* intervals (Trainor & Unrau, 2012).

Aside from infants' differentiation of various consonant and dissonant intervals, they also perceive more general qualities that distinguish consonance from dissonance. Like adults, they perceive specific harmonic intervals, or simultaneous tone combinations, as being similar to other harmonic intervals on the basis of conventional consonance or dissonance classifications rather than interval magnitude (Schellenberg & Trainor, 1996). For example, infants and adults perceive the perfect fifth interval (seven semitones) as more similar to the perfect fourth interval (five semitones) than to the tritone (six semitones).

There have been suggestions, moreover, of an innate preference for consonant intervals arising from findings of longer listening to consonant than to dissonant intervals on the part of newborns (Masataka, 2006), 2-month-olds (Trainor, Tsang, & Cheung, 2002), and 6-month-olds (Trainor & Heinmiller, 1998). This perspective has intuitive appeal for Western listeners, but it is inconsistent with the emergence of explicit preferences for consonance (i.e., judgments of liking) at about 9 years of age (Valentine, 1962). It is also inconsistent with a number of other factors, including the influence of musical exposure or training on adults' preferences for consonance (McDermott, Lehr, & Oxenham, 2010; McLachlan et al., 2013), differences in preferences and musical practices in Western music over the centuries (Tenney, 1988), and favorable attitudes toward dissonant sound combinations in several non-Western cultures (Maher, 1976; Vassilakis, 2005). Adding to the uncertainty are recent findings that failed to confirm 6-month-olds' longer listening to consonant than to dissonant musical patterns (Plantinga & Trehub, 2014). Instead, infants' familiarization with consonant or dissonant stimuli immediately before the test phase resulted in longer listening to the familiar patterns, whether consonant or dissonant. These more recent findings from infants, along with the cross-cultural and historical evidence, lend credence to the view that listening dispositions and preferences are influenced by exposure. Regardless of interpretive problems regarding preference or liking, the infant findings indicate differentiation of consonant from dissonant intervals, which has also been demonstrated in European starlings (Hulse, Bernard, & Braaten, 1995), newborn domestic chicks (Chiandetti & Vallortigara, 2011), and Japanese monkeys (Izumi, 2000).

Some adult–infant similarities such as relational pitch processing reflect skills that may be present from birth or shortly thereafter. Undoubtedly, the ultimate skill level will be affected by the quality and extent of musical exposure. In general, musical exposure and training lead to improvement in the detection of contour and interval information (Fujioka et al., 2004). At times, however, naïve music listeners outperform adult listeners who have had long-term exposure to music (Trainor & Trehub, 1992; Trehub, Schellenberg, & Kamenetsky, 1999). For example, Western infants and adults can detect a semitone change in one note of a tonal melody when the changed note is outside the key of the original melody, but infants detect other changes that many adults fail to notice, such as those remaining within the key and implied harmony of the original melody (Trainor & Trehub, 1992). Infants' superiority in this instance stems from their ignorance of culture-specific musical conventions such as key membership and harmony. Musical enculturation proceeds rapidly in some respects and slowly in others, with children exhibiting sensitivity to key membership by 4 or 5 years of age and to implied harmony by about 7 years of age (Corrigall & Trainor, 2014; Trainor & Trehub, 1994).

Unlike Western adults, who are more sensitive to tuning changes in melodies based on familiar scales (e.g., major) than on unfamiliar scales (e.g., Javanese pelog), young Western infants are equally sensitive to changes in Western and non-Western scales (Lynch et al., 1990; Trehub, Schellenberg, & Kamenetsky, 1999). Adults' implicit knowledge of the tonal and harmonic conventions of their culture interferes with their detection of subtle pitch differences in foreign contexts, just as knowledge of their native language interferes with the perception of some foreign speech sounds (Werker & Tees, 1984). By 12 months of age, Western infants show some signs of culture-specific processing of pitch patterns, as indicated by their greater sensitivity to tuning changes in melodies based on the major scale than on the Javanese pelog scale (Lynch & Eilers, 1992).

Precocious listening skills: Rhythmic patterns

When adults listen to music, they group the unfolding auditory events into meaningful chunks, detecting relations among the chunks, and generating expectations about what sounds are likely to follow and when they will occur. There are indications that infants do likewise. For example, 6- and 8-month-old infants group the component tones of auditory patterns on the basis of similarities in pitch, loudness, and timbre, as do 5-year-old children and adults (Fitzgibbons, Pollatsek, & Thomas, 1974; Thorpe et al., 1988; Thorpe & Trehub, 1989). Moreover, 8-month-olds generally perceive a long-duration note as a boundary between groups or phrases (Trainor & Adams, 2000). Infants display sensitivity to musical phrasing by listening longer to a musical piece with a pause added *between* phrases, which maintains the integrity of phrases, than to the same piece with a pause added *within* a phrase, which disrupts the phrasing structure (Jusczyk & Krumhansl, 1993; Krumhansl & Jusczyk, 1990).

Just as infants respond primarily to relative pitch cues, they respond primarily to relative duration cues. Accordingly, they treat sound patterns as equivalent when those patterns have comparable rhythmic groups (e.g., 3–1 or 2–2) despite changes in tempo (Chang & Trehub, 1977b; Lewkowicz, 2003; Trehub & Thorpe, 1989). Nonetheless, they are capable of detecting changes in tempo (Pickens & Bahrick, 1995).

Metrical aspects of rhythm enable adults and children to synchronize their motor behavior (e.g., singing, dancing, clapping) with the music they hear and with others. The universality of synchronized movement to music implies that listeners readily discern the metrical structure. In fact, adults tend to perceive strong–weak patterns even in sequences with no durational cues or accents (Brochard et al., 2003). Infants are also sensitive to metrical cues. For example, 10-month-olds distinguish musical performances that differ only in the performer's intended meter (Palmer, Jungers, & Jusczyk, 2001). After limited exposure to different rhythms that induce the same meter, 7-month-olds listen longer to novel rhythms that induce a novel meter than to novel rhythms that induce the meter heard previously (Hannon & Johnson, 2005).

The presence of metrical variations across cultures makes it possible to explore the consequences of musical exposure on meter perception. Simple duration ratios (1:1 and 2:1) and isochrony (i.e., a uniform underlying pulse) characterize most Western music, but more complex duration ratios and complex meters occur, along with simple meters, in Eastern Europe, South Asia, Africa, and the Middle East (London, 1995). For example, many dance tunes from Bulgaria and Macedonia consist of short and long durations that alternate in a 2:3 ratio. After two minutes of exposure to unfamiliar Balkan or Macedonian tunes, North American adults differentiate variations that disrupt the metrical structure of the original from those that preserve the metrical structure, but only for simple meters (Hannon & Trehub, 2005a). By contrast, 6-month-old Western infants are like Bulgarian and Macedonian adults in differentiating meter-disrupting from meter-preserving variations in complex as well as simple metrical contexts (Hannon & Trehub, 2005a). These findings challenge the widespread belief of innate biases for the simple meters that prevail in Western music. Instead, young infants seem to be relatively flexible in their perception of meter, unlike adults, who tend to assimilate the music they hear into familiar metrical frameworks. Nevertheless, infants exhibit enhanced processing of metric over non-metric (irregular) rhythms (Bergeson & Trehub, 2006; Trehub & Hannon, 2009).

Listening biases for culture-specific meters can emerge after relatively limited exposure to music. As early as 4 months of age, infants listen longer to metrical structures from the local musical culture than to those from a foreign musical culture (Soley & Hannon, 2010). By 12 months of age, Western infants are like their adult counterparts in failing to differentiate meter-preserving from meter-disrupting variations in the context of complex meters, even though they can do so in the context of simple meters (Hannon & Trehub, 2005b). However, after two weeks of daily exposure to music with complex meter, 12-month-olds perform as well on complex meters as on simple meters, but adults show no improvement (Hannon & Trehub, 2005b). It is likely that long-term exposure to the music of a particular culture generates entrenched representations of metrical structure that are somewhat resistant to change.

Entrenched representations may also account for adults' inability to detect subtle pitch changes in unfamiliar musical scales (Lynch & Eilers, 1992; Trehub, Schellenberg, & Kamenetsky, 1999) and some phoneme differences in foreign speech (Werker & Tees, 1984). The available evidence is consistent with greater flexibility in younger than in older brains (Overy et al., 2004; Zatorre, Belin, & Penhune, 2002), which may support greater perceptual flexibility for infants and young children.

Music perception obviously involves interpretation as well as hearing, but it may involve much more. The tendency to move our bodies while listening to music influences how we perceive and remember the music. In the early months of life, parents often rock or bounce infants while singing to them. How do such movements affect infants' perception of the music? When 7-month-old infants hear two minutes of a drum rhythm that is ambiguous because of the absence of intensity or duration accents (Phillips-Silver & Trainor, 2005), their perception is influenced by the pattern of movements that they experience. Infants who are bounced on every second beat subsequently listen longer to the pattern presented in duple meter (intensity accents on every second beat) rather than triple meter (accents on every third beat), and those who are bounced on every third beat listen longer to the version in triple meter. In other words, infants listen longer to the version that matches the previous pattern of bouncing. Merely watching an adult bounce on every second or third beat has no consequences. In short, infants integrate the sounds they hear with the movement they experience, and adults do likewise (Phillips-Silver & Trainor, 2007). In what could be considered a precursor to dance, infants exhibit some rhythmic movement when listening to rhythmic sounds, with their tempo of movement being faster for music with faster tempo (Zentner & Eerola, 2010).

Memory for music

Infants lack the extended listening experience that enables adults to recognize familiar tunes after hearing the first few notes (Dalla Bella, Peretz, & Aronoff, 2003; Filipic, Tillmann, & Bigand, 2010). Nevertheless, they remember complex musical passages after relatively limited exposure. After two weeks of brief daily exposure to portions of a Mozart sonata, infants can distinguish it from an unfamiliar Mozart sonata (Saffran, Loman, & Robertson, 2000). Similarly, a week of exposure to a synthesized rendition of an English folk melody enables 6-month-old infants to distinguish it from a contrasting folk melody (Trainor, Wu, & Tsang, 2004). Nevertheless, 6-month-olds do not respond differently to the melody presented at the original pitch level or at a novel pitch level (Plantinga & Trainor, 2005), which implies that melodic structure is salient in long-term memory but pitch level is not. Like adults, however, infants remember more information from musical performances that are ecologically valid or relevant to their experience. After two weeks of daily exposure to recordings of an unfamiliar, expressively sung lullaby, 7-month-old infants listen longer to the lullaby sung at a novel pitch level, whether higher or lower, than at the original pitch level (Volkova, Trehub, & Schellenberg, 2006). Aspects of the original performance, including its pitch level, seem to be part of infants' long-term representation of expressive vocal music but not synthesized instrumental music. The relative contributions of vocal music, performance expressiveness, and specific musical materials (e.g., lullabies vs. other musical genres) remain unclear.

Neural responses to music: The case of sleeping newborns

The neuroscience of music, a burgeoning field, is shedding light on the neural mechanisms that underlie music processing (Peretz & Zatorre, 2005; Trainor, 2012; Trainor & Unrau, 2012; Zatorre, Chen, & Penhune, 2007), including structural and functional changes in the brain that result from music training (Habib & Besson, 2009; Hyde et al., 2009). One intriguing but perplexing facet of this research involves newborns' electrophysiological responses to musical stimuli. Electrodes placed on the scalp of sleeping newborns can be used to measure differences between responses to standard or recurring musical events and those to deviant or infrequent musical events (e.g., Carral et al., 2005; Virtala et al., 2013). The presumption is that the brain forms transient representations of the recurring musical patterns such that it detects salient changes or mismatched events. Surprisingly, sleeping newborns show distinctive neural responses to changes in interval size (one semitone vs. seven semitones) and pitch direction (ascending vs. descending) regardless of the absolute pitches of component tones (Carral et al., 2005; Stefanics et al., 2009) and to changes in pitch independent of changes in timbre (Háden et al., 2009). These methods have also revealed differentiated responses to consonant vs. dissonant chords and major vs. minor chords (Virtala et al., 2013) and to violations of the beat of rhythmic sound sequences (Winkler et al., 2009).

How can we interpret these seemingly astounding abilities of sleeping newborns? Unquestionably, the newborn brain registers the changes in question, but some caution is clearly warranted (Trehub, 2013). These change-detection responses are automatic, involving perception without awareness, so the very same changes that elicit distinctive neural responses may not elicit behavioral responses in awake, alert infants. In general, adults' mismatch responses to auditory events are correlated with their behavioral responses, but dissociations are sometimes evident. For example, adults with congenital amusia (Peretz, 2001) exhibit substantial deficits in musical pitch processing on a variety of behavioral tasks, but they show neural mismatch responses to very small pitch changes (Moreau, Jolicoeur, & Peretz, 2013; Peretz et al., 2009). In other words, amusic adults have no awareness of some of the pitch changes that their brain registers.

There are further interpretive issues in the findings from sleeping newborns. For example, newborns' apparent sensitivity to pitch invariance in the context of changing timbre (Háden et al., 2009) is inconsistent with adults' difficulty comparing pitches that differ in timbre (Borchert, Micheyl, & Oxenham, 2011). It is also unclear why distinctive neural responses to major and minor chords are evident in sleeping newborns (Virtala et al., 2013) but not in fully awake 13-year-olds (Virtala et al., 2012). Moreover, infants' apparent perception of the invariance of interval size across changes in component pitches (Carral et al., 2005) was evaluated with only two intervals that were highly contrastive in magnitude (one vs. seven semitones) and consonance/dissonance, raising the possibility that infants were responding to cues other than interval identity. Despite these unresolved issues in research with sleeping newborns, the use of neural measures with older infants has provided insights into age-related changes in responsiveness to music, effects of musical exposure, and plasticity of the infant brain (see Trainor, 2012). Neural and behavioral perspectives can complement one another in advancing our understanding of early musical development.

Musical environment of infants

Do infants make use of their exceptional music listening skills in everyday life? They do, indeed. Caregivers around the world—mothers, fathers, grandparents, and siblings—commonly speak to pre-verbal infants. This infant-directed speech differs from conventional, adult-directed speech in its high pitch register, sustained vowels, rhythmicity, repetitiveness, and expanded pitch contours (Cooper, 1997; Fernald, 1991; Papoušek, Papoušek, & Symmes, 1991). The result is quasi-musical speech or sing-song that falls somewhere between speech and music (Corbeil, Trehub, & Peretz, 2013). When speaking to infants, mothers use a small set of individually distinctive pitch patterns or *signature tunes* that are unrelated to conventional musical scales (Bergeson & Trehub, 2007). These distinctive vocal patterns are accompanied by equally distinctive visual gestures. As a result, adults and even 6-month-old infants can match the infant-directed speech of unfamiliar women with silent video renditions of their speech (Trehub et al., 2013). Mothers' multimodal interactions with infants facilitate the sharing of feelings and intentions and the strengthening of interpersonal bonds.

Vocal emotion sharing is unavailable to some deaf caregivers who communicate primarily by sign language. These deaf, signing mothers add expressiveness to their infant-directed communications by increasing the rhythmicity, repetitiveness, and fluidity of their manual gestures (Erting, Prezioso, & O'Grandy Hynes, 1990; Masataka, 1992). The result is graceful, dance-like movements that are visually interesting to deaf infants (Masataka, 1996) and even to hearing infants who have had no previous exposure to sign language (Masataka, 1998).

Regardless of their culture of origin, most infants experience music-like input from the incomprehensible but pleasant-sounding speech of their hearing mother or from the visually pleasing manual gestures of their deaf mother. They also experience "real" music in the form of sung performances by their mother or primary caregiver (Custodero, Britto, & Brooks-Gunn, 2003; Trehub & Trainor, 1998). Except for unusual circumstances involving extreme stress or illness, mothers across cultures sing to their infants in the course of providing routine care (Brakeley, 1950;

Trehub & Schellenberg, 1995; Tucker, 1984), although *what* they sing and *how* they sing differ (Trehub & Trainor, 1998).

Every culture has a dedicated genre of music for infants, which usually includes lullabies and play songs (Trehub & Trainor, 1998; Trehub, Unyk, & Trainor, 1993a). North American mothers typically sing play songs to their infants (Trehub, Hill, & Kamenetsky, 1997), often with accompanying movements (Eckerdal & Merker, 2009), but mothers in more traditional cultures typically sing lullabies (Trehub & Schellenberg, 1995; Trehub & Trainor, 1998). One source of difference in song choice is the widespread (but non-North American) practice of mothers remaining in close physical contact with infants, even during sleep (Morelli et al., 1992; Super & Harkness, 1986). Another source of difference involves divergent conceptions of infants. North American mothers typically provide stimulation aimed at optimizing infant development (LeVine, 1988), including lively songs, speech, and physical play. They expect infants to respond with smiling, laughter, or other overt signs of pleasure. By contrast, mothers in traditional cultures strive for infant contentment, which accounts for their provision of soothing rather than arousing interactions and almost constant physical contact (Toda, Fogel, & Kawai, 1990).

The distinctiveness of infant-directed singing goes beyond the repertoire, or *what* the mother sings, to *how* she sings. When North American mothers sing to their infants, they tend to raise their usual pitch level and decrease their usual tempo (Trainor, 1996; Trainor et al., 1997; Trehub et al., 1997; Trehub, Unyk, & Trainor, 1993b). These maternal adjustments reflect maternal expressiveness, with elevated vocal pitch linked to joyful feelings (Bachorowski & Owren, 1995; Murray & Arnott, 1993) and slow tempo to affection and tenderness (Fonagy & Magdics, 1963). There may be intuitive didactic aspects of maternal sung performances. For example, mothers' expressive variations in dynamics highlight the pitch structure of their songs (Nakata & Trehub, 2011), and their expressive timing variations (Delavenne, Gratier, & Devouche, 2013) emphasize the hierarchical temporal structure (Longhi, 2009). Depressed mothers, unlike their non-depressed counterparts, do not show comparable reductions in tempo in their infant-directed singing, which may reflect their lesser sensitivity to infants' needs (de l'Etoile & Leider, 2011).

Singing in the course of caregiving often extends beyond infancy, providing opportunities for observing age-appropriate tuning of performances. When mothers sing the same song to their infant and preschool child, their renditions are about a semitone higher for infants than for preschoolers, and the lyrics are pronounced more precisely for preschoolers (Bergeson & Trehub, 1999). In general, adult listeners readily distinguish performances for infants from other informal performances, even when they are unfamiliar with the language and culture of the singers (Trehub et al., 1997; Trehub, Unyk, & Trainor, 1993b). The transparency of infant-directed performances arises largely from their warm vocal tone. The mere presence of an infant has emotional consequences for the mother, which, in turn, affects the expressiveness of her spoken or sung communications. Maternal performances are also affected by the interactive context. For example, mothers sing more expressively when their infant is fully in view rather than obscured by an opaque curtain (Trehub, Plantinga, & Russo, 2011). Mothers also smile more when singing to pre-verbal infants than when talking to them (Plantinga, Trehub, & Russo, 2011).

Expressive singing to infants is not exclusive to mothers or to experienced caregivers. Preschool siblings also sing more exuberantly than usual in the presence of their infant siblings (Trehub, Unyk, & Henderson, 1994). Fathers' singing has been more difficult to study because of Western men's self-consciousness about aspects of caregiving. In general, fathers are disinclined to permit observations of their vocal play with infants, in contrast to their public displays of physical play.

In parks and playgrounds, it is common to see fathers tossing infants in the air, much to mothers' chagrin and infants' delight. When fathers do sing, however, they adjust their sung performances for infants much as mothers do, elevating their usual pitch level and slowing their tempo (Trehub et al., 1997). Although mothers tend to sing similarly to infant sons and daughters, fathers often provide more arousing performances for baby boys and more soothing performances for baby girls (Trehub, Hill, & Kamenetsky, 1997).

One intriguing aspect of maternal singing is its stereotypy, which may facilitate infants' recognition of specific songs and singing voices. When mothers sing the same song to their infant on different occasions, their renditions are nearly identical in pitch level and tempo (Bergeson & Trehub, 2002) so long as the infant is comparably content. Not surprisingly, changes in infant state are typically accompanied by appropriate adjustments in singing style, with soothing renditions offered for sleepy infants and lively renditions for alert, playful infants.

Aside from live expressive performances from parents (Trehub et al., 1997) or siblings (Trehub, Unyk, & Henderson, 1994), infants are increasingly experiencing other kinds of music. For example, contemporary parents expose their infants to musical toys, commercial audio recordings, audio-visual recordings, and television programs that target infant audiences (Young, 2008). Moreover, infants overhear some of the recorded music intended for parents or siblings. In general, infants receive musical or quasi-musical input (e.g., infant-directed speech) for much of their waking time. In contrast to the recorded music that dominates adults' experience, live, improvised performances still dominate the experience of most infants (Custodero, Britto, & Brooks-Gunn, 2003). In a sense, mothers function as infants' first musical mentors. Their singing may not meet professional standards of tuning or timing, but it is unsurpassed in its warmth and meaning for the intended listener.

Responsiveness to infant-directed speech and song

Infants respond to infant-directed speech with greater attentiveness and more positive affect than they accord to adult-directed speech (Cooper, 1997; Fernald, 1991; Werker, Pegg, & McLeod, 1994). The various aspects of maternal speech that attract and maintain infants' attention have not been established definitively. Maternal speech has a larger pitch range and greater dynamic range (whisper to loud) than ordinary adult speech, which undoubtedly contribute to its expressiveness. There are indications, however, that the emotional expressiveness of maternal speech, especially its happy-sounding quality, is highly engaging for infants (Singh, Morgan, & Best, 2002). Emotional expressiveness may also account for infants' greater interest in infant-directed over adult-directed sign language (Masataka, 1996), even for hearing infants with no prior exposure to sign language (Masataka, 1998).

Infants also listen longer to infant-directed singing than to other styles of informal singing in the newborn period (Masataka, 1999) and at 6 months of age (Trainor, 1996). The elevated pitch level of maternal singing may add to its engaging quality for infants. For example, infants listen longer to higher-pitched versions of the same song performed by the same singer (O'Neill, Trainor, & Trehub, 2001; Trainor & Zacharias, 1998), but their choice of higher-pitched singing is largely restricted to lively performances. For lullabies sung at a slow tempo, infants listen longer to lower- than to higher-pitched versions (Tsang & Conrad, 2010; Volkova, Trehub, & Schellenberg, 2006). Perhaps infants are responsive to the more expressive of two performances, which would account for their choice of higher-pitched play songs and lower-pitched lullabies. As noted, the happy-sounding quality of adult vocalizations is engaging to infant listeners (Singh, Morgan, & Best, 2002). When given a choice of speech or singing, infants listen longer to the happier-sounding stimulus regardless of its status as speech or song (Corbeil, Trehub, & Peretz, 2013).

For audio-visual performances of their own mothers' speech and singing, 6-month-old infants show more sustained interest in singing than in speech (Nakata & Trehub, 2004). During the sung performances, infants exhibit dramatic reductions in movement, and they stare at their mother's on-screen image for extended periods. Audio-visual samples of maternal speech are also engaging, but they are not nearly as engaging as are the singing samples. Maternal singing is particularly effective in regulating infant arousal, as reflected in changing levels of a stress-related hormone (cortisol) that is measurable in infants' saliva (Shenfield, Trehub, & Nakata, 2003). For infants with slightly elevated arousal levels, maternal singing promotes subtle decreases in arousal. For those with lower arousal levels, maternal singing promotes subtle increases in arousal. Presumably, an important function of maternal singing is to optimize infant arousal or mood. The arousal-modulating consequences of music may account for its increasing use in neonatal intensive care (Cassidy & Standley, 1995; Lorch et al., 1994).

Studies of infants' responsiveness to speech and singing have typically focused on awake, alert infants (e.g., Corbeil, Trehub, & Peretz, 2013; Nakata & Trehub, 2004). What about infants who are distressed rather than content? When mothers attempt to relieve the acute distress of their 10-month-old infants, multimodal singing (i.e., singing accompanied by face-to-face contact and touch) has considerably greater efficacy than does multimodal speech (Ghazban, 2013). Specifically, such singing reduces infant skin conductance levels, which index arousal, as well as negative facial and vocal expressions. Surprisingly, play songs are more effective than lullabies at alleviating infant distress, either because of the distracting effects of lively, rhythmic singing or because of Western infants' greater familiarity with play songs.

Early musical enculturation

The aforementioned evidence is consistent with claims of infant musical precocity (Trehub, 2000, 2003b). Well before their first birthday, infants discern subtle melodic and rhythmic distinctions in music, whether that music originates from their musical culture-to-be or from another musical culture (Hannon & Trehub, 2005a; Lynch et al., 1990). They link the sounds that they hear to the movements that they feel, with implications for their perception of musical rhythm (Phillips-Silver & Trainor, 2005). In some situations, infants' music perception skills outstrip those of adults (Hannon & Trehub, 2005a; Trehub, Schellenberg, & Kamenetsky, 1999), especially when novel or unusual music is involved. Infants' relative inexperience may generate a kind of open-mindedness that enables them to notice subtle distinctions that are missed by experienced or expert listeners. The duration of this window of perceptual flexibility remains unclear. What is clear is that the process of musical enculturation begins much earlier than previously thought (Cuddy & Badertscher, 1987; Krumhansl, 1990), as evidenced by culture-specific metrical processing biases and pitch processing biases by 12 months of age (Hannon & Trehub, 2005b; Lynch & Eilers, 1992). One important difference in the musical biases of 12-month-olds and adults is their apparent ease of reversibility in the case of infants. Undoubtedly, adults are likely to learn the subtleties of complex Balkan meters with sufficient exposure, but such learning is impeded by their entrenched knowledge, albeit implicit, of Western metrical structure. Perhaps dancing or moving to novel music would facilitate adults' acquisition of its metrical structure, as it does for infants (Phillips-Silver & Trainor, 2005). An important challenge for future research is to identify the ways in which familiarity with the music of one's culture assists and impedes the acquisition of skills and structures relevant to other musical cultures.

Beyond the precocious perceptual skills that characterize the early months of life is infants' incredible interest in music. Although mothers are seemingly unaware of infants' musical abilities, they intuitively provide them with a daily diet of live, expressive performances—simple songs that are playful or soothing. Infants react with rapt attention, which is likely to encourage maternal encores. Regardless of their ignorance of culture-specific musical conventions and ideals, infants qualify as culture-general connoisseurs of music on the basis of their keen music perception skills, their interest in music, and their ease of learning. It is not unreasonable to regard them as musical prodigies, who become the protégés of their adoring caregivers. For their part, caregivers indulge infants with intimate musical performances that enhance their overall well-being and nurture their interest in music.

Little is known about the course of perceptual development or about the "natural" musical environment in the years between infancy and school entry. Research in that period has focused largely on production skills (e.g., Flowers & Dunne-Sousa, 1988; Gérard & Drake, 1990) and, increasingly, on the non-musical benefits of music training (Moreno et al., 2011; Rauscher & Zupan, 2000). Preschoolers' music perception skills undoubtedly exceed those of 12-month-olds in various respects, but some aspects of musical enculturation proceed slowly (Trainor & Hannon, 2013). For example, children's understanding of implied harmony (Corrigall & Trainor, 2010, 2014; Trainor & Trehub, 1994) and the tonal hierarchy (Krumhansl & Keil, 1982) is limited until about 7 years of age, and this knowledge continues to be refined for several years (Costa-Giomi, 2003; Lamont & Cross, 1994). Nevertheless, preschoolers outdo older children in their unbridled enthusiasm for music, which is apparent in the spontaneity and inventiveness of their chants and songs in playgrounds throughout the world (Kartomi, 1980; Marsh, 2008; Opie & Opie, 1969). Perhaps their relative freedom from the constraints of social conventions contributes to their inventiveness (Gardner, Phelps, & Wolf, 1990).

Early music training

Increasing awareness of infants' perceptual capabilities and enthusiasm for music is prompting many educators to advocate systematic exposure to *good* music and *appropriate* musical activities as early as possible (Feierabend, 1996; Gordon, 1996; Tafuri, 2009). In their view, musical aptitude should be nurtured by guided listening, guided movement to music, and guided music-making. Many parents are responding to these appeals for early music training, in some instances for the anticipated musical consequences and in others for the cognitive consequences that are often heralded in the popular media (see Adachi & Trehub, 2012). Despite the absence of scientific support for long-range musical or non-musical benefits of *very early* training, music programs for infants and toddlers are increasing in number and popularity. Some of these programs provide positive experiences for parents, including opportunities for meeting other parents, revitalizing adults' joy in music-making, and increasing their repertoire of children's songs and games. Other programs may be misguided in their attempt to replace parents' intuitive, playful approach to music with prescriptions for "proper" music and activities. Perhaps educators have important lessons to learn from the informal and sensitive musical mentoring that many parents provide for their infants and toddlers.

Music educators' promotion of very early instruction implies a critical or sensitive period during which music training has unique benefits. To date, the only music-related skill that is known to depend on early music training (before 6 years of age) is *absolute pitch* (Takeuchi & Hulse, 1993; Trainor, 2005). Adult musicians with absolute pitch typically began music lessons before 6 years of age, but most musicians with comparable early training do not have absolute pitch, which suggests that genetic predispositions are also implicated (Baharloo et al., 1998). Although absolute pitch is often regarded as a sign of musical giftedness, its value may be overrated. The essence of music involves relative aspects of pitch and timing, and there are indications that musicians with absolute pitch are poorer at relative pitch processing than are musicians without absolute pitch (Miyazaki, 1995). Sensorimotor integration (e.g., synchronized tapping to auditory rhythms) is thought to be enhanced by early music training, as reflected in better synchronization to sound and better rhythm reproduction for musicians whose lessons began before 7 years of age rather than later (Penhune, 2011). Because the age of onset of music training is not random but determined instead by a variety of factors that may affect long-term outcomes, it is impossible to conclude that early music lessons *cause* the later timing advantages.

The proliferation of parent–infant music programs also poses problems for the assessment of outcomes. Although there are numerous claims about the benefits of such programs, as indicated by better outcomes for infants who participate over those who do not (e.g., Gerry, Faux, & Trainor, 2010; Tafuri, 2009), parents of participating and non-participating infants are likely to differ in a number of respects, as do parents whose children take music lessons and those whose children do not (Schellenberg, 2011). Claims that the musical interventions *cause* or promote differential outcomes necessitate random assignment to programs. In one study that involved random assignment of parents and their 6-month-old infants to two programs that met weekly for six months, infants who completed a Suzuki program involving active music engagement (e.g., moving to expressive music, singing, repetition, at-home continuation of program activities) showed greater sensitivity to tonality at program completion than those who completed a program featuring passive musical exposure (e.g., synthesized recordings as background music during play activities) (Gerry, Unrau, & Trainor, 2012). It is possible that active music programs exert their primary effects on parents, who subsequently alter infants' at-home musical experiences. It is also possible that such differences in systematic exposure to music in infancy merely accelerate the appearance of some musical skills relative to the usual course of musical enculturation.

It remains to be determined whether formal musical exposure or training beginning in infancy or in the preschool period promotes higher levels of ultimate musical achievement or engagement than would otherwise be the case. There are indications that a supportive early home environment, one that encourages spontaneous expressiveness, is especially important for optimizing musical achievement (Manturzewska, 1990; Moore, Burland, & Davidson, 2003). A home environment of that nature is also likely to optimize social and emotional development. The challenge for music educators is to sustain the joy of music and the musical creativity that are so clearly evident in the years that precede formal musical instruction.

Summing up

Infants readily meet the criteria for musical connoisseurship, as defined in this chapter. Their ability to perceive pitch and rhythmic patterns provides them with a broad but firm foundation for musical enculturation. Such enculturation begins in the prenatal period (Parncutt, Chapter 1; Ullal-Gupta et al., 2013), continuing through infancy and into the school years. Infants remember some of the music that they hear, especially the music heard frequently. Their listening choices are often influenced by exposure, but some choices, especially those involving emotive vocal performances, may be independent of exposure. Fortunately, caregivers satisfy infants' intense interest in expressive music by singing and talking melodiously to them. In so doing, caregivers nurture their children's enduring love of music.

Reflective questions

1 Is it possible to assess infants' taste in music, for example, which musical selections they like and which they dislike?
2 Music from various cultures differs in its pitch patterning. Why, then, do infants exhibit perceptual advantages for melodies based on the major triad?
3 There are suggestions that infants recognize the rhythms of their native language-to-be before they recognize other aspects of language. Is it likely that musical rhythms have priority over pitch patterns in early infancy?
4 What can we learn from responses to music that are measurable in the brains of human newborns?
5 How early should music training begin if the goal is a) to promote overall well-being or b) to maximize long-term musical achievement?

Reference list

Adachi, M., & Trehub, S. E. (2012). Musical lives of infants. In G. McPherson & G. Welch (Eds.), *Oxford handbook of music education* (pp. 229–47). Oxford: Oxford University Press.

Bachorowski, J. A., & Owren, M. J. (1995). Vocal expression of emotion: Acoustical properties of speech are associated with emotional intensity and context. *Psychological Science*, **6**, 219–24.

Baharloo, S., Johnston, P. A., Service, S. K., Gitschier, J., & Freimer, N. B. (1998). Absolute pitch: An approach for identification of genetic and nongenetic components. *American Journal of Human Genetics*, **62**, 224–31.

Bergeson, T. R., & Trehub, S. E. (1999). Mothers' singing to infants and preschool children. *Infant Behavior and Development*, **22**, 51–64.

Bergeson, T. R., & Trehub, S. E. (2002). Absolute pitch and tempo in mothers' songs to infants. *Psychological Science*, **13**, 72–5.

Bergeson, T. R., & Trehub, S. E. (2006). Infants' perception of rhythmic patterns. *Music Perception*, **23**, 345–60.

Bergeson, T. R., & Trehub, S. E. (2007). Signature tunes in mothers' speech to infants. *Infant Behavior and Development*, **30**, 648–654.

Borchert, E. M. O., Micheyl, C., & Oxenham, A. J. (2011). Perceptual grouping affects pitch judgments across time and frequency. *Journal of Experimental Psychology: Human Perception and Performance*, **37**, 257–69.

Brakeley, T. C. (1950). Lullaby. In M. Leach & J. Fried (Eds.), *Standard dictionary of folklore, mythology, and legend* (pp. 653–4). New York: Funk & Wagnalls.

Brochard, R., Abecasis, D., Potter, D., Ragot, R., and Drake, C. (2003). The "ticktock" of our internal clock: Direct brain evidence of subjective accents in isochronous sequences. *Psychological Science*, **14**, 362–6.

Burns, E. M. (1999). Intervals, scales, and tuning. In D. Deutsch (Ed.), *The psychology of music* (pp. 215–64). San Diego: Academic Press.

Carral, V., Huotilainen, M., Ruusuvirta, T., Fellman, V., Näätänen, R., & Escera, C. (2005). A kind of auditory "primitive intelligence" already present at birth. *European Journal of Neuroscience*, **21**, 3201–4.

Cassidy, J. W., & Standley, J. M. (1995). The effect of music listening on physiological responses of premature infants in the NICU. *Journal of Music Therapy*, **32**, 208–27.

Chang, H. W., & Trehub, S. E. (1977a). Auditory processing of relational information by young infants. *Journal of Experimental Child Psychology*, **24**, 324–31.

Chang, H. W., & Trehub, S. E. (1977b). Infants' perception of temporal grouping in auditory patterns. *Child Development*, **48**, 1666–70.

Chiandetti, C., & Vallortigara, G. (2011). Chicks like consonant music. *Psychological Science*, **22**, 1270–3.

Cooper, R. P. (1997). An ecological approach to infants' perception of intonation contours as meaningful aspects of speech. In C. Dent-Read & P. Zukow-Goldring (Eds.), *Evolving explanations of development: Ecological approaches to organism–environment systems* (pp. 55–85). Washington, D.C.: American Psychological Association.

Corbeil, M., Trehub, S. E., & Peretz, I. (2013). Infants prefer speech to singing only when speech sounds happier. *Frontiers in Psychology*, **4**, 372.

Corrigall, K. A., & Trainor, L. J. (2010). Musical enculturation in preschool children: Acquisition of key and harmonic knowledge. *Music Perception*, **28**, 195–200.

Corrigall, K. A., & Trainor, L. J. (2014). Enculturation to musical pitch structure in young children: Evidence from behavioral and electrophysiological measures. *Developmental Science*, **17**, 142–58.

Costa-Giomi, E. (2003). Young children's harmonic perception. *Annals of the New York Academy of Sciences*, **999**, 477–84.

Cuddy, L. L., & Badertscher, B. (1987). Recovery of the tonal hierarchy: Some comparisons across age and levels of musical experience. *Perception and Psychophysics*, **41**, 609–20.

Custodero, L. A., Britto, P. R., & Brooks-Gunn, J. (2003). Musical lives: A collective portrait of American parents and their young children. *Journal of Applied Developmental Psychology*, **24**, 553–72.

Dalla Bella, S., Peretz, I., & Aronoff, N. (2003). Time course of melody recognition: A gating paradigm study. *Perception and Psychophysics*, **65**, 1019–28.

Delavenne, A., Gratier, M., & Devouche, E. (2013). Expressive timing in infant-directed singing between 3 and 6 months. *Infant Behavior and Development*, **36**, 1–13.

de l'Etoile, S. K., & Leider, C. N. (2011). Acoustic parameters of infant-directed singing in mothers with depressive symptoms. *Infant Behavior and Development*, **34**, 248–56.

Eckerdal, P., & Merker, B. (2009). Music and the "action song" in infant development: An interpretation. In S. Malloch & C. Trevarthen (Eds.), *Communicative musicality: Exploring the basis of human companionship* (pp. 241–61). New York: Oxford University Press.

Erting, C. J., Prezioso, C., & O'Grandy Hynes, M. (1990). The interactional context of deaf mother–infant communication. In V. Volterra & C. J. Erting (Eds.), *From gesture to language in hearing and deaf children* (pp. 97–106). Berlin: Springer.

Feierabend, J. M. (1996). Music and movement for infants and toddlers: Naturally wonder-full. *Early Childhood Connections*, **2**, 19–26.

Fernald, A. (1991). Prosody in speech to children: Prelinguistic and linguistic functions. *Annals of Child Development*, **8**, 43–80.

Filipic, S., Tillmann, B., & Bigand, E. (2010). Judging familiarity and emotion from very brief musical excerpts. *Psychonomic Bulletin and Review*, **17**, 335–41.

Fitzgibbons, P. J., Pollatsek, A., & Thomas, I. B. (1974). Detection of temporal gaps within and between perceptual tonal groups. *Perception and Psychophysics*, **16**, 522–8.

Flowers, P. J., & Dunne-Sousa, D. (1988). Pitch-pattern accuracy, tonality, and vocal range in preschool children's singing. *Journal of Research in Music Education*, **38**, 102–14.

Fonagy, I., & Magdics, K. (1963). Emotional patterns in intonation and music. *Zeitschrift für Phonetik*, **16**, 293–326.

Fujioka, T., Trainor, L. J., Ross, B., Kakigi, R., & Pantev, C. (2004). Musical training enhances automatic encoding of melodic contour and interval structure. *Journal of Cognitive Neuroscience*, **16**(6), 1010–21.

Gardner, H., Phelps, E., & Wolf, D. P. (1990). The roots of adult creativity in children's symbolic products. In C. N. Alexander & E. J. Langer (Eds.), *Higher stages of human development: Perspectives on adult growth* (pp. 79–96). London: Oxford University Press.

Gérard, C., & Drake, C. (1990). The inability of young children to reproduce intensity differences in musical rhythms. *Perception and Psychophysics*, **48**, 91–101.

Gerry, D. W., Faux, A. L., & Trainor, L. J. (2010). Effects of Kindermusik training on infants' rhythmic enculturation. *Developmental Science, 13*, 545–51.

Gerry, D. W., Unrau, A., & Trainor, L. J. (2012). Active music classes in infancy enhance musical, communicative, and social development. *Developmental Science, 15*, 398–407.

Ghazban, N. (2013). Emotion regulation in infants using maternal singing and speech (Unpublished doctoral dissertation). Ryerson University, Toronto, Canada.

Gordon, E. E. (1996). Music aptitude and music achievement. *Early Childhood Connections, 2*, 11–13.

Habib, M., & Besson, M. (2009). What do music training and musical experience teach us about brain plasticity? *Music Perception, 26*, 279–85.

Háden, G. P., Stefanics, G., Vestergaard, M. D., Denham, S. L., Sziller, I., & Winkler, I. (2009). Timbre-independent extraction of pitch in newborn infants. *Psychophysiology, 46*, 69–74.

Hannon, E. E., & Johnson, S. P. (2005). Infants use meter to categorize rhythms and melodies: Implications for musical structure learning. *Cognitive Psychology, 50*, 354–77.

Hannon, E. E., & Trehub, S. E. (2005a). Metrical categories in infancy and adulthood. *Psychological Science, 16*, 48–55.

Hannon, E. E., & Trehub, S. E. (2005b). Tuning in to musical rhythms: Infants learn more readily than adults. *Proceedings of the National Academy of Sciences, 102*, 12639–43.

Hulse, S. H., Bernard, D. J., & Braaten, R. F. (1995). Auditory discrimination of chord-based spectral structures by European starlings. *Journal of Experimental Psychology: General, 129*, 409–23.

Hyde, K. L., Lerch, J., Norton, A., Foregard, M., Winner, E., Evans, A. C., & Schlaug, G. (2009). Musical training shapes structural brain development. *Journal of Neuroscience, 29*, 3019–25.

Izumi, A. (2000). Japanese monkeys perceive sensory consonance of chords. *Journal of the Acoustical Society of America, 108*, 3073–8.

Jusczyk, P. W., & Krumhansl, C. L. (1993). Pitch and rhythmic patterns affecting infants' sensitivity to musical phrase structure. *Journal of Experimental Psychology: Human Perception and Performance, 19*, 627–40.

Kartomi, M. J. (1980). Childlikeness in play songs—a case study among the Pitjantjara at Yalata, South Australia. *Miscellanea Musicologica, 11*, 172–214.

Krumhansl, C. L. (1990). *Cognitive foundations of musical pitch*. New York: Oxford University Press.

Krumhansl, C. L., & Jusczyk, P. W. (1990). Infants' perception of phrase structure in music. *Psychological Science, 1*, 70–3.

Krumhansl, C. L., & Keil, F. C. (1982). Acquisition of the hierarchy of tonal functions in music. *Memory and Cognition, 10*, 243–51.

Lamont, A., & Cross, I. (1994). Children's cognitive representations of musical pitch. *Music Perception, 12*, 27–55.

LeVine, R. A. (1988). Human parental care: Universal goals, cultural strategies, individual behavior. *New Directions in Child Development, 40*, 3–12.

Levitin, D. (1994). Absolute memory for musical pitch: Evidence from the production of learned melodies. *Perception and Psychophysics, 56*, 414–23.

Lewkowicz, D. J. (2003). Learning and discrimination of audiovisual events in human infants: The hierarchical relation between intersensory temporal synchrony and rhythmic pattern cues. *Developmental Psychology, 39*, 795–804.

London, J. (1995). Some examples of complex meters and their implications for models of metric perception. *Music Perception, 13*, 59–77.

Longhi, E. (2009). "Songese": Maternal structuring of musical interaction with infants. *Psychology of Music, 37*, 195–213.

Lorch, C. A., Lorch, V., Diefendorf, A. O., & Earl, P. W. (1994). Effect of stimulative and sedative music on systolic blood pressure, heart rate, and respiratory rate in premature infants. *Journal of Music Therapy, 31*, 105–18.

Lynch, M. P., & Eilers, R. E. (1992). A study of perceptual development for musical tuning. *Perception and Psychophysics*, **52**, 599–608.

Lynch, M. P., Eilers, R. E., Oller, D. K., & Urbano, R. C. (1990). Innateness, experience, and music perception. *Psychological Science*, **1**, 272–6.

Maher, T. E. (1976). "Need for resolution" ratings for harmonic musical intervals: A comparison between Indians and Canadians. *Journal of Cross-Cultural Psychology*, **7**, 259–76.

Manturzewska, M. (1990). A biographical study of the life-span development of professional musicians. *Psychology of Music*, **18**, 112–39.

Marsh, K. (2008). *The musical playground: Global tradition and change in children's songs and games.* Oxford: Oxford University Press.

Masataka, N. (1992). Motherese in a signed language. *Infant Behavior and Development*, **15**, 453–60.

Masataka, N. (1996). Perception of motherese in a signed language by 6-month-old deaf infants. *Developmental Psychology*, **32**, 874–9.

Masataka, N. (1998). Perception of motherese in Japanese sign language by 6-month-old hearing infants. *Developmental Psychology*, **34**, 241–6.

Masataka, N. (1999). Preference for infant-directed singing in 2-day-old hearing infants of deaf parents. *Developmental Psychology*, **35**, 1001–5.

Masataka, N. (2006). Preference for consonance over dissonance by hearing newborns of deaf parents and of hearing parents. *Developmental Science*, **9**, 46–50.

McDermott, J. H., Lehr, A. J., & Oxenham, A. J. (2010). Individual differences reveal the basis of consonance. *Current Biology*, **20**, 1035–41.

McLachlan, N., Marco, D., Light, M., & Wilson, S. (2013). Consonance and pitch. *Journal of Experimental Psychology: General*, **142**, 1142–58.

Miyazaki, K. (1995). Perception of relative pitch with different references: Some absolute-pitch listeners can't tell musical interval names. *Perception and Psychophysics*, **57**, 962–70.

Moore, D. G., Burland, K., & Davidson, J. W. (2003). The social context of musical success: A developmental account. *British Journal of Psychology*, **94**, 529–49.

Moreau, P., Jolicoeur, P., & Peretz, I. (2013). Pitch discrimination without awareness in congenital amusia: Evidence from event-related potentials. *Brain and Cognition*, **81**, 337–44.

Morelli, G. A., Rogoff, B., Oppenheim, D., & Goldsmith, D. (1992). Cultural variation in infants' sleeping arrangements: Questions of independence. *Developmental Psychology*, **28**, 604–13.

Moreno, S., Bialystok, E., Barac, R., Schellenberg, E. G., Cepeda, N. J., & Chau, T. (2011). Short-term music training enhances verbal intelligence and executive function. *Psychological Science*, **22**, 1425–33.

Murray, I. R., & Arnott, J. L. (1993). Toward the simulation of emotion in synthetic speech: A review of the literature on human vocal emotion. *Journal of the Acoustical Society of America*, **93**, 1097–108.

Nakata, T., & Trehub, S. E. (2004). Infants' responsiveness to maternal speech and singing. *Infant Behavior and Development*, **27**, 455–64.

Nakata, T., & Trehub, S. E. (2011). Expressive timing and dynamics in infant-directed singing. *Psychomusicology: Music, Mind, and Brain*, **21**, 45–53.

O'Neill, C., Trainor, L. J., & Trehub, S. E. (2001). Infants' responsiveness to fathers' singing. *Music Perception*, **18**, 409–25.

Opie, I., and Opie, P. (1969). *Children's games in the street and playground.* Oxford: Clarendon Press.

Overy, K., Norton, A. C., Cronin, K. T., Gaab, N., Alsop, D. C., Winner, E., & Schlaug, G. (2004). Imaging melody and rhythm processing in young children. *NeuroReport*, **15**, 1723–6.

Palmer, C., Jungers, M. K., & Jusczyk, P. W. (2001). Episodic memory for musical prosody. *Journal of Memory and Language*, **45**, 526–45.

Papoušek, M., Papoušek, H., & Symmes, D. (1991). The meanings of melodies in motherese in tone and stress languages. *Infant Behavior and Development*, **14**, 415–40.

Penhune, V. B. (2011). Sensitive periods in musical development: Evidence from musical training. *Cortex,* **47,** 1126–37.

Peretz, I. (2001). Brain specialization for music. New evidence from congenital amusia. *Annals of the New York Academy of Sciences,* **930,** 153–65.

Peretz, I., Brattico, E., Jarvenpaa, M., & Tervaniemi, M. (2009). The amusic brain: In tune, out of key, and unaware. *Brain,* **132,** 1277–86.

Peretz, I., & Zatorre, R. (2005). Brain organization for music processing. *Annual Review of Psychology,* **56,** 89–114.

Phillips-Silver, J., & Trainor, L. J. (2005). Feeling the beat: Movement influences infant rhythm perception. *Science,* **308,** 1430.

Phillips-Silver, J., & Trainor, L. J. (2007). Hearing what the body feels: Auditory encoding of rhythmic movement. *Cognition,* **195,** 533–46.

Pickens, J., & Bahrick, L. E. (1995). Infants' discrimination of bimodal events on the basis of rhythm and tempo. *British Journal of Developmental Psychology,* **13,** 223–36.

Plantinga, J., & Trainor, L. J. (2005). Memory for melody: Infants use a relative pitch code. *Cognition,* **98,** 1–11.

Plantinga, J., & Trainor, L. J. (2009). Melody recognition by two-month-old infants. *Journal of the Acoustical Society of America,* **125,** EL58–62.

Plantinga, J., & Trehub, S. E. (2014). Revisiting the innate preference for consonance. *Journal of Experimental Psychology: Human Perception and Performance,* **40,** 40–9.

Plantinga, J., Trehub, S. E., & Russo, F. (2011, June). Multimodal aspects of maternal speech and singing. *Presented at the Neurosciences and Music IV,* Edinburgh, Scotland.

Rauscher, F. H., & Zupan, M. A. (2000). Classroom keyboard instruction improves kindergarten children's spatial–temporal performance: A field experiment. *Early Childhood Research Quarterly,* **15,** 215–28.

Saffran, J. R. (2003). Absolute pitch in infancy and adulthood: The role of tonal structure. *Developmental Science,* **6,** 35–43.

Saffran, J. R., & Griepentrog, G. J. (2001). Absolute pitch in infant auditory learning: Evidence for developmental reorganization. *Developmental Psychology,* **37,** 74–85.

Saffran, J. R., Loman, M. M., & Robertson, R. R. W. (2000). Infant memory for musical experiences. *Cognition,* **77,** B15–B23.

Saffran, J. R., Reeck, K., Niebuhr, A., & Wilson, D. (2005). Changing the tune: The structure of the input affects infants' use of absolute and relative pitch. *Developmental Science,* **8,** 1–7.

Schellenberg, E. G. (2011). Examining the association between music lessons and intelligence. *British Journal of Psychology,* **102,** 283–302.

Schellenberg, E. G., & Trainor, L. J. (1996). Sensory consonance and the perceptual similarity of complex-tone harmonic intervals: Tests of adult and infant listeners. *Journal of the Acoustical Society of America,* **100,** 3321–8.

Schellenberg, E. G., & Trehub, S. E. (1996). Natural musical intervals: Evidence from infant listeners. *Psychological Science,* **7,** 272–7.

Schellenberg, E. G., & Trehub, S. E. (2003). Good pitch memory is widespread. *Psychological Science,* **14,** 262–6.

Shenfield, T., Trehub, S. E., & Nakata, T. (2003). Maternal singing modulates infant arousal. *Psychology of Music,* **31,** 365–75.

Singh, L., Morgan, J. L., & Best, C. T. (2002). Infants' listening preferences: Baby talk or happy talk? *Infancy,* **3,** 365–94.

Soley, G., & Hannon, E. E. (2010). Infants prefer the musical meter of their own culture: A cross-cultural comparison. *Developmental Psychology,* **46,** 286–92.

Stefanics, G., Háden, G. P., Sziller, I., Balázs, L., Beke, A., & Winkler, I. (2009). Newborn infants process pitch intervals. *Clinical Neurophysiology*, **120**, 304–8.

Super, C. M., & Harkness, S. (1986). The developmental niche: A conceptualization at the interface of child and culture. *International Journal of Behavioral Development*, **9**, 545–69.

Tafuri, J. (2009). *Infant musicality: New research for educators and parents*. Farnham, UK: SEMPRE/ Ashgate.

Takeuchi, A. H., & Hulse, S. H. (1993). Absolute pitch. *Psychological Bulletin*, **113**, 345–61.

Tenney, J. (1988). *A history of consonance and dissonance*. New York: Excelsior Music.

Thorpe, L. A., & Trehub, S. E. (1989). Duration illusion and auditory grouping in infancy. *Developmental Psychology*, **25**, 122–7.

Thorpe, L. A., Trehub, S. E., Morrongiello, B. A., & Bull, D. (1988). Perceptual grouping by infants and preschool children. *Developmental Psychology*, **24**, 484–91.

Toda, S., Fogel, A., & Kawai, M. (1990). Maternal speech to three-month-old infants in the United States and Japan. *Journal of Child Language*, **17**, 279–94.

Trainor, L. J. (1996). Infant preferences for infant-directed versus noninfant-directed playsongs and lullabies. *Infant Behavior and Development*, **19**, 83–92.

Trainor, L. J. (2005). Are there critical periods for musical development? *Developmental Psychobiology*, **46**, 262–78.

Trainor, L. J. (2012). Musical experience, plasticity, and maturation: Issues in measuring developmental change using EEG and MEG. *Annals of the New York Academy of Sciences*, **1252**, 25–36.

Trainor, L. J., & Adams, B. (2000). Infants' and adults' use of duration and intensity cues in the segmentation of tone patterns. *Perception and Psychophysics*, **62**, 333–40.

Trainor, L. J., Clark, E. D., Huntley, A., & Adams, B. (1997). The acoustic basis of preferences for infant-directed singing. *Infant Behavior and Development*, **20**, 383–96.

Trainor, L. J., & Hannon, E. E. (2013). Musical development. In D. Deutsch (Ed.), *The Psychology of Music* (3rd ed., pp. 423–98). London, UK: Elsevier.

Trainor, L. J., & Heinmiller, B. M. (1998). The development of evaluative responses to music: Infants prefer to listen to consonance over dissonance. *Infant Behavior and Development*, **21**, 77–88.

Trainor, L. J., & Trehub, S. E. (1992). A comparison of infants' and adults' sensitivity to Western musical structure. *Journal of Experimental Psychology: Human Perception and Performance*, **18**, 394–402.

Trainor, L. J., & Trehub, S. E. (1993). What mediates infants' and adults' superior processing of the major over the augmented triad? *Music Perception*, **11**, 185–96.

Trainor, L. J., & Trehub, S. E. (1994). Key membership and implied harmony in Western tonal music: Developmental perspectives. *Perception and Psychophysics*, **56**, 125–32.

Trainor, L. J., Tsang, C. D., & Cheung, V. H. W. (2002). Preference for sensory consonance in 2- and 4-month-old infants. *Music Perception*, **20**, 187–94.

Trainor, L. J., & Unrau, A. J. (2012). Development of pitch and music perception. In L. Werner, R. R. Fay, & A. N. Popper (Eds.), *Springer handbook of auditory research: Human auditory development* (pp. 223–54). New York: Springer.

Trainor, L. J., Wu, L., & Tsang, C. D. (2004). Long-term memory for music: Infants remember tempo and timbre. *Developmental Science*, **7**, 289–96.

Trainor, L. J., & Zacharias, C. A. (1998). Infants prefer higher-pitched singing. *Infant Behavior and Development*, **21**, 799–805.

Trehub, S. E. (2000). Human processing predispositions and musical universals. In N. L. Wallin, B. Merker, & S. Brown (Eds.), *The origins of music* (pp. 427–48). Cambridge, MA: MIT Press.

Trehub, S. E. (2003a). Absolute and relative pitch processing in tone learning tasks. *Developmental Science*, **6**, 46–7.

Trehub, S. E. (2003b). The developmental origins of musicality. *Nature Neuroscience*, **6**, 669–73.

Trehub, S. E. (2012). Behavioral methods in infancy: Pitfalls of single measures. *Annals of the New York Academy of Sciences*, **1252**, 37–42.

Trehub, S. E. (2013). Music processing similarities between sleeping newborns and alert adults: Cause for celebration or concern? *Frontiers in Psychology*, **4**, 644.

Trehub, S. E., & Hannon, E. E. (2009). Conventional rhythms enhance infants' and adults' perception of musical patterns. *Cortex*, **45**, 110–18.

Trehub, S. E., Hill, D. S., & Kamenetsky, S. B. (1997). Parents' sung performances for infants. *Canadian Journal of Experimental Psychology*, **51**, 385–96.

Trehub, S. E., Plantinga, J., Brcic, J., & Nowicki, M. (2013). Cross-modal signatures in maternal speech and singing. *Frontiers in Psychology*, **4**, 811.

Trehub, S. E., Plantinga, J., & Russo, F. (2011, June). Maternal vocal expressiveness: Face-to-face and other contexts. Presented at the Society for Research in Child Development, Montreal, Canada.

Trehub, S. E., & Schellenberg, E. G. (1995). Music: Its relevance to infants. *Annals of Child Development*, **11**, 1–24.

Trehub, S. E., Schellenberg, E. G., & Kamenetsky, S. B. (1999). Infants' and adults' perception of scale structure. *Journal of Experimental Psychology: Human Perception and Performance*, **25**, 965–75.

Trehub, S. E., & Thorpe, L. A. (1989). Infants' perception of rhythm: Categorization of auditory sequences by temporal structure. *Canadian Journal of Psychology*, **43**, 217–29.

Trehub, S. E., Thorpe, L. A., & Morrongiello, B. A. (1985). Infants' perception of melodies: Changes in a single tone. *Infant Behavior and Development*, **8**, 213–23.

Trehub, S. E., Thorpe, L. A., & Morrongiello, B. A. (1987). Organizational processes in infants' perception of auditory patterns. *Child Development*, **58**, 741–9.

Trehub, S. E., & Trainor, L. J. (1998). Singing to infants: Lullabies and play songs. *Advances in Infancy Research*, **12**, 43–77.

Trehub, S. E., Unyk, A. M., & Henderson, J. L. (1994). Children's songs to infant siblings: Parallels with speech. *Journal of Child Language*, **21**, 735–44.

Trehub, S. E., Unyk, A. M., Kamenetsky, S. B., Hill, D. S., Trainor, L. J., Henderson, J. L., & Saraza, M. (1997). Mothers' and fathers' singing to infants. *Developmental Psychology*, **33**, 500–7.

Trehub, S. E., Unyk, A. M., & Trainor, L. J. (1993a). Adults identify infant-directed music across cultures. *Infant Behavior and Development*, **16**, 193–211.

Trehub, S. E., Unyk, A. M., & Trainor, L. J. (1993b). Maternal singing in cross-cultural perspective. *Infant Behavior and Development*, **16**, 285–95.

Tsang, C., & Conrad, N. J. (2010). Does the message matter? The effect of song type on infants' pitch preference for lullabies and playsongs. *Infant Behavior and Development*, **33**, 96–100.

Tucker, N. (1984). Lullabies. *History Today*, **34**, 40–6.

Ullal-Gupta, S., Vanden Bosch der Nederlanden, C. M., Tichko, P., Lahav, A., & Hannon, E. E. (2013). Linking prenatal experience to the emerging musical mind. *Frontiers in Systems Neuroscience*, **7**, 48.

Valentine, C. W. (1962). Musical intervals and attitudes to music. In C. W. Valentine, *The experimental psychology of beauty* (pp. 196–227). London: Methuen & Co. Ltd.

Vassilakis, P. N. (2005). Auditory roughness as means of musical expression. *Selected Reports in Ethnomusicology, Vol. 12: Perspectives in Systematic Musicology*, **12**, 119–44.

Virtala, P., Houtilainen, M., Partanen, E., Fellman, V., & Tervaniemi, M. (2013). Newborn infants' auditory system is sensitive to Western music chord categories. *Frontiers in Psychology*, **4**, 492.

Virtala, P., Houtilainen, M., Putkinen, V., Makkonen, T., & Tervaniemi, M. (2012). Musical training facilitates the neural discrimination of major versus minor chords in 13-year-old children. *Psychophysiology*, **49**, 1125–32.

Volkova, A., Trehub, S. E., & Schellenberg, E. G. (2006). Infants' memory for musical performances. *Developmental Science*, **9**, 584–90.

Werker, J. F., Pegg, J. E., & McLeod, P. J. (1994). A cross-language investigation of infant preference for infant-directed communication. *Infant Behavior and Development*, **17**, 323–33.

Werker, J. F., & Tees, R. C. (1984). Cross-language speech perception: Evidence for perceptual reorganization during the first year of life. *Infant Behavior and Development*, **7**, 49–63.

Winkler, I., Háden, G. P., Ladinig, O., Sziller, I., & Honing, H. (2009). Newborn infants detect the beat in music. *Proceedings of the National Academy of Sciences*, **106**, 2468–71.

Young, S. (2008). Lullaby light shows: Everyday musical experience among under-two-year-olds. *International Journal of Music Education*, **26**, 33–46.

Zatorre, R. J., Belin, P., & Penhune, V. B. (2002). Structure and function of auditory cortex: Music and speech. *Trends in Cognitive Sciences*, **6**, 37–46.

Zatorre, R. J., Chen, J. L., & Penhune, V. B. (2007). When the brain plays music: Sensory–motor interactions in music perception and production. *Nature Reviews Neuroscience*, **8**, 547–58.

Zentner, M., & Eerola, T. (2010). Rhythmic engagement with music in infancy. *Proceedings of the National Academy of Sciences*, **107**, 5768–73.

Chapter 3

The child musician's brain

Donald A. Hodges

The child musician's brain: Introduction

Music fills the lives of children. Mothers sing their babies to sleep, children move and dance to the music that fills their favorite television programs, and teenagers with their ubiquitous earbuds often seem consumed by music. The purpose of this chapter is to examine relationships between brain growth and development and the emerging musicality of children. For the purposes of our discussion, the following age ranges will be used: fetal (conception to birth), infant (birth to 2 years), children (3–12 years of age and sometimes referring to birth to 18 years of age), and adolescence (13–18 years of age). I organized the chapter into two major sections: one a general overview of brain growth and development, and the other a review of neuroimaging studies on children and music.

Specific aspects of brain growth and development

The adult human brain weighs about three pounds and contains more than 100 billion neurons with trillions of interconnections (Carey, 2008). The journey from conception to the fully realized brain is not linear; rather, it progresses in fits and starts, with different regions of the brain increasing or decreasing at faster or slower paces at varying times. Here, I review four specific aspects of brain growth and development that are critical in understanding human musicality: synaptogenesis, myelination, pruning and plasticity, and critical and optimal periods.

Two comments precede these discussions. First, in spite of substantial progress in understanding brain growth and development, we still have a great deal to learn before claiming anything approximating full knowledge. The brain is the most complex entity in the known universe and we are only at the beginning stages of unraveling its mysteries. Second, brain growth and development require both nature and nurture. Genetic instructions and environmental experiences influence each other in a symbiotic relationship. Considering the brain a social organ recognizes that human beings must interact with others in order to achieve full potential.

Synaptogenesis

A neuron consists of a cell body, multiple dendrites, a single axon, and potentially thousands of synapses (Andreassi, 2007). The body of a brain cell is about one-hundredth the size of the period at the end of this sentence (Brotherson, 2005), and 100 million neurons can fit in one cubic inch (Zull, 2002). The cell body contains the nucleus, which controls cellular activity. Numerous dendrites bring information into the cell body, while a single axon carries information away from it. A synapse is the connection between two neurons. Neurons do not physically touch; rather, they are separated by a synaptic cleft only 200 nanometers wide (Cohen, 1996). Information is ferried across this gap by neurotransmitters such as acetylcholine and dopamine. Each neuron can connect with as many as 15,000 other neurons.

Synaptogenesis is the formation of synaptic connections between neurons. The brain grows very rapidly during gestation, with brain cells proliferating at the rate of 580,000 per minute, leading to 160% brain growth during the first 29 weeks of gestation (Brotherson, 2005). From 19 to 20 gestational weeks until birth, the volume of the whole brain enlarges from 22 ml to 367 ml, an increase of 17 times (Huang et al., 2006). This is in comparison to ages 5–6 where the brain volume is 1,258 ml and adults where the average size is approximately 1,350 ml. The brain dramatically overproduces synapses such that the brain of a 2-year-old has 50% more synapses than the brain of an adult (Lenroot & Giedd, 2006). This is a means of maximizing learning potential. For example, the brain is prepared to learn whatever language or languages the child encounters in the home (Kuhl & Rivera-Gaxiola, 2008). Gradually, many of these synapses will be pruned away because of disuse, as described in the subsequent section on plasticity and pruning.

The brain continues to grow rapidly during the first year and then slows down in the second. Knickmeyer et al. (2008) found that total brain volume increased by 101% in the first year, but only 15% in the second. The majority of this growth was in gray matter (149% growth in the cortex), while white matter (axons that transfer information throughout the core of the brain) only increased by 11%. Cerebellum volume increased by 249%. After birth, the cortex increases until about age 8; from then on it becomes systematically streamlined, as the volume of the cortex is much smaller in adults than in 8-year-olds. Total brain volume is about 95% at age 6 and reaches a peak for girls at age 11.5 and 14.5 for boys (Lenroot & Giedd, 2006). After the brain reaches its peak volume, gray matter decreases as a result of neural pruning, although white matter increases until young adulthood and does not begin to decrease until the fourth decade. Although male brains are approximately 9% larger, there is no cognitive advantage in this size differential (Giedd, 2004).

Myelination

The inner core of the brain contains the axons that carry information throughout the brain (Filley, 2005). Myelination is a process of coating the neuronal axons with a fatty sheath that improves message transfer with respect to accuracy and speed, up to 100 times faster (Zull, 2002). Because myelin is white, the inner core of the brain is called white matter. Myelination begins in the fourth month of gestation and continues for the next 30 years (Lenroot & Giedd, 2006). It occurs in different brain regions at different times and, in general, proceeds from bottom to top and from back to front. The brainstem and cerebellum come first and the frontal lobes last. Myelination is related to cognitive functioning (Webb, Monk, & Nelson, 2001) and because the process is not a smooth, continuous one, development of cognitive functioning is not a smooth, continuous process.

Myelination is influenced by both genetics and learning. The more one practices a specific cognitive (e.g., mathematical times tables) or motor function (e.g., playing the violin), the more the axons connecting the neural networks responsible for the behavior are coated with myelin. In a specific musical example, researchers documented that the number of hours spent practicing the piano in childhood, adolescence, and adulthood correlated positively with white matter development (Bengtsson et al., 2005). Thus, learning influences myelination, and information processing becomes more rapid and more efficient. Conversely, as specific neural pathways become myelinated, what is learned places greater restrictions upon what can be learned (Quartz, 2003). For example, the more a child learns a specific language and a specific musical style, the more difficult it becomes to learn different languages (Pons et al., 2009) or musical styles (Patel, Meltznoff, & Kuhl, 2004).

Pruning and plasticity

A key concept is that brain development is self-organizing (Lewis, 2005). A neuroscience axiom says that, "Neurons that fire together, wire together. Neurons that fire apart, stay apart." Genetic instructions and life experiences work together to sculpt the brain (Doidge, 2007). Plasticity refers to the notion that brain structures are not rigidly defined, rather that they are malleable. Plasticity is influenced by both negative (e.g., injury) and positive (e.g., learning) experiences (Gottesman & Hanson, 2005). Thus, it is not just a response to brain injury, but also a central feature of brain development and learning that persists throughout life as experiences change the brain. Mounting evidence suggests that musicians' brains are models of neuroplasticity (Münte, Altenmüller, & Jäncke, 2002).

Neural pruning is the process by which unused synaptic connections are deleted. From ages 7–11 and 9–13, up to 50% of brain tissue can be lost in specific regions (Thompson et al., 2000), along with up to 80% of cortical neurons and synapses (Stiles, 2000). In experience-expectant systems (e.g., language or music), development is based on expectations that experience will provide the necessary influences to select the appropriate subset of synaptic connections (Lewis, 2005). Experience-dependent systems (e.g., vocabulary or specific musical skills) are unique to each individual as a result of specific learning experiences.

Again, as the brain learns it imposes restrictions on itself, such that what is learned influences what can be learned. In other words, neural systems lose degrees of freedom as they develop (Lewis, 2005). Another key aspect of neural pruning is the influence of emotions, as learning is always accompanied by feelings (Zull, 2002). Learning activates reward centers in the brain, and positive musical experiences are known to increase levels of serotonin (Evers & Suhr, 2000) and dopamine (Menon & Levitin, 2005; Salimpoor et al., 2011) that contribute to feelings of well-being and pleasure.

Critical and optimal periods

Critical periods are times when stimulation is necessary for normal growth and development (Berk, 2004). For example, researchers have identified periods during which normal development of vision occurs (Hooks & Chen, 2007). In behavioral terms, appropriate stimulation from the environment in terms of sensory experiences and interactions, especially with other human beings, is necessary for proper development (Carey, 2008). Lack of appropriate stimulation during a critical period may lead to deficits. For example, physical, social, and emotional growth can be severely stunted when children do not have appropriate opportunities to engage with the environment (Chugani et al., 2001).

In contrast to critical periods, optimal, sometimes called sensitive, periods are growth phases during which time learning may come more easily and more quickly. If appropriate experiences do not occur during optimal periods, learning may still occur at a later time, though it may be more difficult. Thus, for music learning, earlier is better than later (Raufschecker, 2001) and elite musicians nearly always start their musical training at an early age (Moore, Burland, & Davidson, 2003). However, it is never too late to learn music to some degree (Holt, 1978).

Neuromusical research

The vast majority of brain imaging studies concerned with musicality has focused on adults. For obvious reasons, it is difficult to place a child into a scanner to monitor brain responses to musical tasks. Nevertheless, a slowly growing body of literature is beginning to give us a clearer picture of how musicality develops in the child's brain. Literature reviews are organized into fetal and infant stages, childhood, and adolescence.

Neuromusical research in prenatal stages and infancy

Although there is a limited number of neuroimaging studies of fetal and infant responses to music, researchers are beginning to make exciting new discoveries as they investigate how the newborn brain responds to music. Hearing, of course, is central to most musical experiences. Although we come into the world ready to hear and respond to sounds, including music, there are significant and dramatic developmental changes in auditory brain regions.

A fetus responds to sounds as early as gestational weeks 20–27 and is capable of responding to the sound of the mother's voice and to music up to six weeks before birth (Joseph, 2000). Auditory evoked responses tracked in fetuses between 27-weeks gestational age and neonates demonstrated neurological maturation as latency in responses decreased (Govindan et al., 2008). This development continues as demonstrated in significant differences in cerebral blood flow in the auditory cortices between 7 and 13 months after birth (Wang et al., 2008).

After birth, there is a rapid burst of synaptic development in the auditory cortex between months 3 and 4, reaching 150% of their eventual adult levels between 4 and 12 months (Johnson, 1998). The cortex, about 2.7 mm in thickness, consists of six layers. Neural activity in the auditory cortex that is functional and mature is restricted largely to the top, outer layer (layer I) of gray matter before 4 months of age; infants' ability to process auditory information is thus most likely due to brainstem analysis (Moore, 2002; see Figure 3.1). By age 2, axons are beginning to reach deeper layers (layers IV, V, and VI), and interconnections increase significantly over the next few years.

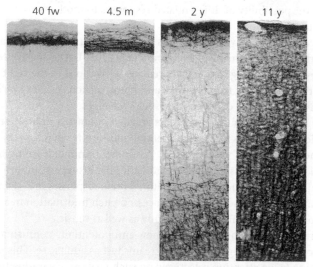

Fig. 3.1 Neurofilament-immunostained sections of cortical tissue. At the fortieth fetal week (fw) and at 4.5 months' postnatal age, mature axons are present only in marginal layer. By 2 years of age, mature neurofilament-expressing axons are entering deeper cortical layers. By 11 years, mature axons are present with adult-like density in all cortical layers.

Reprinted from Moore, J., Maturation of human auditory cortex: Implications for speech perception, *The Annals of Otology, Rhinology & Laryngology*, 111 (1), p. 8, Figure 2 © 2002, SAGE Publications.

This development from 6 months to age 5 reflects transmission of information from inner ear and brainstem to the auditory cortex and results in increasing perceptual skills (e.g., for language and music). From age 5 to 11 or 12, mature axons appear in layers II and III connecting the two hemispheres and areas within hemispheres (e.g., auditory association areas, regions of the brain responsible for placing sounds in a broader context).

Although 2-month-old infants can discriminate between standard and altered patterns, a clear developmental path was seen in that discrimination abilities similar to adults were found in 31% of infants at 3 months, 58% at 4 months, and in most infants by 6 months (Trainor et al., 2003). At 2 weeks, absolute threshold (the softest sound one can hear) is as much as 50 dB poorer than adults; at 3 months the gap is 15–30 dB, and from 6 to 12 months it is 10–15 dB. These differences are also reflected in frequency and intensity discriminations, with 6-month-olds requiring twice the frequency difference and intensity level as adults to detect changes (Aslin, Jusczyk, & Pisoni, 1998). Saffran, Werker, & Werner (2006) provided an extensive overview of research concerning the development of auditory processing capabilities in infancy. (Also of note is an extensive chapter in the same volume on Development in the Arts: Drawing and Music by Winner.)

It is natural to wonder just how much and how well an infant can respond to music. How early does it start—even before birth? Is it something we are born with, or something we learn? Can newborns or even fetuses respond to key characteristics of sound such as pitch, timbre, and rhythm? Many mothers report feeling their babies respond to sounds while still in the womb. Earlier studies monitoring heart rate and movement confirmed this (e.g., Lecanuet, 1996), but now neuroscientists have the ability to obtain even more detailed information using brain scans. For example, Jardi et al. (2008) asked women to undergo fMRI scanning during their third trimester of pregnancy and found that three of eight fetuses (33 gestational weeks) responded to sounds with activations in the left auditory cortex. Cortical responses beyond subcortical brainstem responses indicate the possibility of differentiated responses to mother's voice, music, and other sounds heard regularly.

Immediately after birth, 1–3-day-old newborns respond to music with bilateral activations, but more predominantly in the right hemisphere (Perani et al., 2010). Altering Western tonal melodies by changing key or by creating dissonances reduces activations in the right hemisphere and increases them in the left inferior frontal cortex and limbic structures. Very early in life, infants' brains are responsive to tonal and consonant–dissonant changes.

Moving beyond music generically, researchers are also interested in how well newborns can process musical elements such as pitch. An essential question is what aspects of music we can process at birth and what aspects we must learn. Assuming minimal learning has occurred, the presence of specific music processing abilities soon after birth suggests inborn mechanisms are responsible. Stefanics and colleagues (2009) monitored brain responses in 2–3 day-old newborns. Their findings indicated that these newborns processed pitch information in adult-like fashion. This has implications for processing speech prosody as well as music.

Virtually all the sounds a newborn hears are new and potentially confusing. However, newborns are already capable of segregating sound streams just as adults are. This means they come into the world able to focus attention selectively on such tasks as separating the sound of their mothers' voices from background noise. Infants respond differentially to musical expressions of sadness, fear, and joy (Schmidt, Trainor, & Santesso, 2003). Stefanics et al. (2009) found that newborns can process pitch intervals at adult-like levels. A further refinement is the ability to separate pitch from other attributes of sound, such as timbre. This is important in speech perception, as in tracking pitch changes in both mother's and father's voice, and has musical consequences as well. Further confirmation of neonates' auditory processing capabilities came when 2–3-day-old newborns were able to track pitches across changes in timbre (Háden et al., 2009). Electrophysiological brain data indicated that the newborns processed pitch and timbre separately.

Rhythm perception is important not only for music, but also for speech perception and for social interactions. While babies do not have sufficient control over limb and body movements to be highly rhythmical, the question remains how well they can process rhythm in sound. Neonates, 2–3 days old, were able to detect the beat in rhythmic sound patterns (Winkler et al., 2008). In far less than one second (from 200 to 600 ms), a newborn's brain registers that a down-beat is missing from a rhythmic sound pattern. Such results support the contention that this ability is innate rather than learned. Even here, however, "innate" may mean that such responses are present at birth, not that they are solely the result of genetic instructions without any learning having taken place.

Adults listen to music with expectations, making predictions that are often unconscious about what will happen next in the music. With specific pieces or genres that are highly familiar, predictability aids understanding, as when we track phrases, phrase endings, and so on. Unfamiliar musical styles (e.g., Chinese opera for most Americans) are often confusing because we cannot recognize patterns; we may not be able to find the beat or to know when one musical idea ends and another one begins. Many of these same issues occur in language, too, as we understand sentence structure in our own language but not in an unfamiliar one. Researchers are interested in knowing how early we are able to recognize patterns in sound.

Carral and colleagues (2005) recorded brain responses in newborns as they listened to ascending and descending tone pairs. Most of the tone pairs (87.5%) were ascending, and descending pairs were considered irregular. Within 50–450 ms of the second tone, infants were able to discriminate the deviant patterns, indicating an emerging processing capability that is critical for language acquisition.

A number of studies focused on sound and music processing capabilities of newborns that presumably reflect innate processes. In a review article, Hannon & Trainor (2007) summarized the effects of informal (i.e., hearing music in the environment) and formal music learning experiences. Babies encounter certain sounds (e.g., speech, music, etc.) in their environment more frequently than others. In a process called statistical learning, frequent occurrence of particular tonal and rhythm patterns, and timbres, builds up neural representations such that infants become increasingly adept at processing sounds that contain these patterns. For example, 8-month-old infants performed as well as adults in identifying patterns embedded in 7-minute-long pitch streams (Saffran et al., 1999). Thus, everyday exposure to frequently heard linguistic and musical auditory patterns creates culture-specific neural networks. Formal training further enhances domain-specific (i.e., linguistic or musical) refinements.

In summary, the auditory cortex matures over a considerable period. Some processing capabilities appear to be innate, while others are learned. Beginning at the third trimester of pregnancy, the fetal brain shows activation in the primary auditory cortex to both externally and internally generated sounds. Both hemispheres in newborns respond to music and speech. Although there is a tendency toward left-hemisphere dominance for language, there are significant individual variances. Newborns can process pitch information nearly as well as adults. They can also extract pitch from complex sound stimuli. Newborns display sophisticated awareness of rhythms, indicating that this ability may be innate. They have an awareness of patterns in sound that are critical to both music and speech. Both informal music listening experiences and formal musical training have an effect on the developing auditory cortex.

Neuromusical research in childhood

Musical development in childhood relies on many general brain developments, such as executive functioning (Best, Miller, & Jones, 2009; Garon, Bryson, & Smith, 2008), auditory and motor skills, and emotional maturity. While these developments take place naturally in children who do not take music lessons, it is known that active music making is associated with greater changes in the brain than passive listening (Hannon & Trainor, 2007). Also, throughout this discussion, it must be clear that musical experiences do not occur in a vacuum. That is, musical training is more likely to be provided to children by parents who value education in general and who have financial resources to support the purchase of instruments, private lessons, attending concerts, and so on. Thus, it is difficult to separate the causal effects of music alone from the social context.

Of interest is knowing whether and how musical training might cause changes in both brain structure and function. Previously, investigations of adult musicians inferred that musical learning during childhood resulted in both structural and functional changes lacking in those who did not study music (e.g., Zatorre, Chen, & Penhune, 2007). However, it was unclear whether those changes were the result of genetic inheritance or due to the study of music. More recently, however, studies with children themselves are accumulating.

Children aged 5 and 9 listened to music that contained infrequent, inappropriate chords (Koelsch et al., 2003). Brain responses indicated that the younger children already processed the music according to music-syntactic regularities. Interestingly, there was a gender difference, as boys had prominent left lateralized signals that were bilateral in girls. Hyde et al. (2009) found that structural changes seen in adult musicians are likely a result of training-induced plasticity. Thirty-one children around 6 years old were divided into instrumental and control groups. Brain changes after 15 months of instrumental music study included increases in motor control areas, corpus callosum (responsible for communications between the left and right hemispheres), and auditory regions, as well as bilateral frontal regions and the left posterior pericingulate region (involved in the integration of visual information and limbic system such as in musical notation and emotional responses). These neural changes were reflected in music-related behavioral tasks. The lack of brain differences between instrumental and control groups at the beginning and the lack of changes in the control group after 15 months, other than maturational changes which were factored out of both groups, indicate that music learning experiences were likely the cause of changes in the instrumental group.

Hyde et al. (2009) also found near transfer but no far transfer effects. Near transfer refers to tasks closely related to the training domain (e.g., music training and fine motor tasks); far transfer refers to minimal relationships between, for example, musical rhythm processing and a task involving fractions in math. Although it makes common sense that music would be more likely to influence nonmusical behaviors that share certain features (e.g., auditory processing in both music and language), research data are critical in confirming or contradicting our expectations.

Forgeard et al. (2008) obtained results that are more nuanced than a simple division between near and far transfer tasks. Children who participated in three years of instrumental music study had higher scores than control counterparts in four of six near transfer tasks (i.e., auditory discrimination and fine motor skills) and two of ten far transfer tasks (i.e., vocabulary and nonverbal reasoning skills). Because length of training predicted outcomes, the overall conclusion was that musical training was responsible for changes in the music students' brains.

In an investigation of differences between maturational and training effects, researchers collected data on participants ranging in age from 5 to 33 years, whose duration of musical training ranged from none to 21,000 hours (Ellis et al., 2012). This is one of the first studies to show that both age and musical training have effects on brain plasticity. Even without specific music training, most individuals will improve in their ability to discriminate pitches and rhythms as a factor of maturation. However, those individuals who receive music training in childhood show significantly greater changes. In particular, a portion of the secondary auditory cortex in the left hemisphere was selectively changed by musical training.

White matter tracts are axons that carry information from one region of the brain to another. In terms of plasticity, it is important to learn whether musical experiences cause changes in white matter. Researchers found that piano practicing in childhood can induce white matter plasticity if it occurs in a period when the involved fiber tracts are still under maturation (Bengtsson et al., 2005). A key finding is that a large number of brain regions correlated with childhood practicing, although the total number of hours practiced in childhood was considerably lower than in later life. This illustrates both the importance of early practicing for white matter plasticity and the limited malleability of the system in adulthood. Changes in white matter influence the efficiency of message transmission throughout the brain.

Evidence is mounting that musical training changes the brain in ways that have long-lasting effects. For example, Skoe and Kraus (2012) demonstrated that adult musicians had stronger auditory brainstem responses to sound than those with no formal music training. Even as few as three years of musical training in childhood had effects that persisted into adulthood. The authors believe that these results have significant implications for education policy makers and for developing auditory training programs that will have beneficial effects that last beyond school years. Another example concerns gamma band responses, brain waves in the 30–100 Hz frequency range that are associated with executive functions such as attention, expectation, memory retrieval, and integration of top-down, bottom-up, and multisensory processes (Trainor, Shahin, & Roberts, 2009). Data from both children and adults indicate that musical training increases gamma band responses.

A simplistic view of hemispheric specialization was popularized in the late 1960s. According to this idea, the left hemisphere monitored language and the right hemisphere controlled music. Abundant research since then has led to a much more complex and sophisticated understanding. Although there are some differences in how the two hemispheres process information, there is no clean division. Kotilahti et al. (2010) recorded responses to speech and music in the auditory cortices of newborns. Considering the group as a whole, both hemispheres were activated by speech and music, although there were individual variations. Speech registered more strongly in the left hemisphere, indicating lateralization had begun, but lateralization for music had not occurred yet. Overy and colleagues (2004) found that children around the age of 6 had differential processing for melody and rhythm similar to but less extensive than adults. Compared to a silent condition, melodic and rhythmic tasks activated auditory regions in both hemispheres. Adult musicians show left hemisphere dominance for rhythm and right hemisphere preference for pitches. These results suggest that left–right differences in music processing develop with age.

Further evidence of neuroplasticity was found when researchers examined three groups of children, aged 5–7, some who practiced a lot, some who practiced only a little, and some who did not take music lessons (Schlaug et al., 2009). The amount of practice time predicted the amount of change found in the corpus callosum. Early, extensive, and intensive music practicing caused changes in the part of the brain responsible for connecting various cortical regions.

Koelsch et al. (2005) investigated the developmental aspects of musical training. Children and adults with varying levels of musical training judged whether chord sequences ended on regular or irregular chords. Neural patterns for irregular chord judgments were similar for children and adult nonmusicians. Adult musicians relied more strongly on working memory-based pitch processing than the others. It should be noted, however, that children and adults without musical training were still able to process music effectively. If this were not so, then people without training would not understand the music of their culture (e.g., in movies and television), whereas clearly they do.

Language skills increase enormously between the ages of 2 and 12. Since this is also a time when many children begin formal music lessons, it is natural to wonder what effects music training might have on language development. Several researchers have explored this issue. As shown in the Foregeard et al. (2008) study on near and far transfer, musical training had an effect on vocabulary. Others have also studied the effects of musical training on a variety of language skills. According to Chen, Ho, and Cheung (1998), adults who received music training before the age of 12 have a better memory for spoken words than those who did not have such training. Music training in childhood may therefore have long-term positive effects on verbal memory.

The effects of music training on verbal memory implied that what adult musicians did as children accounted for the difference. Musical training made a difference in 8-year-old children, as the musicians outperformed controls in pitch processing of both musical and linguistic stimuli (Magne, Schön, & Besson, 2006). Such effects can take place with as little as eight weeks of musical training (Moreno & Besson, 2006). Primary school children (average age = 7 years) participated in weekly instrumental music lessons or in natural science training (Roden, Kreutz, & Bongard, 2012). Testing three times over an 18-month period revealed that music students significantly outperformed controls in tests of verbal memory. Nine-year-old children, divided into those with at least four years of musical training and those without, participated in passive and active processing of speech sounds (Chobert et al., 2011). Musician children performed significantly better in actively discriminating acoustical features of speech.

In a study that examined children directly, researchers gathered electroencephalography (EEG) data before speech segmentation training in which children matched syllable–pitch phrases, and again after one and two years (François et al., 2012). Those children who received musical training performed significantly better on speech segmentation tasks than those in a painting group. Brain responses for familiar and unfamiliar words were greater for the music group. Thus, musical training played a role in facilitating children's language development.

Researchers also examined whether musical training influences linguistic and musical syntax, that is, the manner in which children organize discrete elements that are combined into structured sequences (Jentschke & Koelsch, 2009). Children with musical training had more strongly developed neurophysiological markers for processing and sustaining linguistic syntax. Overlapping neural networks subserve both language and music syntactic processing, along with parallel and distinct networks (Brown, Martinez, & Parsons, 2006). This was confirmed when children with specific language impairment also had difficulties in musical syntactic processing (Jentschke et al., 2008).

In summary, neuroimaging studies are beginning to give us a more complete understanding of what transpires in the brains of those who study music during childhood. Musical training causes changes in auditory and motor cortices, and the corpus callosum. Structural changes seen in adult musicians are most likely a result of musical training during childhood. Musical training is more likely to affect those behaviors that are similar to music (near transfer; e.g., auditory discrimination) and less likely to affect dissimilar behaviors (far transfer; e.g., mathematics). Some developmental changes are due to age and maturation (e.g., working memory operations) and some are due to musical training (e.g., spectrotemporal pattern matching and auditory-motor coordination). Extensive piano practice during childhood increased white matter development.

Brain changes that occur as a result of musical training in childhood are retained in adulthood, even if music practicing ceases. Musical training affects brain processes (e.g., gamma band oscillations) associated with attention, expectation, memory retrieval, and integration of top-down, bottom-up, and multisensory processes. Children show very little of the hemispheric differences for musical processing (i.e., melody and rhythm) that adults have, suggesting that such specialization may develop with age and training. Specific changes in cortical structures following musical training are likely due to experience, rather than to inherited characteristics. Music processing tasks activated cerebral structures in trained children with patterns that were similar for adults and children with no formal musical training. This indicated that they were able to gain complex musical knowledge without formal training. Musical training has an effect on language skills, including verbal memory, speech segmentation, and syntactical processing.

Taken as a whole, these findings indicate that children are endowed with the capacity to understand music naturally, that is, as a result of daily living and without formal training. However, when they do engage in musical training, significant brain changes occur and these have implications for cognitive functioning. Moreover, the effects of childhood musical training continue into adulthood, even if active music making does not.

Neuromusical research in adolescence

Unfortunately, adolescents have rarely been participants in neuromusical research. In contrast, it is hardly an overstatement to say that music is a primary factor in the social behaviors of teenagers. Not only that, but also it is clear that teens are influenced by a sense of their own popularity, and responding favorably to the music of the peer group is an important factor in acceptance and popularity. Researchers in one study were interested in examining the neural mechanisms involved in teenagers' likability ratings of music (Berns et al., 2010). They identified brain regions involved in the role of music in socially influenced decision making. Twenty-seven teenagers were scanned as they rated music; results revealed broad neural networks involved in visual and auditory processing. The higher the individual rated a particular song, the greater the activity in the caudate nucleus, an area of the brain previously correlated with intensely pleasurable musical experiences.

Suzuki instruction involves very young children and it is natural to wonder what effects starting music lessons at such an early age might have on developing brains. In one experiment, researchers compared Suzuki students (4–5 years old) to children and teenagers (4–15 years old) who did not receive formal music training (Shahin, Roberts, & Trainor, 2004). The Suzuki students produced specific brain wave patterns comparable to children about three years older. This demonstrates that specific musical experiences influence neural functioning.

Studying individuals who have undergone selective removal of brain tissue is a medical model that allows researchers to determine what behavioral deficits result. Researchers examined children and adolescents who had either their left or right hemispheres removed for intractable epilepsy to determine what the effects of the surgery were on musical perception (Dennis & Hopyan, 2001). Several years after surgery, patients discriminated rhythms equally well whether they had a left or right temporal lobectomy. However, those with right hemisphere removal had higher melody scores than the others and these scores increased with age. These results are consistent with those of adults and confirm the notion that melody and rhythm are processed by distinct neural networks.

In summary, teenagers who change their likability ratings of music to conform to popular opinions were less involved in active listening and were more inclined to feel anxious about not fitting in with their peers. Musical training in the form of Suzuki instruction modifies the auditory cortex (particularly secondary more so than primary) such that the brain responses of younger musicians are similar to controls who are three years older. Children and adolescents who have undergone a temporal lobectomy show differential effects: removal of the right temporal lobe impaired melodic discrimination. Individuals with a left or right lobectomy performed equally well on rhythm discrimination tasks. These few neuroimaging studies do not do full justice to the immense role that music plays in the lives of teenagers.

Summary

The brain undergoes enormous changes from conception to age 18. Explosive growth, directed by genetic instructions and life experiences, is later counterbalanced by deletion of cortical connections in a sometimes severe process of neural pruning. From the last trimester before birth throughout childhood, music plays a significant role in this process of development. Natural maturation leads to some improvements in music processing. Everyday living, including passive listening to music, brings about other changes. Informal music making and formal musical training lead to further significant changes.

Intensive and extensive music practice during childhood leads to specific changes in brain structure and function that persist through adulthood. Some of these changes have effects on nonmusical domains, such as language. We may not yet understand all the intricacies of this phenomenon, but significant inroads have been made, such that we can say with all confidence that we are born to be musical and our musicianship makes a difference in the quality of human life.

Reflective questions

1 Have you experienced directly (i.e., been pregnant) or observed a fetus moving in the womb in response to external sounds or music? If so, how would you characterize the connection between fetal movements and external sounds?
2 What behaviors of infants and toddlers can you identify that demonstrate an emerging musicality?
3 Remembering that no developmental process is completely driven by genetic instructions or by learning experiences, discuss the roles of nature and nurture in childhood musicality.
4 What are the key markers of musicality that occur from birth through adolescence?
5 As you think about brain growth and development in the first two decades of life, along with budding musicality, can you describe how the two might influence each other? That is, what changes in the brain allow for new musical behaviors and what musical experiences might change the brain?

Key sources

Hannon, E., & Trainor, L. (2007). Music acquisition: effects of enculturation and formal training on development. *Trends in Cognitive Sciences*, **11**, 466–72.

Hyde, K., Lerch, J., Norton, A., Forgeard, M., Winner, E., Evans, A. C., & Schlaug, G. (2009). Musical training shapes structural brain development. *Journal of Neuroscience*, **29**(10), 3019–25.

Lenroot, R., & Giedd, J. (2006). Brain development in children and adolescents: Insights from anatomical magnetic resonance imaging. *Neuroscience and Biobehavioral Reviews*, **30**, 718–29.

Perani, D., Saccuman, M., Scifo, P., Spada, D., Andreolli, G., Rovelli, R., Baldonli, C., & Koelsch, S. (2010). Functional specializations for music processing in the human newborn brain. *Proceedings of the National Academy of Sciences*, **107**(10), 4758–63.

Skoe, E., & Kraus, N. (2012). A little goes a long way: How the brain is shaped by musical training in childhood. *Journal of Neuroscience*, **32**(34), 11507–10.

Reference list

Andreassi, J. (2007). *Psychophysiology: Human behavior and physiological response* (5th ed.). Mahwah, NJ: Lawrence Erlbaum Associates.

Aslin, R., Jusczyk, P., & Pisoni, D. (1998). Speech and auditory processing during infancy: Constraints on and precursors to language. In E. Kuhn & S. Siegler (Eds.), *Handbook of child psychology*, Vol. 2 (5th ed., pp. 147–98). New York: John Wiley & Sons.

Bengtsson, S., Nagy, Z., Skare, S., Forsman, L., Forssberg, H., & Ullén, F. (2005). Extensive piano practicing has regionally specific effects on white matter development. *Nature Neuroscience*, **8**(9), 1148–50.

Berk, L. (2004). *Development through the lifespan* (3rd ed.). New York: Allyn & Bacon.

Berns, G., Capra, C., Moore, S., & Noussair, C. (2010). Neural mechanisms of the influence of popularity on adolescent ratings of music. *NeuroImage*, **49**, 2687–96.

Best, J., Miller, P., & Jones, L. (2009). Executive functions after age 5: Changes and correlates. *Developmental Review*, **29**, 180–200.

Brotherson, S. (2005). Understanding brain development in young children. Retrieved from: <http://www.ag.ndsu.edu/pubs/yf/famsci/fs609.pdf>.

Brown, S., Martinez, M., & Parsons, L. (2006). Music and language side by side in the brain: A PET study of the generation of melodies and sentences. *European Journal of Neuroscience*, **23**, 2791–803.

Carey, J. (2008). *Brain facts*. Washington, D.C.: Society for Neuroscience.

Carral, V., Huotilainen, M., Ruusuvirta, T., Fellman, V., Näätänen, R., & Escera, C. (2005). A kind of auditory "primitive intelligence" already present at birth. *European Journal of Neuroscience*, **21**, 3201–4.

Chen, A., Ho, Y.-C., & Cheung, M.-C. (1998). Music training improves verbal memory. *Nature*, **396**, 128.

Chobert, J., Marie, C., François, C., Schön, D., & Besson, M. (2011). Enhanced passive and active processing of syllables in musician children. *Journal of Cognitive Neuroscience*, **23**(12), 3874–87.

Chugani, H., Behen, M., Muzik, O., Juhász, C., Nagy, F., & Chugani, D. (2001). Local brain functional activity following early deprivation: A study of postinstitutionalized Romanian orphans. *NeuroImage*, **14**, 1290–301.

Cohen, D. (1996). *The secret language of the mind*. San Francisco: Chronicle Books.

Dennis, M., & Hopyan, T. (2001). Rhythm and melody in children and adolescents after left or right temporal lobectomy. *Brain and Cognition*, **47**, 461–9.

Doidge, N. (2007). *The brain that changes itself*. New York: Penguin.

Ellis, R., Norton, A., Overy, K., Winner, E., Alsop, D., & Schlaug, G. (2012). Differentiating maturational and training influences on fMRI activation during music processing. *NeuroImage*, **60**, 1902–12.

Evers, S., & Suhr, B. (2000). Changes of the neurotransmitter serotonin but not of hormones during short time music perception. *European Archives of Psychiatry and Clinical Neuroscience*, **250**(3), 144–7.

Filley, C. (2005). White matter and behavioral neurology. In J. Ullmer, L. Parsons, M. Moseley, & J. Gabrieli (Eds.), *White matter in cognitive neuroscience. Annals of the New York Academy of Sciences*, **1064**, 162–83. New York: The New York Academy of Sciences.

Forgeard, M., Winner, E., Norton, A., & Schlaug, G. (2008). Practicing a musical instrument in childhood is associated with enhanced verbal ability and nonverbal reasoning. *PLoS ONE*, **3**(10), 1–8.

François, C., Chobert, J., Besson, M., & Schön, D. (2012). Music training for the development of speech segmentation. *Cerebral Cortex*, **23**(9), 2038–43.

Garon, N., Bryson, S. E., & Smith, I. M. (2008). Executive function in preschoolers: A review using an integrative framework. *Psychological Bulletin*, **134**, 31–60.

Giedd, J. (2004). Structural magnetic resonance imaging of the adolescent brain. *Annals of the New York Academy of Sciences*, **1021**, 77–85. New York: The New York Academy of Sciences.

Gottesman, I., & Hanson, D. (2005). Human development: Biological and genetic processes. *Annual Review of Psychology*, **56**, 263–86.

Govindan, R., Wilson, J., Preissl, H., Murphy, P., Lowery, C., & Eswaran, H. (2008). An objective assessment of fetal and neonatal auditory evoked responses. *NeuroImage*, **43**, 521–7.

Háden, G., Stefanics, G., Vesterrgaard, M., Denham, S., Sziller, I., & Winkler, I. (2009). Timbre-independent extraction of pitch in newborn infants. *Psychophysiology*, **46**, 69–74.

Hannon, E., & Trainor, L. (2007). Music acquisition: Effects of enculturation and formal training on development. *Trends in Cognitive Sciences*, **11**, 466–72.

Holt, J. (1978). *It's never too late: My musical life story*. New York: Delacorte.

Hooks, B., & Chen, C. (2007). Critical periods in the visual system: Changing views for a model of experience-dependent plasticity. *Neuron*, **56**(2), 312–26.

Huang, H., Zhang, J., Wakana, S., Zhang, W., Ren, T., Richards, L., Yarowsky, P., Donohue, P., Graham, E., van Zijl, P., & Mori, S. (2006). White and gray matter development in human fetal, newborn and pediatric brains. *NeuroImage*, **33**, 27–38.

Hyde, K., Lerch, J., Norton, A., Forgeard, M., Winner, E., Evans, A. C., & Schlaug, G. (2009). Musical training shapes structural brain development. *Journal of Neuroscience*, **29**(10), 3019–25.

Jardi, R., Pins, D., Houfflin-Debarge, V., Chaffiotte, C., Rocourt, N., Pruvo, J.-P., Steinling, M., Delion, P., & Thomas, P. (2008). Fetal cortical activation to sound at 33 weeks of gestation: A functional MRI study. *NeuroImage*, **42**, 10–18.

Jentschke, S., & Koelsch, S. (2009). Musical training modulates the development of syntax processing in children. *NeuroImage*, **47**, 735–44.

Jentschke, S., Koelsch, S., Sallat, S., & Friederici, A. (2008). Children with specific language impairment also show impairment of music-syntactic processing. *Journal of Cognitive Neuroscience*, **20**(11), 1940–51.

Johnson, M. (1998). The neural basis of cognitive development. In E. Kuhn & S. Siegler (Eds.), *Handbook of child psychology*, Vol. 2 (5th ed., pp. 1–49). New York: John Wiley & Sons.

Joseph, R. (2000). Fetal brain behavior and cognitive development. *Developmental Review*, **20**, 81–98.

Knickmeyer, R., Gouttard, S., Kang, C., Evans, D., Wilber, K., Smith, J., Hamer, R., Lin, W., Gerig, G., & Gilmore, J. (2008). A structural MRI study of human brain development from birth to 2 years. *Journal of Neuroscience*, **28**(47), 12176–82.

Koelsch, S., Fritz, T., Schulze, K., Alsop, D., & Schlaug, G. (2005). Adults and children processing music: An fMRI study. *NeuroImage*, **25**, 1068–76.

Koelsch, S., Grossmann, T., Gunter, T., Hahne, A., Schröger, E., & Friederici, A. (2003). Children processing music: Electric brain responses reveal musical competence and gender differences. *Journal of Cognitive Neuroscience*, **15**(5), 683–93.

Kotilahti, K., Nissilä, I., Näsi, T., Lipiäinen, L., Noponen, T., Merläinen, P., Huotilainen, M., & Fellman, V. (2010). Hemodynamic responses to speech and music in newborn infants. *Human Brain Mapping*, **31**(4), 595–603.

Kuhl, P., & Rivera-Gaxiola, M. (2008). Neural substrates of language acquisition. *Annual Review of Neuroscience*, **31**, 511–34.

Lecanuet, J.-P. (1996). Prenatal auditory experience. In I. Deliège & J. Sloboda (eds), *Musical Beginnings* (pp. 3–34). Oxford: Oxford University Press.

Lenroot, R., & Giedd, J. (2006). Brain development in children and adolescents: Insights from anatomical magnetic resonance imaging. *Neuroscience and Biobehavioral Reviews*, **30**, 718–29.

Lewis, M. (2005). Self-organizing individual differences in brain development. *Developmental Review*, **25**, 252–77.

Magne, C., Schön, D., & Besson, M. (2006). Musician children detect pitch violations in both music and language better than nonmusician children: Behavioral and electrophysiological approaches. *Journal of Cognitive Neuroscience*, **18**(2), 199–211.

Menon, V., & Levitin, D. (2005). The rewards of music listening: Response and physiological connectivity of the mesolimbic system. *NeuroImage*, **28**, 175–84.

Moore, J. (2002). Maturation of human auditory cortex: Implications for speech perception. *The Annals of Otology, Rhinology, and Laryngology*, **111**, 7–10.

Moore, D., Burland, K., & Davidson, J. (2003). The social context of musical success: A developmental account. *British Journal of Psychology*, **94**, 529–49.

Moreno, S., & Besson, M. (2006). Musical training and language-related brain electrical activity in children. *Psychophysiology*, **43**, 287–91.

Münte, T., Altenmüller, E., & Jäncke, L. (2002). The musician's brain as a model of neuroplasticity. *Nature Neuroscience*, **3**, 473–8.

Overy, K., Norton, A., Cronin, K., Gaab, N., Alsop, D., Winner, E., & Schlaug, G. (2004). Imaging melody and rhythm processing in young children. *NeuroReport*, **15**, 1723–5.

Patel, A., Meltznoff, A., & Kuhl, K. (2004). Cultural differences in rhythm perception: What is the influence of native language? In S. Lipscomb, R. Ashley, R. Gjerdingen, & P. Webster (Eds.), *Proceedings of the 8th International Conference on Music Perception and Cognition* [CD-ROM]. Evanston, IL: Northwestern University.

Perani, D., Saccuman, M., Scifo, P., Spada, D., Andreolli, G., Rovelli, R., Baldonli, C., & Koelsch, S. (2010). Functional specializations for music processing in the human newborn brain. *Proceedings of the National Academy of Sciences*, **107**(10), 4758–63.

Pons, F., Lewkowicz, D., Soto-Faraco, S., & Sebastián-Gallés, N. (2009). Narrowing of intersensory speech perception in infancy. *Proceedings of the National Academy of Sciences*, **106**(26), 10498–602.

Quartz, S. (2003). Learning and brain development: A neural constructivist perspective. In P. Quinlan (Ed.), *Connectionist models of development* (pp. 279–309). New York: Psychology Press.

Raufschecker, J. (2001). Cortical plasticity and music. In R. Zatorre & I. Peretz (Eds.), *The biological foundations of music. Annals of the New York Academy of Sciences*, **930**, 330–6. New York: The New York Academy of Sciences.

Roden, I., Kreutz, G., & Bongard, S. (2012). Effects of a school-based instrumental music program on verbal and visual memory in primary school children: A longitudinal study. *Frontiers in Psychology*, **3**(572). Ddoi: 10.3389/fpsyg.2012.00572.

Saffran, J., Johnson, E., Aslin, R., & Newport, E. (1999). Statistical learning of tone sequences by human infants and adults. *Cognition*, **70**, 27–52.

Saffran, J., Werker, J., & Werner, L. (2006). The infant's auditory world: Hearing, speech, and the beginnings of language. In D. Kuhn & R. Lerner (Eds.), *Handbook of child psychology*, Vol. 2 (6th ed., pp. 58–108). Hoboken, NJ: John Wiley and Sons.

Salimpoor, V., Benovoy, M., Larcher, K., Dagher, A., & Zatorre, R. (2011). Anatomically distinct dopamine release during anticipation and experience of peak emotion to music. *Nature Neuroscience*, **14**(2), 257–64.

Schlaug, G., Forgeard, M., Zhu, L., Norton, A., Norton, A., & Winner, E. (2009). Training-induced neuroplasticity in young children. *The Neurosciences and Music III: Disorders and Plasticity. Annals of the New York Academy of Sciences*, **1169**, 205–8. New York: The New York Academy of Sciences.

Schmidt, L., Trainor, L., & Santesso, D. (2003). Development of frontal electroencephalogram (EEG) and heart rate (ECG) responses to affective musical stimuli during the first 12 months of post-natal life. *Brain and Cognition*, **52**, 27–32.

Shahin, A., Roberts, L., & Trainor, L. (2004). Enhancement of auditory cortical development by musical experience in children. *NeuroReport*, **15**(12), 1917–21.

Skoe, E., & Kraus, N. (2012). A little goes a long way: How the brain is shaped by musical training in childhood. *Journal of Neuroscience*, **32**(34), 11507–10.

Stefanics, G., Háden, G., Sziller, I., Balázs, L., Beke, A., & Winkler, I. (2009). Newborn infants process pitch intervals. *Clinical Neurophysiology*, **120**, 304–8.

Stiles, J. (2000). Neural plasticity and cognitive development. *Developmental Neuropsychology*, **18**(2), 237–72.

Thompson, P., Giedd, J., Woods, R., MacDonald, D., Evans, A., & Toga, A. (2000). Growth patterns in the developing brain detected by using continuum mechanical tensor maps. *Nature*, **404**(9), 190–3.

Trainor, L., McFadden, M., Hodgson, L., Darragh, L., Barlow, J., Matsos, L., & Sonnadara, R. (2003). Changes in auditory cortex and the development of mismatch negativity between 2 and 6 months of age. *International Journal of Psychophysiology*, **51**, 5–15.

Trainor, L., Shahin, A., & Roberts, L. (2009). Understanding the benefits of musical training effects on oscillatory brain activity. *The Neurosciences and Music III—Disorders and Plasticity. Annals of the New York Academy of Sciences*, *1169*, 133–142. New York: The New York Academy of Sciences.

Wang, Z., Fernández-Seara, M., Alsop, D., Liu, W.-C., Flax, J., Benasich, A., & Detre, J. (2008). Assessment of functional development in normal infant brain using arterial spin labeled perfusion MRI. *NeuroImage*, *39*, 973–8.

Webb, S., Monk, C., & Nelson, C. (2001). Mechanisms of postnatal neurobiological development: Implications for human development. *Developmental Neuropsychology*, **19**(2), 147–71.

Winkler, I., Háden, G., Ladining, O., Sziller, I., & Honing, H. (2008). Newborn infants detect the beat in music. *Proceedings of the National Academy of Sciences*, **106**(7), 2468–71.

Winner, E. (2006). Development in the arts: Drawing and music. In D. Kuhn & R. Lerner (Eds.), *Handbook of child psychology*, Vol. 2 (6th ed., pp. 859–904). Hoboken, NJ: John Wiley and Sons.

Zatorre, R., Chen, J., & Penhune, V. (2007). When the brain plays music: Auditory–motor interactions in music perception and production. *Nature Reviews Neuroscience*, **8**, 547–58.

Zull, J. (2002). *The art of changing the brain: Enriching the practice of teaching by exploring the biology of learning*. Sterling, VA: Stylus Publishing.

Chapter 4

Musicality

Susan Hallam

Musicality: Introduction

The term "musicality" refers to the state of being "musical" which, in turn, is defined as being fond of, or skilled in, music. In the literature "musicality" is often used interchangeably with a range of other terms including "musical ability," "musical aptitude," "musical potential," and "musical talent," although the term "musicality" is often adopted in relation to whether being musical is a species-specific characteristic of human beings. Overall, there are no universally agreed definitions of these terms. Meanings are socially constructed and reflect the cultural, political, economic, and social factors pertaining in the time and place that they are adopted (Blacking, 1973). In this chapter the terminology adopted will reflect that of the research to which it refers.

Musicality as species specific

The potential to make and engage with music is generally accepted as a species-specific trait of humankind that is as universal as linguistic ability (Wallin, Merker, & Brown, 2000). There has been much speculation as to why humans have this propensity and existing theories are often contradictory. Some suggest that music, along with the other arts, has no evolutionary significance or practical function and simply exists because of the pleasure that it provides (Pinker, 1997). Others have suggested a range of evolutionary origins, including supporting mate selection, social cohesion, group effort, perceptual development, motor-skill development, conflict reduction, a means of passing time safely, and trans-generational communication (see Huron, 2003). More recently, Perlovsky (2011) has suggested that as spoken language evolved, cognitive dissonances were created between knowledge and instincts. Differentiated emotions were needed for resolving these and music provided a means of developing such a differentiated and refined emotionality. Adopting a more holistic approach, Cross (2003) suggests that music has a "transposable aboutness" (p. 51), i.e., it has many meanings which can change from situation to situation. From a developmental perspective, this suggests that music can play a role in forming connections and interrelations between the social, biological, and mechanical domains, as musical activity can simultaneously relate to movement, mood, emotion, and mastery. Music provides the opportunity to explore how these various elements are linked.

Whatever the evolutionary purposes of music, the capacity for processing it develops very early, three to four months before birth. After 28 to 30 weeks of gestation, fetuses can reliably react to external sounds and their heart rates vary as a result of exposure to music (Parncutt, 2006). The process of musical enculturation begins from the point at which brain development is influenced by auditory stimulation. As a young infant, the complex skills required for understanding and analyzing music within any particular culture develop as a result of ongoing exposure to the music of that culture. Each individual therefore develops different internal representations of music in the brain depending on the particular tonality and genre of music to which they are exposed, in the same way that different languages are learned. These early developing musical representations provide the framework for the child's ongoing musical learning. Rich musical environments and greater exposure will lead to more complex, more detailed, and stronger musical representations providing stronger potential for future learning.

Exceptional abilities and deficits of musical ability

Heritability research

While there is now a general acceptance that human beings as a species are pre-programmed to acquire musical skills in the same way that they are pre-programmed to acquire language, there continue to be heated debates about the extent to which there are individual differences in inherited musical ability. Early studies focused on comparisons of measured musical ability between identical and fraternal twins and other family relationships, the evidence from this research being mixed (e.g., Shuter-Dyson, 1999). Recent advances in our understanding of genetics have now made it possible to explore the relationship between measured perceptual abilities in music and specific genes.

Pulli and colleagues (2008), using molecular and statistical approaches, studied 15 Finnish multigenerational families (with a total of 234 family members) with the aim of establishing the biological background of music perception. Three tests were used to assess musical aptitude: a test for auditory structuring ability (Karma Music Test; KMT) commonly used in Finland, and the Seashore pitch and time discrimination subtests (SP and ST, respectively). Significant evidence of linkage was obtained for chromosome 4q22 (LOD 3.33) and suggestive evidence of linkage for 8q13–21 (LOD 2.29). Heritability estimates for the three tests ranged from 21% to 57%, with a combined estimate of 48%. The results showed that there was a genetic contribution to assessed musical perception. However, this seemed to be regulated by several predisposing genes or variants rather than a single gene. Pulli and colleagues concluded that musical ability as assessed by aural perception varies between individuals, and seems to be expressed at the population level in such a way that both extremes (extremely capable or incapable individuals) are rare. Most individuals demonstrate moderate perceptual abilities. Pulli and colleagues argue that this is a typical feature of a complex trait influenced by several underlying genes, environmental factors, and their interactions. There are, however, as Pulli and colleagues acknowledge, examples of individuals who exhibit extremes of musical ability: savants and those with Williams syndrome, prodigies, those who have absolute pitch, and those with poor music perception.

Musical savants

Musical savants are children whose general cognitive functioning is below normal levels, but who nevertheless are able to undertake some activities with ease and exceptional skill, for instance, drawing, calculating calendar dates, and playing music.

As many as 10% of individuals with autistic disorder exhibit such exceptional skills to varying degrees, although savant syndrome occurs in other developmental disabilities or where there are other types of central nervous system injury or disease. Whatever the particular savant skill, it is always linked to exceptional memory (Treffert, 2009).

Autism is characterized by enhanced perceptual processing, with autistic individuals having superior performance in low-level cognitive operations, for instance, discrimination in the visual and auditory modalities. Many musical savants exhibit absolute pitch (Bonnel et al., 2003; Heaton, 2003), enabling them to make confident, rapid judgments about individual pitches and complex chords. They are also sensitive to rules reflecting harmonic relationships and the structure of musical compositions (Sloboda, Hermelin, & O'Connor, 1985; Young & Nettelbeck, 1995). Mottron, Dawson, and Soulieres (2009) suggest that in autistic children, enhanced detection of patterns, including similarity within and among patterns, is one of the mechanisms responsible for their abilities, as they easily process highly structured and non-arbitrary human codes, one of which is music. Mottron and colleagues (2009) go on to suggest that processing in pattern-rich, highly structured domains is emotionally rewarding for people with autism.

While it is clear that there is an underlying genetic basis for these skills, environmental influences should not be underestimated, not least in explaining the range of different skills, for instance, musical, artistic, mathematical, which savants can exhibit. Many musical savants have sight and language disorders, which may lead to increased development of auditory processing skills. Hearing music, which is based on highly structured codes, may give rise to a focused interest which then serves to reward engagement with particular patterns and leads to their repetition (Grelotti et al., 2005; Miller, 1989; Sloboda, Hermelin, & O'Connor, 1985). Over time, practice leads to the development of high levels of musical expertise. Having the opportunity to actively engage with making music to develop their skills is as important for savants as for other children. Heaton (2009) has shown that there are autistic children with high musical perception scores developed through listening to music who do not develop high-level performing skills because the environmental conditions do not provide the right opportunities.

Williams syndrome

Individuals with Williams syndrome have low measured intelligence and difficulties with mathematical and spatial reasoning, but are more adept than might be expected in language and music, the development of the latter depending on access to appropriate musical opportunities. Levitin and colleagues (Levitin & Bellugi, 1998; Levitin & Menon, 2003; Levitin et al., 2007) have shown that these children are typically as musically accomplished, engaged, and interested as ordinary children, but display greater emotional responses to music, become interested at a younger age, spend more time listening to music, instinctively experience music much more fully than others, and possess a highly sensitive emotional attachment to music.

Musical prodigies

Prodigies display exceptional talent from an early age. Often cited musical examples include Mozart, Bach, Beethoven, and Mendelssohn. As for savants, whatever the underlying gene combination which leads to accelerated learning in particular domains, the environmental conditions have to be conducive. In music, this means exposure from an early age and opportunity to actively engage with it. For example, McPherson describes a young female pianist, Tiffany, who at the age of 2 tried to copy, on a toy piano, music that she had heard. At the age of 4.5 she began formal piano lessons, and after three years of learning was practicing for three or four hours a day and capable of performing at Grade 8 Associated Board standard. Her mother reported that during the early stages of learning she would play games with her daughter that helped her focus on repetition and mastery. This provided a playful learning environment in which there was much very positive verbal feedback. The mother–child relationship supported the development of motivation to achieve at a continually higher level. Tiffany also had high-level self-regulatory skills and acquired an aural representation of what she wanted to learn before playing it, selecting repertoire that she wanted to learn. Her motivation was being able to play particular pieces of music (McPherson & Lehmann, 2012).

It seems that key factors for the accelerated development seen in prodigies are the support of parents and teachers, extensive practice, and motivation which has been described as the "rage to master" (Vandervert, 2009a, b). The importance of stimulation and activation early in life in prodigious development is supported by Shavinina (2009). The developing child selectively responds to stimuli in ways that heighten his or her cognitive, emotional, and social sensitivities. This provides the foundations for their accelerated learning (Shavinina, 2007).

Vandervert suggests that the "rage to master" can be explained as a result of domain-specific high attentional control that begins in infancy. This originates and then accelerates connections between the cerebral cortex (where mental modeling construction and repetition occurs) and the cerebellum (where model formation occurs), such that cerebellar control models feedback to the working memory areas of the cortex. In this way working memory becomes faster, more concentrated, and more efficient (Vandervert, 2007). This phenomenon occurs in the development of all expertise, but in prodigies it is accelerated. This requires appropriate environmental conditions, but is also likely to have some genetic underpinning. Like the savants, the area of expertise developed will depend on opportunity, although the areas developed in prodigies and savants are remarkably similar, e.g., mathematics, music.

There are some similarities in the development of and overt musical behaviors of savants, Williams syndrome individuals, and prodigies, even though their neurodevelopmental trajectories differ. Neuro-constructivists suggest that typical and atypical development can be viewed as different trajectories in a continuum of possibilities. Typical and atypical developing trajectories affect the interactions of others with the child and the kind of experiences that the child seeks out, which further impact on the trajectory (Mareschal et al., 2007). For example, when parents believe that their child has musical ability, whether as a prodigy, savant, or Williams syndrome child, they are more likely to support musical activities by providing opportunities and rewarding engagement. These, in turn, will encourage further musical activity supporting skill development and the consequent changes in neural structures which facilitate future learning (Altenmüller & Gruhn, 2002; Hodges, 2006).

Absolute pitch

There has been considerable debate about the origins of absolute pitch, which is generally defined as the ability to identify or produce isolated pitches in the absence of a reference pitch. Absolute pitch is rare in the general population, and infrequent amongst professional musicians; typically only 4–8% of musicians possess it (Dowling, 1999). While initially, there was an assumption that individuals either possessed absolute pitch or did not, it is now acknowledged that there is diversity in the labeling, accuracy, consistency, and speed of labeling responses. Absolute pitch varies when the attributes of the aural stimuli are manipulated (Takeuchi & Hulse, 1993). Responses are consistently more accurate for tones which are familiar, suggesting that knowledge of pitch is acquired incrementally over time as the result of ongoing experience (Bahr, Christensen, & Bahr, 2005). While this suggests that ongoing musical learning is critical for acquisition, there is support for it having a genetic basis: that it is present very early in life; that it is acquired very quickly; that it is acquired without effort; that it runs in families (Bahr, Christensen, & Bahr, 2005); that it is present in autistic children who have had no musical training (Heaton, 2009); and that not all who receive equivalent musical training at an early age acquire it (Bermudez & Zatorre, 2009). Some have argued that as a species we are predisposed to attend to absolute rather than relative pitch (Saffran, 2003). Support for this comes from evidence that adults can typically approximate the pitch levels of familiar songs (Levitin, 1994). Takeuchi and Hulse (1993) call this "residual absolute pitch." It may be that we are all predisposed to develop absolute pitch, but require an appropriate environment at the right time for it to develop.

Tone deafness (amusia)

It has long been known that some individuals experience difficulties with pitch production in singing. Colloquially they have been referred to as being 'tone deaf'. Recently, research has demonstrated that hereditary factors play a role in tone deafness (Peretz, Cummings, & Dube, 2007), with some individuals exhibiting profound impairments in processing music despite otherwise normal auditory functioning (Stewart et al., 2006). Tone deafness has been estimated to affect around 4% of the general population (Sloboda, Wise, & Peretz, 2005) and is characterized by an impaired ability to acquire frequency information from pitched materials (Loui & Schlaug, 2012). It may also affect phonological awareness (Jones et al., 2009).

Tone deafness emerges in early life and persists throughout adulthood (Peretz, Champod, & Hyde, 2003), with individuals showing impaired performance on basic musical tasks including melodic discrimination and recognition (Sloboda, Wise, & Peretz, 2005), although detection of time changes in music may be unimpaired (Hyde & Peretz, 2004). Most individuals exhibiting tone deafness are aware of their inability to sing in tune (Cuddy et al., 2005), but are frequently unaware of their inability to perceive pitch. While it might be expected that hearing and producing pitch are inextricably linked, this is not always the case (Loui et al., 2008). Some tone-deaf individuals, who cannot consciously perceive pitch differences smaller than a semitone, can produce these pitch intervals in the right direction (Loui et al., 2008).

Overall, advances in research exploring the genetic basis of musical ability, to date, have not greatly increased our knowledge of the inherited characteristics which lead to the development of high-level musical skills. Musical perception itself does not seem to be related to specific gene pairs but several. Those who exhibit generative musical skills (performance, composition, improvisation) need to draw on a range of different gene combinations related to physique, cognition, and emotion, not only those relating to music perception. In addition, whatever genetic inheritance an individual has can be developed and changed through interaction with the environment.

Reframing conceptions of musicality

Historically, musical ability was conceptualized in terms of aural perception, which was typically assessed by musical aptitude tests. In retrospect, the different conceptions proposed seem remarkably similar, although at the time they were bitterly contested. For instance, Seashore (1938) proposed that musical ability was a set of loosely related basic aural discrimination skills, which had a genetic basis and did not change over time. He believed that musical ability included a number of clearly defined characteristics which were unrelated to each other. In contrast, Wing (1981) believed in a general inherited ability to perceive and appreciate music rather than in a profile. More recently, Gordon (2007) used the term "audiation" to describe the ability to give meaning to what is heard. In his most current conceptualization he identified six stages of "audiation": 1) momentary retention; 2) imitating and audiating tonal patterns and rhythm patterns, and recognizing and identifying a tonal center and macrobeats; 3) establishing objective or subjective tonality and meter; 4) retaining in audiation tonal patterns and rhythm patterns that have been organized; 5) recalling tonal patterns and rhythm patterns organized and audiated in other pieces of music; and 6) anticipating and predicting tonal patterns and rhythm patterns (p. 20). Several types of audiation are also identified relating to combinations of listening, reading, writing, recalling, performing, creating, and improvising (p. 15). What all of these conceptions have in common is a focus on aural perception.

The earlier sections of this chapter have focused on inherited perceptual skills (at the species and individual levels) which have underpinned most historical conceptions of musical ability. While perceptual skills are important for reaching high levels of attainment in a wide range of musical activities, they are not sufficient. As a result, there has been an increasing need to reframe what constitutes musical ability. In addition, the rapid technological changes which have taken place over the last 100 years have changed the nature of the music profession and the skills needed to be a member of it, also impacting on conceptions of what it means to be musical. Some careers are easily identified as requiring musical ability, for instance, performing (including conducting), improvising, composing, and teaching. For others, however, the need for musical skills is less visible, for instance, instrument building and maintenance, music therapy, musical research, arts management, sound production, music publishing and work in libraries, broadcasting, and journalism (see Hallam & Gaunt, 2012 for a detailed account). While all of these careers require what has traditionally been thought of as musical ability, i.e., aural skills, they also require a wide range of different professional and personal skills in different combinations. In addition to this, music has become increasingly accessible to listeners through a wide range of media, and there is now the potential for individuals to make and create their own music and publicize it widely through social media outlets. These changes mean that conceptualizing musical ability in terms of aural skills alone is insufficient to reflect the role that music currently plays in people's lives and society more generally.

Some research has attempted to address this issue by exploring public and professional perceptions of what defines musical ability. Hallam and Prince (2003) asked a sample of musicians, student musicians, educators, and the general public (n = 411) to complete the statement "musical ability is." Of the respondents, 71% viewed musical ability as being able to play a musical instrument or sing, suggesting that musical ability is often identified on the basis of the acquisition of practical skills. Alongside this, 28% of the sample mentioned aural skills as indicative of musical ability, 32% included listening and understanding, 24% having an appreciation of music, and 15% being responsive to music, these being activities in which the majority of people engage on a daily basis. Musicians themselves recognized the importance of motivational factors, personal expression, and metacognition (understanding learning and being able to learn how to learn).

A follow-up study (Hallam & Shaw, 2002) developed a series of statements from the original qualitative research which were used with rating scales to illicit responses about the nature of musical ability. Across the whole sample (n = 653) musical ability was conceptualized in relation to rhythmic ability, organization of sound, communication, motivation, personal characteristics, the integration of a range of complex skills, and performing in a group. Overall, rhythm was given the highest ratings, which may reflect its central role in much popular music. Having a musical ear ranked lower in responses than might have been expected given its prominent position with regard to musical ability historically. High ratings were given to motivation and personal commitment, demonstrating their perceived importance in developing high-level skills. Musicians expressed the strongest agreement that musical ability was related to communication, being able to play in a group, and emotional sensitivity, indicating that these skills are crucial at the highest levels of performing expertise. Overall, the conceptions of musical ability generated by the research were complex and multifaceted, and reflected the wide range of expertise that is found in the music professions in the twenty-first century.

There has also been a recognition that different musical skills are required for different musical activities. For instance, McPherson (1995/6) distinguished between visual (i.e., sight-reading, performing rehearsed music from notation), aural (i.e., playing from memory and by ear), and creative (i.e., improvising) aspects of music performance. He found that different musical skills were involved in developing each of these ways of performing music, that there was no automatic transfer between them, and that each needed to be developed separately and in combination to maximize potential.

There has also been increasing recognition of the importance of executive meta-cognitive skills, concerned with the planning, monitoring, and evaluation of learning. These skills are crucial to all music professionals and have been shown to develop over time as musical expertise is acquired (e.g., Hallam, 2001a,b; Hallam et al., 2012; McPherson & Renwick, 2001), although there are also individual differences among musicians and novices at the same level of competence (Austin & Berg, 2006; Nielsen, 1999, 2001).

Table 4.1 sets out the kinds of skills which those wishing to engage in musical activities may require. Some are applicable to all musical activities, others apply selectively to particular tasks, while others also apply to a wide range of non-musical activities.

Table 4.1 Musical and related skills and attributes

Skills and attributes	Musical- and professional-related activities
Aural skills	Rhythmic accuracy and a sense of pulse; Intonation; Creating internal musical representations from notation; Playing by ear; Memorization of music; Improvisation; Critical listening.
Literacy skills (musical and non-musical)	Reading and writing musical notation; Transposition; Understanding keys, harmony, and musical structure; Understanding different musical styles, and their cultural and historic contexts.
Physical attributes	Instrument-specific skills; Acquiring and maintaining technique.
Expressive skills	Conveying musical meaning; Communicating with an audience.
Creative skills	Interpretation; Improvisation; Composition.
Communication skills	Verbal; Non-verbal.
Evaluative skills	Critical listening; Describing and discussing music; Critically assessing personal performance, improvisation, and composition; Monitoring progress.
Self-regulatory skills	Managing the process of learning; Managing practice; Enhancing concentration; Enhancing motivation.
Organizational skills	Managing time; Managing professional commitments.
Social skills	Working in musical groups; Networking.

Learning to be musical

The processes that underpin learning in music are shared across cultures and are part of natural learning processes. Human beings are pre-programmed to learn. This can occur deliberately and intentionally, or incidentally (without our conscious awareness) (Blakemore & Frith, 2000). Musical expertise begins to develop without conscious awareness in the womb and continues through infancy as the individual is encultured into the musical language of his or her particular culture. The enculturation process means that the prerequisites for the development of expertise in music in its many forms begin long before engagement with active music-making. Once the individual begins to actively engage with music, aural perception is enhanced and scores on tests of musical ability improve (see Shuter-Dyson, 1999).

Recent studies in neuroscience have demonstrated the plasticity of the brain and how it can continue to change throughout the lifespan. As we engage with different learning experiences over long periods of time, permanent changes occur in the brain. These changes reflect the way expertise is developed in each individual. These processes have been demonstrated in much research concerned with the development of musical expertise; the longer the engagement with musical learning, the greater the neurological changes (Pantev et al., 2003). Changes are also specific to the particular musical learning undertaken. For instance, processing of pitch in string players is characterized by greater surveillance and more frontally distributed event-related potentials (ERPs), while drummers generate more complex memory traces of the temporal organization of musical sequences, and conductors demonstrate greater surveillance of auditory space (Munte et al., 2003). It seems that when we learn, the cerebral cortex self-organizes, reflecting the "learning biography" of each individual (Altenmuller, 2003, p. 349).

Such neural changes have been demonstrated in children who have been learning to play an instrument for a relatively short time. Schlaug and colleagues (2009) explored the impact of different levels of musical practice on the development of the corpus callosum (the structure which connects the right and left brain). Thirty-one children, divided into three groups (high, low, and no practice) aged 5–7, were compared after 29 months of instrumental music training. While no differences in the corpus callosum were seen prior to the musical training, differences emerged in the high-practicing group in the anterior midbody, which connects the pre motor and supplementary motor areas of the two hemispheres. The amount of musical engagement predicted the degree of change and also improvement on a motor sequencing task. Early, intensive, and prolonged skill learning led to significant structural changes in the brain, which were associated with changes in related skilled behavior.

The expertise paradigm

The main challenge to the role of inherited musical ability in the acquisition of high-level musical skills has come from the expertise paradigm which is characterized by exploration of the ways in which individuals acquire specific skills and knowledge in a domain, and how thinking and learning processes change as expertise develops. The expertise paradigm suggests that the length of time engaged in activities is a better predictor of the level of expertise attained than inherited ability. Developing even moderate levels of expertise in any field of study requires considerable time. For instance, it has been demonstrated that classical Western musicians need to have accrued up to 16 years of active engagement with music to achieve levels leading to international standing in playing an instrument, usually starting to play at an early age and increasing the amount of practice up to about 50 hours a week by adolescence (Sosniak, 1990).

A number of common characteristics have been identified in relation to expert performance (Glaser & Chi, 1988).

1 Experts excel mainly in their own domains, with little transfer to other domains. In music, even learning to perform within a different genre can be time-consuming and difficult (Sudnow, 1993).

2 Experts perceive large, meaningful patterns in their domain as in sight-reading music, where groups of notes are processed together (Goolsby, 1994).

3 Experts process material much faster than novices (Ericsson & Lehmann, 1996).

4 Experts have superior short- and long-term memory in their domain (Ericsson & Lehmann, 1996; Halpern & Bower, 1982).

5 Experts see and represent problems in their domain at a deeper level than novices (Chaffin, Imreh, & Crawford, 2002; Hallam, 2001a).

6 Experts have strong self-monitoring skills (Chaffin, Imreh, & Crawford, 2002; Hallam, 2001a).

7 High levels of expertise can lead to inflexibility and rigidity (see Hallam, 2010).

Within the expertise paradigm, much research in music has focused on the relationship between attainment and time spent practicing. For instance, Ericsson, Krampe, and Tesch-Romer (1993) suggested a monotonic relationship between "deliberate practice" (which they define as goal-oriented, structured, and effortful practice that is influenced by motivation, resources, and attention) and an individual's acquired performance. This relationship was supported by Sloboda et al. (1996), who, comparing five groups of young musicians of different capabilities, found greater levels of practice at all ages from the "best" group, increasing over time to lead to large cumulative differences.

While there is general acknowledgment that time spent in individual deliberate practice makes an important contribution to attainment, not all of the evidence supports a monotonic relationship. There is considerable evidence of wide individual differences in the amount of practice undertaken to achieve similar levels of expertise (Ericsson et al., 1993; Hallam et al., 2012; Sloboda et al., 1996), and even where there are statistically significant relationships between deliberate practice, level of expertise, or performance on particular tasks, the amount of variance explained varies considerably (Hallam, 1998; Hambrick et al., 2013; McPherson, 2005). There are also considerable differences in the amount of practice undertaken between those playing different instruments (Hallam, in preparation; Jorgensen, 2002). Several studies have suggested that the age of starting to play an instrument (Jorgensen, 2001; Sosniak, 1990) and the overall length of time learning are better predictors than practice itself (Hallam, 1998; Hallam et al., 2012; McPherson, Bailey, & Sinclair, 1997). Where data on the amount of practicing undertaken is collected retrospectively, there are issues relating to its reliability (Madsen, 2005).

Another criticism has been the lack of account taken of those who may have undertaken considerable amounts of practice but have dropped out of music instruction. While Sloboda and colleagues (1996) demonstrated that those who had dropped out had undertaken less practice and achieved less than those who continued, in much of the research on dropouts no single explanatory factor emerges. There seem to be complex relationships between prior knowledge, motivation, effort, and perceived efficacy which influence decisions to continue or discontinue learning (Hallam, 1998; Sloboda et al., 1996). When a child begins to learn an instrument, prior musical knowledge affects facility of learning and the time needed to achieve mastery. While undertaking additional practice may compensate for a lack of prior knowledge, this has a time cost and requires perseverance. If a task proves too challenging, then a child may perceive that the effort required to succeed is too great and may give up learning altogether.

A further challenge to the relationship between time spent practicing and learning outcomes relates to the quality of performance at any particular level of expertise. The amount of practice undertaken is not a strong predictor of quality (Hallam, 1998, 2013; Hallam et al., 2012; Williamon & Valentine, 2000). Sloboda and Howe (1991) also showed that learners identified as having greater musical ability by their teachers had undertaken less practice on their main instrument, their practice time having been spread more equally across three instruments.

A further issue is that measures of time spent practicing do not take account of the effectiveness of the practice undertaken. There are certainly differences in the practicing strategies adopted by students, their meta-cognitive skills, and their concentration levels, with some beginners adopting ineffective strategies and wasting time in unproductive activities (Hallam et al., 2012; McPherson & Renwick, 2001).

Perhaps the greatest weakness of the paradigm as it has been applied in music is the lack of account it takes of other musical activities that a learner may engage with which are not "deliberate" practice, for instance, listening, improvising, and participating in group activities where learning and consolidation of skills occur in an informal learning context (e.g., Kokotsaki & Hallam, 2011). This has been demonstrated to particularly be the case in popular music, where there is little emphasis on "deliberate" practice and much reliance on informal learning in peer groups (Green, 2001). Overall, a range of musical activities makes a contribution to an individual's musical skills and their developing expertise.

Summary and conclusions

The methodological and technological advances underpinning recent research in genetics suggest that observed differences in musical ability in children and adults are the result of an interaction between genetic inheritance and the opportunities for learning afforded in the environment. There is abundant evidence that humans as a species are "musical," that we share similar brain structures which respond to music, and that exposure to music and engagement with it improves measured musicality. Evidence from genetic studies to date does not indicate the presence of a "musical" gene, but that the acquisition of all forms of musical expertise depends on complex interactions between a range of skills and experiences which are likely to have equally complex genetic bases.

Narrow conceptions of musicality, which view it in terms of aural perception assessed by musical ability tests, are not sufficient to predict an individual's future musical progress or attainment. While aural abilities are undeniably important, they do not provide the basis from which to accurately assess a child's current or future musical potential or to take decisions about the musical opportunities that they should be able to access. Equally, the focus on "deliberate" practice in the expertise paradigm fails to take account of many of the other musical activities which contribute to the development of musical expertise. Clearly, to develop high-level musical skills the learner must engage with musical activities which are relevant to their goals and aspirations. This requires them to be highly motivated, have strong self-beliefs about their ability and potential to learn, have support from their family, and be given the opportunity to engage with music (Hallam, 2013).

Ideally, we should provide all children, from the earliest age, with opportunities to develop their musical skills. If resources are limited and selection has to be made, interest in music and motivation to engage with it may prove to be the best predictors of success. If motivational criteria are used for selection, the musical skills developed are likely to be well utilized in the long term in some aspect of musical activity. In a society where it is not possible, or desirable, for everyone to become professionally engaged in music, this is surely the most valuable educational outcome.

Reflective questions

1 To what extent do people within your culture believe that musical ability is inherited and cannot be developed?
2 What are the different explanations for child prodigies? Which do you think are the most convincing?
3 Can musicality be measured? What issues arise from such measurements?
4 What skills do professional musicians need? Can these be learned?
5 How important is practice for developing musical skills? What are the educational implications of this?

Reference list

Altenmuller, E. O. (2003). How many music centres are in the brain? In I. Peretz & R. Zatorre (Eds.), *The cognitive neuroscience of music* (pp. 346–56). Oxford: Oxford University Press.

Altenmüller, E., & Gruhn, W. (2002). Brain mechanisms. In R. Parncutt & G. E. McPherson (Eds.), *The science and psychology of music performance: Creative strategies for teaching and learning* (pp. 63–81). New York: Oxford University Press.

Austin, J. R., & Berg, M. H. (2006). Exploring music practice among 6th grade band and orchestra students. *Psychology of Music*, **34**(4), 535–58.

Bahr, N., Christensen, C. A., & Bahr, M. (2005). Diversity of accuracy profiles for absolute pitch recognition. *Psychology of Music*, **33**(1), 58–93.

Bermudez, P., & Zatorre, R. J. (2009). Behavioural assessment of absolute pitch (AP). *Music Perception*, **27**(2), 89–101.

Blacking, J. (1973). *How musical is man?* Seattle: University of Washington Press.

Blakemore, S. J., & Frith, U. (2000) *The implications of recent developments in neuroscience for research on teaching and learning*. London: Institute of Cognitive Neuroscience.

Bonnel, A., Mottron, L., Peretz, I., Trudel, M., Gallun, E., & Bonnel, A. M. (2003). Enhanced pitch sensitivity in individuals with autism: A signal detection analysis. *Journal of Cognitive Neuroscience*, **15**, 226–35. doi: 10.1162/089892903321208169.

Chaffin, R., Imreh, G., & Crawford, M. (2002). *Practicing perfection: Memory and piano performance*. Mahwah, NJ: Erlbaum.

Cross, I. (2003). Music, cognition, culture, and evolution. In I. Peretz & R. Zatorre (Eds.), *The cognitive neuroscience of music* (pp. 42–56). Oxford: Oxford University Press.

Cuddy, L. L., Balkwill, L. L., Peretz, I., & Holden, R. R. (2005). Musical difficulties are rare: A study of "tone deafness" among university students. *Annals of the New York Academy of Sciences*, **1060**, 311–24.

Dowling, W. J. (1999). The development of music perception and cognition. In D. Deutsch (Ed.), *The psychology of music* (2nd ed., pp. 603–25). London: Academic Press.

Ericsson, K. A., Krampe, R. T., & Tesch-Romer, C. (1993). The role of deliberate practice in the acquisition of expert performance. *Psychological Review*, **100**(3), 363–406.

Ericsson, K. A., & Lehmann, A. C. (1996). Expert and exceptional performance: Evidence on maximal adaptations on task constraints. *Annual Review of Psychology*, **47**, 273–305.

Glaser, R., & Chi, M. T. H. (1988). Overview. In M. T. H. Chi, R. Glaser, & M. J. Farr (Eds.), *The nature of expertise*. Hillsdale, NJ: Lawrence Erlbaum Associates.

Goolsby, T. W. (1994). Profiles of processing: Eye movements during sightreading. *Music Perception*, **12**, 97–123.

Gordon, E. E. (2007). *Learning sequences in music: A contemporary music learning theory*. Chicago: GIA Publications.

Green, L. (2001). *How popular musicians learn: A way ahead for music education*. London and New York: Ashgate.

Grelotti, D. J., Klin, A. J., Gauthier, I., Skudlarski, P., Cohen, D. J., Gore, J. C., Volkmar, F. R., & Schultz, R. T. (2005). fMRI activation of the fusiform gyrus and amygdala to cartoon characters but not to faces in a boy with autism. *Neuropsychologia*, **43**, 373–85. doi: 10.1016/j.neuropsychologia.2004.06.015.

Hallam, S. (1998). The predictors of achievement and drop-out in instrumental music tuition. *Psychology of Music*, **26**(2), 116–32.

Hallam, S. (2001a). The development of metacognition in musicians: Implications for education. *The British Journal of Music Education*, **18**(1), 27–39.

Hallam, S. (2001b). The development of expertise in young musicians: Strategy use, knowledge acquisition, and individual diversity. *Music Education Research*, **3**(1), 7–23.

Hallam, S. (2010). Transitions and the development of expertise. *Psychology Teaching Review*, **16**(2), 3–32.

Hallam, S. (2013). What predicts level of expertise attained, quality of performance, and future musical aspirations in young instrumental players? *Psychology of Music*, **41**(3), 265–89.

Hallam, S., & Gaunt, H. (2012). *Preparing for success: A practical guide for young musicians*. London: Institute of Education Press.

Hallam, S., & Prince, V. (2003). Conceptions of musical ability. *Research Studies in Music Education*, **20**, 2–22.

Hallam, S., Rinta, T., Varvarigou, M., Creech, A., Papageorgi, I., & Lani, J. (2012). The development of practising strategies in young people. *Psychology of Music*, **40**(5), 652–80.

Hallam, S., & Shaw, J. (2002). Constructions of musical ability. *Bulletin of the Council for Research in Music Education*, *153/4*(20), Summer/Fall, 102–8.

Hallam, S. (In preparation). Differences in practising between players of different instruments. *Psychology of Music*.

Halpern, A. R., & Bower, G. M. (1982). Musical expertise and melodic structure in memory for musical notation. *American Journal of Psychology*, **95**(1), 31–50.

Hambrick, D. Z., Oswald, F. L., Altmann, E. M., Meinz, E. J., Gobet, F., & Campitelli, G. (2013). Deliberate practice: Is that all it takes to become an expert? *Intelligence*, <http://www.sciencedirect.com/science/article/pii/S0160289613000421>.

Heaton, P. (2003). Pitch memory, labelling, and disembedding in autism. *Journal of Child Psychology and Psychiatry*, **44**, 543–51.

Heaton, P. (2009). Assessing musical skills in autistic children who are not savants. *Philosophical Transactions of the Royal Society*, 364, 1443–7. doi: 10.1098/rstb.2008.0327.

Hodges, D. A. (2006). The musical brain. In G. E. McPherson (Ed.), *The child as musician: A handbook of musical development* (pp. 51–68). Oxford: Oxford University Press.

Huron, D. (2003). Is music an evolutionary adaptation? In I. Peretz & R. Zatorre (Eds.), *The cognitive neuroscience of music* (pp. 57–77). Oxford: Oxford University Press.

Hyde, K. L., & Peretz, I. (2004). Brains that are out of tune but in time. *Psychological Science*, **15**, 356–60.

Jones, J. L., Lucker, J., Zalewski, C., Brewer, C., & Drayna, D. (2009). Phonological processing in adults with deficits in musical pitch recognition. *Journal of Communication Disorders*, **42**(3), 226–34. doi: 10.1016/j.jcomdis.2009.01.001.

Jorgensen, H. (2001). Instrumental learning: Is an early start a key to success? *British Journal of Music Education*, **18**, 227–39.

Jorgensen, H. (2002). Instrumental performance expertise and amount of practice among instrumental students in a conservatoire. *Music Education Research*, **4**, 105–19.

Kokotsaki, D., & Hallam, S. (2011). The perceived benefits of participative music making for non-music university students: A comparison with music students. *Music Education Research*, **13**(2), 149–72.

Levitin, D. J. (1994). Absolute memory for musical pitch: Evidence from the production of learned melodies. *Perception and Psychophysics*, **56**(4), 414–23.

Levitin, D. J., & Bellugi, U. (1998). Musical abilities in individuals with Williams syndrome. *Music Perception*, **15**(4), 357–89.

Levitin, D. J., Cole, K., Chiles, M., Lai, Z., Lincoln, A., & Bellugi, U. (2007). Characterizing the musical phenotype in individuals with Williams syndrome. *Child Neuropsychology*, **10**, 223–47.

Levitin, D. J., & Menon, V. (2003). Musical structure is processed in "language" areas of the brain: A possible role for Brodmann Area 47 in temporal coherence. *NeuroImage*, **20**, 2142–52 [PubMed: 14683718].

Loui, P., Guenther, F. H., Mathys, C., & Schlaug, G. (2008). Action–perception mismatch in tone-deafness. *Current Biology*, **18**, R331–R332 [PubMed: 18430629].

Loui, P., & Schlaug, G. (2012). Impaired learning of event frequencies in tone deafness. *Annals of the New York Academy of Sciences. The Neurosciences and Music IV: Learning and Memory*, **1252**, 354–60.

Madsen, C. (2005). A 30-year follow-up study of actual applied music practice versus estimated practice. *Journal of Research in Music Education*, **52**, 77–88.

Mareschal, D., Johnson, M. H., Sirois, S., Spratling, M. W., Thomas, M. S. C., & Westerman, G. (2007). *Neuroconstructivism: How the brain constructs cognition*, Vol. 1. Oxford: Oxford University Press.

McPherson, G. E. (1995/6). Five aspects of musical performance and their correlates. *Bulletin of the Council for Research in Music Education, Special Issue, The 15th International Society for Music Education*. University of Miami, Florida, 9–15 July 1994.

McPherson, G. E. (2005). From child to musician: Skill development during the beginning stages of learning an instrument. *Psychology of Music*, **33**, 5–35.

McPherson, G. E., Bailey, M., & Sinclair, K. (1997). Path analysis of a model to describe the relationship among five types of musical performance. *Journal of Research in Music Education*, **45**, 103–29.

McPherson, G. E., & Lehmann, A. (2012). Exceptional musical abilities: Musical prodigies. In G. E. McPherson & G. Welch (Eds.), *The Oxford handbook of music education: Volume 2* (pp. 31–50). Oxford: Oxford University Press.

McPherson, G. E., & Renwick, J. (2001). Longitudinal study of self-regulation in children's music practice. *Music Education Research*, **3**(1), 169–86.

Miller, L. K. (1989). *Musical savants: Exceptional skill in the mentally retarded*. Hillsdale, NJ: Erlbaum.

Mottron, L., Dawson, M., & Soulieres, I. (2009). Enhanced perception in savant syndrome: Patterns, structure, and creativity. *Philosophical Transactions of the Royal Society*, **364**, 1385–91. doi: 10.1098/rstb.2008.0333.

Munte, T. F., Nager, W., Beiss, T., Schroeder, C., & Erne, S. N. (2003). Specialization of the specialised electrophysiological investigations in professional musicians. In G. Avanzini, C. Faienza, D. Minciacchi, L. Lopez, & M. Majno (Eds.), *The neurosciences and music* (pp. 112–117). New York: New York Academy of Sciences.

Nielson, S. G. (1999). Learning strategies in instrumental music practice. *British Journal of Music Education*, **16**(3), 275–91.

Nielsen, S. G. (2001). Self-regulating learning strategies in instrumental music practice. *Music Education Research*, **3**, 155–67.

Pantev, C., Engelien, A., Candia, V., & Elbert, T. (2003). Representational cortex in musicians. In I. Peretz & R. Zatorre (Eds.), *The cognitive neuroscience of music* (pp. 382–95). Oxford: Oxford University Press.

Parncutt, R. (2006). Prenatal development. In G. E. McPherson (Ed.), *The child as musician: A handbook of musical development* (pp. 1–32). Oxford: Oxford University Press.

Peretz, I., Champod, A. S., & Hyde, K. (2003). Varieties of musical disorders: The Montreal Battery of Evaluation of Amusia. *Annals of the New York Academy of Sciences*, **999**, 58–75.

Peretz I., Cummings, S., & Dube, M.-P. (2007). The genetics of congenital amusia (tone deafness): A family-aggregation study. *American Journal of Human Genetics*, **81**, 582–8.

Perlovsky, L. (2011). Music. Cognitive function, origin, and evolution of musical emotions, *WebmedCentral Psychology*, **2**(2), WMC001494.

Pinker, S. (1997). *How the mind works*. New York: W. W. Norton.

Pulli, K., Karma, K., Norio, R., Sistonen, P., Goring, H. H. H., & Jarvela, I. (2008). Genome-wide linkage scan for loci of musical aptitude in Finnish families: Evidence for a major locus at 4q22. *Journal of Medical Genetics*, **45**, 451–6. doi: 10.1136/jmg.2007.056366 451.

Saffran, J. R. (2003). Absolute pitch in infancy and adulthood: The role of tonal structure. *Developmental Science*, **6**(1), 35–43.

Schlaug, G., Forgeard, M., Zhu, L., Norton, A., Norton, A., & Winner, E. (2009). Training-induced neuroplasticity in young children. *Annals of the New York Academy of Sciences*, July, **1169**, 205–8. doi: 10.1111/j.1749–6632.2009.04842.x.

Seashore, C. E. (1938). *The Psychology of Music*. New York: McGraw Hill.

Shavinina, L. V. (2007). On the advancement of the expert performance approach via a deep understanding of giftedness. *High Ability Studies*, **18**, 79–82.

Shavinina, L. V. (2009). *The international handbook on giftedness*. Amsterdam: Springer Science and Business Media.

Shuter-Dyson, R. (1999). Musical ability. In D. Deutsch (Ed.), *The psychology of music* (pp. 627–51). New York: Harcourt Brace and Company.

Sloboda, J. A., Davidson, J. W., Howe, M. J. A., & Moore, D. G. (1996). The role of practice in the development of performing musicians. *British Journal of Psychology*, **87**, 287–309.

Sloboda, J., Hermelin, B., & O'Connor, N. (1985). An exceptional musical memory. *Musical Perception*, 3, 155–70.

Sloboda, J. A., & Howe, M. J. A. (1991). Biographical precursors of musical excellence: An interview study. *Psychology of Music*, **19**, 3–21.

Sloboda, J. A., Wise, K. J., & Peretz, I. (2005). Quantifying tone deafness in the general population. *Annals of the New York Academy of Sciences*, **1060**, 255–61.

Sosniak, L. A. (1990). The tortoise and the hare and the development of talent. In M. J. A. Howe (Ed.), *Encouraging the development of exceptional skills and talents*. Leicester: The British Psychological Society.

Stewart, L., von Kriegstein, K., Warren, J. D., & Griffiths, T. D. (2006). Music and the brain: Disorders of musical listening. *Brain*, **129**, 2533–53.

Sudnow, D. (1993). *Ways of the hand: The organisation of improvised conduct*. London: Routledge and Kegan Paul.

Takeuchi, A. H., & Hulse, S. H. (1993). Absolute pitch. *Psychological Bulletin*, **113**, 345–361.

Treffert, D. A. (2009). The savant syndrome: An extraordinary condition. A synopsis: Past, present, future. *Philosophical Transactions of the Royal Society B*, **364**, 1351–7. doi: 10.1098/rstb.2008.0326.

Vandervert, L. R. (2007). Cognitive functions of the cerebellum explain how Ericsson's deliberate practice produces giftedness. *High Ability Studies*, **18**, 89–92.

Vandervert, L. A. (2009a). The appearance of the child prodigy 10,000 years ago: An evolutionary and developmental explanation. *Journal of Mind and Behavior*, **30**(1/2), 12–32.

Vandervert, L. A. (2009b). Working memory, the cognitive functions of the cerebellum, and the child prodigy. In L. V. Shavinina (Ed.), *International handbook of giftedness* (pp. 295–316). New York: Springer.

Wallin, N., Merker, B., & Brown, S. (2000). *The origins of music*. Cambridge, MA: MIT Press.

Williamon, A., & Valentine, E. (2000). Quantity and quality of musical practice as predictors of performance quality. *British Journal of Psychology*, **91**, 353–376.

Wing, H. D. (1981). *Standardised tests of musical intelligence*. Windsor, England: National Foundation for Educational Research.

Young, L., & Nettelbeck, T. (1995). The abilities of a musical savant and his family. *Journal of Autism and Developmental Disorders*, **25**(3), 231–47.

Chapter 5

Music cognition in childhood

Kathleen A. Corrigall and Glenn E. Schellenberg

Music cognition in childhood: Introduction

Music is ubiquitous in children's lives. Caregivers sing lullabies to soothe their upset infants, and sing playsongs to create fun and excitement (Rock, Trainor, & Addison, 1999). Music is also used to teach concepts in daycares and school classrooms, and musical interludes are common in children's television programming. Although it is clear that infants possess sophisticated musical knowledge (see Trehub & Degé, Chapter 2), such knowledge develops over many years (see Stalinski & Schellenberg, 2012; Trainor & Corrigall, 2010; Trainor & Hannon, 2013 for reviews). In this chapter, we focus on the acquisition of musical knowledge during early and middle childhood, when children become increasingly sophisticated at understanding aspects of musical structure that are common to all musical systems. This time in development is also important for musical *enculturation*: the acquisition of knowledge about structural aspects that are particular to a given musical system. Our focus is primarily on children's developing sensitivity to Western music (e.g., music that is prevalent in western Europe, Australia, and much of North America), because there is little research on musical development in non-Western cultures. As we will see, much of children's developing sensitivity to music is a consequence of informal listening experience and general cognitive development. In some instances, enriched musical experience through formal training accelerates the acquisition of musical knowledge and improves children's ability to demonstrate explicit knowledge of musical structure.

Acquisition of musical pitch structure

Much of the research on children's understanding of structure in music has focused on pitch. Some aspects of pitch perception are culture-general, such as the ability to process pitch in a relative way, sensitivity to melodic contour, and the expectation for subsequent notes in a melody to be proximate in pitch. These aspects are also acquired early in development. By contrast, other aspects of pitch structure are specific to Western music structure—such as sensitivity to key membership and harmony—and take years to develop.

Culture-general aspects of pitch processing: Absolute vs. relative pitch

Pitch information in melodies can be processed in two ways: in absolute pitch processing, the exact pitch level of each note is encoded and stored in memory; by contrast, relative pitch processing involves encoding and storing information about the *relations* between subsequent pitches in a melody. Although adults are likely to process melodic information according to both an absolute and a relative pitch code (e.g., Schellenberg, Stalinski, & Marks, 2014), relative pitch is typically more salient because it allows an individual to recognize the same tune presented at different pitch levels (i.e., in different keys). Only a small minority of individuals—those with *absolute pitch*—can name an isolated tone without the help of a reference tone, produce the correct pitch of a musical tone (e.g., middle C), and retain an isolated pitch in memory for long durations even when interfering tones are heard in the interim (Ross et al., 2004; Takeuchi & Hulse, 1993). This rare ability appears to result from a genetic predisposition, early music training, and learning to speak a tone language (for reviews see Chin, 2003; Deutsch, 2013; Takeuchi & Hulse, 1993; Trainor, 2005; and Zatorre, 2003).

Some researchers suggest that infants and young children are biased toward processing pitch in absolute terms, whereas older children and adults are biased toward processing pitch in relative terms (Takeuchi & Hulse, 1993). For example, Sergeant and Roche (1973) found that 3- to 4-year-olds were more accurate than 6-year-olds at singing familiar melodies' absolute pitches, but worse at producing relational aspects of the melody, such as the correct intervals between subsequent notes and staying within a key. In another study, Stalinski and Schellenberg (2010) asked 5- to 12-year-olds and adults to rate how similar pairs of melodies sounded. Adults rated melodies that shared a relative pitch code as sounding more similar than melodies that had the exact same pitches but in a different order; 5- to 9-year-olds showed the opposite pattern. A similar focus on absolute pitch cues has also been reported in infants (Saffran, 2003; Saffran & Griepentrog, 2001; Volkova, Trehub, & Schellenberg, 2006). The results from these studies fit nicely with general theories of child development: across domains, with increases in age children focus less on concrete, surface-level features and more on abstract, relational features (e.g., Piaget, 1966; Vygotsky, 1934/86).

Other evidence suggests, however, that this developmental shift from absolute to relative pitch processing is oversimplified. First, adults retain some information about the absolute pitch level of previously unfamiliar melodies even after only two exposures (Schellenberg et al., 2014), and memory for key is especially long-lasting for recordings that are highly familiar and always heard in the same key (e.g., TV theme songs, pop songs; Levitin, 1994; Schellenberg & Trehub, 2003). Second, several studies have shown that 6- to 11-month-old infants exhibit relative pitch because they recognize a melody when it is transposed (Plantinga & Trainor, 2005; Schellenberg & Trehub, 1999; Trainor & Trehub, 1992; Trehub, Bull, & Thorpe, 1984), whereas memory for the absolute pitch of an isolated tone decays after a few seconds and is disrupted by tones heard in the interim, which implies that infants' absolute pitch processing abilities are not particularly precocious (Plantinga & Trainor, 2008). Moreover, 8-month-olds are able to use relative pitch cues when they are more informative than absolute pitch cues (Saffran et al., 2005). It appears, then, that infants are capable of flexibly using absolute or relative pitch cues depending on task demands and the structure of the stimulus.

Finally, evidence that young children preferentially process pitch according to an absolute pitch code is mixed. Although the results of Stalinski and Schellenberg (2010) suggest that 5- to 9-year-olds focus less on relative pitch cues than older children and adults, other evidence suggests that children's memory for the absolute pitch level of familiar songs is no better than that of adults. In some studies, children's memory for the key of familiar songs did not change from 5 to 10 years of age (Trehub, Schellenberg, & Nakata, 2008), or from 9 to 12 years of age (Schellenberg & Trehub, 2008). In a sample from Japan, however, *older* children remembered the pitch level of familiar songs better than their younger counterparts (Trehub, Schellenberg, & Nakata, 2008). Memory for the absolute pitch of familiar songs may be influenced by particular experiences, such as early experience with using consistent labels for specific pitches (as in a "fixed do" system). Although learning to speak a tone language improves the likelihood of developing absolute pitch (Deutsch et al., 2006), it has little effect on memory for the pitch level of recordings

(Schellenberg & Trehub, 2008). In sum, relative pitch processing becomes more salient with age, but listeners of *all* ages process pitch both absolutely and relatively.

Culture-general aspects of pitch processing: Melodic contour

Another culture-general aspect of melodic processing is pitch contour—whether successive notes go up in pitch, down in pitch, or stay the same. Sensitivity to contour requires understanding directional pitch changes without necessarily encoding specific pitch intervals (i.e., exact distances between tones). Knowledge of contour can be implicit or explicit. Studies that examine implicit knowledge of contour typically test whether listeners are better able to perceive a melodic change if it violates the contour than when it alters the melody's intervals but maintains the contour. Even 5- to 11-month-old infants are sensitive to changes in contour (Chang & Trehub, 1977a; Trehub, Bull, & Thorpe, 1984), as are 5- to 6-year-old children (Morrongiello et al., 1985; Trehub, Morrongiello, & Thorpe, 1985). When asked to sing back a melody, young children between the ages of 3 and 5 are better at reproducing melodic contour than they are at producing exact pitches or intervals (Flowers & Dunne-Sousa, 1990). These kinds of processing biases suggest that contour may be one of the most basic and salient dimensions of melodic processing. Although musically trained children are better than untrained children at detecting contour-violating as well as contour-preserving changes in unfamiliar melodies (Morrongiello, Roes, & Donnelly, 1989), it is unclear whether music training actually improves such abilities. Children with naturally better listening skills may be more likely to take music lessons in the first place.

Explicit knowledge of contour requires listeners to identify pitch direction with verbal labels such as *up, down,* and *same.* Children who are able to demonstrate implicit knowledge of contour (e.g., 5- and 6-year-olds) do not necessarily associate terms such as *high/higher/up* and *low/lower/down* with pitches or pitch changes, and may describe pitch changes with terms such as *louder/softer* and *faster/slower* (e.g., Flowers & Costa-Giomi, 1991; Hair, 1981; Van Zee, 1976). Nevertheless, with extensive training (i.e., over several days), children as young as 5 years show improvements in their ability to describe pitch changes of sine tones (Soderquist & Moore, 1970). In fact, when Stalinski, Schellenberg, and Trehub (2008) used piano tones and only minimal training (a few minutes), 5-year-olds could identify whether the second of three notes went up or down in pitch even when the pitch change was less than a semitone.

Learning to associate pitch changes with *spatial* labels is likely to be a source of difficulty for young children. When French-speaking children are taught to label pitch changes either with spatial terms (*haut* and *bas,* equivalent to *high* and *low*), or with terms that specifically describe pitch (*aigu* and *grave,* no equivalent terms in English), those who are taught the music-specific terms perform better on subsequent pitch-direction tests than children who are taught spatial terms, which have multiple meanings (Costa-Giomi & Descombes, 1996). Thus, development of explicit knowledge of contour may differ across cultures because of language influences.

Culture-general aspects of pitch processing: Melodic expectations

Many years ago, Meyer (1956) proposed that expectations form the basis of emotional responses to music as well as the perception of musical meaning, a theory that was further elaborated by Huron (2006). Meyer argued that musical interest arises from the interplay between unexpected events that produce a feeling of tension and expected events that produce a feeling of relaxation. As such, expectations are fundamental to music appreciation and aesthetics.

Some of these musical expectations stem from culture-general grouping principles that are relevant in vision as well as audition. For example, across cultures and levels of music training, adults' melodic expectations are influenced by two principles (Schellenberg, 1996, 1997): an expectation that subsequent tones will be close to the last tone heard in terms of pitch (pitch proximity), and an expectation for pitch to change direction, either toward the penultimate tone or after a large interval (pitch reversal). Although both of these principles are culture-general, expectations based on pitch reversal are more complex and take longer to develop because they are based on the interval size and contour of the two previous tones, whereas pitch-proximity expectations are based solely on the previous tone (Schellenberg et al., 2002). When Schellenberg et al. (2002) asked children and adults either to judge how well a test tone continued a melodic fragment, or to sing a continuation of a melody, even 5-year-olds expected the next tone to be proximate in pitch. By contrast, expectations based on pitch reversal became stronger with age. Pitch-reversal expectancies may emerge from accumulating exposure to music, as well as from developmental improvements in general cognitive capabilities (e.g., working memory). Children's ability to predict melodic patterns using culture-general principles may facilitate their later acquisition of culture-specific aspects of pitch processing, and the ability to interpret emotions expressed musically.

Culture-specific aspects of pitch processing: Enculturation to Western pitch structure

Musical systems differ across cultures in their use of different musical scales upon which pieces are based, such as the major and minor scales used in Western music (Huron, 2006; Schellenberg & von Scheve, 2012). Most scales are organized around a central reference tone, such as the *tonic* in Western music (i.e., *do* in moveable *do* systems), which also identifies the key of a piece. Knowledge of key membership involves understanding which notes from the chromatic scale belong in a key and which notes do not. Enculturated listeners also acquire sensitivity to the *tonal hierarchy*: the relative frequency, stability, and importance of each note in a scale. *Harmony* is an added dimension of complexity in pitch structure in Western music, but otherwise rare across cultures. Harmony refers to rules and conventions governing the simultaneous combinations of notes that form chords, and how one chord follows another. For enculturated listeners, harmonies are over-learned, such that they can be implied by a single-line melody (i.e., when they are not actually present). Children learn to form expectations based on tonality and harmony by accumulating listening experience with the music of their culture. One possible mechanism is that they implicitly track the statistical probabilities of certain notes and chords heard sequentially (McMullen Jonaitis & Saffran, 2009). For example, in Western music, a dominant-seventh chord near the end of the piece has a high probability of being followed by a tonic chord.

Implicit knowledge of key membership and harmony has been tested in different ways. Change-detection paradigms are based on the premise that culturally familiar pitch schemas facilitate the processing of musical structure, such that a change will be easier to detect if a pattern is typical rather than atypical of Western music. For example, 10- to 13-year-olds have more difficulty detecting mistunings in a melody when it is based on an unfamiliar Javanese pelog scale compared to when the melody is based on familiar major and minor Western scales (Lynch & Eilers, 1991). The advantage for the Western melodies is greater in musically trained than untrained children, which suggests that increased musical experience—whether from formal music instruction or because musically trained children also have more informal exposure to music—accelerates enculturation to musical pitch structure. Even children as young as 4 or 5 years old are better able to detect a semitone change to a melody based on the familiar major triad than to a melody based on less familiar augmented or diminished triads (Schellenberg & Trehub, 1999; Trehub et al., 1986).

By contrast, 6- to 11-month-old infants detect changes to culturally typical and atypical melodies equally well because none is particularly familiar (Lynch et al., 1990; Schellenberg & Trehub, 1999; Trehub et al., 1986; Trehub, Schellenberg, & Kamenetsky, 1999). In general, infants' and young children's performance on change-detection tasks appears to be influenced primarily by culture-general factors, such as how simple the melodies are (e.g., with many repeated tones), rather than by culture-specific factors, although this pattern changes with increasing exposure to music (Schellenberg & Trehub, 1999). In some instances, however, evidence of the onset of enculturation to culture-typical pitch structures can be evident between 6 and 12 months of age (Cohen, Thorpe, & Trehub, 1987; Lynch & Eilers, 1992).

Trainor and Trehub (1994) found that 7-year-olds, like adults, perform equally well at detecting deviant notes in a melody that go outside the key or the implied harmony, but they have difficulty detecting changes that preserve both the key and the harmony. At 5 years of age, children detect only the changes that go outside the key, because unlike 7-year-olds and older listeners, they are not yet sensitive to harmonic relationships within a given key. At 8 months of age, infants detect both in-key and out-of-key changes equally well (Trainor & Trehub, 1992). In other words, enculturation to culture-specific pitch structures influences melody perception sometime between infancy and the preschool years (i.e., before 5 years of age), with additional exposure (from 5 to 7 years) having even greater influence.

Implicit knowledge of Western pitch structure can also be tested using reaction times. The rationale is that enculturated listeners will be slower to make speeded judgments and will make more errors about unexpected chords (those that violate key membership or harmony), even when the task involves unrelated questions such as whether a chord is played in one timbre or another (e.g., piano or trumpet). The method has been used extensively with adults (see Bigand & Poulin-Charronnat, 2006 for a review), but not frequently with children, most likely because of children's difficulty with making speeded judgments and completing many trials. In one instance, however, 6- to 11-year-olds had implicit knowledge of harmony, as evidenced by faster and more accurate judgments of a sung vowel, instrumental timbre, or consonance when the target chord was more stable in the key of the piece (i.e., the tonic rather than the sub-dominant; Schellenberg et al., 2005).

Production tasks can also reveal implicit knowledge of key membership and harmony, although it is difficult to know whether an inability to sing in key reflects a lack of knowledge, a lack of motivation to perform well, difficulty in controlling the motor movements of the vocal apparatus, or cognitive constraints such as memory limitations. Studies on children's singing accuracy also tend to lack controlled and objective measures (see Tsang, Friendly, & Trainor, 2011 for a review), which leads to results that are difficult to interpret. For example, one study found that 3- to 5-year-olds had difficulty maintaining a consistent key while singing (assessed by subjective ratings of tonality), but there was a non-significant trend for 4-year-olds to perform better than 5- and 3-year-olds (Flowers & Dunne-Sousa, 1990). Another study that also used a subjective rating scale found that fourth- and fifth-grade children were better at staying in key compared to third- and sixth-grade children (Mizener, 1993). Future studies could compare singing accuracy in tonal compared to atonal contexts to examine whether tonality influences performance accuracy, ideally using objective measures (e.g., by recording and measuring the exact pitches produced). Measures of motivation and cognitive ability could also be assessed to examine whether they influence performance.

Knowledge of Western pitch structures can also be examined using neurophysiological methods such as EEG, which measures ERPs. When Western adults hear a chord that violates the established key or the most expected harmony in a chord sequence, their brains respond differently than when an expected chord occurs. Two specific brain responses are elicited in response to these violations (e.g., Koelsch et al., 2000, 2001; see Koelsch, 2009 for a review). One (the early right anterior negativity, or ERAN) is automatic because it is elicited even when listeners focus their attention on something other than the music (e.g., watching a silent film; Koelsch et al., 2001; Koelsch, Schröger, & Gunter, 2002), which makes it particularly useful for studying young children, who often have difficulty focusing on a task for long periods of time. The second brain response (the N5) differs because it is more influenced by attentional focus (e.g., Koelsch et al., 2000). Nevertheless, both brain responses are sensitive to the degree of harmonic violation, with larger responses elicited in response to stronger violations (e.g., Koelsch et al., 2000, 2003). In other words, brain-activation patterns tell us when listeners hear a chord that sounds wrong in a musical context, and even when they hear a chord that sounds particularly bad, but *not* whether "bad chords" are actually perceived as such.

The ERAN can be elicited in children as young as 5 years of age in response to strong violations of key structure (Koelsch et al., 2003) and to harmonic violations (Jentschke et al., 2008). The ERAN also tends to be larger in musically trained 11-year-olds compared to untrained children of the same age (Jentschke & Koelsch, 2009), which implies that it strengthens with additional exposure to Western music. But even an immature ERP response can be elicited in much younger children. Corrigall and Trainor (2014) examined 4-year-olds' and adults' ERP responses to violations of key membership and harmony in chord sequences. Among adults, the typical brain responses were elicited in both violation conditions. Among 4-year-olds, an immature brain response (an early *positivity*, thought to be an immature ERAN) was elicited in response to both kinds of violations. Other ERP responses also exhibit a developmental shift from an immature to a mature response during infancy (e.g., He, Hotson, & Trainor, 2009; Tew et al., 2009; Trainor et al., 2003). One goal for future research could be to examine at what age these components emerge in response to violations of key membership and harmony. Although one study reported that an immature early positivity response was elicited in 3-year-olds (Corrigall & Trainor, 2012), another study found that children as young as 2.5 years of age had brain responses comparable to those of adults (Jentschke, Friederici, & Koelsch, 2014). The apparent maturity of the brain response is likely to be influenced by individual differences in cognitive development and exposure to music, how strongly the stimuli establish harmonic expectations, and how strongly deviant chords violate those expectations.

Considered jointly, the results reviewed suggest that children do not become enculturated listeners until the preschool and school years, with the process beginning at around 3 or 4 years of age. There is some evidence, however, that active participation in music classes for infants between 6 and 12 months of age can accelerate the enculturation process (Gerry, Unrau, & Trainor, 2012; Trainor et al., 2012). Even infants who do not participate in any specialized music classes exhibit processing biases that provide the foundation for later acquisition of key membership and harmonic knowledge. For example, 9-month-olds' better processing of unequal-step scales compared to equal-step scales (Trehub et al., 1999) prepares them to learn the particular unequal-step scales of their culture. Moreover, infants' processing advantages and preferences for consonant intervals (related to harmonic relaxation) compared to dissonant intervals (related to harmonic tension) may form the basis for later harmony perception (Masataka, 2006; Schellenberg & Trehub, 1996a,b; Trainor & Heinmiller, 1998; Trainor, Tsang, & Cheung, 2002; Zentner & Kagan, 1998; but see Plantinga & Trehub, 2014). Finally, infants' and children's ability to process pitch relatively allows them to understand and attend to pitch patterns rather than absolute frequencies, abilities that are essential for the acquisition of abstract knowledge of key membership.

As with sensitivity to other musical aspects such as contour, explicit knowledge of key membership and harmony takes longer to develop than implicit knowledge. Explicit knowledge is usually tested by judging how well particular notes and chords continue a particular melody or chord sequence, how good a melody sounds, or whether music is played correctly or incorrectly. Western adults show a reliable pattern of rating in-key notes and chords higher than out-of-key notes and chords, but they also differentiate between notes and chords within a given key by providing the highest rating to the tonic (based on the first note of the scale) and the second highest rating to the dominant (the fifth note; Cuddy & Badertscher, 1987; Krumhansl, 1990; see Krumhansl & Cuddy, 2010 for a review). When rating tasks are simplified to be appropriate for children, similar but cruder patterns emerge by around 6 years of age (Cuddy & Badertscher, 1987; Speer & Meeks, 1985), with continued development between 6 and 11 years of age (Costa-Giomi, 2003; Krumhansl & Keil, 1982; Lamont & Cross, 1994).

Rating scales are difficult for preschoolers because they require them to keep track of several points at once, which taxes young children's memory and attentional capacity. Age-appropriate methods designed to be engaging for young children allowed Corrigall and Trainor (2014) to assess 4- and 5-year-olds' explicit knowledge of Western pitch structure, in the context of both melodies and chord sequences. Four- and 5-year-olds watched videos of pairs of puppets playing the piano. One puppet played an unfamiliar but typical Western melody or chord sequence; the other puppet played an identical sequence with one violation (Corrigall & Trainor, 2014). Children awarded a prize to the puppet that played the best song, and their tendency to award the puppet that played the "correct" song was assessed. Five-year-olds were sensitive to key membership in both melodies and chord sequences, but they were not yet sensitive to harmonic violations (those that remained in key but were not the highly expected tonic). Four-year-olds failed to show sensitivity to either type of violation despite evidence that they understood the task. When tested with a *familiar* song, however, even 4-year-olds could identify when the melody alone, the melody accompanied by chords, or the chords alone were played correctly (Corrigall & Trainor, 2010). As one would expect, formal music training enhances children's explicit knowledge of pitch structures (Corrigall & Trainor, 2009; Lamont, 1998).

Findings from implicit and explicit tests of enculturation to Western pitch structures allow for several conclusions: 1) sensitivity to key membership and harmony takes many years to become adult-like; 2) knowledge of key membership develops before knowledge of harmony; 3) implicit knowledge of pitch structures develops before explicit knowledge; and 4) children demonstrate explicit knowledge of the pitch structure of familiar songs before they do so with unfamiliar songs. Future research could examine in greater detail how listening experience and general cognitive abilities influence the enculturation process. Although Corrigall and Trainor (2014) found that there was no association between children's scores on a short-term memory task and their performance on the test of explicit knowledge of Western pitch structure, other measures of cognitive functioning could be measured, such as attention. The same researchers also found that girls, who were more likely to have taken early informal music or dance classes, performed better than boys on the music task, but the role of listening experience has yet to be tested directly. To our knowledge, moreover, there is no published research on children's understanding of pitch structure in the context of the *minor* mode. This would be a particularly interesting avenue to pursue because the use of minor mode in popular music has increased dramatically since the 1960s (Schellenberg & von Scheve, 2012).

Acquisition of the temporal structure of music

The temporal structure of music includes *rhythm*, which refers to the sequence of sound events and silence, and *meter*, which refers to the underlying alternation of strong and weak beats. Meter must be abstracted from the rhythmic structure because it is not always present in the physical stimulus (Lerdahl & Jackendoff, 1983). Rhythm and meter may be the most fundamental aspects of music because some musical genres (e.g., drum circles) do not exhibit pitch patterning, and because adults readily entrain—or synchronize their movements—to the musical beat (Iversen & Patel, 2008; Repp & Su, 2013). Despite its importance in the experience of music, very little research has been conducted on children's temporal perception and production abilities. One challenge is to develop tasks that are engaging and age-appropriate, avoiding those that rely on sophisticated motor responses, such as the ability to tap along to music.

Culture-general aspects of temporal processing

Implicit measures reveal that 2- to 5-month-old infants discriminate two simple rhythms (Chang & Trehub, 1977b; Demany, McKenzie, & Vurpillot, 1977), and that 7- to 9-month-olds recognize rhythmic patterns even when the tempo and key are varied (Trehub & Thorpe, 1989). As with pitch processing, there are several aspects of temporal processing that may be universal. Drake and Bertrand (2001) proposed five such aspects, which should be evident early in development.

The first proposed universal involves rhythmic grouping. Similarities based on pitch and timbre or temporal proximity allow listeners to perceive musical phrases as well as the break between phrases (Drake & Bertrand, 2001). For example, the last note of a phrase is typically longer in duration than earlier notes. Even 4- to 9-month-old infants appear to group musical phrases similarly to adults (Krumhansl & Jusczyk, 1990; Thorpe & Trehub, 1989; Trainor & Adams, 2000), at least implicitly. There is little to no research on preschoolers' and school-aged children's knowledge of grouping structure, however, and the acquisition of explicit knowledge is likely to follow a protracted developmental trajectory.

A second proposed temporal universal is that the more regular a rhythmic sequence is, the easier it is to process, and that our perceptual systems tend to regularize irregular temporal intervals if they fall within a given window of tolerance (Drake & Bertrand, 2001). Regularity refers to the duration of each temporal interval in a sequence. A completely regular sequence is entirely isochronous, with all note durations identical, whereas a highly irregular sequence comprises many different durations. Regular sequences may also comprise binary subdivisions and multiples of a regular beat, which correspond to the use of eighth notes, quarter notes, half notes, and so on. Five- to 7-year-olds are more accurate at tapping regular sequences than less regular sequences (Drake & Gérard, 1989); when asked to reproduce irregular sequences, they tend to distort temporal intervals toward a more regular pattern.

The third temporal processing universal concerns metrical rather than rhythmic processing. Drake and Bertrand (2001) proposed that we actively search for a regular pulse (the musical beat), and we use this organization to facilitate processing of other aspects of the sequence. Research using both electrophysiological measures (Winkler et al., 2009) as well as behavioral measures (Bergeson & Trehub, 2006; Patel et al., 2011) suggests that even infants perceive the beat in music from the time they are born. In fact, beat *perception* may be one of the most fundamental musical processing abilities, even though the ability to synchronize to a beat takes much longer to develop. For example, infants and toddlers under the age of 4 years do not usually synchronize their sucking rate or their body movements with an auditory beat (Bobin-Bègue et al., 2006; Eerola, Luck, & Toiviainen, 2006; Zentner & Eerola, 2010), although they move more rhythmically to music (or isochronous drum beats) compared to speech (Zentner & Eerola, 2010), and they adjust their movements if the tempo changes (Bobin-Bègue et al., 2006; Zentner & Eerola, 2010).

Preschoolers and toddlers as young as 2 years of age can synchronize to a beat if it matches their *spontaneous motor tempo*—the tempo at which they are most comfortable moving to periodically—but they have difficulty if the beat is slower or faster (Drake, Jones, & Baruch, 2000; Provasi & Bobin-Bègue, 2003). This finding is in line with Drake and Bertrand's (2001) fourth proposed universal, which suggests that processing is best at an intermediate or preferred tempo compared to tempi that are too slow or too fast. Young children have a faster preferred tempo than adults, corresponding to around 140–150 and 100 beats per minute, respectively (e.g., Drake, Jones, & Baruch, 2000; Eerola, Luck, & Toiviainen, 2006; Fitzpatrick, Schmidt, & Lockman, 1996; McAuley et al., 2006; Provasi & Bobin-Bègue, 2003). With age, children's preferred tempo slows down and they become better at synchronizing with a wide range of tempi, due to improvements in cognitive processing (e.g., attention and working memory), motor control, coordination, and planning (Drake, Jones, & Baruch, 2000). Music training improves beat-keeping abilities (Slater, Tierney, & Kraus, 2013), which implicates a role for experience. Finally, 2- to 4-year-old children demonstrate more accurate auditory–motor synchronization abilities when they drum along with a human social partner compared to drumming along with an auditory beat alone or with a robot-like drum machine that provides visual cues (Kirschner & Tomasello, 2009). Two-year-olds can also synchronize with a beat outside their preferred tempo range if they drum along with a social partner (Kirschner & Tomasello, 2009). In other words, the social context plays a role in the motivation and ability to move in synchrony with music.

Drake and Bertrand (2001) proposed a fifth processing bias based on duration ratios, with better processing of binary ratios, in which one temporal interval is twice as long as another, compared to ternary or more complex ratios. For example, 5- and 7-year-olds are quite good at reproducing simple rhythms based on a binary subdivision of the beat (e.g., 2/4 time), but not at rhythms based on a ternary subdivision (e.g., 6/8 time; Drake, 1993). Recent research suggests, however, that this finding may reflect enculturation to Western metrical structures rather than a universal processing bias (Hannon & Trehub, 2005a).

Culture-specific aspects of temporal processing: Enculturation to Western metrical structure

As listeners acquire knowledge of the pitch structure of their culture's music, they also learn about typical metrical structures. In Western cultures, simple isochronous structures dominate, with accented beats occurring every two or (less commonly) three beats and at regular intervals. In other musical systems (e.g., from parts of South Asia, Africa, the Middle East, and parts of south-eastern Europe), complex, non-isochronous meters are common, with accented beats occurring periodically but not at regularly spaced intervals. For example, a complex meter might include two accented beats of unequal length per measure, in which the first beat is subdivided into two but the second beat is subdivided into three, such as in 5/4 time. Although complex meters are difficult for Western adults to perceive or reproduce, adults from cultures that frequently use complex meters show equivalent abilities with simple and complex meters (Hannon & Trehub, 2005a; Snyder et al., 2006).

Implicit knowledge of culture-specific meters develops rapidly during infancy. Hannon and Trehub (2005a,b) created different versions of musical pieces composed in either simple or complex meters. Deviants either changed the surface rhythm but preserved the metrical structure, or changed the rhythm *and* the meter. North American 6-month-olds detected meter-disrupting changes just as easily in simple meters as in complex meters (Hannon & Trehub, 2005a), whereas 12-month-olds exhibited a processing advantage for simple metrical structures that typify most

Western music (Hannon & Trehub, 2005b). Moreover, North American 4- to 8-month-olds *prefer* to listen to simple meters compared to complex meters, but Turkish infants—who are exposed to both kinds of metrical structure—exhibit no such preference (Soley & Hannon, 2010). These findings are inconsistent with Drake and Bertrand's (2001) proposal that simple duration ratios are inherently easier to process than complex duration ratios. Rather, they suggest that infants are born equally ready to process either type of meter, and that perceptual specialization for culture-specific meters begins during the first year of life. Nevertheless, there are constraints on how well young infants process very complex meters. For example, 5-month-olds who notice metrical disruptions in simple and complex meters fail to do so with highly complex meters that are not used in music from *any* culture (Hannon, Soley, & Levine, 2011). Moreover, both North American and Turkish infants prefer to listen to simple or complex meters compared to artificial, highly complex meters (Soley & Hannon, 2010). Thus, although there is a processing bias for simple ratios to some degree, young listeners readily learn meters that are actually used in the music they hear.

Measures of enculturation to metrical structure in infancy examine implicit knowledge, such as the type revealed by processing biases. Very little research has been done on preschool- and school-aged children's ability to make explicit perceptual judgments about the musical beat in culturally familiar or unfamiliar contexts. In a notable exception, Einarson and Trainor (2015a,b) adapted Iversen and Patel's (2008) Beat Alignment Task for children, using videos of puppets similar to those developed by Corrigall and Trainor (2014). North American 5-year-olds watched pairs of videos in which one puppet drummed along with the beat, but the other puppet drummed too fast or too slow (i.e., at a different tempo than the musical beat), or too early or too late (i.e., out of phase from the musical beat). Children were asked to award a prize to the puppet that drummed better, and performance was compared between excerpts that were composed in simple or complex meters. The drumming had no intensity accents, being comprised solely of isochronous woodblock taps in both simple and complex meters. Five-year-olds performed at chance at choosing the puppet that drummed better in the context of complex meters, but they were significantly above chance levels in the context of simple meters.

Although implicit measures reveal enculturation to musical meter during the first year of life (Hannon, Soley, & Levine, 2011; Hannon & Trehub, 2005a,b; Soley & Hannon, 2010), it is unknown whether *explicit* judgments of beat perception would show a bias for simple meters in children younger than 5 years. Moreover, beat perception has yet to be examined in children from cultures with musical systems that frequently use complex meters. Both of these questions would help to determine the role of experience in the development of meter perception. Evidence of a sensitive period for the perception of meter implies that experience with different metrical structures plays a greater role during early compared to later stages of development. For example, when Hannon and Trehub (2005b) provided North American 12-month-olds and adults with one to two weeks of exposure to music with complex meters, 12-month-olds regained their ability to notice meter-disrupting changes in complex metrical structures, but adults did not. Similarly, after two weeks of exposure to music composed in complex meters, North American 5-, 7-, and 9-year-olds showed a reduction in their bias for simple meters, but 11-year-olds and adults did not (Hannon, Vanden Bosch der Nederlanden, & Tichko, 2012). In short, experience with music plays a particularly important role during infancy and early childhood.

Development of sensitivity to musical emotion

People choose to listen to music in order to experience and regulate emotions, and because listening to music is enjoyable (Juslin & Laukka, 2004). Meyer (1956), and later Huron (2006), proposed that expectations are central to the experience of musical emotion. Because enculturation plays a role in the development of musical knowledge and expectations (see Hannon & Trainor, 2007 for a review), it is reasonable to ask whether young children perceive and experience musical emotion in the same way as adults do, even though they may not possess the same degree of culture-specific musical knowledge. To date, research has focused largely on children's *perception* of emotions expressed through music rather than on their actual emotional responses.

Nevertheless, the experience *and* perception of emotion begin in infancy. For example, infant- and child-directed speech—with exaggerated pitch contours, a higher overall pitch, and a slower rate—is essentially *musical* speech (e.g., Trainor et al., 1997), which communicates emotion and promotes infant–caregiver bonding (e.g., Trainor, 1996; Trehub & Trainor, 1998). Moreover, 6-month-old infants respond differently to lullabies compared to playsongs (Rock, Trainor, & Addison, 1999), and music listening affects infants' arousal levels during the first year of life (Schmidt, Trainor, & Santesso, 2003). Although it remains unclear whether infants perceive the positive or negative emotional valence of music, in some cases they associate an emotion expressed through music with its concordant facial expression (Nawrot, 2003).

Culture-general cues to emotion

Because infants and young children are generally not yet sensitive to many culture-specific aspects of musical structure, they use different cues to emotion compared to fully enculturated adults. In real music, a wide variety of culture-general and culture-specific cues to emotion are incorporated. For example, tempo is a culture-general cue: a fast tempo is typically associated with high arousal, whereas a slow tempo is associated with low arousal. By contrast, mode is a culture-specific cue: in Western music, major mode is a cue to positive valence, whereas minor mode is a cue to negative valence. Among adults, cues to musical emotions tend to be perceived in an additive and probabilistic manner (Juslin & Laukka, 2003). Among children, culture-general cues are often sufficient for them to decode emotions that are not subtle or nuanced. For example, even 4- or 5-year-olds identify certain emotions (such as happiness) when real music is used instead of experimentally controlled stimuli (e.g., Cunningham & Sterling, 1988; Doherty et al., 1999; Dolgin & Adelson, 1990; Terwogt & van Grinsven, 1991). Children have more difficulty than adults, however, at identifying other emotions such as fear and anger (e.g., Brosgole & Weisman, 1995; Dolgin & Adelson, 1990; Robazza, Macaluso, & D'Urso, 1994; Terwogt & van Grinsven, 1991), presumably because fear and anger are both high-arousal emotions with negative valence.

Most research on children's perception of emotion in music examines explicit knowledge by asking children to identify the emotion expressed by a short piece of music. Emotion perception can also be measured implicitly, such as when 5- to 6-year-olds' interpretation of an emotionally neutral story is influenced by prior listening to happy- or sad-sounding music (Ziv & Goshen, 2006). This finding implies that children spontaneously perceive the emotional tone of music even when they are not asked about it directly. Children also use *nonmusical* cues to interpret the emotional content of music. For example, when 7- and 8-year-olds perform a happy or sad dance to emotionally ambiguous music, they tend to interpret the emotional content of the music such that it matches their expressive body movements (Maes & Leman, 2013). Under some circumstances, nonmusical cues are actually more influential than musical cues. For example, children have a difficult time ignoring the emotional content of lyrics when asked to identify the emotion expressed by music (Morton & Trehub, 2007).

Other research has tried to pinpoint which cues to emotion children use at different ages. One common finding is that 4- and 5-year-olds rely primarily on tempo to identify the emotion expressed by music, associating a fast tempo with happiness and a slow tempo with sadness (Dalla Bella et al., 2001; Dolgin & Adelson, 1990; Mote, 2011). Even older children (6–12 years) rely more on culture-general than culture-specific cues when making emotional judgments about music (Kratus, 1993), associating excitement with high rhythmic activity and a triple meter, and calmness with low rhythmic activity and a duple meter. They also associate happiness with high rhythmic activity and the use of staccato notes, and sadness with low rhythmic activity and legato notes.

Children also rely on culture-general cues when they are asked to express emotions by singing. For example, 4- to 12-year-olds convey happiness with a faster tempo, a louder singing voice, and a higher overall pitch, but sadness with a slower tempo, a softer singing voice, and a lower overall pitch (Adachi & Trehub, 1998). One interesting finding is that 8- to 10-year-olds are more accurate than adults at perceiving the intended emotion conveyed by their same-aged peers' singing (Adachi & Trehub, 2000; Adachi, Trehub, & Abe, 2004). Presumably, adults focus on culture-specific cues when judging children's expressed emotion through song, even when these cues are unreliable.

One study examined the degree to which adults and 5-, 8-, and 11-year-old children like excerpts of music that convey happiness, peacefulness, fear, and sadness, and how well the listeners could identify the intended emotion (Hunter, Schellenberg, & Stalinski, 2011). The design allowed the researchers to examine the effect of arousal (high or low) as well as valence (positive or negative) on listeners' responses. All age groups were better at identifying high-arousal (i.e., happiness and fear) than low-arousal (i.e., peacefulness and sadness) emotions, but this difference was exaggerated in the younger age groups compared to 11-year-olds and adults. Again, this finding highlights younger children's reliance on tempo as a cue to emotion, because tempo is linked with arousal (faster tempo = higher levels of arousal). Children of all ages also showed greater liking for high-arousal compared to low-arousal excerpts, whereas adults preferred excerpts that conveyed positive (i.e., happiness and peacefulness) rather than negative (i.e., fear and sadness) emotions. In short, culture-general cues such as tempo influence children's perception of musical emotions as well as their music preferences, even during late childhood.

Culture-specific cues to emotion and the role of experience

As children accumulate listening experience, they become increasingly sensitive to culture-specific cues in the identification of musical emotions. By 6 to 8 years of age, children associate the major mode with happiness and the minor mode with sadness (Dalla Bella et al., 2001; Gerardi & Gerken, 1995; Gregory, Worrall, & Sarge, 1996), although younger children may make this link under certain circumstances (Kastner & Crowder, 1990). Because of the long developmental trajectory to acquire knowledge of tonality and harmony (e.g., Costa-Giomi, 2003; Krumhansl & Keil, 1982; Lamont & Cross, 1994), it is unsurprising that children begin to use mode as a cue to emotion during middle childhood.

In many instances, girls outperform boys at the identification of emotions conveyed through music (Cunningham & Sterling, 1988; Giomo, 1993; Hunter et al., 2011; Terwogt & van Grinsven, 1991). One possibility is that girls' better verbal ability (e.g., Fenson et al., 1994) positively influences their performance on emotion-identification tasks. Another possibility is that girls are better at emotion perception in general (e.g., McClure, 2000). A third possibility is that girls accumulate more informal and formal experience with music (e.g., Corrigall & Trainor, 2014), which may enhance their ability to identify musical emotions, at least during childhood.

Despite their superior music-cognition abilities, musically trained children do *not* typically outperform untrained children at the identification of emotions expressed through music

(Adachi, Trehub, & Abe, 2004; Robazza, Macaluso, & D'Urso, 1994; Terwogt & van Grinsven, 1991). In some instances, musically trained children have an advantage (Yong & McBride-Chang, 2007); in others, they have a disadvantage (Giomo, 1993). Because even young children can sometimes identify the emotion expressed through music using culture-general cues alone (Cunningham & Sterling, 1988; Dolgin & Adelson, 1990; Terwogt & van Grinsven, 1991), music training may enhance children's sensitivity to culture-specific cues to emotion, which are not always necessary. In fact, cross-cultural research suggests that both children and adults are relatively accurate at identifying the emotion expressed in an unfamiliar culture's music (Adachi, Trehub, & Abe, 2004; Balkwill & Thompson, 1999; Balkwill, Thompson, & Matsunaga, 2004; Fritz et al., 2009), which implies that culture-general cues are sufficient for the most part. Note, however, that research on the perception of emotions expressed musically typically focuses on the identification of basic emotions (e.g., happiness, sadness, fear), using excerpts that clearly express a particular emotion. One avenue for future research would be to examine the effect of development, cultural familiarity, and music training on the perception of more subtle expressions of emotion in music, or on the perception of so-called aesthetic emotions (e.g., wonder, nostalgia; Zentner, Grandjean, & Scherer, 2008).

Conclusions

Several themes emerge when reviewing the literature on the development of music cognition. First, the use of ecologically valid stimuli—materials that approximate what is found in the real world, such as piano tones rather than sine tones, or real music rather than highly controlled, experimentally created stimuli—typically leads to better performance. As such, there is often a trade-off between stimulus control and ecological validity. Second, children have limited cognitive skills such as shorter attention spans and smaller memory capacities, which make it difficult to study their actual knowledge (i.e., competence) rather than their ability to perform a task on a given day. In order to maximize performance, these limitations can be taken into account by designing engaging and child-friendly tasks, limiting the number of trials that children are required to complete, providing feedback on each trial, keeping instructions simple, and limiting the number of response options that children are offered (e.g., two alternatives rather than a more complex rating scale). Finally, infants and children often reveal knowledge through implicit tasks before they can show explicit knowledge of the same concept.

Research on the development of music perception and cognition is still in its infancy, and some areas remain virtually unexplored. For example, although a good deal of research has been conducted with infants under 12 months, and with children 4 years of age and older, toddlers' music abilities are undocumented for the most part. This gap in the literature is likely due to difficulties in designing procedures that are age-appropriate, a limitation that future research could attempt to resolve. Another area of research that has received little attention is cross-cultural comparisons of children's musical knowledge. Pitch and metrical structures differ across cultures, but our knowledge of children's enculturation to these aspects of music structure comes primarily from children raised in Western cultures. Finally, more research is needed to obtain a better understanding of how music perception and cognition develop naturally during childhood. This knowledge also has potential practical applications, such as helping music educators to design music lessons that build on children's existing skills, although many laboratory-based studies do not have pedagogical implications for real-world settings.

Infants are born with abilities that allow them to acquire musical knowledge (see Trehub & Degé, Chapter 2). They show sensitivity to relative pitch, melodic contour, and musical meter, which provide the foundation for developing more sophisticated skills. In particular, these early processing biases pave the way for the acquisition of culture-specific knowledge such as harmony perception and the ability to move to the beat of music. Enculturation happens primarily during early and middle childhood as cognitive abilities improve. With the accumulation of listening experience, children gain a better understanding of the structure of their culture's music, as well as its emotional content and meaning.

Author note

Preparation of this chapter was assisted with funding from the Natural Sciences and Engineering Research Council of Canada and from the Social Sciences and Humanities Research Council of Canada.

Reflective questions

1 Western music is based on either the major or the minor mode. When do children acquire sensitivity to the minor mode?
2 What are the relative contributions of informal musical experience and general cognitive development to the acquisition of musical knowledge?
3 What can we conclude about children's musical knowledge when there is a discrepancy between their performance on implicit compared to explicit measures?
4 What aspects of musical knowledge are acquired during the toddler years?
5 When and how do children in non-Western cultures acquire sensitivity to aspects of their culture's musical system?

Key sources

Hannon, E. E., & Trainor, L. J. (2007). Music acquisition: Effects of enculturation and formal training on development. *Trends in Cognitive Sciences*, **11**, 466–72.

Stalinski, S. M., & Schellenberg, E. G. (2012). Music cognition: A developmental perspective. *Topics in Cognitive Science*, **4**, 485–97.

Trainor, L. J., & Corrigall, K. A. (2010). Music acquisition and effects of musical experience. In M. R. Jones, R. R. Fay, & A. N. Popper (Eds.), *Music perception* (pp. 89–128). New York: Springer.

Trainor, L. J., & Hannon, E. E. (2013). Musical development. In D. Deutsch (Ed.), *The psychology of music* (3rd ed., pp. 423–98). London, UK: Elsevier Inc.

Reference list

Adachi, M., & Trehub, S. E. (1998). Children's expression of emotion in song. *Psychology of Music*, **26**, 133–53.

Adachi, M., & Trehub, S. E. (2000). Decoding the expressive intentions in children's songs. *Music Perception*, **18**, 213–24.

Adachi, M., Trehub, S. E., & Abe, J. I. (2004). Perceiving emotion in children's songs across age and culture. *Japanese Psychological Research*, **46**, 322–36.

Balkwill, L. L., & Thompson, W. F. (1999). A cross-cultural investigation of the perception of emotion in music: Psychophysical and cultural cues. *Music Perception*, **17**, 43–64.

Balkwill, L. L., Thompson, W. F., & Matsunaga, R. (2004). Recognition of emotion in Japanese, Western, and Hindustani music by Japanese listeners. *Japanese Psychological Research*, **46**, 337–49.

Bergeson, T. R., & Trehub, S. E. (2006). Infants' perception of rhythmic patterns. *Music Perception*, **23**, 345–60.

Bigand, E., & Poulin-Charronnat, B. (2006). Are we "experienced listeners"? A review of the musical capacities that do not depend on formal musical training. *Cognition*, **100**, 100–30.

Bobin-Bègue, A., Provasi, J., Marks, A., & Pouthas, V. (2006). Influence of auditory tempo on the endogenous rhythm of non-nutritive sucking. *European Review of Applied Psychology*, **56**, 239–245.

Brosgole, L., & Weisman, J. (1995). Mood recognition across the ages. *International Journal of Neuroscience*, **82**, 169–89.

Chang, H. W., & Trehub, S. E. (1977a). Auditory processing of relational information by young infants. *Journal of Experimental Child Psychology*, **24**, 324–31.

Chang, H. W., & Trehub, S. E. (1977b). Infants' perception of temporal grouping in auditory patterns. *Child Development*, **48**, 1666–70.

Chin, C. S. (2003). The development of absolute pitch: A theory concerning the roles of music training at an early developmental age and individual cognitive style. *Psychology of Music*, **31**, 155–71.

Cohen, A. J., Thorpe, L. A., & Trehub, S. E. (1987). Infants' perception of musical relations in short transposed tone sequences. *Canadian Journal of Psychology*, **41**, 33–47.

Corrigall, K. A., & Trainor, L. J. (2009). Effects of musical training on key and harmony perception. *Annals of the New York Academy of Sciences*, **1169**, 164–8.

Corrigall, K. A., & Trainor, L. J. (2010). Musical enculturation in preschool children: Acquisition of key and harmonic knowledge. *Music Perception*, **28**, 195–200.

Corrigall, K. A., & Trainor, L. J. (2012). Three-year-olds are sensitive to key membership and harmony: Evidence from electrophysiology. Poster presented at the McMaster Institute for Music and the Mind NeuroMusic Conference, Hamilton, ON.

Corrigall, K. A., & Trainor, L. J. (2014). Enculturation to musical pitch structure in young children: Evidence from behavioral and electrophysiological measures. *Developmental Science*, **17**, 142–58.

Costa-Giomi, E. (2003). Young children's harmonic perception. *Annals of the New York Academy of Sciences*, **999**, 477–84.

Costa-Giomi, E., & Descombes, V. (1996). Pitch labels with single and multiple meanings: A study with French-speaking children. *Journal of Research in Music Education*, **44**, 204–14.

Cuddy, L. L., & Badertscher, B. (1987). Recovery of the tonal hierarchy: Some comparisons across age and levels of musical experience. *Perception and Psychophysics*, **41**, 609–20.

Cunningham, J. G., & Sterling, R. S. (1988). Developmental change in the understanding of affective meaning in music. *Motivation and Emotion*, **12**, 399–413.

Dalla Bella, S., Peretz, I., Rousseau, L., & Gosselin, N. (2001). A developmental study of the affective value of tempo and mode in music. *Cognition*, **80**, B1–B10.

Demany, L., McKenzie, B., & Vurpillot, E. (1977). Rhythm perception in early infancy. *Nature*, **266**, 718–19.

Deutsch, D. (2013). Absolute pitch. In D. Deutsch (Ed.), *The psychology of music* (3rd ed., pp. 141–82). San Diego: Elsevier.

Deutsch, D., Henthorn, T., Marvin, E., & Xu, H.-S. (2006). Absolute pitch among American and Chinese conservatory students: Prevalence differences, and evidence for a speech-related critical period. *Journal of the Acoustical Society of America*, **119**, 719–22.

Doherty, C. P., Fitzsimons, M., Asenbauer, B., & Staunton, H. (1999). Discrimination of prosody and music by normal children. *European Journal of Neurology*, **6**, 221–6.

Dolgin, K. G., & Adelson, E. H. (1990). Age changes in the ability to interpret affect in sung and instrumentally-presented melodies. *Psychology of Music*, **18**, 87–98.

Drake, C. (1993). Reproduction of musical rhythms by children, adult musicians, and adult nonmusicians. *Perception and Psychophysics*, **53**, 25–33.

Drake, C., & Bertrand, D. (2001). The quest for universals in temporal processing in music. *Annals of the New York Academy of Sciences*, **930**, 17–27.

Drake, C., & Gérard, C. (1989). A psychological pulse train: How young children use this cognitive framework to structure simple rhythms. *Psychological Research*, 51, 16–22.

Drake, C., Jones, M. R., & Baruch, C. (2000). The development of rhythmic attending in auditory sequences: Attunement, referent period, focal attending. *Cognition*, 77, 251–88.

Eerola, T., Luck, G., & Toiviainen, P. (2006). An investigation of preschoolers' corporeal synchronization with music. In M. Baroni, A. R. Addessi, R. Caterina, & M. Costa (Eds.), *Proceedings of the 9th International Conference on Music Perception and Cognition* (CD-ROM; pp. 472–6). Bologna, Italy: Università di Bologna.

Einarson, K. M., & Trainor, L. J. (2015a). *Hearing the beat: Young children's perceptual sensitivity to beat alignment varies according to metric structure.* Manuscript submitted for publication.

Einarson, K. M., & Trainor, L. J. (2015b). The effect of visual information on young children's perceptual sensitivity to musical beat alignment. *Timing & Time Perception*, 3, 88–101.

Fenson, L., Dale, P. S., Reznick, J. S., Bates, E., Thal, D. J., & Pethick, S. J. (1994). Variability in early communicative development. *Monographs of the Society for Research in Child Development*, 59 (5, Serial No. 242).

Fitzpatrick, P., Schmidt, R. C., & Lockman, J. J. (1996). Dynamical patterns in the development of clapping. *Child Development*, 67, 2691–708.

Flowers, P. J., & Costa-Giomi, E. (1991). Verbal and nonverbal identification of pitch changes in a familiar song by English- and Spanish-speaking preschool children. *Bulletin of the Council for Research in Music Education*, 101, 1–12.

Flowers, P. J., & Dunne-Sousa, D. (1990). Pitch-pattern accuracy, tonality, and vocal range in preschool children's singing. *Journal of Research in Music Education*, 38, 102–14.

Fritz, T., Jentschke, S., Gosselin, N., Sammler, D., Peretz, I., Turner, R., Friederici, A. D., . . . et al. (2009). Universal recognition of three basic emotions in music. *Current Biology*, 19, 573–6.

Gerardi, G. M., & Gerken, L. (1995). The development of affective responses to modality and melodic contour. *Music Perception*, 12, 279–90.

Gerry, D. W., Unrau, A., & Trainor, L. J. (2012). Active music classes in infancy enhance musical, communicative, and social development. *Developmental Science*, 15, 398–407.

Giomo, C. J. (1993). An experimental study of children's sensitivity to mood in music. *Psychology of Music*, 21, 141–62.

Gregory, A. H., Worrall, L., & Sarge, A. (1996). The development of emotional responses to music in young children. *Motivation and Emotion*, 20, 341–8.

Hair, H. I. (1981). Verbal identification of music concepts. *Journal of Research in Music Education*, 29, 11–21.

Hannon, E. E., Soley, G., & Levine, R. S. (2011). Constraints on infants' musical rhythm perception: Effects of interval ratio complexity and enculturation. *Developmental Science*, 14, 865–72.

Hannon, E. E., & Trainor, L. J. (2007). Music acquisition: Effects of enculturation and formal training on development. *Trends in Cognitive Sciences*, 11, 466–72.

Hannon, E. E., & Trehub, S. E. (2005a). Metrical categories in infancy and adulthood. *Psychological Science*, 16, 48–55.

Hannon, E. E., & Trehub, S. E. (2005b). Tuning in to musical rhythms: Infants learn more readily than adults. *Proceedings of the National Academy of Sciences*, 102, 12639–43.

Hannon, E. E., Vanden Bosch der Nederlanden, C. M., & Tichko, P. (2012). Effects of perceptual experience on children's and adults' perception of unfamiliar rhythms. *Annals of the New York Academy of Sciences*, 1252, 92–9.

He, C., Hotson, L., & Trainor, L. J. (2009). Maturation of cortical mismatch responses to occasional pitch change in early infancy: Effects of presentation rate and magnitude of change. *Neuropsychologia*, 47, 218–29.

Hunter, P. G., Schellenberg, E. G., & Stalinski, S. M. (2011). Liking and identifying emotionally expressive music: Age and gender differences. *Journal of Experimental Child Psychology*, 110, 80–93.

Huron, D. (2006). *Sweet anticipation: Music and the psychology of expectation*. Cambridge, MA: MIT Press.

Iversen, J. R., & Patel, A. D. (2008). The Beat Alignment Test (BAT): Surveying beat processing abilities in the general population. In K. Miyazaki, M. Adachi, Y. Hiraga, Y. Nakajima, & M. Tsuzaki (Eds.), *Proceedings of the 10th International Conference on Music Perception and Cognition (ICMPC10)* (CD-ROM; pp. 465–8). Adelaide, Australia: Causal Productions.

Jentschke, S., Friederici, A. D., & Koelsch, S. (2014). Neural correlates of music-syntactic processing in two-year-old children. *Developmental Cognitive Neuroscience*, 9, 200–8.

Jentschke, S., & Koelsch, S. (2009). Musical training modulates the development of syntax processing in children. *NeuroImage*, 47, 735–44.

Jentschke, S., Koelsch, S., Sallat, S., & Friederici, A. D. (2008). Children with specific language impairment also show impairment of music-syntactic processing. *Journal of Cognitive Neuroscience*, 20, 1940–51.

Juslin, P. N., & Laukka, P. (2003). Communication of emotions in vocal expression and music performance: Different channels, same code? *Psychological Bulletin*, 129, 770–814.

Juslin, P. N., & Laukka, P. (2004). Expression, perception, and induction of musical emotions: A review and a questionnaire study of everyday listening. *Journal of New Music Research*, 33, 217–38.

Kastner, M. P., & Crowder, R. G. (1990). Perception of the major/minor distinction: IV. Emotional connotations in young children. *Music Perception*, 8, 189–201.

Kirschner, S., & Tomasello, M. (2009). Joint drumming: Social context facilitates synchronization in preschool children. *Journal of Experimental Child Psychology*, 102, 299–314.

Koelsch, S. (2009). Music-syntactic processing and auditory memory: Similarities and differences between ERAN and MMN. *Psychophysiology*, 46, 179–90.

Koelsch, S., Grossmann, T., Gunter, T. C., Hahne, A., Schröger, E., & Friederici, A. D. (2003). Children processing music: Electric brain responses reveal musical competence and gender differences. *Journal of Cognitive Neuroscience*, 15, 683–93.

Koelsch, S., Gunter, T., Friederici, A. D., & Schröger, E. (2000). Brain indices of music processing: "Nonmusicians" are musical. *Journal of Cognitive Neuroscience*, 12, 520–41.

Koelsch, S., Gunter, T. C., Schröger, E., Tervaniemi, M., Sammler, D., & Friederici, A. D. (2001). Differentiating ERAN and MMN: An ERP study. *NeuroReport*, 12, 1385–9.

Koelsch, S., Schröger, E., & Gunter, T. C. (2002). Music matters: Preattentive musicality of the human brain. *Psychophysiology*, 39, 38–48.

Kratus, J. (1993). A developmental study of children's interpretation of emotion in music. *Psychology of Music*, 21, 3–19.

Krumhansl, C. L. (1990). *Cognitive foundations of musical pitch*. New York: Oxford University Press.

Krumhansl, C. L., & Cuddy, L. L. (2010). A theory of tonal hierarchies in music. In M. R. Jones, R. R. Fay, & A. N. Popper (Eds.), *Music perception* (pp. 51–87). New York: Springer.

Krumhansl, C. L., & Jusczyk, P. W. (1990). Infants' perception of phrase structure in music. *Psychological Science*, 1, 70–3.

Krumhansl, C. L., & Keil, F. C. (1982). Acquisition of the hierarchy of tonal functions in music. *Memory and Cognition*, 10, 243–51.

Lamont, A. (1998). Music, education, and the development of pitch perception: The role of context, age, and musical experience. *Psychology of Music*, 26, 7–25.

Lamont, A., & Cross, I. (1994). Children's cognitive representations of musical pitch. *Music Perception*, 12, 27–55.

Lerdahl, F., & Jackendoff, R. S. (1983). *A generative theory of tonal music*. Cambridge, MA: MIT Press.

Levitin, D. (1994). Absolute memory for musical pitch: Evidence from the production of learned melodies. *Perception and Psychophysics*, 56, 414–23.

Lynch, M. P., & Eilers, R. E. (1991). Children's perception of native and nonnative musical scales. *Music Perception*, **9**, 121–31.

Lynch, M. P., & Eilers, R. E. (1992). A study of perceptual development for musical tuning. *Perception and Psychophysics*, **52**, 599–608.

Lynch, M. P., Eilers, R. E., Oller, D. K., & Urbano, R. C. (1990). Innateness, experience, and music perception. *Psychological Science*, **1**, 272–6.

Maes, P. J., & Leman, M. (2013). The influence of body movements on children's perception of music with an ambiguous expressive character. *PLoS ONE*, **8**(1), e54682.

Masataka, N. (2006). Preference for consonance over dissonance by hearing newborns of deaf parents and of hearing parents. *Developmental Science*, **9**, 46–50.

McAuley, J. D., Jones, M. R., Holub, S., Johnston, H. M., & Miller, N. S. (2006). The time of our lives: Life span development of timing and event tracking. *Journal of Experimental Psychology: General*, **135**, 348–67.

McClure, E. B. (2000). A meta-analytic review of sex differences in facial expression processing and their development in infants, children, and adolescents. *Psychological Bulletin*, **126**, 424–53.

McMullen Jonaitis, E., & Saffran, J. R. (2009). Learning harmony: The role of serial statistics. *Cognitive Science*, **33**, 951–68.

Meyer, L. B. (1956). *Emotion and meaning in music*. Chicago: University of Chicago Press.

Mizener, C. P. (1993). Attitudes of children toward singing and choir participation and assessed singing skill. *Journal of Research in Music Education*, **41**, 233–45.

Morrongiello, B. A., Roes, C. L., & Donnelly, F. (1989). Children's perception of musical patterns: Effects of music instruction. *Music Perception*, **6**, 447–62.

Morrongiello, B. A., Trehub, S. E., Thorpe, L. A., & Capodilupo, S. (1985). Children's perception of melodies: The role of contour, frequency, and rate of presentation. *Journal of Experimental Child Psychology*, **40**, 279–92.

Morton, J. B., & Trehub, S. E. (2007). Children's judgements of emotion in song. *Psychology of Music*, **35**, 629–39.

Mote, J. (2011). The effects of tempo and familiarity on children's affective interpretation of music. *Emotion*, **11**, 618–22.

Nawrot, E. S. (2003). The perception of emotional expression in music: Evidence from infants, children, and adults. *Psychology of Music*, **31**, 75–92.

Patel, A. D., Iversen, J. R., Brandon, M., and Saffran, J. (2011). Do infants perceive the beat in music? A new perceptual test. Paper presented at the meeting of the Society for Music Perception and Cognition, Rochester, New York.

Piaget, J. (1966). *The psychology of the child*. Paris, France: Presses Universitaires de France.

Plantinga, J., & Trainor, L. J. (2005). Memory for melody: Infants use a relative pitch code. *Cognition*, **98**, 1–11.

Plantinga, J., & Trainor, L. J. (2008). Infants' memory for isolated tones and the effects of interference. *Music Perception*, **26**, 121–8.

Plantinga, J., & Trehub, S. E. (2014). Revisiting the innate preference for consonance. *Journal of Experimental Psychology: Human Perception and Performance*, **40**, 40–9.

Provasi, J., & Bobin-Bègue, A. (2003). Spontaneous motor tempo and rhythmical synchronisation in 2½-and 4-year-old children. *International Journal of Behavioral Development*, **27**, 220–31.

Repp, B. H., & Su, Y. H. (2013). Sensorimotor synchronization: A review of recent research (2006–2012). *Psychonomic Bulletin and Review*, **20**, 403–52.

Robazza, C., Macaluso, C., & D'Urso, V. (1994). Emotional reactions to music by gender, age, and expertise. *Perceptual and Motor Skills*, **79**, 939–44.

Rock, A. M., Trainor, L. J., & Addison, T. L. (1999). Distinctive messages in infant-directed lullabies and play songs. *Developmental Psychology*, **35**, 527–34.

Ross, D. A., Olson, I. R., Marks, L. E., & Gore, J. C. (2004). A nonmusical paradigm for identifying absolute pitch possessors. *Journal of the Acoustical Society of America*, **116**, 1793–9.

Saffran, J. R. (2003). Absolute pitch in infancy and adulthood: The role of tonal structure. *Developmental Science*, **6**, 35–43.

Saffran, J. R., & Griepentrog, G. J. (2001). Absolute pitch in infant auditory learning: Evidence for developmental reorganization. *Developmental Psychology*, **37**, 74–85.

Saffran, J. R., Reeck, K., Niebuhr, A., & Wilson, D. (2005). Changing the tune: The structure of the input affects infants' use of absolute and relative pitch. *Developmental Science*, **8**, 1–7.

Schellenberg, E. G. (1996). Expectancy in melody: Tests of the implication-realization model. *Cognition*, **58**, 75–125.

Schellenberg, E. G. (1997). Simplifying the implication-realization model of melodic expectancy. *Music Perception*, **14**, 295–318.

Schellenberg, E. G., Adachi, M., Purdy, K. T., & McKinnon, M. C. (2002). Expectancy in melody: Tests of children and adults. *Journal of Experimental Psychology: General*, **131**, 511–37.

Schellenberg, E. G., Bigand, E., Poulin-Charronnat, B., Garnier, C., & Stevens, C. (2005). Children's implicit knowledge of harmony in Western music. *Developmental Science*, **8**, 551–66.

Schellenberg, E. G., Stalinski, S. M., & Marks, B. M. (2014). Memory for surface features of unfamiliar melodies: Independent effects of changes in pitch and tempo. *Psychological Research*, **78**, 84–95.

Schellenberg, E. G., & Trehub, S. E. (1996a). Children's discrimination of melodic intervals. *Developmental Psychology*, **32**, 1039–50.

Schellenberg, E. G., & Trehub, S. E. (1996b). Natural musical intervals: Evidence from infant listeners. *Psychological Science*, **7**, 272–7.

Schellenberg, E. G., & Trehub, S. E. (1999). Culture-general and culture-specific factors in the discrimination of melodies. *Journal of Experimental Child Psychology*, **74**, 107–27.

Schellenberg, E. G., & Trehub, S. E. (2003). Good pitch memory is widespread. *Psychological Science*, **14**, 262–6.

Schellenberg, E. G., & Trehub, S. E. (2008). Is there an Asian advantage for pitch memory? *Music Perception*, **25**, 241–52.

Schellenberg, E. G., & von Scheve, C. (2012). Emotional cues in American popular music: Five decades of the Top 40. *Psychology of Aesthetics, Creativity, and the Arts*, **6**, 196–203.

Schmidt, L. A., Trainor, L. J., & Santesso, D. L. (2003). Development of frontal electroencephalogram (EEG) and heart rate (ECG) responses to affective musical stimuli during the first 12 months of postnatal life. *Brain and Cognition*, **52**, 27–32.

Sergeant, D., & Roche, S. (1973). Perceptual shifts in the auditory information processing of young children. *Psychology of Music*, **1**, 39–48.

Slater, J., Tierney, A., & Kraus, N. (2013). At-risk elementary school children with one year of classroom music instruction are better at keeping a beat. *PLoS ONE*, **8**(10), e77250.

Snyder, J. S., Hannon, E. E., Large, E. W., and& Christiansen, M. H. (2006). Synchronization and continuation tapping to complex meters. *Music Perception*, **24**, 135–46.

Soderquist, D. R., & Moore, M. J. (1970). Effect of training on frequency discrimination in primary school children. *Journal of Auditory Research*, **10**, 185–92.

Soley, G., & Hannon, E. E. (2010). Infants prefer the musical meter of their own culture: A cross-cultural comparison. *Developmental Psychology*, **46**, 286–92.

Speer, J. R., & Meeks, P. U. (1985). School children's perception of pitch in music. *Psychomusicology*, **5**, 49–56.

Stalinski, S. M., & Schellenberg, E. G. (2010). Shifting perceptions: Developmental changes in judgments of melodic similarity. *Developmental Psychology*, **46**, 1799–803.

Stalinski, S. M., Schellenberg, E. G., & Trehub, S. E. (2008). Developmental changes in the perception of pitch contour: Distinguishing up from down. *Journal of the Acoustical Society of America*, **124**, 1759–63.

Takeuchi, A. H., & Hulse, S. H. (1993). Absolute pitch. *Psychological Bulletin*, **113**, 345–61.

Terwogt, M. M., & van Grinsven, F. (1991). Musical expression of moodstates. *Psychology of Music*, **19**, 99–109.

Tew, S., Fujioka, T., He, C., & Trainor, L. (2009). Neural representation of transposed melody in infants at 6 months of age. *Annals of the New York Academy of Sciences*, **1169**, 287–90.

Thorpe, L. A., & Trehub, S. E. (1989). Duration illusion and auditory grouping in infancy. *Developmental Psychology*, **25**, 122–7.

Trainor, L. J. (1996). Infant preferences for infant-directed versus noninfant-directed playsongs and lullabies. *Infant Behavior and Development*, **19**, 83–92.

Trainor, L. J. (2005). Are there critical periods for musical development? *Developmental Psychobiology*, **46**, 262–78.

Trainor, L. J., & Adams, B. (2000). Infants' and adults' use of duration and intensity cues in the segmentation of tone patterns. *Perception and Psychophysics*, **62**, 333–40.

Trainor, L. J., Clark, E. D., Huntley, A., & Adams, B. A. (1997). The acoustic basis of preferences for infant-directed singing. *Infant Behavior and Development*, **20**, 383–96.

Trainor, L. J., & Heinmiller, B. M. (1998). The development of evaluative responses to music: Infants prefer to listen to consonance over dissonance. *Infant Behavior and Development*, **21**, 77–88.

Trainor, L. J., Marie, C., Gerry, D., Whiskin, E., & Unrau, A. (2012). Becoming musically enculturated: Effects of music classes for infants on brain and behavior. *Annals of the New York Academy of Sciences*, **1252**, 129–38.

Trainor, L., McFadden, M., Hodgson, L., Darragh, L., Barlow, J., Matsos, L., & Sonnadara, R. (2003). Changes in auditory cortex and the development of mismatch negativity between 2 and 6 months of age. *International Journal of Psychophysiology*, **51**, 5–15.

Trainor, L. J., & Trehub, S. E. (1992). A comparison of infants' and adults' sensitivity to Western musical structure. *Journal of Experimental Psychology: Human Perception and Performance*, **18**, 394–402.

Trainor, L. J., & Trehub, S. E. (1994). Key membership and implied harmony in Western tonal music: Developmental perspectives. *Perception and Psychophysics*, **56**, 125–32.

Trainor, L. J., Tsang, C. D., & Cheung, V. H. (2002). Preference for sensory consonance in 2- and 4-month-old infants. *Music Perception*, **20**, 187–94.

Trehub, S. E., Bull, D., & Thorpe, L. A. (1984). Infants' perception of melodies: The role of melodic contour. *Child Development*, **55**, 821–30.

Trehub, S. E., Cohen, A. J., Thorpe, L. A., & Morrongiello, B. A. (1986). Development of the perception of musical relations: Semitone and diatonic structure. *Journal of Experimental Psychology: Human Perception and Performance*, **12**, 295–301.

Trehub, S. E., Morrongiello, B. A., & Thorpe, L. A. (1985). Children's perception of familiar melodies: The role of intervals, contour, and key. *Psychomusicology*, **5**, 39–48.

Trehub, S. E., Schellenberg, E. G., & Kamenetsky, S. B. (1999). Infants' and adults' perception of scale structure. *Journal of Experimental Psychology: Human Perception and Performance*, **25**, 965–75.

Trehub, S. E., Schellenberg, E. G., & Nakata, T. (2008). Cross-cultural perspectives on pitch memory. *Journal of Experimental Child Psychology*, **100**, 40–52.

Trehub, S. E., & Thorpe, L. A. (1989). Infants' perception of rhythm: Categorization of auditory sequences by temporal structure. *Canadian Journal of Psychology*, **43**, 217–29.

Trehub, S. E., & Trainor, L. J. (1998). Singing to infants: Lullabies and playsongs. *Advances in Infancy Research*, **12**, 43–77.

Tsang, C. D., Friendly, R. H., & Trainor, L. J. (2011). Singing development as a sensorimotor interaction problem. *Psychomusicology: Music, Mind, and Brain*, **21**, 31–44.

Van Zee, N. (1976). Responses of kindergarten children to musical stimuli and terminology. *Journal of Research in Music Education*, **24**, 14–21.

Volkova, A., Trehub, S. E., & Schellenberg, E. G. (2006). Infants' memory for musical performances. *Developmental Science*, **9**, 583–9.

Vygotsky, L. (1934/86). *Thought and language* (trans. A. Kozulin). Cambridge, MA: MIT Press (Original work published 1934).

Winkler, I., Háden, G. P., Ladinig, O., Sziller, I., & Honing, H. (2009). Newborn infants detect the beat in music. *Proceedings of the National Academy of Sciences*, **106**, 2468–71.

Yong, B. C. K., & McBride-Chang, C. (2007). Emotion perception for faces and music: Is there a link? *Korean Journal of Thinking and Problem Solving*, **17**, 57–65.

Zatorre, R. J. (2003). Absolute pitch: A model for understanding the influence of genes and development on neural and cognitive function. *Nature Neuroscience*, **6**, 692–5.

Zentner, M., & Eerola, T. (2010). Rhythmic engagement with music in infancy. *Proceedings of the National Academy of Sciences*, **107**, 5768–73.

Zentner, M., Grandjean, D., & Scherer, K. (2008). Emotions evoked by the sound of music: Characterization, classification, and measurement. *Emotion*, **8**, 494–521.

Zentner, M. R., & Kagan, J. (1998). Infants' perception of consonance and dissonance in music. *Infant Behavior and Development*, **21**, 483–492.

Ziv, N., & Goshen, M. (2006). The effect of "sad" and "happy" background music on the interpretation of a story in 5- to 6-year-old children. *British Journal of Music Education*, **23**, 303–14.

Chapter 6

Musical agency

Jackie Wiggins

Musical agency: Introduction

From the work of ethnomusicological and music education researchers (e.g., Addo, 1997; Barrett, 2005; Bjørkvold, 1989; Campbell, 2011; Campbell & Wiggins, 2013; Davies, 1992; Flohr, 1985; Marsh, 2008; Moorhead & Pond, 1978; Sundin, 1998; Young, 1995), it is clearly evident that, across cultures, young children incorporate music-making into their play and ways of being. Indeed, Trevarthen (2002) and others who have studied the musicality of infants note the essential communicative and enculturational roles musical interactions play in human development. Barrett (2005) describes this work as evidence of the roots of individuals' sociocultural and musical agency as meaning-makers and Burnard (2013), as evidence that children's spontaneous music-making is agentive.

In the data examples captured and shared by these researchers, one can easily see the initiation of musical ideas and musical material by even the youngest children. Burnard (2013) describes children as initiators of musical activities, Wiggins (2007) describes them as initiators of musical ideas, and Marsh (2008) as musical innovators. In teaching music, Burnard (2013), Marsh (2008), and Wiggins (2015) advocate engaging music learners deeply in musical experiences in the context of a music learning community that fosters and nurtures their musical and personal agency—engaging them in what Burnard (2013) describes as "experiences that fill children with a sense of agency, that endow them with creativity, motivation, courage, and belief in their own capacity as musical thinkers, makers, and creators" (pp. 2–3).

In the context of music as process (Elliott, 1995; Small, 1998) and as embodied experience (see, e.g., Bowman, 2004; Stubley, 1996; and Wiggins, 2011c), this chapter is about human capacity as music-makers and human capacity to see oneself as initiating and sharing musical ideas—ideas articulated in music and ideas about music—but mostly, ideas articulated through music-making. This vision of musical agency as capacity to conceive of music and act musically is connected to Elliott's (1995) notion of "musical knowing-in-action" (p. 61).

It is generally accepted in the field of music education that capacity to learn music is dependent upon and rooted in capacity to know music "in-action." Musical learning is fostered and enabled by musical engagement—informed engagement in authentic musical processes of performing, creating, and listening (e.g., Wiggins, 2015). It is also generally understood that music learners bring to music learning situations their lifetime of musical experience as listeners and creators of music. It is therefore beneficial to understand the breadth, depth, and sophistication that young music learners bring to learning situations.

The vignette that follows is an example of emergence and assertion of musical agency as two young children engage in music-making as part of their play at home.

> On a warm summer day, on the back porch of their house, six-year-old Adam is playing his father's conga drums while three-year-old Josh strums a toy guitar with a pick. The guitar hangs over Josh's

shoulder with a strap and he is strumming with some of the style he has seen guitarists display in the media, but also bouncing up and down with the underlying pulse of his brother's drumming.

Grinning at his brother, Adam is playing his drums loudly, chanting his rhythm just as loudly [see Figure 6.1]:

Boom_ boom! Sha-ka - la-ka-la-ka boom!   Boom boom! Sha-ka - la-ka-la-ka boom!

Fig. 6.1 Musical example 1

His rhythm is based on one he has heard in a pop song. He chants and plays this idea four times in all. Josh joins him on the third repetition, chanting along while he strums his guitar. On the fourth repetition, Josh stops strumming and interrupts:

"Adam! Adam! Like this!"

He returns to bouncing and strumming, saying loudly [see Figure 6.2]:

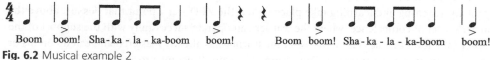

Boom boom! Sha-ka - la - ka-boom boom!   Boom boom! Sha-ka - la - ka-boom boom!

Fig. 6.2 Musical example 2

Adam nods and happily joins him.

Moments of music-making like the one captured in this vignette are dramatic examples of the strength of young children's *musical agency*––their sense that they can initiate and carry out their own musical ideas and ideas about music.[1] Children's belief in their own capacity for initiating and carrying out musical ideas can serve as the basis for further music learning (see, e.g., Blair, 2006). Conversely, ignoring or negating children's belief in this capacity can hamper their music learning (see, e.g., Ruthmann, 2006). It is essential for music educators to understand and respect the musical knowledge and experience that learners bring to music-learning settings, be they classrooms or studios.

Further, and perhaps even more important, the centrality of *learner agency* in the human learning process makes it a quality that cannot be ignored in teaching processes. Human learning is a socially constructive process (Rogoff, 1990; Vygotsky, 1978; Wenger, 1998; Wertsch 1985). As individuals engage in learning experiences (formal and informal), they actively construct their own understanding within social contexts—that is, through direct interaction with others, through what they have learned from others previously, or through interacting with the ideas of others. Learning is an act of the individual, even when that individual is an infant. Both engagement in experience and constructing understanding of experience require initiative on the part of the individual. To engage in meaning-making and learning, "we need to conceive of ourselves as 'agents' impelled by self-generated intentions" (Bruner, 1996, p. 16).

Capacity to take initiative requires *personal agency*—a belief in self, a sense that one has the capacity to engage, initiate, and intentionally influence one's life circumstances (Bandura, 2006). Learning requires personal agency (Bruner, 1996; Rogoff, 1990). Music learning requires both personal agency and musical agency, that is, belief in one's capacity to engage, initiate, and intentionally influence one's life circumstances and also belief in one's capacity to engage musically, initiate musical ideas, and intentionally influence one's musical life circumstances. Embedded in this construct is a belief/trust on the part of the individual that others in shared situations will value the ideas initiated and interactions that result.

Learner agency

The centrality of learner agency to human learning process is clearly evident in Vygotsky's (1978) vision of learning as taking place within what he described as the *zone of proximal development* (ZPD): "the distance between the actual developmental level as determined by independent problem solving and the level of potential development as determined through problem solving under adult guidance, or in collaboration with more capable peers" (p. 86). Engaging and interacting *below* a learner's ZPD means working at a level of difficulty and proficiency that the learner has already mastered. Teaching at a level that lies below a learner's ZPD means teaching something the learner already understands or knows how to do. Engaging and interacting *above* a learner's ZPD means working at a level of difficulty and proficiency that the learner is not ready to pursue. Teaching at a level that lies above a learner's ZPD means teaching something the learner does not have the prerequisite experience or knowledge to understand or know how to do. For Vygotsky, teaching and learning take place *within* the ZPD—at a point that lies just above the learner's level of competence, where the learner can operate successfully with the support of the teacher (at a level that lies just above what the learner has already mastered and can do on his or her own without teacher support). This vision of learning/teaching process makes it clear that, in the process of learning something new, a learner must operate at a level that is just above his or her level of competence—a situation that requires learner willingness to take risks (Rogoff, 1990). Willingness to take risks and enter into a situation of working above one's level of competence requires personal agency (self-belief in capacity to engage, initiate, and intentionally influence one's life circumstances). Learners who do not believe themselves capable will not enter the situation; they will disengage or resist the teacher's efforts. Learning is an act of the individual that requires personal initiative, engagement, and agency. Without the presence of these qualities in the learner, learning cannot take place.

If learning process requires personal agency and music learning requires musical engagement, it follows that music learning process requires personal and musical agency. Let us begin by exploring scholars' understandings of the constructs of personal and musical agency.

Personal agency

Scholars from different fields define *agency* in slightly different ways, but the core issues central to the construct seem to be consistent. Sociologists tend to conceive of agency in terms of the power of individuals within the social structures that constitute society, rooted in the work of Max Weber (1978) who defined power as the ability to exert one's will in spite of obstacles. Post-modern sociologist Anthony Giddens (1991) also describes agency in terms of power, suggesting that "body plus power equals agency" (p. 57). In this relationship, Giddens privileges neither societal structure nor individual agency, describing each as contributing to the creation of the other. Thus, agency is never located solely within individuals but rather in the relationships among individuals and between individuals and societal structures like institutions. In this view, agency is never static; it is not something one has or does not have, but rather something that emerges in circumstances and situations (Giddens, 1984).[2] Going further, sociologist Barry Barnes (2000) rejects all notions of duality between "human beings and the natural order in which they are set" (p. x), arguing that humans are social agents, socially accountable to each other, and that all human decisions and actions are socially embedded. Social constructivists Wertsch, Tulviste, and Hagstrom (1993) take a similar stance, proposing a vision of agency that "extends beyond the skin" in that it is "often socially distributed or shared" and always culturally embedded (p. 352).

Psychologists draw heavily on Albert Bandura, who has written extensively about *self-efficacy* as central to human agency. Bandura (1989) describes self-efficacy as "capacity to exercise control over one's own thought processes, motivation, and action" (p. 1175) and agency as intentionally influencing one's functioning and life circumstances (Bandura, 2006). Individuals need to believe themselves capable of action to be able to engage in action; knowing how is not enough. Bandura (1982) describes perceived self-efficacy as concerned with "judgments of how well one can execute courses of action required to deal with prospective situations" (p. 122), noting that "judgments of self-efficacy . . . determine how much effort people will expend and how long they will persist in the face of obstacles or aversive experiences" (p. 123). Little et al. (2002) offer a similar view, defining personal agency as "the sense of personal empowerment, which involves both knowing and having what it takes to achieve one's goals" (p. 390), and describing individuals who have a sense of agency as striving for "ambitious goals and persist[ing] in their pursuits even in the face of obstacles" (p. 390). Bandura (1982) notes that "people often do not behave optimally, even though they know full well what to do . . . because self-referent thought . . . mediates the relationship between knowledge and action" (p. 122). Sociologists would attribute this self-referent thought to sociological influences.

Like Giddens's (1984) view of agency, Bandura sees efficacy as an emergent interactive phenomenon, not fixed, but involving internal generative capability. Post-modern sociologists would see this internal capability as developed in relation to social influences. In Bandura's more recent writings (2000, 2001, 2006), the construct *agency* appears more frequently, even replacing his earlier use of *self-efficacy* in some statements. He continually refers to *agentic behavior* in the context of individuals' assertion of self-efficacy, even characterizing humans as a "sentient agentic species" (2006, p. 164). Bandura's recent writings (2000, 2001) take a more sociological perspective, proposing a construct of *collective efficacy*, rooted in his understanding of the growing interdependence of human functioning and based on his earlier model of *emergent interactive agency* (Bandura, 1986). In these more recent works, Bandura describes people as both products and producers of their environment, and acknowledges that "people create social systems and these systems, in turn, organize and influence people's lives" (2006, p. 164).

Psychologists Ryan and Deci (2002) express a similar socio-psychological view in their self-determination theory, offering an agentic vision of humans. They pose that, because individuals are "endowed with an innate striving to exercise and elaborate their interests," they "tend naturally to seek challenges, to discover new perspectives, and to actively internalize and transform cultural practices" (p. 3). By their own actions, "people actualize their human potentials" and, through what they experience, construct a "coherent sense of self" (p. 3). However, "the foundations of self-determination theory reside in a dialectical view which concerns the interaction between an active, integrating human nature and social contexts that either nurture or impede the organism's active nature" (p. 6). Little et al. (2002) note that agency underlies the synergy among the constructs that self-determination theorists consider the basic needs for healthy human functioning: competence, autonomy, and relatedness (p. 391).

From a sociocultural perspective (Rogoff, 1990; Vygotsky 1978; Wertsch, 1985) that sees learning as an act of the individual within social contexts—dependent upon and influenced by those social contexts—the centrality of learner agency to learning process becomes clear. Good teaching relies on understanding the nature and role of learner agency within the process, as well as the nature and role of social interaction within the process. These ideas lie at the heart of a social constructivist vision of learning and teaching.

Musical agency

In the field of music education, scholars in psychology and sociology of music learning, ethnomusicology, music education philosophy, and music education research have written directly about musical agency or implied its presence and importance. This includes writings in areas of musical identity (MacDonald, Hargreaves, & Miell, 2002), the nature of musical communication (Miell, MacDonald, & Hargreaves, 2005), and social and cultural psychologies of music education (Barrett, 2011; Hargreaves & North, 1997) that have been highly influential in the field.

From a psychological perspective, musical agency is rooted in and emanates from one's musical identity or, more accurately, identities, which are "forged from a combination of personal, individual musical experiences on the one hand, and membership in various social groups . . . on the other hand" (Green, 2011, p. 1). In their work on musical identity, music psychologists Hargreaves, Miell, and MacDonald (2002) describe self-identity as the overall view we have of ourselves, within which self-esteem is an evaluative component. They describe self-image as developing through a "process of monitoring our own behaviour and making social comparisons" (p. 8). All of what Hargreaves et al. call our self-systems contribute to and influence our sense of agency, including self-efficacy, as described by Bandura.

Sociologists DeNora (2000, 2001), Froelich (2007), and Small (1998) write about some of the agentic roles music plays in human and social experience. DeNora (2000) talks about the role of music "in dynamic relation with social life, helping to invoke, stabilize, and change the parameters of agency, collective and individual" (p. 20). She suggests that, "if music can affect the shape of social agency, then control over music in social settings is a source of social power; it is an opportunity to structure the parameters of action" (p. 20). Froelich (2007) describes musical choice as an expression of self that resides in both personal and social contexts, where personal decision can be a result of social context (e.g., adolescents choosing music preferred by peers). Small (1998) warns that power relationships in educational settings can distort the interconnection between musical and social meanings for learners.

Ethnomusicologist Becker (2001) suggests that there are social components of both personal and musical agency, describing musical events as setting up "an aural domain of coordination that envelops all those present" (p. 151).[3] DeNora (2000) notes that music provides a "resource in and through which agency and identity are produced" (p. 5). She describes the role of music in the development of an aesthetic self or of the individual as an *aesthetic agent*, noting that music is "a resource for modulating and structuring the parameters of aesthetic agency––feeling, motivation, desire, comportment, action style, energy" (p. 53). In this context, DeNora (2001) defines agency as "a capacity for, and ability to, formulate action and experience" (p. 162). Persson (2001) identifies self-expression as a component of musical agency, and surely it is also part of the self-system that supports our personal agency.

Music education philosophers Gould et al. (2009) and Woodford (2005) argue for the music education classroom to be a place where learners' political and social agency is fostered and nurtured, e.g., through thoughtful choice of musical materials used in learning/teaching and through employing democratic approaches to learning/teaching. Allsup, Westerlund, and Shieh (2012) consider philosophically how studying music can foster development of critical and creative agency, and conclude that, for education to be useful to adolescents, it "must help them become critical authors of their present and imagined future lives" (p. 461). Barone (2000) offers a similar perspective, calling for education to enable learners to become "strong poets"—people who refuse to accept, as useful, descriptions of their lives written by others, people who are strong storytellers, continuously revising their life stories in the light of their own experience and imagination (p. 125).

Karlsen (2011) used the term *musical agency* to describe individuals', but more so, social groups', sociological and personal uses of music. Building on Small's (1998) descriptions of the collective value of music, she proposed a collective dimension of musical agency in social groups' use of music, that music's importance for the "creation of meaningfulness and for negotiating a position-in-the-world on the individual level" may be less profound than its importance on the collective level (Karlsen, 2011, p. 114). Looking at learners' collective musical agency in particular classroom settings, Karlsen (2012) notes that the musical agency of learners with cultural and musical backgrounds different from those prevalent in the classroom can be hampered. Conversely, incorporating music of the children's culture can be empowering.

Researchers who have studied children's musical play in the settings in which it occurs (e.g., Addo, 1997; Campbell, 2011; Harwood, 1998; Koops, 2010; Marsh, 2008) have analyzed and described the processes through which children teach music to one another in these settings and contrasted these processes with prevalent music teaching practices. Musical agency underlies capacity to teach music to someone else. Marsh's extensive work in this area describes the creativity and complexity of children's musical games and the ways in which they seek and embrace musical challenge. Both Marsh and Harwood note children's awareness of their own level of capability, and those of their peers, and their capacity to scaffold one another as they engage together, with Marsh finding that children create constant challenges for themselves. Marsh (2008) explains that "self-imposed challenge is a characteristic of children's musical play" (p. 316) and, given opportunity to generate their own variants, they "increase the level of difficulty at their own pace and introduce and follow different musical directions" (p. 313).

Harwood and Marsh (2012) offer suggestions for fostering learner agency in music classroom settings, including a) providing learners control over some repertoire to be learned, b) raising the level of expectation for individual creation and performance, and providing regular opportunities for learners to work independently from the teacher, c) including popular music and repertoire requested by learners and ensuring that the repertoire and associated activities are cognitively challenging, d) allowing for learners' creative manipulation of repertoire over time, e) allowing learners to choose friendship groups for group projects, and f) providing opportunities for peer coaching (paraphrased and excerpted from p. 337).

In studies of musical activity of young children, Barrett (2005) describes children as "active social agents who internalize cultural meanings through interaction with knowledgeable others" (p. 261). Drawing on Wenger (1998), she has explored children's musical interactions in communities of musical practice—musical "communities in which children [were] active agents in the determination of the location, the participants, and the nature and range of the activities involved" (p. 261). Researchers like Barrett (2005) and Marsh (2008) describe the ways in which children appropriate and adapt components of adult music-making and popular media into their invented songs and musical games. Barrett (2005) finds that "children exercise considerable autonomy and agency" in their musical communities, "drawing on a range of communicative practices in producing and negotiating meaning" (pp. 276–7).

In studies of music education practice, researchers have studied learner agency in the applied studio, in becoming instrumental musicians, in music listening experiences, in composing original music, in music teacher education, and in connections between self-efficacy and success in musical performance. In an autoethnographic study, Manovski (2012, 2014) explored ways in which embodied life experience can impede or foster personal and musical agency, describing how his experiences in a caring, supportive, constructivist voice studio served to enable him as a singer. Davis (2008, 2011, 2013, 2014) described the importance of beginning instrumentalists having "a musical say" in their learning experiences, capturing and analyzing the development and emergence of their capacity to engage in agentic musical acts, such as figuring out how to play familiar music by ear and interpreting music for performance as integral parts of their classroom learning experiences.

Hause (2014) studied the experiences of fifth-grade students, who were considered to be "at-risk," as they engaged in an extra-curricular African ensemble. As students' musical skills, understandings, and sense of community grew, they began taking responsibility for and ownership of their own musicianship and musical process, and musical leaders emerged within the group. Development of these capacities influenced their ways of being throughout their school experiences, and in meeting with some of these students three years after the study, Hause could see they had become self-assured, productive students with life goals they could articulate.

Analyzing learners' processes when engaged in collaborative, problem-solving, listening experiences, Blair (2006, 2009) found that coming to understand how others hear music enhances individual perspectives, understanding, and musical agency. She describes the agency of music learners as functioning as musicians while engaging in listening, creating, and performing, developing their own "musician voice," and becoming empowered to further their own musical understanding—where musical growth fuels their musical agency and vice versa, in a "never-ending cycle, a synergistic energy that internally propels students forward" (Blair, 2006, p. 238).

Studies of learners' experiences composing original music in classroom settings (Claire, 1993/4; Espeland, 2007; McGillen & McMillan, 2005; Ruthmann, 2006, 2008; Wiggins, 2011a, 2015; Wiggins & Espeland, 2012; Wiggins & Medvinsky, 2012) are rife, with examples of musically agentic acts and products. In Laurence's (2010) sociological analysis of children's songwriting experiences, she identified learner agency as moving participants to take a highly empathetic stance, choosing to write song lyrics that were about the feelings of others. In a study of listening and composing experiences of students in university general education music courses, White (2012) found that enabling learners to have "a musical say" (Davis, 2008, 2011, 2013, 2014) in their learning by "thinking-in-music-with-music" fostered transformational connections between music and students' lives.

In Abrahams's (2013) study of prospective music teachers learning to conduct, learners expressed that they felt less agentic each time they began to study a new technique and more agentic as they came closer to mastering the technique. Studying his own efforts to become a more constructivist ensemble conductor–teacher, Busch (2013) noted the importance of surfacing and confronting perspectives developed through a lifetime of musical experience. Both these studies captured the importance of the role of reflection (Dewey, 1916; Schön, 1983) in the development of capacity to act in an agentic manner. O'Neill (2012) proposes a theory of transformational engagement in which learners are engaged as "active agents of their own musical development" (p. 163) by working to develop musical competencies, reflecting on the meaning and nature of these competencies, and using what they have learned to foster further learning.

Studies of performance anxiety (e.g., Papageorgi et al., 2010; Sinden, 1999; Steptoe, 2001; Wilson, 1997) often speak of the debilitating effects of lack of self-efficacy and/or agency in particular settings or circumstances. McCormick and McPherson (2003) and McPherson and McCormick (2006) found that self-efficacy was the best predictor of the nature and success of performance. McPherson and Zimmerman (2002) looked at the nature of self-regulation, which Bandura characterizes as part of self-efficacy, in instrumental learning. In a psychological analysis of music performance process, Davidson (1999) notes that self-esteem affects personal motivation, with negative self-appraisal sometimes serving to de-motivate. Wiggins (2011b) described learners' vulnerability in music learning settings and the importance of music teachers' fostering of learners' musical and personal agency in such settings.

Several music education researchers (e.g., Freer, 2009) have looked at the role of Csikszentmihalyi's (1990) concept of *flow* in music learning. Csikszentmihalyi describes flow as the feeling one experiences in moments when "body or mind is stretched to its limits in a voluntary effort to accomplish something difficult and worthwhile" (p. 3). He characterizes this as *optimal experience*, noting that "optimal experience is . . . something that we *make* happen" (p. 3). Csikszentmihalyi italicizes "make"; in the context of this chapter, I would move the italics to "we," to emphasize that our best efforts are agentic in nature. They are the results of our own intentional efforts. Voluntary effort (choosing to act) is part of agency (Barnes, 2000); voluntary effort also implies underlying belief in the potential effectiveness of those efforts. In this sense, elements that contribute to what Csikszentmihalyi (1990) describes as *flow* also contribute to agency. Freer (2009) applied these ideas to music education, talking about choral music students' sense of personal control in a learning setting.

With these ideas in mind, let us look more closely at some instances of active musical agency in children to understand more about how it manifests itself, what it can look like, and how it can contribute to and enable music learning.

Instances of musical agency in children

Instances of children's assertion of musical agency abound in music education literature, including those captured and shared by researchers such as Campbell (2011) and Marsh (2008). To this rich body of examples, I add a few more here, for the purposes of this discussion.

> Sitting in a shopping cart, waiting for family members to finish shopping, six-year-old Adam and three-year-old Josh were more than ready to head home. Josh initiated the musical conversation notated below. I was told it was Josh who had invented the opening theme, that he sang it all the time, and that the theme had developed into an extended musical work to which other family members contributed regularly. This accounts for its high level of organization and the fact that Adam and the boys' father appeared to spontaneously sing the same melody at one point. [See Figure 6.3.]

> It was clearly evident in Josh's facial expressions as he began to sing that he was issuing both a musical and a social invitation to his family members. In his knowing smile, he trusted that the others would join him and contribute their usual parts, or some variation on what they had done in the past. His initial invitation and contribution were his ways of organizing the social structure of the moment, but once the others joined him, he took a different role, listening carefully to their contributions and punctuating their ideas with his own, altering his idea to fit with theirs.

This instance of a 3-year-old initiating a collaborative musical event is a prime example of a child's experiencing himself as a social and musical agent.[4] Bruner (1996) notes that agency reflects belief in a "possible self" and that possible self regulates aspiration, confidence, and optimism (p. 36), all evident in this musical initiation and interaction. Further, Bruner suggests that the "agentive mind is not only active in nature, but it seeks out with other active minds" (p. 93). That Josh's socio-musical invitation was accepted and acted upon by people he valued, in a way that produced the musical result he was seeking, brought him unmitigated joy, clearly evident in his facial expression throughout the event. Also, note how the initial idea and the event that transpired reflect a stylistic awareness rooted in the participants' musical enculturation and experience.

Fig. 6.3 Musical example 3—"Shopping Cart Jam"

In music classroom settings, music learners initiate musical ideas and ideas about music all the time, sometimes as part of the lesson in progress and sometimes in spite of it. Part of good music teaching is noticing, recognizing, enabling, and attending to music learners' attempts to share their musical ideas and ideas about music. They emerge everywhere. Here, I share some instances drawn from data collected in general music class settings over many years.[5]

> Nine-year-old students were accompanying their singing of a popular song by playing a whole-note bass line that followed the chord structure of the song. Some were playing classroom xylophones and some electronic keyboards, with pairs of students sharing each instrument as they played and sang. The teacher was playing the full chords on a keyboard that was located near the students' keyboards. A student standing near the teacher was watching the teacher's hands as she played. The student began to imitate what the teacher was playing, without saying a word. When the song ended, the student asked whether she could show the other students how to play the chords. Within about five minutes, at this student's initiation, many other students in the class could accompany with chords. The students decided to reorganize themselves such that those who could play the chords were on keyboards and those who preferred to play the bass line were on xylophones. Because the teacher was open to learner curiosity and initiative, the nature of the students' performance became more sophisticated and, in reality, much stronger musically.

Here, in a formal music learning setting, we again see an individual taking musical initiative that was accepted and embraced by valued others and led to a larger musical event. In this case, the larger event was organized by the group of learners, acting with a shared, collective agency (Bandura, 2000, 2001; Karlsen, 2011; Wertsch, Tulviste, & Hagstrom, 1993) that they understood would be accepted and valued in this formal learning setting. Further, the collaborative efforts of the learners actually took the music learning experience to a level that was higher and more complex than the teacher had planned for or expected to occur in the context of this lesson. Marsh (2008) finds that children engaged in informal music-making in playground settings also seek and value complexity and challenge.

In the instance that follows, learners were also working in a formal music learning setting where learner-initiated musical ideas were encouraged, embraced, and readily incorporated into the flow of the lesson.

> Eight-year-old students had just finished writing a set of lyrics for a collaborative original song about Thanksgiving.[6] They had decided to write about Thanksgiving dinner "from the point of view of a piece of celery stuck in the stuffing," as one student described the idea. (They had been studying author's point of view in their language arts curriculum.) They were just beginning to think about how to set the lyrics, when Eric popped up from his seat saying, "I know! I know!" and then, swinging his arms from side to side in front of his body, swaying to the macrobeat of the meter, he sang [see Figure 6.4]:

Fig. 6.4 Musical example 4

> From there, they were off. The rest of the song just flowed, following the meter, key, and feel that Eric had established in sharing his initial idea.

Once again, in this vignette we see a young child clearly capable of conceiving and initiating a musical idea which, when accepted and embraced by peers and teacher, took the musical event and product to a higher level than anticipated by the teacher. As in the other vignettes shared here, this learner's action in this situation reflected his level of musical skill and knowledge. Bruner (1996) explains, "[s]ince agency implies not only the capacity for initiating, but also for completing our acts, it also implies skill or know-how" (p. 36).

Individuals' awareness of their own skills and knowledge as well as those of their peers is evident in the vignette that follows.

> Two ten-year-olds were close friends outside of school. Bill was in the school's program for gifted students, Mark in a program for students with learning disabilities. In music class, they generally chose to be partners. In their work together, Bill always tried to anticipate the places where Mark might need some assistance or support to be successful. Where Mark did need the help, he always accepted it, but whenever help was offered where he did not need it, he would quickly reject the support while demonstrating to Bill that he knew how.

Learners' awareness of their own capacity, skill level, and knowledge makes them excellent assessors of their own competence (Harwood & Marsh, 2012; Marsh, 2008). In this situation, Mark makes clear that he prefers to work above his level of competence. He strives to and prefers to engage in more complex action and interaction. He is not complacent. He is confident in and proud of the skills he has mastered, strives to do what he does not yet know how to do, and welcomes Bill's peer scaffolding that enables him to achieve at higher levels.

In the vignette that follows, we are able to gain some insight into a music learner's process of conception and initiation of an original musical idea.

> Ten-year-old Lynn was working with four peers composing a piece that would be in ABA form. She had chosen the big red conga and was working on a rhythm that could serve as the introduction to the piece. In her work, she verbally articulated her ideas before playing them. She said to the group, "And then everyone will go 'dong' [on a semi-sung sustained pitch]. Like this. Watch—one, two, ready, go [and she spoke the rhythm in Figure 6.5 to complete her sentence].

Bum bu bum bu - bu - bu - bu - bu - bu - bu - bum.

Fig. 6.5 Musical example 5

> After speaking the rhythm, she played it accurately on the drum, and then continued to explain and demonstrate (by performing on the drum) her idea to the group.

Note the holistic nature of Lynn's conception and expression of her musical ideas. Also note the intentional and cognitive nature of her process—that she conceived and articulated the musical idea before playing it on the drum. Certainly, her conception and sharing of ideas were not haphazard or happenstance. Further, her confidence in her ideas and skill in executing and sharing them enabled her to take a leadership role in the work of this small group as they composed a musical work together.

In initiating and sharing musical ideas, music learners also provide us windows into the musical skill and knowledge they have developed and constructed through their non-school musical experiences.

> For many years, I taught in a primary school that served a relatively wealthy community and also served a small section of a very poor community. In this context, William was a student who came to school in the same pair of pants every day. While peers made it clear that they liked William, he was

rarely a member of their friendship circles and mostly kept to himself. In music class, he often chose to be a non-participant.

We had arrived at the point in the school year when we would begin work to produce our annual songbook of original songs composed by the children in the school. As students formed groups to begin writing songs, William wandered from group to group and eventually found a keyboard no one was using and began to fiddle. In the next class period, once everyone was working, he approached me saying he had written his song at home and was ready to share it with me. He produced a wrinkled paper covered with words and, in the sweetest soprano voice, sang what sounded like a jazz love song filled with improvisatory, melismatic lines that wandered way up in his register and then back down to rejoin the melody. The song was very long (four verses) and he patiently sang them all to me, a cappella, with a good deal of consistency in sound and style, and expression reflective of the lyrics.

I asked him to tell me about how he had thought of the song. He replied that his aunt, who lived with them, was a jazz singer and that, late at night, she would sit at the piano and practice her songs. He said he always stayed awake to listen to her. His song, he said, was like her songs.

William's pride in his composition was strongly rooted in his highly valued relationship with his aunt and his valuing of her music. He had produced an extended musical work deeply rooted in his informal learning of the musical culture in which he had been raised. William's composing of this song was the most productive work I had seen him generate during that school year. For whatever reasons, the setting of this particular project seemed to motivate in him a desire to participate not only actively in the project, but also to produce one of the more sophisticated products I had seen children produce.

In the vignette that follows, we see a music learner who seeks and achieves musical success in a setting where her language comprehension was minimal.

Maria was new to our school, having just arrived in the U.S. and speaking Spanish, but almost no English. In her first day of music class, we were beginning a project where students would analyze Ives' Variations on "America," learn to play the melody of "America," and then work in groups to compose their own variations. The plan was that each group would work with classroom instruments to compose one variation and then we would assemble them all into one large theme and variations. Maria sat quietly as her classmates listened to and discussed what was happening in the Ives work. In the next class, the students were going to learn how to play the melody of "America." They had access to a notated version, for those who could read it, and also a graphic representation of the melody. As general music students, their capacity to read both versions was heavily scaffolded by their knowledge of how the melody sounded.

Maria worked together with another girl who spoke some Spanish but, as I learned later, the girl's efforts to teach Maria to play the song had been unsuccessful. At the end of class, they told me (explaining together) that Maria did not know the song and therefore could not figure out how to play it. I apologized to Maria for assuming she knew it and lent her a recording of the song to take home. In the next class period, she returned the recording smiling and nodding and got to work immediately with the same classmate. By the end of the work time, the pair had learned to play the melody on a bass xylophone and created a variation. It was not the most spectacular variation produced by members of that class, but Maria's performance of the work showed clearly that she knew how to play the melody and absolutely understood the concept of variation. She played it proudly when her turn came in the context of the whole class performance.

This vignette demonstrates a somewhat opposite situation from William's writing of a jazz song. William's agency was rooted in and fostered by his extensive experience with the musical ideas he sought to replicate (much in the same way as jazz performers talk about knowing how to speak the language of a style in which they play). On the other hand, initially Maria was disadvantaged by not having the knowledge base needed to engage in the musical activity and event. Once she had opportunity to gain the requisite knowledge, she was quite successful in her creative work and participation in the musical event. These vignettes demonstrate the role of prior experience and knowledge in capacity for musical agency. Capacity for musical ideas is rooted in and developed through musical experience and engagement. Musical agency, then, is also rooted in and developed through musical experience and engagement.

In the vignettes shared here, we can see musical agency reflected in children's initiation of musical ideas and interactions. In these settings, efforts succeeded when the initiated ideas were accepted, valued by, and sometimes taken up by others. The agentic efforts were also rooted in the children's musical skill and knowledge, developed through prior musical experience and engagement. In the actions of many of the children, it was clear that they also were aware of their own capacity, skill level, and knowledge. Their actions were often holistic in nature, highly expressive, always intentional, often asserted with confidence, and always reflective of their musical understanding and knowledge.

The following vignette describes a situation in which the actions of a well-meaning teacher undermined and negated a learner's musical agency.

Three orchestral musicians sat in the front of the classroom while twelve-year-old students were working together to compose what they would play. (This was part of an outreach project of a local community orchestra.) One student suggested, "The violas could go [sang Figure 6.6]:

Doo____ doo doo doo   doo   doo

Fig. 6.6 Musical example 6

something like that." Her voice was clear and focused, her pitch excellent.

The teacher sang the beginning of her melody and then turned to the student and asked, "Do you want it longer? Slower?"

She replied a little uncertainly, "Uh . . . a little slower."

The teacher continued. "Do you want to elongate it (gestures with his hand)? What if we really (sings the first half of the melody at about half the tempo) change the tempo completely?" (To the violist) "Try that." He did not let the violist finish playing. Facing the violist, he asked the student over his shoulder: "Did you want that extra note in there?" Without waiting for the student to respond, he arranged it so the viola was playing a different melody [see Figure 6.7]:

Fig. 6.7 Musical example 7

From this point forward, the learner withdrew from the learning situation, ceasing all participation for the rest of the session.

This instance of a teacher negating a music learner's agency is included as a reminder of the important role educators play in fostering and enabling both personal and musical agency in music learners.

Qualities of musical agency

In the literature, it is clear that young children's spontaneous music-making is a form of meaning-making (Barrett, 2005; Campbell, 2011), is evidence of their creativity (Burnard, 2013; Marsh, 2008), has communicative and enculturational significance (Trevarthen, 2002), and is evidence of sociocultural and musical agency (Barrett, 2005). Children are initiators of musical ideas and material (Wiggins, 2007, 2015), reflective of their capacity for musical knowing-in-action (Elliott, 1995). Agency plays a critical role in human learning because learning is a socially embedded process of the individual that requires learner initiative and engagement (Bruner, 1996; Rogoff, 1990; Vygotsky, 1978). Agency is defined as belief in self, a sense that one has the capacity to engage, initiate, and intentionally influence one's life circumstances (Bandura, 2006)—a reflection of belief in a possible self that regulates aspiration, confidence, optimism, and their opposites (Bruner, 1996). Agency is also a social construct in that it resides within individuals in the context of social structures, and thus is not static, but rather emerges in circumstances and situations (Giddens, 1984). Musical agency is rooted in musical identities, which are developed through musical and (socio-)musical experience. Musical engagement can be a source of social agency (DeNora, 2000) and enculturation (Barrett, 2005). Musical agency can be a form of social power (DeNora, 2000), an expression of self (Froelich, 2007; Persson, 2001), and part of the development of the aesthetic self (DeNora, 2000).

In music learning environments, providing opportunity for learners to come to understand the perspectives of others (Blair, 2006, 2009; White 2012) and to better understand themselves (Manovski, 2012, 2014; White, 2012) fosters individual musical and personal agency. In some settings (Abrahams, 2013; Blair, 2006, 2009; Busch, 2013; O'Neill, 2012; White, 2012), researchers note the importance of opportunity for reflection in and on action (Dewey, 1916; Schön, 1983) to the development of agency. Opportunity to assert musical agency plays a role in musical growth in learners (Blair, 2006, 2009; Davis, 2008, 2011), in generating an empathetic perspective in learners (Laurence, 2010), and in fostering collective agency of minority social groups (Karlsen, 2011). Self-esteem affects personal motivation (Davidson, 1999; Hause, 2014), self-efficacy can predict the nature and success of musical performance (McCormick & McPherson, 2003), and lack of musical agency can contribute to performance anxiety (e.g., Papageorgi et al., 2010). Voluntary effort, described by Csikszentmihalyi (1990) as a component for achieving flow, is part of agency (Barnes, 2000).

From analysis of the instances of musical agency shared here, we can see that

- Children certainly have the desire and capacity to initiate and carry out their own musical ideas.

- Children's agentic musical actions are intentional, highly expressive, asserted with confidence, holistic in nature, and reflective of their musical understanding and knowledge.

- Musical agency requires, is rooted in, and emerges from knowledge constructed through prior musical experience—including musical enculturation, informal music learning, and formal music learning.

- Music learners seem to be well aware of their own level of musical proficiency, understanding, and values and seek to function musically at a level above their competence, seeking and striving for more complex experiences and for opportunities to function as more proficient musicians, seeking skills and understandings needed to engage in and take responsibility for musical events.

- Music learners' willingness to assert musical and personal agency is dependent upon opportunity and upon their belief that their ideas will be accepted and valued.

Music educators in all kinds of music learning settings need to understand the role and importance of learners' sense of and capacity for personal and musical agency, and how the musical actions they can precipitate facilitate and enable music learning.

> Ten-year-old students were composing what would be their final instrumental composition of the school year. Matthew was working with two peers, with all three sharing one large keyboard synthesizer. In two thirty-minute class periods, these three students composed what I considered to be the most complex and sophisticated instrumental piece students had ever produced in the context of my classroom. At the end of the second class period, the group shared their music with the class. When they finished playing, the class was silent for a moment, soaking in the effect, and then alive with cheers, compliments, and recommendations that we include the piece as part of our upcoming spring concert. The students then prepared to return to their regular classroom, still discussing and praising the work, and complimenting their peers.
>
> As the others prepared to leave the music room, Matthew approached to speak with me privately. He explained that the musical idea that had formed the basis for his group's composition was his idea. He had conceived the theme and suggested it to the group.[7] During their process of composing together, he said, he had thought of so many things he could have done with the theme that the others did not want to use in the collaborative work. He said the ideas were still in his head and asked whether he might be able to come back to the music room during his upcoming lunch period so that he could work out his own ideas for his theme. I said yes, of course, smiling outwardly and also deep inside. When he returned to the room, he produced a solo keyboard piece that was by far the most sophisticated piece a student in my classroom had ever composed. The piece just flowed from his body within about twenty minutes of "figuring it out," as he described his process.

Some might interpret this situation as the collaborative composing standing in the way of Matthew's independent work, but, having witnessed the processes that gave rise to both works and also having analyzed the two pieces musically afterwards, I have no doubt that it was Matthew's experiences during the collaborative process that engendered and supported his capacity to conceive and create the solo work. To this day, I can still feel the experience of the musical agency and independence in these learners that enabled the creation of these two works: their belief in their possible musical selves and their capacity to act on this belief through the skills and knowledge they had developed through their experiences in our music curriculum and classroom. For me, experiences like this spur my own agency as a music educator and music teacher educator. The process is interactive and cyclical. Fostering and enabling learner musical agency and independence are at the core of what music education is all about.

Reflective questions

1 Can you recall instances of musical agency in your own musical growth? Are you able to identify what fostered and empowered that agency?

2 Can you recall instances where your own musical agency may have been impeded in a music learning situation? How might these situations have been more engendering for you musically?

3 Why is musical agency important in music learning?

4 How can music learning situations foster and support learners' musical agency?

5 How might music learning situations hinder or deter learners' musical agency?

Notes

1 Based on Bruner's (1996) definition of agency as capacity to initiate and carry out ideas (p. 35).

2 I am grateful to sociologist George Sanders for this insightful description of Giddens's perspective.

3 Becker (2001) also reminds us to bear in mind that the whole notion of agency of individuals within society is a Western viewpoint—that we must take into account that there are cultural differences in how people perceive themselves in relation to others. Further, ethnomusicologist Emberly (2012) raises the interesting point that, because of their relationship to and dependency upon the adults in their lives, children's agency can never be fully realized and therefore must be considered within the context of the dynamic relationships between children and adults.

4 Campbell (2011) shares a similar story about a toddler initiating a family rhythmic improvisation by hitting his spoon on the dinner table.

5 These instances are mostly drawn from my own qualitative studies of learning in music classrooms, with some emanating from my experiences as a practitioner teaching music to children.

6 American national holiday usually celebrated with a turkey dinner that includes turkey stuffing/dressing.

7 From extensive study of students' group composition process, I know that particular musical ideas are most often conceived by individuals and contributed to the group.

Key sources

Barrett, M. S. (Ed.) (2011). *A cultural psychology for music education*. London, UK: Oxford University Press.

Bruner, J. (1996). *The culture of education*. Cambridge, MA: Harvard University Press.

Campbell, P. S. (2011). *Songs in their heads: Music and its meaning in children's lives* (2nd ed.). New York: Oxford University Press.

Marsh, K. (2008). *The musical playground: Global tradition and change in children's songs*. New York: Oxford University Press.

Wiggins, J. (2015). *Teaching for musical understanding* (3rd ed.). New York: Oxford University Press. (Originally published in 2001, McGraw-Hill.)

Reference list

Abrahams, D. A. (2013). Fostering musical and personal agency in beginning conductors (Unpublished doctoral dissertation). Oakland University.

Addo, A. O. (1997). Children's idiomatic expressions of cultural knowledge. *International Journal of Music Education*, **30**, 15–25. doi: 10.1177/025576149703000103.

Allsup, R. E., Westerlund, H., & Shieh, E. (2012). Youth culture and secondary education. In G. E. McPherson & G. Welch (eds), *Oxford Handbook of Music Education* (pp. 460–77). New York: Oxford University Press. doi: 10.1093/oxfordhb/9780199730810.013.0028.

Bandura, A. (1982). Self-efficacy mechanism in human agency. *American Psychologist*, **37**(2), 122–47. doi: 10.1037/0003–66X.37.2.122.

Bandura A. (1986). *Social foundations of thought and action: A social cognitive theory*. Englewood Cliffs, NJ: Prentice-Hall.

Bandura, A. (1989). Human agency in social cognitive theory. *American Psychologist*, **44**(9), 1175–84. doi: 10.1037/0003–66X.44.9.1175.

Bandura, A. (2000). Exercise of human agency through collective efficacy. *Current Directions in Psychological Sciences*, **9**(3), 75–8. doi: 10.1111/1467–8721.00064.

Bandura, A. (2001). Social cognitive theory: An agentic perspective. *Annual Review of Psychology*, **52**, 1–26.

Bandura, A. (2006). Toward a psychology of human agency. *Perspectives on Psychological Science*, **1**(2), 164–80. doi: 10.1111/j.1745–6916.2006.00011.x.

Barnes, B. (2000). *Understanding Agency: Social Theory and Responsible Action*. London, UK: Sage.

Barone, T. (2000). Breaking the mold. In T. Barone, *Aesthetics, Politics, and Educational Inquiry* (pp. 119–34). New York: Peter Lang.

Barrett, M. S. (2005). Musical communication and children's communities of musical practice. In D. Miell, R. A. R. MacDonald, & D. J. Hargreaves (Eds.), *Musical communication* (pp. 261–80). Oxford, UK: Oxford University Press.

Barrett, M. S. (Ed.). (2011). *A cultural psychology for music education.* London, UK: Oxford University Press.

Becker, J. (2001). Anthropological perspectives on music and emotion. In P. N. Juslin & J. A. Sloboda (Eds.), *Music and emotion: Theory and research* (pp. 135–60). Oxford, UK: Oxford University Press.

Bjørkvold, J. (1989). *The muse within: Creativity and communication, song and play from childhood through maturity* (trans. W. H. Halverson). New York: Harper Collins.

Blair, D. V. (2006). Look at what I heard! Music listening and student-created musical maps (Unpublished doctoral dissertation). Oakland University.

Blair, D. V. (2009). Learner agency: To understand and to be understood. *British Journal of Music Education,* **26**(2), 173–87. doi: 10.1017/S0265051709008420.

Bowman, W. (2004). Cognition and the body: Perspectives from music education. In L. Bresler (Ed.), *Knowing bodies, moving minds: Towards embodied teaching and learning* (pp. 29–50). The Netherlands: Kluwer.

Bruner, J. (1996). *The culture of education.* Cambridge, MA: Harvard University Press.

Burnard, P. (2013). Teaching music creatively. In P. Burnard & R. Murphy (Eds.), *Teaching music creatively* (pp. 1–11). Abingdon, Oxon, UK: Routledge.

Busch, J. C. (2013). Old dogs and new tricks: One teacher's struggle to develop a more student-centered choral classroom (Unpublished doctoral dissertation). Oakland University.

Campbell, P. S. (2011). *Songs in their heads: Music and its meaning in children's lives* (2nd ed.). New York: Oxford University Press. (Originally published in 1998.)

Campbell, P. S., & Wiggins, T. (Eds.) (2013). *The Oxford handbook of children's musical cultures.* New York: Oxford University Press.

Claire, L. (1993/4). The social psychology of creativity: The importance of peer social processes for students' academic and artistic creative activity in classroom contexts. *Bulletin of the Council for Research in Music Education,* 119, 21–8.

Csikszentmihalyi, M. (1990). *Flow: The psychology of optimal experience.* New York: Harper & Row.

Davidson, J. W. (1999). The solo performer's identity. In R. A. R. MacDonald, D. J. Hargreaves, & D. Miell (Eds.), *Musical identities* (pp. 97–113). Oxford, UK: Oxford University Press.

Davies, C. (1992). Listen to my song: A study of songs invented by children aged 5–7 years. *British Journal of Music Education,* **9**(1), 19–48. doi: 10.1017/S0265051700008676.

Davis, S. G. (2008). Fostering a musical say: Enabling meaning making and investment in a band class by connecting to students' informal music learning processes (Unpublished doctoral dissertation). Oakland University.

Davis, S. G. (2011). Fostering a "musical say." In L. Green (Ed.), *Learning, teaching, and musical identity: Voices across cultures* (pp. 267–80). Bloomington, IN: Indiana University Press.

Davis, S. G. (2013). Informal learning process in an elementary general music classroom. *Bulletin of the Council for Research in Music Education,* 198, 23–50.

Davis, S. G. (2014). Instrumental ensemble learning and performance in primary and elementary schools. In G. McPherson & G. Welch (Eds.), *Oxford handbook of music education* (pp. 417–34). New York: Oxford University Press

DeNora, T. (2000). *Music in everyday life.* Cambridge, UK: Cambridge University Press.

DeNora, T. (2001). Aesthetic agency and musical practice: New directions in the sociology of music and emotion. In P. N. Juslin & J. A. Sloboda (Eds.), *Music and emotion: Theory and research* (pp. 161–80). Oxford, UK: Oxford University Press.

Dewey, J. (1916). *Democracy and education.* New York: Macmillan.

Elliott, D. J. (1995). *Music matters: A new philosophy of music education.* New York: Oxford University Press.

Emberly, A. (2012). Venda children's musical culture in Limpopo, South Africa. In P. S. Campbell & T. Wiggins (Eds.), *The Oxford handbook of children's musical cultures* (pp. 77–95). New York: Oxford University Press. doi: 10.1093/oxfordhb/9780199737635.013.0005.

Espeland, M. (2007). Compositional process as discourse and interaction: A study of small group music composition processes in a school context (Doctoral dissertation). Danish University of Education, Copenhagen (2006), published by Høgskolen Stord/Haugesund (Stord/Haugesund University College).

Flohr, J. (1985). Young children's improvisations: Emerging creative thought. *The Creative Child and Adult Quarterly,* **10**(2), 79–85.

Freer, P. (2009). Boys' descriptions of their experiences in choral music. *Research Studies in Music Education,* **31**(2), 142–60. doi: 10.1177/1321103X09344382.

Froelich, H. C. (2007). *Sociology for music teachers.* Upper Saddle River, NJ: Pearson Prentice Hall.

Giddens, A. (1984). *The constitution of society: Outline of the theory of structuration.* Berkeley, CA: University of California Press.

Giddens, A. (1991). *Modernity and self-identity: Self and society in the late modern sge.* Cambridge, UK: Blackwell.

Gould, E., Countryman, J., Morton, C., & Rose, L. S. (Eds.) (2009). *Exploring social justice: How music education might matter.* Toronto, CA: Canadian Music Educators Association.

Green, L. (Ed.) (2011). *Learning, teaching, and musical identity: Voices across cultures.* Bloomington, IN: Indiana University Press.

Hargreaves, D. J., Miell, D., & MacDonald, R. A. R. (2002). What are musical identities, and why are they important? In R. A. R. MacDonald, D. J. Hargreaves, & D. Miell (Eds.), *Musical Identities* (pp. 1–20). Oxford, UK: Oxford University Press.

Hargreaves, D. J., & North, A. C. (Eds.) (1997). *The social psychology of music.* Oxford, UK: Oxford University Press.

Harwood, E. (1998). Music learning in context: A playground tale. *Research Studies in Music Education,* **11**, 52–60. doi: 10.1177/1321103X9801100106.

Harwood, E., & Marsh, K. (2012). Children's ways of learning inside and outside the classroom. In G. E. McPherson & G. Welch (Eds.), *Oxford handbook of music education* (pp. 322–40). New York: Oxford University Press. doi: 10.1093/oxfordhb/9780199730810.013.0020.

Hause, D. (2014). Unity through transformation (Layimbu wunni lebgi-ra): Community building with at-risk students through participation in an African music ensemble (Unpublished doctoral dissertation). Oakland University.

Karlsen, S. (2011). Using musical agency as a lens: Researching music education from the angle of experience. *Research Studies in Music Education,* **33**(2), 107–21. doi: 10.1177/1321103X11422005.

Karlsen, S. (2012). Multiple repertoires of ways of being and acting in music: Immigrant students' musical agency as an impetus for democracy. *Music Education Research,* **14**(2), 131–48. doi: 10.1080/14613808.2012.685460.

Koops, L. H. (2010). "Deñuy jàngal seen bopp" (They teach themselves): Children's music learning in the Gambia. *Journal of Research in Music Education,* **58**(1), 20–36. doi: 10.1177/0022429409361000 2010.

Laurence, F. (2010). Listening to children: Vice, agency and ownership in school musicking. In R. Wright (Ed.), *Sociology and music education* (pp. 242–62). Surrey, UK: Ashgate.

Little, T. D., Hawley, P. H., Heinrich, C. C., & Marsland, K. W. (2002). Three views of the agentic self: Developmental synthesis. In E. L. Deci & R. M. Ryan (Eds.), *Handbook of self-determination research* (pp. 389–404). Rochester, NY: University of Rochester Press.

MacDonald, R. A. R., Hargreaves, D. J., & Miell, D. (Eds.) (2002). *Musical identities.* Oxford, UK: Oxford University Press.

Manovski, M. P. (2012). Finding my voice: [Re]living, [re]learning, and [re]searching becoming a singer in a culture of marginalization (Unpublished doctoral dissertation). Oakland University.

Manovski, M. P. (2014). *Arts-based research, autoethnography, and music education*. Walnut Creek, CA: Left Coast Press.

Marsh, K. (2008). *The musical playground: Global tradition and change in children's songs*. New York: Oxford University Press.

McCormick, J., & McPherson, G. E. (2003). The role of self-efficacy in a musical performance examination: An exploratory structural equation analysis. *Psychology of Music*, **31**(1), 37–51. doi: 10.1177/0305735603031001322.

McGillen, C., & McMillan, R. (2005). Engaging with adolescent musicians: Lessons in song writing, cooperation and the power of original music. *Research Studies in Music Education*, **25**(1), 1–20. doi: 10.1177/1321103X050250010401.

McPherson, G. E., & McCormick, J. (2006). Self-efficacy and music performance. *Psychology of Music*, **34**(3), 322–36. doi: 10.1177/0305735606064841.

McPherson G. E, & Zimmerman, B. J. (2002). Self-regulation of musical learning: A social cognitive perspective. In R. Colwell & C. Richardson (Eds.), *The new handbook of research on music teaching and learning* (pp. 327–47). Reston, VA: MENC.

Miell, D., MacDonald, R. A. R., & Hargreaves, D. J. (Eds.) (2005). *Musical communication*. Oxford, UK: Oxford University Press.

Moorhead, G. E., & Pond, D. (1978). *Music of young children*. Santa Barbara, CA: Pillsbury Foundation for Advancement of Music Education. (Originally published 1941, 1942, 1944, and 1951.)

O'Neill, S. A. (2012). Becoming a music learner: Toward a theory of transformative music engagement. In G. E. McPherson & G. Welch (Eds.), *Oxford handbook of music education* (pp. 163–86). New York: Oxford University Press. doi: 10.1093/oxfordhb/9780199730810.013.0010.

Papageorgi, I., Haddon, E., Creech, A., Morton, F., De Bezenac, C., Himonides, E., Potter, J., Duffy, C., Whyton, T., & Welch, G. (2010). Institutional culture and learning II: Inter-relationships between perceptions of the learning environment and undergraduate musicians' attitudes to performance. *Music Education Research*, **12**(4), 427–46. doi: 10.1080/14613808.2010.520432.

Persson, R. S. (2001). The subjective world of the performer. In P. N. Juslin & J. A. Sloboda (Eds.), *Music and emotion: Theory and research* (pp. 276–89). Oxford, UK: Oxford University Press.

Rogoff, B. (1990). *Apprenticeship in thinking: Cognitive development in social context*. New York: Oxford University Press.

Ruthmann, S. A. (2006). Negotiating learning and teaching in a music technology lab: Curricular, pedagogical, and ecological issues (Unpublished doctoral dissertation). Oakland University.

Ruthmann, S. A. (2008). Whose agency matters? Negotiating pedagogical and creative intent during composing experiences. *Research Studies in Music Education*, **30**(1), 43–58. doi: 10.1177/1321103X08089889.

Ryan, R. M., & Deci, E. L. (2002). Overview of self-determination theory: An organismic dialectical perspective. In E. L. Deci & R. M. Ryan (Eds.), *Handbook of self-determination research* (pp. 3–33). Rochester, NY: University of Rochester Press.

Schön, D. A. (1983). *The reflective practitioner: How professionals think in action*. New York: Basic Books.

Sinden, L. M. (1999). Music performance anxiety: Contributions of perfectionism, coping style, self-efficacy, and self-esteem (Unpublished doctoral dissertation). Arizona State University. ProQuest, UMI Dissertations Publishing, 1999. 9923872.

Small, C. (1998). *Musicking: The meanings of performing and listening*. Hanover, NH: Wesleyan University Press.

Steptoe, A. (2001). Negative emotions in music making: The problem of performance anxiety. In P. N. Juslin & J. A. Sloboda (Eds.), *Music and emotion: Theory and research* (pp. 292–307). Oxford, UK: Oxford University Press.

Stubley, E. V. (1996). Being in the body, being in the sound: A tale of modulating identities and lost potential. *Journal of Aesthetic Education*, **28**(4), 93–105.

Sundin, B. (1998). Musical creativity in the first six years. In B. Sundin, G. E. McPherson, & G. Folkestad (Eds.), *Children composing* (pp. 35–56). Malmö, Sweden: Malmö Academy of Music, Lund University.

Trevarthen, C. (2002). Origins of musical identity: Evidence from infancy for musical social awareness. In R. A. R. MacDonald, D. J. Hargreaves, & D. Miell (Eds.), *Musical identities* (pp. 21–38). Oxford, UK: Oxford University Press.

Vygotsky, L. S. (1978). *Mind in society: The development of higher psychological processes* (ed. M. Cole, V. John-Steiner, S. Scribner, & E. Souberman). Cambridge, MA: Harvard University Press.

Weber, M. (1978). *Economy and society: An outline of interpretive sociology* (ed. G. Roth and C. Wittich). Berkeley, CA: University of California Press. (Originally published in 1956.)

Wenger, E. (1998). *Communities of practice: Learning, meaning, and identity*. New York: Cambridge University Press.

Wertsch, J. V. (Ed.). (1985). *Culture, communication and cognition: Vygotskian perspectives*. New York: Cambridge University Press.

Wertsch, J. V., Tulviste, P., & Hagstrom, F. (1993). A sociocultural approach to agency. In N. M. Ellice, A. Forman, & C. Addison Stone (Eds.), *Contexts for learning: Sociocultural dynamics in children's development* (pp. 336–56). New York: Oxford University Press.

White, P. A. (2012). Thinking-in-music-with-music: Students' musical understanding and learning in two interactive online music general education courses (Unpublished doctoral dissertation). Oakland University.

Wiggins, J. (2007). Compositional process in music. In L. Bresler (Ed.), *International handbook of research in arts education* (pp. 453–70). Amsterdam, The Netherlands: Springer.

Wiggins, J. (2011a). When the music is theirs: Scaffolding young songwriters. In M. Barrett (Ed.), *A cultural psychology for music education* (pp. 83–113). London, UK: Oxford University Press.

Wiggins, J. (2011b). Vulnerability and agency in being and becoming a musician. *Music Education Research*, **13**(4), 355–67. doi: 10.1080/14613808.2011.632153.

Wiggins, J. (2011c). Feeling it is how I understand it: Found poetry as analysis. *International Journal of Education and The Arts*, **12**(LAI 3). Retrieved from <http://www.ijea.org/v12lai3/>.

Wiggins, J. (2015). *Teaching for musical understanding* (3rd ed.). New York: Oxford University Press. (Originally published in 2001, McGraw-Hill.)

Wiggins, J., & Espeland, M. (2012). Creating in music learning contexts. In G. E. McPherson & G. Welch (Eds.), *Oxford handbook of music education* (pp. 341–60). New York: Oxford University Press.

Wiggins, J., & Medvinsky, M. (2012). Scaffolding student composers. In M. Kaschub & J. Smith (Eds.), *Composing our future: Preparing music educators to teach composition* (pp. 109–25), New York: Oxford University Press.

Wilson, G. (1997). Performance anxiety. In D. J. Hargreaves & A. C. North (Eds.), *The social psychology of music* (pp. 229–45). Oxford, UK: Oxford University Press.

Woodford, P. G. (2005). *Democracy and music education: Liberalism, ethics, and the politics of practice*. Bloomington, IN: Indiana University Press.

Young, S. (1995). Listening to the music of early childhood. *British Journal of Music Education*, **12**, 51–58. doi: 10.1017/S0265051700002394.

Chapter 7

The potential impact of autism on musical development

Adam Ockelford

The potential impact of autism on musical development: Introduction

This chapter explores the relationship between autism and musical development. It is suggested that autism creates an "exceptional early cognitive environment," which presents challenges for children's language acquisition and use, and affects their ability to apprehend the functional significance of everyday sounds, which may well be processed primarily in terms of their perceptual qualities. At the same time, music is ubiquitous in the lives of many young children, and (unlike language) it is self-referencing in nature; the meaning of music lies in the relationships between sounds rather than in their capacity to convey symbolic information. These factors work together to create a tendency among some children with autism for *all* sounds to be processed as music. This cognitive style has a number of consequences, including an unusually high incidence of absolute pitch among those on the spectrum, and the tendency of such children to teach themselves to play by ear, given access to an appropriate instrument.

Autism

Autism is a neurological condition that was initially identified by the American psychiatrist Leo Kanner in 1943 and the Austrian pediatrician Hans Asperger in 1944. It usually manifests itself within the first two or three years of childhood (Boucher, 2009; Frith, 2003; Happé, 1995; Hobson, 1993; Wing, 2003). The effects of autism can be profound, pervading the whole of a child's development. In medical terms, though, it is an elusive phenomenon. Autism is not *one* condition that is attributable to a particular area of the brain that has evolved anomalously. Rather, it exists on a *spectrum*, which is identified solely on the basis of observable behaviors. These can vary widely both between and within individuals in different contexts and at varying stages of their maturation, a position that is complicated by the fact that many people on the spectrum have additional needs, such as learning difficulties and mental health issues. Diagnostically, the best that clinicians can currently do is to say that if a child exhibits certain combinations of internationally accepted attributes, then he or she can be described as having an "autism spectrum condition." It seems quite likely, therefore, as our understanding of brain function becomes more refined, that the concept of "autism" will ultimately be resolved into a number of more specific conditions. At present, though, it is thought that, in developed countries, the incidence of autism as presently defined may be somewhat greater than 1 in 100 people.

Experience of observing the diversity of children's interests, abilities, and developmental trajectories at specialist schools, centers, and units for those on the spectrum suggests the supposition that autism is not "one thing" may well be correct. For example, one child (typically a boy) may approach you and, as if in mid-conversation, address you animatedly and eloquently on a topic that appears to bear no relation to the immediate environment or the people in it. In contrast, another child may completely ignore you, self-absorbedly flicking his fingers in front of the pattern of parallel light and dark stripes made by the window blind. You may notice a third child sitting at a desk, concentrating intently on drawing tiny geometric shapes that fit together to form intricate patterns. Meantime, a fourth child is sitting in the corner of the room—hands over his ears, eyes closed, rocking, and vocalizing in a constant drone.

Pending the advent of more sensitive diagnostic tools, all these children are likely be classed as "autistic" according to the criteria published by the World Health Organization (WHO, 1993) and the American Psychiatric Association (APA, 2013), which are internationally accepted and the most widely used. The WHO and the APA define autism in terms of three broad characteristics: a) qualitative impairment in social interaction; b) qualitative impairment in communication; and c) restricted, repetitive, and stereotyped patterns of behavior, interests, and activities.

From the 1990s, three theories have dominated academic thinking about the causes of autism, each of which has been associated with one of the main characteristics of the WHO/APA definition. Specifically, defective "theory of mind"—the ability to attribute mental states to oneself and others, and to understand that others may have ideas that differ from one's own (see, e.g., Baron-Cohen, 1995, 2000, 2009; Baron-Cohen, Leslie, & Frith, 1985; Frith, 2001; Tager-Flusberg, 2001)—was held to be responsible for impairment in "social interaction." "Weak central coherence"—the tendency to think about things in terms of their parts rather than as a whole (see, e.g., Frith & Happé, 1994; Happé, 1996; Happé & Booth, 2008)—has been linked to communication difficulties (as well, more positively, as accounting for enhanced perception of detail and some "savant-like" abilities). "Executive dysfunction"—a problem with the domain of processing that regulates and controls other cognitive functions (see, e.g., Hill, 2004; South, Ozonoff, & McMahon, 2007; Turner, 1997)—was thought to lead to rigid and repetitive behaviors.

While this swathe of thinking has proved to be of great value to those working with children on the autism spectrum, it is more descriptive than explanatory, and this can lead to a certain circularity of reasoning. For example, while impaired social interaction may be presented as evidence of a weak "theory of mind," it is equally possible to assert that metaphorically being unable to put oneself in someone else's shoes is testimony to poor social interaction. Recently, psychologists have turned to more "general purpose" (rather than domain-specific) cognitive mechanisms, such as those relating to "primary intersubjectivity" (a basic sense of self in relation to other, which develops very early in childhood), on the grounds that these fundamental areas of processing may offer a more coherent explanation of the "autistic mind" (see, e.g., Boucher, 2011). This is still very much work in progress, however, and it may be that, if autism is indeed not a single condition, but an umbrella term for many different types of atypical cognitive development, then the search for a single neurological cause is in any case likely to be frustrating.

What seems beyond doubt, though, is that autism, in all its manifestations, is for life; there is no "cure." Indeed, many "high functioning" adults with Asperger syndrome regard the notion of being "cured" as pertaining to an outmoded medical model based on the notion of deficit (see, e.g., Waltz, 2005). Rather, as a society, the contention is that we should be celebrating difference. In music, proponents of this view point to a range of figures, such as the composers Wolfgang Amadeus Mozart and Erik Satie, and the Canadian pianist Glenn Gould, as evidence that an exclusively "neurotypical" artistic community would be far less rich than one with a smattering of exceptional (if eccentric) minds.

While this assertion may be unarguable, there are many children on the autism spectrum with little or no language, who resist social contact, and who are locked into narrow routines for most of their waking hours, to which the instinctive adult reaction is to try to remediate things—to enhance the children's quality of life by encouraging them to communicate, to form reciprocally warm relationships with other people, and to broaden their range of experiences. Here, there is only one thing that has consistently been shown to have a positive effect, and that is systematic and sustained programs of education. Just as autism exists on a spectrum, so too do the pedagogical approaches that have grown up to meet its perceived challenges. Some of these use "applied behavior analysis" ("ABA") (see, e.g., Fox, 2008; Kearney, 2007), while others, such as "PECS" ("Picture Exchange Communication System"), focus on augmentative communication (see, e.g., Bondy & Frost, 2011; Charlop-Christy et al., 2002). "TEACCH" ("Treatment and Education of Autistic and related Communication handicapped Children") aims to improve skills by modifying the environment to mitigate the impact of what are deemed to be cognitive deficits (Mesibov, Shea, & Schopler, 2005; Panerai, Ferrante, & Zingale, 2002).

Until very recently, however, the field of special education has had little if anything to say about the potential role of organized sound and music in teaching and learning. Elsewhere (Ockelford, 2013), I assert that this may be a serious omission, since at least 1 in 20 children on the autism spectrum are thought to have exceptional musical abilities (Rimland & Fein, 1988). (Indeed, the figure may well be higher than this, though it is difficult to be precise, since children's latent musicality may be masked by a welter of behavioral and communicative challenges.) Furthermore, for many of the remaining children, music appears to be particularly important as a source of educational and therapeutic potential to promote wider learning and development and to foster a sense of well-being (Alvin, 1992; Whipple, 2004). However, it is the exceptional musical development of the 5% to which this chapter is devoted, for two reasons: first, music is critically important for these 1 in 20, sometimes constituting the *only* way of initially reaching into a severely autistic child's psyche; and second, by focusing on the *exceptional* abilities and needs of a minority, we may be better placed to understand the musical development of the majority of children.

An ecological model of auditory processing

To contextualize the discussion that follows, I will return to the "ecological" model of auditory processing first set out in Miller and Ockelford (2005). This builds on the work of Gaver (1993), who suggested that there are essentially two ways in which we hear sounds: through "musical" listening, which focuses on perceptual qualities such as pitch and loudness; and via "everyday listening," which is concerned with attending to events such as a dog barking or a car driving by. To these two categories I added the perception and cognition of speech sounds, which, while sharing some neurological resources with music, appear to have dedicated processing pathways (see, e.g., Patel, 2012). It is not known how these three types of auditory processing—pertaining to speech, everyday sounds, and music—become defined in the brain's architecture following the initial development of hearing around four to three months before birth (Lecanuet, 1996). However, the development of singing and speech, at least, appear to be following distinct paths from around the beginning of the second year of life (Papousek, 1996). Hence, the ecological model of auditory perception can be represented as follows (see Figure 7.1), in which it is assumed that the three functions of sound come to have gradually more distinct neurological correlates in the first 12 months of postnatal brain development. This does not, of course, exclude the possibility of the three categories of sound being combined, as in songs, for example, some pieces of "musique concrète," and movie soundtracks.

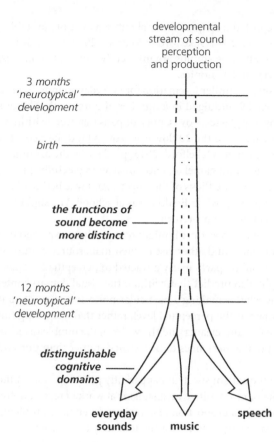

developmental
stream of sound
perception
and production

3 *months*
'neurotypical'
development

birth

**the functions of
sound become
more distinct**

12 *months*
'neurotypical'
development

**distinguishable
cognitive
domains**

**everyday
sounds**   **music**   **speech**

Fig. 7.1 Visual representation of the ecological model of auditory processing

An atypical interest in everyday sounds

Initial evidence that some children may attach particular importance to everyday sounds and that, in certain cases (presumably as a result), auditory perceptual skills may become heightened in this domain, came from my studies of young people who had been born blind or had lost their sight in the first few months of life (Ockelford et al., 2006; Ockelford & Matawa, 2009). Parents reported that almost all in this group had a special interest in day-to-day sounds (around three times as many as those who were fully sighted).

It seems that, in the absence of vision, sound has a distinctive appeal and offers a ready source of stimulation. For instance, the mother of a five-year-old boy noted that "he loves repetitive sounds—[he] will press toys which make noises over and over to hear the sounds" (Ockelford et al., 2006, p. 17). As in this case, such auditory pleasure sometimes seems to have become a fixation. For example, one mother wrote of her 6.5-year-old son with retinopathy of prematurity being

> obsessed with the noise of the microwave, so much so that he becomes upset if he can't make it into the kitchen before it is finished. More recently he has become interested in the tumble drier. He lies on the floor and listens to it and gets upset when it stops. He also loves the noises of the vacuum cleaner, washing machine and dishwasher (Ockelford & Matawa, 2009, p. 16).

Similarly, a 3-year-old boy was reported to be passionate about "any type of fan (table fan, exhaust fan, pedestal, box fan, computer fan etc.)" (Ockelford & Matawa, 2009, p. 16). It is of interest to note (following Gaver, 1993) that all these sounds are inherently "musical," comprising distinct pitches and tone colors that are rich in harmonics.

Some children with autism display a similar fascination for everyday sounds. Take, for example, a pupil of mine, Freddie, who, aged 9, indulged in a number of pursuits that bemused his parents, including habitually flicking any glasses, bowls, pots, or pans that were within reach. Things reached a head when, one day, he removed the 20 flowerpots or so (and their contents) from the patio and brought them into the kitchen (Ockelford, 2013, p. 13). Freddie arranged these on all available surfaces, like some earthenware gamelan, and ran around gleefully, playing his newly constructed instrument with characteristic flicks of the fingers. And woe betide his mother if she tried, even minimally, to tidy the pots up while Freddie was at school! Any slight rearrangement would instantly be noticed and rectified on his return.

How can we account for behaviors such as this? It might reasonably be expected that blind children, deprived of the visual input that would otherwise be their main source of information about their immediate environment, would be particularly attracted to perceptually salient features in the *auditory* landscape. We might also predict that, without the visual data to contextualize the sounds that are heard—to know *what* is making a particular noise and *why*—that at least some auditory information would remain at the perceptual level, rather than acquiring functional significance. Hence, the hum of the vacuum cleaner and the whirr of the tumble drier would remain as ends in themselves, as perceptual experiences to be relished, rather than portending a clean carpet or dry laundry.

But why do some children on the autism spectrum apparently process sound in the same way? Can we assume that there are the same cognitive mechanisms at work here, or different ones that have similar consequences? Certainly, a proportion of autistic children have problems in processing visual information, which may partly account for the tendency to behave in some respects as though they were visually impaired. It is also the case that many autistic children have difficulties with "sensory integration": linking incoming data from different sensory modalities (Iarocci & McDonald, 2006). That is, the process of "binding" (Huron, 2006, p. 124; Roskies, 1999), through which incoming streams of perceptual information in the domains of sight, sound, touch, smell, and taste (as well as balance and proprioception) are typically linked in cognition to produce single, coherent experiences and concepts, appears not to be fully functional. It may be that this cognitive anomaly is linked to "weak central coherence," in which, as we have seen, there is a tendency to focus attention on parts of things rather than wholes. Hence, a child on the autism spectrum may be facing the double challenge of finding it difficult to link information received in *different* sensory channels, as well as successively in *one* domain.

Exceptional Early Cognitive Environments ("EECEs")

This way of handling perceptual data is a consequence of what I term the "exceptional early cognitive environment" ("EECE") that is produced by (and to an extent defines) autism (Ockelford, 2013, p. 211). EECEs have a number of consequences, one of which is that certain sounds, especially those that are particularly salient or intrinsically pleasing (acknowledging that what is pleasurable to one ear may be irritating to another), acquire little or no functional significance. Rather, they tend to be processed purely in terms of their sonic qualities: that is, *in musical terms* (see Figure 7.2). Similarly, other everyday sounds that involve repetition (like the beeping of the microwave or the ticking of clocks or timers) may, I believe, be processed *in music–structural*

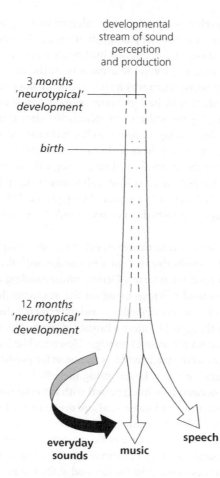

developmental
stream of sound
perception
and production

3 months
'neurotypical'
development

birth

12 months
'neurotypical'
development

everyday
sounds

music

speech

Fig. 7.2 The tendency of
everyday sounds to be
processed as music

terms, since, as I argue at length elsewhere (for example, Ockelford, 2009, 2012a), all music is ultimately organized through the constant reiteration of the qualities of sounds or the relationships between them.

It seems likely that the tendency to hear everyday sounds in this way is reinforced by the prevalence of music in the environment, estimated to be present around 80% of the time in the lives of babies (Lamont, 2008): as well as computers, the TV, and radio, young people are often surrounded by electronic games and gadgets, toys, mobile phones, MP3 players, iPads, and so on, all of which make use of music to a greater or lesser extent. In the wider environment too—shops, restaurants, cafés, cinemas, and waiting rooms, in cars and airplanes, and at many religious gatherings and ceremonies—music is ubiquitous. Hence, given that children are bombarded by *non*-functional (that is, musical) sounds (designed, in one way or another, to influence emotional, behavioral, or what are believed by some to be spiritual states), perhaps we should not be surprised that the *functional* sounds with which they are often jumbled together should become processed in the same way.

I first observed this confusion many years ago when working with the then 10-year-old Derek Paravicini (Ockelford, 2008). Despite being blind, having severe learning difficulties, and being on the autism spectrum, Derek was a prodigiously talented young pianist. On this occasion, he was playing through a Chopin waltz on the piano with his usual fluency, when he stopped, briefly and unexpectedly in mid-phrase, and drummed his fingers vigorously on the music rack above the keyboard, before continuing to play in the usual way. At the time, Derek's language was not sufficiently developed for me to ascertain why he had suddenly stopped playing the waltz in mid-flow, so I could only conclude that he had for some reason become distracted. However, when, a few days later, I heard him play the waltz again, exactly the same thing occurred. Evidently, he had *intended* to include the finger-flapping sound in his performance. But why? I asked the pianist who taught Derek classical pieces at the time, but she was mystified too, so we looked over the score to see if that would offer clarification. And sure enough, the reason became clear: the point at which Derek interrupted his playing coincided with a page turn, and it seemed that he had not only absorbed the music as he listened to the piece being played, but also the extraneous sound of his teacher flicking the page over (which, of course, would have meant nothing to him because of his blindness).

It struck me then that while he may in many respects have been a sophisticated young musician (he had recently performed at the Barbican Centre in London with the Royal Philharmonic Pops Orchestra, for example), in functional terms, Derek's understanding of sound was still in some respects naïve. For him, the sound of a page being turned was as much a part of the musical narrative as the notes that Chopin had prescribed: he evidently did not distinguish between the two.

Another pupil, Romy Smith, aged 11, offers a further example. She is on the autism spectrum, and has limited receptive and no expressive language. However, like Derek, she evinces an exceptional musicality, including absolute pitch, and has a passion for playing the piano. She engages in improvised musical dialogues with glee, largely using melodic fragments from the one hundred or so pieces she has learnt, occasionally interspersed with material that she has invented herself. Motifs tumble over one another in rapid succession and are connected using imitation in whole or in part. This approach enables Romy to control what goes on—something that she is unable to do through speech—and is consequently a source of huge satisfaction for her. Musically, *she* initiates things, and expects her musical partner to continue what she begins (either alone, or simultaneously with her as she continues playing, in the key and at the tempo that she determines), or to provide an accompaniment, typically using material that she dictates.

Romy too is in the habit of introducing everyday sounds into her playing, though in a different way from that adopted by Derek at a similar age. As soon as Romy hears certain sounds, including her father's cellphone ringtone and airplanes as they come in to land (one of the rooms we use for sessions is only a few miles from London's Heathrow Airport), she reproduces them on the piano, incorporating them into her improvised dialogues with me. The extraneous sounds *become* a strand in the music. But unlike, for example, Beethoven's cuckoo in his Pastoral Symphony, Romy's extramusical interjections are not intended to have a residual symbolic meaning, borrowed from their original contexts (cf. Ockelford, 2005a). Her aim is not to create a piece about, say, a plane coming in to land (she has no experience of an airplane landing and therefore, presumably, no such concept): the whine of the jet engines is pure sound as far as she is concerned—like the ringtones, grist to the mill of her musical creativity.

Absolute pitch

It appears that the inclination to attend to each sound as a phenomenon in its own right means that young children may develop an unusually strong focus on "absolute" perceptual qualities. This is particularly noticeable in relation to pitch, where children on the autism spectrum are around five hundred times more likely to develop "absolute" recognition and reproduction skills than those in the general Western population (it is estimated that around 1 in 20 autistic people have absolute pitch [see Rimland and Fein, 1988] as opposed to around 1 in 10,000 of "neurotypicals" [see Profita & Bidder, 1988]). For some of the latter, particularly those who develop absolute pitch beyond the early years, the ability is often limited to the timbre of one instrument (usually the piano), constrained to a "central" range of pitches, adversely affected by factors such as fatigue, and may well operate only in a recognition rather than a production mode. However, such restrictions do not, in my experience, appear to apply to children on the autism spectrum who have absolute pitch. Such children have a "universal" form of the ability, which functions expressively and receptively in relation to all timbres across a very wide pitch range, and is not compromised by considerations such as tiredness.

Strange as it may seem, it is quite likely that neither the children themselves nor those educating or caring for them will be aware of their unusual skill. On one occasion, following a public lecture I gave on the impact of autism on the development of auditory perception, I was approached by a middle-aged man who, through the examples I had provided of people with universal absolute pitch finding certain types of everyday sound distinctive and memorable, had come to realize, for the first time, that he himself had absolute pitch. He could recall, for example, the pitch of a buzzing fluorescent light in his kitchen. However, he had never been taught the names of the notes in music, and so, having lacked the vocabulary to talk about what he heard, he had been unaware that the way he perceived sound was unusual.

This account shows, contrary to the views of some (for example, Miyazaki, 2004), that being able to label pitches is *not* an essential element in absolute pitch. This is in any case obvious to anyone who works with very young children on the autism spectrum, since absolute pitch almost invariably develops before the acquisition of music–theoretical concepts and their associated vocabulary. Indeed, I strongly suspect that there are many young autistic people who, having little or no language, and, therefore, no immediate way of demonstrating their special skill, have undetected absolute pitch (cf. Lenhoff, Perales, & Hickok, 2001, who found a similar situation exists in the case of individuals with Williams syndrome, described later). It is often the case that, when I visit schools and centers specializing in autism spectrum conditions, I encounter pupils and students who are obsessively interested in certain music-like sounds in the environment (to which they appear to be acutely sensitive), or who, like Freddie, enjoy rearranging everyday objects according to the different sounds that they make, or who are habitually singing, humming, or even whistling snatches of melody in a particularly tuneful way. When I see children behaving like this, I immediately wonder whether they may have absolute pitch: whether there is a latent musicality waiting to be released through the development of the necessary technical skills, which would enable the young people concerned to express themselves through playing or singing, and, above all, be equipped to engage with the wider world of musical interaction with others.

Of the thousands of autistic (and blind) children I have encountered, those with absolute pitch had invariably manifested this ability around the age of 2, according to the accounts of parents and teachers and, on some occasions, through my own observations. The effects can be striking. For instance, around 30 years ago a mother brought her 12-month-old baby boy to see me who was totally blind, with a condition known as *Leber Congenital Amaurosis* or "LCA" (Leber, 1869; Ockelford et al., 2015; Stone, 2007). It later emerged that he was on the autism spectrum and had severe learning difficulties too. Mother and child came to the school for the blind where I was then Head of Music. When they arrived, a teenage boy (who, coincidentally, also had LCA, learning difficulties, and autism) was practicing on the organ. On hearing the sound, the little boy stilled in his mother's arms, transfixed. He listened, engrossed, for around quarter of an hour, while the organ music continued. I thought at the time (and mentioned it to his mother) that here was a child who evidently showed signs of exceptional musical *interest*, which may or may not translate into exceptional musical *ability* as he grew up. In any case, it seemed important to ensure that he was exposed to a wide range of music in the coming months and years, that he was given access to instruments to explore freely and to play with, and that he had plenty of enjoyable musical interactions with his adult carers.

I came across the little boy again a year later, when he was 2, having heard that he had started to teach himself to play the piano. As he sat on his mother's knee in my music room, I hummed *Twinkle, Twinkle, Little Star* in A major. What would he do? Would he be able to replicate the piece, and if so, would he do it in the correct key? In the event, not only did he reproduce the tune in the correct key—starting on A—but it also appeared with a rudimentary accompaniment (comprising individual notes) in the left hand. Further simple copying games, involving single pitches, as well as chords comprising two or three notes, confirmed that the boy did, indeed, have absolute pitch.

This ability to disaggregate two musical sounds or more that occur simultaneously is often associated with absolute pitch (Miller, 1989). In its absence, the task appears to be very difficult. Indeed, most people struggle even to hear *how many* notes there are in a chord or cluster, let alone identify which they are (Huron, 1989; Parncutt, 1989). With extensive experience or conscious practice or both, musicians without absolute pitch can learn to disembed the different components of a chord, particularly if they are used to playing with other musicians, and so get to know how each part sounds from hearing it performed by a colleague, distinct from others. In contrast, many children with absolute pitch—whether they are on the autism spectrum or not—seem to be able to disaggregate chords with no conscious effort. Those who have expressive language and have learnt the names of the notes will be able to say which pitches are present when they are presented with chords. Others, who cannot or will not talk about what they can hear, may be persuaded to reproduce chords on a piano or other keyboard.

Indeed, some autistic people are highly skilled in this way. Derek Paravicini publicly demonstrated his capacity for chordal disaggregation on CBS's *60 Minutes* program in the U.S.A. The host, Lesley Stahl, played large, complex combinations of notes on the piano, and Derek was able to imitate them all immediately without apparent error. Subsequent tests showed that Derek actually achieved a little over 90% accuracy, even with nine- or ten-note chords. Beyond this, with only ten fingers to play with, testing becomes more problematic, although on another television program (*Extraordinary People* in the U.K.), Derek did attempt to reproduce the sounds of a whole symphony orchestra by scurrying rapidly up and down the keys!

A striking feature of the way that Derek, other musical savants, and the most skillful "neurotypical" musicians with absolute pitch appear to process chords, is from the "bottom up." That is to say, their attention seems to be drawn most strongly to the lowest pitches in harmonies, with relatively less importance being placed on higher notes. The evidence for this comes from the work of Mazzeschi et al. (2011), who undertook an experiment in which six musical savants and 17 advanced music students (all with absolute pitch) attempted to reproduce a series of 120 chords of four, five, six, seven, eight, and nine notes on the piano, purely by ear. All the savants and around half the music students formed a relatively high-scoring group, whose approach was characterized by "bottom-up" listening. The remaining music students constituted a relatively low-scoring group, who exhibited a strong tendency to get the top notes correct, but were not as good at hearing "further down" into each of the clusters. This, of course, is the strategy that most listeners adopt in everyday listening, and one that is constantly reinforced, since melodies—typically the prime source of musical identity and interest— are usually placed topmost in the texture. To sum up, Mazzeschi's data suggested that two different listening strategies were in play, and that one ("bottom-up") was more effective than the other ("top-down").

To grasp the significance of this in musical terms, it is important to appreciate that the lowest note in a chord has a special significance in determining the nature of harmony that is heard, including its inversion, and in defining its function in relation to neighboring sonorities. That is, the lowest note carries greatest structural weight, and so "bottom-up" hearing implies a deep harmonic understanding. Interestingly, this runs contrary to the tendency, observed in other contexts, of the autistic mind to be attracted primarily to surface detail. And it could be, unlike many other domains of human engagement and activity, that music perception is not adversely affected by "weak central coherence" (cf. Happé & Frith, 2006; Heaton, 2003; Heaton, Pring, & Hermelin, 2001).

This proclivity for structural hearing can also be seen in other aspects of the savants' chordal processing style: even Derek, who consistently managed to replicate nine out of ten notes in the most complex combinations, was better at dealing with some groups of sounds than others. In particular, "conventional" chords, which formed recognizable auditory "shapes," were more likely to be reproduced entirely correctly than clusters of pitch that were irregular or unusual or both. And this was true to an even greater extent with the other participants, including all the savants. In other words, the savant musicians, just like their "neurotypical" counterparts with absolute pitch, were perceiving the "Gestalts" of the chords to which they were exposed *as well as* their individual components. Again, this appears to imply a form of music-perceptual processing in these exceptional autistic people that diverges from the general principle of weak central coherence (cf. Mottron, Peretz, & Ménard, 2000).

Savants are very rare, and so (by definition) they are in some ways atypical of the autism spectrum as a whole. However, there is case-study evidence that the "bottom-up" auditory processing strategy that seems to be favored by musical savants may be used by other children on the autism spectrum (or who have broadly comparable neurodevelopmental conditions). Here is a description of a session that I had with Avni, a 7-year-old girl with Williams syndrome (a neurodevelopmental genetic disorder characterized by cognitive impairment in areas such as reasoning and spatial cognition, and relatively preserved skills in social domains and music). The account is taken from Powell (2011, p. 48).

> The following week, when Adam suggested that they play *Somewhere Over the Rainbow*, Avni began to pick out a bass line in the lower register of the piano. She was playing in C major and it was not very clear what she intended to do. Adam started to play the melody in E♭ major (as he had done in the previous week) to remind her of the tune but Avni stopped him and instructed him to start on C, while she continued to pick her way through a bass line in C major. It seemed that she had assimilated the overall harmonic structure of the piece rather than just the melody, and she was eager to reproduce this harmonic bass line. Avni's mother informed us that, in fact, she had played several different arrangements of *Somewhere Over the Rainbow* to Avni during the previous week, which explained why she had learned the piece in a different key. Her eagerness to play the bass line, rather than the melody, in the first instance, demonstrates Avni's keen sense of harmony, and the facility that she has in reproducing that harmony.

What does this form of pitch perception mean for children on the autism spectrum? For some of them, at least, it seems that the experience of music is likely to be different from that of the majority: more vivid, more powerful, more exhilarating, and more enervating. Having absolute pitch may make each pitch appear as a familiar friend in an otherwise confusing world. For example, when Freddie comes downstairs in the morning, he first goes to his piano and will sit for an extended period, playing individual notes, clusters, and tiny fragments of melody to himself, with evident pleasure—each key-stroke greeting him with a consistency that his fellow humans can never match. That is, while saying "hello" to a family member is likely to evoke a different response on each occasion, middle C and its 87 neighbors are comfortingly consistent!

Moreover, these individual notes and chords have the power to elicit a powerful reaction in Freddie, who often becomes physically and vocally demonstrative during his private "recitals." The "neurotypical" ear, in contrast, would not tend to respond with such emotional intensity to isolated sounds like these, divorced from a musical narrative. To evoke responses of the potency experienced by Freddie, composers typically select notes at the extremes of the usual range of pitches, such as the hushed low Cs played on double basses, contrabassoon, bass drum, and organ that open the introduction to Richard Strauss's *Also Sprach Zarathustra* (popularized in Stanley Kubrick's *2001: A Space Odyssey*) or the pellucid top C to which the highest voice in Allegri's *Miserere* soars.

It is of little wonder, then, that children such as Freddie and Romy will play notes or chords or fragments of melody again and again to get the emotional "kick" that they engender. When he was younger, Derek would strike particular notes on the piano relentlessly and with such force that the hammer or the string would eventually give way. Whereas "neurotypical" brains tend to habituate to such stimuli (whereby their impact diminishes with repeated exposure), children with autism seem to hear them afresh on each occasion—as though listening for the first time. And when, as supporting adults, initial boredom with a child's latest auditory obsession is far in the past, his or her level of emotional arousal appears, if anything, to have increased.

Experience suggests that the same may be true of *everyday* sounds, which, as we have seen, young people on the autism spectrum may process musically. For them, the cluttered soundscape of the shopping center, the airport, or the classroom may be overwhelming. Each stream of auditory information—the humming of the air-conditioning, the ticking of the clock, the musical tones that precede each announcement on the PA system, the babble of people chatting—has its own, distinct characteristics, and the child may not be able to "switch them off" mentally and so escape from them. Through Gestalt perception, most of us instinctively draw some stimuli into the foreground of our attention, while pushing others into the background, where they can be ignored (Bregman, 1990). However, as Romy's reaction to airplanes and cellphones shows, this may be difficult (perhaps impossible) for some children with autism. We may surmise that, for a proportion of children on the autism spectrum, being assailed with an unfiltered jumble of perceived sounds is the cognitive norm. For them, "multi-tracking" appears to be unexceptional and, indeed, they may even seek out high levels of auditory complexity: for instance, both Freddie and Romy enjoy having other music sounding (even from two or three sources, such as the radio, an iPad, and a noisy toy) as they play the piano (in contrast to their music teacher who finds it difficult to cope with the resultant cacophony!).

The capacity to "hear sounds in our heads," without the presence of any physical correlate, is widespread if not universal, and indeed, most people are thought to have "earworms" from time to time—fragments of tunes that go round and round unstoppably in our minds (Halpern & Bartlett, 2011; Williamson et al., 2012). The possession of absolute pitch suggests that the mental imagery of sounds may be more vivid than for those who are reliant on relative pitch alone, since in the former scenario the "inner sounds" one hears are memories of percepts themselves, rather than having to be reconstructed via remembered relationships between notes. Having observed hundreds of children on the autism spectrum over the years, I have come to the conclusion that earworms are a relatively common feature among this population, particularly in those with absolute pitch, for whom, I suspect, internally constructed (or reconstructed) fragments of music may form potent elements in their streams of consciousness. Evidence of this phenomenon includes the frequency with which children repeatedly hum, sing, or whistle snippets of tunes, presumably as an expression of what they can hear in their heads, often with fingers plugging the ears in an effort to block out external distractions. On occasion, pupils have continued to hum or sing while they play a *different* piece on the piano: further testimony to the auditory "multi-tracking" of which they appear to be capable. These two "inner" and "outer" worlds may converge in unexpected ways: for example, both Freddie and Romy will *pretend* to play the piano, by touching the appropriate keys but without them sounding. Freddie, in particular, sometimes sings the pitches of the notes that he is touching. Evidently, there is a sense in which physically causing a pitch to occur when an intense mental image of it has already been generated is tautological—grating, even, if the piano is slightly out of tune. Making the notes on instruments sound when performing is just another thing that "neurotypical" people do that children on the autism spectrum with absolute pitch have to get used to!

The consequences of absolute pitch for musical engagement

One line of thinking is that absolute pitch is something that we all possess as babies, but lose early on, as relative pitch processing comes to dominate (Saffran & Griepentrog, 2001). This is thought to occur since key information, such as the vocal inflections that modulate speech and the identity of musical messages, is largely about pitch *differences* rather than absolute values. If this theory is correct, then we can surmise that a feature of auditory perception prominent in some people on the autism spectrum—absolute pitch—is shared by all of us in the first few months of life. The difference is that the exceptional early cognitive environments of those with autism mean that they have a far higher probability than most of us have of retaining their absolute pitch abilities.

Another contention is that the development of absolute pitch is contingent on music education—in particular, instrumental tuition (Chin, 2003). Of course, it may be the case that, for some children, learning to play a pitched instrument early in childhood has an impact on the development of their absolute pitch perception abilities. However, given that young children are thought to be exposed to music around 80% of the time (Lamont, 2008) whether or not they have music lessons, and since it is not necessary to play an instrument to develop absolute pitch, it is reasonable to question the extent to which specialist music input actually plays a part. Indeed, one could argue the converse, that those young children who are attracted to play instruments (or whose parents consider that they should) are those that have well-developed auditory skills.

Whatever the merits of this argument, for the great majority of children on the autism spectrum with absolute pitch, observation suggests that the ear leads the hand as far as learning to play an instrument is concerned. That is to say, it is absolute pitch perception that drives them toward trying to pick out tunes and harmonies on instruments that they may encounter at home, in the nursery, or at school (typically the keyboard or piano)—something that often occurs with no adult intervention. According to Happé and Frith (2009), it is the autistic child's eye for detail (in this case, *ear* for detail) that catalyzes the development of special talents. I would add that it is absolute pitch that fuels savant abilities in the domain of music (Ockelford, 2013, p. 229). Let us consider how this works.

Take a typical playground chant (Figure 7.3). Neurotypically, in terms of pitch, this is likely to be encoded, stored, and retrieved principally as a series of differences between notes (although absolute pitch memories will exist within a range). However, for children such as Freddie and Romy, who have absolute pitch, the position is rather different, since they have the capacity to encode the pitch data from music directly, rather than as series of intervals. Hence, in seeking to remember and repeat groups of notes over significant periods of time, they have certain processing

Fig 7.3 A playground chant

advantages over their neurotypical peers, who extract and store information at a higher level of abstraction (note that such representations may be more parsimonious, however, since they are able to take advantage of the redundancy inherent in musical structures).

In my view, it is this capacity that explains why children on the autism spectrum with absolute pitch are able to develop instrumental skills at an early age with no formal tuition, since for them, reproducing groups of notes that they have heard is merely a question of remembering a series of one-to-one mappings between given pitches as they sound and (typically) the keys on a keyboard that produce them. These relationships are invariant: once learnt, they can service a lifetime of music-making, through which they are constantly reinforced. On the other hand, were a child with "relative pitch" to try to play by ear, he or she would have to become proficient in the far more complicated process of calculating how the intervals that are perceived map onto the distances between keys, which, due to the asymmetries of the keyboard, are likely to differ according to what would necessarily be an arbitrary starting point.

For example, the interval of a minor 3rd that exists between the first two notes of the playground chant shown in Figure 7.3 can be produced through 12 distinct key combinations, comprising one of four underlying patterns. Moreover, the complexity of the situation is compounded by the fact that virtually the same physical leap between other keys may sound different (a major 3rd) according to its position on the keyboard (see Figure 7.4).

That is not to say that children with absolute pitch who learn to play by ear do not rapidly develop the skills to play melodies beginning on different notes too, and it is not unusual for them to learn to play pieces fluently in every key (a capacity that, as a teacher, I strongly encourage). This may appear contradictory, in the light of the processing advantage conferred by being able to encode pitches as perceptual identities in their own right, each of which, as we have seen, maps uniquely onto a particular note on the keyboard. However, the reality of almost all pieces of music is that melodic motifs and, to an even greater extent, major and minor harmonies variously appear at different pitches, and so to make sense of music, young children with absolute pitch need to learn to process pitch relatively as well as absolutely (cf. Stalinski & Schellenberg, 2010). This begs the question of how the two forms of processing evolve and interact in the musical development of children with absolute pitch.

Let us return to the case of Romy, who today, aged 12, has a repertoire of over a hundred song excerpts and fragments of other pieces from a wide range of styles that she uses as material for improvised interactions on the piano (Ockelford, 2012b). In recreating these motifs, she tends to play the melody alone with the right hand, although she sometimes supplies a bass line in the left, occasionally adding chords and, in the case of the opening of the theme from the second movement of Beethoven's *Pathétique* sonata, a moving inner part.

Apart from being a joyous, unfettered musician with whom to work, Romy is fascinating from a music-developmental point of view because, despite her unusual talents, she does not always get things right, and it is in her pattern of errors that one can obtain a rare glimpse into the workings of an exceptional musical mind—in particular, the relationship between absolute and relative pitch processing, which, in her case, is still evolving. For example, one of her current passions (obsessions) is the theme from *Vltava* by Smetana's orchestral suite *Má Vlast*. I first played Romy the tune in E minor (the key in which it initially appears in the symphonic poem), and she quickly picked it up using her absolute pitch ability, invariably reproducing the outline of the melody correctly, and sometimes adding new details of her own (see Figure 7.5).

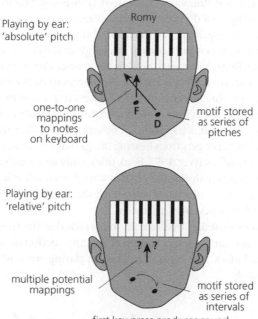

Playing by ear:
'absolute' pitch

Romy

one-to-one
mappings
to notes
on keyboard

motif stored
as series of
pitches

Playing by ear:
'relative' pitch

multiple potential
mappings

motif stored
as series of
intervals

first key press produces sound
mental calculation of interval from this sound
(initial) trial and error to find second key (to match the interval)
there are 12 possibilities: four different patterns
confounding factor: the same pattern and similar ones produce different *intervals*

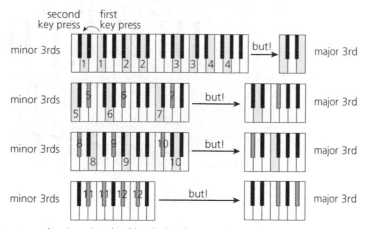

second   first
key press   key press

minor 3rds   but!   major 3rd

minor 3rds   but!   major 3rd

minor 3rds   but!   major 3rd

minor 3rds   but!   major 3rd

Fig. 7.4 Different mechanisms involved in playing by ear using "absolute" and "relative" pitch abilities

Figure 7.5 A typical rendition of the *Vltava* theme in E minor by Romy

This is relatively straightforward. But Romy is a compulsive transposer. She will play the same motif over and over again, starting on a different note each time, and sometimes even suddenly changing key *within* a particular appearance of the musical fragment concerned. As she likes me to provide an accompaniment, this is particularly challenging! It may be, though, that it is this very challenge that explains Romy's maverick modulations, since they ensure that she keeps control of the shared musical narrative. This is a subtle development of the influence that she previously had exerted through playing material in different keys to *prevent* me from joining in (Ockelford, 2012c). On the contrary, she is now content for me to participate in her creative flow provided that she feels in charge of what is happening. I believe that another reason for Romy's constant key changes is the buzz that she gets from hearing things that are at once well known and novel: "so familiar and yet so strange" (Kayzer, 1995, book title). Only someone with her powerful sense of absolute pitch could experience shifts of key in this way: she will often leap up and shriek with excitement as she hears the impact of a motif with which she is familiar appearing as a fresh set of pitches—seeing old friends in a new light, as it were.

And yet she sometimes makes mistakes that remain uncorrected at the time and which are repeated on future occasions. For example, in her version of the introduction of the *Vltava* melody in F minor, she plays a B instead of a C; see Figure 7.6. This is a glaring error, which observers in Romy's lessons notice immediately.

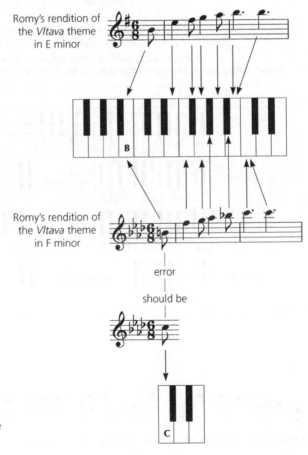

Fig. 7.6 Romy's uncharacteristic error in her transposition of the *Vltava* theme

It seems inconceivable that, in some sense, Romy does not realize that something is awry, given her advanced pitch-processing abilities. At the same time, we can assume that she intends to play things correctly (she rarely makes mistakes, and tends to be intolerant of new harmonies that I may from time to time try to introduce as I accompany her). What, then, is going on? To answer this question, we will take a step back and think again about the neurotypical child's reproductions of the playground chant (Figure 7.3), since this is liable to be sung on different occasions using *intervals*. Now, imagine that the child concerned is at the stage of beginning to sing the first note. Without thinking, he or she chooses a pitch (which is likely to approximate to the ones used in earlier renditions of the same motif). We can surmise that a representation of this opening note will be held in working memory and become a reference point for those that follow, functioning as a temporary "absolute" in the domain of pitch. In much the same way, information on the second note will be retained, as a benchmark for those that follow. So the third note will have two possible points of reference, the fourth three, and so on: the unfolding network of relationships creating an embryonic pitch "framework" (Ockelford, 2008, p. 102) through which the notes are mentally locked together. There are no conflicts, and the structure is self-sustaining (although, as amateur choirs may know to their cost, temporary "absolute pitch" markers can drift over time without the singers being aware of it).

How does this differ from the situation with Romy? We have assumed that she initially encoded the *Vltava* theme as a series of pitches pertaining to E minor (and therefore starting on B, the dominant). When retrieving the melody at this absolute level of pitch, the task appears (for her) to be straightforward, and she recreates it without error (Figure 7.5): it seems that she accesses her absolute pitch memories (which are, of course, not unique to this melody) and reifies these on the piano using the set of pitch-space mappings that she acquired autonomously as a little girl aged 3, experimenting with her first keyboard. It is not clear whether Romy *also* encoded the melody in relative terms, distinct from her "absolute" pitch memories, although (as we shall see) the error she makes casts doubt on this notion.

Let us assume for the time being that the pitches were stored only as *absolute* values. Given a series of data in this form, we can postulate that there are two strategies that Romy could have adopted when she sought to transpose the melody. First, she could have drawn into working memory her long-term representations of absolute pitches, and calculated a transposed version of each. It seems likely that this would have produced interference, since the values being calculated anew would have conflicted with those being recalled, yielding the potential for confusion and, therefore, error (see Figure 7.7). Similar incompatibilities would have arisen had Romy attempted to extract information concerning intervals from the series of absolute pitches as they were recalled.

However, if relative data, in either of these two forms, had been *dissociable* from the absolute, then conflicts would not have arisen, and errors would have been less likely. Hence, one potential explanation for Romy's mistakes in transposition is the absence—or partial lack—of discrete relative encoding of pitch in her long-term memory.

Experience suggests that most children with absolute pitch sooner or later find ways of resolving potential conflicts like this, between the absolute and relative encoding of pitch. Freddie, for example, learnt to play major and minor scales in every key on the piano by ear, requiring only C major and minor as models. In terms of pitch, these provided him with all the information he required. When he was asked to play the scales on other notes, I could hear him singing the next pitch that was required, and then finding the relevant key on the piano, which he could do very rapidly since, as we have seen, his absolute pitch meant that he knew precisely what each note sounds like. Any mistakes that he made (largely due to difficulties with fingering, which he

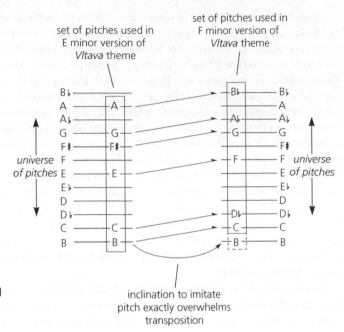

set of pitches used in
E minor version of
Vltava theme

set of pitches used in
F minor version of
Vltava theme

universe
of pitches

universe
of pitches

Fig. 7.7 The conflict between absolute memories recalled and transposed is thought to result in confusion and induce error

inclination to imitate
pitch exactly overwhelms
transposition

continues to learn much more painstakingly through physical demonstration and support) were immediately corrected. Hence, we can assume that Freddie initially encoded the scale of C in absolute terms, abstracted the necessary information about pitch differences from those traces, and subsequently drew on this when transposing, plugging the nodes of the intervals back into his absolute pitch framework (at a different level from the original) (see Figure 7.8).

To sum up, despite the conflicts that may arise from retrieving pitches encoded relatively and absolutely, there is little doubt that the possession of absolute pitch confers a huge advantage on the musical development of children on the autism spectrum, particularly those with learning difficulties, for whom many of the more conventional ways of learning (through emulating peers working in social groups or through being taught using notation, for example) may not be feasible or appropriate.

Music and language

A further potential consequence of the exceptional early cognitive environment that autism engenders pertains to language, and that is "echolalia." This distinctive form of speech is widely reported among children on the autism spectrum (Sterponi & Shankey, 2013). It was originally defined as the meaningless repetition of words or groups of words, occurring either immediately after the language in question has been heard or at some point in the more distant future (Fay, 1967). Prizant (1979) was among the first to observe that echolalia can actually fulfill a range of functions in verbal interaction, such as turn-taking and affirmation, and often finds a place in non-interactive contexts too, where it can serve as a self-reflective commentary or rehearsal strategy (Prizant & Duchan, 1981). It is also a feature of normal language acquisition in young children (Mcglone-Dorrian & Potter, 1984), when the urge to imitate what they hear outstrips

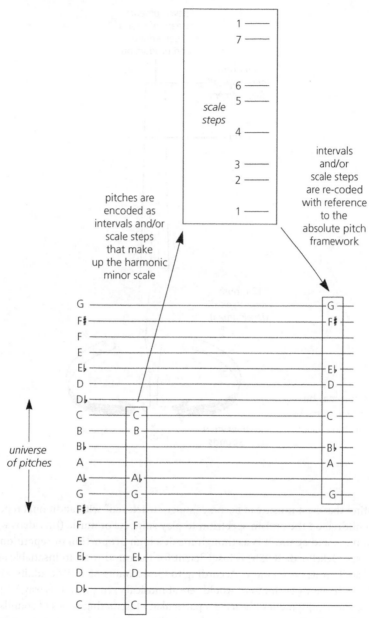

Figure 7.8 Example of Freddie's hypothesized mental processing in transposing a scale

semantic understanding. As I contend elsewhere (Ockelford, 1999, 2009, 2012a), imitation lies at the heart of musical structure, so one could argue that one cause of echolalia is the organization of language (in the absence of semantics and linguistic syntax) through the kind of structure (repetition) that is present in all music. It is as though the words (bearing little or no meaning) become musical objects in their own right, to be manipulated purely through their sounding qualities (see Figure 7.9).

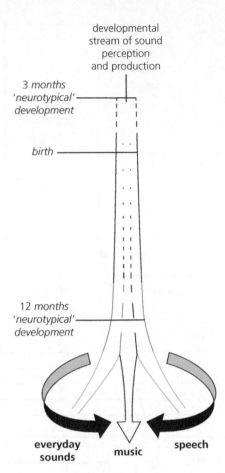

developmental
stream of sound
perception
and production

3 *months*
'neurotypical'
development

birth

12 *months*
'neurotypical'
development

**everyday
sounds**   **music**   **speech**

Fig. 7.9 Speech too may be processed in musical terms by some children on the autism spectrum

It is worth noting that even music can become "super-structured" with additional repetition: it is common for children on the autism spectrum to play snippets of music (or videos with music) again and again . . . and again. It is as though music's high proportion of repetition (typically around 80%—see Ockelford, 2005b) is insufficient for the mind with an insatiable appetite for structure, and so it creates even more. According to the accounts of autistic adults who are now able to verbalize why they (as children) would repeat musical excerpts in this way, it appears that (apart from the sheer enjoyment of hearing a particularly fascinating series of sounds again and again) their main motivation was to enable them to hear more and more in the sequence concerned. Given that most music is highly complex, with many events occurring simultaneously (and since even single notes generally comprise multiple pitches in the form of harmonics), to the child with finely tuned auditory perception, there are a host of different features to attend to in even a few seconds of music, and myriad relationships between sounds to fathom. So, while listening to a passage a hundred times may be extremely tedious to the "neurotypical" ear, which can only detect half a dozen composite events, each fused in perception, to the mind of the autistic child, which can break down the sequence into a dozen different melodic lines, the stimulus may be engrossing.

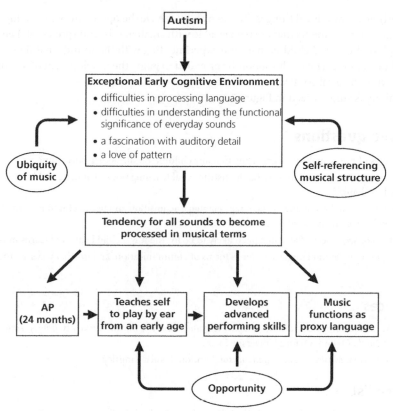

Fig. 7.10 The supposed impact of "exceptional early cognitive environments" ("EECEs") caused by autism on musical and wider auditory development

Conclusion

This chapter rehearses a theory of autism and music, whereby autism creates what is termed an EECE. This can pose challenges in terms of language and in grasping the functional importance of everyday sounds, which are more likely to be processed for their perceptual qualities. To this mix should be added the ubiquity of music in early childhood, and music's self-referencing structure (requiring no symbolic understanding). This leads to a tendency for *all* sounds to be processed as though they were inherently musical, and in terms of musical structure (repetition). A number of consequences follow. Critically, as we have seen, it is estimated that something over 5% of children on the autism spectrum develop absolute pitch. The fact that absolute pitch tends to appear around 24 months of age—the same time as language would generally emerge—has been noted by researchers such as Miller (1989), who investigated the abilities of a number of musical savants with limited verbal communication skills, and led to the suggestion that music can come to function in some respects as a proxy for verbal communication in the auditory domain. Indeed, I have worked with a number of children for whom this is the case, including some instances where music substitutes *entirely* for language (as it does, for example, for Romy).

It seems that absolute pitch plays a particularly important—perhaps an essential—part in the propensity of some children to teach themselves to play an instrument (typically the keyboard) by ear at an early age. The critical thing is that such abilities have the opportunity to develop, through access to musical instruments that are manageable with small hands, and (preferably) encouragement to explore them, and children have fun experimenting with the sounds that they can make. It is crucial that appropriate adult support be provided to guide the development of technique and a love of playing in social contexts.

This thinking is summarized in Figure 7.10.

Reflective questions

1 What qualities of music make it so appealing to many children on the autism spectrum?
2 Why might some "traditional" approaches to instrumental teaching not suit autistic children? What would need to change?
3 What strategies might be suitable to encourage language acquisition and use in children on the autism spectrum with special musical abilities?
4 What are the consequences of absolute pitch likely to be for the way a child hears and learns music?
5 In what ways do music and language differ as forms of communication, and in what ways are they similar?

Key sources

Ockelford, A. (2012a). *Applied musicology: Using Zygonic Theory to inform music psychology, education and therapy research*. Oxford: Oxford University Press.

Ockelford, A. (2013). *Music, language and autism*. London: Jessica Kingsley.

Reference list

Alvin, J. (1992). *Music therapy for the autistic child* (2nd ed.). Oxford: Oxford University Press.

American Psychiatric Association (2013). *Diagnostic and statistical manual of mental disorders*. Arlington, VA: American Psychiatric Association.

Baron-Cohen, S. (1995). *Mindblindness: An essay on autism and theory of mind*. Cambridge, MA: MIT Press.

Baron-Cohen, S. (2000). Theory of mind and autism: A fifteen-year review. In S. Baron-Cohen, H. Tager-Flusberg, & J. Donald (Eds.), *Understanding other minds: Perspectives from developmental cognitive neuroscience* (2nd ed., pp. 3–20). New York: Oxford University Press.

Baron-Cohen, S. (2009). Autism: The empathizing–systematizing (E–S) theory. *Annals of the New York Academy of Sciences*, The Year in Cognitive Neuroscience 2009, **1156**, 68–80.

Baron-Cohen, S., Leslie, A., & Frith, U. (1985). Does the autistic child have a "theory of mind"? *Cognition*, **21**(1), 37–46.

Bondy, A., & Frost, L. (2011). *A picture's worth: PECS and other visual communication strategies in autism* (2nd ed.). Bethseda, MD: Woodbine House, Inc.

Boucher, J. (2009). *The autistic spectrum: Characteristics, causes and practical issues*. London: Sage Publications Ltd.

Boucher, J. (2011). Redefining the concept of autism as a unitary disorder: Multiple causal deficits of a single kind. In D. Fein (Ed.), *The neuropsychology of autism* (pp. 469–82). New York: Oxford University Press.

Bregman, A. S. (1990). *Auditory scene analysis: The perceptual organization of sound*. Cambridge, MA: MIT Press.

Charlop-Christy, M., Carpenter, M., Le, L., LeBlanc, L., & Kellet, K. (2002). Using the picture exchange communication system (PECS) with children autism: Assessment of PECS acquisition, speech, social-communicative behaviour, and problem behavior. *Journal of Applied Behavior Analysis*, **35**(3), 213–31.

Chin, C. (2003). The development of absolute pitch: A theory concerning the roles of music training at an early developmental age and individual cognitive style. *Psychology of Music*, **31**(2), 155–71.

Fay, W. (1967). Childhood echolalia: A group study of late abatement. *Folia Phoniatrica et Logopaedica*, **19**(4), 297–306.

Fox, R. (2008). Applied behavior analysis treatment of autism: The state of the art. *Child and Psychiatric Clinics of North America*, **17**(4), 821–34.

Frith, U. (2001). Mind blindness and the brain in autism. *Neuron*, **32**(6), 969–79.

Frith, U. (2003). *Autism: Explaining the enigma* (2nd ed.). Oxford: Blackwell Publishing.

Frith, U., & Happé, F. (1994). Autism: Beyond "theory of mind." *Cognition*, **50**(1–3), 115–32.

Gaver, W. W. (1993). What in the world do we hear? An ecological approach to auditory event perception. *Ecological Psychology*, **5**(1), 1–29.

Halpern, A., & Bartlett, J. (2011). The persistence of musical memories: A descriptive study of earworms. *Music Perception*, **28**(4), 425–43.

Happé, F. (1995). *Autism: An introduction to psychological theory*. London: UCL Press Ltd.

Happé, F. (1996). Studying weak central coherence at low levels: Children with autism do not succumb to visual illusions. *Journal of Child Psychology and Psychiatry*, **37**(7), 873–7.

Happé, F., & Booth, R. (2008). The power of the positive: Revisiting weak coherence in autism spectrum disorders. *The Quarterly Journal of Experimental Psychology* [Special Issue: A Festschrift for Uta Frith], **61**(1), 50–63.

Happé, F., & Frith, U. (2006). The weak coherence account: Detail-focused cognitive style in autism spectrum disorders. *Journal of Autism and Developmental Disorders*, **36**(1), 5–25.

Happé, F., & Frith, U. (2009). The beautiful otherness of the autistic mind. *Philosophical Transactions of the Royal Society B*, **364**(1522), 1345–50.

Heaton, P. (2003). Pitch memory, labeling and disembedding in autism. *Journal of Child Psychology and Psychiatry*, **44**(4), 543–51.

Heaton, P., Pring, L., & Hermelin, B. (2001). Musical processing in high functioning children with autism. *Annals of the New York Academy of Sciences*, **930**, 443–4.

Hill, E. (2004). Executive dysfunction in autism. *Trends in Cognitive Sciences*, **8**(1), 26–32.

Hobson, P. (1993). *Autism and the development of mind*. Hove, East Sussex: Lawrence Erlbaum Associates.

Huron, D. (1989). Voice denumerability in polyphonic music of homogeneous timbres. *Music Perception*, **6**(4), 361–82.

Huron, D. (2006). *Sweet anticipation: Music and the psychology of expectation*. Cambridge, MA: MIT Press.

Iarocci, G., & McDonald, J. (2006). Sensory integration and the perceptual experience of persons with autism. *Journal of Autism and Developmental Disorders*, **36**(1), 77–90.

Kayzer, W. (1995). *Vertrouwd en a zo Vreemd: Over Geheugen en Bewustzijn*. Amsterdam: Uitgeverij Contact.

Kearney, A. (2007). *Understanding applied behavior analysis: An introduction to ABA for parents, teachers and other professionals*. London: Jessica Kingsley.

Lamont, A. (2008). Young children's musical worlds: Musical engagement in 3.5-year-olds. *Journal of Early Childhood Research*, **6**(3), 247–62.

Leber, T. (1869). Über Retinitis pigmentosa und angeborene Amaurose. *Archive für Ophthalmologie*, **15**(30), 1–25.

Lecanuet, J.-P. (1996). Prenatal auditory experience. In I. Deliège & J. Sloboda (eds), *Musical Beginnings* (pp. 3–34). Oxford: Oxford University Press.

Lenhoff, H., Perales, O., & Hickok, G. (2001). Absolute pitch in Williams syndrome. *Music Perception*, **18**(4), 491–503.

Mazzeschi, A., Ockelford, A., Welch, G., Bordin, A., Taddei, S., & Sirgatti, S. (2011). Musical savants: A new study in the capacity to disaggregate pitches presented simultaneously. *Proceedings of the Neurosciences and Music IV: Learning and Memory*. Edinburgh.

Mcglone-Dorrian, D., & Potter, R. (1984). The occurrence of echolalia in three year olds' responses to various question types. *Communication Disorders Quarterly*, 7(2), 38–47.

Mesibov, G., Shea, V., & Schopler. E. (2005). *The TEACCH approach to autism spectrum disorders*. New York: Springer Science and Business Media, Inc.

Miller, L. (1989). *Musical savants: Exceptional skill in the mentally retarded*. Hillsdale, NJ: Lawrence Erlbaum.

Miller, O., & Ockelford, A. (2005). *Visual Needs*. London and New York: Continuum.

Miyazaki, K. (2004). How well do we understand absolute pitch? *Acoustical Science and Technology*, 25(6), 426–32.

Mottron, L., Peretz, I., & Ménard, E. (2000). Local and global processing of music in high-functioning persons with autism: Beyond central coherence? *Journal of Child Psychology and Psychiatry*, 41(8), 1057–65.

Ockelford, A. (1999). *The cognition of order in music: A metacognitive study*. London: Roehampton Institute.

Ockelford, A. (2005a). Relating musical structure and content to aesthetic response: A model and analysis of Beethoven's Piano Sonata Op. 110. *Journal of the Royal Musical Association*, 130(1), 74–118.

Ockelford, A. (2005b). *Repetition in music: Theoretical and metatheoretical perspectives*. London: Ashgate.

Ockelford, A. (2008). *Music for children and young people with complex needs*. Oxford: Oxford University Press.

Ockelford, A. (2009). Zygonic theory: Introduction, scope, prospects. *Zeitschrift der Gesellschaft für Musiktheorie*, 6(1), 91–172.

Ockelford, A. (2012a). *Applied musicology: Using Zygonic Theory to inform music psychology, education and therapy research*. Oxford: Oxford University Press.

Ockelford, A. (2012b). Music: A proxy language for autistic children. *OUPblog*, <http://blog.oup.com/2012/12/music-proxy-language-autisic-children/>.

Ockelford, A. (2012c). Songs without words: Exploring how music can serve as a proxy language in social interaction with autistic children. In R. MacDonald, G. Kreutz, & L. Mitchell (Eds.), *Music, health, and well-being* (pp. 289–323). Oxford: Oxford University Press.

Ockelford, A. (2013). *Music, language and autism*. London: Jessica Kingsley.

Ockelford, A., Gott, S., Risdon, J., & Zimmermann, S. (2015). *Focus on music 3: Exploring the musicality of children and young people with leber congenital amaurosis*. London: Institute of Education.

Ockelford, A., & Matawa, C. (2009). *Focus on music 2: Exploring the musical interests and abilities of blind and partially sighted children with retinopathy of prematurity*. London: Institute of Education.

Ockelford, A., Pring, L., Welch, G., and Treffert, D. (2006). *Focus on music: Exploring the musical interests and abilities of blind and partially sighted children with septo-optic dysplasia*. London: Institute of Education.

Panerai, S., Ferrante, L., & Zingale, M. (2002). Benefits or the treatment and education of autistic and communication handicapped children (TEACCH) programme as compared with a non-specific approach. *Journal of Intellectual Disability Research*, 46(4), 318–27.

Papoušek, M. (1996). Intuitive parenting: A hidden source of musical stimulation in infancy. In I. Deliège & J. Sloboda, *Musical Beginnings* (pp. 88–112). Oxford: Oxford University Press.

Parncutt, R. (1989). *Harmony: A psychoacoustical approach*. Berlin: Springer-Verlag.

Patel, A. (2012). Language, music, and the brain: A resource-sharing framework. In P. Rebuschat, M. Rohrmeier, J. Hawkins, & I. Cross (Eds.), *Language and music as cognitive systems* (pp. 204–23). Oxford: Oxford University Press.

Powell, A. (2011). Music and Williams syndrome: A single-case study exploring emerging savant musical ability (Unpublished MSc thesis). University of Roehampton, London.

Prizant, B. (1979). An analysis of the functions of immediate echolalia in autistic children. *Dissertation Abstracts International*, **39**(9-B), 4592–3.

Prizant, B., & Duchan, J. (1981). The functions of immediate echolalia in autistic children. *Journal of Hearing and Speech Disorders*, **46**(3), 241–9.

Profita, J., & Bidder, T. (1988). Perfect pitch. *American Journal of Medical Genetics*, **29**(4), 763–71.

Rimland, B., & Fein, D. (1988). Special talents of autistic savants. In L. Obler & D. Fein (Eds.), *The exceptional brain: Neuropsychology of talent and special abilities* (pp. 474–92). New York: The Guilford Press.

Roskies, A. (1999). The binding problem. *Neuron*, **24**(1), 7–9.

Saffran, J., & Griepentrog, G. (2001). Absolute pitch in infant auditory learning: Evidence for developmental reorganization. *Developmental Psychology*, **37**(1), 74–85.

South, M., Ozonoff, S., & McMahon, W. (2007). The relationship between executive functioning, central coherence, and repetitive behaviors in the high-functioning autism spectrum. *Autism*, **11**(5), 437–51.

Stalinski, S., & Schellenberg, G. (2010). Shifting perceptions: Developmental changes in judgements of melodic similarity. *Developmental Psychology*, **46**(6), 1799–1803.

Sterponi, L., & Shankey, J. (2013). Rethinking echolalia: Repetition as interactional resource in the communication of a child with autism. *Journal of Child Language*, published online at <http://dx.doi.org/10.1017/S0305000912000682>.

Stone, E. (2007). Leber congenital amaurosis—A model for efficient genetic testing of heterogeneous disorders: LXIV Edward Jackson Memorial Lecture. *American Journal of Ophthalmology*, **144**(6), 791–811.

Tager-Flusberg, H. (2001). A reexamination of the theory of mind hypothesis of autism. In J. Burack, T. Charman, N. Yurmiya, & P. Zelzao (Eds.), *The development of autism: Perspectives from theory and research* (pp. 157–75). Mahwah, NJ: Lawrence Erlbaum Associates.

Turner, M. (1997). Towards an executive dysfunction account of repetitive behaviour in autism. In J. Russell (Ed.), *Autism as an executive disorder* (pp. 57–100). New York: Oxford University Press.

Waltz, M. (2005). Reading case studies of people with autistic spectrum disorders: A cultural studies approach to issues of disability representation. *Disability and Society*, **20**(4), 421–35.

Whipple, J. (2004). Music in intervention for children and adolescents with autism: A meta-analysis. *Journal of Music Therapy*, **41**(2), 90–106.

Williamson, V., Sagar, R., Jilka, J., Finkel, S., Müllensiefen, D., & Stewart, L. (2012). How do "earworms" start? Classifying the everyday circumstances of involuntary musical imagery. *Psychology of Music*, **40**(3), 259–84.

Wing, L. (2003). *The autistic spectrum: A guide for parents and professionals*. London: Robinson Publishing.

World Health Organization (1993). *The ICD-10 classification of mental and behavioural disorders: Diagnostic criteria for research*. Geneva: World Health Organization.

Section 2

Engagement

Chapter 8

Music and nonmusical abilities

Glenn E. Schellenberg

Music and nonmusical abilities: Introduction

In this chapter, I examine claims about nonmusical consequences of exposure to music. Over the past 20 years, the possibility that *music makes you smarter* has sparked the imagination of researchers, the popular press, and the general public. But is there any truth to this idea? If so, what is the evidence? Could music also improve social skills? Although definitive answers are elusive for the most part, my goal is to provide an overview of what is known from behavioral studies, focusing primarily on those published since 2000.

At the outset, we might ask why people care about nonmusical benefits of exposure to music. Do we have similar concerns about other subjects, such as mathematics, English, or chemistry? Would we value physics *less* if we knew that it did *not* lead to improvements in drama? Although the question is tongue-in-cheek, it highlights the fact that all academic disciplines are not considered equal. Somehow, music's status as an art form reduces its status as a discipline, which means that music is more likely than other subjects to be eliminated from school curricula when budgets are cut. Indeed, in the neo-conservative, belt-tightening climate of the late twentieth century, government-supported education programs in music were often slashed or threatened. Consequently, the idea that music might have collateral benefits was welcomed with open arms as a way of saving or reviving programs. It suggested that music could be *more* than just an art form. In fact, music could be a conduit for improvements in other domains.

These historical and contextual factors helped to exaggerate the timeless and universal appeal of quick fixes to complex problems. Consider intelligence as measured by IQ tests. Competition for admission to the best schools and universities is stiff, and a few extra IQ points could make a difference. In fact, IQ is predictive of academic achievement, job performance, income, health, longevity, and dealing successfully with the demands of everyday life (e.g., Deary, 2012; Kulkofsky & Ceci, 2006; Nisbett et al., 2012). Thus, it is no wonder that the public paid attention to media reports that simply exposing oneself to music leads to a boost in IQ. It is difficult to imagine a simpler fix (music) to such a complex problem (intelligence).

In contemporary Western society, exposure to music typically takes one of two forms: listening and performing. Music listening is everywhere, both by design and by accident. People buy CDs, they watch and hear music videos on TV, they listen to music on the radio, they download MP3 files and stream music from the Internet, and they attend concerts. Much of the time, music is playing in the background while the person does something else, like studying or driving a car. People also *overhear* music without choosing to do so or having any say in what they hear, while shopping, eating in restaurants, and so on. By contrast, performing music is relatively rare in Western society. Although many children take lessons for a year or two, only a small minority studies music year in and year out, practicing regularly on a daily basis. The stark contrast between simply listening to music on the one hand, and actively pursuing a musical education or performing music regularly on the other hand, makes it highly unlikely that the two activities would have similar effects on nonmusical aspects of human behavior. As I have argued previously (Schellenberg, 2005), it is important to treat these two forms of exposure to music separately. Accordingly, associations with nonmusical abilities will be examined first in respect to music listening, and then in respect to music training. Although this handbook focuses on children and music, issues examined in the present chapter are applicable across the lifespan. Hence, relevant research with adults is also considered, particularly in the case of music listening. In the case of music training, which is typically initiated in childhood, it matters less whether the sample comprises children or adults.

Music listening

Studies of effects of music listening on intellectual functioning typically ask one of two questions: whether performance on some kind of task is influenced *after* listening to music or *while* listening to music. The former question asks whether music might put you in the right frame of mind for subsequent intellectual activity, whereas studies of background music ask whether music helps or hinders performance on the foreground (i.e., *primary*) task that takes place concurrently.

Performance after listening

Contemporary interest in nonmusical benefits of exposure to music was instigated by the publication of an article in *Nature* in 1993 (Rauscher, Shaw, & Ky, 1993). The researchers tested the spatial abilities of undergraduates after exposure to ten minutes of classical music, relaxation instructions, or silence. The students were administered three subtests from a widely used test of IQ. Performance was better after listening to music than in the other two conditions. Because the music was a recording composed by Mozart, the effect became known as the *Mozart effect*. The effect was short-lived (ten to fifteen minutes), meaning that it lasted about as long as the actual music listening that occurred before the tests.

Why did these findings create such a fuss, which included widespread coverage in the popular media and state-wide policy changes in daycare centers? One likely reason is that the authors reported their results as IQ scores, suggesting a very simple fix to a complex problem, namely that listening to Mozart increases intelligence. Another reason is that the authors did not consider well-established findings from psychology or neuroscience to explain the link between music listening and test performance. Instead, they suggested that passive listening to "complex" music (e.g., the Mozart piece they used as a stimulus) enhances abstract reasoning in general, including spatial reasoning. In other words, they proposed a direct causal link between listening to Mozart and spatial abilities, which the media extended to intelligence in general.

Researchers subsequently tried to replicate and extend the effect using a variety of outcome measures and different pieces of music. They were successful in some instances, but not in others. A meta-analysis of almost forty studies and over three thousand participants found evidence for small, short-term improvements in performance on spatial tasks after listening to Mozart compared to no music (typically silence; Pietschnig, Voracek, & Formann, 2010). Nevertheless, an effect of similar magnitude was evident for studies that compared spatial abilities after listening to other music (i.e., *not* composed by Mozart) to no music. Thus, the authors concluded that "there is little evidence left for a specific, performance-enhancing Mozart effect" on spatial abilities (p. 314). For example, spatial abilities can also improve after listening to music composed by Bach (Ivanov & Geake, 2003) or Yanni (Rideout, Dougherty, & Wernert, 1998). The effect does not extend to minimalist music composed by Philip Glass (Rauscher, Shaw, & Ky, 1995), however, which many listeners dislike because of its use of repetition.

My colleagues and I (Husain, Thompson, & Schellenberg, 2002; Nantais & Schellenberg, 1999; Schellenberg & Hallam, 2005; Schellenberg et al., 2007; Thompson, Schellenberg, & Husain, 2001) conducted a series of studies that sought to 1) replicate the original effect and 2) make systematic alterations to the method in order to highlight what was driving it. (For a more detailed overview of this research and the historical context, see Schellenberg, 2012.) We hypothesized that the effect was due to between-condition differences in affective state, specifically arousal levels (how alert participants are) and mood (how pleasant they feel). A wide body of research confirms that affective states influence cognitive performance (e.g., Beal et al., 2005; Cassady & Johnson, 2002; Dutton & Carroll, 2001; Eich & Forgas, 2003; Grawitch et al., 2003), and that music listening is an efficient way (but not the only way) to influence how you feel (Juslin & Västfjäll, 2008; van Goethem & Sloboda, 2011; Västfjäll, 2001/2). In fact, people listen to music precisely for its emotional impact (Lonsdale & North, 2011). From this viewpoint, the link between Mozart and spatial abilities is just one example of how a stimulus that makes you feel good can also improve performance on a variety of tests.

We initially confirmed that spatial abilities were better after ten minutes of exposure to music composed by Mozart than after ten minutes of sitting in silence (Nantais & Schellenberg, 1999). We also found a virtually identical advantage when music composed by Schubert was compared to silence. When we contrasted listening to Mozart with listening to a narrated story, the effect disappeared, but there was an interaction between participants' preferences and the listening condition. Listeners who preferred Mozart did better on the spatial test after listening to Mozart; those who preferred the story did better after listening to the story. In short, because we found a "Schubert effect" and a "story effect," we clarified that the so-called Mozart effect was not specific to Mozart in particular or to music in general.

Our second study included another comparison of Mozart with silence, plus a comparison of a piece written by Albinoni with silence (Thompson, Schellenberg, & Husain, 2001). We also measured listeners' arousal levels and moods. The Mozart sonata (used previously by Nantais & Schellenberg, 1999, and Rauscher, Shaw, & Ky, 1993) is an up-tempo, happy-sounding piece in a major key. Albinoni's *Adagio* is a slow-tempo, sad-sounding piece in a minor key. The results from the affective measures showed that after listening to Mozart, arousal levels increased and mood improved, but after listening to Albinoni, arousal levels decreased and mood declined. As expected, there was no advantage on the spatial task after listening to Albinoni compared to silence, but we successfully replicated the Mozart effect once again. When we used statistical means to hold constant participants' changes in arousal and mood, the Mozart advantage on the spatial task disappeared.

We then examined which features of the Mozart sonata cause changes in arousal and mood, which, in turn, lead to enhanced cognitive performance (Husain, Thompson, & Schellenberg, 2002). We created four versions of the same Mozart sonata, which varied in tempo (fast or slow) and mode (major or minor), and we measured arousal and mood before and after listening. Spatial abilities were better among listeners who heard the fast rather than the slow versions, and for those who heard the major rather than the minor versions. The tempo manipulation influenced arousal but not mood; the mode manipulation influenced mood but not arousal. As in Thompson, Schellenberg, & Husain (2001), changes in arousal and mood accounted for most of the variance in performance on the spatial task, with higher scores associated with higher levels of arousal and more positive moods.

In order to show that the Mozart effect generalized to tests that do *not* measure spatial abilities, in the next study we used tests of processing speed and working memory after participants listened to Mozart or Albinoni (Schellenberg et al., 2007). We again found improvements in arousal and mood after listening to Mozart, but decreases in arousal and mood after listening to Albinoni. Increases in arousal and more positive moods were accompanied by better performance on the test of processing speed, but not on the test of working memory. In other words, although tests of some abilities may be more susceptible than others to affective states, whether the test measures spatial abilities is irrelevant.

The type of music that puts listeners in an optimal emotional state is almost certain to depend critically on who the listeners are. In line with this view, we showed that cognitive benefits are more likely after 10- and 11-year-olds listen to popular music than to Mozart (Schellenberg & Hallam, 2005). We then sought to generalize the findings even further by examining the creative abilities of Japanese 5-year-olds (Schellenberg et al., 2007). The children made drawings after a musical experience that consisted of listening to Mozart or Albinoni (i.e., the pieces used earlier), listening to familiar children's songs, or singing children's songs. Compared to the children who heard classical music, those who sang or listened to familiar songs spent a longer time drawing, and their drawings were judged by independent raters to be more creative, energetic, and technically proficient.

To summarize, effects of music on spatial abilities do not depend on music composed by Mozart, as Pietschnig, Voracek, & Formann's (2010) meta-analysis confirmed. Specific characteristics of music affect arousal and mood, which, in turn, affect performance on many tasks. Nonmusical stimuli that lead to better affective states compared to control conditions can show similar effects. The best music for improving how listeners feel and consequently how they perform depends on who the listeners are. Although listening to music composed by Mozart can indeed make a listener feel good and perform well, the term "the Mozart effect" is misleading because the effect does not depend on listening to Mozart, or even on listening to music. Moreover, the claim of a special causal link between listening to complex music and spatial abilities is without merit.

Performance while listening

The majority of music listening occurs while listeners are doing something else at the same time (Sloboda, O'Neill, & Ivaldi, 2001). For example, activities such as driving are accompanied by music listening around 90% of the time (North, Hargreaves, & Hargreaves, 2004). The term "background music" means that music listening is a secondary activity, with the "foreground" activity assuming more importance, which is why it is called the *primary* task. Whether background music has enhancing, detrimental, or no effects on the primary task is important because the stakes can be high. A mother may rightfully ask whether her teenage son can learn anything when he is studying for an exam with Metallica playing at full volume. Similarly, a police officer could ask whether listening to music in the car played a role in a traffic accident. As we will see, the available literature does not allow us to give definitive answers to these questions.

At the most basic level, effects of background music on the primary task are the consequence of two independent factors. First, we need to consider how music makes listeners feel. If a driver is getting sleepy, listening to up-tempo dance or rock music could have an arousing effect such that it improves performance on the primary task (i.e., driving in this case), and reduces the chance of falling asleep and getting into an accident. In the Mozart-effect studies reviewed here, music usually had a *positive* influence on the listeners' affective state, primarily because the goal was to examine whether music listening could *improve* performance on a task performed subsequently. In principle, researchers could have asked instead whether music might impair performance, particularly if the music was disliked or made listeners feel sleepy. Similar positive or negative effects could be evident with background music. For example, when a driver is agitated or nervous, up-tempo dance or rock music could be over-stimulating. By contrast, a piece of music that sounds peaceful or boring could increase the chance that a driver suffering from fatigue falls asleep at the wheel. Clearly, the match between music and listeners—including their current emotional state—is a crucial factor.

We also need to consider that regardless of how we are feeling, working memory has a finite capacity, which means that there is a limited amount of information people can process at any point in time (Cowan, 2005; Engle, 2002; Kane et al., 2004). In some instances, the presence of music could mean that there is less than an optimal amount of cognitive resources left for the primary task. In other words, a bottleneck limits the total amount of information that can be processed simultaneously. When music is difficult to ignore because it is loud or because it has lyrics, it is likely to take up more of the available information that can pass through the bottleneck. The likelihood of exceeding cognitive capacity decreases, however, when the primary task is over-learned or habitual. Such routine activities take up fewer cognitive resources than unfamiliar tasks. For example, people who take the same route to work for years on end use only a small percentage of their total cognitive resources while driving, which allows them to carry on detailed conversations or listen closely to music at the same time. When it rains or snows heavily, however, the primary task becomes more effortful and drivers often instinctively turn down the radio or end the conversation. In general, the more difficult the primary task, the more cognitive resources it will use, leaving fewer resources for music listening and a greater chance of a bottleneck.

Whether background music creates a processing bottleneck is independent of its emotional effect on listeners. In other words, music's emotional impact can be small or large, or negative or positive, whether or not the demands of the primary task, combined with listening to background music, exceed capacity. People could listen to a well-liked, up-tempo song that makes them feel good while they are reading relatively complicated text. The music may enhance their affective state, but it could also overtax their cognitive resources such that they are less likely to comprehend and remember what they read. According to Hallam and MacDonald (2009), a complete account of the effect of background music must also consider basic demographic variables (e.g., age, personality), the specific primary task (i.e., subject matter), the specific piece of music, the music's volume and familiarity, and whether the listener is alone and/or in a familiar environment.

These different factors help to explain why background music can have positive, negative, or no effects on the primary task. Indeed, in a meta-analytic review of studies conducted with adults, there was no effect of background music on a variety of primary tasks, even though individual studies reported effects ranging from strongly negative to strongly positive (Kämpfe, Sedlmeier, & Renkewitz, 2011). More detailed analyses in the same review showed that background music tends to have a small disruptive influence on reading comprehension and memory, even though it typically improves affective states and athletic performance. Another conclusion was that performance on the primary task is quicker or slower if the tempo of the music is fast or slow, respectively.

Let us turn now to empirical studies that examined effects of background music on cognitive performance, in order to illustrate some of the contradictions in the literature that preclude general conclusions that apply across listeners, contexts, tasks, and different kinds of music. In one study, my colleagues and I examined the influence of background music on reading comprehension in a sample of college students (Thompson, Schellenberg, & Letnic, 2012). The question is important because students often listen to music while studying, typically with the explicit goal of understanding and remembering what they are reading. Our participants listened to instrumental classical music while reading short passages of text. They subsequently answered multiple-choice questions about the text in silence. Students who listened to a loud and fast version of the sonata showed performance decrements compared to a control group of students who read in silence. The most interesting finding, however, was that reading comprehension was unaffected while listening to quiet and slow, quiet and fast, or loud and slow versions of the same sonata. In other words, the bottleneck effect was observed only when the music had many notes in relatively rapid succession that could not be ignored because of the volume.

Other researchers documented that background music with lyrics disrupts adults' performance on a low-level test of attention, whereas instrumental versions of the same music have no effect (Shih, Huang, & Chiang, 2012). In this case, additional resources required to process the words lead to a bottleneck effect. Differential effects on attention have also been observed as a function of how much listeners like the music. In one instance, background music that was strongly liked or disliked led to decreases in performance (Huang & Shih, 2011). Presumably, deeper emotional engagement meant that more attention was directed toward the music and away from the primary task. Individual differences in personality also play a role, with introverts more likely than extraverts to show detrimental effects of background music (Cassidy & MacDonald, 2007; Dobbs, Furnham, & McClelland, 2011). Introverts have higher baseline levels of arousal compared to extroverts, which make them less likely to seek out external social stimulation. They are therefore more likely to become over-aroused by the presence of background music, which leads them to perform poorly on the primary task.

What do we know about effects of background music in childhood and the early teenage years? Anderson and Fuller (2010) examined whether background music affected reading comprehension among seventh and eighth graders. The method involved reading passages of text and answering multiple-choice questions (as in Thompson, Schellenberg, & Letnic, 2012), either in silence or while listening to hit recordings presented at a moderate volume. The results showed that background music hindered reading comprehension and that a detrimental effect was evident in 75% of the students. The marked difference compared to relatively benign effects observed with college students could be due to multiple factors: the music had lyrics, it was presented while reading *and* while answering the comprehension questions, the students were younger and tested in groups, and the same students were tested in silence *and* with background music. In any event, the discrepancy across studies that asked the same question highlights the difficulty in making broad conclusions about background music on cognitive performance. Moreover, other studies of 10-year-olds (Bloor, 2009) and 11- and 12-year-olds (Furnham & Stephenson, 2007) failed to find *any* effect of background music on reading comprehension. Nevertheless, because positive findings are rare, the results highlighted here imply that Kämpfe, Sedlmeier, & Renkewitz's (2011) conclusion (i.e., that background music has a small negative effect on reading comprehension among adults) extends to younger listeners.

Another study of eighth-grade students reported no effect of background music (i.e., pop songs) on a memorization task (Pool, Koolstra, & van der Voort, 2003). In a study of college students, however, performance on a memory test was negatively impacted by the presence of background music (Perham & Vizard, 2011), whether it was liked (e.g., Lady Gaga, Arcade Fire) or disliked (thrash metal). Thus, we have another discrepancy except that the negative finding was evident among the college students instead of the eighth-graders. Other studies of young adults reported a small positive effect of background music on memory (de Groot, 2006), no effect (Jäncke & Sandmann, 2010), or a negative effect when the background music was highly arousing (e.g., heavy metal; Cassidy & MacDonald, 2007). In one sample of 11- to 12-year-olds, calming background music improved memory compared to silence, whereas music considered unpleasant (i.e., a jazz piece by John Coltrane) hindered memory (Hallam, Price, & Katsarou, 2002). Because negative findings tend to be more common and stronger than positive findings, at least among adults, Kämpfe, Sedlmeier, & Renkewitz (2011) concluded that background music has a small negative effect on memory. There is no reason to doubt that a similar effect extends to younger listeners.

Bloor (2009) reported that performance on an arithmetic test was better in silence than when listening to Mozart for 10-year-olds, who were unlikely to have developed an appreciation for classical music. In another study of the arithmetic abilities of 10- and 11-year-olds, the children completed more items in the presence of calming music compared to silence, but the number of correct answers did not differ across conditions (Hallam, Price, & Katsarou, 2002). In a study of emotionally disturbed 9- and 10-year-olds, however, calming music improved arithmetic performance, presumably because it also reduced the number of disruptive incidents (Hallam & Price, 1998). Calming background music can also improve pro-social responding (i.e., endorsing altruistic acts) among 11- to 12-year-olds, whereas unpleasant music has the opposite effect (Hallam, Price, & Katsarou, 2002). For children, calming background music is likely to lower arousal levels, which could improve concentration, attention, cooperation, and good behavior more generally. Because calming music tends to be slow with relatively few notes per second, it is unlikely to create a cognitive bottleneck with the primary task.

In sum, whether background music has positive, negative, or no effects on the primary tasks depends on multiple factors. In general, background music appears to be slightly detrimental for reading comprehension or memory. Positive effects are most likely when the music puts listeners in an optimal emotional state for learning, such as when calming music reduces arousal levels in active children.

Music lessons

I will now examine whether music *lessons* are associated with nonmusical abilities. At the outset, it is important to highlight a few critical issues. We know that our personal experiences change us—how we think or feel, what we believe to be true, how we look at things (works of art, legal contracts), and so on. It should come as no surprise, then, that taking music lessons is associated positively not only with music-performance abilities, but also with music-listening skills. Such perceptual and cognitive advantages include: 1) better discrimination of pure tones (Parbery-Clark et al., 2009; Schellenberg & Moreno, 2010), complex tones (Bidelman, Hutka, & Moreno, 2013; Ruggles, Freyman, & Oxenham, 2014), and tone sequences (Bidelman, Hutka, & Moreno, 2013; Forgeard et al., 2008); 2) an ability to detect smaller mistunings to familiar melodies (Schellenberg & Moreno, 2010); 3) enhanced memory for familiar and unfamiliar music (Cohen et al., 2011); 4) faster pitch processing (Bidelman, Hutka, & Moreno, 2013; Jakobson, Cuddy, & Kilgour, 2003; Schellenberg and& Moreno, 2010) and faster temporal processing (Rammsayer & Altenmüller, 2006); and 5) better identification of melodies accompanied by anomalous chords, even after only eight months of music lessons (Corrigall & Trainor, 2009). Although such skills are useful for musicians, the benefits are logical outcomes of taking music lessons and playing music. A more provocative question is whether music lessons are accompanied by improvements in one or more nonmusical domains.

A second point involves the *specificity* of observed links between music lessons and cognitive abilities. If the claim that taking music lessons makes you smarter is to have any real meaning, it is important to show that music is special in this regard, because if reading, chess, ballet, and swimming lessons confer similar benefits, it would be more accurate to say that out-of-school activities *in general* have cognitive benefits. The issue of specificity also applies to the nonmusical outcome variable. If benefits of music lessons are hypothesized to be stronger in some domains (e.g., language) than in others (e.g., spatial abilities), researchers need to show that any observed associations are not simply the consequence of general abilities (e.g., IQ or working memory), and that differential associations (e.g., for language but not for visuospatial abilities) are evident in the same sample of participants.

A third point is that taking music lessons is associated with basic demographic variables. For example, children who take music lessons tend to come from families with higher than average incomes, and their parents tend to have more education than the average parent (Corrigall, Schellenberg, & Misura, 2013; Norton et al., 2005; Roden, Könen et al., 2014; Schellenberg, 2006, 2011a,b; Southgate & Roscigno, 2009). Musically trained individuals may also differ in terms of ethnicity and cultural background compared to participants with no training (Schellenberg, 2011a,b; Southgate & Roscigno, 2009). These associations are problematic because socio-economic status (SES) is correlated positively with IQ (Corrigall et al., 2013; Schellenberg, 2006, 2011a; Schellenberg & Mankarious, 2012), cultural background is predictive of academic abilities (Campbell & Xue, 2001; Chen & Stevenson, 1995; Schellenberg & Trehub, 2008; Southgate & Roscigno, 2009), and linguistic background (e.g., native vs. non-native speaker) can influence verbal abilities (Schellenberg, 2011b). In short, associations between music lessons and cognitive functioning could stem from other variables.

A fourth problem is that even when potential confounding variables are held constant by statistical means, partial associations between music lessons and cognitive abilities do not allow us to conclude that music lessons are actually *causing* increases in abilities. In fact, the direction of causation could be in the opposite direction: children with better cognitive abilities might be more inclined than other children to take music lessons, as Roden, Könen et al. (2014) documented. All correlational studies and quasi-experiments have this limitation. Correlational studies examine whether two or more continuous variables (e.g., duration of musical training and intellectual abilities) increase and decrease in tandem. Quasi-experiments compare children or adults who are categorized into groups based on pre-existing differences (e.g., musically trained or untrained, musicians or nonmusicians). Either way, because individuals are not assigned at random to music training, no inferences about causation can be made.

The only way to infer causation is to conduct a true experiment with random assignment of children to music lessons. The random assignment assures that it is extremely unlikely that extraneous variables (e.g., SES, involvement in nonmusical activities) would differ between conditions. Even then, the extent of the inferences is limited by the particular comparison conditions. For example, one could recruit a sample of children and randomly assign half of them to music lessons, with the other half receiving no lessons. After a year or two of lessons, the music group might have higher scores on one or more tests of intellectual abilities. One could then infer appropriately that music lessons caused the difference between groups. It would remain unclear, however, whether *music* played a central role. Because the comparison group received no additional lessons of any kind, it is possible that nonmusical aspects of the lessons (e.g., additional contact with an adult instructor) were the source of the effect, and that similar results would be evident for other out-of-school activities.

In light of these rather far-reaching problems, let us turn to the available research. What do we know about nonmusical benefits of music lessons? As a first pass, we might ask whether musical abilities tend to be correlated with other abilities. Gardner's (2006) theory of *multiple intelligences* implies that musical abilities (i.e., which he calls musical *intelligence*) are distinct and independent from other abilities (or other intelligences). Accordingly, if the human mind has autonomous and independent mechanisms handling specific types of input (i.e., linguistic, musical, and so on;

Peretz & Coltheart, 2003), improvements in musical abilities are unlikely to be accompanied by improvements in nonmusical domains.

When researchers examine whether music *aptitude* (natural musical ability) is associated with other cognitive skills, participants are usually selected without regard to music training and administered two or more tests (for a detailed review see Schellenberg & Weiss, 2013). At least one of the tests measures aptitude and at least one other test measures a nonmusical ability. Aptitude is typically quantified by asking participants over several trials whether two unfamiliar musical patterns have the same melody or rhythm. Performance on these types of task tends to be correlated positively with general intelligence (Helmbold, Troche, & Rammsayer, 2006; Norton et al., 2005) and auditory short-term memory (Hansen, Wallentin, & Vuust, 2013; Wallentin et al. 2010), as well as with verbal abilities, including acquisition of a second language (Milovanov & Tervaniemi, 2011; Posedel et al., 2012; Slevc & Miyake, 2006), reading ability (Anvari et al., 2002; Huss et al., 2011), and phonological awareness (Anvari et al., 2002; Forgeard, Schlaug, et al., 2008; Huss et al., 2011; Loui et al., 2011; Peynircioğlu, Durgunoğlu, & Öney-Küsefoğlu, 2002; Tsang & Conrad, 2011).

Because music aptitude is associated with a variety of other abilities including general intelligence, the simplest explanation is that intelligent children perform well on a wide variety of tests. In some instances, however, associations between music aptitude and language abilities are evident even when general cognitive ability is held constant (Anvari et al., 2002; Milovanov et al., 2010). The situation is also complicated by the fact that some populations (e.g., individuals with Williams syndrome or autism spectrum disorder) tend to have better music skills than one would expect from their general abilities (Heaton, 2009; Levitin et al., 2004). Moreover, other populations have impaired musical abilities but otherwise normal cognitive functioning (Peretz, 2008). In short, if one were to consider only atypically developing individuals, one might conclude that musical abilities are relatively autonomous and distinct from other abilities. For typically developing individuals, however, music aptitude tends to co-vary with general cognitive abilities, although it may have particularly strong associations with language abilities. Such associations are particularly problematic for determining causation because high-aptitude individuals would be more likely than their low-aptitude counterparts to take music lessons, particularly for extended durations of time.

Some theorists hold that taking music lessons is associated with benefits in specific nonmusical abilities, rather than with cognitive abilities in general. According to Patel (2011), mental representations of music (e.g., melodies) and language (e.g., words) are distinct, but the operations that are used to manipulate and order these representations are shared across domains. In principle, then, music training could lead to improvements in linguistic ability. Other scholars propose that taking music lessons, particularly keyboard lessons, causes improvements in spatial and mathematical abilities (Rauscher & Hinton, 2011).

My review begins with correlational and quasi-experimental studies, which seek to document associations between music training and nonmusical abilities that exist in the real world. I then review experimental studies to evaluate the possibility that music lessons *cause* improvements in nonmusical abilities.

Correlational studies and quasi-experiments

When considered as a whole, correlational and quasi-experimental studies provide evidence that is consistent with the *general* hypothesis (i.e., music lessons affect intellectual abilities generally). They are also consistent with the possibility that children with high IQs—who do well on many outcome measures—are more likely than other children to take music lessons and to come from families with relatively high SES (e.g., Roden, Könen et al., 2014).

In the language domain, an abundance of evidence confirms that musicians are better than non-musicians on tasks that measure speech perception (for reviews see Asaridou & McQueen, 2013; Strait & Kraus, 2011), such as the ability to understand speech in a noisy environment (Parbery-Clark et al., 2009; Parbery-Clark, Strait, & Kraus, 2011; c.f. Ruggles, Freyman, & Oxenham, 2014). In other words, the good listening skills of musically trained individuals extend beyond music to speech. Musically trained individuals also show advantages at remembering 1) short excerpts of speech (Cohen et al., 2011), 2) lists of words that they read (Brandler & Rammsayer, 2003) or hear (Franklin et al., 2008; Hanna-Pladdy & Gajewski, 2012; Hansen, Wallentin, & Vuust, 2013; Ho, Cheung, & Chan, 2003; Jakobson et al., 2008; Roden et al., 2014; Roden, Kreutz, & Bongard, 2012), and 3) lyrics that are spoken or sung (Kilgour, Jakobson, & Cuddy, 2000).

Musically trained adults are also better than their untrained counterparts at pronouncing irregularly spelled words (e.g., cellist, simile, thyme; Jakobson et al., 2008; Stoesz et al., 2007), making grammaticality judgments (Patston & Tippett, 2011), and comprehending and remembering relatively complicated passages of text (Thompson, Schellenberg, & Letnic, 2012). Among children 8 to 11 years of age, music training is predictive of a larger vocabulary (Forgeard, Winner et al., 2008). Among 6- to 9-year-olds, duration of music training predicts performance on a test of reading comprehension (i.e., identifying a missing word in a sentence or paragraph), even when IQ is held constant (Corrigall & Trainor, 2011). Similarly, 8- and 9-year-old boys who play a musical instrument make fewer spelling mistakes compared to other boys, even when IQ is held constant (Hille et al., 2011). In a long-term longitudinal study that monitored children from 6 to 12 years of age, those who took music lessons had larger improvements than other children in second-language abilities (re: comprehension, pronunciation, and vocabulary), even when SES was held constant (Yang et al., 2014). In short, musically trained individuals show enhanced performance on a variety of measures of language ability.

Performance advantages for musically trained individuals extend beyond language, however, to tasks that measure the capacity of auditory working memory (Franklin et al., 2008; George & Coch, 2011; Parbery-Clark et al., 2009; Parbery-Clark et al., 2011; Strait et al., 2012; c.f. Bailey & Penhune, 2012). In some instances, an advantage for musically trained individuals is evident with auditory stimuli (verbal or otherwise), but *not* with visuospatial stimuli (e.g., buildings on a map, line drawings, abstract art, spatial locations; Brandler & Rammsayer, 2003; Cohen et al., 2011; Hansen, Wallentin, & Vuust, 2013; Ho, Cheung, & Chan, 2003; Parbery-Clark et al., 2011; Roden, Kreutz, & Bongard, 2012; Strait et al., 2012; Tierney, Bergeson, & Pisoni, 2008), which is consistent with the idea that musically trained individuals are particularly good listeners.

In other instances, musicians show an advantage on tests of auditory *and* visuospatial memory (George & Coch, 2011; Jakobson et al., 2008), or on tests of working memory for orally *and* visually presented verbal stimuli (Ramachandra, Meighan, & Gradzki, 2012). Psychophysical measures of temporal discrimination also show advantages for musicians over nonmusicians whether the stimuli are auditory or visual (Rammsayer, Buttkus, & Altenmüller, 2012). In one instance, older musicians outperformed same-age nonmusicians on a test of visuospatial memory, but *not* on tests of auditory memory (Hanna-Pladdy & MacKay, 2011). In a study of younger adults, musicians performed better than nonmusicians on a visuospatial test, but nonmusicians performed better on a test of vocabulary (Bailey & Penhune, 2012). Music training has also been associated with enhanced visuospatial working memory in samples of adults (Bidelman, Hutka, & Moreno, 2013; Oechslin et al., 2013) and children (Roden, Grube et al., 2014). Other ways of measuring visuospatial abilities (e.g., visual search, visual attention, copying line drawings) reveal similar advantages for musicians over nonmusicians (Patston & Tippett, 2011; Rodrigues, Loureiro, & Caramelli, 2013; Stoesz et al., 2007).

An illustrative example comes from a quasi-experiment conducted with 10-year-olds (Degé et al., 2011). The children came from different classes at the same school. Some of them registered in an extended music curriculum that was provided in their school for two years, others did not. The extended curriculum involved weekly training on one or more instruments, three music classes, and between two and four hours practicing in the school choir or orchestra. The normal curriculum had one music class per week. The variables of interest were tests that measured visual memory for colors and auditory memory for sounds. At the beginning of the study, the two groups did not differ in sex, IQ, SES, or music aptitude. Improvements over the two-year period on *both* memory tests were greater among the children in the extended curriculum. When considered in conjunction with the research reviewed here, it is clear that positive associations between music training and cognitive performance are *not* limited to language or even to the auditory domain.

Indeed, a series of meta-analyses from 2000 concluded that taking music lessons is predictive of improved reading (Butzlaff, 2000), visuospatial (Hetland, 2000), and mathematical (Vaughn, 2000) abilities. The issue of associations between music training and mathematics is particularly interesting because of the widespread belief that the two domains are intimately linked. In actual fact, empirical evidence is inconsistent. In one study, high-school students completed a self-report measure of musicianship and tests of mathematical abilities (Bahr & Christensen, 2000). Although effect sizes were medium to large in magnitude ($ds \approx .7$), positive associations between musicianship and mathematical skills were at the cusp of statistical significance (i.e., just under or over) depending on the subject matter. In a longitudinal study that followed children from 6 to 12 years of age, taking music lessons had no association with performance on a standardized test of mathematical abilities (Yang et al., 2014). In a study of adults, highly skilled mathematicians (i.e., university professors) were no more musical than professors from the humanities (Haimson, Swain, & Winner, 2011).

Despite some inconsistencies with mathematics, music training tends to be associated with general cognitive abilities. The most compelling evidence in this regard comes from studies showing that musically trained children and adults tend to score higher than untrained individuals on IQ tests (Corrigall, Schellenberg, & Misura, 2013; Degé, Kubicek, & Schwarzer, 2011; Degé et al., 2014; Gibson, Folley, & Park, 2009; Hille et al., 2011; Roden, Könen et al., 2014; Schellenberg, 2006, 2011a,b; Schellenberg & Mankarious, 2012). When music training is treated as a continuous variable, a dose–response association can emerge: as duration of music training increases, so do IQ scores (Corrigall, Schellenberg, & Misura, 2013; Degé et al., 2014; Degé, Kubicek et al., 2011; Schellenberg, 2006). The association between music training and IQ remains evident after accounting for possible confounding variables (e.g., SES) (Corrigall, Schellenberg, & Misura, 2013; Degé, Kubicek et al., 2011; Schellenberg, 2006, 2011a,b; Schellenberg & Mankarious, 2012), and it is evident across the component subtests, which measure a broad range of different cognitive abilities (Schellenberg, 2006, 2011a,b; Schellenberg & Mankarious, 2012).

Because associations between music training and IQ are not always large, significant associations are more likely in large samples (e.g., $N \geq 90$) (Corrigall, Schellenberg, & Misura, 2013; Degé et al., 2014; Hille et al., 2011; Degé, Kubicek et al., 2011; Roden, Könen et al., 2014; Schellenberg, 2006) than in small samples ($30 < N < 40$) (Parbery-Clark et al., 2011; Strait et al., 2012). For the children tested by Corrigall and Trainor (2011), the correlation between duration of training and IQ had a medium effect size ($r \approx .3$) (Cohen, 1992), but it was only marginally significant because of the small sample ($N = 46$). Similarly, in Skoe and Kraus (2012), adults with six or more years of training in childhood had IQs that were 5.6 points higher (more than one-third of an *SD*) than untrained adults, but the difference was not significant because of the small samples (15 per group). Nevertheless, in some comparisons of musically trained and untrained individuals with samples of 40 or more (half trained, half untrained), an IQ advantage for the trained participants is significant and substantial in magnitude (e.g., half of an *SD* in Gibson, Folley, & Park, 2009 and Hille et al., 2011; two-thirds of an *SD* in Schellenberg, 2011a; one *SD* in Schellenberg & Mankarious, 2012).

Positive associations have also been identified between music training and the set of domain-general cognitive abilities called *executive functions*, which include working memory as well as any other mental activity that involves conscious control of thought, such as selective attention, mental flexibility, planning, inhibiting unwanted responses, and so on. Positive associations with music training have been reported for tasks that measure selective attention (e.g., responding to a high pitch sung with the word "low") among younger adults (Bialystok & DePape, 2009), and set shifting among older adults (Bugos et al., 2007). Could individual differences in executive functions explain the link between music training and higher-level cognitive functioning, as some scholars (Hannon & Trainor, 2007; Schellenberg & Peretz, 2008) have proposed?

In one study of 9- to 12-year-olds (Degé, Kubicek et al., 2011), children who varied in duration of music training were tested on five measures of executive functioning: selective attention (listening to a list of words and responding only to the word "red"), task shifting (sorting "animal" cards on the basis of one feature such as number, then on another feature such as color, and then another feature, and so on), planning (drawing the hands on a clock to correspond to a given time, telling the time from a clock without numbers), inhibition (saying "square" when a circle is presented and vice versa, saying "up" when an arrow pointing down is presented and vice versa), and fluency (connecting dots with lines in different ways). Performance on all five tests was correlated positively with duration of training and with IQ. More importantly, the link between duration of training and IQ disappeared when performance on the executive functions was held constant. Mediation analyses revealed that the link between music training and IQ was due to the fact that music training improved performance on the measures of selective attention and inhibition, which in turn led to improvements in IQ.

In another study with a similar design and children of the same age, musically trained and untrained 9- to 12-year-olds did *not* differ on measures of executive functions (except for working memory), even though the groups differed substantially in IQ (Schellenberg, 2011a). Some of the measures were arguably more complex than those used by Degé, Kubicek et al. (2011) (e.g., Tower of Hanoi is a complicated higher-level planning task), but some were quite similar (e.g., saying "sun" for moon and vice versa), so there is no obvious reason for the discrepancy. Moreover, in a longitudinal study that followed 7- to 8-year-olds over a period of 18 months, improvements on a test of selective attention were greater for a control group receiving training in natural sciences than for children taking music lessons, although the music group showed greater improvement on a test of processing speed (Roden, Könen et al., 2014). At present, then, it is unclear whether executive functions explain links between music training and general cognitive ability.

Another point of contention involves *how* IQ is measured. The associations described here came primarily from measures of IQ that include subtests of crystallized intelligence (e.g., defining words) *and* fluid intelligence (e.g., pattern recognition). When the test is a relatively pure measure of fluid intelligence (e.g., Raven's or Cattell's test), associations are less reliable and several null findings have been reported (Bialystok & DePape, 2009; Bidelman, Hutka, & Moreno, 2013; Franklin et al., 2008; Helmbold, Rammsayer, & Altenmüller, 2005; Lima & Castro, 2011b;

Oechslin et al., 2013; Schellenberg & Moreno, 2010; Sluming et al., 2002; Yang et al., 2014). In one instance (Brandler & Rammsayer, 2003), nonmusicians had higher scores than musicians on each of the four subtests from Cattell's test. Null findings have also been evident when the Matrix Reasoning subtest from the Wecshler tests—which is similar to Raven's test—is used to estimate fluid intelligence (Parbery-Clark et al., 2012; Patston, Hogg, & Tippett, 2007; Patston & Tippett, 2011; Strait et al., 2010).

In other instances, however, music training is associated positively with fluid intelligence among adults (Bailey & Penhune, 2012; Thompson, Schellenberg, & Husain, 2004; Trimmer & Cuddy, 2008) and children (Degé, Kubicek et al., 2011; Forgeard, Winner et al., 2008; Hille et al., 2011). Moreover, musically trained individuals often show similar advantages on the crystallized *and* fluid subtests of IQ tests (Schellenberg, 2006, 2011a,b; Schellenberg & Mankarious, 2012). To complicate matters further, most of the null findings with fluid intelligence compared highly trained (or professional) musicians to equally educated and experienced nonmusicians. In short, associations with IQ tend to be evident primarily when musically trained children or adults are compared with their untrained counterparts. When actual musicians are compared to nonmusicians, such associations are unreliable.

If taking music lessons in childhood and adolescence is associated with general cognitive ability, we should except to see similar associations with performance in school. Indeed, in childhood, average grade in school tends to increase as duration of out-of-school music training increases (Corrigall, Schellenberg, & Misura, 2013; Degé et al., 2014; Schellenberg, 2006). This dose–response association is also evident for scores on a standardized test of educational achievement (Schellenberg, 2006). For third to sixth graders, children who take private music lessons outside of school have higher grades than other children in all school subjects except for sports (Wetter, Koerner, & Schwaninger, 2009). When college freshmen are asked about their final year of high school, duration of music training in childhood is associated positively with average grade (Schellenberg, 2006). Such associations remain evident when family differences in SES are held constant (Corrigall, Schellenberg, & Misura, 2013; Schellenberg, 2006; Wetter, Koerner, & Schwaninger, 2009).

One provocative finding is that for children in elementary school, duration of music training is associated with average grade, even when IQ is held constant (Corrigall, Schellenberg, & Misura, 2013; Schellenberg, 2006). Because musically trained children are better students than would be expected based on IQ alone, other individual differences, such as personality, must be playing a role. In line with this view, as duration of music training increases, so does academic self-concept, even when IQ, SES, and grades in school are held constant (Degé et al., 2014). More conventional dimensions of personality are also likely to be implicated, particularly *conscientiousness*, the dimension that best predicts performance in school, and *openness-to-experience*, the dimension that is most closely linked to IQ. Conscientiousness is self-explanatory. Openness-to-experience refers to intellectual curiosity, preference for novelty, and interest in the arts.

Corrigall, Schellenberg, & Misura (2013) tested large samples of 10- to 12-year-old children and college freshmen. For the freshmen, duration of music training was associated at least as strongly with personality—primarily openness-to-experience—as it was with cognitive ability. For the children, the link between music training and cognitive ability disappeared when conscientiousness and openness-to-experience were held constant. Moreover, the unexplained link between music training and performance in school (i.e., with IQ held constant) disappeared when individual differences in conscientiousness were held constant. Earlier in development (7 to 9 years), the parents' openness-to-experience and the child's agreeableness are the best predictors of music training (Corrigall & Schellenberg, 2015). These findings raise the possibility that many of the associations with cognitive abilities reviewed here may have disappeared if personality were held constant.

Other researchers have asked whether taking music courses in *school* is associated with performance in other subjects. In one sample of 14- to 17-year-olds, students who took a music course performed better than other students across the various subjects taught in high school (Cabanac et al., 2013). In another sample of 150,000 students in twelfth grade, scores on a standardized test of academic achievement were analyzed as a function of whether the students took a music course in eleventh grade (Gouzouasis, Guhn, & Kishor, 2007). The music students went on to have higher grades than other students on the mathematics and biology subtests, but not in English. By contrast, taking a visual arts course in eleventh grade had no association with performance in twelfth grade.

A study of over fifteen thousand ninth- to twelfth-grade students included more than nine hundred students enrolled in an instrumental music ensemble (Fitzpatrick, 2006). The design was *retrospective*, with the goal of predicting performance on a standardized test of achievement when the students were in fourth, sixth, or ninth grade. At all three time points, future music students had higher grades in science, mathematics, and reading compared to the other students. In short, good students were more likely to enroll subsequently in a music ensemble. This pattern held for students from both low- and high-SES backgrounds. Southgate and Roscigno (2009) examined performance *prospectively* in reading and mathematics, following over four thousand kindergarteners to fifth grade, and almost eight thousand eighth graders through high school. Taking school music courses was predictive of future reading achievement in both samples, and of future mathematics achievement in the younger sample, even after controlling for SES, ethnic background, and prior achievement. By controlling for prior achievement, the analyses ruled out the possibility that observed associations arose solely because good students were particularly likely to take music classes, as the Fitzpatrick study suggested.

In a recent study of this sort, Elpus (2013) examined a sample of over thirteen thousand American students to determine whether taking music courses in high school was predictive of scores on college entrance exams (either the SAT or the ACT). In general, exam performance was better for students who had completed and passed at least one music course compared to other students. Performance also improved as the number of music credits increased. Neither association remained significant after holding constant demographic variables, grade-point average, and whether students were receiving special education. In other words, individual differences in cognitive ability and demographics appear to determine who takes music courses and who does well academically. In line with this view, Miksza (2010) reported that high-school students who enrolled in band classes tend to exhibit more pro-social behaviors and to have better school attendance, in addition to having higher scores on a standardized test of mathematics achievement. Even before entering high school (i.e., in sixth or eighth grade), good students from high-SES families are more likely than other students to enroll in band classes (Kinney, 2008).

Might associations with music training extend to other nonmusical abilities such as social skills or emotional competence? In general, there is little convincing evidence in this regard. In some cases (Lima & Castro, 2011b; Thompson, Schellenberg, & Husain, 2004) but not others (Trimmer & Cuddy, 2008), music training is associated positively with the ability to understand the emotional meaning of prosody in speech. Similarly, in some instances (Lima & Castro, 2011a) but not others (Resnicow, Salovey, & Repp, 2004), music training is associated with the ability to decode emotions expressed by instrumental music. When emotional intelligence is tested in adulthood, musically trained and untrained participants do not differ (Schellenberg, 2011b). When emotion comprehension is tested among 7- and 8-year-olds, the performance advantage for musically trained over untrained children disappears when IQ is held constant (Schellenbeg & Mankarious, 2012). Parental reports also suggest that social skills are unrelated to music training among 6- to 11-year-olds (Schellenberg, 2006). The vast majority of the training in these studies involved *private* music lessons, however, and it is possible that *group* lessons could be associated with social skills or emotional intelligence.

In sum, correlational and quasi-experimental studies reveal many associations between music training and nonmusical abilities without informing us about the direction of causation. In many instances, such associations might not remain evident if variables such as personality were measured and held constant in the analyses. Regardless, the available data show clearly that music training tends to be associated with cognitive abilities in general (but not with social–emotional abilities), and that such associations often remain evident when SES is held constant. Longitudinal studies without random assignment (e.g., Degé, Wehrum et al., 2011; Roden, Grube et al., 2014; Roden, Könen et al., 2014; Roden, Kreutz, & Bongard, 2012; Yang et al., 2014) provide evidence that is consistent with causation but inconclusive because genetically determined individual differences that are not evident earlier in development may emerge later due to maturation.

True or almost-true experiments

I will now review experiments that assigned children randomly to a music intervention or to a control condition. These studies allow for inferences of causation and are relatively few in number, so they are discussed in some depth. Because random assignment of individual children to different conditions is often difficult or impractical, researchers sometimes opt to assign entire classes to a music intervention and compare them to other classes with a different or no intervention. Compared to true random assignment, results from these "random group" experiments are more prone to the influence of extraneous effects, such as the particular teacher, the particular class, and/or the particular school.

Several studies examined whether music training causes improvements in linguistic abilities, including phonological awareness, vocabulary, and reading. In one study, classrooms of kindergarteners were assigned to four months of music training and compared to same-age children from other schools (Gromko, 2005). The children with music training showed larger improvements on a test of phonological awareness over the four-month interval, but not on tests of identifying letters or reading nonsense words. Another longitudinal study of phonological awareness assigned kindergarteners individually to intensive training (20 weeks, five days/week, ten minutes/day) in music, sports, or phonological skills (Degé & Schwarzer, 2011). Improvements over the course of the intervention (i.e., 100 sessions) were substantial for the phonological-skills group, as one would expect. A more surprising finding was that identical improvements were evident in the music group. The role of maturity was ruled out because similar improvements were not apparent in the sports group.

Other researchers examined language abilities before and after instruction in music or visual arts. In one study, 8-year-olds were assigned to music or painting lessons so that the groups were similar in IQ, verbal working memory, and reading ability when the study began (Moreno et al., 2009). In both groups, the training involved two 75-minute lessons per week for 24 weeks. Only the music group showed improvement from pre- to post-test on tasks that required them to read irregularly spelled words or to detect subtle pitch violations in speech. In a follow-up study, younger children 4 to 6 years of age were assigned to four weeks of daily training in music listening or visual arts (Moreno et al., 2011). The groups were matched initially in SES, previous training in the arts, and IQ. Before and after the training session, children were tested on measures of vocabulary and visuospatial ability, and on a test of executive function (selective attention) that required them to attend to geometric figures that varied in color while ignoring variation in shape. Only the music group showed significant improvement from pre- to post-test on measures of vocabulary and selective attention. Neither group showed improvement in visuospatial ability. The ability to match unfamiliar visual symbols with familiar words—a skill required for reading—also improved more for the music group than for the visual-arts group (Moreno, Friesen, & Bialystok, 2011).

In a similar experiment with a longer intervention, 8-year-olds were assigned to two years of music or painting lessons (François et al., 2013). Lessons were 45 minutes, twice weekly in the first year (October to May), and once a week in the second year. As in the studies by Moreno and colleagues (Moreno et al., 2009; Moreno et al., 2011), the two groups were initially formed to be similar in terms of demographics and general ability. The outcome measures included a comprehensive battery of cognitive measures, as well as a speech-segmentation task that required children to listen to a long string (five minutes) of sung nonsense syllables, and subsequently to identify which syllables tended to follow one another when the syllables were spoken rather than sung. Although improvement over time was similar across groups on the cognitive tests, performance on the speech-segmentation task showed greater improvement for the music group. Nevertheless, sung presentation at initial exposure—with each syllable matched with a distinct pitch—may have provided a mnemonic cue that was more useful for the music group than for the painting group.

Rauscher and Zupan (2000) tested a different hypothesis—that music lessons lead to improvements in visuospatial abilities. They assigned two classes of kindergarten children to receive 20-minute keyboard lessons twice a week for eight months. Two other classes received no lessons. All children were pre- and post-tested on three tests of spatial skills. Compared to the control classes, the keyboard classes had significantly larger increases over the course of the intervention on all three tests. These effects disappeared a year later for children who stopped taking lessons, but they continued to increase for children who continued taking music lessons (Rauscher, 2002). In fact, children who took lessons continuously from kindergarten through third grade proved to have better spatial skills than children who started lessons in second grade. These results suggest that music training, particularly training that begins early in life, may improve visuospatial abilities. It is unclear, however, whether similar benefits would be found for verbal or mathematical abilities, or for general intelligence. It is also unclear whether other types of training (in drama, gymnastics, etc.) would have similar benefits.

Rauscher and Hinton (2011) reviewed the method and results from a longitudinal but unpublished study that assigned at-risk preschoolers (i.e., from Head Start programs) randomly to two years of music (piano, singing, or rhythm), computer, or no lessons. Children in the music groups showed greater improvements from pre- to post-test on measures of auditory, spatial, and arithmetic abilities. Such beneficial effects were still evident in second grade, two years after the lessons had ended. Although these findings are impressive, it is impossible to evaluate them thoroughly because the review article simply summarized the method.

In another experimental study (Costa-Giomi, 1999), 9-year-old children from low-income families received three years of weekly piano lessons taught individually, or no lessons. The original sample included 117 children, but only 78 attended all of the testing sessions and were included in the analyses. A test of cognitive abilities, which provided an overall score as well as separate scores for verbal, quantitative, and visuospatial abilities, was administered at the beginning of the study and each year thereafter. Although the groups did not differ at the beginning or end of the study, there was a small advantage for the music group on the overall score after the second year, and on the visuospatial subtest after the first and second years. There were no group differences in academic achievement (measured by a standardized test or by report cards), except that children who took piano lessons had higher grades in music (Costa-Giomi, 2004). Studying children who begin music lessons at an earlier age might yield results that are stronger, more interpretable, and less temporary.

In a large-scale field experiment, I assigned 144 6-year-olds randomly to a year of weekly keyboard or Kodály (primarily voice) music lessons, or to control groups that received drama or no lessons (Schellenberg, 2004). All lessons were taught in groups of six children, and an IQ test was administered before and after the interventions. IQ scores increased from pre- to post-test in all four groups, but these increases were larger in the music groups (i.e., seven points), which did not differ, than in the control groups (four points), which also did not differ. The large sample and small levels of attrition (i.e., only 12 children dropped out mid-way through the study) meant that the difference between the music and control groups was statistically significant. Importantly, the advantage for the music groups was evident across the 12 subtests that measure different aspects of cognitive ability.

Follow-up studies sought to test the generalizability of these findings by recruiting samples of children from different cultures. In one study that assigned Greek kindergartners to a year of weekly keyboard lessons (Zafranas, 2004), the children improved significantly on five of six subtests of an IQ test, but there was no control group and hence no way to rule out the role of maturity or test/re-test effects. In a sample of Iranian 5- and 6-year-olds (Kaviani et al., 2014), 30 were assigned to a three-month intervention that provided them with music lessons taught weekly for 75 minutes (12 lessons in total, Orff method). Another 30 children matched for sex, age, and SES received no training of any sort. Before and after the training, all children were administered four subtests from an IQ test, which measured visuospatial, quantitative, and verbal abilities as well as short-term memory. The music group had a significant increase in IQ (calculated from all four subtests) from pre- to post-test, but the control group did not. For three of four subtests (all but quantitative ability), the pre- to post-test increase was greater for the music group.

In a study conducted in Israel, 81 6- to 12-year-olds were recruited from after-school programs designed for children considered to be at-risk because of low SES and problems at school (Portowitz et al., 2009). Children from three different centers were assigned to a two-year music intervention. Children from a fourth center served as controls. Each week, children in the music groups had lessons for two to three hours, they attended a music-appreciation class for one hour, and they performed in a group ensemble. Although the music and control groups performed similarly on a test of fluid intelligence (Raven's) before the intervention, the increase from pre- to post-test was greater for the music groups. The music groups but not the control group also showed significant improvements on a test of visuospatial abilities. In the Iranian (Kaviani et al., 2014) and Israeli (Portowitz et al., 2009) studies, the control groups had no additional training of any sort, so it is impossible to attribute the positive results to music per se, although the results are consistent with those reported by Schellenberg (2004).

As in the quasi-experiments discussed previously, increases in IQ as a consequence of music training are rare in experiments with small samples ($N = 24$: Chobert et al., 2014, and François et al., 2013; $N = 32$: Moreno et al., 2009). In one instance, the increase in IQ from pre- to post-test was 5 points higher (1/3 of an SD) in the music group compared to the painting group (Moreno et al., 2009). The lack of statistical significance stemmed from the small sample as well as from large individual differences that arose because of the short interval (six months) between testing sessions, which meant that increases in IQ were unusually large for both groups (12 points for the music group, seven points for the painting group).

Another study assigned almost eighty 4-year-olds randomly to 45-minute music or visual-arts classes, which were taught once a week for six weeks, or to a no-lessons control group (Mehr et al., 2013). After the intervention, there was *no* difference between groups on tests of vocabulary, discriminating different numbers of dots, and visuospatial abilities. Because of the young age of the children, the music lessons did not involve conservatory-style instrumental training, but focused instead on singing and moving to music with a parent. The lessons in visual arts were similarly free-form. Thus, the null findings could be a consequence of the short training program (4.5 hours total), the curriculum, and/or the age of the children.

Social rather than cognitive benefits may be more likely when music interventions, such as that used by Mehr et al. (2013), are designed specifically to be interactive. For example, Gerry, Unrau, and Trainor (2012) assigned 6-month-olds to six months of weekly music lessons that focused on singing and movement with a parent. A control group of same-age infants had an equivalent amount of passive exposure to music. Social–emotional improvements were greater among the infants in the interactive group. In another study, 4-year-olds were trained in a ten-minute game that required synchronizing movements with an experimenter and another child, either with or without the presence of music (Kirschner & Tomasello, 2010). Children in the music condition subsequently exhibited higher levels of cooperation and helping. Small improvements in empathy and emotional intelligence were also evident when 8- to 11-year-olds were assigned to a short-term music intervention that emphasized interactions with other children (Rabinowitch, Cross, & Burnard, 2013).

Such social–emotional advantages are rarely evident, however, for interventions that use more typical pedagogies. In a study of 9-year-olds from low-income families, the music and control groups did not differ significantly in self-esteem at any time during the study (Costa-Giomi, 2004). Similarly, at-risk 7- to 9-year-olds who took part in a two-year music program did not differ from other children in self-esteem at the beginning or the end of the intervention (Portowitz et al., 2009). In my study, with random assignment of children to one year of keyboard, Kodály, drama, or no lessons, there were no group differences at pre- or post-test for maladaptive social skills, but children in the *drama* group showed significant improvement in adaptive social skills, which distinguished them from children who had music lessons or no lessons (Schellenberg, 2004). In other words, drama lessons conferred benefits in social behavior, but music lessons did not.

In sum, the experimental evidence highlights that music lessons can lead to small improvements in cognitive abilities. In some instances there are domain-general improvements, as reflected in measures of IQ. In other instances, music lessons promote the development of visuospatial abilities and, particularly, listening skills, which may lead to improvements in language development more generally (e.g., vocabulary or reading skills). Associations between typical music lessons and social skills are rarely evident, although these could emerge when music training takes place in an interactive social context.

Conclusions

Music listening can change how you feel, and how you feel can influence performance on a variety of tasks. The particular music or genre of music that makes listeners feel good depends on the particular context and who the listeners are. Sometimes, effects of music on arousal levels and mood linger for a while, such that performance on tests administered immediately afterward is influenced by the previous listening experience. When tests are administered concurrently with music listening, the situation is complicated by other factors, such as the capacity of working memory, familiarity with the music, the characteristics of the music, the difficulty of the test, individual differences in personality and age, and so on. Thus, one can make few generalizations about effects of background music that apply across individuals and contexts. Nevertheless, for children and for adults, it is more common to find negative effects on reading comprehension and memory than it is to find positive effects.

Music training and nonmusical abilities are a different issue. Correlational and quasi-experimental studies reveal associations that can be large in magnitude and domain-general, yet observed associations in experimental studies tend to be small or task-specific. Does music training cause improvements in cognitive abilities, are high-functioning children more likely than other children to take music lessons, or do other variables (e.g., personality) account for some or all of the observed associations? Although it is common to believe that only one of these views holds true, there is no logical reason preventing all three from co-occurring.

The best evidence for causation comes from my study with random assignment of 6-year-olds to music, drama, or no lessons (Schellenberg, 2004). Random assignment necessitated providing the lessons for free, however, which meant that the children practiced very little, typically less than 30 minutes per week. In other words, although the experimental and longitudinal design was ideal for determining causation, it created an artificial context that bore little resemblance to the real world. Other positive evidence from experimental studies had very restricted outcome variables, like pronouncing irregularly spelled words (Moreno et al., 2009), remembering strings of nonsense syllables (François et al., 2013), or phonological awareness (Degé & Schwarzer, 2011). In one instance, the intervention involved very short-term but intensive training in listening rather than instrumental or vocal lessons (Moreno et al., 2011).

In correlational and quasi-experimental studies, cognitive differences between musically trained and untrained children are often much too large and general to be attributable to any environmental factor (e.g., Gibson, Folley, & Park, 2009; Hille et al., 2011; Schellenberg, 2011a; Schellenberg & Mankarious, 2012). If long-term interventions (e.g., Head Start) designed specifically to enhance general abilities meet with only modest success (Love et al., 2013), it would be miraculous for music lessons to be causing such associations. In fact, the view that *smarter, more conscientious, and open kids take music lessons* explains most of the available data parsimoniously. Music lessons may exaggerate these pre-existing differences, however, perhaps especially for memory, some language abilities, and visuospatial skills.

It is almost certain that music lessons improve listening abilities, even in nonmusical contexts, with potential consequences for language. But with a few exceptions (Degé & Schwarzer, 2011; François et al., 2013; Moreno et al., 2009; Moreno et al., 2011; Moreno, Friesen, & Bialystok, 2011), most of the available evidence is correlational and irrelevant to the issue of causation (for reviews see Asaridou & McQueen, 2013; Strait & Kraus, 2011). Presumably, like any ability, listening abilities would be a consequence of nature and nurture, and normally distributed. One would also expect that performance on tests of music aptitude—designed to measure natural listening abilities—would be correlated with performance on other listening tests, such as those that measure different aspects of speech perception (Schellenberg, 2015). If so, individuals with low levels of music aptitude and poor listening skills would be unlikely to take music lessons, particularly for long durations of time, which guarantees an association between listening abilities and music training *before* the training begins. The bottom line is that it is counter-productive to focus solely on nature or nurture as a contributing factor to any ability. A complete understanding of musical abilities and their association with nonmusical abilities requires careful consideration of interactions between genes and the environment (Schellenberg, 2015).

The major take-home points about music training and nonmusical abilities can be summarized as follows:

- Music training is associated with listening abilities, language abilities, visuospatial abilities, general intelligence, and academic achievement, and these associations often remain evident when SES is held constant.
- Associations are much less consistent when real musicians are studied, except for listening abilities, performance on some language tasks, and visuospatial abilities.
- The role of executive functions in the associations is unclear.
- *Group* music lessons may be associated with improved social–emotional skills.
- Music training is also associated with personality variables. In fact, associations with personality may be as strong or stronger than associations with cognitive abilities, which can disappear when personality is held constant.
- There is some experimental evidence that music lessons cause small increases in general cognitive abilities, but an abundance of real-world evidence indicating that taking music lessons has a strong association with cognitive abilities. Considered jointly, these findings suggest that high-functioning children are more likely than other children to take music lessons, which may exaggerate their initial advantages.

On a theoretical level, associations between music training and different cognitive abilities, including IQ, provide little support for proposals of modularity for music, music as a distinct intelligence, or "special" links between music and sub-domains of cognitive functioning such as language or mathematics. On a more practical level, if a child seems "musical" and is interested in learning music, taking lessons might have some nonmusical benefits. It cannot hurt. As for public policy, advocating for inclusion of music in school curricula on the basis of positive nonmusical benefits may be misguided, because this position tacitly admits that music is not valuable in its own right. A better message might be that music training promotes skill development and creativity in an inherently pleasurable context, and that it is eminently reasonable to teach children about the only thing that makes people everywhere dance, dream, and connect with one another.

Author note

Preparation of this chapter was supported by the Natural Sciences and Engineering Research Council of Canada and the Social Sciences and Humanities Research Council of Canada. Correspondence should be sent to Glenn Schellenberg, Department of Psychology, University of Toronto at Mississauga, Mississauga, ON, Canada L5L 1C6 (email: g.schellenberg@utoronto.ca).

Reflective questions

1 How can we explain the so-called Mozart effect?
2 Does background music improve or impair performance on the primary task?
3 Is there a special link between music training and language abilities?
4 How do children who take music lessons differ from other children?
5 Do music lessons *cause* the observed associations with cognitive abilities?

Reference list

Anderson, S. A., & Fuller, G. B. (2010). Effect of music on reading comprehension of junior high school students. *School Psychology Quarterly*, *25*, 178–87.

Anvari, S. H., Trainor, B. J., Woodside, J., & Levy, B. A. (2002). Relations among musical skills, phonological processing and early reading abilities in pre-school children. *Journal of Experimental Child Psychology*, **83**, 111–30.

Asaridou, S. S., & McQueen, J. M. (2013). Speech and music shape the listening brain: Evidence for shared domain-general mechanisms. *Frontiers in Psychology*, **4**, 321. doi: 10.3389/fpsyg.2013.00321.

Bahr, N., & Christensen, C. A. (2000). Interdomain transfer between mathematical skill and musicianship. *Journal of Structural Learning and Intelligent Systems*, **14**, 187–97.

Bailey, J., & Penhune, V. B. (2012). A sensitive period for musical training: Contributions of age of onset and cognitive abilities. *Annals of the New York Academy of Sciences*, **1252**, 163–70.

Beal, D. J., Weiss, H. M., Barros, E., & MacDermid, S. M. (2005). An episodic process model of affective influences on performance. *Journal of Applied Psychology*, **90**, 1054–86.

Bialystok, E., & DePape, A. M. (2009). Musical expertise, bilingualism, and executive functioning. *Journal of Experimental Psychology: Human Perception and Performance*, **35**, 565–74.

Bidelman, G. M., Hutka, S., & Moreno, S. (2013) Tone language speakers and musicians share enhanced perceptual and cognitive abilities for musical pitch: Evidence for bidirectionality between the domains of language and music. *PLoS ONE*, **8**(4), e60676. doi: 10.1371/journal.pone.0060676.

Bloor, A. J. (2009). The rhythm's gonna get ya—Background music in primary classrooms and its effect on behaviour and attainment. *Emotional and Behavioural Difficulties*, **14**, 261–74.

Brandler, S., & Rammsayer, T. H. (2003). Differences in mental abilities between musicians and non-musicians. *Psychology of Music*, **31**, 123–38.

Bugos, J. A., Perlstein, W. M., McCrae, C. S., Brophy, T. S., & Bedenbaugh, P. H. (2007). Individualized piano instruction enhances executive functioning and working memory in older adults. *Aging and Mental Health*, **11**, 464–71.

Butzlaff, R. (2000). Can music be used to teach reading? *Journal of Aesthetic Education*, **34**(3/4), 167–78.

Cabanac, A., Perlovsky, L., Bonniot-Cabanac, M.-C., & Cabanac, M. (2013). Music and academic performance. *Behavioral Brain Research*, **256**, 257–60.

Campbell, J. I., & Xue, Q. (2001). Cognitive arithmetic across cultures. *Journal of Experimental Psychology: General*, **130**, 299–315.

Cassady, J. C., & Johnson, R. E. (2002). Cognitive test anxiety and academic performance. *Contemporary Educational Psychology*, **27**, 270 95.

Cassidy, G., & MacDonald, R. A. R. (2007). The effect of background music and background noise on the task performance of introverts and extraverts. *Psychology of Music*, **35**, 517–37.

Chen, C., & Stevenson, H. W. (1995). Motivation and mathematics achievement: A comparative study of Asian-American, Caucasian-American, and East Asian high school students. *Child Development*, **66**, 1215–34.

Chobert, J., François, C., Velay, J. L., & Besson, M. (2014). Twelve months of active musical training in 8- to 10-year-old children enhances the preattentive processing of syllabic duration and voice onset time. *Cerebral Cortex*, **24**, 956–67.

Cohen, J. (1992). A power primer. *Psychological Bulletin*, **112**, 155–9.

Cohen, M. A., Evans, K. K., Horowitz, T. S., & Wolfe, J. M. (2011). Auditory and visual memory in musicians and nonmusicians. *Psychonomic Bulletin and Review*, **18**, 586–91.

Corrigall, K. A., & Schellenberg, E. G. (2015). Predicting who takes music lessons: Parent and child characteristics. *Frontiers in Psychology*, **6**, 282. doi: 10.3389/fpsyg.2015.00282.

Corrigall, K. A., Schellenberg, E. G., & Misura, N. M. (2013). Music training, cognition, and personality. *Frontiers in Psychology*, **4**, 222. doi: 10.3389/fpsyg.2013.00222.

Corrigall, K. A., & Trainor, L. J. (2009). Effects of musical training on key and harmony perception. *Annals of the New York Academy of Sciences*, **1169**, 164–8.

Corrigall, K. A., & Trainor, L. J. (2011). Associations between length of music training and reading skills in children. *Music Perception*, **29**, 147–55.

Costa-Giomi, E. (1999). The effects of three years of piano instruction on children's cognitive development. *Journal of Research in Music Education*, **47**, 198–212.

Costa-Giomi, E. (2004). Effects of three years of piano instruction on children's academic achievement, school performance and self-esteem. *Psychology of Music*, **32**, 139–52.

Cowan, N. (2005). *Working memory capacity*. Hove, UK: Psychology Press.

Deary, I. J. (2012). Intelligence. *Annual Review of Psychology*, **63**, 453–82.

Degé, F., Kubicek, C., & Schwarzer, G. (2011). Music lessons and intelligence: A relation mediated by executive functions. *Music Perception*, **29**, 195–201.

Degé, F., & Schwarzer, G. (2011). The effect of a music program on phonological awareness in preschoolers. *Frontiers in Psychology*, **2**, 124. doi: 10.3389/fpsyg.2011.00124.

Degé, F., Wehrum, S., Stark, R., & Schwarzer, G. (2011). The influence of two-years school music training in secondary school on visual and auditory memory. *European Journal of Developmental Psychology*, **8**, 608–23.

Degé, F., Wehrum, S., Stark, R., & Schwarzer, G. (2014). Music lessons and academic self-concept in 12- to 14-year-old children. *Musicae Scientiae*, **18**, 203–15.

de Groot, A. M. B. (2006). Effects of stimulus characteristics and background music on foreign language vocabulary learning and forgetting. *Language Learning*, **56**, 463–506.

Dobbs, S., Furnham, A., & McClelland, A. (2011). The effect of background music and noise on the cognitive test performance of introverts and extraverts. *Applied Cognitive Psychology*, **25**, 307–13.

Dutton, A., & Carroll, M. (2001). Eyewitness testimony: Effects of source of arousal on memory, source-monitoring, and metamemory judgments. *Australian Journal of Psychology*, **53**, 83–91.

Eich, E., & Forgas, J. P. (2003). Mood, cognition, and memory. In A. F. Healy & R. W. Proctor (Eds.), *Handbook of psychology: Experimental psychology: Vol. 4* (pp. 61–83). New York: Wiley.

Elpus, K. (2013). Is it the music or is it selection bias? A nationwide analysis of music and non-music students' SAT scores. *Journal of Research in Music Education*, **61**, 175–94.

Engle, R. W. (2002). Working memory capacity as executive attention. *Current Directions in Psychological Science*, **11**, 19–23.

Fitzpatrick, K. (2006). The effect of music participation and socioeconomic status on Ohio fourth-, sixth-, and ninth-grade proficiency test performance. *Journal of Research in Music Education*, **54**, 73–84.

Forgeard, M., Schlaug, G., Norton, A., Rosam, C., Iyengar, U., & Winner, E. (2008). The relation between music and phonological processing in normal-reading children and children with dyslexia. *Music Perception*, **25**, 383–90.

Forgeard, M., Winner, E., Norton, A., & Schlaug, G. (2008). Practicing a musical instrument in childhood is associated with enhanced verbal ability and nonverbal reasoning. *PLoS One*, **3**(10), e3566. doi: 10.1371/journal.pone.0003566.

Franklin, M. S., Moore, K. S., Yip, C.-Y., Jonides, J., Rattray, K., & Moher, J. (2008). The effects of musical training on verbal memory. *Psychology of Music*, **36**, 353–65.

François, C., Chobert, J., Besson, M., & Schön, D. (2013). Music training and the development of speech segmentation. *Cerebral Cortex*, **23**, 2038–43.

Furnham, A., & Stephenson, R. (2007). Musical distracters, personality type and cognitive performance in school children. *Psychology of Music*, **35**, 403–20.

Gardner, H. (2006). *Multiple intelligences: New horizons in theory and practice*. New York: Basic Books.

George, E. M., & Coch, D. (2011). Music training and working memory: An ERP study. *Neuropsychologia*, **49**, 1083–94.

Gerry, D., Unrau, A., & Trainor, L. J. (2012). Active music classes in infancy enhance musical, communicative and social development. *Developmental Science*, **15**, 398–407.

Gibson, C., Folley, B. S., & Park, S. (2009). Enhanced divergent thinking and creativity in musicians: A behavioral and near-infrared spectroscopy study. *Brain and Cognition*, **69**, 162–9.

Gouzouasis, P., Guhn, M., & Kishor, N. (2007). The predictive relationship between achievement and participation in music and achievement in core grade 12 academic subjects. *Music Education Research*, **9**, 81–92.

Grawitch, M. J., Munz, D. C., Elliott, E. K., & Mathis, A. (2003). Promoting creativity in temporary problem-solving groups: The effects of positive mood and autonomy in problem definition on idea-generating performance. *Group Dynamics*, **7**, 200–13.

Gromko, J. E. (2005). The effect of music instruction on phonemic awareness in beginning readers. *Journal of Research in Music Education*, **53**, 199–209.

Haimson, J., Swain, D., & Winner, E. (2011). Are mathematicians more musical than the rest of us? *Music Perception*, **29**, 203–13.

Hallam, S., & MacDonald, R. A. R. (2009). The effects of music in community and educational settings. In S. Hallam, I. Cross, & M. Thaut (Eds.), *The Oxford handbook of music psychology* (pp. 471–80). Oxford, UK: Oxford University Press.

Hallam, S., & Price, J. (1998). Can the use of background music improve the behaviour and academic performance of children with emotional and behavioural difficulties? *British Journal of Special Education*, **25**, 88–91.

Hallam, S., Price, J., & Katsarou, G. (2002). The effects of background music on primary school pupils' task performance. *Educational Studies*, **28**, 111–22.

Hanna-Pladdy, B., & Gajewski, B. (2012). Recent and past musical activity predicts cognitive aging variability: Direct comparison with general lifestyle activities. *Frontiers in Human Neuroscience*, **6**, 198. doi: 10.3389/fnhum.2012.00198.

Hanna-Pladdy, B., & MacKay, A. (2011). The relation between instrumental musical activity and cognitive aging. *Neuropsychology*, **25**, 378–86.

Hannon, E. E., & Trainor, L. J. (2007). Music acquisition: Effects of enculturation and formal training on development. *Trends in Cognitive Sciences*, **11**, 466–72.

Hansen, M., Wallentin, M., & Vuust, P. (2013). Working memory and musical competence of musicians and non-musicians. *Psychology of Music*, **41**, 779–93.

Heaton, P. (2009). Assessing musical skills in autistic children who are not savants. *Philosophical Transactions of the Royal Society B*, **364**, 1443–7.

Helmbold, N., Rammsayer, T., & Altenmüller, E. (2005). Differences in primary mental abilities between musicians and nonmusicians. *Journal of Individual Differences*, **26**, 74–85.

Helmbold, N., Troche, S., & Rammsayer, T. (2006). Temporal information processing and pitch discrimination as predictors of general intelligence. *Canadian Journal of Experimental Psychology*, **60**, 294–306.

Hetland, L. (2000). Learning to make music enhances spatial reasoning. *Journal of Aesthetic Education*, **34**(3/4), 179–238.

Hille, K., Gust, K., Bitz, U., & Kammer, T. (2011). Associations between music education, intelligence, and spelling ability in elementary school. *Advances in Cognitive Psychology*, **7**, 1–6.

Ho, Y.-C., Cheung, M.-C., & Chan, A. S. (2003). Music training improves verbal but not visual memory: Cross sectional and longitudinal explorations in children. *Neuropsychology*, **17**, 439–50.

Huang, R.-H., & Shih, Y.-N. (2011). Effects of background music on concentration of workers. *Work*, **38**, 383–7.

Husain, G., Thompson, W. F., & Schellenberg, E. G. (2002). Effects of musical tempo and mode on arousal, mood, and spatial abilities. *Music Perception*, **20**, 151–71.

Huss, M., Verney, J. P., Fosker, T., Mead, N., & Goswami, U. (2011). Music, rhythm, rise time perception and developmental dyslexia: Perception of musical meter predicts reading and phonology. *Cortex*, **47**, 674–89.

Ivanov, V. K., & Geake, J. G. (2003). The Mozart effect and primary school children. *Psychology of Music*, **31**, 405–13.

Jakobson, L. S., Cuddy, L. L., & Kilgour, A. R. (2003). Time tagging: A key to musicians' superior memory. *Music Perception*, **20**, 307–13.

Jakobson, L., Lewycky, S., Kilgour, A., & Stoesz, B. (2008). Memory for verbal and visual material in highly trained musicians. *Music Perception*, 26, 41–55.

Jäncke, L., & Sandmann, P. (2010). Music listening while you learn: No influence of background music on verbal learning. *Behavioral and Brain Functions*, **6**(3). doi: 10.1186/1744–9081–6–3.

Juslin, P. N., & Västfjäll, D. (2008). Emotional responses to music: The need to consider underlying mechanisms. *Behavioral and Brain Sciences*, **31**, 559–621.

Kämpfe, J., Sedlmeier, P., & Renkewitz, F. (2011). The impact of background music on adult listeners: A meta-analysis. *Psychology of Music*, **39**, 424–48.

Kane, M. J., Hambrick, D. Z., Tuholski, S. W., Wilhelm, O., Payne, T. W., & Engle, R. W. (2004). The generality of working memory capacity: A latent-variable approach to verbal and visuospatial memory span and reasoning. *Journal of Experimental Psychology: General*, **133**, 189–217.

Kaviani, H., Mirbaha, H., Pournaseh, M., & Sagan, O. (2014). Can music lessons increase the performance of preschool children in IQ tests? *Cognitive Processing*, **15**, 77–84.

Kilgour, A. R., Jakobson, L. S., & Cuddy, L. L. (2000). Music training and rate of presentation as mediators of text and song recall. *Memory and Cognition*, **28**, 700–10.

Kinney, D. W. (2008). Selected demographic variables, school music participation, and achievement test scores of urban middle school students. *Journal of Research in Music Education*, **56**, 145–61.

Kirschner, S., & Tomasello, M. (2010). Joint music making promotes prosocial behavior in 4-year-old children. *Evolution and Human Behavior*, **31**, 354–64.

Kulkofsky, S., & Ceci, S. (2006). Intelligence, schooling, and occupational success. In J. Greenhaus & G. Callanan (Eds.), *Encyclopedia of career development* (pp. 391–4). Thousand Oaks, CA: SAGE Publications, Inc.

Levitin, D. J., Cole, K., Chiles, M., Lai, Z., Lincoln, A., & Bellugi, U. (2004). Characterizing the musical phenotype in individuals with Williams syndrome. *Child Neuropsychology*, **10**, 223–47.

Lima, C. F., & Castro, S. L. (2011a). Emotion recognition in music changes across the life span. *Cognition and Emotion*, **25**, 585–98.

Lima, C. F., & Castro, S. L. (2011b). Speaking to the trained ear: Musical expertise enhances the recognition of emotions in speech prosody. *Emotion*, **11**, 1021–1031.

Lonsdale, A. J., & North, A. C. (2011). Why do we listen to music? A uses and gratifications analysis. *British Journal of Psychology*, **102**, 108–34.

Loui, P., Kroog, K., Zuk, J., Winner, E., & Schlaug, G. (2011) Relating pitch awareness to phonemic awareness in children: Implications for tone-deafness and dyslexia. *Frontiers in Psychology*, **2**, 111. doi: 10.3389/fpsyg.2011.00111.

Love, J. M., Chazan-Cohen, R., Raikes, H., & Brooks-Gunn, J. (2013). What makes a difference: Early head start evaluation findings in a developmental context. *Monographs of the Society for Research in Child Development*, **78**, 1–173.

Mehr, S. A., Schachner, A., Katz, R. C., & Spelke, E. S. (2013). Two randomized trials provide no consistent evidence for nonmusical cognitive benefits of brief preschool music enrichment. *PLoS ONE*, **8**(12), e82007. doi: 10.1371/journal.pone.0082007.

Miksza, P. (2010). Investigating relationships between participation in high school music ensembles and extra-musical outcomes: An analysis of the Education Longitudinal Study of 2002 using a bioecological development model. *Bulletin of the Council for Research in Music Education*, **186**, 7–25.

Milovanov, R., Pietilä, P., Tervaniemi, M., & Esquef, P. A. A. (2010). Foreign language pronunciation skills and musical aptitude: A study of Finnish adults with higher education. *Learning and Individual Differences*, **20**, 56–60.

Milovanov, R., & Tervaniemi, M. (2011). The interplay between musical and linguistic aptitudes: A review. *Frontiers in Psychology*, **2**, 321. doi: 10.3389/fpsyg.2011.00321.

Moreno, S., Bialystok, E., Barac, R., Schellenberg, E. G., Cepeda, N. J., & Chau, T. (2011). Short-term music training enhances verbal intelligence and executive function. *Psychological Science*, **22**, 1425–33.

Moreno, S., Friesen, D., & Bialystok, E. (2011). Effect of music training on promoting preliteracy skills: Preliminary causal evidence. *Music Perception*, **29**, 165–72.

Moreno, S., Marques, C., Santos, A., Santos, M., Castro, S. L., & Besson, M. (2009). Musical training influences linguistic abilities in 8-year-old children: More evidence for brain plasticity. *Cerebral Cortex*, **19**, 712–23.

Nantais, K. M., & Schellenberg, E. G. (1999). The Mozart effect: An artifact of preference. *Psychological Science*, **10**, 370–3.

Nisbett, R. E., Aronson, J., Blair, C., Dickens, W., Flynn, J., Halpern, D. F., & Turkheimer, E. (2012). Intelligence: New findings and theoretical developments. *American Psychologist*, **67**, 130–59.

North, A. C., Hargreaves, D. J., & Hargreaves, J. J. (2004). Uses of music in everyday life. *Music Perception*, **22**, 41–77.

Norton, A., Winner, E., Cronin, K., Overy, K., Lee, D. J., & Schlaug, G. (2005). Are there pre-existing neural, cognitive or motoric markers for musical ability? *Brain and Cognition*, **59**, 124–34.

Oechslin, M. S., Van De Ville, D., Lazeyras, F., Hauert, C.-A., & James, C. E. (2013). Degree of musical expertise modulates higher order brain functioning. *Cerebral Cortex*, **23**, 2213–24.

Parbery-Clark, A., Anderson, S., Hittner, E., & Kraus, N. (2012). Musical experience offsets age-related delays in neural timing. *Neurobiology of Aging*, **33**, 1482, e1–1483.e4.

Parbery-Clark, A., Skoe, E., Lam, C., & Kraus, N. (2009). Musician enhancement for speech-in-noise. *Ear and Hearing*, **30**, 653–61.

Parbery-Clark, A., Strait, D. L., Anderson, S., Hittner, E., & Kraus, N. (2011). Musical experience and the aging auditory system: Implications for cognitive abilities and hearing speech in noise. *PLoS ONE*, **6**(5), e18082. doi: 10.1371/journal.pone.0018082.

Parbery-Clark, A., Strait, D. L., & Kraus, N. (2011). Context-dependent encoding in the auditory brainstem subserves enhanced speech-in-noise perception in musicians. *Neuropsychologia*, **49**, 3338–45.

Patel, A. D. (2011). Why would musical training benefit the neural encoding of speech? The OPERA hypothesis. *Frontiers in Psychology*, **2**, 142. doi: 10.3389/fpsyg.2011.00142.

Patston, L. L., Hogg, S. L., & Tippett, L. J. (2007). Attention in musicians is more bilateral than in non-musicians. *Laterality*, **12**, 262–72.

Patston, L. M., & Tippett, L. J. (2011). The effect of background music on cognitive performance in musicians and nonmusicians. *Music Perception*, **29**, 173–83.

Peretz, I. (2008). Musical disorders: From behavior to genes. *Current Directions in Psychological Science*, **17**, 329–33.

Peretz, I., & Coltheart, M. (2003). Modularity of music processing. *Nature Neuroscience*, **6**, 688–691.

Perham, N., & Vizard, J. (2011). Can preference for background music mediate the irrelevant sound effect? *Applied Cognitive Psychology*, **25**, 625–31.

Peynircioğlu, Z., Durgunoğlu, A., & Öney-Küsefoğlu, B. (2002). Phonological awareness and musical aptitude. *Journal of Research in Reading*, **25**, 68–80.

Pietschnig, J., Voracek, M., & Formann, A. K. (2010). Mozart effect–Shmozart effect: A meta-analysis. *Intelligence*, **38**, 314–23.

Pool, M. M., Koolstra, C. M., & van der Voort, T. H. A. (2003). The impact of background radio and television on high school students' homework performance. *Journal of Communication*, **53**, 74–87.

Portowitz, A., Lichtenstein, O., Egorova, L., & Brand, E. (2009). Underlying mechanisms linking music education and cognitive modifiability. *Research Studies in Music Education*, **31**, 107–28.

Posedel, J., Emery, L., Souza, B., & Fountain, C. (2012). Pitch perception, working memory, and second-language phonological production. *Psychology of Music*, **40**, 508–17.

Rabinowitch, T.-C., Cross, I., & Burnard, P. (2013). Long-term musical group interaction has a positive influence on empathy in children. *Psychology of Music*, **41**, 484–98.

Ramachandra, V., Meighan, C., & Gradzki, J. (2012). The impact of musical training on the phonological memory and the central executive: A brief report. *North American Journal of Psychology*, **14**, 541–8.

Rammsayer, T., & Altenmüller, E. (2006). Temporal information processing in musicians and nonmusicians. *Music Perception*, **24**, 37–48.

Rammsayer, T. H., Buttkus, F., & Altenmüller, E. (2012). Musicians do better than nonmusicians in both auditory and visual timing tasks. *Music Perception*, **30**, 85–96.

Rauscher, F. H. (2002). Mozart and the mind: Factual and fictional effects of musical enrichment. In J. Aronson (Ed.), *Improving academic achievement: Impact of psychological factors on education* (pp. 267–78). San Diego: Academic Press.

Rauscher, F. H., & Hinton, S. C. (2011). Music instruction and its diverse extra-musical benefits. *Music Perception*, **29**, 215–26.

Rauscher, F. H., Shaw, G. L., & Ky, K. N. (1993). Music and spatial task performance. *Nature*, **365**, 611.

Rauscher, F. H., Shaw, G. L., & Ky, K. N. (1995). Listening to Mozart enhances spatial- temporal reasoning: Towards a neurophysiological basis. *Neuroscience Letters*, **185**, 44–7.

Rauscher, F. H., & Zupan, M. A. (2000). Classroom keyboard instructions improve kindergarten children's spatial-temporal performance: A field experiment. *Early Childhood Research Quarterly*, **15**, 215–28.

Resnicow, J. E., Salovey, P., & Repp, B. H. (2004). Is recognition of emotion in music performance an aspect of emotional intelligence? *Music Perception*, **22**, 145–58.

Rideout, B. E., Dougherty, S., & Wernert, L. (1998). Effect of music on spatial performance: A test of generality. *Perceptual and Motor Skills*, **86**, 512–14.

Roden, I., Grube, D., Bongard, S., & Kreutz, G. (2014). Does music training enhance working memory performance? Findings from a quasi-experimental longitudinal study. *Psychology of Music*, **42**, 284–98.

Roden, I., Kreutz, G., & Bongard, S. (2012). Effects of a school-based instrumental music program on verbal and visual memory in primary school children: A longitudinal study. *Frontiers in Psychology*, **3**, 572. doi: 10.3389/fpsyg.2012.00572.

Roden, I., Könen, T., Bongard, S., Frankenberg, E., Friedrich, E. K., & Kreutz, G. (2014). Effects of music training on attention, processing speed and cognitive music abilities—Findings from a longitudinal study. *Applied Cognitive Psychology*, **28**, 545–57.

Rodrigues, A. C., Loureiro, M. A., & Caramelli, P. (2013). Long-term musical training may improve different forms of visual attention ability. *Brain and Cognition*, **82**, 229–35.

Ruggles, D. R., Freyman, R. L., & Oxenham, A. J. (2014). Influence of musical training on understanding voiced and whispered speech in noise. *PLoS ONE*, 9(1), e86980. doi: 10.1371/journal.pone.0086980.

Schellenberg, E. G. (2004). Music lessons enhance IQ. *Psychological Science*, **15**, 511–514.

Schellenberg, E. G. (2005). Music and cognitive abilities. *Current Directions in Psychological Science*, **14**, 317–320.

Schellenberg, E. G. (2006). Long-term positive associations between music lessons and IQ. *Journal of Educational Psychology*, **98**, 457–68.

Schellenberg, E. G. (2011a). Examining the association between music lessons and intelligence. *British Journal of Psychology*, **102**, 283–302.

Schellenberg, E. G. (2011b). Music lessons, emotional intelligence, and IQ. *Music Perception*, **29**, 185–94.

Schellenberg, E. G. (2012). Cognitive performance after music listening: A review of the Mozart effect. In R. A. R. MacDonald, G. Kreutz, & L. Mitchell (Eds.), *Music, health and well-being* (pp. 324–38). Oxford, UK: Oxford University Press.

Schellenberg, E. G. (2015). Music training and speech perception: A gene–environment interaction. *Annals of the New York Academy of Sciences*, **1337**, 170–7.

Schellenberg, E. G., & Hallam, S. (2005). Music listening and cognitive abilities in 10- and 11-year-olds: The Blur effect. *Annals of the New York Academy of Sciences*, **1060**, 202–9.

Schellenberg, E. G., & Mankarious, M. (2012). Music training and emotion comprehension in childhood. *Emotion*, **12**, 887–91.

Schellenberg, E. G., & Moreno, S. (2010). Music lessons, pitch processing, and *g*. *Psychology of Music*, **38**, 209–21.

Schellenberg, E. G., Nakata, T., Hunter, P. G., & Tamoto, S. (2007). Exposure to music and cognitive performance: Tests of children and adults. *Psychology of Music*, **35**, 5–19.

Schellenberg, E. G., & Peretz, I. (2008). Music, language and cognition: Unresolved issues. *Trends in Cognitive Sciences*, **12**, 45–6.

Schellenberg, E. G., & Trehub, S. E. (2008). Is there an Asian advantage for pitch memory? *Music Perception*, **25**, 241–52.

Schellenberg, E. G., & Weiss, M. W. (2013). Music and cognitive abilities. In D. Deutsch (Ed.), *The psychology of music* (3rd ed., pp. 499–550). Amsterdam: Elsevier.

Shih, Y.-N., Huang, R.-H., & Chiang, H.-Y. (2012). Background music: Effects on attention performance. *Work*, **42**, 573–8.

Skoe, E., & Kraus, N. (2012). A little goes a long way: How the adult brain is shaped by musical training in childhood. *Journal of Neuroscience*, **32**, 11507–10.

Slevc, L. R., & Miyake, A. (2006). Individual differences in second language proficiency: Does musical ability matter? *Psychological Science*, **17**, 675–81.

Sloboda, J. A., O'Neill, S. A., & Ivaldi, A. (2001). Functions of music in everyday life: An exploratory study using the experience sampling method. *Musicae Scientiae*, **5**, 9–32.

Sluming, V., Barrick, T., Howard, M., Cezayirli, E., Mayes, A., & Roberts, N. (2002). Voxel-based morphometry reveals increased gray matter density in Broca's Area in male symphony orchestra musicians. *Neuroimage*, **17**, 1613–22.

Southgate, D., & Roscigno, V. (2009). The impact of music on childhood and adolescent achievement. *Social Science Quarterly*, **90**, 13–21.

Stoesz, B., Jakobson, L., Kilgour, A., & Lewycky, S. (2007). Local processing advantage in musicians: Evidence from disembedding and constructional tasks. *Music Perception*, **25**, 153–65.

Strait, D., & Kraus, N. (2011). Playing music for a smarter ear: Cognitive, perceptual, and neurobiological evidence. *Music Perception*, **29**, 133–46.

Strait, D., Kraus, N., Parbery-Clark, A., & Ashley, R. (2010). Musical experience shapes top-down auditory mechanisms: Evidence from masking and auditory attention performance. *Hearing Research*, **261**, 22–9.

Strait, D., Parbery-Clark, A., Hittner, E., & Kraus, N. (2012). Musical training during early childhood enhances the neural encoding of speech in noise. *Brain and Language*, **123**, 191–201.

Thompson, W. F., Schellenberg, E. G., & Husain, G. (2001). Arousal, mood and the Mozart effect. *Psychological Science*, **12**, 248–51.

Thompson, W. F., Schellenberg, E. G., & Husain, G. (2004). Decoding speech prosody: Do music lessons help? *Emotion*, **4**, 46–64.

Thompson, W. F., Schellenberg, E. G., & Letnic, A. K., (2012). Fast and loud background music hinders reading comprehension. *Psychology of Music*, **40**, 700–8.

Tierney, A., Bergeson, T., & Pisoni, D. (2008). Effects of early musical experience on auditory sequence memory. *Empirical Musicology Review*, **3**, 178–86.

Trimmer, C. G., & Cuddy, L. L. (2008). Emotional intelligence, not music training, predicts recognition of emotional speech prosody. *Emotion*, **8**, 838–49.

Tsang, C. D., & Conrad, N. J. (2011). Music training and reading readiness. *Music Perception*, **29**, 157–63.

van Goethem, A., & Sloboda, J. (2011). The functions of music for affect regulation. *Musicae Scientiae*, **15**, 208–28.

Västfjäll, D. (2001/2). Emotion induction through music: A review of the musical mood induction procedure. *Musicae Scientiae*, **5**, 173–212.

Vaughn, K. (2000). Music and mathematics: Modest support for the oft-claimed relationship. *Journal of Aesthetic Education*, **34**(3/4), 149–66.

Wallentin, M., Nielsen, A. H., Friis-Olivarius, M., Vuust, C., & Vuust, P. (2010). The Musical Ear Test, a new reliable test for measuring musical competence. *Learning and Individual Differences*, **20**, 188–96.

Wetter, O. E., Koerner, F., & Schwaninger, A. (2009). Does musical training improve school performance? *Instructional Science*, **37**, 365–74.

Yang, H., Ma, W., Gong, D., Hu, J., & Yao, D. (2014). A longitudinal study on children's music training experience and academic development. *Scientific Reports*, **4**, 5854. doi: 10.1038/srep05854.

Zafranas, N. (2004). Piano keyboard training and the spatial-temporal development of young children attending kindergarten classes in Greece. *Early Child Development and Care*, **174**, 199–211.

Chapter 9

Musical literacy: Reading traditional clef notation

Janet Mills and Gary E. McPherson

What do we mean when we say that a child is "musically literate"? How can musical literacy be defined and what types of competencies might it infer? Because this term is widely used, it makes sense to address it in this book. As will become evident during the discussion to follow, our view, consistent with approaches to language literacy, is that *literacy* in situations related to Western classical music occurs as a result of children having developed their capacity to make music, reflect on the music in which they are engaged, express their views on music which they play, hear, or create, speak about and listen to music in order to form judgments, and read, write, comprehend, and interpret staff notation. Each of these aspects of literacy has been dealt with elsewhere in this volume, so most of our comments in this chapter will detail the fundamental aspects of learning how to use staff notation, even though we recognize that this is only one dimension of the literacy acquisition process, and that staff notation is only one type of music notation.

Literacy or literacies?

An obvious way to define and thereby understand what "musical literacy" means is to draw parallels with the ways that children become "literate" as they learn to read and write their spoken mother tongue. A common assumption is that literacy involves the simple ability to read and write, through processes involved in decoding letters, and groups of letters, into sounds and vice versa. However, literacy in language development is far more complex.

Although researchers still debate the best methods and techniques for teaching children to read language, and teachers find that each child needs an individual mix of methods and techniques, they agree that language reading is best achieved through speech, after the basic structure and vocabulary of the language has first been established (Cooper, 2003). There is also an increasing recognition of the importance of communication in real-world situations and the need to develop children's capacities to speak, listen, read, write, and think (Cooper, 2003). Thus, literacy in reading and writing can involve developing a large set of structures "ranging from individual skills, abilities, and knowledge to social practices and functional competencies to ideological values and political goals" (Soares, 1992, pp. 8–10). This is why some language researchers prefer the term *literacies* in recognition that there is no single unitary literacy (Soares, 1992), but rather a complex of abilities (Harris & Hodges, 1995). One of the fundamental assumptions in this literature is that children should be exposed to a wide variety of literacy experiences and considerable direct or explicit instruction, beginning with experiences in listening and speaking which in due course lead on to, and continue to develop alongside, reading and writing (Cooper, 2003).

Much of this parallels theoretical conceptions of musical development where an expanded view of musical literacy is the norm (McPherson & Gabrielsson, 2002). This is one reason why some music educators (including the authors of this chapter) try to avoid using the term "musical literacy," because it is so easily misunderstood. There are usually other ways of saying whatever it is that you want to say when describing a child as musically literate—or as not musically literate.

Ask anyone who uses the term "musical literacy" to say what they mean by it, and they will often speak—in effect—of the ability to function fluently as a musician. But delve deeper to find out what is meant by "function," "fluently," or "musician," and it becomes clear that views of "musical literacy" often focus exclusively on the ability to decode written staff notation and turn it "accurately" into sound. And this is where problems start to emerge, for while many musicians around the world can decode written staff notation fluently:

1   There are many modes of music-making in which notation plays no part.

2   No child needs to be able to decode staff notation accurately *before* starting to learn to make the sorts of music where staff notation is used customarily.

3   Learning to read music before, or separately from, learning to make music can lead to misunderstandings.

4   Too early an exposure to staff notation can lead people to overlook the features of music that are not its focus. Staff notation of a melody provides Western classical musicians with information about which note (from the Western classical scale) to play, when it should start, and (provided that the tempo remains constant) when the next note should start. It says little about timbre, articulation, how long a note should be sustained within the space of time allotted to it, dynamics, tempo change, and so forth. And this is just what it does not say about melody. Bring harmony or any of the other dimensions of music into the equation, and the partial nature of the information provided by staff notation becomes even more apparent.

5   Undue emphasis on staff notation can lead to atrophy of musicians' creative abilities, and their ability to memorize.

6   Some people who do not read music at all nevertheless become fluent even within the realm of the music where composers and performers customarily use staff notation. Examples include adults who sing complex Western classical choral works entirely from memory, or who can sit down at a piano to "improvise" or play pieces in the style of named Western classical composers that they recall from aural and physical memory.

Contexts involving musical literacy

Traditionally, many Western classical performing musicians have developed their literacy skills through childhood instrumental lessons that addressed instrumental skills, music reading skills, and related skills as part of the same package. However, as highlighted in other chapters and also in other writing (e.g., Mills, 2005), children who grow up in a culture where music is valued and plentiful, and where there are role models of people who describe themselves, and are described by others, as "musicians," often grow up to be musicians themselves, in effect at their mother or somebody else's knee, just as they learn to speak, to walk, to wash themselves, or to make friends, and so forth. We are not suggesting here that becoming a musician is (literally) innate, or that one becomes a musician simply by being in the right place for the right length of time. Growing up to be a musician involves engaging, in some way, with musicians, just as growing up to speak a foreign language involves engagement with other people who can speak it. There is tuition, of a kind, involved, but it is not necessarily the sort that must take children out of their culture in order to give them trumpet lessons in a distant studio, or piano lessons in their school.

Farrell (2001) writes of the *gharanas* (literally "households") of India that are based on familial lineage and have musical styles that are distinct, but adapt with the times. Wiggins (1996) writes of the challenge, when learning Ghanaian drum music in Ghana, of keeping up with teenage boys who have grown up with it around them, and who cannot understand why he finds it so challenging to play. Green and Bray (1997) write of Cheryl who is aged 13. Cheryl, who lives in England, plays in her father's folk band but has had no formal music training. Despite this, she is the most accomplished member of the band. Cheryl is a fluent musician, arguably "literate" in the music she is playing, who has learnt through engagement with other, older, musicians—and who has developed skills that surpass theirs. Her fluency as a musician—her musical literacies—has been shaped by factors including:

- developing an ability to play by ear;
- development of her musical memory;
- the absence of any curb on her creative and expressive abilities;
- the familiar music of her father's folk band;
- the physical characteristics and timbral possibilities of the instruments available to her; and
- other people, especially her participation and involvement with older musicians.

Cheryl's school music education truly acknowledged neither the unique abilities she brought to lessons nor the musicianship she had developed outside school. In many countries it is possible to visit classrooms where a well-meaning teacher tries to teach young children what is seen as the basics of staff notation, although they have no immediate musical need for it given that they learn songs aurally, remember their compositions or record them using invented symbols or electronically, and so forth. One also sometimes sees early instrumental lessons in which equally well-meaning instrumental teachers inadvertently give children the impression that a musician cannot play a note that has not first been decoded from the printed page, or where children are being distracted from listening to, enjoying, and refining the sounds that they are making through being required to simultaneously decode staff notation.

So, given all these caveats, how do children learn to read staff notation? While there are respects in which music is not a language, there may nevertheless be lessons here from the ways in which children learn to read their own verbal language, be it English or a language that uses another alphabet or symbol system.

Parallels between language and music literacy development

The most important principle we have observed from studies on written verbal language development is that children should become competent with spoken verbal language before they grapple with written verbal language (Adams, 1994; Kirby, 1988). In most countries children speak for as long as five years before being obliged to start learning to read on entry to school, and only after they have gained a great deal of prior experience with their native language and reached the mental age necessary to maximize their success as readers (Adams, 1994; McPherson & Gabrielsson, 2002; Mills, 1991a). By this age, the home experiences of most children of having been read to by their mothers and having seen their parents and others reading will have prepared them about the nature of how words and thoughts can be represented in symbols (Adams, 1994). They are thus ready to begin to read for themselves.

It does not follow from this that children should engage formally with music aurally for as long as five years before being introduced to some form of staff notation, as they will come to their first formal lessons having heard a great deal of music during their infancy and early childhood. Even so, it may be unwise to introduce children to music reading in their early music lessons, especially if they are learning an instrument and still working out the basics of sound production. Rather, children should be encouraged to experience and enjoy music first, so that the acquisition of formal musical skills can occur *inductively* as a natural outcome of this process (Hargreaves, 1986). An activity that can prepare young beginners for learning to read staff notation is to encourage them to invent their own notations to represent pieces they already know. This provides them with the metamusical awareness that will enhance their progress toward understanding why staff notation looks and works the way it does (McPherson & Gabrielsson, 2002; Upitis, 1990, 1992).

Most 5- or 6-year-old children's knowledge about how music can be represented in any form of notation will be below their level of understanding of how verbal language can be represented in print. Thus, children younger than 6 probably learn an instrument best when teaching emphasizes learning to play pieces that they already know by sound, and rote learning of unfamiliar pieces, in order to establish ear-to-hand coordination skills that lay a foundation for introducing notation later and which also keep their imaginative skills alive (McPherson & Gabrielsson, 2002).

We know from studies with young learners that the functional literacy of knowing where to put your fingers after having seen a visual cue on a score, represents a very limited form of comprehending staff notation (McPherson, 1993, 2005; Schleuter, 1997). The knowledge of letter names and note patterns needs therefore to be practiced in various contexts, leading from familiar patterns to more challenging, previously unknown patterns.

Another important principle is that even after children have learnt to read and write verbal language, they still speak it. As they become fluent users of staff notation, and when they have achieved fluency, they still need opportunities to work free of staff notation, in order to develop and sustain the full range and depth of their musical literacy.

As mentioned earlier, children are exposed to a great deal of written verbal language in their environment for several years before they learn to read it. They see when adults use it, and when they do not, such as when a mother helps her infant by pointing to the words as she reads the story. This is related to the practice within the Anglican choral tradition whereby a new chorister may be paired with an older chorister who is expected to point to the music as he or she sings, with younger choristers joining in sections that they can recall, long before they have learned to read music autonomously (Mills & Barrett, 2006).

Finally, in their early stages as readers of spoken verbal language, children learn to read words that they already know. Long before they can read fluently, they may pick out words such as their name on birthday cakes or cards (Mills, 2005). When their formal reading begins, they first learn to read simple words that are already in their spoken vocabulary. The opportunity to cross-check material that they are reading with material that they know, and to relate it within an aural system that they already understand, could be useful also in music. This is why the general rule recommended by McPherson and Gabrielsson (2002) is for children to learn to read pieces they already know by ear, before pieces they do not know which require more sophisticated levels of processing. This principle underpinned some of the early published band methods (Brittin & Sheldon, 2004).

The mechanics of reading music notation

When reading aloud we are saying the words from one section while reading the words from the section that immediately follows. Likewise, when performing and interpreting music from notation our eyes may run ahead of what is actually being played (Sloboda, 2005). Studies show that expert sight-readers are able to recognize "chunks" or patterns of up to seven notes after the music has been removed (Dodson, 1983; Schleuter & Schleuter, 1988; Sloboda, 1988, 2005). Most importantly, the evidence also suggests that reading skills are developed through experience and familiarity with the symbols being read, such that it is easier to look ahead and anticipate the flow of the music when the notation contains predictable or straightforward patterns (Sloboda, 2005). Problems involving visual processing, therefore, do not always explain poor reading ability. As with reading text, poor readers of musical notation are probably the tail end of a continuous distribution, rather than a peculiar group whose reading processes are different from more efficient readers. By this we mean that they probably display deficits on skills that more able readers can do better, rather than employ processes that are entirely different (Meadows, 1993).

In the very beginning stages of learning to read staff notation, a young child will need to learn that music is read by moving your eyes from left to right, top to bottom on the page. As a child learns to distinguish common familiar patterns in the pieces being studied, he or she becomes more capable of integrating a more varied array of patterns into his or her repertoire, and begins to differentiate and predict patterns from the overall shape or start of the particular pattern. It is advantageous in all stages of development for the child to have the sound of the music in his or her mind, because this will enable the young musician to draw on these aural recollections in order to "read ahead."

Many children exposed to a traditional approach to music instruction begin learning notation from the very first lessons. Without being taught to link the sound of musical patterns with notated patterns these children will probably learn to rely on sight vocabulary, going directly from the visual image to the fingering required to execute this on their instrument. These are what Schleuter (1997) refers to as "button pushers" to whom notation indicates only what fingers to push down. In such cases the player goes from eye to hand, without necessarily connecting this with his or her ear, or from visual perceptions to the reproduction of the written notation on the instrument (King, 1983). Being aware of the sound of the music and also of being able to link this auditory perception with the visual perception, however, is especially important if the child is to be able to develop the repertoire of musical patterns required to perform more difficult passages. Establishing each of the links between eye, ear, and hand is also necessary if the child is to develop the capacity to deal with unfamiliar patterns when performing a new piece of music (King, 1983).

It is probably true also that there are various stages leading up to the skilled ability to read notation and that the nature of reading staff notation, as with most other musical skills, changes substantially during the first five or six years of the formal learning process. For example, McPherson's (1993, 1994a, 2005) studies with beginner- to advanced-level children learning musical instruments show wide differences between sight-reading ability occurring even within the first 12 months, and that the main predictor of the children's ability to process notation was the strategies they used to aid their performance (see further McPherson, Davidson, & Evans, Chapter 22).

In summary, the mechanics of reading notation involve the coordination of a number of differing skills. Highly developed readers of notation display an ability to link the sound with the notation (McPherson, 1993, 1994b, 2005; Schleuter, 1997). Young instrumentalists, however, may have more trouble with reading rhythm than pitch, because "pitch production with many instruments is possible without internalization of pitch, while rhythm production is difficult without auditory coding" (Dodson, 1983, p. 4). As an example, McPherson (1993, 1994a) examined a group of wind instrumentalists, all of whom had been studying their instrument for more than two years. He found that students of all ability levels made approximately three times as many rhythm errors as compared to pitch errors. These results can be interpreted as follows: Sight-singing involves processes whereby the child will need to comprehend both pitch and rhythm in order to success-fully "sing" the passage being performed. In this sense, the task of sight-singing demands an abil-ity to inwardly "hear," or what Gordon (2003) refers to as "audiate" (i.e., comprehend), both pitch and rhythm. However, when sight-reading on an instrument, the player does not need to audiate pitch at the same level as is needed to bring meaning to the rhythm. When most children see the passage "F-G-E-F," for example, they know that this is fingered in a certain way on their instru-ment. They therefore do not necessarily need to be able to hear the passage in their mind, in order to be able to perform it on their instrument. But with rhythm, they will need to know how the pattern sounds. There are therefore subtle differences between sight-singing and sight-reading in the way that musicians process pitch and rhythm. The ability to self-correct errors is important for efficient sight-reading and sight-singing (Mills, 1983).

Hierarchical levels

There are few studies that help us conceptualize how young children develop their ability to read unfamiliar melodies from staff notation. One, by Cantwell and Millard (1994), involves an attempt to identify the different hierarchical levels at which reading traditional staff notation can be analyzed. These researchers speculated that processing staff notation has similarities with pro-cessing text and used Kirby's (1988) work on processing text to construct an eight-level hierarchy of operational levels that they believe are required when children process staff notation. Cantwell and Millard's (1994) theoretical synthesis of Kirby's work can be abbreviated as follows:

1 *Features*: the markings on the page that form the basis of notation. These involve awareness of the features of the lines and curves of the musical symbols and notes, and knowledge that they are both systematic and meaningful.

2 *Letters/musical notes and signs*: Consistent interpretation of features allows the child to attend to and recognize basic symbol units such as individual notes, clef signs, time signatures, dynamic markings, sharps, flats, and so forth.

3 *Syllables/intervals*: Structural analysis of melodic patterns involves recognizing the systematic relationships between adjoining notes (e.g., intervals).

4 *Words/groups*: The transition from individual notes to groups of notes occurs via structural analysis of the component intervals, or by visual scanning of the whole musical idea (e.g., chord, scale run). This represents the first level of musical meaning; however, at this level, the meanings attached to individual clusters are decontextualized and isolated.

5 *Word groups/motifs or note grouplets*: Combinations of clusters form a *motif* or *motif grouplet*, a level of musical meaning equivalent to understanding individual phrases and clauses in text. These may vary in length according to their musical function.

6 *Idea/musical phrase or figure*: In music, an individual idea is expressed by combining motifs into a musical phrase.

7 *Main idea/musical idea*: The combination of musical phrases yields a musical idea, equivalent in text-processing terms to the construction of a main idea from a paragraph.

8 *Themes/musical subject*: Understanding of the musical subject involves imposing a sense of musicality onto the score such that the component musical phrase and subject are taken beyond technical proficiency to include variations of sound, mood, dynamics, and so forth in ways that allow for individualized interpretation of the score (Cantwell & Millard, 1994, pp. 47–9).

This hierarchy suggests that children first become aware of the features of staff notation as they start to develop a sense of what reading notation is all about, and begin to learn how music is notated on the score. Next, consistent interpretation of the features of staff notation allows the child to attend to basic symbol units of the medium. In staff notation, this includes being able to recognize individual notes, clef signs, time and key signatures, dynamic markings, sharps, flats, and so forth. During this stage the size of the notation is important, as children learn to process the notation and focus their eyes on the line of the staff notation. If the symbols are too close together, then they may have difficulty perceiving differences, or may even skip over important details such as a flat or sharp.

From here, further development will be hampered unless the child has already learnt to link the auditory sound with the visual notation. They will need to develop their capacity to recognize motifs and patterns, such as sequences, and cope with pulse, meter, and rhythm as well as key, tonality, and pitch. These relationships form the basis for learning to comprehend or "audiate" what is seen in notation, and of being aware of the syntax of the music being performed. At the most sophisticated level, the child will learn how to use what he or she has seen in the notation to enhance the expression of their performance.

A number of implications arise from this hierarchy, two of which are highlighted by Cantwell and Millard (1994). The first involves the need for teachers to explicitly cue their students to focus their processing operations at a higher level on the hierarchy than they are currently working. For example, young learners could be cued to translate the individual notes and patterns that they are learning to read into a meaningful entity of a melody or phrase, such as by singing the melody while following the notation before they commence to play it on an instrument. Focusing children's attention on the flow of a melody and the expressive detail in a score, or even encouraging them to play the passage with a different kind of expression, can help them develop a more sophisticated awareness of the broader purpose of notation. As they develop further, students can then be encouraged to focus their attention on the upper two levels (*musical ideas* and *themes*), so that they understand how notation can help them develop a personalized conception of the musical score.

A second implication of the study concerns ways in which "deep" rather than "surface" levels of processing can be encouraged during teaching, based on the premise that the development of deeper processing skills when reading notation is just as important as the development of technical skill on an instrument.

Practice leads to automaticity, allowing children to quickly and accurately discern key features in the staff notation, and then use these to coordinate motor movements that allow them to either sing or play the melody represented in notation. Such automaticity allows musicians to direct their attention to higher levels, such as the expressive detail or the overall flow of the melody and how it might be interpreted. Practice, in the form of drill and practice exercises, can help a child to react quickly to the symbols they see in notation. But drill and practice activities can also be boring and frustrating for learners, and not necessarily the most efficient form of learning. Guided meaningful reading of a range of musical repertoire in which the student's attention is directed to relevant technical and expressive characteristics that are embedded in the music itself helps to instill confidence and knowledge that can be applied in other contexts. Allied with these experiences are kinaesthetic relationships such as being able to recognize the "key terrain" of the piece. On the piano, for example, each key has a kinaesthetically distinct feel (E major being quite different from C major, for example). A child will have a better chance of learning how to read staff notation if he or she is able to recognize the "key terrain" of the passage of the piece being learned.

As an extension of these points, McPherson and Gabrielsson (2002) propose that children need to acquire some knowledge of how to attend to individual details and decode the basic elements of pitch and rhythm. They will need to learn, for example, that a quarter note (or crotchet) is one beat in length in many contexts and that music is represented by notes on a five-line staff which can be more easily remembered using mnemonic aids (e.g., "F-A-C-E" for the spaces on a treble clef; this is levels 1 and 2 on the hierarchy). However, learning can be extremely tedious and frustrating if the process concentrates too much on these types of fine detail such that a child's attention is constantly focused on learning the names of individual notes and rhythmic patterns divorced from the sound of the music itself. This is especially evident in situations where knowledge of this kind is not immediately put into practice so that it can be integrated into the child's growing awareness of how the actual music really sounds.

Following on from this it would be incorrect to assume that children need to memorize a wide range of "facts" before they will be successful in learning how to read and comprehend notation. The process of reading music can be extremely slow and tortuous for children when the learning process introduces elements of music that are not immediately applied in the musical examples performed or studied by the children themselves. Thus, the old style of instrumental "method" books, which displayed all the rhythmic patterns (from whole notes leading down to quarter, sixteenth, and thirty-second note values) and a full range of pitches within as well as above and below the musical stave, have long been dismissed by music educators as a very ineffective way of introducing children to notation. Most contemporary method books for teaching children to play an instrument now include only the information needed at the time of learning to play a specific melody, so that the child does not have to learn information which is not immediately put into practice.

Children will not always acquire efficient reading skills by exclusively starting on letter name/note duration and then working up. Right from the start, they need to operate at a higher level of abstraction to extract the sense of the passage they are attempting to read. Equally important are the small-scale predictions built up through a knowledge of form, style, and larger units such as chords, measures, beats, and phrases, which must be understood before music reading becomes meaningful (Sloboda, 2005). In this sense, unless the beginner knows the music through repeated hearings and has been able to form a mental blueprint internally, then it will be more difficult and frustrating to try to read it note by note.

Finally, and as mentioned previously, it is important to remind ourselves that children will vary widely in their progress toward fluent reading. As shown in McPherson's (1993, 2005) longitudinal studies with young beginners (see Chapter 22, this volume), wide differences in reading abilities appear in the first weeks of learning, with some children struggling to read while others pick up notation skills relatively easy. Unfortunately, children who have problems often do not receive the type of supportive instruction that will improve their abilities, with the result that they often cease instruction. Educators would not allow such wide differences to occur in everyday instruction of children learning to read their spoken language, and nor should we allow them to occur in music. Learning to read staff notation involves a complex of skills, and no two students will follow exactly the same line of development.

In summary, then, a key principle of effective learning is that any new concept or piece of information about staff notation should be linked wherever possible to structurally meaningful entities such as phrases and melodies (i.e., the upper levels of the hierarchy) rather than individual notes, so that the child's focus of attention is on the main reason for learning: access to music-making. In the very early stages of learning, unless the sound of the melody the child is trying to read or perform is in his or her mind, then the act of reading the notation is more likely to be frustrating and tedious.

An example of the music-reading process

With the previous section as our guide, we now turn to a practical example of the very earliest stages of learning to read musical notation. If reading staff notation is in any way similar to reading words, then at its most basic level there are probably two distinct ways in which a child can decode notation. First, the child could break down the individual notes and sound them out before they are blended together to form a meaningful whole. In this method the child would see, for example (see Figure 9.1), and try to decode this by breaking it down into individual notes (see Figure 9.2):

Fig. 9.1 A meaningful whole

A major problem with this approach is that the emphasis is on moving from symbol to action

Figure 9.2 Individual notes

(fingerings) to sound, rather than from symbol to sound to action (McPherson & Gabrielsson, 2002; see also Mainwaring, 1933, 1941, 1951). This is how many young beginners who are taught to read music from the very first lessons often practice at home—by stumbling over individual notes as they continue playing, sometimes so slowly and hesitantly that they no longer are able to perceive the music they are attempting to perform (McPherson, 1993; McPherson & Gabrielsson, 2002; McPherson & Renwick, 2001). In such situations children may have insufficient cognitive resources left to devote to manipulating their instrument and listening to what they are playing because so much of their attention is focused on reading notation (McPherson & Gabrielsson, 2002). This is particularly important to note, given that vision tends to dominate and inhibit the processing of signals from other modalities (Posner, Nissen, & Klein, 1976; Smythe, 1984). As Bamberger (1996, 1999) explains, beginners find these types of learning experiences extremely frustrating, especially when they are taught to look at the smallest objects such as single notes and to classify these without any knowledge of their context or functional meaning. Asking beginners to focus on notation too early, according to Bamberger (1996), means asking them to "put aside their most intimate ways of knowing—figures, felt paths, context and function" (p. 44). Too early an emphasis on notation can therefore lead to a decreased aural sensitivity for the natural unified patterns that children spontaneously observe when listening to music.

A second, more direct method would be for the child to link the patterns of a group of notes directly to the overall sound that is represented in the notation. This is more like the processes that seem to be used by children who are given the opportunity to play by ear, for example:

> Amy [age 32 months] is not one to "plink-plonk" on the piano, but loves to watch her father play. He shows her how to play E-D-C: she copies him and says 'That's *Three Blind Mice*.' She works out how to continue *Three Blind Mice*, playing E-D-C E-D-C G-F-E G-F-E. She then stops abruptly, and goes off to play with some toys. (Mills, 2005, p. 164)

In a related approach to music reading, the child would be encouraged to learn to comprehend groups of notes (see Figure 9.3):

Fig. 9.3 Comprehending patterns

and to associate these with the aural image already formed of a well-known piece of music, such as the repeated pattern at the beginning of *Three Blind Mice*. Obviously, this is a more direct and musical way of working, as young readers work more holistically to connect what they see with the sound of each pattern or phrase. This *direct* or holistic way of processing notation is how many children exposed to rote teaching techniques would learn to process notation. For example, in the Suzuki method children learn a large repertoire of pieces by rote before learning to perform the same repertoire when notation is introduced. In this approach they already have a mental image of what the music sounds like and how it can be reproduced on their instrument, and therefore only need to learn how to link the symbol of what they see with this mental image. In contrast to the first method, the emphasis is more musical, as the young musician learns to work from symbol to sound to action (McPherson & Gabrielsson, 2002).

There may be times when all children will use both methods for analyzing notation, depending on the level of difficulty of the music being performed. For example, young musicians who are skilled readers will tend to work at the holistic level, performing with ease the musical patterns that they have come to know and internalize. However, when they encounter a difficult or unusual rhythmic or pitch pattern they may stumble before breaking the pattern down into simpler units and then gradually piecing it together in order to perform it as a whole. However, it is important to note that research in reading words (Kirby, 1988) suggests that poor readers find it difficult to rely exclusively on a "phonological approach," whereby they break a word down into individual letters before sounding it out and eventually blending it together. Reading staff notation can cause a similar type of problem, because when individual notes are broken down into isolated units, and divorced from the meter or key in which they operate, their meaning can be destroyed. This is why Gordon (2003) and others stress the importance of learning to read notation in context, and why staff notation will only have relevance when the child learns to feel the beat or tonality of the patterns he or she is trying to reproduce from notation. It is also the reason why teachers will often use rhythmic and tonal syllables as an aid to reading development and why young children learning an instrument will often be taught to tap out the beat using large motor movements as an aid to learning to feel the rhythm of a pattern they are about to learn to perform. However, tapping out rhythms, rather than a pulse, can be problematic, as we will see in the next section.

Common problems

Learning to decipher staff notation can be very confusing for a child. Music uses a number of ordinary-sounding words that mean something different from their usage in everyday life: high and low being just one pair of examples. The relationship between hearing and comprehending high and low pitch in music and physically learning how to play it on an instrument can be very mystifying. On the piano high and low notes go from right to left, on the guitar the highest string is at the bottom, and on the cello the sound goes up as you slide your hand down a string.

The common practice of teaching children to read rhythms by tapping or clapping is also very problematic. Rhythms have durations as well as onsets, but a "long" tap or clap is the same length as a "short" tap or clap: only the silence after the tap or clap changes in length. The first author (Mills, 1991b, c) worked with children aged 8 to 10, to learn more about the information they pick up from rhythms that are clapped or played to them. She based her experiment on a simple rhythmic pattern used in earlier research by Bamberger (1988) (see Figure 9.4):

Fig. 9.4 Experimental rhythmic pattern

The response of one child was typical of many of the children who took part in the Bamberger research (see Figure 9.5). Lucy had recently started learning the violin:

> After listening to the clapped rhythm, she drew her hand and showed, through labelling the fingers from "beat 1" to "beat 5" that she had spotted that the rhythm repeated, and also that the repeating cell consisted of five claps. She also showed that "beats 3–5" were a group of some sort (Figure 9.5a). [The researcher] asked Lucy if she could think of another way of drawing the rhythm. She drew five teddy bears that she numbered 1–5, labelling clasps 3–5 "fast." Alice's response seemed reasonable . . . there is a sense in which "beats 3–5" sound like a group. However, the US research had judged responses like Lucy's to be immature, and to suggest that she had not heard the rhythm properly. (Mills, 2005, pp. 101–103)

In a subsequent session a couple of weeks later, the researcher returned with a very simple electronic keyboard so that she could investigate how Lucy might respond to rhythms that were sustained. Instead of clapping rhythms, Lucy was taught to play them on a single note using the electronic keyboard that would sustain the sound until the key was lifted. After learning the rhythm shown in Figure 9.5b, Lucy was asked to draw something that would remind her of the rhythm that she had just learned.

> Lucy drew ten pigs, which she numbered from one to ten. She labelled pigs 2, 3, 7 and 8 as "fast." Next . . . without prompting, she clapped the rhythm and labelled pigs 4 and 9 "fast" too. It was as though the rhythm that she was hearing had changed into one that could be written more accurately using the notation shown below the pigs. Thereafter, Lucy gave up drawing until she had first clapped a rhythm that she had learnt to play on the keyboard. (Mills, 2005, p. 103)

Her responses to three further rhythms are shown in Figures 9.5c–e.

Finally, the researcher returned to the original rhythm (see Figure 9.5f). Lucy's response was the same as when she had not used the sustaining instrument, except that she produced squares instead of teddies, and wrote out the repetition of the first "bar." Her notation could be interpreted as:

- inaccurate, duration-based notation of the rhythms;
- notation based on something other than duration;
- accurate, duration-based notations of rhythms reconstructed from the previously clapped rhythms.

Given that in the rhythm shown in Figure 9.5b Lucy changed her accurate notation after clapping, the third of these interpretations is the most sensible:

> A long clap is no longer than a short clap: only the silence between varies in length. So Lucy is entitled to reconstruct the clapped rhythms like this if she wishes.

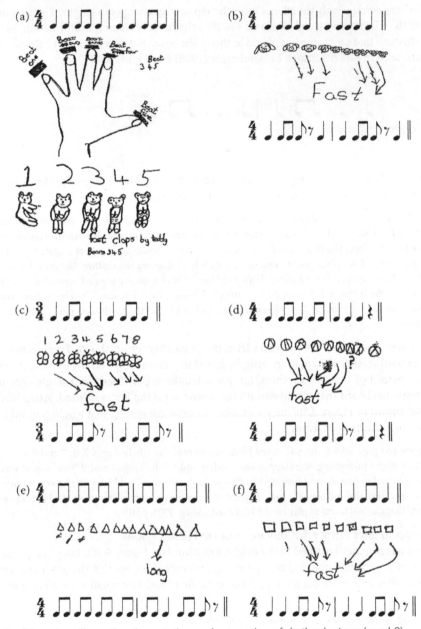

Fig. 9.5a–f Drawings illustrating the notation and perception of rhythm by Lucy (aged 8)

Why did Lucy clap?

The answer is that her violin teacher has trained her to clap rhythms before playing them. When Lucy plays a rhythm, her teacher cannot tell whether any mistakes result from inaccurate rhythmic perception or technical difficulties such as plucking a string, or changing bow, at the moment intended. Asking Lucy to sing the rhythm on a single note does not work either, because Lucy learns in a group, and the teacher cannot tell whether an individual is, for example, sustaining a crotchet for the duration of a minim. Asking Lucy to clap makes things easier for the teacher, who can see if Lucy is not clapping in the right place, even when she is clapping in a group.

> The problem is that Lucy's teacher had not noticed that clapping changes Lucy's rhythmic perception. There is nothing intuitive about an assumption that a clap represents a note which lasts until the next clap is heard. When the teacher claps a rhythm she may, as [adult musicians often] do, "hear" a tone that sustains until the onset of the next clap. But Lucy seems not to do this. She may learn to. (Mills, 2005, pp. 103–4)

But it is unlikely that clapping rhythms before she has played them will prove helpful. Problems such as Lucy's are embedded deeply within systems of music education. For example, syllabuses sometimes suggest activities such as clapping the rhythm of a known song, or clapping short rhythmic patterns. What, exactly, is the rhythm of a song? How can a clap be anything other than short?

Coda

This chapter has considered how children develop into "literate" musicians. As has become evident in the discussion and other chapters in this volume, any conception of what it is to be "musically literate" is fraught with problems related to defining what is meant by music and the various situations in which children might be engaged musically. Consequently, one of the main purposes of this chapter has been to disentangle some issues related to literacy as it applies to music, and to do so in ways that will help readers understand one of the most easily misunderstood areas of a child's musical development.

In the final analysis, it is important to acknowledge how many children learn to read staff notation and achieve a level of proficiency that enables them to function musically. Equally, however, many children are failed by the ways in which they are taught to read music, and give up playing completely. Reading staff notation is not a prerequisite for successful engagement with and appreciation of music, and exclusive concentration on reading has held back the progress of countless learners, while putting many others off completely (McPherson, 1993, 2005; Mills, 1991b,c, 2005; Priest, 1989; Schenck, 1989).

Author note

Janet Mills passed away in 2007, which is the reason why this chapter is a reproduction of Chapter 8 from the first edition of the book, with the addition of five reflective questions.

Reflective questions

1 Reflect on how you learned to read traditional staff notation. How successful was it, and if you had the opportunity to learn again, what could have been done differently that would have helped you master traditional staff notation more quickly?

2 Think about how children learn to read and write language, and draw parallels for how they learn to read and notate music. What are the key similarities and differences? To what degree is it valid to even make these comparisons?

3 List the positives and negatives for introducing notation from the very first instrumental lesson. What are the short- and long-term consequences for the learner?

4 List the ways you could encourage "deep" rather than "surface" levels of processing during your teaching. How might this approach enhance the acquisition of technical skill on an instrument?

5 To what degree do you think traditional staff notation will be important in music education approaches in the future, given that many of the world's music traditions are not notated? How would you defend the teaching of staff notation to the population of students you teach?

Reference list

Adams, M. J. (1994). *Beginning to read: Thinking and learning about print*. Cambridge, MA: MIT Press.

Bamberger, J. (1988). Les structurations cognitives de l'apprehension et de la notation de rhythmes simples. In H. Sinclair (Ed.), *La production de notations chez le jeune enfant* (pp. 99–121). Paris: Presses Universitaires de France.

Bamberger, J. (1996). Turning music theory on its ear. *International Journal of Computers for Mathematical Learning*, **1**(1), 33–55.

Bamberger, J. (1999). Learning from the children we teach. *Bulletin of the Council for Research in Music Education*, **142**, 48–74.

Brittin, R., & Sheldon, D. C. (2004). An analysis of band method books: Implications of culture, composer and type of music. *Bulletin of the Council for Research in Music Education*, **161**/2, 47–56.

Cantwell, R. H., & Millard, Y. (1994). The relationship between approach to learning and learning strategies in learning music. *British Journal of Educational Psychology*, **64**, 45–63.

Cooper, D. (2003). *Literacy: Helping children construct meaning* (5th ed.). New York: Houghton Mifflin.

Dodson, T. A. (1983). Developing music reading skills: Research implications. *Update*, **1**(4), 3–6.

Farrell, G. (2001). India. In D. J. Hargreaves & A. C. North (Eds.), *Musical development and learning: The international perspective* (pp. 56–72). London: Continuum.

Gordon, E. E. (2003). *Learning sequences in music: Skill, content and patterns*. Chicago: GIA Publications.

Green, S., & Bray, D. (1997). *Differentiation: A guide for music teachers*. Northampton: NIAS.

Hargreaves, D. J. (1986). *The developmental psychology of music*. Cambridge: Cambridge University Press.

Harris, T. L., & Hodges, R. E. (Eds.) (1995). *The literacy dictionary: The vocabulary of reading and writing*. Newark, DE: International Reading Association.

King, D. W. (1983). Field-dependence/field-independence and achievement in music reading (Doctoral dissertation). University of Wisconsin, Madison.

Kirby, J. R. (1988). Style, strategy, and skill in reading. In R. R. Schmeck (Ed.), *Learning strategies and learning styles* (pp. 229–73). New York: Plenum Press.

Mainwaring, J. (1933). Kinaesthetic factors in the recall of musical experience. *British Journal of Psychology*, **XXIII**(3), 284–307.

Mainwaring, J. (1941). The meaning of musicianship: A problem in the teaching of music. *British Journal of Educational Psychology*, **XI**(3), 205–14.

Mainwaring, J. (1951). Psychological factors in the teaching of music. *British Journal of Educational Psychology*, **XXI**, 105–21.

McPherson, G. E. (1993). Factors and abilities influencing the development of visual, aural, and creative performance skills in music and their educational implications (Doctoral dissertation). Dissertation Abstracts International, 54/04-A, 1277 (University Microfilms No. 9317278). University of Sydney, Australia.

McPherson, G. E. (1994a). Factors and abilities influencing sight-reading skill in music. *Journal of Research in Music Education*, **42**(3), 217–31.

McPherson, G. E. (1994b). Improvisation: Past, present and future. In H. Lees (Ed.), *Musical connections: Tradition and change* (pp. 154–62). Proceedings of the 21st World Conference of the International Society for Music Education. Tampa, Florida, USA.

McPherson, G. E. (2005). From child to musician: Skill development during the beginning stages of learning an instrument. *Psychology of Music*, **33**(1), 5–35.

McPherson, G. E., & Gabrielsson, A. (2002). From sound to sign. In R. Parncutt & G. E. McPherson (Eds.), *The science and psychology of musical performance: Creative strategies for music teaching and learning* (pp. 99–115). Oxford: Oxford University Press.

McPherson, G. E., & Renwick, J. M. (2001). A longitudinal study of self-regulation in children's musical practice. *Music Education Research*, **3**(2), 169–86.

Meadows, S. (1993). *The child as thinker: The development and acquisition of cognition in childhood.* London: Routledge.

Mills, J. (1983). Identifying potential orchestral musicians (Unpublished doctoral dissertation). Oxford University, Oxford, UK.

Mills, J. (1991a). *Music in the primary school.* Cambridge: Cambridge University Press.

Mills, J. (1991b). Clapping as an approximation to rhythm. *Canadian Music Educator*, **33**, 131–8.

Mills, J. (1991c). Out for the count: Confused by crotchets—part 2. *Music Teacher*, **70**(6), 12–15.

Mills, J. (2005). *Music in the school.* Oxford: Oxford University Press.

Mills, J., & Barrett, M. S. (2006). Raising boys' achievement?: Music as everyday life. In W. Sims, & R. Tahir (Eds.), *Proceedings of the 27th International Society for Music Education World Conference* (pp. 861–7). 27th International Society for Music Education World Conference, Kuala Lumpur, Malaysia, 16–21 July 2006.

Posner, M. I., Nissen, M. J., & Klein, R. M. (1976). Visual dominance: An information-processing account of its origins and significance. *Psychological Review*, **83**(2), 157–71.

Priest, P. (1989). Playing by ear: Its nature and application to instrumental learning. *British Journal of Music Education*, **6**(2), 173–91.

Schenck, R. (1989). Above all, learning an instrument must be fun! *British Journal of Music Education*, **6**(1), 3–35.

Schleuter, S. (1997). *A sound approach to teaching instrumentalists* (2nd ed.). New York: Schirmer Books.

Schleuter, S., & Schleuter, L. (1988). Teaching and learning music performance: What, when, and how. In C. Fowler (Ed.), *The Crane symposium: Toward an understanding of the teaching and learning of music performance* (pp. 63–87). New York: Potsdam College of the State University of New York.

Sloboda, J. A. (1988). *Generative processes in music: The psychology of performance, improvisation, and composition.* Oxford: Clarendon Press.

Sloboda, J. A. (2005). *Exploring the musical mind: Cognition, emotion, ability, function.* Oxford: Oxford University Press.

Smythe, M. M. (1984). Perception and action. In M. M. Smythe & A. M. Wing (Eds.), *The psychology of human movement* (pp. 119–52). London: Academic Press.

Soares, M. B. (1992). Literacy assessment and its implication for statistical measurement. Paper prepared for UNESCO, Division of Statistics, Paris.

Upitis, R. (1990). Children's invented notations of familiar and unfamiliar melodies. *Psychomusicology*, **9**(1), 89–106.

Upitis, R. (1992). *Can I play you my song? The compositions and invented notations of children.* Portsmouth, NJ: Heinemann Educational Books.

Wiggins, T. (1996). The world of music in education. *British Journal of Music Education*, **13**(1), 21–9.

Chapter 10

Musical literacy: Music as language

Chris Philpott

Music as language: Introduction

Bennett Reimer famously premised his philosophy of music education on the assumption "that the nature and value of music education are determined primarily by the nature and value of music" (1989/2003, p. ix). This chapter examines the nature of music as a basis for understanding what it means for a child to be musically literate. In particular, the chapter sets out the way in which music makes meaning in a foundational musical literacy that underpins a wider conception of musical *literacies*. The central assertion is that music functions as language, and that to understand what it means for the child to be musically literate we need to consider the ways in which music as language works to make meaning through bodily, cognitive, and social processes. Furthermore, an understanding of music as language has important hierarchical implications for the sequence of musical development in children *from* a foundational (intuitive) literacy *to* what can be regarded as technical and analytical literacies.

In what sense can we think of music as language? This is not music as being the same as "language" in the specific sense of when we speak, read, and write words. Nor is music some kind of universal language that transcends cultures. Here the notion of music as language is taken from what Kress calls a "mode," which "is a socially shaped and culturally given semiotic resource for making meaning" (2010, p. 79).

> Instances of commonly used *modes* are *speech; still image; writing; gesture; music; action; colour.* Each offers specific potentials and is therefore in principle particularly suited for specific representational/communicational tasks. (Kress, 2010, p. 28)

For Kress, all modes have the potential for making meanings that have been shaped by cultures and societies over a long period of time, and all modes arising out of the same culture and society are likely to embody shared meanings, i.e., they give material expression to the same sociocultural circumstances. Kress argues that at a lower level of generality, modes of signification can be uniquely distinguished by their offer "affordances," i.e., their material nature and potential for meaning making. For example, the materiality of the *image* as mode is very different from that of *music*. However, at a higher level of meaning making it is possible to see how modes share similar semiotic processes.

It is in this context that music can be regarded as language, one in which while its "affordances" are a unique social and cultural appropriation of sound and silence, as a mode of signification music shares common semiotic processes with other modes for the making of meaning. It is in the combination of specific, unique resources and generic semiotic processes that we can view music as language located within the wider context of meaning making in society. Understanding both the materiality and structure of meaning making in music can reveal important features of what it means for a child to be literate in music and the subsequent implications for the conduct of music education.

In light of this, the following sequence of questions will be used to structure the chapter:
Part 1: Developing a foundational musical literacy.

- What does it mean for music to function as language?
- How does music as language work to make meaning?
- What is the significance of the body in making musical meaning?
- What is the nature of the meanings held by music as language?

Part 2: How a conception of music as language articulates with wider musical literacies.

- What conceptions of musical literacy arise out of music as language?
- What are the implications of this analysis for music education?

Part 1: Developing a foundational musical literacy

Introduction

What does it mean for a child to be musically literate? There is the sense of being literate in common usage when we "speak" music and "listen" to music, and also in the sense of when we codify (notate) music during the acts of "reading" and "writing." Musical literacy includes each of these senses, and while both are significant across cultures and traditions, being musically literate is not contingent upon being able to codify or notate. "Reading" and "writing" music (in the sense of deciphering notations) are not defining features of musical literacy and yet it is inconceivable for a child to be musically literate without them being able to understand it through the acts of "speaking" or "listening," i.e., through performance, composition, improvisation, and audition. It could be that music shares this distinction with all modes of signification and meaning.

In this context, it is increasingly clear that being musically literate is a complex and socially constructed concept, often with a plurality of senses within the same culture, and thus it is perhaps more appropriate to refer to *musical literacies*. There are different dimensions to a child's musical literacy depending upon social context, for example, when "jamming" with friends, playing in a formal concert, singing along at a gig, or listening to a CD. There are also what we might refer to as technical and analytical literacies, e.g., technique, technology, and when notating and codifying music. All of these "literacies" are subject to social and cultural processes and thus are always open to a critical sociological and cultural analysis.

Indeed, the history of music education is littered with ideological tensions associated with what it means to be literate, for example between being literate in the sense of "speaking and listening" musically (the oral and the aural) and when "reading and writing" music. The most recent manifestation of this tension can be found in discussions surrounding the role of formal and informal moments of learning in music. For example, and as we shall see later, the literacies surrounding what Folkestad (2005, 2006) calls an orientation to playing and making music can be distinguished from those that are focused on learning *how* to play music.

In the context of musical *literacies*, how can a conceptualization of music as language enable us to understand what it means for a child to be musically literate? In particular, what is the nature of a foundational literacy that underpins music as language?

What does it mean for music to function as language?

Attempts to consider music as language have previously been riven with problems. Typically, such analyses have been premised on the assumption that the fundamental characteristic of meaning

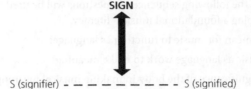

Fig. 10.1 Determinist, casual
semiotics after Saussure

making (semiosis) in any mode of signification is a causal link between, for example, words and sounds (as signifiers) and the object of meaning (the signified). The origin of this "logical" view of semiotics has its roots in the work of Sausurre (1916), where he suggests that the *signifier* (the sound, word, or picture, for example) has an object of meaning which he called the *signified*. Together, the sound/word and the object of meaning form what Saussure called the *sign* or concept (see Figure 10.1). In this account Saussure proposed that meaning is made from a deterministic and causal relationship between the *signifier* and the *signified*.

This "logical" view of music as language underpinned a celebrated attempt by Cooke (1959) to provide a "vocabulary" for musical meaning. Cooke suggested that composers are able to communicate emotions through music by using a vocabulary that links musical ideas (signifiers) to emotional meanings (signifieds), thus proposing music as a language of the emotions. The basis of the causal link proposed by Cooke is the play between major and minor elements which are related, after Freud, to various gradations of pleasure and pain. On the face of things this is an attractive proposal for music educators who, in order to bring about the musically literate state, could teach children to understand the vocabulary of music when they play, compose, and listen in the same way that a teacher might teach the vocabulary of the English language. However, attempts at writing such a vocabulary for music are problematic. For example, why is it that "major" can also feel sad? Can music only communicate emotions? It is also the case that the musical vocabulary proposed by Cooke has little validity outside of the Western classical tonal tradition. Further criticisms have argued that music is a non-discursive, non-referential symbolic mode (see Langer, 1942) and that while spoken and written language can be metaphorical *and* denotational, music can only be metaphorical (Bernstein, 1976).

In short, music does not construct its meanings through causal denotations between signifiers and signifieds; it is impossible to conceive of music having specific, translatable referents such as "this chair," "this animal," or "this number." Bowman captures the issues here when he suggests that "the rigorous aspirations and rule governed nature of semiotics is ill suited to the ambiguity, the multiplicity of potential meanings, the indefinite variability, and the diversity of musical phenomena and practices" (1998, p. 239).

Furthermore, and as we shall see, it can be argued that this is not the way in which *any* modes of signification construct meaning, including what has been regarded as the paradigm case of spoken and written language itself.

The failure to make a case for music as language on this basis has led to further attempts to ascribe epistemological status to music as a *type* of language. Langer (1942) argued that while music is not ultimately referential, it "logically resemble(s) certain dynamic patterns of human experience" (p. 226) and "reflect(s) . . . the morphology of feeling" (p. 238). Langer also argues that music is significant to us and makes its meaning through sharing the shapes of our conscious experience, e.g., growth and decay, ebb and flow, tension and resolution, and asserts that these "rhythms of life are the prototypes of musical structures" (p. 227). Similarly, Meyer (1956) suggests that the reason music means something to us is related to the way that it either conforms to or confounds our expectations.

Such arguments for music as a "type" of language have underpinned various philosophies of music education (see Reimer, 1989/2003; Swanwick, 1979). However, these philosophies have not always promoted a rich understanding of what it means to be musically literate through a) focusing on music as a "type" of language for our inner and subjective worlds, and b) being inextricably linked with a Western classical aesthetic.

If we are to develop a foundational musical literacy for the child that is underpinned by a notion of music as language, we need a different way of accounting for the way in which music works to make meaning, knowledge, and understanding. Perhaps there is a possibility for a more fruitful account for music as language alongside other modes of signification following Wittgenstein's enigmatic assertion that "[u]nderstanding a sentence is much more akin to understanding a theme in music than one may think" (1953, p. 143). Is the "logical" semiology an adequate account of the way in which meaning is made in any mode? What possibilities arise if we explore more recent semiotic and cultural theory to understand the ways in which all modes of signification create meaning? Such explorations can enable us to understand the implications for how music works as language, and thus what it means for a child to be musically literate.

What are the characteristics of "music as language"?

A careful analysis of the assumptions behind the "logical" view of signification calls it into question as an adequate account of meaning making in *any* mode, including what has been considered the paradigm example: spoken and written language. For example, more recent developments in the field of semiotics have argued that the relationship between the word/sound (signifier) and the object of meaning (the signified) is a) open to a multitude of cultural, ideologically delineated influences, and b) is an ever-shifting and unstable horizon, where any signifier is open to many interpretations of its meaning. Such a vision of meaning making for all modes has the potential to provide a more fruitful account of music as language, i.e., where multiple and complex relationships between signifiers and the signified exist.

Barthes (1957/1973), starting from a causal, denotative semiotics, also maintained that all signs can be seen as a connotation for something else that are influenced by sociocultural processes. He called these signs "myths," and this led Barthes to the view that almost anything can be what he called a "system of communication" (1957/1973, p. 117). He explored the significance of myth systems from wrestling to red wine in French culture. There is some heritage here with the multimodality proposed by Kress.

By introducing connotation, Barthes raised the possibility that a different account of the relationship between signifier and signified in producing signs was possible. In pursuing this idea, Hodge & Kress (1988) in the field of multimodality and Nattiez (1987) for music turned to the work of C. S. Peirce. The position of Peirce is summed up by Bowman:

> According to Peirce, a sign is something that becomes connected with something else (another sign, its "object") in such a way that it draws in a third element (the "interpretant") into a relationship with that same object. But the signified-signifier-interpretant relationship is not a simple, closed system; its meaning is never exhausted in that three-way connection. For the interpretant also functions as a sign, mediated by still other potential interpretants that relate to the object in still different ways, and so forth, ad infinitum (1998, p. 214).

For Peirce, then, the act of making meaning is a dynamic and interpretative process although not simply a free-for-all, being limited by materiality and cultural "habits" (see Figure 10.2). The

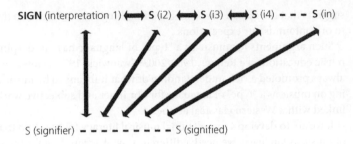

Fig. 10.2 Dynamic, interpretative semiotics after Peirce and Nattiez

upshot of this vision for semiotics and the making of meaning is that all modes of signification can be characterized as producing complex webs of meaning that are not causal and deterministic but often indeterminate and potentially unstable.

The work of C. S. Peirce has been appropriated by Nattiez (1987) for music where for him, meaning "is not to be construed along lines of message transmission . . . [but] . . . is a slippery and transient affair that arises among the dynamically related sites within Peirce's web of inter-pretants" (Bowman, 1998, p. 241). Philpott (2001) has further highlighted the consequences and importance of this "shift" for music (and indeed all modes of signification) made by Peirce and Nattiez, arguing that "the sign (interpretation) sparks off many other signs (interpretations) and each interpretation adds to a web of musical meaning . . . The web is part of a complex inter-pretative process . . . " (p. 39).

A conception of music which, as with other modes of signification, is characterized by complex webs of meaning and multiple interpretants provides a more cogent underpinning for music as language. The notion that music as language shares a process of meaning making with all modes of signification, even if unique in what Kress (2010) calls its "affordances," is fundamental to our account of musical literacy and what it means to be musically literate.

How, then, does music as language work to make meaning in a foundational musical liter-acy? After Nattiez and Peirce, and given the complexity surrounding the construction of webs of musical meaning, being musically literate is bound up with a dynamic and hermeneutical (interpretative) relationship between music and the child. In this sense music is not a "universal" language, but *languages* that are socially, culturally, and historically located. Furthermore, this hermeneutic relationship can be characterized by a dynamic and playful process that is, as we shall see, intimately related to the human (child) body.

How does music as language work to make meaning?

There are three important themes for the ways in which music as language makes meaning, and these can be illustrated by drawing on wider work in the field of semiotics and post-structural theory. As we have seen, Peirce characterizes the process of meaning making as one of "dynamic interpretation" and this is particularly important in relation to music as language. In this regard we shall explore three dynamic themes related to how music (and indeed other modes of signi-fication) works to make meaning that further enable us to characterize music as language. The three dynamic themes are:

- the dynamic role of *differánce* in the construction of musical meaning;
- the dynamic, hermeneutic (interpretative) process as we come to understand music;
- the dynamic and playful role of metaphor in meaning making in music.

The role of *differánce* in the construction of musical meaning

The concept of *differánce* is taken from the post-structural literary theory of Jacques Derrida and this is explained succinctly by Sarup in the following way:

> Derrida has developed a concept which he calls "differánce" and which refers "to differ" – to be unlike or dissimilar in nature, quality or form – and to "defer" – to delay, to postpone (the French verb *differer* has both these meanings) . . . Language is thus a play of differences . . . (Sarup, 1988, p. 48).

Derrida himself also explains that "each element is . . . related to something other than itself but retains the mark of a past element and already lets itself be hollowed out by the mark of its relation to a future element" (1996, p. 450).

It is interesting to see how the concept of *differánce* can be applied to the dynamic and playful process of making meaning in music. Music is indeed constructed through a relationship of parts, for example the dynamic relationship between sounds, tones, phrases, and structural units. Our understanding arises out of the differences and similarities that exist between these parts. Furthermore, our understanding is endlessly deferred; never achieving a final authoritative version, but constantly shifting, changing, and moving as past and present interact with musicians and audience. This is *differánce* in action: a dynamic and playful process as part of a complex web of interrelated interpretations. In short, *differánce* is at the heart of a dynamic and interpretative semiotics.

The dynamic, hermeneutic process

As we have seen, the act of understanding music is one of interpretation and this is central to the work of Gadamer (1975), who argues that understanding is always a dynamic interpretative act. Gadamer emphasized the primacy of "play" during the act of interpretation. In addition to there being "play" within the music itself (as described by *differánce*), there is play between audience (the child) and the musical work.

Furthermore, each piece of music (whether we are performing, creating, or listening to it) comes, he suggests, with an "attitude" and engages in a dynamic dialogue with our own (the child's) values, culture, ideology, and beliefs (which Gadamer calls "prejudices") to construct meaning. Gadamer developed the concept of "fusions of horizons" to describe this process of interpretation. It is here at the "fusions of horizons" that we find a dynamic process in the construction of meaning in music. "It is thus of the very nature of dramatic or musical works that their performance at different times and on different occasions is, and must be, different . . . The viewer of today not only sees in a different way, but he also sees different things" (Gadamer, 1975, p. 130). Here, meaning is a complex web of interpretative interactions during the fusions of horizons.

The themes of dynamism and play in the making of musical meaning during interpretation are also important features of the third theme: metaphor in music as language.

The role of metaphor and play in making musical meaning

We have seen that in the "logical" semiotics of Saussure, denotation and metaphor (connotation) are seen as different dimensions to the making of meaning. However, the approaches we have been drawing on here suggest that the relationship between signifier and signified is *always* metaphorical, i.e., in that we are always seeing one thing in terms of another as argued by Kress, when he suggests that "[m]etaphors provide (usually unnoticed) guides and framings for thinking . . . All signs are metaphors. All signs are always newly made . . . " (2010, p. 30).

Importantly on this account our cognitive relationship with the world through modes of signification is metaphorical. For example, Sarup argues that spoken and written language "works by means of transference from one kind of reality to another and is thus essentially metaphorical . . . meaning shifts around, and metaphor is the name of the process by which it does so" (1988, p. 52).

This account resonates in much writing about music. For example, Langer suggests that music is a metaphor for our felt world, and Scruton also proposes that "our experience of music involves an elaborate system of metaphors of space, movement, and animation" (1997, p. 80). Furthermore, Swanwick argues that in music, metaphorical processes take place when we "hear 'tones' as though they were 'tunes,' sound as expressive shapes; when we hear these expressive shapes assume new relationships as if they had a 'life of their own'" (1999, p. 13).

Of particular importance to our account here is the way in which metaphor underpins our interpretations of music as we recognize the dynamic shift to something new. The dynamic, playful, interpretative, and metaphorical processes of music underpin the notion of music as language, to a foundational musical literacy and thus what it means to be musically literate.

Given what we have said thus far about the significance of dynamic interpretation in music, at the center of the process of children learning to become literate in music as language is the body in the mind.

What is the significance of the body in making musical meaning?

To summarize, we have argued thus far that:

◆ music constructs meaning through the play of *differánce*;

◆ understanding music is a dynamic, hermeneutic process;

◆ music as language is underpinned by playful and dynamic metaphorical processes.

Given that dynamic, playful, and interpretative processes are at the core of music as language (and indeed all modes of signification), the importance of the child's body in becoming musically literate should be no surprise, i.e., these processes of meaning making are rooted in the dynamic body. We know from the work of Piaget, Bruner, and Merleau Ponty (and many others) that cognition and learning (and thus music) are rooted in our sensuous bodily experiences. When applying some of this theory to children's musical development and engagement, Swanwick (1988) argues that not only is musical understanding rooted in the body, but also our sense of body is always and fundamentally present during *all* musical experiences. In this sense the mind is always founded on the body and the body is always in the mind, where "knowing in any humanly meaningful sense is emergent from and grounded in bodily experience, and continuous with the cultural production of meaning" (Bowman, 2004, p. 48).

The work of the philosopher Mark Johnson is interesting in this regard and provides a link with our analysis of music as language. Johnson asserts that the link between the body and mind is metaphor. As we have seen, metaphor is a device of transference "by which we project patterns from one domain of experience in order to structure another domain of a different kind" (1987, xv). Johnson suggests that metaphor is a device through which our bodily understandings are held in our minds: "Through metaphor, we make use of patterns that obtain in our physical experience to organise our more abstract understanding . . . our bodily movements and interactions in various physical domains of experience are structured . . . and that structure can be projected by metaphor onto abstract domains" (1987, xv).

The point here is that our bodily experience of the world structures the very nature of our cognition. Cognition relies on dynamic metaphorical processes which "move" us to understand, i.e., the "play" of seeing one thing in terms of another.

However, there is a further sense in which music seems to actually thematize the dynamic nature of cognition in creating meaning. All of our engagement with music as language is rooted in the notions of play, movement, and dynamism; music is "moving" on so many different levels. Furthermore, music seems to "play" with metaphor for its own sake when constructing its own metaphorical meanings. In other words, music creates metaphors for metaphorical processes and thus has a very special relationship with the body in the mind: a consequence of the material "affordances" of music that distinguish it from other modes of signification. In short, in becoming musically literate we know music, we understand music, and we practice music through the unique relationship that music has to our body and minds. Bowman makes this same point when he suggests that:

> On the enactive, embodied account of cognition . . . knowing is inseparable from action: knowing is doing, and always bears the body's imprint . . . Part of what I have been urging here is that we recognize the profundity of the somatic/corporeal moment in human cognition, generally, and that we recognize music in particular as a kind of special celebration of this moment—of our here-and-now, embodied, action based mode of being (2004, p. 46).

In this sense it could be argued that music is a paradigm example of human cognition, knowledge, and understanding.

The body and musical literacy

When considering the nature and development of musical literacy in children, the earlier analysis has some significant implications for the practice of music education itself. Most obviously, children become musically literate by learning how to engage with the dynamic, playful, and interpretative processes of making meaning in music. Furthermore, they engage with music as language by listening to it and making it (in all senses), and the body is *always* present with such learning and experience.

Following our semiotic analysis, Kress makes the important point that "[a]ll signs . . . are always embodied, for maker and remake alike. In this way the meaning potentials of the mode in which a sign is made become embodied. No sign remains, as it were, simply or merely a 'mental,' 'conceptual,' a 'cognitive' resource" (2010, p. 77).

Similarly, children know and develop musically through their bodies with the body ever present in all musical experience, pointing to an imperative that the body comes first when learning to be musically literate. Furthermore, the developmental work of Swanwick would suggest that even experienced musicians return exclusively to sensuous bodily learning when they engage with a totally new musical experience. Swanwick's spiral (1988) outlines a developmental journey for children from a sensory literacy with the materials of music through the expressive power of materials, to structural literacy and alighting at a literacy of musical values and identity. While this sequence moves from the body to the mind, the early developmental layers are swept up (after Bruner) such that the body is always in the mind. Bowman further summarizes this position when he remarks that:

> Musical experience is no mere response to an aural stimulus, nor is it in any straightforward sense an act of symbolic representation. Musical experience is, however, invariably an embodied practice. When we hear a musical performance, we do not just "think," nor do we just "hear": we participate with our whole bodies; we construct and enact it. We feel melodies in our muscles as much as we process them in our brains—or perhaps more accurately, our brains process them as melodies only to the extent our bodily extended schemata render that possible (2004, p. 47).

For Jaques-Dalcroze, the body and music are almost synonymous with each other, and he understood the relationship between music and the bodies of youngsters.

He saw feet tapping, heads nodding, bodies responding to the nuances of the music, following a crescendo, marking an accent. They were allowing the music literally to penetrate them through and through, they were responding to it *in movement* . . . He realised that to music and rhythm he must add movement, thereby acknowledging the body as man's first instrument of self expression. (Dutoit, 1971, p. 9)

Jaques-Dalcroze saw that all types of musical movement (rhythmic, harmonic, tonal, expressive, structural) were closely related to life itself and that musical experience is a physical and bodily experience. He believed that the "movement" of music "finds its nearest prototype in our muscular system," and that all of the nuances of music "can be 'realised' by our bodies, and the acuteness of our musical feeling will depend on the acuteness of our bodily sensations" (Jaques-Dalcroze, 1921/80, p. 60). For Jaques-Dalcroze, the primacy of the body in all musical experience meant that learning in music is always founded upon physical experience. We need to "be" the pulse before we understand it and we need to "live" the rhythm before we can learn how to read it or write it.

By way of example, developing the technical literacy of written notation without "the body in the mind" of the child is to invert the sequential and cognitive implications of all that we know about becoming literate in music as language. In the sequence of becoming musically literate, the body underpins all musical development and learning. The work of music educators from Jaques-Dalcroze to Kodaly to Paynter through to Green also confirms this sequence with the implication that a foundational musical literacy for children develops (in all cultures) through bodily immersion in music as language when making and engaging with music. Music teachers who have ignored such wisdom have often been beset by poorly motivated children, whose heads and bodies have literally been disconnected.

In short, the body is always at the center of a foundational musical literacy for children and is underpinned by the dynamic semiotics of music as language. Given this analysis of how meaning is constructed, what sorts of meanings can be held by music as language?

What is the nature of the meanings held by music as language?

Green (1988) has provided a useful theoretical framework for understanding the construction of meaning in music as language. She proposes two types of meaning that are inextricably linked: inherent meaning and delineated meaning. Inherent meaning is constructed directly through the "temporal musical experience" (p. 25) of musical materials as they sound and play out for us.

In relation to our analysis, this is the play of *differánce* in music and the metaphors created by inherent meaning when we hear tones and tunes, and sounds as expressive shapes. However, music "must mean something apart from itself" (p. 26), for "[n]o sooner do the first sounds of any music reach our ears, than we begin to assimilate them within a web of meanings in the social world: our past, our future, our friends, family, taste" (p. 27).

In keeping with a semiotic analysis of music it is important to recognize the social construction of meaning making in all signs and in all modes. Kress argues that a mode "is a socially shaped and culturally given semiotic resource for making meaning" (2010, p. 79), and that "[t]he genesis of signs lies in social actions . . . signs are always newly *made* in social interaction; signs are *motivated*, not *arbitrary* relations of meaning and form . . . [arising] out of the *interest* of makers of signs" (2010, pp. 54–5).

This for Green is delineated meaning, as music not only points to itself, but also out from itself to social meanings and social relations, and as such is subject to wider ideological and cultural processes. For music as language is a dynamic, playful, and hermeneutic process, as delineated meanings are constructed during composition, improvisation, performance, and audition. This is not music as a "universal" language, but *languages* that are culturally and historically located.

In this view of the meanings that can be held by music as a language, we must accept that while meanings are never fully clinched in any language, music has the metaphorical power to engage with the full range of human ideas—both savory and unsavory (see Philpott, 2012a).

Understanding the full gamut of meanings in music here is, as we have suggested, a dynamic, playful, and interpretative act that is mediated by social, psychological, and cultural processes. Children can be musically literate by engaging in the acts of meaning making and understanding either in the audition, creation, or recreation of music, and this literacy is foundational to what can be regarded as technical and analytical literacies.

How does this analysis of a foundational basis for musical literacy play alongside these wider musical literacies and the ensuing issues and debates in music education?

Part 2: How a conception of music as language articulates with wider musical literacies

What conceptions of musical literacy arise out of music as language?

The previous analysis points to a conception of musical literacy that arises out of the notion of music as language. This foundational musical literacy is an intuitive literacy that results as a consequence of being immersed in music as language within culture(s). Here, music as language functions, as with all modes of signification, through a dynamic and interpretative semiology that is centered on the body in the mind. In this sense it is almost impossible to imagine any child not being literate, to a certain extent at least. Such literacy is based upon an intuitive understanding of how music works as language and represents what Reid (1986) calls our knowledge "of" music. Children derive meaning out of the music that surrounds them by acquaintance, even if they do not actually make it themselves, and this is a foundational engagement with music as language. On this account, all children have the potential to be musically literate.

Following Swanwick (1988), this is a literacy that can be differentiated into several layers (the left hand of his developmental the spiral) from a sheer sensory engagement with sound through sound as expression, expression as structure to music as personal symbolic significance. Here music makes sense to children as a dynamic and interpretative mode. Such intuitive understanding does not necessarily need to manifest itself further than a child's individual subjectivity, although it is rare for it to remain completely private. For example, children move to music, dance to it, talk about music, draw to music, sing along to music. In other words, they "get" the meanings of music as language at an intuitive level and this is a primordial musical literacy. There is also a creative dimension here, as children undertake the hermeneutic act of interpretation since they literally create and recreate the music in their bodies and minds. As music educators we forget this foundational dimension to musical literacy at our peril and it is crucially important that we establish its essential nature.

This elemental and foundational literacy underpins other aspects of musical literacy when children engage with music as language. From this essential base, becoming musically literate can also mean a developmental engagement with the technical and analytical dimensions of musical literacy (the right-hand side of Swanwick's spiral). Such "know-how" can come in a variety of forms, for example, technical literacy, technological literacy, perceptual literacy, notational literacy, and analytical literacy. It is often the case that these technical and analytical dimensions to musical literacy are integrated with and arise out of a child's foundational, intuitive, and encultured

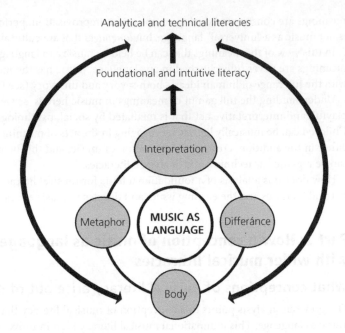

Analytical and technical literacies

Foundational and intuitive literacy

Interpretation

Metaphor

MUSIC AS LANGUAGE

Differánce

Body

Fig. 10.3 Musical literacy and music as language

literacy. However, while the latter is not contingent upon the former in defining what it means to be musically literate, technical literacy is certainly contingent upon the encultured and intuitive.

What we have suggested thus far can be found summarized in Figure 10.3. At the center of musical literacy is music as language, and while this can be differentiated into intuitive and analytical literacies, learning for children (and us all and in all cultures) moves from the former to the latter with the intuitive always being foundational. However, in *all* cultures it is possible to develop a foundational literacy in music without any technical or analytical know-how. A sense of perspective is important here.

In music education there has been a long history of tension between intuitive and analytical literacies, and certain conceptions of literacy have taken on an ideological significance. Indeed, the history of music education is littered with controversy and debate over the relative importance of both broad types of literacy and the developmental sequence of learning for children that each demands.

In relation to the arguments in this chapter, and what counts as musical literacy, it is possible to identify some of the dichotomous ideological tensions inherent in the history of music education (see Table 10.1). For example, while we have argued for a conception of literacy that is founded on "speaking and listening," literacy in the sense of "reading and writing" Western notation has often been accorded a status as being self-evidently "good" for us and a transcendental measure of a child being musically literate. Such a conception of what counts as musical literacy is closely related to the appearance of Western classical music as having a universal and autonomous value (Spruce, 1999). For Spruce, this perspective on literacy denies the social and cultural construction of what counts as musical literacy, and does not recognize itself as being ideological.

The tensions identified here represent some of the ideological fault lines in the recent history of music education. These tensions can most recently be seen in the formal–informal debate, where authors promoting the informal, as a reaction to a perceived alienation amongst youngsters in the

Table 10.1 Some dichotomous tensions in music education

Intuitive, informal, cultural literacies	Formal, technical, analytical literacies
Oral/Aural	Notation
Practice	Theory
Informal	Formal
Enculturation	Training
Encounter	Instruction
Knowledge "of" music	Knowing the "about" and "how" of music
Intuition	Analysis
Creativity	Re-creativity

music classroom (see Green, 2008), are countered by those espousing the values and importance of more formal learning for children (see Cain, 2013). It is to this debate that we now turn by way of a case study, to further understand the conception of musical literacy being developed here.

What are the implications of this analysis for music education?

In drawing out the implications of a foundational, dynamic, and interpretative literacy, and to develop a framework for multiple literacies based on this, Folkestad's writing on the relationship between formal and informal musical learning is important.

Folkestad (2005, 2006) has recognized that the relationship between the formal and the informal is hugely complex. An appreciation of the relationship between the formal and informal moments of learning for children is crucial to an understanding of musical literacy, and he proposes the following distinction: formal leaning, he suggests, can be characterized as the intentional predetermined sequencing of learning activities by "a person who takes on the task of organising and leading the learning activity" (2006, p. 141); informal learning can be characterized as being "not sequenced beforehand" and occurs during "*self chosen and voluntary activity*" (2006, p. 141).

For Folkestad, the crucial issue here is the intentionality of the learner. Formal learning is found when the minds of pupils and teachers are directed towards learning *how to play music*; informal learning is found when minds are directed towards *playing and making* music. Furthermore, "what characterises in most learning situations is the instant switch between these learning styles and the dialectic interaction between them" (2006, p. 142).

We can characterize this dialectic as "flipping" along a continuum (see Philpott, 2012b). This can be seen in most situations where musical learning takes place, for example, when a group improvises freely over a riff, but then stops while they learn how to play a guitar chord from one of the members. In this analysis, the formal–informal continuum of musical learning is characterized by constant "flipping" between the orientations of a focus on how to play and a focus on making and playing music.

Most musicians of all types will have experienced this "flipping," although the "formal" moment (and associated literacies) is so frequently prioritized in music education that this experience often lies buried in the collective consciousness (see Finney & Philpott, 2010). And so for Folkestad, the relationship of formal to informal is not a dichotomy but a continuum, and

Table 10.2 A continuum of musical literacies after Folkestad

The *informal* moment of learning—intentionality is orientated to playing and making music (in the widest possible sense)	"Flipping" ← →	The *formal* moment of learning—intentionality is orientated to learning how to play music
Intuitive literacy		Analytical literacy
Knowledge "of" music		Knowledge "about" music
Encultured literacy		Technical literacy ("know-how" in music)
Acquaintance knowledge		
Holistic understanding		Reductionist understanding
Creative literacy		Re-creative literacy
Informal (foundational) literacies		Formal (technical and analytical) literacies

"in most learning situations, both of these aspects of learning are in various degrees present and interacting" (2006, p. 143).

In keeping with the analysis in this chapter, it is argued that "flipping" along the continuum is always underpinned by and grounded in the foundational literacy that arises out of the informal moment of learning for children. Table 10.2 illustrates the ways in which different musical literacies align with Folkestad's analysis.

It has been important in this chapter to establish the foundational importance of what might be termed the intuitive, encultured, or informal literacies in music as language. It has been argued that analytical, technical, or formal literacies provide important developmental differentiation to intuitive literacies for children, but these are not necessarily a defining feature. In drawing out the implications of this case study example for music education, the following points can be made by way of summary:

1 The foundational intuitive literacy of music as language underpins all other literacies, and indeed can exist in isolation from the analytical, e.g., as in the case of a child who *only* consumes and listens to music;

2 Where children learn other musical literacies, there are sequential implications of moving from the intuitive to the analytical as these develop;

3 While notation is an aspect of analytical literacy it is not essential to it, but is in any case subject to the same developmental sequence;

4 The developmental need and motivation for children to move from the intuitive to the analytical most readily arises out of the former, i.e., where an intentionality is focused on learning *how* to play music enhances the intentionality of making and playing music;

5 In this sense, if children "own" the "flip" from the informal to the formal, they are more likely to form an un-alienated relationship with formal aspects of musical literacy, i.e., when they can trust that formal literacies are important to their informal, intuitive literacy. In short, formal literacies ("know-how") are most likely to be learned and accepted when they are perceived to be needed by the children themselves arising out of their interests (focused on playing and making music) and thus *owned* by them (see Philpott, 2012b).

These are important implications for a music education where our aim is for *all* children to have their musical literacy recognized and developed.

Summary and conclusion

In this chapter, and in answer to our initial questions, it has been argued that being musically literate is a complex and diverse notion, but that it is based around a conception of music as language. While being musically literate can include both intuitive and analytical literacies, the former is an elemental and foundational dimension to literacy that *can* be free-standing from the latter.

Music as language shares with other modes of signification certain processes of semiosis. In this sense it is part of, and integrated with, a multimodal conception of the ways in which we make and hold meaning. At the center of the ways in which children learn to construct meaning in music as language is the body in the mind, and these meaning-making processes are dynamic, hermeneutic, and metaphorical in nature. Diverse meanings can be held by music as language, and these are subject to social and cultural processes.

Conceptions surrounding the nature of musical literacy arising from this analysis are ideological. Indeed, the ideology arising out of different conceptions of musical literacy and the meanings held by music have for a long time been at the heart of debates in music education, most recently exemplified in issues surrounding the formal and informal. The implications of this chapter for the conduct of music education are to place making and responding to music (in the widest possible sense) at the heart of what it means for the child to become musically literate, with the development of "formal" knowledge surrounding the analytical literacies arising out of a foundational literacy.

Why is this important? The aim of this chapter has been to achieve a perspective on the nature of musical literacy and what it means to achieve the musically literate state. Such a perspective is essential for maximizing the musical achievement and motivation of all children throughout the world, and as such is important to social justice in music education. There is no doubt that a child learning technical and analytical musical literacies bestows many important advantages, such as the huge benefits of musical independence. However, such literacies can take on a significance that buries the essential nature of musical understanding and in doing so poses a threat to ambitions for social justice in music classrooms. In order to facilitate musical development that *is* socially just, music teachers need to recognize the foundational and intuitive dimension to musical literacy. They also need to recognize the developmental relationship between musical literacies, and understand the trust and ownership required when children move from the intuitive to the analytical. Understanding the nature of a musical literacy that derives from music as language and the consequent implications for practice will enable us to fashion a more socially just music education that provides access to musical achievement for all children.

Reflective questions

1 Do you agree that meaning making is at the core of a foundational musical literacy?

2 In what ways, other than those suggested here, is the body in the mind when children learn to be musically literate?

3 To what extent has the treating of technical and analytical literacies as if they are themselves foundational, been an issue in music education? In what other ways have tensions between various literacies been manifest in music education?

4 Once children have developed sophisticated analytical and technical literacies, what is the ongoing relationship between these and a foundational literacy?

5 In what ways can children demonstrate a foundational musical literacy without having developed any technical and analytical literacies?

Reference list

Barthes, R. (1957/1973). *Mythologies*. London: Paladin.

Bernstein, L. (1976). *The unanswered question*. Cambridge, MA: Harvard University.

Bowman, W. D. (1998). *Philosophical perspectives on music*. New York: Oxford University Press.

Bowman, W. D. (2004). Cognition and the body: Perspectives from music education. In L. Bresler (Ed.), *Knowing bodies, moving minds: Towards embodied teaching and learning* (pp. 29–50). Dordrecht: Kluwer Academic Publishers.

Cain, T. (2013). Passing it on: Beyond formal or informal pedagogies. *Music Education Research*, 15(1), 74–91.

Cooke, D. (1959). *The language of music*. Oxford: Oxford University Press.

Derrida, J. (1996). Differánce. In R. Kearney & M. Rainwater (Eds.), *The continental philosophy reader* (pp. 441–64). London: Routledge.

Dutoit, C.-L. (1971). *Music movement therapy*. Croydon: Dalcroze Society.

Finney, J., & Philpott, C. (2010). Informal learning and meta-pedagogy in initial teacher education in England. *British Journal of Music Education*, 27(1), 7–19.

Folkestad, G. (2005). Here, there and everywhere: Music education research in a globalised world. *Music Education Research*, 7(3), 279–87.

Folkestad, G. (2006). Formal and informal learning situations or practices vs formal and informal ways of learning. *British Journal of Music Education*, 23(2), 135–45.

Gadamer, H. G. (1975). *Truth and method*. New York: Seabury Press.

Green, L. (1988). *Music on deaf ears: Musical meaning, ideology and education*. Manchester: Manchester University Press.

Green, L. (2008). *Music, informal learning and the school: A new classroom pedagogy*. Aldershot: Ashgate.

Hodge, H., & Kress, G. (1988). *Social semiotics*. Cambridge: Polity Press.

Jaques-Dalcroze, E. (1921/80). *Rhythm, music and education*. Croydon: Dalcroze Society.

Johnson, M. (1987). *The body in the mind*. Chicago: University of Chicago Press.

Kress, G. (2010). *Multimodality: A social semiotic approach to contemporary communication*. London: Routledge.

Langer, S. (1942). *Philosophy in a new key*. Cambridge, MA: Harvard University Press.

Meyer, L. B. (1956). *Emotion and meaning in music*. Chicago: University of Chicago Press.

Nattiez, J.-J. (1987). *Music and discourse: Towards a semiology of music*. Princeton, NJ: Princeton University Press.

Philpott, C. (2001). Is music a language? In C. Philpott & C. Plummeridge (Eds.), *Issues in music teaching* (pp. 32–47). London: Routledge.

Philpott, C. (2012a). The justification for music in the curriculum: Music can be bad for you. In C. Philpott & G. Spruce (Eds.), *Debates in music teaching* (pp. 48–63). London: Routledge.

Philpott, C. (2012b). Assessment for self-directed learning in music education. In C. Philpott & G. Spruce (Eds.), *Debates in music teaching* (pp. 153–68). London: Routledge.

Reid, L. A. (1986). *Ways of understanding and education*. London: Heinemann.

Reimer, B. (1989/2003). *A philosophy of music education*. Englewood Cliffs, NJ: Prentice-Hall.

Sarup, M. (1988). *An introductory guide to post-structuralism and postmodernism*. London: Harvester Wheatsheaf.

Saussure, F. (1916). *A course in general linguistics* (trans. R. Harris). London: Duckworth.

Scruton, R. (1997). *The aesthetics of music*. Oxford: Oxford University Press.

Spruce, G. (1999). Music, music education and the bourgeois aesthetic: Developing a music curriculum for the new millennium. In R. McCormick & C. Paechter (Eds.), *Learning and knowledge* (pp. 71–87). London: Oxford University Press.

Swanwick, K. (1979). *A basis for music education*. London: Routledge.

Swanwick, K. (1988). *Music, mind and education*. London: Routledge.

Swanwick, K. (1999). *Teaching music musically*. London: Routledge.

Wittgenstein, L. (1953). *Philosophical investigations*. Oxford: Blackwell.

Chapter 11

Engaging in a sound musicianship

Andrew R. Brown

A child born today may well live to the end of the century. For these children, the world presents a range of opportunities and challenges for music-making with increasing access to a variety of musical heritages through enhanced travel and the distribution of audio-visual materials over the Internet. The efforts of science continue to expand what we know about the physics of sound, the operation of the musical mind, how to monitor our expressive bodily gestures and physiological responses. Digital technologies allow us to amplify our musicality through new mobile devices and apps, and social networking technologies enable fluid communication about music and how it relates to our life and culture. Some of these trends have only become apparent in recent decades, and there will certainly be more change ahead for today's young musician. As Robinson and Aronica (2009) remind us,

> Children starting school this year [2009] will be retiring in 2070. No one has any idea of what the world will look like in ten years' time, let alone in 2070. There are two major drivers of change—technology and demography . . . These driving cultural and technological forces are producing profound shifts in the world economies and increasing diversity and complexity in our daily lives, and especially in those of young people. (pp. 17–19)

This chapter helps readers navigate these changes. It outlines *modes of creative engagement* that provide a taxonomy of musical activities that a child can undertake. Second, it describes *contexts for meaning* which highlight the value of creative activities when undertaken in private, social, and cultural settings. Third, four perspectives of a *sound musicianship*—the sonic, psychological, embodied, and cultural—outline various dimensions of a child's musicality and highlight the types of skills and understandings that can be developed through meaningfully engaging with music.

These connections between technology and culture are deep and impossible to disentangle. This is why the contemporary context can be described as a technoculture; the culture that emerges from the impacts of mechanization and computation (Green, 2002; Sangüesa, 2011). These various frameworks interlock to provide a robust foundation on which musical practices can be understood in our current technocultural context.

Music and technoculture

Children in the developed countries today live in a technoculture, in a world saturated with digital technologies, where information and entertainment alike are largely mediated by computing technologies. With touchscreen mobile devices for accessing the Internet, children can play games and make video calls to their grandparents. Access to these experiences is often time limited and they are interspersed with more traditional and physical interactions. But this does not reduce the significance or pervasiveness of digital experiences.

One effect of these technological interactions is increased access to media other than text. Digital devices have microphones, cameras, and gesture sensors. These allow the capture, manipulation, and transmission of multiple and integrated media forms, including drawings, photos, videos, audio recordings, and—of course—music. It is not that these media types did not exist prior to the emergence of the technoculture, but resistance of analog media to integration and transmission provided a degree of friction in earlier eras that moderated their cultural influence.

Children today have tools that provide an increasing capacity for media creation. Easy and inexpensive apps for mobile devices and expanding storage and sharing facilities play a part in allowing the current generation of children to be more focused on generating content than on consuming it. Moreover, as this content expands across media forms it is not dominated, as in the past, by textural literacy as the means of expression. As Lessig (2008), the notable lawyer and theorist of digital culture, notes: "These other forms of 'creating' are becoming an increasingly dominant form of 'writing.' The internet didn't make these other forms of 'writing' (what I will call simply 'media') significant. But the internet and digital technologies opened these media up to the masses" (p. 69). On a positive note, music is one of the media that is elevated by digital infrastructure and it is already evident that the access to music creation with digital tools is moving composition (music production) forwards from being only a minority activity to being almost as accessible as performance and consumption.

An obvious challenge for the development of a child as musician in a technoculture is how to incorporate digital literacy and competency into musical studies. It is also clear that the impact of digital technologies will vary between musicians, like any other element. However, there is a growing number of musicians for whom working with music technology is a core skill. In particular, for those musicians whose instrument is the computer and where the creative workflow from conception to distribution is digital. Hugill (2012) has identified this particularly contemporary form of practice as requiring a "[d]igital musicianship—a different kind of artistry—[that] is largely a disembodied form of knowledge made evident through a set of technical skills and critical judgments" (p. 52).

And, as if the reforms of human creative activities were not enough to navigate through, computing technologies can make their own claims on creative agency as a result of automated and adaptive processes programmed into them. Presently these are not convincing claims, but they may be important philosophically. Musical instruments have always amplified human musicality, but "smart" digital music systems can enable new levels of scaffolding for inexperienced musicians and provide creative leverage and collaborations for the experienced. In the same way that a Google web search enhances a person's capacity for research, so an interactive music system enhances a person's musical expression. Scholars have highlighted a future life with intellectual prostheses of this kind for some decades (Clark, 2008; Perkins, 1993). But, like a fish in water, these capabilities may simply be second nature, perhaps invisible, to musicians of the future.

So what are some of the effects of the technoculture on the child as musician? One effect is increasing diversity and complexity in available music, there is an expansion in the range of musical styles and genres that children are exposed to or can learn to master. Also expanding is the range of methods for accessing musical experience and the varied contexts in which music is encountered. In particular, mobile and networked technologies provide an almost endless variety of music to listen to and apps to make music with.

As the range of musical practices expands through internationalization and technological development, new musical opportunities are opened up. These include access to musical genres from all over the world with their particular traditions, instruments, and sounds. They include new musical practices enabled by technologies, such as DJing, chip tunes, glitch music, live coding, and more. While musical genres share many common elements, each musical practice has its own ecosystem of knowledge and skills, its own definitions of quality and virtuosity, and its own cultural habits and conventions. Add to these the rich history of music-making in the West, such as classical and popular music, jazz, and the twentieth-century avant-garde that we are already familiar with, and the diversity is great indeed.

The expectations around musical experiences for twenty-first-century children expanded well beyond instrumental performance or concert attendance. Digital technologies have allowed them to increasingly emphasize a broader range of tasks including creation and production, distribution and promotion, and analysis and review. As music and other arts are framed as part of the creative industries, the expectations for musicians to understand aspects of business, law, and economics intensify and there is greater recognition of music careers beyond composing and performing. This trend is underscored by books on music careers like those from Beeching (2010), Cann (2007), and D'Eith (2013).

Reframing musical experience

In the face of the challenges of an expanding array of musical experiences and expectations driven by changes in technology and culture, the ways in which we think about engaging with music are adapting. Robinson and Aronica (2009) suggest that the key to managing this situation is a shift in focus from particular aspects of the field on to the child's interests and capability, to create links with their aptitude and passion. While motivation and amplification of capacity are certainly key to engagement and learning, I suggest that these alone may be too abstract to help reorient understanding of musical experience and development. To achieve this reorientation, I suggest that we reframe our thinking about music around more generalized descriptions of music activities, what I call *modes of engagement*, to help focus our developmental efforts in a new direction, and to frame the selection and pruning of musical experiences based on relevance and context.

Modes of creative engagement

Engagement involves immersion in a dynamic process of interpretation and action. The modes of creative engagement outline different classes of creative behaviors. They are articulated here as types of actions undertaken during creative practice. These modes have been derived from studies of expert musicians (Brown, 2003), but have been shown to be a useful guide to understanding children's experiences (Hirche, 2011). A well-rounded musical life includes all the modes of creative engagement, and a broad range of developmental activities should enable children to encounter them.

A child or adolescent can be engaged with music by:

◆ Attending—paying careful attention to creative works and analyzing their representations;

◆ Evaluating—judging aesthetic value and cultural appropriateness;

◆ Directing—crafting creative outcomes and leading creative activities;

◆ Exploring—searching through artistic possibilities;

◆ Embodying—being engrossed in fluent creative expression.

The order of the modes as listed does not imply a particular hierarchy; rather, individuals can encounter modes in any order and shift between modes during a single creative activity. It is for pragmatic reasons that the modes are described as activities; this makes it straightforward to talk about a child being engaged in a particular mode.

As well as being activities, these modes of engagement also relate to different phenomenological experiences that include, or promote, varying degrees of intuitive and analytic knowledge—and working styles (Spinosa, Flores, & Dreyfus, 1997). As a result, the modes of engagement promote a broad range of musical experiences and understandings without being tied to particular musical genres, repertoire, or technologies.

As a phenomenological category, "engagement" with creative activities has similarities to the notion of "flow." The state of flow is described by Csikszentmihalyi (1992) as one in which people are so involved in an activity that nothing else seems to matter; flow is a type of "optimal experience." This is clearly a high bar for any experience to aspire to, and is certainly a desirable target for a child "engaged" in music-making. It also raises an important point concerning the modes of engagement.

As the term is used here, engagement is measured by degree, ranging from short periods of attention and action through to the flow state and the mastery of a skill. Engagement is not seen as a binary state where a child switches between being engaged or disengaged, but rather it is viewed as a continuum, which increases as a child is drawn further into an experience and develops expertise. It follows, then, that it is possible to be simultaneously engaged to varying extents in more than one mode. It is also common that within one task a person switches between modes, perhaps quite frequently.

However, despite the fluidity and flexibility of these ways of engaging, most musical tasks tend to favor one mode of engagement in particular. For example, listening to recorded music is most likely to engage someone in *attending*, even though a listener may also be writing a review which would lead them toward *evaluating*, or they may dance to the music or play along with it, which would lead them toward *embodying*.

These tendencies for correlations between activities and modes of engagement allow the modes of engagement to be applied to activity planning and participatory experience. Taking on board the suggestion made earlier, that a well-rounded musical life involves access to each of the modes of engagement, an activity plan or a review of a child's musical activities can be interrogated to see the extent to which each of the modes of engagement is likely to be, or have been, part of their experience. Modifications can then be made to musical tasks, if required, to rebalance access to the modes of engagement.

The meaningful engagement matrix

Engagement with music can be experienced in different contexts. In particular, the difference between private and public contexts is seen to be significant and has been implicated in the development of personal identity (e.g., Connell & Gibson, 2013; Ruud 1997). In his work on meaning and music education, Steve Dillon (2001, 2007) highlighted three contexts and the opportunities for meaning they provide:

- Personal—the intrinsic enjoyment of creative activities;
- Social—the development of artistic relationships with others;
- Cultural—the feeling that one's creative actions are valued by the community.

The modes of engagement and contexts for meaning can be combined to form a *meaningful engagement matrix* (MEM), as shown in Table 11.1. The matrix results in cells where modes of engagement and contexts for meaning intersect. For example, conducting a choir rehearsal provides meaningful engagement in the directing + social cell of the matrix. It creates an opportunity for the conductor to exercise musical leadership, to feel a sense of accomplishment at assisting others in their musical expression, and to develop friendships with the members of the ensemble. A young child playing alone at home with a xylophone or iPad music app can experience

Table 11.1 The meaningful engagement matrix (MEM)

	Appreciating	Evaluating	Directing	Exploring	Embodying
Personal					
Social					
Cultural					

Table 11.2 The MEM with exemplary musical activities in each cell

	Appreciating	Evaluating	Directing	Exploring	Embodying
Personal	Listen, Read, Watch	Analyze, Select	Compose, Produce	Improvise, Experiment	Practice, Play
Social	Share files	Discuss, Share playlists	Conduct, Lead	Jam	Rehearse, Record
Cultural	Attend events, Patronage	Curate, Publish reviews	Promote, Manage	Publish research	Perform

meaningful engagement in the exploring + person and the embodying + personal cells of the matrix. The child can experience the pleasure of sound, and can marvel at their ability to have agency in the world and to develop coordination between their physical actions and visual and sonic acuity.

The MEM has the capacity to act as a visualization tool for categorizing and examining musical practices. Activities or experiences can be plotted on the matrix allowing areas of concentration or absence to become visible.

Just as musical activities can be seen to promote particular modes of engagement, so too can they be classified according to the context in which meaning arises. As a demonstration of this, Table 11.2 has a variety of music activities plotted on the MEM. The addition of contexts for meaning as a second dimension helps to further differentiate musical activities (and their associated experiences) to provide a useful map of experience that can help guide thinking about a child's or an adolescent's musical life.

For more detail about the notion of meaningful engagement and discussion of its basis in philosophical and psychological literature, see other publications by Brown and Dillon (Brown, 2003, 2014; Brown & Dillon, 2012; Dillon, 2001, 2007).

A sound musicianship

Along with rethinking the categories of activity that define children's engagement with music, it follows that our understanding of musicianship be broadened as well. During the twentieth century the focus of musicianship was on the development of aural and notational skills required by Western instrumental and vocal repertoire. Despite musicianship being narrowly defined in some quarters, it has long been understood amongst musicians that the skills and abilities required to be an active creative artist were many and varied. Musicianship, understood more broadly, extends even beyond the actual practice of music-making and appreciation to include interpersonal and entrepreneurial expertise that assists artists to operationalize their talents within society. Around the turn of the century this socio-economic perspective gathered momentum through the redefinition of the creative arts as the creative industries (Caves, 2000). The positioning of music as part of the creative industries has had its advocates and its skeptics. Because of this controversial history the concept of creative industries could not be considered a broadly accepted framework suitable for the contemporary reconceptualization of musicianship.

Our understanding of musicianship should evolve to accommodate changes in musical practices arising from globalization and technology. A review is important because the way we understand musicianship informs the way it guides the development of children as musicians. Concepts of musicianship shape the kind and range of activities that are seen as a valid part of a musical life, and provide horizons and boundaries for the knowledge and understandings that are considered necessary in being a musician.

I propose the concept of a *sound musicianship* that adopts a humanistic perspective on music but also considers the broader physical and cultural contexts within which people make and experience music. A sound musicianship does not limit itself to notational literacy or decontextualized aural competencies, but embraces the broader demands of musical activities relevant to the child or adolescent living in a technoculture. These demands include developing skills and understanding that use sound-making techniques, an understanding of music perception and contextualized aural awareness, the acquisition of appropriate motor skills for gestural expression, and awareness of the role of music in the community and one's interrelatedness with others through music.

As a way of reframing our thinking about musicianship, four distinct perspectives will be discussed: music and sound, music and cognition, music and the body, and music and culture. These perspectives respect the multi-dimensional nature of music and highlight important aspects of the lived impressions of musical experiences. Music is a sonic art form and, therefore, understanding the characteristics of music as sound is fundamental to musical awareness. Musicians employ both their cognitive and bodily capabilities to make and experience music; therefore, the psychological and embodied aspects of musicianship both need attention. Music is, along with other art forms, a cultural expression. It has social and community dimensions and there is an economy and an industry that surrounds it. Appreciating and navigating these cultural considerations is a critical part of operating in the world as a musician. In the sections that follow, each of these four perspectives on musicianship will be examined in more detail.

Music and sound

Understanding music as sound involves exploring music from a scientific angle, particularly in terms of understanding music as acoustical vibrations, audio recordings, and digital representations. Music and sound are also central to hearing and listening, although aural training and awareness will be considered more fully from the perspective of cognition and interpretation in a later section.

Musical acoustics is concerned with the motion of sound in physical materials and in the air. The vibrations of acoustic instruments and voices produce sounds, organized and expressed as music by musicians. Given the generality of these phenomena, they form a critical aspect of every person's musicianship. Being aware of how sounds are produced and how materials affect sound production can assist musical expression. Principles of the physics of sound, in particular the harmonic series and the temporal aspects of periodic motion, are fundamental to understandings of timbre, pitch, harmony, pulse, and meter that appear across all music systems.

Musical sounds are heard and felt by musicians. Therefore, being aware of how hearing and perception operate to filter and transform sound is useful. A re-engagement with the purely sonic within musical discourse was driven in the second half of the twentieth century by experiments in electronic music, experimental endeavors in composition by the likes of John Cage and Pierre Schaeffer that focused on sound objects and their organization, and the concerns about acoustic ecology and increasing awareness of the natural sound world led by R. Murray Shafer, Hildegard Westerkamp, and others.

For over a century sound recording has transformed musical practices. The ability to store and manipulate sound is fundamental to music-making in a technoculture. A musicianship training that includes sound-recording practices would prepare children with technical, aesthetic, and industry skills. Increasingly, sound-recording and distribution processes are digital. It follows that an awareness of how sound is stored as digital data and how this enables transformation, replication, and communication of music can assist musicians to appreciate the possibilities and limitations of digital audio. For a musician engaging with music expressed in digital form, fluency with these processes would be a critical part of their musicianship. As Borgo (2012) points out, digital musicianship in the twenty-first century is more than simply literacy—rather, in an age where knowledge is expressed as data, we are entering an era of musical data virtuosos.

The skills of musicianship also relate to instrument making, whether or not those instruments are acoustic, digital, or both in combination. Instrument making is often included as part of a child's musical experience as a way of encouraging them to play with sound and better appreciate sound-making devices. Often this aspect of musicianship is ignored in later music education, only to come back into focus for those adults who regain an interest in instrument design and construction. This need not be the case. There is good reason to continue instrument-making practices as part of developing sound musicianship. It can continue to underscore the relationship between technologies of sound making and the skills of controlling them for musical expression. In a technoculture the opportunities to develop software instruments and musical apps has re-energized instrument making, albeit in a new way.

Music and cognition

Music occurs in the mind. It occurs through our interpretation of heard sounds and in our imagination. We respond to music intellectually and emotionally. Also, we develop mental models, or theories, of musical patterns and how musical practices and processes are organized. All of these and more are subjects of a psychological perspective on musicianship.

In the past century there have been significant developments in the study of human cognition, and the psychology of music more specifically (Deutsch, 1999). It is now quite clear what an important role the mind plays in understanding musical patterns and structures. In more recent times neuroscience research has added to the data about how our mind functions during musical activities. All this information can inform our appreciation of how we are musical beings and about our musical tendencies, capacities, and limits. This knowledge can certainly inform definitions of musicianship and can assist in shaping the ways we assist children to develop it.

Aural training and awareness have played, and will continue to play, a significant role in musicianship. How a mind interprets the sound stimulus it receives is a complex and marvelous phenomenon. Musicianship includes the ability to identify elements such as notes and other sound objects, to stream these into coherent parts and voices, to chunk them over time into phrases, riffs, and patterns, to identify subtle changes in timbre, pitch, volume, and location, and to aggregate all of this (and more) into an expressive and meaningful whole.

Aural training has traditionally included identification, memorization, transcription, and theorization. There seems good reason to continue these activities as part of developing the child as a musician, so long as the content is relevant to the child's musical interests or future and the sonic materials are authentic and contextualized. In addition to aural awareness being based in features of musical repertoire, these skills can be enhanced by carefully attending to any sonic context. This was an important insight in the development of "soundwalks" and "ear cleaning" exercises during the 1970s that emphasized how aural acuity should be exercised in any place and at any time, not just in "musical" settings.

Emotional response to music and sounds is another important aspect of music and cognition, as highlighted by Schubert and McPherson (Chapter 12). According to Sloboda (1985), music's "emotional factor is . . . transcultural. It seems unlikely that music could have penetrated to the core of so many different cultures unless there were some fundamental human attraction to organised sound which transcends cultural boundaries" (p. 1). There are two ways in which music and emotions are linked, and understanding the sometimes-subtle distinctions between them is important: music can *elicit* emotions, and music can *express* emotions. When music moves us it is eliciting emotions in us, and there can be a number of reasons for this. These may have to do with considerations within the music, such as its expressive nature or its impressive construction, or it may be a result of external associations indicated by the lyrical content of a song, or triggering memories of events or people the music reminds us of.

On the other hand, when we make a claim about music expressing emotions we usually mean that music expresses sadness, happiness, exuberance, pensiveness, or otherwise—even if it does not make us feel that way. Schubert and McPherson (Chapter 12) attribute these emotional impressions to a balancing of schematic and veridical processes that varies with different stages of a child's musical development, meaning that emotional reading of musical stimulus may be due to sonic qualities, such as tempo or texture, that seem to align with particular emotional states. Or it may be that the music has characteristics that have become synonymous with an external referent, such as a particular event, person, or mood, or with associated emotive associations. These links tend to be personally or culturally bound. Developing an understanding of how music's internal features and its external referents have emotive effect is an important factor in a musician harnessing these for their expressive potential.

The emotive power of music and of musical experiences also plays a role in the link between music and well-being, and in therapeutic applications of music. These connections with health, in particular mental health, also extend into the sociocultural aspects of music explored in a later section.

Many more topics central to cognitive psychology are also relevant to musicianship; these include interpretation, representation, memory, and learning. Music psychologists have studied not only how we perceive music as sound, but also how we represent and read it as notation. Memory plays an important part in how our musical expectations arise, how we can play or sing a tune without reference to a score, and how training memory through repetition has a significant role in developing musicianship.

Some psychologists are quick to emphasize that the contemplation of representations in the mind does not necessarily explain all our behavior (Brunswick, 1952; Gibson, 1966), whilst others caution that we are not simply cognitive beings, but rather our minds and body act together to produce musical competency. In his book on situated cognition, Clancey (1997) reminds us that:

> All human action is at least partially improvisatory by direct *coupling* of perceiving, conceiving, and moving—a coordination mechanism unmediated by descriptions of associations, laws or procedures. This mechanism complements the inferential process of deliberation and planning that form the backbone of theories of cognition based on manipulation of descriptions. (p. 2)

With this in mind, the next section examines how human movement and gesture contribute to the physicality of music-making and experience.

Music and the body

From the embodied perspective, human movement and music are intertwined. This is clearly evident in the way musical sounds are produced through physical gestures and how people are compelled to move to music they hear or imagine. The most prominent example of embodied musicianship is performance capability. However, musicianship can be expressed in many ways, including through singing, tapping a pulse or rhythm, conducting an ensemble, playing an instrument, or dancing to music. Performance gestures and motion synchronization can be associated with many musical elements including pulse, pitch or volume contour, emotive intensity, rise and fall of expectation or intensity, and so on.

In acknowledgment of the coupling of sound and motion, many music activities emphasize participation through singing, playing, and moving. The developmental interaction between mind and body is a deliberate part of many early childhood music programs, of music education methods such as Dalcroze Eurhythmics, and of many community and therapeutic music activities. Research, as well as experience, suggests that there is significant value in gestural participation in music-making for the development of embodied cognition, that movement is a valid indicator of musical understanding, and that these tendencies transcend cultural contexts (Davidson, 2012; Luck & Toiviainen, 2012).

The relationship between music and the body extends beyond the connection between movement and sound; it relates to a sense of intuitive or embodied knowledge and understanding. This is often developed through repeated action to the point where responses become unconscious or automatic. Embodied musicality involves a tight interaction between thought, action, and environment. Competency emerges through processes of feedback and adjustment during practice. Embodiment, when understood this way, is concerned with *being* a musician. It emphasizes musicianship beyond competency and deliberate effort, but strives for fluency and virtuosity.

With a focus on developing embodied expertise through repetition and reinforcement, Davies suggests (1998) that there are "degrees of understanding which might be attained only through years of hard work and there are kinds of music which yield their richest rewards only to listeners so prepared" (p. 80). This certainly seems true and reinforces the notion that the development of musicianship is iterative and developmental. It is also certain that these "rewards" will be conferred to modes of engagement other than listening and to musical genres other than the Western classical canon that Davies focuses on.

A final aspect of embodiment that needs to be emphasized is that musicians are situated in an environment. An awareness of the environment and the skill of interacting with that environment to musical ends are important aspects of an embodied musicianship. An environment may include natural or man-made structures. The ways in which musical instruments are fashioned from pieces of wood and from electronic components are examples of effective utilization of environmental resources. A situated view of embodiment can also manifest itself in how sounds are positioned in space, either physically in the world or through virtual positioning via loudspeakers. An embodied musicianship includes both an awareness of the surround-sound context and an ability to construct one as a creative act. One musical practice where situated embodiment is particularly evident is eco-composing—a practice which emphasizes the design of musical experiences via the construction of sonic ecologies and interactive environments (Keller, 2012). Typically eco-composition uses sound recordings of the natural world and combines them with other materials in an immersive soundscape experience.

Developing a child's embodied awareness of musical contexts is critical, but can extend beyond the physical environment to include the sociocultural environment. This perspective of social and cultural competency is the topic of the next section.

Music and culture

Culture includes the social, political, and economic context in which we make music (and do everything else), and the accumulated ideas, customs, and social behaviors of a community. Musical culture includes previous musical actions, accumulated expertise and innovations, and a community's musical conventions, wisdom, and habits. Culture is both a source of inspiration and an object of study for the child as musician. As they mature it can become a foil against which to rebel in order to articulate an individual identity and make a unique contribution, thus influencing cultural evolution.

Understanding the cultural functions and roles that music serves in a community enhances musicianship. Music can also be used to mediate and facilitate relationships between people in a society. The culturally aware musician understands why musical practices act to reinforce or disrupt these social structures.

Music notation systems are a significant artifact of musical culture, and are used to record and transmit music ideas and creations. Understanding these notations allows children to access this history and participate in musical communities. There is a range of notational literacies, each with a community with various geographic or stylistic traditions. There are also many aural musical traditions, and the increased ubiquity of sound recording is playing a role in preserving and sharing these traditions.

Another feature of musical culture is commentary and critique. In an age of pervasive social media, there are more opportunities than ever for people to share ideas and opinions about the music they encounter and about their music-making activities. When formalized, these conversations amount to music criticism. A sound musicianship should include the ability to think critically and communicate articulately about one's own music and that of others.

One of the larger impacts of globalization is increased access to musical cultures from around the world. Migration and travel mean that these encounters may not only be with the artifacts of those cultures, but also with the musicians making them. This increased access and the diversity of multicultural communities present ethical and educational challenges and opportunities.

Cultures are not only geographically defined, but also exist within particular demographic and interest groups. Of particular interest, for readers of this volume, is the identification of distinctive children's and youth musical cultures with their own conventions, social relations, and sound (Emberly, 2012). This suggests that for the child as musician opportunities exist not only to learn the ways of musical cultures they encounter, but also to become culture creators within their own peer group.

Another meeting place in which particular musical cultures can develop is the Internet. The online space enables a freeing-up of geographic-centrality in cultural discussions and supports the coming together of like-minded musicians and audiences. Online spaces have become sites for music production and distribution, and these are often disruptive to established production and business models as new technologies and evolving online practices reshape musical practices. There is also an argument that online platforms promote a participatory culture often called user-generated content, driven by the democratization of music production through the use of digital media tools (Jenkins, 2009).

The cultural impacts of our technoculture are also felt in the dissolution of music's boundaries as a discipline—particularly its blending with visual media practices. The interoperability of digital data between media forms and the convergence of media tools to a singular computational platform have meant that previous cultural distinctions between art forms have dissipated and new inter-media forms have emerged. As a result, the child today might be less likely than in any previous generation in the Western world to see music as separate from other art forms. This questions the very notion of musicianship as sonic capability alone, challenging us, again, to reconsider the range of skills and sensibilities that might come together in a child's unique creative output.

Finally, cultures and societies include economic and organizational structures that support, or suppress, musical activities. The recasting of the creative arts as the creative industries in the early years of the twenty-first century drew this fact into sharp relief. As a result, the contemporary musician is characterized not only as an artist, but also as an entrepreneur. With this shift comes an expansion of the definition of musicianship to explicitly include aspects of project development and management, economics, marketing, law, and career planning.

Musical diversity and identity

As we are well aware, musical features and functions can vary from one style to another and differ between cultures (and within subcultures). As a result, there is not just one kind of musicianship. The range and variety of skills and abilities involved can be as varied as are musicians themselves. Also, each musical style has its own array of skills and knowledge, habits, and tools. Making decisions about which skills and knowledge are relevant to any particular child's musicianship will depend on the particulars of their personal circumstances and interests.

Allowing for diversity in the ways that a child can be a musician is quite consistent with observations of the diversity of musicianship in experts. Marcus (2012) observed this diversity in his investigation of musical expertise where he noticed enormous variations between experts and in their expertise: "Some could read music, many couldn't. Some could play blisteringly fast, others not. Some had an encyclopedic knowledge of the history of the music that preceded them, others only had an intuitive notion of the music they themselves wanted to create" (p. 161).

Allowing for diversity, however, is not the same as saying all sets of musical skills and knowledge are of equal value. Rather, the benchmark for the utility of a set of musical skills is a child's ability to operate effectively in a chosen musical context. There will be many abilities and understandings that are shared between musical styles and roles, allowing for peer learning and for the transference of competencies from one musical domain to another. What should be avoided, however, is the imposition of the competency values from one style or culture onto musicians wishing to operate in another. This would be both unfair and unproductive. As each child engages with meaningful musical activities they develop their particular musicianship as a part of their individual identity.

Conclusion

The twenty-first century is well upon us and the globalized technoculture in which we find ourselves calls for a re-examination of the musical life of today's child, whose musical activities may continue into the twenty-second century. It is also timely that we take the opportunity to revisit the frameworks that guide children's music activities and our thinking about them. This chapter presents several frameworks that may assist us to meet these challenges.

The *modes of creative engagement* outline the range of musical activities that a child can undertake. The *contexts for meaning* highlight the value of these activities when undertaken in private, social, and cultural settings. The four perspectives of a *sound musicianship* outline various perspectives on musicality and highlight the types of skills and understandings that a child can develop through meaningful engagement with music.

The MEM brings together the modes and contexts to provide a conceptual landscape on which to map the child's musical activities. Doing so will assist in better understanding the extent of the child's musical experiences and highlight ways of extending or rebalancing their musical lives.

The view of musicianship presented here is intentionally broad. It considers the sonic, cognitive, embodied, and cultural aspects of musicianship. The child as musician may develop these skills and understandings through an equally broad range of musical activities and experiences that cover different modes of engagement. However, each child's musical profile will be a unique and personal one, which can arise by prioritizing aspects of musicianship relevant to the child's cultural context and personal interests.

Reflective questions

1 What are new opportunities and challenges faced by the child musician today compared to previous generations?
2 How might you define the term technoculture?
3 What are the activity descriptors for the five modes of engagement?
4 What are the three contexts for meaning that are part of the meaningful engagement matrix (MEM)?
5 How might your understanding of musical development be shaped through a consideration of the four perspectives of a sound musicianship proposed in this chapter?

Reference list

Beeching, A. (2010). *Beyond talent: Creating a successful career in music*. New York: Oxford University Press.

Borgo, D. (2012). Embodied, situated and distributed musicianship. In A. R. Brown (Ed.), *Sound musicianship: Understanding the crafts of music* (pp. 202–12). Newcastle upon Tyne: Cambridge Scholars Publishing.

Brown, A. R. (2003). *Music composition and the computer: An examination of the work practices of five experienced composers* (Doctoral dissertation). The University of Queensland, Brisbane.

Brown, A. R. (2014). *Music technology and education: Amplifying musicality*. New York: Routledge.

Brown, A. R., & Dillon, S. (2012). Meaningful engagement with music composition. In D. Collins (Ed.), *The act of musical composition: Studies in the creative process* (pp. 79–110). Surrey, UK: Ashgate.

Brunswick, E. (1952). *The conceptual framework of psychology*. Chicago: University of Chicago Press.

Cann, S. (2007). *Building a successful 21st century music career*. Sydney: Cengage Learning.

Caves, R. E. (2000). *Creative industries: Contracts between art and commerce*. Harvard: Harvard University Press.

Clancey, W. J. (1997). *Situated cognition: Human knowledge and computer representations*. Cambridge: Cambridge University Press.

Clark, A. (2008). *Supersizing the mind: Embodiment, action and cognitive extension*. Oxford: Oxford University Press.

Connell, J., & Gibson, C. (2013). *Sound tracks: Popular music identity and place*. New York: Routledge.

Csikszentmihalyi, M. (1992). *Flow: The psychology of happiness*. London: Rider Books.

Davidson, J. (2012). Demonstrating musical knowledge. In A. R. Brown (Ed.), *Sound musicianship: Understanding the crafts of music* (pp. 156–66). Newcastle upon Tyne: Cambridge Scholars Publishing.

Davies, S. (1998). Musical understanding and the musical kinds. In P. Alperson (Ed.), *Musical worlds: New directions in the philosophy of music* (pp. 69–82). University Park, PA: The Pennsylvania State University Press.

D'Eith, B. (2013). *A career in music: The other 12 step program.* Vancouver, Canada: CreateSpace Independent Publishing Platform.

Deutsch, D. (1999). *The psychology of music.* San Diego: Academic Press.

Dillon, S. (2001). The student as maker: An examination of the meaning of music to students in a school and the ways in which we give access to meaningful music education (Doctoral dissertation). La Trobe University, Melbourne.

Dillon, S. (2007). *Music, meaning and transformation: Meaningful music making for life.* Cambridge: Cambridge Scholars Publishing.

Emberly, A. (2012). The roles of music and culture in children's lives. In A. R. Brown (Ed.), *Sound musicianship: Understanding the crafts of music* (pp. 241–50). Newcastle upon Tyne: Cambridge Scholars Publishing.

Gibson, J. J. (1966). *The senses considered as perceptual systems.* Boston: Houghton Mifflin.

Green, L. (2002). *Technoculture: From alphabet to cybersex.* Crows Nest, NSW: Allen & Unwin.

Hirche, K. (2011). Meaningful musical engagement: The potential impact of generative music systems on learning experiences (Master of Arts thesis). Queensland University of Technology, Brisbane, Australia.

Hugill, A. (2012). Musicianship in the digital age. In A. R. Brown (Ed.), *Sound musicianship: Understanding the crafts of music* (pp. 52–61). Newcastle upon Tyne: Cambridge Scholars Publishing.

Jenkins, H. (2009). *Confronting the challenges of participatory culture: Media education for the 21st century.* Cambridge, MA: MIT Press.

Keller, D. (2012). Sonic ecologies. In A. R. Brown (Ed.), *Sound musicianship: Understanding the crafts of music* (pp. 213–26). Newcastle upon Tyne: Cambridge Scholars Publishing.

Lessig, L. (2008). *Remix: Making art and commerce thrive in the hybrid economy.* New York: Penguin.

Luck, G., & Toiviainen, P. (2012). Movement and musical expression. In A. R. Brown (Ed.), *Sound musicianship: Understanding the crafts of music* (pp. 167–77). Newcastle upon Tyne: Cambridge Scholars Publishing.

Marcus, G. (2012). *Guitar zero: The new musician and the science of learning.* New York: The Penguin Press.

Perkins, D. (1993). Person-plus: A distributed view of thinking and learning. In G. Salomon (Ed.), *Distributed cognitions: Psychological and educational considerations* (pp. 88–110). Cambridge: Cambridge University Press.

Robinson, K., & Aronica, L. (2009). *The element: How finding your passion changes everything.* London: Allen Lane, The Penguin Press.

Ruud, E. (1997). Music and identity. *Nordic Journal of Music Therapy,* **6**(1), 3–13.

Sangüesa, R. (2011). *Technoculture and its democratization: Noise, limits and opportunities of the "labs."* Presented at the Center for Organizational Innovation, Columbia University. Retrieved from <http://www.gridspinoza.net/sites/gridspinoza.net/files/anguesaLabDemocratizadors.pdf>.

Sloboda, J. A. (1985). *The musical mind: The cognitive psychology of music.* Oxford: Clarendon Press.

Spinosa, C., Flores, F., & Dreyfus, H. L. (1997). *Disclosing new worlds: Entrepreneurship, democratic action, and the cultivation of solidarity.* Cambridge, MA: MIT Press.

Chapter 12

Underlying mechanisms and processes in the development of emotion perception in music

Emery Schubert and Gary E. McPherson

Underlying mechanisms and processes in the development of emotion perception in music: Introduction

At what age can children perceive emotion in music? How might this evolve as they mature? These two questions form the focus of this chapter, which examines the perception of emotion in music from birth to adolescence. Because there is scant understanding about how the capacity to identify emotion in music develops over ontogenetic time (Nieminen et al., 2011), we draw on available evidence to propose a theoretical framework of how children develop their abilities to perceive emotion in music. We begin by providing a definition for emotion and identifying the processes for connecting emotion and music, before surveying the general development of emotional perception throughout childhood. Importantly, the main part of our chapter draws on literature that helps explain how children perceive emotion in music rather than the emotion a child experiences in response to music or emotion involved in the performance of music (about which see, e.g., Adachi & Trehub, 1998, 2000, 2011). The theoretical position we propose suggests that throughout childhood different mental processing styles work in parallel to form a spiral-like pathway in which the decoding of emotional information from music involves a dynamic combination of one-to-one (veridical) connections, such as hearing a particular melody and associating it with a particular mood, and general (schematic) associations, where responses to general principles of emotion in music are both learnt and innate. This view is expanded in our examination of the methodological issues, where we discuss limitations concerning how this topic has been previously studied, and our conclusions that provide a speculative model for understanding the development of the perception of emotion in music from infancy to adolescence.

What is an emotion?

Defining precisely what is meant by emotion is challenging (Izard, 2010; Solomon, 1993), but it can be simplified if we begin by separating its *function* from its *structure*. There are numerous ways of thinking about the *function* of emotion. Most show that emotional states occur spontaneously rather than as a result of conscious effort and can produce physiological changes (such as an increase in heart rate when feeling angry). The emotion producer does not have to focus on the emotion-inducing event or situation, because the emotion itself serves as an identifying marker with its own set of predetermined patterns (such as crying or laughing or being worried). Emotions can also be captured from others involuntarily (via "emotional contagion"; Hatfield, Rapson, & Le, 2009) and are generally difficult to change voluntarily (Dezecache et al., 2013). Accordingly, emotions can be defined as a temporally elongated marker of the state of the individual for the purpose of communicating to others and reinforcing the state of the individual to him- or herself. So if one feels happy, markers associated with happiness, such as smiling (which signals to others this emotional state), will be generated (Izard, Kagan, & Zajonc, 1984; Mandler, 1984, 1990; Oatley & Jenkins, 1996; Rolls, 2002). Likewise, because it is able to portray an emotion (a state) in a mode that is almost exclusively auditory, music that sounds happy can be viewed as an indication of the state displayed by the music from the perspective of the listener (Schubert, 2013).

Emotions can also be defined *structurally* as a collection of entities (such as happiness, sadness, anger, and fear) (Izard et al., 2000) or alternatively as dimensional constructs, lying along scales of negative to positive emotion (i.e. the valence dimension), activity to sleepiness (i.e. the arousal dimension), and so forth (Russell, 1997, but see also Schimmack, 2002; Schimmack, Oishi, & Diener, 2002 regarding some complications of this simplified view of emotional structure).

In sum, emotions are often connected with other actions, associations, behaviors, and environmental stimuli. For example, Lang (1979) demonstrated how emotions can be triggered through a network of interacting nodes representing the emotion-inducing stimulus (such as seeing a snake), the representations of physiological states (increased heart rate), and the associated thought patterns which occur as a result (such as running away). Bower (1981) further developed this way of understanding emotion by suggesting that emotion nodes (one representing happiness, another sadness, another anger, and so on) are able to activate memory structures (e.g. the memory of a snake, or even a piece of music), and vice-versa. These network-based models help to bring together the functional and structural understandings we have of emotion.

Cognitive organization of music

Such network models have been used to explain musical expectation (for a review, see Rohrmeier & Koelsch, 2012). Bharucha (1987, 1994) described two processes through which musical information is primed during the listening process: when listening to a melody, what do we expect the next note to be? One process is the *veridical* (one-to-one) expectation, where a node which represents a single note of a melody then activates a node representing the next node of that melody. We expect to hear the next note of the melody because its node is being prepared ("primed") by the currently activated node. Here, a melody (or piece of music) is well known, and rehearing it produces the expectation of the note which follows. For example, if you heard the notes C4 C4 G4 G4 A4 A4, the veridical memory of *Twinkle, Twinkle, Little Star* would facilitate an expectation of a G4—the next note of that tune.

Another process is referred to as *schematic* expectancy. Here, the listener has acquired (without any necessary conscious attention) the rules of music in a particular style and can therefore predict the next note of a melody of that style when the melody is unfamiliar. A typical example is the leading tone toward the end of a musical phrase. There are so many examples in which we hear this note rise to the tonic in Western music (e.g. B4 to C5 in the key of C major) that when a new piece is heard coming to the end of the phrase with a leading tone, we have a deeply engrained, schematic expectation that the next note will be the tonic. Bharucha (1987) argues that these schematic expectancies emerge through exposure. We adapt these processes into our model of mental processing styles to explain how emotion is connected to and extracted from music by the listener.

Two mental processing styles for connecting emotion with music

Meyer's (1956) landmark monograph, *Emotion and Meaning in Music*, describes two broad ways in which emotions and music can be connected by listeners. The first—*referentialism*—is where meaning comes from direct associations made with the music and situations, mood, and so forth. In this explanation, something outside the music is connected and associated with the music. The second—*absolutism*—is where the meaning in music comes from within the structure of the music itself, without any need to make reference to something outside the music.

Meyer's explanation shares remarkable similarities with Bharucha's (1987) notion of veridical and schematic expectation. Veridical (or referentialist) connections occur between a distinct life event and (in our case) a specific piece of music. Examples might include a song or piece of music that reminds an individual of a particular event that he or she danced to as a child or heard on a first date as an adolescent. In contrast, when many exemplars of a particular mood are connected with similar musical structures (such as music in minor keys representing general sadness or negative emotions), we can say that there is a general, or schematic (absolute), representation of emotion and music: general principles have emerged. In this way, absolutism (and therefore schemata) may be understood as a subconscious abstraction of musical and extra-musical rules, such that the listener *thinks* that the connection with emotions is part of the musical structure, but in actual fact this has emerged from multiple hearings of different veridical connections.

As will become evident later in this chapter, these two processing styles—veridical and schematic—can be used to provide a framework for answering the two aims of the chapter, which are to understand how children perceive emotion in music and how their perceptions evolve as they mature. But first, it is relevant to note that the dichotomy of absolute-expressionism and referentialism can be illustrated further by comparing them with Juslin and Västfjäll's (2008) six mechanisms of emotion in music (see Table 12.1). The comparison will be exemplified with the scenarios and the developmental model that follow.

Consider the following scenarios.

In the first, we see a young boy sitting in front of a TV watching a cartoon in which a villain is creeping around a corner. The associated soundtrack outlines a minor triad, such as the one shown in Figure 12.1.

Each step taken by the villain is mimicked by each note in the soundtrack (so-called Mickey-Mousing), which provides the context for the child to pair the villain's movements with the

Table 12.1 Conceptualizing Juslin and Västfjäll's (2008) emotion mechanisms according to Absolute Expressionism-Schematic (AE) and Referentialism-Veridical (R) processing styles

Mechanism	Processing Style
(1) brainstem reflexes	AE
(2) evaluative conditioning	AE
(3) emotional contagion	AE
(4) visual imagery	R
(5) episodic memory	R
(6) musical expectancy	AE

Fig. 12.1 Example of a tune associated with a cartoon villain

character of the melody in the soundtrack. The emotion evoked by the situation may be suspenseful fear, and if the connection is strong, then later hearings can evoke the image (visual imagery—Table 12.1, row 4), situation, or the emotional feelings (episodic memory, Table 12.1, row 5) made in the initial, veridical connections, even in the absence of the villain. The music itself is sufficient to evoke the emotion. This form of association occurs because humans are acculturated into the norms of emotional meaning in music through conscious or unconscious exposure (Zajonc, 2000) during the early years of their life, and well beyond. Juslin and Västfjäll refer to this kind of pairing between music and emotional-event as episodic memory (Table 12.1, row 5).

In the second scenario, the boy previously mentioned has seen so many cartoons and films where similar pairings occur that the emotional connotation conveyed by the music is thoroughly absorbed. The child has, without deliberate attention or explicit knowledge, learnt the rule that the minor chord harmony (of the kind outlined in Figure 12.1) presents a schematic, general connection to the negative emotion that was once only associated with a particular villain. We refer to this kind of association as *schematic*,[1] because it corresponds to Juslin and Västfjäll's evaluative conditioning mechanism (Table 12.1, row 2).

The apparently *intrinsic* ability of music to convey emotional information can also occur in other ways. One of the earliest and more important examples is an infant who is startled by an unexpected *subito forte* chord while being exposed to an orchestral work. In Table 12.1 (row 1), this would correspond to a brainstem reflex mechanism. Because this type of reflexive response to an acoustic signal can occur as a hard-wired connection that is phylogenetically present (Gaston, 1951; Masterson & Crawford, 1982), our current definition of schematic expectation (the emergence of the general from numerous veridical connections) needs to be extended so that schematic associations are defined as emotions that are subconsciously or *intrinsically* connected with musical structures. An intrinsic schematic connection of this type would be present at birth and enable general, possibly universal, rules of music and emotion to be known. As we shall see later, these intrinsic, schematic rules have evolutionary explanations.

Previous research on the perception of emotion in music has described what children can do at different ages, and so the framework we provide here is intended to help explain patterns in the data (for other theories and reviews of children's emotional responses to music and art see, e.g. Nieminen et al., 2011; Nieminen et al., 2012; Parsons, 1976; Perani et al., 2010; Trainor & Corrigall, 2010). Establishing the corresponding developmental paths for *veridical* and *schematic* activation is important for understanding how children develop their capacity to perceive emotion in music. While both veridical and schematic associations can operate in parallel, a more interesting question concerns the extent to which one may dominate over the other at various stages of a child's development. Before turning to this question, however, it is important to understand how emotional perception develops throughout childhood.

Perception of emotion in general: birth to late childhood

In their first ten weeks of life, infants are able to show interest, distress, disgust, and contentment, and in the subsequent weeks and months of their development, leading up to around 7 months, they extend these to include happiness, sadness, anger, joy, surprise, and fear (Izard et al., 1995). Researchers believe that these primary (basic) emotions are biologically programmed because they emerge in normal infants from all cultural backgrounds at around the same age (Camras, 1992; Malatesta et al., 1989). By 7 months infants are also able to identify and distinguish facial emotional expressions (Walker-Andrews & Dickson, 1997) and by 10 months to use social cues to decide how to act in ambiguous situations (Striano & Rochat, 2000). Furthermore, infants internalize many features associated with emotion because they are able to mimic actions they observe in the environment, such as lip and tongue positions as well as vocalization (Kuhl & Meltzoff, 1996; Meltzoff & Moore, 1977). Since these mimicry acts are considered foundational to emotional contagion (Niedenthal & Brauer, 2012; Preston & De Waal, 2002), it suggests that the rudiments of the circuits required for emotional contagion are present in infancy. This is why we classify Juslin and Västfjäll's (2008) emotional contagion mechanism (the capturing of emotion portrayed by the music—Table 12.1, row 3) as a schematic processing style, since the rules for capturing an emotion from music may well be hard-wired and begin to mature from infancy. Furthermore, emotional contagion is a function of general musical features/characteristics, rather than idiosyncrasies of individual pieces.

Secondary (complex) emotions, such as embarrassment, shame, guilt, envy, and pride, begin to appear in the second year as young infants start to experience situations when they feel self-conscious and begin to gain an understanding of rules and standards for evaluating their own and other people's conduct (Shaffer, 1999). These types of emotions depend on infants having developed some understanding of themselves. Because they are more sophisticated than primary emotions, these secondary emotions are also more culturally specific, in that they tend to vary more than primary emotions, depending on the social setting and the types of human interactions which govern what is appropriate in any given culture (Bee, 1997).

By 3 years of age infants are able to display nearly the entire range of adult emotions (Lewis, 2000), and their capacity to do this is part of a more generalized ability that allows them to make decisions through social referencing (Feinman, 1982). Infants of this age are able to make inferences about situations in their environment based on emotional information they gain from others, particularly their mothers. For example, a child's examination of a parent's emotional response to a stranger or a toy (such as a fearful expression) determines the way the child responds in the new situation and can impinge on their response at a later time (for example, a fearful response to the stranger or toy at a later interaction). Social referencing of this type suggests a high level of interpretation about events, and emotional information from the caretaker is used as a key or a kind of glue for associating information about new people and objects.

Between 3 and 6 years of age, children's understanding of the external causes and consequences of their emotions continues to improve, and, in the years that follow, they become increasingly better at integrating the perceptions and cues they learn (from observing other people) into a more complete understanding of their own and others' emotional reactions (Shaffer, 1999). By the age of 4, children are able to verbally explain the emotional states of others but tend to describe them as consequences of external events ("He is sad because the other boy took his ball away"), rather than internal states. From the age of 4, children's ability to attribute emotion to both external and internal causes continues to improve (Levine, 1995), with a gradual shift toward them being able to decode accurately complex emotional situations (Lagattuta, Wellman, & Flavell, 1997). For example, at around 4 years of age, children tend to simply use the content of spoken messages to decipher emotional information, even if the "paralinguistic" (i.e. emotions and other messages transmitted via inflections and prosody) contradict the message (e.g. saying "What a beautiful day" with an angry voice). Morton and Trehub (2001) demonstrated that in these situations

4-year-olds are probably processing both language content and paralinguistic emotional cues (even though they are responding only to the content) because their reaction times in these conditions are longer than when content and paralinguistic cues are concordant. That is, the reaction time increase provides evidence of the difficulty of the task. By the time the child has reached the Piagetian concrete operational stage at around the age of 6 or 7, they have not only acquired the ability to understand the consequences of emotions but are also able to appropriately interpret and resolve many such complex emotional situations.

There are still some limitations in children's emotion-perception skills, however, that take time to develop to the level of the typical adult. For example, as children approach the age of 6 years, they become aware of the thoughts and feelings different people have but often confuse them. In contrast, children over 7 years of age are normally able to understand when more than one emotion is present simultaneously and subsequently are able to hide socially undesirable emotions. This increasing sophistication in emotion recognition is also reflected by more refined categories of emotion. For example, although infants are able to recognize "happy" expressions, older children and adults are able to recognize more specific, narrow kinds of happiness. Furthermore, recognition of negative emotions, such as fear and disgust, can be particularly difficult for younger children to distinguish (Balconi & Carrera, 2007). During the period from 7 to 12 years of age children are able to empathize and take the perspective of different people in a self-reflective manner. For example, if a child is teasing another in a joking way, but the other child takes the joke seriously and becomes upset, the first child is able to identify what has happened and to provide an understanding explanation, such as "I was only joking, I'm sorry that I upset you." Selman (1977) refers to this as "self-reflective perspective taking." Improvements in children's perception of complex emotional situations and dilemmas therefore result as a consequence of increasing levels of sophistication and socialization (Gurucharri & Selman, 1982; Selman, 1977). It should be pointed out that much of the research on the development of emotion perception is based on social interactions/situations and recognition of facial and vocal expressions (e.g. Grossmann, 2010; Vieillard & Guidetti, 2009). In fact, since our first review of the development of emotion perception of music (Schubert & McPherson, 2006), relatively few studies have been located that address the question of emotion perception in music, so we are currently severely lacking in both data and theory (Nieminen et al., 2011; Nieminen et al., 2012; Volkova et al., 2013). In the following sections, we group the music-perception literature according to what we know about the development of the child.

Infancy to 2 years

Musical interactions between a mother and her infant emerge out of an evolutionary necessity for bonding and as such are a critical and biologically programmed part of infant (and parent) functionality (Dissanayake, 2000; Trehub, 2009). During the months before birth, the developing fetus hears a range of nuances expressed in his or her mother's voice, such as the changes in vocal quality when she is happy or sad, excited or relaxed. Immediately after birth, newborn babies show an awareness of the various emotional signals they perceive from their caregivers through their own vocalizations and hand movements (Malloch, 1999/2000; Malloch et al., 2012; Nadel & Butterworth, 1999; Trainor et al., 1997). The slow, high-pitched utterances involved in infant-directed speech help them attend to and grasp messages in their parents' tone of voice long before they are capable of understanding what is actually being said (Fernald, 1992, 1993; Trehub & Nakata, 2001), and the pitch variations associated with infant-directed speech facilitate the communication of emotional messages (Slaney & McRoberts, 2003). In the weeks and months that follow birth, the infant's innate communicative capacities, supported by his or her parent's intuitive behavior, provide the catalyst for an intimate dialogue between parent and infant. This typically involves a type of turn taking, in which parent and child respond to each other in a way that is responsive to the infant's communicative needs. Malloch (1999/2000; Malloch et al., 2012) describes this process as *communicative musicality* (see also Preti & Welsch, 2004, 2011), because the parent–child interaction has a music-like rhythmic and melodic quality.

Communication occurs not necessarily as a result of the infant understanding the words said to it by the mother but rather through the inflections of these words and the effect they evoke, as expressed through the "music-like" qualities of their joint vocalizations and the "dance-like" gestures of their facial expressions and bodily movements. Infants are able to distinguish between gross pitch differences—the high pitches found in infant-directed speech versus growling and low pitches that are more typical of adult-directed speech—even though they prefer higher-pitched vocalizations, which can even make learning vowels more difficult (Trainor & Desjardins, 2002). This preference for higher-pitched sounds may have an evolutionarily basis given that infants have a predisposition to understanding emotional messages through pitch and pitch contour (Trainor & Desjardins, 2002).

A central question in the research on infant-directed speech has been to determine the extent to which an infant gains cues about its caregiver's emotional state through vocal communication, including the musical elements used while singing. Evidence shows that infants have a distinct preference for infant-directed "motherese" compared to normal adult speech inflection patterns because emotional information through this type of prosody is the only verbal channel available to the pre-linguistic, speech-listening infant in the absence of knowledge about the meaning of words (Cooper et al., 1997; Kitamura & Burnham, 1998; Trehub & Nakata, 2001; Werker & McLeod, 1989). So it stands to reason that musical signals that share characteristics of speech also share its meaning (Trehub & Schellenberg, 1995), or, as Fernald (1992) puts it:

> The communicative force of the mother's vocalizations derive not from their arbitrary meanings in a linguistic code, but more from their immediate musical power to arouse and alert, to calm and to delight. Through this distinctive form of vocal communication the infant begins to experience emotional communion with others, months before communication through symbols is possible. (p. 148)

Other studies suggest that infants are biologically predisposed to extracting emotional meaning not only from vocal signals but also from lullabies because of the soothing nature of the melodic, dynamic, rhythmic, and tempo features of the music which characterize this genre (Trehub & Schellenberg, 1995; Trehub & Trainor, 1998; Trehub, Unyk, & Trainor, 1993).

If infants are predisposed to extracting emotional information from auditory signals, the question remains whether the baby is processing the various elements of the signal (such as contour variations, tempo) and quickly developing a repertoire of emotional associations based on an analysis of these signals, or whether emotional perception is hard-wired and automated as though the auditory signal is processed as an emotional whole (or "gestalt"), without the need for prior processing of the auditory parameters. The prevailing view is that:

> emotion perception occurs as soon as the child learns to attend to the relevant stimulus cues and to decode the specified emotion. Emotion cognition is thought to develop later, as the child gains more sophisticated cognitive skills, has more experience in social interactions, and begins to acquire culture-specific display rules. (Boone & Cunningham, 1998, p. 1008)

This view is in accord with the emotion-perception latency argument that some musical features *can* be reliably detected by infants under 12 months of age (Trehub, 2001; Trehub & Degé,

Chapter 2; Trehub & Schellenberg, 1995). For example, even though hearing is relatively under-developed, in that infants are not capable of detecting subtle changes in loudness and duration until 5 to 8 years of age (Trehub & Schellenberg, 1995), in comparison with other nonmusical parameters they are fairly sensitive. This includes contour, where infants can detect alternations in pitch as small as a semitone from 7 months of age (Trainor & Trehub, 1992a; Trehub et al., 1986). The infant auditory system is therefore highly sophisticated, even though not fully developed, at a very early age.

While keeping this in mind, it may also be the case that infants process musical and prosodic information as an emotional gestalt (Levi, 1978) and that this occurs before they are able to perceive separate musical parameters. So, a more radical interpretation would be that emotional understanding is innate and that this form of understanding is more important for an infant than being able to abstract musical and acoustic features from an auditory signal (see Gentile, 1998). Evidence that the human affect processing system develops before the cognitive processing system supports this view (Zajonc, 1984).

In summary, we believe that infants are born with basic kinds of processing styles that enable them to interpret the emotional meaning of sounds in the environment and, in particular, from their caregiver. This suggests the presence of a strong absolutist, hard-wired processing style that may well provide the young infant with an evolutionary advantage. While the situation with music is made more complex because of the problem of musical feature detection versus emotion abstraction primacy, we conclude from studies on infants' perception of emotion in music, and from the infant-directed speech literature, that it is likely that some acoustic signals also signal emotional meaning to the infant. That is, the processing style for emotional detection by the infant is primarily, though not exclusively, schematic.

The critical ages from 3 to 7

From the age of 3, children are already able to identify the emotions of sadness and happiness in music and by 4 can perceive the basic emotional labels of happiness, sadness, anger, and fear (Boone & Cunningham, 2001; Cunningham & Sterling, 1988). The age of 4 marks the beginning of a period of increasing sophistication, as children develop their capacity to encode verbally emotional meaning across a range of nonverbal modalities, including the face and voice (Boone & Cunningham, 2001).

In a pioneering study by Adachi and Trehub (1998), performances (as distinct from perception) by children were recorded on video for later analysis. They found that children as young as 4 manipulate the tempo, dynamics, and pitch of familiar songs when they are asked to present them in a happy or sad way. However, while older children used appropriate musical devices, the 4-year-olds tended to use more idiosyncratic and varied devices such as physical gestures to facilitate the emotional communication. This parallels the perception of emotion in culturally appropriate responses (both production and perception) commencing around this age, which reach their full potential around the age of 7 or 8 years (see further Trehub & Degé, Chapter 2).

Gardner (1973; Gardner & Perkins, 1989) asserts that infants have developed enough knowledge and maturation to be able to start manipulating symbols by reading and writing from the age of 3 years. For example, children around the age of 3 can describe music in terms of simplified musical features such as loud, fast, and so on as part of a "pre-conventional" stage of creative development, whereas by the age of 7 they are more likely to use descriptive adjectives (conventional stage) (Gardner & Perkins, 1989; Gardner, Phelps, & Wolf, 1990).

One of the most fascinating changes in children's perception of emotion in music in Western culture from the ages of 3 to 7 is the gradual development of the major–*happy*, minor–*sad* connection. The literature suggests that infants are able to perceive happiness in music (Gentile, 1998; Nawrot, 2003). However, up to the age of 4, the young child does not appear to use the mode relationship to do so (Kastner & Crowder, 1990). In fact, responses are significantly less accurate in decoding happy and sad emotions from music in comparison to adult responses. The reason appears to be because 4-year-olds' decisions tend to rely too heavily on other musical parameters such as tempo, rather than mode (major/minor) (Crowder, Renznick, & Rosenkrantz, 1991; Dalla Bella et al., 2001). With a few exceptions (Dolgin & Adelson, 1990), the literature suggests that the major–*happy*, minor–*sad* relationship is only beginning to be made at 4 years of age, even though it has become firmly established by the age of 7 or 8 (Dalla Bella et al., 2001; Gerardi & Gerken, 1995; Kratus, 1993; Trunk, 1981).

Research on nursery songs confirms the weak link between emotional message and musical mode. The vast majority of nursery songs in Western literature are in a major key, even those with negative or sad stories such as *Who Killed Cock Robin* and *Humpty Dumpty* (Gregory, Worrall, & Sarge, 1996). And of those common nursery songs in a minor key, several have a happy message, such as *Old King Cole Was a Merry Old Soul*. This suggests that very young children will not be able to use mode to decipher sad/happy emotions because the generational/evolutionary process has not put pressure on streamlining nursery songs into major–*happy* and minor–*sad* categories. In other words, children's insensitivity to mode means that there is little pressure to produce songs with the major–happy, minor–sad relationship. The lack of a clear relationship between mode and meaning in nursery songs also suggests a possible delay in the learning of an association between emotion and mode (Gregory et al., 1996), such that over the next five years, the child learns to associate major and minor key with happiness and sadness, respectively.

It is important to keep in mind that this refers to the child's limited use of musical features to decode culturally encoded emotional meaning from music (that is, with respect to adult responses) and does not mean that the child's emotional response is trivial, because although they may not be as sophisticated as adults in analyzing harmony, they may well have the same emotional reactions. This is why Kastner and Crowder (1990) speculate that the effect of age may result from children's "enhanced ability to perceive emotional connotations of the major and minor modes" or "from effects of learning superimposed on whatever tendency was present at three years of age" (p. 197). Yet another possibility is that older children are more capable of understanding the types of tasks being used in studies and therefore focusing their attention on it (Kastner & Crowder, 1990).

Even though this evidence does not "resolve the learned-versus-intrinsic controversy" (Kastner & Crowder, 1990, p. 200), evidence from other studies (e.g. Dalla Bella et al., 2001; Gregory et al., 1996) seems to point toward a dominant contribution of a veridical processing style in the mode–emotion connection, such that repeated exposure to positive–major, negative–minor exemplars help develop increasingly stronger associations over the period from 3 to 7 years of age.

Several other factors also emerge between the ages of 3 and 7. Children commence the period being better at recognizing emotion in the human voice but by the end of the period can achieve consistent interpretation of emotion in melodies presented on musical instruments (Dolgin & Adelson, 1990). While they can judge emotions of happiness and sadness in music before the age of 3, some research demonstrates that fear and anger are more easily confused. Music expressing anger can be interpreted as being angry or fearful throughout this age bracket and beyond, in the same way that adults have difficulty deciphering these two emotions (Robazza, Macaluso, & Durso, 1994; Terwogt & van Grinsven, 1991; Trunk, 1981).

Recent evidence also addresses how emotion categories become more refined with age, as already discussed (Perception of Emotion in General: Birth to Late Childhood). Consistent with previous research, Stachó et al. (2013) demonstrated that 3–7-year-olds could differentiate happy and sad music at adult levels but also demonstrated a weakness in the young participants' ability to differentiate among negative emotions, confusing, for example, adult-judged fear-expressing-music with sadness. Adults are able to make more refined distinctions in emotion categories, and the confusions for younger participants are generally linked to emotions that are similar along valence dimensions (such as anger and fear) and arousal (such as anger and happiness), as suggested by Widen and Russell (2008).

The infant–child literature helps to crystallize, and to some extent substantiate, Meyer's view about the cultural context required for learning major–*happy* minor–*sad* relationships. This evidence suggests that during infancy, absolutist (schematic) processes are at work in determining the emotional content of musical and auditory signals. We therefore speculate that this could be the period when children begin to develop emotional responses when schematic expectations are disrupted (Meyer, 1956; Table 12.1, row 6). For example, we would predict that in this age range children would "get" musical jokes that consist of disruptions of expectations (Huron, 2004). We therefore speculate that loudness, tempo, and pitch may be connected with emotion in a schematic, possibly hard-wired (innate) way. By the same token, the infant is slowly developing new ways of connecting emotional information through exposure to and participation in cultural norms, such that by the age of 7 years we see the major–*happy* minor–*sad* connotations of Western culture becoming firmly established. This age corresponds to a shift to the Piagetian concrete operational stage, where cognitive processing starts to resemble that of adults. The end of this stage is signified by several music cognition landmarks, such as the ability to sing with a sense of tonal stability and reduced reliance on contour mapping for the storage of melodic information (Hargreaves & Zimmerman, 1992). In Gardner's (1973) view, 7-year-old children display all the characteristics necessary to actively participate in the artistic process and are therefore ready to perceive emotion in music in a manner not unlike adults, because the essential cultural connections between emotions and music can and have been made and are layered on top of those established from birth (see also Hargreaves, 1996).

8 to 12 years

Emotional perception of happy from major mode and sadness from minor mode is firmly established by the age of 8. In fact, in parallel to their vocabulary and emotional empathy at this age, children have acquired a significant collection of musical experiences and connections that are so thoroughly absorbed that the emotional identification of music becomes apparently natural, automated, and increasingly consistent with adult responses.

Our view is that schematic processing also comes from the openness children show to different styles between the ages of 6 and 9 (Hargreaves & North, 1999; Kopiez & Lehmann, 2008), and at the same time, their ability to detect correctly different musical and other artistic styles (Hasenfus, Martindale, & Birnbaum, 1983; Silverman et al., 1975; Walk et al., 1971). At these ages, many children have built up a sizeable repertoire of musical examples and styles, without showing a strong bias toward, or rejection of, any particular style. This suggests an absolutist value in music, because referentialism (veridical connection) is closely connected with specific exemplars of emotion–music connections. In contrast, this phase of openness suggests that many different styles of music can be valued intrinsically. The veridical connections built up between 3 and 7 years become highly internalized and generalized to many kinds of music and may well be fully integrated with the schematic connections made during infancy.

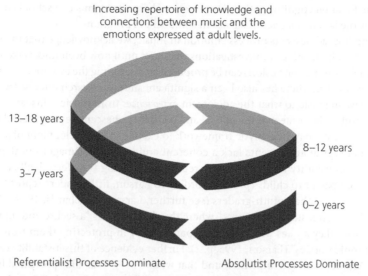

Increasing repertoire of knowledge and connections between music and the emotions expressed at adult levels.

13–18 years

8–12 years

3–7 years

0–2 years

Referentialist Processes Dominate   Absolutist Processes Dominate

Fig. 12.2 Spiral model of developmental of emotion perception in music

The model shows the dominating process of acquiring the ability to perceive emotion in music from birth to the end of adolescence. From birth the dominant method is through schematic connections (on the right-hand side of the diagram), but from the age of 3 veridical connections are favored between emotions and music (that is, through the absorption of cultural norms as shown on the left-hand side of the diagram). The dominant processing style swings back round toward schematic processes but builds on what has been previously learnt (hence the spiral) from the age of 7 until the beginning of adolescence, and so forth. The model does not claim one process is in force at the exclusion of the other, only which one appears to be dominant at different ages, as assessed from the current literature.

All of this helps us bring into focus a picture of the development of emotional perception of music from birth to the end of childhood. At birth, the principle processing style of emotion in music is schematic. As shown in Figure 12.2, this then spirals into a layer where veridical association is the dominant processing style, and the spiral comes full circle back to schematic association up until the age of about 12. The spiral nature of the proposed model accounts for the cumulation of musical–emotional information at each of these three stages and reminds us that emotional connections to music occur over a long period, are cumulative, and build on elements that are both schematic and veridical, without any necessary exclusion of one form of meaning acquisition from the other. With this in mind, we now examine the literature for evidence of any further transitions from late childhood to adolescence.

Adolescence (13–18 years)

There exist numerous theories of why music is important during adolescence (see Hargreaves, North, & Tarrant, Chapter 16), and while the predominant explanations stem from social psychological research, the connection between emotion and music is an inextricable element in the relationship between teenage development and music. North, Hargreaves, and O'Neill (2000) identify the reasons for the importance of music to adolescents as being to "portray an 'image' to the outside world and . . . satisfy their emotional needs" (p. 255). Even when emotion is not specified as an explicit reason, the connections between emotion and enjoyment (Schubert, 1996), and emotions associated with social settings such as positive emotions experienced as part of a feeling of belonging, and negative from rejection, are undeniable and essential. In fact, Behne (1997) even argues that the focus on cognitive rather than emotional aspects of music in school curricula may be a reason for the lack of success music has in some school programs.

In examining how adolescents process emotion in music, we acknowledge that the literature is seriously restricted in the kinds of investigations that have until now been undertaken (Miranda, 2013). Nevertheless, some conclusions can be proposed by examining the evidence that is available. As shall become evident, there has also been a significant shift in research interest from what the child can *perceive* in music to what the adolescent *experiences* from music. This latter dimension is best understood in the context of the critical and complex pubescent developmental processes.

Larson (1995) used a psychoanalytic framework to examine the development of self-concept. He suggests that typical adolescents lack a coherent and integrated imagery of themselves, at "a time when responsibility for emotion self-regulation is being transferred, albeit sometimes precariously, from parent to child" (p. 2). According to Larson, fifth-graders report being happy much more of the time than ninth-graders (see further, Larson & Richards, 1989). This earlier age is a period of "naïve, stable happiness," where the child still has "a secure and unquestioning acceptance of who they are, as well as the role parents play in protecting them from emotional threats and chronic worries" (Larson, 1995, p. 2). Further evidence of this instability can be found in a study by Mulder et al. (2010), who found that when 12–17-year-olds presented lists of their favorite artists, there was agreement (overlap) less frequently (21% of cases) than for lists of favorite artists of older age group participants (36% for 18–22-year-olds and 39% for 23–29-year-olds).

During adolescence popular music listening increases substantially, while TV watching decreases (Larson, 1995; Roberts & Foehr, 2008). The reason for this is connected with the need for developing autonomy, identity, love, and sexuality (see Marcia et al., 1993). Music listening provides adolescents with the opportunity to discover things about themselves without the guidance and interaction of parents in the family lounge-room and serves as a tool for managing their emotions (Christenson & Roberts, 1998). In contrast, TV watching time is correlated with time spent with parents (regardless of whether the TV is on or off), although TV watching does allow adolescents to be in the presence of parents without having to make conversation (Larson, 1995). It should be noted, too, that television and other screen-viewing devices (computers, iPads, tablets, etc.) can aid in facilitating further social separation from caregivers when they are highly portable or located in the adolescent's bedroom. But even so, music listening time continues to increase during this period of development (Roberts & Foehr, 2008). Furthermore, personal, portable sound devices such as iPods allow complete immersion into music through headphones, providing the adolescent with great flexibility in choosing whom they socially engage with (e.g. sharing songs) (Herbert, 2012). Thus, the portable sounds system is another way that music is used as a marker for personal space, such that the adolescent clearly shifts toward matters critically connected with their emotional and personal development (Krause & Hargreaves, 2012). New songs shared by friends, or discovered in the privacy of the bedroom to manage mood, are all forming new mental connections between music, mood, and situations (Schubert, Hargreaves, & North, 2014).

In analyzing his psychologically disturbed patients, Wooten (1992) reports a referentialist link when asserting that the "connection between drug use and heavy metal music may substantiate the concerns that teenagers are over-identifying with this music and its musicians" (p. 96). From this perspective the emotional connections made with the musicians are significant, and the music may act simply as a veridical reference to the image of the performer. In Western culture the idea of "over-identifying" is characterized by the increasing tendency to idolize an individual, such as a sporting champion, movie celebrity, or rock star. This behavior peaks in early adolescence (from 10–11 years of age) and is decreasing by the ages of 16–17 years (Raviv et al., 1996). Idolization reflects a strong emotional connection made by the adolescent with the individual being idolized. While the music of the idolized rock star is a prime example of a veridical connection between the emotions associated with that individual, any piece of music can be connected with any idol. Further, having such strong connections with a piece of music can support an individual in being able to identify with peers of a sub-culture (Willis, 1978).

One of the few studies to specifically examine emotional responses to music from a music-perception perspective was reported by Watson in 1942. He tested emotional responses of children from the sixth-grade level (age of 11 or 12) through to adulthood (in two-year intervals) and music experts, using an adjective checklist response format (instead of basic emotions used in most childhood studies) in which subjects were asked to rate the music they heard. Watson reports a consistent growth in ability to discriminate between musical meanings from sixth-grade through to college levels. If adolescents are responding to emotion in music at adult levels, there should be no change in emotion from the age of 12 through to adulthood. The Watson study therefore suggests that there still are some changes, and this supports the view that emotional connections with music are still being fine-tuned, despite the implication of more recent research which suggests that by this age, emotion in music is perceived essentially at the same level as adults. Additional evidence of how perception of emotion in music develops through adolescence comes from studies where a test group, such as a group of adolescents with autism spectrum disorder, is compared with a typically developing group of adolescents (e.g. Quintin et al., 2011).

The evidence from the literature on adolescents points to a dominance of veridical association between emotion and music. In a study of associations with rap music made by African American children, Hall (1998) demonstrated a shift from a general understanding of rap music toward a better understanding of the specific message of particular songs. Thus, by the age of 12, the ability to extract general information about music is superimposed with a new dimension and ability (and perhaps even a need) to form specific, veridical links with music and its meaning. In doing so, adolescents use music for the purpose of identifying with others, in developing their own sense of identity, and in managing their emotions. Connections are being formed between pieces of music and the new, complex emotional changes that the adolescent experiences. So just before the teenage years, individuals start to move once again around the spiral from schematic to an additional level of veridical connectivity between music and emotion, completing the pattern of the way in which veridical and schematic processes fluctuate in dominance from birth to the end of adolescence (Figure 12.2).

Methodological issues

The spiral model shown in Figure 12.2 provides a framework to help explain the data on the development of emotional perception in music. However, readers need to be cognizant of the methodological problems and limitations that, if mitigated, may result in revisions to this model.

A general issue is the lack of specificity regarding the locus (in the listener versus in the music) and structure of emotion. In this chapter we have attempted to limit our attention to the ability of the listener to observe (or perceive) emotion in music, as distinct from experiencing the emotion. However, this restriction was nearly impossible to maintain because (1) some studies are not explicit about whether they refer to the perception or experiencing of emotion, and (2) studies of adolescents are predominantly interested in the experiential aspect of emotion. This is a fairly serious limitation given the complex relationships that exist between the perception versus the experience of emotion in music (Gabrielsson, 2001; Schubert, 2013).

Regarding the issue of structure, many studies make an implicit assumption that emotions are categorical, simply because of the focus on forced choice responses from a subset of basic emotions (such as happy and sad). Quite often, a dimensional perspective of emotion can identify some of the problems of categorical responses that may otherwise be overlooked. The dimensional model of emotion refers to a collection of more-or-less independent continua, such as positive to negative valence, excited to sleepy, dominant to submissive (Plutchik, 1962). For example, in the infant research "looking-time" paradigm, a "happy" and a "sad" video are used to determine the infants association with a piece of music. If infants look at the allegedly happy video, then we might conclude that they are associating the music with happiness (Nawrot, 2003). However, the happy video may contain a higher degree of activity than the sad video, and indeed it might be that the infant is responding to this activity dimension rather than (or in addition to) the valence dimension (see Widen & Russell, 2008, p. 351). The fact that in Nawrot's (2003) study most of the infants' time was spent looking at the happy video (regardless of the musical stimulus) suggests that the happiness and/or the *activity* in the video was more interesting to them than the sad/ low-activity video. Despite some problems with the dimensional approach in its simplest forms (Schimmack, 2002; Schimmack et al., 2002), this technique nevertheless provides a useful perspective in dealing with the structure of emotion (Eerola & Vuoskoski, 2011; Widen & Russell, 2008) and has been adopted by McManis et al. (2001) for ratings of pictures by children. In the present case, the dimensional paradigm of emotion provides researchers with a tool for matching the amount of activity in the two videos to try to eliminate the possibility of this dimension skewing or confabulating the results.

In the child research literature, the frequent absence of the dimensional paradigm of emotional structure also appears to be responsible for some methodological problems. In studies with children, researchers are able to use language to measure response. However, since linguistic skills are developing over this time, and particularly in early childhood, the limitations of language need to be overcome (for further information see Durbin, 2010; Rodriguez, 2001). The use of facial expressions is an important tool in dealing with the problem of limited language. The use of faces simplifies the task for the child, who is instructed to point at the face that corresponds to the emotion the music is conveying (and in some studies to also verbalize his or her answer). However, these studies have not always been able to demonstrate an isomorphic relationship between a facial expression and its corresponding verbal labels. For example, Kastner and Crowder (1990) used four schematic faces for testing 3- to 12-year-olds. Of the four facial expressions with intended emotions—happiness, contentment, sadness, and anger—the contented face was described as "plain" by many participants. In one of the largest (N = 658) studies of children's emotional responses to music, Kratus (1993) used schematic drawings of facial expressions and is one of the few researchers (Giomo, 1993, is another) who has applied information about the dimensional structure of emotion, thus ensuring that the facial expressions chosen optimize the range of emotions along the valence (positive–negative) and arousal (active–sleepy) dimensions. However, the face Kratus used for excited seems to have a strong negative valence component (fear) due to the eyebrow position. This may have skewed poles to negative–calm, rather than the intended excited–calm. It has also been demonstrated that "excited" actually contains some positive valence (Russell, 1980), contrary to the Kratus sketch. An additional, though related problem, is that if all emotions are developed by childhood, including sophisticated strategies for interpreting social situations by children as young as 8, then we need to be moving beyond the identification of two or four emotions during this time. For example, Stachó et al. (2013) provided five emotion faces to be used as a response interface (representing emotions of sadness, happiness, fear, anger, and neutral) to conclude that it is still happiness and sadness that produce the most reliable, adult-level emotional responses by 3–7-year-olds. This is consistent with the general developmental views of emotion which assert that emotion categories are less refined in younger listeners. Finally, no research has measured children's emotional responses to music continuously. While continuous response measurement, where children move a dial or mouse connected to a computer, is in its infancy (Schubert, 2001, 2010; Schubert et al., 2013), important questions about differences in adult versus child response patterns remain to be addressed.

A recent instrument developed by Schubert et al. (2013) has been designed to find a compromise between the growing interest in dimensional approaches and the commonly used categorical emotions in research using children. The technique is able to collect data from a wide age range of participants because it exploits the categorical perception of emotion found in the research on children's emotional response to music, as reported earlier. The interface uses categorical emotional expressions of line-drawn faces which the participant can select while the music unfolds. So far, this emotion-face clock has been piloted on adults, with results from younger participants under way.

In the adolescent research the focus is usually on social and psychological development, meaning that we have insufficient data on their perception of emotion in music. An exception is the Watson (1942) study, already discussed, which suggests that the development of emotional perception is not as complete and adult-like as the late childhood literature might suggest. So it is hard to tell whether there really is a veridical processing style dominating during adolescence or that researchers (apart from Watson) have simply not investigated schematic connections, which may be equally present. That is, conscious attributions of why young people identify with music is not necessarily causal. For example, we know very little about whether a preference response to a piece of popular music is due to identification with the performer in the video clip or due to the structure and qualities of the song, because the conscious attribution reported by the participant is probably filtered by the need to vindicate a badge or group membership (Zillman & Gan, 1997). Zillman and Mundorf (1987) report, for example, that increasing the amount of sexual and violent content in a video clip increases the musical enjoyment, which suggests a schematic, conscious *attribution* when in fact only a veridical alteration was made. An important research question, therefore, is to determine the way in which adolescents perceive emotion in music because evidence is still required to confirm or reject a weakly supported veridical explanation.

Summary and conclusions

Our view of the development of the perception of emotion in music from infancy to adolescence commences with infants who have a developed auditory perception system that is highly attuned to detecting emotion information from lullabies and nursery songs and prosodic information from their mother. They are able to detect basic emotions such as happiness in music, though the cues they use for doing so are not yet the same as for adults. Since this auditory system is probably present at birth, the dominant process for connecting emotional meaning to music or musical information is schematic (that is, more or less, innate). Veridical (one-to-one) connections between emotion and music only appear to become dominant from the age of around 3 years and continue to dominate until the age of around 7. Over this time, cultural associations such as the Western major–*happy* and minor–*sad* are developed and fully internalized.

From the age of 8, culturally determined musical styles and rules are so firmly established that connections between emotion perception and music are once again dominated by a schematic process. Children are able to identify numerous styles of music but are also open to them, suggesting that they can find meaning within the various styles and structures. This period lasts until about the age of 11 or 12, at which time a new layer of veridical connections is made.

As the child moves to adolescence, music can become the most profoundly important non-human stimulation they can receive, providing meaning that appears not so much to be tied to the intrinsic value of the music but to the way they use the music to develop their sense of identity and social bonding. The value of music for these individuals is strongly connected with factors outside the music itself. While the veridical process may not be exclusive in this period, it does appear to be dominant. We speculate that as the individual moves out of adolescence, both veridical and schematic processes have an equal footing. The young adult has developed such a long and rich set of experiences that they will be primed to extract intrinsic musical meaning but at the same time continue to form strong associative connections between music and other stimuli, situations, and emotions (Davies, 1978). The model shown in Figure 12.2 therefore depicts a development that involves layers of associative and intrinsic connections.

One of the implications of the theoretical framework is that we should not be concerned about valuing one process over another. Schematic and veridical processes are important and different ways of building up knowledge about music and emotion in a given culture. Apart from innate connections between auditory and emotional information, all truly new musical experiences are necessarily veridically connected, and with time these connections may merge into schematic representations as the associations become thoroughly absorbed and assimilated. Our model also suggests that from early childhood both veridical and schematic processing styles are in place, and so while there may be some value in exposing the child to music which is familiar and comfortable, they should also be challenged and exposed to new musical styles and stimuli to ensure that they can maximize their next period of openness and renewed schematic meaning. This is of critical importance because this window of openness may close in the adolescent stage, where individuals tend to become restricted in the way they regulate their musical exposure. For some adolescents this may be a period of restriction that opens up again during early adulthood. Our conclusion for understanding musical development is, therefore, that early childhood up to adolescence can be regarded as the most critical time during which individuals should have many, varied, and positive musical experiences.

Despite all of this, we have not been able to conclude whether changes are dependent on age or stage. That is, there is no clear evidence that the developmental landmarks of being able to recognize sadness in music, for example, is a process of maturation which occurs at a certain age or whether the recognition can be delayed or fast tracked. Some research suggests that the latter, more fluid, developmental stages are more likely to be the case (Gembris & Davidson, 2002). If this is true, then there is a degree of fluidity in that it may be possible for our spiral to be compressed or expanded. Future research should therefore seek to clarify whether the order of schematic and veridical dominance alterations occurs in a rigid way.

Author note

This chapter was written with support from an Australian Research Council (ARC) Discovery Project held by both authors (DP1094998), and earlier work was supported by an ARC Discovery Project (DP0452290) held by the first author.

Reflective questions

1 The lack of success of some school programs has been explained by too much focus on formal rather than emotional aspects of music in school curricula. Using information gleaned from this chapter, what might a music educator do to cater for the emotional needs of learners during each stage of childhood?

2 The spiral model provided in this chapter suggests that from early childhood both veridical and schematic processing styles are in place. To what extent, therefore, should music educators devise activities that expose 3- to 7-year-old children to music that is familiar and comfortable versus exposing them to new musical styles and stimuli to ensure they can maximize their next period of openness and renewed schematic meaning, particularly before adolescence? How might music educators try to deal with or accommodate the adolescent stage where individuals tend to become restricted in the way they regulate their musical exposure?

3 In what ways is early childhood up to adolescence the most critical time during which individuals should have many, varied, and positive musical experiences?

4 What are the reasons for our limited understanding of the perception of emotion in music, and what could researchers do to mitigate some of the problems?

5 Discuss the advantages and disadvantage of the spiral model described in the chapter. What does it help us to explain, and why is it important? In what way is the model a simplification of a highly complex process? What might be the advantages of other approaches, such as developmental steps (instead of the smooth transition of the spiral)?

Note

1 We make the connection between schematic connections and absolutisim, but it is worth noting that Meyer actually refers to emotional meaning that is instrinsic to musical structure as *absolute expressionism*. While this may be viewed as a subset of absolutism, the term absolutism is frequently used to mean what Meyer refers to as absolute expressionism (e.g. Trainor & Trehub, 1992b). For a further discussion of this nomenclature, see Hargreaves (1986, p. 8).

Key sources

Hallam, S., Cross, I., & Thaut, M. (2009). *The Oxford handbook of music psychology*. Oxford: Oxford University Press.

Hargreaves, D. J. (1986). *The developmental psychology of music*. Cambridge: Cambridge University Press.

Juslin, P. N., & Sloboda, J. A. (Eds.) (2010). *Handbook of music and emotion: Theory, research, applications*. Oxford: Oxford University Press.

Reference list

Adachi, M., & Trehub, S. E. (1998). Children's expression of emotion in song. *Psychology of Music*, 26(2), 133–53.

Adachi, M., & Trehub, S. E. (2000). Decoding the expressive intentions in children's songs. *Music Perception*, 18(2), 213–24.

Adachi, M., & Trehub, S. E. (2011). Canadian and Japanese preschoolers' creation of happy and sad songs. *Psychomusicology: Music, Mind & Brain*, 21(1), 69–82.

Balconi, M., & Carrera, A. (2007). Emotional representation in facial expression and script: A comparison between normal and autistic children. *Research in Developmental Disabilities*, 28(4), 409–22.

Bee, H. L. (1997). *The developing child* (8th ed.). New York: Longman.

Behne, K. E. (1997). The development of "Musikerleben" in adolescence: How and why young people listen to music. In I. Deliège & J. Sloboda (Eds.), *Perception and cognition of music* (pp. 143–59). East Sussex, UK: Psychology Press.

Bharucha, J. J. (1987). Music cognition and perceptual facilitation: A connectionist framework. *Music Perception*, 5(1), 1–30.

Bharucha, J. J. (1994). Tonality and expectation. In R. Aiello & J. Sloboda (Eds.), *Musical perceptions* (pp. 213–39). Oxford: Oxford University Press.

Boone, R. T., & Cunningham, J. G. (1998). Children's decoding of emotion in expressive body movement: The development of cue attunement. *Developmental Psychology, 34*(5), 1007–16.

Boone, R. T., & Cunningham, J. G. (2001). Children's expression of emotional meaning in music through expressive body movement. *Journal of Nonverbal Behavior, 25*(1), 21–41.

Bower, G. (1981). Mood and memory. *American Psychologist, 36*(2), 129–48.

Camras, L. A. (1992). Expressive development and basic emotions. *Cognition and Emotion, 6*(3–4), 269–83.

Christenson, P. G., & Roberts, D. F. (1998). *It's not only rock & roll: Popular music in the lives of adolescents.* Cresskill, NJ: Hampton.

Cooper, R. P., Abraham, J., Berman, S., & Staska, M. (1997). The development of infants' preference for motherese. *Infant Behavior and Development, 20*(4), 477–88.

Crowder, R., Reznick, J. S., & Rosenkrantz, S. (1991). Perception of the major/minor distinction: V. Preferences among infants. *Bulletin of the Psychonomic Society, 29*(3), 187–8.

Cunningham, J. G., & Sterling, R. S. (1988). Developmental change in the understanding of affective meaning in music. *Motivation & Emotion, 12*(4), 399–413.

Dalla Bella, S., Peretz, I., Rousseau, L., & Gosselin, N. (2001). A developmental study of the affective value of tempo and mode in music. *Cognition, 80*(3), B1–B10.

Davies, J. B. (1978). *The psychology of music.* Stanford, CA: Stanford University Press.

Dezecache, G., Conty, L., Chadwick, M., Philip, L., Soussignan, R., Sperber, D., & Grèzes, J. (2013). Evidence for unintentional emotional contagion beyond dyads. *PloS One, 8*(6), e67371.

Dissanayake, E. (2000). Antecedents of the temporal arts in early mother–infant interaction. In N. L. Wallin, B. Merker, & S. Brown (Eds.), *The origins of music* (pp. 389–410). Cambridge, MA: MIT Press.

Dolgin, K. G., & Adelson, E. H. (1990). Age changes in the ability to interpret affect in sung and instrumentally-presented melodies. *Psychology of Music, 18*(1), 87–98.

Durbin, C. E. (2010). Validity of young children's self-reports of their emotion in response to structured laboratory tasks. *Emotion, 10*(4), 519–35. doi: 10.1037/a0019008.

Eerola, T., & Vuoskoski, J. K. (2011). A comparison of the discrete and dimensional models of emotion in music. *Psychology of Music, 39*(1), 18–49.

Feinman, S. (1982). Social referencing in infancy. *Merrill-Palmer Quarterly, 28*(4), 445–70.

Fernald, A. (1992). Human maternal vocalizations to infants as biologically relevant signals: An evolutionary perspective. In J. H. Barkow, L. Cosmides, & J. Tooby (Eds.), *The adapted mind: Evolutionary psychology and the generation of culture* (pp. 391–428). New York: Oxford University Press.

Fernald, A. (1993). Approval and disapproval—infant responsiveness to vocal affect in familiar and unfamiliar languages. *Child Development, 64*(3), 657–74.

Gabrielsson, A. (2001). Emotion perceived and emotion felt: Same or different? [Special issue]. *Musicae Scientiae,* 123–47.

Gardner, H. (1973). *The arts and human development.* New York: John Wiley.

Gardner, H., & Perkins, D. N. (Eds.). (1989). *Art, mind, and education: Research from project zero.* Urbana, IL: University of Illinois Press.

Gardner, H., Phelps, E., & Wolf, D. P. (1990). The roots of adult creativity in children's symbolic products. In C. N. Alexander & E. J. Langer (Eds.), *Higher stages of human development: Perspectives on adult growth* (pp. 79–96). New York: Oxford University Press.

Gaston, E. T. (1951). Dynamic factors in mood change. *Music Educators Journal, 37*(4), 42–4.

Gembris, H., & Davidson, J. (2002). Environmental influences. In R. Parncutt & G. McPherson (Eds.), *The science and psychology of music performance* (pp. 17–30). Oxford: Oxford University Press.

Gentile, D. (1998). *An ecological approach to the development of perception of emotion in music* (Unpublished doctoral dissertation). University of Minnesota.

Gerardi, G. M., & Gerken, L. (1995). The development of affective responses to modality and melodic contour. *Music Perception, 12*(3), 279–90.

Giomo, C. J. (1993). An experimental study of children's sensitivity to mood in music. *Psychology of Music*, **21**(2), 141–62.

Gregory, A. H., Worrall, L., & Sarge, A. (1996). The development of emotional responses to music in young children. *Motivation & Emotion*, **20**(4), 341–8.

Grossmann, T. (2010). The development of emotion perception in face and voice during infancy. *Restorative Neurology and Neuroscience*, **28**(2), 219–36.

Gurucharri, C., & Selman, R. L. (1982). The development of interpersonal understanding during child-hood, preadolescence, and adolescence: A longitudinal follow-up study. *Child Development*, **53**(4), 924–7.

Hall, P. D. (1998). The relationship between types of rap music and memory in African American children. *Journal of Black Studies*, **28**(6), 802–14.

Hargreaves, D. J. (1986). *The developmental psychology of music*. Cambridge: Cambridge University Press.

Hargreaves, D. J. (1996). The development of artistic and musical competence. In I. Deliege & J. Sloboda (Eds.), *Musical beginnings: Origins and development of musical competence* (pp. 145–70). Oxford: Oxford University Press.

Hargreaves, D. J., & North, A. C. (1999). Developing concepts of musical style. *Musicae Scientiae*, **3**(2), 193–216.

Hargreaves, D. J., & Zimmerman, M. P. (1992). Developmental theories of music learning. In R. Colwell (Ed.), *Handbook of research on music teaching and learning* (pp. 377–91). New York: Schirmer.

Hasenfus, N., Martindale, C., & Birnbaum, D. (1983). Psychological reality of cross-media artistic styles. *Journal of Experimental Psychology: Human Perception & Performance*, **9**(6), 841–63.

Hatfield, E., Rapson, R. L., & Le, Y.-C. L. (2009). Emotional contagion and empathy. In J. Decety & W. Ickes (Eds.), *The social neuroscience of empathy* (pp. 19–30). Cambridge, MA: MIT Press.

Herbert, R. (2012). *Young people's use and subjective experience of music outside school*. Proceedings of the 12th International Conference on Music Perception and Cognition (ICMPC) Thessaloniki, Greece: Aristotle University, July 23–28, 2012.

Huron, D. (2004). *Music-engendered laughter: An analysis of humor devices in PDQ Bach*. Proceedings of the 8th International Conference on Music Perception and Cognition. Evanston, IL.

Izard, C. E. (2010). The many meanings/aspects of emotion: Definitions, functions, activation, and regula-tion. *Emotion Review*, **2**(4), 363–70.

Izard, C. E., Ackerman, B. P., Schoff, K. M., & Fine, S. E. (2000). Self-organization of discrete emotions, emotion patterns, and emotion–cognition relations. In M. D. Lewis & I. Granic (Eds.), *Emotion, devel-opment, and self-organization: Dynamic systems approaches to emotional development* (pp. 15–36). New York: Cambridge University Press.

Izard, C. E., Fantauzzo, C. A., Castle, J. M., Haynes, O., Rayias, M., & Putnam, P. (1995). The ontogeny and significance of infants' facial expressions in the first 9 months of life. *Developmental Psychology*, **31**(6), 997–1013.

Izard, C. E., Kagan, J., & Zajonc, R. B. (1984). Introduction. In C. E. Izard, J. Kagan, & R. B. Zajonc (Eds.), *Emotions, cognition, and behavior* (pp. 1–14). Cambridge: Cambridge University Press.

Juslin, P. N., & Västfjäll, D. (2008). Emotional responses to music: The need to consider underlying mech-anisms. *Behavioral and Brain Sciences*, **31**(5), 559–75.

Kastner, M. P., & Crowder, R. G. (1990). Perception of the major/minor distinction: IV. Emotional conno-tations in young children. *Music Perception*, **8**(2), 189–201.

Kitamura, C., & Burnham, D. (1998). The infant's response to vocal affect in maternal speech. In C. Rovee-Collier & L. Lipsitt (Eds.), *Advances in infancy research* (pp. 221–36). Norwood, NJ: Ablex.

Kopiez, R., & Lehmann, M. (2008). The "open-earedness" hypothesis and the development of age-related aesthetic reactions to music in elementary school children. *British Journal of Music Education*, **25**(2), 121–38.

Kratus, J. (1993). A developmental study of children's interpretation of emotion in music. *Psychology of Music*, **21**(1), 3–19.

Krause, A. E., & Hargreaves, D. J. (2012). myTunes: Digital music library users and their self-images. *Psychology of Music*, **41**(5), 531–44. doi: 10.1177/0305735612440612.

Kuhl, P. K., & Meltzoff, A. N. (1996). Infant vocalizations in response to speech: Vocal imitation and developmental change. *The Journal of the Acoustical Society of America*, **100**(4 0 1), 2425–38.

Lagattuta, K. H., Wellman, H. M., & Flavell, J. H. (1997). Preschoolers' understanding of the link between thinking and feeling: Cognitive cuing and emotional change. *Child Development*, **68**(6), 1081–104.

Lang, P. J. (1979). A bio-informational theory of emotional imagery. *Psychophysiology*, **16**(6), 496–512.

Larson, R. (1995). Secrets in the bedroom: Adolescents' private use of media. *Journal of Youth and Adolescence*, **24**(5), 535–50.

Larson, R. W., & Richards, M. H. (Eds.) (1989). The changing life space of early adolescence [Special Issue]. *Journal of Youth and Adolescence*, **18**(6), 501–626.

Levi, D. S. (1978). Expressive qualities in music perception and music education. *Journal of Research in Music Education*, **26**(3), 425–35.

Levine, L. J. (1995). Young children's understanding of the causes of anger and sadness. *Child Development*, **66**(3), 697–709.

Lewis, M. (2000). The emergence of human emotions. In M. Lewis & J. M. Haviland-Jones (Eds.), *Handbook of emotions* (pp. 265–80). New York: Guilford Press.

Malatesta, C. Z., Culver, C., Tesman, J. R., & Shepard, B. (1989). The development of emotion expression during the first two years of life. *Monographs of the Society for Research in Child Development*, **54**(1–2), 1–104.

Malloch, S. (1999/2000). Mothers and infants and communicative musicality. *Musicae Scientiae* (Special issue on rhythm, musical narrative, and origins of human communication), 29–57.

Malloch, S., Shoemark, H., Črnčec, R., Newnham, C., Paul, C., Prior, M., Coward, S., Burnham, D. (2012). Music therapy with hospitalized infants—the art and science of communicative musicality. *Infant Mental Health Journal*, **33**(4), 386–99.

Mandler, G. (1984). *Mind and body*. New York: Norton.

Mandler, G. (1990). A constructivist theory of emotion. In N. S. Stein, B. L. Leventhal, & T. Trabasso (Eds.), *Psychological and biological approaches to emotion* (pp. 21–34). Hillsdale, NJ: Lawrence Erlbaum.

Marcia, J. E., Waterman, A. S., Matteson, D. R., Archer, S. L. & Orlofsky, J. L. (Eds.) (1993). *Ego identity: A handbook for psychosocial research*. New York: Springer-Verlag.

Masterson, E. A., & Crawford, M. (1982). The defense motivation system: A theory of avoidance behavior. *The Behavioral and Brain Sciences*, **5**(4), 661–96.

McManis, M. H., Bradley, M. M., Berg, W. K., Cuthbert, B. N., & Lang, P. J. (2001). Emotional reactions in children: Verbal, physiological, and behavioral responses to affective pictures. *Psychophysiology*, **38**(2), 222–31.

Meltzoff, A. N., & Moore, M. K. (1977). Imitation of facial and manual gestures by human neonates. *Science*, **198**(4312), 75–8.

Meyer, L. B. (1956). *Emotion and meaning in music*. Chicago: University of Chicago Press.

Miranda, D. (2013). The role of music in adolescent development: Much more than the same old song. *International Journal of Adolescence and Youth*, **18**(1), 5–22.

Morton, J., & Trehub, S. E. (2001). Children's understanding of emotion in speech. *Child Development*, **72**(3), 834–43.

Mulder, J., Ter Bogt, T. F., Raaijmakers, Q. A., Gabhainn, S. N., & Sikkema, P. (2010). From death metal to R&B? Consistency of music preferences among Dutch adolescents and young adults. *Psychology of Music*, **38**(1), 67–83.

Nadel, L., & Butterworth, G. (Eds.) (1999). Immediate imitation rehabilitated at last. In L. Nadel & G. Butterworth (Eds.), *Imitation in infancy* (pp. 1–5). New York: Cambridge University Press.

Nawrot, E. S. (2003). The perception of emotional expression in music: Evidence from infants, children and adults. *Psychology of Music*, **31**(1), 75–92.

Niedenthal, P. M., & Brauer, M. (2012). Social functionality of human emotion. *Annual Review of Psychology*, **63**(1), 259–85.

Nieminen, S., Istók, E., Brattico, E., & Tervaniemi, M. (2012). The development of the aesthetic experience of music: Preference, emotions, and beauty. *Musicae Scientiae*, **16**(3), 372–91.

Nieminen, S., Istók, E., Brattico, E., Tervaniemi, M., & Huotilainen, M. (2011). The development of aesthetic responses to music and their underlying neural and psychological mechanisms. *Cortex*, **47**(9), 1138–46.

North, A. C., Hargreaves, D. J., & O'Neill, S. A. (2000). The importance of music to adolescents. *British Journal of Educational Psychology*, **70**(2), 255–72.

Oatley, K., & Jenkins, J. M. (1996). *Understanding emotions*. Oxford, UK: Blackwell.

Parsons, M. J. (1976). A suggestion concerning the development of aesthetic experience in children. *The Journal of Aesthetics and Art Criticism*, **34**(3), 305–14.

Perani, D., Saccuman, M. C., Scifo, P., Spada, D., Andreolli, G., Rovelli, R., Baldoli, C., Koelsch, S. (2010). Functional specializations for music processing in the human newborn brain. *Proceedings of the National Academy of Sciences*, **107**(10), 4758–63.

Plutchik, R. (1962). *The emotions: Facts, theories and a new model*. New York: Random House.

Preston, S. D., & De Waal, F. (2002). Empathy: Its ultimate and proximate bases. *Behavioral and Brain Sciences*, **25**(01), 1–20.

Preti, C., & Welch, G. F. (2004). Music in a hospital setting: A multifaceted experience. *British Journal of Music Education*, **21**(3), 329–45.

Preti, C., & Welch, G. F. (2011). Music in a hospital: The impact of a live music program on pediatric patients and their caregivers. *Music and Medicine*, **3**(4), 213–23.

Quintin, E.-M., Bhatara, A., Poissant, H., Fombonne, E., & Levitin, D. J. (2011). Emotion perception in music in high-functioning adolescents with autism spectrum disorders. *Journal of Autism and Developmental Disorders*, **41**(9), 1240–55.

Raviv, A., Bar-Tal, D., Raviv, A., & Ben-Horin, A. (1996). Adolescent idolization of pop singers: Causes, expressions, and reliance. *Journal of Youth and Adolescence*, **25**(5), 631–50.

Robazza C., Macaluso C., & Durso V. (1994). Emotional-reactions to music by gender, age, and expertise. *Perceptual and Motor Skills*, **79**(2), 939–44.

Roberts, D. F., and Foehr, U. G. (2008). Trends in media use. *The Future of Children*, **18**(1), 11–37.

Rodriguez, C. X. (2001). Issues in the use of verbal data to assess children's affective responses to music. *Research Studies in Music Education*, **16**(1), 57–65.

Rohrmeier, M. A., & Koelsch, S. (2012). Predictive information processing in music cognition. A critical review. *International Journal of Psychophysiology*, **83**(2), 164–75.

Rolls, E. T. (2002). A theory of emotion, its functions and its adaptive value. In R. Trappl, P. Petta, & S. Payr (Eds.), *Emotions in humans and artifacts* (pp. 11–34). Cambridge, MA: MIT Press.

Russell, J. A. (1980). A circumplex model of affect. *Journal of Social Psychology*, **39**, 1161–78.

Russell, J. A. (1997). How shall an emotion be called? In R. Plutchik & H. R. Conte (Eds.), *Circumplex models of personality and emotions* (pp. 205–20). Washington, DC: American Psychological Association.

Schimmack, U. (2002). Experiencing activation: Energetic arousal and tense arousal are not mixtures of valence and activation. *Emotion*, **2**(4), 412–17.

Schimmack, U., Oishi, S., & Diener, E. (2002). Cultural influences on the relation between pleasant emotions and unpleasant emotions: Asian dialectic philosophies or individualism–collectivism? *Cognition & Emotion*, **16**(6), 705–19.

Schubert, E. (1996). Enjoyment of negative emotions in music: An associative network explanation. *Psychology of Music, 24*(1), 18–28.

Schubert, E. (2001). Continuous measurement of self-report emotional response to music. In P. N. Juslin & J. A. Sloboda (Eds.), *Music and emotion: Theory and research. Series in affective science* (pp. 393–414). Oxford: Oxford University Press.

Schubert, E. (2010). Continuous self-report methods. In P. N. Juslin & J. A. Sloboda (Eds.), *Handbook of music and emotion: Theory, research, applications* (pp. 223–53). Oxford: Oxford University Press.

Schubert, E. (2013). Emotion felt by the listener and expressed by the music: Literature review and theoretical perspectives. *Frontiers in Psychology, 4*, 837. doi: 10.3389/fpsyg.2013.00837.

Schubert, E., Ferguson, S., Farrar, N., Taylor, D., & McPherson, G. E. (2013). The six emotion-face clock as a tool for continuously rating discrete emotional responses to music. In M. Aramaki, M. Barthet, R. Kronland-Martinet, & S. Ystad (Eds.), *From sounds to music and emotions* (Vol. Lecture Notes in Computer Science, pp. 1–18). Berlin, Germany: Springer Berlin Heidelberg.

Schubert, E., Hargreaves, D. J., & North, A. C. (2014). A dynamically minimalist cognitive explanation of musical preference: Is familiarity everything? *Frontiers in Psychology, 5*(38). doi: 10.3389/fpsyg.2014.00038.

Schubert, E., & McPherson, G. E. (2006). The perception of emotion in music. In G. E. McPherson (Ed.), *The child as musician: A handbook of musical development* (pp. 193–212). Oxford: Oxford University Press.

Selman, R. L. (1977). A structural–developmental model of social cognition: Implications for intervention research. *Counseling Psychologist, 6*(4), 3–6.

Shaffer, D. R. (1999). *Developmental psychology: Childhood and adolescence* (5th ed.). Pacific Grove, CA: Brooks/Cole.

Silverman, J., Winner, E., Rosentiel, A. K., & Gardner, H. (1975). On training sensitivity to painting styles. *Perception, 4*(4), 373–84.

Slaney, M., & McRoberts, G. (2003). Baby ears: A recognition system for affective vocalizations. *Speech Communication, 39*(3), 367–84.

Solomon, R. C. (1993). The philosophy of emotions. In M. E. Lewis & J. M. E. Haviland (Eds.), *Handbook of emotions* (pp. 3–15). New York: The Guilford Press.

Stachó, L., Saarikallio, S., Van Zijl, A., Huotilainen, M., & Toiviainen, P. (2013). Perception of emotional content in musical performances by 3–7-year-old children. *Musicae Scientiae, 17*(4), 495–512. doi: 10.1177/1029864913497617.

Striano, T., & Rochat, P. (2000). Emergence of selective social referencing in infancy. *Infancy, 1*(2), 253–64.

Terwogt, M. M., & van Grinsven, F. (1991). Musical expression of moodstates. *Psychology of Music, 19*(2), 99–109.

Trainor, L. J., Clark, E. D., Huntley, A., & Adams, B. A. (1997). The acoustic basis of preferences for infant-directed singing. *Infant Behavior and Development, 20*(3), 383–96.

Trainor, L. J., & Corrigall, K. A. (2010). Music acquisition and effects of musical experience. In M. Riess-Jones & R. R. Fay (Eds.), *Springer handbook of auditory research: Music perception* (Vol. 36, pp. 89–128). Heidelberg: Springer.

Trainor, L. J., & Desjardins, R. N. (2002). Pitch characteristics of infant-directed speech affect infants' ability to discriminate vowels. *Psychonomic Bulletin & Review, 9*(2), 335–40.

Trainor, L. J., & Trehub, S. E. (1992a). A comparison of infants' and adults' sensitivity to Western musical structure. *Journal of Experimental Psychology: Human Perception & Performance, 18*(2), 394–402.

Trainor, L. J., & Trehub, S. E. (1992b). The development of referential meaning in music. *Music Perception, 9*(4), 455–70.

Trehub, S. E. (2001). Musical predispositions in infancy. *Annals of the New York Academy of Sciences, 930*(1), 1–16.

Trehub, S. E. (2009). Music lessons from infants. In S. Hallam, I. Cross, & M. Thaut (Eds.), *The Oxford handbook of music psychology* (pp. 229–34). Oxford: Oxford University Press.

Trehub, S. E., Cohen, A. J., Thorpe, L. A., & Morrongiello, B. A. (1986). Development of the perception of musical relations: Semitone and diatonic structure. *Journal of Experimental Psychology: Human Perception & Performance*, **12**(3), 295–301.

Trehub, S. E., & Nakata, T. (2001). Emotion and music in infancy. *Musicae Scientiae*, **5**(1), 37–61.

Trehub, S. E., & Schellenberg, E. (1995). Music: Its relevance to infants. *Annals of Child Development*, **11**(1), 1–24.

Trehub, S. E., & Trainor, L. (1998). Singing to infants: Lullabies and play songs. In C. Rovee-Collier & L. Lipsitt (Eds.), *Advances in infancy research* (pp. 43–77). Norwood, NJ: Ablex.

Trehub, S. E., Unyk, A. M., & Trainor, L. J. (1993). Adults identify infant-directed music across cultures. *Infant Behavior & Development*, **16**(2), 193–211.

Trunk, B. (1981). *Children's perception of the emotional content of music* (Unpublished doctoral dissertation). The Ohio State University: Columbus.

Vieillard, S., & Guidetti, M. (2009). Children's perception and understanding of (dis)similarities among dynamic bodily/facial expressions of happiness, pleasure, anger, and irritation. *Journal of Experimental Child Psychology*, **102**(1), 78–95.

Volkova, A., Trehub, S. E., Schellenberg, E. G., Papsin, B. C., & Gordon, K. A. (2013). Children with bilateral cochlear implants identify emotion in speech and music. *Cochlear Implants International*, **14**(2), 80–91.

Walk, R. D., Karasaitis, K., Lebowitz, C., & Falbo, T. (1971). Artistic style as concept formation for children and adults. *Merrill-Palmer Quarterly*, **17**(4), 347–56.

Walker-Andrews, A. S., & Dickson, L. R. (1997). Infants' understanding of affect. In S. Hala (Ed.), *The development of social cognition. Studies in developmental psychology* (pp. 161–86). Hove, UK: Psychology Press.

Watson, K. B. (1942). The nature and measurement of musical meanings. *Psychological Monographs*, **54**(2), i–43.

Werker, I. E., & McLeod, P. J. (1989). Infant preference for both male and female infant-directed talk: A developmental study of attentional and affective responsiveness. *Canadian Journal of Psychology*, **43**(2), 230–46.

Widen, S. C., & Russell, J. A. (2008). Young children's understanding of other's emotions. In M. Lewis, J. M. Haviland-Jones, & L. F. Barrett (Eds.), *Handbook of emotions* (pp. 348–63). New York: Guilford Press.

Willis, P. (1978). *Profane culture*. London: Routledge and Kegan Paul.

Wooten, M. A. (1992). The effects of heavy metal music on affects shifts of adolescents in an inpatient psychiatric setting. *Music Therapy Perspectives*, **10**(2), 93–8.

Zajonc, R. B. (1984). On the primacy of affect. *American Psychologist*, **39**(2), 117–23.

Zajonc, R. B. (2000). Feeling and thinking: Closing the debate over the independence of affect. In J. P. Forgas (Ed.), *Feeling and thinking: The role of affect in social cognition* (pp. 31–58). Cambridge: Cambridge University Press.

Zillman, D., & Gan, S. (1997). Musical taste in adolescence. In D. J. Hargreaves & A. C. North (Eds.), *The social psychology of music* (pp. 161–87). Oxford, UK: Oxford University Press.

Zillman, D., & Mundorf, R. (1987). Image effects in the appreciation of video rock. *Communication Research*, **14**(3), 316–34.

Chapter 13

Felt experiences of popular musics

David J. Elliott and Marissa Silverman

Felt experiences of popular musics: Introduction

In what ways do young people's felt experiences of popular musics contribute to their musical development? We consider this question from our perspective as philosophers of music and music education. Our thoughts are based on the large body of research during the last 20 years in many domains related to our topic, including emotion studies, music psychology, embodied–enactive music cognition, affective neuroscience, and music philosophy (Bicknell, 2009; Damasio, 2000; Davies, 1994; Elliott & Silverman, 2012, 2014; Juslin & Västfjäll, 2008; Krueger, 2009; LeDoux, 1996, 2002; Robinson, 2005; Thompson, 2007).

To anticipate major themes of this chapter, we posit that an emotion is a *process* (e.g., Damasio, 2003; Johnson, 2006; LeDoux, 1996, 2002) that arises from multiple external and internal personal–ecological factors. Also, emotions differ from feelings, not only because emotions are public and feelings are personal, but also because feelings usually follow emotions (Damasio, 2000, 2003; Johnson, 2006; Thompson, 2005, 2007).

As a prelude to the theoretical sections of this chapter, we examine concrete, real-world descriptions of the natures and contexts in which two adolescents respond to and discuss their experiences of popular musics. We follow this with concepts of emotion and feeling, and link these concepts to psychological and philosophical explanations of why and how a wide range of musical–social variables can arouse felt musical experiences of popular musics (Davies, 1994; Elliott & Silverman, 2012, 2015; Juslin & Västfjäll, 2008; Krueger, 2009; Schellenberg & von Scheve, 2012). Next, we connect these conceptualizations to a holistic concept of embodied–enactive personhood and cognition (e.g., Johnson, 2006; Krueger, 2009; Noë, 2004, 2009). We utilize this approach because of the possibilities it holds for understanding a) youth as multi-dimensional beings who interact with the ecological circumstances of their worlds, and b) young people's felt experiences of popular musics, which we suggest can contribute to their musical development. Implicit in this approach is our premise that in addition to being a matter of elaborate mental–cognitive musical processes that develop over time (see Schubert & McPherson, Chapter 12), musical–emotional experiences are also *unified* body, brain, mind, conscious, and non-conscious experiences (Elliott & Silverman, 2015; Noë, 2004, 2009; Thompson, 2007) that operate and grow in dynamic relation to all factors of people's environments.

Notably here, the concept of "popular music" is notoriously difficult to unravel because it is an ever-changing, culturally situated, multi-dimensional, and value-laden category term that is challenging to explain succinctly. As Fisher (2011) says: "there is no *one* answer to the question 'What is popular music?' . . . Further complicating the issue is the fact that the categories 'popular' and 'folk' both evolved as ways of referring to 'the people,' although from different perspectives" (pp. 406–7). Bowman (2004) is more specific, and writes that popular musics may exhibit the following tendencies:

> (a) breadth of intended appeal, (b) mass mediation andcommodity character, (c) amateur engagement, (d) continuity with everyday concerns, (e) informality, (f) here-and-now pragmatic use and utility, (g) appeal to embodied experience, and (h) emphasis on process. (pp. 36–7)

Although some scholars tend to interchange the terms popular music(s) and youth music(s), doing so is not completely justified: "popular music is not a commodity or mass music for those who care most about and are most intimately involved with it, nor is it always 'youth' music, nor is it invariably connected to everyday concerns, and so on" (Bowman, 2004, p. 37).

Given this, it is more appropriate to use the term popular musics. Doing so, we follow Nettl (2007) and Cross (2011), who favor the term "musics" over "music" because the former implies a phenomena that is variegated, contingent, always fluid, and irreducible to precise definition. As such we will not circumscribe narrowly the galaxy of popular musics, thereby allowing for wide variations in musical style characteristics. Put another way, when we refer to popular (or pop) musics, we mean it as an open and porous concept, which acknowledges that genres are continuously changing, emerging, and crossing over, depending on the music-makers, listeners, and the various contextual circumstances in which they are made, used, or abused.

Arielle and Ahmed: felt experiences of popular musics

To begin our discussion of popular musics and young people's musical development, consider two narratives provided by our former students, which are taken from a larger study (Elliott & Silverman, in press). These narratives provide a realistic starting point for our journey through the themes of this chapter.

When Arielle[1] was 14 years old, she began to deepen her felt emotional attachment to the musics, lyrics, and contexts of punk rock. Her older sister (who was 18) and her sister's boyfriend (who was 22) invited Arielle to hear a band called Bouncing Souls, which performed at the Highline Ballroom in New York City. Upon hearing "Born Free" at that concert, Arielle "fell in love" with punk rock. To her, no other music expressed her "unique sense of self." Arielle puts it this way:

> I like being me. And it's cool that I found myself in this music. I never was one who did things she was told. And I didn't like "belonging." I am me and I'm proud of it. And I don't care what other people think or say.

Despite Arielle's conviction that punk rock allowed her to be an "individual," she describes how her individuality is closely tied to many other facts, including the people at the concert and specific details of the context in which everyone is participating:

> Imagine it. You are in the mosh pit, and it's so loud that you can't really understand the lyrics. At least I couldn't at my first show. But as I'm swept away by the raw energy of the music and the people standing, jumping, and shouting, I hear something that speaks directly to me and to everyone else, too. The lines: "Peace and love are on the way out/Why can't they just let me be?/How I live is up to me/Don't forget that you're born free." The Bouncing Souls helped me realize that I wasn't the only one who felt the need to be left alone, to be able to be my own person.

Elaborating Arielle's description, it seems fair to suggest that in a specific musical place and space that might *seem* isolated, many people are in fact connected musically and emotionally, and integrated socially, corporeally, and culturally by the combination of numerous musical qualities, lyrics, the "raw energy," the persona of the performers, their voices and instruments, and the emotional bonding of the crowd.

For Arielle, there is something contagious about the emotionality of this music, about feeling completely at peace with her own individuality, yet knowing that there are people "out there" who can "rage *their* way" to show their "true" selves to each other. From that first show onwards, Arielle "became more and more invested in the world of punk rock." When she was asked about her favorite songs, she said:

> Too many to say. But, this is just a taste of my favorites: "Jaded" by Operation Ivy, from *Operation Ivy (Energy)*; "American Jesus" by Bad Religion, from *Recipe for Hate*; "Suburban Home" by Descendants, from *Milo Goes to College*; "Anesthesia" by Paint It Black, from *CVA*; "Regress, No Way" by 7 Seconds, from *Walk Together, Rock Together*; "Call It What You Will" by Larry and His Flask, from *All That We Know*; "Jigsaw Youth" by Bikini Kill, from *Yeah Yeah Yeah Yeah*; "One Day" by Cobra Skulls, from *American Rubicon*; "There's no 'I' in Team" by Good Riddance, from *Bound by Ties of Blood and Affection*. This list is sort of all over the place and is in no way a complete list of the best punk songs ever (because really, that list would never end, ha!). It is also a bit more contemporary, but that's OK.

The second narrative from Ahmed begins with his description of Tupac Shakur, otherwise known as 2Pac, who died in 1996. In the hearts and minds of many urban youth such as Ahmed, 2Pac's records continue to live and "live strong." Ahmed is a 17-year-old in a large urban high school, a straight-"A" student, captain of the swim team, and "looking forward to attending college for political science." When asked about his favorite musics, his eyes light up: "Rap. I love all music . . . but rap, I love it because of what it does for me."

Related to his strong feelings about rap, Ahmed explains that his family is particularly conservative. They moved to the United States from Pakistan to seek "a better life." Yet, says Ahmed, although his mother and father worked exceedingly hard—all day and night—to make sure he and his brother achieved happy and successful futures, he felt something was terribly wrong. After watching his mother faint in front of him from over-work—she worked three jobs, his father worked two—he vowed he would help his family escape their situation by being the first to attend college. One of the strongest motivational factors in his decision was his first encounter with 2Pac's "Changes."

> I was 8 years old when that song came out on his "greatest hits" album. I was immediately "shown the light" by this track. It really spoke to me and continues to speak to me in ways that are undeniable. When I was younger, my brother and I had to take care of ourselves because our parents were always working. We didn't realize there was anything unusual about our circumstances. But when I started listening to rap, especially to 2Pac, he helped me see my world from other perspectives, including differences between right and wrong. And the older I got, the more I realized how very political his messages were.
>
> Right there in "Changes" he [2Pac] says: "I see no changes. All I see is racist faces. Misplaced hate makes disgrace to races we under. I wonder what it takes to make this one better place . . . "
>
> I wondered why my mom and dad had to work so hard and couldn't get anywhere. I wondered why my friends at school were in similar situations. I wondered why there was such inequality in such a rich country. I wondered if there was a way to do something about it. And I was pissed off that there were no answers to my questions. This is what rap music does. It makes you question reality, for good and for bad.

These quotations provide a glimpse of how some young people might interpret, feel, grow, and transform themselves through their interactions with multiple musical–emotional variables, including the intrinsic and extrinsic variables involved in perceiving and responding to pieces, performances, and the contexts in which youth experience popular musics, including the personal and musical personalities of the performers of popular musics, whether or not these experiences occur in situ, or via recordings, YouTube viewings, and so forth. Specifically, several keywords and phrases testify to the positive developmental and transformative moments that accompany felt musical experiences—conceptual, social, and political—that impacted each teenager consciously and non-consciously. Recall Arielle's felt corporeal reactions to and "cognitive monitoring" of the music and lyrics of "Born Free":

> it's cool that I found *myself* in this music . . . I'm swept away by the *raw energy* of the music . . . I hear something that *speaks* directly to me and to everyone else . . . The Bouncing Souls helped me realize that I wasn't the only one who felt the need to be left alone, to be able to be my own person.

Similarly, Ahmed says,

> I was immediately "shown the light" by this track ["Changes"]. It really spoke to me and continues to speak to me in ways that are undeniable. I realized how very *political* his messages were. Right there in "Changes" he [2Pac] says: "I see no changes. All I see is racist faces. Misplaced hate makes disgrace to races we under. I wonder what it takes to make this one better place . . . "

So, now, what human processes underlie and propel these kinds of felt musical experiences?

Emotions and feelings

To explain how musics arouse and express emotions and, concomitantly, why making and listening to popular musics become passionate engagements for youth, we must explain the nature of emotions, the differences between emotions and feelings, and the nature of musical emotions.

As stated at the outset, an emotion is a process. Specifically, an emotion involves i) a non-cognitive appraisal of a situation (Damasio, 2000) that causes ii) physiological responses (e.g., changes in heart rate, skin temperature; Hodges, 2009), iii) brain stem and cortical activation (Blood & Zatorre, 2001; Menon & Levitin, 2005), iv) action tendencies (e.g., a desire to move to musics, or focus intently; Frijda, 2007), v) overt expressions of emotions (e.g., crying, smiling, frowning; Gabrielsson, 2001), vi) subjective feeling (Becker, 2004; Gabrielsson, 2001), vii) self-regulation (using musics to calm, stimulate, or comfort oneself; Becker, 2004; Juslin & Sloboda, 2001), viii) synchronization among all these components, and ix) more discriminating cognitive monitoring of felt emotions and the circumstances triggering the emotional process (Elliott & Silverman, 2015; Juslin et al., 2008).

An emotion is not something that happens to us. Events trigger emotions (LeDoux, 1996, p. 19). An emotion is a process by which the brain instantly, non-consciously, and automatically assesses and responds to the qualities of all types of events and patterns in our environment: sounds, sights, threats, objects, social interactions, personal and cultural artifacts, musical sounds and performances, and so on, ad infinitum (Damasio, 2000, 2003; Johnson, 2006; Juslin & Västfjäll, 2008; LeDoux, 1996, 2002; Schubert & McPherson, Chapter 12). Our embodied–enactive sensory–cognitive systems (for more details, see the following section, Persons and Personhood: Embodied and Enactive) process our environmental and bodily changes and activate the chemical–neural brain systems responsible for emotional processing (e.g., Damasio, 2000, 2003). Emotional responses cause an avalanche of profound changes in our body–brain landscapes (Damasio, 2000); the body–brain "changes quite remarkably over the ensuing hundreds of milliseconds," seconds, and, in some cases, minutes (Damasio, 2000, p. 2).

This brings us to the difference between emotions and feelings. Feelings occur when we become consciously aware of changes in our non-conscious emotional states. A feeling is a conscious perception of an emotional process: "Feelings emerge after all processes of emotional arousal run their course" (Damasio, 2003, p. 88). LeDoux (1996) agrees: "Feelings result when we become consciously aware that an emotion system of the brain is active" (p. 302); "a feeling is the conscious experience of an emotion" (LeDoux, 2002, p. 225). Emotions and sensations underlie and precede feelings. "Feelings are consciously experienced bodily processes" (Johnson, 2007, p. 59). A conscious feeling of (say) fear, joy, or sadness occurs as part of an elaborate chain of responses that we call an emotion.

Emotions and feelings are central to intersubjectivity and intercommunication. Emotions can display themselves outwardly, in public. We read (we see, hear, and interpret) people's emotions in details of their facial expressions, gait, and posture and in the qualities of people's voices. We notice and interpret others' emotions constantly, as we must, because reading others' emotions is crucial to social relationships and developing empathy for others. If someone looks or sounds frightened, angry, or joyful, we assume from outward physical changes that s/he is feeling something (fear, anger, or joy), which allows us to act in our own best interests for others' best interests.

Although learning to interpret others' emotions is a natural part of youth development, paying keen attention to the emotional expressions of others is fundamental to developing young people's musical ability to recognize expressions of emotions in pieces and performances and perform and compose pieces that arouse and express emotions (Davies, 1994; Elliott & Silverman, 2015; Schubert & McPherson, Chapter 12). Developing young people's awareness of emotional expressiveness in everyday life opens pathways for the creation of strategies that enable them to express their developing emotions in narrative or story-telling lyrics that they compose in their own songs. Of course, this does not hold for all young people, including those with autistic spectrum disorders (Heaton, Hermelin, & Pring, 1999).

Becoming more and more aware of the nature of emotions and how music can arouse and express emotions seems central to both young people's social and emotional development, and also their creative musical development and musical–personal engagement.

Psychological perspectives on felt experiences of musics

Depending on a number of variables (e.g., the specific music, the listener, and the situation), a large body of research (Juslin & Laukka, 2004; Juslin et al., 2011; Kreutz et al., 2008; Sloboda, 1992) supports the claim that "music can induce just about any emotion that may be felt in other realms of human life" (Juslin, 2009, p. 133). Huron (2006) agrees: "Listening to music can give rise to an enormous range of emotions" (p. 25). Based on numerous studies, researchers argue that the most prevalent musical–emotional experiences reported by listeners (in laboratory or everyday situations) are happiness, sadness, excitement, calm, nostalgia, love, pleasure, awe, pride, anxiety, and anger, as well as "chills and shivers" (Juslin et al., 2011; Juslin & Västfjäll, 2008).

Related to this, in an analysis of more than one hundred empirical studies of emotional expression in musics, Juslin and Laukka (2004) conclude that many listeners perceive emotions in musical patterns and "listeners are generally consistent in their judgment of emotional expressions in music" (p. 218), meaning that perceived emotions seem to be stable across a range of listeners. More specifically, an analysis of 79 studies by Gabrielsson and Juslin (2003) concludes that listeners most consistently and reliably perceive and describe musical–emotional expressions as happy, joyful, gay, sad, mournful, gentle, relaxing, agitated, and angry. Less consistent musical emotion descriptors include: playful, soothing, tranquil, humorous, yearning, nostalgic, dignified, reverent, sentimental, and solemn. This does not mean, however, that listeners necessarily feel the same emotion(s) they perceive in a musical piece or passage. Listeners may hear a passage as being expressive of happiness and feel happy as a result, or they may not.

In sum, the emotions aroused and expressed by musics are not a special category of "purely" musical or "aesthetic" emotions. According to Huron (2006), they are the same felt emotions we experience in everyday life when we respond to something that is intensely important to us personally, including the people we care about. It seems fair to say, then, that youth are motivated powerfully to make and listen to pop musics and pop performances because they provide actual and virtual means, "tools," or "affordances" to express, affirm, inform, share, and feel their individual and peer-related social, cultural, political, romantic, and many other dimensions of their embodied personhood. Becker's (2004) emphasis on the situated, social, and cultural nature of listening extends the last point: "A *habitus of listening* suggests that the stance of the listener is not a given, not *natural*, but necessarily influenced by place, time, the shared context of culture, and the intricate and irreproducible details of one's personal biography" (p. 71).

Philosophical perspectives on felt experiences of musics

The writings of Peter Kivy and Stephen Davies hold an important place in music philosophy generally and in music education philosophy particularly (e.g., Bowman, 1998; Elliott & Silverman, 2015; Higgins, 1991; Regelski, 2004; Robinson, 2005). Thus, they add another layer of research that enhances our understanding of adolescents' felt experiences of popular musics.

Among his many contributions to music philosophy in the last 30 years, Peter Kivy is best known for his *cognitivist* theory of musical expression, which others call enhanced formalism, the contour theory,[2] or the "doggy theory." Kivy (1980) builds on a basic distinction between "expressing" an emotion and "being expressive *of*" an emotion (p. 12). Kivy uses the example of a Saint Bernard's face to explain the difference. He suggests that the droopy, downward contour of a Saint Bernard's face gives it a sad-looking quality. Does this mean that the dog is constantly feeling sad? If so, her face is *expressing* her own felt sadness. But if she is not perpetually sad (which is most likely the case), then her face is *expressive of* sadness. We perceive or recognize sadness in the contours of her face because it *resembles* the look of a sad human face. We know that the dog is not actually sad. And because of these factors, Kivy argues, our response is cognitive, not emotional.

According to Kivy (1990), certain features of musical structure correspond to (and thus remind us of) features of emotional behavior, such as facial expressions, bodily gestures, movements, posture, and speech patterns. He argues that music can be expressive of "garden-variety emotions" (p. 175) such as fear, grief, happiness, and anger because they have "*standard* behavioral responses" (p. 180) that musical structures can capture. Music can be expressive of joy, for example, because joy has a standard *behavioral expression* that can be mimicked by energetic, "expansive" music. However, music cannot be expressive of complex emotions like pride because "there is no standard behavioral manifestation of pride" (Robinson, reviewing Kivy, 2005, p. 302). The only way we might perceive something like pride in music is if we were certain of a composer's intentions. Clearly, Kivy's theory depends partly on the idea that we naturally "animate" our environments by investing and "reading" emotions in the looks, gestures, and utterances of things.

To explain what his doggy theory means for music, consider Kivy's words in relation to Coldplay's "Fix You":

> We hear sadness in this . . . musical line, we hear it as expressive of sadness, because we hear it as a musical resemblance of the gesture and carriage appropriate to the expression of our sadness. It is a "sound map" of the human body under the influence of a particular emotion (1989, p. 53).

Note Kivy's use of the words *"hear sadness in"* the musical line: we perceive sadness in the musical line (as we perceive sadness in the contour of the dog's face). But, according to Kivy (1990), this does not mean necessarily that the sad-sounding structure of the vocal line makes us feel sad ourselves. If we are moved by this passage it is because we perceive how Coldplay's "Fix You" is expressive of sadness: "a piece of sad [sounding] music might move us (in part) because it is expressive of sadness, but it does not move us by making us sad" (p. 153).

Kivy calls his theory "cognitivist" because he believes that music can be expressive of emotions without arousing them; a passage of music can be expressive of (say) sadness, but it does not cause sadness in the listener. Kivy (1990) is emphatic: "There are no behavioral symptoms of listeners actually experiencing [emotions] when attending to music" (p. 151). In other words, Kivy is a cognitive-judgment theorist. His reasoning goes as follows: when "garden-variety" emotions (p. 175) like fear, grief, happiness, or anger arise in daily life, it is because we are fearful, sad, happy, or angry *about* something; however, when we listen to music, there is nothing to be fearful, sad, happy, or angry about. In short, Kivy rejects the idea that music is an emotional stimulus: music "is not a stimulus object but a cognitive one" (pp. 40–1).

Kivy (1990) has modified his view slightly during the last 25 years. He acknowledges that "good music" can arouse listeners' emotions under three circumstances. First, the beauty of a piece of music or a musician's performance might move us. In these cases, listeners might experience pleasure, admiration, awe, and so on. Two other ways are obvious. A piece of music might imitate something real (e.g., the sound of weeping) or remind us of something meaningful ("lost love"). In both cases, the music–image *association* can arouse whatever emotion(s) we attribute personally to these links. Kivy (2001) modifies his view again. He accepts that

> the expressive properties of music have a *tendency* to arouse, upon perception, the corresponding emotions, but that for a significant group of listeners, to which I [Kivy] belong, that tendency . . . does not prevail. In a word, we are not aroused. But there is another group of listeners . . . who are aroused to melancholy by melancholy music, to happiness by happy music, and so on. (p. 86)

In short, Kivy does not completely deny that musical expressions of emotions can arouse emotions, just not for him and "a significant group of listeners."

The cognitivist theory offers some constructive ideas about musical expressiveness. It is plausible that specific musical patterns correspond to specific emotional behaviors that cause us to hear these patterns as expressive *of* certain emotions. It is also reasonable to argue that composers, arrangers, and producers of music (consciously or non-consciously) use musical patterns that have accrued emotive identities over years of repetition and association during the history of popular musics generally, or the evolution of one style of popular music specifically. Such patterns cause listeners to hear these patterns as expressive of specific emotions.

The cognitivist theory is problematic in several ways. First, although Kivy admits that beautifully crafted music can move listeners, his claim that musical structures and musical expressions of emotions do not arouse emotions in a "significant group of listeners" is highly questionable. As Kivy (1990) says emphatically, "there are no behavioral symptoms of listeners actually experiencing [emotions] when attending to music" (p. 151). And, when he re-evaluates his position, Kivy (2001) maintains that the properties in music—"pure instrumental music, *sans* text, title, program or dramatic setting" (p. 119)—"are not dispositions to arouse the garden-variety emotions" (p. 120). Moreover, in making his assertions, Kivy omits almost all contextual details including, for example, who is performing, where the music-makers are performing, for whom they are performing, and so forth. Psychological research denies Kivy's assertion.

Another problem with this theory is its focus on a narrow range of basic emotions such as fear, joy, and grief. Is this all that music can be emotionally expressive of? Also, his concept of emotional expression relies mostly on examples of melodic contour from vocal music and short phrases of instrumental music (Kivy, 1980). But surely harmonic changes can also play an important role in musical expression, as Stokes (2002) observes. And even when Kivy (1990) does examine longer examples of music (i.e., J. S. Bach's *2nd Brandenburg Concerto*), he does not consider how expressions of different emotions seem to transform into one another or why such alterations might be musically or emotionally satisfying (Robinson, 2005, p. 303).

Fourth, Kivy claims that music is expressive *of* emotions *not* because performers or composers try to express anything, but rather because listeners perceive certain patterns *as* expressive. But this is one-sided. The reason people tend to see a behavior like smiling as expressive of happiness is that smiling is what people normally do when they are happy. Similarly, observes Robinson (2005), "When a composer expresses some emotion in his music, it is primarily something that he *does* or that he makes it *appear* that he does" (p. 304).

Stephen Davies' concept of musical expressiveness is similar to Kivy's.[3] Davies (1994) believes that music can be expressive of emotions because listeners perceive resemblances between musical elements and emotion-characteristics as displayed in passionate speech, facial expressions (he refers to a basset hound's sad-looking face), "the dynamic character of music and human movement" (p. 229), and so forth (p. 228). In short, "the expressiveness of music consists in its presenting emotion characteristics in its [aural] appearance" (p. 228). Like Kivy, Davies also acknowledges that convention plays an important role in musical expressiveness: "Naturally expressive elements are taken up within traditions of musical practice and style . . . that are highly conventionalized" (p. 242).

So how do Davies and Kivy differ? Although Davies (1980) originally argued that "only those emotions which may be expressed naturally in behavior can be mirrored by emotion-characteristics in appearances [e.g., the garden-variety emotions]" (p. 85), he qualified his viewpoint later by proposing that musical movement, "like human action and behavior, and unlike random process" (1994, p. 229), can present an unfolding sense of unity and intention. Thus, Davies (1994) thinks it might be possible for music to convey more complex emotions such as "hope, embarrassment, puzzlement, annoyance, and envy" (p. 226). In fact, he believes it is possible for composers to create sufficiently long and complex sequences of musical emotion-characteristics that, in combination and over time, can present aural appearances of emotions "which form a progression in which hope [for example] occurs naturally" (p. 262). Additionally, as Robinson (2005) notes, Davies argues that musical patterns not only present aural appearances of emotions, but these appearances (expressions of emotion) can also "comment" on the expressions themselves (p. 307). That is, since composers and performers can intentionally select "sounds with one expressive potential rather than another," then "it is not inappropriate that we find significance in the appropriations that occur" (Davies, 1994, p. 265).

In terms of arousal, Davies believes musical patterns can not only be expressive of emotions, but also arouse emotions in a group of listeners. Davies (1994) argues that just as we tend to respond empathetically to—or *mirror*—the emotional behaviors or features that people (and other things) display, we tend to respond emotionally to the emotion-characteristics we perceive or recognize in musical patterns (p. 315).

Just as we might feel pleased when we see someone smile, or feel sad when we see someone crying, we might feel happy or sad when we experience musical patterns that resemble these behaviors. Davies believes that such musical–emotional mirroring is more fundamental than other, more cognitive responses to music. Of course, Davies (1980) understands that listeners may not respond to musical expressions of emotions with the corresponding felt emotions (listening is highly personalized, as we have noted, see Juslin, 2009), and he also understands that our emotional responses to music may depend on the emotional nature of unfolding musical structures. He sums these points as follows:

> The mirroring response may not, *in the full context of the work*, be appropriate, for the work may provide reasons for over-ruling the mirroring response ... the mirroring response is ontologically prior to the more sensitive and sophisticated response and to be disregarded it must be over-ruled. (pp. 83–4)

Davies' theory seems right on several counts. First, based on new scientific research on mirror neurons and person-to-person emotion recognition and response (e.g., de Waal, 2007; Gallese, 2003; Ramachandran, 2000), musical patterns can resemble and remind us of the emotional appearances of everyday, garden-variety emotions such as happiness and sadness (Huron, 2006). Second, it is also reasonable to claim (as many empirical studies do) that a common response to perceiving emotional appearances in music is to actually feel the emotions we perceive (e.g., Elliott & Silverman, 2015; Juslin, 2009). As Higgins (1991) says, many Western listeners "go to" musics with the expectation that music is a communicative medium that involves a range of musical–emotional expressions such that listening to and/or making musics will move us emotionally. Moreover, it is surely the case that many music-makers (e.g., pop performers, composers, and arrangers) deliberately intend (and have the musical skills and understandings) to communicate musical expressions of emotion that will cause us to actually feel one or more emotions or some combination of them ourselves. In other words, many listeners approach music with a willingness, if not a deep desire, to have "felt" experiences, even before they begin engaging with music (Higgins, 1991, p. 130): "We are open to undergoing, through empathy, a course of [truly felt] emotional experience that parallels the one we recognize in the music" (Higgins, 1991, p. 130).

Davies' theory is valuable as far as it goes, but it does not go far enough. First, while Davies' theory is broader than Kivy's, it still deals in a fairly narrow range of emotions. Second, although Davies is to be commended for trying to make a case that music can express more complex emotions, his theory is not sufficiently deep to persuade us this is possible, let alone explain completely how music can "comment" on other musical expressions of emotions. Third, as Robinson (2005) points out, Davies' theory does not explain the difference between musical expressions of garden-variety emotions and "emotional *expressiveness* in music" (pp. 309–10). That is, the basset hound's face looks sad because it resembles sad-looking human faces, but as Robinson says, "a sad *expression* is not necessarily very *expressive*" (p. 310). Although something may look or sound sad (happy, and so on), such expressions (like a smiley face) may not be very expressive. It depends partly on the artistry of the pop music composer or arranger, or the performers' musical–gestural interpretations. Indeed, Davies pays no attention to the emotions we experience in relation to how performers actually interpret and perform certain song lyrics and pieces (Higgins, 1991).

Personhood: A brief discussion

Musics are made by and for *persons*. Every *person* is musical to one degree or another. If so, then all instances of felt musical experiences, and the concomitant development of creative popular music-making and listening, involve multiple factors that include, but go beyond, mental–cognitive processing. These factors include collective social–sonic actions and events; interpersonal spaces and places; personal and interpersonal emotions; and relationships between all of these and the ecological circumstances and needs of young people living with and for others. Put another way, each adolescent is embedded (to lesser of greater degrees) in his or her preferred pop musical practices and life values (Stetsenko, 2013, p. 184).

Thus, the roots of young people's felt musical experiences of popular musics and musical development trace back to the fundamental issue of what it means to be the kind of living entity that possesses, undergoes, enacts, and performs his or her personhood. But what, more precisely, does it mean to be a person who possesses personhood?

Common sense and everyday discussions about persons and personhood assume that "person" and "human being" are synonymous. However, recent research in philosophy, sociology, anthropology, and neuroscience tells us that these two concepts are not identical. In fact, "human being" is a biological term. The concepts of person and personhood acknowledge that human beings are also part of a social–cultural–moral community in which we live for and with one another. Such relationality is at the heart of personhood. As Diamond (1991) argues:

> What makes us human is that we have certain properties, but these properties, making us members of a certain biological species, have no moral relevance. If, on the other hand, we define being human in terms which are not tied to biological classification, if (for example) we treat as the properties which make us human the capacities for reasoning and self-consciousness, then indeed those capacities may be morally relevant, but if they are morally significant at all, they are significant whether they are the properties of a being who is a member of our species or not. And so it would be better to use a word like "person" to mean a being that has these properties, to bring out the fact that not all human beings have them and that non-human beings conceivably have them (p. 35).

Thus, when we use the words "person" or "personhood," we insert "human being" in the social, cultural, gendered, political, and experiential dimensions of living and life. This is an important point, because anyone who makes, listens to, or thinks about popular musics to any degree understands (as Arielle and Ahmad do) that it is impossible to separate the music and lyrics of pop musics from cultural, political, gendered, and other meanings that pop musicians and pop songs communicate. Stated in different terms, because popular musics and personhood are anchored and felt *in the worlds* of people (young and old), and because musical development is not purely accidental but nurtured non-formally, informally, and/or formally, musical development is what contemporary cognitive scientists and philosophers of mind called "embodied and enactive," as explained next.

Persons and personhood: Embodied and enactive

A holistic, embodied–enactive concept of personhood receives support from numerous scholars in a variety of fields (e.g. Damasio, 1994; Di Paolo, Rohde, & De Jaegher, 2010; Johnson, 2007; LeDoux, 1996; Noë, 2009; Prinz, 2012; Thompson, 2007; Varela, Thompson, & Rosch, 1991). A holistic concept of personhood is *nondualist* and social–cultural. Holistic concepts of personhood reject past and current assumptions that you equal your brain, and that consciousness, cognition, perception, emotion, and so forth are disembodied, all centered "in the head." From modern versions of dualism, education should be brain-centered, and that everything we need to know about personhood and musical development will be explained when neuroscientists locate the "neural correlates" (the smallest brain mechanisms) that cause our conscious experiences of "Jaded," "American Jesus," "So What," "Short Ride in A Fast Machine"—of everything people think, feel, and do.

These disembodied and localized views are not only simplistic, but they also overlook the fact that persons are much more than brains alone. Each person's brain operates in and for "a living, purposive body, in continual engagement with complex environments that are not just physical but social and cultural as well" (Johnson, 2007, p. 175). As Johnson (2006) says, "what we can experience and think, and also how we think, that is, how we conceptualize and reason" is embodied (p. 49). Personhood includes and combines "a functioning human brain, in a living human body, interacting with complex physical, social, and cultural environments, in an ongoing flow of experiences" (Johnson, 2007, p. 279).

What does the enactive component of personhood involve? Since the late 1990s, more and more scholars of consciousness, perception, and cognition have argued that researchers concerned with perception and cognition—and musical perception and cognition—should turn away from computational, "cold-cognition," information-processing concepts of consciousness and turn toward much more holistic concepts that conceive all so-called mental processes as body-based and world-related, as shaped by the body-in-the-world. In contrast to dualists, a growing cadre of scholars maintain that "the human mind is embodied in our entire organism and embedded in the world, and hence is not reducible to structures inside the head" (Thompson, 2005, p. 409).

The embodied–enactive concept of action and perception emphasizes that "cognition is not the representation of a pre-given world by a pre-given mind but is rather *the enactment of a world* and a mind on the basis of a history of the variety of *actions that a being in the world per-forms*" (Varela et al., 1991, p. 9). This view acts as a much-needed corrective to dualistic, materialist, computational, and representational theories of mind, cognition, and perception, and it moves phenomenological concepts of musical experience nearer the center of our musical experiences.

Seminal work on the enactive approach (Noë, 2004, 2009) argues that the mind does not drive perception, cognition, and action. Rather, the body–brain–mind is fused such that "the mind" is actually a complex combination of know-hows that allow us to achieve our moment-to-moment and long-term goals in our environment. McGann (2010) states it this way: "Though the mind is driven by the autonomy of the agent, all of its activities occur in engagement with those aspects of the world around it . . . The description of either an agent or its environment will therefore always perforce involve reference to the other" (p. 72). The person and his or her environment "are inextricably entwined and an analysis must appreciate not just one element or the other, but how the two interact and are interrelated" (p. 72). Likewise, Thompson (2007) argues that perception and cognition involve the "exercise of skillful know-how in situated and embodied action" (p. 14). The embodied–enactive concept of mind and perception are forms of active doing:

> Perceptual experience acquires content thanks to our possession of bodily skills. *What we perceive* is determined by *what we do* (or what we know how to do); it is determined by what we are *ready* to do . . . we *enact* our perceptual experience; we act it out. (Noë, 2004, p. 1)

In other words, how we listen to and make music is anchored in and unified by our music cognition processes plus all our other body–brain–mind processes, including our sensorimotor apparatuses, which allow us to *actively create our worlds* (Krueger, 2009, p. 100). Thought and experience, says Krueger (2009), "emerge from embodied action . . . [and] the situated subject's temporally-extended, exploratory activity" (p. 100) allows each of us to navigate and shape the social structures and dynamics of our environment. Krueger continues: "crucially, subject and world are conceived of as dynamically coupled and reciprocally determining; both are co-implicated in the structure of various cognitive processes" (p. 100). Krueger (2009) argues that "music listening episodes are, in fact, doings" (p. 98). Music listening is a matter of "robust sensorimotor engagements with and manipulations of sonic structures within musical pieces" (p. 98). Music, therefore, is experiential in the full-blooded sense of phenomenological couplings between our entire beings (not just our brains) and the musical meaning-making opportunities or affordances of pieces of music that flow in time and across time.

Thus, the embodied–enactive view fits with our social–cultural, holistic concept of youth, popular musics, and felt musical experiences insofar as popular musics and musical development are *embodied* and *encultured* processes. The music and lyrics of popular musics "*play* across our memory, embodiment and situated consciousness, and includes multisensory experiences and actions that lead to our perceptions of sounds" (Matyja & Schiavio, 2013, p. 353), songs, and their meanings. Popular musics are "*actively* constructed by the listener, rather than passively transferred from performer to listener within the given culture and context" (p. 353).

So, in enactive–phenomenological terms, pieces of music "beckon for an active response" (Krueger, 2009, p. 103). To clarify what this means, Thompson (2007) explains that we need to distinguish between our experience of a melody "proceeding in time, and our simultaneous experience of our listening act unfolding in time" (p. 327). The same holds for the actions of performing pop musics. That is, when we say that we make or listen to music, what this actually means is that we make and listen to it "but we also subjectively live through our listening" (p. 327). Our making and listening has "a subjective character that makes it immediately manifest, without observation or inference, as one's own experience. In this way, we experience our listening implicitly, without it becoming an object of awareness" (p. 328).

Related to everyone's musical experiences, but especially in the case of youth, who (we posit) tend to be especially emotionally and corporeally grounded, the experiences of musicing and listening are "rainbow-like" (Thompson, 2007). Why? Because our unified embodied–enactive powers of mind–perception–cognition are not receptive but *active*—they are engaged with the musical patterns and lyrics of popular musics that we create "on the fly" in virtue of our musical, bodily perceptual "knowing-hows." A continuous music-listening experience, which we create for ourselves, is an instance of "a standing-streaming living present . . . the living present is streaming because it is the continuous transformation . . . of the about-to-happen into the happening into just-happened" (Thompson, 2007, p. 326). And yet, at the same time, the real-time, living present "is standing" because our *self*-awareness remains as an unchanging dimension. "It stands . . . permanent, like the rainbow on the waterfall, with its own quality unchanged by the events that stream through it" (p. 326). Herein lies a partial explanation of one of the most captivating and exhilarating dimensions of felt experiences of music.

A concept of felt musical–emotional experiences

Here we outline a brief, provisional concept of musical experience that posits eleven processes or mechanisms that contribute variously to young people's moment-to-moment felt musical experiences. This concept draws heavily on a psychological model of musical emotions proposed by Juslin et al. (2010, pp. 615–28). Our eleven-dimensional concept includes seven mechanisms put forth by Juslin and his colleagues: brain stem reflex, rhythmic entrainment, evaluative conditioning, emotional contagion, visual imagery, associations/episodic memory, and musical expectancy. We add cognitive monitoring–naming, corporeality, musical persona, and social attachment.

Our addition of the latter four dimensions arises from our predisposition as philosophers to conceive music as an embodied, social–cultural praxis, rather than pieces of music alone. This does not mean we disagree with Juslin and his colleagues, who also emphasize the social nature of music listening. It only points out that whereas our work (Elliott, 1995; Elliott & Silverman, 2015) takes a praxial (a social/cultural and pragmatic) view of music, Juslin and his fellow researchers assume a psychological stance. To us, following Juslin and his colleagues and adding our views, adolescents' powerful feelings of and attachments to pop-music performers and songs do not arise from musical patterns or brain responses alone. Instead, musical–emotional experiences arise from *all* of these processes and more, considered in relation to the sociality of music.

The *brain stem* anchors many body–brain sensory and motor functions, including the control of emotional arousal, auditory perception, heart rate, and so forth. A brain stem reflex is an automatic process that arouses an emotion. Characteristics of musical sounds can instantly activate basic emotion circuits. The brain stem automatically interprets several basic acoustic qualities of music as signals of potentially significant negative or positive, threatening or pleasing, events: "Sounds that are sudden, loud, dissonant, or feature fast temporal patterns induce arousal" (Juslin & Västfjäll, 2008, p. 564). Think of the throbbing beats and high volumes of most rock and hip-hop songs. Other features of musical sounds (e.g., very high, very low, and dissonant sounds) activate brain stem reflexes to cause other emotions. How? Since emotional systems are widely distributed in tree-like structures, "music is bound to access these emotional systems at many levels" (Panksepp & Bernatzky, 2002, p. 137).

Humans are the only species that can spontaneously synchronize or entrain their body–minds to a musical beat (Patel, 2008, p. 100). Rhythmically induced synchronization—the *sine qua non* of popular musics and many children's and adolescents' passionate involvements with pop musics—engages brain stem and cortical regions automatically, thereby activating motor behaviors and emotional responses, especially pleasurable feelings (Juslin & Västfjäll, 2008).

Unsurprisingly, then, people across cultures make and listen to "movement music" of various kinds for a variety of purposes, including emotional arousal. For example, highly rhythmic music for dancing, trancing, sporting events, and celebrations; steady, stately parade music; slow, dignified music for ceremonial processions (e.g., religious/ritual occasions; academic parades); gentle, rocking lullabies; and work songs. In short, we are innately predisposed to synchronize our bodies with and respond emotionally to musical rhythms. Moreover, rhythm is a fundamentally infectious and contagious corporeal–emotional dimension of music, as illustrated clearly by Arielle's felt emotions in the mosh pit of a punk rock show.

When a specific piece of music is repeatedly paired with other positive or negative stimuli, it can arouse specific emotions through simple, non-conscious *conditioning*. The same holds for a specific pop-song performer or song lyric. A particular piece may make you feel happy because "it has occurred repeatedly together in time with a specific event that always makes you happy, such as meeting one of your friends. Over time, through repeated pairings, the music itself will eventually evoke happiness even in the absence of the friendly interaction" (Juslin et al., 2010, p. 622). Juslin identifies several characteristics of this kind of musical–emotional arousal: a) it arises from non-cognitive processes; b) it tends to resist extinction; and c) it can happen in social situations where listening, while present, is not the main activity. Indeed, music often occurs in social situations, so that musical sounds and social interaction cannot reasonably be separated.

We said earlier that when we see sadness, happiness, and other emotions expressed in someone's physical behavior, in his or her voice, or in other sounds he or she makes (e.g., a moan, a scream), we tend to respond empathetically. We have a specialized set of neurons in our brains called *mirror neurons*. These automatically map the expressed emotions of other people in our body–brains. This mapping can result in the activation of our own emotions of sadness, happiness, and so forth. This process is called *musical–emotional contagion*. Thus, de Waal (2007) argues that emotional contagion processes "have deep evolutionary roots in primates and other highly social species, whereby they help foster social bonds which promote survival in a group setting" (p. 49). Given the importance of facial, bodily, and vocal gestures in conveying human emotions, de Waal argues that it is plausible that people also experience emotional contagion from the sounds of expressive voices and instrumental music. As evidence from emotion theory and music psychology suggests, it is common for listeners to unconsciously mirror, mimic, internalize, and feel the emotions they perceive in musical patterns (Juslin et al., 2010). Also, of course, the movements and gestures of pop-musics performers activate emotional contagion among pop-music listeners at live concerts or in videos of live performances.

The *personal associations and autobiographical memories* we attach to the musical patterns and lyrics of pop songs and pop musicians can strongly influence our emotions (Juslin, 2009). Personal attribution is the key. This is partly why specific pieces of music—Arielle's emotional attachment to "Born Free"; Justin Timberlake's painful break-up song, "Cry Me A River"—cause certain listeners to feel energized, sad, melancholy, and/or happy. Also, it is very common for people to musically "self-regulate" by deliberately selecting music to remind themselves of important events in their lives (DeNora, 2001). Thus, music serves an important "nostalgic function" in everyday life (Juslin, 2009, p. 137). Indeed, because pop musics often play an essential formative role in the personal–social–musical development of adolescents, it is not surprising that adults experience particularly strong autobiographical–musical emotions related to music from their adolescence (Schulkind, Hennis, & Rubin, 1999).

Since most readers of this volume are familiar with Leonard Meyer's theory of the relationships between musical *expectancy* and musical emotions, we will keep our discussion of this topic very brief. However, we will add two points that are rarely mentioned in regard to his theory. The key to Meyer's theory is musical expectation. He holds that listeners perceive musical patterns as tending toward resolution and closure. But, he says, composers have ways of stimulating and challenging our perceptual expectations in order to influence our emotional responses. That is, because we come to listening experiences with informal or formal musical knowledge of how Western tonal music unfolds, we appraise musical events in relation to our expectations about how musical patterns usually occur. As long as a piece of music unfolds predictably and fulfills our stylistic structural expectations immediately, we will have no intellectual or emotional reaction. But if something happens in instrumental music that we do not expect, we react, either intellectually or emotionally.

Meyer (1956) argues that we may feel surprised, bewildered, uncertain, puzzled, or anxious when we hear such things as (say) unresolved cadences, unusual melodic sequences, and sudden key changes; or we may feel relieved and satisfied when (say) harmonic sequences eventually return to the tonic (and so on, and on): "While the trained musician consciously waits for the expected resolution of a dominant seventh chord the untrained, but practiced, listener feels the delay as affect" (p. 67). Although some scholars still depend heavily on Meyer's theory, the fact is that expectancy is only one among many processes that contribute to the arousal of musical emotions. Indeed, says Huron (2006), while Meyer's approach was pioneering, it "was written at a time when there was little pertinent psychological research to draw on" (p. 2).

Moreover, Meyer's theory is weakened by the fact that the range of emotions he links to musical expectations is extremely limited; his tendency–inhibition theory is too simple to account either for the range of people's everyday emotional lives or for the range of musical emotions people can and do experience. Huron (2006) agrees: "Listening to music can give rise to an enormous range of emotions" (p. 25); for example, nostalgia, love, awe, tragic grief, pride, anxiety, anger, and betrayal (Elliott & Silverman, 2015, p. 323; Juslin, 2009; Juslin & Västfjäll, 2008).

In addition, when scholars and students focus exclusively on Meyer's analyses of musical patterns as they relate to emotional arousal, they tend to overlook an exceptionally important amendment that he adds to his theory. That is, Meyer argues that musical–emotional profundity has more to do with *associations* than it does with musical structure: "Music in which structure is of greater interest for the *associations* it suggests than for its internal resolutions—is great music" (p. 78). Importantly, then, Meyer acknowledges exactly what researchers now argue about how importantly numerous so-called extra-musical associations, conditions, social contexts, and other variables play in musical–emotional arousal and expression.

In our discussion of emotions and feelings we wrote that after an initial non-cognitive appraisal of a situation and immediate physiological reactions, our cognitive processes kick in to modify our initial appraisals and emotional responses. The same holds for musical emotions. Popular musics engage the attention, the conscious and non-conscious responsiveness, and the emotions of teenagers—like adult listeners—because (among other variables) listeners' *cognitive monitoring* of the *narrative contents* of pop songs, and people's *naming of emotions* in songs, can continuously readjust listeners' initial emotional reactions to the musical patterns of pop songs. Moreover, the facial features, vocal intonations, and movements (dancing, prancing) that pop performers accentuate or dramatize during their performances of song lyrics, and the musical–social contexts related to any of these dimensions of pop singing (e.g., light shows, backup singers and dancers, elaborate stage sets, etc.), can expand and intensify musical–emotional stimuli.

Let us examine briefly the lyrics of three award-winning pop songs by well-known pop and rock stars. In 2010, at the Hiro Ballroom in New York, Corinne Bailey Rae, a jazzy, neo-soul singer from the UK, began to sing and play "The Sea." Her husband, Jason Rae, composed the song shortly before he died. Rae sang the song as a powerful meditation on the grief she felt about the death of her husband, and her gradual recovery: "it was enough to make the crowd feel protective." Ms. Rae sang: "The sea/the majestic sea/breaks everything/cleans everything/crushed everything/takes everything from me." From the front row of the audience, one fan called out: "It's okay, honey." Another shouted: "We love you!" (Maerz, 2010).

In "You Oughta Know," Alanis Morissette (1995) vents her anger as she ambushes her ex at dinner: "Did you forget about me Mr. Duplicity?/I hate to bug you in the middle of dinner/It was a slap in the face how quickly I was replaced." Arguably, Morissette articulated the emotions, if not the exact words, of more than a few jilted lovers in the lives of young and old alike.

In "I Used to Love Him," Lauryn Hill performs a song that is both a despairing, tortured "break up song," says critic Christine Duong (2013), and ultimately a "very empowering and motivational one about realizing you deserve better, and moving on from a relationship that only caused you pain": "I chose a road of passion and pain/Sacrificed too much and waited in vain/Gave up my power ceased being a queen/Addicted to love like the drug of a fiend." Once again, it seems plausible to say that Hill's music, lyrics, and YouTube performance musically and visually represent the deep pain that many adolescents experience and, therefore, respond to emotionally themselves.

Regarding the linguistic-narrative-naming nature of the content of song lyrics, LeDoux (1996) emphasizes that in contrast to the brains of other species, humans' emotions and feelings are different because we are able to classify the world linguistically and name emotional reactions to our experiences: "The difference between fear, anxiety, terror, apprehension, and the like would not be possible without language" (p. 302). Indeed, human beings not only respond emotionally to important events in their lives, they also tend to reflect upon them (Robinson, 2005, p. 79). Thus, to some degree, our musical emotions are influenced by the ways we identify them to ourselves and others. If and when we name a musical emotion sad, rather than joyful, our emotional action tendencies and behaviors will likely be different after such naming. Thus, we may feel differently than if we had labeled our emotion "bitter" (p. 82). Put succinctly, cognitive-musical-narrative monitoring processes and acts of emotional naming enable us to reflect on and interpret our ongoing musical–emotional experiences. Accordingly, we propose that children and youth may achieve an increasingly rich level of musical–emotional experiences when language comes into play, because language enables our feelings and movements to be named and communicated to ourselves and others.

Musical-narrative songs and performances may also cause listeners to "dream up" a visual image that may arouse a wide range of emotions (Juslin & Västfjäll, 2008, p. 566). The processes involved are still not understood, but psychological research suggests that listeners might conduct a "metaphorical non-verbal mapping between the music and 'image-schemata' grounded in bodily experience" (Juslin et al., 2010, pp. 622–3), which echoes our earlier references to body mapping. In the context of popular musics, "dreaming up" can be even deeper. The music, the lyrics, the nature of a specific singer's dramatic portrayal of the words she or he is singing, or a combination of all of these factors may engage young people's imaginations to the point that they may empathize with a singer's narrative, or "become one" with the singer's emotions, as Corinne Bailey Rae's fans did.

Indeed, neurobiological research suggests that music activates attachment by stimulating release of the neurotransmitter oxytocin. Emotional contagion also plays a significant part in facilitating social interaction and affiliation (Lakin et al., 2003; Preston & de Waal, 2002). Contagion helps to explain adolescents' use of popular musics in courting, peer and romantic bonding, and the emotional impact of experiencing anthems, folk songs, and popular music in social groups.

For example, in March 2002 Justin Timberlake broke up with Britney Spears after a three-year relationship (Cragg, 2013). As the story goes, Spears had cheated on Timberlake. In 2011 "Timberlake admitted that he had written 'Cry Me a River' after an argument with Spears: 'I was on a phone call that was not the most enjoyable,' after which he said, 'I can't believe she did that to me.'"

Given the numerous awards "Cry Me A River" and Timberlake received over many years (a Grammy Award, a MTV video award, and numerous international awards), it seems reasonable to suggest that several features of Timberlake's hit aroused and expressed the emotions of a significant number of his worldwide teenage fans, who may have experienced similar gut-wrenching periods in their lives and who may have empathized with and projected themselves into his personal–musical narrative. The melodic and rhythmic qualities of the song; its "dark" instrumental–vocal arrangement; Timberlake's passive–aggressive lyrics; the specific characteristics of his sensuous male vocal performance; his masculine mannerisms and clothing; and the voyeuristic characteristics of the video—he sings in the pouring rain while spying on his former lover—may have combined to "play to" his fans and arouse many dimensions of their personhood. As Bowman and Powell (2007) write: "Bodies in states of music are multiply sensed and strongly connected to the world" (p. 1099).

Of course, individual listeners can turn on or turn off emotion-producing mental images that a piece or lyrical passage induces, or choose specific pieces to deliberately stimulate emotion-producing images of important events from their past, or things they may wish to hear, see, and feel in the future. Thus, says Larson (1995), adolescents use music to simulate strong emotional responses that allow them to explore "possible selves" and their musical identities.

Mention of emotion-producing images brings us to Cone's (1974) suggestion that all instrumental and vocal musics are dramatic in one way or another, and that pieces can be heard as personal narratives. On this view, listeners can (if they wish) listen to music "as if" each piece is, in some way, the emotional expression of the composer or the performers' actual emotions, just as actors portray the personalities and emotions of the characters in a play (p. 5). This aligns with what we said about "Cry Me A River" and 2Pac's "Changes." Cone argues that musical patterns can carry emotional meanings that can be heard, expressed, and felt as the emotional "utterances" of a composer's voice, or a performer's "true personalities," or the people and relationships portrayed in the lyrics of a popular song. Once again, we propose that children and adolescents may not only feel but also understand consciously and/or non-consciously (to greater and lesser degrees) what is happening musically and dramatically during performances of popular songs.

One further example comes to mind. Standing before 15,000 of her adoring fans (mostly teen-age girls) at the Staples Center in Los Angeles, which was glistening with glow sticks and multi-colored visual displays, the teenage sensation Taylor Swift sang her trad-country-rock-pop hits (e.g., "Our Song") while traversing catwalks between alternate stages (Roberts, 2013). Taken together, the rich combination of her show's many alternating mood songs and lyrics, her on- and off-stage gesturing and dancing, her musical arrangements and her backup musicians func-tioned to induce continuous entrainment and contagious emotions that drove Swift's screaming audience (of largely young girls) into an electrified frenzy. Arguably, such youthful displays and engagements—fed by expert marketing, branding, and pop journalism—create elaborate rites of felt emotional "passage" for the young women who constitute Swift's fan base. Her audiences, swept up emotionally by many dimensions of her extravagant shows, bond with Swift as an ideal-ized version of themselves, in ways that are similar to fans of Timberlake, Morissette, and Hill. Swift's affecting and infectious musical–textual expressions of love, loss, pain, assertiveness, and playfulness are (we suggest) *probably* intended as and perceived and felt by her audiences as com-munications of empathy and, possibly, "guidance" related to what young women have already experienced, or may experience in their future lives.

Felt experiences of popular musics and child and adolescent development

Why are felt experiences of popular musics important in the development—musical, emotional, and social—of the child musician? Since human beings are emotional beings—since emotions affect everything everyone says, does, and experiences throughout life (Damasio, 1994; Juslin, 2009; LeDoux, 2002)—and since popular musics (like all musics) arouse, express, and communi-cate a wide range of felt human emotions, we may infer that a) young people's felt experiences of popular musics not only move and express a wide variety of emotions that they feel, but also b) felt experiences of popular musics impact (in a variety of ways) the psychological and emotional devel-opment of children and youth, and their musical, personal, social, and cultural identities. Indeed, research by Panksepp and Pasqualini (2005) suggests that the maturation of emotional relatedness and emotional–musical skills "promote the harmonious blending of these disparate sources of influence on our emotional lives, so that the borderlands between the biological, psychological, and sociological become replete with rich commerce as opposed to unthoughtful antagonism" (p. 24).

But, in general, do the daily lives of children and adolescents in formal school music situations promote such blending? We suggest that if dynamic and meaningful musical experiences include creative experiences with popular musics that arouse and express young people's emotions posi-tively, then it is more likely that young people will have opportunities to develop positive "harmo-nious obsessions" for making and listening to the musics they love.

We say this because it is important for music teachers (of all kinds) to keep in mind that advan-cing the musical development of children and youth is coextensive with strengthening their feel-ings of well-being, musical meaningfulness, safety, and personal dignity. A young person's sense of belonging, security, and self-confidence during popular musicing and listening provide the scaf-folding needed to promote their positive feelings of joyful persistence, self-discipline, the devel-opment of creative skills of engagement, commitment, responsibility, and the self-confidence needed to deal with short- and long-term musical challenges (Goldstein & Brooks, 2013, p. 194).

Developing the skills and sensibilities needed to craft personal narratives and marry these with emotionally expressive popular musics can foster educative and ethical interactions—peer-to-peer, adult-to-youth. However, the "music itself"—sounds alone—will not advance fully most young people's "musicianship and listenership" (Elliott, 1995; Elliott & Silverman, 2015) in and for popular music-making. Doing so requires a positive and holistic relationality within informal and formal music-teaching situations.

Practically speaking, and given the philosophical and scientific research cited in preceding sections of this chapter, it seems reasonable to suggest that musicing and listening experiences can and should endeavor to enhance the musical–emotional skills and experiences of children and adolescents. This means that musical development depends on encouraging youth to focus on their musical emotions while making and listening to popular musics and while watching and listening to popular music performers. The aim is to make young people increasingly aware of the musical and narrative details of popular songs and performers that seem to be responsible for their musical–emotional effectiveness or ineffectiveness. In the process, young music-makers are more likely to build sets of musical understandings and strategies they can use in their own popular song writing and performing efforts. In the same vein, we should engage youth in listening *with* their emotions as a way of understanding why and how popular musicians craft emotional musical–visual, musical–social, and musical–movement experiences. Third, we should encourage adolescents to use "emotion words" to name, describe, and discuss composers' and performers' compositions and performances. These strategies are likely to contribute to empowering and engaging students in creating musical expressions of emotions as performers, composers, and arrangers of popular musics, and motivating them to engage in life-long music-making and listening and, eventually, become more aware of the many ways in which music arouses, comforts, bonds, and creates who we are as embodied, social beings.

Reflective questions

1 How do emotions and feelings differ?
2 What does it mean to say that persons are embodied and enactive beings?
3 Describe eleven ways music can arouse and express felt emotional experiences of popular musics.
4 Other than the purely musical qualities of popular songs, what other factors contribute to adolescents' felt emotional experiences of and passionate attachment to individual performers' songs and performance contexts?
5 Provide three reasons why felt experiences of popular musics are important in the development of the child musician.

Notes

1 The names of the two students have been altered for the purposes of this discussion. The larger study from which these students' experiences are drawn met IRB approval.
2 Kivy pays special tribute to Mattheson as the progenitor of the contour theory.
3 In *Deeper Than Reason*, Robinson notes that Davies and Kivy developed their theories independently but at the same time: by Kivy in *The Corded Shell* (1980), and by Davies in a journal article, "The Expression of Emotion in Music," *Mind, 89*.

Reference list

Becker, J. (2004). *Deep listeners: Music, emotion, and trancing*. Bloomington, IN: Indiana University Press.

Bicknell, J. (2009). *Why music moves us*. New York: Palgrave Macmillan.

Blood, A., & Zatorre, R. (2001). Intensely pleasurable responses to music correlate with activity in brain regions implicated in reward and emotion. *Proceedings of the National Academy of Sciences of the USA, 98*(20), 11818–23.

Bowman, W. (1998). *Philosophical perspectives on music*. New York: Oxford University Press.

Bowman, W. (2004). Pop goes . . . ? Taking popular music seriously. In C. X. Rodriguez (Ed.), *Bridging the gap: Popular music and music education* (pp. 29–49). Reston, VA: National Association for Music Education.

Bowman, W., & Powell, K. (2007). The body in a state of music. In L. Bresler (Ed.), *International handbook of research in arts education* (pp. 1087–106). Dordrecht, Netherlands: Springer.

Cone, E. T. (1974). *The composer's voice*. Berkeley: University of California Press.

Cragg, M. J. (2013). Timberlake's "Cry Me A River," the ultimate break-up record. *The Guardian*. Accessed March 1, 2014. <http://www.theguardian.com/culture/2013/feb/08/justin-timberlake-cry-me-a-river>.

Cross, I. (2011). Music and biocultural evolution. In M. Clayton, T. Herbert, & R. Middleton (Eds.), *The cultural study of music* (pp. 17–27). London: Routledge.

Damasio, A. (1994). *Descartes' error: Emotion, reason, and the human brain*. New York: Putnam Publishing.

Damasio, A. (2000). Emotion, consciousness, and decision-making. The London School of Economics and Political Science, January 24, 2000.

Damasio, A. (2003). *Looking for Spinoza: Joy, sorrow, and the feeling brain*. Orlando, FL: Harcourt.

Davies, S. (1980). The expression of emotion in music. *Mind*, **89**(353), 67–86.

Davies, S. (1994). *Musical meaning and expression*. Ithaca, NY: Cornell University Press.

DeNora, T. (2001). *Music in everyday life*. Cambridge: Cambridge University Press.

de Waal, F. (2007). The "Russian doll" model of empathy and imitation. In S. Braten (Ed.), *On being moved: From mirror neurons to empathy* (pp. 49–69). Amsterdam: John Benjamins.

Diamond, C. (1991). The importance of being human. In D. Cockburn (Ed.), *Human beings*. Cambridge: Cambridge University Press.

Di Paolo, E., Rohde, M., & De Jaegher, H. (2010). Horizons for the enactive mind: Values, social interaction, and play. In J. Stewart, O. Gapenne, & E. Di Paolo (Eds.), *Enaction: Towards a new paradigm for cognitive science* (pp. 33–87). Cambridge, MA: MIT Press.

Duong, C. (2013). Top 10 sad break-up songs: Lauryn Hill. Accessed August 4, 2014, <http://popinsomniacs.com/2013/06/01/top-10-sad-break-up-songs/>.

Elliott, D. J. (1995). *Music matters: A new philosophy of music education*. New York: Oxford University Press.

Elliott, D. J., & Silverman, M. (2012). Rethinking philosophy, re-viewing musical–emotional experiences. In W. Bowman & A. L. Frega (Eds.), *The Oxford handbook of philosophy in music education* (pp. 37–62). New York: Oxford University Press.

Elliott, D. J., & Silverman, M. (2015). *Music matters: A philosophy of music education* (2nd ed.). New York: Oxford University Press.

Fisher, J. A. (2011). Popular music. In T. Gracyk & A. Kania (Eds.), *The Routledge companion to philosophy and music* (pp. 405–15). New York: Routledge.

Frijda, N. (2007). *The laws of emotion*. Mahwah, NJ: Lawrence Erlbaum.

Gabrielsson, A. (2001). Emotions in strong experiences with music. In P. N. Juslin & J. A. Sloboda (Eds.), *Music and emotion: Theory and research* (pp. 431–49). New York: Oxford University Press.

Gabrielsson, A., & Juslin, P. N. (2003). Emotional expression in music. In H. H. Goldsmith, R. J. Davidson, & K. R. Scherer (Eds.), *Handbook of affective sciences* (pp. 503–34). Oxford: Oxford University Press.

Gallese, V. (2003). The manifold nature of interpersonal relations: The quest for a common mechanism. *Philosophical Transactions of the Royal Society of London*, **358**(1431), 517–528.

Goldstein, S., & Brooks, R. B. (2013). *Understanding and managing children's classroom behavior: Creating sustainable, resilient classrooms*. Hoboken, NJ: John Wiley & Sons.

Heaton, P., Hermelin, B., & Pring, L. (1999). Can children with autistic spectrum disorders perceive affect in music? An experimental investigation. *Psychological Medicine*, **29**(6), 1405–10.

Higgins, K. (1991). *The music of our lives*. Philadelphia: Temple University Press.

Hodges, D. (2009). Bodily responses to music. In S. Hallam, I. Cross, & M. Thaut, (Eds.), *The Oxford handbook of music psychology* (pp. 121–30). Oxford: Oxford University Press.

Huron, D. (2006). *Sweet anticipation: Music and the psychology of expectation*. Cambridge, MA: MIT Press.

Johnson, M. (2006). Mind incarnate: From Dewey to Damasio. *Daedalus*, **135**(3), 46.

Johnson, M. (2007). *The meaning of the body: Aesthetics of human understanding*. Chicago, IL: The University of Chicago Press.

Juslin, P. N. (2009). Emotional responses to music. In S. Hallam, I. Cross, & M. Thaut, (Eds.), *Oxford handbook of music psychology* (pp. 131–40). Oxford: Oxford University Press.

Juslin, P. N., & Laukka, P. (2004). Expression, perceptions, and induction of musical emotions: A review and a questionnaire study of everyday listening. *Journal of New Music Research*, **33**(3), 217–38.

Juslin, P. N., Laukka, P., Liljeström, D., Västfjäll, D., & Lundqvist, L. (2011). Emotional reactions to music in a nationally representative sample of Swedish adults: Prevalence and causal influences. *Musicae Scientiae*, **15**(2), 174–207.

Juslin, P. N., Liljeström, D., Västfjäll, D., Barradas, G., & Silva, A. (2008). An experience sampling study of emotional reactions to music: Listener, music, and situation. *Emotion*, **8**(5), pp. 668–83.

Juslin, P. N., Liljeström, D., Västfjäll, D., & Lundqvist, L. (2010). How does music evoke emotions? Exploring the underlying mechanisms. In P. N. Juslin & J. A. Sloboda (Eds.), *Handbook of music and emotions* (pp. 605–42). Oxford: Oxford University Press.

Juslin, P. N., & Sloboda, J. A. (2001). Psychological perspectives on music and emotion. In P. N. Juslin & J. A. Sloboda (Eds.), *Music and emotion: Theory and research* (pp. 71–104). Oxford: Oxford University Press.

Juslin, P. N., & Västfjäll, D. (2008). Emotional responses to music: The need to consider underlying mechanisms. *Behavioral and Brain Sciences*, **31**(5), 559–621.

Kivy, P. (1980). *The corded shell: Reflections on musical expression*. Princeton, NJ: Princeton University Press.

Kivy, P. (1989). *Sound sentiment: An essay on the musical emotions*. Philadelphia: Temple University Press.

Kivy, P. (1990). *Music alone: Philosophical reflections on the purely musical experience*. Ithaca, NY: Cornell University Press.

Kivy, P. (2001). *New essays on musical understanding*. New York: Oxford University Press.

Kreutz, G., Teichmann, D., Osawa, P., & Viatl. D. (2008). Using music to induce emotions: Influences of musical preference and absorption. *Psychology of Music*, **36**(1), 101–26.

Krueger, J. (2009). Enacting musical experience. *Journal of Consciousness Studies*, **16**(2–3), 98–123.

Lakin, J. L., Jeffers, V. E., Cheng, C., & Chartrand, T. L. (2003). The chameleon effect as social glue: Evidence for the evolutionary significance of nonconscious mimicry. *Journal of Nonverbal Behavior*, **27**(3), 145–62.

Larson, R. (1995). Secrets in the bedroom: Adolescents' private use of media. *Journal of Youth and Adolescence*, **24**(5), 535–50.

LeDoux, J. (1996). *The emotional brain: The mysterious underpinnings of emotional life*. New York: Simon & Schuster.

LeDoux, J. (2002). *Synaptic self: How our brains become who we are*. New York: Viking.

Maerz, M. (2010). After a death, embracing life's diversity. *The New York Times*. Accessed August 9, 2014, <http://www.nytimes.com/2010/01/17/arts/music/17maerz.html?scp=1&sq=baiely%20rae&st=cse&_r=0>.

Matyja, J., & Schiavio, A. (2013). Enactive music cognition. *Constructivist Foundations*, **8**(3), 351–7.

McGann, M. (2010). Perceptual modalities: Modes of presentation or modes of interaction? *Journal of Consciousness Studies*, **17**(1–2), 72–94.

Menon, V., & Levitin, D. J. (2005). The rewards of music listening: Response and physiological connectivity of the mesolimbic system. *Neuroimage*, **28**(1), 175–84.

Meyer, L. (1956). *Emotion and meaning in music.* Chicago: University of Chicago Press.

Morissette, A. (1995). You oughta know. *Jagged little pill.* Accessed August 4, 2014, <http://www.azlyrics.com/lyrics/alanismorissette/yououghtaknow.html>.

Nettl, B. (2007). Music. *Grove Music Online. Oxford Music Online.* Oxford University Press, accessed August 4, 2014, <http://www.oxfordmusiconline.com/subscriber/article/grove/music/40476>.

Noë, A. (2004). *Action in perception.* Cambridge, MA: MIT Press.

Noë, A. (2009). *Out of our heads: Why you are not your brain, and other lessons from the biology of consciousness.* New York: Hill and Wang.

Panksepp, J., & Bernatzky, G. (2002). Emotional sounds and the brain: The neuron-affective foundations of musical appreciation. *Behavioral Processes,* **60**(2), 133–55.

Panksepp, J., & Pasqualini, M. (2005). The search for the fundamental brain/mind sources of affective experience. In J. Nadel & D. Muir (Eds.), *Emotional development: Recent research advances* (pp. 5–30). New York: Oxford University Press.

Patel, A. D. (2008). *Music, language, and the brain.* New York: Oxford University Press.

Preston, S. D., & de Waal, F. B. M. (2002). Empathy: Its ultimate and proximate basis. *Behavioral and Brain Sciences,* **25**(1), 1–72.

Prinz, J. (2012). *The conscious brain.* New York: Oxford University Press.

Ramachandran, V. S. (2000). Mirror neurons and imitation learning as the driving force behind "the great leap forward" in human evolution. *Edge.* Retrieved from <http://www.edge.org/3rd_culture/ramachandran/ramachandran_p1.html>, July 9, 2009.

Regelski, T. (2004). Social theory, and music and music education as praxis. *Action, Criticism, and Theory for Music Education,* **3**(3). Retrieved from <http://act.maydaygroup.org/articles/Regelski3_3.pdf>, June 2, 2014.

Roberts, R. (2013). Taylor Swift sticks to the script; it reads, "thrill fans." *Los Angeles Times.* Retrieved from <http://www.latimes.com/entertainment/music/posts/la-et-ms-taylor-swift-review-20130821,0,4224199.story#ixzz2wGehnYdh>, February 16, 2014.

Robinson, J. (2005). *Deeper than reason: Emotion and its role in literature, music, and art.* Oxford: Oxford University Press.

Schellenberg, G., & von Scheve, C. (2012). Emotional cues in American popular music: Five decades of the Top 40. *Psychology of Aesthetics, Creativity, and the Arts,* **6**(3), 196–203.

Schulkind, M., Hennis, L. K., & Rubin, D. C. (1999). Music, emotion, and autobiographical memory: They are playing our song. *Memory and Cognition,* **27**(6), 948–55.

Silverman, M., & Elliott, D. J. (In press). Arts education as/for artistic citizenship. In D. Elliott, M. Silverman, & W. Bowman (Eds.), Artistic citizenship: Artistry, social responsibility, & ethical praxis. New York: Oxford University Press.

Sloboda, J. A. (1992). Empirical studies of emotional response to music. In M. Reiss-Jones & S. Holleran, (Eds.), *Cognitive bases of musical communication* (pp. 33–46). New York: American Psychological Association.

Stetsenko, A. (2013). Theorizing personhood for the world in transition and change. In J. Martin & M. H. Brickland (Eds.), *The psychology of personhood* (pp. 181–203). Cambridge: Cambridge University Press.

Stokes, A. (2002). *Resemblance theory and the problem of musical meaning: Defining the relationship between form and feeling* (Doctoral dissertation). Brandeis University.

Thompson, E. (2005). Sensorimotor subjectivity and the enactive approach to experience. *Phenomenology and the Cognitive Sciences,* **4**(4), 407–27.

Thompson, E. (2007). *Mind in life: Biology, phenomenology, and the sciences of mind.* Cambridge: Harvard University Press.

Varela, F., Thompson, E., & Rosch, E. (1991). *The embodied mind.* Cambridge: MIT Press.

Chapter 14

Children, popular music, and identity

Sharon G. Davis

Children, popular music, and identity: Introduction

Popular music is important in the lives of children and plays an important sociocultural role (Bosacki et al., 2006; Campbell, 2010; Christenson, 1994; Clements & Campbell, 2006; Davis, 2005, 2013; Lum, 2008; Marsh, 1999; Marsh & Millard, 2000; Minks, 1999; Roberts & Christenson, 2001; Woody, 2007). Engagement with music develops early in a child's life through shared social interaction with parents, caregivers, and companions. These early shared experiences shape identity as children come to understand and interpret their capacity for exchange in meaningful musical experiences (MacDonald, Hargreaves, & Miell, 2002; Trevarthen, 2002). Trevarthen (2002) defines one of the primary features of musicality as the behavior infants display as they interact in these early communicative encounters and argues that as they realize they are active participants, they begin to establish an identity as a group member, a *social identity*.

Social and cultural influences play a critical role in the formation of identity. While children's musical interactions begin with family, as they develop, these interactions expand to include friends, community, and virtual communities that are so much a part of modern culture (Barrett, 2005; Campbell, 2010; Lamont, 2002; Lum, 2008; Lum & Marsh, 2012). The ubiquitous nature of popular music in our society provides a palate of timbres and rhythms for musical consumption for children at the earliest age. Engagement with mediated mass music comes in many forms and continues to evolve at an ever-increasing rate. Children are enculturated into popular music styles through television, radio, movies, music videos, and games, and through personal music devices and social media.

This chapter will consider the nature of children's learning processes when engaged with popular music in performing ensembles and in general music settings, and is divided into three sections: the first section deals with sociocultural roles of popular music in children's lives and how this involvement works to affect their conceptual and emotional views of music; the second section focuses on popular music as shared experience, detailing ways in which children engage in and negotiate popular music with family and friends and the importance of dance to their musical understanding; the final section will focus on the influences of peer and family on the ways that children consider popular music. Highlighted throughout will be children's use of informal processes, both personally and through collaborative opportunities in ensemble situations, and how children's use of these processes informs the development of their musical identities.

Along with extant research I consider datasets from a four-year study collected in my own elementary music classroom. As teacher–researcher, I observed children engaged in popular music-making and carried out lessons using popular music and informal processes in both general music and choral ensemble settings. Additional data were derived from interviews with many of the children over the course of this study.[1]

Sociocultural roles of popular music in the lives of children

Social interaction is a main component of knowledge construction. The origins of sociocultural theory, through the works of George Mead (1934) and Lev Vygotsky (1978), illuminate the role that social situations and cultural contexts have in individual thought, growth, and learning. For Vygotsky (1978) the social construction of learning develops in two ways: first, at the social or interpsychological level, between people; and then within individuals or at the intrapsychological level. This social construction takes place within cultural contexts and is mediated by symbolic tools, language, and other artifacts (Huong, 2003; Wertsch, Tulviste, & Hagstrom, 1993). In this way, children are enculturated not only into the music of their environment, but also into the "associated values, norms, roles, and identities that facilitate sociocultural reproduction and transformation" (Welch, 2000, p. 1).

Much has been written about the importance of music to adolescents in various parts of the world, for American youth (Arnett, 1995; Campbell, Connell, & Beegle, 2007), and British and European youth (Boal-Palheiros & Hargreaves, 2001; Ivaldi & O'Neill, 2008; Lamont et al., 2003; North, Hargreaves & O'Neill, 2000; Tarrant, Hargreaves, & North, 2002; Tarrant, North & Hargreaves, 2000, 2001; Stålhammar, 2006), but as Christenson (1994) points out, association with popular music does not begin abruptly at the onset of adolescence, but rather "evolves over the years from early childhood to adolescence" (p. 136). Listening forms the basis of many early interactions between children and family and plays a crucial role in this *evolution*.

Listening

In his study of first-grade children in Singapore, Lum (2008) found that popular music styles formed the central focus of listening in the home. Engagement through a plethora of mediated sources provided daily interactions amongst the children and their family members and assisted in providing a "common space for bonding and communication" (Lum, 2008, p. 113). Listening to popular music is an important activity in children's lives (Bosacki et al., 2006), and they are adept at operating digital devices, making musical choices, and constructing musical preferences in personal and social situations (Mercier-De Shon, 2012). Barrett (2003) describes contemporary children as "meme engineers" as they access and control their listening experiences rather than being "passive recipients of those offered to them through adult-mediated action in the spaces of popular, media, and institutional cultures" (Barrett, 2003, p. 197).

In my conversations with elementary school children about their musical backgrounds, I expected to hear about instrumental lessons or singing in the choir, but instead many mentioned listening first before any other musical engagement. Here is one such response:

SD: Tell me about your musical background.
MADELINE: I have been listening to music since I was pretty little. My older brother's guitar teacher would come to our house. He would have guitar lessons and I was 3 and I would also listen. . . . In the car I like to listen to the radio. When I was four or five my mom realized that I really like music . . . then I started to play the violin cause my mom knew a friend that did violin lessons and she also did piano too. Basically two weeks into violin I started piano.

Siblings have a large influence on the musical interactions within the home (Bosacki et al., 2006; Campbell, 2010) and, as described here, Madeline was an active observer of live instrumental instruction as a toddler, and at 9 is a violinist, pianist, singer, and also a prolific songwriter.

Although she takes traditional instrumental lessons Madeline writes songs in a pop style. In detailing some of her favorite listening experiences she describes a variety of reasons that she listens to particular artists. She likes Rihanna for the quality of her voice, Taylor Swift because of her artistry and for the personal nature of her songwriting, the song "Jukebox Hero" because it is a favorite of her dad's, but it is Kelly Clarkson who has created a meaningful influence in Madeline's life:

MADELINE: I like the song "Stronger" by Kelly Clarkson. I like this song because it's an inspirational song and this is where I kinda got my inspiration for writing music.

SD: So, this song made you want to write music?

MADELINE: Yeah, because I really like pop and country and this is really a pop song but I like her singing in it.

SD: You mean her voice?

MADELINE: Yeah, her voice and stuff and if you see the music video . . . I like it.

SD: But you said that this song inspired you to write songs?

MADELINE: Yeah.

SD: So what was it about the song that inspired you to write?

MADELINE: Well it's kinda like the first song that I ever heard that's like that, the title really goes with it and her voice and the background music really goes with it and I like it.

SD: So you heard that song and–

MADELINE: (interrupting) and I'm like, *I have to write music.*

SD: So do you see yourself as a songwriter?

MADELINE: Yes.

Madeline is a songwriter and often enters music class and asks if she can perform her songs. She started performing on the violin and piano for her classmates in first grade and has performed her original songs at school functions. The school chorus has also performed her songs as she accompanied them on the piano. Listening is not a passive activity for her but has contributed to her musicianship and formed the foundation for her compositional processes. She listens to music with a discerning ear, for vocal quality, for aspects that she defines as artistic, and for music that entertains and facilitates her identity as a singer–songwriter.

Hargreaves, Miell, and MacDonald (2002) distinguish musical identity in two ways: as identities in music, and as music in identities. Identities in music are the manner in which musicians are "socially defined within given cultural roles and musical categories" (p. 2), for example in the role of performer or composer. Music in identities refers to the ways music can influence or modify one's personal identity. When Madeline was asked what it meant to be a musician she explained that playing an instrument is important, but songwriting is the way to "communicate in music with other people." Songwriting differentiates her from other members of her family who are also involved in music, as she has mentioned many times, "I'm the only one in my family that writes songs."

Kaschub and Smith (2009) describe composition as a "powerful act of self" (p. 6) and propose "novice composers are eager to create music that represents their musical identity" (p. 239). Popular music guides Madeline's songwriting form and style and she is inspired by the piano, but admits that she is motivated to write music because she enjoys "showing people my talent" and influencing her friends to also write songs. Drawing upon her sociocultural influences, popular music gives form to Madeline's songwriting and "reflects membership of particular cultural communities and awareness of the values and behaviors appropriate to the contexts of these communities" (Barrett, 2003, p. 201). The female singer–songwriters whom Madeline admires have influenced her values as a musician, provided tools with which to construct her own songs and influenced her ideas about what constitutes a musician. Composing in this pop style *represents* Madeline's developing musical identity.

O'Neill (2002) describes the ways in which young people come to define being a musician or not, and the different ways in which music is produced, distributed, and received play a key role in this understanding. She posits, "As children and adolescents negotiate a sense of self and identity in relation to music, they respond in ways that sustain and perpetuate these differences" (p. 79). Playing an instrument and creating songs are Madeline's view of being a musician and clearly she sees herself in this role. Despite her traditional piano lessons and ability to read and write music in notation form, Madeline's process of writing songs remains aurally based and her approach reflects the informal processes ascribed to by popular musicians.

Listening is learning

Informal learning is the root of learning and is a part of everyday life long before formal schooling begins. Informal learning processes play a significant part of children's interactions as they collaborate together on the playground and engage in meaningful games and chants (Campbell, 2010; Harwood, 1994; Harwood & Marsh, 2012; Marsh, 2008). In recent years there has been much research on informal learning processes in music (Davis, 2012, 2013; Folkestad, 2006; Green, 2002, 2008; Harwood & Marsh, 2012; Jaffurs, 2004; Johansen, 2010; Mans, 2009), the effectiveness of aural learning (Baker & Green, 2013; Kohut, 1985; McPherson & Gabrielsson, 2002; Priest, 1989; Shively, 1995) and the importance of valuing aural learning in music education. Green's (2002) seminal work on the informal processes of popular musicians outlined five key areas of informal music practices of which copying by ear plays a main role. I have already described the importance of listening as more than a passive activity, one that is certainly not a barrier to learning as described in this vignette:

> It was a typical Monday morning and Mrs. Wood's fourth grade class was making their way into the music room when Cynthia excitedly approached me, recorder in hand, and enthusiastically exclaimed, "Hey, listen to what I figured out over the weekend." She began to play the opening chorus of "I gotta feelin" by the Black Eyed Peas, much to the delight of her classmates and teacher. "I can play most the chorus, but there is something I don't get about the ending." Before I could grab my recorder and iPod to cue up the tune, Cynthia had begun to play the song again from the beginning and students were already gathered around her, watching her fingers and trying it out for themselves.

Children often spend time at home fiddling with music by ear with available instruments and they enjoy sharing this music with classmates at school. This example is representative of children's processes heard throughout the course of the school year and an example of how children approach music-making. Consider Cynthia's statement: "I can play most of the chorus, but there is something I don't get about the ending." Instead of waiting for the teacher to show her she begins to play from the beginning again, at the part she has already told us she understands. That children prefer to start over from the beginning of a game or a song has been found to be a consistent characteristic of children's ways of being in learning and in play practices around the world (Blacking, 1995; Campbell, 2001; Harwood & Marsh, 2012; Marsh, 2008; Wiggins, 1994). Children seem to understand working with contextual wholes rather than breaking down music into smaller sequences. Notice also that children gather around the music-maker and try to aurally copy. The immediate response is to participate and *do* music.

In a recent field experience I observed four young girls working on a popular song for a project in their chorus ensemble. One girl was playing bass guitar and singing and the other three were singers. Their tools included a lyric sheet, an iPod, and an electric bass. Their main method of working was repeatedly singing the song from the beginning. If the song broke down or they stopped singing, much conversation and laughter would ensue and then rehearsal would begin again from the start. When I inquired as to why they always stopped and went back to the beginning, Kit the bass player, replied:

KIT: If we got stuck on a part we would just go back and do it over again. Most of the time we just stayed with the part that we knew. And we would talk about it, we were like, this part is a little confusing so let's go back to this part and keep going.

SD: So you went back to the beginning?

KIT: Yeah, we went back to the beginning and started all over again.

SD: So it helps you to go back to the beginning?

KIT: I find it very helpful.

SD: Why is that?

KIT: Well when you start from the beginning you know where to start. If you keep starting from like, one certain point [that wasn't the beginning] you might think, ooh it starts from there.

SD: So you can't start in the middle?

KIT: Well from time to time if it's just one thing that's bad you can start from a place just before that, but I wouldn't say, practicing it over and over from there.

SD: So is that what you did to learn a song, just do it over and over?

KIT: Yes, well, we communicated too . . . I would say my question or my statement and we would start again and if someone had a question they would like say what they meant.

Kit considers herself a musician and is no stranger to playing popular music on her bass. She takes bass guitar lessons and reads music quite well, but her preferred method of working is by ear. From her explanation we see that repeating from the beginning provides an anchor and a secure entrance point. Breaking down a section for rehearsal is not out of the question, but repetitive entrances from a locale that is not from the beginning is confusing. Through conversation they were able to discuss the solutions needed to repair a troublesome section, but the process of repair had to occur within the process of whole, in other words returning to the anchor point and work through the problem spot and, as Kit describes, "to keep going." Children do not like to stop the flow of their work and attempt to repair their mistakes in real time, on the fly. A much preferred method rather than stopping and starting from a non-anchor point such as the middle of a piece.

Popular music is a constant companion for Kit, and her iPod touch is always within reach. Her method of learning songs, even for her private lessons, is to figure it out by ear first. She approaches this by first singing the lyrics repeatedly until these words are secure. In this process she records herself singing on her cell phone voice recorder and then evaluates her accuracy. Once she is satisfied with this part she begins to figure out the bass line on her instrument. Guitar tabs found on the Internet are only used as a last resort. Her ear is her guide.

John, the immersion learner

John loves learning new songs and the Internet is his constant source for learning. He often uses YouTube lyric videos or connects his Karaoke machine up to the Internet to begin his process.

Lyrics are the first obstacle to overcome when learning a song, but are learned in real time with attention to rhythm.

SD: Why is tempo so important in learning a new song?

JOHN: Well, do you know "The Devil Went Down to Georgia" (taps a fast beat on the table) that is a fast song but if I just looked at the lyrics I would think it was a slow song. [By listening] then I know that song is fast and I have to sing it fast. I need to learn that first [real time].

SD: So singing at tempo is what helps you?

JOHN: Yes. If I learn the lyrics, then I can get the song.

John's process of learning a song is repeating it over and over while listening or watching the lyric video on YouTube. This, according to John, does not take very much time. Embedded in this process is the importance of focusing on the rhythm and the tempo, as this supports the lyric acquisition process. Again, as in these examples, children prefer to learn from contextual wholes, rather than breaking down songs into pieces or slowing down the tempo.

Children are drawn to and engage quickly with music that is familiar (Davis, 2013). While they may appreciate and enjoy the music of their particular faith or ethnicity, as is evident in this section, popular music seems to be the most pervasive music in their everyday activities and therefore the most familiar. For children who take private instrumental lessons, classical music plays a role in their musical experience and they have some appreciation for it. Beethoven and Mozart were the most familiar composers, and the piano piece *Für Elise*, the most popular piece both requested in class and performed by students. The music of the *Nutcracker* also fared well, as children had heard the music in advertisements or had attended or performed in the ballet. But as a rule, the children with whom I spoke did not seek out classical music to listen to and said they found it boring. Classical music was heard rarely if ever in their homes and in my discussions with them they described classical music as "too like . . . throwback," "too slow," "not upbeat enough," and otherwise lacking "crazy" rhythm and beats, for their taste.

Knowledge is culturally and socially mediated and learning is influenced by the environment and participation in which children are able to access. In each of these scenarios children were in control of their own learning processes. They chose the music they wanted to learn, and their preferred learning mode was through aural processes. The students used assessment procedures to further their learning, evaluate their accuracy in learning a song, and to judge whether the song met their criteria. Informal learning in music-making can foster musical agency (see Wiggins, Chapter 6) and can be a critical aspect of musical-identity development. Incorporating and valuing authentic informal processes can draw upon rather than alienate students' musical experiences.

Popular music as a shared experience

How children and adolescents use popular music in their lives can be conceived as signaling a "transition from parent orientation toward peer orientation" (Christenson, 1994, p. 136). For children this transition contains a melding of the music that is important to parents, peers, and the children's personal choices. Popular music listening accompanies many activities within the home, and children are influenced by their parents' music (Bosacki et al., 2006) and enjoy sharing and being involved in their parents' music. For many children listening to music their parents enjoy helps them feel connected. Radio listening in the car provides almost daily interaction for some, and with the variety of stations, satellite radio, and iPods, children come to know the music that their parents appreciate currently and also enjoyed in their adolescence. Children are also keenly aware of the music their parents disapprove of and, while they may seek to honor parental discretion, they are also negotiating potential conflicts within their own listening experiences as evidenced in these comments from 9- and 10-year-old children.

JILLIAN: My taste in music has been influenced by my parents. . . . My parents listen to this band called Tegan and Sara and they are a kind of rock band/pop. That has definitely changed my taste. I don't listen to rapping. I don't listen to Ke$ha or people that say bad words.

MADELINE: Yeah, I like clean music.

JILLIAN: I like Bruno Mars but sometimes he has bad stuff and I only listen to the good songs. I like Taylor Swift and Christina Perri.

*

AVERY: I share most of the music with my mom because she doesn't want me to listen to anything inappropriate. But I listen to country songs a lot and I put my iPod on and put the headphones in my ears and I just like sit there and listen to the words, 'cause country music always has a story. . . . It's like a mixture of reading and listening to music. And I love to read too.

*

LILLY: My mom and I don't always agree on the same kinds of music. She grew up in the 80s and now likes a cappella groups who make their own music with their voices. I like more popular songs that are on the radio or in movies. We do like some of the same channels on the radio and XM [satellite radio] but our personal playlists on our iTunes shows how different our tastes are.

While Jillian and Madeline say they do not listen to rap music, they were very well acquainted with it. Earlier in the year they formed a band with a few other students and regularly performed in music class and at school events. They are very good singers, but recognized that when they performed slow songs or covers from artists such as Adele or Taylor Swift, the reaction amongst some students, especially boys, was not so favorable. They enjoyed performing songs that had a slower tempo because they were easier to learn and facilitated finding harmonies, but in order to drum up more interest in their band they decided to create a parody of a popular rap. They explained their decision to do so was because "we wanted people to think we were funny and not boring, slow-mo singers." They used the theme of Field Day, an all-school outdoor activity hosted by the physical education department. They engaged in a little marketing research around the playground to find out what other students enjoyed most about field day in order to incorporate these activities into their lyrics. When they performed their finished product they were an instant hit, performing their rap at several school activities. The parody was well crafted and was enjoyed by their peers, especially the boys. All their peers had a stake in the rap and were delighted when their favorite game was mentioned during the performance. Catering to the tastes of their audience generated cultural capital amongst their peers, and as Arthur (2005) describes, "Children's popular media culture is part of children's social repertoire and generates cultural capital that is valued within children's peer groups. Popular media culture creates a shared frame of reference that children draw on in their musical play" (p. 167, as noted in Lum, 2008, p. 107).

For Lilly, the difference in listening preferences between her mother and her were qualified through musical characteristics, such as "the beat feels old" or "I don't like the main singer's voice."

Lilly enjoyed a lot of rap music and admitted that her mother did not appreciate this genre and tired easily of its repetition. But Lilly offered an olive branch as she discussed the music upon which they can agree:

> A song that my mom and I can agree on is "Fifty Ways To Say Goodbye" by Train. We both like the lyrics and the singer's voice. Next time you think you can't agree on music with your parents, try listening to different radio stations to find songs you both like.

Roberts and Christenson (2001) note that lyrics are a "primary gratification" for many adolescents and while children may interpret lyrics more concretely than teens, lyrics play a significant role and may work to inform their "decision-making processes" (Bosacki et al., 2006). Certainly adult themes, explicit language, and violence are of great concern for parents and educators and, as Bosacki et al. (2006) point out, because of the significant role of popular music in the lives of children, there is a need for "critical media literacy programs to foster metacognitive skills such as critical thinking and reflective thought in children across various ages and socioeconomic backgrounds" (p. 381). In this transition period of late childhood to adolescence it seems that children desire to share and experience popular music with their parents, and perhaps this may be the prime time to instigate discussions about lyric content to foster critical thinking.

Media

Understanding the ways children use popular music provides a portal into popular culture as viewed by children and into ways in which it influences their lives (Campbell, 2010; Fitzpatrick, 2012; Harwood & Marsh, 2012; Lum, 2008; Lum & Marsh, 2012). Children are proficient with handheld digital devices, and YouTube provides access to learning songs from their favorite groups either through karaoke versions, or viewing music videos or instructional videos. Through immediate access children can follow their favorite artists through social media, which often provide a seemingly insider's view into the artists' personal lives.

For many young children, popular music is heard as a soundtrack to their favorite television shows and cartoons and, unlike the fleeting sounds of many popular tunes on the top billboard charts, television shows provide theme music that can be heard for years and through these sources children can come to establish long relationships with artists. Disney Channel, an American cable/satellite channel, is an entertainment channel that caters to children through early adolescence (ages 2–14 years old). The Disney website features interactive possibilities for viewers and, from my experience in an American general music classroom, many children are familiar with this channel and draw their love of popular music through watching this and other similar channels that are customized for children. Consider this vignette of two second-grade girls discussing their favorite artist:

SD: So, tell me about Selena Gomez.

KENNEDY: I started listening to her when I was four.

JORDAN: And she's like our favorite artist.

KENNEDY: She's my favorite artist out of all.

JORDAN: She's on the Disney channel and the Wizards of Waverly place. I heard her sing and I went on the computer and I saw that she had all these songs and I started to hear them and I really liked her.

SD: Is she still on the show, Wizards of Waverly place?

JORDAN AND KENNEDY:	Yes.
SD:	You started watching her when you were four. How old are you now?
KENNEDY:	Eight.

Upon hearing this singer on television, Jordan immediately researched additional songs that the singer recorded to add to her listening experiences. She and Kennedy were influenced by the singer and in music class, patterned several of their musical compositions after her songs, and also tried to emulate her singing style.

The ease with which children can search the Internet and research their musical interests promotes autonomy, discrimination, and self-discovery of their musical tastes (O'Neill, 2012) and, as evident in Jordan's comments, the process of musical self-socialization (Arnett, 1995; Mueller, 2002). Musical self-socialization transpires through the musical choices that people make with regard to listening, becoming a music fan, or participation in a group or ensemble, and these self-selected choices contribute to an individual's social identity (Arnett, 1995; Mueller, 2002). These choices became a part of the girls' shared experiences, but also contributed to their identity construction as they took on the musical attributes of the pop artist through performance and creating projects.

Dancing

Children are rarely still, and one way they come to know and understand their world is through movement. For young children, engagement with popular music is most easily experienced through movement and dance. The rhythm invites participation and it is through these experiences that musical meaning-making can unfold. Physical engagement with music enables children to have a "fuller intellectual and emotional experience" (Campbell, 2010, p. 239) and can also explicitly demonstrate what they are hearing and musically thinking (p. 240). Dance also provides children with an "enhanced form of listening" and a more "concentrated *sense of the music*" (Frith, 1996b, p. 223).

Rhythmic engagement provides entrance-level participation and involves decision-making processes regarding when to move, which is dictated by tempo and repetitive patterns, some of the hallmark characteristics of popular music. Children are more than capable of demonstrating with their bodies not only the beat and rhythm of the song, but also the subtle nuance of expression (Cohen, 1997). Rhythmic play formed the basis of much of the everyday engagement of children in Lum and Campbell's (2007) study of one American elementary school. Rhythmic play was described as a fusion of "music and movement" or activities involving regular rhythmic movement "frequently but not always accompanied by vocalization in the form of speech-inflected chant" (p. 36). The body is the main source of performance acquisition on the playground where "learning is 'by feel' rather than step by step instruction" (Harwood & Marsh, 2012).

Dance is an important aspect of engagement with popular music, as Frith (1996b) describes:

> Dance matters not just as a way of expressing music but as a way of listening to it, a way into the music *in its unfolding*—which is why dancing to music is both a way of losing oneself in it, physically, and a way of thinking about it. (p. 142)

In my observations of young children dancing and moving to their favorite pop songs, part of the *unfolding* that I witness results in enjoyment and social interaction but also evidence of thinking in motion. Initial physical enactment includes moving to the beat and gesturing with their arms, but because of its familiarity and the children's experience with the song both aurally and also visually through music video, children can bring a depth of bodily understanding.

Consider the following vignette where students have been asked to create movements or dance to reflect the musical form of a popular song of their choice.

> The song "Love You Like a Love Song" (Armato & James, 2011), sung by Selena Gomez, is playing as the second graders enter the room. It is one of their favorites and they have requested that we listen to it in music class. Upon entering the room they begin to smile and move their bodies to the beat. The form of the song is a typical pop song format, and at the chorus, the part that is familiar to most, they all join in and sing together the following:
>
> > I, I love you like a love song baby
> > I, I love you like a love song baby
> > I, I love you like a love song baby
> > And I keep hitting repeat, peat, peat, peat, peat, peat.
>
> Melodically the first two lines are identical and line three has some melodic variation on the last three words but it is the last line, the hook, with the novel repetition of "peat, peat, peat" that the children enjoy the most. Here they catch eye contact with their friends and gesture in sync to the rhythm of phrase. From their experiences in the music curriculum the children were familiar with call and response and binary form, and without taking class time to analyze the song's form, the teacher asked them to create some movements that reflected the form of this song. Given free reign to create, it was obvious from their movements that they understood the differences between the verse, chorus, and bridge.
>
> One dance was simply not enough for the children and as the class continues they join together in friendship groups. As they engage with the song again, while they know the words to the verses fairly well, the volume level escalates at the chorus when the majority joins the singing. Their motions are littered with dance moves and acting out synchronized motions that change with each section of the song. For most of the children dancing is a form of social interaction and as they engage together, they join hands, spin in circles, and acquiesce to each other's desired moves. They include each other and with each repetition their movements become more elaborate and fluid. At the bridge, when the tempo slows to a half-time feel, the children change their moves immediately to graceful motions that reflect the change in tempo and feel in the song.

While this experience was very social, it was also highly individual. Dancing to this music provided a way of playacting or acting out the role of the singer or instrumentalist in the song. Some children pretended to have a microphone and perfectly emulate the words of the song as if they were the performer. Dancing is a form of "self-actualization—physical, emotional and intellectual" (Bresler, 2004, p. 148) and as Frith (1996b) describes, "When dancing we subject our body movements to musical rules . . . and yet in our very self-consciousness we seem to reveal more clearly our physical sense of ourselves; we are more self-expressive" (p. 220). Dancing can enhance children's awareness of the world and their experience in it.

After the dance moves were over the teacher queried the children, "Why do you like that song so much?" and the children replied, "Peat, peat, peat, peat, peat." This song features a *hook*, a memorable part of the song, of which students were aware and took great pleasure in acting out and dancing to. Hooks are the infrastructure of popular music and consist of repetitive musical devices to catch the listener's attention. These devices can range from melodic phrases of varying lengths, to harmonic progressions or expressive textures, but in theory, a hook should involve one or more of the following: "a) a driving, danceable rhythm; b) a melody that stays in people's minds;

c) a lyric that furthers the dramatic action, or defines a person or place" (Kasha & Hirschhorn, 1979, pp. 28–9, as cited in Burns, 1987, p. 1).

The driving dance rhythm encouraged the children to move immediately and continuously throughout the song, and while they demonstrated an understanding of the musical form through their movements, they delighted in showing gestures for the part of the hook that was very novel, the words "peat, peat, peat, peat, peat." The longer they moved, the more in sync their motions became, as they used similar rhythmic gestures that imitated the exact rhythm and articulation of this small motive. It was evident from the children's movements and gestures that they understood the changes in the musical form as the song moved from the verse through the chorus and bridge sections, yet in their discussions following the dancing, the children had difficulty verbally articulating these formal aspects, preferring instead to show with their body rather than tell.

Many have written on bodily knowing and gesture and its role in musical understanding (Juntunen & Hyvönen, 2004; Small, 1998; Stubley, 1998; Trevarthen, 1999/2000). The function of gesture, investigated by scientists in a biochemistry lab, was found to enable group conceptualization and communications about molecule theories (Becva, Holland, & Hutchins, 2005). The use of hand gesture has visual, spatial, and dynamic elements, which could be employed immediately in explaining details of the subject matter. A key aspect of this study for educators is that the use of gestures calls upon "embodied schematic knowledge about our bodies and our interactions with the material world. By using gestures to represent an abstract concept, perceptual processes can replace or support cognitively difficult conceptual processes" (p. 108).

Dance provided a *visual, spatial, and dynamic* component to the children's engagement as the music and their experience unfolded. To musick, writes Small (1998), is to "take part, in any capacity, in a musical performance, whether by performing, by listening, by rehearsing or practicing, by providing material for performance (what is called composing), or by dancing" (p. 9). Through musicking, their embodied understanding gave rise to symbolic meaning, as the teacher was then able to explain the formal names of the musical sections they had physically described. For some children the ability to bring their own dance moves to a song was an important criterion for choosing certain types of music. The experience of engaging in music that was a part of the fabric of their musical worlds also provided a form of social bonding. As Overy and Molnar-Szakacs (2009) describe,

> The experience of being synchronized together in time, and yet with a musical, human flexibility and variety creates a powerful sense of togetherness, and demonstrates to listeners the cooperation and strength of a social group. It thus seems likely that imitation, synchronization, and affective, shared experience are key elements of musical behavior, which may be crucial or at least important in music education and music therapy. (p. 495)

The freedom of moving and dancing to their favorite song, a song that was very familiar to them, provided a space for identity making both individually and collectively. They used their bodies to reflect not only what they were hearing and feeling, but also in this way created, transformed, and magnified their *physical sense of self* (Frith, 1996b).

Peer and family influences

Parental support, particularly in the formative years, has a great impact on the musical achievement of children (Borthwick & Davidson, 2002; Creech & Hallam, 2003; Davidson, 2002; Davidson, Howe, & Sloboda, 1995; McPherson, 2008; McPherson & Davidson, 2006). The work of Borthwick and Davidson (2002) underscores the effect that family interactions can have on a child's musical identity. Children's identity is influenced by the "responses and values" expressed by the immediate family members through expectations of musical involvement (p. 76). In the development of a child musician certainly the social influences of peers, teachers, and role models also have a great deal of impact on their musical identity (Davidson & Burland, 2006).

"Jillian the singer" is how she is known at school. Jillian came to understand herself as a musician partially through responses she received from her school peers and through her analysis of meaningful popular songs, the performers' voices, and how they related to her own voice. Jillian does not take private musical lessons, but she is a good musician with excellent aural ability. Her father is a musician and both parents are very supportive of her musical endeavors.

Jillian has been involved in the school chorus and many school productions since she was in first grade. In fourth grade she formed a band made up of friends in her school and they wrote their own songs, created parodies, and performed pop songs. In a project for her general music class in which students were asked to discuss and share the music that was most meaningful to them, Jillian took great care to discuss three songs that were representative of her musical identity. The order of her choices was a) a song her father performed, b) a popular song that made an early impression, and c) a current popular song. I found the order that she presented the songs as well as the commentary on each song insightful, and through several interviews, Jillian very eloquently disclosed her understanding of self, and in so doing, an avenue of her musical identity. The order chosen was in direct relation to her connection to the music. Her father's song was one which she felt very close to, but it was the second song that was the impetus that propelled her along her singing path. As Jillian explains:

> The first time that I heard "Our Song," I was in kindergarten. I liked it immediately because it was really catchy and had a great tune. I also liked the sound of Taylor Swift's voice. This song means a lot to me because it was the first Taylor Swift song that I ever heard and now she is my favorite singer. It makes me feel happy and makes me believe that I can be a successful singer someday too. My favorite part is the chorus because I like how she sings it really fast and it makes me want to dance. I would definitely share this song with my friends because most of them like Taylor Swift too. I would also share it with my family because they would ask me to sing along to it.

In a later interview I asked her about her comments on the song and she clarified that "Our Song" was the reason she had started singing. Her love for the song and desire to sing it propelled her budding singer identity. Several telling meanings lie behind Jillian's commentary. First was the young age at which she discovered this song, in kindergarten (age 5), and the emotion she felt upon hearing the song, and second, her knowledge that sharing this song with her family would invite a performance. Davidson (2002) noted the influence that early experiences can have in the development of the solo performer. Drawing upon experiences in her early life, Davidson describes the effect of hearing a choral performance in school, which caused her to immediately recreate the music for her family. In this experience she describes the notion of performance as "central to my enjoyment and understanding of the music itself" (p. 98). As Jillian's father was a professional musician, exposure to live performance was frequent in her young life, but upon hearing a song at age 5, she decided that she wanted to be a singer and she endeavored to do just that in her school experiences, emulating many of her favorite artists at school performances.

The last song in Jillian's trilogy revealed more about the developmental aspects of seeing oneself as a performer. Upon hearing the song "A Thousand Years" by Christina Perri, she was enthralled with the emotion in the voice and smooth sound. This song inspired her to change her vocal technique and to work on singing with a "relaxed sound." She was also moved by the way this artist blended and harmonized with the background vocals, but mentioned that while this song was obviously important to her, she would prefer to sing it in her room, as she does not normally share slow songs with friends.

While this song was important to her, she explained that she really could not relate to the words necessarily, but it was the sonic qualities of the singer's voice that drew her to it. These timbres meet the criterion of her search as she reaches out to discover what it is that she likes and strives vocally to do. She is motivated by harmony in a song and seeks to discover this in music that she engages in. The last statement drew my attention, and in a later interview Jillian explained her meaning more precisely. I was interested in why this was a song she would sing alone in her room.

JILLIAN: Most people don't expect me to sing slow songs like that.
SD: And it's important what most people think?
JILLIAN: NO, NO, I definitely stepped out of my comfort zone since that time and I probably wouldn't have trouble doing it now, but then I wasn't so YEAH YEAH let's do this (confident). But now I would.
SD: Why are you able to step out of your comfort zone now?
JILLIAN: 'Cause I realized even though I mess up on a bunch of stuff people still like my singing and I realized that a lot of people compliment me more than I would think.
SD: So that helps?
JILLIAN: So that makes me feel like, OK, they like that . . . and that connects to this so I'll try that; if they like that I'll go to this.

Discussing the aesthetics of popular music, Frith (1996a) first describes identity as a process, as something *mobile*, something in flux, not something that is static, and second, how the experiences of music-making and listening are experiences through this "self as process" (p. 109). In her self-reflective analysis, Jillian is aware of her "presentation of self to others" (DeNora, 2000) and she has drawn upon this knowledge to forge a way forward. Jillian is a perfectionist and her concept of "messing up" means perhaps interchanging or leaving out a word. She is certainly performance-ready whenever she sings, so I was curious if she could describe herself before she was able to step out of her comfort zone.

SD: Can you describe yourself as a singer before you stepped out of that comfort zone.
JILLIAN: I think I was always able to step out of my comfort zone, it was just for me to be ready, like for me to have the right effort and for people to push me in the right way. Just to be ready for that.
SD: So you were always ready to step out?
JILLIAN: Yes. I just needed the push.

The positive encouragement of family and friends is certainly important for any developing musician (Davidson & Burland, 2006) and can change the course of a performer's perception of him/herself as a musician (Davis, 2013). As O'Neill (2006) describes, "the quality of both formal and informal musical activities matters, as well as peer groups and communities that pay attention to, and show an interest in, musical activities" (p. 469). Jillian's identity as a singer has evolved through listening discernment, recognition from her peers, and from identifying with and learning from vocal timbres that she desires to emulate.

Many children described admiring pop artists for their vocal quality, qualities that they wanted to emulate or recognized as similar to theirs. For John, who has been singing publicly since the first grade, Bruno Mars was his pop artist of choice because he enjoys the way that Bruno Mars moves and dances, but he likes to sing his songs because:

> His voice is always the right pitch to match mine. It kinda sounds the same and he sings on the right note so I can hit it.

Hargreaves, MacDonald, & Miell (2012) suggest that our perception of our abilities helps to shape our identities both personally and musically, and the degree to which we view ourselves as a musician "is an essential aspect of our musical identities" (p. 132). Monk's (2003) longitudinal study revealed that in adolescence, a vocal identity "reveals a close relationship with their sense of self" (p. 253). In these examples we see that identification of vocal timbre and the ability to perform songs that matched a sense of self was one way in which children's musical identity evolved. Through their own analysis and synthesis the children were able to engage in the practices of popular music-making, an important aspect of their musical development. Musical meaning is socially determined as a result of the cultural activities that people deem important. The evolution of a musical identity occurs within these social situations and musical interactions (MacDonald et al., 2002; Turino, 2008; Wenger, 1998) and is a complex and emerging process (DeNora, 2000; Frith 1996a; Hargreaves et al., 2012).

Conclusions

Popular music plays a significant role in the lives of children. It is one aspect of family life that provides communal time with parents and siblings and a platform for shared understandings and cultural capital amongst playmates and peers. As popular music is ubiquitous in the media it forms a large part of children's daily listening experiences and is influential in establishing what it means to be a musician. Listening was underscored throughout this chapter as more than a passive activity for children, establishing a foundation for compositional skills for some and as vocal models for others. Musical-identity construction is facilitated through engagement with popular music as children realize themselves in such socially defined roles as singer or songwriter and are recognized as such amongst family and peers.

Popular music is embraced by children and seen as music that is within their grasp to learn without adult intervention. Informal processes, and in particular aural learning, are familiar and preferred methods of engaging with music. Children's strategies for learning pop music include listening, and repetitive performances, through which evaluation, usually through recording devices, is the norm. For many children, physical engagement is a natural response to popular music, which provides an important way to understand music in real time, but also promotes social interaction and provides a bodily sense of self as the music unfolds. Children use popular music as a leisure activity but also as a tangible tool for furthering their musical understanding and engaging in musical self-socialization, contributing to their social identities and personal musical identities.

Certainly popular music is not the only music that children enjoy, but its importance in their lives should not be overlooked. Their musical tastes and interests should be considered in curricular choices. In understanding the child as musician, educators should consider the importance of the inclusion of popular music and popular culture in the musical experiences planned for children.

Reflective questions

1 What music is currently on your playlist and what does this reveal about your musical identity?
2 Listening is such an active part of learning music for children. Have you ever learned an entire song by listening? How was this process different than learning a song from notation?

3 Do you notice that you use certain kinds of music in certain situations or in certain roles in your life?

4 Consider events in your early life that were meaningful and from which you can pinpoint as creating or adding to your own musical identity.

5 How do children's musical tastes factor into the curricular choices in your classroom?

Note

1 All names are pseudonyms.

Key sources

DeNora, T. (2000). *Music in everyday life*. Cambridge, UK: Cambridge University Press.

Frith, S. (1996). Music and identity. In S. Hall & P. du Gay (Eds.), *Questions of cultural identity* (pp. 108–27). London, UK: Sage Publications.

Green, L. (Ed.) (2011). *Learning, teaching, and musical identity: Voices across cultures*. Bloomington: Indiana University Press.

MacDonald, R., Hargreaves, D., & Miell, D. (Eds.) (2002). *Musical identities*. Oxford, UK: Oxford University Press.

Turino, T. (2008). *Music as social life: The politics of participation*. Chicago and London: University of Chicago Press.

Reference list

Armato, A., & James, T. (2011) Love you like a love song [Recorded by Selena Gomez and The Scene]. *On when the sun goes down* [CD]. Burbank, CA: Hollywood Records.

Arnett, J. J. (1995). Adolescents' uses of media for self-socialization. *Journal of Youth and Adolescence*, 24(5), 519–33.

Arthur, L. (2005). Popular culture: Views of parents and educators. In J. Marsh, (Ed.), *Popular culture, new media and digital literacy in early childhood* (pp. 165–82). New York: Routledge Falmer.

Baker, D., & Green, L. (2013). Ear playing and aural development in the instrumental lesson: Results from a "case-control" experiment. *Research Studies in Music Education*, 35(2), 141–59. doi: 10.1177/1321103X13508254.

Barrett, M. (2003). Meme engineers: Children as producers of musical culture. *International Journal of Early Years Education*, 11(3), 195–212. doi: 10.1080/0966976032000147325.

Barrett, M. S. (2005). Musical communication and children's communities of musical practice. In D. Miell, R. MacDonald, & D. Hargreaves (Eds.), *Musical communication* (pp. 261–80). Oxford, UK: Oxford University Press.

Becva, L. A., Holland, J., & Hutchins, E. (2005). Hands as molecules: Representational gestures for developing theory in a scientific laboratory. *Semiotica: Journal of the International Association for Semiotic Studies*, 156(1/4), 89–112.

Blacking, J. (1995). *Music, culture and experience*. Chicago and London: University of Chicago Press.

Boal-Palheiros, G. M., & Hargreaves, D. J. (2001). Listening to music at home and at school. *British Journal of Music Education*, 18(2), 103–18. doi: 10.1017/S0265051701000213.

Borthwick, S. J., & Davidson, J. W. (2002). Developing a child's identity as a musician: A family "script" perspective. In R. MacDonald, D. J. Hargreaves, & D. Miell (Eds.), *Musical identities* (pp. 60–78). Oxford, UK: Oxford University Press.

Bosacki, S., Francis-Murray, N., Pollon, D. E., & Elliott, A. (2006). "Sounds good to me": Canadian children's perceptions of popular music. *Music Education Research*, 8(3), 369–85. doi: 10.1080/14613800600957495.

Bresler, L. (2004). Dancing the curriculum: Exploring the body and movement in elementary schools. In L. Bresler (Ed.), *Knowing bodies, moving minds: Towards embodied teaching and learning* (pp. 127–52). Dordrecht, The Netherlands: Kluwer Academics.

Burns, G. (1987). A typology of "hooks" in popular records. *Popular Music*, **6**(1), 1–20.

Campbell, P. S. (2001). Unsafe suppositions? Cutting across cultures on questions of music's transmission. *Music Education Research*, **3**(2), 215–26. doi: 10.1080/14613800120089269.

Campbell, P. S. (2010). *Songs in their heads: Music and its meaning in children's lives* (2nd ed.). New York: Oxford University Press.

Campbell, P. S., Connell, C., & Beegle, A. (2007). Adolescents' expressed meanings of music in and out of school. *Journal of Research in Music Education*, **55**(3), 220–36. doi: 10.1177/002242940705500304.

Christenson, P. (1994). Childhood patterns of music uses and preferences. *Communication Reports*, **7**(2), 136–44. doi: 10.1080/08934219409367596.

Clements, A. C., & Campbell, P. S. (2006). Rap, rock, race, and rhythm: Music and more in a methods class. *The Mountain Lake Reader*, **4**, 16–22.

Cohen, V. W. (1997). Explorations of kinesthetic analogues for musical schemes. *Bulletin of the Council for Research in Music Education*, **131**(Winter), 1–13.

Creech, A., & Hallam, S. (2003). Parent–teacher–pupil interactions in instrumental music tuition: A literature review. *British Journal of Music Education*, **20**(1), 29–44.

Davidson, J. (2002). The solo performer's identity. In R. MacDonald, D. Hargreaves, & D. Miell (Eds.), *Musical identities* (pp. 97–116). Oxford, UK: Oxford University Press.

Davidson, J. W., & Burland, K. (2006). Musician identity formation. In G. E. McPherson (Ed.), *The child as musician: A handbook of musical development* (pp. 475–90). Oxford, UK: Oxford University Press.

Davidson, J., Howe, M. J. A., & Sloboda, J. (1995) The role of parents and teachers in the success and failure of instrumental learners. *Bulletin of the Council for Research in Music Education*, **127**(Winter), 40–4.

Davis, S. G. (2005). That thing you do! Compositional processes of a rock band. *International Journal of Education and the Arts*, **6**(16). Retrieved from <http://www.ijea.org/v6n16/>.

Davis, S. G. (2012). Instrumental ensemble learning and performance in primary and elementary schools. In G. E. McPherson & G. Welch (Eds.), *The Oxford handbook of music education* (pp. 417–34). Oxford, UK: Oxford University Press.

Davis, S. G. (2013). Informal learning processes in an elementary music classroom. *Bulletin of the Council for Research in Music Education*, 198(Fall), 23–50. doi: 10.5406/bulcouresmusedu.198.0023.

DeNora, T. (2000). *Music in everyday life*. Cambridge, UK: Cambridge University Press.

Fitzpatrick, K. (2012). Cultural diversity and the formation of identity: Our role as music teachers. *Music Educators Journal*, **98**(4), 53–9. doi: 10.1177/00274321112442903.

Folkestad, G. (2006). Formal and informal learning situations or practices vs formal and informal ways of learning. *British Journal of Music Education*, **23**(2), 135–45. doi: 10.1017/S0265051706006887.

Frith, S. (1996a). Music and identity. In S. Hall & P. du Gay (Eds.), *Questions of cultural identity* (pp. 108–27). London, UK: Sage.

Frith, S. (1996b). *Performing rites: On the value of popular music*. Cambridge, MA: Harvard University Press.

Green, L. (2002). *How popular musicians learn: A way ahead for music education*. Hampshire, UK: Ashgate.

Green, L. (2008). *Music, informal learning and the school: A new classroom pedagogy*. Aldershot, Hampshire, UK: Ashgate.

Hargreaves, D. J., MacDonald, R., & Miell, D. (2012). Musical identities mediate musical development. In G. E. McPherson & G. Welch (Eds.), *The Oxford handbook of music education* (pp. 125–42). Oxford, UK: Oxford University Press.

Hargreaves, D., Miell, D., & MacDonald, R. (2002). What are musical identities, and why are they important? In D. Hargreaves, D. Miell, & R. MacDonald (Eds.), *Musical identities* (pp. 1–20). Oxford, UK: Oxford University Press.

Harwood, E. E. (1994). Miss Lucy meets Dr. Pepper: Mass media and children's traditional playground song and chant. In H. Lees (Ed.), *Musical connections: Tradition and change* (pp. 187–93). Auckland, NZ: International Society for Music Education.

Harwood, E., & Marsh, K. (2012). Children's ways of learning inside and outside the classroom. In G. E. McPherson & G. Welch (Eds.), *The Oxford handbook of music education* (pp. 322–40). Oxford, UK: Oxford University Press.

Huong, L. P. H. (2003). The mediational role of language teachers in sociocultural theory. *English Teaching Forum*, **41**(3). Retrieved from <http://exchanges.state.gov/forum/vols/vol14/no3/p32.htm>.

Ivaldi, A., & O'Neill, S. (2008). Adolescents' musical role models: Whom do they admire and why? *Psychology of Music*, **36**(4), 395–415. doi: 10.1177/0305735607086045.

Jaffurs, S. E. (2004). The impact of informal music learning practices in the classroom, or how I learned how to teach from a garage band. *International Journal of Music Education*, **22**(3), 189–201. doi: 10.1177/0255761404047401.

Johansen, G. (2010). Modernity, identity and musical learning. In R. Wright (Ed.), *Sociology and music education* (pp. 155–64). Surrey, UK: Ashgate.

Juntunen, M. L., & Hyvönen, L. (2004). Embodiment in musical knowing; how body movement facilitates learning within Dalcroze Eurhythmics. *British Journal of Music Education*, **21**(2), 199–214.

Kaschub, M., & Smith, J. (2009). *Minds on music: Composition for creative and critical thinking*. Lanham, MD: Rowman & Littlefield Education.

Kasha, A., & Hirschhorn, J. (1979). *If they ask you, you can write a song*. New York: Simon and Schuster.

Kohut, D. (1985). *Musical performance: Learning theory and pedagogy*. Englewood Cliffs, NJ: Prentice-Hall.

Lamont, A. (2002). Musical identities and the school environment. In R. MacDonald, D. Hargreaves, & D. Miell (Eds.), *Musical identities* (pp. 41–59). Oxford, UK: Oxford University Press.

Lamont, A., Hargreaves, D., Marshall, N. A., & Tarrant, M. (2003). Young people's music in and out of school. *British Journal of Music Education*, **20**(3), 229–41. doi: 10.1017/S0265051703005412.

Lum, C.-H. (2008). Home musical environment of children in Singapore: On globalization, technology, and media. *Journal of Research in Music Education*, **56**(2), 101–17. doi: 10.1177/0022429408317517.

Lum, C.-H., & Campbell, P. S. (2007). The sonic surrounds of an elementary school. *Journal of Research in Music Education*, **55**(1), 31–47.

Lum, C.-H., & Marsh, K. (2012). Multiple worlds of childhood: Culture and the classroom. In G. E. McPherson & G. Welch (Eds.), *The Oxford handbook of music education* (pp. 381–98). Oxford, UK: Oxford University Press.

MacDonald, R., Hargreaves, D., & Miell, D. (Eds.) (2002). *Musical identities*. Oxford, UK: Oxford University Press.

Mans, M. (2009). Informal learning and values. *Action, Criticism and Theory for Music Education*, **8**(2), 80–93.

Marsh, K. (1999). Mediated orality: The role of popular music in the changing tradition of children's musical play. *Research Studies in Music Education*, **13**(1), 2–12. doi: 10.1177/1321103X9901300102.

Marsh, K. (2008). *The musical playground: Global tradition and change in children's songs and games*. Oxford, UK: Oxford University Press.

Marsh, J., & Millard, E. (2000). *Literacy and popular culture: Using children's culture in the classroom*. London, UK: Paul Chapman.

McPherson, G. E. (2008). The role of parents in children's musical development. *Psychology of Music*, **37**(1), 91–110. doi: 10.1177/0305735607086049.

McPherson, G. E., & Davidson, J. W. (2006). Playing an instrument. In G. E. McPherson (Ed.), *The child as musician: A handbook of musical development* (pp. 331–52). Oxford, UK: Oxford University Press.

McPherson, G. E., & Gabrielsson, A. (2002). From sound to sign. In R. Parncutt (Ed.), *The science of psychology of music performance* (pp. 99–116). Oxford, UK: Oxford University Press.

Mead, G. H. (1934). *Mind, self and society*. Chicago and London: University of Chicago Press.

Mercier-De Shon, M. (2012). *Music is waiting for you: The lived experience of children's musical identity*. Middle-Secondary Education and Instructional Technology Dissertations. Paper 100. Retrieved from <http://digitalarchive.gsu.edu/msit_diss/100>.

Minks, A. (1999). Growing and grooving to a steady beat: Pop music in fifth-graders' social lives. *Yearbook for Traditional Music*, **31**, 77–101.

Monks, S. (2003). Adolescent singers and perceptions of vocal identity. *British Journal of Music Education*, **20**(3), 243–56.

Mueller, R. (2002). Perspectives from the sociology of music. In R. Colwell & C. Richardson (Eds.), *The new handbook of research on music teaching and learning* (pp. 584–603). Oxford: Oxford University Press.

North, A. C., Hargreaves, D. J., & O'Neill, S. (2000). The importance of music to adolescents. *British Journal of Educational Psychology*, **70**(2), 255–72.

O'Neill, S. A. (2002). The self-identity of young musicians. In R. MacDonald, D. Hargreaves, & D. Miell (Eds.), *Musical identities* (pp. 79–96). Oxford: Oxford University Press.

O'Neill, S. A. (2006). Positive youth musical engagement. In G. E. McPherson (Ed.), *The child as musician: A handbook of musical development* (1st ed., pp. 461–74). Oxford, UK: Oxford University Press.

O'Neill, S. A. (2012). Becoming a music learner: Toward a theory of transformative music engagement. In G. E. McPherson & G. Welch (Eds.), *The Oxford handbook of music education* (pp. 163–86). Oxford, UK: Oxford University Press.

Overy, K., & Molnar-Szakacs, I. (2009). Being together in time: Musical experience and the mirror neuron system. *Music Perception*, **26**(5), 489–504.

Priest, P. (1989). Playing by ear: Its nature and application to instrumental learning. *British Journal of Music Education*, **6**(2), 173–91.

Roberts, D., & Christenson, P. (2001). Popular music in childhood and adolescence. In D. Singer & J. Singer (Eds.), *Handbook of children* (pp. 395–413). Thousand Oaks, CA: Sage.

Shively, J. L. (1995). *A framework for the development and implementation of constructivist learning environments for beginning band classes* (Unpublished doctoral dissertation). University of Illinois, Urbana-Champaign.

Small, C. (1998). *Musicking: The meanings of performing and listening*. Middletown, CT: Wesleyan University Press.

Stålhammar, B. (2006). *Musical identities and music education*. Aachen, Germany: Shaker Verlag.

Stubley, E. (1998). Being in the body, being in the sound: A tale of modulating identities and lost potential. *Journal of Aesthetic Education*, **32**(4), 93–105.

Tarrant, M., Hargreaves, D., & North, A. C. (2002). Youth identity and music. In R. MacDonald, D. Hargreaves, & D. Miell (Eds.), *Musical identities* (pp. 134–50). Oxford, UK: Oxford University Press.

Tarrant, M., North, A. C., & Hargreaves, D. (2000). English and American adolescents' reasons for listening to music. *Psychology of Music*, **28**(2), 166–73. doi: 10.1177/0305735600282005.

Tarrant, M., North, A. C., & Hargreaves, D. (2001). Social categorization, self-esteem, and the estimated musical preferences of male adolescents. *The Journal of Social Psychology*, **141**(5), 565–81.

Trevarthen, C. (1999/2000). Musicality and the intrinsic motive pulse: Evidence from human psychobiology and infant communication. *Musicae Scientiae*, *Special Issue*, 155–215.

Trevarthen, C. (2002). Origins of musical identity: Evidence from infancy for musical social awareness. In R. MacDonald, D. Hargreaves, & D. Miell (Eds.), *Musical identities* (pp. 21–38). Oxford, UK: Oxford University Press.

Turino, T. (2008). *Music as social life: The politics of participation*. Chicago and London: University of Chicago Press.

Vygotsky, L. S. (1978). *Mind in society: The development of higher psychological processes*. Cambridge, MA: Harvard University Press.

Welch, G. F. (2000). The ontogenesis of musical behaviour: A sociological perspective. *Research Studies in Music Education*, 14(1), 1–13.

Wenger, E. (1998). *Communities of practice: Learning, meaning, and identity.* Cambridge, UK: Cambridge University Press.

Wertsch, J. V., Tulviste, P., & Hagstrom, F. (1993). A sociocultural approach to agency. In E. A. Forman, N. Minick, & C. A. Stone (Eds.), *Contexts for learning: Sociocultural dynamics in children's development* (pp. 336–56). New York: Oxford University Press.

Wiggins, J. (1994). Children's strategies for solving compositional problems with peers. *Journal of Research in Music Education*, 42(3), 232–52. doi: 10.2307/3345702.

Woody, R. (2007). Popular music in school: Remixing the issues. *Music Educators Journal*, 93(4), 32–7.

Chapter 15

The child as music critic

Paul Woodford

A key idea that has long been foundational to music education philosophy and practice in Western schools is that children should develop musical critical thinking ability, that is, that they should learn how to think like expert music critics who can *perceive, analyze, evaluate, judge,* and *appreciate* the quality of music for themselves unmediated, or, so it seems, by history, politics, or other modes of experience (Broudy, 1958; Colwell, 1992; Reimer, 1970, 1989; Richardson, 1996; Schippers, 2010; Swanwick, 1979, 1994, 2011). The development of these perceptual and evaluative abilities coupled with a corresponding receptivity and responsiveness to the structural and expressive qualities of music are still regarded by many music educators as almost synonymous with musical intelligence (Dalby 2005; Hallam, 2006; Hope, 2002; Trehub, 2006; Younker, 2002; Zakaras & Lowell, 2008). But if so, it is a blind intelligence because children never learn of music's social and historical contingency and how much of what they think of as musical knowledge is based on illusion, myth, conventional knowledge, ideology, or deliberate fabrication by other people for their own ends.

For example, and as is explained in more detail shortly, this traditional idea of the music critic as an educational model for children was itself an invention of late eighteenth- and nineteenth-century Germany. The decline of the aristocracy and changing economic conditions in that region during that period gave rise to the music critic as professional propagandist to shape public opinion about the nature and value of music in order to create a paying public for composers' music and to teach audiences how to listen to their music for its own sake, for the quality of its construction, rather than, as had formerly been the case under the patronage of the aristocracy, for any extra-musical functions or associations (Goehr, 1992; Taruskin, 2007). Composers and critics (they were often one and the same) drew on the aesthetic myth of music's autonomy from politics and other domains of experience to bolster the claim that learning how to listen this way, that is, aesthetically, contributed to the development of those "technical, intellectual, and emotional resources" that individuals required to exercise their freedom (Applegate, 1998, p. 295). Whatever freedom they might have obtained by those musical means, though, was constrained by a government emphasis on the development of a pan-German character and identity that stifled political dissent. The authorities understood that by allowing the masses a measure of freedom and equality in music, art, and religion they would "not seek it in political life" (p. 295).

The history of Western music and education is replete with examples of the power of myth, illusion, ideology, conventional knowledge, and propaganda in shaping musical consciousness and identity for political or other purposes in ways that most children and adults probably fail to understand, because the historical and socio-political origins and meanings of musical and pedagogical practices remain obscure to them, and because music is typically taught *as if* divorced from worldly problems. This, of course, is only an illusion. Nor are children in schools or elsewhere usually encouraged to seriously question tradition and the status quo, and including conventional historical accounts (Ferguson, 2011; Woodford, 2014). Perhaps the greatest challenge for those wishing to develop in children some measure of intellectual and musical freedom and independence is thus to help them develop critical awareness of the ubiquity and significance of the music in their lives, by going beyond the notes and any pedagogical methods to critically examine the origins and provenance of inherited myths or ideas surrounding or embedded in them that will continue to shape their thought and behavior so long as their mythic or illusory "character remains unperceived" (Small, 1998, p. 101). Musical propaganda and other forms of manipulation should similarly lose much of their sway over children once they become more aware of the intentions of those wielding the various musical or other mechanisms of social control in their lives.

This chapter accordingly historicizes and politicizes some of the discourses and ideas in music and music education that continue to exert power over the lives of children by tracing and critiquing their origins and provenance to reveal some of their mythic or illusory qualities, propagandistic functions, or habits of mind instilled in them from birth through constant reiteration and modeling in the home, school, and ubiquitous media that are assumed as natural, but that may have unnecessarily constrained their freedom and creativity because neither perceived nor understood as historically contingent and politically charged (Taruskin, 2007). The chapter proper begins with a short history and critique of the German aesthetic myth of musical autonomy with its corollary notion of the music critic as perceiver of objective musical truth, because they are central tenets of one of the most influential narratives in the history of Western music education and remain embedded in the academic culture and language of schools and universities. As Schippers (2010) has recently observed, even in this age of globalization and multiculturalism, "most formal music education . . . can be regarded as still following nineteenth century German ideas and values" in that it remains "predominantly atomistic, notation-based, and relatively static in its approach to tradition, authenticity, and context" (p. 104). Musical materials may have changed as non-Western music and instruments have been introduced into those institutions, but lessons therein tend to be "marketed and conducted in the same way as piano or violin" (p. 11; see also Fautley & Murphy, 2013; Garnett, 2013; Volk, 1998).

The German aesthetic tradition presents a fascinating story that, like the other historical vignettes and critical analyses provided in this chapter, is intended to exemplify the kinds of historical research and critical analyses in which pre-service teachers and children might engage when confronting sacred myths, propaganda, and doctrinaire thought. This is followed with a description and explanation of a more holistic and current conception of the music critic as possibly (but not necessarily) possessing strong perceptual or musical skills while also realizing that music and music teaching and learning are in the profoundest sense "unintelligible without some understanding of the economic, social, and political institutions which devised them, paid for them, [and] executed them" (Ferguson, 2011, p. 2). Much of the remainder and bulk of the chapter is given to critique of recent and current music education practice and reforms that may obstruct or hinder the development of critical thought and awareness in children by failing to ensure that they are provided with the intellectual environments and conditions that can provoke, foster, and sustain them. The chapter concludes with a brief practical suggestion for re-organizing music teacher training and the school music curriculum to achieve a better balance between performance and other subjects and to re-vivify music teaching and learning by using historical research and study as critical tools for challenging conventional accounts and practices (Dewey, 1934).

The music critic and *The Imaginary Museum of Musical Works*

As traditionally defined and understood in the Western world, a *music critic* is a professional who makes value judgments about the degrees of excellence of compositions and concert performances, typically in journalistic venues (Griffiths, 2004). The etymology of the word critic can be traced back to the late sixteenth-century "Latin *criticus*, from Greek *kritikos*, from *krites*, 'a judge,' from *krinein* 'judge, decide'" (*The Oxford Dictionary of English*; see Soanes & Stevenson, 2006). Within the classical music tradition, these value judgments were usually based on an assessment of the quality of a composition's structural properties and performers' fidelity to the score. Extra-musical associations were typically glossed over or treated as only of secondary importance to the musical experience. This understanding of the music critic as a professional and concerned exclusively or primarily with evaluation of musical structure and performances thereof is an old idea, the origins of which can be traced back at least as far as the early nineteenth century to the German *werktreue* or "work" ideal of "being true or faithful to" composers' musical intentions as represented in the score or musical work (Goehr, 1992, p. 1). The work ideal first arose in response to particular social, political, and economic circumstances occurring around the turn of that century. Following Kant's 1790 *Critique of Judgement* (Kant, 1790/1987) and Hegel's 1770–1831 lectures on aesthetics (Hegel, 1975), it became fashionable among the intelligentsia to talk about music as one would paintings or other works of fine art, as objects possessing an independent existence of their own and that should be judged and appreciated for their own sakes, for their beauty, and not for any extra-musical associations (Goehr, 1992). Fine art and music were idealized as existing in isolation from everyday experience and as means of gaining access to transcendental or spiritual truths. All listeners had to do was to exercise aesthetic judgment with respect to those works by parsing composers' musical intentions as represented in the score, thereby gaining an appreciation of the latter's God-like genius!

These ideas about musical works as objects akin to paintings and statuary and as providing access to ultimate truths were, of course, only illusions. Music literally does not exist except in the imagination or when it is being performed, whether live or via recordings. But even then, and because it is a temporal art, it exists only in the fleeting moment and consequently, if it is to be appreciated at all by the listener, any sense of the phrase or larger structure must be constructed in the mind (Small, 1998). Nor does it exist in isolation from the world or provide access to ultimate truths, or at least not in any way that can be demonstrably proved. And yet, as Goehr (1992) observed in her landmark book *The Imaginary Museum of Musical Works*, the *werktreue* ideal with its related notions of the music critic as aesthetic judge par excellence, the composer as creative genius, the conductor as maestro and servant of composers' wishes, and of music teaching and learning as divorced from politics, eventually came to dominate musical and educational praxis for the next century and a half and more. As already suggested, as the twentieth century progressed, it was also applied hegemonically as a regulative ideal to the teaching and learning of jazz, popular, and non-Western music (Schippers, 2010).

Goehr's historical analysis of the origins of the *werktreue* ideal demonstrates the power of illusion, myth, and ideology in shaping musical consciousness—people's conceptions and perceptions of reality and truth with regard to the nature and value of music, and thus also of music teaching and learning—and how claims thereof may be shaped by individuals and groups for their own ends. The development of the work concept, although described by nineteenth-century philosophers, composers, and musicians as natural to the art of music and as representing objective truth, presents a classic example of the latter in that it was driven, at least in part, by composers seeking a greater measure of professional autonomy from the aristocracy and a corresponding improvement in their social status. For our immediate purposes, it is enough to know that this concept required the creation of an interested and paying public that could appreciate composers' works for their own sakes, for their structural or formal properties alone, and that this necessitated the invention of the music critic as professional musical propagandist who could train audiences how to listen.

Many nineteenth-century music critics were themselves composers. Pianist and journalistic critic Eduard Hanslick (b. 1825–d. 1904), however, was probably most influential in contributing to the cult of the composer's genius by helping to create a language of music analysis based on the idea of musical greatness that subsequently became foundational to the study of music theory and music education philosophy in schools and universities for many generations to come. In his own day, Hanslick was widely regarded as the quintessential music critic, and the definition of the music critic presented at the beginning of this section remains indebted to him. Importantly for present purposes, this Platonic conception of the music critic as perceiver of objective musical truths, outlined in his classic 1854 book *On The Musically Beautiful* (Hanslick, 1854/1986), eventually gave rise to the model of connoisseurship that undergirded the aesthetic education movement that arose in the United States during the early years of the Cold War and that was later also influential elsewhere (Horsley, 2005; Swanwick, 1979). Whereas the term critic usually referred to professionals, the connoisseur was an aficionado who, like the critic, was "a discerning listener" possessing "keen perceptual skills" and thereby capable of "distinguishing musical compositions and performances of high quality from those of lesser quality" (Trehub, 2006, p. 33). This was considered the most appropriate educational model for children for the reason that the connoisseur was a consumer and not a maker of music (Broudy, 1958; Colwell, 1992). Listening was deemed the most practical and effective way for the vast majority of children to experience music aesthetically, that is, to perceive its structural subtleties and to thereby respond to its intrinsic meanings. Ultimately, those meanings were said to be spiritual in *nature* (Reimer, 1970). The purpose of music education became to develop all children's aesthetic potential and critical thinking ability through exposure to great music and to thereby experience some form of transcendence from everyday reality.

This was thought to be humanizing and an argument that would convince the government of the day that music was a serious subject, because it purportedly developed the intellectual skills that children needed to exercise their freedom; but, similar to what had happened in nineteenth-century Germany, that freedom was constrained by anti-communist hysteria and a government emphasis on national unity that was intended to stifle political dissent so that the country could better fight the Cold War (Woodford, 2012). Any sense of freedom that children obtained by listening to music for its intrinsic meanings was thus likely to have been illusory, as was the romantic notion that individuals could achieve spiritual transcendence by listening to great music. Indeed, Dewey (1934), one of the founders of the modern critical thinking movement, had previously rejected these conceptions of the critic and connoisseur as educational models for children because they contributed to art's segregation from society by spiritualizing it "out of connection" with daily living, thereby contributing to their intellectual and political passivity (pp. 11, 238).

Probably few American teachers associated with the rise of the aesthetic education movement during the late 1940s and 1950s gave much thought to how the myth of the music critic and connoisseur as politically neutral and the illusion of musical experience as involving "a response to the spiritual nature inherent in great music" (Wis, 1992, p. 65) were legacies of a nineteenth-century pan-German nationalism that had eventually culminated in the Third Reich (Applegate, 1998). During the 1930s and throughout the war, Hitler propagandized nineteenth- and early twentieth-century "masterworks" as objective proof of German cultural superiority and as a musical model for the world to emulate (Eichner, 2012; Kertz-Welzel, 2005; Spotts, 2003). After World War Two, American musicologists and teacher educators turned to the German universities for inspiration and enthusiastically adopted their analytical and educational methods and ideas about musical greatness in order to demonstrate the superiority of the "American way" (DeLapp, 2004). The success of that political project, however, required that academics and teachers turn a blind eye and deaf ear to that music's elitist, nationalist, and racist "overtones" or associations (Applegate, 1998, p. 276). Teachers were advised by their professional leaders that music teaching and learning should have nothing to do with politics (Reimer, 1959). Rather, the country needed more expert musicians and musically educated audiences to support them, and teaching for associated political or other meanings would only foster "musical delinquency" among children (Leonhard & House, 1959/72, p. 113).

The salient points here are that these notions of the nature of music and of music teaching and learning as apolitical and of critical thinking as a form of abstract thinking ability that could be honed through study of "great music" were themselves to a significant extent politically driven and in ways that most teachers and children probably failed to realize or understand, and, once embedded in the academic culture and language of universities and schools, they proved remarkably enduring. This move toward increased educational specialism and the development of expertise in children and students of all ages was given renewed impetus by the 1958 National Defense Education Act, resulting in changes in public policy that necessitated that music, like the sciences and other subjects that were deemed important to national security, be redefined as a discipline and taught "as an objective and unbiased producer of knowledge for its own sake" (Efland, 1988, p. 264).

The growing prevalence of science in German and American universities during the nineteenth and latter half of the twentieth centuries, respectively, also had something to do with the longevity of the aesthetic legacy in academia insomuch as music scholars were obliged to define their own work in positivist and scientific terms, which worked to discourage social criticism of so-called great music (Applegate, 1998). It remained until the early 1980s before the American music historian Joseph Kerman (1980) linked the "masterpiece status" of many nineteenth-century German works with ideological or uncritical worship of the "great German tradition" (p. 314) and complained that this only stifled musicological research and understanding of music's social significance by needlessly restricting analysis to the level of the notes and their interrelations. "Articles composed after 1950," he facetiously wrote, "appear sometimes to mimic scientific papers in the way that South American bugs and flies will mimic the dreaded carpenter wasp" (p. 313). Notwithstanding whatever validity or explanatory power those analytic methods might have had when applied to that and similar music, they were "less important for other music that we value" (p. 320). Other critical methods or approaches were needed that could take into account relevant social, political, or other information in order to help "explain, validate, or just plain illuminate these other traditions" (p. 320).

That nineteenth-century German and much later American and other musicians and teachers might have been guilty of hypocrisy, self-delusion, or the pursuit of self-interest in claiming music's autonomy, quasi-scientific status, and transcendental qualities is beside the point of the foregoing discussion, which, as Goehr (1992) helps to explain and illustrate, is that "music as an end could never, on aesthetic grounds alone, fully justify the social or political means involved in its composition, performance, and reception" (p. 285). Music is inevitably and "inextricably connected to the ordinary and impure conditions of our human affairs" (p. 286). Thanks to Kerman and to British music scholars before him in the 1970s (e.g., Blacking, 1973; Shepherd et al., 1977; Small, 1977/80), who together laid a foundation for the sociological and post-modern turns in musical scholarship in the 1980s and 1990s, music historians, theorists, and even some professional music critics now conceive of music criticism more holistically, as involving listening and appreciation of music's formal and aesthetic qualities but also the transcending of disciplinary boundaries to locate music and music education within broader social, cultural, and political contexts or webs of knowledge (Alperson, 2010; Cox, 2002; Cox & Stevens, 2010).

The late Edward Said (1993), former music critic to *The Nation*, and Alex Ross (2007), music critic at large to *The New Yorker*, epitomize the modern-day conception of the music critic as public intellectual in revealing music and arts' social and historical contingency and how composition, performance, and appreciation are inseparable from political considerations. Small (1998) even went so far as to assert that composing, performing, conducting, teaching, learning, listening, and critiquing music are all ultimately political acts: They are all expressions of, or metaphorically represent, human interests and relationships and are therefore rife with issues of power and control. Many academics, and including some music education scholars (e.g., Allsup, 2010; Elliott, 1995; Lamb, 2010), now agree with Small (1998) that music is better described and understood as a verb rather than as a noun or matter of fact. There is no such *thing* as music per se, as value-neutral and an object to be appreciated strictly for its own sake and in isolation from culture, politics, and other modes of experience. Music literally does not exist except when played: It is something that we "do." For these and other reasons, today's music academics are less likely to assume the superiority of the classical or any other musical tradition or genre as inherently and objectively superior or unsullied by politics and worldly problems (Goehr, 1992, 2007).

Nevertheless, and despite the aforementioned sociological and post-modern turns in musical scholarship, there remains a strange reluctance among many music teachers to grapple with the social, political, and moral complexities of music and pedagogy in the music education of children (Jorgensen, 2004). This problem is explored toward the conclusion of this chapter. For now it will suffice to simply observe that music teacher education programs tend to emphasize performance and related pedagogical methods at the expense of upper-level courses in music history, philosophy, sociology, and the liberal arts in which undergraduates are more likely to "encounter the big, tough questions about themselves and their place in the country and in the world" and thereby also gain a better appreciation of how music education too is shaped by history and politics (Colwell, 2012, p. 608). Further, and even when university students take the required introductory music history and theory survey courses, the content and general methodological and pedagogical approaches employed in those classes tend, for reasons of large enrolment, lack of student knowledge of the Western classical canon, and the uncomfortable fact that music history pedagogy is only in its infancy, to be more or less the same as they were before the emergence of the new musicology in the 1980s (Briscoe, 2010; Lowe, 2010; Natvig, 2002). The emphasis in those courses is on isolated facts and historical figures and less so "about why and how their predicaments arose" (Ferguson, 2011, p. xiv). Performance, as music historian Richard Taruskin (2007) has recently declared, "is not the only area [of music education] that needs liberation from the tyranny of aesthetic autonomy" (p. viii).

An important purpose of the foregoing discussion has thus been to emphasize the importance in music education of going far beyond performance or other musical activities to help children realize that much of what they learn about music in school and everyday life is only fiction or historical artifact and not objective fact. Although often necessary to successful functioning in particular socio-musical contexts, the kinds of musical or other knowledge and skills learned in educational institutions, the home, or elsewhere do not constitute absolute or immutable truths. As Goehr (1992) explains, this is a liberating idea that can help them make more intelligent musical or other choices and decisions by overcoming "that deep-rooted desire to hold the most dangerous of beliefs, that we have at any time got our practices absolutely right" (p. 284). By developing critical awareness of music's social *and* historical contingency, and how it helps to "produce the discourses and representations of which it is the product" (Kramer, 1990, p. 17), children will be more likely to realize that they can exercise their musical or educational freedom and creativity to a greater extent than they had previously thought possible. For those teachers wishing to promote musical critical awareness among children, the task will be to create, foster, and sustain "a critical practice meant to affiliate music richly with things beyond itself without *either* allowing it to fade into a mere echo of those things *or* [italics his] succumbing to the illusion that it has any genuine identity apart from them" (Kramer, 2002, p. 6). As is explained next, however, and as already suggested by the lack of access of teachers-in-training to appropriate courses and pedagogical methods that are important to understanding music's social significance, this goal of developing critical awareness in children is far more difficult to achieve than one might suppose.

Developing critical musical awareness in children: Problems and possibilities

The first difficulty of teaching for critical awareness in children is that it is a state of mind: It is an existential goal and difficult to assess. Critical theorists refer to this state of mind as critical consciousness. Among the many challenges that teachers wishing to develop critical consciousness in children and youth will have to face is that, because the latter have been indoctrinated into their beliefs through long association with family, friends, church, school, or the media, or in the case of older students, because they have also modeled themselves after former teachers, it will likely be difficult for them to make explicit and to critically examine their own beliefs and assumptions.

Psychologists employ the term "confirmation bias" to explain why and how people become confirmed in their beliefs and prejudices through constant reiteration and modeling within their social and cultural environments: They often prefer to associate with like-minded individuals and to "seek out information that fits with their currently held views while not attending deeply to information that does not" (Joordens, 2010, p. 12). They may also be defensive when challenged in their beliefs, although this defensiveness may be construed as a positive sign insomuch as they are at least personally invested in whatever issue is at stake and therefore more likely to engage in dialogue with teachers and their peers. Among the tasks for teachers and parents wishing to stimulate critical thinking in children so that they are less susceptible to received knowledge and confirmation bias will be to find or create age-appropriate instructional materials and strategies that help to allay their fear of controversy and possible change while creating educational spaces in which they can learn to participate safely in a "culture of questioning that demands far more confidence than rote learning and the application of acquired skills," both of which predominate in traditional performance-based music programs (Giroux, 2010a, p. 3, quoted in Spruce, 2012, p. 189). Within this space, children should learn what is at stake for them; that the alternative to critical thinking, and whether in performance, listening, or other musical activities, is likely deference to arbitrary authority resulting, as Dewey (1938/69) said, in passivity, gullibility, conformity, and a lack of creativity.

Yet another, and related, difficulty of teaching children how to think critically is that critical pedagogy resists codification, formulaic "training techniques, methods, and primers" (Spruce, 2012, p. 190). Rather, the development of critical consciousness in children requires a change in the relationship between teachers and learners "from one where the teacher teaches a predefined body of knowledge to one where, through a dialectical process, students and teachers together negotiate and construct knowledge, curriculum, and pedagogy as a manifestation of the critical consciousness of our worlds" (p. 191). Within this educational scheme, teachers and children are no longer objects or passive receivers of knowledge, but rather subjects and co-creators of knowledge. Freire describes this critical process as involving continuous questioning or problem posing "in relation to the world of the learners *and* teachers" (Spruce, 2012, p. 193; italics his). This implies that music teachers and children should begin this critical process by examining the musical and pedagogical practices in their own everyday experience. "The problem-posing education," Freire (1970/2011) writes, "which accepts neither a well-behaved present nor a pre-determined future—roots itself in the dynamic present and becomes revolutionary" (p. 84). Among the difficulties with this conception of critical pedagogy and thinking is that critical consciousness is conceived as a personal achievement and a relationship between the subject and the world. Foucault appears to be raising much the same concern as I am when he asked, "What if understanding were a complex, multiple, non-individual formation, not 'subjected to the subject,' which produced effects of truth?" (Chomsky & Foucault, 2006, p. 17).

Critical pedagogues acknowledge—insist—that individuals are shaped by society, history, and culture. As Freire once said in an interview, "we have to understand how history is walking with us and because of us, while at the same time conditioning us to walk like this" (quoted in Olson, 1992, p. 9). However, because the emphasis is on children's own lives, their own personal "consciousness and . . . historicity" (Spruce, 2012, p. 191), they are likely to be preoccupied with the present while looking to the future and therefore they may not realize why and how their own problems and understandings of current practice have arisen in the first place, let alone realize how the past remains in and has some bearing on the present. This was Foucault's (2007) archaeological history of knowledge project, and later his genealogy of the subject, which was to uncover when and how certain social, cultural, and institutional ideas and ideals eventually "came to be seen as true" (p. 152), and how they led to the creation of discourses and technologies (i.e., social practices) that shaped Western ideas of the subject. The salient question for Foucault was,

> which techniques and practices constitute the Western concept of the subject, giving it its characteristic split of truth and error, freedom and constraint. I think it is here that we will find the real possibility of constructing a history of what we have done and, at the same time, a diagnosis of what we are. (p. 152)

That history should also allow us to better appreciate "what has been *done to us*" (Woodford, 2014, pp. 30-31).

The *werktreue* ideal and the related notions of the music critic and connoisseur that we explored earlier in this chapter [there are of course many more] are just two examples of technologies and related discourses that contributed through time to the shaping of the musical subject in Western society. The literature on the informal learning practices of popular musicians that has been capturing the imaginations of music teachers in Britain and elsewhere for the past decade or so (Green, 2001, 2008, 2009) is another example of a discourse that has been increasingly playing a role in the shaping of the musical subject in schools, but that, because focused almost exclusively on performance in the present, may cause children and youth to mistakenly assume that they are free of ideological control, or of what Foucault called regimes of truth and power. Giroux (2010b) has written extensively about how Disney and other major corporations, for example, control and use the media and music to seduce children to consumer culture via an "insidious" form of public pedagogy that "commercializes and infantilizes most of what it touches" (p. 415). Chomsky (1987), and of course long before him Dewey (1927/46) and critical theorists such as Horkheimer (1972), similarly complained of schools and universities operating as almost subsidiaries of the capitalist system and as expressly designed to maintain the status quo by preventing children and adults "from seeing what we observe, from knowledge and understanding of the world in which we live" (Chomsky, 1987, p. 136).

Children in school and everyday life seldom learn how to distinguish truth from propaganda, needs from wants, and the real from the merely illusionary because that would be perceived as a threat to capitalism and to the consumer society on which it is based (Chomsky, 2006). But if children learn popular or any other music as a practical activity without much, if any, recognition of its many and often shifting social meanings, or of the externalities that literally shape their musical and other interests, in this case by corporate and political efforts to educate them to become "consuming subjects [read objects] rather than civic minded and critical citizens" (Giroux, 2010b, p. 415), then they are not likely to develop much capacity for critical awareness and self-determination.

Critical theorists address the problem of musical ideology and hegemony by conceptualizing music as a form of praxis concerned with "how people engage with music: how they produce, transmit (and who does the transmitting) and receive (use) music" (Spruce & Matthews, 2012, p. 124). Teaching music as praxis is thought to promote critical consciousness in children, and thereby help them to resist the musical hegemony of dominant cultural groups and to develop their own musical voices by encouraging them to "recognize musical ideologies not as immutable 'givens' but rather as belief systems that can be engaged with and challenged" (p. 131). As already suggested, this places the emphasis in music teaching and learning on pedagogy over content, "as children are no longer distanced from music as objectified [and pre-existing knowledge], existing independently of them but rather are immersed in music as active participants in the construction of musical knowledge" (p. 131). As is thought to be the case with Green's (2001, 2008, 2009) informal learning pedagogy, "pedagogies . . . emerge naturally as reflections of musical practices rather than being artificially imposed as manifestations of a particular ideology" (Spruce & Matthews, 2012, p. 131). And by learning music this way, while exploring the various musical practices found in their own society, children can gain a better appreciation of other people and cultures in their communities.

Adorno, however, famously warned against assuming that culture, and by extension pedagogy, "arises spontaneously" or naturally "from the masses themselves" (Lowenthal, 1979, quoted in Giroux, 1983, p. 24). Barthes (1957/2012) similarly declared his impatience with artists and others who invoked nature "to dress up" reality, causing people to confuse nature with history. His project was "to expose in the decorative display of what-goes-without-saying the ideological abuse I believed was hidden there" (p. xi). Adorno coined the term "culture industry" to refer to the "concentration of economic and political determinants that control the cultural sphere in the interest of social and political domination" and also to draw much-needed attention to the social mechanisms of rationalization, standardization, and pseudo-individualization that dominant groups utilized via popular music to maintain the status quo (Giroux, 1983, p. 24; Adorno, 1941, p. 25).

Thus, and although popular music and pedagogy are often associated with the pursuit of freedom, that too may only be illusory. This is not to reduce popular or any other music or pedagogy to a crude determinism: Not all children will necessarily respond in precisely the same ways to the music they perform and hear or to the pedagogy employed (Paddison, 1982). Individuals negotiate the musical world in complex ways that are sometimes difficult to understand or predict. But neither am I willing to accept what Giroux (2000) describes as a "bloodless formalism, and the nonthreatening, if not accommodating, affirmation of indeterminancy as a transgressive aesthetic" (p. 28). We read much in the professional literature nowadays about personal engagement and transformation for children through musical experience, but not enough about moral guidance, critical awareness (except in mostly abstract terms), and critical self-reflection for children and youth so that they are able to "make sense of their possibilities for agency within the power-regulated relations of everyday life" (p. 28). The danger here is that, if the informal learning pedagogy of popular musicians that is being employed in schools emphasizes performance to the virtual exclusion of all else, then it is ultimately not all that different from the traditional pedagogy based on the classical tradition that focused exclusively on music's inherent meanings while studiously avoiding questions about its "embeddedness in networks of nonmusical forces" (Kramer, 1995, p. 17). In short, popular music and pedagogy are likely to appear to children as commonsensical and politically neutral when neither is true (McPhail, 2013).

Probably most children and youth are unaware or prefer to live in ignorance or denial of the cultural politics and social forces involved in the commodification of popular (or any) music, just as they are likely to be unaware of popular music's particular vulnerability to co-option or to historical or political revisionism by those who would use or abuse it for their own economic or other ends. Much the same observation applies to pedagogy, that when lacking knowledge of its origins and provenance, teachers and their pupils are not likely to realize when and how specific practices may have been employed in the past as social and political, as much as musical, tools to shape their understandings of the world while possibly teaching them to passively submit (McMurray, 1991). Adorno knew that performance alone can all too easily be used to indoctrinate children to potentially dangerous ideologies while promoting escapism. When performance is over-emphasized at the expense of critical consciousness and self-reflection, it will likely have diversionary and tranquilizing effects (Kertz-Welzel, 2005). This was Hedges' (2009) concern as expressed in his book *Empire of Illusion*, in which he warned that an overly narrow education is likely to result in historical amnesia which infantilizes children by causing them to think that they are "unique in history and have nothing to learn from the past" (p. 98)!

These criticisms, of course, are not meant to imply that children cannot benefit at all from informal music pedagogies such as those associated with popular music. It is just that, as Taruskin (2004) has observed, even academics who acknowledge music's social contingency often continue—presumably through force of habit instilled in them through their own early training—to ignore or give short shrift to music's "morally or politically dubious aspects," which only contributes to the erroneous belief that the quality of music-making is all that matters (p. 33). The point here is that, while it would be naïve were some music teacher educators and practicing teachers to assume that popular or any other music pedagogy was free of ideological control, those claiming to be critically informed would be remiss in their duty to children if they continued to gloss over the sometimes problematical aspects of popular music and pedagogy and the social, political, or economic mechanisms that undermine whatever liberatory potential they might have.

Philpott (2010) is making a similar point about informal music pedagogy in observing that, although intended to allow children a greater measure of musical autonomy through self-directed learning, it is already being packaged in formulistic ways that may result in its reification and commodification, thereby causing it to be "appropriated by the status quo" (p. 88). As Philpott warns, if radical pedagogical initiatives are not to be co-opted by politicians, business people, or others in ways that subvert their intended purposes, teachers need to be critically aware of the social "mechanisms which can confound or sustain these changes" (p. 90). Much the same admonition applies to the teaching of children, that they too should develop critical awareness of how music and pedagogy are shaped by all manner of people via various social and political mechanisms so that they can have some hope of intellectually defending their own interests and thereby of exerting at least a modicum of control over their own musical lives.

Are music and music education history bunk?

This goes once more to the question of the many meanings of music and education. If, as Green (1988) says, music is a medium of social communication, then teachers should encourage children to attempt to take into account the intentions of all concerned in musical praxis, including those of performers, listeners, teachers, politicians, and corporate advertisers, but also those of composers that are notated in the score, although, as Goehr (1992, 2007) and Small (1998) have already suggested, that does not mean that they must slavishly conform to the composer's or anyone else's wishes and vice versa. Nevertheless, children should learn that they "have an obligation to the dead, the living, and the unborn; the past, present, and future" (Woodford, 2009, p. 55).

This point bears reiteration and some elaboration because it goes to the crux of the argument being presented here, which is that there is a danger that praxialists, because they prefer the living to the dead, and "place music-making at the heart of the music experience" (Green, 2008, p. 60), overemphasize performance and other musical activities in the here and now at the expense of broader knowledge of history and politics that is essential if children are to understand music's social significance and avoid being imprisoned "in an eternal present" (Stivers, 2007, p. 134). Freire (1970/2011), for example, describes the banking model of education whereby teachers conceive of children as empty vessels to be filled with pre-existing knowledge, in our case with the music of the Western classical canon, as "necrophilic" (p. 77). This is an unfortunate descriptor because it contributes to a prejudice that an interest in the past is somehow morbid, when its study can illuminate the full range of human experience, including the "long, hard path of human striving for dignity" (Nash, Crabtree, & Dunn, 1997, p. 9) but also our own inhumanity. Musical examples of the latter are all too easily obtained, such as occurred in the period immediately before the Rwandan crisis of 1994, when a prominent popular musician composed and used his own music as a deliberate incitement to genocide. The past is sometimes described as a foreign country that can be difficult to understand, but its study can be revelatory, sometimes horrifying, often intriguing, and profoundly humanizing (Lowenthal, 1985).

Freire (1970/2011), however, would have us believe that there is nothing positive or constructive to be learned from the past other than the roots and conditions of current oppression. Individuals should instead relentlessly "move forward and look ahead . . . immobility represents a fatal threat" (p. 84). There is a certain truth to Freire's observation that dominant groups have historically tended to be conservative and, in the not too distant past, they relied on the music of the dead to maintain social power and control. But the current and overwhelming emphasis in the vast majority of music education literature on the present, on "doing," "making," or "exploring" today's music, can be seen as a form of confirmation bias that needlessly constricts praxis while thwarting the development of critical consciousness in teachers and children alike by contributing to the illusions that current music practices are ahistorical and fixed in the present (because they are all that matter to children), and that what they *think of* as their own music and associated practices and behaviors are unique and thus beyond reproach.

Goehr's (1992) comment made with regard to the music of the dead, white European males of the classical tradition, that music is inevitably and "inextricably connected to the ordinary and impure conditions of our human affairs" (p. 286), also applies to the music of today in all of its varieties and permutations, and particularly in our increasingly globalized, hyper-commercialized, and technologically driven world in which appearances are all too often mistaken for truth. Indeed, today's politicians, and including conservatives, are far more likely to utilize popular rather than classical music to maintain the status quo owing to the former's immediacy and seductive appeal to the masses, just as, owing to the emphasis on copying recordings of pre-existing tunes in popular music pedagogy, there are bound to be problems with authority and over-conformity as children emulate popular music traditions in classical music's stead (Jorgensen, 2012).

Particularly when knowledge is viewed as a personal achievement to be constructed in the fleeting present, there is a danger that teachers and children might conclude that, in the words of automobile magnate Henry Ford, "history is more or less bunk. It's tradition. We don't want tradition. We want to live in the present, and the only history that's worth a tinker's damn is the history that we make today" (<http://www.phrases.org.uk/meanings/182100.html>). But, as Ferguson (2011) remonstrates, "although the past is over, . . . it is indispensable to our understanding of what we experience today and what lies ahead of tomorrow and thereafter" (pp. xix–xx). There is much that children can learn about music, art, politics, character, and moral judgment from the study of their forbearers. This understanding of the importance of history in music education resonates with Alperson's (2010) "robust praxial view" of music education, which "calls into question the hard distinction between intrinsic and instrumental values of music" and that, in addition to attending to music's structural properties, attempts to examine the "personal, cultural, and social significance of music that have been a part of music practice since antiquity" (p. 183). By ignoring or downplaying the importance of history in schools and universities, music teachers and teacher educators may have been restricting the range of musical and other meanings and possible choices available to children, when their aim should be to "embrace the full measure of musical meaning and value" (p. 191). Virtually everything that is taught and learned in school and everyday life is already history in the sense that the specific practices and ideas encountered more often than not have an ancient lineage and have already been done many times before, albeit perhaps involving countless variations thereupon. It would thus be folly to ignore the collective experience, wisdom, and advice of previous generations (Wilentz, 1997)!

As the late Christopher Small (1998) demonstrated, history is the most integrative and therefore also potentially the most liberating discipline of all, as, for historians, "nothing is beyond notice in the quest to understand the nature and meaning of change, the complexities of human behavior, and the multitude of connections between the past and our world today" (Nash et al., 1997, p. 9). Small's (1998) and Goehr's (1992) contribution to understanding music as praxis was to provide *new* historical and interpretive frameworks for understanding music's social and political significance through time. Having said that, however, Small (1998) should bear some portion of the responsibility for the music teaching profession's continued lack of interest in the past, for while acknowledging that performers "work always from a base in the firmly known sets of musical relationships we call a tradition . . . and most of what they do will already have been done many times before" (p. 216), he ultimately advised teachers and children that they were free to do as they pleased; "The performer's obligation" was only "to his own enjoyment and to that of his or her listeners" (p. 217).

My purpose here is not to disparage Small, who had a profound impact on the music teaching profession. It is to simply point out that he was a progressive music educator and that, in reacting to what he perceived to be the rigidity of the Western classical musical and pedagogical traditions, he went to the opposite extreme with his advice by recommending that teachers and children could more or less ignore the past. Their present musical experience, he wrote, should not be "mediated through the judgment of generations" (1977/80, p. 203), which Foucault would likely have said was an impossibility. There is in Small's work, and that of many progressives, a "Rousseauian belief in the innately wise child, the conviction that children gain more from immediate experience than from learning about things that are distant in time and space" (Grant & Mirel, 2001, para. 7) and that, because they already possess the native intelligence to make their own aesthetic or other judgments, they might be better off learning music in more informal music settings, such as community centers, "as and when it suits them ('user-directed') . . . and where instruction is offered as the need is felt for it" (Small, 2010, p. 288). This, of course, presumes that children always know what they want and need and are capable of distinguishing between the two (Jorgensen, 2012), that music instructors in those venues can go beyond performance to connect music teaching and learning to the wider world and its problems, and that those venues are accessible to all children. It goes almost without saying that community music schools often favor the middle class, which suggests that, if politicians actually followed Small's advice and removed music from state schools (as many of today's politicians are actually wont to do), many children would have no access to music education at all beyond those public pedagogies already available to them via the ubiquitous media that are more likely to infantilize than educate (Odendaal & Westerlund, 2012; Pitts, 2012).

It was in response to this romantic progressivism that Dewey, regarded as the father of the progressive education movement, began to distance himself from progressive education in the late 1930s, complaining that "many progressive educators, particularly those who emphasized a child-centered approach, attended to students' individual interests and needs without engaging [them] in critical analysis of social issues" (Westheimer & Kahne, 1998, p. 4). Dewey loathed this avoidance of politics and history in education because it was likely to result in their political emasculation. Although he agreed that teachers should begin with the child's own interests, he warned that the "simple pursuit of these interests, which were often vague and chaotic," would produce trivial results (Westbrook, 1991, p. 504). It was similarly a grave mistake for progressive educators to assume that their schools or other venues could ignore the past, because it was "bound to result in adoption of superficial measures which in the end will only render existing problems more acute and more difficult to solve" (Dewey, 1938/69, p. 77). Nor should they eschew structure, organized subject-matter, and adult direction altogether, as Small appears to be suggesting, as an "invasion of individual freedom" (p. 22). Rather, the task for progressive educators was to help "the young become acquainted with the past in such a way that the acquaintance is a potent agent in appreciation of the living present" (p. 23).

This brings us to the final point of this chapter, and of this all too brief discussion and critique of Small's (1998) work, which is that it would be a mistake were music educators to focus exclusively on his conclusions and recommendations for practice for the reasons that some of them are arguably dubious because overly romantic, and because they would be overlooking his most significant contribution of all, which was to spark much-needed controversy and debate among academics—but unfortunately not among children—about the nature and value of music and music education in contemporary society. Small's work exemplifies how historical research and study can function as critical tools for challenging conventional accounts by provoking controversy and critical thought and self-reflection among children and undergraduates so that they can gain a better understanding of how their own musical or other thinking might sometimes be based on a foundation of lies or on doctrinaire conceptions of practice that have seldom been questioned in school and teacher education. Among the most enduring and damaging of those conceptions for music education has been the "scientistic, fact-oriented model of education" that Small critiqued in the late 1970s but that is *still* "disastrously failing young people" (Small, 1977/80, p. 220).

Thankfully, owing to the aforementioned sociological and post-modern turns in musical academia, there is now a wealth of research and theorizing in the fields of music history, popular music and media, gender studies, and the politics of music, to name only a few subjects, some of it deliberately controversial like Small's (1998), but also integrative because crossing disciplinary boundaries, that teachers can now draw upon to provoke children to think more critically about music and pedagogy so that they can, to the extent that it is possible, judge for themselves music's significance in their lives (Laurence, 2010). This, however, implies reform of music teacher education in order to allow undergraduate music education majors more access to the appropriate academic courses, which would likely be at the expense of performance courses. Small (2010), for the reasons outlined, was in the end pessimistic about the possibility of initiating music education reform that could prepare future teachers to resist the economic and technocratic ideologies "that were gaining an ever tighter hold on the schools" (p. 288). But this pessimism too might be attributable to his romantic educational emphases on music-making in the moment and the pursuit of personal enjoyment that left little time or room in school and university curricula for critical self-reflection and the study of history and other relevant academic subjects, both of which are essential to the development of critical consciousness and the exercise of political resistance.

As was demonstrated and explained throughout this chapter and elsewhere (e.g., Woodford, 2005, 2009, 2010, 2012, 2014), music educators have a long history of ignoring music's moral and political difficulties while also downplaying its critical and creative potential for productive political or other change. But, if the recent book by Pellegrino and Lee (2012), *Let the Music Play: Harnessing the Power of Music for History and Social Studies Classrooms*, is any indication, history and social studies teachers are beginning to recognize music's potential for confronting rather than escaping reality and are drawing on history to raise children's awareness of music's important, and oft times central, roles in social and political struggles while helping them to empathize with and learn from the experiences of their ancestors. The book provides useful explanation and resources for teachers wishing to relocate music instruction within broader contexts involving social, historical, and political controversy and unrest, including, for example, the progressive and civil rights movements, 1960s counterculture, black militancy and power, and the rise of Punk rock and hip-hop in the 1980s partly as a response to neoliberal Reaganomics (p. 136). Music teacher educators have long resisted "reducing" music education to social studies, which may be a sign of their own continued educational indoctrination to the German aesthetic tradition and the political status quo. But if we admit Small's (1998) argument that there is no such thing as music per se, that music-making is a form of socialization, and also his vision of education as helping children to achieve some form of integration of thought and experience leading to "fuller and freer apprehension of reality" (1977/80, p. 219), then music education might be better conceived in terms of social studies in which music instruction is intertwined with the study of history, politics, and other subjects to allow for the synthesis of experience and controversy and debate that children require to function as music critics and to thereby make better sense of their musical and wider worlds (Dewey, 1934; Fallace, 2009). Within this educational scheme, performance and other musical activities would of course continue to play a part, but music instruction would no longer function in schools as an isolated mode of experience with the rehearsal room treated as the modern-day equivalent of the medieval convent and monastery, or, at the other extreme, the dance club or Disneyland theme park.

Reflective questions

1 Who and what are some of the people, things, and events that have literally shaped children's musical perceptions and understandings of music and its many uses since World War Two? Can you think of some examples in recent history of confirmation bias in the music education of children?

2 What are some examples of previously taken for granted musical or other relevant "facts" that have influenced your own music-making and listening but that in hindsight you realized were only based on myth or illusion?

3 Recall that Foucault's project was to identify "regimes of truth and power" that shaped Western notions of the subject. What, other than those already identified in this chapter, are some of the technologies (i.e., discourses or social practices) and regimes of truth that may be shaping the identities and musical interests and thought patterns of children today?

4 Describe and explain some of the mechanisms of indoctrination and other forms of musical manipulation, including by whom and to what ends, that you have experienced in your own everyday life.

5 As was explained in this chapter, music educators have a long history of political avoidance. Reflect on your own music education and whether, to what extent, or in what ways your teachers, parents, or peers engaged you in discussion of controversial social issues relating to music and politics or, alternatively, whether they encouraged you to use music as a medium for expressing political or other potentially controversial beliefs (see, e.g., Elliott, 2012).

6 The importance of knowledge of history and other subjects to the development of critical awareness in children has been a central theme of this chapter. Describe your own music education during childhood, including how and to what extent historical or other knowledge was deemed important by your teachers, parents, and peers to musical understanding and, thereby, to understanding its social and political significance. Were you ever encouraged to question your teachers about musical or pedagogical practices and their origins and provenance in your classes or lessons?

Key sources

Giroux, H. A. (2000). *Stealing innocence: Youth, corporate power, and the politics of culture*. New York: St. Martin's Press.

Goehr, L. (1992). *The imaginary museum of musical works: An essay in the philosophy of music*. Oxford: Clarendon Press.

Kramer, L. (2002). *Musical meaning: Toward a critical history*. Berkeley: University of California Press.

Small, C. (1998). *Musicking: The meanings of performing and listening*. Hanover, NH: Wesleyan University Press.

Spruce, G. (2012). Musical knowledge, critical consciousness and critical thinking. In C. Philpott & G. Spruce (Eds.), *Debates in music teaching* (pp. 185–96). London: Routledge.

Reference list

Adorno, T. W. (1941). On popular music. *Studies in Philosophy and Social Sciences*, **11**, 17–48.

Allsup, R. E. (2010). Philosophical perspectives of music education. In H. F. Abeles & L. A. Custodero (Eds.), *Critical issues in music education: Contemporary theory and practice* (pp. 39–60). New York: Oxford University Press.

Alperson, P. (2010). Robust praxialism and the anti-aesthetic turn. *Philosophy of Music Education Review*, **18**(2), 171–93.

Applegate, C. (1998). How German is it? Nationalism and the idea of serious music in the early nineteenth century. *19th-Century Music*, **21**(3), 274–96.

Barthes, R. (1957/2012). *Mythologies*. New York: Farrar, Straus and Giroux.

Blacking, J. (1973). *How musical is man?* Seattle, WA: University of Washington Press.

Briscoe, J. R. (Ed.) (2010). *Vitalizing music history teaching*. Hillsdale, NY: Pendragon Press.

Broudy, H. S. (1958). A realistic philosophy of music education. In N. B. Henry (Ed.), *Basic concepts in music education* (pp. 62–87). Chicago: National Society for the Study of Education.

Chomsky, N. (1987). The manufacture of consent. In J. Peck (Ed.), *The Chomsky reader* (pp. 121–36). New York: Pantheon Books.

Chomsky, N. (2006). *Failed states: The abuse of power and the assault on democracy*. New York: Henry Holt & Company.

Chomsky, N., & Foucault, M. (2006). *The Chomsky–Foucault debate on human nature*. New York: The New Press.

Colwell, R. (1992). Goodness and greatness: Broudy on music education. *Journal of Aesthetic Education*, **26**(4), 37–48.

Colwell, R. J. (2012). Pride and professionalism in music education. In G. E. McPherson & G. F. Welch (Eds.), *The Oxford handbook of music education* (Vol. 2, pp. 607–11). New York: Oxford University Press.

Cox, G. (2002). *Living music in schools, 1923–1999: Studies in the history of music education in England.* Aldershot: Ashgate Publishing Limited.

Cox, G., & Stevens, R. (2010). *The origins and foundations of music education: Cross-cultural historical studies of music in compulsory schooling.* London: Continuum International Publishing Group.

Dalby, B. (2005). Toward an effective pedagogy for teaching rhythm: Gordon and beyond. *Music Educators Journal*, **92**(1), 54–60.

DeLapp, J. (2004). Review of the book *Music on the frontline: Nicolas Nabokov's struggle against communism and middlebrow culture*, by I. Wellens. *American Music*, **22**(2), 317–19.

Dewey, J. (1927/46). *The public and its problems: An essay in political inquiry.* Chicago: Gateway Books.

Dewey, J. (1934). *Art as experience.* New York: Perigee Books.

Dewey, J. (1938/69). *Experience and education.* London: Collier Books.

Efland, A. D. (1988). How art became a discipline: Looking at our recent history. *Studies in Art Education*, **29**(3), 262–74.

Eichner, B. (2012) *History in mighty sound: Musical constructions of German national identity, 1848–1914.* Woodbridge: Boydell Press.

Elliott, D. J. (1995). *Music matters: A new philosophy of music education.* New York: Oxford University Press.

Elliott, D. J. (2012). Music education as/for artistic citizenship. *Music Educators Journal*, **99**(1), 21–7.

Fallace, T. (2009). John Dewey's influence on the origins of the social studies: An analysis of the historiography and new interpretation. *Review of Educational Research*, **79**(2), 601–24.

Fautley, M., & Murphy, R. (2013). Editorial. *British Journal of Music Education*, **30**(2), 157–9.

Ferguson, N. (2011). *Civilization: The West and the rest.* London, UK: Penguin Books.

Foucault, M. (2007). *The politics of truth: A history of the present* (S. Lotringer, Ed.). Los Angeles: Semiotext(e).

Freire, P. (1970/2011). *Pedagogy of the oppressed* (M. Bergman Ramos, Trans.). New York: Continuum International Publishing.

Garnett, J. (2013). Beyond a constructivist curriculum: A critique of competing paradigms in music education. *British Journal of Music Education*, **30**(2), 161–75.

Giroux, H. A. (1983) *Theory & resistance in education: A pedagogy for the opposition*, foreword by P. Freire. South Hadley, MA: Bergin & Garvey Publishers.

Giroux, H. A. (2000). *Stealing innocence: Youth, corporate power, and the politics of culture.* New York: St. Martin's Press.

Giroux, H. A. (2010a). Lessons from Paulo Freire. *Chronicle of Higher Education*, **59**(9), B15–16.

Giroux, H. A. (2010b). Stealing childhood innocence—Disney and the politics of casino capitalism: A tribute to Joe Kincheloe. *Cultural Studies, Critical Methodologies*, **10**(5), 413–16.

Goehr, L. (1992). *The imaginary museum of musical works: An essay in the philosophy of music.* Oxford: Clarendon Press.

Goehr, L. (2007). *The imaginary museum of musical works: An essay in the philosophy of music* (rev. ed.). Oxford: Oxford University Press.

Grant, G., & Mirel, J. (2001). Distorting Dewey: Progressive ideals, lost in translation [Reviews of the book *Left behind: A century of failed school reforms*, by D. Ravitch]. *Educationnext*, **1**(1), 1–4. Retrieved from <http://educationnext.org/distorting-dewey/≥>.

Green, L. (1988). *Music on deaf ears: Musical meaning, ideology, and education.* Manchester, UK: Manchester University Press.

Green, L. (2001). *How popular musicians learn.* Aldershot and Burlington, UK: Ashgate.

Green, L. (2008). *Music, informal learning and the school: A new classroom pedagogy.* Aldershot, UK: Ashgate Publishing Limited.

Green, L. (2009). Response to special issue of "Action, Criticism and Theory for Music Education" concerning "Music, informal learning and the school: A new classroom pedagogy." *Action, Criticism and Theory for Music Education, 8*(2), 121–32. Retrieved from <http://act.maydaygroup.org/articles/Green8_2.pdf≥.

Griffiths, P. (2004). *The Penguin companion to classical music.* London: Penguin Books.

Hallam, S. (2006). Musicality. In G. E. McPherson (Ed.), *The child as musician* (pp. 93–110). Oxford, UK: Oxford University Press.

Hanslick, E. (1954/86). *On the musically beautiful* (G. Payzant, Trans.). Indianapolis: Hackett Publishing Co.

Hedges, C. (2009). *Empire of illusion: The end of literacy and the triumph of spectacle.* Toronto: Alfred A. Knopf.

Hegel, G. W. F. (1975). *Aesthetics: Lectures on fine art* (T. M. Knox, Trans.). Oxford: Clarendon Press.

Hope, S. (2002). Policy frameworks, research, and K-12 schooling. In R. Colwell & C. Richardson (Eds.), *The new handbook of research on music teaching and learning* (pp. 5–16). New York: Oxford University Press.

Horkheimer, M. (1972). *Critical theory: Selected essays* (M. J. O'Connell and others, Trans.). New York: Herder & Herder.

Horsley, S. M. (2005). An historical and critical analysis of the music education advocacy efforts of the Canadian Music Educators Association, the Coalition for Music Education in Canada, and the National Symposium on Arts Education (Unpublished master's thesis). University of Western Ontario, London, Canada.

Joordens, S. (2010). The challenge of teaching critical thinking. *Academic Matters,* October–November, 11–14.

Jorgensen, E. R. (2004). *Pax Americana* and the world of music education. *Journal of Aesthetic Education, 38*(3), 1–18.

Jorgensen, E. R. (2012). On informalities in music education. In W. Bowman & A. L. Frega (Eds.), *The Oxford handbook of philosophy in music education* (pp. 453–71). Oxford, UK: Oxford University Press.

Kant, I. (1790/1987). *Critique of Judgement* (W. S. Pluhar, Trans.). Indianapolis: Hackett Publishing Co.

Kerman, J. (1980). How we got into analysis, and how to get out. *Critical Inquiry, 7*(2), 311–31.

Kertz-Welzel, A. (2005). The pied piper of Hamelin: Adorno on music education. *Research Studies in Music Education, 25*(1), 1–12.

Kramer, L. (1990). *Music as cultural practice, 1800–1900.* Berkeley: University of California Press.

Kramer, L. (1995). *Classical music and postmodern knowledge.* Berkeley, CA: University of California Press.

Kramer, L. (2002). *Musical meaning: Toward a critical history.* Berkeley: University of California Press.

Lamb, R. (2010). Music as sociocultural phenomenon: Interactions with music education. In H. Abeles & L. A. Custodero (Eds.), *Critical issues in music education: Contemporary theory and practice* (pp. 23–38). New York: Oxford University Press.

Laurence, F. (2010). Listening to children: Voice, agency and ownership in school musicking. In R. Wright (Ed.), *Sociology and music education* (pp. 243–62). Farnham, UK: Ashgate Publishing Ltd.

Leonhard, C., & House, R. W. (1959/72). *Foundations and principles of music education.* New York: McGraw Hill Book Company.

Lowe, M. (2010). Teaching music history today: Making tangible connections to here and now. *Journal of Music History Pedagogy, 1*(1), 45–59.

Lowenthal, L. (1979). Theodor Adorno: An intellectual memoir. *Humanities in Society, 2*(4), 387–99.

Lowenthal, D. (1985). *The past is a foreign country.* Cambridge, UK: Cambridge University Press.

McMurray, F. (1991). Part 2: Variations on a pragmatic theme. In R. J. Colwell (Ed.), *Basic concepts in music education, II* (pp. 54–70). Niwot, CO: University Press of Colorado.

McPhail, G. (2013). Informal and formal knowledge: The curriculum conception of two rock graduates. *British Journal of Music Education*, **30**(1), 43–57.

Nash, G. B., Crabtree, C., & Dunn, R. E. (1997). *History on trial: Culture wars and the teaching of the past.* New York: Alfred A. Knopf.

Natvig, M. (Ed.) (2002). *Teaching music history.* Aldershot, UK: Ashgate.

Odendaal, A., & Westerlund, H. (2012). Christopher Small. *Philosophy of Music Education Review*, **20**(1), 93.

Olson, G. A. (1992). History, praxis, and change: Paulo Freire and the politics of literacy. *Journal of Advanced Composition*, **12**(1), 1–14.

Paddison, M. (1982). The critique criticized: Adorno and popular music. *Popular Music*, **2**, 201–18.

Pellegrino, A. M., & Lee, C. D. (2012). *Let the music play! Harnessing the power of music for history and social studies classrooms.* Charlotte, NC: Information Age Publishing.

Philpott, C. (2010). The sociological critique of curriculum music in England: Is radical change really possible? In R. Wright (Ed.), *Sociology and music education* (pp. 81–92). Farnham, UK: Ashgate Publishing Limited.

Pitts, S. (2012). *Chances and choices: Exploring the impact of music education.* Oxford, UK: Oxford University Press.

Reimer, B. (1959). What music cannot do. *Music Educators Journal*, **46**(1), pp. 40–5.

Reimer, B. (1970). *A philosophy of music education.* Englewood Cliffs, NJ: Prentice-Hall Inc.

Reimer, B. (1989). *A philosophy of music education* (2nd ed.). Englewood Cliffs, NJ: Prentice Hall Inc.

Richardson, C. P. (1996). Understanding the critical process: A model of the music critic's thought. *Journal of Aesthetic Education*, **30**(1), 51–61.

Ross, A. (2007). *The rest is noise: Listening to the twentieth century.* New York: Farrar, Straus & Giroux.

Said, E. W. (1993). *Culture and imperialism.* New York: Vintage Books.

Schippers, H. (2010). *Facing the music: Shaping music education from a global perspective.* New York: Oxford University Press.

Shepherd, J., Virden, P., Vulliamy, G., & Wishart, T. (1977). *Whose music? A sociology of musical languages.* London: Latimer.

Small, C. (1977/80). *Music, society, education* (2nd ed.). London: John Calder.

Small, C. (1998). *Musicking: The meanings of performing and listening.* Hanover, NH: Wesleyan University Press.

Small, C. (2010). Afterword. In R. Wright (Ed.), *Sociology and music education* (pp. 283–90). Farnham, UK: Ashgate Publishing Limited.

Soanes, C., & Stevenson, A. (Eds.) (2006). Critic. In *The Oxford Dictionary of English* (2nd ed., revised). Oxford, UK: Oxford University Press.

Spotts, F. (2003). *Hitler and the power of aesthetics.* Woodstock, NY: The Overlook Press.

Spruce, G. (2012). Musical knowledge, critical consciousness and critical thinking. In C. Philpott & G. Spruce (Eds.), *Debates in music teaching* (pp. 185–96). London: Routledge.

Spruce, G., & Matthews, F. (2012). Musical ideologies, practices and pedagogies. In C. Philpott & G. Spruce (Eds.), *Debates in music teaching* (pp. 118–34). London: Routledge.

Stivers, R. (2007). Vulgar music and technology. *Bulletin of Science, Technology & Society*, **27**(2), 133–5. doi: 10.1177/0270467606298220.

Swanwick, K. (1979). *A basis for music education.* Windsor, Berks, UK: NFER Publishing Company Ltd.

Swanwick, K. (1994). *Musical knowledge: Intuition, analysis and music education.* London: Routledge.

Swanwick, K. (2011). Musical development: Revisiting a generic theory. In R. Colwell & P. R. Webster (Eds.), *MENC handbook of research on music learning* (Vol. 1, pp. 140–72). New York: Oxford University Press.

Taruskin, R. (2004). The poietic fallacy. *The Musical Times, 145*(1886), 7–34.

Taruskin, R. (2007). Foreward. In L. Goehr, *The imaginary museum of musical works: An essay in the philosophy of music* (rev. ed.). Oxford: Oxford University Press.

Trehub, S. E. (2006). Infants as musical connoisseurs. In G. E. McPherson (Ed.), *The child as musician: A handbook of musical development* (pp. 33–49). Oxford, UK: Oxford University Press.

Volk, T. M. (1998). *Music, education and multiculturalism: Foundations and principles.* New York: Oxford University Press.

Westbrook, R. B. (1991). *John Dewey and American democracy.* Ithaca: Cornell University Press.

Westheimer, J., & Kahne, J. (1998). Education for action: Preparing youth for participatory democracy. In W. Ayers, J. A. Hunt, & T. Quinn (Eds.), *Teaching for social justice: A democracy and education reader* (pp. 1–20). New York: Teachers College Press.

Wilentz, S. (1997). Don't know much about history: A battle report from the front lines of the culture wars [Review of the book *History on trial: Culture wars and the teaching of the past*, by G. B. Nash, C. Crabtree, & R. E. Dunn]. *New York Times*, November 30. Retrieved from <http://www.nytimes.com/books/97/11/30/reviews/971130.30wilentt.html>.

Wis, R. (1992). Aaron Copland (1900–1990). In B. Reimer & J. Wright (Eds.), *On the nature of musical experience* (pp. 61–8). Niwot, CO: University Press of Colorado.

Woodford, P. (2005). *Democracy and music education: Liberalism, ethics, and the politics of practice.* Bloomington: Indiana University Press.

Woodford, P. (2009). Democracy, pragmatist aesthetics and the choral experience. *Musikpaedagogik, 42*(2), 53–9.

Woodford, P. (2010). What does music mean, and can music education really matter? In P. Schmidt & C. Benedict (Eds.), *The place of music in the 21st century: One hundred-eleventh 2012 National Society for the Study of Education Yearbook, 111*(1), 34–50. New York: Teachers College Press.

Woodford, P. (2012). Music education and social justice: Towards a radical political history and vision. In C. Philpott & G. Spruce (Eds.), *Debates in music teaching* (pp. 85–101). London: Routledge.

Woodford, P. (2014). The eclipse of the public: A response to David Elliott's "Music education as/for artistic citizenship." *Philosophy of Music Education Review, 20*(1), 22–37.

Younker, B. A. (2002). Critical thinking. In R. J. Colwell & C. P. Richardson (Eds.), *The new handbook of research on music teaching and learning* (pp. 162–70). New York: Oxford University Press.

Zakaras, L., & Lowell, J. F. (2008). *Cultivating demand for the arts: Arts learning, arts engagement, and state arts policy.* Santa Monica, CA: The Rand Corporation.

Chapter 16

How and why do musical preferences change in childhood and adolescence?

David J. Hargreaves, Adrian C. North,
and Mark Tarrant

How and why do musical preferences change in childhood and adolescence?: Introduction

We hear music in many different circumstances and contexts in twenty-first-century life—in shops, restaurants, workplaces, dental surgeries, on recorded phone messages, as well as in the concert hall and through the media. Because it fulfils so many different functions in our lives, and because most music listening is an active and creative rather than a passive activity, our musical tastes and preferences are in a constant state of flux.

In this chapter we look for regularities in the complex and ever-changing pattern of individual preferences, with a particular focus on age changes from early childhood through to adolescence. These questions are of vital concern to musicians, teachers, and audiences, and in this chapter we approach them from our own perspective as psychologists. If any such developmental patterns can be identified, it is our job to try to explain rather than merely to describe them. We will review the nebulous and scattered literature on the development of taste and preference, and try to explain the main findings in terms of four main approaches. Two of these approaches could be described as "theoretical" as they adopt clear, underlying theoretical frameworks: these are experimental aesthetics, and the social identity perspective, which we will describe later. The other two approaches are based on distinct methodologies or on the types of phenomena that they deal with rather than with specific theories: they are developmental approaches, in which we will include some qualitative and experience sampling method studies, and what is becoming known as neuroaesthetics: the last of these, and the qualitative research, were not present in the first version of this chapter in 2006, and this gives some idea of how the field has changed since then.

We use the term *preference* to refer to a person's liking for one piece of music as compared with another at a given point in time, and *taste* to refer to the overall patterning of an individual's preferences over longer time periods (for a further discussion of these issues of definition, and the relationship with other terms such as *attitudes, emotional responses, opinions*, and *behavioral intentions*, see Hargreaves, 1986). We also suggest that any explanation of taste and preference must take into account the characteristics of the three main components of any listening situation, namely the *person* (e.g., age, gender, cultural group, musical training), the *music* (e.g., structure, style, complexity, familiarity), and the *listening situation* (e.g., work, leisure, entertainment situations, presence/absence of others), and we start the chapter with a brief description of a "reciprocal feedback" model of musical processing that enables us to specify how these different factors may interact in giving rise to a preference response, which may then feed into longer-term patterns of taste. This is a reformulation by Hargreaves (2012) of an earlier model of musical communication which combined two constituent models of response and performance, and it derives from a view of music listening as a creative activity.

The rest of the chapter is organized around these four approaches. We first review research in the field of *experimental aesthetics*, which has traditionally focused on the characteristics of the musical stimulus itself, and on how these give rise to different types of response in the listener. The two main types of explanation within experimental aesthetics are those that explain preferences in terms of the levels of arousal that different stimulus configurations arouse in the listener, and the opposing "preference for prototypes" model. We compare and contrast these two approaches, and summarize their relative contributions to the explanation of developmental issues. We look next at the emerging field of *neuroaesthetics*, which stems from the rapid recent growth of research in the neurosciences of music, and which is beginning to investigate the neural basis for music perception, cognition, and emotion, and we also outline some of its potential pitfalls.

The study of musical preference and taste has been dominated by traditional positivist paradigms and by quantitative methods of data collection, as Lamont and Greasley (2009) argue, and some *qualitative studies* are now emerging which redress this balance to a certain extent: the next section consequently deals with these alongside the quantitative studies. A body of *developmental research* has tried to describe and explain age-related changes in musical preference, and we next review those studies that have looked specifically at age changes in musical preference and taste, mostly in childhood and adolescence (though there are also smaller research literatures on prenatal preferences, and those in old age). One of the main problems with this undertaking is that any regular individual developments are likely to be swamped by the massive influence of social and cultural factors arising from the media, from popular culture, and many other external sources, such that current sociocultural research on the development of preferences is more likely to investigate specific social groups, musical styles, or situations.

This leads on to the final area of our review, which draws on the social identity perspective (Tajfel & Turner, 1986; Turner et al., 1987) to understand adolescents' musical behavior. The social identity perspective encourages us to think about what happens when we categorize ourselves in terms of our social group memberships. At the heart of this perspective is the claim that our group memberships, and associated social identities, frame the way in which we make sense of the social world—and also the way in which we respond to it. We review research which has examined the relationship between adolescents' musical preferences and tastes and their social identities, considering how music is used by adolescents both to express their identities and also to create new identities. Finally, we explore the potential of music to contribute a "curative" function in contexts where problems with social identity can undermine people's health and well-being.

A reciprocal feedback model of music processing

The ways in which we process music are determined by the variables involved in the three interacting components of any given musical experience, namely the *person* (*listener, composer, improviser*, or *performer*), the *music*, and the *listening situation*. The original version of this model, which is elaborated and described in more detail by Hargreaves, Miell, and MacDonald (2005), was a model of musical communication which combined two constituent models of response and performance, and the response model was used in the original version of this chapter. Figure 16.1 shows the revised version (Hargreaves, 2012), which has been recast as a model of music processing, and which combines elements of musical production and perception with a central core of *imagination* ("creative" cognitive processing). We describe it as a "reciprocal feedback" model

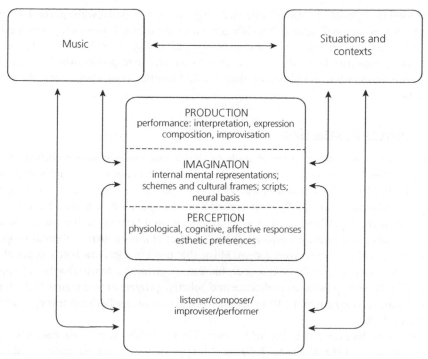

Fig. 16.1 Revised reciprocal-feedback model of music processing

Reproduced from David J. Hargreaves, Musical imagination: Perception and production, beauty and creativity, Psychology of Music, 40 (5), p. 554, Figure 3, doi: 10.1177/0305735612444893 © 2012, The Author.

because each of the three components can exert a simultaneous influence upon each of the other two, and because these mutual influences are bidirectional in each case.

The *music* itself can be characterized, and be seen to vary, in several different ways. As we shall see in the next section, research in experimental aesthetics describes the different "collative variables" of a given stimulus, such as its complexity, familiarity, or orderliness, and others emphasize its *prototypicality*—the extent to which a piece is typical of the genre or style that it represents. Listeners' immediate reactions in terms of style or genre can sometimes have a more powerful influence on preference than the piece itself (North & Hargreaves, 1997).

Listeners/composers/improvisers/performers vary with respect to "individual difference" factors such as age, gender, personality, and specific musical training, knowledge, and experience, and these will all determine preference responses. The revised version of the model emphasizes the point that music listening is a creative process (see also Hargreaves, Hargreaves, & North, 2012): the reciprocal feedback relationship between the music and the listener can explain how individuals' immediate responses to new stimuli are shaped by their longer-term taste patterns, but significant new responses can correspondingly change those longer-term patterns, as the system is in a constant state of change and evolution.

Situations and contexts, which complete the triangle, might include features of the listener's immediate situation (e.g., the presence or absence of others, or simultaneous engagement in other ongoing activities), the immediate social or institutional context (e.g., concert hall, shop, restaurant, workplace, school classroom, consumer or leisure environment), and also broader factors relating to regional or national influences (e.g., music associated with sports clubs, political movements, or national figures). This is a general model of music processing which extends well beyond preference responses, of course, and can explain many other phenomena. It nevertheless provides a perspective from which we can explain preference responses, which in turn shape people's longer-term tastes, and ultimately their musical identities (see Hargreaves, MacDonald, & Miell, 2002).

Experimental aesthetics

In recent years, research on experimental aesthetics has focused on one issue, namely the relative importance of two theories concerning arousal-mediating and cognitive variables respectively (see, e.g., Boselie, 1991; Hekkert & Snelders, 1995; Konečni, 1996). The arousal-based approach is best associated with Berlyne (1971), who argued that when people hear music, they collate several of its informational properties, such as its complexity and familiarity. Berlyne claimed that liking for the music is determined principally by the effect of these collative stimulus properties on activity in the autonomic nervous system. Music that possesses intermediate degrees of what has been termed *arousal potential* is supposedly liked most, giving rise to what has been termed an "inverted-U" relationship between preference and collative properties (see Figure 16.2). Indeed, numerous studies carried out in the 1970s supplied broad support for Berlyne's theory (see review in Hargreaves, 1986).

The next major development in the field occurred in the 1980s, when other researchers (e.g., Martindale & Moore, 1988) began to challenge this approach. They argued instead that preference is determined by the extent to which a particular stimulus is typical of its class. Explanations of this have tended to invoke neural network models of human cognition: this approach claims that preference is positively related to prototypicality because typical stimuli give rise to stronger activation of the salient cognitive categories, and allow the perceiver to make greater sense of the world.

Consequently, by the mid-1980s there were essentially two competing camps. One comprised adherents to Berlyne's theory who argued that the collative properties of art works were most important because preference was determined by arousal of the autonomic nervous system.

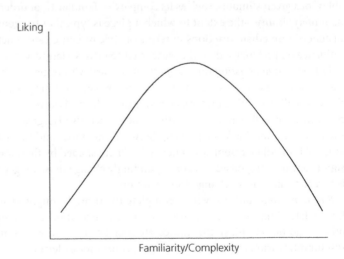

Fig. 16.2 The inverted-U relationship between liking for music and its arousal-evoking qualities

These researchers had clearly been influenced by elements of the behavioral approach, favoring precise manipulations of artificial stimuli followed by measurement of their observable physical effects. The other camp comprised a younger group of cognitive psychologists who argued that the prototypicality of a given art work of the more general category to which it belonged was most important, and that this was because preference was determined by the activation of cognitive categories in the mind of the perceiver. Although these researchers continued the tradition of careful manipulation of (usually artificial) artistic stimuli, they had far fewer concerns about discussing the effect of these on mental states and abstract cognitive constructs.

The degree of conflict was increased by the nature of much of the research on what might be termed the *preference for prototypes* model. Understandably, a considerable portion of this considered the relative extent to which prototypicality and stimulus arousal potential were able to explain liking for aesthetic objects. The consistent conclusion of this research was that variations in preference are more closely associated with stimulus prototypicality. For example, Martindale and Moore (1989) report that complexity accounted for 4% of the variance in participants' preference for classical music themes, whereas 51% was accounted for by typicality measures (see similar findings by Hekkert & van Wieringen, 1990; Martindale, Moore, & Borkum, 1990; Moore & Martindale, 1983; Whitfield, 1983; Whitfield & Slatter, 1979). Martindale, Moore, and West (1988) argued that results such as these "suggest that collative variables are probably a good deal less important in determining preference than Berlyne thought them to be. Furthermore, they probably determine preference via mechanisms different than those proposed by Berlyne" (p. 94).

Taken at face value, this implies that Berlyne's theory should be discarded. However, as two of us have argued elsewhere (North & Hargreaves, 2000), this is not necessarily the case. Although there are other arguments we could cite, perhaps the most compelling is that variations in the arousal potential of a piece of music (i.e., an arousal-mediating variable) also affect the typicality of a piece of music of the class from which it is drawn. For example, some of Stockhausen's music would score very highly on measures of arousal potential, and supporters of Berlyne's theory would argue that this explains its unpopularity relative to, say, Beethoven, although this may raise some deeper issues for musicologists. Nevertheless, the same erratic nature that gives this music its arousal potential also makes it untypical of the category "classical music." In short, arousal-mediating variables contribute to the prototypicality of a stimulus: in other words, both approaches can consider the same aspects of music as being important. The discrepancy still remains, however, concerning the causal mechanisms proposed by the two theories, with one focusing on the autonomic nervous system and the other focusing on unobservable cognitive mechanisms. However, even this apparent distinction presupposes that the nervous system arousal and cognitive functioning are wholly unrelated. This of course is certainly not the case, and there is no evidence of which we are aware to suggest that just because a piece of music produces nervous system arousal it cannot also affect the listener's cognitive processing. Consequently, the battle between the two theories may to some extent constitute a "red herring" for those concerned with more practical issues.

Nevertheless, this degree of theoretical confusion perhaps explains why so little research has considered specifically developmental issues. Consequently, it is worthwhile speculating on how the two theories may be applied in future research aiming to understand young people's developing musical preferences. Although it is possible to formulate numerous hypotheses, we focus on two that seem particularly likely to bear fruit.

First of all let us consider research that might be carried out overtly within the approach of Berlyne's theory. One concept that remains almost entirely unresearched concerns increasing acculturation over the lifespan to a broad range of musical styles. As we noted earlier, technological advances mean that music is perhaps more prevalent in our everyday lives now than at any previous point in time. It is important to remember that not all this exposure to music is voluntary, as we also hear music in the context of other media (e.g., television advertising) and in numerous places outside the home (e.g., restaurants). This means that over the course of the lifespan there is a continuous growth in the number of hours we have been exposed to a variety of musical styles. For example, a pop-music-loving 5-year-old will have heard less classical music than a pop-music-loving 15-year-old, who in turn will have heard less classical music than a pop-music-loving 35-year-old.

This increasing exposure over the lifespan has interesting implications in terms of Berlyne's theory. The more we hear a particular piece of music or musical style, the easier it is to understand it. In short, the music becomes less erratic and varied to our own individual ear, and this of course means that it should be perceived as less complex. Thus with increasing age, a piece of music or musical style moves from right to left along the inverted-U relationship between liking and arousal potential. The process is demonstrated in Figures 16.3a and 16.3b. Figure 16.3a shows the position of three pop songs at one particular point in time, and Figure 16.3b shows

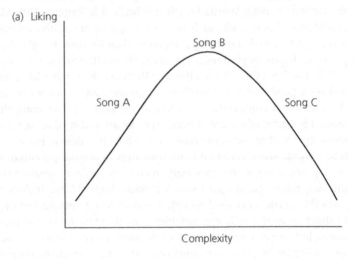

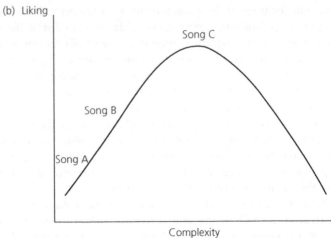

Figs. 16.3a and 16.3b The effect of increasing familiarity over time on the subjective complexity of three songs

how the position of these songs on the inverted-U should change following repeated exposures. This suggests one interesting model for how musical preferences could evolve through the lifespan. Increasing age could well be associated with a preference for increasingly complex music. Whereas Song B might be moderately arousing to young ears (see 16.3a), it could be too simplistic to older ears (16.3b); Song C might seem uninterpretable to children (16.3a), but could be moderately arousing to older people (16.3b). Such a process could only occur for music common to our culture, but does suggest one means by which liking for individual pieces or even entire styles (with their characteristic levels of complexity) might evolve as people age.

Similarly, the preference for prototypes theory may also be able to shed light on the development of musical taste across the lifespan. Holbrook (1995) found that preferences for several types of musical and other stimuli tended to peak for those "encountered during a *critical period* of development associated with late adolescence or early adulthood" (p. 57), and consistent with this are data concerning specifically pop music reported by North and Hargreaves (1995). Two hundred and seventy-five participants aged 9–78 years were asked to nominate their most eminent pop musicians. The "top 10" list for each age group showed one very interesting pattern: Although there was a tendency for all age groups to nominate the "greats" of pop music such as The Beatles, the remaining nominations seemed to be awarded to artists who were themselves at the peak of their fame during the participants' adolescence/early adulthood.

In direct contrast to the idea proposed earlier, this suggests that our notion of what constitutes "music" does not evolve over time, and instead becomes fixed during the adolescence/early adulthood "critical period." If this central category of "music" does not change, then any new piece of music should be evaluated according to the extent to which it corresponds with that which we heard when in adolescence/early adulthood. In short, today's music will always be evaluated by yesterday's criteria. Such an argument might explain why many aspects of our musical preferences remain consistent throughout life.

Neuroaesthetics

As is clear from the previous section, the great majority of research in experimental aesthetics has taken an approach based on physiological arousal, categorization processes, and/or social psychology. However, one of the most notable trends in research in aesthetics over recent years has been the rise of neuroaesthetics (see Brattico & Pearce, 2013). The neurosciences of music have become a prominent subdiscipline of cognitive neuroscience in the past two decades, and they attempt to explain the neural basis of music perception, music cognition, and musical emotion. Music perception and cognition have been studied in an analogous way to the processing and understanding of language, and the neuroscience of music has made significant strides in this respect. However, what is becoming known as the neuroaesthetics of music—the study of its affective and emotional effects—is much less advanced. Brattico and Jacobsen (2009) concluded that "a consensus on the nature of affective states during music listening has not been reached," but that "subjective affective states can be triggered by various and even opposite musical events" (p. 308). In their paper they review recent studies on the determinants of subjective affective processes of music and contrast these with the neural processes linked to the objective universal properties of music, dealing with how people make evaluative judgments of music which are based on its aesthetic and structural values, and on music-specific emotions that are felt by listeners, and conscious liking for different pieces.

One study by Muller et al. (2009), for example, compared groups of musicians and nonmusicians when making either aesthetic ("beautiful" or "not beautiful") or cognitive ("correct" or "incorrect") judgments of five-chord tonal cadences. By recording event-related potentials they were able to show that the main difference between the two groups was in the slow late positive potentials (LPP) localized in the posterior regions of the scalp. At 600 to 1200 ms. from the onset of the ending chord of the cadence, this LPP was larger in response to the correctness judgments than in response to the aesthetic judgments in nonexperts, whereas there was no difference between these two potentials for the music experts.

This demonstrated a clear difference between the cognitive and affective aspects of the response to music: and Brattico and Pearce (2013) suggest that "[a]lthough much is known about the frontotemporal brain mechanisms underlying perceptual and cognitive musical processes, and about the limbic and paralimbic networks responsible for musical affect, there is still a great deal of work to be done in understanding the neural chronometry and structures determining aesthetic responses to music" (p. 48), and a certain amount of subsequent attention has been paid to these aesthetic, emotional, and affective responses. For example, Brattico, Brattico, and Jacobsen (2009) have reviewed the literature on the origins of the aesthetic enjoyment of music in biological evolution, trying to approach this issue from the points of view of evolutionary psychology, cognitive science, and systems neuroscience; and Brattico, Bogert, and Jacobsen (2013) have made a first effort to establish a neural chronometry of the aesthetic experience of music which is mediated by internal and external context factors such as intentionality, background mood, attention, and expertise. Cross-modal neural processes are required to produce aesthetic emotions, aesthetic judgments, and conscious liking.

There seems to be consensus amongst the researchers in this area that the three principal aesthetic responses to music, as they are termed, are emotions, judgments, and preferences, and this is consistent with our own definitions outlined earlier in this chapter. We are gratified that Brattico and Pearce (2013) agree with us that it is important to take into account the interacting properties of the music, of the listener, and of the listening situation in explaining aesthetic experiences. As far as the development of preferences and taste in children and adolescents is concerned, the neuroaesthetic approach has not produced a great deal of empirical evidence, although a paper by the neuroscientists Nieminen et al. (2011) puts forward the view that the development of aesthetic responses to music is an important and under-explored topic which involves both cognitive and affective processes, and that further empirical investigation should be a primary concern. We await these developments with great interest.

In the meantime, we can conclude that the field of neuroaesthetics undoubtedly has clear promise. For instance, it provides a clear bridge between the arousal-based models that dominated research in the 1960s and 1970s and the more overtly cognitive models that have been proposed since, many of which we have reviewed in the current chapter. However, we would highlight a small number of other challenges that the approach will need to address. First, one possibility is that neurological phenomena are only the physical manifestation of what is really a psychological phenomenon. For instance, the true cause of one person attacking another may be racism or a heightened state of aggression in response to a temporary setback, whereas the neurological manifestations of both would be similar. In the same way, it is possible that the true cause of musical taste and preference is more psychological than a strictly neurological model would allow, resulting from, for instance, conformity to a peer group or the culture in which one is raised. Research might, for instance, identify a neurological basis for the effect of conformity on preference, but this arguably would not shed much light on the true cause of the behavior in question.

A second possible problem follows from this and concerns the reliance of neuroaesthetics on physical causation. In short, if a factor in an individual's aesthetic judgment cannot be reduced to a physical cause, then it will be difficult to explain via neuroaesthetics (just as, conversely, a social psychological theory finds it difficult to account for direct physical influences on aesthetics). As such, we believe that there is greater long-term potential for accounts which contain a neuro-logical component, but which are able to express these and other influences in cognitive terms. For instance, a more cognitive approach could easily explain the link between violence and both racism and a temporary setback, and also the impact of conformity to a group on an individual's musical preference and taste.

A third potential long-term issue with neuroaesthetic approaches follows from this. We have argued elsewhere on several occasions that musical taste exists on a variety of social levels. Intra-individual level variables exist within the person concerned, and include factors such as gender, age, or personality. It is easy to see how such factors could eventually become subsumed within a neuroaesthetic approach that conceptualizes them in physical terms. However, as we proceed to higher levels of this social hierarchy, it becomes increasingly difficult to conceptualize the relevant variables in terms of neurology. At the next level of the hierarchy, inter-personal factors, we find research on topics such as the impact of musical taste on inter-personal attraction, for instance; at the next, inter-group, level we find factors such as conformity to peer group preferences; and at the highest, cultural, level we find factors such as the system of musical norms to which one was subjected during one's upbringing. For each of these levels it becomes increasingly difficult to regard a neurological explanation as a necessary and sufficient account of musical taste, and social and cognitive accounts appear better suited.

Developmental approaches: Quantitative and qualitative studies

Age changes in the perception, production, and performance of music are of great interest to musicians and educators as well as to psychologists, and a good deal of research has looked at this. The general idea of Piagetian-style developmental stages is rejected by many contemporary developmental psychologists in the UK and elsewhere (e.g., Goswami, 2001), and the postulation of age-related stages or phases in musical development is similarly problematic. Considerations of age developments in competencies, skills, or abilities may be less likely to apply to musical pref-erences and tastes, as likes and dislikes are presumably less dependent on the maturation of com-petencies and skills than performing or composing abilities, for example. This is not necessarily true, however: one of the more prominent explanations of age-related changes in preferences is that the putative cognitive structures underlying musical behavior at different ages do exert a dir-ect influence upon individual likes and dislikes. The notion of general "cognitive aesthetic devel-opment" was used by one of us, for example, in summarizing the findings of several empirical investigations of developmental changes in children's aesthetic judgments about visual art works (see Hargreaves & Galton, 1992).

Bearing this in mind, it is useful to evaluate the literature on the development of musical pref-erence and taste by keeping a clear distinction in mind between the capabilities that appear to be involved in making a particular preference decision, and the actual content of that deci-sion. Research on what has become known as "musical style sensitivity" (see, e.g., Hargreaves & North, 1999) suggests that although some age-related changes in stylistic discrimination and knowledge do seem to exist, their manifestation is strongly dependent on the range of genres under investigation, the degree of contrast between the style exemplars that are selected, and on the experimental procedures employed. The best way to explain this, following the conclusions of our own study, is to distinguish between the cognitive and affective components of responses to musical styles—i.e., between people's abilities to understand and discuss them on the one hand, and their subjective responses to them, including likes and dislikes, on the other. There may be more consistent age-related changes in the former—in stylistic knowledge, for example, which will increase through acculturation and learning, than in the latter—but both aspects are influenced directly by the social and cultural connotations of the particular pieces under investigation.

As we suggested in the Introduction, the study of musical preference and taste has been dominated by traditional positivist paradigms and by quantitative methods of data collection, although some qualitative studies are now emerging which redress this balance to a certain extent: we will look next at some of these. The most significant development in this still small field is probably the growing number of studies which use different adaptations of the Experience Sampling Method (ESM), first described by Csikszentmihalyi and Lefevre (1989), in which people's everyday experiences are sampled in different ways at random intervals over a particular time period: this method can be used to generate quantitative as well as qualitative data. The first of these studies to look at the functions of music in everyday life was that by Sloboda, O'Neill, and Ivaldi (2001), in which eight adult nonmusicians between the ages of 18 and 42 carried an electronic pager with them over a one-week period. At random intervals, once in every two-hour period between 8 a.m. and 10 p.m., participants were asked to stop what they were doing as soon as possible and to complete a diary of self-report forms with open-ended and scaled items recording their "on the spot" thoughts and feelings in real-life everyday situations. The authors suggest that this method comes as close as can possibly be obtained to direct observation of daily musical life without intervention, thus giving ecologically valid data.

The second ESM study, which was based on a much larger sample of participants because of its use of mobile phone technology, was that of North, Hargreaves, and Hargreaves (2004), who used a mobile phone text messaging Internet site to send one text message per day over a period of 14 days to their 346 adult participants who owned a mobile phone. On receiving this message, participants were asked to complete a questionnaire about any music they could hear, or had heard since their previous message. Numerous detailed questions about the "who, what, when, where and why" of people's everyday music listening emerged from this, but some of the more striking findings were that there was a high general incidence of exposure to music; that liking for the music was dependent on who the participant was with, where they were listening, and whether or not they had chosen to hear that music. Music was involved in some way in these participants' lives on 39% of the occasions on which they were texted, and this is comparable with the equivalent figure of 44% from Sloboda et al.'s (2001) study.

These two studies provide a wealth of information about the detailed background to adult music listening in everyday life, but a third ESM study by Lamont (2008) investigated preschoolers' engagement with music in everyday life. Thirty-two children aged between 3.2 and 3.9 years took part in the study with their families, nursery teachers, and other caregivers, who answered a series of questions about dimensions of the child's music listening including its location, social situation, source of the music, and who selected it, up to a maximum of three times per day over seven consecutive days. Amongst many other results, Lamont found that the level of exposure to music was extremely high in these children's lives, taking up a massive 81% of their waking hours. It seems hardly surprising that music has been shown to have so many powerful effects on children's development in different areas, given this very high proportion of exposure.

Greasley and Lamont (2011) also used ESM to study the differences in people's everyday engagement with music by recruiting three different types of listener: those who were identified as having low, moderate, or high engagement with music. They collected quantitative and qualitative data from 25 young adults aged between 18 and 30 over a period of seven days, and carried out retrospective interviews to generate accounts of their musical experiences. The data revealed two different kinds of listener: those described as "less engaged" listened for fewer hours per week (an average of 12 hours), and tended to use music to help to pass the time and to feel less lonely, and those who were "more engaged" listened to a greater number of hours (average of 21 hours), and were more likely to be hearing self-chosen music and to use it to evoke specific moods or to create a particular atmosphere.

Finally, another qualitative study which did not use ESM was carried out to explore other aspects of everyday listening by Lamont and Webb (2010), who investigated the question of what constitutes a "favorite" piece of music over short-term and long-term time spans by carrying out a diary- and interview-based study of nine undergraduates over a period of one month, which indicated that these favorites tended to be subject to rapid changes, and that they were highly context-dependent. What they identified as "magpie" listeners had a large number of mostly short-term favorites, whereas "squirrels" had a larger number of longer-term pieces from which to select their favorites, and long-term favorites were more likely to be associated with intense emotional events in the listeners' lives. These studies do not deal with the development of musical preferences as such, but they do throw a great deal of light on some of the critical factors which govern people's everyday music listening which cannot be gained from quantitative studies, showing, for example, that the media which are used in order to play the music can exert a significant influence upon the way in which it is perceived (see also Krause and Hargreaves' (2013) study, which used listeners' iTunes records as very precise and detailed records of their listening preferences).

This takes us on to the more extensive body of research on the *content* of the musical preferences of different age groups, which was comprehensively reviewed by LeBlanc (1991), and which is largely based on quantitative data. LeBlanc's (1991) review was specifically devoted to the effects of "maturation/ageing" on music listening preference, and we drew extensively upon it in the original version of the present chapter: Table 16.1 updates this, summarizing the participants, musical stimuli, and results of most of the studies reviewed by LeBlanc, and also includes those that have been conducted in the intervening years.

LeBlanc (1991) used the concept of "open-earedness," a term that was first used in the psychological research literature by Hargreaves (1982) in explaining the overall pattern of these results, and which has been used more formally in a growing body of research since then, especially in Germany. The term was originally used as a shorthand way of conveying the impression that younger children were more readily able to listen to and maybe also enjoy unconventional or unusual (e.g., "avant garde," aleatory, or electronic) musical forms, as they may "show less evidence of acculturation to normative standards of 'good taste' than older children" (Hargreaves, 1982, p. 51). LeBlanc then proposed four generalizations on the basis of his review: that "younger children are more open-eared . . . open-earedness declines as the child enters adolescence . . . there is a partial rebound of open-earedness as the listener matures from adolescence to young adulthood . . . open-earedness declines as the listener matures to old age" (pp. 36–8).

A closer look at Table 16.1 shows that with one or two exceptions, LeBlanc's generalizations receive general support. The "dip" in open-earedness in later childhood seems to occur at around the age of 10 or 11 years, and this typically shows itself in very strongly expressed preferences for a narrow range of pop styles, and strong general dislike for all other styles. After this, there seems to be a general decline in liking for popular music styles across the rest of the lifespan, and a corresponding general increase in "classical" styles—although this does not necessarily seem to apply to more contemporary art music (e.g., Taylor, 1969). There may be some kind of interaction with the familiarity or complexity of the music (Hargreaves & Castell, 1987), and several of the studies suggest that age and musical training are associated with preference for more "serious" music, but there is insufficient evidence to propose any causal links between these findings.

Table 16.1 Summary of empirical studies of age differences in musical preference

	Participants	Music	Results
Rogers (1957)	635 grades 4, 7, 9, 12	"seriously classical," "popular classical," "dinner," "popular"	preference for classical > with age, diversity of preferences > between grades 4 and 12
Baumann (1960)	1410 12–20 y	range of styles within "art music," "popular," "traditional"	popular preference > with age, classical preference < with age
Taylor (1969)	800 8–11 y	paired excerpts of art music by composers from six historical periods	preference for twentieth-century composers > with age, for later baroque composers < with age
Meadows (1970)	982 grades 7–college students	30 excepts from 10 "popular" and "art music" styles	art music preference < with age
Greer, Dorow, & Randall (1974)	134 grades K–6	"top 20 rock" and "non-rock" styles, operant listering task	older Ps preferred "rock," becoming significant at grade 2
Bragg & Crozier (1974)	12 at each of 8–9, 14–15, 20+ y	random electronic stimuli at six complexity levels: studies I, II, III with different preference tasks	I older Ps preferred more complex on verbal rating scale task: II no age effect on paired comparison task: III no age effect on untimed task
Eisenstein (1979)	64 grades 2–6	Webern tone "ows	younger Ps listened for longer than older
May (1985)	577 grades 1–3	24 pieces representing 9 generic styles including art music, popular music, non-Western music	overall preference > with age, decline for "rock" and "country" styles less than for other styles
Hargreaves and Castell (1987)	96, 16 in each of grades K, 2, 4, 6, 9, college	familiar/unfamiliar real melodies, near/far approximations to music	preference for approximations > with age; preference for real melodies suggest inverted-U preference function with age
Haack (1988)	108 25–54 y	pop song titles 1945–82: selection of "top 10 of all time"	preference for music popular in mid-20s
LeBlanc et al. (1988)	926 grades 3, 5, 7, 9, 10, 11, 12, college	24 trad. jazz pieces at different tempo levels	preferences summed over tempo levels: U-shaped curve with age
LeBlanc et al. (1993)	2262 6–91 y	"art music," "trad. jazz, rock	preference > in adolescence, < in adulthood, > in old age

Table 16.1 (continued) Summary of empirical studies of age differences in musical preference

	Participants	Music	Results
Hargreaves, Comber, & Colley (1995)	278 grades 7, 11	ratings of 12 style category labels	overall liking > with age, especially for "serious" styles
Holbrook & Schindler (1989)	108 adults 16–86 y	preference ratings of 28 music examples from Billboard Top 100 1932–86	use of song-specific ages: inverted-U preference curve over age with peak at 23.5 years
North & Hargreaves (1995)	275 9–78 y	nominations of 30 most eminent pop artists 1955–94	general preference for artists from late adolescence/ early adulthood: The Beatles/Elvis nominated by all
Hargreaves & North (1999)	275 9–78 y	ratings of liking for self-nominated styles	liking for rock/pop styles > with age, for classical < with age: "cross over" in middle age?
Gembris & Schellberg (2003)	591 grades K–6	popular, classical, avant garde, ethnic	overall preference > with age: grade 1 most positive, grade 6 most negative, overall preference for pop
Kopiez & Lehmann (2008)	186 6–10 y	preference ratings of eight sound examples in five different styles	decline of "open-earedness" for "unconventional" styles: effect disappeared when "classical" was excluded
Muller et al. (2009)	238 Dutch 12–17, 18–22 and 23+ y	nominations of favorite three artists/bands and genre ratings at three points in time over 21 months	high turnover of favorite artists: general consistency in genre preferences
Nieminen et al. (2012)	38 6–7 y; 40 8–9 y	3 piano pieces: major, minor, free tonal	major piece preferred to minor, and also received higher happiness ratings: only 8–9s found minor pieces more sad than major
Hemming (2013)	473 6–86 y	25 examples from German top 10 1960–2008	follow-up to Holbrook & Schindler (1989): their inverted-U peak shifted to 17.36 years

The studies by Haack (1988), Holbrook and Schindler (1989), North and Hargreaves (1995), and Hemming (2013) demonstrate a general preference for artists/musicians who were popular during the listeners' late adolescence/early adulthood: a third of these studies also reveal the intriguing finding that some popular artists, Elvis Presley and The Beatles in particular, are consistently rated as eminent by all age groups over the last 30 years or so. Given that the studies in Table 16.1 vary widely with respect to their theoretical rationales, their participant groups and age ranges, the actual genres and styles under investigation, and the assessment techniques employed, it is perhaps surprising that LeBlanc's generalizations do seem to hold true.

These generalizations about age differences in "open-earedness" with respect to "popular" and "classical" or "serious" styles may be valid because they work at a high level of generality: they refer to broad genres rather than to specific styles within those genres, and thus side-step the problems of cohort or historical effects, although Holbrook and Schindler (1989) circumvented this problem by introducing what they called song-specific ages, which is defined as the year of release of the song minus the listener's year of birth. Kopiez and Lehmann (2008) found that the decline in "open-earedness" with increasing age in their results disappeared when classical music was excluded from their analyses, which led them to suggest that factors other than open-earedness may also have influenced their results. Nevertheless, by obtaining the eminence rankings of participants aged between 9 and 78 years for specific popular musicians over the last half of the last century, North and Hargreaves (1995) produced clear evidence for such effects: and it was possible to make generalizations about preferences that were not bound to specific historical periods. Investigating preferences for specific current popular styles presents huge practical problems because those styles themselves are changing and evolving more rapidly than ever in today's post-modern and increasingly globalized society.

Expressing and constructing social identities through music

A growing body of research highlights the important ways in which musical "behavior" (including musical performance, listening habits, and preference expressions) during adolescence informs a developing sense of self which is defined through psychological connections to other people. The social identity perspective, comprising social identity and self-categorization theories (Tajfel & Turner, 1986; Turner et al., 1987), maintains that people derive an important sense of self from their social group memberships. When individuals define themselves in terms of a particular group membership—be that their gender, nationality, hobby group, or any other meaningful social category—that membership frames the way in which they interact with the social world. Moreover, when a social identity is salient, group members internalize and seek to conform to the typical ways of behaving (group norms) and expected roles (e.g., goals, attitudes, and behaviors) of the group (see Turner, 1999). By acting *as group members* in this way, individuals derive positive psychological benefits from their group membership, including a sense of belonging and well-being.

Music research in this area broadly falls into two categories: that which emphasizes the role of music in the expression of existing social identities, and that which considers how music contributes to the construction (and reconstruction) of social identity. Central to all this work is the observation that music is an integral part of what it means to belong to a group during adolescence—that it helps define the *content* of adolescents' social identity and, accordingly, describes and prescribes the values of the group and actions of its members (see Turner, 1999). We now briefly review each of these lines of research.

Some of our own early work in this area explored ways in which adolescents make statements about music as a means of distinguishing their own peer groups (or "ingroups") from other groups ("outgroups"). In one study (Tarrant, Hargreaves, & North, 2001), we asked a sample of adolescents to rate different styles of music according to how much they were associated with an ingroup and an outgroup. As expected, and consistent with predictions from social identity theory, the study showed that music which was valued positively by the group (namely, popular forms of music) was associated more strongly with the ingroup than it was with the outgroup. At the same time, participants associated music which they valued negatively (e.g., classical music, country music) more strongly with the outgroup than with the ingroup (for a detailed discussion, see Tarrant, North, & Hargreaves, 2002). Reflecting the reduction in "open-earedness" which is observed in late childhood (see Table 16.1), a follow-up study demonstrated that adolescents relied more closely on music to express their social identity than they did other activities or attributes, such as sports ability (Tarrant et al., 2001). This finding indicates that a focus on discrete styles of music during adolescence may help to define social identity, framing the development and expression of adolescents' values, and potentially also behavior (see similar findings by Rentfrow & Gosling, 2003).

Several other studies in this vein have explored how adolescents and young people use music to publicly communicate their group affiliations and to express their personalities and values. As well as showing that statements about musical preferences influence how adolescents are perceived by others (e.g., North & Hargreaves, 1999; Zillmann & Bhatia, 1999), recent studies have established that young people hold clear and distinct stereotypes about the fans of different types of music—and that these stereotypes may be shared by people across different cultural contexts (Rentfrow, McDonald, & Oldmeadow, 2009). While such stereotypes are very often innocuous, in some (e.g., racial) contexts they can underscore deeper feelings of group-based prejudice (Reyna, Brandt, & Viki, 2009; also Rentfrow & Gosling, 2007).

It is seen then that adolescents' expressions of their own musical preference, and their judgments about others' preferences, are important to the functioning of their social groups, enabling them to derive positive psychological benefits from these memberships. We turn now to the second line of research, referred to earlier, which indicates that music is also valuable to the construction or reconstruction of new social connections—that music contributes to *group formation*. We start with a review of research showing that music can help promote harmonious relations between different social groups.

One particularly promising line of research in this regard has drawn upon predictions of the common ingroup identity model (Gaertner et al., 1993). This model holds that bias in inter-group perceptions can be reduced through interventions which encourage people to cognitively recategorize an ingroup and outgroup in terms of an inclusive social identity (i.e., moving from an "us" and "them" distinction to a "we" categorization). Bakagiannis and Tarrant (2006) conducted an experiment to examine whether statements about music could influence adolescents' perceptions of different social groups. Participants in the study were first assigned to social groups which were especially created for the purpose of the experiment (see Tajfel et al., 1971). After this, they were led to believe that the two groups either had very similar or very different musical preferences; a third group was not told anything about the groups' musical preferences (this group acted as the control group). Participants then rated each group along a series of trait adjectives. Compared with participants who were not told anything about the groups' musical preferences, those who believed the groups had very similar preferences were significantly less likely to perceive that the groups were different along the trait adjectives—suggesting that they came to cognitively represent the two groups in terms of a new common, or shared, social identity.

Clearly, more research is needed to determine whether such findings extend to contexts where there are real divisions between different social groups. Nevertheless, these findings indicate a potential role for music in social interventions aimed at changing people's group-based perceptions. In this regard, it is worth highlighting the case of the West-Eastern Divan Orchestra, formed in the late 1990s and involving musicians from across the Middle East, including from Israel and Palestine. The initiative is intended to help break down cultural and political barriers at the heart of the Arab–Israel conflict. No doubt, bringing different groups together in this way to perform music is not going to be without its challenges, particularly when there is a history of conflict and distrust between groups, as in the Arab–Israel conflict. Indeed, research has shown that group members sometimes react against interventions which promote the formation of a common ingroup identity (Crisp, Stone, & Hall, 2006). Particularly when they are strongly attached to their existing (subgroup) identities, such interventions can actually make relations between groups *worse* (Tarrant, Calitri, & Weston, 2012). Such challenges should not be insurmountable, however (Crisp et al., 2006), and we are greatly encouraged that researchers and practitioners are starting to acknowledge and explore music's potential in this regard.

A final domain in which we are starting to see a promising application of music to identity-related "problems" is in the area of health research. There is growing interest in the potential benefits of music, and the arts more generally, on well-being and quality of life, both amongst healthy populations and those with long-term health conditions (Stuckey & Nobel, 2010). This work builds on the observation that collectively participating with others in musical activities (e.g., group singing or playing) can promote "joint attention": the coordinated sharing and understanding of a common point of reference (O'Donnell, MacDonald, & Davies, 1999). Thus, music may help to bring people together in new group contexts, working towards a common (health) outcome. For example, making music with others who share health symptoms (e.g., of disability) may promote a sense of group belonging, collective identity, and feelings of social support— foundations for building confidence and self-efficacy (Bandura, 1997; Resnick et al., 2002) which may have translational value outside of the group setting. In this regard, music may act as a kind of "social glue" through which new connections—new identities—can be formed, and through which interrupted or "damaged" identities can be reconstructed.

Conclusions

The purpose of this chapter has been to review the fundamental mechanisms governing the development of preference and taste from the psychological point of view, as well as to review the research literature on the course of development of those preferences. Our main contention forms the essence of the model presented in Figure 16.1: that any adequate explanation of these developments must take into account the interactions between the person, the music, and their social and cultural context. Although the model operates at a very broad and imprecise level, it nevertheless provides a framework within which we can conceptualize the interplay between different theoretical approaches. Experimental aesthetics deals mainly with "the music" in the model, albeit at a very general level, and would benefit enormously from further contributions from music theory. Neuroaesthetics deals with the neural mechanisms within individuals which underlie aesthetic and affective responses, and developmental approaches focus on one important "listener variable," age, which of course interacts with many other aspects of individual differences. The social identity approach deals specifically with the ways in which one important aspect of "situations and contexts," psychological connections to significant others, directly affects the listener's immediate responses, and thereby incorporates much more long-term and deep-seated aspects of personal identity.

Given the immense importance of musical taste and preference in the everyday lives and social identities of young people, and the commercial significance of the music business, we suggest that the issues raised in this chapter have profound implications for education and social policy. The power of music is increasingly apparent in all of our lives, and the development of psychological theory and research in this area has the potential to tell us much more about how this influence works, and about how it might be used to promote social and educational well-being.

Reflective questions

1 What are the differences between people's preferences, tastes, attitudes, emotional responses, opinions, and behavioral intentions in relation to music?

2 What are relative contributions of quantitative and qualitative research methods to the study of the development of musical preferences?

3 What are the strengths and weaknesses of the approach of neuroaesthetics to the study of people's responses to music?

4 What is "open-earedness," and how does it develop and change over the lifespan?

5 How does our membership of particular social groups influence our identities and our musical preferences?

Reference list

Bakagiannis, S., & Tarrant, M. (2006). Can music bring people together? Effects of shared musical preference on intergroup bias in adolescence. *Scandinavian Journal of Psychology*, **47**(2), 129–36.

Bandura, A. (1997). *Self-efficacy: The exercise of control*. New York: W. H. Freeman.

Baumann, V. H. (1960). Teen-age music preferences. *Journal of Research in Music Education*, **8**(2), 75–84.

Berlyne, D. E. (1971). *Aesthetics and psychobiology*. New York: Appleton-Century-Crofts.

Boselie, F. (1991). Against prototypicality as a central concept in aesthetics. *Empirical Studies of the Arts*, **9**(1), 65–73.

Bragg, B. W. E., & Crozier, J. B. (1974). The development with age of verbal and exploratory responses to sound sequences varying in uncertainty level. In D. E. Berlyne (Ed.), *Studies in the new experimental aesthetics: Steps towards an objective psychology of aesthetic appreciation*. Washington, DC: Hemisphere.

Brattico, E., Bogert, B., & Jacobsen, T. (2013). Toward a neural chronometry for the aesthetic experience of music. *Frontiers in Psychology: Hypothesis and Theory Article*, **4**(206), 1–21.

Brattico, E., Brattico, P., & Jacobsen, T. (2009). The origins of the aesthetic enjoyment of music—a review of the literature. *Musicae Scientiae, Special Issue*, 15–39.

Brattico, E., & Jacobsen, T. (2009). Subjective appraisal of music: Neuroimaging evidence. *Annals of the New York Academy of Sciences*. Neuroscience and Music III—Disorders and Plasticity, **1169**(July), 308–17.

Brattico, E., & Pearce, M. (2013). The neuroaesthetics of music. *Psychology of Aesthetics, Creativity, and the Arts*, **7**(1), 48.

Crisp, R. J., Stone, C. H., & Hall, N. R. (2006). Recategorization and subgroup identification: Predicting and preventing threats from common ingroups. *Personality and Social Psychology Bulletin*, **32**(2), 230–43.

Csikszentmihalyi, M., & Lefevre, J. (1989). Optimal experience in work and leisure. *Journal of Personality and Social Psychology*, **56**(5), 815–22.

Eisenstein, S. R. (1979). Grade/age levels and the reinforcement value of the collative properties of music. *Journal of Research in Music Education*, **27**(2), 76–86.

Gaertner, S. L., Dovidio, J. F., Anastasio, P. A., Bachman, B. A., & Rust, M. C. (1993). The common ingroup identity model: Recategorization and the reduction of intergroup bias. In W. Stroebe & M. Hewstone (Eds.), *The European Review of Social Psychology* (Vol. 4, pp. 1–26). Chichester: Wiley.

Gembris, H., & Schellberg, G. (2003). *Musical preferences of elementary school children* (p. 324). Abstracts of the 5th ESCOM conference, University of Hanover, Germany.

Goswami, U. (2001). Cognitive development: No stages please—we're British. *British Journal of Psychology*, 92(1), 257–77.

Greasley, A. E., & Lamont, A. M. (2011). Exploring engagement with music in everyday life using experience sampling methodology. *Musicae Scientiae*, 15(1), 45–71.

Greer, R. D., Dorow, L. G., & Randall, A. (1974). Music listening preferences of elementary school children. *Journal of Research in Music Education*, 22(4), 284–91.

Haack, P. A. (1988). *An exploratory study of popular music preferences along the age continuum*. Paper presented at the meeting of the Music Educators National Conference, Indianapolis, Indiana, USA.

Hargreaves, D. J. (1982). The development of aesthetic reactions to music. *Psychology of Music, Special Issue*, 51–4.

Hargreaves, D. J. (1986). *The developmental psychology of music*. Cambridge: Cambridge University Press.

Hargreaves, D. J. (2012). Musical imagination: Perception and production, beauty and creativity. *Psychology of Music*, 40(5), 539–57.

Hargreaves, D. J., & Castell, K. C. (1987). Development of liking for familiar and unfamiliar melodies. *Council for Research in Music Education Bulletin*, 91(Spring), 665–9.

Hargreaves, D. J., Comber, C. J. F., & Colley, A. M. (1995). Effects of age, gender, and training on the musical preferences of British secondary school students. *Journal of Research in Music Education*, 43(3), 242–50.

Hargreaves, D. J., & Galton, M. (1992). Aesthetic learning: Psychological theory and educational practice. In B. Reimer & R. A. Smith (Eds.), *1992 N.S.S.E. yearbook on the arts in education* (pp. 124–50). Chicago: N.S.S.E.

Hargreaves, D. J., Hargreaves, J. J., & North, A. C. (2012). Imagination and creativity in music listening. In D. J. Hargreaves, D. E. Miell, & R. A. R. MacDonald (Eds.), *Musical imaginations* (pp. 156–72). Oxford: Oxford University Press.

Hargreaves, D. J., MacDonald, R. A. R., & Miell, D. E. (2002). What are musical identities, and why are they important? In R. A. R. MacDonald, D. J. Hargreaves, & D. E. Miell (Eds.), *Musical identities* (pp. 1–20). Oxford: Oxford University Press.

Hargreaves, D. J., Miell, D. E., & MacDonald, R. A. R. (2005). How do people communicate using music? In D. E. Miell, R. A. R. MacDonald, & D. J. Hargreaves (Eds.), *Musical communication* (pp. 1–25). Oxford: Oxford University Press.

Hargreaves, D. J., & North, A. C. (1999). Developing concepts of musical style. *Musicae Scientiae*, 3(2), 193–213.

Hekkert, P., & Snelders, H. M. J. J. (1995). Prototypicality as an explanatory concept in aesthetics: A reply to Boselie. *Empirical Studies of the Arts*, 13(2), 149–60.

Hekkert, P., & van Wieringen, P. C. W. (1990). Complexity and prototypicality as determinants of the appraisal of cubist paintings. *British Journal of Psychology*, 81(4), 483–95.

Hemming, J. (2013). Is there a peak in popular music preference at a certain *song-specific age*? A replication of Holbrook & Schindler's 1989 study. *Musicae Scientiae*, 17(3), 293–304.

Holbrook, M. B. (1995). An empirical approach to representing patterns of consumer tastes, nostalgia, and hierarchy in the market for cultural products. *Empirical Studies of the Arts*, 13(1), 55–71.

Holbrook, M. B., & Schindler, R. M. (1989). Some exploratory findings on the development of musical tastes. *Journal of Consumer Research*, 16(6), 119–24.

Konečni, V. J. (1996). Daniel E. Berlyne (1924–1976): Two decades later. *Empirical Studies of the Arts*, 14(2), 129–42.

Kopiez, R., & Lehmann, M. (2008). The "open-earedness" hypothesis and the development of age-related reactions to music in elementary school children. *British Journal of Music Education*, 25(2), 121–38.

Krause, A. E., & Hargreaves, D. J. (2013). myTunes: Digital music library users and their self-images. *Psychology of Music*, **41**(5), 531–44.

Lamont, A. (2008). Young children's musical worlds: Musical engagement in 3.5-year-olds. *Journal of Early Childhood Research*, **6**(3), 247–61.

Lamont, A. M., & Greasley, A. E. (2009). Musical preferences. In S. Hallam, I. Cross, & M. Thaut (Eds.), *The Oxford handbook of music psychology* (pp. 160–8). Oxford: Oxford University Press.

Lamont, A. M., & Webb, R. (2010). Short- and long-term musical preferences: What makes a favourite piece of music? *Psychology of Music*, **38**(2), 222–41.

LeBlanc, A. (1991). Effect of maturation/aging on music listening preference: A review of the literature. Paper presented at the Ninth National Symposium on Research in Music Behavior, Canon Beach, Oregon, USA.

LeBlanc, A., Colman, J., McCrary, J., Sherrill, C., & Malin, S. (1988). Tempo preferences of different-age music listeners. *Journal of Research in Music Education*, **36**(3), 156–68.

LeBlanc, A., Sims, W. L., Siivola, C., & Obert, M. (1993). Music style preferences of different-age listeners. Paper presented at the Tenth National Symposium on Research in Music Behavior, University of Alabama, Tuscaloosa, Alabama, USA.

Martindale, C., & Moore, K. (1988). Priming, prototypicality, and preference. *Journal of Experimental Psychology: Human Perception and Performance*, **14**(4), 661–70.

Martindale, C., & Moore, K. (1989). Relationship of musical preference to collative, ecological, and psychophysical variables. *Music Perception*, **6**(4), 431–55.

Martindale, C., Moore, K., & Borkum, J. (1990). Aesthetic preference: Anomalous findings for Berlyne's psychobiological theory. *American Journal of Psychology*, **103**(1), 53–80.

Martindale, C., Moore, K., & West, A. (1988). Relationship of preference judgements to typicality, novelty, and mere exposure. *Empirical Studies of the Arts*, **6**(1), 79–96.

May, W. V. (1985). Musical style preference and aural discrimination skills of primary grade school children. *Journal of Research in Music Education*, **33**(1), 7–22.

Meadows, E. S. (1970). The relationship of music preference to certain cultural determiners. *Dissertation Abstracts International*, **31**, 6100A.

Moore, K., & Martindale, C. (1983). *Preference for shapes varying in color, color typicality, size, and complexity*. Paper presented at the International Conference on Psychology and the Arts, Cardiff.

Muller, M., Höfel, L., Brattico, E., & Jacobsen, T. (2009). Electrophysiological correlates of aesthetic music processing: comparing experts with laypersons. *Annals of the New York Academy of Sciences*. Neuroscience and Music III—Disorders and Plasticity, **1169**(July), 355–8.

Nieminen, S., Istók, E., Brattico, E., & Tervaniemi, M. (2012). The development of the aesthetic experience of music: Preference, emotions, and beauty. *Musicae Scientiae*, **16**(3), 107–26.

Nieminen, S., Istók, E., Brattico, E., Tervaniemi, M., & Huotilainen, M. (2011). The development of aesthetic responses to music. *Cortex*, **47**(9), 1138–46.

North, A. C., & Hargreaves, D. J. (1995). Eminence in pop music. *Popular Music and Society*, **19**(4), 41–66.

North, A. C., & Hargreaves, D. J. (1997). Liking for musical styles. *Musicae Scientiae*, **1**(1), 107–26.

North, A. C., & Hargreaves, D. J. (1999). Music and adolescent identity. *Music Education Research*, **1**(1), 75–92.

North, A. C., & Hargreaves, D. J. (2000). Collative variables versus prototypicality. *Empirical Studies of the Arts*, **18**(1), 13–17.

North, A. C., Hargreaves, D. J., & Hargreaves, J. J. (2004). Uses of music in everyday life. *Music Perception*, **22**(1), 41–77.

O'Donnell, P. J., MacDonald, R. A. R., & Davies, J. B. (1999). Video analysis of the effects of structured music workshops for individuals with learning difficulties. In D. Erdonmez & R. R. Pratt (Eds.), *Music therapy and music medicine: Expanding horizons* (pp. 219–28). St. Louis: MMB Music.

Rentfrow, P. J., & Gosling, S. D. (2003). The do re mi's of everyday life: Examining the structure and personality correlates of music preferences. *Journal of Personality and Social Psychology*, **84**(6), 1236–56.

Rentfrow, P. J., & Gosling, S. D. (2007). The content and validity of music-genre stereotypes among college students. *Psychology of Music*, **35**(2), 306–26.

Rentfrow, P. J., McDonald, J. A., & Oldmeadow, J. A. (2009). You are what you listen to: Young people's stereotypes about music fans. *Group Processes and Intergroup Relations*, **12**(3), 329–44.

Resnick, B., Orwig, D., Magaziner, J., & Wynne, C. (2002). The effect of social support on exercise behavior in older adults. *Clinical Nursing Research*, **11**(1), 52–70.

Reyna, C., Brandt, M., & Viki, G. D. (2009). Blame it on hip-hop: Anti-rap attitudes as a proxy for prejudice. *Group Processes and Intergroup Relations*, **12**(3), 361–80.

Rogers, V. R. (1957). Children's musical preferences. *Elementary School Journal*, **57**(8), 433–5.

Sloboda, J. A., O'Neill, S. A., & Ivaldi, A. (2001). Functions of music in everyday life: An exploratory study using the Experience Sampling Method. *Musicae Scientiae*, **5**(1), 9–32.

Stuckey, H. L., & Nobel, J. (2010). The connection between art, healing, and public health: A review of current literature. *American Journal of Public Health*, **100**(2), 254–63.

Tajfel, H., Billig, M. G., & Bundy, R. P., & Flament, C. (1971). Social categorization and intergroup behaviour. *European Journal of Social Psychology*, **1**(2), 149–78.

Tajfel, H., & Turner, J. C. (1986). An integrative theory of intergroup conflict. In S. Worchel & W. G. Austin (Eds.), *Social psychology of intergroup relations* (pp. 2–24). Chicago: Nelson-Hall.

Tarrant, M., Calitri, R., & Weston, D. (2012). Social identification structures the effects of perspective taking. *Psychological Science*, **23**(9), 973–8.

Tarrant, M., North, A. C., & Hargreaves, D. J. (2001). Social categorization, self-esteem, and the estimated musical preferences of male adolescents. *Journal of Social Psychology*, **141**(5), 565–81.

Tarrant, M., North, A. C., Edridge, M. D., Kirk, L. E., Smith, E. A., & Turner, R. E. (2001). Social identity in adolescence. *Journal of Adolescence*, **24**(5), 597–609.

Tarrant, M., North, A. C., & Hargreaves, D. J. (2002). Youth identity and music. In R. A. R. MacDonald, D. J. Hargreaves, & D. Miell (Eds.), *Musical identities* (pp. 134–50). Oxford: Oxford University Press.

Taylor, S. (1969). Development of children aged seven to eleven. *Journal of Research in Music Education*, **17**(1), 100–7.

Turner, J. C. (1999). Some current issues in research on social identity and self-categorization theories. In N. Ellemers, R. Spears, & B. Doosje (Eds.), *Social identity: Context, commitment, content* (pp. 6–34). Oxford: Blackwell.

Turner, J. C., Hogg, M. A., Oakes, P. J., Reicher, S. D., & Wetherell, M. S. (1987). *Rediscovering the social group: A self-categorization theory*. Oxford, UK: Blackwell.

Whitfield, T. W. A. (1983). Predicting preference for familiar, everyday objects. An experimental confrontation between two theories of aesthetic behaviour. *Journal of Environmental Psychology*, **3**(3), 221–37.

Whitfield, T. W. A., & Slatter, P. E. (1979). The effects of categorization and prototypicality on aesthetic choice in a furniture selection task. *British Journal of Psychology*, **70**(1), 65–75.

Zillmann, D., & Bhatia, A. (1999). Effects of associating with musical genres on heterosexual attraction. *Communication Research*, **16**(2), 263–88.

Section 3

Differences

Chapter 17

Motivation

Paul Evans

Motivation: Introduction

Developing and sustaining motivation may be one of the most difficult aspects of learning to play a musical instrument. On the one hand, learning a musical instrument is inherently appealing: Making music is intrinsically enjoyable, it has considerable social appeal, and it is a means of personal and creative expression in an artform linked closely to personal and social identity and sense of self. Yet on the other hand, these most outwardly visible benefits of learning and playing a musical instrument can disguise the efforts required to attain them. What most children encounter shortly after commencing learning is that their skills and abilities develop slowly, and only with considerable effort, compared to the expectations of themselves and their parents.

Studies of musical ability from childhood through to adulthood, and from the most basic levels of accomplishment through to expert performance at the highest level, show that musical performance ability cannot be attained without practice. The more hours of effective practice one accumulates, the better one can expect to perform. The trouble with this is that sustaining practice is hard work. Practice is a deliberate, effortful activity. It usually occurs in isolation, and many students are unfortunately left to their own devices when it comes to working out the most effective ways to utilize practice time. Considering the immense amount of time it takes to accumulate practice alongside the pressures of public performance, niggling doubts about one's abilities, the social and emotional challenges faced throughout childhood and adolescence, and competing interests from other activities that may provide faster routes to mastery, it is not surprising that motivation is a major issue for children learning to play a musical instrument.

A relatively small body of research exists specifically in the area of motivation for music learning, but a complete understanding of motivation in music learning necessarily relies also on theoretical frameworks and empirical work in related fields such as educational psychology. This chapter overviews some of the major motivation frameworks in the music education and educational psychology literature. As such, it is necessarily selective, for a comprehensive review of motivation in music learning is well beyond the scope of this book chapter. I begin by outlining the nature of motivation as a psychological construct, and then review some of the major themes and conclusions in the research on motivation in music learning.

Motivation as a psychological construct

Motivation is a psychological construct that is concerned with the complicated nature of why people do what they do. Throughout the twentieth century, motivation research evolved dramatically. In the early twentieth century, psychologists understood motivation in ways ranging from behaviorist approaches focused on reward and punishment contingencies, to psychoanalytic theories, and theories that focused on innate drives (e.g., for food and sex) or desires. In more recent decades, cognitive approaches to understanding the mind have shifted the emphasis to inner states, with the discovery that beliefs, values, attitudes, and intentions explain a considerable proportion of human behavior. A multitude of theoretical traditions and perspectives on motivation still exist. This considerable range of approaches is evident in reviews of motivation research in music education. For example, Hallam (2002, 2011) has examined a range of influences making a distinction between personal factors (such as goals, self-beliefs, personality, and intelligence) and environmental factors (such as family, friends, social contexts, and place of work or study) which can impact motivation to behave in music-related contexts.

Despite the plurality of research approaches and traditions, psychologists have converged on a number of points of agreement, particularly on an understanding of the importance of cognitive and social aspects of human psychology. The most fruitful of these approaches stem from understanding the importance of not only observed behavior and the environmental stimuli that influence it, but also the social interactions that are so intrinsically linked to psychological health, and the cognitive processes surrounding behavior, including intentions, beliefs, values, attitudes, and self-regulatory processes.

A widely cited definition of motivation in educational psychology literature is "the process by which goal-directed behavior is instigated and sustained" (Schunk, Meece, & Pintrich, 2014). This definition contains a number of features that reveal the way contemporary psychologists think about motivation: first, motivation concerns the entire process of behavior—not only the direct cause of the behavior, but also relevant choices, beliefs, thoughts, social influences, and consequences; second, it explains behavior in terms of the way it is focused on attaining goals, which most conscious, intentional behavior is; third, it concerns all physical and mental activity—the undertaking of behavior and the efforts surrounding it, as well as the cognitive and meta-cognitive processes of planning, evaluating, strategizing, making decisions, and monitoring progress towards goals; finally, it is concerned with how behavior is instigated and sustained, that is, not only the initial effort required to commence activity, but also the nature and quality of its direction in the short, medium, and long term.

Beliefs

Children (and adults) have beliefs about the nature of their abilities in any domain, which guide their thinking and behavior. One strand of research that has examined such beliefs in a range of domains refers to two *self-theories* of intelligence or ability: people either believe their ability or intelligence is a fixed trait that they cannot develop, or that their ability or intelligence is a malleable quality that can incrementally improve with learning and practice. More recently, Dweck (2000; Dweck & Molden, 2005) has referred to these self-theories and their implications as either a *fixed* or a *growth* mindset, citing decades of research on the two ways of thinking and about their tremendous implications for learning. These beliefs are important, because when people encounter setbacks, they will respond based on their beliefs. Those with a fixed, or entity theory are less likely to pursue attempts to overcome difficulties, believing that the effort required is a sign that they simply are not cut out for the task. Those with a growth, or incremental theory are much less likely to experience difficulty as failure, and more likely to pursue solutions to the problem, develop strategies for learning, and see their efforts as a necessary and interesting part of learning or acquiring new skills.

What are the implications of self-theories in music learning? The specific links between ability beliefs and achievement have received relatively little attention by researchers. Broadly speaking, it seems clear that students in Western countries rate their abilities in music as being much lower than their abilities in other subjects (McPherson & O'Neill, 2010), and that these ability beliefs decline faster in music than for other subjects throughout adolescence (Wigfield et al., 1997). Schmidt (2005) found correlations between a success orientation and practice time, and between student's confidence in their abilities and their competence as rated by their teachers. A more elaborate measure of these factors, drawing on work from Dweck (2000), was carried out by Smith (2005), who found relationships between an entity belief and subsequent performance-approach and performance-avoid patterns of behavior, and conversely, between incremental beliefs and mastery patterns of behavior including interest, challenge-seeking, and desire to learn. The latter study, however, was focused on university-level musicians, not children.

Though there are few research studies on fixed and growth mindsets in music education, research on these mindsets in educational psychology more broadly has proliferated in recent years and is so extensive that mindset programs are being implemented in school education systems on a broad scale. The growth mindset is shown to be associated with an increased performance trajectory, while the fixed mindset is associated with declines. There is strong evidence that relatively simple intervention programs (e.g., eight 25-minute activities based on learning how ability can improve with effort) can make substantial differences to students' mindsets and subsequently their achievement trajectories (Blackwell, Trzesniewski, & Dweck, 2007). This appears to extend beyond the academic realm into social–emotional skills, with evidence suggesting that learning that social attributes can be developed results in stronger social resilience and lowered stress in response to victimization (Yeager & Dweck, 2012).

One important feature of the growth or fixed mindsets is that they can be communicated through the things that parents and teachers say and the way they communicate to their children. For example, feedback following performance can provide information about the extent to which children adopt different beliefs about their abilities. The common tendency to praise children after good performances (e.g., "Well done! You must be very talented!," "You are really good at music!," "You must be a natural at playing the drums!") might have the undesirably negative effect of promoting the fixed mindset. This has been observed extensively in research in other learning areas, particularly the effects on children's subsequent enthusiasm to learn (Dweck & Molden, 2005; Mueller & Dweck, 1998). The reason the fixed mindset appears to be particularly prominent in the domain of music (Howe, Davidson, & Sloboda, 1998) may be because of the ubiquity of polished recorded music, the messages conveyed about musical "talent" in reality television competitions, or other aspects of the musical environment that communicate information about the nature of musical ability. Therefore, children learning music may be particularly vulnerable— perhaps more so than learning in other areas—to messages from teachers and parents about their performances. The advice from the research on mindset is to provide informational feedback that links children's performance to their efforts: "You must have practiced really hard to perform that piece!," "I can see that you tried really hard to work on that, and it paid off!," "Look at all the things you can do now that you couldn't do last week!".

The message of the fixed and growth mindsets research is that beliefs about the nature of ability have enormous influence over people's behavior, including children's musical practice behavior and the belief that if they practice effortfully, strategically, and regularly, they can improve their abilities. The conclusions of the research show that although some children show a fixed mindset and experience subsequent degradations in their motivation and performance, the mindset can be shifted relatively easily: Praise linked to efforts, rather than the person, can immediately change a child's desire for learning. Consistent emphasis on efforts can make more lasting changes, and relatively simple and cost-effective programs that instill the belief that abilities can be improved can have enduring positive effects on children's motivation. Still, more research is needed in music education where children may be particularly vulnerable to developing beliefs about talent or ability. Music research with adults suggests that early childhood experiences of music in which messages about a low level of fixed ability were communicated to them resulted in long-term, enduring feelings of anxiety, being "unmusical," feeling like a terrible singer, and deliberately avoiding situations that involved singing or musical performance (Knight, 2011; Ruddock & Leong, 2005).

Values

Values are a kind of belief that guides decision-making. The most prominent construct in the motivation literature that is related to values is *subjective task value*, a component of the Eccles (2005) expectancy-value theory of achievement motivation. According to the theory, achievement-related choices are directly linked to the values individuals attach to the various choices that they perceive to be available to them. Subjective task value employs four dimensions:

1 *Attainment value* is the importance of doing well on a task. Tasks are perceived to be important when people view the task as being closely related to their sense of self. Attainment value, according to expectancy-value theory, is strongly influenced by the social setting: one's sense of self draws on children's perceptions of the things that are important in their social environment, including their parents, and cultural expectations such as gender roles. Attainment value can be measured by asking questions such as, "How important is it for you to do well in music?," "Is the amount of effort it takes to practice and learn music worthwhile?," and "Is it important for you to persist with music?".

2 *Intrinsic interest* value refers to the enjoyment one gains from a task. At a general level there appear to be core differences in intrinsic interest value that are relatively stable, that is, some individuals simply enjoy music activities more than others, perhaps based on personality or other relatively stable traits stemming from genetic differences or experiences of music learning early in life. At a more specific level, intrinsic interest can be influenced by educators varying the challenge level of tasks and the degree to which they arouse curiosity and provide opportunities for attaining competence. Intrinsic interest can be measured by asking questions such as, "Do you find learning music enjoyable?," "Is music practice very boring, or very interesting?," and "Do you like going to music lessons?".

3 *Utility value* is the degree to which a task is useful for attaining some future goal that is important to the self. For example, learning to play a musical instrument may be seen as useful if a child wishes to participate in an orchestra or aspires to become a professional musician. Utility value is a kind of extrinsic motivation because the task is not engaged for the intrinsic benefits, but rather as a means to an end, but as long as the end is aligned with the sense of self, the means will be experienced as relatively internal to the self. Utility value can be measured by asking questions such as, "How useful do you think this practice session will be?" and "Is it useful for you to keep learning your musical instrument?".

4 *Perceived cost* is influenced by how much effort is required to participate in a task, anxiety or stress that will be induced by participating in a task, the mental effort required to sustain involvement, and social costs. In music this can range from the anxiety imposed by a performance in front of a large audience, to the social costs in missing out on lunchtimes in order to rehearse with the orchestra at school.

Music appears to be particularly influenced by subjective task value. In some influential work in academic settings by Wigfield et al. (1997), a three-year longitudinal study of elementary students' values for music, reading, mathematics, and sport was conducted. Valuing of instrumental music declined faster and more dramatically than for any other subject in the study. The authors concluded that in the context of their sample, instrumental music was not experienced until relatively later in elementary school. Thus, those students had reached the developmental capacity to make judgments about activities and the values they attach to them, but for music they were making those judgments with relatively little experience in the domain. The researchers speculated that in other countries, where music commenced earlier and a different style of instruction was used, children may value music differently.

This has turned out not to be the case. In a recent study of over 24,000 students in Brazil, China, Finland, Hong Kong, Israel, Korea, Mexico, and the USA, music was compared to science, mathematics, physical education, language, and art (McPherson & O'Neill, 2010). There were significant overall differences between the countries, but the size of these differences was marginal. In rankings of competence beliefs (students' confidence in their abilities) for music compared with other subjects, music was ranked in the lowest two subjects in Hong Kong, Israel, Mexico, and the USA, and rankings of music's task difficulty was ranked in the bottom two subjects in China, Finland, Hong Kong, and the USA (see Table 17.1). Subjective task values for music placed them among the bottom two subjects in every country except Brazil, where they were fourth (the authors attributed the difference in this to the fact that only schools offering specialist music studies were sampled). Thus, the international trend appears to be that "as students progress through school, many report school music to be increasingly less valuable to them as a school subject, and a subject in which they feel they are less capable than other subjects" (McPherson & O'Neill, 2010, p. 132).

A major concern for music educators is students choosing music as an elective subject when it becomes an optional subject in high school. This issue has been addressed by several research studies using subjective task value. Waters, McPherson, & Schubert (2014) recently examined music elective choice in relation to sport in an all-boys independent school in Australia and found that interest was a significant predictor of elective choice. Students appeared to value music less than sport, and there were greater "impediments" impacting their motivation for music than

Table 17.1 Ranking of music based on scores for subjective task values drawn from McPherson & O'Neill (2010)

| | Ranking of Music Compared with Other Subjects (1=highest, 6=lowest) | | |
	Competence	Values	Task Difficulty
Brazil	1	4	4
China	4	5	6
Finland	3	5	5
Hong Kong*	4	5	4
Israel	5	5	4
Korea	4	5	4
Mexico	6	6	2
USA	5	6	5

*Note: Hong Kong did not include science data; scores for Hong Kong are 1=highest, 5=lowest.

sport, in terms of interest, importance, competence beliefs, enjoyment, and social involvement by friends. A qualitative study of values in an independent school (McEwan, 2012) found that values for choosing music as an elective subject were influenced by the culture of the school, and by implicit family values for music, academic, and sporting achievement. In this case, sport was valued as enjoyable and socially relevant, academic subjects were valued as important, and music was seen to offer "limited academic rigor" (p. 14). Simpkins, Vest, & Becnel (2010) in the United States also examined music and sport motivation longitudinally over a period of seven years, and found that active and consistent participation in an activity had higher values for the activity in subsequent years. Interestingly, children in the study did not vary their participation in music or sport from elementary school: whether they participated in music and not sport, or sport and not music, or both music and sport, that pattern of participation did not tend to change as they progressed through adolescence. The authors therefore recommended that educators and parents should ensure consistent time is invested in music activities (particularly for boys, as they are underrepresented in music), with an early start, and regular activities that reinforce the maintenance of task values for music.

These patterns of involvement reflect the consistent finding in subjective task value research that values are formed early in life and are relatively resilient. That is, even though the initial judgments of value in an activity might be made with relatively little experience in the domain, the values are difficult to change over time (Wigfield, Cambria, & Eccles, 2012; Wigfield et al., 1997). In a longitudinal study from childhood through to young adulthood, Evans (2009) found strong relationships between childhood subjective task values, and adult beliefs about the benefits of music and music learning, but no such relationships between adolescent subjective task values and adult beliefs. Thus, early experiences of music that result in negative judgments of task value have long-lasting consequences that may be difficult to reverse. A recent intervention study (Harackiewicz et al., 2012) showed that it may be possible to turn this around later in adolescence. A relatively simple intervention with parents had a flow-on effect to students in science education: The researchers sent two brochures about the utility value of science to parents and encouraged them to have conversations with their children. The intervention appeared to increase students' selection of advanced science subjects in upper levels of high school compared with a control group.

The underlying message from research on subjective task value appears to be that children's valuing for music as an activity or school subject depends strongly on whether they find it important, interesting, useful, and worth the costs of involvement. Children appear to be able to form these values at a relatively young age (e.g., 7 years old), yet by this age, many school systems provide limited music learning activities, so children may begin to form values of music unfairly, with limited experience and involvement. The problem with this appears to be that these values are resistant to change over time. These results speak to the need for good quality, early music learning experiences that facilitate the development of understanding music as useful, interesting, important, and worth the cost of involvement.

Identity

Who are you? A detailed answer to that question is an indication of your identity—an inner working theory or schema of your own sense of self (Vignoles, Schwartz, & Luyckx, 2011). Identity is particularly important in music learning because of the ubiquity of music in everyday life, the importance of music in social circumstances, and the emotional implications of engagement with music. The kinds of music a child plays and listens to contributes to the way the child sees themselves and the role of music in their social world.

Identity schemas are developed at individual, relational, collective, and material levels (Vignoles et al., 2011). At an individual level, identity involves a sense of who one is from an understanding of things one is good at, and an organized set of beliefs and attitudes about the world. For example, a child could identify as a musician, and derive meaning from his or her engagement with a musical instrument. At a relational level, people understand themselves in terms of the connections they have with others: father, sister, friend, fellow musician, music student, and so on. At the collective level, identity involves those aspects of one's self that set them apart from others, such as identifying with other musicians as distinct from sportspeople, or as a musical theatre specialist rather than a metal guitarist. Musical tastes are also developed and portrayed prominently during this time, and become an integral part of a person's social identity (Macdonald, Hargreaves, & Miell, 2009). Finally, at the material level, people identify and define themselves in terms of places and things such as homes, special places, the clothes they wear, and possessions; for a musician, this could involve the place they made their professional debut or where they had a significant learning experience, and of course the often special relationship that musicians have with their instruments.

Establishing a long-term musical identity from the outset of learning to play a musical instrument may be an important way to regulate motivation. In McPherson's (2001) longitudinal study of 157 children aged 7–9, he asked them, before they began learning, "How long do you think you will continue to play a musical instrument?". Their responses—ranging from "until the end of this year" to "for the rest of my life"—were coded into short-, medium, and long-term commitment. Over the next year, McPherson tracked the students' practice time reported by their mothers, and then administered a standardized performance test. There was a mild relationship, as expected, between practice and achievement. But the more interesting finding that arose from this study was that children's achievement was more fully explained when their commitment was included as a factor. Children who practiced the most over the year achieved the highest, but only if they had also expressed a long-term commitment to learning before they even began playing their instrument.

In a follow-up to this study, Evans and McPherson (2014) examined whether this finding held up for musical achievement beyond the first year of learning. We looked at how powerful this "commitment" was for explaining achievement after three years of learning, and for how long the children persisted with playing a musical instrument after ten years (see Figure 17.1). After three years, the results replicated that of the initial one-year study: Children who practiced more *and* expressed a long-term commitment achieved higher on the standardized performance test. Children who practiced more but had a short-term commitment did no better than children who practiced less. After ten years, achievement tests seemed less relevant, as the children showed vastly different pathways of musical participation on various instruments, styles, and learning experiences. We were more interested in how long children persisted with learning and playing music more generally. We found that after ten years, the same pattern held: More practice in the first three years of learning was not enough to predict whether they would persist with music learning. Practice had to be accompanied by a long-term musical identity to explain why musicians persisted.

Our interpretations of these results led us to an understanding of the potential importance of identity in music learning. Establishing a view of oneself as a musician well into the future appears to be predictive of persistence and achievement. The finding does not mean that thinking about one's future is merely a self-fulfilling prophecy. Rather, the long-term identity goal becomes a schema that comes into play to establish more proximal medium and short-term goals, and to regulate behavior toward achieving them (Markus & Nurius, 1986; Zimmerman, 2002). How is the schema developed? Again, the social environment is the source: Children in our study who persisted the longest came from environments that were more enriched and more active than

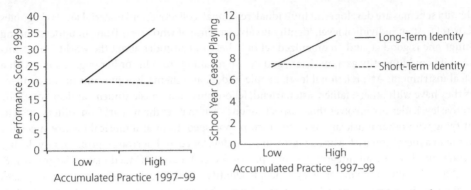

Fig. 17.1 Children's long-term identity—a view of themselves as a musician well into the future—interacted with practice to predict their achievement after three years (left), and their persistence with music learning and playing before they ceased (right).

Adapted from Paul Evans and Gary E. McPherson, Identity and practice: The motivational benefits of a long-term musical identity, Psychology of Music, 43(3) pp. 414–415 Figures 4 and 5, doi: 10.1177/0305735613514471 © 2014, The Author.

those who gave up sooner. These learning environments provide role models, such as older peers who are also in the band program, and through more frequent public performance opportunities they give meaning and purpose to the activity of learning a musical instrument. Contrast this with one boy in our study for whom the learning activity was so foreign and so insignificant that he recalled not comprehending why the students would all gather in a room together, going to such great lengths to learn how to read music to perform on instruments he had never seen before. He gave up learning on the instrument so soon that when we interviewed him ten years later, he had forgotten what instrument it was (Evans, 2009).

These experiences may be an important backdrop to the processes that happen during adolescence. Adolescents are subject to a *moratorium* (Erikson, 1968; Marcia, 1966), a period of time where they can freely explore various kinds of identity-related activities. As they mature, they will be increasingly required to make identity *commitments*—devoting personal resources to an activity and integrating long-term commitments to their sense of self. In a study on musical-identity formation, Evans and McPherson (in press) interviewed students who had high ability, extensive music learning from childhood into adulthood, and a rich level of engagement with music learning. Those who told us about more coherent and cohesive plans seemed to have experiences that allowed them to think about music well into the future. They were able to articulate more precise images of how music would fit into their lives, e.g., as the main focus of their university study or as a hobby alongside another central career focus. Those who had not undergone this examination and consideration of the role of music in their lives experienced anxiety and confusion about their futures and how they would continue to make decisions about their identity pathways.

Needs

Self-determination theory (SDT) is an approach to motivation that has risen to prominence in recent decades. It incorporates a key explanation for the psychological needs people need to have satisfied in order to experience well-being, be motivated in healthy ways, and live fulfilling lives. It is therefore particularly suited to understanding motivation in music learning—the extent to which music learning situations contribute to fulfilling people's needs and creating a motivational orientation that enables them to persist in their music learning.

SDT contends that people are naturally oriented towards growth and experiences that advance their psychological health through the fulfillment of basic psychological needs: the need to feel effective in one's interactions with the environment (competence), the need to feel a sense of belongingness to the social environment (relatedness), and the need to feel as though one's behavior is aligned with and regulated by one's sense of self and identity (autonomy) (Deci & Ryan, 2000). When these needs are fulfilled, regulation is internalized and behavior is perceived to be regulated by the *self*, rather than someone or something in the external environment. Internalized regulation more closely resembles intrinsic motivation—freely engaging in a behavior because of the rewards that naturally arise out of doing the task. When the needs are thwarted, behavior is perceived to be regulated by the external environment—rewards and punishments, and feelings of ego and pride, or guilt and shame.

SDT advances beyond the classic distinction between intrinsic motivation—doing something for its own sake—and extrinsic motivation—doing a task for some reason external to the task itself (e.g., for a longer-term goal or a reward, or to avoid a punishment). Instead, SDT contends that extrinsic motivation actually consists of several types of behavioral regulation: external and introjected regulation, in which behavior is motivated by rewards or punishments and ego contingencies respectively; and identified and integrated regulation, in which behavior is motivated by the understanding of the importance of doing a task, and the alignment of the task with one's sense of self. By making these distinctions between relatively external and relatively internal forms of extrinsic motivation, SDT creates the possibility that some forms of extrinsic motivation can be adaptive, healthy forms of motivation. It addresses the issue that not all behaviors can be intrinsically motivating.

Evans (2015) provides a theoretical overview of SDT applied to music education settings, summarizing the mini-theories of SDT (Vansteenkiste, Niemiec, & Soenens, 2010) and providing examples of related research in music learning. Hypotheses derived from the five mini-theories and examples of their applications are described as follows:

1 Cognitive Evaluation Theory: External motivators such as rewards and punishments do not add to already existing intrinsic motivation for tasks. Rather, external motivators *undermine* intrinsic motivation. For example, parents or teachers providing rewards for practicing or attaining new skills is theorized to undermine, not enhance, intrinsic motivation (Deci, Koestner, & Ryan, 2001).

2 Organismic Integration Theory: Extrinsic motivation can be conceptualized as a continuum, ranging from fully external to internalized motivation. Although not all behaviors can be intrinsically motivating (e.g., practicing scales; hauling a heavy instrument to school each day), they can be understood in relation to their utility for achieving other, more internalized goals (e.g., improving technical ability and playing in a school concert) and for helping develop one's identity (e.g., becoming a better musician).

3 Basic Psychological Needs Theory: People are more psychologically adaptive and have enhanced well-being when their basic psychological needs are met. Music students who do not feel a sense of competence, relatedness, or autonomy will not be able to develop the more internalized forms of motivation outlined here (Evans, McPherson, and Davidson, 2012).

4 Goal Contents Theory: Goals themselves can be intrinsic or extrinsic in quality to the extent that they fulfill basic psychological needs. For example, the goal of attaining fame and notoriety is an extrinsic goal. It is less likely to help motivate effective practice than more intrinsic goals, such as the goal of learning an instrument for its own sake.

5 General Causality Orientations Theory: People differ in their general approach to motivation in day-to-day circumstances. Some people are simply more likely to feel autonomously

motivated on a day-to-day basis, while others might tend to feel more controlled. This "global" orientation is influenced by the summative experiences of motivation people feel in situational settings (e.g., a particular music lesson) and contextually (e.g., at school, in music learning contexts) (Deci & Ryan, 1985).

A further adaptation of General Causality Orientations Theory suggests that motivation is evident at various levels within a hierarchy. Vallerand and Ratelle's (2002) hierarchical model of motivation describes three levels: the global level or general level, which describes a person's overall motivational orientation; the contextual level, which describes broad life contexts such as music or school; and the situational level, which describes motivation in specific life events such as music lessons or practice sessions. According to this model, motivation-related events that occur at the situational level can impact how a person feels more broadly about the context. For example, an individual music lesson that fulfills a person's psychological needs will have a positive impact on a person's motivation in music more broadly. Similarly, if a person feels positively motivated for music as a major context in their life, they will be more likely to be globally more positively motivated. These relationships are depicted in Figure 17.2. This has major implications for the way teachers and parents approach motivation because it suggests that the things that teachers say and do have an impact not only on children's motivation for music learning on a particular day, but also on their motivation in music learning more generally, and subsequently, their overall motivation. In other words, teachers and parents can impact children's motivation for music learning in ways that may affect their psychological health.

The perception of autonomy is central to SDT. In music lessons, the fulfillment of the need for autonomy can occur through the things that parents and teachers say and do. Theoretical coverage of the concept of autonomy has been provided by Renwick and Reeve (2012), emphasizing recommendations for socializers involved in children's music education, summarized as follows:

1　Nurture *inner motivational resources* as much as possible by appealing to students' intrinsic interests in the music itself, creating a sense of challenge by providing material that is difficult but within reach, and explaining the reasons behind choosing learning tasks.

2　Use informational, rather than controlling, language to communicate with students. For example, provide choices for learning activities, and at each stage of instruction explain "why" so that the student understands their progress to longer-term learning goals.

3　Acknowledge and accept students' affect and behavior, rather than seeing them as problematic.

The full breadth of SDT in music education has not yet been examined. However, my work with McPherson and Davidson (Evans, McPherson, & Davidson, 2012) examined the fulfillment of

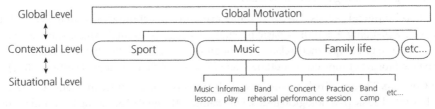

Fig. 17.2 Motivation has both top-down and bottom-up effects between three levels of the hierarchy

Adapted from Vallerand, R. J., & Ratelle, C. F. 'In: Intrinsic and extrinsic motivation: A hierarchical model', in E. L. Deci & R. M. Ryan (eds.), Handbook of self-determination research, pp. 37–64 (Rochester, New York), © 2002, University of Rochester Press.

basic psychological needs in students when they were most active in music learning compared with when they decided to cease music learning. Their psychological needs were overall less fulfilled and more thwarted when they ceased music learning. It is likely that the fulfillment of psychological needs was associated with music being an integral part of their identity and sense of self. When the participants did not experience the fulfillment of their psychological needs, they ceased the activity. This is evident in some of the reasons cited for why they ceased learning:

> The music was unchallenging, the band seemed lax and unfocused compared to my primary school experience, I had no opportunities to improve or make a significant contribution to the band. (Competence)

> I continued to play the clarinet in high school but felt it isolated me socially. (Relatedness)

> I found it boring and the reason I continued all the way through primary school was because my mum wanted me to. I didn't feel like it was something that was relevant or tied in to my life. (Autonomy)

Integrating approaches to motivation

One of the problems with the field of motivation research is that it is conceptually fragmented. Many lines of research are based on individual motivation constructs, which on their own are successful theoretical explanations for components of motivation. One attempt to address this is Martin's (Martin, 2007) integrative approach to measuring motivation and engagement. In his model, adaptive cognitions and behaviors are contrasted with maladaptive cognitions and behaviors on a wheel incorporating 11 dimensions of motivation, as shown in Figure 17.3. The wheel

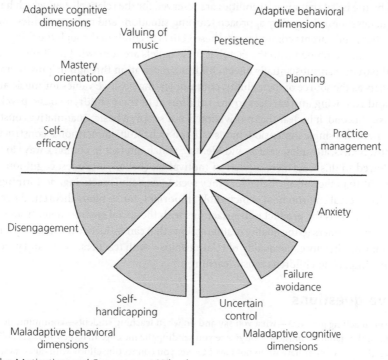

Fig. 17.3 The Motivation and Engagement Wheel

Reproduced with permission from Lifelong Achievement Group (<http://www.lifelongachivement.com>).

was developed in the context of children's motivation for school, but the parallels with music learning are clear. Indeed, the wheel has been examined within the context of children's music learning at school with robust results (Martin, 2008a,b).

The integrative approach to motivation has a number of implications for both theoretical aspects of research as well as practical uses in teaching situations. Because each component is drawn from theoretical work, it is a means by which the fragmented field of motivation can be examined holistically. Researchers and practitioners can also use the Motivation and Engagement Scale (Martin, 2007) to diagnose various aspects of students' engagement in music lessons and practice. The detailed results allow practitioners to provide specific guidance and support based on the motivational factors of interest. For example, teachers could find that a student had positive motivational beliefs, used excellent self-regulatory strategies to plan and persist with their learning, but frequently engaged in self-handicapping skills due to anxiety in meeting performance standards. The teacher could then choose to target the student's anxiety and bring to their attention their use of self-handicapping skills.

Conclusion

Research on motivation in music education has covered a vast range of approaches, including exploratory approaches cataloguing the vast array of personal and environmental influences on music learning (Hallam, 2002, 2011), as well as approaches guided by the psychological study of human motivation more broadly. However, the research appears to converge on several aspects of motivation that are important to understand. Three such conclusions emerge from the literature. First, most children are musical, and it appears that much of the motivation for music learning is constrained by the belief that musical abilities are reserved for the relatively few, which has significant consequences for the way they approach learning situations and music activities and opportunities. Teachers and parents communicate these beliefs to children through the things that they can say or do. This, combined with the fact that these beliefs are somewhat malleable, means that teachers and parents can substantially effect children's motivation through helping them to identify their efforts as the source of their ability, communicating positive values for music and music education, and removing any barriers to the fulfillment of their children's basic psychological needs in music. Second, it is clear that motivation is not simply a basic, quantitative construct that can be measured on a single dimension, but is rather a rich, multi-dimensional construct, including cognitions, beliefs, attitudes, values, and identity, which interact in complex ways to influence behavior. Viewed in this way, these aspects of motivation (beliefs, attitudes, cognitions) may be more important than the specific behaviors they seek to explain (practicing, performing, achieving). Finally, the social environment is incredibly important, for so many theoretical perspectives agree that motivation is the product of transactions with the social environment, from the vicarious observations of others to the quality of interactions that can influence the quantity and quality of our motivation. Therefore, the quality of relationships—with teachers, peers, and parents—has a considerable impact on children's music learning.

Reflective questions

1 What do your teaching practices—what you say and do when teaching students—communicate to your students about the nature of musical ability? Are you sending the message that their musical ability is a "knack" that they may either have or do not have? Or are you connecting efforts with outcomes, helping students to see the fruits of their practice, and promoting the idea that ability can be improved through effort?

2 How do you balance short-term motivational interests (e.g., playing favorite pieces, or learning easy, new pieces quickly) with long-term interests (e.g., developing technique, or learning large, challenging works) when the short-term interests are more enjoyable but impede attainment of long-term interests?

3 What extrinsic rewards and contingencies are being used to motivate a child to practice or learn to play an instrument? How might you help the child capitalize on intrinsically motivating aspects of playing an instrument, or build more internalized forms of motivation?

4 What can teachers do to help children understand and develop a musical identity, that is, to imagine themselves well into the future as a musician? What role will music play in their life?

5 Research has uncovered a vast, potentially infinite, array of influences and factors affecting motivation for music learning and development. How can researchers continually refine and theorize about this range of influences to more parsimoniously understand motivation in children's musical development?

Key sources

Evans, P. (2015). Self-determination theory: An approach to motivation in music education. *Musicae Scientiae*, **19**(1), 65–83. doi: 10.1177/1029864914568044.

Hallam, S. (2011). Motivation to learn. In S. Hallam, I. Cross, & M. Thaut (Eds.), *The Oxford handbook of music psychology*. Oxford, England: Oxford University Press.

Renwick, J. M., & Reeve, J. (2012). Supporting motivation in music education. In G. E. McPherson & G. F. Welch (Eds.), *Oxford handbook of music education* (Vol. 1, pp. 143–62). New York: Oxford University Press.

Ryan, R. M. (2012). *The Oxford handbook of human motivation*. Oxford, England: Oxford University Press.

Reference list

Blackwell, L. S., Trzesniewski, K. H., & Dweck, C. S. (2007). Implicit theories of intelligence predict achievement across an adolescent transition: A longitudinal study and an intervention. *Child Development*, **78**(1), 246–63.

Deci, E. L., Koestner, R. F., & Ryan, R. M. (2001). Extrinsic rewards and intrinsic motivation in education: Reconsidered once again. *Review of Educational Research*, **71**(1), 1–27.

Deci, E. L., & Ryan, R. M. (1985). The general causality orientations scale: Self-determination in personality. *Journal of Research in Personality*, **19**(2), 109–34.

Deci, E. L., & Ryan, R. M. (2000). The "what" and "why" of goal pursuits: Human needs and the self-determination of behavior. *Psychological Inquiry*, **11**(4), 227–68.

Dweck, C. S. (2000). *Self-theories: Their role in motivation, personality, and development*. New York: Psychology Press.

Dweck, C. S., & Molden, D. C. (2005). Self-theories: Their impact on competence motivation and acquisition *Handbook of competence and motivation* (pp. 122–40). New York: The Guilford Press.

Eccles, J. S. (2005). Subjective task value and the Eccles et al. model of achievement-related choices. In A. J. Elliot & C. S. Dweck (Eds.), *Handbook of competence and motivation* (pp. 105–21). New York: The Guilford Press.

Erikson, E. H. (1968). *Identity, youth, and crisis*. New York: Norton.

Evans, P. (2009). *Psychological needs and social–cognitive influences on participation in music activities* (PhD dissertation), University of Illinois at Urbana-Champaign. Available from UMI ProQuest Dissertations and Theses database.

Evans, P. (2015). Self-determination theory: An approach to motivation in music education. *Musicae Scientiae*, **19**(1), 65–83. doi:10.1177/1029864914568044.

Evans, P., & McPherson, G. E. (2014). Identity and practice: The motivational benefits of a long-term musical identity. *Psychology of Music*, **43**(3), 407–422. doi: 10.1177/0305735613514471.

Evans, P., & McPherson, G. E. (in press). Processes of musical identity consolidation during adolescence. In D. Hargreaves, R. A. R. Macdonald, & D. Miell (Eds.), *Oxford handbook of musical identities*. Oxford, England: Oxford University Press.

Evans, P., McPherson, G. E., & Davidson, J. W. (2012). The role of psychological needs in ceasing music and music learning activities. *Psychology of Music*, **41**(5), 600–19.

Hallam, S. (2002). Musical motivation: Towards a model synthesising the research. *Music Education Research*, **4**(2), 225–44.

Hallam, S. (2011). Motivation to learn. In S. Hallam, I. Cross, & M. Thaut (Eds.), *The Oxford handbook of music psychology*. Oxford, England: Oxford University Press.

Harackiewicz, J. M., Rozek, C. S., Hulleman, C. S., & Hyde, J. S. (2012). Helping parents to motivate adolescents in mathematics and science: An experimental test of a utility-value intervention. *Psychological Science*, **23**(8), 899–906.

Howe, M. J. A., Davidson, J. W., & Sloboda, J. A. (1998). Innate talents: Reality or myth? *Behavioral and Brain Sciences*, **21**(3), 399–442.

Knight, S. (2011). Adults identifying as "non-singers" in childhood: Cultural, social, and pedagogical implications. In A. Williamon, D. Edwards, & L. Bartel (Eds.), *Proceedings of the International Symposium on Performance Science*. Utrecht, The Netherlands: European Association of Conservatoires.

Macdonald, R., Hargreaves, D. J., & Miell, D. (2009). Musical identities. In S. Hallam, I. Cross, & M. Thaut (Eds.), *Oxford handbook of music psychology*. Oxford, England: Oxford University Press.

Marcia, J. E. (1966). Development and validation of ego-identity status. *Journal of Personality and Social Psychology*, **3**(5), 551–8.

Markus, H., & Nurius, P. (1986). Possible selves. *American Psychologist*, **41**(9), 954–69.

Martin, A. J. (2007). Examining a multidimensional model of student motivation and engagement using a construct validation approach. *British Journal of Educational Psychology*, **77**(2), 413–40.

Martin, A. J. (2008a). How domain specific is motivation and engagement across school, sport, and music? A substantive-methodological synergy assessing young sportspeople and musicians. *Contemporary Educational Psychology*, **33**(4), 785–813.

Martin, A. J. (2008b). Motivation and engagement in music and sport: Testing a multidimensional framework in diverse performance settings. *Journal of Personality*, **76**(1), 135–70.

McEwan, R. (2012). Secondary student motivation to participate in a Year 9 Australian elective classroom music curriculum. *British Journal of Music Education*, **30**(1), 103–24.

McPherson, G. E. (2001). Commitment and practice: Key ingredients for achievement during the early stages of learning a musical instrument. *Bulletin of the Council for Research in Music Education*, **147**(1), 122–7.

McPherson, G. E., & O'Neill, S. A. (2010). Students' motivation to study music as compared to other school subjects: A comparison of eight countries. *Research Studies in Music Education*, **32**(1), 1–37.

Mueller, C. M., & Dweck, C. S. (1998). Praise for intelligence can undermine children's motivation and performance. *Journal of Personality and Social Psychology*, **75**(1), 33.

Renwick, J. M., & Reeve, J. (2012). Supporting motivation in music education. In G. E. McPherson & G. F. Welch (Eds.), *Oxford handbook of music education* (Vol. 1). New York: Oxford University Press.

Ruddock, E., & Leong, S. (2005). "I am unmusical!": The verdict of self-judgement. *International Journal of Music Education*, **23**(1), 9–22.

Schmidt, C. P. (2005). Relations among motivation, performance achievement, and music experience variables in secondary instrumental music students. *Journal of Research in Music Education*, **53**(1), 134–47.

Schunk, D. H., Meece, J. L., & Pintrich, P. R. (2014). *Motivation in education: Theory, research, and applications* (4th ed.). Englewood Cliffs, NJ: Prentice Hall.

Simpkins, S., Vest, A., & Becnel, J. (2010). Participating in sport and music activities in adolescence: The role of activity participation and motivational beliefs during elementary school. *Journal of Youth and Adolescence*, **39**(11), 1368–86.

Smith, B. P. (2005). Goal orientation, implicit theory of ability, and collegiate instrumental music practice. *Psychology of Music*, **33**(1), 36–57.

Vallerand, R. J., & Ratelle, C. F. (2002). Intrinsic and extrinsic motivation: A hierarchical model. In E. L. Deci & R. M. Ryan (Eds.), *Handbook of self-determination research* (pp. 37–64). Rochester, New York: University of Rochester Press.

Vansteenkiste, M., Niemiec, C. P., & Soenens, B. (2010). The development of the five mini-theories of self-determination theory: An historical overview, emerging trends, and future directions. *Advances in Motivation and Achievement*, 16(1), 105–65.

Vignoles, V. L., Schwartz, S. J., & Luyckx, K. (2011). Introduction: Toward an integrative view of identity. In S. J. Schwartz, K. Luyckx, & V. L. Vignoles (Eds.), *Handbook of identity theory and research* (pp. 1–27). Brighton, UK: Springer.

Waters, S., McPherson, G. E., & Schubert, E. (2014). Facilitators and impediments for elective music and sport in adolescent males. *SAGE Open*, 4(2), doi: 10.1177/2158244014529779.

Wigfield, A., Cambria, J., & Eccles, J. S. (2012). Motivation in education. In R. M. Ryan (Ed.), *Oxford handbook of motivation* (pp. 463–78). Oxford, England: Oxford University Press.

Wigfield, A., Eccles, J. S., Yoon, K. S., Harold, R. D., Arbreton, A. J. A., Freedman-Doan, C., & Blumenfeld, P. C. (1997). Changes in children's competence beliefs and subjective task values across the elementary school years: A 3-year study. *Journal of Educational Psychology*, 89(3), 451–69.

Yeager, D. S., & Dweck, C. S. (2012). Mindsets that promote resilience: When students believe that personal characteristics can be developed. *Educational Psychologist*, 47(4), 302–14.

Zimmerman, B. J. (2002). Becoming a self-regulated learner: An overview. *Theory Into Practice*, 41(1), 64–70.

Chapter 18

Building gifts into musical talents

Gary E. McPherson and Aaron Williamon

Building gifts into musical talents: Introduction

One of the most contentious debates in psychology, education, biology, and other related disciplines centers on the source of exceptional ability. To what extent can the remarkable achievements of eminent musicians, intellectuals, visual artists, writers, and so on be explained through "nature" (genetic endowment) or "nurture" (the environment)? How can these achievements, regardless of their source, be identified and fostered?

In this chapter, we address fundamental issues surrounding the nature/nurture debate in music and, in doing so, scrutinize much of the folklore that typically accompanies remarkable achievement in music. Specifically, we outline a broad structure that distinguishes between "giftedness" and "talent" and discuss, in turn, six core components of this framework:

◆ Giftedness

◆ Intrapersonal factors

◆ Environmental catalysts

◆ The developmental process

◆ Chance

◆ Talent

We then explore the scope and potential for identifying musically gifted children. Throughout, we draw on examples reported by Gagné and McPherson (in press) of highly gifted and talented musicians, including musical prodigies, to elucidate these components.

Defining giftedness and talent

Throughout history there has been an endless fascination with children who display extraordinary abilities in various domains of learning, and this is especially so in music (see de Mink & McPherson, in press; Gagné & McPherson, in press; McPherson & Lehman, 2012). Studying the course of this captivation across the centuries shows that conceptions of giftedness have evolved from a theological view, in which children who display special abilities were regarded as "heavenly" (i.e., a gift from God), through to a metaphysical phase that emphasized individual aptitudes but which also fostered many myths such as the stereotyped "crazed genius," which we see portrayed in many films. Nowadays empirical approaches attempt to focus on the interaction of genetic and environmental factors, domain-specific training, educational measures and individual differences, and how these differ between cultures (Stoeger, 2009).

One of the most immediate problems one encounters when sifting through literature on giftedness and talent is the range of competing definitions used in various sectors; moreover, as these definitions are often theoretical in nature, they can be troublesome to implement in practice (Gagné & McPherson, in press; Gallagher, 1993; Gross, 1994). Frequently, terms used in one field are employed differently in another, with the added complication that some researchers use two or three terms interchangeably without any operational definitions to guide their work.

We also see this problem in school education, where it is common to hear teachers use and regard the terms "gifted" and "talented" as if they were synonyms. In other contexts (Ofsted, 2009), the term "gifted" is used to describe learners with high ability or potential in the academic subjects and "talented" for those with high ability or potential in the expressive or creative arts or sports. And yet in others, giftedness is used to indicate higher order excellence than talent (US Department of Education, 1993). In our view, these types of explanations do not adequately explain the difference between human potential and actual achievement, and lead to the confusion and misunderstandings that can undermine efforts to cater for the needs of this group of special-needs learners. This lack of standardization and agreement also makes it difficult to compare findings from different research traditions or across disciplines (see further Gagné, 2004a).

A final problem with the lack of standardization of terms is that conceptions of giftedness and talent are inevitably culture-specific. Shinichi Suzuki's (1898–1998) Talent Education method for training young violinists and pianists, for instance, is based on the principle that all children can develop requisite musical skills provided they are exposed to the "right" education (Suzuki, 1983). However, this view is very much based on Japanese societal values, in which hard work is often respected above achievement.

For the purposes of this chapter, we choose to differentiate between the terms "giftedness" and "talent" according to the most dominant view internationally, and one that has been adopted by many educational systems around the world. Our explanation is based on the work of the educational psychologist Françoys Gagné (1985, 1993, 2000, 2003, 2004b, 2009a,b, 2010, 2013). This view takes a decidedly "bottom-up" approach to conceptualizing exceptional skills, in that it seeks to explain and identify potential and ability and then to offer direct implications for the education and training of young people. An alternative approach has emerged within the context of psychological research into expert performance and behaviour (for reviews, see Ericsson, 1996; Ericsson & Lehmann, 1996; Howe, Davidson, & Sloboda, 1998; Williamon & Valentine, 2000, 2002). Here, a more "top-down" approach has been adopted, in that much effort has been directed toward studying the performance of established experts, the rationale being that such investigations can shed light on fundamental psychological mechanisms underpinning high-level performance and can eventually be used to inform the training of novices. The former, bottom-up conception fits more organically with the main purpose of this chapter, which is to explain how a child, born with a range of natural abilities that can enhance his or her study of music, may then develop into a talented musician. Nevertheless, we encourage readers to understand both approaches in order to acquire a comprehensive understanding of the topic.

At the heart of Gagné's (2010, 2013) model, which is adapted here for music to identify specific musical talents (see Figure 18.1), is the distinction between domains of ability (*gifts*) and fields of performance (*talent*). Gagné uses the term "giftedness" to describe individuals who are endowed with natural *potential to achieve* that is distinctly above average for their age group in one or more aptitude domains. In this conception, aptitudes are natural abilities that have a genetic origin and that appear and develop more-or-less spontaneously in every individual. The mix of these aptitudes explains the major proportion of differences between individuals when the surrounding environment and practice are roughly comparable. However, aptitudes do not develop purely by maturation alone; environmental stimulation through practice and learning is also essential.

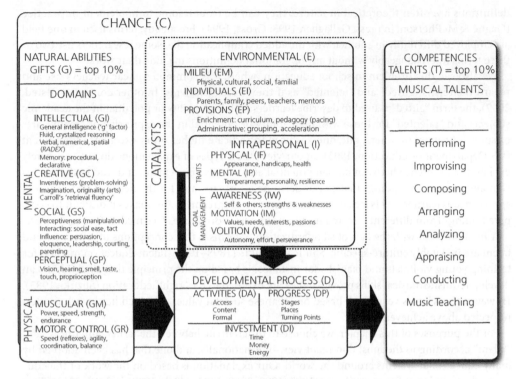

Fig. 18.1 Differentiated model of musical giftedness and talent

Adapted from Gagné, F., "Building gifts into talents: Detailed overview of the DMGT 2.0," in B. MacFarlane & T. Stambaugh (eds.), *Leading change in gifted education: The festschrift of Dr. Joyce VanTassel-Baska*, p. 64 (Waco, TX), © 2009, Prufrock Press.

Talent can be used to describe someone who demonstrates *superior performance* (or *superior skills*) as a result of some type of systematic training in a specific field. In music, it can refer to a range of competencies that encompass the defined talents shown in Figure 18.1: performing, improvising, composing, arranging, analysis, appraising, conducting, and music teaching.

Giftedness

As depicted in Figure 18.1, Gagné (2010, 2013) identifies six domains of natural abilities (*gifts*), four mental (Intellectual, Creative, Social, Perceptual), and two physical (Muscular, Motor Control). The individual blending of these mental and physical "natural" abilities (or aptitudes) is expected to influence the types of musical talents that will eventually evolve. For example, creativity may not be the key component of some particular talents in music—such as performance within the Western art music tradition—yet it is an essential ingredient of some of the more overtly creative sides of the discipline, including improvising and composing (Winner & Martino, 1993, 2000). Likewise, physical natural abilities—such as the muscular and motor control components of power, speed, strength, endurance, reflexes, ability, coordination, and balance—are in varying ways essential in many forms of musical performance, but may be far less important for those who compose or are engaged in the analysis or appraisal of music. One of the great challenges in the discipline is for researchers to sort through this maze and to clarify the particular blend of natural abilities which underpin each form of music-related activity (this is discussed further in the section "Identifying the musically gifted").

Furthermore, as Gagné (2010) explains, these natural abilities "are not innate," but rather develop "through maturational processes and informal exercise" even though such development and level of expression is "partially controlled by the individual's genetic endowment" (p. 83). Obviously, gifts are more easily observed in young children before environmental forces and training moderate their influence, but can also be observed at all ages and, most especially, through the facility and how rapidly a music learner acquires new knowledge, skills, and understanding. In this way, ease and speed of learning define any type of giftedness (Gagné, 2010).

What is the difference between "gifted," "innate," and "precocious"?

As Gagné (2013) suggests, natural abilities develop progressively, mostly during the early years of one's life, but spontaneously without the structured learning or formal training associated with the development described in his model. In contrast, the term "innate" is best used in a very restricted way to imply, at a behavioral level, "hard-wired, fixed action patterns of a species that are impervious to experience. Genetic influence on abilities and other complex traits does not denote the hard-wired deterministic effect of a single gene but rather probabilistic propensities of many genes in multiple-gene systems" (Plomin, 1998, p. 421; see further Gagné, 2013).

Given this, it does not make sense to use expressions such as "David is a born musician." Suggesting that musical talent is "innate" only makes sense metaphorically. Rather, natural mental and physical natural abilities of the type described by Gagné (2013) mean that gifted children can be contrasted with their peers by the rate and speed at which they acquire new skills. The term "precocious," defined as having developed certain abilities or inclinations at an earlier age than is usual or expected, is often used when referring to "gifted" children's ability to learn more rapidly than their peers. For example, saying that "David is a precocious pianist" would imply that David was able to play pieces much earlier and faster than peers of his own age who were also learning the piano. Therefore, the higher David's level of giftedness, the earlier and faster will his mastery of successive stages in his development be achieved (see Gagné & McPherson, in press).

Intellectual natural abilities

Gifted music learners, and most especially musical prodigies, display a number of distinguishing characteristics, but one stands out: their extraordinary ability to memorize music. Mozart, for example, was barely 14 years old when he visited the Sistine Chapel, heard Gregorio Allegri's famous *Miserere*, and then came back home and reproduced the complete 15-minute score in notation. It is believed that he heard the work more than once, and knew the text beforehand, yet this still stands as a remarkable feat of memorization (Keefe, in press; Kopiez & Lehmann, in press).

The literature is full of impressive feats of memorization by young musicians. Some examples include Erwin Nyiregyházi, who reportedly "learned to play Robert Schumann's *Piano Concerto in A minor*, Op. 54 by heart in only 10 days, although he played it through only once a day" (Kopiez & Lehmann, in press), and the 4-year-old Lang Lang whose "teacher was astonished by his memory; he could memorize four big pieces every week" (Solomon, 2012, p. 445). Gagné and McPherson (in press) document multiple examples of extraordinary progress based on powerful memory processes. Whilst some of these historical reports might be questioned or even exaggerated, the consistency of instances among their most famous still demonstrates the highly developed memory systems that distinguish young, highly gifted musicians.

Perceptual natural abilities

Because music is an "aural artform," much of the literature has concentrated on the "perceptual" domain to describe an underlying "trait" of musical potential which might form an integral component of success in all of the eight musical talents listed in Figure 18.1. However, researchers use different frameworks to define this potential. Gardner (1983) refers to a sensitivity to the physical and emotional aspects of sound, while Gordon (2007) talks of the ability to audiate (i.e., comprehend sound inwardly), and Mainwaring (1941, 1947, 1951a,b) places an emphasis on the ability to "think in sound." These earlier conceptions have been extended by Brodsky (2004), who draws on findings by Papoušek (1996) to posit that the extent to which the processing of complex musical structures might be an innate predisposition in infants tends to "fade away" in situations when the developing child is "not sufficiently engaged in auditory and musical interchanges" (Brodsky, 2004, p. 87).

Although music teachers will be able to gauge a child's motor abilities and physical coordination within the first weeks of learning an instrument, evidence from studies on high ability (Winner & Martino, 2000) suggests that a possible basic core ability of musically gifted children is their "sensitivity to the structure of music—tonality, key, harmony, and rhythm, and the ability to hear the expressive properties of music" (p. 102). This sensitivity to structure allows musically gifted children to remember, play back, transpose, improvise and create music—ways of enjoying and studying music that were evident during childhood for many of the great composers and performers throughout history. Another aspect is that musical giftedness can reveal itself as early as 1 or 2 years of age, which is earlier than practically any other domain of skill. Mozart, for example, is reported to have had such delicate ears that he would become physically ill when exposed to loud sounds. In similar extreme cases of extraordinarily gifted prodigies, this intense interest in musical and environmental sounds is also accompanied by an even more sophisticated sense of the "goodness" of tone and timbre, as evident in examples of famous musicians such as Rubinstein and Menuhin who as young children broke their toy violins because the tone was so poor (Winner & Martino, 2000).

A more universal perceptual ability that typifies highly gifted musical children, however, is their ability to sing back heard songs earlier than ordinary children, which can occur even before they learn to talk (Winner & Martino, 2000). While ordinary children start imitating songs at around 2 years (or a little after), singing whole songs by age 4 and reproducing songs accurately by 5, the most musically gifted are able to match pitches accurately by their second year and do this often after just one listening. Associated with this sensitivity to sound is the capacity for musically gifted children to represent musical relations in multiple ways (Bamberger, in press) and to respond positively to the emotional aspects of music (Persson, 1996; Persson, Pratt, & Robson, 1996). Although a young musician may not have sufficient training to follow every detail of musical structure, he or she "can hear and respond to the emotional message of the music" (Winner & Martino, 2000, p. 105). In these ways, traditional measures of assessing musical aptitude that involve examples of telling whether two successive tonal or rhythmic patterns are the same or different may be missing the point; a sharp ear for distinguishing differences in pitch and rhythm "may be no more predictive of musicality than possessing a good eyesight is predictive of good reading ability" (Winner & Martino, 2000, p. 105; see also Davies, 1978; McPherson & Hallam, in press). The two most important core ingredients of musical giftedness, therefore, seem to involve sensitivity to structural and to expressive (in contrast to technical) properties of music.

Csikszentmihalyi (1998) extends this conception by asserting that "children whose neurological makeup makes them particularly sensitive to sounds will be motivated to pay attention to aural stimulation, be self-confident in listening and singing, and likely to seek out training in music" (p. 411), while Brodsky (2004) proposes that potential for processing music develops as children become more aware of sound and start to identify and associate with music according to their own "auditory style." For Brodsky, this predisposition involves a fusion between a *responsiveness* and *preference* for music that links with the child's *awareness* of music. In our conception, however, *responsiveness* and *preference* would be associated with motivation and interest and therefore fall among intrapersonal catalysts.

Absolute (perfect) pitch

As an extension, the degree to which absolute (or perfect) pitch is related to Gagné's (2013) natural *perceptual* abilities, hard wired (innate or genetically determined), or impacted by maturation or environmental stimulation, continues to be an area of fascination. Available evidence suggests that no single factor is predictive of absolute pitch in musicians, but rather that a combination of genetic predisposition (especially family history), commencing an instrument during the sensitive period between 3 and 7 years (with an outside limit of between 9 and 12 years), and early exposure to a pedagogy that emphasizes consistent tone–label associations (e.g., fixed-*do* systems, with continuing use of fixed-pitch instruments such as the piano) provides the strongest explanation (Wilson et al., 2012; see also Elmer et al., 2013). Interestingly, a majority of absolute-pitch musicians play piano, a fixed-*do* instrument where the visual layout of the keyboard reinforces rather than destabilizes long-term absolute pitch templates both at the time of starting the instrument and throughout the rest of the musician's playing career (Wilson et al., 2012). Even though a majority of musical prodigies do seem to possess this ability (Gagné & McPherson, in press), most professional musicians do not, so it is important to keep in mind that absolute-pitch possession (as compared with exceptional relative pitch) is not a prerequisite for achieving musical excellence, or a determining trait that might be used to identify and categorize musically gifted children. Even so, the role of genetic predisposition, commencement age, and appropriate early pedagogy is consistent with Gagné's explanation in that it shows how the natural *perceptual* (aural) abilities of the most gifted and talented child musicians have developed through maturational processes and appropriate education into an acute sense of pitch (whether absolute- or relative-pitch ability) which then feeds into a more sophisticated sense of musical structure and expression.

Mimicry

In their extensive survey of musical prodigies, Gagné and McPherson (in press) cite Solomon (2012), who suggests that "[t]o be a musician, the person has to have a mimetic capacity to reproduce others' techniques" (p. 419). Solomon suggests that this ability to produce exceptionally refined interpretations even at a young age seems to involve both auditory and motor aptitudes, as the musician picks up specific aspects of musicianship to craft an interpretation and then reproduces this through performance. In some ways this is akin to languages: "Some people are apparently born with an ear for languages. A small fraction can continue to pick up new languages, and learn to speak them like a native, even when they are well advanced in age. They are natural mimics" (Harris, 1998, p. 388).

Physical natural abilities

In much of the music literature the physical aspects of performing have been underestimated and little studied, even though it is self-evident that they are essential, as they are in other performing arts. This is remarkable, given that a concert pianist can play at speeds of ten or more notes per second in both hands, in complex changing and spatial patterns, and with multiple patterns of rhythm, dynamics, and articulation (Clarke, 2002, p. 59).

As a very young boy, Michael Jackson reports that he could watch someone do complicated dance steps and know immediately how to do it (Jackson, 2009, p. 136). In this and many other cases of musical prodigies we can observe major individual differences from the earliest phase of music learning which seem to indicate the presence of significant aptitude differences (Gagné & McPherson, in press). Another good example comes from Kenneson (1998), who cites the first cello lesson he gave to 2-year-old Shauna Rolston and how impressed he was by

> that toddler's dexterous left hand that was soon acting out musical ideas on the cello with great agility. Shauna was marvelously coordinated. Her right hand, with its deft sense of touch, showed the promise of an unusual talent for bowing. (. . .) Within a year she drew a tone pure as crystal from her little cello (p. 22).

These examples highlight the two distinct dimensions of motor control abilities: a) the motor dexterity itself, and b) the procedural memorization of these motor sequences. A significant gap in the music literature is the dearth of studies focusing on individual differences in motor control abilities among novice performing students. We find this remarkable given that music teachers are able to gauge a child's motor abilities and physical coordination within the first weeks of learning an instrument.

Intrapersonal catalysts

Intrapersonal catalysts comprise at least five types of physical and mental traits, each partially influenced by genetic endowment (Gagné, 2010). First, *physical traits* associated with one's appearance, any disabilities, and general health help identify young individuals who might succeed because of their build. *Mental traits* cluster around temperament and personality, and can be useful in explaining a musician's basic tendencies as opposed to behavioral styles, plus the resilience they draw on when experiencing failure or in situations where learning is frustrating.

Second, *goal management* dimensions help us understand how learners focus on *what* they want to achieve and *how* they intend to go about reaching their goals. It includes three subcomponents: awareness (being attentive and responsive to personal and others' strengths and weaknesses), motivation (in terms of the identification and reassessment of goals), and volition (the intense dedication and personal willpower necessary to achieving goals).

One line of research—achievement motivation—demonstrates how talented children seek moderate challenges and risks, in that they are attracted to tasks that are neither too hard nor too easy. These types of children are "strivers" in that they constantly seek to improve themselves and become better in those tasks that they choose to study (Sternberg, 2000). Another area of research, on so-called self-efficacy, focuses on children's beliefs in their own personal competence about whether or not they can do a task in a particular situation (Bandura, 1997; see further McCormick & McPherson, 2003; McPherson & McCormick, 2006). A key point, however, is that intrapersonal catalysts affect both the quality and quantity of children's engagement with music (McPherson, Davidson, & Faulkner, 2012).

Many gifted children are highly capable in a number of areas and commit themselves to a range of activities, each of which requires vast amounts of time and energy for continuing success. This sometimes produces high levels of stress and emotional instability (Coleman & Cross, 2000). However, multitalented adolescents tend also to be good at *self-managing* their learning by focusing their efforts on a specific task for hours or even days on end, monitoring and controlling their own learning, sustaining their effort (even when tired), and efficiently planning what they need to do in order to master a new skill (Gagné, 1999, 2000; Gagné et al., 1996).

Some exceptionally gifted children also display *personalities* that are different from other children, such as over-excitabilities in psychomotor, intellectual, sensual, imaginational, and emotional areas of their development. These over-excitabilities, which researchers define as "expanded awareness, intensified emotions, and increased levels of intellectual and/or physical activity" (Coleman & Cross, 2000, p. 204), manifest themselves in many different ways. In music, they explain why some children develop an almost fanatical love of a particular genre or composer, an intense emotional commitment to one or more forms of music, or a deep love for the sound of a particular instrument. Among many examples of the phenomena is the celebrated cellist Jacqueline du Pré, who started her musical education at the age of 4 after hearing the cello performed on the radio and then demanding that her mother arrange lessons (Wilson, 1998). Unfortunately, however, these children's highly developed capacities in music may not always match other aspects of their development, with the complication that they may experience difficulties physically, socially, or emotionally. In addition, the particular blending of the psychological dimensions results in some highly gifted children placing unreasonably high expectations on themselves, which if not tempered can result in stress, burn-out, and unhealthy self-criticism (Coleman & Cross, 2000).

Each of these characteristics was evident in Mozart, who was so passionate about his learning that it was "of little moment to him what he was given to learn; he simply wanted to learn" (cited in Solomon, 1995, p. 39). He was also single-minded, eager, and capable of intense concentration. "Whatever he was given to learn occupied him so completely that he put all else, even music, on one side; e.g., when he was doing sums, the tables, chairs, walls, even the floor was covered with chalked figures" (Solomon, 1995, p. 39). By the age of 3, when his 7-year-old sister began receiving keyboard lessons from their father, Mozart was drawn to music, "perhaps by a desire to emulate his sister and win his share of their father's attention," and spent "endless hours at the keyboard, particularly delighting in 'picking out thirds and sounding them'" (Solomon, 1995, p. 35). Mozart's efforts were so focused and concentrated that soon after he began learning he could master simple musical repertoire in a surprisingly short amount of time (Solomon, 1995). These extraordinary behaviors are not seen to the same degree in the vast majority of musically gifted children, and we need to be careful, therefore, that any conception of giftedness and talent values the uniqueness of each individual learner.

Environmental catalysts

It is impossible to survey the full range of environmental forces that come into play in the development of a gifted child musician. However, it is possible to survey some of the most important environmental catalysts, given available research that asserts the importance of parents and siblings, the influence of teachers, and the types of events in children's lives that can have a profound impact on their subsequent development.

Important environmental influences are the *milieu* in which the child is raised, the *individuals* with whom the learner comes into contact, and the *provisions* which can serve to accelerate progress. According to Gagné (2010), the *milieu* can be studied from a macroscopic level, to understand geographical location and demographic and social issues, and also a microscopic level, to understand issues related to the size of the family, socio-economic status, and neighboring services. For example, living in close proximity to appropriate learning resources supports a young child's learning and can act as a stimulus for a gifted child's musical education, as would having parents who are financially comfortable and prepared to devote large amounts of their time and resources to supporting their child's musical education.

Much of the literature in music and other areas of talent development focuses on the influence of significant *individuals* such as parents, teachers, peers, and siblings within the immediate environment of the young learner. Even though their influence may qualitatively change over time, these significant individuals often provide the emotional and intellectual support necessary for developing skills at the highest level (McPherson, 2009; McPherson, Davidson, & Faulkner, 2012). McPherson and Lehmann (2012) draw on research in sports psychology, for example, to show how the parents' role evolves from direct involvement as an organizer of lessons and encouraging spectator during the *sampling* and *specialist* stages of learning to indirect involvement as a spectator when the child enters the *investment* stage. This can be contrasted to the teacher's role, which for the sampling stage works best if the teacher is a helper and friend, in contrast to the investment stage where the teacher needs to be both an expert musician and a superb role model.

Some researchers such as Sosniak (1985), who studied highly talented pianists, assert that exceptionally talented children typically have at least one parent or relative who cared deeply about their musical development, as confirmed by violinist Isaac Stern:

> There *has* to be someone pushing, a parent or a teacher. Every one of the kids I've guided has someone like that in their lives, pushing them, sometimes gently, sometimes horribly, sometimes, unfortunately, to the point of driving the child away from music. It's the quality of parental pushing that helps determine the eventual outcome of the prodigy. (Winn, 1979, p. 40)

Extending this conception is work by Yun Dai and Schader (2001), which stresses the importance of cultural values and beliefs about learning. They report on a study of children who were taking lessons at eminent conservatory music programs as an extension of their normal schooling. Their findings show that parents of these high-level learners tended to emphasize intrinsic rather than extrinsic rewards for their children's learning, by stressing the appreciation and aesthetic qualities, and enrichment of life as the major reasons for wanting their child to learn music. This result was consistent for both children who were beginning their training and also for those who had been studying for more than ten years. The explanation they provide is that the parents who expressed an intrinsic orientation for their children's learning tended to nurture and foster internal motivations for them, in contrast to parents who expressed a strong extrinsic orientation and who pushed their children to a loss of effort and possible conflict. The authors of this study suggest that a social environment that reduces anxiety and external pressure, and encourages personal growth and task commitment, is essential for sustained, long-term involvement (see also Gottfried, Fleming, & Gottfried, 1994; Kemp, 1996; McPherson, Davidson, & Evans, Chapter 22; Sloboda, 1993). Interestingly, many of the parents of the successful learners did not say they wanted their children to learn merely for musical reasons. Nonmusical benefits relating to the child's holistic development (e.g., self-discipline, diligence, academic achievement) were of utmost concern. In sum, a family's lifestyle is important to a child's development, but there is nonetheless no ideal family, in that gifted children can spring from many and varied backgrounds (Freeman, 2000).

Research also shows that musicians who continue playing are able to differentiate between the "personal" and "professional" qualities of their teachers and that personal warmth is a vital characteristic of a teacher during the initial stages of development. Better students remember their first teacher "not so much for their technical adeptness as for the fact that they made lessons fun. They communicated both their love for music and their liking for their pupil" (Sloboda, 1993, p. 110). Leopold Mozart is perhaps one of the best examples of a teacher who could nurture talent. He "was a supreme teacher who understood how to inspire gifted children to great effort and achievement, instilling a drive for excellence and awaking in them a sense of unlim-ited devotion to his person and a desire to obtain his approval above all else" (Solomon, 1995, pp. 39–40). At the time, Leopold was one of the finest performers and composers in Europe and, by the time Wolfgang was born, had already published a method for teaching the violin (*Versuch einer grundlichen Violinschule*), which had brought him much acclaim (Turner, 1965). Lehmann, Ericsson and Hetzer (2002), in a biographical study of Wolfgang and 21 lesser-known composers at the time, effectively demonstrate that it was predominantly the quality of young Wolfgang's educational opportunities that distinguished him from the others and that, among the others, it was the quality of their early music instruction that correlated with their status as a prodigy.

Leopold Mozart was also aware of the need to showcase his son's remarkable achievements as an added incentive to fostering his development, and by the age of 7 1/2, Wolfgang had travelled thousands of miles across Europe to perform in almost 90 cities (Solomon, 1995). Such exten-sive travelling and exposure to influential patrons and contemporary trends in music-making enriched Wolfgang's musical development in profoundly important ways, also leaving indelible impressions on those who were witness to his abilities. At a brief stay at a Franciscan church in Ybbs, the 6-year-old Mozart played the organ "so well that the Franciscans . . . were almost struck dead with amazement" (Anderson, 1985, p. 6). Certainly, one can begin to imagine how the inev-itable praise to follow such a performance must have left its mark on the young prodigy.

These are brief examples of how parents and teachers impact on a gifted child's musical devel-opment. Although the impact of other significant others such as siblings and peers is not dealt with here, we would predict that in certain situations their impact might be equally influential. Likewise, gaining access to high-quality *provisions* such as music camps, community ensembles, or being chosen to participate in selective schools helps to accelerate the development of a tal-ent or talents. These significant events in a child's life leave a lasting impression on subsequent vocational decisions to engage in a particular activity and are therefore crucial for sustaining involvement.

The developmental process

As can be inferred from the direction of arrows in Figure 18.1, natural abilities (or aptitudes) act as the "raw material" for the emergence of talents (Gagné, 2010), so no amount of giftedness will guarantee success without opportunities for intense, systematic learning and practice. For this reason, Gagné divides his Developmental Processes into three subcategories:

Activities: Access to a musical education, whether by being selected or identified, provides gift-ed children with opportunities to develop musical talents through exposure to purposeful, structured activities within a specific learning context.

Investment: Exceptionally talented music learners are intellectually curious and emotionally engaged. An intense determination fuels their drive to achieve at a high level such that par-ents will often make lifestyle changes to accommodate their child's musical interest.

Progress: Precocious learners are defined by the rate at which they learn and acquire new skills, knowledge, and understanding, and thereby possess a "rage to learn" that is not necessarily driven by a desire to achieve fame, money, or a possible career (McPherson & Lehmann, 2012; Winner & Martino, 2000). Such learners often devote large amounts of time, money, and energy into their learning to acquire expertise.

In the music literature, most studies of the developmental process have demonstrated a close connection between *deliberate* forms of practice and overall achievement, for both young and older musicians (Chaffin & Lemieux, 2004; Ericsson, Krampe, & Tesch-Römer, 1993; Howe et al., 1998). Indeed, the literature discusses the so-called ten-year rule, which suggests that a *minimum* of ten years of dedicated practice are required to become an expert in any field—from music, drama, and dance, to sports and athletics, to business and other cognitive domains (Ericsson et al., 1993; Winner, 1996a,b). In the case of music, the path to eminence can often be much longer, with requisite skills requiring constant development and maintenance (Krampe, 1997; Krampe & Ericsson, 1996). Chaffin and Lemieux (2004) expound on this point further:

> While the idea that practice is integral to success is not likely to surprise anyone, the amount of training involved is striking. It is estimated that more than 10,000 hours of practice is required before a performer is ready to begin a professional career. . . . The young pianists in a study by Sosniak (1985) started their careers as concert soloists after an average of 17 years of training. For composers, the period of preparation is even longer: 20 years from first exposure to music to first notable composition for the 76 major composers whose careers were reviewed by Hayes (1981). After a lifetime of practice, the experienced pianists in Krampe's (1997) study had put in 60,000 hours of practice. (pp. 20–1)

High achievement, however, is not determined by quantity of practice alone, just as it is clear that two individuals who practice for the same amount of time will not produce exactly the same performances. Rather, the acquisition of expert-level skill is cultivated through engagement in the highest *quality* of practice (Ericsson et al., 1993; Williamon, Lehmann, & McClure, 2003; Williamon & Valentine, 2000). Reviews by Chaffin and Lemieux (2004), Jørgensen (2004), and Davidson and King (2004) offer a number of suggestions for the content and form that such practice may take.

To this we could also add historical indications that Mozart's musical practice from a very early age was goal-oriented, structured, and effortful, as described in the literature on *deliberate practice* (e.g., Ericsson, 1996). By the age of 6, Mozart was devoting large chunks of his day practicing pieces and receiving a considerable amount of daily input from his father, who was himself an eminent musician and teacher. Not only did the young Mozart practice repertoire, but he also improvised for hours on end and put these thoughts on paper in the form of compositions. His remarkable learning curve meant that he was able to master all the musical clefs very early in his training, as well as sight-read any type of score on the keyboard. His learning was, therefore, not focused merely on performing other composer's music, but also continually varying and building on what had been previously achieved. Very early in his music education, he was gaining practice in transferring what he had learned in one context to another (see Deutsche, 1966).

We feel it judicious to add a note of caution when interpreting the literature cited immediately above, something that the first author of this chapter has discussed in much greater detail in the opening chapter of his recent book on musical prodigies (Gagné & McPherson, in press). Very recent evidence is questioning the power of deliberate practice as the single most important predictor of performance achievement (see further *Intelligence*, volume 45, 2014; Hambrick et al., 2014; Macnamara, Hambrick, & Oswald, 2014; but see also, Platz et al., 2014), and newly emerging evidence in neuroscience is starting to map out the genetic underpinnings of individual differences on diverse musical phenotypes, including perception, melodic memory, absolute pitch, music creativity, and congenital amusia (Mossing & Ullén, in press; Tan et al., 2014, see also Polderman et al., 2015). Harris (1998, 2006) challenges the notion that children's behaviors are primarily the result of how they were raised or taught, because parents and teachers react and adjust their behavior just as much to the child as does the child to his or her parents or teacher. Furthermore, children relate more to their peers than their parents, and are adept at modifying their behavior so that they can fit in with their peer group.

Given this, we can note that development results from the transformation of outstanding natural abilities or gifts into the highly refined and systematically developed competencies displayed in one or more of the musical talents depicted in Figure 18.1 (Gagné, 2010). A major implication of the discussion thus far is that a child may be gifted without displaying any specific "talent" (but not the reverse). This is because the child may possess the potential for success, but may not be able to act on it due to a number of factors such as a lack of interest.

Chance

Chance can act positively on a child's natural abilities, plus a range of intrapersonal and environmental catalysts in as much as it may bring good fortune, particularly if a child is constantly engaged in exploring the environment or is simply in the "right place at the right time." The influence of this factor should not be underestimated, and we might wonder whether any of the great composers or performers throughout history would have made it to the top of their fields without at least some breaks during their early, developmental years.

The great jazz trumpeter Louis Armstrong, for example, worked from around 6 years of age for two emigrant brothers collecting cast-offs for their junk wagon. Normally, they would ring a bell or shout to attract customers, but one day, the brothers asked Louis to blow a simple tin-horn that was used at the time during celebrations. It worked wonders, and in the space of a short period of time it became a tremendous asset to the business, helping to draw attention to the junk wagon, with Louis playing a number of popular tunes on what was essentially a crude instrument. In his own words, Armstrong explains:

> When I would be on the junk wagon . . . I would blow this long tin-horn without the top on it. Just hold my fingers close together and blow. It was a call for old rags, bones, bottles, or anything that the people and kids had to sell. The kids loved the sound of my tin-horn . . . One day I took the wooden top off the horn, and surprisingly I held up my two fingers close together where the wooden mouthpieces used to be and I could play a tune of some kind. Oh, the kids really enjoyed that. Better than the first time. They used to bring their bottles, Alex would give them a few pennies, and they would stand around the wagon while I would entertain them. (Cited in Bergreen, 1997, pp. 55–6)

According to Bergreen (1997), the chance event of being given a tin-horn to attract attention was "a startling discovery" which made Armstrong realize "that he was capable of pleasing others, white and black, young and old" (p. 56). This event subsequently sowed the seeds "to his revolutionizing jazz, and by extension, American music" (p. 56). Had he been born a decade earlier or later (and had not been exposed to all of the elements of jazz brewing in New Orleans at the time), the entire evolution of jazz may have been different, and we may not have even heard of this remarkable musician.

It would be easy to cite numerous other examples of how chance, such as the luck of being born into a particular family, helps to provide the catalyst for subsequent development. Moreover, it is important to note that Mozart's unique gifts and exemplary talent as a composer were at least partly influenced by his birth into the cultural milieu of eighteenth-century Europe, at a time when his father could take opportunities to travel and showcase his son's remarkable achievements. The type of training, experience, and exposure Leopold gave his son would simply not have been possible had Wolfgang been born decades earlier. The same could be said of many other eminent musicians, for as Atkinson (1978) suggests, all human accomplishments can be ascribed to "two crucial rolls of the dice over which no individual exerts any personal control. These are the accidents of birth and background. One roll of the dice determines an individual's heredity; the other, his formative environment" (p. 221).

Musical talents

Our adaptation of Gagné's (2010) model proposes that there are at least eight distinct types of musical talent: performing, improvising, composing, arranging, analyzing, appraising, conducting, and teaching. All are related to professional occupations and areas of the discipline in which musicians can earn a living. Examples would include professional orchestral musicians, jazz improvisers, composers of original music or arrangers who rework existing pieces for a particular context, professors who teach musical analysis or music critics who write reviews of performances for newspapers, conductors of ensembles, and music teachers.

Part of the reason we define eight distinct talents is our belief that many programs that cater for musically talented children place too much emphasis on performance. A young violinist who can perform a violin concerto is obviously talented, and we must recognize and nurture this type of ability. But there are many other forms of talent that go largely unrecognized, such as the child who can sit at the piano and play "by ear" a variety of popular melodies in any key, or the teenager who can compose a catchy song directly onto a music sequencer without the need to write out the melody using traditional notation. It is here that we are reminded that "the technical skills of Bob Dylan or John Lennon were rudimentary by classical standards, yet few would deny that these two musicians produced work which has had a profound impact on a whole generation, and whose influence is still being felt" (Hargreaves, 1994, p. 358). The point we wish to stress is that all too often children's ability to perform pieces from notation is taken as the defining skill, while the range of abilities needed to develop musically in a broader sense are often neglected (McPherson, 2005).

To add to this, it could be mentioned that while performance skills often develop early, talents in other areas—particularly composition—are rarely seen before late childhood (Winner & Martino, 1993). Simonton (1988, 1991, 2014) shows that the average famous composer begins composing during the late teens and produces unqualified masterpieces before age 30, although Mozart is an obvious exception.

Identifying giftedness and talent

The identification of musical giftedness is essentially a task of trying to predict a child's potential to succeed musically, prior to any formal musical training. However, trying to assess potential prior to formal musical training is no easy matter. Indeed, there are at least three major methodological obstacles that must be overcome in doing so.

First, the measurement of mental and physical gifts is an issue of tremendous debate in and of itself. There are any number of psychometric tests, qualitative methodologies, and experimental procedures that purport to offer insight into these core features of psychological functioning; however, none is completely free of criticism concerning its basic reliability and validity or the operational definitions on which it is based (e.g. see Sternberg & Lubart, 1999 for a critique of psychometric testing in relation to creativity).

Second, beyond perhaps the most obvious examples described here, it is difficult to predict which gifts (or combinations thereof) will lead to which talents. For instance, exactly how creative must one be to excel in composition? To what extent does that level of creativity depend on or interact with other intellectual, social, perceptual, or physical aptitudes? How might an abundance of one gift compensate for a slight deficiency of another? Of course, research has begun to explore the relationships between aptitudes of various types (most notably between creativity and intelligence; see Sternberg & O'Hara, 1999, for a review), but much further grassroots research is needed to determine precisely how these interrelate before one can then move on to studying how their subsequent interactions predict specific musical talents.

Third, it is typically the case that, by the time an individual is seen to be talented in a given area, the pervasive influences of the developmental process, intrapersonal and environmental catalysts and chance (as detailed earlier), may already have begun to mask initial, subtle differences in natural abilities. No doubt, this may be one explanation for why there has, to date, been little success in matching outstanding musical achievement with a clear-cut set of traits (Simonton, 1999, 2001, 2014; Winner, 1996a). From this viewpoint, it is not surprising that much research on expert performance (with its focus on the skills of acknowledged experts, who are usually adults) has offered so little support for the widely held belief that talent has a biological basis. An intriguing paradox here is that, *if* there is a strong genetic component to musical giftedness, then those who achieve the highest of standards will be those with the most suitable genetic make-up; therefore, for those most talented at the top of the profession, the variance in genetic material will be substantially decreased such that the remaining individual differences in heredity would be no longer easy to observe (Gagné, 2003).

These three obstacles are not necessarily insurmountable, and we believe that progress in this area is inevitable, but most likely through programs of longitudinal research that employ a range of quantitative and qualitative methods and that concurrently examine giftedness in children *and* expert performance.

As explained earlier, some researchers have argued for a general trait of musical giftedness involving sensitivity to the structural and expressive dimensions of sound, rather than the physical parameters of sound as suggested by the music psychologists Carl Seashore, Arnold Bentley, and Edwin Gordon (see further, Hallam, Chapter 4; McPherson & Hallam, in press). Research reviewed by Boyle (1992), however, shows that nonmusical factors such as academic achievement, academic intelligence, and socio-economic background will increase the accuracy of prediction (see also Hedden, 1982; Rainbow, 1965). Based on Gagné's model, high aptitudes in music, though observable in older children and adults, are more easily and directly observable in young children, as environmental influences and systematic learning have exerted their moderating influence only to a limited extent. Nevertheless, a salient and robust battery of tests as such has thus far eluded researchers.

There are probably a multitude of indicators, given the nature and scope of the aptitude domains described here, in addition to the fact that some students (including those from minority or disadvantaged groups) often display their potential in ways that are unique or individual (Richardson, 1990) and that success in music may not be totally dependent on only those aptitudes identified by Gordon (1987). Moreover, Gordon (1987) himself states that "[t]here is no one infallible score on any music aptitude test which indicates superior potential for learning music" (p. 56) because it is up to the teacher to make a subjective evaluation of the results from each of the components of the measure. This is yet another reason why "giftedness" should be viewed more broadly in terms of a profile of aptitudes which, as a result of intrapersonal and environmental catalysts in addition to learning and training, may lead to the development of specific fields of talent.

Prevalence, identification, and labeling

Many authorities in the gifted and talented education literature suggest, for school system classifications purposes, that children in the top 10 to 15% of a given population can be labeled as "gifted." Gross (2000), for example, advocates a system whereby the top 15% of any population would fit this category, while Gagné (2010) takes a more conservative view by defining the top 10%. In Gagné's conception children can be described as mildly (1:10), moderately (1:100), highly (1:1,000), exceptionally (1:10,000), or extremely (1:100,000) gifted. As mentioned earlier, measures of musical aptitude focus exclusively on perceptual (aural) discrimination, with the result that other natural abilities required for understanding the full range of musical potential included in our figure are not measured or defined in many conceptions of musical giftedness. This is one of the reasons why no measure of musical aptitude currently exists that can demonstrate the reliability and validity of assessment seen in IQ measures of general cognitive functioning (McPherson & Hallam, in press).

In contrast to difficulties in assessing giftedness, talent measurement is relatively straightforward (Gagné, 2003) because soon after beginning music a child can be compared with peers of similar age and approximate training who are engaged in the same activity (Gagné, 1993; Sisk, 1990). Normative assessment in the form of teacher ratings, achievement tests, competitions, and scholarships (though occasionally criticized as subjective) is one way in which talented young musicians have traditionally been identified. According to Gagné (2003), however, the use of the term *talented* should be reserved for the top 10% of children, with the emerging talent being the major criterion for further selection into advanced programs.

Perhaps more so than any other area of human pursuit, the label *prodigy* is used repeatedly in music to describe the most extreme cases of exceptionally talented childhood musicians. Definitions of prodigies stipulate that they must have developed their skills to an extraordinary high level before the onset of puberty, which normally occurs around 10–11 for girls and 11–12 for boys (McPherson & Lehmann, 2012; Morelock & Feldman, 2000; but see further Gagné & McPherson, in press). Without any doubt the most famous musical prodigy is Wolfgang Amadeus Mozart, who performed at a very young age throughout Europe and went on to compose some of the greatest music ever written. In current times, any Internet search for the "next Mozart" and "musical prodigy" will return thousands of hits, some of the videos of which have received over a million views (de Mink & McPherson, in press). The vast majority of these children are not true prodigies according to research definitions, and as has often been the case throughout history, acquiring skills and expertise in any area of music does not always equate to commercial success or acclaim in later adult life. Most important for our discussion here, however, is that exceptional talent in particular fields, such as performing or creating music, emerge when a child's natural abilities are mediated, not only through the support of intrapersonal and environmental catalysts, but also through systematic learning and extensive practice (Gagné, 1993, 2010). Taking into account Gagné's classification, however, examples such as Mozart and many other recognized child prodigies would occur on the extreme far end of the classification scale, which reinforces the importance of acknowledging and celebrating less distinct and remarkable forms of giftedness that are much more common within any given age group.

Conclusions

In this chapter, we have distinguished between *gifts* and *talents*. Giftedness corresponds to potential that is distinctly above average in at least one aptitude domain, while talent refers to superior performance in a specific field of human activity (Gagné, 2010, 2013).

In conclusion, we believe the most productive means for understanding how naturally occurring human *gifts* blossom into at least eight forms of musical *talent* is by understanding the complex series of interactions through which natural abilities interact with intrapersonal and environmental catalysts, developmental processes, and chance events to produce certain types of musical talent. The most distinctive aspect of this choreography of interactions is that it is unique for each child. For this reason we should therefore celebrate the unique musical profile of each and every child.

Reflective questions

1 Reflect on your own musical development. Using Figure 18.1, how would you explain each aspect of your own musical development?

2 What do you believe has had the most impact on your own musical development? Why?

3 If you were to provide a percentage (e.g., 60–40, 50–50) to explain the impact of nature versus other factors in your own development, what would it be? Is this an appropriate way of thinking about these influences?

4 Have you observed any examples of children who display natural abilities of the type shown in Figure 18.1? If so, how would you describe them? How can you be certain they are natural abilities rather than acquired abilities that result from some sort of environmental exposure?

5 How has the content of this chapter shaped your thinking on musical development?

6 As a result of reading this chapter, what will you do in the future to more adequately cater for the gifted and talented children with whom you come into contact?

Key source

Gagné, F., & McPherson, G. E. (in press). Musical prodigiousness: Analysing its complex origins from a CMTD perspective. In G. E. McPherson (Ed.), *Musical prodigies: Interpretations from psychology, education, musicology and ethnomusicology*. Oxford: Oxford University Press.

Reference list

Anderson, E. (1985). *The letters of Mozart and his family*. New York: Macmillan.

Atkinson, J. W. (1978). Motivational determinants of intellective performance and cumulative achievement. In J. W. Atkinson & J. O. Raynor (Eds.), *Personality, motivation, and achievement* (pp. 221–42). New York: John Wiley.

Bamberger, J. (in press). Growing-up prodigies: The midlife crisis. In G. E. McPherson (Ed.), *Musical prodigies: Interpretations from psychology, education, musicology and ethnomusicology*. Oxford: Oxford University Press.

Bandura, A. (1997). *Self-efficacy: The exercise of control*. New York: Freeman.

Bergreen, L. (1997). *Louis Armstrong: An extravagant life*. New York: Broadway Books.

Boyle, J. D. (1992). Evaluation of musical ability. In R. Colwell (Ed.), *Handbook of research on music teaching and learning* (pp. 247–65). New York: Schirmer.

Brodsky, W. (2004). Developing the Keele Assessment of Auditory Style (KAAS): A factor-analytic study of cognitive trait predisposition for audition. *Musicae Scientiae*, **VIII**(1), 83–108.

Chaffin, R., & Lemieux, A. (2004). General perspectives on achieving musical excellence. In A. Williamon (Ed.), *Musical excellence: Strategies and techniques to enhance performance* (pp. 19–39). Oxford: Oxford University Press.

Clarke, E. (2002). Understanding the psychology of performance. In J. Rink (Ed.), *Musical performance: A guide to understanding* (pp. 59–72). Cambridge: Cambridge University Press.

Coleman, L. J., & Cross, R. L. (2000). Social–emotional development and the personal experience of giftedness. In K. A. Heller, F. J. Mönks, R. J. Sternberg, & R. F. Subotnik (Eds.), *International handbook of giftedness and talent* (2nd ed., pp. 203–12). New York: Elsevier.

Csikszentmihalyi, M. (1998). Fruitless polarities. *Behavioral and Brain Sciences*, **21**(3), 411.

Davidson, J. W., & King, E. C. (2004). Strategies for ensemble practice. In A. Williamon (Ed.), *Musical excellence: Strategies and techniques to enhance performance* (pp. 105–22). Oxford: Oxford University Press.

Davies, J. (1978). *The psychology of music*. London: Hutchinson.

de Mink, F., & McPherson, G. E. (in press). Musical prodigies within the virtual world of YouTube. In G. E. McPherson (Ed.), *Musical prodigies: Interpretations from psychology, education, musicology and ethnomusicology*. Oxford: Oxford University Press.

Deutsch, O. E. (1966). *Mozart: A documentary biography*. London: Adam & Charles Black.

Elmer, S., Sollberger, S., Meyer, M., & Jäncke, L. (2013). An empirical reevaluation of absolute pitch: Behavioral and electrophysiological measurements. *Journal of Cognitive Neuroscience*, **25**(10), 1736–53.

Ericsson, K. A. (Ed.) (1996). *The road to excellence: The acquisition of expert performance in the arts and sciences, sports, and games*. Mahwah, NJ: Erlbaum.

Ericsson, K. A., Krampe, R. T., & Tesch-Römer, C. (1993). The role of deliberate practice in the acquisition of expert performance. *Psychological Review*, **100**(3), 363–406.

Ericsson, K. A., & Lehmann, A. C. (1996). Expert and exceptional performance: Evidence of maximal adaptation to task constraints. *Annual Review of Psychology*, **47**, 273–305. doi: 10.1146/annurev. psych.47.1.273.

Freeman, J. (2000). Families: The essential context for gifts and talents. In K. A. Heller, F. J. Mönks, R. J. Sternberg, & R. F. Subotnik (Eds.), *International handbook of giftedness and talent* (2nd ed., pp. 573–85). New York: Elsevier.

Gagné, F. (1985). Giftedness and talent: Reexamining a reexamination of the definitions. *Gifted Child Quarterly*, **29**(3), 103–12.

Gagné, F. (1993). Constructs and models pertaining to exceptional human abilities. In K. A. Heller, F. J. Monks, & A. H Passow (Eds.), *International handbook of research and development of giftedness and talent* (pp. 69–87). New York: Pergamon.

Gagné, F. (1999). The multigifts of multitalented individuals. In S. Cline & K. T. Hegeman (Eds.), *Gifted education in the twenty-first century: Issues and concerns* (pp. 17–45). Delray Beach, FL: Winslow Press.

Gagné, F. (2000). Understanding the complex choreography of talent development through DMGT-based analysis. In K. A. Heller, F. J. Mönks, R. J. Sternberg, & R. F. Subotnik (Eds.), *International handbook of giftedness and talent* (2nd ed., pp. 67–79). New York: Elsevier.

Gagné, F. (2003). Transforming gifts into talents: The DMGT as a developmental theory. In N. Colangelo & G. A. Davis (Eds.), *Handbook of gifted education* (3rd ed., pp. 60–74). Boston: Allyn and Bacon.

Gagné, F. (2004a). An imperative, but, alas, improbable consensus! *Roeper Review*, **27**(1), 12–14.

Gagné, F. (2004b). Transforming gifts into talents: The DMGT as a developmental theory. *High Ability Studies*, **15**(2), 119–41.

Gagné, F. (2009a). Building gifts into talents: Detailed overview of the DMGT 2.0. In B. MacFarlane & T. Stambaugh (Eds.), *Leading change in gifted education: The festschrift of Dr. Joyce VanTassel-Baska* (pp. 61–80). Waco, TX: Prufrock Press.

Gagné, F. (2009b). Debating giftedness: Pronat vs. Antinat. In L. V. Shavinina (Ed.), *International handbook of giftedness* (pp. 155–204). New York: Springer.

Gagné, F. (2010). Motivation within the DMGT 2.0 framework. *High Ability Studies*, **21**(2), 81–99.

Gagné, F. (2013). The DMGT: Changes within, beneath, and beyond. *Talent Development & Excellence*, **5**(2), 5–19.

Gagné, F., & McPherson, G. E. (in press). Musical prodigiousness: Analysing its complex origins from a CMTD perspective. In G. E. McPherson (Ed.), *Musical prodigies: Interpretations from psychology, education, musicology and ethnomusicology*. Oxford: Oxford University Press.

Gagné, F., Neveu, F., Simard, L., & St Père, F. (1996). How a search for multitalented individuals challenged the concept itself. *Gifted and Talented International*, **11**(1), 4–10.

Gallagher, J. J. (1993). Current status of gifted education in the United States. In K. A. Heller, F. J. Monks, & A. H. Passow (Eds.), *International handbook of research and development of giftedness and talent* (pp. 755–70). New York: Pergamon.

Gardner, H. (1983). *Frames of mind: The theory of multiple intelligences*. New York: Basic Books.

Gordon, E. E. (1987). *The nature, description, measurement and evaluation of music aptitudes*. Chicago: GIA Publications.

Gordon, E. E. (2007). *Learning sequences in music: A contemporary music learning theory*. Chicago: GIA Publications.

Gottfried, A. E., Fleming, J. S., & Gottfried, A. W. (1994). Role of parental motivational practices in children's academic intrinsic motivation and achievement. *Journal of Educational Psychology*, **86**(1), 104–13.

Gross, M. (1994). Radical acceleration. *The Journal of Secondary Gifted Education*, 5(4), 27–34.

Gross, M. (2000). Issues in the cognitive development of exceptionally and profoundly gifted individuals. In K. A. Heller, F. J. Mönks, R. J. Sternberg, & R. F. Subotnik (Eds.), *International handbook of giftedness and talent* (2nd ed., pp. 179–92). New York: Elsevier.

Hambrick, D. Z., Altmann, E. M., Oswald, F. L., Meinz, E. J., & Gobet, F. (2014). Facing facts about deliberate practice. *Frontiers in Psychology*, 5, 751. doi: 10.3389/fpsyg. 2014.00751.

Hargreaves, D. J. (1994). Musical education for all. Is everyone musical?—Peer commentaries. *The Psychologist*, August, 357–8.

Harris, J. R. (1998). *The nature assumption: Why children turn out the way they do*. New York: The Free Press.

Harris, J. R. (2006). *No two alike: Human nature and human individuality*. New York: E. E. Norton.

Hayes, J. R. (1981). *The complete problem solver*. Philadelphia: Franklin Institute Press.

Hedden, S. K. (1982). Prediction of music achievement in the elementary school. *Journal of Research in Music Education*, **30**(1), 61–8.

Howe, M. J. A., Davidson, J. W., & Sloboda, J. A. (1998). Innate talents: Reality or myth? *Behavioral and Brain Sciences*, **21**(3), 399–442.

Jackson, M. (2009). *Moonwalk*. New York: Harmony Books.

Jørgensen, H. (2004). Strategies for individual practice. In A. Williamon (Ed.), *Musical excellence: Strategies and techniques to enhance performance* (pp. 85–103). Oxford: Oxford University Press.

Keefe, S. P. (in press). Mozart the child performer–composer: New musical–biographical perspectives on the early years to 1766. In G. E. McPherson (Ed.), *Musical prodigies: Interpretations from psychology, education, musicology and ethnomusicology*. Oxford: Oxford University Press.

Kemp, A. E. (1996). *The musical temperament*. Oxford: Oxford University Press.

Kenneson, C. (1998). *Musical prodigies: Perilous journeys, remarkable lives*. Portland, OR: Amadeus Press.

Kopiez, R., & Lehman, A. C. (in press). Musicological reports on early 20th century prodigies: The beginnings of an objective assessment. In G. E. McPherson (Ed.), *Musical prodigies: Interpretations from psychology, education, musicology and ethnomusicology*. Oxford: Oxford University Press.

Krampe, R. T. (1997). Age-related changes in practice activities and their relation to musical performance skills. In H. Jørgensen & A. C. Lehmann (Eds.), *Does practice make perfect? Current theory and research on instrumental music practice* (pp. 165–78). Oslo: Norwegian Academy of Music.

Krampe, R. T., & Ericsson, K. A. (1996). Maintaining excellence: Deliberate practice and elite performance in young and older pianists. *Journal of Experimental Psychology: General*, **125**(4), 331–59.

Lehmann, A. C., Ericsson, K. A., & Hetzer, J. (2002). How different was Mozart's music education and training? A historical analysis comparing the music development of Mozart to that of his contemporaries. In C. Stevens, D. Burnham, G. E. McPherson, E. Schubert, & J. Renwick (Eds.), *Proceedings of the seventh international conference on music perception and cognition* (pp. 426–9). Adelaide, Australia: Causal Productions.

Macnamara, B. N., Hambrick, D. Z., & Oswald, F. L. (2014). Deliberate practice and performance in music, games, sports, education, and professions: A meta-analysis. *Psychological Science*, **25**(8), 1608–18. doi: 10.1177/0956797614535810.

Mainwaring, J. (1941). The meaning of musicianship: A problem in the teaching of music. *British Journal of Educational Psychology*, **XI**(3), 205–14.

Mainwaring, J. (1947). The assessment of musical ability. *British Journal of Educational Psychology*, **17**(1), 83–96.

Mainwaring, J. (1951a). Psychological factors in the teaching of music: Part 1: Conceptual musicianship. *British Journal of Educational Psychology*, **21**(2), 105–21.

Mainwaring, J. (1951b). Psychological factors in the teaching of music: Part II: Applied musicianship. *British Journal of Educational Psychology*, **21**(3), 199–213.

McCormick, J., & McPherson, G. E. (2003). The role of self-efficacy in a musical performance examination: An exploratory structural equation analysis. *Psychology of Music*, **31**(1), 37–51.

McPherson, G. E. (2005). From child to musician: Skill development during the beginning stages of learning an instrument. *Psychology of Music*, **33**(1), 5–35.

McPherson, G. E. (2009). The role of parents in children's musical development. *Psychology of Music*, **37**(1), 91–110.

McPherson, G. E., Davidson, J. W., & Faulkner, R. (2012). *Music in our lives: Rethinking musical ability, development and identity*. Oxford: Oxford University Press.

McPherson, G. E., & Hallam, S. (in press). Musical potential. In S. Hallam, I. Cross, & M. Thaut (Eds.), *The Oxford handbook of music psychology*. Oxford: Oxford University Press.

McPherson, G. E., & Lehmann, A. (2012). Exceptional musical abilities—child prodigies. In G. E. McPherson & G. Welch (Eds.), *Oxford handbook of music education* (pp. 31–50). New York: Oxford University Press.

McPherson, G. E., & McCormick, J. (2006). Self-efficacy and performing music. *Psychology of Music*, **34**(3), 325–39.

Morelock, M. J., & Feldman, D. H. (2000). Prodigies, savants and Williams syndrome: Windows into talent and cognition. In K. A. Heller, F. J. Mönks, R. J. Sternberg, & R. F. Subotnik (Eds.), *International handbook of giftedness and talent* (2nd ed., pp. 227–41). Oxford: Elsevier Science Ltd.

Mossing, M. A., & Ullén, F. (in press). Genetic influences on musical giftedness, talent and practice. In G. E. McPherson (Ed.), *Musical prodigies: Interpretations from psychology, education, musicology and ethnomusicology*. Oxford: Oxford University Press.

Office of Standards in Education, Children's Services and Skills (Ofsted, 2009). *Gifted and talented pupils in schools*. Manchester: Ofsted (available as download at <http://www.ofsted.gov.uk>).

Papoušek, H. (1996). Musicality in infancy research: Biological and cultural origins of early musicality. In I. Deliège & J. A. Sloboda (Eds.), *Musical beginnings: Origins and development of musical competence* (pp. 37–55). Oxford: Oxford University Press.

Persson, R. S. (1996). Musical reality: Exploring the subjective world of performers. In R. Monelle & C. T. Gray (Eds.), *Song and signification: Studies in music semiotics* (pp. 58–63). Edinburgh: University of Edinburgh Faculty of Music.

Persson, R. S., Partt, G., & Robson, C. (1996). Motivational and influential components of musical performance: A qualitative analysis. In A. J. Cropley & D. Dehn (Eds.), *Fostering the growth of high ability: European perspectives* (pp. 287–302). Norwood, NJ: Ablex.

Platz, F., Kopiez, R., Lehmann, A. C., & Wolf, A. (2014). The influence of deliberate practice on musical achievement: A meta-analysis. *Frontiers in Psychology*, **5**, 746. doi: 10.3389/fpsyg.2014.00646.

Plomin, R. (1998). Genetic influence and cognitive abilities. *Behavioral and Brain Sciences*, **21**(3), 420–1.

Polderman, T. J. C., Benyamin, B., de Leeuw, C. A., Sullivan, P. F., van Bochoven, A., Visscher, P. M., & Posthuman, D. (2015). Meta-analysis of the heritability of human traits based on fifty years of twin studies. *Nature Genetics*, **47**(7), 702–709. doi: 10.1038/ng.3285.

Rainbow, E. L. (1965). A pilot study to investigate the constructs of musical aptitude. *Journal of Research in Music Education*, **13**(1), 3–14.

Richardson, C. P. (1990). Measuring musical giftedness. *Music Educators Journal*, **76**(7), 40–5.

Simonton, D. K. (1988). Age and outstanding achievement: What do we know after a century of research? *Psychological Bulletin*, **104**(2), 251–67.

Simonton, D. K. (1991). Emergence and realization of genius: The lives and works of 120 classical composers. *Journal of Personality and Social Psychology*, **61**(5), 829–40.

Simonton, D. K. (1999). Talent and its development: An emergenic and epigenetic model. *Psychological Review*, **106**(3), 435–57.

Simonton, D. K. (2001). Talent development as a multidimensional, multiplicative, and dynamic process. *Current Directions in Psychological Science*, **10**(2), 39–43.

Simonton, D. K. (2014). *The Wiley handbook of genius*. Malden, MA: John Wiley & Sons.

Sisk, D. A. (1990). The state of gifted education: Toward a bright future. *Music Educators Journal*, **76**(7), 35–9.

Sloboda, J. A. (1993). Musical ability. In D. Goldstein & J. J. Godfrey (Eds.), *The origins and development of high ability* (pp. 106–18). Wiley, Chichester: Ciba Foundation Symposium 178.

Solomon, M. (1995). *Mozart*. London: Hutchinson.

Solomon, A. (2012). *Far from the tree: Parents, children, and the search for identity*. New York: Scribner.

Sosniak, L. A. (1985). Learning to be a concert pianist. In B. S. Bloom (Ed.), *Developing talent in young people* (pp. 19–67). New York: Ballantine.

Sternberg, R. J. (2000). Giftedness as developing expertise. In K. A. Heller, F. J. Mönks, R. J. Sternberg, & R. F. Subotnik (Eds.), *International handbook of giftedness and talent* (2nd ed., pp. 55–66). New York: Elsevier.

Sternberg, R. J., & Lubart, T. I. (1999). The concept of creativity: Prospects and paradigms. In R. J. Sternberg (Ed.), *Handbook of creativity* (pp. 3–15). Cambridge: Cambridge University Press.

Sternberg, R. J., & O'Hara, L. A. (1999). Creativity and intelligence. In R. J. Sternberg (Ed.), *Handbook of creativity* (pp. 251–72). Cambridge: Cambridge University Press.

Stoeger, H. (2009). The history of giftedness research. In L. V. Shavinina (Ed.), *International handbook of giftedness* (pp. 17–38). New York: Springer.

Suzuki, S. (1983). *Nurtured by love*. New York: Smithtown.

Tan, Y. T., McPherson, G. E., Peretz, I., Berkovic, S. F., & Wilson, S. J. (2014). The genetic basis of music ability. *Frontiers in Psychology*, **5**, 658.

Turner, W. J. (1965). *Mozart: The man and his works*. London: Methuen & Co Ltd.

U.S. Department of Education, Office of Educational Research and Improvement. (1993). *National excellence. A case for developing America's talent*. Washington, DC: U.S. Government Printing Office.

Williamon, A., Lehmann, A. C., & McClure, K. (2003). Studying practice quantitatively. In R. Kopiez, A. C. Lehmann, I. Wolther, & C. Wolf (Eds.), *Proceedings of the fifth triennial ESCOM conference* (pp. 182–5). Hanover, Germany: Hanover University of Music and Drama.

Williamon, A., & Valentine, E. (2000). Quantity and quality of musical practice as predictors of performance quality. *British Journal of Psychology*, **91**(3), 353–76.

Williamon, A., & Valentine, E. (2002). The role of retrieval structures in memorizing music. *Cognitive Psychology*, **44**(1), 1–32.

Wilson, E. (1998). *Jacqueline du Pré*. London: Weidenfeld & Nicolson.

Wilson, S. J., Lusher, D., Martin, C. L., Rayner, G., & McLachlan, N. (2012). Intersecting factors lead to absolute pitch acquisition that is maintained in a "fixed-*do*" environment. *Music Perception*, **29**(3), 285–96.

Winn, M. (1979). The pleasures and perils of being a child prodigy. *New York Times Magazine, 12–19* (December 23), 38–45.

Winner, E. (1996a). *Gifted children: Myths and realities*. New York: Basic Books.

Winner, E. (1996b). The rage to master: The decisive role of talent in the visual arts. In K. A. Ericsson (Ed.), *The road to excellence: The acquisition of expert performance in the arts and sciences, sports, and games* (pp. 271–301). Mahwah, NJ: Erlbaum.

Winner, E., & Martino, G. (1993). Giftedness in the visual arts and music. In K. A. Heller, F. J. Monks, & A. H. Passow (Eds.), *International handbook of research and development of giftedness and talent* (pp. 253–81). New York: Pergamon.

Winner, E., & Martino, G. (2000). Giftedness in non-academic domains: The case of the visual arts and music. In K. A. Heller, F. J. Mönks, R. J. Sternberg, & R. F. Subotnik (Eds.), *International handbook of giftedness and talent* (2nd ed., pp. 95–110). New York: Elsevier.

Yun Dai, D., & Schader, R. (2001). Parent's reasons and motivations for supporting their child's music training. *Roeper Review*, **24**(1), 23–6.

Chapter 19

Inclusive music classrooms: A universal approach

Judith A. Jellison

Introduction

Throughout the history of institutional care for children with disabilities, physicians promoted the use of music for mental and physical health, although there were few opportunities for genuine music education experiences. Years of advocacy, litigation, and legislation worldwide have led to dramatic reforms in educational policies that affect deeply the lives of children with disabilities, increasing their opportunities for a meaningful music education and a meaningful musical life. Many children now benefit from inclusion in regular schools and regular music classes with their typically developing peers.

Policies regarding the education of children with disabilities were addressed globally for the first time at the World Conference on Special Needs Education: Access and Quality held in Salamanca, Spain (UNESCO, 1994). The delegates defined the conference as a "platform to affirm the principle of Education for All" (p. 3) and urged governments to "adopt as a matter of law or policy the principle of inclusive education, enrolling all children in regular schools, unless there are compelling reasons for doing otherwise" (p. 10). Further, UNESCO's guidelines on inclusion (2009) and arts education (2006) support the rights of diverse groups of children to a comprehensive education, including an arts education and cultural experiences.

In light of legislative mandates designed to improve the quality of education of children with disabilities, the important issues among advocates, parents/guardians, and educators have focused on general education programs, including music programs, and access to regular environments in the community. The challenge for music education is to provide appropriate educational opportunities in inclusive classrooms so that children will participate happily and successfully in quality music experiences throughout their lives.

In meeting this challenge, teachers must recognize the significance of sociocultural experiences on children's musical development—inter-personal relations (e.g., with family members, friends, peers, paid professionals), physical environments (e.g., the child's home, music classroom in school, and neighborhood and community events), values, attitudes, and beliefs of people and institutions (e.g., school policies, state and federal laws, culture, tradition), and economic resources (e.g., school's budget for music instruction and resources). Research is conducted with regularity on a wide array of variables in these contexts outside and inside schools. Although a discussion of sociocultural variables on music learning is not included in this chapter, I have discussed in other publications the influences of several of these variables on the musical development of children with disabilities (Jellison, 2012) and all children (Jellison, 2015). I present them as governing principles, proposing that the musical lives of children can be improved when:

> . . . culturally normative music experiences and participation in socially valued roles and socially valued activities with a diverse population of children are part of the routine of daily life.

. . . interactions with same-age peers in inclusive music environments are frequent, positive, and reciprocal.

. . . self-determination is fostered in music environments where children feel safe and secure, and where they experience autonomy, demonstrate competence, and make choices and decisions about music, music making, and other music activities in their lives.

. . . the design, implementation, and evaluation of an individualized music education program involves collaboration and coordinated efforts among parents/guardians, professionals, other significant individuals in the child's life, and the child, when appropriate.

Even as teachers structure learning environments considering the influences of sociocultural variables on their students' development, what principles do they use to guide their curricular and instructional decisions in accomplishing music goals? What knowledge is available to help teachers develop and implement effective strategies for inclusive music classrooms?

Much of the knowledge in this chapter, and from established research on teaching and learning, applies equally to typically developing children and children with disabilities that vary in kind and degree. Well-established principles comprise the foundation of effective educational practices with all children and are transferable across individuals and contexts. In the preface of his book of essays on music teaching, Duke (2011) writes:

> discussions about educational practice that focus primarily on how teachers teach and that fail to consider the basic principles of human learning are fundamentally misguided. There is an expansive, rich body of data that illuminates the processes of knowledge acquisition and skill development. Intelligent teaching is predicated on a deep understanding of these processes—how knowledge and skills are acquired, refined, and applied. (p. vii)

A universal approach in music education is grounded in the basic principles of human learning, and as this well-recognized approach in special education gains greater recognition in music education, increasing numbers of students will benefit.

The literature in psychology and special education provides the basis for many of the ideas I present in this chapter, since there is scant music research to document effective practices in inclusive music education settings (Jellison & Draper, 2015; see also Brown & Jellison, 2012; Jellison, 2000). Research from the fields of psychology, special education, and music education support the notion that all children can develop musically when a meaningful music program is designed to be accessible, equitable, and flexible, instructional practices are effective, individual adaptations are used only as needed, and students' progress is assessed frequently. When music programs are designed in such a way, they can best be described as following a *universal approach*.

I begin with a discussion of quality of life as an overarching principle that has driven laws and advocacy leading to educational reforms for children with disabilities. Other brief discussions follow concerning the definition of disabilities and issues related to labeling and significant developments in educational practices leading to a universal approach. In the main, the focus of the chapter is on principles of a universal approach in inclusive music classes. The chapter closes with summary comments regarding the potential impact of a universal approach on the music development of all children.

Quality of life and access to education

People strive for quality of life for themselves, for their loved ones, and perhaps for others deemed in need. Quality of life, no matter how it is conceptualized, is the cornerstone of thought and action for people with disabilities, their families, and advocates; it is the driving force behind socio-political changes that have positively influenced hundreds of thousands of lives.

The core dimensions associated with quality of life (e.g., living environments, education, employment, recreation) form the bases for laws to ameliorate inequities and discrimination. Essentially, quality of life can be assessed by asking the following questions: 1) where is the person? (home, community, school settings), 2) with whom is the person interacting? (persons with or without disabilities, classmates, acquaintances, friends, paid professionals), 3) what does the person do? (music activities, school curriculum, daily living activities, employment), and 4) how does the person feel? (individual's perceptions of competence, emotional well-being, autonomy).

For decades, music instruction was not accessible to large numbers of children with disabilities. Children with disabilities were not in music classrooms (where), and had few opportunities to interact with their typical peers (with whom) or to learn and increase their ability to make music and use music knowledge (what), which limited opportunities for feelings of competence, accomplishment, and autonomy in music contexts (feelings). Some children are still isolated from the types of meaningful music experiences enjoyed by their typically developing peers.

Among the earliest and most striking victories in the United States were changes in federal and state laws associated with the deinstitutionalization movement during the late 1970s and 1980s. Public awareness of discriminatory practices dramatically increased as a result of books and photography that chronicled the blatant inequities of physical and social segregation (e.g., Blatt & Kaplan, 1966; Shapiro, 1993). Although the initial outcomes of the deinstitutionalization movement were less than ideal, it was an important step toward improving the living conditions and daily routines of children with disabilities. The movement of children back into communities precipitated education reform that continues to have far-reaching consequences for children with disabilities, their parents, and their teachers.

Children with disabilities in the United States began to receive a free appropriate education as a result of the passage of the Individuals with Disabilities Education Improvement Act (IDEA), first signed into U.S. law in 1975 as The Education for All Handicapped Children Act. As a result of amendments to the Act, IDEA requires not only that children with disabilities be educated in regular classrooms with children without disabilities to the maximum extent appropriate, but also that they have access to the regular curriculum, with opportunities to learn the same knowledge and skills as those required for their same-age typical peers.

Although it is uncertain how many children with disabilities are in regular music education classrooms in the United States, in a survey of music teachers, a large percentage reported teaching in inclusive classrooms (VanWeelden & Whipple, 2014). Also, the most current report from the U.S. Department of Education shows that in 2011 over 5.7 million children and youth (ages 6–21) were served under IDEA, and almost 95% of them were educated in regular classrooms for at least some portion of the school day with more than 60% educated in regular classrooms 80% or more of the day (U.S. Department of Education, 2013). Given these reports, it is likely that many children with disabilities are in regular, rather than separate, music education classrooms.

The music activities of typically developing children can be used as a standard by which to evaluate whether and how children with disabilities are participating in the same music activities as their typical peers. To the maximum extent possible, children with disabilities should attend regular music classes and school music concerts or field trips; participate in a variety of activities as part of the regular music curriculum (singing, playing instruments, listening, creating, talking about music, and so on); make choices and communicate their music preferences, ideas, and feelings about music; and demonstrate accomplishments they value and that are valued by others.

Overview: Defining disabilities and issues of labeling

Research in genetics, embryology, fetal development, and the birthing process unveils what can happen before, during, and shortly after birth that may put children at risk of having disabilities. Environmental factors such as poor nutrition, substance abuse, disease, infection, and physical trauma can have dire consequences for the development of the brain, microskeletal systems, organs, and sensory systems. The developing child is also at risk when social–emotional environments are unhealthy and traumatic.

Non-discriminatory and multifaceted evaluation and re-evaluation procedures may be necessary to determine the strengths and weaknesses of a child with a disability. Although the definitions of specific disabilities may vary, most often the broad label of disability implies conditions that are permanent.

Procedures to identify, assess, and categorize disabilities vary among countries, as do methodologies for collecting and reporting national statistics, thus prohibiting a meaningful description of disabilities worldwide. The final determination of a disability rests with the results of evaluations of the child, and the interpretations and decisions of knowledgeable professionals in schools and communities who then identify the disability using accepted categorical labels. In most cases, labels serve no meaningful purpose other than to determine who is eligible to receive specialized medical and educational services and support; appropriate curricular and instructional decisions are based on individual children's strengths and needs.

Irrespective of the different labels that are used to describe children with disabilities, it is likely that most labels have undergone changes over several decades as a result of social values, advocacy, and laws. Some of the first changes appeared with the use of person-first language as a way to focus attention on the commonality among all children—all people—while still acknowledging varying abilities and disabilities as appropriate (e.g., children *with* intellectual disabilities; children *with* learning disabilities; children *with* autism). The term "normal," associated with the statistical normal distribution, now appears infrequently in professional writing; the preferred term of professionals in psychology and special education is "typically developing." Changes are also appearing in legal documents. For example, the U.S. Congress passed a law that changes references in Federal laws from "mental retardation" to "intellectual disability" and "a mentally retarded individual" to "an individual with an intellectual disability."

Spoken and written language can foster negative stereotyping, and children with disabilities are limited in their musical development when educational decisions rely primarily on stereotypic characteristics associated with the concept of disability. There are no specific instruments, songs, or music activities that are more successful for groups of children with the same disability label (e.g., songs for children with intellectual disabilities). Children are additionally stigmatized when they are restricted to particular instruments, music, or activities that are not valued by their typical peers.

Inclusive music education provides opportunities to decrease negative stereotyping and to increase positive attitudes toward classmates with disabilities. Sufficient evidence in the psychological literature (e.g., Pettigrew & Tropp, 2006) shows that inter-group contact can reduce prejudice between members of the different groups. Several early studies in music research are consistent with these findings (Jellison, Brooks, & Huck, 1984; see also Jellison & Taylor, 2007) and consistent with research showing positive social outcomes for all students when teachers structure student interactions in small groups or dyads (Ginsburg-Block, Rohrbeck, & Fantuzzo, 2006; Rohrbeck et al., 2003). Because small groups, dyads, and other peer-assisted learning strategies are flexible strategies, providing opportunities for a variety of tasks, task-levels, and ways for students to respond, these instructional formats are used frequently in a universal approach.

What is a universal approach?

There are many things for teachers to think about and do to develop and implement accessible, effective inclusive music programs. Planning and implementing strategies, albeit a critical part of the music teaching and learning process, must be considered within the multitude of other activities that are necessary for children to accomplish music goals. In another publication (Jellison, 2015), I present and organize this process in a model built around four broad ideas: 1) *Creating a Quality Music Program and Culture of Inclusion* (which includes the four governing principles presented earlier); 2) *Gathering Information* (about the student, teaching environment, and teaching activities); 3) *Planning and Implementing* (determining curricular priorities, and designing and implementing universal strategies and individual adaptations); and 4) *Thinking Ahead* (evaluating students' progress and the effectiveness of strategies).

When teachers develop a quality program, create a culture of inclusion in their classrooms, gather information about their students with disabilities from every possible source (beginning with parents), and consider students' strengths and needs given the teaching environment and demands of various tasks and activities, they are in a position to plan and implement effective strategies, many of which will be universal strategies.

A new way of thinking about strategies

A universal approach is one that moves away from the view of students in separate groups and toward one that views students on a continuum of learners, an approach that is particularly effective in music classrooms that include children with disabilities. Some background on significant changes in curricular and instructional practices with children with disabilities will highlight the contributions this new way of thinking offers for learning in inclusive classrooms.

Until the 1970s, the developmental model dominated curricular and instructional decisions in special education services. Many children were educated in separate settings and there was little thought of providing them with a curriculum similar to that of same-age typically developing peers. On the basis of decades of observing adults with disabilities who experienced this type of education, the developmental model was deemed ineffective by parents and professionals whose views foreshadowed sweeping changes in curricular and instructional practices for children with disabilities (e.g., Brown et al., 1979). Pressed to optimize instructional time, teachers began to prioritize meaningful learning outcomes and remove unnecessary prerequisite skills, basing curricular decisions on a principle of functional value. When applied to music teaching and learning, the principle of functional value is evident when music skills and activities are not only interesting to the child with a disability, but also lead to outcomes that have meaning and relevance for the child now and in the future.

A music curriculum that is functional is also age-appropriate. When applied to music teaching and learning, children with disabilities participate to the maximum extent possible in activities that are identical to those that would (or could) be considered appropriate for their same-age typical peers. When curricular decisions are based on "mental or emotional age," as was the case in institutional settings and still remains the case in some segregated schools and classrooms, history shows that many children will never catch up and learn important skills for adulthood. Careful evaluation of students with disabilities, particularly those with severe disabilities, shows that rarely, if ever, can students move through the number of prerequisites and learning sequences at a rate that would enable them to participate in the activities enjoyed by their same-age peers.

The principle of partial participation, introduced in the 1980s, guided the development of strategies that allowed for even greater numbers of students with disabilities to participate in regular classrooms. Originally proposed for children with severe disabilities (Baumgart et al., 1982), this idea has applications for students who are unable to learn the myriad age-appropriate skills that are required of their typical same-age peers. Earlier practices followed the thinking of "all or nothing," that if a child *could not do all* of the activity, a child *could not do any* of the activity. When applied to music teaching and learning, music instruction and learning environments are arranged in such a way that children with disabilities participate in music activities as independently as possible and in as many different environments as is instructionally possible. This concept led to highly effective practices and encouraged teachers to make curricular modifications to enable increased participation. As an example, when a class is playing three-chord song accompaniments, a guitar could be tuned to one chord for a student who needs a simpler task. Although this is an obvious example of an individual adaptation, the important point is that the student will *participate in the same activity and in the same way, to the degree possible*, an idea that is consistent with a universal approach.

As increasing numbers of children with disabilities were included in classrooms, music teachers increased their skills in the development and implementation of individual adaptations, most often as a result of university instruction, clinics, and books on the topic (e.g., Adamek & Darrow, 2010). The development of appropriate individual adaptations will continue to be of importance since some students will need specific adaptations to meet their individual needs—for movement, for communication, for learning. However, the past decade has seen dramatic changes in legislation, policies, and attitudes related to access for individuals with disabilities, changes that led to alternatives to individual adaptations.

Since individual adaptations have traditionally been the first consideration, teachers are now being advised to consider universal strategies first and then select appropriate individual adaptations as needed. A universal approach involves every student in regular classroom activities; strengths and weaknesses of all students are considered in the development of multiple strategies so that every student will accomplish important music goals. Also, a universal approach guards against overuse and overspecialization of individual adaptations.

The musical development of children can be impeded when adaptations are excessive and when teacher assistants are unaware of how to provide support to students with disabilities (e.g., Bernstorf, 2001; Darrow, 2010). Giangreco (2013, p. 2) talks of the increasing use of teacher assistants in many countries, including the United States, and the problem that "teaching assistants have become almost exclusively *the way*, rather than *a way* to support students with disabilities" in general education classrooms.

Adaptations can result in the unnecessary separation of students from activities and classmates and contribute to negative stereotyping and lower expectations, thus limiting opportunities for music achievement, positive peer interactions, and the development of self-determination. When all students participate successfully in the same activity, experience personal success, and contribute to the success of their classmates, a culture of inclusion is fostered—students feel competent, experience a sense of belonging, and feel good about themselves and their classmates.

Consider an example of multiple strategies for a specific dance activity when movements for everyone may not be easily adapted to accommodate a student who uses a wheelchair. If the student who uses the wheelchair plays a percussion instrument as other classmates dance, the teacher has implemented an individual adaptation for that student. In contrast, the teacher who implements multiple strategies has all students learn instrumental accompaniments for the dance and also create upper-body movements for particular sections. There are now three different actions in one activity (dance, upper-body movements, and accompaniments), different ways for students to respond and show what they have learned. At different times in the activity, typically developing students can participate fully by doing any of the three actions, and the student using the wheelchair partially participates by doing two of the three: accompanying and upper-body movements. With multiple strategies, the student with a disability has more opportunities to participate successfully with classmates and in many of the same ways. Throughout the activity, there is no compromise to the quality of the experience for any student, and the experience is enriched for typically developing students who have opportunities to dance, create movements, and play in the dance band.

From architecture to education: Universal design first

A universal approach in education is grounded in principles of universal design applied to the design of buildings, public spaces, and products. Universal design incorporates many of the ideas and advances from laws and policies that specifically apply to individuals with disabilities, although it has come to benefit all people, not just those with disabilities. Ron Mace, an architect and advocate who coined the term universal design in the late 1980s, used the term to describe the concept of designing all products and built environments to be aesthetic and usable to the greatest extent possible by everyone, regardless of their age, ability, or status in life (Center for Universal Design, 2013). The fundamental idea of universal design is applied in products and environments, including teaching environments, and is studied at several centers in the United States (e.g., Center for Applied Special Technology, 2013).

Universal design in the United States had its beginnings with the barrier-free movement of the 1950s that was driven by World War II veterans with disabilities, other individuals with disabilities in communities, and their advocates. Other movements related to civil and disability rights in the 1970s drove changes in public policies and laws not only related to architecture, but also to all activities of daily living including education. More and more laws protected children and adults against discrimination in public and private sectors, ensuring access to all programs and services that are public *and* private, including music programs and services, many of which were in buildings that were inaccessible.

New laws and financial incentives to address issues of access attracted the attention of professionals in other fields, not only architects. Common examples of designs that were originally intended for people with disabilities proved beneficial to everyone: curb cuts, smooth ground surfaces at entryways, ramp access to buildings and swimming pools, lever-type handles for doors and sink faucets, and light switches with large flat panels. The idea that new designs could be usable by everyone became marketable and popular. It is easier to enter hotel rooms with luggage when entryways are wider, to use kitchen tools with thicker grips, and to know when to walk (and how much time you have remaining) when icons and audio signals are at crosswalks. Icons and audio prompts appear on any number of household items (e.g., ovens and washing machines) and electronics (e.g., computers, phones, televisions), making the completion of tasks easier and more efficient.

As battles in the disabilities movement were being won through new laws and policies, special educators and other professionals developed strategies, structures, and devices to provide more services and programs for students with disabilities. With architectural changes and technology, students began to experience greater access to, and more independence in the physical environments of their schools. With the passage of IDEA, requiring access to the general curriculum, materials, and testing, universal design became an increasingly prominent approach in education.

Ideas of equity, access, barrier-free design, and technological advancements, combined with new policies and laws, led to the idea of universal design in education. Meeting individual needs of children in a single classroom is certainly not new. What is new, however, is the focus of this approach relative to meeting the learning needs of diverse populations. A universal approach moves in a direction that, to the extent possible, increases opportunities for students with disabilities and those who are struggling academically and/or socially to participate successfully in the same types of activities as those experienced and enjoyed by their classmates.

Principles of a universal approach in inclusive music classrooms

Among the more prominent concepts in special education related to universal design are those developed by researchers and professionals at the Center for Applied Special Technology (CAST). This non-profit organization has a history of more than 25 years of research and development expanding learning opportunities for individuals with disabilities. Numerous publications, materials, and services focusing on a universal design for learning (UDL) framework are available through the center's resource pages (Center for Applied Special Technology, 2013). Many of the ideas in this chapter reflect the principles of UDL and are applicable to music teaching in inclusive classrooms as follows:

- Learning differences are viewed on a continuum, expectations are high for all students, and diversity is valued.
- The regular music education program is accessible, equitable, and flexible.
- Universal design is a proactive process, not an afterthought, and requires:
  - knowledge of students' needs and characteristics;
  - knowledge of activity/task requirements for successful performance;
  - strategies built into regular instruction;
  - use of well-established teaching principles; and
  - collaboration and cooperation.
- Flexible strategies in the regular music teaching and learning environment allow all students to be successful and progress in the same music curriculum and with the same performance standard, to the extent appropriate. Strategies may include:
  - a variety of ways to present information, engage and motivate students, and structure ways for students to participate in meaningful ways in the same activity;
  - other adjustments to the learning environment that reduce or eliminate the need for individual adaptations; and
  - individual adaptations, but only as needed.
- Goals, standards, and the quality of the music experience are not compromised for any student.

Strategies should be designed based on students' strengths and needs, although some universal strategies can be developed in the absence of specific student information. Before the first day of class, most experienced teachers are aware of adjustments that they will need to make to structure a positive learning environment for all of their students. For example, they are aware of the fact that many students benefit when information is presented visually as well as aurally, that some students will be more motivated to respond in smaller groups than in front of the entire class, and that many students will be less distracted when seats are turned away from the windows or the entry door. Other strategies are best developed after assessments of teaching environments and activities considering students' specific strengths, characteristics, and needs.

To meet specific needs, universal strategies can be developed by making adjustments to various elements of the teaching environment (modes of communication; curricular goals and performance standards; instructional methods; assessment procedures; physical environment; materials, instruments, and equipment; technology; support from peers and others, as needed). Teachers may design a single strategy based on the needs of one or several students and then apply this same strategy in an activity with all students, or design several strategies for the same activity that may also include individual adaptations as one of those strategies.

Several examples of universal strategies designed by teachers are presented here. They may seem relatively simple, but keep in mind the teachers' thinking—thinking first about ways to use a universal approach and then, as needed, individual adaptations.

- A teacher knows that several of his students will more easily comprehend information when visuals are used and decides to make it a practice to present important information and announcements aurally and visually. Information is posted, announced, and repeated frequently. The same teacher uses several ways for students to express their ideas, to show what they know and can do. Some students improvise music but have difficulty reading music, some read music fluently but have difficulty talking about it, some can use their bodies or draw to show expressiveness in music but cannot read and follow dynamic markings in printed music, and some can compose using computers but have difficulty using writing tools. As often as possible, he plans activities to include multiple ways for students to use their strengths when responding and expressing themselves.

- An orchestra director rewrites parts for many of her students, making the parts less complex for some. One particular student is assessed individually on fewer pieces than his classmates and is assessed only on his modified parts; however, he is still expected to play the parts assessed and other pieces accurately and musically with the entire group. In one particular piece, several students play solo and the student with a disability is one of those students.

- A general education music teacher considers the limited attention span of several students, and chooses shorter listening excerpts so he can move on to the interactive part of the lesson sooner. Knowing that a few students will have difficulty expressing their ideas in a class discussion of the music, he plans to use partners and small group formats and selects partners and group membership based on the students' characteristics and needs.

- When a very loud classroom was carpeted, everyone, not just the student who was sensitive to sound, benefited from the improved acoustics. The behavior of one student in this classroom made the sound problem all the more obvious, and carpeting became a priority.

- A teacher assigns students to electronic keyboards, computers, and MIDI equipment to compose and/or arrange music for a class performance. Assignments are completed in groups, with a partner, or alone, with some students creating melodic lines over a single chord, others playing chord progressions, others in charge of loading audio files, and others imitating melodic material.

- A choir student who had low vision inspired the idea of recordings for all students. All students found recordings of class songs, individual parts, or entire rehearsals useful for learning individual parts; the teacher also used the recordings to help increase his students' auditory discrimination and memory skills.

- A teacher offers her students alternatives (trackballs and joysticks) to the traditional computer mouse. She regularly uses switches of various material and shapes (e.g., slides knobs, buttons) as a way for her students to input a signal to a computer or sound system, or to record and play back speech and music. Equipment is turned on, off, or changed in degree after activation (e.g., dimmer light switches, volume controls, metronome markings, variable speed/pitch controls on keyboards and recorders). She was inspired to bring these into her classroom at the suggestion of her student with severe physical disabilities.

As with all instruction, frequent authentic assessments are necessary to determine students' progress and thus, the effectiveness of universal strategies. "Is the student accomplishing meaningful music goals?" "Is the student participating in a meaningful way and as fully and independently as possible in the same activity as classmates?" "Will successful outcomes transfer to other situations and environments?" "Are there additional positive outcomes for the student as a result of peer interactions?" "What are the student's feelings about participating in this way, using this strategy, or adaptation?" Every meaningful, successful learning outcome for students ultimately contributes to their quality of life, and parents will be particularly eager to hear of their children's successes in school, and in music.

Closing

For years, social and educational policies impeded rather than nurtured the overall development of children with disabilities. Progress has been slow, but across the past several decades changes are clearly evident in research, educational practices, and values in special education. Research that consistently identifies factors influencing learning has led to principles that have widespread applications for children with varying abilities in a variety of music teaching and learning settings. As a result of a substantive research base describing the influence of sociocultural factors on children's development, principles of human learning, and quality of life dimensions, much of what we need to do to improve the musical lives of children with disabilities is known.

Most music teachers are familiar with the idea of developing adaptations to meet students' needs, adaptations that may involve curricular and instructional practices, the physical environment, materials, assistive technology, and other elements of the teaching environment. As increasing numbers of children with disabilities are included in regular music classrooms, teachers will find that a universal approach takes on greater relevance in meeting students' diverse learning needs. Universal strategies are not designed based on group membership (disability, learning needs, or other characteristics such as gender, race, ethnicity, culture, or language spoken), but rather on students' individual strengths and needs and the requirements of activities and tasks. All students are involved when universal strategies are employed; they participate, to the extent possible, in the same activities and in the same way.

A universal approach to music teaching is a new challenge for music teachers, and one that takes thoughtfulness and practice. The outcomes, however, will ultimately lead to positive learning environments for all students—music learning environments where students will not only accomplish meaningful goals, but will also learn to value diversity among their classmates and celebrate each other's successes.

Reflective questions

1 UNESCO's guidelines on inclusion and arts education support the rights of diverse groups of children to a comprehensive education, including an arts education and cultural experiences, yet many children with disabilities still do not experience a meaningful music education program in schools. From your perspective, what are the barriers that prevent children with disabilities from receiving a meaningful music education, and what actions can be taken by teachers, parents, and advocates to remove those barriers?

2 The sociocultural environment of a classroom can influence the overall development of students in those classes: their cognitive, social, emotional, and musical development. Reflecting on the governing principles presented in this chapter, in what ways can meaningful music activities and experiences be designed to increase positive interactions among classmates and foster students' feelings of autonomy and competence?

3 Spoken and written language can foster negative stereotyping. Have you observed examples of negative stereotyping as a result of the assessment and categorical labeling of students with disabilities? In what ways can music teachers create a culture of inclusion in their classrooms through ensemble and classroom activities?

4 What are the benefits of a universal approach in inclusive music classes and under what conditions should teachers consider using individual adaptations?

5 A universal approach is one that moves away from the view of students in separate groups and toward one that views students on a continuum of learners. Consider specific characteristics of several students and design multiple universal strategies for presenting information and content to students, for students to show what they know and can do, and for stimulating interest and motivating students.

Reference list

Adamek, M. S., & Darrow, A. A. (2010). *Music in special education* (2nd ed.). Silver Spring: MD: American Music Therapy Association.

Baumgart, D., Brown, L., Pumpian, I., Nisbet, J., Ford, A., Sweet, M., Messina, R., & Schroeder, J. (1982). Principle of partial participation and individualized adaptations in educational programs for severely handicapped students. *Journal of he Association for Persons with Severe Handicaps, 7*(2), 17–27.

Bernstorf, E. (2001). Paraprofessionals in music settings. *Music Educators Journal, 87*(4), 36–40.

Blatt, B., & Kaplan, F. (1966). *Christmas in purgatory: A photographic essay on mental retardation.* Boston: Allyn & Bacon.

Brown, L., Branston, M. B., Hamre-Nietupski, S., Certo, N., & Gruenwald, L. (1979). A strategy for developing chronological-age appropriate and functional curricular content for severely handicapped adolescents and young adults. *Journal of Special Education, 13*(1), 81–90.

Brown, L. E., & Jellison, J. A. (2012). Music research with children with disabilities and their typical peers: A systematic review. *Journal of Music Therapy, 49*(3), 335–64.

Center for Applied Special Technology (2013). *Transforming education through universal design for learning.* Retrieved from <http://www.cast.org>.

Center for Universal Design (2013). *About the center: Ronald L. Mace.* Retrieved from <http://www.ncsu.edu/ncsu/design/cud/about_us/usronmace.htm>.

Darrow, A. A. (2010). Working with paraprofessionals in the music classroom. *General Music Today, 23*(1), 35–7.

Duke, R. A. (2011). *Intelligent music teaching.* Austin, TX: Learning Behavior and Resources.

Giangreco, M. F. (2013). Teacher assistant supports in inclusive schools: Research, practices and alternatives. *Australasian Journal of Special Education/FirstView* Article/March 2013, 1–14. Retrieved from <http://www.uvm.edu/%7Ecdci/parasupport/reviews/giangreco11.pdf>.

Ginsburg-Block, M. D., Rohrbeck, C. A., & Fantuzzo, J. W. (2006). A meta-analytic review of social, self-concept, and behavioral outcomes of peer-assisted learning. *Journal of Educational Psychology, 98*(3), 732–49.

Jellison, J. A. (2000). A content analysis of music research with children and youth with disabilities (1975–99). In American Music Therapy Association (Ed.), *Effectiveness of music therapy procedures: Documentation of research and clinical practice* (3rd ed., pp. 199–264). Silver Springs, MD: American Music Therapy Association.

Jellison, J. A. (2012). Inclusive music classrooms and programs. In G. E. McPherson & G. Welch. *The Oxford handbook of music education* (Vol. 2, pp. 65–80). London: Oxford University Press.

Jellison, J. A. (2015). *Including everyone: Music classrooms where all students learn*. New York: Oxford University Press.

Jellison, J. A., Brooks, B. H., & Huck, A. M. (1984). Structuring small groups and music reinforcement to facilitate positive interactions and acceptance of severely handicapped students in the regular music classroom. *Journal of Research in Music Education*, 32(4), 243–64.

Jellison, J. A., & Draper, E. A. (2015). Music research in inclusive school settings: 1975–2013. *Journal of Research in Music Education*, **62**(4), 325–31.

Jellison, J. A., & Taylor, D. M. (2007). Attitudes toward inclusion and students with disabilities: A review of three decades of music research. *Bulletin of the Council for Research in Music Education*, **172**(Spring), 9–23.

Pettigrew, T. F., & Tropp, L. R. (2006). Interpersonal relations and group processes: A meta-analytic test of intergroup contact theory. *Journal of Personality and Social Psychology*, **90**(5), 751–83.

Rohrbeck, C. A., Ginsburg-Block, M. D., Fantuzzo, J. W., & Miller, T. R. (2003). Peer-assisted learning interventions with elementary school students: A meta-analytic review. *Journal of Educational Psychology*, **95**(2), 240–57.

Shapiro, J. P. (1993). *No pity: People with disabilities forging a new civil rights movement*. New York: Times Books.

UNESCO (1994). *World conference on special needs education: Access and quality*. Retrieved from <http://unesdoc.unesco.org/images/0011/001107/110753eo.pdf>.

UNESCO (2006). *Road map for arts education*. Paris: UNESCO. Retrieved from <http://www.unesco.org/new/fileadmin/MULTIMEDIA/HQ/CLT/CLT/pdf/Arts_Edu_RoadMap_en.pdf>.

UNESCO (2009). *Policy guidelines on inclusion in education*. Paris: UNESCO. Retrieved from <http://unesdoc.unesco.org/images/0017/001778/177849e.pdf>.

U.S. Department of Education (2013). *35th Annual report to congress on the implementation of the Individuals with Disabilities Education Act, 2013*, Washington, D.C.: U.S. Department of Education.

VanWeelden, K., & Whipple, J. (2014). Music educators perceived effectiveness of inclusion. *Journal of Research in Music Education*, **62**(2), 148–60.

Chapter 20

Music and well-being during illness

Costanza Preti and Katrina S. McFerran

Music and well-being during illness: Introduction

When a child becomes ill, there are psychological and social adjustments that both the child and the family have to deal with in addition to the physical dimensions of illness. The life of all members of the family is disrupted, often only temporarily, but sometimes with consequences that will redefine the dynamics of family interactions, particularly in the event of a long-term or life-threatening illness. This disruption sets the broad hospital context in which musical experiences can be used to foster well-being. There are different ways in which music can be used to support children and their carers when they are in hospitals, ranging from the therapeutic use of music at bedsides or in procedure rooms, through to a more entertaining function such as creating live performances in public spaces. Music therapists, as well as professional and community musicians, have an opportunity to share the role of engaging children, carers, and staff in musical activities within hospital settings. Furthermore, hospital administrators have increasingly recognized the value of the arts as therapeutic allies within a new holistic view of illness, treatment, and recovery (Sternberg, 2009).

The most common use of music in pediatric settings is to improve the well-being of young patients and their carers, including both children and adolescents. The notion of well-being is a multifaceted concept that incorporates physical, psychological, emotional, social, cultural, and spiritual matters. Consequently, this multi-dimensionality makes it difficult to establish a simple definition of well-being, and as Ansdell and DeNora point out, "it is possible to enjoy 'good health' according to some of these measures, while being 'ill' according to others" (Ansdell & DeNora, 2012, p. 106). The difficulty in establishing a definition of well-being is also due to the fact that the notions of health and well-being are culturally constructed and related to different social and cultural contexts (Koen, Barz, & Brummel-Smith, 2008). In order to discuss the impact of music on young patients who are in hospitals, we have adopted an ecological perspective that reflects the relationships between the wider society and the social and personal dynamics unfolding within the family when illness occurs.

The socio-ecological model suggests that individual behavior both influences and is influenced by the social environment and that individual behavior simultaneously shapes and is shaped by such environment (Bronfenbrenner, 1979). The health of a young person is defined in relation to the interaction of the three different levels of family, community, and society (see Figure 20.1). All levels are dependent on each other and influences occur within and between the different levels. In this context, the family (micro level) is nested in the community and wider society (macro level), and all levels are likely to determine the emotional reaction of the family to the illness of their child and the psychological, emotional, and practical changes associated with it. The wider society and the community surrounding the child and the family will also shape their musical preferences and they will define the musical repertoire that the musicians will perform in health

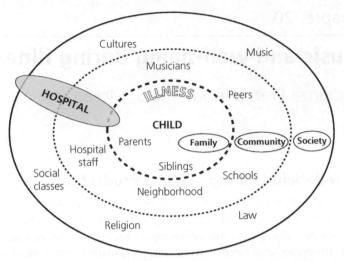

Fig. 20.1 A socio-ecological model of factors involved when music is played in healthcare settings

care settings, such as hospitals (Preti & Welch, 2011). In order to be engaging, the music will have a connection with the sociocultural identity of the child and the family, or for adolescents, with the musical identity of their peers (MacDonald, Hargreaves, & Miell, 2002). Within this model, the hospital (but also more generally, other healthcare settings) is considered a meta level that embraces family and community, and is the expression of the society where the family and community are nested, as illustrated in Figure 20.1.

The chapter starts with an overview of the different reactions of children and families to illness and hospitalization. The shifts of social dynamics within the family will form the basis to redefine the psychological and social needs of both the child and the family and it will also form the basis for planning effective music sessions in hospitals. The use of music in hospitals is analyzed in three different situations where it has been documented to improve the well-being of the child/patient: 1) within the family unit; 2) among peers; and 3) across the hospital population. Although presented separately, each of these aspects has the potential to influence each other. For example, a patient who feels less stressed is more likely to reach out to their peers. Similarly, a parent who feels empowered by contributing to their child's coping is more relaxed, which impacts on all those around. Also, a musical environment that emphasizes the shared musicality between all people may reduce the amount of anxiety felt by a child who is approached by the same doctor who has just played the guitar, or sung a song with them. Different levels can be addressed more easily by music therapists or musicians, depending on their focus and training, as well as on their interests and the conditions in the hospital.

Children's psychological reactions to illness

The medical literature highlights the extent to which children's perception of their illness is at least as important as the illness itself in determining how they cope with being unwell (Hockenberry & Bologna-Vaughan, 1985). For instance, some preschool children perceive illness as a punishment (Melnyk, 2000), and since "animism" is a cognitive characteristic of pre-school children and toddlers, children in this developmental stage may also attribute human characteristics to inanimate objects (such as physiological monitoring devices). As a result, young children may sometimes experience generalized and uncontrolled fear about the hospital environment (Melnyk, 2000). Other authors go further, arguing that the way children respond to being hospitalized can radically affect how they perceive the nature of their illness (Rennick et al., 2002). In a review of the literature on the effect of children's hospitalization in a pediatric intensive care unit, Rennick and Rashotte (2009) concluded that children's personal interpretation of what happened to them while in the hospital affected their subsequent behavioral and emotional response to hospitalization. Feeling a loss of control over their life may lead some children to experience a sense of helplessness. In this respect factors such as the child's age, personality type, illness severity, the number of invasive procedures to which they are exposed, length of hospitalization, and previous hospital experiences can be predictors of coping mechanisms that significantly impact on the health behaviors of the child after their discharge from hospital (Rennick & Rashotte, 2009). In addition to personal factors, inter-personal influences are also important, such as the social context surrounding the child, the parents' emotional state in coping with their child's hospitalization, and the support network that surrounds the family (Lambert, 1984; LaMontagne, 1987).

The practice of providing children with developmentally appropriate information about events and procedures that they will experience while in the hospital has been accompanied by attempts to equip children with positive experiences of hospitalization in order to minimize its negative effects. Pre-hospitalization programs, such as the widespread American *Child Life Program* (American Academy of Pediatrics—Committee on Hospital Care, 2000), aim to prepare children for the procedure that is about to happen by increasing their understanding, confidence, as well as the predictability of the forthcoming experience, which should ultimately lead to better coping outcomes (Johnson et al., 1997).

The child's age is the main predictor of the child's reaction to hospitalization, and it also impacts on the degree of preparation that can realistically be achieved. For this reason, children aged between 6 months and 4 years are considered to be the most vulnerable group (Melnyk, 2000). Vernon and Thompson (1993) argue that the benefits of psycho-educational preparation for hospitalization are considerably less for those up to 6 years old as compared to older children. Such limitation suggests the need for non-verbally based support for hospitalized children and is the reason why music and other forms of play therapy are often incorporated into pediatric hospital contexts. Dahlquist (1999) provides a technical explanation of the distractive power of music, theorizing that because of limited sensory awareness, "the higher the attention demands of a distracting stimulus the more cognition will be consumed with proportionately less left for processing painful stimuli" (Klein & Graham-Pole, 2008, p. 456).

Music is a central feature of children's personal and social identity (Lamont, 2002) and therefore familiar musical repertoire can mitigate threats associated with the hospital environment because such space becomes less intimidating and more familiar once the child's music background becomes part of it (Preti & Welch, 2011). Both music therapists and musicians have developed ways of providing social support for young patients that can impact positively on their coping mechanisms while in the hospital (Preti, 2013). Furthermore, the literature shows that music can significantly reduce children's distress during painful procedures such as venipunctures (Vohra & Nilsson, 2011) and lumbar punctures (Nguyen et al., 2010), as well as impacting on the perception of pain during needle insertion (Caprilli et al., 2007). Building on the effectiveness of using music to alter pain perception, one systematic review has also established a positive relation between the use of music and the reduction of stress and anxiety in children undergoing medical procedures (Klassen et al., 2008). In some cases, music is used prior to medical experiences through engaging techniques such as writing songs and creating CDs prior to radiotherapy (Barry et al., 2010). Other studies have used music-making both before and during procedures such as echocardiograms and tomography scans to reduce or remove the need for sedation (DeLoach Walworth, 2005). Trends toward reduction in anxiety have also been captured during stressful procedures such as dressing changes (Whitehead-Pleaux, Baryza, & Sheridan, 2006). The types of strategies used by music therapists to address anxiety vary depending on the age of participants, with Barrera et al. (2002) describing how younger children were engaged by animated songs and instrument play, whilst older children were engaged through song writing, improvising, and listening to recorded music.

Although many of the positive benefits of music have been investigated in the literature reported above, the majority of the studies do not include a control group and cannot be replicated under similar conditions (Mrazova & Celec, 2010; Treurnicht Nayloret al., 2011). However, randomized controlled designs with matched interventions are difficult to implement in pediatric settings where the age group of children with similar pathologies is mixed, the length of hospitalization varies according to the degree of their illness, and the number of variables to control are often too many (e.g. number of carers present, levels of anxiety and stress, presence of pain, previous hospitalizations, etc.), impacting on the replicability of such studies. Robb and Carpenter (2009) have advocated for the development of reporting guidelines for music-based interventions and have identified eight areas that commonly affect the standardization and reproduction of music interventions: music qualities, intervention materials, intervention components, intervention delivery schedule, interventionist, treatment fidelity, setting, and music delivery method. The desire for standardization in this area of research is also linked to the blossoming of live music programs in hospitals that involve musicians without specific training and sometimes with a lack of understanding of the hospital context, which some music therapists and researchers find concerning (Dileo & Bradt, 2009).

Coping through music, within the family

Despite many negative memories being associated with medical experiences, administrators of pediatric hospitals in Western cultures have focused on creating positive, rather than reducing negative experiences for the patients and their families. Music is often used to minimize the effects of hospitalization and patients have been reported to react significantly better during music therapy and music activities, even when compared to play therapy and other experiences in the hospital (Hendon & Bohon, 2008; Longhi & Pickett, 2008; Longhi, Pickett, & Hargreaves, 2013). In-depth investigations suggest that positive expectations about the potential benefits of music therapy may contribute to the pleasure experienced by pediatric patients. Parents of cancer patients have confirmed this theory both in hospital-based oncology (Kemper & McLean, 2008) and home-based pediatric palliative care (Lindenfelser, Grocke, & McFerran, 2008). Music therapy is frequently described as fun by young people in hospitals (O'Callaghan et al., 2013) and music therapists attribute such comments to their ability to normalize the otherwise unfamiliar hospital environment by incorporating preferred music and providing an alternative focus to hospitalization and illness (Dun, 2011). Robb's research (2000, 2003) emphasizes the value of active music engagement as critical in eliciting positive coping and acquiring new coping capacities when a child is ill.

However, the child does not learn how to cope with their hospitalization in isolation and the whole family unit is required to evolve in response to the hospitalization of a child. The interactions between the child and the parents, as well as within the family, are likely to impact on the child's choice of coping strategies and these are ultimately predictive of health outcomes (Edwards & Kennelly, 2011; Lazarus, 2000). In the context of a child's hospitalization, the family can be seen as a "system" (Roberts & Wallander, 1992), since the events that affect one family member will in turn affect the other family members, influencing other family members' reactions and coping strategies. The idea of family centered care, mostly developed in pediatric medicine at the end of the 1990s (Kovacs, Bellin, & Fauri, 2006), illustrates how the relationship between the child/patient and the family is considered central to the recovery process by many staff in hospitals. The family is recognized as being expert in assessing their child's abilities and needs and therefore its members are asked to make informed decisions about the support and level of care that the child will receive while sick. Music therapists have often worked within family centered models for this reason, and the literature describes processes that include and value the contributions of other family members (Shoemark & Dearn, 2008).

The theory that supports the values of family centered approaches suggests that opportunities for musical communication between family members allows parents to move from being passive observers of their child's treatment to being active participants (Dun, 1999). Parents are then in a position to "hear" their children as they match and imitate the different sounds the child creates, which can be supported and encouraged by the music therapist (Hiscock et al., 2013). Making music together also provides an opportunity to actively reconnect with the healthy parts of the patient, reminding parents of their child's capacity, often through humorous and expressive musical activities (Lindenfelser et al., 2008). Parents describe how valuable it is for music therapists to create activities that the whole family is able to participate in so that they are able to share positive experiences that open up communication between family members (Lindenfelser, Hense, & McFerran, 2012). Although family centered music therapy programs can facilitate deeper interactions, some ways of using music with families in the hospital can be effective simply by offering temporary respite and escape (O'Callaghan, Sexton, & Wheeler, 2007). In other circumstances, music can directly support children during stressful procedures and indirectly support the parents by creating a more relaxed atmosphere, where the child can focus on an alternative activity, like in the following case example:

> Anna was a 3-year-old with leukemia as well as Down's syndrome who was in hospital to undergo a bone marrow aspiration. She had always been responsive to music on the ward and her family asked the medical team to consider active music making during the aspiration procedure to see if it could moderate her distress. In the room, prior to treatment, Anna's mother was supported to sing favourite songs to her daughter, accompanied by the musician. The mother's selection of relaxing songs and lullabies allowed Anna to remain relaxed even though she was aware of what would soon happen (one hour before the procedure, nurses applied a special anesthetic cream on Anna's back). When the time for the aspiration came, the musician continued to accompany her and her mother into the operating theatre, playing the guitar and humming or singing, according to Anna's mood. Although Anna was still frightened, she was able to focus on the music throughout the procedure and did not cry. (Adapted from Preti & Welch, 2004, p. 329).

The constant stress and anxiety can take its toll on parents, and research has highlighted the relationship between the parents' level of stress and their child's anxiety (Lam, Chang, & Morrissey, 2006; Melnyk, 2000). In this case example, music-making helped both Anna and her mother to relax. Her mother was aware of the positive effect that music had on Anna and was using music as a tool to reduce the stress of the procedure. Her familiarity with the musician and with the repertoire contributed to the creation of a relatively safe environment even during a stressful procedure.

The opportunity for parents and children to make choices about what activities, instruments, or songs they prefer is a simple but effective way to increase the degree of control over the hospital environment, which often induces feelings of vulnerability and helplessness (Wolfe et al., 2000). Since young children rely on their family members for support during the treatment process, the use of music can alter the internal experience of the family (Docherty et al., 2013).

Music as a vehicle to foster communication among peers

Family support is important to hospitalized adolescents, but there is also an increased reliance on peer support as the child matures. In the cases of teenagers with long-term chronic illness that require frequent hospital visits, friendships between patients are often established over time, beginning in childhood and becoming more important as time passes. Hospital administrators have built on this expanded support system by emphasizing group programs on adolescent wards that target psychosocial development (Viner & Keane, 1998). A combined focus on promoting connections with peers and identity formation has been found to be an essential target of such programs, with creative arts practitioners being particularly well placed to create mutually empowering conditions for patients to participate in (McFerran & Sawyer, 2003). The presence of arts programs in hospital is especially important for adolescents whose opportunities for social development have been impacted by frequent hospitalizations, creating a need for developmental opportunities even within an acute environment. Medical professionals often describe being conscious that adolescent programs can be too effective, since teenagers whose home lives are complicated and who are also suffering with an ongoing illness may prefer life on the ward compared to home (McFerran & Sawyer, 2003), and may even collude in perpetuating the illness when mental health issues are involved (McFerran, 2005). Despite these necessary cautions, the benefits of participating in music-based group programs have been reported in several studies (Bittman et al., 2001; Burns et al., 2005; Nicholson et al., 2008). The following case example illustrates how a music therapy program can address the inter-personal needs of adolescents in hospitals.

> Alice was diagnosed with Cystic Fibrosis when she was 6 years old. Since that time she has had frequent stays at the hospital, first on the respiratory ward, and more recently on the adolescent ward. Alice participated in a range of music therapy group programs as a younger child but as she moved towards adolescence, she had outgrown the available programs and had started to rely on her growing network of patient-peers for entertainment during her stays, rather than on professional support. The nurses asked the music therapist to make herself known to Alice during a particularly traumatic admission, when one of the cystic fibrosis patients had passed away during the night. Alice expressed minimal interest in the idea and was dismissive of the music therapist when first introduced. Instead of interpreting this reaction as resistance, the music therapist chose to engage Alice in a discussion of her preferred music and offered to become a resource for her in accessing new song material on the ward.
>
> A number of patients left the ward in the intervening 24 hours, and by the time the music therapist returned, Alice's context had changed markedly. She had been informed that her stay would be longer than anticipated, and that other adolescent patients who had not been present at the loss of her friend now surrounded her. In this context, the music therapist provided a link to the experience Alice had had just a few hours earlier and she was now open to the suggestion of writing a song in memory of her friend; an idea that would have likely been rejected the previous day. This also provided opportunities for Alice to connect with the potential support network around her. By the following day, Alice had produced a poem that she wanted set to a drum beat, and it had become clear that two of the other

patients were instrumental players (guitar and drums, respectively). The group of young people on the ward decided to form a band, with Alice singing her poem (supported by the music therapist) and playing the keyboard, while the other two patients played their instruments. Alice was unexpectedly discharged that afternoon, leaving a note for the music therapist to say that she would like to work on the song again next time she came in to the hospital.

This case example illustrates the important role that music can play in fostering connections between patients whilst being conscious of the intense emotional experiences that can be experienced. In this case, music is not used as a substitute form of medication that treats an individual's anxiety; rather, it promotes social connections that are grounded in authentic and creative expression of identity. These kinds of psychosocial support programs are often advocated for young people who have multiple hospitalizations, in contrast to a more acute model that is designed for sudden and short-term cases. It is also particularly pertinent at an age where patients are relying more heavily on peers and placing less demands on the family as the primary form of support, as is expected during a healthy adolescence.

Music as a bridge between different cultures and communities in hospitals

Fostering new relationships, or recreating a familiar environment, are often listed in the literature among the primary benefits of introducing music in hospitals. Researchers have ascribed to music the capacity to distract from stress and anxiety (Barrera et al., 2002) as well as increasing children's compliance with hospital staff (Grasso et al., 2000). In each case there are additional benefits for all those involved in the hospitalization, since families, nurses, and doctors are often able to negotiate with a calmer and more cooperative child (Preti & Welch, 2012).

The use of live music in hospitals encompasses a complex system of interactions surrounding the young patient, making the unseen dynamics visible in sound when the child plays expressively. The child's reactions cannot be isolated from those of the family or the hospital staff surrounding them and the degree to which the family participate actively in the music-making not only reflects, but also predicts how successful the interaction between the musician and the child will be (Preti & Welch, 2011). The opportunity to engage in music-making—either with members of the family or with new friends made at the hospital—creates a space that is mediated by the musician and that allows children to engage in more normal interactions. The musical context provides a secure and alternative framework for the child who has the opportunity to engage cognitive skills such as coordination and concentration and the chance of learning new skills, either musical, social, inter-personal, or a combination of these (Ockelford, 2000; Preti & Welch, 2004).

The importance of turning the hospital into a positive environment where children and their carers can have a chance to encounter and experience the intrinsic benefits of artistic creation whilst being treated physically has been promoted by the European Network "Music in Healthcare Settings"[1] and advocated by the Arts and Health movement (White, 2009). In the past 20 years, particularly in the United States and Europe, there has been a proliferation of associations that recruit musicians to perform in healthcare settings, with a special focus on young patients (Veblen et al., 2013). In addition to standard music therapy services, the variety of programs offered generally includes: 1) bedside music; 2) concerts in common areas (e.g., entrances, corridors, waiting rooms); 3) special music events (e.g., concerts organized by charities involving musicians from established orchestras or pop groups); and 4) artists in residence programs. These activities are often coordinated by the hospital charity or by the resident music therapist who organizes and facilitates the access of musicians in the hospital and assists them with the challenges of performing in such spaces (Curtis, 2011; Kennelly, 2000; Shoemark, 2009). On these occasions music is employed to chiefly impact on children's perception of the hospital environment and to distract their attention from what is otherwise perceived as a threatening space, especially in the light of recurrent hospitalizations (Aasgaard, 2004; Preti & Welch, 2013).

The use of live music in the context of the humanization of hospitals (Oakland, 2012) has chiefly the function of encouraging the communication between different groups of people (children, carers, hospital staff) by bringing into the hospital the musical tradition of different cultures and communities that are represented in the hospital. In so doing, music becomes a bridge between the wider society and the different cultures that are gathered in the hospital at a very special time in their lives. The following case example shows how music is used to distract, connect, and diversify the attention of children, carers, and hospital staff in a pediatric oncology ward:

> Bruno was diagnosed with an aggressive form of cancer when he was 12 years old. He was from a small town in the south of Italy and was travelling a long way to be treated in the hospital. He did not have any friends who could visit him in hospital, nor relatives who could relieve his mother from the long hours, days, and weeks spent in the oncology ward. Bruno did have a CD player in his room however, and often played the music of an Italian pop group called "883" so that many nurses and most of the young patients in the ward had become familiar with those songs and knew some of the refrains. Nurses and doctors used to tease Bruno about his musical "obsession" and the pop group had become a regular topic of conversation between the boy and the medical team.
>
> Naturally, Bruno's existing relationship with music also formed the basis of his relationship with the musicians who regularly visited the ward. Whenever they walked into Bruno's room, he would ask for an "883" song and then sing along at the top of his voice. The sight and sound of this enthusiastic singing and playing often attracted other children to join in and they would walk into his room with their carers when the music began, sometimes drawing nurses into the shared musical experience as well. Occasionally one of the physicians—a keen guitar player—would drop into the room to play a solo on the guitar, pretending to be a famous rock star for the general amusement of the group. The small two-bed ward was often full at music time and the musicians would hand out little percussion instruments to whoever walked into the room so that a range of possibilities for all participants was made available.
>
> Bruno's mother was always very grateful for the break that the music was bringing in her long days in hospital and for the chaotic cheerfulness that the session was able to create in a room that was otherwise silent or populated by TV programs.

Bruno's story shows how the use of music can, even if for a short time, alter the perception of a space where suffering, boredom, loneliness, and anxiety often dominate, to foster positive interactions between children, carers, and hospital staff. In the hospital context music promotes a non-hierarchal level of communication between the nurses and the doctors who gather at the bedside of one of their patients, playing and singing together and engaging with the young patients and their family in a non medicalized way. Shared music-making can provide an occasion for children and their carers to sing together and garner temporary relief from the relentless intensity of hospitalization, as well as be a vehicle to improve socialization among the different groups of people involved in the music-making.

Conclusion

In contrast to traditional images of hospitalization, the introduction of music-making into a pediatric hospital setting promotes a range of possibilities for growth and development. In this chapter we have highlighted the ways in which music can help address negative, personal experiences, as well as to promote positive experiences within the hospital. Although the family is often the primary source of support in the event of a significant illness, the nature of the hospital system means that the shared ward and common spaces are also a social microcosm where meaningful interactions can impact on the child's perception of their illness. Given the important relationship between peer support and positive growth, this close proximity can be appropriated by musicians to promote bonding in the service of coping. Dun (2007) has described how she incorporates the notion of bricolage when appropriating a range of diverse musical strategies to respond to each patient. Rather than *performing* to those in the hospital context, a responsive musician draws on each individual's existing musical interests to create the basis for engaging them and their networks in musicking. Whether it is facilitating shared singing of pop songs or writing original songs in order to express the unique response to the illness, the affordances of music provide opportunities for authentic self-expression in a way that promotes bonding with others who participate in the musical encounter. The potential for development occurs through this transaction and is particularly welcome at a time where there is an assumption that growth will go on hold whilst the illness is being treated.

Reflective questions

1 The literature presented in this chapter about children's psychological reactions to hospitalization discusses the personal and social adjustments that children and their carers experience when they become ill. Using information gathered from this chapter, what might a professional musician or a music educator do to structure their music sessions in healthcare settings?

2 How does the social ecology model inform the organization of music sessions in hospital?

3 How can being in a hospital with a music program provide a child or an adolescent with the opportunity to develop their own musicality?

4 What might be some alternatives to having a music program in a healthcare setting? List the advantages and disadvantages of the non-music programs (e.g. clowns, pets) and compare with music programs. Does music have anything unique to offer?

5 Read through the case studies presented in the chapter again. Consider where things could have gone wrong, and what kinds of factors ensured that the sessions and situations were successful. Was the musical interest of the patient critical, or could anyone benefit from the approaches described in those case studies? Why?

Note

1 <http://www.musique-sante.org/en/projets-en-europe/european-network-%E2%80%9Cmusic-healthcare-settings%E2%80%9D> (retrieved September 10, 2013).

Key sources

Koen, B. D. (Ed.) (2008). *The Oxford handbook of medical ethnomusicology*. New York: Oxford University Press.

MacDonald, R., Kreutz, G., & Mitchell, L. (Eds.) (2012). *Music, health, and wellbeing*. London: Oxford University Press.

Stige, B., Ansdell, G., Elephant, C., & Pavlicevic, M. (Eds.) (2010). *Where music helps: Community music therapy in action and reflection*. Farnham, England: Ashgate Publishing Limited.

Veblen, K. K., Elliott, D., Messenger, S. J., & Silverman, M. (Eds.) (2013). *Community music today*. Lanham, Maryland: Rowman & Littlefield Education.

Reference list

Aasgaard, T. (2004). A pied piper among white coats and infusion pumps: Community music therapy in a paediatric hospital setting. In M. Pavlicevic & G. Andsell (Eds.), *Community music therapy* (pp. 147–66). London: Jessica Kingsley Publishers.

American Academy of Pediatrics—Committee on Hospital Care. (2000). Child life service. *Pediatrics*, **106**(5), 1156–9.

Ansdell, G., & DeNora, T. (2012). Musical flourishing: Community music therapy, controversy, and the cultivation of wellbeing. In R. MacDonald, G. Kreutz, & L. Mitchell (Eds.), *Music, health, and wellbeing* (pp. 97–112). London: Oxford University Press.

Barrera, M. E., Rykov, M. H., Doyle, S. L., & Caldwell-Andrews, A. A. (2002). The effect of interactive music therapy on hospitalized children with cancer: A pilot study. *Psycho-Oncology*, **11**(5), 379–88.

Barry, P., O'Callaghan, C., Wheeler, G., & Grocke, D. (2010). Music therapy CD creation for initial pediatric radiation therapy: A mixed methods analysis. *Journal of Music Therapy*, **47**(3), 233–63.

Bittman, B. B., Berk, L. S., Felten, D. L., Westengard, J., Simonton, O. C., Pappas, J., & Ninehouser, M. (2001). Composite effects of group drumming music therapy on modulation of neuroendocrine-immune parameters in normal subjects. *Alternative Therapies in Health and Medicine*, **7**(1), 38–47.

Bronfenbrenner, U. (1979). *The ecology of human development*. Cambridge, MA: Harvard University Press.

Burns, D. S., Sledge, R. B., Fuller, L. A., Daggy, J. K., & Monahan, P. O. (2005). Cancer patients' interest and preferences for music therapy. *Journal of Music Therapy*, **42**(3), 185–99.

Caprilli, S., Anastasi, F., Grotto, R. P. L., Abeti, M. S., & Messeri, A. (2007). Interactive music as a treatment for pain and stress in children during venipuncture: A randomized prospective study. *Journal of Developmental and Behavioral Pediatrics*, **28**(5), 399–403. doi: 10.1097/DBP.0b013e31811ff8a7.

Curtis, S. L. (2011). Music therapy and the symphony: A university-community collaborative project in palliative care. *Music and Medicine*, **3**(1), 20–6.

Dahlquist, L. M. (1999). *Pediatric pain management*. New York: Springer.

DeLoach Walworth, D. (2005). Procedural-support music therapy in the healthcare setting: A cost-effectiveness analysis. *Journal of Pediatric Nursing*, **20**(4), 276–84.

Dileo, C., & Bradt, J. (2009). On creating the discipline, profession, and evidence in the field of arts and healthcare. *Arts & Health*, **1**(2), 168–82.

Docherty, S. L., Robb, S. L., Phillips-Salimi, C., Cherven, B., Stegenga, K., Hendricks-Ferguson, V., Roll, L., Donovan Stickler, M., & Haase, J. (2013). Parental perspectives on a behavioral health music intervention for adolescent/young adult resilience during cancer treatment: Report from the Children's Oncology Group. *Journal of Adolescent Health*, **52**(2), 170–8.

Dun, B. (1999). Creativity and communication: Aspects of music therapy in a children's hospital. In D. Aldridge (Ed.), *Music therapy in palliative care* (pp. 59–67). London and Philadelphia: Jessica Kingsley Publishers.

Dun, B. (2007). Journeying with Olivia: Bricolage as a framework for understanding music therapy in paediatric oncology. *Voices: A World Forum for Music Therapy*, **7**(1). Retrieved from <http://www.voices.no/mainissues/mi40007000229.php>.

Dun, B. (2011). All in good time: A music therapist's reflection of providing a music therapy program in a pediatric cancer center over 20 years. *Music and Medicine*, **3**(1), 15–19.

Edwards, J., & Kennelly, J. (2011). Music therapy for children in hospital care: A stress & coping framework for practice. In A. Meadows (Ed.), *Developments in music therapy practice: Case study perspectives* (pp. 150–65). Gilsum, NH, United States: Barcelona Publishers.

Grasso, M. C., Button, B. M., Allison, D. J., & Sawyer, S. M. (2000). Benefits of music therapy as an adjunct to chest physiotherapy in infants and toddlers with cystic fibrosis. *Pediatric Pulmonology*, **29**(5), 371–81.

Hendon, C., & Bohon, L. M. (2008). Hospitalized children's mood differences during play and music ther-apy. *Child: Care, Health and Development*, **34**(2), 141–4.

Hiscock, N., O'Callaghan, C., Goodwin, M., & Wheeler, G. (2013). Music, intelligence, and the neurocog-nitive effects of childhood cancer treatment. *Music and Medicine*, **5**(2), 93–8.

Hockenberry, M. J., & Bologna-Vaughan, S. (1985). Preparation for intrusive procedures using non-invasive techniques in children with cancer: State of the arts vs. new trends. *Cancer Nursing*, **8**(2), 97–102.

Johnson, J. E., Fieler, V. K., Jones, L. S., Wlasowicz, G. S., & Mitchell, M. L. (1997). *Self-regulation theory: Applying theory to your practice*. Pittsburgh, PA: Oncology Nursing Press.

Kemper, K. J., & McLean, T. W. (2008). Parents' attitudes and expectations about music's impact on pediat-ric oncology patients. *Journal of the Society for Integrative Oncology*, **6**(4), 146–9.

Kennelly, J. (2000). The specialist role of the music therapist in developmental programs for hospitalized children. *Journal of Pediatric Health Care*, **14**(2), 56–9.

Klassen, J. A., Liang, Y., Tjosvold, L., Klassen, T. P., & Hartling, L. (2008). Music for pain and anxiety in children undergoing medical procedures: A systematic review of randomized controlled trials. *Ambulatory Pediatrics*, **8**(2), 117–28.

Klein, J., & Graham-Pole, J. (2008). Building community within the health-care environment: Marrying art and technology. In B. D. Koen (Ed.), *The Oxford handbook of medical ethnomusicology* (pp. 445–60). New York: Oxford University Press.

Koen, B. D., Barz, G., & Brummel-Smith, K. (2008). Introduction: Confluence of consciousness in music, medicine, and culture. In B. D. Koen (Ed.), *The Oxford handbook 3399of medical ethnomusicology* (pp. 3–17). New York: Oxford University Press.

Kovacs, P. J., Bellin, M. H., & Fauri, D. P. (2006). Family-centered care: A resource for social work in end-of-life and palliative care. *Journal of Social Work in End-of-Life & Palliative Care*, **2**(1), 13–27.

Lam, L. W., Chang, A. M., & Morrissey, J. (2006). Parents' experiences of participation in the care of hospi-talised children: A qualitative study. *International Journal of Nursing Studies*, **43**(5), 535–45.

Lambert, S. (1984). Variables that affect the school-age child's reaction to hospitalization and surgery: A review of the literature. *Maternal Child Nursing Journal*, **13**(1), 1–17.

Lamont, A. (2002). Musical identities and the school environment. In R. MacDonald, D. J. Hargreaves, & D. Miell (Eds.), *Musical identities* (pp. 49–55). Oxford: Oxford University Press.

LaMontagne, L. L. (1987). Factors influencing children's reactions and adjustment to illness: Implications for facilitating coping. In T. Krulik, B. Holaday, & I. M. Martinson (Eds.), *The child and family facing life-threatening illness* (pp. 273–8). Philadelphia: J. B. Lippincott Company.

Lazarus, R. S. (2000). Evolution of a model of stress, coping, and discrete emotions. In V. H. Rice (Ed.), *Handbook of stress, coping, and health: Implications for nursing research, theory, and practice* (pp. 195–222). London: Sage Publications.

Lindenfelser, K. J., Grocke, D., & McFerran, K. S. (2008). Bereaved parents' experiences of music therapy with their terminally ill child. *Journal of Music Therapy*, **45**(3), 330–48.

Lindenfelser, K. J., Hense, C., & McFerran, K. S. (2012). Music therapy in pediatric palliative care: Family-centered care to enhance quality of life. *American Journal of Hospice and Palliative Medicine*, **29**(3), 219–26.

Longhi, E., & Pickett, N. (2008). Music and well-being in long-term hospitalized children. *Psychology of Music*, **36**(2), 247–56. doi: 10.1177/0305735607082622.

Longhi, E., Pickett, N., & Hargreaves, D. J. (2013). Wellbeing and hospitalized children: Can music help? *Psychology of Music*. Published online before print, August 22, 2013. doi: 10.1177/0305735613499781.

MacDonald, R. A. R., Hargreaves, D. J., & Miell, D. (2002). *Musical identities*. Oxford: Oxford University Press.

McFerran, K. (2005). Dangerous liaisons: Group work for adolescent girls who have anorexia nervosa. *Voices: A World Forum for Music Therapy*, **5**(1). Retrieved from <http://www.voices.no/mainissues/mi40005000173.html>.

McFerran, K., & Sawyer, S. M. (2003). From recreation to creative expression: The essential features of an adolescent inpatient psychosocial support program. *ANNALS: Journal of the Singaporean Medical Association (Special Issue on Adolescence)*, 32(1), 64–70.

Melnyk, B. M. (2000). Intervention studies involving parents of hospitalized young children: An analysis of the past and future recommendations. *Journal of Pediatric Nursing*, 15(1), 4–13.

Mrazova, M., & Celec, P. (2010). A systematic review of randomized controlled trials using music therapy for children. *Journal of Alternative and Complementary Medicine*, 16(10), 1089–95. doi: 10.1089/acm.2009.0430.

Nguyen, T. N., Nilsson, S., Hellström, A.-L., & Bengtson, A. (2010). Music therapy to reduce pain and anxiety in children with cancer undergoing lumbar puncture: A randomized clinical trial. *Journal of Pediatric Oncology Nursing*, 27(3), 146–55.

Nicholson, J. M., Berthelsen, D., Abad, V., Williams, K., & Bradley, J. (2008). Impact of music therapy to promote positive parenting and child development. *Journal of Health Psychology*, 13(2), 226–38.

Oakland, J. (2012). Music for health: A thematic evaluation of practitioner experiences of work, training, and professional development. Report: Royal Northern College of Music.

O'Callaghan, C., Dun, B., Baron, A., & Barry, P. (2013). Music's relevance for children with cancer: Music therapists' qualitative clinical data-mining research. *Social Work in Health Care*, 52(2–3), 125–43.

O'Callaghan, C., Sexton, M., & Wheeler, G. (2007). Music therapy as a non-pharmacological anxiolytic for paediatric radiotherapy patients. *Australasian Radiology*, 51(2), 159–62.

Ockelford, A. (2000). Music in the education of children with severe or profound learning difficulties: Issues in current UK provision. A new conceptual framework, and proposal for research. *Psychology of Music*, 28(2), 197–217.

Preti, C. (2013). Live music as a bridge between hospitals and outside communities: A proposed research framework and a review of the literature. *UNESCO Refereed E-Journal, Multi-Disciplinary Research in the Arts*, 3(3), 1–18.

Preti, C., & Welch, G. F. (2004). Music in a hospital setting: A multifaceted experience. *British Journal of Music Education*, 21(3), 329–45.

Preti, C., & Welch, G. F. (2011). Music in a hospital: The impact of a live music program on pediatric patients and their caregivers. *Music and Medicine*, 3(4), 213–23.

Preti, C., & Welch, G. F. (2012). The incidental impact of music on hospital staff: An Italian case study. *Arts & Health: An International Journal for Research, Policy and Practice*, 4(2), 135–47.

Preti, C., & Welch, G. F. (2013). Professional identities and motivations of musicians playing in healthcare settings: Cross-cultural evidence from UK and Italy. *Musicae Scientiae*, 17(4), 359–75.

Rennick, J. E., Johnston, C. C., Dougherty, G., Platt, R., & Ritchie, J. (2002). Children's psychological responses after critical illness and exposure to invasive technology. *Developmental and Behavioural Pediatrics*, 23(3), 133–44.

Rennick, J. E., & Rashotte, J. (2009). Psychological outcomes in children following pediatric intensive care unit hospitalization: A systematic review of the research. *Journal of Child Health Care*, 13(2), 128–49.

Robb, S. L. (2000). The effect of therapeutic music interventions on the behavior of hospitalized children in isolation: Developing contextual support model of music therapy. *Journal of Music Therapy*, 37(2), 118–46.

Robb, S. L. (2003). Coping and chronic illness: Music therapy for children and adolescents with cancer. In S. L. Robb (Ed.), *Music therapy in pediatric healthcare: Research and evidence-based practice* (pp. 101–36). Silver Spring, MD: The American Music Therapy Association, Inc.

Robb, S. L., & Carpenter, J. S. (2009). A review of music-based intervention reporting in pediatrics. *Journal of Health Psychology*, 14(4), 490–501. doi: 10.1177/1359105309103568.

Roberts, M. C., & Wallander, J. L. (Eds.) (1992). *Family issues in pediatric psychology*. Hillsdale, NJ: Lawrence Erlbaum Associates Publishers.

Shoemark, H. (2009). Sweet melodies: Combining the talents and knowledge of music therapy and elite musicianship. *Voices: A World Forum for Music Therapy*, **9**(2). Retrieved from <https://normt.uib.no/index.php/voices/article/viewArticle/347/271>.

Shoemark, H., & Dearn, T. (2008). Keeping parents at the centre of family centred music therapy with hospitalised infants. *Australian Journal of Music Therapy*, **19**(1), 3–24.

Sternberg, E. M. (2009). *Healing spaces. The science of place and well-being*. Cambridge, Massachusetts: The Belknap Press of Harvard University Press.

Treurnicht Naylor, K., Kingsnorth, S., Lamont, A., McKeever, P., & Macarthur, C. (2011). The effectiveness of music in pediatric healthcare: A systematic review of randomized controlled trials. *Evidence-Based Complementary and Alternative Medicine* [Epub ahead of print]. doi: 10.1155/2011/464759.

Veblen, K. K., Elliott, D., Messenger, S. J., & Silverman, M. (Eds.) (2013). *Community music today*. Lanham, Maryland: Rowman & Littlefield Education.

Vernon, D. T. A., & Thompson, R. (1993). Research on the effect of experimental interventions on children's behaviour after hospitalization: A review and synthesis. *Developmental and Behavioural Pediatrics*, **14**(1), 36–44.

Viner, R., & Keane, M. (1998). *Youth matters: Evidence-based best practice for the care of young people in hospital*. London: Action for Sick Children.

Vohra, S., & Nilsson, S. (2011). Does music therapy reduce pain and anxiety in children with cancer undergoing lumbar puncture? *Focus on Alternative and Complementary Therapies*, **16**(1), 66–7.

White, M. (2009). *Arts development in community health: A social tonic*. Oxford: Radcliffe.

Whitehead-Pleaux, A. M., Baryza, M. J., & Sheridan, R. L. (2006). The effects of music therapy on pediatric patients' pain and anxiety during donor site dressing change. *Journal of Music Therapy*, **43**(2), 136–53.

Wolfe, J., Grier, H. E., Klar, N., Levin, S. B., Ellenbogen, J. M., Salem-Schatz, S., Emanuel, E. J., & Weeks, J. C. (2000). Symptoms and suffering at the end of life in children with cancer. *New England Journal of Medicine*, **342**(5), 326–33.

Chapter 21

Adolescent music is not problematic

Katrina S. McFerran

Music and happiness: Introduction

Many commentators claim that music is the golden road to happiness. Contributors within this volume make convincing arguments in the direction of personal growth, suggesting that musical participation leads to personal happiness (Elliot & Silverman, Chapter 13), promotes identity work (Davis, Chapter 14), encourages empathy (Higgins, Chapter 32), and provides a sense of relevance, purpose, and fulfillment (O'Neill, Chapter 33). These connections between music and happiness are well supported by the literature and also in the minds of many teenagers.

When asked about their relationship with music, many young people report that music is "my best friend," or that music "makes me feel better" (Barrera, Rykov, & Doyle, 2002; McFerran & Saarikallio, 2013). The sincerity of these claims is undeniable and research shows that music considered significant during adolescence is the most important of our lives. Adrian North and David Hargreaves (2002) have clarified that it is the music of our late adolescence that has enduring significance and is most likely to remain prominent in our personal listening repertoire for decades to come. This does not suggest that our musical lives end as we reach adulthood, but it does provide a rationale for focusing on the importance of music during adolescence as a passionate illustration of what music means during the subsequent years. As Paul Van Heeswyk (1997) insightfully suggests in describing adolescent development, this may be because adulthood marks the point where "the petrol is getting low and we need to think about saving it for the long, straight road ahead" (p. 3). The passion for music is high and the space for musical engagement is available more during adolescence than in any other period of life. Therefore, research on the relationship between adolescents, music, and happiness potentially provides potent insights into life-long experiences, although there is only a limited amount to date. But is the picture as radiantly positive as many suggest?

In a critical synthesis of research literature examining the relationship between adolescents and their music (McFerran, Garrido, & Saarikallio, 2013), it became apparent that researchers were strongly prejudiced by one of two assumptions: the power of music was either good, or it was bad. Different research methods were favored depending on what beliefs were held by the authors. Those who anticipated that music had a negative influence over teenagers' mental health chose correlational designs, measuring happiness and music tastes separately and then identifying connections (Anderson, Carnagey, & Eubanks, 2003; Hutchison, Baldwin, & Oh, 2006; Kistler et al., 2010). This approach has almost invariably led to the identification of strong correlations between heavier genres of music (such as Rap and Metal music) and darker, anti-conformist personal traits. In contrast, "light" music, as Kelly Schwartz and Gregory Fouts (2003) chose to label pop and dance music, was strongly correlated with well-behaved adolescents, sometimes so attentive to the needs of others that they were driven to anxiety in their attempts to uphold societal expectations.

North and Hargreaves (2008) highlight an important error in the interpretation of this particular group of studies, however. Despite the arguments that are often made once results are taken beyond the scientific context, none provides evidence to support a causal relationship. Certain types of music have not been found to cause unhappiness. Instead, what these correlations suggest is that young people from "vulnerable backgrounds" may be more inclined to engage with more intense forms of music, which are then associated with "problem" behaviors. North and Hargreaves described some of the vulnerable conditions considered to be problematic as "poor school performance, membership of an undervalued social group, a sensation-seeking personality, poor family relationships and poor parenting, low self-esteem, and sex" (2008, pp. 211–12). Recognition of this important distinction promotes a movement away from unsubstantiated beliefs about causality and toward a more accurate understanding of a complex interaction between teenagers and their music. The implication of contextual influences, such as vulnerable conditions, is a critical piece of the puzzle.

The few causal studies that do exist actually find music to be a variable that is more likely to lead to positive outcomes. These studies have often been undertaken with young people who come from vulnerable backgrounds, since music therapists often work in this context and conduct this research. A meta-analysis of music therapy intervention studies with young people who have psychopathology (Gold, Voracek, & Wigram, 2004) identified six studies with adolescents that showed clinically relevant outcomes on psychological measures. Even young people without particularly challenging contexts have been seen to improve significantly more than a control group in ratings of depression and self-esteem from pre- to post-testing after participating in supportive, music-making experiences compared to a control condition (Currie & Startup, 2012).

These findings from pre–post measures are congruent with descriptive reports from qualitative investigations. In contrast to the assumption that some music is bad, authors using qualitative designs have often solicited exclusively positive reports from their informants. The music therapy literature is replete with descriptions from young people who describe how "the group gave me a lot more spirit because I got to be destructive and express my feelings" (McFerran-Skewes, 2000, p. 18), and "it was very good, well worth doing and I would recommend doing it again. I loved it there" (McFerran & Hunt, 2008, p. 49). Similarly, music psychology studies describe how adolescents use music for revival: "After school, it's fun and energizing to listen to music [after a long day at school] and to relax one's neck muscles" (Saarikallio & Erkkila, 2007, p. 97), and for mood improvement: "If you're in a terribly depressed mood, then, in my view, it's much nicer to start listening to something uplifting" (p. 99). In the healthy adult population, even listening to sad music has been described as a positive experience, with explanations such as, it is "very upsetting but a good release of my grief" (Van den Tol & Edwards, 2011, p. 9).

So why do caring adults report concerns about vulnerable young people's music listening habits? Parents frequently describe the ways that their children flounce from the bedroom in a worsened emotional state after they have been listening repeatedly to loud music. Stories abound of young people priming themselves for anti-social behaviors by listening to aggressive music in the moments prior. If music does not cause these behaviors, then why is it so strongly associated with them? The answer defies an either/or dichotomy. Music is not innocent; it is dynamic and powerful and emotional. Nor can everything be explained by context, since many young people come from vulnerable backgrounds and use music successfully to manage and mediate their moods so that they are able to thrive. Yet, as the survey research has shown, there is a significant connection between vulnerable teenagers and "problem" music, as North and Hargreaves (2008) label it in their review. The interaction between the two cannot be sufficiently explained when music is viewed as a stimulus; however, ecological thinking provides a number of key concepts that assist in explaining this complex, human–music interaction. In this chapter, I will argue that music is neither a positive stimulus, nor negative, nor neutral, but it is powerful.

The affordances of music

The notion that music affords various possibilities for action was adopted by music scholars from James Gibson's (1986) initial work in the field of visual perception. The important difference between music as a stimulus and music as affording possibilities for action is that the first assumes that qualities exist in a static way within the object that is music, whilst the second emphasizes the interaction between the person doing the perceiving and the music as subject. It is the interaction that creates conditions wherein particular kinds of actions and reactions are more or less likely to occur. This distinction is most helpfully illustrated by considering the ways that we understand a particular genre of music—Metal music.

Many of the correlational studies I have described have associated Metal music with depression. Whilst the point has been emphatically made that Metal music does not cause depression, the association between the two undeniably exists. The notion of affordances helps to explain that particular qualities (affordances) of Metal music are prominent in the perception of someone who feels depressed—the loud dynamics and distorted guitar sounds, the raw vocals, the driving rhythms. Each of these qualities can be interpreted as mirroring some parts of the experience of being depressed, with intense emotions and resultant isolation. However, Metal music is not a pure expression of a depressed state. The same qualities can afford different meanings to other listeners: the sheer energy of the band can be experienced as invigorating; the lyrics can scream a protest against conformity and passivity; the community of Metal-heads offers acceptance and inclusion. Metal music is not one thing; it affords an array of possibilities for action that are perceived uniquely by different people, and even by the same person at different times and in different contexts. People with depression may well relate to the affordances of Metal music. So might highly energetic people. So might angry and aggressive people. So might non-conformists. So might cold people—after all, the Fins and the Norwegians represent a huge chunk of the consumer and performer market for this genre. This explanation bypasses the need to explore the vast myriad of sub-genres that exist within the Metal scene because it is not the specific features of the genre that are most influential, but the fact that music is particularly good at affording possibilities for action. But music does not dictate the specific action; rather it suggests a number of possibilities.

In critically analyzing the literature reporting associations between a particular genre of music and specific moods or personality traits, this failure to acknowledge that music is more than a direct stimulus became apparent (McFerran et al., 2013). Yet this assumption dominates the research activity, and as a result, the questions that are asked by researchers seek to determine whether the influence of music is positive or negative, and also, to identify the differences in influence between different types of music. This naturally leads to the assumption that a particular harmonic condition, such as a suspended cadence, will result in a predictable change in perception and that all people will experience this change similarly, so long as listeners are "enculturated into specific auditory environments where some events or patterns are more predictable than others," such as culture (Huron, 2006, p. 36).

Whilst these theories are interesting, they are regularly contradicted by individuals' experiences, often seen in music therapy. A particular piece of music may fulfil all the characteristics of being relaxing, for example. The music may be played at a slow tempo, it may have a limited range of notes in the melody, and the harmony and form may be predictable (Grocke & Wigram, 2006).

And yet, if that piece of music is known to the listener, their response may be the opposite of relaxing. If the listener is a musician who studied the piece on her instrument, she may become analytical in listening and therefore miss the effect of the relaxing qualities. If the song was played at a funeral of a loved one, the song may elicit tears and sadness, or even anger (Vuoskoski & Eerola, 2012). Although the music affords a relaxed response, it does not necessarily elicit one, because the context of the individual interplays with the music itself in a dynamic manner.

Karl Popper's (1959/80) theory of falsifiability provides a useful framework for challenging the argument. He claims that theories cannot be proven to be true because of individual examples, but they can be proven to be false. Although it is possible to prove that certain qualities, or genres of music, can be predictably associated with a specific result, it does not confirm the hypothesis that music is a predictable stimulus. A more interesting discovery is that individual examples exist where this is shown not to be true for all people. These individual examples suggest that music has an unpredictable effect—it does not maintain a coherent enough set of features to be considered a direct stimulus, at least in the context of human responses. The construct of affordances therefore provides a fascinating framework with which to try to understand the phenomenon of human experience with music. In this chapter, this will be more specifically refined to explore the question of whether there is, or can be, a problem with the relationship between teenagers and music.

Appropriating the affordances of music

The notion that music affords possibilities for action has been extended within music studies, particularly in Tia DeNora's (2000) explorations of music in the everyday life of adults. Her emphasis on the agency exercised by people as they engage with music (DeNora, 2006) is particularly pertinent when transferred to the relationship between teenagers and music. Another assumption that results from viewing music as a stimulus is that the listener is under the influence, or out of control of their reactions to the music. DeNora argues in direct opposition, providing rich descriptions of people using music purposefully in their own lives, rather than the other way around.

Under Even Ruud's supervision, a number of music researchers have explored a range of possibilities related to the appropriation of music for health by individuals. Marie Skanland (2011) investigated the ways that adult Norwegians use MP3 listening to manage their environments when negotiating everyday life experiences such as travelling to work on public transport. Kari Batt-Rawden (Batt-Rawden, DeNora, & Ruud, 2005) focused on adults with chronic illness and illustrated how simple it is to increase the intentional use of music listening and promote more positive experiences of health. Hege Beckmann (2013) contributed another set of narratives, more specifically focusing on the ways that she conceived young people's health-oriented uses of music in their daily lives. Brynjulf Stige's (Stige & Aarø, 2002a,b, 2012; Stige et al., 2010) contribution to the discourse has been the most extensive, and the now prominent emphasis on music and health within music therapy discourse can be largely attributed to his repeated requests to expand theorizing beyond institutionalized uses of music to influence health and toward more collaborative, community-building initiatives.

Each of these scholars has explored how people appropriate the affordances of music, rather than testing how music acts upon individuals and groups. This perspective is deeply relevant to music therapists whose practices are informed by strengths-oriented and humanistic theories of psychology (Rolvsjord, 2010), and who therefore relate to DeNora's emphasis on individual agency. Music therapists are particularly interested in detailing how possibilities for healthy actions can be promoted. Instead of conceptualizing this process as designing programs for clients, which is traditionally how music therapists have conceptualized their role, Stige has introduced a more empowering language that emphasizes agency and is labeled "appraising affordances" (Stige & Aarø, 2012, p. 184). In practice, what this means is similar to how music therapists have always worked, but instead of assuming a set of languages that emphasizes the expertise of the therapist, the idea of appraising affordances highlights how decisions involve collaborating with the individual and/or group to identify what musical genre or participatory activity appeals. The music therapist negotiates with the individual to discover whether they prefer listening to Western classical music, or learning to play guitar, or writing pop songs. These personal preferences are then considered in identifying what possibilities for healthy action would be most beneficial in the given circumstance. This might involve considering whether the individual or group need opportunities for relaxation, expression, or participation. The final consideration of the music therapist, again reached in collaboration with the participant, is whether the preferred form of musical participation is well suited to the proposed purpose. If listening to Metal music has been nominated, the music therapist reflects on whether it will support emotional release and catharsis. As the music therapy process moves toward conclusion, the focus returns to examining the uses of music in everyday life and considering further, independent possibilities for action.

Strengths-oriented music therapists have always been closely aligned with the emphasis on positive engagement with music. However, colleagues working in the field of mental illness have traditionally adopted different theoretical orientations and these are also relevant to the examination of potential problems with teen music. Psychodynamic perspectives, with an emphasis on unconscious mental processes (Hadley, 2003), are the most common, and the awareness of both conscious and unconscious dynamics means that therapists do not view the relationship between clients and music as simple. It is not assumed that descriptions offered about one's relationship with music will be accurate, for example, since a lack of contact with a shared reality is the defining feature of mental illness. Instead, the psychodynamically informed music therapist embarks on a long journey of exploring the perception of music as a reflection of inner state. In traditional practice in psychiatric institutions, this involves a large number of sessions where music is performed in a way that is unfettered by expectations about genre, often using free, atonal improvisations (Mahns, 2002). Creating music together in a spontaneous fashion affords opportunities for original meaning making, with the presence and carefully responsive practices of the music therapist providing boundaries and safety to the experience (Purdon, 2002). The client projects their internal experience through their external expression of self in the music, and in relationship. Together with the music therapist, they then construct meanings, either verbally or through ongoing musical development. There is no prediction that a particular harmonic progression conveys a single meaning, or that the pace and intensity suggest a specific diagnosis. The free expression affords novel interpretation. The insights that result are thought to enhance personal understanding and support growth and recovery.

More contemporary practices in the field of mental illness have started to take existing musical preferences into account, so that pure improvisation is no longer the only way to appropriate music for meaning making. Resource-oriented practices have developed (Rolvsjord, 2010; Rolvsjord, Gold, & Stige, 2005), again under Even Ruud's tutelage, which emphasize the positive potentials of shared experiences where the collaboration between therapist and client utilizes existing relationships with music. This expansion of traditional practices is much needed, particularly with the current emphasis on recovery in mental health (Jacobson & Greenley, 2001) and the concurrent deinstitutionalization that has already swept across the United States and Australia. Clients do not remain in institutional contexts for the kind of long-term treatment that is required to successfully undertake traditional psychodynamic work. Whilst the parallels between resource-oriented music therapy practices and recovery have been documented (Solli, Rolvsjord, & Borg,

2013), the knowledge accrued from decades of psychodynamic thinking remains critical. An emphasis on appropriating the affordances of music should not be mistaken for naïve positivity. The affordances of music can be utilized toward positive, negative, and neutral ends.

What problems can there be?

A small body of literature exists that documents the ways that music has been appropriated for aggressive purposes. Warriors have long understood how to use music to intimidate the enemy, creating walls of sound that terrified those under attack, particularly through the use of drums (Norris, 2012). These practices continue in some ways today, with the New Zealand tradition of singing and dancing the Haka before a rugby game illustrating the concept powerfully (<http://www.youtube.com/watch?v=Zi0igR4AJ0U>). Hitler provides another clear illustration of the abuse of musical power, with his appropriation of the powerful bonding that occurs when men march together in time, providing a foundation for thoughtless violence that continues to unnerve social commentators (McNeill, 1995). More recent warfare examples exist in the use of sonic torture by American army persons who trapped victims in enclosed spaces and played particular types of music repeatedly to break their spirit (Cusick, 2008). Everyday examples also abound, with the courts frequently being required to intervene in cases of sonic torture described by neighbors who are overwhelmed by loud and repeated playing from adjacent properties (Johnson & Cloonan, 2009).

Music is not only appropriated for violence, but also for fostering unhappiness. A small body of literature is now emerging that explores human proclivity for sad music. Sandra Garrido and Emery Schubert have explored the paradox of what attracts people to the negative emotions expressed in music, despite the fact that these feelings are usually avoided in other contexts (Garrido & Schubert, 2010). Although concluding that many listeners dissociate from actual emotions and instead experience aesthetic versions of these emotions, their qualitative investigations show high degrees of individuality (Garrido & Schubert, 2011). Similarly, studies of emotion-related memory and judgment have shown that the relevance of the music, as well as the personality attributes of the listener, do affect the degree to which sad music induces sad emotions (Vuoskoski & Eerola, 2012). One type of appropriation of sad music that is particularly relevant here is the use of music to ruminate, a tendency that has been evidenced in a correlational study that included people who struggle with depression (Garrido & Schubert, 2013). Rumination is the constant and repetitive return to thoughts in a passive way that does not lead to resolution, but instead reinforces negative thinking. This is distinct from cognitive reappraisal, where a positive outcome results and which has been linked to positive effects on mood (Van den Tol & Edwards, 2014). Recorded music powerfully affords opportunities for ruminative action, since it is repetitive and contributes both emotion and stimulation to the process, potentially extending and deepening experiences of rumination.

The relationship between rumination and repetitive music listening has not been explored in the vast majority of literature that has examined how young people use music to manage their moods. There is an overall inclination to focus on positive processing and cognitive reappraisal (Dickmeis & Roe, 2013; Saarikallio, 2011; Van den Tol & Edwards, 2014), and researchers and informants alike frequently describe how music affords opportunities to resolve issues. However, people who have depression, or who have ruminative features associated with another form of mental illness, may not be able to accurately or honestly reflect on their actual experiences of appropriating music. They may report what they hope will happen, or they may avoid describing the more negative aspects of their experience in an attempt to please the researcher.

Returning to Popper's falsification theory, one published example suggests that the difference between beliefs and reality may be quite different for people struggling with depression. In reflecting upon experiences of music therapy as a teenager with chronic illness, Kelly Baird describes her own tendency to use music to reinforce negative mood states (McFerran & Baird, 2013). Prior to the onset of depression, her tendency to use music as a form of expression was felt to be helpful. However, reflecting on the ways that she uses music listening in a depressed state, she notes that her assumptions about the positive benefits of appropriating music are not substantiated by her experience of listening repeatedly to sad songs. A targeted qualitative analysis of the ways Australian teenagers describe appropriating music when depressed has provided further confirmation of this tendency (McFerran & Saarikallio, 2013). Data collected from in-depth interviews revealed that teenagers assume that music makes them feel better, but that when challenged to describe a time where they felt worse after appropriating music, they were able to identify such experiences. This was particularly true of depressed young people, with one teenager describing how a friend had eventually deleted a "break-up" track from her iPhone because she was using it to repeatedly relive the trauma of her complex break-up experience. Although this illustration does not, at all, provide support for deleting music, the theory resulting from the analysis of the 40 interviews suggests that greater conscious and intentional uses of the power of music by young people is an important public health message.

Intentional playlist creation: A vehicle for better health

The MP3 revolution has created conditions where it is more possible than ever to make a difference in the ways that young people perceive the possibilities for appropriating the affordances of music. It is apparent to any observer that young people are accessing music at speeds that were previously impossible. These possibilities for accessing music are also open to a wider range of young people than before, since most music is freely available if Internet access is accessible. The breadth of repertoire is also exhaustive and young people are no longer restricted to what is being played on radio stations, or available in their older siblings' and parents' collections. Interestingly, the rates of music listening do not seem to have increased substantially. Whilst there is considerable variability, between 2 and 3 hours per day continues to be the norm, but music is now more often used in conjunction with other activities such as gaming (Brown & Bobkowski, 2011). The difference appears to be in access and diversity, not in consumption.

Apple technology has introduced another dimension to the ways that young people appropriate music, through the iTunes application and associated phone apps. The method developed for storing and categorizing songs has been labeled as "playlists," which is essentially the same as desktop folders. Rather than having to store music in alphabetical order, playlists allow for grouping of songs that are then labeled by the user. For a music therapist, the possibilities that are afforded are reminiscent of techniques that have been described as lyric analysis (Grocke & Wigram, 2006; O'Callaghan & Grocke, 2009), where therapists worked with clients to compile lists of songs in order to work toward a specific purpose. The purpose of this practice in music therapy is often to foster understanding and promote development when working with adolescents (McFerran, 2010). What iTunes affords is a mechanism for doing this that makes the process smooth, simple, and potentially more independent.

This possibility has been explored in Australia by Carmen Cheong-Clinch (2013), who investigated the ways that young people appropriate their preferred recorded music in hospital settings during periods of acute mental illness. Whilst her research revealed similar strategies to the ways healthy young people use music to identify with and manage their emotions (Saarikallio, 2011;

Sloboda & O'Neill, 2001), some differences were also apparent. In listening to preferred music with young people as part of the music therapy process, Cheong-Clinch often used playlist creation as a central part of her clinical practice. Supporting young people in crisis to choose and access music had become a point of advocacy in her organization, since mobile phones were taken from the young people upon admission for reasons of confidentiality related to cameras, but this process severed their contact with their own music. As she interviewed young people as part of her study, it became clear that the fervent belief they held in the transformative power of music to help them cope actually made music one of the most important parts of their lives. Fighting for their right to access music became a critical role that she played within the institution. However, it was necessary to pair this advocacy with critical discussions, since the impact of the young people's music listening fluctuated due to the complexity and unpredictability of their mental health difficulties and illness. Young people were not always aware of the ways they were using music, and did not necessarily discern between healthy and unhealthy uses of music. Her role was to promote increased awareness through supportive dialogue, without which she may have been promoting the appropriation of music in ways that actually hindered their recovery.

It is not only music therapists who are using playlist creation with a health orientation. Kari Batt-Rawden, under the supervision of DeNora and Ruud, investigated participatory CD design with adults who have chronic illness (Batt-Rawden, 2010). Once again, the movement into working with vulnerable participants resulted in an emphasis on "learning" to learn to use music for health, healing, and recovery. This contrasts significantly with the assumption that music is naturally geared toward positive outcomes. The important emphasis is on collaboration and intentional decision making, rather than a more humanistic and non-critical valuing of whatever choices the individual might make. In the following section, an example of how this can be applied with teenagers who do not have mental illness is offered as a model to promote musical development.

An example of critically appropriating music with teenagers

The use of music to promote well-being and connectedness in Australian schools has been the focus of a series of investigations conducted during 2012–13. Within this program, called *MusicMatters*,[1] a number of strategies were explored for encouraging increased critical awareness of the healthy and unhealthy uses of music. One project that has been successful in a number of schools is the Mixed Tape Assignment. This assignment was implemented as part of a classroom-based well-being program, and all students were required to complete the playlist creation tasks as well as participate in class discussions and experiential activities. In the first unit of learning, students were introduced to the idea of music being related to health and asked to complete a baseline survey that scored the healthy and unhealthy dimensions of their relationship with music (Saarikallio, McFerran, & Gold, under review). Musical examples were provided by the facilitator throughout the units to stimulate small group discussions, using songs such as Gary Jule's "Mad World" to talk about the dark side of music, and Pharrell Williams' "Happy" to discuss positive associations. Students worked in pairs to devise a list of songs that make them feel good and then in the next unit, to distinguish between listening to music alone and in the company of others. The third unit introduced the notion of knowing when to "press stop" and students began to consider different types of intentional playlists that they might wish to create, such as the "chill-out" playlist, or the "pump me up" playlist. The assignment was marked using a rubric that was based on the descriptive writing and presentational components of the assignment, as well as some scoring for the well-being components. Student and teacher feedback on the value of the assignment was very positive, with many reporting that they had never considered the possibility of negative experiences with music.

Conclusion

By understanding the relationship between music and young people as an encounter where music affords particular possibilities for action that are appropriated more and less consciously, we become alert to benefits and problems. It is too simplistic to judge or blame a particular type of music as causing problems. Similarly, an over-emphasis on challenging contexts within which some people appropriate music is an insufficient explanation for the diverse ways in which young people respond to experiences of music. By focusing on the interaction between music (as subject) and individual teenagers, the observer is likely to experience an increased consciousness about the unique situation, which will result in higher levels of empathy and attentiveness to nuance. In promoting the healthy musical development of adolescents, this is a critical stance to adopt.

Music has the potential to create mutually empowering conditions within which we can support one another and ourselves during difficult times. The MP3 revolution provides a societal context where this is more possible than ever. By introducing discussions about playlist creation and asking young people questions about how they feel after they have listened to music that is meant to make them feel better, we have the opportunity to make a difference not only to their musical development, but also to their overall well-being.

Author note

The *MusicMatters* program was a collaboration devised with Dr. Lucy Bolger and Kate Teggelove, and the Mixed Tape Project was documented in detail by Priscilla Pek and Angela Mallia at Presentation College, Windsor, Australia.

Reflective questions

1 What music do you listen to when you want to improve your mood?
2 Does that music consistently have the effect that you are expecting?
3 What songs do you listen to when you want to connect with negative feelings?
4 Does sad music listening lead to a feeling of release and relief, or does it intensify negative feelings?
5 What music could you compile in a playlist that you associate with positive mood states?

Note

1 A range of other musical strategies were also investigated for this purpose, with the main principles being described elsewhere (McFerran & Rickson, 2014).

Key sources

Batt-Rawden, K. B., DeNora, T., & Ruud, E. (2005). Music listening and empowerment in health promotion: A study of the role and significance of music in everyday life of the long-term ill. *Nordic Journal of Music Therapy*, 14(2), 120–36.

McFerran, K. S., & Saarikallio, S. (2013). Depending on music to make me feel better: Who is responsible for the ways young people appropriate music for health benefits? *The Arts in Psychotherapy*, 41(1), 89–97. Retrieved from <http://www.sciencedirect.com/science/article/pii/S019745561300186X>.

Reference list

Anderson, C. A., Carnagey, N. L., & Eubanks, J. (2003). Exposure to violent media: The effects of songs with violent lyrics on aggressive thoughts and feelings. *Journal of Personality and Social Psychology*, **84**(5), 960–71.

Barrera, M. E., Rykov, M. H., & Doyle, S. L. (2002). The effects of interactive music therapy on hospitalized children with cancer: A pilot study. *Psycho-Oncology*, **11**(5), 379–88.

Batt-Rawden, K. B. (2010). The benefits of self-selected music on health and well-being. *The Arts in Psychotherapy*, **37**(4), 301–10.

Beckmann, H. B. (2013). Music, adolescents and health: Narratives about how young people use music as a health resource in daily life. In L. O. Bonde, E. Ruud, M. S. Skanland, & G. Trondalen (Eds.), *Musical life stories: Narratives on health musicking* (Vol. 6). Norwegian Academy of Music, Oslo: NMG-publikasjoner.

Brown, B. J. D., & Bobkowski, P. S. (2011). Older and newer media: Patterns of use and effects on adolescents' health and well-being. *Journal of Research on Adolescence*, **21**(1), 95–113.

Cheong-Clinch, C. (2013). *Musical diaries: An investigation of the everyday music engagement of young people with mental illness* (Doctoral dissertation), University of Melbourne.

Currie, M., & Startup, M. (2012). Doing anger differently: Two controlled trials of percussion group psychotherapy for adolescent reactive aggression. *Journal of Adolescence*, **35**(4), 843–53. doi: 10.1015/j.adolescence.2011.12.003.

Cusick, S. G. (2008). You are in a place that is out of the world . . . : Music in the detention camps of the global war on terror. *Journal of the Society for American Music*, **2**(1), 1–26.

DeNora, T. (2000). *Music in everyday life*. Cambridge, UK: Cambridge University Press.

DeNora, T. (2006). Music and self-identity. In A. Bennett, B. Shank, & J. Toynbee (Eds.), *The popular music studies reader* (pp. 141–7). Milton Park, UK: Psychology Press.

Dickmeis, A., & Roe, K. (2013). *Adolescents' emotion regulation as a predictor of music importance, and of music as a reflection of identity*. Paper presented at the Music, Mind, and Health Conference, University of Melbourne, November 28.

Garrido, S., & Schubert, E. (2010). Imagination, empathy and dissociation in individual response to negative emotions in music. *Musica Humana*, **2**(1), 54–78.

Garrido, S., & Schubert, E. (2011). Negative emotion in music: What is the attraction? A qualitative study. *Empirical Musicology Review*, **6**(4), 214–30.

Garrido, S., & Schubert, E. (2013). Adaptive and maladaptive attraction to negative emotions in music. *Musicae Scientiae*, **17**(2), 147–66. doi: 10.1177/1029864913478305.

Gibson, J. J. (1986). *The ecological approach to visual perception*. Mahwah, NJ: Lawrence Erlbaum.

Gold, C., Voracek, M., & Wigram, T. (2004). Effects of music therapy for children and adolescents with psychopathology: A meta-analysis. *Journal of Child Psychology and Psychiatry*, **45**(6), 1054–9.

Grocke, D. E., & Wigram, T. (2006). *Receptive methods in music therapy*. London: Jessica Kingsley Publishers.

Hadley, S. (Ed.) (2003). *Psychodynamic music therapy: Case studies*. Phoenixville, PA: Barcelona Publishers.

Huron, D. (2006). *Sweet anticipation: Music and the psychology of expectation*. Cambridge, MA: MIT Press.

Hutchison, S. L., Baldwin, C. K., & Oh, S.-S. (2006). Adolescent coping: Exploring adolescents' leisure-based responses to stress. *Leisure Sciences: An Interdisciplinary Journal*, **28**(2), 115–31.

Jacobson, N., & Greenley, D. (2001). What is recovery? A conceptual model and explication. *Psychiatric Services*, **52**(4), 482–5.

Johnson, B., & Cloonan, M. (2009). *Dark side of the tune: Popular music and violence*. Surrey, England: Ashgate.

Kistler, M., Rodgers, K. B., Power, T., Austin, E. W., & Hill, L. G. (2010). Adolescents and music media: Toward an involvement–mediational model of consumption and self-concept. *Journal of Research on Adolescence*, **20**(3), 616–30.

Mahns, W. (2002). Psychodynamic function of music in analytical music therapy with children. In J. T. Eschen (Ed.), *Analytical music therapy* (pp. 95–103). London: Jessica Kingsley Publishers.

McFerran, K. S. (2010). *Adolescents, music and music therapy: Methods and techniques for clinicians, educators and students*. London: Jessica Kingsley Publishers.

McFerran, K. S., & Baird, K. (2013). Is music really my best friend?: Reflections of two maturing women on one's relationship with music. In L. O. Bonde, E. Ruud, M. S. Skånland, & G. Trondalen (Eds.), *Musical life stories: Narratives on health musicking* (Vol. 6, pp. 117–38). Oslo, Norway: Norwegian Academy of Music.

McFerran, K. S., Garrido, S., & Saarikallio, S. (2013). A critical interpretive synthesis of the literature linking music and adolescent depression. *Youth and Society, Online First*, doi: 10.1177/0044118X13501343.

McFerran, K. S., & Hunt, M. (2008). Learning from experiences in action: Music in schools for coping with grief and loss. *Educational Action Research*, **16**(1), 43–53.

McFerran, K. S., & Rickson, D. J. (2014). Community music therapy in schools: Realigning with the needs of contemporary students, staff and systems. *International Journal of Community Music*, in press (Special Issue on Community Music Therapy).

McFerran, K. S., & Saarikallio, S. (2013). Depending on music to make me feel better: Who is responsible for the ways young people appropriate music for health benefits? *The Arts in Psychotherapy*, **41**(1), 89–97. Retrieved from <http://dx.doi.org/10.1016/j.aip.2013.11.007>.

McFerran-Skewes, K. (2000). From the mouths of babes: The response of six younger bereaved teenagers to the experience of psychodynamic group music therapy. *Australian Journal of Music Therapy*, **11**(1), 3–22.

McNeill, W. (1995). *Keeping together in time: Dance and drill in human history*. Cambridge, MA: Harvard University Press.

Norris, J. (2012). *Marching to the drums: A history of military drums and drummers*. Stround, Gloucestershire: Spellmount.

North, A. C., & Hargreaves, D. J. (2002). Age variations in judgments of 'great' art works. *British Journal of Psychology*, **93**(3), 397–405.

North, A. C., & Hargreaves, D. J. (2008). *The social and applied psychology of music*. New York: Oxford University Press.

O'Callaghan, C., & Grocke, D. (2009). Lyric analysis research in music therapy: Rationales, methods and representations. *The Arts in Psychotherapy*, **36**, 320–8.

Popper, K. (1959/80). *The logic of scientific discovery*. New York: Routledge.

Purdon, C. (2002). The role of music in analytical music therapy: Music as a carrier of stories. In J. Eschen (Ed.), *Analytical music therapy* (pp. 104–15). London: Jessica Kingsley Publishers.

Rolvsjord, R. (2010). *Resource-oriented music therapy*. Gilsum, NH: Barcelona Publishers.

Rolvsjord, R., Gold, C., & Stige, B. (2005). Therapeutic principles for resource-oriented music therapy: A contextual approach to the field of mental health. *Nordic Journal of Music Therapy*, **14**(1), online appendix.

Saarikallio, S. (2011). Music as emotional self-regulation throughout adulthood. *Psychology of Music*, **39**(3), 307–27, doi: 10.1177/0305735610374894.

Saarikallio, S., & Erkkila, J. (2007). The role of music in adolescents' mood regulation. *Psychology of Music*, **35**(1), 88–109.

Schwartz, K. D., & Fouts, G. T. (2003). Music preferences, personality style, and developmental issues of adolescents. *Journal of Youth and Adolescence*, **32**(3), 205–10.

Skanland, M. S. (2011). Use of MP3-players as a coping resource. *Music and Arts in Action*, **3**(2), 15–33.

Sloboda, J. A., & O'Neill, S. A. (2001). Emotions in everyday listening to music. In P. N. Juslin & J. A. Sloboda (Eds.), *Music and emotion: Theory and research* (Vol., pp. 415–30). Oxford: Oxford University Press.

Solli, H. P., Rolvsjord, R., & Borg, M. (2013). Toward understanding music therapy as a recovery-oriented practice within mental health care: A meta-synthesis of service users' experiences. *Journal of Music Therapy*, **50**(4), 244–73, doi: 10.1093/jmt/50.4.244.

Stige, B. (2002a). *Culture-centered music therapy*. Gilsum, NH: Barcelona Publishers.

Stige, B. (2002b). The relentless roots of community music therapy. *Voices: A World Forum for Music Therapy*, **2**(3). Retrieved from <http://www.voices.no/mainissues/Voices2(3)stige.html>.

Stige, B., & Aarø, L. E. (2012). *Invitation to community music therapy*. New York: Ashgate.

Stige, B., Ansdell, G., Elefant, C., & Pavlicevic, M. (2010). *Where music helps: Community music therapy in action and reflection*. Surrey, UK: Ashgate.

Van den Tol, A. J. M., & Edwards, J. (2011). Exploring a rationale for choosing to listen to sad music when feeling sad. *Psychology of Music*, **23**(1), doi: 10.1177/0305735611430433.

Van den Tol, A. J. M., & Edwards, J. (2014). Listening to sad music in adverse situations: How music selection strategies relate to self-regulatory goals, listening effects, and mood enhancement. *Psychology of Music, Online First*, January 29, doi: 10.1177/0305735613517410.

Van Heeswyk, P. (1997). *Analysing adolescence*. London: Sheldon Press.

Vuoskoski, J. K., & Eerola, T. (2012). Can sad music really make you sad? Indirect measures of affective states induced by music and autobiographical memories. *Psychology of Aesthetics, Creativity, and the Arts*, **6**(3), 204–13.

Section 4

Skills

Chapter 22

Playing an instrument

Gary E. McPherson, Jane W. Davidson,
and Paul Evans

Playing an instrument: Introduction

One of the most common and popular ways a child can be involved in music is to play an instrument, so it is important to include a chapter on this aspect of musical development in this volume. Traditionally, literature on this topic has focused on performance skills and the acquisition of technique on particular instruments. More recently, however, this emphasis has been broadened through research dealing with cognitive aspects of learning (such as values and beliefs about music, the reasons children engage with music, and the way they structure their practice) and social aspects of learning (the relationships children have with their teachers, parents, and peers), and how these interact to impact children's ongoing musical development. In this chapter we focus on this latter body of evidence in order to explain some of the underlying principles that govern how children develop their capacity to mature into performing musicians.

The chapter begins with a description of the various catalysts that shape children's initial motives to commence learning and their choice of an instrument when they begin formal training. We then explore what children expect and value from their learning and how this aspect of motivation influences their subsequent musical development. This leads to a discussion of the types of strategies children need to acquire in order to become successful performers, and the playing habits and practice techniques that either enhance or impede their progress. A final section deals with the help and encouragement children need to receive from their parents if they are to develop into successful, self-regulated learners. The chapter reviews instrumental learning within the Western musical tradition, based on the available literature and popularity of these instruments worldwide. It is our hope, however, that some of the basic principles we propose can be extrapolated and applied to the learning of different types of instruments within other musical styles and genres.

Starting age and early experiences

Within reason, the adage "the earlier the better" is probably appropriate as a general guide to when children can start learning an instrument. In practice, however, there are many differences between instruments, with physical maturation and mental attention span often being used by teachers and parents to guide decisions on whether a child is ready to begin formal lessons. Children learning the keyboard can start as early as 2 or 3 years of age, preferably with informal play activities. For strings, some Suzuki teachers recommend no earlier than the age of 3, when smaller-sized instruments ensure that the physique to play these instruments does not cause problems for children with particularly small fingers. But for brass and woodwind instruments which require more physical strength it is unlikely that children will have much success until at least 6 or

7 years of age, when they have acquired the physical ability (and the teeth) to maintain a correct embouchure and move the air through the instrument in order to produce a characteristic tone.

Musical instruments are now commonplace in childhood. While much of the nineteenth century saw advances in manufacturing that enabled widespread piano ownership within the middle classes, the twentieth and early twenty-first centuries have seen the mass production of inexpensive acoustic and electronic instruments such as electronic keyboards, acoustic guitars, ukuleles, toy pianos, and recorders. The adoption of the acoustic guitar and electronic keyboard parallels the broadening of the music curriculum in school systems, particularly in curriculum models such as those in the UK and Australia. These curriculums emphasize music composing and performing with an emphasis on broad access for students, rather than traditional curriculums that tend to be taken up only by those who have the opportunity for specialized training in an instrument. Unfortunately, this has led many schools to adopt the recorder as a means to providing inexpensive and accessible music performance opportunities in schools. The inherently unappealing and shrill sounds produced by these instruments may be the reason children regard them as the least popular of all instruments (O'Neill, 2001), not to mention the ironic difficulty in producing a pleasing tone on the instrument. With a broad curriculum, the keyboard and guitar, combined with informal music-learning pedagogies, have proven more successful (Green, 2008).

Children who play such instruments at a young age often do not take lessons, because they are simply expected to use it in school, or if they possess one at home, it is used for fun rather than for serious study. However, these instruments can provide initial and unthreatening points of departure, and so their merits should not be underestimated. Indeed, Davidson et al. (1998) found that all of their 258 young music learners had played one of these instruments as a way of engaging informally with music in a playful and exploratory way before specializing on their chosen instrument. Looking back on their learning, some students regarded these earliest experiences as a basis for them to experiment with, get to know, understand, and enjoy music. In the case of one particularly enthusiastic student—Carl—the recorder was eventually adopted as the main instrument, and he progressed rapidly (Davidson & Burland, 2006). He became obsessed with achieving and fascinated by the way in which he could manipulate the pitch and timbre of the instrument's sound.

Of course, children who begin learning traditional instruments, such as ensemble instruments or the piano, are generally much more likely to take lessons and participate in a structured learning environment right from the start. They can develop a liking for an initially disliked instrument, or a hatred for one they previously liked. In the work of Sloboda et al. (1996) it was discovered that some of the most successful young learners were those who had been through a range of musical instruments, often settling on a particular instrument for pragmatic reasons. For instance, one of their students—Lisa—changed from violin to viola at the age of 12 years, realizing that she was far more likely to have an orchestral career playing the less commonly learned viola (Davidson & Burland, 2006). In this case, her participation in music was more important than the instrument itself. But, this is not necessarily the case for all individuals.

The decision to begin

In formal music programs offered at schools, the teacher's decision about which instrument might be learned is often dictated by what instruments are available for study, plus also what instruments need to be assigned to maintain a balanced instrumentation in the school's ensembles. Typically, however, a parent's view will often evolve from an entirely different perspective. Many will be concerned about the speed at which their child will be able to learn the instrument. Very often they will also consider more pragmatic issues, such as whether the child will be able to continue learning the same instrument and perform with good ensembles after entering high school. In many cases, parents will also be concerned about the cost involved in learning, both in terms of the expense of ongoing lessons and maintenance of an instrument, as well as the eventual cost of purchasing a quality instrument if the child continues playing.

Market research by Cooke and Morris (1996) helps identify some of the important motivational concerns, from the child's perspective, that impact on long-term success in learning an instrument. They found that English children aged 5 and 6 were the most enthusiastic for expressing a desire to learn. Almost half of their sample of 5- and 6-year-olds (48%) said that they were likely to start learning in the near future. But this enthusiasm is short-lived because by the age of 7 less than half the children surveyed expressed a desire to learn an instrument, and this remained stable at about a quarter of non-playing children until 11 years. By the age of 14 only 4% of the children said that they were likely to start learning an instrument. These results need to be placed in perspective, however, because they depend on the type of instrument and music to be learned. Many rock guitarists, for example, typically do not begin playing until they reach their early teenage years, but then, if they are highly motivated, make progress very quickly as a result of engaging in many hours of practice alone, with friends, and in bands (Gullberg & Brändström, 2004).

Choosing an instrument

Various intrinsic and extrinsic factors impact on why a child will choose one instrument over others. Some are intrinsically attracted to a particular instrument because of a liking for its sounds, or how it looks and feels (e.g., Boyle, DeCarbo, & Fortney, 1993; Delzell & Leppla, 1992; McPherson, Davidson, & Faulkner, 2012; O'Neill & Boulton, 1996). When difficulties such as trying to get a sound out of the instrument, or carrying it around in a large and heavy case become apparent, this genuine intrinsic appeal of the way the instrument sounds, looks, or feels can help to sustain engagement with it.

In other cases, children may begin learning because of extrinsic reasons such as wanting to emulate a model they admire, such as a famous musician. A more common reason is to join with friends who are learning at the same time. Indeed, children will very often become interested in joining a school or community musical ensemble because they wish to keep up with their friends who are also beginning (MacKenzie, 1991; McPherson et al., 2012). Other important extrinsic motivational influences include significant others, including encouragement from a family member or teacher (Sloboda, Davidson, & Howe, 1994). Sosniak's (1985) landmark study of concert pianists, for instance, shows that some of the highest achievers were reluctantly persuaded by a parent to start learning, and it was years before they became passionately committed and intrinsically motivated to continue their own development and decide to become professional pianists. Unfortunately, the opposite can also be true: some children in Evans, McPherson, and Davidson's (2013) study enjoyed being in a band program with their peers in primary school, but by the time their music program in high school did not live up to the same social experience, they had not internalized their motivation for learning and subsequently ceased.

Many children have been grateful in later life for having parents who insisted that they learn a particular instrument. In general terms, where motivation of this type is externally directed, rather than internally driven, sustaining an interest is more difficult. If learning is merely to please a parent or teacher, a child is unlikely to make much progress or to show much enthusiasm beyond the initial stages of development (Evans et al., 2013). This is even more apparent in situations where children encounter difficulties mastering the complex physical and mental skills involved in learning.

In terms of the advice given by teachers to their students, physical factors also appear to have some role in instrumental selection. A very large underbite or protruding or irregularly shaped teeth may cause endless frustration to a wind instrument player, in which case teachers may advise the child to choose an instrument that does not require the use of the embouchure. But advice must be given with caution, for a casual glance at almost any professional ensemble will show that many players do not possess "ideal" physical characteristics for playing their instrument. The wonderful jazz trumpeter Chet Baker managed to play despite having lost many of his teeth, for instance.

It is therefore clear that no single factor will fully explain why a child will decide to learn an instrument. This is why our longitudinal research (McPherson et al., 2012) with beginning instrumentalists across the first three years of their learning has tried to clarify the blend of factors that motivate each individual child to commence learning. Many of our 7- and 8-year-old beginners said they began because they believed learning an instrument might be fun, exciting, or enjoyable. Their observations were often based on evidence of having seen and heard musical ensembles at their school and in the community, or knowing friends and siblings who were also involved as musicians. Indeed, these students who had a strong presence of music ensembles in their school and community were more likely to persist after three years of learning (Evans & McPherson, 2015; McPherson et al., 2012). When asked to explain why they selected their particular instrument, almost a third of the children said that they liked the sound of the instrument, thus confirming the important intrinsic reason already cited. Children also indicated, however, that the choice of instrument was influenced by what they perceived to be easy instruments to play, whether they liked the look of the instrument, whether they felt it was an appropriate size for them, or whether their friends were also playing the same instrument (see also Boyle et al., 1993; O'Neill & Boulton, 1996).

As with other studies, our research has revealed gender associations with boys tending to choose so-called masculine instruments such as trumpets and trombones, and girls selecting more feminine instruments like flutes and clarinets (Abeles & Porter, 1978; Bruce & Kemp, 1993; Conway, 2000; Delzell & Leppla, 1992; Harrison & O'Neill, 2003; O'Neill & Boulton, 1996), even though these types of associations are being increasingly challenged. One such example can be viewed on the TV show "The Simpsons," where Lisa Simpson plays the saxophone.

In summary, the general evidence of our study and other related literature suggests that children not only have a projected belief about which instruments are more or less easy to learn, but also a specific view of themselves in relation to their capacity to successfully master each particular instrument, with these impressions often being influenced by gender stereotypes.

Personal expectations and values

It might be inferred from this that children will either possess the right motivation or not to engage with music learning. To some degree this may be true, with some individuals genuinely being more intrinsically driven on specific tasks than others. In our view, a more appropriate way of thinking about this is to understand the personal beliefs that children hold and that are shaped by their experiences of the world around them. These include the expectations and values children bring to their first instrumental lessons that subsequently shape and influence their future development. For example, in our study we asked the children to explain to us before they began their instrument how long they expected to play (McPherson, 2001). Results show that they were able to differentiate between their interest in learning a musical instrument, the importance to them of being good at music, whether they thought their learning would be useful to their short- and long-term goals, and the amount of effort they felt would be needed to continue improving. Their responses were no different to what we would have expected if they were taking up any other activity. Many seemed intrinsically interested, but did not feel that they would want to play the instrument all of their lives. Others seemed more extrinsically motivated, but recognized the value of learning for their overall education. For most of the children, learning an instrument was something useful to do while they were at school, but something that would be of far less value in later life (Evans & McPherson, 2015; see also Evans, Chapter 17). Only a small number suggested that they wanted to become professional musicians (McPherson, 2001; McPherson et al., 2012), and indeed only one of the 157 students in the study appears to have pursued any professional (albeit part-time) opportunities as a musician 15 years later.

Our results are consistent with research in academic subjects that seek to understand what children expect and value in their learning (Eccles, 2005; Wigfield & Cambria, 2010). This work demonstrated that children are goal-oriented: they choose and gravitate toward activities in which they believe they can achieve and be successful. Their behavior is directly connected to the personal beliefs they hold about the activity, such that their motivation is a product of expectations they hold for attaining success in learning and the subjective values they have for the task. More specifically, value can be understood on the following four dimensions:

- *Interest*—the personal satisfaction gained when playing and practicing alone and with others, plus the love for the repertoire learned.
- *Importance*—the degree to which learning the instrument fits with personal goals about what the child hopes to be good at.
- *Usefulness*—whether learning the instruments is constructive and functional for what the child wishes to do, both now and in the future.
- *Difficulty*—whether the outcomes of the learning process are worth the effort and investment required.

Within the context of a music-performance examination, expectancies for success may be particularly important. McCormick and McPherson's (2007) study of children and young people aged 9 to 19 found that their expectations for success played a vital role in their achievement. As would be expected, those who had received higher grades in earlier examinations attained higher grades. But importantly, the statistical model was stronger when also considering students' beliefs about their success. In other words, the study found that students are accurate in their expectations about what they will achieve, but the beliefs themselves contributed to their success above and beyond their actual prior performance.

More broadly, beyond expectations about success, the length of children's musical engagement seems to be influenced strongly by their expectations for music in their lives more generally. We found this to be the case in two of our studies on children's musical identities. In the first, we asked children, before they began learning, how long they thought they would be playing their instrument for. There was a range of responses: some said they would play their instrument for a few months and then give up, while others articulated a view of their personal identities as musicians well into adulthood. The longer-term view turned out to be very helpful: combined with the amount of practice they did, a long-term musical identity sustained children's involvement for longer compared with a short-term musical identity (Evans & McPherson, 2015). The second of our musical identity studies (Evans & McPherson, in press) was a qualitative interview study of adolescents who were highly engaged in music learning and had high abilities. We found that those who had gone through a process of considering the role of music in their lives well into the future, and those who made firm yet flexible commitments about that role, had more adaptive and coherent plans for their futures. Students who experienced anxiety or pressure in thinking about their future, or were not able to articulate their music learning in terms of its place in their musical identity, tended to have disjointed or vague plans.

Sustaining involvement

As already shown, personal beliefs associated with a desire to achieve not only influence children's motivation to continue playing, but also shape their identities as individuals and their orientations as learners (see also Evans, Chapter 17). Two of the more important of these learning orientations explain why some individuals strive to achieve while others are prone to give up and deliberately avoid activities with which they believe they cannot become competent. The first of these, *adaptive mastery-oriented* students, have a tendency to continue working hard when faced with failure and enjoy putting effort into achieving their goals. These types of learners remain focused on trying to achieve, despite difficulties that might come their way. In contrast, *maladaptive helpless-oriented* students often fail to establish reasonable goals for themselves, or goals that are within their reach. When they feel that the situation is out of their control and that nothing can be done to alleviate the situation, they tend to avoid further challenges, lower their expectations, experience negative emotions, give up, and perform more poorly in the future (Dweck, 2000; O'Neill & McPherson, 2002).

Some evidence of these types of orientations as they might apply in music comes from O'Neill (1997), who studied 6- to 10-year-old children during their first year of learning an instrument. Before beginning instruction, these children were given a problem-solving task and procedure used to assess their motivational patterns (O'Neill & Sloboda, 1997). Some of the children were classified as *maladaptive helpless-oriented* because they avoided challenges, showed low persistence, and performed poorly when faced with failure. Before they commenced learning, this group was compared with another group of children who were defined as *adaptive mastery-oriented*, in that they were more inclined to persist with their efforts following failure or experiencing difficulties.

O'Neill (1997) believes that studying these two motivational patterns is important, because bright and skilled children can display either orientation. Importantly, her results demonstrate how children who displayed mastery-oriented motivational patterns prior to commencing their instrument progressed to a higher level of achievement at the end of their first year of learning than children who displayed maladaptive helpless-oriented motivational patterns. Interpreting these findings, O'Neill suggests that the less successful students learned to feel helpless because of a tendency to focus their attention on their existing level of performance, with the result that they could not see that the difficulties they were having now could be overcome in the future. Because of this, they tended to feel that any further effort would be futile. In contrast, the children with mastery orientations were more focused on how to increase their competence so they could perform better in the future. Consequently, they viewed failure as a normal part of their learning instead of something that should be avoided.

Thus, we can see how children's self-beliefs shape how they see the role of music learning in their lives. This is particularly important in an area as difficult and taxing for young children as learning an instrument, where the physical, mental, and emotional effort needed to sustain long-term engagement requires a great deal of resilience and persistence. The personal beliefs that children hold for their own competence and capacity to master tasks therefore have a major effect on their subsequent ability to persist in the face of difficulties, stressful situations, and competing interests (Bandura, 1997; Hendricks, 2014; McCormick & McPherson, 2007).

In addition to these results, we also compared the comments of the children who continued learning with those who ceased playing across the first three years of learning (McPherson & Davidson, 2002). Children who ceased learning typically had unrealistically high expectations about how much practice they would undertake before commencing lessons. After they started, and the reality of learning set in, they then consistently undertook far less practice than their peers who chose to continue.

The results outlined here demonstrate that children bring many preconceptions to their first lessons, and that their progress is shaped by their expectations for being able to cope and succeed with their learning, combined with the value they place on the activity as something they will enjoy doing. This does not mean, however, that children's initial motivations are fixed and that positive attitudes cannot emerge and evolve over time. As we have seen in the Sosniak (1985) study mentioned earlier, it is only after extensive experience with music that many young learners will develop a lasting desire and commitment for performing beyond their school years.

Task-related cognitive strategies for performing

A hallmark of successful learners is the quality of the mental strategies they apply to monitor and control their learning (Zimmerman, 2008). Being able to choose and apply appropriate task-related strategies may help these individuals learn faster because they are able to integrate new knowledge and skills more quickly.

Identifying the range of musically appropriate mental strategies beginners and intermediate-level students adopt when learning to play an instrument has been a key concern of the first author in his work with beginner- through to advanced-level instrumentalists (McPherson, 2005). At the heart of this research is the search to understand what children are thinking as they solve various kinds of musical problems and how the sophistication of these task-related mental strategies impacts on their overall skill development. In these studies children are typically asked to explain what they are doing in their minds in order to prepare for or complete a variety of tasks, such as performing music that they have rehearsed at home, sight-reading, playing from memory, playing by ear, and improvising.

Importantly, this line of research suggests that many strategies concerned with learning to play an instrument are domain specific and therefore quite different to the strategies children would use to solve problems in other areas of their learning. This explains why some children experience problems very early in their development, as they try to adopt a strategy from another area of their learning or an entirely inappropriate strategy to perform on an instrument (McPherson, 2005). As an example, in one study, the beginners were given a short piece of music to memorize, to assess their ability to process musical notation and perform this from memory once the notation had been removed. A variety of strategies were reported by the children, including many unmusical strategies such as staring at the notation to memorize the contour of the melody or inwardly saying the names of the notes of the phrase over and over to themselves. As an example, one beginner commented:

> I picture the notes in my mind. I take a photograph and keep it in my mind. That's what my mum told me to do with phone numbers.

In contrast, the more successful learners employed more sophisticated, musically appropriate task strategies for each of the styles of performance very early in their development and as a result went on to achieve at a much higher level than their peers (McPherson, 2005). The best strategies children used for playing from memory and by ear, for example, were focused on what the music should sound like, and incorporated the physical actions required to produce the sound on their instrument. This was achieved through a type of mental practice where the instrumentalist worked holistically to sing and mentally "play" through the piece while he or she was studying the score (for the memorization tasks) or listening to the recording (for the ear playing tasks).

In a similar way, the highest-achieving sight-readers were those children who took the most strategic approach, by making themselves aware of the finer details of the piece in the moments before they commenced playing. In a strategic fashion, they typically studied the first measure to get a feel for how the piece started and what tempo might be appropriate, identified the key- and time-signatures, scanned the music to identify possible obstacles, directed and maintained their attention throughout the performance in order to anticipate problems and to observe musical indications such as expression markings and articulation, and monitored and self-evaluated their performance in order to correct errors (McPherson, 1994, 2005).

More broadly based strategies were also identified for children's rehearsal of repertoire they learn during their home practice (McPherson, 2005). In the study with our beginners, for example, the most successful learners were children who actively kept track of what they were learning by using a practice diary to take notes about what they needed to practice and how this might be accomplished. They also organized their practice sessions by focusing on the repertoire they needed to practice first in order to improve their playing before moving on to pieces they could already play or enjoyed playing (in contrast to children who organized their practice by playing for enjoyment first and improvement later).

Additional strategies included a more strategic approach to problems they encountered with the repertoire they were learning, such that better players displayed a more concentrated ability to refine their playing (e.g., "First I play it once and see how good I am, then I practice it again and again until it's at a standard that I can take to my tutor"), in contrast to less capable musicians who reported inefficient task strategies (e.g., "I play my pieces through just once. I want to get them over with"). Finally, more strategic and capable players were also more inclined to self-diagnose and correct their playing (e.g., "I try to think about how my teacher played it, then go back over it slowly and then speed it up"). This is in contrast to poor learners who displayed virtually no evidence of being sufficiently motivated to try to improve their playing (e.g., "I don't try to fix it, I go through everything once") (McPherson, 2005, p. 18).

The quality of children's performance may also be directly related to the quality of their thinking when playing their instrument (McPherson, 2005). Unfortunately, by the end of the third year of learning, there were extremely wide differences between the children's performance abilities across the skills studied. Of particular importance is the finding that children who established *ear-to-hand* coordination skills very early in their development for aural forms of performance such as playing from memory and by ear, and *eye-to-ear-to-hand* coordination skills for visual forms of performance such as sight-reading, went on to achieve at the highest level and experienced far fewer problems with their learning compared to their less strategic peers (McPherson, 2005; McPherson & Gabrielsson, 2002).

Analysis of what the teachers were covering in their lessons and the types of books used in lessons suggests that many children were picking these strategies up implicitly, rather than through direct instruction from their teachers (McPherson, 1994, 2005). This point reinforces the importance for children to be exposed to quality early experiences in music so that they not only establish proper playing habits, but also develop their capacity to think musically as they learn to coordinate their eyes, ears, and hands, and to think in sound (Rostvall & West, 2003). It also highlights the need for instruction that more explicitly links thinking skills and task-oriented strategies with actual physical performance, an element of learning that is often lacking in instrumental tuition.

Engagement with the instrument

Without doubt, one of the most important parts of learning an instrument is the time and effort put into practicing by children to develop their skills between lessons. Dictionaries define practice as involving repetition of exercises to improve and develop skill. But this limited use of the word practice, stressing the repetitive aspect of training, is far from suited to music (Hallam, 1997a). A better approach is to think of practice as encompassing the range of thoughts and behaviors that children engage in "that are intended to influence their motivational or affective state, or the way in which they select, organize, integrate, and rehearse new knowledge and skills" (Jørgensen, 2004, p. 85).

The key function of practice is to develop the internal memory representations necessary to understand and execute a musical task. This involves, as discussed earlier, various elements such as sight-reading, aural, and physical skill and dexterity, coupled with a sense of musical time and intonation in order to bring cohesion and accuracy, in addition to knowledge of musical style and form. The ability to generate and use mental representations efficiently is critical to instrumental learning, and the degree to which these representations have been acquired is clearly reflected in the learner's ability at any given point in time. Indeed, this is true of learning in any domain, where schematic knowledge is increasingly automated, allowing learners to recall mental representations quickly and effortlessly. Consider the following contrasting examples: a beginner piano student's mental representation of a piece of music might consist of a sequence of difficult and laborious fingering combinations, while a more advanced player might also represent the underlying chord progression along with some expressive information, some aural image of the sounds, and perhaps even a visual representation of how the score looks. Of course, the degree of knowledge and experience shapes the performer's goals and level of achievement (the child being far less fluent and expressive than an expert soloist, for example). So, one of the more important aims of practice, therefore, is for the child to acquire as much knowledge and experience as possible, in order to be able eventually to produce technically fluent and musically expressive performances of the literature he or she aims to play.

Generally, skilled musicians exert a great deal more effort and concentration during their practice than less skilled musicians, and are more likely to image, monitor, and control their playing by focusing their attention on what they are practicing and how it can be improved (Ericsson, 1997). In other words, they use current information to develop more sophisticated mental representations about music and how to perform it. Williamon and Valentine (1998) have demonstrated that these individuals are able to enjoy the more pleasurable aspects of practice (e.g., experimenting with phrasing, dynamics, and expressiveness) at the same time as engaging with the taxing requirements of dexterity, coordination, and so on. They therefore appear to be more intrinsically motivated. In other words, the challenges of acquiring technical skill are for the pleasure of the ultimate expressive ends.

Developing self-regulated practice habits

Studies with young learners show that their home practice is very different from the picture depicted here. As with any complex skill, it can take children years to develop to a level where their practice is efficient and effective. Unfortunately, many beginners have great difficulty moving beyond the overwhelming challenges of coordination. It is not surprising, therefore, that after the initial burst of excitement has worn off, practicing a musical instrument can cause a mix of emotions for children, many of which may not seem particularly pleasant. These negative connotations are the reason why some teachers do not use the term "practice," preferring instead to talk about "music time" or "music play" as one way of refocusing this activity to try to make it more interesting and enjoyable for the student.

A growing body of research has helped us to understand some of the processes that young children adopt in their musical practice. In our study with young beginners, a large proportion of practice time (in many cases over 90%) was spent simply playing through a piece from beginning to end, without the child adopting a specific strategy for performance improvement (McPherson & Renwick, 2001). Barry and Hallam (2002) suggest that this is because beginners have not developed appropriate internal representations to identify and correct their own mistakes and are therefore not always aware when they are going wrong. For the same reason, they also are unable to foresee the kinds of long- and short-term practice goals that would help them to structure their learning in order to attain successful and rewarding experiences.

Hallam (1997a,b) has undertaken studies that attempt to clarify the content of individual practice. Ranking student achievements, she has demonstrated that at the least successful level students focus their practice only on the early sections of the music, without completing the task. In the next level they play through the music without stopping to correct their performance. Following this, they stop when a mistake is made, but only to correct and repeat single notes in contrast to the next level, where short sections are repeated before they are able to practice larger sections. Finally, the most sophisticated practice occurs when students are able to play through the work to obtain a general overview before identifying difficult passages that can be isolated for more concentrated attention.

Definitions of effective practice should, according to Hallam (1997a), differ depending on the level of expertise acquired. Beginners need support in order to develop internal aural representations of music that they are learning, and in their early stages of development, repetition helps to develop the basic skills that lay a foundation for more advanced levels of skill development later on. Providing a variety of repertoire and pieces that the learner is already familiar with, plus repertoire that can be easily assimilated aurally, can also help to motivate children to be more strategic with their practice. In this way, repetition may be an effective practice strategy for beginners who are trying to assimilate a variety of complex skills. The adoption of more expert practice habits is probably therefore unrealistic, given the underdeveloped knowledge base of most beginners (Hallam, 1997a,b).

Of critical importance in Hallam's (1997a) opinion is the need for teachers to demonstrate and model the processes of effective practice, such as how to:

◆ obtain an overview of the work,

◆ identify difficulties,

◆ select appropriate strategies,

◆ work on sections and integrate them into a whole,

◆ monitor progress,

◆ set personal goals, and

◆ self-evaluate progress.

According to Hallam (1997a), as students' expertise increases, they can be challenged to perform more difficult and more complex repertoire. As their overall mental representational skills develop, they will be more capable of reflecting on their own style of practice as well as how, and in what ways, they can change their practice habits in order to produce better results. At this time also, they should be encouraged to develop their interpretative abilities, through listening, researching, and analyzing a broad range of music. Obviously, the quality of teaching plays an important facilitative role in making each of these facets of a musician's development possible.

Thus, in order to practice and so develop skills more quickly and effectively, students need to become "self-regulated learners" in the sense that they need to learn how to plan, monitor, and control aspects of their own practice. This need is addressed by an approach known as *self-regulated learning*. This is why the first author's research over the past two decades has concentrated on the context-specific set of processes that children draw upon as they promote their own learning (McPherson & Renwick, 2011; McPherson & Zimmerman, 2011). The normal cycle of development occurs as children gradually acquire the knowledge required to be able to manage their practice and learning independently. Self-regulated learning processes in music may be characterized according to the following dimensions:

Motive: Vicarious or direct reinforcement by others leads to children being able to establish their own personal goals, reinforce their own learning, and develop a sense of purpose and confidence in their own ability to perform.

Method: The strategies that children are taught or observe from others lead to them develop a repertoire of ways for dealing with problems in their playing and also the ability to self-initiate ways of practicing that will enhance their development.

Time: Children's use of time is socially planned and managed through suggestions and reminders from others (such as parents and teachers), leading to them eventually being able to take responsibility for, plan, and manage the amount of time they devote to their practice.

Behavior: Performance is socially monitored and evaluated before children are able to self-monitor and evaluate their own progress.

Physical environment: The physical environment in which practice occurs (e.g., lounge/bedroom, use of music stand) is often structured by parents as a foundation for the child to eventually be able to control and shape the physical conditions in which they feel most comfortable practicing.

Social: Support for practice is provided by significant others such as parents, teachers, and peers who provide emotional and psychological support, leading to the child being able to directly seek help by themselves.

Practicing to improve versus practicing for fun

Another way of understanding why some children make rapid progress while others have difficulties or avoid practice is to examine the actual repertoire practiced. Children can practice repertoire they need to learn for their teacher or the next performance situation as well as pieces they have already mastered and can already play. Some children even report a form of musical doodling: activities that are usually undertaken for the pleasure of the musical experience alone, rather than to refine specific skills.

Sloboda and Davidson (1996) report that high-achieving learners tend to do significantly greater amounts of formal practice, such as scales, pieces, and technical exercises, than their less successful peers. But the same learners also report more informal practice, such as playing their favorite pieces by ear, playing for fun, or improvising. As reported earlier in the section dealing with strategies for performing rehearsed repertoire, children who organize their practice by starting on the repertoire that they need to learn for their next lesson or upcoming performance before moving on to repertoire they enjoy and can already play tend to progress faster than children who organize their practice the other way around. However, children need to find a balance between these two elements—the discipline of practicing to improve versus the freedom of practicing for personal enjoyment (McPherson, 2005). Both aspects of practice are extremely important and relate back to the motivational issues covered earlier: that musical progression is most efficient when learning involves a sense of individual empowerment, such that the child enjoys and values learning and expects to become a successful musician.

We know also, that an important way of fostering positive motivation is to take advantage of the students' own individual goals, interests, and self-perceptions. This was clearly apparent in another phase of our study where we analyzed videotapes of a young child's practice to examine the efficiency of her practice when rehearsing repertoire assigned by her teacher as compared to pieces she chose to learn herself (Renwick & McPherson, 2002). The practice efficiency of repertoire she chose to learn herself was markedly superior to literature she had been assigned by her teacher, with the result that she was able to connect to a more advanced stage of development, as she included more varied strategies into her practice such as silent fingerings, silent thinking, and singing. These findings are consistent with other research showing that children who tend to be more cognitively engaged when practicing, by thinking about what they are playing and actively trying to improve their playing, tend to be more motivated and do more practice (McPherson & McCormick, 1999). A clear finding, however, is that allowing students choice in their repertoire can lead to positive improvements in their intrinsic motivation and task involvement (Renwick & Reeve, 2012). This highlights a major problem that occurs in much teaching: When students are always learning pieces that are selected by their teachers they may start to feel that they are learning these pieces to satisfy their teacher, rather than because they want to learn them. Obviously, in such situations, motivation and efficiency of practice will quickly diminish.

Parental support

An important thread in the educational literature studies connections between the family and the environment in which a child receives instruction (McPherson, 2009). The socialization process is bidirectional because parents convey important messages to their children even though the level at which these messages are accepted, received, and internalized varies between children (Grusec, Goodnow, & Kuczynski, 2000). More recently this literature has focused on two dimensions of the parent–child relationship: *parental practices* and *parental styles* (Spera, 2005). Parental practices refer to specific behaviors used by parents to socialize their children, such as helping with practice or by attending concerts. Parental styles are concerned more with the emotional climate in which parents raise their children and act to moderate the relationship between parenting practices and children's achievement. For example, parents who are authoritarian (i.e., strict, expect obedience, and assert their power) when monitoring homework are more likely to inhibit their child's school performance, whereas parents who foster a mature attitude through bidirectional communication involving explanations of their behavior and encouragement of independence are more likely to facilitate their child's performance (McPherson, 2009).

An important area of research related to parental practices investigates how parents help their children acquire the necessary skills to complete their homework: by modeling the task as the child moves through the assignments, by direct instruction such as questioning and drill and practice activities, and by reinforcement through the use of praise and encouraging comments (Spera, 2005). If this line of research is compared to musical practice, it becomes clear that the only support parents can give to a child who is learning an instrument, especially if they do not play an instrument themselves, is the last of these categories.

The extent to which children rely on their parents' support and encouragement is evident in a number of studies on children's homework, which show that very young children up to grade 2 or 3 tend not to view homework as their own responsibility (Warton, 1997). While young children may possess an understanding of the importance of doing homework as a means of improving their competence, they often fail to realize the importance of taking personal responsibility to initiate practice, preferring instead to rely on their parents' reminders (Warton, 1997). Many children therefore need constant support in the form of reminders and checking from both parents and teachers over a number of years before they can develop the self-regulatory competence needed to take personal responsibility to complete it by themselves. A critical related issue here is that these interactions—reminders, support, checking—need to occur in a way that supports the child's sense of autonomy, rather than in a controlling or demanding way (Grolnick, 2009; McPherson, 2009).

We found very similar evidence in our study of young music learners (McPherson & Davidson, 2002), with one important exception. Whereas many parents will continue to remind their child to do his or her homework for however many years it takes, the support our children received from their parents, in the form of reminders and more general support for their musical practice, tended to drop off toward the end of the children's first year of learning—at the very time they needed ongoing encouragement to continue across the difficult period of adjusting to their instrument and gaining sufficient skill to continue into their second year of learning. Unfortunately, very soon after the children commenced learning, some of their mothers began to form judgments about their child's ability to cope with practice, as well as their own capacity to devote energy to regulating the child's practice through continual reminders and encouragement to practice. Many mothers tended to withdraw their reminders, often because they felt that the child was either not coping emotionally, believing that if the child was really interested he or she would do it anyway, or because they were unwilling to invest their personal time and effort into regulating their child's daily schedule. The overall impression we gained from these interviews was that some mothers had actually given up on the child as a potential musician much sooner than the child had come to feel the same way.

Like children, parents form expectations and values about their child's learning which subsequently impact on how capable they will be of helping their child to take responsibility for his or her learning. Some of our parents reported very active participation, such as sitting with the child during practice sessions, being present to add support, or becoming involved in the parent–teacher committees at the school. In the early months of learning over 80% of the mothers reported actively reminding and encouraging their child to practice. But as for the children themselves, the beliefs the parents held about whether or not their child might be successful on the instrument were directly related to how much practice the children actually completed. Those mothers who expressed concerns that the child would need to be supervised in order to do sufficient practice had children who went on to do significantly less practice than other children (McPherson & Davidson, 2002).

Some mothers had exigent standards and expected some sort of routine and a consistent approach to practice. Their children tended to flourish. In the homework literature (Hoover-Dempsey et al., 2001), parental-role construction has been found to link with parental involvement in children's education. The research seeks to understand why parents believe that they should be involved in homework, the extent to which they believe that their involvement will make a difference, and also whether they feel invited by teachers (or their child) to become involved. In our study, most of the parents felt that they should be involved, but because many parents had no previous musical experience, they were often hesitant to say or do too much for fear of interfering with the teacher–child relationship. Indeed, some had little idea about how to support their children's practice, with the result that they had a very unclear perception of their role as a facilitator of their child's learning. Others actively sought out information that they could use to help their child, such as by attending lessons and ensemble rehearsals, or talking with the teacher to see how their child was progressing and how they could help overcome difficulties by assisting in the practice sessions.

Related to parental style were the interviews in our study that show the mothers had experienced times when they were frustrated with their child's attitude or approach to musical instrument learning. Sometimes these frustrations were on both sides, with the children expressing concerns that they were bored with their practice or did not know how to improve their playing, and the parent feeling frustrated that their child was not making sufficient efforts or they would argue with the child about practice. These displays of negative affect were especially evident in the post-interview discussions we completed with parents and their children who had ceased instruction.

A key finding in the homework literature is that parents who stay positive when helping with homework are more likely to stimulate their child's motivation (Pomerantz, Wang, & Ng, 2005). While helping a child can cause all sorts of frustrations for a mother, it appears that if they are able to stay positive—even in the most frustrating and demanding situations—then their child is much more likely to persist and eventually become more motivated in school, as well as value and enjoy the learning process. This finding seems to have a special relevance for children's musical learning, because a parent's ability to put their own frustrations aside to help focus their child on what is enjoyable about their learning is probably one of the key elements in promoting motivation, persistence, and ongoing musical involvement. In the homework literature there is convincing evidence that parents' homework-involvement practices are directly related to children's learning, achievement, and the time they are willing to devote to their homework (Hoover-Dempsey et al., 2001; Spera, 2005). For musical practice, the results of our studies suggest a similarly strong relationship (McPherson, 2009; McPherson & Davidson, 2002; Sloboda & Davidson, 1996).

Concluding comments

It is clear from the literature reviewed in this chapter that children's learning of a musical instrument is shaped by many factors. Most important among these are the expectations children hold for becoming competent on their instrument, the enjoyment they experience when playing their instrument, the types of self-regulatory strategies they acquire to enhance their learning, and the support and encouragement they receive for their learning from their family, teachers, and peers (McPherson et al., 2012).

Table 22.1 Summary of age-related learning principles in formal learning settings

Age	Choice of Instrument	Learning Processes	Learning Activities	Role of Significant Others
Early childhood	The most obvious choices are scaled-down instruments that children can readily hold and produce sound from. Keyboard and smaller stringed instruments, recorder, plus tuned and untuned percussion are common choices.	The emphasis should be on making music enjoyable, with opportunities for children to explore their own and other instruments. Children should be encouraged to sing and play a variety of musical games as a foundation for developing a sense of pitch and rhythm. Learning about some basic terms allows the child to articulate and expand their learning.	Learning by rote (copying and repetition) is the most important and natural way for very young children to learn. Aural awareness can be developed by learning pieces that are already known or first learnt by heart through repeated singing or hearings, before being reproduced on an instrument. An emphasis on musical sound, rather than notation, is recommended. The repertoire should be interesting and challenging, not difficult and frustrating. The emphasis should be on providing a rich, varied background of experiences that will lay the foundation for future musical success.	Teachers must develop a strong personal nurturing relationship such that the child regards them as warm, caring, and lots of fun to be with. Parents have a particularly special role during this time. Because children will not have developed their self-regulatory abilities, it is advisable for parents to attend lessons so that they will be able to reinforce what has been taught during the rest of the week. They should also try to be actively involved in their children's musical progress, by reminding them to practice, sitting in on their practice, and helping the child to recognize the exciting development of their learning. Parents are also responsible for exposing their children to a variety of music around the home, such as by putting on a recording of music when they go to bed, by playing music during the day, and by singing and playing musical games whenever possible.

Continued

Table 22.1 (continued) Summary of age-related learning principles in formal learning settings

Age	Choice of Instrument	Learning Processes	Learning Activities	Role of Significant Others
Childhood	More choices become available, but choosing a suitable instrument is still dependent on the child's physical capacity, with larger winds still being beyond their control. Wind instruments require a full set of teeth while young children who commence on string instruments will still need to play a smaller sized instrument. Posture will need to be carefully monitored, so that any child who is struggling to maintain a correct hand, lip, or seated position does not fall into habits which may eventually lead to physical injury. In some cases, it is advisable for a child to commence on a more manageable instrument before progressing to more difficult instruments.	The emphasis should still be on making music enjoyable while at the same time ensuring that there is a reasonable amount of progress over time. Children's learning can happen at a rapid pace during this time. During these years a child's interest and motivation can ebb and flow, depending on a variety of extrinsic and intrinsic forces. This is a natural part of growing and learning. It is therefore important to have regular exposure to enriching activities that help motivate the child, such as ensemble activities, attending recitals and concerts, performing in concerts, and attending music camps.	Musical notation should not be emphasized until the child can demonstrate basic ear-to-hand coordination skills. Children should be able to play a repertoire of works by ear. In the initial stages of introducing musical notation, children should be encouraged to invent their own notations to describe well-known songs. Later this can be extended to include traditional forms of notation but only when the child has become capable of coordinating their eyes, with their ears and hands.	The importance of a teacher retaining a strong personal relationship with the child is still paramount. Personal characteristics such as being a good communicator, showing interest, and being easy to talk and relate to the child are important, along with an appreciation of the ability of the teacher as a good musician. Professional characteristics of the teacher, such as being able to demonstrate effectively and provide an appropriate model for the child become increasingly important. Parents should continue to provide ongoing support for their child, through gentle but persistent reminders to practice, and take an active interest in their child's learning, with an emphasis on autonomy support. Increasing economic and practical sacrifices may need to be made by parents for the child's learning, such as transport to lessons, setting up a part of the home where the child can practice in private, finding a more advanced teacher, and assisting with activities such as band camps.

Table 22.1 (continued) Summary of age-related learning principles in formal learning settings

| Adolescence | Almost any instrument is now possible, with opportunities to learn instruments informally with peers increasing. Social acceptance and identity become particularly salient for young adolescence, so they are likely to choose instruments that align with their developing sense of musical, social, and personal identities. If they do not have extensive learning, accomplishments, or internalized motivation for more traditional instruments by this age, they are likely to give these up in favor of more socially appealing activities. | Some may be motivated to learn by ear rather than a desire to become musically literate. In formal settings, however, children are able to pick up music reading skills more quickly than in the past. If intuitive aural skills are not developed, music reading may become more efficient than playing by ear, and students may be inclined to neglect their natural musical intuitions in favor of accomplishing a larger body of rehearsed music. Adolescents will increasingly question tasks in relation to how they are aligned with their personal identity and their utility for the future. | This is a period when children become more independent, demand more autonomy, and in which they will want to perform repertoire that they find stimulating and challenging rather than repertoire that their teacher feels is appropriate for their technical development. | Children at this age are becoming more self-regulated and better able to monitor and control their own learning. Both the personal and professional characteristics of their teacher are important to them. They need to know that the teacher cares and will support them during difficult patches in their learning, but increasingly need to be stimulated by the quality of their teacher's abilities as a musician, in order to become inspired to reach higher levels of achievement. Children of this age are increasingly social, so it is important that the learning environment allows opportunities for group interaction and social experiences that enable them to be immersed in the style and culture of the type of music being learned. This can occur in both formal settings such as a school band or orchestra, and informal settings such as garage bands. |

Table 22.1 shows a number of age-related principles of learning an instrument which we feel confident to propose, based on our understanding of the literature, our longitudinal studies with young musicians, and our own teaching experiences. Our thoughts should not be considered as definitive, as children can vary markedly in both their interests as well as their mental, emotional, and physical readiness to commence and continue learning.

Overall, the principles outlined in Table 22.1 are based on our view that initial experiences in music should involve opportunities for children to:

1 experiment with several instruments before selecting one;

2 test out the instrument in a number of contexts; and

3 consider what might be right both physically and expressively for them.

Later, in order to cope with the many obstacles involved with learning, young learners should be:

1 encouraged and supported in their learning but not forced to learn;

2 provided with ample opportunities to explore the value of instruments and the role that music learning and playing might have for them now and into the future;

3 inspired to set reasonable goals for themselves which provide a balance between their own skill level and the challenge required to master new repertoire and techniques; and

4 exposed to a learning environment that is highly structured with extensive opportunities for psychologically rewarding experiences, but that is also supportive of the child's autonomy— their increasing tendency to make decisions in relation to their identity and sense of self.

Learning a musical instrument can be one of the most enjoyable and rewarding hobbies or pastimes that a child can pursue. However, it can also be one of the most frustrating. With this in mind, teachers and parents need to understand better the many forces which impact on how children align music learning and playing with an ever-more developing sense of who they are. By surveying some of the literature related to these issues, we hope that this chapter has provided a basic framework for understanding some of the more important elements in this process.

Reflective questions

1 What issues discussed in this chapter resonate with your own learning of an instrument?

2 What have you learned that might change your view of instrumental teaching?

3 How might you encourage a child who is starting to learn an instrument to take a longer-term view of his or her learning?

4 Given the significant role of parents, what can be done to make instrumental learning a three-way interaction between teacher, learner, and parent (and in what ways would this be important)?

5 How would you describe your own teachers' abilities to develop your motivation to learn an instrument?

Key source

McPherson, G. E., Davidson, J. W., & Faulkner, R. (2012). *Music in our lives: Rethinking musical ability, development and identity*. Oxford: Oxford University Press.

Reference list

Abeles, H. F., & Porter, S. Y. (1978). Sex stereotyping of musical instruments. *Journal of Research in Music Education*, **26**(2), 65–75.

Bandura, A. (1997). *Self-efficacy: The exercise of control*. New York: Freeman.

Barry, N., & Hallam, S. (2002). Practice. In R. Parncutt & G. E. McPherson (Eds.), *The science and psychology of music performance: Creative strategies for teaching and learning* (pp. 151–65). New York: Oxford University Press.

Boyle, J. D., DeCarbo, N. J., & Fortney, P. M. (1993). A study of middle school band students' instrument choices. *Journal of Research in Music Education*, 41(1), 28–39.

Bruce, R., & Kemp, A. (1993). Sex-stereotyping in children's preferences for musical instruments. *British Journal of Music Education*, 10(3), 213–17.

Conway, C. (2000). Gender and musical instrument choice: A phenomenological investigation. *Bulletin of the Council for Research in Music Education*, 146, 1–17.

Cooke, M., & Morris, R. (1996). Making music in Great Britain. *Journal of the Market Research Society*, 28(2), 123–34.

Davidson, J. W., & Burland, K. (2006). Musician identity formation. In G. E. McPherson (Ed.), *The child as musician: A handbook of musical development* (pp. 475–88). Oxford, England: Oxford University Press.

Davidson, J. W., Moore, J. W., Sloboda, J. A., & Howe, M. J. A. (1998). Characteristics of music teachers and the progress of young instrumentalists. *Journal of Research in Music Education*, 46(1), 141–60.

Delzell, J. K., & Leppla, D. A. (1992). Gender association of musical instruments and preferences of fourth-grade students for selected instruments. *Journal of Research in Music Education*, 40(2), 93–103.

Dweck, C. S. (2000). *Self-theories: Their role in motivation, personality and development*. Philadelphia, PA: Psychology Press.

Eccles, J. S. (2005). Subjective task value and the Eccles et al. model of achievement-related choices. In A. J. Elliot & C. S. Dweck (Eds.), *Handbook of competence and motivation* (pp. 105–21). New York: The Guilford Press.

Ericsson, K. A. (1997). Deliberate practice and the acquisition of expert performance: An overview. In H. Jørgensen & A. C. Lehmann (Eds.), *Does practice make perfect? Current theory and research on instrumental music practice* (pp. 9–51). Oslo, Norway: Norges Musikkhøgskole.

Evans, P., & McPherson, G. E. (2015). Identity and practice: The consequences of a long-term musical identity. *Psychology of Music*, 43(53), 407–22. doi: 10.1177/0305735613514471.

Evans, P., & McPherson, G. E. (in press). Processes of musical identity consolidation during adolescence. In D. Hargreaves, R. A. R. Macdonald, & D. Miell (Eds.), *Oxford handbook of musical identities*. Oxford, England: Oxford University Press.

Evans, P., McPherson, G. E., & Davidson, J. W. (2013). The role of psychological needs in ceasing music and music learning activities. *Psychology of Music*, 41(5), 600–19. doi: 10.1177/0305735612441736.

Green, L. (2008). *Music, informal learning and the school: A new classroom pedagogy*. Aldershot, England: Ashgate Publishing.

Grolnick, W. S. (2009). The role of parents in facilitating autonomous self-regulation for education. *Theory and Research in Education*, 7(2), 164–73, doi: 10.1177/1477878509104321.

Grusec, J. E., Goodnow, J. J., & Kuczynski, L. (2000). New directions in analyses of parenting contributions to children's acquisition of values. *Child Development*, 71(1), 205–11.

Gullberg, A.-K., & Brändström, S. (2004). Formal and non-formal music learning amongst rock musicians. In J. W. Davidson (Ed.), *The music practitioner. Research for the music performer, teacher and listener* (pp. 161–74). Aldershot: Ashgate.

Hallam, S. (1997a). What do we know about practicing? Toward a model synthesising the research literature. In H. Jørgensen & A. C. Lehmann (Eds.), *Does practice make perfect? Current theory and research on instrumental music practice* (pp. 179–231). Oslo, Norway: Norges Musikkhøgskole.

Hallam, S. (1997b). Approaches to instrumental music practice of experts and novices: Implications for education. In H. Jørgensen & A. C. Lehmann (Eds.), *Does practice make perfect? Current theory and research on instrumental music practice* (pp. 89–108). Oslo, Norway: Norges Musikkhøgskole.

Harrison, A. C., & O'Neill, S. A. (2003). Preferences and children's use of gender-stereotyped knowledge about musical instruments: Making judgements about other children's preferences. *Sex Roles*, **49**(7–8), 389 (312).

Hendricks, K. S. (2014). Changes in self-efficacy beliefs over time: Contextual influences of gender, rank-based placement, and social support in a competitive orchestra environment. *Psychology of Music*, **42**(3), 347–65, doi: 10.1177/0305735612471238.

Hoover-Dempsey, K. V., Battiato, A. C., Walker, J. M. T., Reed, R. P, DeJong, J. M., & Jones, K. P. (2001). Parental involvement in homework. *Educational Psychologist*, **36**(3), 195–209.

Jørgensen, H. (2004). Strategies for individual practice. In A. Williamon (Ed.), *Musical excellence: Strategies and techniques to enhance performance* (pp. 85–103). Oxford: Oxford University Press.

MacKenzie, C. G. (1991). Starting to learn to play a musical instrument: A study of boys' and girls' motivational criteria. *British Journal of Music Education*, **8**(1), 15–20.

McCormick, J., & McPherson, G. E. (2007). Expectancy-value motivation in the context of a music performance examination. *Musicae Scientiae*, **11**(2 suppl.), 37–52. doi: 10.1177/10298649070110S203.

McPherson, G. E. (1994). Factors and abilities influencing sight-reading skill in music. *Journal of Research in Music Education*, **42**(3), 217–31.

McPherson, G. E. (2001). Commitment and practice: Key ingredients for achievement during the early stages of learning a musical instrument. *Council for Research in Music Education*, **147**, 122–7.

McPherson, G. E. (2005). From child to musician: Skill development during the beginning stages of learning an instrument. *Psychology of Music*, **33**(1), 5–35.

McPherson, G. E. (2009). The role of parents in children's musical development. *Psychology of Music*, **37**(1), 91–110. doi: 10.1177/0305735607086049.

McPherson, G. E., & Davidson, J. W. (2002). Musical practice: Mother and child interactions during the first year of learning an instrument. *Music Education Research*, **4**(1), 143–58.

McPherson, G. E., Davidson, J. W., & Faulkner, R. (2012). *Music in our lives: Rethinking musical ability, development and identity.* Oxford: Oxford University Press.

McPherson, G. E., & Gabrielsson, A. (2002). From sound to sign. In R. Parncutt & G. E. McPherson (Eds.), *The science and psychology of musical performance: Creative strategies for music teaching and learning* (pp. 99–115). Oxford: Oxford University Press.

McPherson, G. E., & McCormick, J. (1999). Motivational and self-regulated learning components of musical practice. *Bulletin of the Council for Research in Music Education*, **141**, 98–102.

McPherson, G. E., & Renwick, J. M. (2001). A longitudinal study of self-regulation in children's musical practice. *Music Education Research*, **3**(2), 169–86.

McPherson, G. E., & Renwick, J. (2011). Self-regulation and mastery of musical skills. In B. Zimmerman & D. Schunk (Eds.), *Handbook of self-regulation of learning and performance* (pp. 234–48). New York: Routledge.

McPherson, G. E., & Zimmerman, B. J. (2011). Self-regulation of musical learning: A social–cognitive perspective on developing performance skills. In R. Colwell & P. Webster (Eds.), *MENC handbook of research on music learning, volume 2: Applications.* New York: Oxford University Press.

O'Neill, S. A. (1997). The role of practice in children's early performance achievement. In H. Jørgensen & A. C. Lehmann (Eds.), *Does practice make perfect? Current theory and research on instrumental music practice* (pp. 53–70). Oslo, Norway: Norges Musikkhøgskole.

O'Neill, S. A. (2001). *Young people and music participation project: Practitioner report and summary of findings.* Unit for the Study of Musical Skill and Development, Keele University, UK—see <http://www.keele.ac.uk/depts/ps/ESRC/Practitionerimp.doc> (accessed July 28, 2005).

O'Neill, S. A., & Boulton, M. J. (1996). Boys' and girls' preferences for musical instruments: A function of gender? *Psychology of Music*, **24**(2), 171–83.

O'Neill, S., & McPherson, G. E. (2002). Motivation. In R. Parncutt & G. E. McPherson (Eds.), *The science and psychology of musical performance: Creative strategies for music teaching and learning* (pp. 31–46). Oxford: Oxford University Press.

O'Neill, S. A., & Sloboda, J. A. (1997). The effects of failure on children's ability to perform a musical test. *Psychology of Music*, **25**(1), 18–34.

Pomerantz, E. M., Wang, Q., & Ng, F. F. (2005). Mothers' affect in the homework context: The importance of staying positive. *Developmental Psychology*, **41**(2), 414–27.

Renwick, J., & McPherson, G. E. (2002). Interest and choice: Student-selected repertoire and its effect on practising behaviour. *British Journal of Music Education*, **19**(2), 173–88.

Renwick, J. M., & Reeve, J. (2012). Supporting motivation in music education. In G. E. McPherson & G. F. Welch (Eds.), *Oxford handbook of music education* (Vol. 1, pp. 143–62). New York: Oxford University Press.

Rostvall, A., & West, R. (2003). Analysis of interaction and learning in instrumental teaching. *Music Education Research*, **5**(1), 213–26.

Sloboda, J., & Davidson, J. (1996). The young performing musician. In I. Deliege & J. Sloboda (Eds.), *Musical beginnings: Origins and development of musical competence* (pp. 171–90). New York: Oxford University Press.

Sloboda, J. A., Davidson, J. W., & Howe, M. (1994). Is everyone musical? *The Psychologist*, **7**(7), 349–54.

Sloboda, J. A., Davidson, J. W., Howe, M. J. A., & Moore, D. G. (1996). The role of practice in the development of performing musicians. *British Journal of Psychology*, **87**(2), 287–309.

Sosniak, L. A. (1985). Learning to be a concert pianist. In B. S. Bloom (Ed.), *Developing talent in young people* (pp. 19–67). New York: Ballantine.

Spera, C. (2005). A review of the relationship among parenting practices, parenting styles, and adolescent school achievement. *Educational Psychology Review*, **17**(2), 125–46.

Warton, P. M., (1997). Learning about responsibility: Lessons from homework. *British Journal of Educational Psychology*, **67**(2), 213–21.

Wigfield, A., & Cambria, J. (2010). Expectancy-value theory: Retrospective and prospective. In T. C. Urdan & S. A. Karabenick (Eds.), *The decade ahead: Theoretical perspectives on motivation and achievement* (Vol. 16A, pp. 35–70). Bradford, UK: Emerald Group Publishing Limited.

Williamon, A., & Valentine, E. (1998). "Practice makes perfect": The effects of piece and ability level on performance preparation. In S. W. Yi (Ed.), *Proceedings of the 5th international conference on music perception and cognition* (pp. 323–8), August 26–30, 1998, Seoul National University, Korea.

Zimmerman, B. J. (2008). Investigating self-regulation and motivation: Historical background, methodological developments, and future prospects. *American Educational Research Journal*, **45**(1), 166–83.

Chapter 23

Building performance confidence

Margaret S. Osborne

Should we be concerned about performance anxiety in child and adolescent musicians? Studies suggest we should, as up to 75% of students experience some form of performance anxiety (Britsch, 2005). Given that most people learn how to play and perform music during their school years, knowledge of how to cope with music performance anxiety (MPA) at this time is crucial for satisfactory engagement with music, whether or not they wish to continue with a music career. Performance anxiety is the most significant psychological issue for performing musicians of any age (Kenny, 2011), and can be a significant blow to the psychological well-being and optimal performance of a young performer.

Many young people choose to leave formal music education as they enter adolescence (McPherson, Davidson, & Faulkner, 2012). This is at odds with older and more experienced musicians who are more likely to remain engaged in the act of performing even if it feels aversive, rather than avoiding or escaping it, in a phenomenon described by Senyshyn and O'Neill (2001) as "creative yearning." It may be that "creative yearning" reflects a strong personal investment in performing, such that a musician's desire to approach the act of performing (remain in the field) remains stronger than their desire to avoid it (leave the field) (Dollard & Miller, 1950). Sadly, if a young musician becomes overwhelmed by negative emotions due to their inability to control them or play despite them, they may eventually discontinue performing altogether, even if they have not experienced any serious performance breakdowns (Kenny, 2011). Considering that musical identities moderate musical development in young musicians (Hargreaves, MacDonald, & Miell, 2012), the musical identities of child and adolescent musicians may be too fragile to remain in the field alongside the plethora of aversive emotions, thoughts, and physiological responses they may experience with MPA. Therefore, children and adolescents might require less trauma or distressing anxiety to decide that they no longer wish to remain in the performance "field," and choose to avoid performing and/or music learning altogether.

Using a hypothetical case study of a young musician named Louise, this chapter will illuminate both the debilitating and facilitating aspects of performance anxiety. Current methods to conceive and measure MPA are discussed, including the unclear relationship between MPA and performance quality, before moving into a review of psychological strategies to manage MPA in this age group. The chapter finishes with a summary of practical strategies to overcome performance anxiety which can be used by parents, teachers, and students to help young musicians become more confident in managing performance anxiety and achieve their performance potential.

In Year 5, Louise started learning the clarinet. In order to play comfortably and reduce her anxiety she preferred to perform in a group, or pieces that were technically below her standard and very highly practiced to people that she knew well. At the start of high school she was asked to play a solo at school assembly. She had never performed in the school auditorium before to such a large audience who were also her new peers. She was shy and anxious in daily life, which increased as she entered adolescence. Louise was exceedingly worried about her ability to perform well. Her instrumental teacher and parents simply said, "Don't worry, everyone gets nervous performing," and emphasized technical competence: "You'll be fine if you practice hard enough." They did not talk about the physical sensations that Louise was experiencing, and that her attention to those sensations would increase the likelihood of her making a mistake or choking on stage. Louise became so anxious before this performance that she wanted to avoid it altogether. After poor sleep and inadequate preparation she squeaked and struggled through a poor performance. After this, she considered giving up altogether. Instead, she found a new teacher who openly discussed performance anxiety and helped her manage it through knowledge and performance practice, encouraging her to play well despite her anxiety. Louise joined the school band and performed in as many solo concerts as she could. Fears and worries about making mistakes were gradually replaced by the joy of communicating to others through music.

Phenomenology

Anxiety is a normal and healthy reaction to perceived danger that triggers a variety of physical, mental, and behavioral changes in order to facilitate a speedy response (WHO, 2004). Similarly, MPA typically manifests as a constellation of three interactive, yet partially independent factors: cognitions, autonomic arousal, and overt behavioral responses (Craske & Craig, 1984; Salmon, 1990). The cognitions or worries that Louise would have experienced in response to being asked to perform at the school assembly include worry about not being able to perform perfectly, fear of making a mistake, fear of being negatively evaluated by others, overestimations of the likelihood and consequences of a negative evaluation of the music performance, and negative self-evaluation in relation to her own high standards for performance quality (Kenny, 2011; Osborne & Franklin, 2002; Osborne & Kenny, 2008).

On detecting danger, a series of hormones would have been released in Louise's brain including adrenalin and cortisol (the main hormone responsible for the stress response), triggering the sympathetic nervous system (which can occur during excitement *as well as* anxiety) in an almost reflexive urge to escape, or alternatively stand and engage with the threat, which is described in the psychological literature as the "fight-or-flight" response (Barlow, 2002). This elevation in autonomic arousal and tension is characterized by physiological symptoms such as racing heart, dry mouth, rapid breathing, sweating, gastric disturbances, dizziness, and feelings of dread, fear, and panic. Somatic anxiety includes worry about the potential of excessive physiological arousal to negatively effect performance (Gill, Murphy, & Rickard, 2006). Louise most likely demonstrated behaviors such as a frozen expression, signaling her nerves to others and undermining her attempt to effectively communicate her musical repertoire to the audience (Williamon, 2004). Under stress, she would have more difficulty learning, remembering, and executing the complex cognitive (e.g., problem solving) and sensorimotor (i.e., execution and sequencing of controlled body movement) skills required in a music performance (Altenmüller & McPherson, 2008; Kim & Diamond, 2002). The performance-stress model of choking in Figure 23.1 demonstrates how these factors can work together to produce a sub-optimal music performance for Louise in high stress situations, such as a solo at the whole school assembly.

Louise also demonstrated the more explicit behavioral consequences of MPA such as choosing group repertoire over solo, or easier pieces instead of more difficult ones. Whilst this might successfully reduce her performance anxiety, it also results in negative educational consequences, as she resists performing pieces that match her level of skill (Kubzansky & Stewart, 1999), or in the extreme, avoids performing altogether (Fehm & Schmidt, 2006). Like Louise, many young musicians avoid feared performance situations in order to alleviate anxiety, which is a common theme across other types of evaluative situations such as tests and competitions in mathematics

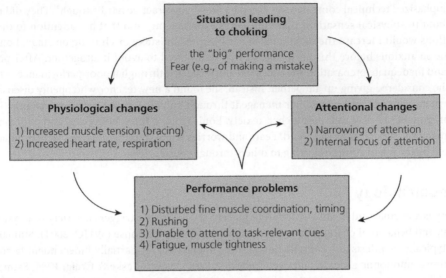

Fig. 23.1 Performance-stress model of choking

Adapted from Jean M. Williams, Robert M. Nideffer, Vietta E. Wilson, Marc-Simon Sagal, and Eric Peper, *Concentration and strategies for controlling it*, in Applied Sport Psychology: Personal Growth to Peak Performance, 6e, p. 343 © 2010, McGraw Hill.

and sport. Unfortunately, this limits Louise's opportunities for performances that could provide positive evidence of her performance capability (to help her reduce worrisome thoughts), and problem solving opportunities to identify areas for skill improvement. Over time, Louise's reper- toire of adaptive coping thoughts and music performance skills disintegrates (Kenny, 2011). This cycle subsequently escalates the likelihood of a future performance catastrophe (the initial feared event and cause for worry), escalating distress and increasing the likelihood of complete disen- gagement from music learning. In this way, anxiety-driven avoidance behavior leads to a lack of motivation to perform (Zeidner & Matthews, 2005).

Avoidance also implies hypervigilance—in order to avoid a threatening stimulus, we continu- ously scan our environment (internal or external) in order to detect the feared event that we wish to avoid, thus making us hypervigilant to anxious and fearful stimuli (Barlow, 2002). Executing a musical task requires minute control over fine motor skills (such as vibrato and bow holds) which can be easily and potentially disrupted by even minor changes in physiological arousal, prompting musicians to become hypervigilant to minor physiological changes and misinterpret them with major significance (Gill et al., 2006). Neurobiologically, hypervigilance to anxious phenomena (e.g., worrying about the potential for making mistakes due to profusely sweating or trembling hands) maintains anxiety by strengthening cellular networks in our brains that are specialized to detect danger and respond with anxiety and the "fight or flight" response (Kasai et al., 2010). The more attention Louise would pay to the potential negative effect of anxiety on musical per- formance, the stronger the connectivity between cells would become, consolidating performance anxiety material into memory and making it more efficiently retrieved in stressful performance situations. Essentially, Louise was *learning* to be anxious about performing. Conversely, if Louise reduced her attentional focus, the connections between cells would deteriorate, making once- consolidated material more difficult to retrieve. Learning to stop paying attention to anxious phenomena reduces anxious thoughts and feelings over time (McLaren, 2004, 2013; Schwartz & Begley, 2002). Therefore, a key point of helping Louise optimize music performance would be to reduce hypervigilance to the mental and physical sensations of anxiety.

Child and adolescent musicians are more likely to be anxious in performance if they tend to be anxious across many stressful situations in daily life (i.e., are trait anxious; Spielberger, 1983) and/or are perfectionists. Louise had high trait-anxiety, responding in highly anxious ways across many stressful situations perceived as dangerous or threatening, which increased her likelihood of having high MPA (Kenny & Osborne, 2006; Maroon, 2003; Osborne & Kenny, 2008; Ryan, 1998; Thomas & Nettelbeck, 2014). In a stressful situation, for example, performing solo in front of expert judges, she would more likely experience all three of the cognitive, physiological, and behavioral features of MPA. On the other hand, low trait-anxious individuals demonstrate elevated heart rate, but not cognitive or behavioral features (Craske & Craig, 1984). Importantly, being female contributed to this relationship: young female musicians with high trait-anxiety are more likely to be highly distressed by MPA than young trait-anxious male musicians. Similarly, females and older students are more likely to have higher levels of both perfectionism and MPA (Kenny & Osborne, 2006; Osborne & Patston, 2013). Children and adolescents who have higher levels of performance anxiety are also greatly concerned about making mistakes and have extreme personal standards for excellence, and therefore submit themselves to intense training and practice in order to meet those standards (Kenny & Osborne, 2006; Osborne, 2008). Further variations in cognitive, physiological, and behavioral manifestations of MPA according to age and gender will now be discussed.

Age

Children as young as 3 years of age can show many of the physical and physiological characteristics of adult MPA, such as significant increases in heart rate between practice and recital, and significant negative correlations between self-esteem (particularly social self-esteem), trait, and state anxiety (Boucher & Ryan, 2011; Ryan, 1998). Like Louise, many anxious children articulate cognitions related to fear of making mistakes in front of people, and the negative impact of physiological arousal on performance. State anxiety is significantly higher on the day of a school concert performance, and is positively related to trait-anxiety (Ryan, 2005).

Preschool children's responses to performance situations provide valuable insight into the experience of MPA in this age group as well as potential innate and developmental contributions (Boucher & Ryan, 2011). Children from two daycare centers participated in weekly group music lessons which culminated in two concerts for their families on two consecutive days. Concert activities included group singing, movement, and instrument playing. All children were more anxious before the concert performances, but this differed according to prior performance experience and performance location. Children with prior performing experience reported less anticipatory anxiety than those without prior experience. Performance location also affected anxiety responses. Children from one daycare center who were very familiar with the performance venue responded with less anxiety than those who had never attended the performance venue. The second performance within a short timeframe elicited much lower anxiety responses than the initial performance for all students. This suggests that performance stress in young children can be reduced through performance practice strategies such as rehearsing in (or at least visiting) the performance venue the day before the actual performance.

Like Louise experienced, MPA increases with age and peaks at around 15 years (Chan, 2011; Osborne & Kenny, 2005; Osborne, Kenny, & Holsomback, 2005). Up to a third of adolescent music students are adversely affected by MPA, which appears to be unrelated to years of playing or musical grade (Fehm & Schmidt, 2006; Rae & McCambridge, 2004). Studies of high school musicians show that MPA is likely to be greater if students have high levels of trait-anxiety, neuroticism, and introversion (Kemp, 1981; Rae & McCambridge, 2004; Smith & Rickard, 2004). Consistent with the social nature of music performance, Louise's anxiety would increase from a solo practice to solo performance in front of a small audience. She was much more anxious performing on her own than in a group, and to adjudicators and/or large audiences than small, familiar ones (LeBlanc et al., 1997; Maroon, 2003). She also used to feel more comfortable playing solo when she was younger (Britsch, 2005). Entering adolescence, the two main triggers to MPA for Louise include cognitions (negative thoughts) and physiological manifestations of anxiety (somatic anxiety) (Osborne & Kenny, 2005, 2008; Papageorgi, 2007).

The increase in MPA in adolescence as experienced by Louise can be explained by the development of formal operational thought (Osborne et al., 2005). The cognitive skill of formal operations is characterized by an increase in retrospection and self-evaluation, particularly in areas of great interest and involvement (Piaget, 1970). The ability to imagine other people's thoughts lead Louise to mistakenly believe that others were as preoccupied about performance failure as she was. This can create anxiety and self-criticism (Kenny, 2000). Adolescence is also characterized by decreased satisfaction with family, encouraging peers to become the focus of attention and increased social–interpersonal anxiety (Kashani et al., 1989). Hence, the new peers were very threatening for Louise. Adolescents are also more likely to evaluate themselves in terms of academic and other achievements (Heaven, 2001). The greater commitment to music exhibited by young people who remain engaged in music learning from childhood to adolescence invites greater expectations from one's self and others regarding performance standard and quality, thereby increasing the likelihood of high performance anxiety (Osborne et al., 2005).

Gender

From late childhood female musicians report higher MPA than their male counterparts (Osborne et al., 2005; Thomas & Nettelbeck, 2014). Social anxiety is common for boys and girls, as peers become the increasing focus of attention, with girls (not boys) becoming increasingly concerned with age (Kashani et al., 1989). Girls also have significantly greater fears of performing in front of others (Essau, Conradt, & Petermann, 1999).

Measures of state anxiety (a person's level of anxiety at any given moment; Spielberger, 1983) in Grade 3 to 7 school students on a concert day show that this can vary according to age. Grade 6 boys report a small decrease in anxiety, and girls a moderate increase. In comparison, Grade 7 boys' anxiety increases, and Grade 7 girls' anxiety decreases (Ryan, 2005). After Grade 4, boys and girls manifest anxiety differently (Ryan, 2004): Girls have substantially higher heart rates than boys immediately prior to but not during a performance, whereas boys' heart rates exceed girls' heart-rate levels during a performance. Interview findings indicate that boys do experience anxiety prior to performing, at which time they claimed to be most anxious (Ryan, 2004, 2005). Boys tend to use physical activity as a coping mechanism to distract them from the impending performance situation, which may also help them to maintain lower heart rates. Boys also demonstrate significantly more somatic anxiety and anxious behavior than girls both prior to and during a recital, such as feet and legs shifting and tapping during playing, shuffling and pacing during measures of rest or in between movements, drying one's hands by touching the body, lip moistening or jaw movements, and adjusting, manipulating, and/or inspecting the instrument when not playing (see Brotons, 1994 for further details on behavioral manifestations of MPA).

On the basis of these findings, we can conclude that MPA increases with age peaking in mid-adolescence, with gender emerging as a distinguishing feature in adolescence. This highlights the need to examine musicians from late primary school and high school according to gender rather than as one homogenous group, potentially requiring gender-specific strategies (Ryan, 2005).

Measuring MPA

Valid, reliable, and easy-to-use measures for child and adolescent MPA are vital for early intervention and prevention of potentially debilitating levels of MPA. One quick and easy-to-use self-report scale that Louise's teacher could have used to start the conversation about the topic is the Music Performance Anxiety Inventory for Adolescents (MPAI-A) (Osborne & Kenny, 2005), which contains 15 questions assessing the somatic, cognitive, and behavioral components of MPA. Table 23.1 outlines the topics that are covered by the scale, which provide clues as to the most important issues of concern for a young musician. The total score indicates students' overall susceptibility to performance anxiety and effectiveness of intervention outcomes. The scale can also be used item-by-item to identify and target strategies to address individual performance anxiety concerns, and has improved our knowledge of the phenomenology and effective

Table 23.1 MPAI-A items by topic

Item	Topic
Somatic and cognitive features	
1	Before I perform, I get butterflies in my stomach
2	I often worry about my ability to perform
4	Before I perform, I tremble or shake
5	When I perform in front of an audience, I am afraid of making mistakes
6	When I perform in front of an audience, my heart beats very fast
7	When I perform in front of an audience, I find it hard to concentrate on my music
8	If I make a mistake during a performance, I usually panic
9	When I perform in front of an audience, I get sweaty hands
12	Just before I perform, I feel nervous
13	I worry that my parents or teacher might not like my performance
15	My muscles feel tense before I perform
Performance context	
3	I would rather play on my own than in front of other people
11	I try to avoid playing on my own at a school concert
14	I would rather play in a group or ensemble than on my own
Performance evaluation	
10*	When I finish performing, I usually feel happy with my performance*

Items are answered on a 7-point Likert scale: *0–Not at all* to *6–All of the time*.

*Item 10 must be reverse scored before summing for a total score (original scale in Osborne & Kenny, 2005).

interventions for MPA in adolescents (e.g., Braden, Osborne, & Wilson, 2015; Chan, 2011; Khalsa et al., 2013; Osborne, 2013; Osborne & Kenny, 2008; Osborne, Kenny, & Cooksey, 2007; Thomas & Nettelbeck, 2014).

Conceptualization

As inferred in the previous section, performance anxiety in children and adolescents varies depending on age, gender, level of trait-anxiety, and type of performance. The challenge, then, is how to best summarize the development and chronicity of MPA across different individuals and performance conditions. Given that by its very nature, abject expressions of MPA cross both the anxiety and performance spectra, the following discussion highlights the main theoretical conceptualizations of anxiety from both performance and clinical foundations. Wilson's (2002) three-dimensional model of artistic performance anxiety and the Individualized Zone of Optimal Functioning (IZOF) approaches elaborate on the facilitative effects of anxiety on performance.

Wilson's three-dimensional model of performance anxiety

Wilson (2002) considers context and individual psychological characteristics in a three-dimensional model specifically for artistic performance anxiety. Distressing anxiety arises from a performer's trait-anxiety, degree of task mastery of the performed piece, and degree of situational stress. The optimal or detrimental effect of performance anxiety depends on the interaction between these three groups of factors. For example, a high trait-anxious individual will perform best playing an easy, well-prepared piece in a relaxed environment, whereas a low trait-anxious performer will perform better with a challenging piece in an evaluative environment, such as an exam or a competition. Wilson's theory accommodates cases where highly anxious performers rarely demonstrate impaired performance, nor performance that is inferior to that of low trait-anxious individuals (Strahan & Conger, 1998).

Individual differences in optimal performance

Performance anxiety can vary across individuals for two reasons: first, small changes in context or task-expectancy can lead to individual differences in stress response due to cognitive appraisals of whether the situation is stressful or not (Bandura, 1991; Salmon, 1991); and second, highly anxious performers are likely to engage in a number of pre-performance preparations, such as over-learning, additional rehearsals, or visiting the venue (Kenny & Ackermann, 2009; Kenny, Davis, & Oates, 2004).

Drawn from the sports performance literature, tools such as Hanin's (2000) IZOF model and emotion-profiling instrument, and Greene's (2012) Performance Success program for musicians and Performance Skills Inventory, acknowledge that successful athletic and musical performance occurs when competition anxiety (nervous energy) approximates the ideal level for that athlete or performer, whether it is low, medium, or high. According to Hanin, when an individual's arousal exceeds their zone of functioning, then performance falters. Similarly in Greene's approach, when a performer is unable to regulate their Performance or Audition Energy to their Optimal Energy level, and the gap between these respective energy levels is substantial, then a performer can struggle to control their energy in high-pressure performance situations, and performance is likely to be less than desirable. The main similarity across both models is that it is not the amount of nervous energy per se that is the problem, but rather identifying what amount is most advantageous for each individual.

Kenny's model of MPA development

Kenny (2011) draws from clinical psychology literature to provide a comprehensive, yet parsimonious model which accounts for the development of MPA. It postulates that MPA in young musicians is developed and maintained as a result of three integrating vulnerabilities:

1 generalized biological (heritable) vulnerability = young performers who are high in trait-anxiety; plus

2 generalized psychological vulnerability = young performers who come from home environments in which expectations for excellence are high but support for achieving excellence is low; plus

3 specific psychological vulnerability = young performers who experience frequent evaluations of their performances in a competitive environment, early in their musical training.

Anxiety may be triggered by conscious, rational concerns or by cues that unconsciously trigger earlier anxiety-producing experiences or somatic sensations. The latter may include earlier aversive performances that drive negative cognitions in subsequent performances. For example, adolescents who report experiencing a traumatic music performance have more negative thoughts about performance than those who have never experienced a traumatic performance (Osborne & Kenny, 2008). Once anxiety is triggered, attention turns inward and is self-evaluative, focusing on somatic sensations and catastrophic self-statements regarding their perceived inadequacy in managing the forthcoming performance. Akin to a self-fulfilling prophecy, the result of attentional focus turning inward to cognitions and somatic sensations, and away from the task of executing the musical piece, increases the likelihood of an impaired performance or performance failure (see Figure 23.1).

This model includes a detailed account of conditioning processes in stressful performances that account for the sequence of negative emotions accompanied by a negative evaluation of the performance by one's self *and* others combined with somatic anticipatory responses, which may or may not be associated with an actual impaired performance or a performance breakdown (interested readers are encouraged to consult Kenny, 2011, pp. 157–65 for details). It accounts for the occurrence of severe MPA in musicians who may or may never have experienced a performance catastrophe. MPA is likely to develop "if not extinguished by appropriate interventions and performance outcomes" (Kenny, 2011, p. 164), and "repeated successful performance may eventually reduce the amount of anxious apprehension experienced before performances so that music performance anxiety does not persist, at least not at severe levels" (p. 162). The model diagram notes this process as "successful performance," with an arrow pointing to "Exit/avoid MPA" (Kenny, 2011, p. 163).

The suggestions that only successful performances can lead to reduced MPA and that MPA can be avoided and eliminated are two potential difficulties with this model. Performers, parents, and educators may misinterpret this framework in their efforts to assist in managing MPA. Certainly, as in Louise's case, many opportunities to perform with minimal adverse consequences helped her learn that performance is an enjoyable and manageable part of learning an instrument. These points are elaborated further in the "Strategies to overcome performance anxiety" section at the end of this chapter.

MPA and performance quality

Much of the early performance anxiety literature posited a simple relationship between physiological arousal and performance quality, notably due to the Yerkes Dodson Inverted-U curve model (Yerkes & Dodson, 1908). According to this model, moderately difficult tasks are best performed under conditions of moderate physiological arousal, and insufficient or excessive arousal impedes performance. Hypervigilance to somatic sensations produces cognitive interference, triggering debilitating anxiety and potentially disrupting the execution of skilled behavior resulting in sub-optimal performance (Zeidner & Matthews, 2005). Over time the Inverted-U relationship has broadened to consider a number of moderating factors, including difficulty of the piece and degree of preparation. For example, Louise would be more likely to deliver a good-quality performance with high physiological arousal by playing a less complex (Tassi et al., 2003) and highly practiced (Kokotsaki & Davidson, 2003) piece. A moderate amount of anxiety may *enhance* her performance when her skill level matches the performance demands of the situation (Jackson & Csikszentmihalyi, 1999), *and* she interprets that anxiety positively (Jones, Swain, & Hardy, 1993).

The relationship between excessive levels of MPA and actual impairment of performance skills is unclear in young musicians. Grade 7 and 8 students in a solo and ensemble contest with high state anxiety do not perform as well as those with lower levels of anxiety in the presence of an adjudicator (Maroon, 2003). There is no evidence for either debilitating or facilitating effects of anxiety in 7- to 18-year-old Hong Kong musicians, although state anxiety scores are significantly lower for students who expect to perform better than their daily practice, compared to those who expect to do worse than their daily practice (Chan, 2011). The relationship between reduced performance anxiety and improved performance quality in judged solo performances following cognitive-behavioral interventions in high school music students is inconclusive (Braden et al., 2015; Osborne et al., 2007). This relationship is complicated by the effect of observer's ratings of manifest MPA on performance quality. If Louise was perceived by judges to be more anxious than her competitors, she would be given poorer performance scores, regardless of how anxious she herself felt (Kubzansky & Stewart, 1999). Yet, despite Louise's perception of conspicuous behavioral manifestations of MPA such as sweating, trembling, hyperventilating, and tense musculature in a solo musical performance, these would not be obvious to highly trained judges (Braden et al., 2015), which is an important psychoeducational point for Louise's teacher to emphasize in helping to manage her performance anxiety.

Interestingly, 12-year-old boys who play piano display more anxious behaviors before performing and still subsequently perform better than their female counterparts (Ryan, 2004). It is possible that these behaviors reduce hypervigilance to negative rumination about the performance, thereby allowing them to perform better. Girls with the least state anxiety perform the worst, and those with very high anxiety perform moderately well. Several of the lower-rated performers exhibited behaviors common to anxious musicians, such as memory slips and false starts. Hence it is difficult to know whether or not differences in recital performance quality can be attributed to variations in anxiety. It is possible that performance problems are due to poor preparation, as adolescents with high MPA like Louise invest less effort in performance preparation (Papageorgi, 2007). What we can conclude is that the relationship between an individual's level of anxiety and quality of music performance is not straightforward. As Louise's case study shows, variability occurs due to a range of antecedents such as level of preparation, gender, performance situation, worrisome thoughts and elevated physiological arousal, and covert or overt anxious and avoidant behavior.

Positive emotions in performance

Ryan's (2004) finding that boys who displayed more anxious behaviors prior to performing subsequently performed better provides tantalizing evidence that the experience of anxiety before or during a music performance is not necessarily associated with negative performance outcomes in young musicians. In a study of gifted 15- to 19-year-old musicians, Fehm and Schmidt (2006) found that although 73% identified anxiety as having a negative influence on their performance, almost half the students reported that it had a somewhat positive influence on their performance (although no details were obtained about what those facilitative effects might be). A positive or negative interpretation of anxiety is mediated by an individual's performance history and previous experience with elevated arousal levels, degree of skill or task mastery, self-confidence, self-belief in one's ability to execute the task correctly, and control over physical and cognitive anxiety symptoms (Gill et al., 2006; Kenny, 2011; Rapee & Medoro, 1994).

If Louise had perceived the music performance as a stressor that was controllable, then the stress hormones cortisol and catecholamine, which stimulate anxious responding, would not have been released (Davis et al., 1999). Even with high anxiety, if Louise also had high self-confidence, she would be more likely to experience anxiety as facilitative, regardless of performance outcome (Hanton, Mellalieu, & Hall, 2004; Jones, Hanton, & Swain, 1994). Therefore, like Louise's teacher had done, interventions to facilitate achievement outcomes in learning and performance should not be directed toward decreasing the degree of negative emotion, but rather increasing the amount of positive emotions directed to the task (Pekrun, Elliot, & Maier, 2009). Indeed, the typical "fight or flight" response in high anxiety states tends to motivate success-oriented students to "fight," that is, to approach a performance situation and undertake the necessary preparation required to achieve optimal performance outcomes (Martin & Marsh, 2008). Success-oriented students tend to be optimistic, proactive, and positively orientated to tasks, and respond to setbacks and failure with optimism and energy (Covington, 1992).

Interventions

Performance psychology techniques drawn from the sports domain have a strong evidence base in performance enhancement in recent years following treatment with athletes for performance anxiety (Murphy, 2012; Williams, 2010). Sport and music performance have many overlapping features: both require high levels of motor control and learning, mastery over mind and body, the necessity for implicit recall and smooth performance, and the presence of an audience which may invoke enjoyment of excellence and/or psychological pressure (Yoshie et al., 2009). Performance psychology techniques address the "cognitive, emotional, behavioural and psychophysiological inhibitors of consistent, excellent performance" to support individuals to "consistently perform in the upper range of their capabilities" (American Psychological Association, 2011, p. 9). Positive psychology draws upon character strengths and positive visualization, encouraging flow, and the close study of what occurs during an optimal performance (Csikszentmihalyi, 1990).

Only a handful of studies have empirically tested whether a psychological intervention is effective in reducing MPA in this age group. A recent study tested a six-week program of three weekly Kripalu-style yoga classes for advanced adolescent musicians (mean age 16 years) participating in a summer residential training program at a prestigious music performance institute, compared to a no-intervention control group (Khalsa et al., 2013). Students who participated in the yoga classes reported significant reductions in MPA during group and solo performances. This study suggests that the physical postures and movements, meditation, attention control, breathing, and deep relaxation activities of yoga may be a useful way to manage MPA in adolescence.

Two other studies have evaluated more comprehensive psychological skills programs in school settings. In the first reported study to empirically evaluate anxiety management techniques for MPA in adolescent musicians, Osborne et al., (2007) implemented a combined group–individual cognitive-behavioral intervention program to reduce MPA and improve performance quality for 23 students (mean age 13.87 years, $SD = 1.22$ years) at the Sydney Conservatorium of Music High School. They were assessed using the MPAI-A, State-Trait-Anxiety Inventory (Spielberger,

1983) and the Anxiety Disorders Interview Schedule for DSM-IV (Child version, ADIS-IV:C, Silverman & Albano, 1996). Physiological measures of heart rate and frontalis muscle tension were also taken. Prior to commencing, students gave an unaccompanied solo performance of 2–3 minutes demonstrating their highest level of musical proficiency. Students were then randomly allocated to the Music Performance Enhancement Program (MPEP) as a cognitive-behavioral performance psychology intervention, or were required to perform the piece of music only as a behavior-exposure-only (BEO) condition.

The MPEP was delivered over seven sessions: three one-hour group sessions (weeks 1, 3, and 5) after school, and four 45-minute individual sessions (weeks 2, 4, 6, and 7) within school time. Group sessions covered the following topics which were followed up with students in their individual sessions: psychoeducation regarding the physiological, cognitive, and behavioral aspects of MPA; relaxation strategies; goal setting; cognitive restructuring and self-talk performance diaries; and performance routines, choking, warm-up decrements and paralysis-by-analysis. Within two weeks of finishing the program all students completed the same self-report and diagnostic interview as pre-intervention, and performed the same piece of music as their first performance with accompanying physiological measurements.

Following the intervention, students who participated in the MPEP reported lower MPAI-A scores and performance fear than students who were in the BEO group. There was no difference between groups in performance quality. Generalized Anxiety Disorder (GAD) diagnoses decreased by 50% for both the MPEP and BEO groups, and Social Phobia (SocP) decreased by 84% for MPEP and 50% for BEO. Students in the MPEP group also demonstrated significantly less performance avoidance than the BEO group. There were even more striking reductions in MPA for the adherent students (see Figure 23.2). Social phobia diagnoses in the adherent group were eliminated entirely after participating in the program, combined with a 67% reduction in GAD, and a greater decrease in performance fear than the non-adherent group.

This study included a concert condition in which all students performed the same piece of music to an audience of friends, relatives, and Conservatorium staff one month after completing the program. At this concert state-anxiety scores for the adherent group reduced dramatically, demonstrating ecological validity (Osborne, 2008). These findings reveal that psychological skills training can significantly reduce MPA and performance avoidance within a school setting, and may also provide psychological benefits in other areas of students' lives.

A subsequent study by Osborne (2013; Braden et al., 2015), "Unleash your Music Potential," evaluated the manualized performance psychology program "Thinking Skills for Peak Performance: Unleash your Potential!" (Brandon & Ivens, 2009) as an early intervention strategy for Year 7, 8, and 9 students at a non-selective Catholic girls school. The program is grounded in cognitive-behavioral, performance, and positive psychology principles to build students' self-knowledge in relation to achieving a peak performance. In this study, a randomized wait-list control design with a larger sample size was used to delineate the effect of time from intervention which was not possible in the Sydney Conservatorium High School study (Osborne et al., 2007). The "Unleash your Music Potential" program included eight sessions covering peak performance, personal strengths, planning and goal setting, motivation, positive self-talk, relaxation, imagery and visualization, stress regulation, and recovery after disappointments or setbacks. Three solo performances performed in front of two judges acted as both a behavioral exposure and an outcome assessment of manifest MPA. Additional outcome measures included self-reported state (pre-performance) and trait (non-performance) MPA, motivation to learn and perform music, and expert ratings of performance quality and observable behavioral manifestations of MPA.

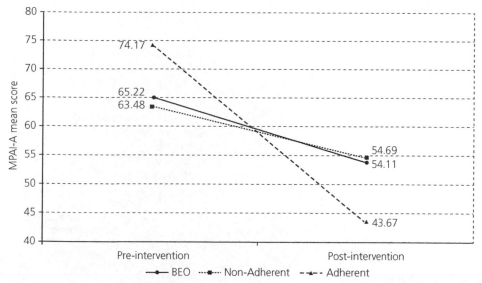

Fig. 23.2 MPAI-A scores pre- and post-intervention by group

Reproduced from Margaret S. Osborne, Dianna T. Kenny, and John Cooksey, Impact of a Cognitive-Behavioural Treatment Program on Music Performance Anxiety in Secondary School Music Students: A Pilot Study, Musicae Scientiae *11*(2) (Special Issue), p. 67, doi: 10.1177/10298649070110S204 © 2007, The Author.

Self-reported MPA reduced significantly for all students after completing the program. MPA scores continued to decline two months after completing the program for the first intervention group, showing both maintenance of gains *and* continued improvement after program completion. There was also evidence of improved performance quality. In contrast, there appeared to be no effect of the intervention on judge-rated behavioral manifestations of MPA.

Significant improvements were also observed in music performance resilience as measured by the Motivation and Engagement Scale for Music (MES-M) (Martin, 2008). Improved self-efficacy scores indicated that students were more likely to want to perform in order to achieve a successful outcome, rather than to avoid failure. Performance preparation improved through increased planning, effort, and persistence, showing improved autonomy in achieving successful outcomes, with a commensurate reduction in self-handicapping and withdrawal behaviors. In short, as a result of the intervention, students' music performance preparation strategies became more self-regulated.

Both studies demonstrate that performance psychology programs, which teach young musicians the mental skills needed to enhance personal confidence and competence to perform at one's best, lead to significant reductions in MPA when delivered within the school environment.

Strategies to overcome performance anxiety and achieve an optimal musical performance

Louise is more likely to achieve music performance excellence when three factors are working in tandem (see Figure 23.3):

1 musical competence (e.g., adequate skill development, practice, and task mastery);

2 physical well-being (e.g., adequate nutrition, sleep, and fitness); and

3 psychological well-being (e.g., positive and realistic self-statements and realistic self-appraisal of performance quality) (Kenny & Ackermann, 2009; Williamon, 2004).

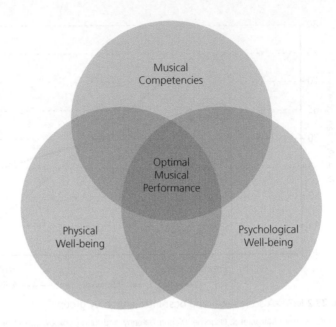

Fig. 23.3 Contributors to optimal music performance

Parents and teachers can support Louise's psychological well-being in music performance by helping her to understand that:

1 an optimal or "peak" performance (one where performers think and feel they are performing at their best) is not a perfect performance. It is one where mistakes are fewest and/or minor problems are recovered from quickly (Williams, 2010). Musicians *do* make mistakes, and this does not necessarily mean performance failure;

2 poor performances provide valuable information on how to learn to improve performance in future events (see, e.g., the achievement and motivation literature on mastery and performance goals by Dweck, 2012 and Martin, 2010);

3 experiencing anxiety prior to, during, or after a performance is not inherently maladaptive and should not be avoided per se; in fact, it is our natural nervous system response providing us with alertness and energy to face any challenging situation; and,

4 anxiety may actually *enhance* performance.

These points lead into four areas in which psychological skills can be integrated with technical practice to increase young musicians' ability to control performance anxiety and optimize musical performance.

1. Manage physiological arousal, but don't expect to give your best performance being relaxed

Breathing and relaxation strategies such as yoga lead to significant reductions in MPA in adolescents, yet incorporating relaxation training into exposure-based treatments for anxiety does not necessarily lead to improved outcomes. The focus of psychological treatment in challenging social-evaluative performances such as oral presentations or music performance is to develop a tolerance for the natural rise in physiological arousal (Velting, Setzer, & Albano, 2004). This is a crucial point to note in managing MPA, because a moderate amount of arousal is necessary for good musical performance. Therefore, it is *not* recommended to advise Louise that she should feel relaxed before performing. The discord between the belief that "I must be relaxed in order to perform well" and the inevitable "fight-or-flight" sensations of elevated heart rate, dry mouth, sweating etc. is likely to inspire a sense of confusion and failure before she has even played the first note. Louise can be put at ease about performance anxiety through education about the natural anxiety response to challenging situations, and identifying her own zone of optimal functioning (see tip 4).

2. Build positive emotions toward performing

Interventions to facilitate achievement outcomes in learning and performance should not be directed toward decreasing the degree of emotion per se, but rather, increasing the amount of *positive* emotion directed to the task (Pekrun et al., 2009). As in Louise's case, this can be done by emphasizing artistic expression, and the purpose of a musical performance as an opportunity to communicate one's unique interpretation of the emotional intent or story composed within the piece, rather than "not making any mistakes" which can facilitate rumination over the potential for errors (Ryan, 2004). Framing errors as an inevitable part of the learning process has a performance-enhancing effect compared to the negative effect of framing errors as events that should be avoided (Andersen, 2009).

3. Performance simulation

Mere exposure to public performance does not automatically lead to a decrease in anxiety. What is required for anxiety management skills training to lead to performance-specific outcomes is to integrate it with performance practice. Louise was encouraged to build up levels of physiological arousal to approximate the levels experienced in actual performance, to enable her to be confident in executing musical skills *despite* elevations in physiological arousal. Through simulation training, she can deliberately practice coping with internal and external performance anxiety triggers so that they are readily engaged in performances (Greene, 2002; Williamon, Aufegger, & Eiholzer, 2014). Adverse consequences associated with early evaluative performances should be minimized by offering frequent, low-stress opportunities to perform so that she can learn that performance is an integral, enjoyable, and manageable part of learning her instrument. The repertoire should be within her technical capability, and well learned before performing.

4. Identify your own IZOF

By working on these elements, Louise can identify her IZOF. IZOF analysis can be as simple as using video recordings of music performances and keeping a performance diary noting each event, recording preparatory and pre-performance thoughts and behaviors, rating level of preparation and anxiety (say, out of 100), and providing her own feedback on performance outcomes (again rating, say, out of 100). Over time this builds an individualized database of thoughts and actions leading to successful performances which can be summarized to generate an individualized "how to" list of constructive behaviors and strategies that can kick-start an optimal music performance.

Conclusion

This chapter has reviewed our knowledge of performance anxiety in child and adolescent musicians and provided information about psychological strategies to manage overwhelming MPA that can be readily incorporated into instrumental/vocal training. Anxiety was discussed as an adaptive reaction to perceived danger, and common manifestations through thoughts, behaviors, and physiological sensations were summarized, including a brief description of the neural mechanisms underpinning these manifestations. The instinctive desire to avoid performances perceived as threatening and thus anxiety provoking was discussed as a maladaptive means to performance success, as this encourages a deterioration of musical skills which can spiral into a self-defeating and self-fulfilling prophecy of performance failure, reinforcing the primary fear of MPA. Conceptualizations of MPA drawing from music and sports performance literature were summarized to show that the experience of MPA is not detrimental to performance per se. Rather, the effect of anxiety as facilitating or detrimental to the quality of a performance depends on the young musician's performance history, their experience and skill in managing the spike of physiological arousal prior to and during a performance, their level of musical skill or task mastery, and self-confidence. Building confidence will improve their ability to perceive anxiety as conducive to good performance. It is hoped that the information presented in this chapter will help in our collective efforts to support young musicians like Louise to understand themselves as performers, and apply strategies to manage performance anxiety so that they feel joy, happiness, and satisfaction as they strive for musical excellence and deliver performances that demonstrate their full potential.

Reflective questions

1 Look back on your own musical development. Can you remember instances where you experienced a "fight or flight" response? What happened to trigger each response? To what extent did you find MPA exhilarating or debilitating?
2 What are the benefits of addressing psychological well-being to enhance music performance?
3 Explain the different ways young musicians experience MPA.
4 What techniques might be used to benefit a child or an adolescent who is experiencing MPA?
5 How can parents, teachers, and educational institutions facilitate a supportive learning and performance environment that minimizes adverse consequences and encourages excellence, particularly in the early stages of music learning?

Key sources

Brandon, C., & Ivens, C. (2009). *Thinking skills for peak performance: Student workbook and coach's manual.* South Yarra: Macmillan Education Australia.

Greene, D. (2012). *11 strategies for audition and performance success: A workbook for musicians* (p. 48). Retrieved January 17, 2014 from <http://psi.dongreene.com/>.

Reference list

Altenmüller, E., & McPherson, G. E. (2008). Motor learning and instrumental training. In W. Gruhn & F. Rauscher (Eds.), *Neurosciences in music pedagogy* (pp. 121–44). New York: Nova Biomedical Books.

American Psychological Association. (2011). *Defining the practice of sport and performance psychology,* Division 47 (Exercise and Sport Psychology), Practice Committee of the American Psychological Association. Retrieved from <http://www.apadivisions.org/division-47/about/resources/defining.pdf>.

Andersen, M. B. (2009). The "canon" of psychological skills training for enhancing performance. In K. F. Hays (Ed.), *Performance psychology in action: A casebook for working with athletes, performing artists, business leaders, and professionals in high-risk occupations* (pp. 11–34). Washington, DC: American Psychological Association.

Bandura, A. (1991). Self-efficacy conception of anxiety. In R. Schwarzer & R. Wicklund (Eds.), *Anxiety and self-focused attention.* New York: Harwood Academic Publishers.

Barlow, D. H. (2002). *Anxiety and its disorders. The nature and treatment of anxiety and panic* (2nd ed.). New York: The Guilford Press.

Boucher, H., & Ryan, C. A. (2011). Performance stress and the very young musician. *Journal of Research in Music Education*, **58**(4), 329–45.

Braden, A. M., Osborne, M. S., & Wilson, S. J. (2015). Psychological intervention reduces self-reported performance anxiety in high school music students. *Frontiers in Psychology*, **6**. doi: 10.3389/fpsyg.2015.00195.

Brandon, C., & Ivens, C. (2009). *Thinking skills for peak performance: Student workbook and coach's manual.* South Yarra: Macmillan Education Australia.

Britsch, L. (2005). Investigating performance-related problems of young musicians. *Medical Problems of Performing Artists*, **20**(1), 40–7.

Brotons, M. (1994). Effects of performing conditions on music performance anxiety and performance quality. *Journal of Music Therapy*, **31**(1), 63–81.

Chan, M.-Y. (2011). *The relationship between music performance anxiety, age, self-esteem, and performance outcomes in Hong Kong music students* (Doctoral dissertation), Durham University, UK. Available at Durham E-Theses Online: <http://etheses.dur.ac.uk/637/>.

Covington, M. V. (1992). *Making the grade: A self-worth perspective on motivation and school reform.* Cambridge: Cambridge University Press.

Craske, M. G., & Craig, K. D. (1984). Musical performance anxiety: The three-systems model and self-efficacy theory. *Behaviour Research and Therapy*, **22**(3), 267–80.

Csikszentmihalyi, M. (1990). *Flow: The psychology of optimal experience.* New York: Harper and Row.

Davis, E. P., Donzella, B., Krueger, W. K., & Gunnar, M. R. (1999). The start of a new school year: Individual differences in salivary cortisol response in relation to child temperament. *Developmental Psychobiology*, **35**(3), 188–96.

Dollard, J., & Miller, N. E. (1950). *Personality and psychotherapy: An analysis in terms of learning, thinking, and culture.* New York: McGraw-Hill.

Dweck, C. (2012). *Mindset: How you can fulfil your potential.* London: Constable & Robinson.

Essau, C. A., Conradt, J., & Petermann, F. (1999). Frequency and comorbidity of social phobia and social fears in adolescents. *Behaviour Research and Therapy*, **37**(9), 831–43.

Fehm, L., & Schmidt, K. (2006). Performance anxiety in gifted adolescent musicians. *Journal of Anxiety Disorders*, **20**(1), 98–109.

Gill, A., Murphy, F., & Rickard, N. S. (2006). A preliminary examination of the roles of perceived control, cortisol and perceptions of anxiety in music performance. *Australian Journal of Music Education*, **1**, 32–47.

Greene, D. (2002). *Performance success: Performing your best under pressure.* New York: Routledge.

Hanin, Y. L. (Ed.) (2000). *Emotions in sport.* Champaign, IL: Human Kinetics.

Hanton, S., Mellalieu, S. D., & Hall, R. (2004). Self-confidence and anxiety interpretation: A qualitative investigation. *Psychology of Sport & Exercise*, **5**(4), 477–95.

Hargreaves, D. J., MacDonald, R. A., & Miell, D. (2012). Musical identities mediate musical development. In G. E. McPherson & G. Welch (Eds.), *The Oxford handbook of music education* (pp. 125–42). New York: Oxford University Press.

Heaven, P. C. L. (2001). *The social psychology of adolescence.* Hampshire, UK: Palgrave.

Jackson, S. A., & Csikszentmihalyi, M. (1999). *Flow in sport.* Champaign, IL: Human Kinetics.

Jones, G., Hanton, S., & Swain, A. (1994). Intensity and interpretation of anxiety symptoms in elite and non-elite sports performers. *Personality & Individual Differences*, **17**(5), 657–63.

Jones, G., Swain, A., & Hardy, L. (1993). Intensity and direction dimensions of competitive state anxiety and relationships with performance. *Journal of Sports Sciences*, **11**(6), 525–32.

Kasai, H., Fukuda, M., Watanabe, S., Hayashi-Takagi, A., & Noguchi, J. (2010). Structural dynamics of dendritic spines in memory and cognition. *Trends in Neurosciences*, **33**(3), 121–9.

Kashani, J. H., Orvaschel, H., Rosenberg, T. K., & Reid, J. C. (1989). Psychopathology in a community sample of children and adolescents. *Journal of the American Academy of Child & Adolescent Psychiatry*, **28**(5), 701–6.

Kemp, A. (1981). The personality structure of the musician: I. Identifying a profile of traits for the performer. *Psychology of Music*, **9**(1), 3–14.

Kenny, D. T. (2000). Psychological foundations of stress and coping: A developmental perspective. In D. T. Kenny, J. G. Carlson, F. J. McGuigan, & J. L. Sheppard (Eds.), *Stress and health: Research and clinical applications* (p. 467). Amsterdam: Gordon Breach/Harwood Academic Publishers.

Kenny, D. T. (2011). *The psychology of music performance anxiety*. Oxford: Oxford University Press.

Kenny, D. T., & Ackermann, B. (2009). Optimizing physical and psychological health in performing musicians. In S. Hallam, I. Cross, & M. Thaut (Eds.), *Oxford handbook of music psychology* (pp. 390–400). Oxford, UK: Oxford University Press.

Kenny, D. T., Davis, P. J., & Oates, J. (2004). Music performance anxiety and occupational stress amongst opera chorus artists and their relationship with state and trait anxiety and perfectionism. *Journal of Anxiety Disorders*, **18**(6), 757–77.

Kenny, D. T., & Osborne, M. S. (2006). Music performance anxiety: New insights from young musicians. *Advances in Cognitive Psychology*, **2**(2–3), 103–12.

Khalsa, S. B., Butzer, B., Shorter, S. M., Reinhardt, K. M., & Cope, S. (2013). Yoga reduces performance anxiety in adolescent musicians. *Alternative Therapies in Health and Medicine*, **19**(2), 34–45.

Kim, J. K., & Diamond, D. M. (2002). The stressed hippocampus, synaptic plasticity and lost memories. *Nature Reviews Neuroscience*, **3**(6), 453–62.

Kokotsaki, D., & Davidson, J. W. (2003). Investigating musical performance anxiety among music college singing students: A quantitative analysis. *Music Education Research*, **5**(1), 45–59.

Kubzansky, L. D., & Stewart, A. J. (1999). At the intersection of anxiety, gender and performance. *Journal of Social and Clinical Psychology*, **18**(1), 76–97.

LeBlanc, A., Jin, Y. C., Obert, M., & Siivola, C. (1997). Effect of audience on music performance anxiety. *Journal of Research in Music Education*, **45**(3), 480–96.

Maroon, M. T. J. (2003). Potential contributors to performance anxiety among middle school students performing at solo and ensemble contest. *Dissertation Abstracts International*, **64**(2-A), 437.

Martin, A. J. (2008). *Motivation and Engagement Scale Music (MES-M) test user manual*. Summer Hill: Lifelong Achievement Group.

Martin, A. J. (2010). *Building classroom success: Eliminating academic fear and failure*. London: Continuum Books.

Martin, A. J., & Marsh, H. W. (2008). Academic buoyancy: Towards an understanding of students' everyday academic resilience. *Journal of School Psychology*, **46**(1), 53–83.

McLaren, S. (2004). *Don't panic: You can overcome anxiety without drugs*. Victoria, Australia: Scribe.

McLaren, S. (2013). More on Mental Control. Retrieved February 20, from <http://www.blog.salleemclaren.com.au/>.

McPherson, G. E., Davidson, J. W., & Faulkner, R. (2012). *Music in our lives: Rethinking musical development, ability and identity*. Oxford: Oxford University Press.

Murphy, S. M. (Ed.) (2012). *The Oxford handbook of sport and performance psychology*. New York: Oxford University Press.

Osborne, M. S. (2008). Music performance anxiety in young musicians: Conceptualisation, phenomenology, assessment and treatment (Doctoral dissertation), University of Sydney, Australia.

Osborne, M. S. (2013). Maximising performance potential: The efficacy of a performance psychology program to reduce music performance anxiety and build resilience in adolescents. In A. Williamon & W. Goebl (Eds.), *Proceedings of the international symposium on performance science 2013* (pp. 303–10). Brussels, Belgium: Association Européenne des Conservatoires.

Osborne, M. S., & Franklin, J. (2002). Cognitive processes in music performance anxiety. *Australian Journal of Psychology*, **54**(2), 86–93.

Osborne, M. S., & Kenny, D. T. (2005). Development and validation of a music performance anxiety inventory for gifted adolescent musicians. *Journal of Anxiety Disorders*, **19**(7), 725–51.

Osborne, M. S., & Kenny, D. T. (2008). The role of sensitising experiences in music performance anxiety in adolescent musicians. *Psychology of Music*, **36**(4), 447–62.

Osborne, M. S., Kenny, D. T., & Cooksey, J. (2007). Impact of a cognitive-behavioural treatment program on music performance anxiety in secondary school music students: A pilot study. *Musicae Scientiae*, **11**(2) (Special Issue), 53–84.

Osborne, M. S., Kenny, D. T., & Holsomback, R. (2005). Assessment of music performance anxiety in late childhood: A validation study of the music performance anxiety inventory for adolescents (MPAI-A). *International Journal of Stress Management*, **12**(4), 312–30.

Osborne, M. S., & Patston, T. (2013, October 24–27). The developmental progression of music performance anxiety and perfectionism: Implications for prevention and early intervention in adolescent musicians. Paper presented at the Australian Association for Cognitive and Behaviour Therapy, 36th National Conference "Innovations in Australasian Mental Health Care," Hotel Grand Chancellor, Adelaide.

Papageorgi, I. (2007). The influence of the wider context of learning, gender, age, and individual differences on adolescent musicians' performance anxiety. In A. Williamon & D. Coimbra (Eds.), *Proceedings of the international symposium on performance science 2007* (pp. 219–24). Utrecht, The Netherlands: AEC.

Pekrun, R., Elliot, A. J., & Maier, M. (2009). Achievement goals and achievement emotions: Testing a model of their joint relations with academic performance. *Journal of Educational Psychology*, **101**(1), 115–35.

Piaget, J. (1970). Piaget's theory. In P. H. Mussen (Ed.), *Carmichael's manual of child psychology* (pp. 703–32). New York: Wiley.

Rae, G., & McCambridge, K. (2004). Correlates of performance anxiety in practical music exams. *Psychology of Music*, **32**(4), 432–9.

Rapee, R. M., & Medoro, L. (1994). Fear of physical sensations and trait anxiety as mediators of the response to hyperventilation in nonclinical subjects. *Journal of Abnormal Psychology*, **103**(4), 693–9.

Ryan, C. A. (1998). Exploring musical performance anxiety in children. *Medical Problems of Performing Artists*, **13**(3), 83–8.

Ryan, C. A. (2004). Gender differences in children's experience of musical performance anxiety. *Psychology of Music*, **32**(1), 89–103.

Ryan, C. A. (2005). Experience of musical performance anxiety in elementary school children. *International Journal of Stress Management*, **12**(4), 331–42.

Salmon, P. (1990). A psychological perspective on musical performance anxiety: A review of the literature. *Medical Problems of Performing Artists*, **5**(1), 2–11.

Salmon, P. (1991). Stress inoculation techniques and musical performance anxiety. In G. D. Wilson (Ed.), *Psychology and performing arts* (p. 323). Lisse, The Netherlands: Swets & Zeitlinger.

Schwartz, J. M., & Begley, S. (2002). *The mind and the brain: Neuroplasticity and the power of mental force*. New York: Harper Collins.

Senyshyn, Y., & O'Neill, S. A. (2001). Subjective experience of anxiety and musical performance: A relational perspective. *Philosophy of Music Education Review*, **9**(1), 42–53.

Silverman, W. K., & Albano, A. M. (1996). *Anxiety disorders interview schedule for DSM-IV: Child interview schedule*. San Antonio: The Psychological Corporation.

Smith, A. J., & Rickard, N. S. (2004). Prediction of music performance anxiety via personality and trait anxiety in young musicians. *Australian Journal of Music Education*, **1**, 3–12.

Spielberger, C. D. (1983). *State-Trait Anxiety Inventory STAI (Form Y)*. Palo Alto, CA: Consulting Psychologists Press, Inc.

Strahan, E., & Conger, A. J. (1998). Social anxiety and its effects on performance and perception. *Journal of Anxiety Disorders, 12*(4), 293–305.

Tassi, P., Bonnefond, A., Hoeft, A., Eschenlauer, R., & Muzet, A. (2003). Arousal and vigilance: Do they differ? Study in a sleep inertia paradigm. *Sleep Research Online, 5*(3), 83–7.

Thomas, J. P., & Nettelbeck, T. (2014). Performance anxiety in adolescent musicians. *Psychology of Music, 42*(4), 624–34. doi: 10.1177/0305735613485151.

Velting, O. N., Setzer, N. J., & Albano, A. M. (2004). Update on and advances in assessment and cognitive-behavioral treatment of anxiety disorders in children and adolescents. *Professional Psychology: Research and Practice, 35*(1), 42–54.

WHO. (2004). *Management of mental disorders* (Vol. 1). Darlinghurst, NSW: World Health Organisation Collaborating Centre for Evidence in Mental Health Policy.

Williamon, A. (Ed.) (2004). *Musical excellence: Strategies and techniques to enhance performance*. Oxford: Oxford University Press.

Williamon, A., Aufegger, L., & Eiholzer, H. (2014). Simulating and stimulating performance: Introducing distributed simulation to enhance musical learning and performance. *Frontiers in Psychology, 5*. doi: 10.3389/fpsyg.2014.00025.

Williams, J. M. (Ed.) (2010). *Applied sport psychology: Personal growth to peak performance* (6th ed.). New York: McGraw-Hill.

Wilson, G. D. (2002). *Psychology for performing artists* (2nd ed.). London, UK: Whurr.

Yerkes, R. M., & Dodson, J. D. (1908). The relation of strength of stimulus to rapidity of habit formation. *Journal of Comparative Neurology and Psychology, 18*, 459–82.

Yoshie, M., Kudo, K., Murakoshi, T., & Ohtsuki, T. (2009). Music performance anxiety in skilled pianists: Effects of social-evaluative performance situation on subjective, autonomic, and electromyographic reactions. *Experimental Brain Research, 199*(2), 117–26.

Zeidner, M., & Matthews, G. (2005). Evaluation anxiety. In A. J. Ellliot & C. S. Dweck (Eds.), *Handbook of competence and motivation* (pp. 141–63). New York: The Guilford Press.

Chapter 24

Singing and vocal development

Graham F. Welch

Singing and vocal development: Introduction

Despite the warmth in the room as they shook the snow off their winter coats and gathered around the kitchen table, there was a collective sense of nervousness and, in some cases, unease that was barely touched by the hostess' cheerful manner and greeting. Outside, the dark of a Newfoundland evening had already descended and the hostess wondered if some of the wind's icy chill was reflected in the body language. This gathering was to be the first of several sessions for the group when things usually unspoken, sometimes hidden for many decades, would be allowed to surface.

> My biggest recollection is school, of course. You went to school, the first thing the nuns would say, — Anybody can sing. You'd go and you were embarrassed to tears because you knew you couldn't sing, and there was no help . . . I can remember, at least a full row, if not two, in the classroom choirs or the singing choir, that you were told to pantomime. You had to go to music, and you had to listen to all the words and be able to mouth it or lip-sync it like everybody else, but you were not allowed to sing and you weren't allowed to turn it down. (Knight, 2010, pp. 108–9, interview with C., aged 50)
>
> I remember playing skipping and singing on the street. I can't remember the tunes now . . . I don't think I ever really thought I couldn't sing until Grade 7 and the teacher and all my friends and I were in glee club and that was a major time, she stopped and said —Somebody is tone deaf here. She said —It's you Vic, you're tone deaf. She said —You don't have any notes, you just can't sing along with the music at all . . . I can see the class, I was sitting second row back and there were kids behind me, you can imagine how embarrassed I felt. From then on I just assumed I was tone deaf . . . I guess obviously it was traumatic, to remember after 30 years. (Knight, 2010, p. 125, interview with V., aged 47)
>
> Then in Grade 6 [age 11] . . . I stood up to sing it and she told me to sit down, that I couldn't sing. Well, I was devastated . . . I'm sure I wanted to cry. Of course you came home, it was no good of telling your parents at the time that something like this had happened to you . . . And she was such a powerful person in the community . . . It stayed with me for so long. It was so degrading at the time. Even in high school, if there was anything to do with music, I hated music . . . I didn't learn it. I couldn't learn it, as I thought . . . I'm sure that [incident] affected it, in a lot of ways . . . maybe she just didn't have the knowledge and it didn't come to her—'I am doing something that's going to affect this child for most of her life.' That's probably the way it was. (Knight, 2010, p. 91, interview with L., aged 42)

Over the next few weeks and months, these adults shared many similar detailed, yet negative, memories, particularly associated with their former schooldays. Despite the passing of time, these episodes of childhood were vividly recalled. A sense of embarrassment, shame, deep emotional upset, and humiliation were commonly evidenced, usually accompanied by reports of a life-long sense of musical inadequacy. For these particular Canadians, as for many other adults around the world in different cultural contexts, the associations between singing and childhood were not positive. Within the local Newfoundland culture, singing competency either as an individual or within a group has always had high status. Consequently, any perceived singing "failure" in childhood has often led to continued self-identify as a "non-singer" (see Knight, 1999) and has reinforced a cultural stereotype of a community that is divided in two: those who "can sing" and those who "cannot"—a status associated with emotional trauma, acceptance, and a sense of "irrevocability" (Knight, 1999, p. 144).

Similar findings have been reported from other studies of adults in North America, the UK, and Scandinavia. Yet, despite such experiences, there are some adults who never give up hope of improvement and there have been several successful examples of specialist choirs being started for adult "non-singers" (Mack, 1979; Richards & Durrant, 2003). These include a new community choir in St. John's, Newfoundland, four "beginners" choirs in one London college that have a 20-year history, various "Singing from Scratch" choirs in the Midlands and South-East of England, and similar initiatives in Sweden, the United States, Canada, Australia, and New Zealand.

The existence of such choirs for adult "non-singers" is one of a number of significant challenges to a bi-polar "can/cannot" categorization of singing behaviors. They are part of the evidence base for singing to be considered as a normal developmental behavior that can be enhanced or hindered, particularly by the events and experiences of childhood. For example, other recent research suggests that such self-labeling in adulthood may be somewhat erroneous. An adult's perceived sense of singing inadequacy, based on their negative childhood experiences, is not necessarily born out empirically when their singing ability is actually assessed. Several studies have reported a mismatch between perceived and actual singing ability in adults, with the behavior often being more competent than the self-perception (Cuddy et al., 2005; Knight, 2010; Wise, 2009). One recent study of singing ability in the general adult population, for example, found that the majority of adult participants were much more pitch accurate when they performed a well-known target melody at slower tempi (Dalla Bella, Giguére, & Peretz, 2007).

Overall, the prime source of singing "failure" for an individual is often a particular moment in childhood and/or adolescence when there is a mismatch between developing singing competences and a set singing task (Cooksey & Welch, 1998; Welch, 1979, 1985, 2000a,b, 2005a). Erroneous adult expectation often creates the problem. This mismatch may then become further "objectified" by continuing inappropriate comments from adults or peers, which suggests that the singing problem is evidence of an underlying disability in music. Arguably, the number of singing "failures" that are socially generated in our communities would be reduced radically if there was a greater awareness of a) how singing mastery develops, b) how children of the same age can be in different phases of development (as is considered normal with other forms of culturally biased behavior, such as reading), and c) how best to provide suitable "developmentally sensitive" singing activities. The narrative that follows reviews the nature of singing development from early childhood through to (and including) adolescence. Particular features are highlighted of how normal development may be fostered, shaped, and sometimes hindered.

Singing as a developmental behavior

Pre-birth and infancy

The foundations of singing development originate in the auditory and affective experiences of the developing fetus during the final months of gestation, particularly in relation to the earliest perception of melodic variations in the mother's voice. The amniotic fluid that surrounds the fetus is an effective transducer of the pitch contours of maternal voicing. As the mother speaks or sings, the prosodic features of her voice (melody and rhythm) are conveyed to the developing fetus by the sound waves that transfer through her body tissue and that also are reflected from surfaces in her immediate environment. At the same time, the mother's affective state as she speaks or sings is encoded hormonally in her bloodstream through neuroendocrine activity. This emotional state is believed to be experienced by the fetus relatively concomitantly with the sound of the mother's voice because of an interfacing of the fetal and maternal bloodstreams (see Welch, 2005a for a more detailed review). The outcome is an interweaving of acoustic (prosodic/melodic) and emotional experiences pre-birth that are likely to underpin the developing infant's subsequent interactions post-birth with the sounds of the maternal culture. For example, our ability to determine particularly strong emotions in vocal behaviors in speech and singing (Johnstone & Scherer, 2000; Loui et al., 2013; Nawrot, 2003; Sundberg, 2000) is likely to originate in these earliest dual-channel (acoustic-affect) experiences and, arguably, to create a certain bias toward the association of particular vocal timbres with positive and negative feelings (termed "emotional capital"—Welch, 2005a). Six-month-olds, for example, exhibit endocrine (cortisol) changes after listening to their mothers singing (Trehub, 2001), becoming calmed when upset and more alert when sleepy.

The first year of life is characterized by a shaping of the infant's vocal production through an interaction with the acoustic characteristics of the maternal culture. Parents, for example, typically incorporate rich musical properties when interacting with infants: they speak and sing at higher pitch levels, use a wider pitch range and longer pauses, often at a slower rate, and use smooth, simple, but highly modulated intonation contours (see Thurman & Welch, 2000; Welch, 2005b; Trehub & Degé, Chapter 2). At birth, neonates continue to be particularly sensitive to the sound of the human voice, whilst demonstrating a certain initial perceptual plasticity toward any language (Eimas, 1985). Two-day-old neonates, for example, listen longer to women singing in a maternal style (Masataka, 1999). Adult singing (both male and female) appears to be especially significant, as demonstrated in its beneficial effects on premature infants' physiological functioning through changes in heart rate and oxygen saturation, alongside a reduction in stressful behaviors (Coleman et al., 1997).

The earliest vocal behavior is crying. It contains all of the ingredients of subsequent vocalization, including singing, with variations in intensity and pitch, as well as rhythmic patterning and phrasing (Vihman, 1996). At the age of 2 months, cooing and vowel-like sounds are already evidenced and being shaped by the maternal culture (Ruzza et al., 2003). Aspects of "musical babbling" that contain definite musical features, such as pitch and rhythmic patterns, are also evidenced from 2 months onwards (Tafuri & Villa, 2002). Their incidence and quality appear to be related positively to the amount of time devoted to daily singing behaviors by the mother; the greater the amount of maternal singing, the increased likelihood of earlier musical babbling. Although maternal singing to infants is primarily a caregiving tool aimed at emotional regulation, it provides a rich musical context for mother–infant interaction where the young child is motivated to imitate and play with vocal sound (see Trehub & Gudmundsdottir, 2014, for a review).

By the age of 3 to 4 months, the infant is able to imitate their mother's exaggerated prosodic contours that characterize infant–mother interaction (Masataka, 1992). Vocal play emerges around the ages of 4 to 6 months (Papousek, 1996). By the age of 1 year, infants are sufficiently cued into the language of the maternal culture for elements to be reflected in their own vocalizations. As examples, French infants babble using French speech units, Russian infants babble using Russian, and Japanese infants using Japanese (Meltzoff, 2002). In general, the first year of life is characterized by increasingly diverse vocal activity. The first vocalizations of infancy, with their communication of affective state (discomfort and distress, then also comfort and eustress), are expanded to include quasi-melodic features (2–4 months), developing vocal control (4–7 months), with vocal pitch behaviors that are directly linked to the prosodic features of the mother tongue.

Early childhood and preschool

Singing development preschool is characterized by an increasing interaction with the sounds of the experienced maternal culture. This interaction is reflected in a mosaic of different singing behaviors that are evidenced between the ages of 1 and 5 years. They relate to the young child's acquisitive, playful, creative, and spontaneous nature as they engage with and make sense of their "local" musical world (e.g., Barrett, 2011). The variety of vocalization includes: 2-year-olds' repetition of brief phrases with identifiable rhythmic and melodic contour patterns (Dowling, 1999); and 3-year-olds' vocal interplay between spontaneous improvisation and selected elements from the dominant song culture, termed "pot-pourri" songs (Moog, 1976) and "outline songs" (Hargreaves, 1996) in which the nature of the figurative shape of the sung melodic contour (its "schematic" contour) is thought to reflect the current level of the young child's understanding of tonal relationships (Davidson, 1994).

There is evidence of increasing sophistication and complexity in relation to the learning of songs from the dominant culture by young children (e.g., Mang, 2005; and see footnote 1 for developmental models by Rutkowski, 1997; Welch, 2002). However, the path of development is not necessarily linear for any particular individual. In a US study of the spontaneous singing of 2-year-olds' first songs, for example, there is evidence that "phrases are the initial musical units" (Davidson, 1994, p. 117). Such phrases are characterized by limited pitch range, a certain disjunction of key/tonality, and a descending contour. In contrast, recent Italian data of 2- to 3-year-old children indicate that some young children appear to be much better at imitating a complete melody modeled by their mother (and also by a specialist course tutor) than matching individual phrases of the same song (Tafuri & Welch, unpublished data, see Figure 24.1; see also Tafuri, 2008). These Italian children had been exposed to regular sessions of their mothers' singing since the final trimester of pregnancy, both at home and in a special infant–parent singing course organized in the local conservatoire. Yet for other children in the same Italian group, with apparently the same levels of exposure to maternal singing, the opposite is the case. Their sung phrase

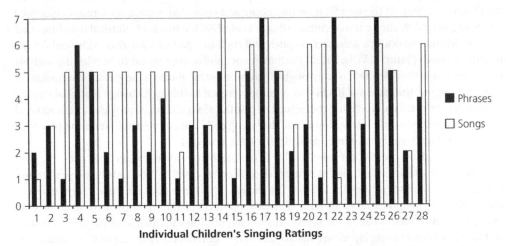

Fig. 24.1 Accuracy ratings of Italian children (n=28) aged 2.6 to 3.3 years in imitating song phrases and complete songs modeled by their mothers. Ratings are based on a 7-point scale of perceived accuracy

Data from Tafuri, J., *Infant Musicality*, 2008.

accuracy is rated as better than their whole song accuracy (Figure 24.1), in line with data from the earlier US (Davidson, 1994) study.

For the youngest children, the boundaries between singing and speaking may be blurred, or at least ambiguous to the adult listener, and are related to the dominance of a particular contour schema (Davidson, 1994) as well as to the influence of the mother tongue. For example, a longitudinal study in Canada of young girls aged 18 to 38 months from monolingual and bilingual backgrounds reported that "intermediate vocalisations" (a type of vocal behavior at the boundary between speech and song) were more prevalent in Mandarin- and Cantonese-speaking children than in English-speaking children (Mang, 2000/1). A follow-up study in Hong Kong with mono- and bilingual 3- and 4-year-olds confirmed these findings and revealed that, regardless of age, the manipulation of vocal pitch was used to distinguish between singing and speaking (Mang, 2002). The mean fundamental frequencies (F0) for songs were reported to be consistently higher than speech, but "own choice" songs were performed at a slightly lower pitch than a criterion song. In addition, the older English monolingual children demonstrated a wider mean F0 differentiation between their singing and speaking behaviors compared to their Cantonese monolingual and bilingual peers. Taken together, such examples from these diverse cultural settings remind us that singing behavior is subject to developmental processes, whilst also being sensitive to sociocultural context (including task). In these examples, context also includes the presence or absence of a pitch-based language as the mother tongue in which meaning is explicitly conveyed by the shaping of melodic contour.

As might be expected from the interaction of enculturation with generative skill development in music (British Educational Research Association Music Education Review Group, 2001; Welch, 2005b), longitudinal data on singing development in early childhood confirm the importance of the prosodic features of the mother tongue. Spontaneous singing is characterized principally by the control of melodic–rhythmic contour patterns (Dowling, 1999; Sundin, 1997). Between the ages of 1 and 2 years, for example, a typically spontaneous infant song consists of repetitions of one brief melodic phrase at different pitch centers. By the age of 3 years, three different phrases are characteristically evidenced and one-phrase singing is rare (Dowling, 1988, 1999). Furthermore, recent case study research with 2- to 3-year-olds in a free-play daycare setting (Young, 2002) celebrates a wide diversity in young children's spontaneous singing that is linked to context and activity, whilst being mediated by age. This diversity includes "free-flow vocalizing" (a wordless vocal creation often associated with solitary play with no defined overall musical shape), "chanting" (often short, repeated phrases), "reworking of known songs" (the utilization of enculturated song fragments), "movement vocalizing" (either of self or objects), singing for "animation" (associated with dramatic play), and the imitation of actual sounds (defined as "comic-strip type noises," usually associated with object play). As children grow older (3 to 4 years) and more sociable, more speaking than singing may be evidenced.

Age is also a factor in young children's perception and expression of emotion in singing; 4- and 5-year-olds are able to express happiness and sadness in their invented songs. In one Canadian study, children used conventional musical devices, such as a major modality and dotted or syncopated rhythms for "happy" songs, contrasted by a reduced pitch range and suppression of melodic contours in "sad" songs (Adachi & Trehub, 2000). Their song texts were also contraposed emotionally, with "happy" songs focused on "friends," "family," and "sweets," but "sad" songs focused more on a negative version of these (e.g., "no family"). In contrast, older children's "sad" songs were dominated by themes related to death (Adachi & Trehub, 1999). Data from Sweden (Gabrielsson & Örnkloo, 2002) confirm the growth of children's expertise with age in the recognition and expression of intended sung emotion, particularly between the ages of 4 and 7 years.

The first years of schooling

It is common for a diverse range of singing abilities to be exhibited by children on entry to compulsory schooling. Within this diversity, it is necessary to distinguish between i) children's (developing) skill in the performance of a taught song (Rutkowski, 1990, 1997; Welch, 1986, 1998, 2000b, 2002; Welch, Sergeant, & White, 1996, 1997, 1998) and ii) children's ability to invent songs (Davies, 1986, 1992, 1994). As with preschool singing behaviors, context and culture are also factors (Mang, 2003; Rutkowski & Chen-Haftek, 2000).

With regard to the first of these categories concerning the skilled performance of a taught song, two major US and UK studies have drawn on developmental theories to propose phased models of singing development (Rutkowski, 1997; Welch, 1998[1]). The US data (Rutkowski, 1997) was generated through systematic evaluation of children's singing behaviors across a period of over 15 years. The emergent nine-phase model (which went through several versions[2]) suggests that children progress from speech-like chanting of the song text, to singing within a limited range ("speaking range singer") to the demonstration of an expanded vocal pitch range that is allied to skilled competency in vocal pitch matching. This model has an affinity with that of another US-based longitudinal study (Davidson, 1994), which suggests that children's singing development is linked to a schematic processing of melodic contour. Data from Harvard University's six-year *Project Zero* study of children aged between the ages of 1 and 6 years indicated five specific levels of pitch development in young children's singing, expanding from an initial melodic contour scheme with a pitch interval of a third to one that embraced a complete octave.

Within the research literature, children are sometimes reported as being more skilled when copying a sung model if they used a neutral syllable rather than attempting the song with its text (e.g. Levinowitz, 1989). This finding has resonances with data from a three-year longitudinal study of 184 children in their first three years of formal education in ten UK primary schools (Welch et al., 1996, 1997, 1998). The research provided detailed evidence of how singing behaviors are age-, sex-, and task-sensitive. Over the three years, the participants as a collective appeared to demonstrate little overall improvement when required to match the sung pitches of the criterion songs (two songs were specially taught and assessed each year) (see Figure 24.2). However, this singing behavior was in marked contrast to their ability to learn the words of the songs, which was extremely good, even in their first term of compulsory schooling at age 5 (Figure 24.2: Year 1 age 5 data). Furthermore, when the pitch elements of the target songs were deconstructed into simpler musical tasks in which the children were required to match individual pitches, echo melodic contours, or copy small melodic fragments, the children were significantly more pitch accurate, as demonstrated by year-on-year improvements. There were no sex differences in their singing of these three types of deconstructed tasks: boys and girls were equally successful and demonstrated similar improvements over time. In contrast, when the *same* boys were faced with the challenge of singing a complete song, their vocal pitch became less accurate and, as a group, they demonstrated little or no improvement in song-singing across the three years. Overall, singing competency appeared to be closely related to the nature of the task, with many boys negatively affected in the task of singing a "school" song.

This is a consistent finding across twentieth-century research literature. In general, girls as a group are reported to be more advanced in their singing development than boys, with recent research indicating that this gender difference gets larger as children get older from age 5 through to 12 (see Welch et al., 2012 for a review).

In line with these longitudinal findings, two recent studies suggest that gender stereotyping may be a factor in the lack of singing development in some young boys (Hall, 2005; Joyce,

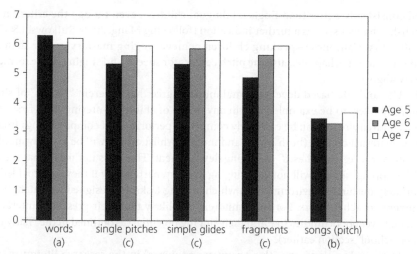

Fig. 24.2 Longitudinal data on 5- to 7-year-old children's (n=184) rated singing abilities (maximum accuracy rating=7) for a) words of target songs (two songs were assessed each year); b) sung pitches of same complete songs; c) deconstructed pitch elements of the same songs (single pitches), simple melodic contours (glides), and simple melodic fragments)

Data from Welch, G. F., Sergeant, D. C., & White, P., The singing competences of five-year-old developing singers. *Bulletin of the Council for Research in Music Education, 127*, pp. 155–162, 1996, Welch, G. F., Sergeant, D. C., & White, P., Age, sex and vocal task as factors in singing "in-tune" during the first years of schooling. *Bulletin of the Council for Research in Music Education, 133*, pp. 153–160, 1997, and Welch, G. F., Sergeant, D. C., & White, P., The role of linguistic dominance in the acquisition of song. *Research Studies in Music Education, 10*, pp. 67–74, 1998.

2005). Australian research into 5-year-old boys' singing (Hall, 2005) indicates that singing may be perceived as a "female" activity. UK research of 9- and 10-year-olds (Joyce, 2005) across three primary schools found that only one-third of boys enjoyed singing (compared with two-thirds of girls) and that boys believed that girls were better singers.

In addition to age, sex/gender, and task, there are also contextual factors that can affect children's singing behaviors. For example, the UK longitudinal study data demonstrated a clear "school effect" (Welch, 2000a). When comparing individual school data, *all* the children in one inner-city school improved their singing skills over the three years, notwithstanding their poor socio-economic environment and generally low academic attainment in other areas of the curriculum, whereas relatively few children made progress in another school, despite them having much higher socio-economic status and attainment levels. A major factor in these differences appears to have been teacher expectation. Progress was most marked where the class teacher expected and worked consistently for singing improvement with all their pupils over a sustained period. Similar findings concerning school effects on singing motivation perceived self-identity as a singer and overall enjoyment of singing as a school activity are also reported by Joyce (2005).

Sociocultural differences have been exampled also in the more advanced singing skills demonstrated by a large class of first-grade Chinese (Hong Kong) children compared with their US peers (Rutkowski & Chen-Haftek, 2000). Similarly, an assessment of the singing behaviors of 120 Hong Kong children aged 7 to 9 years from various language groups (Mang, 2003, 2006), using both the Rutkowski and Welch developmental profiles, reported statistically significant effects for sex (favoring girls) as well as mother-tongue. Chinese monolingual children performed consistently better than English bilingual children, even though the criterion song was in English. This was seen as a further indication (following Mang, 2006; Rutkowski & Chen-Haftek, 2000) that Cantonese-speaking children achieve singing mastery earlier than their English counterparts, perhaps because the pitch centers for speech and singing of the former are more closely aligned.

Both the US- and UK-based developmental models agree that different "phases" of singing competency are likely to be exampled within any group of children entering their first school class. Some children already will be extremely competent performers of complete songs from the experienced maternal culture (both words and music), whilst others will be less advanced and will be in one of the "earlier phases" of singing development. This does not mean that the latter group of "developing" singers will not gain singing mastery, particularly if they are provided with an appropriately nurturing environment in which singing tasks are designed to match, then to extend, current vocal behaviors. For such children, it is likely that their preschool interactions have provided fewer opportunities to fulfill their singing potential (as outlined in the "Early child-hood and preschool" section earlier).

The effects of singing alone or with a group are equivocal in the research literature. Some research evidence suggests that children may become more accurate in reproducing the musical features of a criterion song when singing in a group compared to singing alone (e.g. Buckton, 1982; Greene, 1993). Other research (e.g. Goetze, 1985; Smale, 1988) reports the opposite in favor of increased reproductive accuracy if the young child is assessed when singing alone. It may be possible to reconcile these two positions by assuming that individual singing behavior is likely to be framed by an interaction between current singing competency, the nature of the singing task, the competency of other singers in the group, and an individual's current ability to make sense of the available feedback. There is an internal psychological feedback monitoring system that is essentially outside conscious awareness, which is used for a moment-by-moment self-monitoring of the singing behavior. This system draws on information from internal sense receptors, as well as internal and external auditory information concerning the relative matching of vocal behavior with an external model (see Welch, 1985, 2005a). Where the individual is able to make sense of and use these different feedback channels in combination, then singing as a member of a skilled group may promote more competent behavior. Where the individual is less able to make sense of and use this feedback, such as when surrounded by a less skilled group of singers and/or when it is difficult to "hear" their own voice, then performing in a group context may be more disadvantageous. Data from studies of choral acoustics, for example, indicate that auditory feedback for one's own vocal output is reduced when i) other singers are in close proximity (self-to-other ratio) and ii) when nearby singers are singing, or attempting to sing, the same pitches (Daugherty, 2000; Ternström, 1994).

Nevertheless, it is likely that singing competency will be nurtured through exposure to frequent opportunities for vocal play within an environment that encourages vocal exploration and accurate imitation (Mang, 2003; Welch, 2005a; Young, 2002).

The data from various studies on early singing development were collated into a theoretical protocol "baseline assessment of singing" for use with children on entry to school (Welch & Elsley, 1999). This was evaluated subsequently with a small class of children (n=19) aged from 3 years 8 months to 5 years 10 months (King, 2000). In general, the data supported key features of the model, namely that singing competence is likely to vary at an individual level with musical task, such as in the sung reproduction of melodic contour, pitch intervals, and song text. Any assessment of singing abilities in young children, therefore, should provide a mixture of tasks (such as pitch glides and pitch patterns, as well as song melodies) as a basis for diagnosis and curriculum planning. Furthermore, recent neuropsychobiological data on pitch-processing modules in the brain (Peretz & Coltheart, 2003) support a hierarchical model in which melodic contour (*pace* Davidson, 1994; Rutkowski, 1997; Welch, 1998) is analyzed before the processing of intervals and tonality (see Welch, 2005a for a review).

With regard to children's ability to invent songs, a series of studies (Davies, 1986, 1992, 1994) indicate that 5- to 7-year-olds have a range of song-making strategies; these include narrative songs (chant-like in nature, often with repeated figures), as well as songs that have more conventional features, such as an opening idea and a clear sense of closure, four-phrase structures, repetition, phrases that both "borrow" from the immediate musical culture and which also may be transformed (sequenced, inverted, augmented) in some way. Overall, children in the first years of schooling demonstrate a clear sense of musical form and of emotional expression in their invented songs.

Older childhood

The latter years of childhood are characterized by a general singing competency for the majority. Relatively few children are reported as singing "out-of-tune" at the age of 11 years (Howard, Angus, & Welch, 1994; Welch, 1979, 2000b). For example, evidence from a wide range of studies indicates that approximately 30% of pupils aged 7 years are reported as being relatively "inaccurate" when vocally matching a melody within a Western cultural tradition. However, this proportion drops to around 4% of the same pupil population by the age of 11 (a proportion that is similar to that reported for the adult population—Dalla Bella et al., 2007). Within each of these and the intervening age groups, "out-of-tune" boys outnumber girls by a ratio of 2:1 or 3:1 (Welch, 1979). Culture, however, continues to be significant. Anthropological and ethnomusicological studies, for example, have suggested that young children from the Anang in Nigeria can sing "hundreds of songs, both individually and in choral groups" by the age of 5 (Messinger, 1958, p. 20), Venda children in South Africa were reported as both learning special children's songs and composing new songs for themselves (Blacking, 1967), whereas Herati children in Afghanistan tended to focus on the imitation of adult models, with the children (particularly boys) of professional musicians' families (*sazendeh*) being immersed in the local music culture and often expected to perform professionally by the age of 12 (Doubleday & Baily, 1995).

A large-scale study of children's singing development was undertaken as part of an evaluation of the impact of the UK Government's National Singing Program "Sing Up," which ran in England from 2007 to 2012. Data on the singing ability of 11,258 children aged 5 to 12 years were collected over a period of four years as the program was rolled out across the country. Children's singing was assessed using a protocol that combined the Rutkowski (1997) and Welch (1998) developmental profiles (mentioned previously) to create a normalized singing score (out of 100). Amongst other findings, data analyses revealed a) that older children tended to be more advanced in their singing ability compared to younger children, and b) that those children with experience of "Sing Up" were, on average, two years in advance developmentally compared to their peers outside the program, an impact that was even more marked for the youngest children (see Figure 24.3) (Welch et al., forthcoming). In general—and in line with the research reported earlier—singing ability normally develops with age and can be enhanced if children experience an appropriately rich educational program. Moreover, there are also other potential benefits of successful singing experience, in that children are more likely to have a positive self-concept and sense of being socially included (Welch et al., 2014). Amongst other potential benefits from singing are improved reading skills (Biggs et al., 2008; Welch et al., 2012).

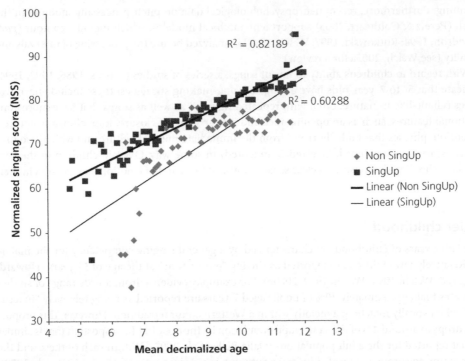

Fig. 24.3 Mean normalized singing scores averages by decimal age and intervention ("Sing Up" versus Non "Sing Up") for n=11,258 children (Welch et al, forthcoming)

One effective means of fostering singing development is by the use of "imitation," which is a core reciprocal feature of early mother–child vocal interactions (Trehub & Gudmundsdottir, 2014). This approach is also evidenced pedagogically as part of an enculturated induction into the skilled practices of expert singers in many different musical cultures, such as exampled in the cathedrals where European sacred music is practiced, as well as in the choral communities of sub-Saharan Africa and Scandinavia. Cathedrals in the UK, for example, typically induct their choristers at the age of 8, so that by the age of 13 they will have had five years' immersion into a weekly (usually daily) ritual of rehearsals, performances, choral singing, and solos, embracing a wide range of compositional styles and musical genres that span over 500 years of Western classical music. Within the cathedral choir, performance skill level is signaled by singer nomenclature (such as "head chorister," "senior corner boy," "probationer") and variations in the dress code, as well as by the degree of performance involvement in particular repertoire. Novices are deliberately placed in between more skilled, older choristers and normally are required to sing only certain items during the cathedral services while they deepen and develop their performance skills through listening and observing their more accomplished peers (see Welch, 2011).

Although the tradition of highly skilled boy singers in the UK may be traced back to the first foundations of English cathedrals in Canterbury (AD 597), Rochester (AD 604), and St. Paul's, London (AD 604), the "all-male" hegemony of cathedral music experienced a major challenge in 1991 with the admittance of girls to Salisbury Cathedral in the West of England. Since then, by 2009, the potential for equally skilled performance by girl choristers has been recognized through the creation of separate girls' choirs in 31 cathedrals and minsters (Welch, 2011),[3] with a small number of others added since. Girl choristers are usually admitted using the same audition criteria as their male counterparts and are expected to perform the same repertoire to the same professional standard.

Evidence of the power of the musical culture in cathedrals in fostering specialist singing skills may be found both in the quality of choral outputs (such as national and international broadcasts by the BBC, commercial recordings, international tours, and concerts) and also in the regular media-fuelled controversies over whether it is possible or not to perceive differences between the singing of older female and male children (Sergeant, Sjölander, & Welch, 2005; Welch & Howard, 2002). With regard to perceived singer gender, a summary of recent research data (Figure 24.4) indicates that, whilst it is possible for an untrained solo singer's sex to be identified relatively accurately from around the age of 8 onwards, it is also equally possible for trained female choristers from the age of 8 to be systematically mistaken as male, depending on the particular piece of music being performed. However, once the female chorister moves into her mid-teens, the voice quality becomes more characteristically identifiable as "female" ("womanly").[4]

A key component of our ability to assign gender accurately to children's sung products relates to changes in vocal timbre as part of the aging process. A recent study of n=320 children aged 4–11 years revealed that, as children get older, there were significant shifts in spectral energy in their singing of the same target song. For the youngest age group (4–5 years), no gender differences were evidenced in the vocal spectrum. In contrast, significant differences emerged between genders for children aged 9–11 years, with spectral energy levels above 5.75 kHz decreasing with age and energies below 5.75 kHz increasing. However, this spectral shift occurred up to two years earlier for girls compared to boys of the same age (Sergeant & Welch, 2009).

In general, children's voices tend to be higher in pitch and have a less complex acoustic make-up than those of adults. Also, there are increases in vocal pitch range, both upwards and

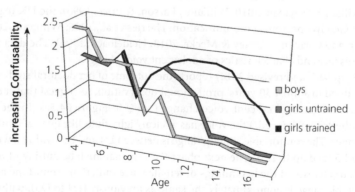

Fig. 24.4 Confusability by age and gender of children and adolescents aged 4 to 16 years. The figure is extrapolated from measured data of perceived confusability for untrained singers (Sergeant et al., 2005) and measured data of perceived confusability for trained singers (Welch & Howard, 2002). Initially, untrained young boys are confused as girls. Then, the sexes become more readily distinguishable from the age of 8/9 years. However, singing training can enable girls from 8/9 years to 14 years to sound "boy-like" in certain pieces from the repertoire. From 14 years onward, singer sex becomes more readily identifiable

Data from Sergeant, D. C., Sjölander, P., & Welch, G. F., Listeners' identification of gender differences in children's singing. *Research Studies in Music Education, 25*, pp. 28–39, 2005 and Welch, G. F., & Howard, D., Gendered voice in the cathedral choir. *Psychology of Music, 30*(1), pp. 102–120, 2002.

downwards, that are closely correlated with advancing chronological age (Sergeant & Welch, 2009). Nevertheless, children are able to achieve similar loudness levels as adults by using relatively more breath until the age of 12, when adult-like breathing patterns are observed (Stathopoulos, 2000).

Puberty and adolescence

The onset of puberty heralds fundamental changes to the nature and quality of the singing voice for both females and males. Whereas the actual dimensions and growth of the vocal instrument are similar across sexes during childhood (Titze, 1994), during puberty the male vocal tract becomes significantly longer and develops a greater circumference. In contrast, the growth of the female vocal tract is less marked, being about 15% to 20% shorter than in the male and with a different internal ratio of resonating spaces, mainly because the female neck (pharynx) is relatively shorter compared to that of the male (Story, Titze, & Hoffman, 1997). Growth typically lasts from 10 to 18 years in females (and can begin at age 7—Herman-Giddens et al., 1997), compared with 12 to 20 years in males (Thurman & Klitzke, 2000). At the turn of the century, the highpoint of pubertal voice change was reported to be around the age of 12 to 14 years in both females and males (Cooksey, 2000; Gackle, 2000), a finding subsequently generally supported in more recent studies (Juul et al., 2006; Willis & Kenny, 2008). Nevertheless, there is also some evidence of a trend for voice change to happen earlier than previously (Ashley & Mecke, 2013; Killian & Wayman, 2010). The mean average onset of voice change is likely to be between 10 and 12 years (e.g., Fisher, 2010), with one study reporting 80% of 11-year-olds showing evidence of voice change (Killian & Wayman, 2010). However, ethnicity is not reported to be a significant factor in voice change (Fisher, 2010).

There are relatively few major empirical studies of singing voice transformation during adolescence reported in the literature, particularly with regard to the female changing voice. Those that are available draw primarily on data from populations in the United States (e.g., Cooksey, 2000; Gackle, 2000; Killian & Wayman, 2010; Williams, Larson, & Price, 1996), the UK (e.g., Cooksey & Welch, 1998; Geddye, personal communication; Harries et al., 1996; Williams, 2010), Japan (Norioka, 1994), and Germany (Ashley & Mecke, 2013; Heidelbach, 1996). The data are consistent about the presence and characteristics of adolescent voice change.

Gackle (2000, updated and revised 2014) reports the outcome of her doctoral studies in Florida (during 1987), allied to almost 30 years' professional observation, to suggest that there are four distinct "phases" in female adolescent voice change (see ♀ in Figure 24.5a). In the first phase (termed "pre-pubertal: unchanged") the voice has a "clear/light, flute-like quality" with no apparent register changes. The comfortable singing range is between D4 and D5, within a wider singing range of Bb3 to F5 (and up to A5). The next phase ("pre-menarchial: beginning of mutation"—Phase IIA) is characteristic of the beginnings of female voice mutation around the ages of 11 to 13. The comfortable range is approximately the same as previously (D4 to D5), within a slightly expanded overall range (A3 to G5). However, there is often breathiness in the tone due to inadequate closure of the vocal folds as a result of growth occurring in the laryngeal area. A singing register transition typically appears between F#4 and A#4, and some girls may have difficulties in singing lower pitches; others will experience a loss of upper range. Singing often becomes uncomfortable and effortful and a breathy voice quality is characteristic across the range. The next phase is the peak of female voice mutation ("post-menarchial: pubertal—high point of mutation"—Phase IIb). Singing is characterized by a limited comfortable range (B3 to C5), discomfort (particularly at upper pitches), distinct voice qualities for each sung register, and with the lower part of the voice often taking on a more "alto" and often husky quality. Register changes appear between F4 and A#4 and also at D5 to F#5. The final phase ("young adult female"—Phase III) has a much-expanded comfortable singing range (A3 to G5), less breathiness, greater consistency in tone quality and registers, and greater singing flexibility and agility. Vibrato often appears at this stage and the voice has a more adult, womanly quality. Ongoing research (Welch, 2004; Welch & Howard, 2002) indicates that adolescent voice change is the same for relatively untrained female singers as for those who have been involved in sustained vocal performance, such as through membership of a female cathedral choir. However, as with adult female singers (Lã & Davidson, 2005), there is always some individual variation in the impact of puberty on the singer's voice related to slight differences in the underlying endocrinological metabolism and physiological functioning.

Male adolescent voice change has a more extensive literature, both in Europe and the United States. One major and influential longitudinal study was conducted by Cooksey (2000), initially based on fieldwork in California in the late 1970s, then drawing on further studies in the United States during the following decade, as well as a London-based cross-cultural investigation in the 1990s (Cooksey & Welch, 1998). Overall, Cooksey reports six "stages" of adolescent male singing voice change (see ♂ in Figure 24.5a) that are characterized by an overall lowering of the sung pitch range. Whilst the rate of voice change is unpredictable for any given individual, it is reliably sequential for all.

In the first male adolescent stage ("unchanged"), the mean sung vocal pitch range is A3 to F5, with the tessitura pitch boundaries C#4 to A#4. The voice quality is perceived as "clear," with relatively little evidence of breathiness in the tone. The beginnings of voice change (termed by Cooksey as Stage I, "Midvoice I") are marked by a reduced vocal range (Ab3 to C5) and instability of sung pitch, particularly for the upper frequencies, which tend to be produced with increased effort, as well as tone quality that is perceived as more effortful, strained, and breathy. The sung range then descends approximately in thirds across the next three stages (see Figure 24.5a), with each stage being characterized by a reduced mean range and relative continuing instability in the production of upper pitches, but contrasted by relative stability for the lower pitches. The pitch ranges are: Stage II ("Midvoice II"), F3 to A4; Stage III ("Midvoice IIa"), D3 to F#4; followed by Stage IV ("New Baritone," also termed "New Voice"), B2 to D#4. Within these, Stage II may be regarded as the mid-point of voice change, and this is when a falsetto register (C5 to B5) first appears and (for some) a whistle register (C6 to C7). Stage III ("Midvoice IIa") is characterized by the greatest vocal instability and the least clear vocal quality. It is only in the final stage of voice change (Stage V, "Settling Baritone," also termed "Emerging Adult Voice" G2 to D4) that the mean sung pitch range opens out again and the voice timbre begins to adopt a clearer, less breathy quality. However, the number and intensity of harmonics do not yet approximate normal adult characteristics. Nevertheless, for each stage of voice change the adolescent male has a (limited) number of pitches that can be produced comfortably and musically (see the darker shaded elements in the ranges for male voices in Figure 24.5a) and it has been possible in recent years to find a greater awareness by publishers to produce repertoire that is specially written as being suitable for these changing voices.

In general, age is a poor predictor for establishing voice change stages, with any given age group likely to encompass several stages. It is possible for an individual to pass through all stages of adolescent voice change in twelve months, but it is also possible for this process to be much slower and to last several years. Nevertheless, a summation of selected UK and Japanese data for over 3,000 males, aged 9 to 14 years, provides some indication of the possible proportions of different categories of voice change by age group (Figure 24.5b), whilst noting that other, more recent research suggests that voice-change onset may be getting younger (Ashley & Mecke, 2013;

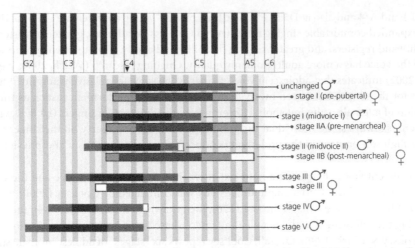

Fig. 24.5a Stages of singing voice change for females (based on Gackle, 2000) and males (based on Cooksey, 2000)

Data from Gackle, L., "Understanding voice transformation in female adolescents," in: L. Thurman, & G. F. Welch (Eds.), *Bodymind and Voice: Foundations of Voice Education*. Revised Edition, pp. 739–744, 2000 and Cooksey, J., "Voice transformation in male adolescents," in: L. Thurman, & G. F. Welch (Eds.), *Bodymind and Voice: Foundations of Voice Education*. Revised Edition, pp. 718–738, 2000.

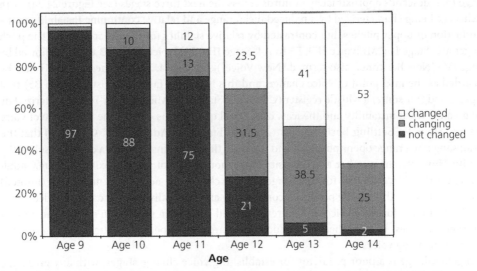

Fig. 24.5b Extrapolated model of adolescent male voice change by age, based on UK (Geddye, personal communication) and Japanese data (Norioka, 1994), total n=3,188

Includes data from Norioka, Y., "A survey of Japanese school aged poor pitch singers," in: G. F. Welch, & T. Murao (Eds.), *Onchi and singing development*, pp. 49–62, 1994.

Killian & Wayman, 2010). As can be seen, the ages of 12 to 14 have significant proportions of males whose voices are perceived to have already "changed," or in the process of "changing," whilst embracing a reducing number that are still "unchanged." Ideally, choral groups of adolescent male singers in this age range are best suited, therefore, to music that has been arranged specifically for them in three parts, using the Cooksey classification guidelines (Unchanged and Stage I on a top line, Stages II and III on a middle line, and Stages IV and V on the bottom line), rather than to attempt traditional four-part music in which the tessiturae often are likely to be mismatched with current singing abilities.

Factors influencing singing development and the realization of potential

As can be seen from the previous text, singing in one form or another is an essential feature of our musical development and behavior. In each age phase (infancy, early childhood, older childhood, adolescence), the human voice has a distinctive underlying anatomy and physiology that is capable of producing a diversity of "singing" behaviors. These increasingly explore and approximate to the particular sonic features of models that are available in the soundworlds of the experienced maternal and global cultures. In the first months of life, these "sung" products are driven by basic human needs, before becoming more exploratory and melodic in nature as vocal skills develop in the acquisition and mastery of musical elements. Throughout childhood and adolescence, singing development is a product of neuropsychobiological activity, potential, and change, interfaced with, and shaped by, particular sociocultural environments in which certain patterns of sound characterize the dominant musical genres. At any age, development can be supported or hindered by a number of factors, such as the appropriateness of a given singing task set by an adult in relation to current singing capabilities, the expectations of peers, and/or the value placed on singing (and certain types of singing behavior) within the immediate culture. Opportunities to engage in vocal play and exploration, to share in singing games with peers and "experts," as well as to improvise and compose their own songs are essential features of musical cultures that foster singing development. Children who exceed the "norms" reported in the research literature are likely to have been provided with a nurturing environment that is designed to match, celebrate, enable, and extend individual singing expertise (such as evidenced in the "Sing Up" evaluation data (Welch et al., in press)). Others, whose singing is perceived to be "lacking" in some way, will not have had such appropriate opportunities. For some, entry to adolescence can confirm their perceived identity as a "non-singer," as someone for whom music is seen as an area of "failure." Yet, everyone has the potential to learn to sing—and indeed, studies of singing in adults suggest that "singing in the general population is more accurate and widespread than currently believed" (Dalla Bella et al., 2007, p. 1188; see also Cuddy et al., 2005). We need, therefore, to continue to seek optimal ways to allow children and adolescents to explore and extend their singing (and musical) birthright. In this, we will reduce the need for "remedial" action in adulthood, such as the establishment of adult choirs for "non-singers." The stories of a life-long sense of singing "disability" should be confined to history.

Reflective questions

1 What is the nature of children's first experiences of singing?
2 Has your own experience of singing been positive, or not?

3 What are the key factors that can influence singing development?

4 What happens to the singing voice during adolescence?

5 How should teachers organize singing in their classes with different age groups?

Notes

1 Rutkowski (1997), *Singing Voice Development Measure (SVDM)*

  1 "Pre-singer" does not sing but chants the song text.

  1.5 "Inconsistent Speaking Range Singer" sometimes chants, sometimes sustains tones and exhibits some sensitivity to pitch, but remains in the speaking voice range (usually a3 to c4 [note: the pitch labels have been altered to bring them in line with modern conventions in which middle C=c4, 256 Hz]).

  2 "Speaking Range Singer" sustains tones and exhibits some sensitivity to pitch but remains in the speaking voice range (usually a3 to c4).

  2.5 "Inconsistent Limited Range singer" wavers between speaking and singing voices and uses a limited range when in singing voice (usually up to f4).

  3 "Limited Range Singer" exhibits consistent use of initial singing range (usually d4 to a4).

  3.5 "Inconsistent Initial Range Singer" sometimes only exhibits use of limited singing range, but other times exhibits use of initial singing range (usually d4 to a4).

  4 "Initial Range Singer" exhibits consistent use of initial singing range (usually d4 to a4).

  4.5 "Inconsistent Singer" sometimes only exhibits use of initial singing range, but other times exhibits use of extended singing range (sings beyond the register lift: b♭4 and above).

  5 "Singer" exhibits use of extended singing range (sings beyond the register lift: b♭4 and above).

Welch (1998) *A revised model of vocal pitch-matching development (VPMD)*

  Phase 1 The words of the song appear to be the initial center of interest rather than the melody, singing is often described as "chant-like," employing a restricted pitch range and melodic phrases. In infant vocal pitch exploration, descending patterns predominate.

  Phase 2 There is a growing awareness that vocal pitch can be a conscious process and that changes in vocal pitch are controllable. Sung melodic outline begins to follow the general (macro) contours of the target melody or key constituent phrases. Tonality is essentially phrase based. Self-invented and "schematic" songs "borrow" elements from the child's musical culture. Vocal pitch range used in "song" singing expands.

  Phase 3 Melodic shape and intervals are mostly accurate, but some changes in tonality may occur, perhaps linked to inappropriate register usage. Overall, however, the number of different reference pitches is much reduced.

  Phase 4 No significant melodic or pitch errors in relation to relatively simple songs from the singer's musical culture.

2 The conceptualization of development as occurring in "phases" is a common outcome of research that is undertaken over a long period with time for researcher reflection and the evaluation of new data. For example, the current author has developed and reviewed a particular model of vocal pitch matching over the past two decades (1986, 2002), which reconceptualizes the evidence and reduces the number of developmental "phases" (rather than the originally labelled "stages") from five to four.

3 The data for 2009 on the numbers of cathedrals with female choristers in UK cathedrals has been collated by Claire Stewart as part of her ongoing doctoral studies at the Institute of Education into their impact on the all-male choral tradition.

4 For a detailed review of the literature on gender and chorister voice, including similarities and differences in the underlying anatomy and physiology for singing, see Welch & Howard (2002). For data on the perceived gender of untrained children's voices, see Sergeant et al. (2005).

Key sources

Dalla Bella, S., Giguére, J.-F. & Peretz, I. (2007). Singing proficiency in the general population. *Journal of the Acoustical Society of America*, **121**(2), 1182–9.

Trehub, S. E., & Gudmundsdottir, H. R. (2014). Mothers as singing mentors for infants. In G. F. Welch, D. M. Howard, & J. Nix. (Eds.), *Oxford handbook of singing*. New York: Oxford University Press.

Welch, G. F. (2005a). Singing as communication. In D. Miell, R. MacDonald, & D. J. Hargreaves (Eds.), *Musical communication* (pp. 239–59). New York: Oxford University Press.

Welch, G. F., Saunders, J., Papageorgi, I., & Himonides, E. (2012). Sex, gender and singing development: Making a positive difference to boys' singing through a national programme in England. In S. Harrison, G. F. Welch, & A. Adler (Eds.), *Perspectives on males and singing* (pp. 37–54). London: Springer.

Reference list

Adachi, M., & Trehub, S. E. (1999). Children's communication of emotion in song. In S. W. Yi (Ed.), *Music, mind and science* (pp. 454–65). Seoul: Seoul National University Press.

Adachi, M., & Trehub, S. E. (2000, April). *Preschoolers' expression of emotion through invented songs*. Paper presented at the meeting of the Society for Research in the Psychology of Music and Music Education, University of Leicester, England.

Ashley, M., & Mecke, A.-C. (2013). "Boys are apt to change their voice at about fourteene yeeres of age": An historical background to the debate about longevity in boy treble singers. *Reviews of Research in Human Learning and Music*, 1(epub2013001). doi: 10.6022/journal.rrhlm.2013001.

Barrett, M. S. (2011). Musical narratives: A study of a young child's identity work in and through music-making. *Psychology of Music*, **39**(4), 403–23. doi: 10.1177/0305735610373054.

Biggs, M. C., Homan, S. P., Dedrick, R., Minick, V., & Rasinski, T. (2008). Using an interactive singing software program: A comparative study of struggling middle school readers. *Reading Psychology*, **29**(3), 195–213.

Blacking, J. (1967). *Venda children's songs*. Johannesburg: University of Witwatersrand Press.

British Educational Research Association Music Education Review Group. (2001). *Mapping music education research in the UK*. Southwell, UK: British Educational Research Association.

Buckton, R. (1982). *Sing a song of six-year-olds*. Wellington, New Zealand: Council for Educational Research.

Coleman, J. M., Pratt, R. R., Stoddard, R. A., Gerstmann, D. R., & Abel, H.-H. (1997). The effects of the male and female singing behaviours and speaking voices on selected physiological and behavioural measures of premature infants in the intensive care unit. *International Journal of Arts Medicine*, 5(2), 4–11.

Cooksey, J. (2000). Voice transformation in male adolescents. In L. Thurman, & G. F. Welch (Eds.), *Bodymind and voice: Foundations of voice education* (revised ed., pp. 718–38). Iowa City, Iowa: National Center for Voice and Speech.

Cooksey, J., & Welch, G. F. (1998). Adolescence, singing development and National Curricula design. *British Journal of Music Education*, **15**(1), 99–119.

Cuddy, L. L., Balkwill, L.-L., Peretz, I., & Holden, R. R. (2005). Musical difficulties are rare. A study of "tone deafness" amongst university students. *New York: Annals of the New York Academy of Sciences*, **1060**, 311–24. doi: 10.1196/annals.1360.026.

Dalla Bella, S., Giguére, J.-F. & Peretz, I. (2007). Singing proficiency in the general population. *Journal of the Acoustical Society of America*, **121**(2), 1182–9.

Daugherty, J. F. (2000). Choir spacing and choral sound: Physical, pedagogical, and philosophical dimensions. In B. A. Roberts & A. Rose (Eds.), *Conference proceedings of the international symposium, sharing the voices: The phenomenon of singing II* (pp. 77–88). St. Johns, Newfoundland, Canada: Memorial University of Newfoundland Press.

Davidson, L. (1994). Songsinging by young and old: A developmental approach to music. In R. Aiello and J. Sloboda (Eds.), *Musical perceptions* (pp. 99–130). New York: Oxford University Press.

Davies, C. (1986). Say it till a song comes: Reflections on songs invented by children 3–13. *British Journal of Music Education,* **3**(3), 279–93.

Davies, C. (1992). Listen to my song: A study of songs invented by children aged 5 to 7 years. *British Journal of Music Education,* **9**(1), 19–48.

Davies, C. (1994). The listening teacher: An approach to the collection and study of invented songs of children aged 5 to 7. In H. Lees (Ed.), *Musical connections: Tradition and change* (pp. 120–7). Auckland, NZ: International Society for Music Education.

Doubleday, V., & Baily, J. (1995). Patterns of musical development among children in Afghanistan. In E. J. Fernea (Ed.), *Children in the Muslim Middle East* (pp. 431–44). Austin: University of Texas Press.

Dowling, W. J. (1988). Tonal structure and children's early learning of music. In J. Sloboda (Ed.), *Generative processes in music* (pp. 113–28). Oxford: Oxford University Press.

Dowling, W. J. (1999). The development of music perception and cognition. In D. Deutsch (Ed.), *The Psychology of Music* (2nd ed., pp. 603–25). London: Academic Press.

Eimas, P. D. (1985). The perception of speech in early infancy. *Scientific American,* **252**(1), 34–40.

Fisher, R. A. (2010). Effect of ethnicity on the age of onset of the male voice change. *Journal of Research in Music Education,* **58**(2), 116–30. doi: 10.1177/0022429410371376.

Gabrielsson, A., & Örnkloo, H. (2002, August). *Children's perception and performance of emotion in singing and speech.* Paper presented at the ISME Early Childhood Conference, Copenhagen, Denmark.

Gackle, L. (2000). Understanding voice transformation in female adolescents. In L. Thurman, & G. F. Welch (Eds.), *Bodymind and Voice: Foundations of Voice Education* (revised ed., pp. 739–44). Iowa City, Iowa: National Center for Voice and Speech.

Gackle, L. (2014). Adolescent girls' singing development. In G. F. Welch, D. M. Howard, & J. Nix (Eds.), *Oxford handbook of singing.* New York: Oxford University Press. doi: 10.1093/oxfordhb/9780199660773.013.22.

Goetze, M. (1985). Factors affecting accuracy in children's singing (Unpublished doctoral dissertation), University of Colorado.

Greene, G. A. (1993). *The effects of unison singing versus individual singing on the vocal pitch accuracy of elementary school children.* Paper presented at the Southern Division of the Music Educators' National Conference.

Hall, C. (2005). Gender and boys' singing in early childhood. *British Journal of Music Education,* **22**(1), 5–20.

Hargreaves, D. J. (1996). The development of artistic and musical competence. In I. Deliege & J. Sloboda (Eds.), *Musical beginnings* (pp. 145–70). Oxford: Oxford University Press.

Harries, M. L. L., Griffin, M., Walker, J., & Hawkins, S. (1996). Changes in the male voice during puberty: Speaking and singing voice parameters. *Logopedics Phoniatrics Vocology,* **21**(2), 95–100.

Heidelbach, U. (1996). Die entwicklung der knabenstimme zur mannerstimme bei chorsangern dargestellt am singstimmfeld (Unpublished MD thesis). Technischen Universität Dresden, Dresden, BRD.

Herman-Giddens, M. E., Slora, E. J. Wasserman, R. C., Bourdony, C. J., Bhapkar, M. V., Kock, G. G., & Hasemeier, C. M. (1997). Secondary sexual characteristics and menses in young girls seen in office practice: A study from the Pediatric Research in Office Settings Network. *Pediatrics,* **99**(4), 505–12.

Howard, D. M., Angus, J. A., & Welch, G. F. (1994). Singing pitching accuracy from years 3 to 6 in a primary school. *Proceedings of the institute of acoustics,* **16**(5), 223–30.

Johnstone, T., & Scherer, K. R. (2000). Vocal communication of emotion. In M. Lewis & J. M. Haviland-Jones (Eds.), *Handbook of emotions* (pp. 220–35). New York: The Guildford Press.

Joyce, H. (2005). The effects of sex, age and environment on attitudes to singing in Key Stage 2 (Unpublished master's dissertation). Institute of Education, University of London.

Juul, A., Teilmann, G., Scheike, T., Hertel, N. T., Holm, K., Laursen, E. M., Main, K. M., & Skakkebaek, N. E. (2006). Pubertal development in Danish children: Comparison of recent European and US data. *International Journal of Andrology,* **29**(1), 247–55. doi: 10.1111/j.1365–2605.2005.00556.x.

Killian, J. N., & Wayman, J. B. (2010). A descriptive study of vocal maturation among male adolescent vocalists and instrumentalists. *Journal of Research in Music Education*, 58(1), 5–19. doi: 10.1177/0022429409359941.

King, R. (2000). An investigation into the effectiveness of a baseline assessment in singing and some influential home-environmental factors (Unpublished master's dissertation). Roehampton Institute London, London.

Knight, S. (1999). Exploring a cultural myth: What adult non-singers may reveal about the nature of singing. In B. A. Roberts & A. Rose (Eds.), *The phenomenon of singing II* (pp. 144–54). St. John's, NF: Memorial University Press.

Knight, S. (2010). A study of adult "non-singers" in Newfoundland (Unpublished doctoral dissertation). Institute of Education, University of London.

Lã, F., & Davidson, J. (2005). Investigating the relationship between sexual hormones and female Western classical singing. *Research Studies in Music Education*, 24(1), 75–87.

Levinowitz, L. (1989). An investigation of preschool children's comparative capability to sing songs with and without words. *Bulletin of the Council for Research in Music Education*, 100, 14–19.

Loui, P., Bachorik, J. P., Li, H. C., & Schlaug, G. (2013). Effects of voice on emotional arousal. *Frontiers in Psychology*, 4(675). doi: 10.3389/fpsyg.2013.00675.

Mack, L. (1979). A descriptive study of a community chorus made up of "non-singers" (Unpublished EdD dissertation). University of Illinois at Urbana-Champaign.

Mang, E. (2000/1). Intermediate vocalisations: An investigation of the boundary between speech and songs in young children's vocalisations. *Bulletin of the Council for Research in Music Education*, 147, 116–21.

Mang, E. (2002). An investigation of vocal pitch behaviours of Hong Kong children. *Bulletin of the Council for Research in Music Education*, 153(4), 128–34.

Mang, E. (2003). Singing competency of monolingual and bilingual children in Hong Kong. In L. C. R. Yip, C. C. Leung, & W. T. Lau (Eds.), *Curriculum innovation in music* (pp. 237–42). Hong Kong: Hong Kong Institute of Education.

Mang, E. (2005). The referent of children's early songs. *Music Education Research*, 7(1), 3–20. doi: 10.1080/14613800500041796.

Mang, E. (2006). The effects of age, gender and language on children's singing competency. *British Journal of Music Education*, 23(2), 161–74. doi: 10.1017/S0265051706006905.

Masataka, N. (1992). Pitch characteristics of Japanese maternal speech to infants. *Journal of Child Language*, 19(2), 213–23.

Masataka, N. (1999). Preference for infant-directed singing in 2-day-old hearing infants of deaf parents. *Developmental Psychology*, 35(4), 1001–5.

Meltzoff, A. N. (2002). Elements of a developmental theory of imitation. In A. N. Meltzoff & W. Prinz (Eds.), *The Imitative Mind* (pp. 19–41). Cambridge: Cambridge University Press.

Messinger, J. (1958). Overseas report. *Basic College Quarterly*, 4(Fall), 20–4.

Moog, H. (1976). *The musical experience of the pre-school child* (trans. C. Clarke). London: Schott.

Nawrot, E. S. (2003). The perception of emotional expression in music: Evidence from infants, children and adults. *Psychology of Music*, 31(1), 75–92.

Norioka, Y. (1994). A survey of Japanese school aged poor pitch singers. In G. F. Welch & T. Murao (Eds.), *Onchi and singing development* (pp. 49–62). London: David Fulton Publishers.

Papousek, M. (1996). Intuitive parenting: A hidden source of musical stimulation in infancy. In I. Deliege & J. Sloboda (Eds.), *Musical beginnings* (pp. 88–112). Oxford: Oxford University Press.

Peretz, I., & Coltheart, M. (2003). Modularity and music processing. *Nature Neuroscience*, 6(7), 688–91.

Richards, H., & Durrant, C. (2003). To sing or not to sing: A study on the development of "non-singers" in choral activity. *Research Studies in Music Education*, 20(1), 78–89.

Rutkowski, J. (1990). The measurement and evaluation of children's singing voice development. *The Quarterly*, 1(1–2), 81–95.

Rutkowski, J. (1997). The nature of children's singing voices: Characteristics and assessment. In B. A. Roberts (Ed.), *The phenomenon of singing* (pp. 201–9). St. John's, NF: Memorial University Press.

Rutkowski, J., & Chen-Haftek, L. (2000, July). *The singing voice within every child: A cross-cultural comparison of first graders' use of singing voice*. Paper presented to the ISME Early Childhood Conference, Kingston, Canada.

Ruzza, B., Rocca, F., Boero, D. L., & Lenti, C. (2003). Investigating the musical qualities of early infant sounds. In G. Avanzini, C. Faienza, D. Minciacchi, L. Lopez, & M. Majno (Eds.), *The neurosciences and music* (Vol. 999, pp. 527–9). New York: Annals of the New York Academy of Sciences.

Sergeant, D. C., Sjölander, P., & Welch, G. F. (2005). Listeners' identification of gender differences in children's singing. *Research Studies in Music Education*, **24**(1) 28–39.

Sergeant, D. C., & Welch, G. F. (2009). Gender differences in Long-Term-Average Spectra of children's singing voices. *Journal of Voice*, **23**(3), 319–36. doi: 10.1016/j.jvoice.2007.10.010.

Smale, M. J. (1988). An investigation of pitch accuracy of four- and five-year-old singers. *Dissertation Abstracts International*, AAT—8723851.

Stathopoulos, E. T. (2000). A review of the development of the child voice: An anatomical and functional perspective. In P. J. White (Ed.), *Child Voice* (pp. 1–12). Stockholm: Royal Institute of Technology, Voice Research Centre.

Story, B. H., Titze, I. R., & Hoffman, E. A. (1997). Volumetric image-based comparison of male and female vocal tract shapes. *National Center for Voice and Speech Status and Progress Report*, **11**, 153–61.

Sundberg, J. (2000). Emotive transforms. *Phonetica*, **57**(2–4), 95–112.

Sundin, B. (1997). Musical creativity in childhood: A research project in retrospect. *Research Studies in Music Education*, **9**(1), 48–57.

Tafuri, J. (2008). *Infant musicality*. Farnham, UK: Ashgate.

Tafuri, J., & Villa, D. (2002). Musical elements in the vocalisations of infants aged 2 to 8 months. *British Journal of Music Education*, **19**(1), 73–88.

Ternström, S. (1994). Hearing myself with others: Sound levels in choral performance measured with separation of one's own voice from the rest of the choir. *Journal of Voice*, **8**(4), 293–302.

Thurman, L., & Klitzke, C. (2000). Highlights of physical growth and function of voices from prebirth to age 21. In L. Thurman, & G. F. Welch (Eds.), *Bodymind and Voice: Foundations of Voice Education* (revised ed., pp. 696–703). Iowa City, Iowa: National Center for Voice and Speech.

Thurman, L., & Welch, G. F. (Eds.) (2000). *Bodymind and voice: Foundations of voice education* (revised ed.). Iowa City, Iowa: National Center for Voice and Speech.

Titze, I. (1994). *Principles of voice production*. Englewood Cliffs, NJ: Prentice-Hall.

Trehub, S. E. (2001). Musical predispositions in infancy. In R. J. Zatorre & I. Peretz (Eds.), *The biological foundations of music* (Vol. 930, pp. 1–16). New York: Annals of the New York Academy of Sciences.

Trehub, S. E., & Gudmundsdottir, H. R. (2014). Mothers as singing mentors for infants. In G. F. Welch, D. M. Howard, & J. Nix. (Eds.), *Oxford handbook of singing*. New York: Oxford University Press.

Vihman, M. M. (1996). *Phonological development*. Oxford: Blackwell.

Welch, G. F. (1979). Poor pitch singing: A review of the literature. *Psychology of Music*, **7**(1), 50–8.

Welch, G. F. (1985). A schema theory of how children learn to sing in tune. *Psychology of Music*, **13**(1), 3–18.

Welch, G. F. (1986). A developmental view of children's singing. *British Journal of Music Education*, **3**(3), 295–303.

Welch, G. F. (1998). Early childhood musical development. *Research Studies in Music Education*, **11**(1), 27–41.

Welch, G. F. (2000a). Singing development in early childhood: The effects of culture and education on the realisation of potential. In P. J. White (Ed.), *Child voice* (pp. 27–44). Stockholm: Royal Institute of Technology.

Welch, G. F. (2000b). The developing voice. In L. Thurman, & G. F. Welch (Eds.), *Bodymind and voice: Foundations of voice education* (pp. 704–17). Iowa: National Center for Voice and Speech.

Welch, G. F. (2002). Early childhood musical development. In L. Bresler & C. Thompson (Eds.), *The arts in children's lives: Context, culture and curriculum* (pp. 113–28). Dordrecht, NL: Kluwer.

Welch, G. F. (2004). Developing young professional singers in UK cathedrals. *Proceedings, 2nd International Physiology and Acoustics of Singing Conference, Denver, USA.* Retrieved 3 June 2005 from <http://www.ncvs.org/pas/2004/pres/welch/welch.htm>.

Welch, G. F. (2005a). Singing as communication. In D. Miell, R. MacDonald, & D. J. Hargreaves (Eds.), *Musical communication* (pp. 239–59). New York: Oxford University Press.

Welch, G. F. (2005b). The musical development and education of young children. In B. Spodek & O. Saracho (Eds.), *Handbook of research on the education of young children* (pp. 251–67). Mahwah, NJ: Lawrence Erlbaum Associates Inc.

Welch, G. F. (2011). Culture and gender in a cathedral music context: An activity theory exploration. In M. Barrett (Ed.), *A cultural psychology of music education* (pp. 225–58). New York: Oxford University Press.

Welch, G. F., & Elsley, J. (1999). Baseline assessment in singing. *Australian Voice, 5,* 60–6.

Welch, G. F., Himonides, E., Saunders, J., Papageorgi, I., & Sarazin, M. (2014). Singing and social inclusion. *Frontiers in Psychology, 5*(803). doi: 10.3389/fpsyg.2014.00803.

Welch, G. F., Himonides, E., Saunders, J., Papageorgi, I., Vraka, M., Preti, C., & Sarazin, M. (forthcoming). Children's singing behaviour and development in the context of Sing Up, a national program in England.

Welch, G. F., & Howard, D. (2002). Gendered voice in the cathedral choir. *Psychology of Music, 30*(1), 102–20.

Welch, G. F., Saunders, J., Hobsbaum, A., & Himonides, E. (2012). *Literacy through music: A research evaluation of the New London Orchestra's Literacy through Music programme.* London: International Music Education Research Centre, Institute of Education, University of London.

Welch, G. F., Saunders, J., Papageorgi, I., & Himonides, E. (2012). Sex, gender and singing development: Making a positive difference to boys' singing through a national programme in England. In S. Harrison, G. F. Welch, & A. Adler (Eds.), *Perspectives on males and singing* (pp. 37–54). London: Springer.

Welch, G. F., Sergeant, D. C., & White, P. (1996). The singing competences of five-year-old developing singers. *Bulletin of the Council for Research in Music Education, 127,* 155–62.

Welch, G. F., Sergeant, D. C., & White, P. (1997). Age, sex and vocal task as factors in singing "in-tune" during the first years of schooling. *Bulletin of the Council for Research in Music Education, 133,* 153–60.

Welch, G. F., Sergeant, D. C., & White, P. (1998). The role of linguistic dominance in the acquisition of song. *Research Studies in Music Education, 10*(1), 67–74.

Williams, J. (2010). The implications of intensive singing training on the vocal health and development of boy choristers in an English cathedral choir (Unpublished doctoral dissertation). Institute of Education, University of London.

Williams, B., Larson, G., & Price, D. (1996). An investigation of selected female singing- and speaking-voice characteristics through comparison of a group of pre-menarchial girls to a group of post-menarchial girls. *Journal of Singing, 52*(3), 33–40.

Willis, E., & Kenny, D. T. (2008). Relationship between weight, speaking fundamental frequency, and the appearance of phonational gaps in the adolescent male changing voice. *Journal of Voice, 22*(4), 451–71. doi: http://dx.doi.org/10.1016/j.jvoice.2006.11.007.

Wise, K. (2009). Understanding tone deafness: A multi-componential analysis of perception, cognition, singing and self-perceptions in adults reporting musical difficulties (Unpublished doctoral dissertation). Keele University.

Young, S. (2002). Young children's spontaneous vocalizations in free play: Observations of two- to three-year-olds in a day care setting. *Bulletin of the Council for Research in Music Education, 152,* 43–53.

Chapter 25

Musical play

Kathryn Marsh and Susan Young

Musical play: Introduction

What do we mean by musical play and in what contexts does it take place? Educational practice and theory, rooted as it is in psychology, reflects a long-held belief that play is a form of growth that is associated positively with learning and development. Most of what we will write about in this chapter emerges from our own backgrounds and interests—and those of our fellow researchers—as music educators in countries belonging to the developed world where the simple divisions between work and play result in a view of play as a trivial, lightweight, random, and somewhat useless activity. One of our aims in this chapter is to show how the complexity and sophistication of children's play goes well beyond many adult preconceptions. To children, play is neither trivial nor useless.

Assumptions about the nature of play have translated into theories that have tended to see play as merely steps on the way to more "serious" or logical forms of thinking. Consequently, accounts of play, particularly those leaning on psychological theory, have tended to assign children's play to broad types and categories, such as "exploratory," "symbolic," "functional," "constructive," "dramatic," and so on (Isenberg & Jalongo, 2000). Such wide-scope categories fail to capture the structural complexity of play and the social dimension of play as it is enacted by children in real-life situations. Brian Sutton-Smith (1997), a psychologist specializing in play, has explored the many theories of play and the definitions of play that they generate. From these different descriptions and versions of play he has arrived at the conclusion that the essential characteristic of play is its variability. Play varies according to the players, their situations, their motivations, and, importantly, according to the interpretive lens of those observing, describing, and theorizing play, thus eluding simplified definitional frameworks. In our own work and much of the work on play we will recount in this chapter, this variability is documented by describing and analyzing the specific detail of children's play in context.

So we define children's musical play as the activities that children initiate of their own accord and in which they may choose to participate with others voluntarily. Like other modes of play, these activities are enjoyable, intrinsically motivated, and controlled by the players. They are free of externally imposed rules, but may involve rules developed by the children who are playing (Isenberg & Jalongo, 2000; Rogers & Sawyers, 1988). They are "everyday" forms of musical activity, happening in the places children inhabit when not engaged in organized educational, recreational, or economic activity. These include the home, daycare, preschool, or nursery, then as children move on to school, the playground, lunchroom, after-school care settings, recreational settings, in the car, or on school buses. In these places certain forms of musical play are possible, even encouraged by adults, and in others play may be severely constrained. The constraints imposed by space, the levels of acceptable noise, what might be used to produce a sound, and availability of others with whom to make music, all influence the ways in which children will play musically. Musical play is thus embedded in and blends across many features of its context.

Musical play: Forms and contexts

As play is assumed in educational theory and research to be a valuable learning experience for young children, in early childhood preschool or nursery settings it is usual practice for free play to be provided for and encouraged. Spontaneous musical play, such as singing, moving rhythmically, and playing with sound-making objects, is viewed positively and supported, for example, by setting out educational percussion instruments. When children reach the age at which formal school begins, usually about the age of 5 or 6 years, the play-based educational provision gradually changes in favor of a more product-oriented, skills-based approach to education. Children's play in the school context thus moves out into the spaces and times between formal classroom learning activities. Forms of musical play in these settings include more stylized genres of play that constitute part of an oral tradition, such as singing games. These are the sung and chanted games that are owned, spontaneously performed, and orally transmitted by children, and incorporate the elements of text, music, and movement. They include games associated with hand clapping, mimetic movement, skipping (or jump rope), counting out or elimination, and ball bouncing, and usually occur in pair, ring, or line formations. Other forms of play include singing and dance routines associated with popular music and sports chants, in addition to more improvised chants, taunts, and rhythmic movements in response to occurrences in the immediate environment (Campbell, 2010; Harwood, 1998a; Harwood & Marsh, 2012; Marsh, 2008).

There are, however, certain characteristics of musical play that persist across all ages. A key characteristic is multimodality: children blend movement with singing and, if available, with making sounds with objects or instruments. The children are therefore as visually and kinaesthetically active as they are aurally (Bishop & Burn, 2013; Harrop-Allin, 2010; Harwood & Marsh, 2012; Young, 2008). Another defining characteristic is its unpremeditated, improvisational character. Among the youngest children, forms of musical play are often spontaneous, made up on the spot. For older children, musical play may be based on more stylized genres that form part of an oral tradition, but nevertheless, performances are not pre-planned. However, analyses of children's musical play show that there are creative processes of transformation that may be quite consciously enacted. Even apparently fixed forms are subject to a continual process of creative change (Bishop, 2014; Marsh, 2008).

An additional characteristic of musical play is its importance as a form of social interaction. Music is a means for playing *with* others. For babies and their caregiving adults, music-like playful interactions are an essential form of communication. Young children share music play ideas, synchronize their rhythmic movements with others, and imitate simple melodic ideas (Moorhead & Pond, 1941/78; Young, 2004). In mid-childhood children suggest new text, music, or movement to their friends, actively teach them new games learnt in other contexts, and jointly create variations for amusement of their playmates. Such activities promote collaboration and cohesiveness within friendship groups (Marsh, 2008). Social rules of turn-taking and hierarchical structures of social importance among friends are literally played out in the playground, reflecting and endorsing enculturated behaviors and social patterns from the wider sociocultural environment (Blacking, 1967/95; Brady, 1975; Burn & Richards, 2014; Eckhardt, 1975; Emberley, 2009; Minks, 2006, 2013; Willett et al., 2013).

There is a perception that collaborative musical play becomes predominantly the province of girls once children enter formal schooling (Factor, 1988; Knapp & Knapp, 1976). What is apparent from observation of musical play in a number of international locations is that many boys continue to participate in musical playground games well into the school years, particularly in genres of musical play that incorporate dance, counting out or elimination through chance or skill, and in contexts where limited space precludes more boisterous play (Harrop-Allin, 2010; Marsh, 2008). Boys participate in hand-clapping games, though they do so less frequently, in fewer numbers, and more privately than girls. Where other musical playground games such as jump rope have been endorsed through educational programs by classroom teachers, boys may continue to play them in the playground, though once again in lesser numbers than girls (Marsh, 2008). Contexts of musical play are therefore extremely important in determining its forms and the ways in which it is enacted.

The many activities that come under the term "children's musical play" are also culturally variable (Young & Ilari, 2012). There are communities in which some adult musical activities are thought of as forms of play (Mans, 2002) or in which children's playful activities are seen as "serious" and equitable to adult music genres. Like many aspects of music, what is understood by children's musical play becomes blurred, with increased awareness of worldwide musical practices in diverse communities (Campbell & Wiggins, 2013; Emberley, 2009; Harrop-Allin, 2010; Lum, 2007; Marsh, 2008; McIntosh, 2006; Minks, 2006). However, most research into children's musical play has been carried out in the developed world. This chapter therefore focuses on play from this perspective.

Investigating musical play

In comparison with other fields of children's musical development, there is relatively little research into children's musical play. Music education researchers tend not to study musical play, focusing their attention on adult-initiated activity in formal educational settings rather than child-initiated activity. Likewise, researchers with an interest in play and early childhood education tend to neglect musical play, considering music to be a specialized area of interest (Littleton, 2002). Add to this the strong cognitive-skills orientation of education and it is of little surprise that musical play has been less central in research on children's musical development than the acquisition of "serious" formal skills such as learning to sing, to play an instrument, or to develop aural skills. One influential researcher in the field of children's folklore has deplored the "pragmatic and utilitarian ideology that emphasizes the 'product' and evaluates the worth of a human action or idea by the profitability of its outcome" (Factor, 1988, p. 31). Play for which there is no obvious "product" in the form of measurable learning is thus seen as trivial and unworthy of serious study. This inability to view children's play as an important object of study has been termed the "triviality barrier" by Sutton-Smith (1970). Yet an understanding of how children choose to make music when left to their own devices, to play musically, reveals important information about children's musical development, their capabilities, and what is significant and meaningful to them.

The background of research on musical play divides into two distinct areas, matching the educational contexts for children in early and mid-childhood. The studies on musical play in early childhood are based on observations of children's spontaneous musical behaviors, largely in care and educational settings that have been designed by adults to promote free play. This work took its impetus from the ecological, observational studies in experimental nurseries of post-Freudian early childhood researchers such as Susan Isaacs in England in the 1930s (Isaacs, 1929). Young children were thought to possess drives and impulses that could give rise to distinct characteristic behaviors if they were allowed to play freely and follow their own inclinations.

In middle childhood, children's musical play activities are squeezed out of educational settings and so children have been mostly observed playing together in outdoor play areas. This research originally constituted a field within folklore studies and ethnomusicology, where researchers were interested in plotting the oral traditions of childhood such as singing games and in collating a corpus of traditional repertoire (Jones & Hawes, 1972/87; Knapp & Knapp, 1976; Opie & Opie, 1977, 1979, 1988; Segler, 1992; Sutton-Smith, 1972).

Research interest in children's musical play then shifted its priorities to explore the musical processes that underlie children's activity (e.g., Harwood, 1998a; Marsh, 1995, 1997, 2006, 2008; Young, 2003a, 2005). An understanding of the intuitive ways in which children make music when left to their own resources has provided vital information for the design of educational activities that can be made more appropriate to children's self-motivated learning styles (Harrop-Allin, 2010; Harwood & Marsh, 2012; Marsh, 2008). These studies have relied on analysis of quite large datasets collected by video recording in naturalistic circumstances. This has enabled detailed analyses of movement and interaction between participants as well as purely sonic information (Marsh, 2008).

Work in the field of children's musical play also made another important shift, as exemplified in the work of Campbell (1998, 2010). Adopting ethnomusicological methods she went in search of children's spontaneous musical activity in a wide range of settings, both within school and outside. Campbell observed and interviewed children between the ages of 4 and early teens, and discovered that they initiated playful musical activity throughout their varied experiences during the day, both alone and in the company of others. She found that children used music in many ways to help maintain emotional and social equilibriums, to entertain themselves, to relieve the boredom of their surroundings, to create and enjoy its sonic forms, and to assist in the formation of identity.

It is still fair to say that the majority of studies of children's various forms of musical play have been restricted to children from developed world societies, but there has been increasing research interest in understanding children's play in diverse societies and in understanding how context and living situations influence the nature of children's musical play (Campbell & Wiggins, 2013; Emberley, 2009; Harrop-Allin, 2010; Lum, 2007; Marsh, 2008; McIntosh, 2006; Minks, 2006, 2013). The work of Blacking (1967/95) on Venda children's songs did much to establish the importance of understanding children's music within the framework of the culture from which it emanates, rather than as a "universal" phenomenon. As discussed later in the chapter, Blacking's study has contributed to ideas about children's musical creativity and to an understanding of the ways in which children's music is transmitted within a culture.

Characteristics of musical play

In the next sections, musical play is discussed in four broad age phases: newborn to 3 years, 3–6 years, over 6 years, and on into adolescence. These age phases are not intended to be taken as specific developmental stages; rather, they reflect the physical maturation of children and changing contexts of care and education in the home or daycare, in play-based care and education settings, and on to formal schooling. In particular, there is no attempt to differentiate between the characteristics of children's play within the age band of 6–12 years. For example, children appear to begin learning and performing singing games from the time they enter school and become adept within varying periods of time. Some 6-year-olds can perform quite complex games, while some 9-year-olds still experience difficulty with coordination of text, music, and movement patterns. Children's preference for singing games seems to diminish in favor of singing and dance routines around the age of 10 years, but children beyond this age still perform clapping games, though less publicly and frequently.

The majority of musical play described in the following sections is vocal. In early childhood settings and in some school settings, depending on the nature of the curriculum, provision will be made for children to explore instruments and initiate play with them or to "play" with recorded music by responding to it with movement or vocalizing. However, musical play for children more usually occurs in the absence of equipment. Again, this can be explained as a situational constraint. Clapping games, when played in the school context, for example, tend to be played during recess and lunchtimes, while waiting for a teacher, or during bus excursions. Played by pairs or small groups of children they easily fit into small spaces and limited time periods, and are therefore eminently transportable both in time and place.

It should be noted, however, that one of the most striking developments in recent years that is impacting on children's musical play is the digitization of music. Miniaturized music-playing devices can be incorporated into all kinds of toys and equipment, much of it portable, so that now music is secreted into the spaces and times of their lives in a way that has never happened before. Musical experiences engendered by digitized music have changed the nature of musical experience in the home, and particularly at times when children may benefit from being occupied and entertained such as travelling and waiting times. Musical items for children are found in the form of toys that incorporate musical tunes, CDs and videos produced for children, children's digital music players, video games such as karaoke and access to Internet-based games that incorporate music, often linked to children's TV programs (Brooks, 2012, 2013a). The common perception is that technology "closes" down children's creativity and improvisational activity by providing ready-made activities, but from the few studies that are beginning to explore the ways that digital music resources are used by children, it would seem that they are providing new possibilities and new musical resources for children to play with (Bickford, 2011, 2013, 2014; Bishop, 2014; Burn & Richards, 2014; Campbell, 2010; Willett, 2014; Young, 2008, 2012a).

Birth to 3

In recent years there has been a considerable upsurge of interest in the musical competencies of babies. Painstaking analysis of infant–caregiver interaction has revealed that successful communication between adult and baby depends on music-like qualities of rhythm, variations in pitch inflexion, and dynamics (Malloch & Trevarthen, 2009; Trevarthen, 2000, 2002a). The adult intuitively adopts infant-directed speech characterized by short rhythmic phrases and expressively contoured variations in pitch, and the baby responds with movements and vocal responses that are coordinated with the adult. These are spontaneous, intuitive, and playful exchanges between adults and babies which, when well matched, strengthen the bond between them and enable adults to support the emotional and physical regulation of the babies they are caring for. Importantly they provide a raft of playful exchanges that enable the babies to access important aspects about the social and physical world around them.

With older babies and toddlers, parents and carers supplement these playful, music-like exchanges with a repertoire of lullabies, playsongs, rhymes, and improvised "ditties" (Street, 2004; Trehub & Trainor, 1998; Trehub, Unyk, & Trainor, 1993; Trevarthen, 2002b). They make use of all available sources for musical material and may well sing a snatch from a contemporary popular song alongside a traditional children's song. These early music play experiences are highly meaningful to very young children, as they are integral to their close relationships with caregiving adults. Early music play provides a rich resource for the development of many skills and understandings, particularly the acquisition of language (Papoušek, 1992).

Becoming more knowledgeable about the musical play experiences of babies and toddlers in the home is difficult for reasons of access, although there are some small studies in which family members have kept diaries of young children's musical play in the home, noting for example vocal play (Forrester, 2010; Papoušek & Papoušek, 1981; Papoušek, 1996), general responses to recorded music (Littleton, 2002), and body movement responses to music (Chen-Hafteck, 2004). Video-recordings of one complete day of home care for 2-year-olds in different international locations revealed a range of music play activities that took place as part of day-to-day life in the home. These playful activities included interactive play between adult and child more in the style of traditional lapgames, alongside musical experiences engendered by toys that often include sound and music, and recorded music from CD players, video, and TV programs (Young & Gillen, 2010).

It is easier to gain access to observe young children in daycare, although here the availability of equipment to play with, more space, freedom to move and make noise, and the higher adult–child ratio will influence the way children play in comparison with the home (Suthers, 2000; Young, 2002). However, what is striking in all contexts is how children actively create their own opportunities for playful musical activity from what is available and show a need to repeat favorite experiences in order to deepen and develop them. For example, a toddler observed in a daycare setting requested a replay of the same recorded popular song many times and bounced rhythmically on cushions during each repetition of the chorus. Thus young children drive their own learning by selecting what they currently need, and what might appear to be arbitrary or repetitious behaviors can hold a key to children's current competencies.

The preschool years

Educational settings

Musical play in the preschool years (the ages of 3 to 6 years approximately) has been the focus of a number of studies dating from 1937 to the present. The underlying premise of the famous Pillsbury study in the United States was that young children possess an innate musicality, and that if allowed freedom to play in a potentially rich environment, they would display this musicality in a coherent form embedded in their general playful behaviors (Moorhead & Pond, 1941/78; Moorhead, Sandvik, & Wight, 1951/78; Pond, 1980). A special nursery was set up, well equipped with musical instruments, and the staff recorded their observations of children's musical activity over a number of years. The Pillsbury study inspired a number of subsequent observational studies in North America in the early 1980s (Cohen, 1980; Miller, 1984; Shelley, 1981; Shelley & Foley, 1979). What all these researchers found was that all young children are prodigious producers of a rich variety of spontaneous musical play and that there are some broad common features of this play. Overwhelmingly the majority of spontaneous musical behaviors found by all these researchers were vocal. Littleton (1991) subsequently grouped types of "pre-schoolers" musical play into three categories: singing; play with instruments and sound-makers; and spontaneous movement to music. It is around these three types of play and their broad common features that discussion continues.

Vocal play Although studies of young children's spontaneous vocalizations during free play are widely separated both chronologically and in geographic location, collectively they reveal a surprising similarity of findings (Bjørkvold, 1989/92; Moorhead & Pond, 1941/78; Sundin, 1960/98). In summary, a general consensus emerges that identifies two broad types of singing among young children: a communicative, chant-like, repetitive singing of short verbal and musical ideas; and a more introverted, solitary, free-flowing, diffuse kind of singing, often on open syllable sounds. Snatches of known songs resurface in children's spontaneous singing of either kind, often with altered words or melodic and rhythmic transformations.

A further theory was proposed by Sundin (1960/98) as a result of his observations of 3–6-year-olds during the "free play" hour in Swedish kindergartens. He suggested that the two types of singing were distinguished by social context: the free-flowing "plainsong" being primarily solo and introverted, and the "chant" (using reiterated short phrases) most often produced in group activity. Interesting comparative studies carried out among children attending preschools in Oslo, Russia, and the United States (Bjørkvold, 1989/92) revealed that the repetitive "chant" (also called "formula song") is the dominant form of song among children in groups. It is possible that there is continuity between the preschool chant and the sociable playground games of mid- and later childhood. There is less evidence for the extension of individual introverted free-flow singing into the later years of childhood, although it may be found when children improvise songs individually (Davies, 1986).

Young children's spontaneous singing is integrated not only with the social environment, but also with their play in all media (Pond, 1981), exemplifying the characteristic of multimodality mentioned earlier. Children typically synchronize singing with movement, either their own physical movement or that of toys; they dramatize their toys with improvised vocalizations and act out role plays that have singing incorporated (Young, 2002).

Spontaneous play with instruments Where instruments or other sound-makers are available, children will enjoy playing with them to explore sounds and create sequences and patterns of sounds. The idea that children are merely exploring the instruments randomly and that sounds that ensue are not "music" but simply noise is still prevalent (Young, 1999), supported by echoes of Piagetian theory that characterize young children's activity as exploratory but without structure. However, by analyzing play with instruments, two researchers (Cohen, 1980; Young, 2003a, b) demonstrated that what might appear, initially, to be random and sporadic play is generated and structured by patterns of bodily movement that are gestural or stimulated by the structure of the instruments. For example, children commonly strike or tap instruments in an ordered way, making regular rhythmic groupings and extending them into sequences.

The complexity and creativity of children's spontaneous play with instruments can often eclipse that found in more teacher-directed activities. In an interesting piece of action research, Smithrim (1997) provided a setting for eight 3- and 4-year-olds to play freely with percussion instruments, a guitar, and a piano. She found that the range, variety, and complexity of the children's musical activity when left to free-play far exceeded anything they would have been able to achieve in a teacher-led class. However, not surprisingly, noise was a consideration, and she acknowledges that the changes in practice it implies would be difficult in many settings.

Movement play Movement is one of the child's earliest self-initiated responses to music and a small group of studies have looked at their responses to recorded music (Chen-Hafteck, 2004; Gorali-Turel, 1999) and to songs (Hicks, 1993). Many have noticed that when recorded music is played, young children typically respond with movement. Gorali-Turel was interested to observe these movements and record them systematically in order to identify any common characteristics that emerged. She found that the youngest children of about 3 years often performed simple twirling or bouncing movements and were highly repetitive in their movements, but also, that they were responsive to the tempi, the intensity, and other generalized characteristics of the music. In the Israeli daycare center where she carried out this research, she also observed the interactions of the adults, and found that if adults modeled movements, the children often attempted to imitate but only if the modeled movements took account of children's natural tempo and movement style. The way that the adult responds and partners the playing child has a crucial impact on how children play.

The adult role When experimental situations were set up to evaluate the differences between a range of teacher interaction styles on children's musical play (Tarnowski & Leclerc, 1994), the children played in the most creative and interesting ways when "observed" by adults and failed to extend or develop play when "entertained" or "directed." Over-intrusive and directive interventions tend to close down children's play, whereas interactions that the children perceive to be responsive and supportive will foster and creatively extend it (Young, 2003c). Such findings demonstrate the motivation that will sustain children's musical play when it is supported by adults who show interest and provide appropriate assistance. For this reason, some have worked carefully in early childhood settings alongside staff to help them recognize the musical learning taking place when children are playing musically so that they have a rationale for play-based approaches and pedagogical knowledge of how to support it (Suthers, 2000; Young, 2003a).

The home

Within the home, musical play of children aged from 3 to 6 years continues to involve adult-generated musical materials, both those that are provided by parents and other relatives and those that more generally permeate the sonic environment of the home. While children in this age group engage in musical play with parents and grandparents in the home setting, particularly with traditional songs such as nursery rhymes (Brooks, 2013b), children's home musical play is increasingly reflective of the mass media's audio-visual stimuli (Lamont, 2008; Lum, 2008, 2009). Lum's (2009) study of a 5-year-old and older sibling in their home environment in Singapore found that media dominated musical play, which included singing, dancing to theme songs from television programs, and fantasy play with toy figures of media characters. Other studies involving home observations of children note that children's patterns of interaction with the media (e.g., singing along with themes) become infused in their play, often continuing post-viewing (Brooks, 2013c; Lum, 2008). In her study of young children's uses of music in screen media, Brooks (2013a, c) observed musical play being invited by television hosts, often resulting in musical interactions between children and a televised partner. Such musical play often involves mimicry and is influenced by the gender of television presenters and repeated viewings.

Mid-childhood

Home play of children in mid-childhood

As in the early childhood years, musical play in the home continues into middle childhood. An international study of music in the home among 7-year-olds revealed a wealth of playful music activity that took place at home (Young, 2012b). With changing notions of parenting among the middle classes (and the children in this study were from middle-class families), parents now understand their role to be about providing ways for children to occupy themselves in the indoor safety of their homes and so they purchase musical items, both material and digital (Ilari, 2011). The children had musical toys and instruments, video games, access to radio, CD players, and TV, and some children could use Internet-linked computers. The production and marketing of musical items for children has become a rapidly increasing international business. What the study also found was that these children often described playing alone in their bedrooms, and the increase of solitary play enabled by digital technologies and commercial media designed for children is one of the transformations of music play that research is starting to discover and explore. Nevertheless, interactive play between children is an important characteristic of musical play for this age group, occurring in the home, community, and school, often in marked contrast to what is happening musically on a formal level in educational settings.

Characteristics of musical play in the playground

The differences between children's spontaneous play and that found in teacher-directed educational settings continue into the middle childhood years. It has long been assumed that children's

Fig. 25.1 Universal childish rhythm proposed by Brailoiu

musical play in the playground is quite rhythmically, melodically, and formally simple. Such assumptions were supported by the work of ethnomusicologist Brailoiu (1954), whose analysis of children's songs and rhymes from Europe, West Africa, Russia, Canada, Japan, and Formosa (currently Taiwan) resulted in his postulation of a universal "childish rhythm" (p. 21): a binary rhythm equal to the value of eight quavers, as shown in Figure 25.1. This "universal" rhythmic structure was subsequently endorsed by studies of Australian Aboriginal children's play (Kartomi, 1980) and Javanese children's play (Romet, 1980).

However, these findings have related to the rhythm of game texts only and have failed to take into account the integral element of movement that accompanies the texts. While it is true that many game texts are in duple meter, the movement patterns often are metrically contrasting. Perhaps the most pervasive set of movements reported in clapping games since the late 1970s is that of a three-beat clapping pattern (Bishop, 2014; Campbell, 1991; Harwood, 1998a; Harwood & Marsh, 2012; Marsh, 2008; Merrill-Mirsky, 1988; Riddell, 1990). This is seen by children in Australia, the United States, England, and Norway as a clapping pattern which is applicable to most texts, despite the fact that it creates a polymetric relationship with the text (Marsh, 2005a). This can be seen in Figure 25.2.

Fig. 25.2 Polymetric relationship between clapping pattern and text of a Sydney playground game

Fig. 25.3 Clapping rhythm of *Slide*

While children are rarely conscious of this polymetric aspect of their performance (to some extent maintaining the textual and movement rhythms independently), it nevertheless exists in sonic form, often highlighted by the regular accents provided by specific handclapping movements (clapping own hands together, for example, having a louder sound than clapping partner's hands). It is evident that the three-beat pattern is generally acquired and ably demonstrated (in conjunction with duple texts) by children at least from the age of 6 years. Children of 8 and 9 years of age have been observed performing, with remarkable fluency, a textless game, which has a seven-beat clapping pattern and additive meters as its structural core (Marsh, 2008; Riddell, 1990). The rhythm of the first three sections of this game is illustrated in Figure 25.3.

A 13-beat clapping pattern identified in the United States by Riddell (1990) and Harwood (1992; Harwood & Marsh, 2012) has also been performed in Sydney by children as young as 7 years (Marsh, 1997, 2008). Similar polymetric relationships between duple text and quintuple movement rhythms of clapping games have been reported in Portugal by Prim (1989).

Environmental influences are clearly reflected in the rhythmic characteristics of playground singing games. Both the African-American game tradition and the influence of popular music, which has global dimensions, have resulted in increased syncopation in text rhythms of games from the last decades of the twentieth century through to the twenty-first century (Campbell, 1991; Gaunt, 2006; Marsh, 1997, 2008; Merrill-Mirsky, 1988), as demonstrated in Figure 25.4.

Studies of musical play in Ghana (Addo, 1995) and South Africa (Blacking, 1967/95; Emberley, 2009) have also revealed that the polyrhythmic characteristics of adult music in these locations are maintained in children's games and songs. Complex combinations of duple and triple rhythms are identified in Balkan children's musical play by Yugoslavian ethnomusicologist Basic (1986), who has decried the "systematic impoverishment of the children's musical creative imagination" (p. 131) by music educators who simplify children's games for classroom use.

There are also melodic differences between children's singing games and songs employed in the classroom. Melodies in children's games frequently have a melodic range of no more than a fifth and rarely exceed an octave (Campbell, 1991; Marsh, 2008), although Segler's (1992) trans-European collection and analysis of children's games includes melodies with a range of a ninth, particularly found in games from northern Europe. The minor third, which is popularly believed to be a "universal" characteristic of children's musical play, is no more dominant in game melodies than both major and minor seconds (Marsh, 2008). In Ghanaian children's games, the melodic patterns have been linked to the speech tones of Ghanaian languages (Addo, 1995).

Of potential interest is the finding of Marsh (2008) that children's songs in an Australian playground have a unique tonality, whereby the first note of the song functions as its tonal center. Standard tonal melodies which are part of a wider musical environment are adapted by children

Fig. 25.4 Syncopation in text rhythms in a Sydney playground game of African-American origin

for performance in a playground context. When held within the repertoire of a group of children for a protracted period of time, however, what may have originated as a tonal melody is frequently transformed into a variant in which the melodic contours have been "flattened." This can be seen in the contrast between the Australian playground version of *See, see my playmate* (Figure 25.2) and the original melody found in a Los Angeles rendition of the song (Figure 25.5) collected by Riddell (1990).

The tessitura of children's games appears to be much lower than that commonly found in published classroom material; a probable explanation for this is the common practice of moving from pitched song to unpitched speech. As the tonal center of children's speech appears to be fairly low,

*Differs from original song

Fig. 25.5 Los Angeles version of *See, see my playmate*

the melodies with which the speech is interwoven are also low in pitch. In some cases melodic renditions can arise directly from exaggerated speech inflexions (Marsh, 2008).

Formally, children's singing games are frequently repetitive and cyclical. Ostinati are found in many movement patterns, but these are often interrupted by mimetic movements or changes to the rhythm pattern of movements at points of textual rest or emphasis. Once again, the structure of games reflects environmental influences. For example, call and response forms may be found in Ghanaian, South African, African-American, and Norwegian games, but not in the musical play of Australian children, unless they have been derived from other sources, such as the classroom or media (Addo, 1995; Emberley, 2009; Harrop-Allin, 2010; Marsh, 2008; Riddell, 1990).

Adolescence

Children in their early teens often continue to play clapping games or chants with younger siblings, but do this less publicly at home rather than in the playground, where cheers or dance routines may be more prominent (Harwood, 1998b). Depending on the school environment, playground play may continue into teenage years. For example, in Norway, children attend primary (elementary) school until they are 13 and have been observed playing jump-rope and circle games at this age because of endorsement by the school and prominence of these forms of play in this environment (Marsh, 2008).

Adolescent musical play has only recently become a focus of research interest. Lill (2014) has explored the phenomenon of two examples of digitally disseminated play found in high schools in the UK and Australia. Both the "Cup Song" (played predominantly by girls) and the "Knife Song" (played predominantly by boys) are played socially by adolescents and younger children in the playground or at home. The "Cup Song," involving a rhythmic ostinato performed with kinaesthetic virtuosity using cups or other objects has been made particularly popular by its appearance in the movie *Pitch Perfect*, but can be played with a variety of songs or with no song. The "Knife Song" involves a series of rhythmic movements with a knife (or object of similar dimensions) pointing between the spread fingers of one hand and accompanied by a song emphasizing the daring nature of this activity. In both cases, multiple versions of these games and tutorials to assist with learning them are found on YouTube and are thus highly accessible as learning aids promoting improvisation.

During early adolescence the boundaries between adult and child activity begin to diminish. What constitutes adolescent play is therefore less easy to define. However, a number of musical activities that are self-initiated, spontaneous, self-regulated, and enjoyable might also be characterized as forms of adolescent musical play. Such activities include downloading music files from the Internet and singing along with them or dancing in spontaneous response to a CD. More creative and organized endeavors such as hip-hop freestyling or participation in garage bands might also be characterized as types of musical play. By this age many children have often developed competence on a musical instrument and may also be observed in solitary "playful" improvisation. Other activities such as computer games have embedded musical soundtracks which form an intrinsic accompaniment or "electronic soundscape" accompanying play (Campbell, 2010, p. 86). Games such as *Guitar Hero* and *High School Musical* promote the playing out of musical skills and characterizations, often developing adolescents' real musical skills in the process (Cassidy & Paisley, 2013).

Teaching and learning in the context of play

From early years through to early adolescence, children collaborate and learn in musical play not only from adults, but also from one another. Competence as musical players is increased by observation of and participation in modeled play behaviors, facilitated by physical proximity to and physical contact with other players (Harwood, 1992, 1998a; Harwood & Marsh, 2012; Marsh, 2002, 2008; Moorhead & Pond, 1941/78; Young, 2004).

In the playground, among older children, games are usually transmitted between age peers and from older to young children (Harwood, 1992, 1998a; Harwood & Marsh, 2012; Marsh, 1999a, 2008). Children may move into a pair formation, sometimes away from the larger group, in order to practice new games or performance skills. Game transmission and skill development are always achieved by observation and attempted performance of the whole game, though hand positions are sometimes maneuvered or demonstrated separately prior to the commencement of a game performance. Song acquisition in this context is therefore achieved by aggregative "catching" of musical, textual, and movement phrases within a musical whole. Skills are also gained within a holistic framework and never fragmented or taught in isolation from the game as a whole (Harwood, 1992, 1998a; Harwood & Marsh, 2012; Marsh, 2002, 2008). However, a recent study of playground game transmission has found that the integration of YouTube clips of games as a source of game learning possibly encourages a more segmented approach to learning, as the clips can be stopped and replayed at various points at will (Bishop, 2014).

It can be seen, then, that the social milieu of the setting, whether with adults or peers, allows for multiple levels of competence to coexist and be incorporated into play activities and for children to learn at their own pace. Children can choose their own level of participation, from observation, to trialing some limited form of participation, such as movements, through to full participation, perhaps joining in with singing play or playing alongside others with instruments or a digital model (Bishop, 2014; Harwood & Marsh, 2012; Marsh, 2008).

Older children may develop collaborative skills to the level at which they can provide careful tuition of novice players, as observed by Marsh (1999a, 2008). Children in the school playground were aware of developmental differences in playing abilities, particularly relating to the performance of movement patterns, and accommodated these differences through a process akin to the notion of "scaffolding" (Wood, Bruner, & Ross, 1976), whereby learners' progress is supported by modeling of behaviors slightly beyond their present level of competence. Older or more adept children switched automatically to easier clapping patterns when playing with younger or less adept players. They then carefully modeled clapping patterns of greater difficulty, physically manipulating the hands of the less able player until some level of competence was reached (Marsh, 1999a, 2008).

Children do not seem to require that one skill or game genre be perfected before moving on to a new one. Rather, they create challenges for themselves by devising and adopting from external sources new variants of movement, music, or text. These variants might then be disseminated through performance with other players or by observation of the performance by child onlookers (Marsh, 1997, 2008). In his study of Venda children's play songs in South Africa, Blacking (1967/95) states that "children's songs are not always easier than adult songs and children do not necessarily learn the simple songs first" (p. 29). For example, more difficult songs may be learnt first by Venda children simply because they have been heard more frequently. A similar phenomenon is demonstrated by children's learning of quite complex popular songs from repeated renditions in the media (Harwood, 1987; Harwood & Marsh, 2012; Marsh, 2008; Young, 2003a).

Creativity in children's musical play

There has been a long-standing assumption derived from developmental models of learning, both generally and in music, that young children's play is aimlessly exploratory. However, careful analysis of young children's play activity reveals creative processes of transformation. Typically, short motifs or ideas are revisited, repeated, and gradually transformed, within themselves, by extending or by combining with other ideas. These processes can be identified in the musical play of even quite young children (Young, 2003a) and continue in more sophisticated and complex ways in the play of older children. This can be seen in the following vignette observed by Young in a daycare setting.

> Ahmed points to a picture of a football and declaims, "Pop-ball!" He repeats the word with a strong accent on the first syllable. He then turns away from the picture book, stomping across the room singing "Pop-ball" four times in a falling interval of a fourth expanding in the last two versions to a wider interval. His rhythmic singing is in time with his stomps. He then starts to repeat the "pop" first to "pop, pop-ball" and then "pop, pop, POP—ball!"—thereby changing the rhythm and using the word not for its specific meaning, but as a rhythmic idea.

Older children's quest for novelty in their games results in the generation of many variants, which are created through a process of combining short textual, melodic, and rhythmic phrases or formulae. This process of formulaic construction, which is characteristic of orally transmitted performance genres, occurs quite spontaneously during the performance of singing games and is termed "composition in performance" (Lord, 1995). In children's generative practices there is no dichotomy between process and product, so that the repertoire is constantly evolving. Within the social safety of their friendship groups, children engage collaboratively in the generation of variants (Marsh, 1995, 2008). This is described by Blacking (1985) as a collective effort that results both in "new cultural forms and a richer experience for the participants" (pp. 46–7). Bishop (2014) refers to this process as "revoicing" (p. 72).

In selecting formulae for use in games, children draw upon raw material from their auditory environment. Musical, textual, and movement formulae are therefore derived from the media, the classroom, and songs or games performed by other children or adults (Harwood & Marsh, 2012; Marsh, 1999b, 2008, 2013; Willett, 2014). As they combine formulae in their play, children consciously consider formal, rhythmic, and melodic appropriateness and demonstrate a sophisticated array of innovative processes. These include reorganization of formulae, elaboration through addition of new material or expansion of known material, condensation through omission or contraction of formulae, and recasting of material, for example, through substitution of new words or movements. It should be noted that these processes occur across the age range and so do not appear to develop in complexity with age, although children become more aware of their own processes of innovation from the age of approximately 8 or 9 (Marsh, 1995, 2008).

Cultural adaptation and appropriation

As previously discussed, globalization, a burgeoning mass-media industry, and large-scale patterns of migration have brought major changes to children's auditory environments since the middle of the twentieth century. Popular music, disseminated through television, radio, the Internet, digital recordings, DVD, and CD, forms a background to many activities and is heard in the home, in shops, and in recreational centers (Campbell, 1998, 2010). The performance of popular music for many years has also included both aural and visual elements that are avidly absorbed and emulated by children in their play.

Electronic recordings of songs provide templates that children can use for repetitive listening and viewing. As with the learning of playground singing games, songs and dance routines are learnt holistically. Even very young children are able to reproduce portions of popular songs, often key phrases and movements (Young, 2002, 2003a), and children in the first years of schooling can reproduce songs in full (Harwood, 1987). Song and dance routines are performed individually by children in front of the television, using karaoke, or among groups of friends well into preteen years (Harwood, 1987; Lum, 2007, 2009; McIntosh, 2006; Willett, 2014; Young, 2012a).

Once adult-generated sources of entertainment are transported into the playground, however, they are immediately reappropriated and subjected to the creative endeavors of the children. Children may invent new dance routines to popular songs or to cheerleaders' chants, drawing on the repertoire of movements learnt from the media or older performers (Bishop & Burn, 2013; Marsh, 2006; Willett, 2014). While children as young as 6 years have been observed performing popular dance routines and sports chants (Marsh, 2005b, 2008), Harwood states that these genres, designated cheers, drill teams, and routines by the performers, are more regularly the province of older children in the preteen and early teen years (1998b).

Younger school-age children are more likely to invent clapping patterns with which to accompany popular songs and sports chants. These may be relatively transient, as in the renditions of the Spice Girls' *Wannabe* reported in an English playground in 1997 by Grugeon (2001), or may become part of a longer tradition, such as that of *See, see my playmate*, derived from the popular song *Playmates* composed in the 1940s (Opie & Opie, 1988), which has become a clapping game still played in the UK, United States, Australia, and many European countries (Marsh, 1997, 1999b; Opie & Opie, 1988; Riddell, 1990; Segler, 1992) (see Figures 25.2 and 25.5).

Popular culture and its icons are also subverted in the playground. Thus *Down, down, baby*, a game linked with a popular song from the 1960s, *Shimmy, Shimmy Ko-Ko-Bop* (Riddell, 1990), becomes a vehicle for the ridiculing of pop star Britney Spears:

> The train goes
> Down down baby down by the riverside
> Sweet sweet baby never let it go again
> Shimmy shimmy coconut shimmy shimmy ah
> Shimmy shimmy coconut shimmy shimmy ah
> I hate coffee, I hate tea
> I hate Britney, she's never with me
> Down by the fire peeling potatoes
> Britney Spears is so crap.
>
> Recorded Keighley, England, 2002 (Marsh, 2005a, 2008)

Parody songs perhaps represent this subversion of adult culture at its zenith. In the middle years of school, children may adapt texts of well-known songs, advertisements, or TV jingles (Harwood, 1994), creating parallel texts which mock adult concerns and reduce "adult order to humorous disorder" (Factor, 1988, p. 153) as an "antithetical reaction to the institutional and everyday hegemonies of the life about them" (Sutton-Smith, 1995, p. 6). Such disorder is aptly illustrated by the following example, which is sung to the melody of the Christmas carol, *Joy to the World*:

> Joy to the world, the school burnt down
> And all the teachers too.
> The principal is dead; we shot her in the head;
> The secretary too, we flushed her down the loo
> And all, and all the teachers too.
>
> Recorded Sydney, Australia, 1994 (Marsh, 1997)

Many other songs learnt either through the media or from other adult sources, such as the classroom, become raw materials for formulaic construction in the playground. In utilizing this material for creative purposes, children exert ownership and control over it and are thus never passive recipients of adult culture. At the same time, their play is inexorably changed by its influences, as exemplified by the syncopation that has permeated the rhythms of playground games. Bishop (2014) notes that children use both the content and mediated form of transmission provided by new media sites such as YouTube to add a cachet of novelty and cultural capital to their "revoicings."

Within the playground, children may also be influenced by the play of children from other cultural backgrounds. The level of cross-cultural transmission seems to vary according to circumstance. For example, where there is a wide diversity of ethnocultural groups within a playground, children appear to engage actively in exchanging games between groups. This can partly be explained by an acceptance of difference, but also by children's interest in novelty and the "nonsense" characteristics of many game texts, which can be transferred readily between games in different languages (Marsh, 2001, 2008). In a monocultural environment there may be less opportunity for or disposition toward cross-cultural transmission. In Marsh's (2005b, 2008) field observation of school children in Busan, southern Korea, the only playground game that directly appeared to transcend cultural boundaries was a textless clapping game that strongly resembled the game *Slide* found in the United States and Australia (see Figure 25.3). In this instance, the absence of text probably contributed to the ease of its transmission.

Other games, such as the Punjabi *Zig Zag Zoo*, may be learnt in children's (or their parents') countries of origin, and then are transplanted to countries of residence and played actively at home and with friends within the ethnocultural group (Curtis, 2000; Marsh, 2008). Studies of games in the United States seem to indicate that games are played more within ethnocultural groups than exchanged between them (Merrill-Mirsky, 1988). However, Merrill-Mirsky also maintains that there has been a strong transcultural influence of African-American musical styles, promulgated both by African-American games and by popular music. Programs such as *Sesame Street* have also broadcast African-American games to an international viewing audience, thus contributing to their wider dissemination (Emberley, 2009; Marsh, 2001, 2008).

Forms of play in the home provide avenues both for cross-cultural sharing and creative generation of songs and games. Two immigrant girls in a Sydney school, 11 and 12 years old, respectively, described how they created new songs in completely new languages by melding the performative influences of Arabic, Persian, Turkish, and Azerbaijani popular singers (observed on YouTube), using selected musical phrases, dance movements, and text, translated with the assistance of Google dictionary functions. The selection of these component parts was also made within the framework of game elements, for example, putting written text or dance movements into a hat and choosing them randomly. The end result was a performance that was completely their own, in a language which only they shared and controlled, creating a performative space of belonging (Marsh, 2013).

Conclusions

In this chapter we have explored the variety and range of children's musical play from birth through to early adolescence. We have shown how children within their play are able to integrate, transform, and generate new ideas that capitalize on the material, digital, and human resources that are available to them in different settings. At any given age children may be engaged in the simultaneous development of a wide range of skills associated with different types of play and different game genres. Progress may be very irregular across different skills and even within skills, and unlikely to accrue in simple linear developmental pathways. Such abilities might be harnessed in educational approaches that create ample opportunities for children to play with music. The significance of play as an essential vehicle for children's musical expression should be acknowledged and encouraged within and beyond educational settings.

Reflective questions

1 What are the major characteristics of children's musical play? Discuss your own or family members' childhood experiences of musical play, alone and with others.

2 How has children's musical play changed over the last decade? What changes have you observed or experienced in home or educational settings?

3 In what ways does children's self-directed musical play differ from provision of formal music activities or experiences in educational settings?

4 What, in your opinion, is the value of musical play to children and how might the value differ to children of different ages?

5 Should musical play be provided for in educational practice—and if so, how?

Key sources

Campbell, P. S. (2010). *Songs in their heads: Music and its meaning in children's lives* (2nd ed.). New York: Oxford University Press.

Gaunt, K. D. (2006). *The games black girls play: Learning the ropes from double-Dutch to hip-hop*. New York: New York University Press.

Harwood, E., & Marsh, K. (2012). Children's ways of learning inside and outside the classroom. In G. McPherson & G. Welch (Eds.), *Oxford handbook of music education* (pp. 322–40). New York: Oxford University Press.

Marsh, K. (2008). *The musical playground: Global tradition and change in children's songs and games*. New York: Oxford University Press.

Young, S. (2003). *Music with the under-fours*. London, UK: RoutledgeFalmer Press.

Reference list

Addo, A. O. (1995). Ghanaian children's music cultures: A video ethnography of selected singing games (Doctoral dissertation, University of British Columbia, Canada, 1995). *Dissertation Abstracts International*, 57/03, AAC NN05909.

Basic, E. (1986). Differences in the authenticity of children's expression and the viewing angle of the adults (II). In I. Ivic & A. Marjanovic (Eds.), *Traditional games and children of today: Belgrade: OMEP Traditional Games Project* (pp. 129–34). Belgrade, Serbia: OMEP.

Bickford, T. (2011). Children's music, MP3 players, and expressive practices at a Vermont elementary school: Media consumption as social organization among schoolchildren (Unpublished doctoral dissertation). Columbia University, New York.

Bickford, T. (2013). Tinkering and tethering in the material world of children's MP3 players. In P. S. Campbell & T. Wiggins (Eds.), *The Oxford handbook of children's musical cultures* (pp. 527–42). New York: Oxford University Press.

Bickford, T. (2014). Earbuds are good for sharing: Children's sociable uses of headphones at a Vermont primary school. In J. Stanyek & S. Gopinath (Eds.), *The Oxford handbook of mobile music studies* (pp. 335–55). Oxford, UK: Oxford University Press.

Bishop, J. C. (2014). "That's how the whole hand-clap thing passes on": Online/offline transmission and multimodal variation in a children's clapping game. In A. N. Burn & C. O. Richards (Eds.), *Children's games in the new media age* (pp. 53–84). Farnham, UK: Ashgate.

Bishop, J. C., & Burn, A. (2013). Reasons for rhythm: Multimodal perspectives on musical play. In R. Willett, C. Richards, J. Marsh, A. Burn, & J. C. Bishop (Eds.), *Children, media and playground cultures: Ethnographic studies of school playtimes* (pp. 89–119). Basingstoke, UK: Palgrave Macmillan.

Bjørkvold, J. (1989). *The muse within: Creativity and communication, song and play from childhood through maturity*, (trans. W. H. Halverson, 1992). New York: Harper Collins.

Blacking, J. (1985). Versus gradus novos ad parnassum musicum: Exemplum Africanum. In D. P. McAllester (Ed.), *Becoming human through music: The Wesleyan symposium on the perspectives of social anthropology in the teaching and learning of music* (pp. 43–52). Reston, VA: Music Educators' National Conference.

Blacking, J. (1995). *Venda children's songs: A study in ethnomusicological analysis*. Chicago, IL: University of Chicago Press. (Original work published 1967.)

Brady, M. (1975). This little lady's gonna boogaloo: Elements of socialization in the play of black girls. In R. Bauman (Ed.), *Black girls at play: Perspectives on child development* (pp. 1–51). Austin, TX: Southwest Educational Development Laboratory.

Brailoiu, C. (1954). The children's rhythm–liminal notions (trans. unknown). In *Les Colloques de Wegmont* (pp. 1–21). Brussels, Belgium: International d'Etude Ethnomusicolique.

Brooks, W. (2012). An introductory analysis of music in infant-directed media. In A. Niland & J. Rutkoski (Eds.), *Passing on the flame: Reflecting on the past, envisioning towards the future of early childhood music education*. Proceedings of the 15th International Seminar of the Commission for the Early Childhood Music Education (ECME). Corfu, Greece: July 9–13, 2012.

Brooks, W. (2013a). Watching music with young children: An investigation of three Australian television productions. Proceedings of the AEC-APSMER Conference, Singapore: July 17–19, 2013. Retrieved from <http://arts2013.sg/full-papers-download.html>.

Brooks, W. (2013b). Taking the music out of nursery rhymes? Changing features and functions of young children's traditional songs. In L. Chen-Hafteck & M. N. Yildiz (Eds.), *Educating the creative mind: Developing capacities for our future*. Conference Proceedings of 2nd Educating the Creative Mind Conference, May 30–31, New Jersey.

Brooks, W. (2013c). Live and mediated music for young children: A case study of Lah-Lah. In *Redefining the musical landscape: Inspired learning and innovation in music education—XIX National Conference Proceedings* (p. 37). Australian Society for Music Education.

Burn, A. N., & Richards, C. O. (Eds.) (2014). *Children's games in the new media age*. Farnham, UK: Ashgate.

Campbell, P. S. (1991). The child-song genre: A comparison of songs by and for children. *International Journal of Music Education*, **17**, 14–23.

Campbell, P. S. (1998). *Songs in their heads: Music and its meaning in children's lives*. New York: Oxford University Press.

Campbell, P. S. (2010). *Songs in their heads: Music and its meaning in children's lives* (2nd ed.). New York: Oxford University Press.

Campbell, P. S., & Wiggins, T. (2013). *The Oxford handbook of children's musical cultures*. New York: Oxford University Press.

Cassidy, G. G., & Paisley, A. M. J. M. (2013). Music-games: A case study of their impact. *Research Studies in Music Education*, **35**(1), 119–38.

Chen-Hafteck, L. (2004). Music and movement from zero to three: A window to children's musicality. In L. Custodero (Ed.), *Proceedings of the ISME Early Childhood Conference "Els Móns Musical Dels Infants" (The Musical Worlds of Children)*, Barcelona, Spain, July 5–10, 2004.

Cohen, V. (1980). The emergence of musical gestures in kindergarten children (Doctoral dissertation, University of Illinois, Champaign Urbana, 1980). *Dissertation Abstracts International*, AAT 8108471.

Curtis, M. (2000). Zig Zag Zoo and other games: The oral tradition of children of Asian origin in Keighley, West Yorkshire. *Folklife, the Journal of Folk Life Studies*, **38**, 71–82.

Davies, C. (1986). Say it till a song comes (reflections on songs invented by children 3–13). *British Journal of Music Education*, **3**(3), 279–93.

Eckhardt, R. (1975). From handclap to line play. In R. Bauman (Ed.), *Black girls at play: Perspectives on child development* (pp. 57–99). Austin, TX: Southwest Educational Development Laboratory.

Emberley, A. (2009). *"Mandela went to China . . . and India too": Musical cultures of childhood in South Africa* (Unpublished doctoral dissertation). University of Washington, Seattle.

Factor, J. (1988). *Captain Cook chased a chook: Children's folklore in Australia*. Ringwood, Victoria, Australia: Penguin Books.

Forrester, M. A. (2010). Emerging musicality during the pre-school years: A case study of one child. *Psychology of Music*, **38**(2), 131–58.

Gaunt, K. D. (2006). *The games black girls play: Learning the ropes from double-Dutch to hip-hop*. New York: New York University Press.

Gorali-Turel, T. (1999). Spontaneous movement response of young children to musical stimulation as indicator of the hidden cognitive process. Unpublished paper. *Cognitive Processes of Children Engaged in Musical Activity*, Urbana-Champaign, IL: School of Music, University of Illinois.

Grugeon, E. (2001). "We like singing the Spice Girl songs and we like Tig and Stuck in the Mud": Girls' traditional games on two playgrounds. In J. C Bishop & M. Curtis (Eds.), *Play today in the primary school playground: Life, learning and creativity* (pp. 98–114). Milton Keynes, UK: Open University Press.

Harrop-Allin, S. (2010). *Recruiting learners' musical games as resources for South African music education, using a Multiliteracies approach* (Unpublished doctoral dissertation). University of the Witwatersrand, Johannesburg, South Africa.

Harwood, E. (1987). *The memorized song repertoire of children in Grades 4 and 5 in Champaign, Illinois* (Doctoral dissertation, University of Illinois Champaign Urbana, 1987). *Dissertation Abstracts International*, AAT 8721651.

Harwood, E. (1992). Girls' handclapping games: A study in oral transmission. *Bulletin of the International Kodály Society*, **17**, 19–25.

Harwood, E. (1994). Miss Lucy meets Dr Pepper: Mass media and children's traditional playground song and chant. In H. Lees (Ed.), *Musical connections: Tradition and change* (pp. 187–94). Proceedings of the 21st World Conference of the International Society for Music Education, Tampa, Florida, USA.

Harwood, E. (1998a). Music learning in context: A playground tale. *Research Studies in Music Education*, **11**, 52–60.

Harwood, E. (1998b). Go on girl! Improvisation in African-American girls' singing games. In B. Nettl & M. Russell (Eds.), *In the course of performance: Studies in the world of musical improvisation* (pp. 113–25). Chicago, IL: University of Chicago Press.

Harwood, E. & Marsh, K. (2012). Children's ways of learning inside and outside the classroom. In G. McPherson & G. Welch (Eds.), *Oxford handbook of music education* (pp. 322–40). New York: Oxford University Press.

Hicks, W. K. (1993). An investigation of the initial stages of preparation audiation (Doctoral dissertation, Temple University, USA). *Dissertation Abstracts International*, **54**(4A), 1277.

Ilari, B. (2011). Twenty-first-century parenting, electronic media, and early childhood music education. In S. L. Burton & C. C. Taggart (Eds.), *Learning from young children: Research in early childhood music* (pp. 195–214). Lanham: Rowan & Littlefield and MENC.

Isaacs, S. (1929). *The nursery years: The mind of the child from birth to six years*. London, UK: Routledge.

Isenberg, J. P., & Jalongo, M. R. (2000). *Creative expression and play in the early childhood curriculum* (3rd ed.). New York: Macmillan.

Jones, B., & Hawes, B. L. (1987). *Step it down. Games, plays, songs & stories from the Afro-American heritage*. Athens, GA: Brown Thrasher Books, The University of Georgia Press. (Original work published 1972.)

Kartomi, M. (1980). Childlikeness in play songs—a case study among the Pitjantjara at Yalata, South Australia. *Miscellanea Musicologica*, **11**, 172–214.

Knapp, M., & Knapp, H. (1976). *One potato, two potato . . . : The folklore of American children*. New York: W. W. Norton.

Lamont, A. (2008). Young children's musical worlds: Musical engagement in 3–5-year-olds. *Journal of Early Childhood Research*, **6**(3), 247–61.

Lill, A. (2014). From local to global: The evolution of musical play in secondary schools. *International Journal of Play*, **3**(3), 251–66.

Littleton, D. (1991). *Influence of play settings on preschool children's music and play behaviours* (Doctoral dissertation). The University of Texas at Austin, USA. Retrieved from *Dissertation Abstracts International*, **52**(4), 1198 (University Microfilms Order No. 91–28294).

Littleton, D. (2002). Music in the time of toddlers. *Zero to Three*, **23**, 35–8.

Lord, A. B. (1995). *The singer resumes the tale*. Ithaca, NY: Cornell University Press.

Lum, C.-H. 2007. Musical networks of children: An ethnography of elementary school children in Singapore (Unpublished doctoral dissertation). University of Washington, Seattle.

Lum, C.-H. (2008). Home musical environment of children in Singapore: On globalization, technology, and media. *Journal of Research in Music Education*, **56**(2), 101–17.

Lum, C.-H. 2009. Musical behaviours of primary school children in Singapore. *British Journal of Music Education*, **26**(1), 27–42.

Malloch, S., & Trevarthen, C. (Eds.) (2009). *Communicative musicality: Exploring the basis of human companionship*. Oxford, UK: Oxford University Press.

Mans, M. (2002). Playing the music—comparing performance of children's song and dance in traditional and contemporary Namibian education. In L. Bresler & C. M. Thompson (Eds.), *The arts in children's lives: Context, culture and curriculum* (pp. 71–86). Dordrecht: Kluwer Academic Publishers.

Marsh, K. (1995). Children's singing games: Composition in the playground? *Research Studies in Music Education*, **4**, 2–11.

Marsh, K. (1997). Variation and transmission processes in children's singing games in an Australian playground (Unpublished PhD thesis). University of Sydney, Sydney.

Marsh, K. (1999a). Young children's negotiation of difference in playground singing games. *Australian Research in Early Childhood Education*, **6**(2), 217–27.

Marsh, K. (1999b). Mediated orality: The role of popular music in the changing tradition of children's musical play. *Research Studies in Music Education*, **13**, 2–12.

Marsh, K. (2001). The influence of the media, the classroom and immigrant groups on contemporary children's playground singing games in Australia. In J. C. Bishop & M. Curtis (Eds.), *Play today in the primary school playground: Life, learning and creativity* (pp. 80–97). Milton Keynes, UK: Open University Press.

Marsh, K. (2002). Children's song acquisition: An ethnomusicological perspective. In C. Stephens, D. Burnham, G. McPherson, E. Schubert, & J. Renwick (Eds.), *Proceedings of the 7th international conference on music perception and cognition* (pp. 265–8). Adelaide: Causal Productions (CD-ROM).

Marsh, K. (2005a). A cross-cultural study of the musical play practices of children in school playgrounds. In V. Rogers & D. Simonds (Eds.), *The legacy of John Blacking: Essays on music, culture and society* (pp. 152–66). Crawley, Australia: University of Western Australia Press.

Marsh, K. (2005b). Worlds of play: The effects of context and culture on the musical play of young children. *Early Childhood Connections*, **11**, 32–6.

Marsh, K. (2006). Cycles of appropriation in children's musical play: Orality in the age of reproduction. *The World of Music*, **48**(1), 8–23.

Marsh, K. (2008). *The musical playground: Global tradition and change in children's songs and games*. New York: Oxford University Press.

Marsh, K. (2013). Music in the lives of refugee and newly arrived immigrant children in Sydney, Australia. In P. S. Campbell & T. Wiggins (Eds.), *Oxford handbook of children's musical cultures* (pp. 492–509). New York: Oxford University Press.

McIntosh, J. A. (2006). Moving through tradition: Children's practice and performance of dance, music and song in South-Central Bali (Unpublished doctoral dissertation). Queen's University, Belfast.

Merrill-Mirsky, C. (1988). Eeny meeny pepsadeeny: Ethnicity and gender in children's musical play (Doctoral dissertation, University of California, Los Angeles). *Dissertation Abstracts International*, AAT 8826013.

Miller, L. W. (1984). Music in early childhood: Naturalistic observation of young children's musical behaviours (Doctoral dissertation, University of Kansas). *Dissertation Abstracts International*, **44**(11), 3316. (University Microfilms No. 84–03616.)

Minks, A. (2006). Interculturality in play and performance: Miskitu children's expressive practices on the Caribbean coast of Nicaragua (Unpublished doctoral dissertation). Columbia University, New York.

Minks, A. (2013). Miskitu children's singing games on the Caribbean coast of Nicaragua as intercultural play and performance. In P. S. Campbell & T. Wiggins, *The Oxford handbook of children's musical cultures* (pp. 218–31). New York: Oxford University Press.

Moorhead, G. E., & Pond, D. (1941, reprinted 1978). Music of young children: 11. General observations. *Music of young children: Pillsbury foundation studies*. Santa Barbara, CA: Pillsbury Foundation for Advancement of Music Education.

Moorhead, G. E., Sandvik, F., & Wight, D. (1951, reprinted 1978). Music of young children: IV. Free use of instruments for musical growth. *Music of young children: Pillsbury foundation studies*. Santa Barbara, CA: Pillsbury Foundation for Advancement of Music Education.

Opie, I., & Opie, P. (1977). *The lore and language of schoolchildren*. Oxford, UK: Oxford University Press. (Original work published 1959.)

Opie, I., & Opie, P. (1979). *Children's games in street and playground*. Oxford, UK: Oxford University Press.

Opie, I., & Opie, P. (1988). *The singing game*. Oxford, UK: Oxford University Press. (Original work published 1985.)

Papoušek, M. (1992). Early ontogeny of vocal communication in parent–infant interactions. In H. Papoušek, U. Jürgens, & M. Papoušek (Eds.), *Nonverbal vocal communication: Comparative and developmental approaches* (pp. 230–61). Cambridge, UK: Cambridge University Press.

Papoušek, M. (1996). Intuitive parenting: A hidden source of musical stimulation in infancy. In I. Deliège & J. Sloboda (Eds.), *Musical beginnings: Origins and development of musical competence* (pp. 88–112). Oxford, UK: Oxford University Press.

Papoušek, M., & Papoušek, H. (1981). Musical elements in the infants' vocalisation: Their significance for communication, cognition and creativity. In L. P. Lipsitt (Ed.), *Advances in infancy research* (Vol. 1 pp. 163–224). Norwood, NJ: Ablex.

Pond, D. (1980). The young child's playful world of sound. *Music Educators' Journal*, **76**(7), 38–41.

Pond, D. (1981). A composer's study of young children's innate musicality. *Bulletin of the Council for Research in Music Education*, **68**, 1–12.

Prim, F. M. (1989). The importance of girls singing games in music and motor education. *Canadian Journal of Research in Music Education*, **32**, 115–23.

Riddell, C. (1990). Traditional singing games of elementary school children in Los Angeles (Doctoral dissertation, University of California, Los Angeles) (University Microfilms No. 9023293).

Rogers, C. S., & Sawyers, J. K. (1988). *Play in the lives of children*. Washington, DC: National Association for the Education of Young Children.

Romet, C. (1980). The play rhymes of children—a cross-cultural source of natural learning materials for music education. *Australian Journal of Music Education*, **27**, (October), 27–31.

Segler, H. (1992). *Tänze der Kinder in Europa*. Hannover, Germany: Moeck Verlag.

Shelley, S. (1981). Investigating the musical capabilities of young children. *Bulletin of the Council for Research in Music Education*, 68, 26–34.

Shelley, S., & Foley, J. R. (1979). Observing the nature of young children's musicality, *Current Issues in Music Education: Music of Young Children*, **12**, 44–54.

Smithrim, K. (1997). Free musical play in early childhood. *Canadian Music Educator*, **38**(4), 17–24.

Street, A. (2004). Singing to infants: How maternal attitudes to singing influence infants' musical worlds. In L. Custodero (Ed.), *Proceedings of the ISME Early Childhood Conference "Els Móns Musical Dels Infants" (The Musical Worlds of Children)*, Barcelona, Spain, July 5–10, 2004.

Sundin, B. (1960, translated into English 1998). Musical creativity in the first six years. In B. Sundin, G. E. McPherson, & G. Folkestad (Eds.), *Children composing: Research in music education 1998* (pp. 35–56). Lund, Sweden: Malmo Academy of Music, Lund University.

Suthers, L. (2000). Music experiences for toddlers: Responses of daycare staff members. *Music within every child. Proceedings of the International Society of Music Education, Early Childhood Seminar*. Kingston, Ontario, Canada: Queen's University.

Sutton-Smith, B. (1970). Psychology of childlore: The triviality barrier. *Western Folklore*, **29**, 1–8.

Sutton-Smith, B. (Ed.) (1972). *The folkgames of children*. Austin, TX: University of Texas Press.

Sutton-Smith, B. (1995). Introduction: What is children's folklore? In B. Sutton-Smith, J. Mechling, T. W. Johnson, & F. McMahon (Eds.), *Children's folklore: A source book* (pp. 3–9). New York: Garland.

Sutton-Smith, B. (1997). *The ambiguity of play*. Cambridge, MA: Harvard University Press.

Tarnowski, S., & Lerclerc, J. (1994). Musical play of pre-schoolers and teacher–child interaction. *Update: Applications of Research in Music Education*, **13**, 9–16.

Trehub, S. E., & Trainor, L. J. (1998). Singing to infants: Lullabies and play songs. *Advances in Infancy Research*, **12**, 43–77.

Trehub, S. E., Unyk, A. M., & Trainor, L. J. (1993). Maternal singing in cross-cultural perspective. *Infant Behavioral Development*, **16**, 285–95.

Trevarthen, C. (2000). Musicality and the intrinsic motive pulse: Evidence from human psychobiology and infant communication. *Musicae Scientiae: Journal of the European Society for the Cognitive Sciences of Music: Special Issue* 1999–2000, **3**(1) (Suppl.), 155–215.

Trevarthen, C. (2002a). Musicality and music before three: Human vitality and invention shared with pride. *Zero to Three*, **23**, 10–18.

Trevarthen, C. (2002b). Origins of musical identity: Evidence from infancy for musical social awareness. In R. MacDonald, D. J. Hargreaves, & D. Miell (Eds.), *Musical identities* (pp. 21–38). Oxford, UK: Oxford University Press.

Willett, R. (2014). Remixing children's cultures: Media-referenced play on the playground. In A. N. Burn, & C. O. Richards (Eds.), *Children's games in the new media age* (pp. 133–51). Farnham, UK: Ashgate.

Willett, R., Richards, C., Marsh, J., Burn, A., & Bishop, J. C. (2013). *Children, media and playground cultures: Ethnographic studies of school playtimes*. Basingstoke, UK: Palgrave Macmillan.

Wood, D., Bruner, J. C., & Ross, G. (1976). The role of tutoring in problem solving. *Journal of Child Psychology and Psychiatry*, **17**(2), 89–100.

Young, S. (1999). Just making a noise? Reconceptualising the music-making of early childhood. *Early Childhood Connections (USA)*, **5**, 14–22.

Young, S. (2002). Young children's spontaneous vocalisations in free-play: Observations of two- to three-year-olds in a day-care setting. *Bulletin of the Council for Research in Music Education*, **152**, 43–53.

Young, S. (2003a). *Music with the under-fours*. London, UK: RoutledgeFalmer.

Young, S. (2003b). Time–space structuring in spontaneous play on educational percussion instruments among three- and four-year-olds. *British Journal of Music Education*, **20**(1), 45–59.

Young, S. (2003c). The interpersonal dimension: A potential source of musical creativity for young children? *Musicae Scientiae Special 10th Anniversary Conference Issue, ESCOM: European Society for the Cognitive Sciences of Music*, **7**(1) (Suppl.), 175–9.

Young, S. (2004). Musical collaboration between three- and four-year-olds in self-initiated play with instruments. In S. D. Lipscomb, R. Ashley, R. O. Gjerdingen, & P. Webster (Eds.), *Proceedings of the 8th International Conference on Music Perception and Cognition (ICMPC8)*. Evanston, IL: Northwestern University School of Music, CD-ROM.

Young, S. (2005). Adults and young children communicating musically. In D. J. Hargreaves, D. Miell, & D. MacDonald (Eds.), *Musical communication* (pp. 281–99). Oxford: Oxford University Press.

Young, S. (2008). Lullaby light shows: Everyday music of under-two-year-olds. *International Journal of Music Education*, **26**(1), 33–46.

Young, S. (2012a). Theorizing musical childhoods with illustrations from a study of girls' karaoke use at home. *Research Studies in Music Education*, **34**(2), 113–27.

Young, S. (2012b). MyPlace, MyMusic: An international study of musical experiences in the home among seven-year-olds. *Min-Ad, Israel: Israeli Studies in Musicology Online*, **10**. Retrieved from <http://www.biu.ac.il/hu/mu/min-ad/>.

Young, S., & Gillen, J. (2010). Musicality. In J. Gillen & C. A. Cameron (Eds.), *International perspectives on early childhood research: A day in the life*. Basingstoke: Palgrave Macmillan.

Young, S. & Ilari, B. (2012). Musical participation from zero to three: Towards a global perspective. In G. McPherson & G. Welch (Eds.), *Oxford handbook of music education* (pp. 279–95). New York: Oxford University Press.

Chapter 26

The individual and social worlds of children's musical creativities

Pamela Burnard and Hsu-Chan Kuo

Introducing creativities as a pluralist sociocultural construct

There are many ways in which creativity in music may be understood and its meaning constructed. The concept does not possess the same meaning from one cultural context to another or from one individual to another. It is not surprising, therefore, that children manifest and liberate themselves in the use and function of creativity in music in ways which defy traditional psychological definitions (Amabile, 1996). Taking time to reflect on how children, from early childhood through to adolescence, constitute their own types of musical creativities (and musical culture making) is as necessary as for adults to reflect on their constructions of what musical creativities are, where they happen, with whom, and how. The vignettes that follow illustrate how a child's personal and social worlds interface within cultural contexts to shape creativities.

Tania's first memory of music is of hearing her mother singing. Her next recollection is her parents' CD collection, sitting in front of the television watching videos on YouTube where video, images, and sounds are interactively used as the medium for new media musicianship, musical expression, and creativity. From as early as she can remember, she would sing and dance with her mum and friends. Her recollections are of her singing and humming, bobbing and bouncing in play immersion. As soon as she closes the front door of the house to leave for school, the mobile phone is never switched off. While she sleeps, she puts her mobile next to her pillow on her bed while the battery recharges. At primary school, Tania sang in all the choirs, played in several instrumental groups, performed solos in concerts and was recognized as "creative." Now, at 14, her mobile phone is the principal driving force in her life. Her ambition is "to be like Beyoncé." She does not consider herself to be a high-achieving performer, but in explaining significant events and crystallizing digital media experiences, it is clear she has had many. She digitally records all her music. She explores, practices, and proclaims the expressive virtues of various different cultures, all of which are deeply rooted in the vernacular of her many favorite singers and groups. She shifts between personal time and sharing time–space with family and friends, between online and offline and public and private. The Internet is where her song writing, as she explains, is "influenced by loads of singers and bands."

Tosh's significant musical memories, recalled at 16, relate to his most recent involvement with like-minded peers as new producers, designers, and creators of musical environments, building, designing, remixing, and making musical instruments, games, and new music. Tosh is a member of numerous sub-cultures that offer him opportunities for, and agency in, techno, hip-hop, rap, DJ-ing, and more. Tosh is not into school music. His home environment is interpenetrated by digital and networked technologies, unlike his school which he considers irrelevant. He redefines himself with a high profile within his peer group. Like his friends, Tosh is immersed in new technologies that open up the potential for new types of social and musical engagement. There is no separation. His bedroom plugs into multiple digital media sources which emulate a recording studio. There is nothing ambivalent about his relationship to digital music. Digital technology enables his learning. Tosh is not simply a consumer; he is an impassioned producer, innovator, and creator of new kinds of music and musical creativities.

For Tania and Tosh, who share attendance at the same schools, their personal, social, and cultural biography is central to how their development in creativity proceeds. Development does not exist exclusively in the child. Their creative development stems from membership within various social and cultural units such as parents and carers within the nuclear culture of the family, or occurs at the interface of social contexts with friends and peers in school and out-of-school communities and as members of multiple cultures. It is these social and cultural realities that largely determine the possibility or lack of possibilities for developing creativity (Feldman, 1999; Partti, 2012). Development in diverse musical creativities occurs as children live and interact with the inevitable influences which these units have upon their musical ideas, values, and behaviors (Campbell, 2002; Harris, 2014; Richardson, 1983). It is the child's individual and social worlds that interact to create the cultural dynamic of developmental change (Kuo, 2014).

Let us give another two vignettes outlining the different developmental pathways in musical creativities of two enthusiastic music teachers—Ingret and Angelina—who both teach music in primary and secondary school settings and have abundant music-relevant knowledge.

Recalling her personal development of musical creativity, Ingret argues that her musical creativity has experienced highs and lows. From primary school (aged 7–12) to high school (aged 16–18), the development did not follow a linear curve but fluctuated with important events. She argues that the music courses within school, extra-curricular private music tutoring, both mental and economic support from her family, and discussions with fellow students have had a very positive impact on her music creativity. "I always regard myself as a creative musician." She claims that all of her teachers and fellow students think she is a talented and creative musician. However, she found that her musical creativity declined at every single moment when she needed to take music tests. "Even though the peer support was significant, my fellow students never stopped encouraging me to be myself, to be creative, and I quite enjoyed the feeling of being adored or envied by peers. However, tests still had a dominant influence on my music performance, which, I believe, negatively impacted on my creativity." She recalled that her music journey was like an adventure, which encountered a wide range of gatekeepers. "Music test scores were extremely important for us—music majored students—because we needed to pass the examination (to gain better opportunities) to enter better schools, which means that we can have more options. Therefore, rather than performing my own music, I'd ask my teachers what kind of performances, or how to interpret the songs, so I can get better results. Then, I repetitively practiced the songs based on the examiners' tastes. Following their preferences, to some extent, was like killing my music creativity." She expressed the belief that from childhood to adolescence, her musical creativity had increased most dramatically when she studied in high school (aged 16–18) because her music teacher was open-minded. "Rather than telling me the 'correct' way to play songs, she asked me to try, to create, to play my music, and gave me the opportunities to choose what I preferred. For me, it was very personal and phenomenal; my musical expression, skills, and aesthetic sense thus rocketed to a peak at high school."

The most significant parts of Angelina's musical memories through childhood (aged 3–12) to high school (aged 16–18) were her family's support and the experience of learning with music teachers. Living in an average-income family, her father's income needed to fund Angelina and her three brothers' studies. She argues that it was because of the family's economic support and her parents' sacrifices that she could study music. "Studying music was a huge investment for my family; my mother even mortgaged our house to fund my music study in a private school . . . " When discussing her creativity, Angelina argues that her motivation to play music and the levels of her musical skills both influenced her musical creativity. "Recalling the crucial moments directly influencing the development (of musical creativity), I believe they were the changes of relationships with my music teachers." She claims that emotional conflicts with her teachers had a very negative impact on her confidence and musical creativity. "One of my music teachers was a very emotional person; she always revealed her emotion directly to me. As an elementary school kid, she shouted loudly at me, gave me punishments if I did not play 'correctly' as she asked." Angelina argues that for a very long period of time in her childhood (especially in middle to late childhood), playing music made her nervous and she only played to avoid being punished. What killed her musical creativity were the times she had issues with teachers: "My motivation to play music declined whilst the tensions (between me and teachers) appeared; so also my musical creativity, because I just did not want to play . . . " When discussing the positive stimuli that improved her musical creativity, she responded: "Motivation must have played a dominant role in my development, and I think good relationships between me and teachers and the necessity to take tests are the most important sources. . . . Tests helped me to increase my musical skills and creativity, because I was always asked to play very difficult songs in the tests, and in order to play those difficult songs I had to improve my skills, I had to practice, listen to teachers and fellow students' suggestions, and then find the best way or creative solutions to perform them well. As my musical skills increased, I had more weapons and options to create my own songs." Additionally, Angelina mentioned that the good apprenticeship with her third teacher ignited her passion for music, and the encouragement and valuable suggestions provided by the teacher really improved her musical creativity; "the teacher empowered me to love music again," she said.

As soon as a child is born, adults and other knowledgeable individuals begin to contribute to the child's socialization by arranging the environment and the musical stimuli encountered within it. The developing child is located within the working orbit of particular parents, carers, friends, peers, teachers, artists, and pedagogical, community, and cultural practices. This serves to guide children's attention to, and participation in, the community (or communities) of which they are a part. Children may participate in, and become members of, a number of musical communities to creatively use music as a soundtrack for their everyday lives. These variously situated practices integrate with and draw upon the child's individual and social interests. For Ingret and Angelina, individual differences, including personalities, social skills, and personal interpretations of events, all played important roles influencing the development of their musical creativity. Their reaction to music tests was very different. While Ingret claims that music tests constantly killed her creativity, because she needed to meet the many examiners' expectations, Angelina believes that the challenges inherent in the tests ignited her motivation to improve her musical skills as well as her creativity. Angelina's argument that "musical skills and musical creativity are closely related" echoes comments by Coulson and Burke (2013), whose investigation of 118 children, aged 5–11 years, shows that students produce more creative and original music when they are more confident with their musical skills. Reflecting on Ingret and Angelina we find some similarities that potentially contribute to the development of musical creativity: *good apprenticeships between students and teachers, encouragement from significant others* (such as teachers, parents, and fellow students), *formal and extra-curricular music courses/training, support from family* (both economic and mental), and *motivation to play music.*

With socialization, schooling, and enculturation, the child's world continues to expand out into ever-widening networks. Thus, the development of children's diverse musical creativities occurs through their active participation in a network of cultural systems. They can be members of the "super-culture," such as "children," several "sub-cultures," such as family members or Caribbean or Asian children, boys or girls, and "inter-cultures" such as players, collectors of or listeners to particular types of music, classrooms, groups, or clubs in or out of school (Campbell, 2002). They may come from Muslim families who disapprove of girls and boys making music together in the same room or even making music in single-sex groups (Halstead, 1994). It is the established norms and practices in our society and culture that identify and distinguish between ways of understanding creativity, in terms of societal judgments and values.

Csikszentmihalyi's (1999) advancement of a *Systems View of Creativity* offers support for these observations. Csikszentmihalyi conceptualizes creativity as something that is not simply contained within the mind of the person, but is also a cultural construct which is given meaning by what others have to say about it. Creativity involves interaction between a *domain* discipline (for example, music, mathematics, chess playing), a *person* (individual creator), and a *field* (including specialists and appropriate observers who are familiar with the domain who make judgments about what constitutes quality in the domain). What is important about this systems perspective of creativity is that creative endeavor and achievement in a domain ultimately arise from, and become accepted in, a particular cultural setting *as products of societal judgments*. Thus it is the affordances and constraints constructed by and contained within specific learning communities that stimulate and fertilize diverse creativities (Feldman, 1993, 1999). Importantly, if the individual creator is to make a significant contribution to a domain (or practice), his or her endeavors must be judged by members of the cultural community (or field).

Csikszentmihalyi's (1999) work has helped us to understand that definitions of creativity must take into account the fact that creativity is a cultural construct. It is a concept dependent upon the judgment of observers, or so-called gatekeepers. It is a concept dependent on cultures to enhance and constrain what is possible, what is supported, what is accessible, what is valued, and what is not.

In contrast to research concerned with the development of *extreme talent* in individual creativity (Feldman, 1999; Gardner, 1993), this view treats the ever-widening child's world of diverse musical creativities as irrefutably a *cultural construct* related to how *individuals* construe themselves within a multiplicity of *cultural networks* (an idea conceptualized as a "cultural organism" in relation to extreme talent by Feldman in 1993). As we see it, a child's musical creativity develops not as something solitary (that is, in relation only to themselves), but rather in relation to others. According to this view, and as illustrated in earlier observations (Burnard, 1999a, b, 2000a, b, 2004), it is the dialectic (in which *individual* and *social worlds* interact) that provides the tacit messages; these are culturally embedded in and supported by multiple cultures, each of which has its own musical affiliations (Campbell, 2002).

Considering Tania, Tosh, Ingret, and Angelina, we know they are embedded in a complex web of digital networks, social groups, and immersive digital communities in contexts that are dynamic and fluid and which are enmeshed in an ever-widening cultural network. They all reflect the particular cultures within which they are raised. Their musical interests and involvements inside and outside the school are distinctive. At the same time, what is consistent is that they are musically knowledgeable; they make connections in the search for meaning within their musical lives; their individual creative endeavors are recognized and valued; and what they do musically is construed—in some ways—as expanding frontiers (that is, where the new and familiar co-exist) as members of multiple musical cultures, each of which has its own musical affiliations. So, how can creativities be understood in relation to children's musical development? What specific lines of development interact to create the dynamics of change in children's musical creativities? What counts as music and making informed judgments about children's creativities?

How should we understand creativities in relation to music?

Past research (e.g., Webster, 1992, 2002) has characterized the conceptual base for "creativity" in music as a set of *enabling conditions* (these include motivation, divergent–convergent thinking, environment, and personality) and *enabling skills* (these include musical aptitudes, conceptual understanding, craftsmanship, and aesthetic sensitivity) and provides a plausible framework for describing the "product intention" and the making of the "creative product." At the center of his conceptual model of creative thinking are two types of thinking: divergent (which leads to many solutions) and convergent (leading to a single solution). From this starting point, Webster developed his model of "creative thinking" in music as a way of looking for differentiated factors that seem to shape "creative thinking" in music as a distinct process of thought. The larger the storehouse of enabling conditions and skills that children possess, the better equipped they will be to think creatively in music.

Importantly, this line of argument recognizes how person-based individual differences occur in the development of creative thinking in music; but it does not articulate a position that includes roles for (and connects agents of) the cultural networks in creative development. In contrast, the systems view of creativity, as advanced by Csikszentmihalyi (1999), represents a fundamental shift from a view that defines creativity developmentally, or as a fixed entity, to one that is dependent upon people's judgments. This is important because music educators (and researchers) often find themselves in the role of assessing and judging the creativity of children's musical endeavors. Judgments about the nature and achievement of musical creativity will depend upon the relationships that hold between the *domain* discipline (musical opportunities and constraints, the accessibility to musical knowledge, and the opportunities for children to acquire musical skills), the *person* (the child creator), and the *field* (usually music teachers or researchers who make judgments about what constitutes quality in the domain). Judgments about what constitutes development in musical creativity will depend upon the relationships that hold between the domain, the person, and the field.

In the music education literature, Elliott (1995, 2009) has discussed the role of societal judgments as "tangible products or achievements that people deem valuable, useful, or exceptional in some regard" (1995, p. 216), the function of which is a process of induction into particular musical practice. The assumption made by Elliott and others is that a creative achievement in music "has its roots in specific communities of practitioners who share and advance a specific tradition of musical thinking" (1995, p. 67). This emphasizes that there are children's discourses of creative music-making, particularly when framed within the context of children's musical worlds, as occurs, for example, in analyses of the studies of children's musical play and improvisation (Addo, 1997; Coulson & Burke, 2013; Marsh, 1995, 1997; Pond, 1981; Sundin, 1998) and music-making with computer-based digital tools (Folkestad, 1996; Kim, 2013; Nilsson & Folkestad, 2005). These studies provide us with evidence of children being able to position themselves as experts. The musical playground provides us with a powerful example of children positioning themselves as creative decision-makers who make judgments from within the field and are the experts in that domain. Importantly, this line of argument recognizes that what may be a creative endeavor and achievement in a child's musical world may not necessarily be viewed, judged, or defined as "creative" within the adult musical world in which the child is situated. What constitutes a creative achievement where the creative activity involves the musical practices of hip-hopping or rapping, may prove highly problematic within the school setting, but not beyond it.

This raises an important issue about creative exclusion (and lack of opportunities for creative choice) where a systems view of creativity excludes creative endeavor that is *not* created with an understanding of the field. How do we make sense of, and actively contribute to, educational programs aimed at raising the overall creative endeavors and achievements of the least educationally advantaged populations of children in our formal educational systems? Forms of engagement in and judgments about musical creativity are inevitably based on, and reflect, the rules, traditions, and practices identified and practiced within the dominant culture. Crucially, how do teachers work creatively with children of migrants and travelers in areas where there is the risk of social exclusion? What about creative endeavors that are not valued as creative by observers? This is of great concern among music educators.

Indeed, if we argue that diverse *musical creativities take place as contextualized activity* and need to be understood in different contexts, then we need to locate them both within the *individual world* of the child and where cultural dynamics interact within the *social worlds* of the child in which the child's diverse musical creativities develop. To illustrate, from infancy through to adolescence, children construct and enact any number of possibilities as vehicles for musical creativity. These can range from child's play explorations, to creative exchanges between adults and babies (Trevarthen, 1993), to how music happens and is played out in nurseries, playgrounds, schools, and garages (Marsh & Young, 2006), to young people as hip-hoppers and rappers who busily (re-)construct repertoires from the interactive possibilities and (re-)experiences of mixing and downloading Internet files as representations and expressions of innovative musical style-practices. Children engage creatively in music from within a wide range of communities of practice. These communities may range from those within a school classroom, to a community band, to their "peer worlds" of leisure time, to forms of creative activity which happen in the home between the child and parents, to playgrounds and recreational settings, to any number of other musical communities with which the child interacts. For children (as with adults), whether in relation to performance, improvisation, perception, listening, arranging, or compositional practices, the kind of creative music-making that we come to hold in high regard is contextual and situational (Burnard, 2012; Burnard & Murphy, 2013; Sawyer, 1997).

Contextual influences

Whilst there appears to be no suggestion that there are universal schematized levels, themselves developmentally achieved, particular changes in children's creative engagement with music are discernible within and across cultural contexts. In the following sections we highlight the contextual influences during early childhood, middle to late childhood, and adolescence.

Contextual influences during early childhood

From infancy, with the earliest vocal and gestural musical responses, as displayed in a baby's selective orientation to musical sound, we see an innate psychological foundation for both creative behavior and creativity. These innate and culturally significant creative behaviors begin, according to Trevarthen (1993), as "a music-like composition, an improvised song or dance of companionship with someone we trust, whom we admire, and who admires us" (p. 135). We see these creative behaviors in the production of songs and action games as infant–parent "playful sharing."

In early childhood, children's musical creativities are characterized within a wide variety of contexts that may involve spontaneous song-making, singing, dancing, and playing together, and improvising with instruments (Campbell, 2002; Woodward, 2005). It is through the process of enculturation that young children learn the musical culture of their environment (Small, 1977). Studies of musical play have also shown that the emergence of young children's spontaneous music-making is embedded within solitary and social play settings and demonstrates how musical creation from early infancy onwards is not fortuitous, but rather sophisticated and constantly evolving (Custodero, 2002; Littleton, 1998). A preschooler (4- or 5-year-old), for example, might sustain long periods of purposeful inventiveness and exploration in sound making, involving spontaneous vocal, instrumental, and movement play, with structures arising from a very rich variety of patterning, sequences, repetition, and transformations of patterns (see Marsh & Young, 2006).

At the same time, how children shape their own development is clear, particularly in infancy, with much evidence to support the saliency of the social dimension of creativity, shaped largely by the people who surround them, like their parents, carers, family, and friends. What comes across most strongly from studies of young children is the sense of primacy of relationships and interactions between child and adult, social contexts that are shaped largely by family circumstances (Young, 2003). As an example, for most preschoolers, music is created in "music specific" (domain-specific) and "non-music" (domain-general) play settings in which musical play behaviors, such as voice play and instrumental "sounding" and "sound making" (in which objects or instruments are used musically), arise equally from long episodes of solitary play and socially within-group play, often started by the child and taken up by the parent, carer, or other children. More often, as Addo (1997) suggests with specific reference to West African singing games, young children's creative undertakings are as much connected to the sociocultural context as the learning environment in which the child is immersed.

In a seminal study of children's spontaneous musical creativity, set in a nursery school, Moorhead and Pond (1941/78) observed creativity as a process characterized by originality, adaptiveness, and realization in a child's private and social worlds of sound. The following observations by Moorhead and Pond (1941/78) testify how far this claim can be justified.

> One variety of instrumental music was flexible and asymmetrically measured rhythmically; it endeavoured to explore wide intervals in pitch and contrasting tone colours. Another was rigidly and symmetrically "rhythmical"; it seemed indifferent almost to melody or to colour variation; it was insistent and savage. One was most frequently quiet and produced in solicitude, the other raucous, and associated very often with physical activity and belonging to the group. So also with vocal music. One variety was unfettered and free rhythmically like plainsong; the voice wandered over a large compass, the singer sang to himself alone, quietly, of everyday things, as though the melody not the words were more important. Another variety was rhythmic, like a ritual chant; the voice clung to one note around which it wove a melodic pattern limited in scope and insistent in form; it was sung most often in the group, usually loudly, repeated over and over again, rising often to a high emotional pitch. (1978, p. 8)

Clearly, very young children enter into the creative musician's experience of making music, exploring sounds, acquiring expressive vocabulary, and developing manipulative skills in response to specific cultural environments. Some longitudinal empirical studies shed the light on the development of musical creativity in early childhood children. For instance, Forrester (2010) documents a child's emergence of musicality through the ages of 1 year to 3 years 10 months. It is found that there is an interrelationship between musicality, early word use, interpretational skills, and narrative development. Three stages with distinctive developmental milestones of musicality are identified. While social affective/emotional expression appears in phase one (age 1.5 to 2 years), music-like word-play, repetitive imitation, and song alteration skills mainly develop in phase two (age 2 to 2.5 years). Finally, narrative-related and multifunctional expressions of musicality emerge in phase three (age 2.6 to 3.5 years).

Barrett (2011) reports the dynamic relationship between a 2-year-old child's musical narratives, identity, and music-making. By documenting one child's engagement with known and invented song and music-making for one year, she found that music is a rich resource of insights into children's meaning making and connections with music—critical for understanding choices and decisions that impact children's lives. The engagement provides the child with a platform to act multiple roles, such as listener, instrumentalist, dancer, singer, and song maker. The activity of music-making contributes to the development of a young child's communicative musicality and narrative skills. This finding echoes the results identified in previous research: in particular, that music-making can be regarded as a means to develop communication skills and emotional expression (Campbell, 2002) and self-regulation of emotional states (Barrett, 2009). Koops (2013) investigated ten preschool children and six parents to explore the factors enhancing and inhibiting children's musical play. This study indicates that children's musical play developed more rapidly when they had more freedom to choose and take control of music-making. Furthermore, the use of technology and video-sharing activity may help teachers and parents regularly readjust their involvements, connect to other teachers and families, and extend the learning community from school to out-of-school contexts.

Contextual influences at middle to late childhood

In order to explore children's perceptions about creativity in middle to late childhood, Coulson and Burke (2013) conducted a year-long quantitative research project involving 118 elementary school children (aged 5–11 years). Results reveal that students identified three main characteristics of creativity in music: i) *creativity as variety* (playing different notes, using different times and tempos, adding different endings to their improvisations, and playing a variety of instruments); ii) *creativity as originality* (music should contain aspects that make it unique and different); and iii) *creativity as personally appealing* (can it make children feel enjoyment and interest?). The results indicate that developing improvisational creativity is a good approach to promote students' creativity.

Between 5 and 7 years of age, children's experience of diverse creativities widens further with more and more contact in social contexts, including teacher-led and peer-led experiences. In the context of playgrounds, Marsh (1995, 1997), with the illustration of children's improvisations and variations on playground chants, provides us with another valuable perspective on children's musical creative development. In a study of children's complex playground music-making, Marsh shows how children draw socially and culturally on many musical worlds as they give voice to their own ways of transmitting culture and operating creatively in music. They effortlessly discover, explore, and negotiate polyrhythms and syncopations in highly sophisticated social music-making, driven by, and creatively influenced by, their cultural musical biography.

Griffin (2009) claims that in-school and out-of-school contexts are both important for the development of children's musical abilities. By investigating the experiences of 20 grade 2–3 students (aged 7–8), Griffin surprisingly found that the majority of talk that children shared was in relation to their experiences outside of school. For non-music specialized children, they seemed more likely to refer to music as a place, as in music class, as opposed to music as a thing, something different from school music. In other words, both in-school and out-of-school contexts are important sources for middle childhood children to acquire musical knowledge, expand their horizons of the sound world, and make meanings of music. Griffin thus stresses the need to honor children's voices in all discussions of music curricula.

Rozman (2009) sampled a total of 118 children aged from 8.5 to 9 years old in Slovenia to explore their perceptions of creative musical activities. The interesting findings from this study demonstrated that individual differences matter; most students (43.2%) enjoyed creating movements to music activity, 24.5% felt excited when expressing music through painting activities, 16.2% of the students liked to create rhythmical accompaniments, and 8.5% of the participants enjoyed the activity of creating lyrics to a melody. Even though the students had different preferences, all four activities are indicated as meaningful and helpful approaches to promote students' musical creativity. However, Rozman argues that most teachers do not have a comprehensive understanding of creativity and creative thinking.

With preadolescents, creative music-making in musical partnerships and small groups feature more prominently. Children aged 8–12 musically and creatively come into contact with and are compared with peers of similar ages and abilities; in the process they come to recognize and develop more situated perspectives that focus on interactive systems (that is, collaborative musical creativity) that include individuals as participants, interacting with each other as well as materials and representational systems (Burnard, 2002a,b). This implies that older children draw upon an increasingly sophisticated range of sources and resources, including the dual informal practices of peer learning (and peer critique), as they manipulate and create ideas (Jaffurs, 2004; Savage, 2003). At the same time, children experience an *awareness of audience* that can function in a way that is similar to a particular *field of judges* (Burnard, 1999b; Burnard & Murphy, 2013).

A good deal of the research suggests that developmental differences in children's musical creativity have their origins linked to and differentiated by the kinds of musical background and contexts in which music-making and creating takes place (Stauffer, 2002; Younker, 2003). For example, the opportunity to learn to play an instrument can result in children composing for their own instruments. The child's instrumental proficiency and fluency may well determine their composing pathways using compositional thought processes that are rooted in the performance technique of the particular instrument at hand (Burnard & Younker, 2002, 2004). Children who have prior experience of formal instrumental music tuition and who are advanced on their instruments, and who are then offered open opportunities to compose their own music, may approach composing as composers from the outset (Glover, 2000).

In Western countries, for children without formal musical training or children who are just beginning to acquire some technical playing skills, the media world at home and school (that is, the arrival of new digital technologies) opens new possibilities. The new technologies give them the opportunity to mediate the creative process and instill new meaning in their creative music-making (Nilsson & Folkestad, 2005; Seddon & O'Neill, 2001, 2003; Wiggins, 2002). The research is extensive in its use of digital data, generated automatically by the computer and saved as a progressive series of files, as research data. In Asia, Kim (2013) investigates the effects of a technology-mediated teaching and learning program on 16 elementary school children (aged 11–12) in South Korea. Results indicate that the digital technology-mediated approach can enhance students' self-motivated engagement and collaboration in music classes, because it gives students more freedom to compose fun and interesting music, use technological devices to create music instantly, and learn practical skills.

Key studies of children aged 8–12 (late childhood) similarly track progression toward the technical mastery of musical composition. Each of these studies applies fundamentally different developmental frameworks, with particular foci on the development of different skills. Similarly, each incorporates variously defined criteria for labeling something as a developmental change (Barrett, 1996, 2001; Glover, 2000; Kratus, 1989; Swanwick & Tillman, 1986). A common finding is that children become increasingly enculturated into various musical discourses as they absorb the musical vocabulary that they experience in and out of school. In a study of sixth-grade composers, Stauffer (2002) emphasizes the relationship between children's own musical and life experiences and composing development for this age group. Similarly, Swanwick and Tillman (1986) found that around the age of 10 or 11 children move into a "speculative" stage, whereupon they begin to introduce features that deviate from the more accepted conventions and norms. What emerges is an awareness of personal and public expressiveness where both the individual and social worlds of preadolescent children appear concurrently with the development of their wider awareness of their own musical creativity. This suggests considerable differences in the ways children experience, explain, and immerse themselves in a creative activity (Hickey, 2003).

Contextual influences at adolescence

During adolescence, the development of musical creativity occurs in the context of differences in opportunities and participation in music (Cope & Smith, 1997). What also characterizes this phase is that complex social interactions take place within creative participation that results in even greater prominence being given to identity development (Fautley, 2004).

Research findings continually indicate that young people lay claim to different identities associated with musical creativity, marking out relationships and establishing and maintaining social standing from within the peer group (MacDonald & Miell, 2000a, b). Whilst some young people prefer to work alone to author creative products (drawing upon the image of the individual inscribed as a "lone artist"), others prefer to engage collaboratively whereupon their identity is more bound up with being a group member responsible for joint creative work (Miell & MacDonald, 2002). The differences are made visible, as creative activity is considered the locus of culturally significant acts, events, and meanings as observed in the ways young people engage differently in, and acquire situated and contextual understandings of, musical creativity (Lamont et al., 2003).

What, then, does musical creativity look like during adolescence? Several studies have documented the impact new technologies have had on young people's engagement with, and achievements in, musical creativity (Dillon, 2004; Folkestad, 1998; Jennings, 2003; Savage & Challis, 2001). For example, Seddon (2004) reports ICT has been effective in supporting creative learning in schools. It was found that music e-learning environments provide new opportunities for, and direct access to, ideas enabling collaborative composition between young people within and between schools across a global community. This allows and motivates young people to produce creative and professional products—especially those young people who would not otherwise be engaged. The common impression of the use of music technologies as one of individual work at a computer has equally been debunked through the interactive musical systems developed by Brown and Dillon (2009), where networked computers are used as a vehicle for real-time improvisation using digital instruments connected via electronic networks drawn from a selection of school- and community-based learning spaces. Typically, in these projects, key features of the creative work are: the *immediacy* given to the trial and error, without the fear of losing or spoiling work; the *interaction* between "the maker" and "the made" in which musical ideas develop through feedback and reflection; and the nature of the *collaborative creativity* between the pairs or groups of students in designing, creating, and discussing the ways in which they could use the features of the software package to develop and present their ideas.

Cassidy and Paisley (2013) indicate that music-games can be regarded as a platform to connect formal and informal music participation in the twenty-first century. By investigating three 15- to 16-year-old adolescents, results reveal that the approach can deepen participants' musical understanding, improve their fundamental skills, and allow them to become more focused on rhythmic and melodic forms. Cassidy and Paisley argue that music-games have the potential to attract a wider world of learners, produce positive impact on musical learning in school contexts, promote music engagement and academic and personal well-being, enable learners to examine the relevance of the music curriculum to personal experiences, and stimulate the acquisition of some transferable skills like eye–hand coordination, rhythmic and melodic awareness, and ensemble and listening skills.

Young people's informal cultural competencies (as consumers and users of digital multimedia technology in the context of leisure) and the ever-widening range of music technologies increasingly enable them to draw on their own musical experience and access any number of highly desirable sound worlds which support their composing skills (Fung, 1997). Other features of adolescent musical creativity include the facilitative effects of friendship (MacDonald, Meill, & Mitchell, 2002), where socializing and learning are closely connected as young people cultivate and coordinate their actions with those of others (Kuo, 2014).

Conclusion: Widening the lens on the social and digital bases of diverse musical creativities

There are as many cultural sites and types of creativities as there are ways of doing and making sense of children's musical development. There are also as many different views of musical creativity as there are things about which creative decisions can be made. Therefore, recasting our understanding of children's musical development in relation to diverse creativities reasserts the child into multiple narratives and asserts the need for richer and more complex mappings of multiple creativities. The focus here has been to understand the ways in which children's diverse musical creativities can be conceptualized, gained, shared, and evaluated, all issues which are massively influenced within and by cultural and contextual factors.

From here we can begin to contemporize the issues and ask questions about how children in the twenty-first century understand their own creativities, and what constitutes and changes children's beliefs about what it takes to be and succeed creatively in music. This means observing and talking with children (and their teachers) to understand how creative practices are differently constructed and situated in cultural, historical, and institutional settings. These are questions we need to continually ask ourselves if we are to identify how diverse creativities are central to our understanding children's musical development.

Reflective questions

1 What are your own experiences of diverse musical creativities?
2 In what ways have your own creativities been stimulated, developed, and diversified in professional and/or personal practices?
3 What learning culture and teaching principles will best foster diversity in musical creativities in your practice?
4 What are the problems that teachers face in the assessment of distinct forms of creativity? How might teachers (and music teacher education programs prepare teachers to) teach and assess children's diverse musical creativities?
5 How do communal and collaborative, empathic and intercultural creativities in music interact and feed each other as distinctive forms of musical creativity in the development of children?

Key sources

Burnard, P. (2012). *Musical creativities in practice*. Oxford: Oxford University Press.
Burnard, P., & Murphy, R. (2013). *Teaching music creatively*. London: Routledge.

Reference list

Addo, A. O. (1997). Children's idiomatic expressions of cultural knowledge. *International Journal of Music Education*, **30**(1), 15–25.

Amabile, T. M. (1996). *Creativity in context: Update to the social psychology of creativity*. Boulder, CO: Westview.

Barrett, M. (1996). Children's aesthetic decision-making: An analysis of children's musical discourse as composer. *International Journal of Music Education*, **28**(1), 37–62.

Barrett, M. (2001). Constructing a view of children's meaning-making as notators: A case-study of a five-year-old's descriptions and explanations of invented notations. *Research Studies in Music Education*, **16**(1), 33–45.

Barrett, M. S. (2009). Sounding lives in and through music: A narrative inquiry of the "everyday" musical engagement of a young child. *Journal of Early Childhood Research*, **7**(2), 115–34.

Barrett, M. S. (2011). Musical narratives: A study of a young child's identity work in and through music-making. *Psychology of Music*, **39**(4), 403–23.

Brown, A. R., & Dillon, S. (2009). Networked improvisational musical environments; learning through on-line collaborative music making. In J. Finney & P. Burnard (Eds.), *Music education with digital technology* (pp. 96–106). London: Continuum.

Burnard, P. (1999a). Into different worlds: Children's experience of musical improvisation and composition (Unpublished PhD thesis). University of Reading, England.

Burnard, P. (1999b). Bodily intention in children's improvisation and composition. *Psychology of Music*, **27**(2), 159–74.

Burnard, P. (2000a). Examining experiential differences between improvisation and composition in children's music making. *British Journal of Music Education*, **17**(3), 227–45.

Burnard, P. (2000b). How children ascribe meaning to improvisation and composition: Rethinking pedagogy in music education. *Music Education Research*, **2**(1), 17–23.

Burnard, P. (2002a). Investigating the emergence of musical interaction in group improvisation. *British Journal of Music Education*, **19**(2), 157–72.

Burnard, P. (2002b). Into different worlds: What improvising and composing can mean to children. *Music and Movement Education Quarterly*, **34**(4), 22–8.

Burnard, P. (2004). "A damaged dream?" Adolescent realities and changing perspectives on school music. In P. Shand (Ed.), *Music education entering the 21st century* (pp. 25–34). The University of Western Australia: Uniprint.

Burnard, P. (2012). *Musical creativities in practice*. Oxford: Oxford University Press.

Burnard, P., & Murphy, R. (2013). *Teaching music creatively*. London: Routledge.

Burnard, P., & Younker, B. A. (2002). Mapping pathways: Fostering creativity in composition. *Music Education Research*, **4**(2), 245–61.

Burnard, P., & Younker, B. A. (2004). Problem-solving and creativity: Insights from students' individual composing pathways. *International Journal of Music Education*, **22**(1), 59–76.

Campbell, P. S. (2002). The musical cultures of children. In L. Bresler & C. Thompson (Eds.), *The arts in children's lives: Context, culture and curriculum* (pp. 57–69). Netherlands: Kluwer.

Cassidy, G. G., & Paisley, A. M. J. M. (2013). Music-games: A case study of their impact. *Research Studies in Music Education*, **35**(1), 119–38.

Cope, P., & Smith, H. (1997). Cultural context in musical instrumental learning. *British Journal of Music Education*, **14**(3), 283–90.

Coulson, A. N., & Burke, B. M. (2013). Creativity in the elementary music classroom: A study of students' perceptions. *International Journal of Music Education*, **31**(4), 428–41.

Csikszentmihalyi, M. (1999). Implications of a systems perspective for the study of creativity. In R. Sternberg (Ed.), *Handbook of creativity* (pp. 313–38). Cambridge, England: Cambridge University Press.

Custodero, L. (2002). Connecting with the musical moment: Observations of flow experience in pre-school-aged children. *Children's musical connections* (pp. 68–74). Proceedings of the 10th International conference of the Early Childhood Commission of the International Society for Music Education, August, Copenhagen, Denmark, 2002.

Dillon, T. (2004). What does it mean to compose collaboratively and creatively when using music technologies? Paper presented at a conference *Musical Collaboration* of the Society for Education, Music and Psychology Research (SEMPRE), Open University, Milton Keynes, United Kingdom, April 2004.

Elliott, D. (1995). *Music matters: A new philosophy of music education*. Oxford: Oxford University Press.

Elliott, D. (2009). *Praxial music education: Reflections and dialogues*. New York: Oxford University Press.

Fautley, M. (2004). Teacher intervention strategies in composing processes. *International Journal of Music Education: Practice*, **22**(3), 201–18.

Feldman, D. H. (1993). Cultural organisms in the development of great potential. In R. H. Wozniak & K. W. Fisher (Eds.), *Development in context: Acting and thinking in specific environments* (pp. 225–51). New Jersey: Lawrence Erlbaum.

Feldman, D. H. (1999). The development of creativity. In R. J. Sternberg (Ed.), *Handbook of creativity* (pp. 169–88). Cambridge: Cambridge University Press.

Folkestad, G. (1996). Computer-based creative music making: Young people's music in the digital age (Unpublished doctoral dissertation). Goteborg, Acta Universitatis Gothoburgensis.

Folkestad, G. (1998). Music learning as cultural practice: As exemplified in computer-based creative music making. In B. Sundin, G. E. McPherson, & G. Folkestad (Eds.), *Children composing* (pp. 97–134). Lund, Sweden: Malmö Academy of Music, Lund University.

Forrester, M. A. (2010). Emerging musicality during the pre-school years: A case study of one child. *Psychology of Music*, **38**(2), 131–58.

Fung, C. V. (1997). Effect of a sound exploration programme on children's creative thinking in music. *Research Studies in Music Education*, **9**(1), 13–18.

Gardner, H. (1993). *Creating minds*. New York: Basic Books.

Glover, J. (2000). *Children composing: 4–14*. London: RoutledgeFalmer.

Griffin, S. M. (2009). Listening to children's music perspectives: In- and out-of-school thoughts. *Research Studies in Music Education*, **31**(2), 161–77. doi: 10.1177/1321103X09344383.

Halstead, J. M. (1994). Muslim attitudes to music in schools. *British Journal of Music Education*, **11**(2), 162–78.

Harris, A. (2014). *The creative turn: Toward a new aesthetic imaginary*. Rotterdam: Sense Publishers.

Hickey, M. (2003) (Ed.). *Why and how to teach music: A new horizon for music education*. Reston, VA: MENC.

Jaffurs, S. (2004). The impact of informal music learning practices in the classroom or how I learned how to teach from a garage band. *International Journal of Music Education: Practice*, **22**(3), 189–200.

Jennings, K. (2003). "Toy Symphony": An international music technology project for children. *Music Education International*, **2**, 3–21.

Kim, E. (2013). Music technology-mediated teaching and learning approach for music education: A case study from an elementary school in South Korea. *International Journal of Music Education*, **31**(4), 413–27.

Koops, L. (2013). Enjoyment and socialization in Gambian children's music making. In P. S. Campbell & T. Wiggins (Eds.), *The Oxford handbook of children's musical cultures* (pp. 166–280). Oxford: Oxford University Press.

Kratus, J. (1989). A time analysis of the compositional processes used by children ages 7–11. *Journal of Research in Music Education*, **37**(1), 5–20.

Kuo, H. C. (2014). An investigation of the perceived impact of the programme of creativity and imagining the futures in education (PhD thesis). Faculty of Education, University of Cambridge, UK.

Lamont, A., Hargreaves, D., Marshall, N., & Tarrant, M. (2003). Young people's music in and out of school. *British Journal of Music Education*, **20**(3), 229–42.

Littleton, D. (1998). Music learning and child's play. *General Music Today*, 12(1), 8–15.

MacDonald, R., & Miell, D. (2000a). Creativity and music education: The impact of social variables. *International Journal of Music Education*, 36(1), 58–68.

MacDonald, R., & Miell, D. (2000b). Musical conversations: Collaborating with a friend on creative tasks. In R. Joiner, K. Littleton, D. Faulkner, & D. Miell (Eds.), *Rethinking collaborative learning* (pp. 65–78). London: Free Association Books.

MacDonald, R., Miell, D., & Mitchell, L. (2002). An investigation of children's musical collaborations: The effect of friendship and age. *Psychology of Music*, 3(2), 148–63.

Marsh, K. (1995). Children's singing games: Composition in the playground? *Research Studies in Music Education*, 4(1), 2–11.

Marsh, K. (1997). Variation and transmission processes in children's singing games in an Australian playground (Unpublished PhD thesis). University of Sydney.

Marsh, K., & Young, S. (2006). Musical play. In G. E. McPherson (Ed.), *The child as musician: A handbook of musical development* (pp. 289–310). Oxford: Oxford University Press.

Miell, D. E., & MacDonald, R. (2002). *"The lone artist or the group?" Staking claims of ownership of creative products through retelling the story of the compositional process.* Conference proceedings of the European Society for the Cognitive Sciences of Music (ESCOM), University of Liege, April, 51–2.

Moorhead, G. E., & Pond, D. (1941, reprinted 1978). *Music of young children: Pillsbury foundation studies.* Santa Barbara: Pillsbury Foundation for Advancement of Music Education.

Nilsson, B., & Folkestad, G. (2005). Children's practice of computer-based composition. *Music Education Research*, 7(1), 21–38.

Partti, H. (2012). *Learning from cosmopolitan digital musicians.* Sibelius Academy: Studia Musica 50.

Pond, D. (1981). A composer's study of young children's innate musicality. *Bulletin of the Council for Research in Music Education*, 68(Fall), 1–12.

Richardson, C. P. (1983). Creativity research in music education: A review. *Research in Music Education, Bulletin of the Council for Research in Music Education*, 74(Spring), 1–21.

Rozman, J. Č. (2009). Musical creativity in Slovenian elementary schools. *Educational Research*, 51(1), 61–76.

Savage, J. (2003). Informal approaches to the development of young people's compositional skills. *Music Education Research*, 5(1), 81–6.

Savage, J., & Challis, M. (2001). Dunwich revisited: Collaborative composition and performance with new technologies. *British Journal of Music Education*, 18(2), 139–50.

Sawyer, K. (1997) (Ed.), *Creativity in performance.* London: Ablex.

Seddon, F. (2004). Cross-cultural collaborative computer-mediated composition in cyberspace. Paper presented at a conference *Musical Collaboration* of the Society for Education, Music and Psychology Research (SEMPRE), Open University, Milton Keynes, United Kingdom, April.

Seddon, F. A., & O'Neill, S. A. (2001). An evaluation study of computer-based compositions by children with and without prior experience of formal instrumental music tuition. *Psychology of Music*, 29(1), 4–19.

Seddon, F. A., & O'Neill, S. A. (2003). Creative thinking processes in adolescent computer-based composition: An analysis of strategies adopted and the influence of instrumental music training. *Music Education Research*, 5(2), 125–37.

Small, C. (1977). *Music, society, education.* New York: Schirmer Books.

Stauffer, S. L. (2002). Connections between the musical and life experiences of young composers and their compositions. *Journal of Research in Music Education*, 50(4), 301–22.

Sundin, B. (1998). Musical creativity in the first six years: A research project in retrospect. In B. Sundin, G. E. McPherson, & G. Folkestad (Eds.), *Children composing* (pp. 35–56). Malmö: Malmö Academy of Music.

Swanwick, K., & Tillman, J. (1986). The sequence of musical development: A study of children's composition. *British Journal of Music Education*, 3(3), 305–39.

Trevarthen, C. (1993). The self born in intersubjectivity: The psychology of an infant communicating. In U. Neisser (Ed.), *The perceived self: Ecological and interpersonal sources of self-knowledge* (pp. 121–73). New York: Cambridge University Press.

Webster, P. (1992). Research on creative thinking music: The assessment literature. In R. Colwell (Ed.), *Handbook of research on music teaching and learning* (pp. 266–78). Reston, VA: MENC.

Webster, P. (2002). Creative thinking in music: Advancing a model. In T. Sullivan & L. Willingham (Eds.), *Creativity and music education* (pp. 16–34). Canada: Britannia Printers and Canadian Music Educators' Association.

Wiggins, J. (2002). Creative process as meaningful musical thinking. In T. Sullivan & L. Willingham (Eds.), *Creativity and music education*. In L. R. Bartel (Series Ed.), Canadian Music Educators' Association as the first in the Biennial Series, *Research to Practice* (pp. 78–88). University of Alberta.

Woodward, S. (2005). Critical matters in early childhood music education. In D. Elliott (Ed.), *Praxial music education: Reflections and dialogues* (pp. 249–66). London: Oxford University Press.

Young, S. (2003). Time–space structuring in spontaneous play on educational percussion instruments among three- and four-year-olds. *British Journal of Music Education*, 20(1), 45–60.

Younker, B. A. (2003). Fifth grade students' involvement in composition: A teacher's intentionality. *Music Education International*, 2, 22–35.

Chapter 27

Computer-based technology

Peter R. Webster

Computer-based technology: Introduction

Few would argue that computer-based technology plays a major role in how children come to understand their worlds (McHaney, 2011). This is especially true in countries with high standards of living and major sources of wealth. In a recent major survey of students, teachers, parents, and others administered by Project Tomorrow,[1] over 400,000 respondents in the United States indicated that nearly 90% of all high school students have access to Internet-connected smartphones and that 50% of students in grades three to five have access to similar devices. Results from this survey work also documented the recent rise of Internet connectivity, use of video for classwork and homework, and the rise of gaming and social media in learning. Research in other countries is likely to show similar if even more dramatic evidence that computer-based technologies play a major role in learning and, in turn, development. This chapter considers the impact of this technology on the musical development of our youth.

In earlier writing on this topic, it was argued that "the connection between music technology and our understanding of musical development in children has yet to be fully bridged" (Webster & Hickey, 2006, p. 391). We further urged that more research should be done to link developmental theory in music with specific uses of music technology to help better understand the development of musical developments. Some ten years later, we still have little direct empirical evidence of any links between the use of specific types of technology and substantial theory of musical development in children. Certainly this could be the basis for a recommendation for future research, but because computer-based music technology is now so fundamentally embedded in the day-to-day experiences of a child's musical life, such experimentation may seem unnecessary to many. Computer-based technology that is considered here represents a basic tool set in the age of the digital millennial student and functions much like other tools such as pencils, paper, and markers for a whiteboard. Its connection to any number of developmental theories can be defended on the basis of logic and common sense.

For example, even the most casual review of classic general theories of child development can be conceptually linked to the affordances offered by technology and more specifically to computer-based music technology. Vygotsy, Montessori, and Piaget each stressed the importance of active and interactive learning in a social context. The importance of play is stressed and the notion of allowing children time to experiment and explore is valued (Mooney, 2013). As will be argued, music software designed for child use has moved more dramatically toward a constructivist, sociocultural posture that embraces these classic theories.

Perhaps what remains to be better understood is how best to leverage technology's potential for supporting the development of musical development both in terms of learning and research. In his recent chapter on better understanding technology's role in music teaching and learning, Himonides concluded that "technology is not something that we can decide to become estranged from; it is part of our human condition" (2012, p. 452).

Musical experience as a basis for musical development

Barrett and Webster (2014) have written that:

> Music itself is often considered an inherently human construction of sound, unfolding in time, intentionally designed to be expressive. Those engaged in the teaching of music consider four human behaviors as fundamental to its understanding: (1) performance of the music of others, (2) performance of one's own music (improvisation in its many forms), (3) composition of music, and (4) music listening. Music experience . . . is the result of active engagement in the construction of music in its many forms. It includes the development of skills, knowledge, attitudes, and values that lead to deeper understandings of music as art. At its core are the intrinsic and affective quality of sounds and the construction of personal meaning that comes from the creative engagement with musical experiences themselves. (pp. 1–2)

For the purposes of this chapter, I claim that patterns of musical development are guided by the centrality of musical developments in the lives of children. As stated previously, "the line between musical development that occurs naturally and that development that is encouraged or facilitated by the environment is always a difficult one to draw" (Webster & Hickey, 2006, p. 375). Music technology used as a way to encourage music learning is an experience that should support the natural growth pattern of children (McDowall, 2008). Just as parental engagement in musical development has been shown to be so critical (McPherson, 2009), so too are the environmental supports of technology.

New age of music engagement with technology

The role of computer-based music technology in both formal and informal musical developments (Green, 2008) has vastly increased in recent years to include far more Internet-based software programs (often free) and far more affordable mobile computing devices on which children can make and listen to music. Recent books by d'Escriván (2012), Dorfman (2013), and Bauer (2014) all serve as sources of current data about contemporary music technology.

Part of the narrative about the new age of music engagement involves broadening our conceptions of musical development and understanding. For example, Thibeault (2012) reviews the development of media from the 1930s to modern times, placing emphasis on the challenges that face music education in what he terms as a "postperformance world":

> I contend that much more attention should be devoted to understanding the ramifications of the decoupling of music from performance via the rise of media. Media also offers expanded notions of learning, inviting educators to participate in the wider nets cast by those who are interested in music in everyday life, in traditionally excluded music, in the uses and purposes of music, and in understanding music as a cultural practice embedded in multiple discourses. (p. 527)

Another example of the changing scene is the consideration of music in video games as an avenue for music learning (Tobias, 2012). Gower and McDowall (2012) provide some preliminary data on the role that interactive music video games might play in musical development. They conclude that such games should be considered as alternative ways for music to be learned, particularly in more informal settings.

Another remarkable hallmark of the new age of music engagement with technology is economy of scale. The majority of the software titles I will highlight reside as free or inexpensive software applications ("apps") on mobile devices or as freely available Internet-based programs that can be used by any appropriate computer anywhere.

Finally, if there are any lingering doubts about the new environment and how researchers and educators might use computer-based technology for their work, one needs only to watch how current children of all ages engage in musical developments. Consider the following scenarios with references from Internet sources:

Scenario 1: A 4-year-old is given a tablet computer and is shown how to draw patterns on the screen that produce sounds. Colorful patterns are drawn like finger painting on a canvas. The software is written to allow manipulation of pitch and rhythm and also instrument timbres drawn from different musical cultures. The child begins to experiment with the tablet and finds that one can reverse the sounds' order by clicking on an icon, or flip the sounds upside down. Patterns can be erased or can be saved for playing later. *Pitch Painter* (<https://itunes.apple.com/us/app/morton-subotnicks-pitch-painter/id519738403?mt=8>)[2] Example of use: <http://youtu.be/YLFUGDtY0IM>.

Scenario 2: A 7-year-old works with a set of circles or "pads" on a tablet computer that creates an expressive sound that is a cross between an exotic string instrument and a percussion sound. The quality of the sound can be controlled by touch and different adjacent circles create different pitches. Multiple sounds can be played together, with rhythm controlled by touch. Touching the pads continuously creates a completely different timbre, and with little effort, complex polyphonic music is created. *Ophion* (<http://www.orphion.de/>). Example of use: <https://www.youtube.com/watch?v=laAbRsWykw8>.

Scenario 3: Two eighth-grade students, working as a team, create a soundtrack with a computer sequencing program and a music keyboard. They experiment with chords, octave placement, and other musical parameters, deciding what sounds best. *Garageband* (<https://www.apple.com/mac/garageband/>). Example of use: <http://www.youtube.com/watch?v=C3Gf9LQgTCM>.

Scenario 4: A group of high school sophomores gather on consecutive days after school to "cover" a new pop song that they all like. Using their own instruments, they begin to experiment with playing the song, with each member of the group working out different parts. They listen several times to the original and work out the chords and melody on their own by successive experimentation. Each person helps the others when necessary until they have it worked out. When they arrive at a solution that they like, it is uploaded to a sound file sharing location on the Internet. *SoundCloud* (<https://soundcloud.com/>). Example of use: <https://soundcloud.com/groups/acoustic-covers-remakes-of-classic-songs>.

Scenario 5: The same group of students discovers a new site on the Internet that encourages creative collaboration. The goal is to create a weekly cable TV show based on a theme. Through interaction with the Internet site for the project, they contribute a sound track that they hope will be used by the cable show producers. Others contribute graphics, live video, and stories that might be used as well. The students are contributing to a collaborative production company of sorts (<http://www.hitrecord.org/>).

Scenario 6: A group of high school students with special needs (autism) work with a high school band director to compose and perform their own music using iPads. Students find the iPad and the music software that it runs to be a powerful way for them to make music together in ways not as easily accomplished with traditional, analog instruments. Students learn much about music theory and music performance skills while also interacting socially in the ensemble in ways not always possible for them otherwise (<http://www.npr.org/blogs/ed/2014/06/11/320882414/ipads-allow-kids-with-challenges-to-play-in-high-schools-band>).

In each of these six scenarios drawn from reality, individuals, through actions of their own and with some help as needed from adults, are developing deep musical understanding related to the musical developments of creating, performing, responding, and connecting. Technology of the sort that is displayed in these scenarios is naturally suited to musical development because it is so much a part of how today's youth experience the world (Finney & Burnard, 2007).

An important purpose of this chapter is to review selected work on musical development in terms of many of these musical developments and make conceptual links to current computer-based music technology. After a brief introduction to modern computer-based technology, selected software is noted in a table for those interested in experimenting with such titles in research and practice. The heart of the chapter is an accounting of selected work on musical development that shares a link with computer-based music technology. Note is made of how the aforementioned scenarios might relate. The chapter ends with a final note.

Music technology past and present

The rise of new media technology (e.g., computers and the internet) and the emergence of new musical styles contribute to an increasing variety of musical development in the fields of composition, performance, listening, and preferences. Therefore, parents and teachers should be aware that the children's and student's musical development may differ considerably from their own. (Gembris, 2002, pp. 489–90)

The quotation from Gembris reminds us of the fact that not only is it wise to consider how current technology might support what we know about development, but also how technology itself has a role in framing and perhaps even effecting this development.

It is fair to say that the history of music technology has not been fundamentally driven by any interest in musical development and learning with its attendant literature. Instead, music technology's growth has been guided by: 1) practical needs in music production (music notation, sound recording, and reproduction); 2) certain technical achievements in hardware (faster, smaller, and cheaper processors, laser disc technology); and 3) the Internet as a medium of communication. This is beginning to change. This is especially true now that more musicians and educators are engaged in formal and informal software development. After reading this short section, those interested in a bit more detail about the history of music technology as it relates to music teaching and learning as well as development might find the summaries and citations in *Experiencing music technology* (Williams & Webster, 2008) of some interest.

Certainly computers and related technology devoted to music learning existed before the age of the 1970s and the age of the personal computer, but we start this short overview with the development of relatively affordable personal computers and continue with Internet development and mobile/cloud computing. Each of these time periods features technological developments that are meaningful for the development of musical experiences.

Personal computer (1970–90)

The period starting in the mid 1970s to perhaps 2007 might be considered the age of the integrated circuit. The growth of small and powerful personal computer systems marks this important time. Because of the effectiveness of the integrated circuit and the computer chip, number machines and electronic instruments became smaller while increasing their ability to process digital information.

As this computer technology developed, so did electronic music instruments. The MIDI (Music Instrument Digital Interface) protocol was developed in the mid-1980s and allowed music devices to transmit codes that described sound. The sound resources inside these devices have improved dramatically in recent years, as sampling technology captured in chips has allowed the internal sounds of MIDI hardware to rival some of the best acoustic instruments. Since the beginning of the 1990s, music educators have used these MIDI-based devices to assist in music composition, performance, and listening.

In terms of software for computer-assisted instruction, more behavioristic, drill-and-practice titles gave way to more personalized, simulation, and creative exploration software. In 1990, *Band-in-a-Box* (<http://www.pgmusic.com/>) became the first commercial software to provide automated accompaniments for improvisation. *Practica Musica* (<https://www.ars-nova.com>) was first published in 1987 as one of the first music theory/aural skills programs to incorporate options for students and teachers, creating a kind of "flexible-practice" software that could be adapted to individual learning needs.

In addition to these more flexible computer-assisted instruction titles, the first programs for music notation were published, including the popular *Finale* (<http://www.finalemusic.com/>) software in 1988. Software for music sequencing such as *Performer* (<http://www.motu.com/>) was first released in 1985 (now known as *Digital Performer*), allowing arrangers and composers to develop scores and sound files more effectively for commercial music, television, and film. Such software was used by music educators as well as commercial musicians to help students experiment with music production. This tradition continues today.

Hypermedia and web development (1990–2007)

A couple of decades earlier, in 1965, the term "hypermedia" was coined by Ted Nelson (<https://archive.org/details/TedNelsonHypermedia>), building on an idea of interrelated text sources. Nelson's idea was to create environments where text and other forms of content such as graphics and sound could be integrated without regard to hierarchy. This was to become critically important for music technology development.

It was during this latter half of the 1980s that the installation of audio CD players into personal computers greatly influenced the development of multimedia software production. This was to lead in 1989 to Robert Winter's interactive program on Beethoven's *Symphony No. 9* from the Voyager company (<http://vimeo.com/7581651>), using a CD recording controlled by a software program. This was among the first commercial products in music to use the hypermedia idea. The software program at the base of this product was Apple's *HyperCard*, a toolkit for the development of hypermedia programs (<http://arstechnica.com/apple/2012/05/25-years-of-hypercard-the-missing-link-to-the-web/>). HyperCard was a conceptual breakthrough for music software (and many other information-rich programs) because it allowed music educators and researchers without significant computer programming experience to create high-quality interactive software on their own that used audio recordings on CD. This, together with Apple's development of *QuickTime* technology, which allowed the capture and playback of digital video as part of computer software, inspired a number of professionally created interactive CD-ROMs devoted to music subjects.

With the recent and continued decline of the audio CD medium, multimedia software has gravitated toward the Internet. Software for music pedagogy intended to run on personal computers has included titles that encourage simulation and guided instruction. *Making Music* and *Making More Music* (<http://creatingmusic.com/>), both authored by famed electronic music composer, Morton Subotnik, were significant music titles for music composition. (The *Pitch Painter* software that is featured in Scenario 1 is a new mobile app version of *Making Music*.) These programs assume no knowledge of music notation and allow the student to discover musical structures using a drawing metaphor. The role of a composer is simulated in ways that help teach the processes of composition.

Music Ace (<http://www.harmonicvision.com/>) used guided instruction to help students understand music theory and aural skills in an interactive environment using animation. Children were guided in their discovery of important music facts, and opportunities are provided to test mastery with games and a composing space.

Music technology support for music performance was significantly increased in this same period. Software such as SmartMusic (<http://www.smartmusic.com/>) has been and continues to be successful in providing accompaniment support for instrumentalists and vocalists as well as providing diagnostic and assessment assistance. Digital audio recording capabilities on modern personal computers increased in quality during this period to a point where educators could take advantage of software that records performances directly to disc. Software such as *Audacity* (<http://audacity.sourceforge.net/>) was developed and used to record and process sound with an impressive array of special effects. Music could be easily recorded, processed, and "burned" to audio CD or other storage formats in the basement of one's home using software such as ProTools (<http://www.avid.com/>) and Audition (<http://www.adobe.com/>).

Returning to the notion of hypermedia, another significant development during this time period was the development of the World Wide Web (or simply "web") as we know it today. Tim Berners-Lee in 1989 proposed a universal linked information system that was to eventually lead to the conceptual and technical base for the web running as a service on the Internet (<http://en.wikipedia.org/wiki/Tim_Berners-Lee>). During the period from 1990 to the present day, concurrent with the development of software for personal computers of the kind noted for music, the Internet (and the web that is hosted by the Internet) has grown significantly to include over 40% of the world's total population (<http://www.internetworldstats.com/>). The Internet as a system of interconnected devices and the web have come to affect nearly every part of our personal and professional lives, including the availability of music and information about music for people of all ages.

Mobile devices and the cloud (2007–present)

The details of this time period are still unfolding. Cell phones, pagers, and other such devices were in development years before 2007, but Apple's first iPhone was released in 2007 using the iOS operating system, and other companies such as Nokia and Samsung followed soon after with devices that use the Android operating system (<http://en.wikipedia.org/wiki/Smartphone>). These "smartphones" are designed to provide multiple services that include email, web browsing, messaging, and calendaring, as well as phone communication. In addition, the operating system is designed to execute specially written apps that extended the usefulness of the device even further. Tablet devices such as Apple's iPad and the Samsung Galaxy Tab were released in 2010 (<http://en.wikipedia.org/wiki/History_of_tablet_computers>). Tablets offer more screen viewing area and more flexible apps that rival personal computers.

These small devices offer flexibility and affordability, but their real power resides in the apps they run. Smartphones and tablets offer platforms for new software to contribute significantly to music learning in terms of creating, performing, responding, and connecting. Literally thousands of free and low-cost apps are now available for both smartphones and tablets for iOS and Android, with hundreds more added each month.

Another stunning development in recent years is the number of Internet-based applications that run completely from remote servers or "clouds." Programs for music theory and aural skills, music notation, audio recording and sequencing, music performance support, and any number of other music-based programs are being developed exclusively for use over the Internet. Little or no installed software is necessary for personal computers, smartphones, or tablets to run these apps.

Given this outline of the history, Table 27.1 displays the titles of selected music software that support musical developments at various ages and are rendered by personal computers, smartphones, tablets, and Internet-based servers. Examples chosen have a record of successful use and can function as supportive of research and teaching noted in the following section.

Selected literature on musical development

Many scholars have contributed to the literature on musical development over the years in significant ways (e.g. Bamberger, 1991; Deliege & Sloboda, 1996; Hargreaves, 1986; Hargreaves & North, 1999, 2001; Sloboda, 1985). These classic sources and others included here are recommended in order to gain a comprehensive understanding of the field.

The intent of the sections that follow is to highlight some of the more salient aspects of the literature, particularly when matches to music software usage by teachers and researchers seem appropriate. The work is organized around the musical developments of creating, performing, and responding/connecting; an introductory section on preschool development is also included. When appropriate, software from Table 27.1 is paired with the ideas in the literature and linkages to the six scenarios are made.

Preschool development

Music awareness begins a few months before birth as the auditory system is formed. Infants become accustomed to structures in music and prefer patterns that conform to known structures by at least the end of the first year of life (Adachi & Trehub, 2012; Trehub, Hill, & Kamenetsky, 1997). Babbling in the early months progresses to formed songs during this period (Deliege & Sloboda, 1996; Hargreaves, 1996; McDonald & Simons, 1989; Moog, 1976; Moorhead & Pond, 1978). A more recent study by Gerry, Unrau, and Trainor (2012) has demonstrated that systematic participation in musical experiences beginning at 6 months of age leads to more sensitive awareness of Western tonality.

The time between 1 month and 5 years of age is marked by incredibly rapid growth in all areas of musical development. The ages from 1 to 3 years point to a time of major experimentation and play with sounds in the environment. This development can be enhanced by exposure to rich musical environments for experimentation and growth (Morehouse, 2012). Scenario 1 suggests at least one way that very young children can use some of the more recent apps on mobile devices

Table 27.1 Exemplar software by age and music experience

Music Experience	Preschool	Elementary	Middle and High School
Creating (Composition and Improvisation)	Bloom (iOS) Keezy (iOS) Pitch Painter (iOS) Singing Fingers (iOS) SoundBrush (iOS)	Bloom (iOS) Garageband (iOS) Hyperscore (W) Keezy (iOS) Mixcraft (W) Pattern Music (iOS) SoundBrush (iOS) Tonematrix (I) MadPad (iOS) moxMatrix (iOS) Loopesque (iOS) Orphion (iOS) Isle of Tune (I/iOS/A) Figure (iOS) MelodyMorph (iOS) NodeBeat (iOS/A) Notation-Based NotateMe (iOS) NoteFlight (I)	Ableton Live (M/W) Audacity (M/W) Audiotool (I) Beatlab (G) Figure (iOS) Figure (iOS) Garageband (iOS/M) GroveMixer (A) Hyperscore (W) Indaba.com (I) Jamestudio (I) Logic Pro (M/W) Loopesque (iOS) Mixcraft (W) moxMatrix (iOS) ProTools (M/W) Rebirth (iOS) Sector (iOS) Soundation (I) ToneCraft (I) Notation-Based NoteFlight (I) Scorio (iOS/G/I)
Responding	Apple Radio (iOS, M) Impromptu (M, W) Pandora (I, iOS, A) Pitch Painter (iOS) Singing Fingers (iOS) SoundBrush (iOS)	Apple Radio (iOS, M) Educreations (iOS/I) Impromptu (M, W) MusicTheory.net (I) Pandora (I, iOS, A) Practica Musica (M/W) Shamza (iOS/A,I) Soundcloud (I) Spotify (I)	Apple Radio (iOS, M) MusicTheory.net (I) Pandora (I, iOS, A) Practica Musica (M/W) Notation-Based Finale (M/W) MuseScore (M/W) Shamza (iOS/A,I) Soundcloud (I) Spotify (I)

Continued

Table 27.1 (continued) Exemplar software by age and music experience

Music Experience	Preschool	Elementary	Middle and High School
Performing	AirVox (iOS) AUMI (iOS) EAMIR Note (iOS) Garageband (iOS, M) iKaossilator (iOS)	Crystal Synth (iOS) EAMIR Note (iOS) Garageband (iOS, M) iKaossilator (iOS) Synthesia (iOS) Theremin (I) ThumbJam (iOS)	ChordMapMidi (iOS) Garageband (iOS, M) iKaossilator (iOS) JAM with Chrome (G) Rockmate (iOS) Seline Ultimate (iOS)	SmartMusic (I) SynthZ (iOS) ThumbJam (iOS) Voice Analyzer Pro (iOS) Voice Coach (iOS)

Note: iOS = Apple operating system (iPhone or iPad)

AD = Android operating system for other tablets and phones

G = Google app (works with Google-based software)

I = Internet-based (cloud) (works with most browser software)

M = Macintosh computer

W = Windows computer

All software can be referenced by title on the Internet to find more information. Most are free or are offered at minimal charge; computer-based software tends to be more expensive. The author gratefully acknowledges Jesse Rathgeber (PhD student at Arizona State University) for his expert advice on selected software.

like *Pitch Painter* to explore creation of sound patterns. Researchers might find software such as *Bloom* or *AirVox* of additional interest as stimuli for data collection.

Studies indicate that children around age 5 understand diatonic scale structure and even begin to be sensitive to harmonic properties (Dowling, 1988; Lamont & Cross, 1994). The ability to distinguish between fast and slow tempi seems to also emerge between the third and fourth year, although comparative judgments (slow and slower) are more difficult and the language used to express this distinction may be not developed.

Another perspective of preschool development relates to cross-modal perception. Meltzoff, Kuhl, & Moore (1991) have speculated that important to the development of musical perception are the connections between auditory stimuli, visual stimuli, and touch. There is credible evidence that children by the age of 3 or 4 can identify fundamental expressivity in music and can match certain pictures correctly to music (Kastner & Crowder, 1990). Work with *iKassilator* might be particular useful for researchers with these interests.

Barrett and Tafuri (2012) remind us too of our emerging understanding of infants and young children's meaning making and identity formation.

> Learning environments that support and extend children's creative music-making provide opportunities for children to engage with a range of musical styles and genres, and to take on the role of engaged listener, performer, music maker. (p. 309)

Supporting this conceptual frame and all these data, software such as *Singing Fingers, SoundBrush,* and *Keezy* help practitioners and researchers explore the power of affordable and elegantly conceived technology in individual and group settings.

> The infant perceives the acoustical characteristics of the maternal voice (melody, contour, tempo, rhythmical structure, timbre) as synchronous with and analogous to his or her own sensory perception, to visual experiences, and to the movements of the mother. The development of such cross-modal perceptual schemata is likely to play an important role for the perception of musical expression. (Gembris, 2002, p. 491)

Creating

The importance of encouraging children of all ages to create their own music continues to be supported by several studies. Summaries of research on this topic can be found in recent chapters and books (Odena, 2012; Wiggins & Espeland, 2012).

Studies of very young children by Moorhead and Pond (1978) and Flohr (1984) showed that children beginning about age 3 enthusiastically explore sounds on musical instruments, mostly using motor energy, and also show a fascination for timbre. Flohr found that children as young as 3 were able to repeat musical patterns in their improvisations—showing early understanding and ability to develop basic forms.

Kratus (1996) proposed a seven-level approach to improvisation development, beginning with exploration-based behavior with novices and ending with the highest level of personal improvisation that is transformational for the genre. Intermediate stages include: 1) improvisation that is product based in which the individual becomes aware of the audience and traditions within a genre; 2) fluid improvisation, where a student has mastered certain technical aspects of the genre; and 3) structural improvisation in which more expressive and more technically advanced improvisations are noted.

Pressing (1988) defined improvisation and surveyed teaching techniques, offering a model that utilizes intuition, memory, and decision-making skills combined with motor processes. Berliner's definitive ethnographic work (1994) on jazz improvisation offers still further insight into the development of improvisation from the jazz perspective, including the critical role of music listening and developing a vocabulary of patterns.

Sawyer's recent text that summarizes the research on creativity offers excellent conceptual bases for the social construction of musical understanding in terms of both composition and improvisation (Sawyer, 2012). Improvisation and its role in musical development are also summarized in a recent chapter by MacDonald, Wilson, and Miell (2012). Both sets of writings underscore the importance of the further study of improvisation because it can help us understand "how individual creativity is qualified or constrained by participation in the social creativity of improvisation" (MacDonald, Wilson, & Miell, 2012, p. 253).

In terms of improvisation, software such as *Pattern Music, Tonematrix*, and *MelodyMorph* are ideal for elementary-aged children, and *moxMatrix, Beatlab, GrooveMixer, ToneCraft*, and *Band-in-a-box* are all excellent choices for elementary-school and middle-school children. Since most of these programs are executed on mobile devices, groups of children can participate in music-making. Researchers interesting in studying improvisational development in many styles of music will find software noted here helpful in studying individuals or subjects working in groups. The 7-year-old in Scenario 2 is an example of how improvisation development might be studied with the aid of software such as *Orphion*.

In addition to the growing interest in improvisation and its role in musical development, compositional thinking as a strategy for teaching music has become a major force in countries such as Australia, the UK, and the United States (McPherson & Dunbar-Hall, 2001; Wiggins, 2002). Hickey (2002) has suggested a developmental sequence for teaching composition that involves exploration of sound followed by the study of form. The cycle might move to concentration on musical elements and then the larger issues of tension, unity, and balance. This model may be useful in the study of musical development using such programs as *Garageband* or *Mixcraft*.

The four-stage model of composition development that has been suggested by Swanwick and Tillman (1986) based on a sequence that involves the mastery of basic music materials followed by stages based on imitation, more formal property development, and meta-cognitive decision-making common with more adult behaviors continues to represent a useful model in considering the use of compositional experiences supported by software. Each stage begins with activities that are egocentric in nature and concludes with a sense of social sharing. Similar models have been proposed by Hargreaves and Galton (1992) and Lamont (1998), and relate to general musical understanding as well as creation. Interestingly, movement through these stages is highly dependent on enculturation and formal training, especially latter stages that involve movement from more figural and imitative to more formal understanding (Swanwick et al., 2004).

Webster (2002) has proposed a model of creative thinking in music that speculates on the role of enabling skills and conditions and a process of thinking that moves through cycles of divergent and convergent thinking. Based on the growing empirical, philosophical, and practical literature on creative thinking and children, the model offers a perspective on developmental issues and is intended as a springboard for such research. There are no claims in the Webster model about developmental sequence, however.

These theoretical perspectives are important bases for qualitative and quantitative research on generative thinking for children separately and in groups. Accessible software such as *Hyperscore, Garageband*, and *Mixcraft* hold special promise for detailed qualitative or quantitative work on child development in music from a compositional perspective. Scenario 3 that features eighth-graders working to create music with a computer and keyboard is a clear example of the kind of setting that might hold significant promise.

In thinking more broadly about creative work in social contexts, the book by Burnard (2012) is particularly significant. This work summarizes much of Burnard's thinking about expanding conceptions of creativity to form multiple forms of "creativities." In doing so, she reinforces the work of Sawyer (2012) and applies a broad social context lens to creative work of a number of individuals such as singer–songwriters, DJs, live coders, and interactive sound designers—nearly all using computer-based music technology. The implications for this broader view are significant for musical development and for deepening our understanding of musical developments.

New pedagogical writings on composition and creative musical experiences have emerged in the United States to accompany the long-established traditions of this topic in other countries. Books by Hickey (2012), Kaschub and Smith (2009), and Randles and Stringham (2013), among others, offer examples of including composition and improvisation in both individual and group settings. These resources also include references to the use of technology, including the possible use of *Noteflight, Soundation Garageband, Audacity, Audiotool*, and *Ableton Live*. Of course, more classic and more costly programs such as *Pro Tools, Finale*, and *Logic* are in play here as well.

Responding

Classic research on response supports the idea that dynamics and timbre develop first in infants, while pitch, rhythm, texture, and harmony develop later in the growth process. By the age of 6, nearly all students have developed the ability to perceive and discriminate differences in all of these areas (McDonald & Simons, 1989; Trainor & Trehub, 1992). Dowling (1999) has shown that melodic perception in its early stages is linked to contour only, and then to more specific interval-lic details as age increases. This is particularly true if children are involved in formal and active music instruction, such as playing a musical instrument. Hair (1977) and Webster and Schlentrich (1983) have shown that pitch perception in younger students cannot be judged by words or gestures alone and that their real perception of subtle pitch change may be more accurate at a young age than might be otherwise imagined.

As the child in Scenario 1 is working with *Pitch Painter*, a close study of how the child makes musical decisions about the sounds can be fascinating to study. One can imagine how this might be extended by using both *Singing Fingers* and *SoundBrush*.

Piagetian notions of "conservation" (coordinating several different aspects of perception with children aged 7 or older) have inspired work in musical development. For example, Pflederer and Sechrest (1968), in an older but classic work, showed that 8-year-old children can identify different melodies as variations of the same melody when rhythmic, melodic, or tonal changes were made.

An interesting line of investigation in music perception is graphic representation of music. As a way to uncover the mental representation of sound, researchers have asked children to notate the music they hear with invented notation (Bamberger, 1991; Gromko, 1994; Smith, Cuddy, & Upitis, 1994). In terms of rhythm, before the age of 6, children tend to notate a sequentially ordered series of symbols in a more figural (or what Bamberger called "intuitive") way. Older children, especially those with more musical experience, tend to order notation in a more formal or "metric" way. Hargreaves (1986) has commented that this movement from more figural (6- to 7-year-olds) to more metric listening (11- to 12-year-olds) may be related to other kinds of musical development by saying that it "is very clearly paralleled in the progression from 'outline' to 'first draft' songs . . . as well as in that from pitch contours to tonal scale intervals in melodic processing" (p. 99). Bamberger's notions of figural and formal notational representation based on what is heard resulted in her own software, *Impromptu*, which was part of her research and other writings (Bamberger, 2000). This software can be used in both research and teaching settings to better understand music listening.

Children above the age of 6 seem to prefer harmonization that is more consonant (Zenatti, 1993). Enculturation into Western tonal systems seems important here and it raises an interesting question if familiarity on a regular basis with more dissonant and perhaps atonal materials in younger years might create different results.

Schellberg (1998) has determined that, by age 6, most children can perceive different instruments by their sound. Again, it is reasonable to assume that continued exposure to formal study of timbre in the early grades in general music settings and experience with music performance ensembles would further the discrimination of timbre. *Garageband*, with its many optional kits for non-Western instruments, and *Pitch Painter* and other software authored by Morton Subotnick (Stauffer, 2002) that allow changes in scales and harmonies, are all software products that can be adapted for teaching and research.

Finally, on a more gestalt level for music listening, Dunn (2011) provides a comprehensive summary of research on music learning, while providing his own models of music listening that hold promise for research on music-listening development. Hargreaves, Hargreaves, & North (2012), in an edited volume on musical imaginations, provide helpful work on listening as active construction of meaning from a number of disciplinary perspectives. These notions hold significant promise for the role of imagination in better definitions of the creative listening product.

An important key to the study of musical preference and listening skill is understanding the role of culture and context. Musical learning through listening can happen informally as well as formally (Hargreaves, Hargreaves, & North, 2012; Serafine, 1988; Upitis, 1987). More whole, contextualized listening experiences (as opposed to isolated or de-contextualized fragments) will provide children with richer and more authentic learning experiences.

What is perhaps more interesting for teachers is the growing body of research related to clear adolescent preference and identity with popular music and its associated culture. Adolescent self-esteem and self-confidence are clearly linked to their musical tastes—their "badges" of identity (North & Hargreaves, 1999; Tarrant, North, & Hargreaves, 2002). Music serves as an important social function for teenage youth and benefits to self-identity and self-esteem often occur only through peer interaction in the type of unsupervised musical activities that typically take place outside of school (Green, 2001).

Much of the music software in Table 27.1 may assist in both the research on music listening and its instruction. Software that supports music theory and specific aural skills still play a significant role in musical development; sites such as musictheory.net (<http://www.musictheory.net/>) offer online and mobile solutions that are worth considering. Of particular importance are various Internet-based music server sites such as *Pandora, SoundCloud*, and *Spotify*. Again, video sites such as *YouTube* are becoming increasingly important for music listening. Finally, it is not difficult to understand the critical role that responding plays in each of the scenarios described in the opening of this chapter.

Performing

Singing skills develop rapidly between birth and 6 years. In the second year, children can sing short phrases and spontaneous improvisations—moving toward more accurate intervals consistent with the diatonic system (Moog, 1976). By the age of 6, most children's sense of key is stabilized and can sing most songs (in the appropriate range) fairly accurately (McDonald & Simons,

1989). Learning to sing as a soloist or in a choir presents a complex array of factors for success or failure. Because the body is the instrument, singers cannot necessarily see the physical issues to readily fix problems that arise, and the self-identity and emotion and feeling states of the person are essentially wrapped together with the singing voice.

From a recent perspective, Phillips and Doneski (2011) provide an extensive review of research on singing, as well as a number of conclusions for both elementary and secondary-level students that help inform our understanding of musical development. Under the Performance category in Table 27.1, applications of some interest for singing include *MagicSinger, Voice Coach,* and *Voice Analyzer Pro.*

In formal settings, children who learn to play musical instruments often start either very young (such as in the Suzuki talent education program) and learn to play by ear, or begin about the age of 12 or 13 when they have opportunities to join a school band or chorus. While Suzuki learning emphasizes playing by ear, children who learn instruments in the more traditional ways are confronted with the confounding factor of having to read notation. Studies indicate that the most efficient way to teach notation when learning an instrument is to teach "sound before symbol"; that is when children begin to learn an instrument they should learn to play by ear first and later be introduced to the notation system (Haston, 2004; McPherson, 1993; McPherson & Gabrielsson, 2002). McPherson, Bailey, and Sinclair (1997) found that providing students with "enriching" activities such as composition and improvisation had a positive impact on student's ability to play by ear and improvise, while their ability to play by ear had a strong effect on their ability to sight-read. From Table 27.1, *Smartmusic, Noteflight, Logic Pro, Garageband, iKaossilator,* and *Synthz* all may play a role in instrumental instruction and research in various ways, including group performances using such software alone or in combination with acoustic instruments. Performance instruction delivered by video websites such as *YouTube* and *Vimeo* are also worth noting and can play a role in developmental research.

More is known today about music practice. Barry and Hallam (2002) summarized research on practice and noted the important need for models of good practice at various stages of development and the wisdom of creating practice strategies. Self-regulation of music learning is the subject of a recent chapter that includes references to some of the most important research on music practice (McPherson & Zimmerman, 2011). Lehmann and Jorgensen (2012) summarized still more research on practice with attention to teaching and learning strategies. The *Smartmusic* software is a fine example of technology support for music practice and assessment, providing powerful tools to monitor development. Such software also plays a role in the study of musical development.

Webb and Seddon (2012) provide summaries of recent research on digital settings for instrumental music teaching and for virtual learning (teaching from remote sites with the aid of differing technologies). They also provide a perspective on emerging alternative performance ensembles with digital support as well as comment on the changing scene in applied teaching that holds special significance for development.

> Various types of pedagogical bricolage (where any of a range, and even all, of the available and known means of transmission are being alternated and combined) are now employed to motivate and meet the needs of today's students. This development is taking place within the broader arena of musical pluralism. The related flow into music education of new kinds of instrumental ensemble is presenting opportunities for the expanding of current conceptions of musicianship. (p. 765)

Various video conference programs such as *Skype, FaceTime,* and other more advanced software apply here.

Consider Scenarios 4 and 5. In each of these settings, students are using musicianship skills with the aid of technology to perform and create music that is deeply meaningful to them. In each of these instances, not only is the music itself of interest in studying development, but also the socio-cultural role in the creation and performance of the music is of prime importance.

Finally, computer-based music technology is being used in significant ways today in working with children with special needs. There is increasing evidence that such use has a profound effect on the development of music understanding as well as the sociocultural development (Houringan, 2008; McCord, 2002; Swingler & Brockhouse, 2009). Scenario 6 is a touching, powerful, and critically important example of how advances in technology are making a major difference in understanding musical development and understanding.

Final word

The intent here is to highlight what seems to be some of the more salient work on musical development and learning from the standpoint of the musical developments that help define the art. Cascaded against this are a few software exemplars that are readily available today for personal computers, mobile devices, and Internet-based sources. Not unlike pairing fine wines with gourmet foods, there are no long-established traditions that make the matches suggested here definitive or even widely acceptable. Other conceptual content might be imagined and other contemporary software and hardware might be suggested. What seems clear, however, is that there is a match between many of the more exciting research findings and conceptual writings about musical development and the kinds of technology that are becoming readily available for our use in research and practice.

The rather condensed review of music technology in the last 40 years reveals a movement to a more constructionist posture for developers, researchers, and educators. Software based on structured ways of rote learning, memorization, and patterns of convergent thinking that were commonly found in the early days of personal computers are now more likely to be augmented or even replaced with methods of discovery learning, problem-solving, and divergent thinking with more powerful and inexpensive hardware resources. Software is now more diverse in nature and reflective of a wider array of music styles and traditions.

All of this seems well matched with much of the more sophisticated writings on musical development, in which attention is paid to more nuanced topics in creating, performing, responding, and connecting to music. The role of social context is now more widely considered and a more democratic and diverse focus is given to the subjects of study. Certainly attention to the student voice and agency is greatly valued. In all of this, technology seems to be moving toward supportive postures, particularly in the hands of fine teachers and researchers.

Evidence for all this might be found in a careful consideration of the scenarios like the ones that begin this chapter. Perhaps this is the best inspiration for the future study of musical development and music technology. By placing into the hands of developing children the technology tools like the ones noted here and by allowing children to make their own aesthetic decisions—to experiment, explore, create, and imagine with our guidance and encouragement—perhaps then we can more clearly understand the developmental processes that really matter.

Reflective questions

1 Have you had an opportunity to observe young people working with music and computer-based technology like the scenarios portrayed here? What did you observe happening and how might it contribute to musical development?

2 Considering the titles listed in Table 27.1, how might a few of these be used to study musical development? Briefly describe a research project that you might design using this software.

3 Choose a musical experience (creating, responding, performing) and describe how you might design a set of learning experiences for students that would include the use of computer-based music technology in a constructivist manner. How might this relate to your continued assessment of musical development in the student subjects?

4 Using material in this chapter and in other chapters in this handbook, select a theory of child development—either a general one or one related specifically to music. How would you imagine computer-based technology in music relating to the major tenants of this theory?

5 It is likely that you know or are close to someone with physical, emotional, or learning difficulties. What role might computer-based technology in music play in the remediation and enhancement of the life of this person?

Notes

1 Project Tomorrow is an independent, non-profit organization which studies and advocates for education in the United States (<http://www.tomorrow.org/>). Results from the most current national survey are published at <http://www.tomorrow.org/speakup/SU13DigitalLearningPlaybook_StudentReport.html>.

2 The convention followed for documenting software is to cite the title in italics and to include the URL for its location on the Internet.

Key sources

McHaney, R. (2011). *The new digital shoreline*. Sterling, VA: Stylus Publishing.

Mooney, C. (2013). *Theories of childhood: An introduction to Dewey, Montessori, Erikson, Piaget, and Vygotsky* (2nd ed.). St. Paul, MN: Redleaf Press.

Swingler, T., & Brockhouse, J. (2009). Getting better all the time: Using music technology for learners with special needs. *Australian Journal of Music Education*, **2**, 49–57.

Tobias, E. (2012). Let's play! Learning music through video games and virtual worlds. In G. E. McPherson & G. Welch (Eds.), *The Oxford handbook of music education* (Vol. 2, pp. 532–48). New York: Oxford University Press.

Williams, D. B., & Webster, P. R. (2008). *Experiencing music technology* (3rd ed.). Boston, MA: Cengage Higher Education.

Reference list

Adachi, M., & Trehub, S. (2012). Musical lives of infants. In G. E. McPherson & G. Welch (Eds.), *The Oxford handbook of music education* (Vol. 1, pp. 229–47). New York: Oxford University Press.

Bamberger, J. (1991). *The mind behind the musical ear: How children develop musical intelligence*. Cambridge, MA: Harvard University Press.

Bamberger, J. (2000). *Developing musical intuitions*. New York: Oxford University Press.

Barrett, M., & Tafuri, J. (2012). Creative meaning-making in infants' and young children's musical cultures. In G. E. McPherson & G. Welch (Eds.), *The Oxford handbook of music education* (Vol. 1, pp. 296–316). New York: Oxford University Press.

Barrett, J., & Webster, P. (Eds.) (2014). *The musical experience*. New York: Oxford University Press.

Barry, N., & Hallam, S. (2002). Practice. In R. Parncutt & G. E. McPherson (Eds.), *The science and psychology of music performance: Creative strategies for teaching and learning* (pp. 151–66). New York: Oxford University Press.

Bauer, W. (2014). *Music learning today*. New York: Oxford University Press.

Berliner, P. (1994). *Thinking in jazz*. Chicago, IL: University of Chicago Press.

Burnard, P. (2012). *Musical creativities in practice*. Oxford, England: Oxford University Press.

Deliege, I., & Sloboda, J. (Eds.) (1996). *Musical beginnings: Origins and development of musical competence*. New York: Oxford University Press.

d'Escrivan, J. (2012). *Music technology*. Cambridge, UK: Cambridge University Press.

Dorfman, J. (2013). *Theory and practice of technology-based music instruction*. New York: Oxford University Press

Dowling, J. (1988). Tonal structure and children's early learning of music. In J. Sloboda (Ed.), *Generative processes in music: The psychology of performance, improvisation, and composition* (pp. 113–28). New York: Oxford University Press.

Dowling, J. (1999). The development of music perception and cognition. In D. Deutsch (Ed.), *The psychology of music* (pp. 603–25). San Diego, CA: Academic Press.

Dunn, R. (2011). Contemporary research on music listening: A holistic view. In R. Colwell & P. Webster (Eds.), *MENC handbook of research on music learning* (Vol. 2, pp. 3–60). New York: Oxford University Press.

Finney, J., & Burnard, P. (Eds.) (2007). *Music education with digital technology*. London, UK: Continuum.

Flohr, J. (1984). Young children's improvisations: A longitudinal study. Paper presented at the Music Educators National In-Service Conference (49th, Chicago, IL, March 23, 1984).

Gembris, H. (2002). The development of musical abilities. In R. Colwell & C. Richardson (Eds.), *The new handbook of research on music teaching and learning* (pp. 487–508). New York: Oxford University Press.

Gerry, D., Unrau, A., & Trainor, L. J. (2012). Active music classes in infancy enhance musical, communicative and social development. *Developmental Science, 15*(3), 398–407. doi: http://dx.doi.org/10.1111/j.1467–7687.2012.01142.x.

Gower, L., & McDowall, J. (2012). Interactive music video games and children's musical development. *British Journal of Music Education, 29*(1), 91–105. doi: http://dx.doi.org/10.1017/S0265051711000398.

Green, L. (2001). *How popular musicians learn: A way ahead for music education*. Hampshire, England: Ashgate Publishing.

Green, L. (2008). *Music, informal learning and the school: A new classroom pedagogy*. Hampshire, England: Ashgate Publishing.

Gromko, J. E. (1994). Children's invented notations as measures of musical understanding. *Psychology of Music, 22*(2), 136–47.

Hair, H. I. (1977). Discrimination of tonal direction on verbal and nonverbal tasks by first-grade children. *Journal of Research in Music Education, 25*(3), 197–210.

Hargreaves, D. J. (1986). *The developmental psychology of music*. New York: Cambridge University Press.

Hargreaves, D. J. (1996). The development of artistic and musical development. In I. Deliege & J. A. Sloboda (Eds.), *Musical beginnings: Origins and development of musical competence* (pp. 145–70). Oxford, UK: Oxford University Press.

Hargreaves, D. J., & Galton, M. J. (1992). Aesthetic learning: Psychological theory and educational practice. In B. Reimer & R. A. Smith (Eds.), *The arts, education, and aesthetic knowing* (pp. 124–50). Chicago, IL: National Society for the Study of Education, distributed by University of Chicago Press.

Hargreaves, D., Hargreaves, J., & North, A. (2012). Imagination and creativity in music listening. In D. Hargreaves, D. Miell, & R. MacDonald (Eds.), *Musical imaginations* (pp. 156–72). Oxford, England: Oxford University Press.

Hargreaves, D. J., & North, A. C. (1999). Developing concepts of musical style. *Musicae Scientiae: Journal of the European Society for the Cognitive Sciences of Music, 3*(2), 193–216.

Hargreaves, D. J., & North, A. C. (2001). Complexity, prototypicality, familiarity, and the perception of musical quality. *Psychomusicology, 17*(1–2), 77–80.

Haston, W. (2004). Comparison of a visual and an aural approach to beginning wind instrument instruction (Unpublished doctoral dissertation). Northwestern University, Evanston, IL.

Hickey, M. (2002). Creative thinking in the context of music composition. In M. Hickey (Ed.), *Why and how to teach music composition: A new horizon for music education* (pp. 31–54). Reston, VA: MENC.

Hickey, M. (2012). *Music outside the lines.* New York: Oxford University Press.

Himonides, E. (2012). The misunderstanding of music-technology education: A meta perspective. In G. E. McPherson & G. Welch (Eds.), *The Oxford handbook of music education* (Vol. 2, pp. 433–56). New York: Oxford University Press.

Hourigan, R. (2008). Teaching strategies for performers with special needs. *Teaching Music, 15*(6), 26–9.

Kaschub, M., & Smith, J. (2009). *Minds on music.* Lanham, Maryland: Rowman & Littlefield.

Kastner, M. P., & Crowder, R. G. (1990). Perception of the major/minor distinction. IV: Emotional connotation in young children. *Music Perception: An Interdisciplinary Journal, 8*(2), 189–201.

Kratus, J. (1996). A developmental approach to teaching music improvisation. *International Journal of Music Education,* (26), 27–37.

Lamont, A. (1998). Music, education, and the development of pitch perception: The role of context, age and musical experience. *Psychology of Music, 26*(1), 7–25.

Lamont, A., & Cross, I. (1994). Children's cognitive representations of musical pitch. *Music Perception, 12*(1), 27–55.

Lehmann, A., & Jorgensen, H. (2012). Practice. In G. E. McPherson & G. Welch (Eds.), *The Oxford handbook of music education* (Vol. 1, pp. 677–93). New York: Oxford University Press.

MacDonald, R., Wilson, G., & Miell, D. (2012). Improvisation as a creative process within contemporary music. In D. Hargreaves, D. Miell, & R. MacDonald (Eds.), *Musical imaginations* (pp. 242–59). Oxford, England: Oxford University Press.

McCord, K. (2002). Children with special needs compose using music technology. *Journal of Technology in Music Learning, 1*(Fall/Winter), 3–14.

McDonald, D. T., & Simons, G. M. (1989). *Musical growth and development: Birth through six.* New York: Schirmer Books.

McDowall, J. (2008). Music technology: A vehicle for young children's music learning. *Australian Journal of Music Education, 2,* 41–50.

McHaney, R. (2011). *The new digital shoreline.* Sterling, VA: Stylus Publishing.

McPherson, G. E. (1993). Factors and abilities influencing the development of visual, aural and creative performance skills in music and their educational implications (Unpublished doctoral dissertation). University of Sydney, Sydney, Australia.

McPherson, G. E. (2009). The role of parents in children's musical development. *Psychology of Music, 37*(1), 91–110. doi: http://dx.doi.org/10.1177/0305735607086049.

McPherson, G. E., Bailey, M., & Sinclair, K. E. (1997). Path analysis of a theoretical model to describe the relationship among five types of musical performance. *Journal of Research in Music Education, 45*(1), 103–29.

McPherson, G. E., & Dunbar-Hall, P. (2001). Australia. In D. J. Hargreaves & A. C. North (Eds.), *Musical development and learning: The international perspective* (pp. 14–26). New York: Continuum.

McPherson, G. E., & Gabrielsson, A. (2002). From sound to sign. In R. Parncutt & G. E. McPherson (Eds.), *The science and psychology of music performance: Creative strategies for teaching and learning* (pp. 99–116). New York: Oxford University Press.

McPherson, G. E., & Zimmerman, B. (2011). Self-regulation of musical learning: A social cognitive perspective on developing performance skills. In R. Colwell & P. Webster (Eds.), *MENC handbook of research on music learning* (Vol. 2, pp. 130–75). New York: Oxford University Press.

Meltzoff, A. N., Kuhl, P., & Moore, M. K. (1991). Perception, representation, and the control of action in newborn and young infants towards a new synthesis. In M. J. S. Weiss & P. R. Zelazo (Eds.), *Newborn attention: Biological constraints and the influence of experience* (pp. 377–411). Norwood, NJ: Ablex.

Moog, H. (1976). The development of musical experience in children of pre-school age. *Psychology of Music, 4*(2), 38–45.

Mooney, C. (2013). *Theories of childhood: An introduction to Dewey, Montessori, Erikson, Piaget, and Vygotsky* (2nd ed.). St. Paul, MN: Redleaf Press.

Moorhead, G. E., & Pond, D. (1978). *Music of young children*. Santa Barbara, CA: Pillsbury Foundation.

Morehouse, P. (2012). Investigating young children's music-making behavior: A development theory (Unpublished doctoral dissertation). Claremont Graduate University, Claremont, CA.

North, A. C., & Hargreaves, D. J. (1999). Music and adolescent identity. *Music Education Research*, 1(1), 75–92.

Odena, O. (Ed.) (2012). *Musical creativity: Insights from music education research*. Surrey, England: Ashgate.

Pflederer, M., & Sechrest, L. (1968). Conversation-type responses of children to musical stimuli. *Bulletin of the Council for Research in Music Education*, **13**, 19–36.

Phillips, K., & Doneski, S. (2011). Research on elementary and secondary singing. In R. Colwell & P. Webster (Eds.), *MENC handbook of research on music learning* (Vol. 2, pp. 176–232). New York: Oxford University Press.

Pressing, J. (1988). Improvisation: Methods and models. In J. Sloboda (Ed.), *Generative processes in music: The psychology of performance, improvisation and composition* (pp. 129–78). New York: Oxford University Press.

Randles, C., & Stringham, D. (Eds.) (2013). *Musicianship: Composing in band and orchestra*. Chicago, IL: GIA.

Sawyer, K. (2012). *Explaining creativity*. New York: Oxford University Press.

Schellberg, G. (1998). *Zur entwicklung der klang farben-wahrnehmung von vorschulkindern*. Münster, Germany: Lit Verlag.

Serafine, M. L. (1988). *Music as cognition: The development of thought in sound*. New York: Columbia University Press.

Sloboda, J. (1985). *The musical mind: The cognitive psychology of music*. New York: Oxford University Press.

Smith, K. C., Cuddy, L. L., & Upitis, R. (1994). Figural and metric understanding of rhythm. *Psychology of Music*, **22**(2), 117–35.

Stauffer, S. L. (2002). Connections between the musical and life experiences of young composers and their compositions. *Journal of Research in Music Education*, **50**(4), 301. doi: 10.2307/3345357.

Swanwick, K., Hallam, S., Lamont, A., O'Neill, S., Green, L., Cox, G., Hennessy, S., Farrell, G., & Welch, G., (2004). Mapping music education research in the UK. *Psychology of Music*, **32**(3), 239–90.

Swanwick, K., & Tillman, J. (1986). The sequence of musical development: A study of children's compositions. *British Journal of Music Education*, **3**(3), 305–39.

Swingler, T., & Brockhouse, J. (2009). Getting better all the time: Using music technology for learners with special needs. *Australian Journal of Music Education*, **2**, 49–57.

Tarrant, M., North, A. C., & Hargreaves, D. J. (2002). Youth identity and music. In R. MacDonald, D. J. Hargreaves, & D. Meill (Eds.), *Musical identities* (pp. 134–50). New York: Oxford University Press.

Thibeault, M. (2012). Music education in the postperformance world. In G. E. McPherson & G. Welch (Eds.), *The Oxford handbook of music education* (Vol. 2, pp. 517–30). New York: Oxford University Press.

Tobias, E. (2012). Let's play! Learning music through video games and virtual worlds. In G. E. McPherson & G. Welch (Eds.), *The Oxford handbook of music education* (Vol. 2, pp. 532–48). New York: Oxford University Press.

Trainor, L. J., & Trehub, S. E. (1992). The development of referential meaning in music. *Music Perception*, **9**(4), 455–70.

Trehub, S. E., Hill, D. S., & Kamenetsky, S. B. (1997). Parents' sung performances for infants. *Canadian Journal of Educational Psychology*, **51**(4), 385–96.

Upitis, R. (1987). Children's understanding of rhythm: The relationship between development and music training. *Psychomusicology*, **7**(1), 41–60.

Webb, M., & Seddon, F. (2012). Musical instrument learning, music ensembles, and musicianship in a global and digital age. In G. E. McPherson & G. Welch (Eds.), *The Oxford handbook of music education* (Vol. 1, pp. 752–68). New York: Oxford University Press.

Webster, P. (2002). Creative thinking in music: Advancing a model. In T. Sullivan & L. Willingham (Eds.), *Creativity and music education* (pp. 16–33). Edmonton, AB: Canadian Music Educators' Association.

Webster, P., & Hickey, M. (2006). Computers and technology. In G. E. McPherson (Ed.), *The child as musician* (pp. 375–95). New York: Oxford University Press.

Webster, P., & Schlentrich, K. (1983). Discrimination of pitch direction by preschool children with verbal and nonverbal tasks. *Journal of Research in Music Education*, **30**(3), 151–61.

Wiggins, J. (2002). Creative process as meaningful musical thinking. In T. Sullivan & L. Willingham (Eds.), *Creativity and music education* (pp. 78–88). Edmonton, AB: Canadian Music Educators' Association.

Wiggins, J., & Espeland, M. (2012). Creating in music learning contexts. In G. E. McPherson & G. Welch (Eds.), *The Oxford handbook of music education* (Vol. 1, pp. 341–60). New York: Oxford University Press.

Williams, D. B., & Webster, P. R. (2008). *Experiencing music technology* (3rd ed.). Boston, MA: Cengage Higher Education.

Zenatti, A. (1993). Children's musical cognition and taste. In T. J. Tighe & W. J. Dowling (Eds.), *Psychology and music: The understanding of melody and rhythm* (pp. 177–96). Hillsdale, NJ: Erlbaum.

Section 5

Contexts

Chapter 28

Historical perspectives

Gordon Cox

Historical perspectives: Introduction

There are two particular challenges for historians of childhood: to tease out the relationship between ideas about childhood and the experience of being a child, and how it has changed over time; and to unearth source material on past childhoods, as children themselves leave few records (Cunningham, 2005). It is my intention in this chapter to focus on the changes and continuities that comprise musical childhoods by assembling four exemplars presented chronologically: the English medieval song schools, private instrumental instruction in eighteenth- and nineteenth-century England, school music teaching in late nineteenth-century Europe, and recapitulation and musical childhood in twentieth-century America and Britain. My contention is that the changing ideas about what childhood is like and how children develop have influenced the nature of formal music education, whether in church, the studio, or school.

Bearing the foregoing challenges in mind, I hope we will be able to hear children's musical voices, albeit somewhat faintly at times, through such diverse evidence as cathedral records, travelers' observations, official reports produced by school inspectors, instructional manuals, and polemical works generated by debates concerning musical childhoods.

Song schools in medieval England

The popular view is that children in the medieval period were regarded as small adults, and that childhood was impoverished and disregarded by modern standards. Much of this stems from the work of Philippe Ariès (1962), who believed that medieval children lived very dissimilar lives from their early modern successors. The publication of his work sparked off a widespread interest into the history of childhood (Kok & Boynton, 2006). More recent historians, however, have rebutted Ariès's assertions, and have gathered copious evidence to demonstrate that medieval people did have concepts of what childhood was: the arrival of children in the world was a notable event, and their upbringing and education were taken seriously (Orme, 2003).

Opinions within the medieval Christian tradition were sharply polarized on whether children were channels of diabolical or divine influence. The belief in original sin, which could only be remitted through baptism, has to be balanced with the belief, rooted in the Christian tradition, in the original innocence of children (Heywood, 2001). The Church was an all-powerful force, and in medieval England music education derived strength and privilege from its place within the liturgy. Indeed, until the Reformation, song schools were necessities for all monasteries and cathedrals (Orme, 2006). But what kind of musical education did pre-Reformation choristers receive in such institutions?

We have been provided with a detailed picture by Flynn (2003), drawing upon the evidence of indentures of Masters of Choristers in 11 major English and Scottish choral institutions dating from the mid-fifteenth century. The aim of choristers' training was not primarily musical; it was focused upon the liturgy, the performance of which demonstrated practically the way to live a virtuous Christian life. In addition to acquiring musical skills, choristers learned to read and write English and Latin, and their morals were based upon Christian teaching. The training was practical rather than academic: lessons were designed to reinforce the knowledge and expertise necessary for participation in the liturgy. The boys practiced their lessons as a group, usually in one room, reciting and listening to others, and being corrected by the master.

From the evidence available, Flynn has listed the musical skills acquired by pre-Reformation choristers, which suggests a progressive order of attainment:

- "Plainsong." All students in the song schools, not only choristers, began their education at around 7 years of age with "song," a combination of Latin grammar and chant. They learned to read and write, and memorized the psalms with their psalm tones and other liturgical texts such as Canticles. Solmization (singing by sol-fa syllables introduced by Guido at the beginning of the eleventh century) helped them to memorize intervals which they learned to sing in tune. They did not need to learn the letter names of notes or how to read music in the early stages. However, the more advanced choristers would find the ability to read music preferable to additional memorizing. They learned how to read music by using the "gamut," the sequence of note names over the three octaves of the human voice which beginners had to commit to memory.

- "Pricksong." The boys learned the note values and ligatures characteristic of mensural music (polyphonic music with specific time values as opposed to plainchant with free rhythm). In order to reinforce such learning, some ligature shapes (in which two or more notes were combined) were painted on one of the walls of the classroom at St. George's Chapel, Windsor. A well-used way of learning mensuration was to sing canons.

- "Figuration." This was the singing of chant, in equal notes and regular mensuration for others to improvise against.

- "Faburden." Singing in faburden, a form of improvisation on a chant, involved little more than doubling the chant a fourth above in the top voice and a third below in the third voice except at cadences. The cantus firmus was in the middle voice.

- "Descant" was another, more varied form of improvisation less dependent on parallelism. The boys began learning note-against-note counterpoint, whilst more advanced descanters would improvise two or more notes against each note of the chant, sometimes involving imitation.

- "Square-note," apparently improvisation on a "square." A square originated as the lowest part in a polyphonic composition, and was used as the basis for an improvisation or a new notated composition.

- "Counter." That is, improvising a melody below a chant, suitable for choristers who were older, singing in the lower range.

- "Organ." Older choristers learned to play the organ, in the course of which they applied to the keyboard descant skills originally acquired through vocal music.

It would be misleading to imply that these various disciplines were part of some kind of fixed and universal medieval curriculum. However, it is significant that things appear to have been taught in a more or less fixed order; teaching was certainly progressive. A student began with pre-existing material, first learning largely by memory, then by reading notation; next, others improvised while the student provided the part for them to improvise against ("figuration"); then the student learned to improvise himself, beginning with the most straightforward method ("faburden"). All this was achieved through the mind and the voice. The final stage was technology—the organ.

This outline shows that in the finest song schools usually connected with the great cathedrals, boys acquired a sophisticated musical education through a way of sequencing material so that they were able to develop their musical competence as quickly as possible, even though we are unsure about the extent to which their practice exemplified their teachers' intentions. We gain a rare glimpse, however, of the day-to-day realities of life in such institutions from a sermon preached on Christmas Day 1558 by the Boy Bishop, John Stubbs, himself a chorister at Gloucester. He admonished his fellow choristers for their behavior in church:

> I kan not let this passe ontouched how boyyisshly thei behave themselves in the church, how rashly thei cum into the quere without any reverence; never knele nor cowntenaunce to say any prayer or Pater Noster, but rudely squat down on ther tayles and justle with ther fellows for a place. (Mould, 2007, p. 72)

The song schools were not only placed in the grand institutions, but they were also kept in many of the parishes of the land, frequently in humble circumstances. For example, one London parish church, St. Mary at Hill, had a choir school which was conducted in a separate chamber in 1523. The school had one or two forms and a desk, and the floor was covered with rushes. Some of the children were sent at the expense of the parishioners who paid for clothing, boots, and board in addition to tuition (Hanawalt, 1993; Littlehales, 1905).

Song schools thus provided opportunities for boys, often from humble backgrounds, to specialize in music (Marsh, 2013). We must recollect that only a tiny minority of boys would receive such instruction, and that essentially it provided an induction into the adult musical world, in which mastery of specialist skills was paramount. Whereas the Church recruited boys to do duties such as singing the liturgy in cathedrals, colleges, monasteries, friaries, or parish churches, girls could be utilized only in nunneries, of which there were never more than 146 throughout England and Wales (Orme, 2003).

In England the Dissolution of the Monasteries between 1536 and 1542 saw the demise of the majority of song schools, apart from those connected with cathedrals. According to Rainbow, "the long eclipse of music teaching in English schools had begun" (Rainbow, with Cox, 2006, p. 65). These song schools had provided a musical education based upon the comprehensive religious organizations that were the backbone of social life, although for only a small minority of children they provided musical instruction sometimes of the highest order to a range of pupils from diverse social backgrounds.[1]

Private music instruction in eighteenth- and early nineteenth-century England

Some account of developments in educational thinking and practice which preceded the eighteenth century is necessary here in order to provide some context. In 1693 John Locke had published *Some Thoughts Concerning Education*, which was highly secular in tone. Central was the notion of habit formation in terms of the gradual applicability of reason, so that as the child became more capable of thinking for himself, he would eventually submit his will to his own reason. Gone were the old assumptions about inherent childhood evil. The child was to be "considered only as white paper or wax to be moulded and fashioned as one pleases" (in Fletcher, 2008, p. 7). The clear implication was that childhood was a definite stage apart, and the central image was the child as a plant. Somewhat ironically it was the same John Locke who famously (or infamously) in 1684 had allocated music the last place in his list of educational accomplishments (see Mark, 2013, p. 22).

A curriculum of what Fletcher (2008) calls "female politeness" was already apparent in the early seventeenth century. Typical training might include tuition in "accomplishments" such as French, needlework, dancing, and music. Instruction in these subjects was generally only available to the gentry, who were keen that their daughters gained such "accomplishments" as a means of setting them apart from the lower orders. Robert Burton writing in 1621 in his *Anatomy of Melancholy* noted that music was "[a] thing . . . frequently used, and part of a Gentlewoman's bringing up, to sing, and dance, and play on the Lute, or some such instrument . . . 'tis the next way their parents thinke to get them husbands" (Marsh, 2013, p. 200).

Training in "musical accomplishments" really took off after 1700 and private music instruction began to flourish (Fletcher, 2008). Drawing on the work of Kassler (1976, 1979), I shall focus upon textbooks and manuals published up until the early nineteenth century in order to demonstrate how in the early stages of learning, young upper-class children were taught the rudiments of music, and their first steps in singing and playing a musical instrument.

Charles Burney writing in 1779 had pointed out:

> A child is not thought capable of profiting from the instructions of a music-master till five or six years old, though many have discovered an ear capable of being pleased with musical tones, and a voice that could imitate them much sooner . . . in music the undirected efforts of an infant must be . . . circumscribed: for without the aid of reason and perseverance he can only depend on memory and a premature delicacy and acuteness of ear for his guides. (Kassler, 1976, p. 70)

Hence music teachers were concerned primarily to communicate facts suitable for impressing "simple ideas" on their young pupils' memories. Since the mind at this early stage was thought to be passive, various educational tools were devised to assist teachers in "imprinting" these simple musical ideas. The most numerous were music instruction books. For infants these covered such elements as the stave, lines and spaces, leger lines, names of notes in different clefs, accidentals, rests, proportions, etc.

Along with musical facts, infants were to acquire physical dexterity by singing, playing an instrument, or copying music. Instruction books included material pertaining to the body and the mind: fingering, sitting, scales, and arpeggios. The musical education of infants was patterned after their education in language, the elements being taught grammatically. In music, infants learned the different kinds of single elements (etymology), their union into larger structures (syntax), and writing correctly (orthography). These books may be called the "ABCdaria" (after ABC books), for they taught the musical alphabet. Kassler (1979) cites Keith's *A Musical Vade Mecum* (*c.* 1820) as an example of the genre. Some ABCdaria were in the form of a catechism, either as dialogue or question and answer. These tutors might also contain pictures and verses. There was, however, no room for rhetorical ornament. Universal concerns in all the instructional materials focused upon musical ciphers, the reduction of the number of musical characters and substituting them for symbols of a more universal application. The reform of musical notation was undertaken so that infants could remember more easily simple musical ideas.

Music instruction, therefore, was patterned after the study of language where elementary grammar consisted of two domains: knowledge and practice. Musical knowledge pertained to the mind, practice to the body. The child learned by having the elements merely impressed on the memory by having the model placed before the senses. Further explication beyond naming was not required. In the practice of music children were encouraged by the teacher to inculcate correct bodily habits. Music instruction books and mnemonic aids impressed this musical knowledge on the mind.

Musical games connected with instruction have not been located before the 1790s, when new developments in educational theory held that the child should be amused as well as interested. Play was being prioritized: the earliest instructive game appears to be musical dominoes in 1793. Anne Gunn's *Instructions for Playing Musical Games* (1801) described how following each throw of the dice, two players were to compete by arranging on their separate boards the notes, clefs, chords, and key signatures called for. The intent was to make the learning of music rudiments amusing and instructive (Ghere & Amram, 2007; Rainbow, 2009, pp. 79–82). There were also mechanical aids to assist good bodily habits in musical performance. The Hand Director or Chiroplast, as featured in Logier's *Companion to the Royal Patent Chiroplast* of 1815, was based on the physiological theory that part of the body cast into a mold while soft and tender will be better formed than if left to chance (Rainbow, 2009, pp. 114–25).

In summary, with the Age of Reason came a more egalitarian outlook and the powerful notion of the child's mind as a tabula rasa. All this raised questions concerning nature vs. nurture. Musical knowledge was impressed upon the infant's memory, and instruction became highly systematized and modeled upon language teaching.

Observing the teaching of school music in Europe in the late nineteenth century

An essential factor in the universalizing of childhood was the introduction of compulsory schooling. Beginning in some European states in the eighteenth century, it spread to some other parts of the world, and by the late 1800s had been adopted by Europe's industrial leaders—France, The Netherlands, and Britain (Cox & Stevens, 2011). My intention in this section is to focus upon what children were actually doing in their compulsory music lessons.

In Britain, the 1870 Education Act made both free and compulsory education possible, and "singing" became a compulsory subject in 1872 governed by specific codes (Cox, 2011). It is not surprising, therefore, that officials were dispatched to countries on the continent to see what lessons could be learnt or avoided. An independent and influential observer of school music abroad was John Spencer Curwen (1847–1916), who was the oldest son of John Curwen, the founder of the Tonic Sol-fa movement. J. S. Curwen succeeded his father as president of the Tonic Sol-fa College in 1880, and thereafter was responsible for the exponential growth of the "movement" (McGuire, 2009). He made a number of independently organized visits to observe the teaching of music in schools over a period of 19 years between 1879 and 1901, ranging through Europe, Scandinavia, and North America (see Rainbow, 2009, pp. 264–70). His intention was "to ascertain what was the highest level reached in the subject in Europe; to know whether our children have as good capacity for singing as the children of other countries; [and] to find whether the difficulties which our teachers meet in teaching singing were met with abroad" (Curwen, 1901, p. iii). Curwen's accounts were intended for the information of supporters of the Tonic Sol-fa movement at home. Finally, these were assembled into the book *School Music Abroad* (1901). I shall draw upon his observations in Europe in order to present a picture of nineteenth-century music education, focusing on what children were learning and how they were learning. Curwen was very precise about the ages of pupils, and so I will present this material in order from the youngest to the oldest.

In Paris, Curwen found that the syllabus for communal schools was minutely laid down, and based on the fixed-doh system (i.e., "doh" is always "C"). For 6–8-year-olds notation was explained in small doses, so that by the end of the second year in school, children were singing songs in unison by ear, and singing from notation those they had already learned by ear. They would also know the common signs of the staff, being still in the key of C. The 8–9-year-olds were required to sing easy solfeggios (vocal exercises using sol-fa syllables) in unison, and easy two-part and unison songs. The keys of G and F major, and E and D minor were specified, with dictation exercises and the introduction of the three-pulse measure. By the end of the following year pupils were supposed to sing at sight an easy piece containing simple-time divisions and two changes of key.

The weekly one-hour lessons included ten minutes each of instruction on theory and dictation plus 20 minutes each on blackboard exercises and solfeggios, and songs with words. For 10–11-year-olds, singing in two and three parts was required, as well as knowledge of such details as compound time, less-used signs, and the enharmonic scale. Every lesson at this stage it was stated should start with singing a major, a minor, and a chromatic scale.

To sample what Curwen saw in practice, I shall focus upon his visits to Swiss and German schools. Whilst he found that the public schools on the continent did not generally include an infant department, an agreeable exception was *l'Ecole Enfantine de Malagnon* in Geneva. The head teacher was doing all she could to carry out Froebel's principles with her children who were aged 3 to 7. Curwen observed a class of 24 children of 6- to 7-year-olds who began to sing "with tiny soft sweet tone" (Curwen, 1901, p. 140). He remarked on the absence of a piano. The singing was all by imitation, there were no exercises, and the lesson was mixed with games and with the topics of the stories and pictures. The songs were appropriate to the season, and the teachers "headed the children in their marches and evolutions, singing with them and inspiring their organised play." For Curwen, "it was a pretty sight, and one which dwelt in my mind" (Curwen, 1901, p. 140).

Curwen noted that the Chevé system had been taught in Geneva for 40 years. It was based on cipher notation (Madurell, 2011). Indeed, it was Rousseau, a Genevan himself, who was the first to produce such a notation of figures. It depended upon the representation of the degrees of the rising major scale by the figures 1–7, where the figure 1 always referred to the keynote of a major key (Rainbow, 2009, pp. 71–8; Rousseau, 1742/1982). This is shown in Figure 28.1.

Curwen found the influence of Chevé and cipher notation in the music teaching he witnessed in a girls' high school on the Quai de la Poste, Geneva, a "Secondary and Superior School for Young Ladies," where he observed a class of 12–13-year-olds. The teacher was M. Henri Kling, a distinguished horn player and teacher. The blackboard behind the teacher's desk had two octaves of crotchets on the treble stave painted on it. Below this were a number of phrases painted in the Chevé figures. The girls sang phrases from the staff in C, then from the figures. M. Kling next sang to "la" a phrase of 18 notes in C, which the girls wrote down in the Chevé notation. Curwen observed that the dictation of time was found by the girls to be more difficult than the tune. The passage was finally copied into notebooks into staff notation. This dictée took 20 minutes. The last quarter of an hour was devoted to singing two-part songs from a collection in the Chevé notation. Four songs were given, and "The Loreley" was sung in German, the first foreign language song the French–Swiss learnt.

In Zürich, Curwen visited a girls' secondary school close to the Grossmunster, and observed a class of 30 pupils aged 13–15 in an impressive lesson. After they had sung from their books a two-part solfeggio to alphabetical names, the pupils sight-read a simple E minor melody from the blackboard, and then tried it in the major key. A two-part song was sung, and then the girls stood up one by one and answered questions on notes, rests, and intervals. This class was followed by one of 20 girls aged 15–17, who began with long holding tones to "laa," ascending by semitones, then the minor scale to alphabetical names. A difficult melody was written on the blackboard, with a tricky syncopation. The teacher accompanied well on the piano, but talked little himself. Intervals were discussed, followed by three-part singing exercises to "laa." The girls received two hours of music per week.

Fig. 28.1 Rousseau's cipher notation from his *Dictionnaire de la Musique*

Curwen was critical of those schools which did not focus upon the teaching of sight-singing skills. In Berlin's Victoria Schule, a high school for girls, Curwen heard 18-year-olds singing in four parts: "the voices were pure and soft, and the lowest part of all seemed to me more resonant than we find in England" (Curwen, 1901, p. 9). Great expenditure of time was spent in rehearsing the separate parts, the different parts having only their own score, which led Curwen to comment acerbically that "[b]linkers on a horse prevent his seeing too much, and these single voice parts are the expression of feeble reading power" (Curwen, 1901, p. 9). The teacher agreed that the girls could hardly read music at all. Their motets were unaccompanied. But while the single parts were being rehearsed, "the rest are yawning, whispering, nudging or staring" (Curwen, 1901, p. 9).

At the Training College for Men Teachers in Hamburg he observed a class of 25 "lads" who were 18 years old. They took up Bertalotti's solfeggios, which had sol-fa syllables printed under the staff. F sharps were very "sore places" even after much prompting with the violin. The tune "God speed the right" came next, sung to a drinking song. There were two tenor parts and two bass parts. There was a lot of repetition over a short phrase: "time after time the violin led them through this passage, and rasped out the right notes against their wrong ones a second apart." The students "began to gape and look bored" (Curwen, 1901, p. 26). The situation reminded Curwen of Herbart's observation: "Weariness is the cardinal sin of instruction" (Curwen, 1901, p. 26). There evidently was plenty of weariness in the class while this piece was being learnt. The "lads" had soft, rich voices and the feeling for singing, but their reading power was practically nil—although Curwen noted that they had entered the school when they were 7. If the eleven years produced this result, a shorter time would do still less. Curwen admitted "sight-reading is not the whole business of the teacher of singing, but choral music will never spread widely where new music has to be taught laboriously by ear" (Curwen, 1901, p. 27).

What do we conclude from all this? That for the most part children were receiving a structured program of tuition characterized by the imperatives of regimentation and drill. We should recollect that this reflected the general trend that pedagogical methods were governed by imperatives of codes and examinations, size of classes, attitudes about the status of children, and philosophies about what education should be preparing children for in adult life.

Most systematic instruction appeared to be based upon the fixed-doh, but also included influences from Chevé. In those schools which proved musically effective in Curwen's eyes, the pupils must have felt a progression through their school musical life, so that by the time they were 18 some of them were in classes singing in four parts. Curwen was convinced that the fixed-doh system itself was unsuitable for such teaching, compared to the tonic sol-fa method based upon the movable-doh. However, he also found a tendency in some schools to aim for vocal performance without sufficient background knowledge of notation, which meant the loss of musical independence. Curwen characterized this tension as "the old conflict between technic and sensibility, which will never be settled" (Curwen, 1901, p. iv). We will find this tension at the heart of our discussion of twentieth-century notions of music and childhood.

Rediscovery of the primitive child in the twentieth century

A number of authorities have regarded the late nineteenth and early twentieth centuries as significant in the construction of modern childhood (Heywood, 2001). I shall focus on one particularly influential model as far as music education is concerned, derived from evolutionary theory: racial recapitulation. It is not surprising that Darwin's theory of evolution should have profoundly influenced views of childhood. It came to be believed that in their embryonic development, individuals passed through stages similar to those through which their ancestors had evolved. The idea of racial recapitulation was thus developed. It stated that the ontogenesis of the individual, or the development of the individual, is a short and quick repetition (recapitulation) of phylogenesis, or the development of the tribe to which it belongs: ontogeny recapitulates phylogeny (Gould, 1980).

This theory soon appeared as a basis for piano teaching (Zon, 2012) and the school curriculum. One suggestion was that curriculum materials in each school grade should draw the child along the path travelled by the race. By 1900 the doctrine of recapitulation was an unchallenged truth in the influential Child Study Movement and championed by its leader, the American psychologist G. Stanley Hall (1844–1924) (Selig, 2004). Underlying Hall's drive to study the basic emotional and mental characteristics of child behavior was the belief, in his own phrase, that "[e]very child is a little savage" (Savage, 2007, p. 68). More specifically, Hall propounded that young people pass through three distinct stages: the primitive (children from infancy to 6 or 7 years of age), the barbaric (youths from 8 to 12 years of age), and the civilized (adolescents from 13 years of age) (Southcott, 2009).

Hall devoted a chapter to "The Pedagogy of Music" in his two-volume work, *Educational Problems* (1911). He believed sound to be the most primitive of man's contacts with self and the environment. Furthermore, it was a pivotal element in humankind's mental constitution, and the best and truest expression of the pre-intellectual stage, comprising feeling, instinct, and impulse.

It was Hall who wrote the foreword to the first edition of the book by the American music educator Satis N. Coleman (1878–1960), *Creative music for children: A plan of training based on the natural evolution of music including the making and playing of instruments, dancing, singing, poetry* (1922). Coleman was an innovative music educator who later worked at the progressive Lincoln School in New York (see also Boston, 1992; Cremin, 1964; Southcott, 2009; Volk, 1996). While not attempting to support or discuss what she called "the once popular Recapitulation Theory," Coleman nevertheless believed that most primitive peoples were musical, and the music employed by them was a necessity of life. In our midst, she continued, it is the children who are the primitives, they are musical in the beginning, but this tendency does not always survive their training. She believed that her young pupils were little savages, and this gave Coleman her mission:

> Being little savages, they can understand savage music. I shall find the child's own savage level, and lift him gradually up to higher forms . . . The natural evolution of music shall be my guide in leading the child from the simple to the complex. (Coleman, 1922, p. 29)

In her book Coleman describes how by their own creative work children shall experience the most important stages in the evolution of music. Her experiment proper began in October 1918 after a summer of preliminary experimentation with two children aged 5 and a half, and 7 and a half. Others aged 3–9 joined them. There was a weekly lesson of one hour, but some children came four times a week, others twice. After the first year, Saturday lessons were also scheduled.

The children made percussion instruments first "as primitive peoples do" (Coleman, 1922, p. 39), then ventured into making amongst others the Pipes of Pan, Shepherd's pipe, Ocarinas, Squash leaf oboes, Petunia blossom oboes, cornstalk fifes, Cocoa nut fiddles, and dulcimers. Coleman then emphasized movement and rhythm: "Many dances of primitive peoples are excellently suited to little children" (p. 84). The children invented new steps and pantomimes, improvised to music almost daily, made dance dramatizations of fairy tales, poems and original stories, and impersonated natural phenomena.

After a clear rhythmic grounding came singing and voice control for the children. Coleman (1922) believed that although the union of song and dance was almost universal among primitive peoples, all primitive music stressed rhythm rather than melody. In its turn, singing was more elemental than playing: "Most savage children are trained in keenness of ear perception" (Coleman, 1922, p. 103). She drew on the writings of a British music historian, J. F. Rowbotham, whose key work was *A history of music to the time of the troubadours* (1885) (see Zon, 2000, pp. 193–201). Rowbotham believed that the story of vocal music commenced with a one-note stage, and he cited the inhabitants of Tierra del Fuego as living examples of primitive peoples emerging from that period: he claimed this was followed historically by a two-note period, later the third note was added, and so on. As an "evolutionist" he followed the fashionable anthropological method of treating contemporary "primitive" music as a survival from the past, "a kind of living fossil" (Blacking, 1989, p. 8).

These ideas permeated Coleman's thinking and practice. For instance, after improvising chants, her pupils "naturally" began to sing Mother Goose rhymes to melodies of three notes, then progressed to a five-note scale (see Figure 28.2).

Coleman employed numerical names: "'Do-re-mi' is a foreign language to the young child, and complicates his singing progress" (Coleman, 1922, p. 107). Indeed, she believed that notation should be postponed until after the child has had wide experience in making music. As the child plays by imitation and by ear, no symbols whatever are needed in the beginning. The first thought of written signs usually comes when a child had made up a little song "which he plays and would like to remember, and thinks he might forget" (p. 118). Composing was a definitely prescribed

Fig. 28.2 Dorianne's *Goosey Gander*

activity in each phase of the work. Song improvisations really began in mere singing conversations, making up songs on the spot.

Coleman (1922) is worth quoting in this summary of her philosophy:

> Those early years of the child's development correspond to the stage of primitive music and the simplest of instruments. The music of the childhood of the race belongs to him while he is yet a little child . . . Heretofore in most of our instrumental training for children we have forced the child to skip a very important and a very broad stage in his indigenous evolution. We have urged him while still in swaddling clothes to take on adult culture, as one who would try to teach a savage to drive an automobile before he has had any simpler experiences with machinery. (p. 154)

Skipping 40 years or so, we find that in the opinion of Steven Gould, recapitulation "became the strongest argument for child-centered education" (Gould, 1980, p. 155), which reached its climax in the 1960s and 1970s.

In English music education, this was most apparent in the educational writings of Wilfrid Mellers (1914–2008). It was Mellers, a distinguished academic and composer, who founded the Department of Music at the University of York in 1964 which subsequently gained an international reputation for its adventurous curriculum. This curriculum embraced music education particularly through the work of John Paynter (1931–2012), who was highly influential in encouraging the development of creative music-making in schools. In this regard, his book *Sound and silence: Classroom projects in creative music* (Paynter & Aston, 1970) was seminal (see Finney, 2011a,b).

Mellers wrote three articles for the *Musical Times* in 1964 under the heading "Music for 20th Century Children," in which he expounded his beliefs in the nature of childhood and musical experience. In the first of these Mellers (1964a) addressed "magic and ritual in the junior school." His main point was that "as children, we start as little savages, and must do if we are to grow to consciousness. If we miss out the savage phase in childhood, it will find an outlet later on, at the wrong time, in the wrong place" (Mellers, 1964a, p. 342).

He pointed out that a return to primitive intuition had been one of the mainsprings of music since Wagner's Tristan. Stravinsky and Bartók used rhythm in a directly corporeal manner. The

New World avant-garde from Varèse to Partch, Cage, and Feldman manifested "aboriginal child-ishness still more unequivocally" (Mellers, 1964a, p. 343). Children recognized in Cage's prepared piano music an experience parallel to their own, and indeed his later music was of a type that the child, given appropriate facilities, would create from his or her own subconscious.

Carl Orff, according to Mellers, explored the rebirth of melody and achieved a liberation of corporeal rhythm. *Schulwerk* is music as inseparable from action:

> The mythology of the child's world, of the rune and nursery rhyme, is the only wonder-creating magic that is still available to us in our urban society . . . Orff's children's music is thus a necessary and blessedly innocent renewal of pagan delight, whereby the senses are enriched and the limbs rejoiced. (Mellers, 1964a, p. 344)

After the first and "pagan" phase of children's musical awareness, Mellers (1964b) considered the dramatic conflict characteristic of Christianity. Orff's undulating organum-like triads are har-mony before puberty, while the homophonic part songs of Peter Maxwell-Davies are an embry-onic consciousness in which the parts move in restricted compass and in very close harmony (note the evolutionary correspondences), as though the music were half eager to escape from the innocence of the monodic state, "and this must be why children, growing through puberty, could recognise it as particularly their music" (Mellers, 1964b, p. 422).

In his final article for the series, "The Teenager's World," Mellers (1964c) asked, what happens as we cross the borderline from childhood to adolescence, and then to an adult state? He concluded that neither Orff, nor Kodály, nor Britten really addressed the teenager's world. Orff's music for adolescents seemed inadequate, Kodály's music was inseparable from his own creativity and the culture in which he lived and worked, while the popularity of Britten's beautiful and moving music for children was largely a middle-class phenomenon. Instead, Mellers concluded, we should look to jazz and blues as urban folk arts whose creative essence lay in their honesty.

Some years later in *Life Cycle*, a fascinating and ambitious cantata for young people written for two choirs and orchestra, Mellers attempted to express in compositional terms the ideas he had been thinking about in his *Musical Times* articles (see Mellers, 1969).

We see in all this discussion a linking of the child with the primitive. It develops the idea that teaching should follow the child's innate and natural development, but this view of the child was also central to the modernist view of "primitivism." Musically, this accords with Mellers' view of musical childhood, which he connects with the music of those "American aboriginals" (his words) of the twentieth century, John Cage and Harry Partch.

Mellers' writings on education appear to have had an impact upon the thinking that lay behind the so-called creative music movement in UK schools and then elsewhere in the 1960s and 1970s. For example, the influential writer on music education, Christopher Small (1927–2011), aligned himself with reformers such as Mellers and Paynter, stating that they were bearing out the biolo-gist's truism that "ontogeny recapitulates phylogeny." The individual showed the various phases of the evolution of the species. As music teachers we must cooperate with the recapitulative process: "We are trying to do nothing less than re-establish the lifeline to the subconscious and harness its energies" (Small, 1968, p. 304). Interestingly, Mellers was still preaching the same message in the 1990s, writing about the musical evolution of children "who are by nature small savages" (Mellers, 2013, p. 146).

However, as Kathryn Marsh in her landmark study *The musical playground* (2008) points out, the "child as primitive" idea that underpinned the work of Coleman and Mellers is now discred-ited. Neither children nor societies are simple, and the notion of musical primitivism as applied to non-Western musics is now regarded as erroneous. However, Marsh detects some assumptions relating to cultural and developmental evolution associated with recapitulation theory embedded in the work of Carl Orff with his "elemental" music, and Zoltan Kodály's adherence to musical evolutionism. She calls for the need to question the underlying philosophical and methodological tenets of the educational works of both men.

More generally, Amanda Minks (2006) makes the point that whilst Western children might have recapitulated the stages of human development from primitive to civilized, non-Western others were condemned to occupy a state of arrested development.

In spite of such critiques, it is surprising that the racial theory of recapitulation should have had such a long-lasting influence on music education. Indeed, Southcott (2009) believes that "although unstated . . . [it] still underpins much current practice" (p. 31).

This offshoot of the romantic conception of childhood attempted to establish a connection between the primitive and the child. It resulted in a movement that tried to establish a flowering of creativity and expressive freedom for children, and also a relationship with contemporary musical developments. But we need to bear in mind that although as a racial theory recapitulation is no longer respected, the innate/learned question remains central to considering the nature of creativity and its place in musical experience.

Conclusions

What I have attempted to demonstrate in these examples from the historical record is that the character of institutionalized music education is always related to ideas about what childhood is like and how the child develops. Cultural ideas about childhood will have a structuring effect on educational practices: different cultural ideas about childhood will produce significantly different educational ideas and practices. However, we also need to bear in mind that institutional arrangements construct as much as reflect childhood and perspectives on it, so the ideas and the institutions are always in some kind of tension. An exploration of ways in which changes in music education both mirror and shape the shifts in the historical constructions of musical childhoods should help music educators to become more aware of the cultural influences that impinge on the construction of childhood, and more specifically to better understand how children can be encouraged to fulfill their musical potential.

Reflective questions

1 To what extent might some of the very different notions about music education described in this chapter be reconciled?

2 Discuss some of the ways in which changing ideas about childhood are reflected in the ways in which music was and is taught.

3 How do you feel about the tension Curwen observed in the teaching of music between technique and sensibility?

4 What historical practices in the teaching of music do you find most compelling in regard to your own practice?

5 In what ways do you think such historical perspectives might be able to tell us "a story about the present, using items from the past?"

Note

1 For comparative examples of the musical education of pre- and post-Reformation choristers, see Boynton and Cochelin (2006) on the Abbey of Cluny, Borgerding (2006) on Spanish cathedrals, and Munro (2010) on Scottish song schools.

Key sources

Boynton, S., & Kok, R.-M. (Eds.) (2006). *Musical childhoods & the cultures of youth*. Middletown, CT: Wesleyan University Press.

Cox, G., & Stevens, R. (Eds.) (2011). *The origins and foundations of music education: Cross-cultural historical studies of music in compulsory schooling*. London and New York: Continuum.

Mark, M. L. (2013). *Music education: Source readings from Ancient Greece to today*. New York and London: Routledge.

Rainbow, B., with additional chapters by Cox, G. (2006). *Music in educational thought and practice: A survey from 800 BC* (2nd ed.). Woodbridge: Boydell Press.

Rainbow, B. (2009). *Four centuries of music teaching manuals 1518–1932*. Woodbridge: Boydell Press.

Reference list

Ariès, P. (1962). *Centuries of childhood* (R. Baldick, trans.). London: Jonathan Cape.

Blacking, J. (1989). *"A commonsense view of all music": Reflections on Percy Grainger's contribution to ethnomusicology and music education*. Cambridge: Cambridge University Press.

Borgerding, T. M. (2006). Imagining the sacred body: Choirboys, their voices, and corpus christi in early modern Seville. In S. Boynton & R.-M. Kok, (Eds.) *Musical childhoods & the cultures of youth* (pp. 25–48). Middletown, CT: Wesleyan University Press.

Boston, S. (1992). Satis N. Coleman (1878–1961): Her career in music education (Doctoral dissertation). University of Maryland, College Park.

Boynton, S., & Cochelin, I. (2006). The sociomusical role of child obates at the Abbey of Cluny in the eleventh century. In S. Boynton & R.-M. Kok, *Musical childhoods & the cultures of youth* (pp. 3–24). Middletown, CT: Wesleyan University Press.

Coleman, S. N. (1922). *Creative music for children: A plan of training based on the natural evolution of music including the making and playing of instruments, dancing, singing, poetry*. New York and London: G. P. Putnam's Sons.

Cox, G. (2011). Britain: Towards "a long overdue renaissance?" In G. Cox & R. Stevens (Eds.), *The origins and foundations of music education: Cross-cultural historical studies of music in compulsory schooling* (pp. 15–28). London and New York: Continuum.

Cox, G., & Stevens, R. (Eds.) (2011). *The origins and foundations of music education: Cross-cultural historical studies of music in compulsory schooling*. London and New York: Continuum.

Cremin, L. A. (1964). *The transformation of the school: Progressivism in American education 1876–1957*. New York: Alfred A. Knopf.

Cunningham, H. (2005). *Children and childhood in Western society since 1500* (2nd ed.). London: Pearson Education.

Curwen, J. S. (1901). *School music abroad: A series of reports on visits to schools in Prussia, Saxony, Bavaria, Austria, Switzerland, France, Belgium, Holland, Sweden, Norway, Denmark, Italy and America during the years 1882 to 1901*. London: J. Curwen. [Reproduced as a Classic Text in Music Education #5, Boethius Press, now available from Boydell Press, Woodbridge, Suffolk, UK.]

Finney, J. (2011a). John Paynter: Music in education and the creativity of coincidence. *British Journal of Music Education*, **28**(1), 11–26.

Finney, J. (2011b). *Music education in England 1950–2010: The child-centred progressive tradition*. Farnham: Ashgate.

Fletcher, A. (2008). *Growing up in England: The experience of childhood 1600–1914*. New Haven and London: Yale University Press.

Flynn, J. (2003). The education of choristers in England during the sixteenth century. In J. Morehen (Ed.), *English choral practice 1400–1650* (2nd ed., pp. 180–99). Cambridge: Cambridge University Press.

Ghere, D., & Amram, F. (2007). Inventing musical games. *British Journal of Music Education,* **24**(1), 55–75.

Gould, S. J. (1980). *Ontogeny and phylogeny.* Cambridge, MA: The Belknap Press of Harvard University Press.

Hall, G. S. (1911). *Educational problems* (2 vols). New York: D. Appleton.

Hanawalt, B. (1993). *Growing up in medieval London: The experience of childhood in history.* New York: Oxford University Press.

Heywood, C. (2001). *A history of childhood: Children and childhood in the West from medieval to modern times.* Cambridge: Polity.

Kassler, J. C. (1976). Music made easy to infant capacity. *Studies in Music,* **10**, 67–78.

Kassler, J. C. (1979). *The science of music in Britain, 1714–1830: A catalogue of writings, lectures and inventions* (2 vols). New York: Garland.

Kok, R.-M., & Boynton, S. (2006). Preface. In S. Boynton & R.-M. Kok, *Musical childhoods & the cultures of youth* (pp. ix–xvi). Middletown, CT: Wesleyan University Press.

Littlehales, H. (Ed.) (1905). *The medieval records of a London city church (St. Mary at Hill) A.D. 1420–1559.* London: published for the Early English Text Society by Kegan Paul, Trench, Trübner & Co.

Madurell, F. (2011). France: An uncertain and unequal combat. In G. Cox & R. Stevens (Eds.), *The origins and foundations of music education: Cross-cultural historical studies of music in compulsory schooling* (pp. 29–44). London and New York: Continuum.

Mark, M. L. (2013). *Music education: Source readings from Ancient Greece to today* (4th ed.). New York and London: Routledge.

Marsh, C. (2013). *Music and society in early modern England.* Cambridge: Cambridge University Press.

Marsh, K. (2008). *The musical playground: Global tradition and change in children's songs and games.* Oxford and New York: Oxford University Press.

McGuire, C. E. (2009). *Music and Victorian philanthropy: The tonic sol-fa movement.* Cambridge: Cambridge University Press.

Mellers, W. (1964a). Music for 20th-century children: 1: Magic and ritual in the junior school, *Musical Times,* May, 342–5.

Mellers, W. (1964b). Music for 20th-century children: 2: From magic to drama, *Musical Times,* June, 421–7.

Mellers, W. (1964c). Music for 20th-century children: 3: The teenager's world, *Musical Times,* July, 500–5.

Mellers, W. (1969). *The resources of music: Vocal score* [of *Life Cycle*] *and commentary.* Cambridge: Cambridge University Press.

Mellers, W. (2013). Music: The breath of life. In P. Dickinson (Ed.), *Music education in crisis: The Bernarr Rainbow lectures and other assessments* (pp. 145–9). Woodbridge: Boydell Press.

Minks, A. (2006). Afterword. In S. Boynton & R.-M. Kok, *Musical childhoods & the cultures of youth* (pp. 209–18). Middletown, CT: Wesleyan University Press.

Mould, A. (2007). *The English chorister: A history.* London: Hambledon Continuum.

Munro, G. (2010). "Sang Schwylls" and "music schools": Music education in Scotland, 1560–1650. In R. E. Murray Jr., S. Forscher Weiss, & C. J. Cyrus (Eds.), *Music education in the Middle Ages and the Renaissance* (pp. 65–83). Bloomington: Indiana University Press.

Orme, N. (2003). *Medieval children.* New Haven: Yale University Press.

Orme, N. (2006). *Medieval schools: From Roman Britain to Renaissance England.* New Haven: Yale University Press.

Paynter, J., & Aston, P. (1970). *Sound and silence: Classroom projects in creative music.* Cambridge: Cambridge University Press.

Rainbow, B., with additional chapters by Cox, G. (2006). *Music in educational thought and practice: A survey from 800 BC* (2nd ed.). Woodbridge: Boydell Press.

Rainbow, B. (2009). *Four centuries of music teaching manuals 1518–1932.* Woodbridge: Boydell Press.

Rousseau, J.-J. (1742/1982). *Project concerning New Symbols for Music*. Translated and introduced by Bernarr Rainbow. Kilkenny: Boethius. Classic Texts in Music Education #1. [Now available from the Boydell Press, Woodbridge, Suffolk, UK.]

Rowbotham, J. F. (1885). *A history of music to the times of the Troubadours*. London: Trübner & Co.

Savage, J. (2007). *Teenage: The creation of youth 1875–1945*. London: Chatto & Windus.

Selig, D. (2004). Granville Stanley Hall. In P. Fass (Ed.), *Encyclopedia of children and childhood in history and society* (p. 413). New York: MacMillan Reference.

Small, C. (1968). Music in a liberal education forum—3. *Music in Education*, **31**, November/December, 302–4.

Southcott, J. (2009). The seeking attitude: Ideas that influenced Satis N. Coleman. *Journal of Historical Research in Music Education*, **XXXI**(1), 20–36.

Volk, T. (1996). Satis Coleman's "creative music." *Music Educators Journal*, May, pp. 31–3 & 47.

Zon, B. (2000). *Music and metaphor in nineteenth-century British musicology*. Aldershot: Ashgate.

Zon, B. (2012) Recapitulation and the musical education of Victorian children: *The child's pianoforte book* (1882) by H. Keatley Moore. In B. Zon (Ed.), *Music and performance in nineteenth-century Britain* (pp. 299–326). Farnham: Ashgate.

Chapter 29

Child as musical apprentice

Frank Abrahams and Daniel Abrahams

Child as musical apprentice: Introduction

In this chapter, we present traditional, cognitive, and sociotransformative approaches to apprenticeships and describe how each may have a positive impact on the child as a developing musician. While there are some characteristics that overlap among and between the three models, each has distinctive differences and connects to different psychologies. Traditional apprenticeship (Collins, Brown, & Newman, 1989; Rogoff, 1990; Schön, 1983, 1987) relies on demonstration and imitation, as we later describe in the example of the high school drum major learning to conduct. Within the one-on-one relationship between the mentor and the apprentice, the child acquires the skills necessary for membership within a community of practice; however, in this model of apprenticeship, there is limited dialogue between child and mentor. Instead, this model of apprenticeship is teacher-centered and grounded in behaviorist practices where power rests with the mentor as the one in control of the apprentice. Specifically, the mentor evokes the stimulus, and the apprentice provides the response. This is replicated until the apprentice masters the task. Thus, the apprentice remains dependent on the mentor until the mentor deems the apprentice proficient. In the traditional model, the apprentice is expected to observe, imitate, and practice, and gains membership in the community of practice only after the mentor grants entry. As a result, the child acquires a view of himself or herself that is limited to the boundaries of the specific musical learning task.

Cognitive apprenticeship (Lave & Wenger, 1991) expands upon the traditional model by providing the apprentice opportunities to question, clarify, predict, summarize, and connect their learning to experiences situated within the context of the "real world" (Abrahams & Abrahams, 2010, 2012; Palinscar & Brown, 1984). Framed in cognitive psychology, mentors applying the cognitive apprenticeship perspective use modeling, coaching, and fading to assist the child's mastery of music skills and musical concepts. However, as described through our examples of the piano classroom, ensemble rehearsals, and drum circle, students engage in dialogue with their mentor. This dissipates the issues of power encountered with traditional apprenticeship, but only slightly. The mentor is still the pedagogical authority who makes assumptions that the apprentice is one who should be taught rather than serve as a peripheral participant in a community (Lave & Wenger, 1991). This perspective might lead to issues of miscommunication, lack of trust, unclear identity, and so forth between the apprentice and mentor, and could inhibit an apprentice from feeling accepted into a community of practice by his or her peers.

Sociotransformative apprenticeship is a constructivist approach that addresses issues such as power and emerging musical identity that are neglected within the other two models. As we describe in two different scenarios, mentor with child and child with mentor develop a collegial relationship through dialogic conversation that builds mutual trust. Through culturally relevant and authentic activities it fosters the abilities in both child and teacher to acquire the characteristics of a critical consciousness.

Jerome Bruner (1986) wrote, "I have come increasingly to recognize that most learning in most settings is a communal activity, a sharing of the culture. It is not just that the child must make his knowledge his own, but that he must make it his own in a community of those who share his sense of belonging to a culture" (p. 127). Similarly, in *Pedagogy of the Oppressed* (1970), Paulo Freire wrote that learners exist in a cultural context and insisted that students learn to think reflectively about themselves. He taught that true and meaningful development took place when the learning was a catalyst for a change in the student's perception of reality. We contend that children working as apprentices with a mentor, singly or in groups, is an appropriate way to ensure meaningful musical development.

In Freire's classes, students made meaning of themes and learned to decode them in an act of becoming *critically conscious*, a state of deep knowing and understanding of the world. They could then take action against those forces that might oppress or inhibit such knowings and understandings. Like Freire's model, the apprentice framework considers the actions of both the children and teacher, who in the process of working together as apprentices and mentor are changed as a result.

> As the learner develops a schema [mental structures that represent individual understanding of experiences that frame a person's conceptualization of reality] that begins to incorporate the intricacies of the environment, they will be more capable of performing similarly to their peers. Once the trainer recognizes this, the student will become accepted as a peer; at this point, as the new worker tackles problems through their new and previously existing schema, their individual talents may start to be applied within the group practices. In this way, apprenticeship retains fresh information and ideas within a common body of knowledge. (Educational Theory of Apprenticeship, para. 3)

As early as 1993, Gardner suggested that children learn best when serving as apprentices to master teachers. He believed that learning in an apprenticeship model provided a framework for children to engage in experiential learning that recognized children's individual and collective potentials. He states:

> In an apprenticeship, you see a young person hanging around a very knowledgeable adult—an expert, someone who really knows what he or she is doing—watching that person, day after day, as he uses his knowledge. The master challenges his apprentice at the level the apprentice can handle. He doesn't give her something she could do six months ago; he doesn't give her tasks that are way too difficult. He's always calibrating the challenge for about where the student is. And I think that if you hang around an expert, not only will you develop requisite skills, you'll know when to use them and when not to use them. (Quoted in Brandt, 1993, p. 5)

In this chapter, we focus primarily on engagements in formal music instruction and musical experiences in schools, because it is there that children have regular interactions with the music teacher as their mentor.

The nature of apprenticeship

When knowledge is passed from expert to novice, as in an apprenticeship, children learn naturally. Though he was not talking about children, Schön said that apprenticeship "offers direct exposure to real conditions of practice and patterns of work" (1987, p. 37). This exposure affords children insight into the methods needed to be successful in a particular domain. Through an apprenticeship, children learn the processes used by expert mentors to formulate questions, pose and solve problems, and acquire the knowings, understandings, skills, and applications needed to complete domain-specific tasks (Collins, Brown, & Newman, 1989; Rogoff, 1990; Schön, 1983, 1987).

The apprenticeship model involves active learning, where the mentor supports, challenges, and guides apprentices as they move from novice to expert and from uninformed to critically conscious. By studying how craftsmen in African societies learn, Lave and Wenger (1991) developed the theory of situated learning, which has become central to the cognitive framework of apprenticeship. As a learning theory, it posits that children learn through interactions with individuals in a culture or community of practice. For example, the student musician who learns by playing in an ensemble or by participating in a classroom group activity interacts not only with the mentor, but with a peer group as well. This is called *situated cognition*. In short, they suggest that children enter into an apprenticeship by first observing the mentor, which they call *legitimate peripheral participation*. The child is on the peripheral of the community or culture—looking in as he or she observes the mentor. The literature by Lave and Wenger is vast, and we are only providing highlights here.

Apprentices also participate in a community of practice (Wenger, 1998) because they share a common craft or profession. A middle-school band is an example of a community of practice. In the context of apprenticeship, one might say that the members of the band are apprentices to the conductor, who serves as their mentor, teacher, guide, or facilitator. Together, all work toward a common goal, namely presenting a polished performance. A drum circle and a mariachi ensemble are also communities of practice.

Children refine ideas by observing and conversing with the mentor and with their peers. By completing practical assignments that become progressively more difficult and engaging in dialogue and reflection with the mentor, the apprentice acquires a professional identity. The mentor ensures that the members of the group meet learning outcomes and benchmark standards and that the practices of the group are authentic. That is, using music as an example, the group acts as musicians do while engaging in musicking.

Within the context of education, apprenticeship involves the development of schema, which Freire (1970) spoke of when he argued for the ability of students to read and write the world. For him, reading and writing the world meant having a deep understanding of content in ways that were broader than the literal and rooted in context and culture. Such meanings and understandings may be acquired through formal and informal interactions between the apprentice and the mentor. For example, a child studying voice may watch a video on singing technique, but will probably find it difficult to apply such informal training on stage in a recital. By working with a voice teacher who can formally sequence the requisite skills and knowings, the apprentice singer acquires the competence suitable for a voice recital.

Three forms of musical apprenticeships

In this chapter, we focus on three forms of musical apprenticeship that can have a positive impact on the child as a developing musician: traditional, cognitive, and sociotransformative. An apprentice is one who wishes to learn a particular craft or skill and works for a period of time with someone who is an expert at that craft or skill.

Traditional apprenticeship

Burwell (2013) reports that the "notion of apprenticeship seems to be at least as old as the notion of education" (p. 277). Historically, it was the exclusive way students mastered a craft. During the middle ages, cohorts of apprentices in like crafts formed guilds, fraternities, or societies throughout Europe (Baillie, 1956). The society of masons is one famous example. By the nineteenth century, the guild model had moved inside the traditional music conservatory, where students learned to be singers or instrumentalists by working one-on-one with a master teacher (Persson, 2000) in what we call a traditional apprenticeship. Essential features of the traditional apprenticeship model include demonstration or modeling and imitation (Jørgensen, 2000).

Today, examples of traditional musical apprenticeship in schools still exist in many conservatories and are found in the applied teacher–student model. Typically, a student, the apprentice, learns to play the trumpet by working one-on-one with a trumpet teacher who models through demonstration and monitors the student's weekly progress. The apprentice advances from a peripheral legitimate participant to full participant by working with the mentor, practicing, and reflecting on his or her own practice, in the process acquiring the competency to make meaningful contributions as a member of the community of practice. Mentoring is continuous in this model, but is not considered an activity on its own. The experiences the mentor provides for the apprentice are not grounded in real-world experiences; rather, they are confined to the domain of the particular skill or proficiency being developed.

Consider also how the high school drum major learns to conduct the high school marching band. Historically, musicians learn to conduct by imitating or emulating the practice of ensemble conductors with whom they perform or observe. In so doing, they attempt to mimic first, and then, through guided assistance with a mentor, refine their skills. Throughout the process, the mentor sequences each skill, moving from simple to complex, and then slowly fades out of the picture, leaving the apprentice conductor to perform more and more independently. Through this process, the apprentice slowly and deliberately moves toward expertise. The focus of traditional apprenticeship, in this instance, is to develop the physical and skill processes of the domain through guided experience. The sequence of traditional apprenticeship is demonstration by the mentor in one-on-one tutoring, practice by the apprentice, and then remediation by the mentor. The cycle repeats until the apprentice has mastered the skill well enough that the mentor deems him or her proficient.

Cognitive apprenticeship

During the late 1980s and early 1990s, cognitive psychologists, as a response to behaviorism, suggested a framework of apprenticeship that recognized the importance of learning as a social activity. As with traditional apprenticeships, in cognitive apprenticeships children learn by watching and imitating masters who coach students and over time wean the apprentice from dependence on the mentor. However, unlike traditional apprenticeships, skills and concepts situate themselves within the context of "real-world" experiences (Brown, Collins, & Duguid, 1989). For the young musician, this may mean understanding why a composer chose to set a piece in a particular key or how to remedy out-of-tune playing by the brass section in the school band. Rogoff (1990) suggests "all human activity is embedded in context; there are neither context-free situations nor decontextualized skills" (p. 27). Important in this type of apprenticeship is that the mentor models the desired skill or concept within a contextually situated experience. In addition, the rote experience of observing the modeling of the mentor and then practicing is modified by the inclusion of explanations by the mentor as the apprentice listens and observes the mentor explaining what he or she is doing and thinking, all the while developing a conceptual framework of the processes involved. The apprentice then attempts those processes, with the mentor observing and providing remediation as appropriate.

The child musician observes experts who model processes of a domain-specific task. This affords the child an opportunity to experience, in a holistic way, an exemplar of the desired learning outcome. The sequence of experiences for children in the framework of a cognitive apprenticeship consists of modeling, coaching, scaffolding, articulation, reflection, exploration, and fading (Collins, Brown, & Newman, 1989).

Children attempt the activity with coaching (Bruner, 1996; Schön, 1987). The teacher guides the apprentice toward finding solutions to musical problems posed by the mentor/teacher. Such problems may be as simple as which classroom instruments to choose to accompany a song, or as complex as which rhythm would make the best track on a piece composed using GarageBand. The mentor, like a coach, would monitor student performance, correct errors, and guide children toward correct responses (Schön, 1987). In this model, mentor and apprentice enter into what Rogoff (1990) describes as shared problem solving, where children determine the kinds of questions to formulate or how to begin the process of solving a problematic situation by gaining access to the skills and inner thoughts of the teacher. Children develop the skills of predicting, summarizing, questioning, and clarifying—abilities borrowed from the domain of language literacy and known as reciprocal teaching (Palinscar & Brown, 1984). Inclusion of predicting, summarizing, questioning, and clarifying by the mentor is at the core of the cognitive apprenticeship model as well as the sociotransformative model.

Embedded inside coaching is the concept of scaffolding. Scaffolding comes from Bruner's (1978) description of an expert assisting a novice or an apprentice. In scaffolding instruction, the mentor provides supports, or scaffolds, to facilitate the learner's development. The scaffolds foster the ability of the apprentice to build on prior knowledge and to process and internalize new information. Typically, the activities provided in scaffolded instruction are just beyond the level of what the learner can do alone (Olson, Platt, & Dieker, 2007). The mentor provides the scaffolds so that the apprentice can accomplish (with assistance) the tasks that he or she could otherwise not complete on his or her own. For example, to teach students the *Nocturne in E-flat Major, Op. 9, No. 2* by Frédéric Chopin, piano teacher Ingrid Clarfield (2002) scaffolds the learning into four stages. In stage one, the student learns background information about the piece and, with Clarfield, develops shorthand to write notes to themselves into the score. These notes become triggers to engage imagery while practicing the piece. In this stage, the student also plays exercises that prepare him or her for the technical challenges inside the piece. Clarfield has options for small hands and larger hands, adapting the exercises to accommodate each student apprentice. Together, piano student and piano teacher/mentor discuss articulation, dynamics, and pedaling. Clarfield encourages the student to predict the challenges he or she will face in the process of mastering the piece. In stage two, the student begins to play the piece slowly, applying the principles mastered in stage one and presented in a preparation and practice score prepared by the mentor. Together they discuss a variety of practice techniques. In stage three, the student polishes the piece and readies it for performance. Teacher and student reach closure on articulation, dynamics, and pedaling. Clarfield even suggests lyrics for the melody to guide imagery for the student as he or she plays. She provides an artistic performance score, including suggested YouTube clips for the student to watch. These clips are of various pianists playing the Nocturne. In these experiences, the mentor provides the necessary scaffolds, or steps, and the schema to challenge the student to engage the cognitive processes of questioning, predicting, summarizing, and clarifying throughout. While this is done one-on-one as in the traditional model, the mentor, in the kind of scaffolds and schema described, presents challenges to the student that integrate cognitive processes. In the case of the Chopin piece, mastering this particular Nocturne provides entry into the community of pianists who have the same Nocturne in their repertoire.

The next step in the sequence, articulation, includes the ways children speak about the content, explain and defend their point of view, and describe the steps they used to solve a particular problem (Collins, Brown, & Newman, 1987). There are three types of articulation: inquiry teaching, where teachers ask children a series of questions that prompt students to paraphrase, re-explain, summarize, and clarify; thinking aloud, where students articulate their thoughts while in the process of solving a problem; and role reversal, where the student apprentice becomes the teacher or mentor to a peer in group-learning situations.

Reflection provides students with opportunities to think deeply and introspectively and to internalize their learning, an idea that was inspired by the work of Collins et al. (1987). Within the school ensemble rehearsal, students might examine the similarities of and differences between their in-class performances of a work with that of a more advanced ensemble.

Within the exploration phase, students gain an understanding of how to investigate, research, and develop hypotheses. Such explorations are ripe for problem posing and problem solving. Under the tutelage of the mentor, children acquire expertise and formulate the habits of mind of thinking critically, and posing and solving problems. As this expertise advances, the scaffolding provided by the mentor is progressively withdrawn. This is called *fading*. Finally, the learner is able to complete the task or master the concepts independently (Chang, Chen, & Sung, 2002). The goal in this endeavor is for the apprentice to become independent of the mentor. The drum circle is an example of how exploration is operationalized. The mentor acts as facilitator, but as they continue to work together, over time the members make the musical decisions.

Sociotransformative apprenticeship

Our research working with children in music classes and musical ensembles suggests that children learn best within an apprenticeship framework that is sociotransformative (Abrahams, 2005; Rodriquez & Berryman, 2002). What distinguishes this model from the others is that in addition to the apprentice learning to master a skill or concept or body of content, the model aims for a change in perception on the part of the apprentice. This transformative perceptual change involves the apprentice discovering how the acquired skill, knowledge, or understanding is situated beyond the community of practice and in a broader context of the world. Such realization is evidence that the learner has not only constructed his or her own meaning, but has also acquired a critical consciousness (Freire, 1973) such that he or she can apply that meaning more globally. An example of this comes from our colleague Paul Head writing of his daughter, who is an example of one who has such a critically conscious habit of mind that enables her to make sophisticated musical decisions on her own. He writes,

> As the father of three teenage children, I have a good sense of what an adolescent child considers a meaningful musical experience. One daughter in particular has been especially diligent in building her music collection according to the new rules of the digital age—a process that was markedly different twenty or so years ago when I became an avid consumer of commercial music. She will spend hours on end surfing the Internet, seeking out not only the latest commercially available releases available for purchase but also working her way through a labyrinth of blogs and personal Web pages that give detailed accounts of live performances by her favorite artists, along with video and audio clips that provide much fodder for the infinite discussion that proliferates daily in cyberspace—all contributed by devoted fans who not only desire to chronicle their experiences but who also wish to share their reflections and reactions to the nuance of a particular performance, the sub text of the lyrics, and the unique and genuine qualities (or lack thereof) of the performer. (Head, 2011, p. 21)

Sociotransformative instruction is an orientation toward teaching and learning that is sensitive to how issues of power, gender, and equity influence both the subject matter and how it is taught. In the traditional and cognitive models of apprenticeship, the issues of power are clear and conventional. The mentor is in the position of power, and the apprentice is in a subservient position and vulnerable to abuses of power, marginalization, and hegemony. This is especially true if the mentor is male and the apprentice is female. Instead, in the sociotransformative model, mentors and their apprentices interact with each other in ways that are empowering and lead both to deeper understandings of the subject content matter and to skills in ways that stimulate critical thinking and action in socially relevant ways. Drawing from the theories of Vygotsky (1978), the sociotransformative framework suggests that knowledge and the application of such knowledge are socially constructed and thus the relationship of mentor with apprentice is reconceptualized.

There are four components to the sociotransformative model of apprenticeship: *dialogic conversation, authentic activity, metacognition*, and *reflexivity*. Each takes place through the natural social interaction of mentor with apprentice and apprentice with mentor in groups inside the classroom.

Dialogic conversation

During dialogic conversation the mentor engages with the apprentice in conversation to create "context-relevant meaning" (Rodriguez & Berryman, 2002, p. 1021). In this scenario, the apprentice not only hears what is being said, but also attends to the reasons why the mentor may choose a particular strategy or instructional schema. Dialogic conversation establishes trust between the mentor and the apprentices as well as creates a safe space for the scaffolding of learning experiences.

Authentic activity

Dewey (1938) described authentic activity when he wrote:

> An experience may be immediately enjoyable and yet promote the formation of a slack and careless attitude; this attitude then operates to modify the quality of subsequent experiences so as to prevent a person from getting out of them what they have to give. . . .[E]xperiences may be lively, vivid, and "interesting," yet their disconnectedness may artificially generate dispersive, disintegrated, centrifugal habits. (p. 26)

Such activities or experiences must be socially relevant and connected to the apprentice's everyday life. For example, in an elementary music classroom where the population is primarily Mexican American, students work with mentors to master the mariachi tradition rather than learning to play songs like "Hot Cross Buns" on recorders.

Metacognition

Metacognition happens when the apprentice takes control of his or her own learning. The acquisition of the skill or knowledge of the content or the ability to do something one has worked on over time, and do it at a high level of competence, is a goal for the apprentice and a desired outcome for the mentor. Metacognition is an extension of the concept of fading, described in the cognitive model; however, in the sociotransformative model the mentor fades only when he or she is convinced that the apprentice has not only mastered the skill, but has also acquired the personal agency and habits of mind to understand the concept or perform the skill in ways that demonstrate a critical consciousness. Mentors nurture apprentices to think about why what they are doing is important, how and why the strategies they use are important, and what other methods they might find effective.

Reflexivity

Reflexivity is an important component of the sociotransformative model of apprenticeship. It is connected to how the apprentice will act on the skill or concept taught by the mentor to demonstrate a value-added component. What makes this useful, important, and of value? Freire (1973) argued for the necessity of children acquiring a critical consciousness. Students, he believed, should be able to perceive the world in such a way that they can identify and act upon generative themes, which Freire identifies as "iconic representations that have a powerful emotional impact in the daily lives of learners" (1970, pp. 96–7).

Learning styles

In the sociotransformative model of apprenticeship, the mentor aligns to the apprentice's preferred learning style. In the 1980s educational psychologist Bernice McCarthy (1987, 2012) identified four distinct learning styles and labeled them type 1—imaginative learner, type 2—analytic learner, type 3—common sense learner, and type 4—dynamic learner. Our research (Abrahams, 1992; Abrahams & Abrahams, 2010, 2012; Abrahams & Head, 2005) has studied how these different learning types inform children's music learning and how children, as apprentices, interact with their mentors.

Type 1: Imaginative learners

Type 1 learners are imaginative learners who enjoy listening and sharing ideas. They are interested in people and culture and believe in their own experience. These learners rely on their feelings and thrive in environments rich with discussion. For imaginative learners and their mentors, learning is a social process where learners learn from more capable others who provide guidance or collaboration (Brown et al., 1989; Bruner, 1996; Rogoff, 1990; Vygotsky, 1978). As for the apprentice, classrooms are laboratories for musical imagination (Greene, 1995), where children work together to offer assistance and to solve musical problems. Children interact with each other, relating prior knowledge to new knowledge. Type 1 students want to make a strong personal connection with their mentor. This is important in the sociotransformative model of apprenticeship. Mentors for these children focus on facilitating individual growth, and helping their apprentices become more self-aware.

To best support this objective, mentors should include activities that involve social interaction and group work such as playing classroom instruments in an ensemble, movement and dance, and circle games.

Type 2: Analytic learners

Analytic learners, those labeled type 2, learn best by gathering data and thinking critically about ideas. Even in music, they enjoy traditional classrooms where they can watch, listen, and work alone. As musical people, they enjoy the theoretical aspects of the art form and love studying "about" music. Unlike type 1 learners, who may select a mentor because they like that person or think that the mentor likes them, the type 2 apprentices seek out mentors who will set clear expectations, set structured parameters, pay attention to detail, and strive for accuracy from themselves and from their apprentices.

Gardner (2006) spoke of minds that are both disciplined and synthesizing. In his definition, the disciplined mind is skilled at prediction and "knows how to work steadily over time to improve skill and understanding" (p. 3). The synthesizing mind "takes information from disparate sources, understands and evaluates that information objectively, and puts it together in ways that make sense to both the person and to others" (p. 3). Together, these characteristics combine to define musical intellect. The development of intellect is a desired outcome for type 2 learners.

Musicologists, for instance, engage musical intellect as they deconstruct various musics, while ethnomusicologists explore the characteristics of music from many places in the world. Gardner (2006) would describe these processes as synthesizing in that they incorporate "new findings and delineating new dilemmas is part and parcel of the work of any professional" (p. 6). Elementary school children who can recognize the recurring theme in a rondo or identify the oboe when listening to symphonic music evidence their musical intellect as well. Priorities for mentors of type 2 learners include a desire to transmit knowledge, to be accurate, and to work from structured plans rich with detail and facts.

Type 3: Common sense learners

As apprentices, children who are common sense learners, type 3, test theories and ideas, want to know how things work, and do best with hands-on experiences. In music classes, these youngsters like participatory experiences. While this is similar to the type 1 learner, these children are actually the opposite of the type 1 learner. What they do with their hands, playing instruments and the like, is for practical reasons. These are called "common sense" learners because they are pragmatists. Teachers and mentors of these children value productivity and competence and want to give their apprentices the skills they will need later in life. Mentors for these children encourage practical applications and design-measured rewards.

Best (1992) wrote, "virtually everyone should be able to think in and think up music, given the right training" (p. 4). While this statement may apply to all types of learners, this resonates well with common sense apprentices and their mentors. They do not want to waste time, but instead want the "right training." Creativity, Gardner (2006) suggests, is the ability to pose new questions or problems. He writes that a creative mind "conjures up fresh ways of thinking" (p. 3) and "arrives at unexpected answers" (p. 3). Csikszentmihalyi (cited in Gardner, 2006) refines this idea when he posits that "creativity occurs when—and only when—an individual or group product generated in a particular domain is recognized by the relevant field as innovative and, in turn, sooner or later, exerts a genuine, detectable influence on subsequent work in that domain" (p. 81). But, Gardner adds the caveat that such new creation "must find acceptance among knowledgeable consumers" (p. 3). This could also be about common sense learners. These children use the tools of music-making that are learned in one context and apply them in unique, innovative, and original ways such that they influence future musical efforts. It is transforming and liberating for the creator.

Type 4: Dynamic learners

McCarthy (1987, 2012) labels type 4 learners "dynamic." By this, she means that they learn by trial and error and are more likely to take risks than their peers of types 1, 2, and 3. These children rely on their natural instincts to arrive at conclusions. In music classes they like to try new things and love composing and improvising, and all forms of creative expression. Their mentors are interested in student self-discovery, experimental learning, experiences, and activities that appeal to the interests of their student apprentices.

For the type 4 children, musical performance is quite attractive because it presents opportunities that re-create the musical ideas of others. Musical performance is empowering when it triggers an emotional response from the performer or listener or both. In the school setting, musical performance provides the vehicle for the teacher to assess musical growth and understanding on the part of those performing. The sixth-grade chorus singing at the annual holiday concert is one obvious example. Nevertheless, the street musician playing his violin for patrons eating outside at a restaurant or for those waiting for the train on the subway platform is also an example.

Reciprocal teaching

The ability of children to predict, question, clarify, and summarize are elements of reciprocal teaching, an effective literacy strategy applied in the sociotransformative apprenticeship model. First identified by Palinscar and Brown (1984), reciprocal teaching is a process where children assist each other in finding solutions to problematic situations within the context of language literacy, and particularly reading. We extended the model and contextualized the learning in music, and Daniel Abrahams added "connecting" to the skill set (Abrahams & Abrahams, 2010, 2012).

Questioning is the first strategy of reciprocal teaching. In an apprenticeship setting, mentor and apprentice question each other, often the mentor posing a problem, and the apprentice solving the problem so that the apprentice, as in the case of Paul's teenage daughter (Head, 2011), can find ways to solve the problem on his or her own. Once this happens, the mentor fades into the background, and the apprentice is on his or her own to find the resources necessary to provide answers.

Clarifying is the next strategy of reciprocal teaching. In the sociotransformative apprentice–mentor relationship, each clarifies for the other. When called upon by the mentor, the apprentice demonstrates the appropriate skill or competency in question to the mentor. Alternatively, when questioned, the mentor clarifies for the apprentice. The mentor scaffolds experiences, helping the apprentice develop the requisite schema. For example, students in a middle-school band rehearsal might pose questions to the mentor concerning difficult or unfamiliar rhythms. Through the strategy of clarifying, the mentor might model aloud his or her process of figuring out a problematic rhythmic pattern using a variety of strategies. The learner, through the strategy of clarifying, gains access to and awareness of the mentor's thought processes and actions in figuring out a solution to the problematic rhythm. Once the apprentice uncovers the processes of the mentor, the student is more capable in attempting to perform, identify, and problem-solve other examples of difficult rhythmic patterns during the rehearsal process.

Predicting is central to reciprocal teaching. Through working collaboratively with the mentor and with peers, the apprentice learns to predict. Predictions are often mediated by culture. Children learn to expect the dominant chord to lead to a tonic chord because of the situated learning they have experienced. Teachers who advocate using Edwin Gordon's music learning theory often sing segments of a melody and stop toward the end, asking students to predict the resolution or to sing the root or tonic tone. In a framework of apprenticeship, the mentor scaffolds exercises for the apprentice to hone the ability to predict and test those predictions for accuracy.

Another component of reciprocal teaching is summarizing. To summarize is a higher-level thinking skill and central to the development of musical apprentices. Summarizing is the student's ability to identify and integrate the most important information within the music. An apprentice realizing that a certain element of music—such as meter, texture, or timbre—is the principal musical element in a particular piece or that issues of style are the most prominent challenge in a piece of music are examples of summarizing. Here is an example:

> For choirs, this aspect [summarizing] of reciprocal teaching engages students in the ability to summarize the text across sentences, paragraphs, or whole passages because understanding and communicating the text is paramount. A singer's initial focus will be on the text within musical phrases and then grow to encompass musical periods, then musical sections. (Abrahams & Abrahams, 2012, pp. 242–3)

Studying reciprocal teaching within the context of secondary-school large ensembles, we added connecting to the list of reciprocal teaching skills because the components of reciprocal teaching acted in ways that were interlocking and holistic (Abrahams & Abrahams, 2010, 2012). Within the sociotransformative apprenticeship model the apprentice learns to make these connections, seeing the schemas intersect, and, with guidance in the form of dialogue and reflection with the mentor, learns to act upon them. Action on the part of the apprentice leads to him or her creating meaningful connections between newly acquired musical knowledge, skills, and understandings and his or her environment and bringing about a critical consciousness that dramatically alters the apprentice's perspective. As a result of connecting, the apprentice is capable of applying meaning more globally and moving beyond the community of practice and into the broader context of the world.

Sociotransformative apprenticeship model in action

What follows are examples of how teachers have applied the sociotransformative model. The actual scenarios have been fictionalized; however, they are typical of the process. The names of the teachers and the schools are real; the children's names have been changed. The teachers edited their students' quotes before they were sent to us.

High school music mentors

Each year at the high school where she teaches, Suzanne (Schmidt, 2008) selects her top students to participate in a music mentor program. Once per week the students travel to a nearby elementary school to work with a small cohort of children who have been identified by their classroom teacher as worthy of experiences in music that are not provided in the regularly scheduled music classes.

In her own music classes, Suzanne prepares the student mentors who serve as her apprentices. She models appropriate teaching behaviors and coaches the student-mentor candidates as they peer teach in simulated situations that mirror the authentic activities they will enact when they go into the elementary school and work with the children assigned to them. Suzanne sequences or scaffolds each experience for them, moving from simple to complex, suggesting the schema, or mental structures, her future music mentors will need when they work with their own children apprentices. Woven into the experience is dialogic conversation, where she has substantial and significant discussions with her mentor candidates. Throughout the experience Suzanne and her students question what is important, why children should know or be able to do a particular task, and how best to provide meaningful critique. Suzanne's music mentors keep a reflective journal and share entries with her and the other members of the music mentoring team by posting to an online discussion board. The music mentor candidates work toward metacognition as they master the skills and strategies they will need when they work with the elementary children. Suzanne's theoretical framework is the sociotransformative apprenticeship model. Her candidates will replicate that model when they work with their own charges at the nearby primary school.

Beatrice is a high school senior. She plays French horn in the school band, sings in the choir, and has played piano since she was 5 years old. At the high school, Beatrice is also in Suzanne's advanced music theory class and was thrilled when Suzanne invited her to become a music mentor. Beatrice watched carefully as Suzanne modeled scaffolds. She participated thoughtfully with Suzanne and the others in the program in simulations, dialogic conversations, and reflective journaling. Now, Suzanne's role fades into the background, and she will watch Beatrice from the sidelines as she begins her term as a music mentor.

There are four children in Beatrice's third-grade cohort. On the first day, she meets Eric, a 9-year-old rapper who, with his cousin, has formed a group they call Revolution. Already, they have the rhythm scheme and dance moves secured for a rap and have selected a backbeat from YouTube. Unfortunately, their music teacher was not interested, telling them that "rap was not real music." But Eric does not agree and has different ideas. Unfortunately, he has become a discipline challenge for the music teacher during music class, claiming that those classes are not relevant. Beatrice performs her own rap for Eric and asks the other children to be the human backbeat. Over time, her goal for Eric is to find ways to use his love for rap and his creative energy as a crosswalk to other types, styles, and genres of music. She is particularly interested in showing him how others tell their stories in different musical formats and how these musical stories connect to the individual composers' lives.

Ryasia loves to sing. She has a beautiful voice but does not understand musical line or how to sing expressively. Beatrice wants to help Ryasia learn to sing with musicality, using her voice in ways that are both artistic and vocally healthy.

Courtland wants to play with his iPad mini. Beatrice wants to show him how the iPad can be a musical instrument and downloads apps that will enable him to write his own music. She quickly learns that Courtland succeeds when directions are clear and instructions are sequential. Courtland bonds with Beatrice because it is obvious to him that Beatrice knows her stuff.

Angela does not speak English very well. She recently moved from Puerto Rico. Her family speaks Spanish at home, and Angela struggles with communication. Beatrice wants to teach her some folk songs and music games in English to help her language skills improve.

Beatrice also wants to include group experiences where she can engage the children in some conversation, provide authentic musical experiences for them using the classroom instruments and technology in the room, and help the children, even at their young age, see how music opens up their world in exciting and significant ways.

Beginning band

Ryan John was in his first year of teaching band to 9- and 10-year-old children at Léman Manhattan Preparatory School, a private school in the financial district of New York City. He was hired to start an instrumental program in the lower school and to organize beginning bands for the fourth-grade (9-year-olds) and fifth-grade (10-year-olds) pupils. In addition to the band rehearsals, which occurred twice weekly for 45 minutes each, Ryan met all of the students weekly for 30–45-minute lessons in small groups of like instruments. Because of some conflicts with the school schedule, a few of the students also studied privately with him. All were first-year beginners.

Ryan accepted the position because the philosophy of the school centers on the importance of musical training and its connection to professional achievement (from the school website). The curriculum "is designed to empower all students with the requisite skills and understanding for future success in all areas of musical study. In the arts, it focuses specifically on developing instrumental and vocal performance capabilities, fluency of audiation, and increasing depth of musical literacy."[1] In a televised news report highlighting the new string program, one student said, "In violin you have to listen very well to see if you are playing the right notes or the right melody and that sort of helps me listen better in school."[2]

The curriculum for beginning band, in place when Ryan arrived, guides students to develop the fundamental skills of playing their instruments, a disposition toward being an ensemble player, and the habits of mind a musician needs to think reflectively and critically.

Ryan's role in the band class was the mentor, and he viewed the novice instrumentalists as apprentices inside a community of practice (Wenger, 1998). Throughout the group lessons and band rehearsals, he applied principles of the sociotransformative apprenticeship model by adapting schema to meet individual student learning styles and developed scaffolds that engaged the apprentices in reciprocal teaching. His goal was to nurture the children's journey to become young musicians.

The four components of the sociotransformative apprenticeship model (dialogic conversation, authentic activity, metacognition, and reflexivity) were present throughout the curriculum. For instance, while the focus of each instrumental class was on skill acquisition, opportunities for dialogic conversation in the form of critique by the mentor with the child after he or she played was a regular part of the class routine. In addition, students engaged in dialogic conversation to become active members of their community (Rodriguez & Berryman, 2002) by completing reflective blogs. Engaging students in summarizing, predicting, clarifying, questioning, and connecting, elements of reciprocal teaching, were the schemas Ryan used for dialogic conversation and ways the cohort of apprentices could scaffold each other's learning.

For example, in one of the group lessons for the flutes, Rachel began taking high, shallow breaths as she played her flute. When she finished playing, Ryan asked, "Did you notice anything in your breathing?" She replied, "I wasn't paying attention to it. I was focused on the notes." Using modeling, Ryan said, "Let me show you. It's an exaggeration," and he demonstrated what she was doing. "The shoulders. You are raising them when you inhale. Try breathing lower." He demonstrated a proper diaphragmatic breath. "I wasn't focused on that so much," said Rachel. She then played the excerpt again with focus on her breathing. This was an issue that was best addressed through teacher observation, modeling, coaching, and scaffolding. By bringing attention to Rachel's breathing issue, the other members of the class became more attentive to their breathing when it was their turn to play.

In another class lesson, Keith, a saxophone player, had difficulty keeping a steady tempo. At the conclusion of Keith's playing, Ryan asked, "What did you think about your playing?" Keith replied, "I played the hard parts slower." Using coaching that included strategies from reciprocal teaching, Ryan scaffolded Keith's thinking to assist him in gaining understanding of his problem and to engage in problem solving. Ryan asked Keith, "What do you think you might do to correct the problem?" Keith responded, "I could play the whole piece slower." Engaging in problem solving, Keith continued, "I could practice the hard parts more times than the easy ones." Ryan replied, "Yes!"

It was Ryan's goal to intentionally develop opportunities for the children to learn to play their instruments within a social context, with individuals and groups of peer practitioners to provide scaffolding. Students coached each other in excerpts from the lesson books and band music. At one point toward the December holidays, more advanced students had the opportunity to conduct the band in rehearsal. That too, constituted an authentic activity that moved the learning from the abstract to the concrete. Ryan created scaffolds that encouraged a meta-cognitive approach. His apprentices always connected what they were doing and how they were learning to concerns for relevance and value-added experience. Reflection happened at each step, with Ryan and his students keeping introspective journals and sharing reflections with each other. Several class sessions were video recorded, and each young musician received feedback from his or her peers in the class and from the mentor/teacher. Consistent with sociotransformative characteristics, students constantly switched roles between player and evaluator, allowing the mentor to fade more into the background.

Throughout Ryan's engagement as mentor, his apprentices exhibited evidence of metacognition through revealing comments in their journals. For example, at the beginning of the semester, one 10-year-old student wrote: "I always loved watching those guys on the street playing drums on garbage buckets. They made it look so easy. But when I started lessons, I began to realize that there was a lot to learn. Keeping the beat going for an entire song was hard." Ryan was pleased to see that by the end of the term, the student had acquired some basic skills and used more appropriate vocabulary to describe them. After the first concert, the student wrote:

> We have made lots of progress since the beginning of the year. We have turned from blasting out random notes to synchronized and masterful musicians. Over the months, our Band group has done an excellent job at melody and harmony.

The term "masterful musicians" was one Ryan frequently used with his pupils.

Throughout the year, each apprentice in the class engaged in problem posing and problem solving within a context authentic to practice. By mastering each schema and scaffold, the child apprentices acquired mastery of the large musical concepts that occurred contextually within the practice of learning a musical instrument and playing as a member of the ensemble. Examples included the importance of phrasing and shaping a musical line, keeping a steady tempo, and following a conductor.

After students had mastered the ability to play several different notes, Ryan used actual musical excerpts of familiar songs for students to play together in the band. As expected, and consistent with each one's learning style and skill proficiency, the students had different entry points to assess their work. In a reflection, Ryan wrote:

> I began class by having the children work in pairs with another child who had chosen the same instrument. Applying the strategies of reciprocal teaching, together, the students predicted, clarified, questioned, summarized, and connected by sharing insights they had found while preparing the musical excerpt individually. Some of them found the same challenges, and some had different ideas about how phrases might be played.

Ryan noticed that when playing in the band, each child was a better player than when he or she had worked alone in individual or small group lessons. As their mentor, this was exactly what Ryan wanted to happen. In all, everyone brought something different to the community and had an individual perspective on his or her work. Their individual learning styles mediated part of this. Scott asked his older brother, who also played trombone, to show him how a piece should sound. As a type 1 imaginative learner, Scott needed to understand context. Rich was a type 3 common sense learner and only practiced the hard parts; he thought that would be practical. Michelle and Tia were type 2 analytic learners and methodically practiced each line five times before moving to the next. Thus, there were multiple perspectives and multiple solutions to mastering the challenges in each musical excerpt.

After four months, children had learned enough pieces to play a public concert. They were nervous, as was Ryan. Ryan believed that moving from the security of the band rehearsal room to the public concert hall was a test of his success as the mentor. Students appeared to gain a deeper understanding of their individual and collective roles in the ensemble and applied their newly acquired knowledge in a socially relevant way. In a reflection, Trish describes some of her struggles with playing clean attacks on her trumpet. At the beginning of the semester she wrote:

> The first day we used instruments we didn't do very good, we sounded like a dying goat or an ensemble that didn't really know what it was doing. I was nervous because I hadn't played trumpet in a while and only just learned a little at my other school last year.

After the concert she wrote:

> We have made a lot of progress since the beginning of the year. I have learned how to play pitches on my instrument using the correct fingerings and reading the notes on the page. In the trumpet section, we have learned how to play in unison, which is when we play the same note for a consistent time and sound like one person. Some of the other musical concepts we have covered this fall are whole notes, half notes, and quarter notes and keeping a steady tempo. My favorite part of band is the challenge of getting to learn how to play an instrument. When I can't get a note right, I have to work to get it right and push myself a little to succeed.

Ryan was pleased that his students connected what they accomplished as solo players in private lessons to members of a performing community of practice they called band. As a group, students gained a better understanding of the preparation they needed to be effective contributors during the rehearsal process and began to see the role of the ensemble player more globally. This global view and the ability to see oneself inside this view were a goal of Freire's (1973) teaching and a component of critical consciousness. This was also a goal of the sociotransformative apprenticeship model, and the insights Ryan's students provided confirmed its success.

Ryan worked as a mentor analyzing the experiences of the students, his apprentices in a beginning instrumental program that functioned as a community of practice. Everyone mentored one another as the students negotiated learning to become young musicians in an instrumental ensemble. Ryan's experiences revealed that the apprentices navigated along a continuum, with one end rooted in their practice as instrumental music performers and the other end rooted in a community of practice. Spiraling around the continuum were the authentic band experiences or scaffolds in which learners engaged. As Ryan's interaction with them as formal mentor evolved, his students took action to problem solve and interact more with each other. They were changed by their membership in the community. By applying the tenets of the sociotransformative apprenticeship model, which included observation, modeling, scaffolding, and the building of schema, students began to feel empowered as young musicians and as members of a community of practice.

Conclusions

Beatrice, the young music mentor, experienced similar positive results at the end of her time with Eric, Ryasia, Courtland, and Angela. The topics of Eric's raps changed from superheroes to home, family, friends, and real things in his life. Ryasia sang with improved breath support and began listening to better role models through recordings of children singing appropriately that Beatrice chose for her. Courtland composed an instrumental piece on his iPad mini and Angela's classroom teacher reported that her reading level had improved and her vocabulary had significantly expanded. And even as fourth and fifth graders, Ryan's band members were able to articulate their transformation, as evidenced by Kyle, who wrote: "We masterful musicians have gained such confidence in our instruments that we can even play at a concert."

Whether music teachers acknowledge it or not, or whether they label the relationships they have with their students as one of apprentice and mentor, the traditional and cognitive models are seen frequently. Through our investigation of three forms of apprenticeship—traditional, cognitive, and sociotransformative—we found that children and their teachers are most changed when mentors apply instructional strategies from the literature on reciprocal teaching and align instruction to each student's learning style.

Today, within a sociotransformative apprenticeship model children can move from feeling powerless to one of empowerment as they journey with their mentor to master musical skills and become musicians and life-long musical people.

Reflective questions

1 Of the three models of apprenticeship presented in this chapter, which model do you believe best serves your personal teaching philosophy and practice?

2 Were you ever the apprentice to a mentor? If so, which type of mentor was he or she?

3 In what ways might you apply the sociotransformative apprenticeship model in your own music teaching?

4 How might you apply strategies of reciprocal teaching to differentiate instruction for students of different learning styles? What scaffolds might you apply to foster a critical consciousness among your students?

5 What do you think is your learning style? How might that influence your teaching style and the interactions you have mentoring own students?

Notes

1 Léman Manhattan Preparatory School website. Retrieved from <http://www.lemanmanhattan.org/podium/default.aspx?t=204&nid=690183&sdb=1&bl=/default.aspx>, para. 5.

2 Retrieved from <http://www.lemanmanhattan.org/podium/default.aspx?t=204&nid=690183&sdb=1&bl=/default.aspx>. Also available at <http://www.youtube.com/watch?v=UqX1QSOrRw0>.

Key sources

Abrahams, F., & Abrahams, D. (2012). The impact of reciprocal teaching on the development of musical understanding in high school student members of performing ensembles: An action research. In K. Swanwick (Ed.), *Music education: Major themes in education* (Vol. 3, pp. 239–59). New York: Routledge.

Burwell, K. (2013). Apprenticeship in music: A contextual study for instrumental teaching and learning. *International Journal of Music Education*, 31(3), 276–91. doi: 10.1177/0255761411434501.

Collins, A., Brown, J. S., & Newman, S. E. (1989). Cognitive apprenticeship: Teaching the crafts of reading, writing, and mathematics. In L. B. Resnick (Ed.), *Knowing, learning, and instructional essays in honor of Robert Glaser* (pp. 453–92). Hillsdale, NJ: Erlbaum.

Freire, P. (1973). *Education for critical consciousness*. New York: Continuum.

Lave, J., & Wenger, E. (1991). *Situated learning: Legitimate peripheral participation*. New York: Cambridge University Press.

Wenger, E. (1998). *Communities of practice: Learning, meaning and identity*. New York: Cambridge University Press.

Reference list

Abrahams, F. (1992). Using a learning styles approach to help "at risk" youth in music. *General Music Today*, 6(1), 22–6.

Abrahams, F. (2005). The application of critical pedagogy to music teaching and learning: A literature review. *Update—Applications of Research in Music Education*, 23(2), 12–22.

Abrahams, F., & Abrahams, D. (2010). The impact of reciprocal teaching on the development of musical understanding in high school student members of performing ensembles: An action research. *Visions of Research in Music Education*, 15, 1–33.

Abrahams, F., & Abrahams, D. (2012). The impact of reciprocal teaching on the development of musical understanding in high school student members of performing ensembles: An action research. In K. Swanwick (Ed.), *Music education: Major themes in education* (Vol. 3, pp. 239–59). New York: Routledge.

Abrahams, F., & Head, P. D. (2005). *Case studies in music education* (2nd ed.). Chicago, IL: GIA.

Baillie, H. (1956). A London gild of musicians, 1460–1530. *Proceedings of the Royal Musical Association*, 83rd session (pp. 15–28). Oxford, UK: Oxford University Press on behalf of the Royal Musical Association.

Best, H. M. (1992). Music curricula in the future. *Arts Education Policy Review, 94*, 2–7.

Brandt, R. (1993). On teaching for understanding: A conversation with Howard Gardner. *Educational Leadership, 50*(7), 4–7.

Brown, J. S., Collins, A., & Duguid, P. (1989). Situated cognition and the culture of learning. *Experimental Researcher, 18*(1), 32–42.

Bruner, J. (1978). The role of dialogue in language acquisition. In A. Sinclair, R. J. Jarvella, & W. J. M. Levelt (Eds.), *The child's conception of language* (pp. 241–56). New York: Springer-Verlag.

Bruner, J. (1986). *Actual minds, possible worlds.* Cambridge, MA: Harvard University Press.

Bruner, J. (1996). *The culture of education.* Cambridge, MA: Harvard University Press.

Burwell, K. (2013). Apprenticeship in music: A contextual study for instrumental teaching and learning. *International Journal of Music Education, 31*(3), 276–91. doi: 10.1177/0255761411434501.

Chang, K., Chen, I., & Sung, Y. (2002). The effect of concept mapping to enhance text comprehension and summarization. *The Journal of Experimental Education, 71*(1), 5–23.

Clarfield, I. J. (2002). *Nocturne in E-flat major, Op. 9, No. 2 by Frédéric Chopin.* Van Nuys, CA: Alfred Publishing.

Collins, A., Brown, J. S., & Newman, S. E. (1987). *Cognitive apprenticeship: Teaching the craft of reading, writing and mathematics* (Technical Report No. 403). Cambridge, MA: BBN Laboratories, Centre for the Study of Reading, University of Illinois.

Collins, A., Brown, J. S., & Newman, S. E. (1989). Cognitive apprenticeship: Teaching the crafts of reading, writing, and mathematics. In L. B. Resnick (Ed.), *Knowing, learning, and instructional essays in honor of Robert Glaser* (pp. 453–92). Hillsdale, NJ: Erlbaum.

Dewey, J. (1938). *Experience and education.* New York: Macmillan.

Educational Theory of Apprenticeship. (n.d.). In Wikipedia. Retrieved from <http://en.wikipedia.org/wiki/Educational_Theory_of_Apprenticeship>.

Freire, P. (1970). *Pedagogy of the oppressed.* New York: Optimum.

Freire, P. (1973). *Education for critical consciousness.* New York: Continuum.

Gardner, H. (2006). *Five minds for the future.* Boston, MA: Harvard Business Review Press.

Greene, M. (1995). Art and imagination: Reclaiming the sense of possibility. *Phi Delta Kappan, 76*(5), 378–82.

Head, P. D. (2011). Hearing between the lines: Promoting choral artistry in rehearsal and performance. In F. Abrahams & P. D. Head (Eds.), *Teaching music through performance in middle school choirs* (pp. 23–36). Chicago, IL: GIA.

Jørgensen, H. (2000). Student learning in higher instrumental education: Who is responsible? *British Journal of Music Education, 17*(1), 67–77.

Lave, J., & Wenger, E. (1991). *Situated learning: Legitimate peripheral participation.* New York: Cambridge University Press.

McCarthy, B. (1987). *The 4MAT system: Teaching to learning styles with right/left mode techniques.* Barrington, IL: EXCEL.

McCarthy, B. (2012). *The learning cycle, the 21st century and millennial learners.* Wauconda, IL: About Learning.

Olson, J., Platt, J., & Dieker, L. A. (2007). *Teaching children and adolescents with special needs* (5th ed.). Upper Saddle River, NJ: Pearson.

Palinscar, A. S., & Brown, A. L. (1984). Reciprocal teaching of comprehension—fostering and comprehension-monitoring activities. *Cognition and Instruction, 1*(2), 117–75.

Persson, R. S. (2000). Survival of the fittest or the most talented? *Journal of Secondary Gifted Education, 12*(1), 25–39.

Rodriguez, A. J., & Berryman, C. (2002). Using sociotransformative constructivism to teach for understanding in diverse classrooms: A beginning teacher's journey. *American Educational Research Journal, 39*(4), 1017–45.

Rogoff, B. (1990). *Apprenticeship in thinking: Cognitive development in social context*. New York: Oxford University Press.

Schmidt, S. M. (2008). Impact of a music peer mentoring and cross-age tutoring program on the emerging musicianship of advanced high school music theory students: A case study of students participating in a music mentors program at one suburban high school (Unpublished master's thesis). Rider University, Lawrenceville, NJ.

Schön, D. A. (1983). *The reflective practitioner: How professionals think in action*. New York: Basic Books.

Schön, D. A. (1987). *Educating the reflective practitioner: Toward a new design for teaching and learning in the profession*. San Francisco, CA: Jossey-Bass.

Vygotsky, L. S. (1978). *Mind in society: The development of higher psychological processes*. Cambridge, MA: Harvard University Press.

Wenger, E. (1998). *Communities of practice: Learning, meaning and identity*. New York: Cambridge University Press.

Chapter 30

Global practices

Patricia Shehan Campbell

Global practices: Introduction

Children are learning the music of their heritage, and of children's culture, from their earliest childhood experiences. Across the globe, they know similarities in their early developing musical expressions and interests, and in the manner through which they acquire music. Yet even as they grow musically in ways that are common across cultures, they are also musically enculturated so as to reflect the local facets of their homes, families, and neighborhood communities. They are trained and entrained, educated and schooled, according to national policies and cultural preferences.

This chapter examines the acquisition by children of musical knowledge in selected environments, with attention to the role of music within their society, and the means of transmission that are traditionally practiced by adults in the process of passing on musical repertoire and techniques, behaviors, and values. In exploring global practices of children's learning of music, and through music their learning of social mores, reference will be made to the cultural underpinnings of children's own playful repertoire, as well as to their musical heritage of adult-influenced culture in which they are enculturated and schooled. Attention will be drawn to cases of music learning engagements among children and youth in Ireland, Japan, The Philippines, Thailand, within North American First Nations circumstances, and in a selection of societies spread across eastern and western Africa. While the promise of a full global scope on the subject is tantalizing, it was necessary to select and only briefly sample musical cultures, with the aim of highlighting events and behaviors in the process of transmitting and acquiring music. The writer's own North American perspective may surface here in references to geographic places and peoples "off the beaten track" in the Americas, yet the fieldwork of notable scholars (often American ethnomusicologists) of various music cultures across the world is consulted and cited for issues and insights. Similarities and distinctions will be evident, and prominent techniques will be traced to their use in formal settings such as school and the one-on-one private lesson where musical training is known for its successful process of teacher–student interactions.

Music learning by degrees of formality

There are constructs to consider in a discussion of children's global practices in music learning, each of them definitive yet also somewhat overlapping and adding meaning to the other. A spectrum of learning may be found, extending from the most formal means to the non-formal processes found beyond institutionalized settings, all the way to completely informal, indirect, and unintentional forms of learning. Learning may be defined through a differentiation of it as a) formal, occurring through a teacher's intervention in highly structured settings such as school, b) non-formal and only partly guided, occurring outside institutionalized settings through the prompting of non-consecutive directives, frequently by expert musicians to novices, and c) encul-turative, occurring naturally, non-consciously, and without direct instructional activity of any sort (Campbell, 1998/2010, 2001).

The first realm of learning is thoroughly linked to the standard processes evidenced in formal institutions where teachers' selection, presentation, and rehearsal of students are in operation to ensure that explicit knowledge and skills are learned, while the second, non-formal process may be a father's occasional coaching at home of his daughter in the bar chords on a guitar, or a neighbor's infrequent modeling for a youngster of repertoire and techniques at the piano. In the last realm, enculturative learning, the psychic structure of a societal group is passed from one generation to the next through a cultural immersion process, so that a child develops an implicit understanding of the knowledge and values of a repertoire by nature of his membership and participation in that society. Language and communications, including self-identity, gender role, kinesthetics (body language), and daily rhythms are learned but not taught; they are acquired in ways that are automatic and outside children's own conscious awareness. These cultural patterns appear always to have been there as part of the ambience of a people's lifestyle, permeating the manner and style of their thought, expression, and behavior (Hall, 1992).

Further differentiations and descriptions of learning have been offered: apprenticeships and live-in private study with a teacher (as in the case of Thai *piphat* houses or Indian *gharanas*) out-side of institutionalized settings, growth-oriented experiences that are arranged within a commu-nity (such as Suzuki instruction), and socialization, the process by which a group shares its beliefs and values in a learner- (rather than teacher-) constructed learning experience (Jorgensen, 1997). There may be further gradations than these, yet it is useful to consider them as degrees of formal-ity in the means by which music is transmitted and acquired. These spectral points of music learn-ing, along with particular techniques of pedagogy and reception by children and other learners, will find their illustration in the selected cultures described in the next section.

Multiple bases for the study of children

Through a diversity of disciplines, music learning as global practice can be explored, and a con-ceptualization of its features can be understood. Scholars of anthropology, ethnomusicology, sociology, and (music) education are only beginning to awaken to the study of children from their own perspective, and as such are discovering their perceived beliefs, interests, and needs (Boynton & Kok, 2006; Campbell & Wiggins, 2013; Lum & Whiteman, 2012). Even while Rousseau's *Emile* drew attention two centuries ago to the unique conditions of children and childhood, as a group they have always existed on the sidelines and in the margins of disciplines. A movement is afoot to know children as they naturally are within their local social and cultural environments, with intent to piece their culture-specific cases together in order to develop a broader and more glo-bal understanding of them. The recent emphases given by these various disciplinary fields to the study of children are worthy of consideration prior to a review of culture cases that probe music learning practices, if only to explain the scant attention which children have received in the past concerning their own cultural, artistic, and specifically musical expressions. In many instances, they have been swept together with adult novices and beginning students in a discussion of the transmission of a musical tradition, even when there may be reason to believe that children learn in ways that are unique to them.

Tracing the evolution of children's music and its relationship (or not) to adult culture is a task ahead that may require the expertise of scholars from multiple disciplines. How does the music of a Malay child differ from that of children in Labrador, or Yoruba culture? Will these children sound alike as members of child culture, or will they vary by way of their sociocultural influences? In fact, will Malay children differ also in the music that they express, based upon the region in which they live, and the economic and social condition of their families? What features of the mature "adult" music of a culture are found in children's music? How is children's music more alike than different, cross-culturally? When does children's music end and youth music begin? How do the unique facets of contemporary children's music and culture hang on and shape adult music? Such questions are likely directives for scholarly study of children and their expressive selves.

Children, their developmental processes and practices, and their means of growing into the knowledge systems of their culture and society, were never central to the scholarly concerns of anthropologists. They were marginalized in anthropological descriptions of social organization and kinship, individual personality, and collective culture, and have even been dismissed altogether by adult "outsiders" to their culture (Lancy, 2008; Schwartzman, 2001). Where children did surface in the literature, it was often as a means of gauging their imitation of adults or tracing the origin and development of adult behaviors. Typically, anthropologists were concerned with what adults do to children, and what adults give to children or make for children. An "anthropology of children" is a fairly recent phenomenon within the field, in which children are increasingly examined for who they are within culture, and even as their own culture (Goldman, 1998; Hardman, 1973; Montgomery, 2009; Stephens, 1995). Where anthropologists once used children as specimens for examining, collecting, and measuring culture, frequent and more rigorous "child-focused studies" (Benthall, 1992) in anthropology are beginning to be aimed at understanding children themselves. In the last decade, studies of children for their family and peer relationships, household activity, school achievement, spiritual development, and religious beliefs reflect and foreshadow a deeper commitment to the study of children by anthropologists.

Likewise, an "ethnomusicology of children" is only just beginning to emerge (Campbell, 1998/2010; Minks, 2002). Early studies of musical culture assumed that children passively received the artistic and linguistic expressions from adults, participating in the song and dance that came "from above to below." Children were left out of descriptions of a musical culture, as they were viewed by ethnomusicologists as incomplete in their representation of adult expressive practices. Diffusionist scholars, mostly active as folklorists (if not anthropologists at the edge of ethnomusicology), collected children's songs to examine as the source of understanding not just the concept of "child as primitive," but also the "primitive as child." A study of their songs was considered a way for knowing children as early "stages" of human development, thus a means of examining theories of sociocultural evolution. Cross-cultural comparisons of children's musical expressions surfaced occasionally in ethnomusicology, if only to seek a more homogenous child culture that transcends specific music cultures (Brailiou, 1984; Herzog, 1950; Whiteman & Campbell, 2012). Socialization of music-cultural norms has been of interest to scholars who contribute to an enculturative paradigm, where adult-to-child sociocultural education is examined for its influences in raising (musical) citizens within communities (Blacking, 1967/1995; Waterman, 1956). In the last decade, however, border crossings by music educators employing an ethnomusicological method have brought attention to children's musical expressions as a means of studying their patterns of thought and social behavior (Campbell, 2003).

As in anthropology and ethnomusicology, children were less ignored by sociologists than minimalized and moved to the rim of more central concerns. They were considered more for what can be known about adult society than for who they are in their current lives, their needs, and their desires (Corsaro, 1997; Lancy, 2008). Rather than viewing children in the process of constructing their own social worlds, sociologists typically examined their socialization, the processes by which they are shaped by family and passively developed into adult members of their society. Early work of a behavioristic mode gave way to a study of their cognitive development (best represented in the work of Jean Piaget), after which a sociocultural view was formulated of their internalization of culture (as in Vygotsky's approach). (While the two theorists were contemporaries, it was not until Vygotsky's work was translated into English that his perspective on broader cultural contexts of children became influential beyond a Russian-speaking readership.) Piagetian thought emphasized developmental outcomes, however, with little attention to the complexity of children's own social structures, their collective activities, and their membership as active participants in both children's and adults' cultures.

An understanding of children as children, as having their own identities, growing in the midst of their own peer culture, in the locus of their roles within the family, and under the influence or through interaction with mediated forces, is yet to be discovered within the realm of sociological method. Some sociologists are providing frameworks for studying the status of children and childhood, constructing relevant metatheories and suitable methodologies (James, Jenks, & Prout, 1998; Mayall, 2002; Montgomery, 2009). Such perspectives would be well suited to music-education research, in which the study of children at musical play and in non-formal learning circumstances might lend insight to their academic and social–emotional behaviors at school. A sociological approach would be likely to shed light on children's musical experiences within families and peer groups, and a pastiche of local cases might provide a global understanding of their socio-musical nature.

Research by music teacher-scholars

Music education scholarship has been concerned with the musical achievement of children and adolescents, and the instructional procedures and curricular values of teachers within elementary and secondary school music courses and in tertiary programs of music and music teacher education. Topics for study in the field have included children's development of music perception abilities, their singing skills, and their capacities as instrumentalists, composers (and improvisers), and eurhythmic "movers" and dancers. Secondary-school students have been less likely subjects than elementary students, although some attention is paid to skill development and attitudes of students in choral and instrumental ensembles. Research has also concentrated on the pre-service training of university students as musicians and teachers, and of practicing teachers' attitudes and in-service training. Clearly, music education scholarship has been centered on the outcomes of formal instruction, with attention to teachers as curriculum designers, communicators, conductors, and facilitators, and their students as beneficiaries of this instruction. Much less attention has been paid to their non-formal and informal music-learning processes and children's natural means of learning through socialization and play (Campbell, 1998/2010; Harwood, 1998; Marsh, 1997, 2008). British scholars working within the overlaps of sociology, psychology, and education are notable for their attention to children's socialization in music and informal music learning processes, as well as to their emergent identities as performing musicians, listeners, and consumers of popular forms of mediated music (Hargreaves & North, 1997; Juslin & Sloboda, 2001; MacDonald, Hargreaves, & Miell, 2002). The examination of children's "musical incubation" and musical engagement at home and in school has been a developing interest among Scandinavian scholars, too, notably Bjorkvold's *The muse within* (1992). Yet global practices of children's music and music learning have not been addressed systematically. An understanding of children's natural inclinations and interests, and their interactions with siblings, peers, and various adults in (and beyond) musical venues, may lead to understanding effective avenues for their in-school learning of musical skills, repertoire, and overall knowledge.

Questions of children's views, experiences, and behaviors are increasingly being put to children by disciplinary scholars, so as to investigate their sense of themselves, and of the society and culture in which they live. Adjustments of theoretical and methodological orientations are beginning to bring out the expressive voice of children on their thoughts and actions. Such developments are long overdue, however, such that an understanding of cross-cultural patterns of children's music learning now comes largely through the scholarship on music and its transmission among adults. This adult-oriented perspective will become clear in a recounting of culture-cases that address the manner in which music learning unfolds for young people, and by extension how it is taught and transmitted in a selection of traditions and locations in the world. Running through the descriptive text as a central strand are fieldwork observations of children at the edge of adult culture, learning by doing, living in musical worlds that are steered and directed by adults, listening intently, or lapping up the soundscape into their daily lives. There is an acknowledgement of music across the world as an aural expression, too, and thus the aural–oral components will be noted as prominent in the means by which it is transmitted to and acquired by children. Despite the mostly marginal mention of children in the extant scholarship on music in and as culture, a careful telling and interpretation of it may offer provocative points in the study of global practices of the child as musician.

Lilting the legacy of a cultural heritage (Ireland)

Irish tunes, from sung ballads to the jigs, hornpipes, and reels of flutes and fiddles, have long been learned by ear. The traditional transmission and learning process is a social one, where novice and accomplished musicians alike have continued a traditional give-and-take process through the socio-musical realm of the group session, and in the fashion of a personalized lesson with an expert musician. Musical elders act as role models, offering to young and less-experienced singers and players the musical repertoire and the stylistic nuances and technicalities of their performance. They pass on social behavior and history as well, in which the "Celtic Tiger" character of a post-modern and economically successful Ireland can be viewed as but a recent development away from the rich traditions of a long-standing rural agrarian society.

Children are naturally there in the midst of family music-making in traditional Ireland, in those families with members who have for decades and even centuries fiddled, played flute, pipes, harp, or concertina, or sung *sean-nos* style. They are there also for celebrations of weddings, christenings, holidays, and family reunions at which music and dance are prominent features. They may participate in the equally festive occasions of the wake, when the memory of the deceased is honored in the family home and tribute is paid through song and sessions lasting long into the night and over several days. Like the air they breathe, music surrounds the children of professional and amateur musicians in Ireland, and the melodies become a part of their natural sonic fabric. In the changing scene of a contemporary Ireland, adults and children, including those with no past family history in musical practice, are finding their musical selves as an important component of their Irish identity (O'Suilleabhain, 2004).

Professional performers recall house parties as one important context of their musical learning. Mary McNamara, a concertina player growing up in the west-coast county of Clare, recalled that her father would take the children to his sessions: "he would go to different houses . . . maybe twice a week and we'd sit down and we'd listen to these musicians. And listen to the stories they had to tell, listen to them playing. We'd have the tea and the corncake and all the rest, and then we'd play a few tunes with them, might dance a set" (Hast & Scott, 2004, p. 44). As in the case of so many Irish musicians who grew up with music as part of their family activity, her participation as a child at these musical house parties consisted mostly of listening. The music was just part of a scene that mixed well with visits with family and neighbors, conversation, dancing, and tea.

Just as it is natural to listen, it follows that children living within an environment where Irish traditional music is actively performed also "pick up" instruments to play. Pennywhistles are sometimes played by children as an entry-point to instrumental music, as they are useful in un-loading the tunes that settle in the ear from countless listening occasions. Some pick up the fiddle, or transfer tunes from pennywhistle to the Irish flute, and girls might be drawn to the concertina as an acceptable woman's instrument. Years of listening to the elders in their informal playing together form the basis of their repertoire and sense of style, so that performance can advance more rapidly than if they had not absorbed the music. Children may graduate into lessons with more expert players, and of course continue to learn within the socio-musical realm of the session.

With the growth of Irish national identity in the early part of the twentieth century, the markers of Irish culture—its Gaelic language and its Catholic religion—were promoted in government-sponsored schools for children and youth. This promotion of the Irish national language as part of state policy led to the support of traditional Irish song. By the early 1930s Irish song and the litur-gical repertoire of the Catholic Church were widespread in the national schools (McCarthy, 1999). Pennywhistles were an additional development in school music instruction, so that Irish song and common tunes could be performed together in class groups of students playing monophonically *en masse* under the tutelage of their teacher. Thus it was that children at large and far beyond the families of musicians came to know in a formal fashion a standard musical repertoire. Such a system of musical education is continuing in some schools, even as curricular changes have also entered the scene to include Western art music and occasionally other world traditions as well.

One of the strongest contemporary supports for the continuation of traditional music outside school, and a means of musically training children and youth of Ireland in their cultural music, is the organization known as *Comhaltas Ceoltoiri Eireann* (or just "Comhaltas"). Established in 1951, the organization seeks to promote Irish traditional music, dance, and language nationally and abroad, by motivating the young to remain actively involved in learning these traditions. The funding of more than 400 branches in Ireland and internationally is based largely on govern-ment grants, which thus finance the competitions that occur at county, regional, provincial, and all-Ireland levels. The competitions include all major traditional instruments, "lilting" (singing vocables to the dance tunes), Irish and English singing, and are divided into age levels to suit those children under 12 years, youth from 12 to 15, from 15 to 18, and over 18. The Comhaltas branches are responsible for organizing the community schools, arranging sessions, teaching the music, and preparing the young musicians for competitions. The songs and tunes are selected by Comhaltas, and so both the musical content and its means of transmission are in the hands of the organization to preserve or modify.

Living old and new "traditions" (Japan)

In Japan, where Westernization has been an integral part of Japanese identity since the late nine-teenth century, children have within their school music repertoire a set of Western orchestral and chamber works to perform and appreciate songs translated to Japanese from English, French, German, and other languages of the world. In after-school programs, many opt for experiences in wind band performance, where musical standards are high and competition can be fierce. Their knowledge of their own Japanese musical traditions and song repertoire has been minimal, due to priorities set by the Ministry of Education to promote "basic musical skill" and "encourage children's love of music" through a Western-styled repertoire that has been a measure of excellence in musical education for nearly a century (Takizawa, 1997). Yet some path-breaking developments by Japanese educators and ethnomusicologists are beginning to redirect materials and methods of teaching to musical genres, repertoire, and processes beyond the West, including Japan's own unique instrumental, musical theatre, and *minyo* (folk song) traditions. Thus, despite the enormous success of Western art music in Japanese schooling, a curricular shift is now in progress to raise young people to understand their Japanese musical identity as well as to know a broader and more global view of musical cultures.

When Americans first arrived to Japan in 1868 and for the following several decades of frequent exchanges between Japan and the West, a grand assortment of musical instruments, styles, and explicit pieces were introduced to children in Japanese schools. Japanese educator Seiji Izawa invited American educator Luther Whiting Mason to Japan for a period in the 1880s, and a curriculum was forged for elementary school music classes that was to bring Japanese schoolchildren the songs of not only their American peers, but also of European traditions. This musical transformation came rapidly, too, so that by the turn of the century, young women in preparation as future teachers (and mothers) were also taught these multicultural children's songs (Howe, 1997). The Japanese Ministry of Education developed *shoka*, a specific way of school singing in which Western song melodies were imbued with Japanese moral and patriotic texts. The aim of these curricular actions was to radically alter the culture by influencing the children and the women who would work with them, in music and through music (Manabe, 2013).

Yet even while *shoka* singing and Western songs were the musical mainstay in Japanese schools at the end of the nineteenth century, children continued a traditional repertoire of children's songs, singing games, and chants (called collectively *warabe-uta*) when off on their own and at play. By the 1920s composers and poets were creating new songs of high artistic quality for children with texts thought to be relevant to their needs and interests (Gottschewski, 1998). These songs merged Japanese and Western musical and textual sensibilities, which became the center point of a school-based repertoire for much of the twentieth century (Manabe, 2013). Yet when post-war Japan was in search of its own identity, *warabe-uta* were "re-discovered" and viewed as central not only to children's culture, but also to the Japanese spirit (Suzuki, 2003). These traditional children's songs were even seen as having been a musical foundation or inspiration for other genres such as the *nagauta* (the "long songs" of *kabuki* theatre) and instrumental music for koto, shamisen, and shakuhachi. Traditional children's songs continue to be sung by Japanese children today, even in the midst of Western art music, Japanese traditional music, and the ubiquitous sounds of mediated popular music.

The study of traditional Japanese instruments by beginners of all ages typically transpires through highly stylized individual lessons beyond school, where the teacher's own musical competence is useful in modeling appropriate techniques. Verbal explanations are rare, while demonstration and the physical interaction of teacher and student in clarifying finger and arm positions are common practices. Pieces for koto, as well as shamisen and shakuhachi, are learned through mnemonics—semantically meaningless aural cues that use pitched or rhythmic syllables to represent the music. Japanese teachers transmit phrases of melody and rhythm orally, singing or chanting them to the student who immediately repeats them; they may sing and chant together before or during their performance of these phrases on the instrument. Even as notation is available, learning by rote or at least in a combination of rote and note is preferable, so that notation becomes a trigger for remembering what had transpired in aural and kinaesthetic terms within the lesson. The beauty of the physical execution of the music is a key aesthetic component in Japanese traditional music, and a teacher's modeling of posture and graceful movement is yet another component of the student's efforts at observation and imitation (Campbell, 1991). Instrumental study in Japan typically commences in childhood, and while there is a steady stream of young people in piano and violin lessons, a significant number are drawn also to the traditional instruments both for its sonic appeal as for the performance rituals that are embraced by the teacher and the culture at large.

Formal schooling in the traditional music of Japan typically emphasizes listening and appreciation. As in any music curriculum, there are some pieces and genres that are "fixed" and others that "go missing." The song, "Sakura," is a constant among teaching materials in Japan, and a handful of minyo are typically spread through textbooks. Koto music, especially "Rokudan," a shakuhachi piece called "Shika No Tone," a kabuki nagauta selection, and the *gagaku* court ensemble piece, "Entenraku," are commonly featured. The musical canon in Japanese school texts does not feature, however, music of the fourteenth-century *noh* theatre, Buddhist *shomyo* chant, *biwa* lute music, or *gidayu* (the duo of musicians that perform in the *bunraku* puppet theatre) (Takizawa, 1997). Where Japanese traditional music is taught in schools, the emphasis is frequently given to understanding musical structure, cultural and historical context, and aesthetic values. Still rare for children in Japanese schools is the mass-class performance-based study of traditional instruments or vocal music beyond select minyo and warabe-uta.

Of maystros and kulintangs (The Philippines)

While continuing a long history of European and American-styled systems of schooling in The Philippines that includes both Western content and pedagogical processes, a movement is in motion for the rediscovery in curriculum and courses of indigenous musical expressions that comprise the unique identity of the Filipino people. The urban concert scene, and the content of music within established conservatories and university departments of music, is overwhelmingly Western in flavor. Still, there are folk ensembles, vocal forms, and instrumental genres that reflect the indigenous, colonial, and immigrant groups that comprise the nation, and which are increasingly becoming a presence in formal studies of Filipino music (Castro, 2011). The local music genres are often the first sounds that children may hear, and are likely to be the sounds that remain closest to them even as they grow into adulthood; these are now finding further validation through their inclusion in educational settings.

The Western tradition of established conservatories is tied to Western standard pedagogical methods, but within communities and schools, the *maystro* works to revive folk ensembles that have known a considerable history in The Philippines, and which continue to be important in rural areas and provincial towns. From the Spanish *maestro* (master or teacher) comes the maystro system, where individual musician-educators teach, arrange, and conduct music for school-age members of *banda* (band) and *rondalla* (string) ensembles. The maystro prepares music arrangements in staff notation, many players are taught by rote. Every banda and rondalla player knows the melodic line by heart, and can sing it, and thus shares this identical aural and kinetic referent so that no one can get lost in the ensemble. Solfege is frequently utilized in learning melody and parts, so that a comprehensive musicianship develops in players that goes beyond keys and bowings (Trimillos, 1989).

The maystro system provides a template for social relationships in and through music. The maystro is coach and mentor of the students, and he typically takes on the role of a family member when he offers his home as the location of instructional sessions and rehearsals. Student players learn to help novice players, and to seek out the advice and support of players more expert than themselves. In the case of improvisation, which is standard practice within the rondalla ensemble, young students learn the idiomatic ways of their instrument and a certain technical proficiency through the experience of playing the maystro's arrangements and from listening to others. On cue from the maystro, adolescent and adult musicians are expected to take off from the arrangements, trying out new harmony parts and counter-melodies (Atabug, 1984). The maystro, as authority figure and benefactor, provides encouragement and guidance and is viewed as the source of all early knowledge of the instruments and its repertoire.

Within The Philippines is the large island of Mindanao, where the Maranao reside and retain their brilliant Muslim traditions. The Maranao have a signature vocal form, *bayok*, a love song of artistic merit sung by artists called *onor* from either gender. The onor must be prepared intellectually and artistically for the task of performing bayok, and so the cultivation begins in childhood when onors learn Arabic language, Qur'anic recitation, Maranao social ethics, the principal Maranao epic, called Darangen, performance techniques, and repertoire for the *kulintang* (set of knobbed gongs). The skill of a performing onor is measured by how well the onor delivers an improvised musical discourse with high literary value, using classical Maranao language, proverbs, humor, and poetic devices. The training requires long tutorial sessions filled with rote learning, with texts to be memorized in set melodic phrases. The Maranao bayok is highly specialized, and thus requires rigorous lessons and practice sessions before a public performance is permitted (Santos, 1996).

The Yakan people, an Islamic community of Basilan Island in the Sulu archipelago, perform instrumental music that is related to their agricultural cycle. Their instruments include small graduated bossed gongs that are laid in a row (*kwintangan*), hanging log beams (*kwintangan kayu*), a bamboo xylophone (*gabbang*), a percussion plank with jar resonator (*tuntungan*), a bamboo clapper (*kopak-kopak*), and a digging stick topped by a clapper (*daluppak*). They are played solo and ensemble, and their music is created through improvisation on one of hundreds of *lebad* (nuclear melodies) from which to select. The lebad are learned from childhood, as are the instruments, when children learn within the immediate family circle or surrounding neighborhood; in fact, many of the Yakan instrumental ensembles are comprised of family members. Children study with known masters and artists as arranged by their parents, and the process is kinaesthetically driven where the teacher holds the hands of the student and performs the music on the instrument at the proper performance speed. This is done repeatedly until the sound and feel of the music are comprehended, at which point the teacher steps away, observes, and provides commentary.

The kulintang is by far the ultimate national musical symbol of The Philippines, exoticized by the renown folkloric ensemble known as Bayanihan (Castro, 2011), and is fast becoming the instrument of choice for many young Filipinos living there and abroad. Kulintang is both the name of the ensemble as it is also a single instrument, which appears as an oblong wooden box with cords strung within it so as to support eight kettle-shaped embossed bronze gongs. Two long light-wood mallets are used to play the gongs, each with a small head of wrapped yarn and cloth. The ensemble includes this instrument along with several hanging gongs and a single-headed barrel drum, and plays a percussive melody along with punctuating rhythms that drive the sound forward and motivate listeners to want to dance. The transmission of Filipino kulintang music occurs through an oral/aural process where demonstration and imitation are prominently featured, and singing the melody line may spontaneously occur while attempting to play it. The visual-kinesthetic channels of information are critical to learning, too, so that young players watch as much as listen to other players perform at high speed and then reproduce the gestures of the hands as they fly across the gongs. In early listening and performing attempts, student players "catch" the motifs and partial phrases and realize the general ideas of melodic contour, but may take many trials before they can fill in the details that replicate the music as it is meant to be played (Campbell, 2001). Kulintang music is rhythmically sophisticated, and the ensemble of instruments sounds in interlocking fashion where one rhythm fits in between or surrounds another one to create a complex musical groove that is immensely appealing to Filipino youth.

Varied venues for learning music (Thailand)

Thailand is considered a gong-chime culture, but it is not only the resonant tuned gongs that provide a soundscape for children growing up Thai. There are as well wooden xylophones, stringed instruments, flutes, quadruple-reed instruments, and various drums, wood blocks, and cymbals that comprise the classical court music ensembles; these are heard in elaborate public ceremonies to honor the royal family, to commemorate important national events, to perform for tourists, to play for dance and theatre shows, and to continue the long-standing Thai musical identity (Douglas, 2009). Children hear the music of the classical *pi phat* and *mahori* ensembles on TV, if not live, and grow to expect their sounds in conjunction with performances by dancers, actors, and even puppets reenacting the *Ramakien* legend. They are immersed in the popular songs imported from Hong Kong, Japan, Taiwan, Great Britain, and the United States that are played in restaurants and shops. They are also grounded in Thai folk songs and singing games, many passed on by the generations before them, and they know the music of weddings, funerals, and other landmark events in their lives. Three musical streams—classical, popular, and folk—are prominent in the lives of children in modern Thailand, filling needs and functions over the course of their growing up in cities, towns, and villages (Phaosavadi & Campbell, 2003).

Alongside the more informal and non-formal learning, there appear to be three venues for children's formal learning of traditional Thai music. Piphat houses (*ban piphat*) were once the primary means of musical training for classical musicians, where as many as 50 or 60 disciplines, usually boys or young men, lived with a master teacher to study traditional instruments and play daily in the house ensemble. Although the houses are nearly all gone today, the pedagogical approach of a ban piphat master parceling out small phrases from a larger work to teach to his student by rote continues on in private lessons. Community institutes are a second venue for instrumental tuition, developed over the last several decades to serve tuition-paying students who wish to study stringed instruments, particularly *khim* (a hammered dulcimer), after school and on Saturdays. Teaching techniques include the use of written notation, including staff notation, solfege notation, numerical notation, and tablature, even while the oral/aural process is also very much in play (Miller, 1992). In public schools, children may sing Thai folk songs and, depending upon the teacher's interest, perform the basic movements of Thai classical and folk dances, play Thai melodies together on recorder-like *khlui*, or join together in playing *angklung* ensembles of bamboo idiophones. The establishment of Thai Music Clubs gives students in some schools opportunities to study traditional instruments and singing style; they follow the model of such clubs at universities where campus piphat and mahori ensembles perform competitively (Campbell, 1995).

An important element in the learning of Thai music is the custom of *wai kru*, or honoring the teacher (Wong, 2001). Children learn to show the sign of salutation (*wai*) by the time they enter school, raising both hands, joining palm to palm, and lightly touching the body somewhere between the face and chest. Schooldays, lessons, and even performances begin with this gesture of respect. Yet the wai kru is more than this: it is a ceremony to mark the time at which, following a trial period of study, the child or youth becomes a student of a particular teacher for life. The student brings gifts of food and money to the teacher when he (or she) has agreed to open the riches of his musical knowledge to the student. Since Thai classical music was once learned only through oral means, the teacher's acceptance of the student is a significant event. For young people wishing to devote themselves to learning this revered music, the teacher's selection of a student is the gateway to labor-intensive practice that may lead to musical excellence.

Yet while few Thai children will follow a pathway to classical music studies, they all know a repertoire of singing games and rhythmic chants that are frequently the focal point of their play. Children sing songs of the elephant ("Chaang"), imitating its lumbering movement and swinging "trunk," and of the blind fisherman with a trap ("Poong Paang") meant to catch the fish swimming near him. They chant in games that resemble "Drop the handkerchief" and "London Bridges," their language sounding rich with melodic nuances due to the five-tone nature of Thai language. There are clapping games, circle games, and double-line games, all in which children's live music-making is prominent (Phaosavadi & Campbell, 2003). Along with this playful song repertoire they trade among themselves, there are also the heritage songs passed to children from parents and grandparents. This is the music close to the heart of the Thai, music that cuts across age, class, and gender, the folk music of their history, customs, and beliefs that all are invited to sing.

Musical grooves from infancy onward (West Africa)

Much has been written about the musical engagement of children and youth in West Africa. Children of the Ewe (Agawu, 1995) and the Dagara (Wiggins, 2013) of Ghana, the Yoruba of Nigeria (Waterman, 1991), the Wolof of The Gambia (Koops, 2013), and the Kpelle of Liberia (Stone, 2004) are naturally enculturated into social worlds in which music plays a high-profile and prominent role in their daily lives. They sing, dance, and play from their earliest childhoods. In the arms of their mothers, or strapped to their mothers' backs, children learn from infancy the rhythms and tunes of their culture. In rural societies, they continue as infants and toddlers in a cultural practice of listening and feeling the rhythmic movement and sound vibrations of their mothers at work, walking, talking, chopping, stirring, stamping, and singing. Their sound worlds are extended beyond infancy as they come under the watchful eye of older siblings and neighbor-children, who teach them songs, stories, and games through which they may learn useful life skills and initial understandings of their cultural roles.

West African societies perceive music, dance, and even drama as a tightly bound complex of the performing arts. The Kpelle people of Liberia describe a beautifully performed song, drum pattern, or dance with the same term, "sang," a deliberate choice of word that reflects the blending of the arts into one entity. In illustration of the term, a drummer comments upon a dancer's performance that might be "The dance she spoke," just as a dancer might say of a drummer, "The music he moved" (Stone, 2004, p. 21). Children generally see the arts as blended, too, and in West African societies they are encouraged to hold this concept into adolescence and adulthood, as song, speech, movement, and instrumental music are viewed as part of an artistic continuum.

The performance practice of West African musicians typically encompasses both tradition and creative change. Among the Yoruba of Nigeria, the point is not to create a perfect imitation of music that has come before, but rather to catch the "feel" of music for specific functions and to portray it with new energy (Waterman, 1991). The performance practice influences the manner of its learning, so that a combination of informed listening with mimesis, or learning through imitation, is a powerful one. This is the way they learn stories and riddles, songs and dances, often combining the interspersing spoken and sung interludes in their stories, interjecting with their spontaneous exclamations, and dancing as it suits the story and the song. Yoruba children learn signing games at play with their peers in this manner, as they also learn their church hymns, the rhythms of the *dundun* (talking drum) and drumming ensembles, and the grooves of popular music such as *juju* and *fuji*.

Even as they sing their clapping games and counting songs, young children are perfecting some of the essential characteristics of the music of their culture. Where non-overlapping call and response structure is a key musical component, children infuse it within their songs. They have heard adults performing call and response songs as they plant rice, chop wood, cut and harvest sugar cane, pound maize into powder, and weave straw into baskets. They themselves learn as children to pound cassava in a mortar, or to ground recently harvested rice in order to remove the husks, all the while incorporating interactive rhythmic exchanges between them (Agawu, 1995). The call and response melodies and rhythms of ensembles of xylophones, drums, flutes, horns, harps, and lutes have surrounded them, too, so that this organizing element comes easily to them as they sing familiar and spontaneously created songs. Children learn the timing and turn-taking of call and response, even so far as to understand the importance of an equal balance in some genres between the length of the call phrase and the response phrase (Stone, 2004).

There are important social groups in some areas of West Africa that function as secret societies, in which older children are expected to leave their homes to live for a time in Poro (for males) and Sande (for females) enclosures in the forest. There they receive instruction in the traditions and values of their culture, which is an intensive training for the adult roles they will one day play. Music and dance are featured within this training for all students, and for the talented there is even specialized training for becoming solo singers, instrumentalists, or dancers in their communities (Stone, 2004). Everyone performs the dances they learned in Poro and Sande as a part of their graduation exercise, after they are declared ready to take on some of the challenges of the adult lives into which they will grow.

In describing their life history, Wolof griots of Senegal offer detailed accounts of their childhoods as prominent in their growth as musicians and tellers of tales (Tang, 2001). Most learn their drumming early, and the critical period of developing their drumming talent falls between the ages of 2 and 10 years. Children are exposed to drums and drummers from infancy, so that an immersion phenomenon occurs. With drums in the home and yard, babies may grab them to steady themselves when learning to walk, or might be offered a turn on the drum to appease and reward them. Young Wolofs watch and then imitate the adult drummers, sometimes playing on empty cans and plastic containers when they are just 3 and 4 years old (Koops, 2013). Since they are brought to adult gatherings that feature music, children hear characteristic rhythms and complicated phrases, and may chant them and dance to them. They then apply the music to their toy drums the next morning, sometimes alone or together in small groups. If a child is observed to be particularly talented, he will be taken under the wing of a male relative and trained until sufficiently skilled to contribute his minor part in a public festival. While Wolof griots may describe the music they know as inherited, it is often the presence of the music within their environment that allows them to know it intimately.

Ngoma to grow on (East Africa)

East African societies in Kenya, Tanzania, Uganda, and the Cape Horn countries of Ethiopia, Eritrea, Somalia, and Djibouti embrace the participation of all their members, including children, in traditional music and dance. *Ngoma* (in as many translations as there are languages) is the combined music–dance form of performance that spreads across the region, where singers dance, dancers sing, and instrumentalists may sing and move as they play. Traditional ngoma serves important rituals and routines throughout East Africa, including music for education, entertainment, and funerals, in work and as therapy, and for communication (through metalinguistic drumming from one village to another) and timekeeping (as in calling villagers to worship where no church bells chime). It serves didactic and educational purposes as well in village Uganda (Barz, 2004), and surfaces in the Christian worship services and festivals of the Wagogo of Tanzania (Mapana, 2013). Music is viewed as an appropriate means of handling social problems, where stories are sung as warnings to villagers of wrongdoings and encouragement to individuals to mend their ways. It is used for coping with diseases such as HIV/AIDS, so that songs, dances, and dramatic performances of people suffering and dying are presented so that they might be more thoughtful about the issues.

Some genres function in multiple ways, including as means for enhancing the quality of young workers as well as for entertaining them. *Bugobogobo* is a genre of the Sukuma of Tanzania found in the context of field labor and as a refined stage art (Gunderson, 1999). It was initially intended as music made by youth and adult laborers to facilitate their work in harvesting, hauling, and planting. The benefits of music-making for those engaged in this physical labor are multiple: to create a desire to work together, to work longer hours without being tired, to calm listeners and focus their mental energies and organizational skills, to cast off worries and create joy, and to pass on important life testimonies and teaching within the songs. The music and dance of Bugobogobo are carefully synchronized, and even as it has risen from the field to become a refined performance art, the origins of the form are seen in the young dancers who demonstrate the motions of hoeing the earth and spreading seeds. A popular genre in clubs throughout East Africa due to its pulsive, energetic, and colorful nature, Bugobogobo serves as a symbol of Tanzanian national identity. Performers are not "taught" how to perform it, but they have been imitating their elders—both farmers and performers—since early in their childhoods. As early as 5 and 6 years of age, children witness the workers and the performance troupes, and commence playing the intricate rhythms of Bugobogobo on discarded tin cans and wooden sticks (Barz, 2004). This active participation thus assures their place on the receiving end of the process of transmission of traditional culture, and often motivates their fuller involvement in Bugobogobo later in their lives.

At home and in the Islamic schools of Kenya, children learn to recite the Qur'an in Arabic. They can be heard performing their devotional chants in school choirs, with texts from the Qur'an, called *kaswida*, that enhance the religious sentiment. They do not perform *nyimbo* (songs), as their more melodic styles would be considered a distraction from the religious beliefs of the texts (Barz, 2004). In the same rehearsal, the girls may take to performing *chakacha*, a traditional ngoma that is sung, danced, and drummed exclusively by women. The dance features the rhythmicized rotation of the hips, which is accented by the women tying their *hijab* headscarves at the hips of their traditional Muslim black robes. Its virtuosically played drum rhythms and sensual movements have contributed to its popularity as the national musical symbol of Kenya across the generations (Campbell & Eastman, 1984).

In much of East Africa, as in sub-Saharan Africa at large, girls are typically discouraged from playing musical instruments. The gender roles are often clearly delineated from childhood onward, such that while everyone sings, only men play instruments and women more typically dance. In some villages, women are discouraged from touching or even passing near musical instruments; to do either is considered a transgression of a social taboo. This value system is changing in urban centers such as Nairobi, Kampala, Dar-es-Salaam, and Mogadishu, where boys and girls are taught in schools on many different musical instruments. Yet even while youth understand and appreciate the changes, the older generation still maintains these beliefs about gender (Ephrem, 2004).

One way of understanding the socio-musical life of children is to learn from the reflections of a performer well attuned to his own development as well as that of others whom he now teaches. Centurio Balikoowa, a performer of the *ntongooli* (a multistring bowl-lyre) of Uganda, recalled beginning his musical education by playing musical games as early as 3 years of age (Barz, 2004). He learned the ntongooli by observing his father, who had in turn learned by observing his grandfather. He remembered also playing *endere* (flute) by ear, having heard the melodies played by shepherds as they took care of the grazing cows in the neighboring field. Like all children in his village, Balikoowa learned to play *embaire* (xylophone). Because there was no electricity, a communal embaire was constructed by the adults, who would take turns playing it through the evenings. Since there was no television, radio, or videos, one resident after another in the village would play for a period of time, and sometimes residents in neighboring villages would contribute their own complementary performances, too. For the master and professional musicians with whom he is associated, learning happens through a combination of listening, imitation, and repetition.

Keeping culture through traditional song (North American First Nations)

Among the people of the First Nations, or Native Americans, of North America (including Canada and the United States), music is a communal event as it is also a deeply personal phenomenon. Its transmission may be a matter of one's age, gender, and rank within a community, or it may be a result of a personal journey that leads to spiritual inspiration. Music is deeply embedded in ritual and social customs of the clan or tribe, in coming-of-age ceremonies, and in coming to terms with the supernatural, the ancestral spirits, and the spirits of nature and of living creatures. Some songs are group-owned and intended for all to know, while others are considered personal property, to be sung only by those whose songs they are or by permission given for their use. For many people of the First Nations, song is the equivalent of the Bible's Genesis and Leviticus in the moral lessons it holds, and those without knowledge of song are considered "poor," uneducated, or lacking an important piece of who they are.

For children growing up in their Native American communities, music is a part of their personal and social identities. Concepts of traditional indigenous knowledge to be passed to the young allow for the music as a way of recounting history, predicting the future, passing on local wisdom, reflecting on meaningful places and contexts, and clarifying one's role within a nation and a clan (Diamond, 2008). Modern indigenous music and dance has emerged even as older layers are continued, so that a group of unaccompanied singers and dancers can still hold its own even as wired rock and country music bands perform their own blend of contemporary and indigenous expressions. Inter-tribal celebrations are raising new issues of ownership, borrowing, and sharing, as songs cross groups and become fused with different cultural expressions. Meanwhile, young people are often caught in the middle of contemporary cultural revitalization that is occurring, trying to make sense of older layers of culture, including music, in their changing world.

Families are responsible for teaching songs and dances to family members in order to perpetuate their traditions. The Spokane and Coeur d'Alene tribes of the interior of the American Northwest assert the primary place of song in their development as children. They remember it as the sound they awakened to and to which they would go to sleep, when mothers, fathers, grandparents, and other family members sang alone and together. From birth to death, songs are there for points through the day and through their lives, from the morning song, the song for the birth of a child, of becoming a man or woman, of being in love, for marriage, for sickness and death. There are welcoming songs, songs for learning dances, for being a warrior, and for battle itself (Sijohn, 1999).

The Coast Salish groups who live along the Pacific Rim of the United States and Canada continue to pass on the lessons of their culture to young people through their songs. While stories are significant in that they contain metaphors, and important cultural knowledge about ancestors, family, animals, and plants, the elders believe that "You have to sing the most important teaching of a story for children to remember it" (Miller, 1999, p. 31). Singing is often reserved for the moral of the story, the bottom-line lessons to be learned, the story's most important turn of events. One account of the song-learning among the Snohomish people underscores the means of ensuring that the substance of stories and songs is learned.

> My great-grandmother would sing the songs that went with the stories. Then somewhere during the story, my great-grandmother would stop and pretend to try to remember what came next (it was a test). One of the older children, who had heard the song many times before, would have to say 'Kaya [grandmother], this is what they did' (Miller, 1999, p. 30).

A singer of the Makah Nation remembered the importance of repeated listening: "My dad . . . would make us sit down and listen to a new song 'til we were very tired of it! He'd just play the drum and sing the song, every day" (Swan, 1999, p. 86). Although the oral method continues to be practiced by the Makah, children now learn songs via tape recordings given to them by their elders. However, since children may no longer be "forced" to sit and listen repeatedly to their parents and grandparents, they do not practice regularly. The same is true of the dance, where videotapes are available, but the viewing by First Nations' children is sporadic when left to chance. With no one there to help them out physically and to correct their errors, children and youth know less of the traditional repertoire than they once did.

For the Mescaleros, as well as other Apaches of the American Southwest, a coming-of-age ceremony combines ritual with song, prayer, rattles, and ritual in order to prepare young adolescent girls for marriage and child-bearing ahead in their future. An older woman serves as sponsor of the girl, who is selected by the family because of her knowledge of Apache traditions, including the puberty rite and its songs. The ceremony brings the girl into womanhood over a period of five days, when powwow dancing occurs outside even as the girl is taking instruction by her sponsor within her specially constructed private tipi (thought to be the home of the goddess). The sounds of the girl's tin-cone jingles, sewn into her ceremonial dress, can be heard as she dances. Male ritual singing is punctuated by female ritual cries, and supportive singing is offered by women who know the rituals. On the fourth night, the singing and dancing extend until dawn, when the girls are painted with red and white clay. Adolescent Mescalero girls remain largely silent through the ceremony, but they hear the music and prayers that swirl around them (Shapiro & Talamantez, 1986). Some of them later become sponsors, drawn to the music, beginning their learning of it at their very own puberty rite.

As in many First Nations cultures, Navajo children learn the songs of their adult culture from adults by joining in as singing participants in the rituals and social functions in which adults play prominent roles. They may also sing the adult songs, or parts of them, away from adults, sometimes converting them into their own new expressions, adding interactive movements, or combining them with games they know or invent. Among the Oglala Sioux of the Dakotas, the word for "compose" is *yatun*, literally "to give birth to a song," and yet the connotation of *tun* is "to give rise to something that has already existed in another form" (Powers, 1980, p. 33). Thus it appears that there may be an unconscious recycling of songs that occurs from person to person, with the singer uncertain of the song's evolution. Since country, rock, rap, gospel, and other popular forms have become embedded in the ambience of their communities, these styles are also influential in the music children make. There are, of course, traditional children's songs, too, and singing games, lullabies, and humorous songs, which are all part of the oral tradition passed on to them by adults (McAllester, 1996).

The traditional music continues, despite an attempt that was under way in the nineteenth century to "civilize" the children of First Nations communities. Indigenous people in Canada and the United States were banned from practicing their Native rituals, religious celebrations, and extended family gatherings, and children and youth were sent to boarding schools where traditional practices, including heritage songs and dances, could be replaced by the curricular content of mainstream schools. By the 1890s these schools were mandatory for all Native children, where they were subjected to studies that were far afield from their tribal life, and they were clothed in uniforms. Their hair was cut short, and they were housed in barracks-style halls and fed a new menu of foods foreign to them. Many schools were run like military academies, and wind and brass bands similar to those found in the military were established (Swan, 1999). These actions were intended to bring assimilation to Native American children, and to focus attention away from the culture they would have known at home that would not serve to bring them into the mainstream of society. Yet in summer, when school was out and the children were back at home, the traditions, including the music, crept back into their lives. They serenaded one another, sang and danced with their families, and (depending upon the particular tribe) found drums to beat, rattles to shake, and flutes to play. People of the First Nations survived the boarding schools, and gradually the government-sponsored schools closed and children were returned to their families to be educated in their local schools, where curricular subjects today include Native American cultural studies and celebrations of music and dance with standard public-school fare.

Living and learning music

The manner by which children and youth learn music may vary from culture to culture, and yet in interesting ways this learning by individuals may also be seen as transpiring across a continuum of aural–oral techniques and formal, non-formal, and informal processes. Children's musical involvement may encompass active and engaged learning at times, and more passive, receptive, and indirect modes at other times. Further, as surely as they acquire music, children are also involved in transmitting it (often to other children), thus preserving it. In examining settings and situations of music learning by young people across cultures, comparisons may be made of the strategies employed by children in the process of knowing music well enough to be able to perform it, to create it anew, and to understand its meaning. As they live, children learn, and many are keen to know the music that suits them and their view of the world—as well as to reflect the musical values of adults who are influential in shaping their cultural identities.

Across the globe, childhood is a period of life in which learning one's membership in a cultural group is a crucial accomplishment (Campbell & Wiggins, 2013). This learning transpires within the immediate family group and in the wider community, and includes language (and dialect), social skills, religious beliefs and rituals, values, and culturally based artistic expression to adhere to and strive for as children progress into adolescence and toward adulthood. Children pledge their allegiances to family, friends, and community values, and gradually they shift their focus toward achieving competence in economically useful skills they will use in their future. They acquire leisure skills, too, that include sport and the arts, some of which become life-long pursuits that fill and fulfill them. Stretching from childhood into adolescence is the period of exploration in how best one might participate in one's collective culture, as well as to learn how to shape oneself in the direction of one's individual future; here, too, music is often a choice that young people make to engage in, and to be engaged by, its performance. Children's social lives evolve as they graduate from a dependence upon adults exclusively as caregivers to one of an interdependence with family members, other children, and adults (teachers, youth leaders, relatives, and others within their community). Children come to an understanding of self in relation to others, and they learn their roles and responsibilities, and their strengths in the contributions they will make to their culture and society. Through the stages of children's growth, their musical expressions and interests are evident and often significant means of their learning.

Music is emblematic of personal and collective identity, so that whether or not they study it and specialize in its performance, children and youth are at least subconsciously aware of its expressive power and symbolism. A few will become highly competent in music so as to choose it for their life's work, while the vast majority will find music a component of their life within family, social, and religious communities. As children, they sing because they must, they move because the music prompts them, and they dabble with instruments and sound-sources out of curiosity and a need for tactile experience, and because it "feels good" to do so. It is this dabbling that may lead to ever-deepening involvement in instrumental play, even when it begins with mere whistling, tooting, tapping, key-clicking, and other exploratory behaviors. Children learn the role of music within their society simply by living in their culture, and the musical grammar they develop is a direct result of what sounds come into their ears. As they grow, children are developing a sense of their musical heritage, for it is apt to be their own soundscape of live and mediated expressions. Their inventions of a musical nature derive from this musical sound-surround.

As music is a human phenomenon, it is also a learned behavior. Children are to an extent similarly "wired," regardless of where they live, so that some facets of the manner in which they perceive, receive, and grow to know music are evident across cultures. Yet if there is variance in musical expression from one culture to another, it follows also that the manner in which it is learned may be affected by the music itself, and by the ways, means, and values of the locality concerning the transfer of knowledge. The function of music, including the role it plays in the daily lives of people, may influence the circumstances of its transmission, as do also the values placed upon the music by a society as either the rare endowment of expert artists or a characteristic shared by all its citizens. Who learns the music and how it is learned are thus reflective of its internal content and the collective cultural thought about it. However, a central interest is the extent to which music learning is similar in process regardless of its content and the context of its learning.

Clearly, music moves from teacher to learner, from master to apprentice, from adult to child. It also moves from child to child, even from child to adult, and from mediated sources to anyone who will listen. Sensory avenues are exercised by children in "getting the music," and learning may embrace aural, visual, and kinesthetic/tactile capacities. Beginners may need to listen, observe, and then imitate the teacher, and so students across many traditions use their ears and eyes in learning the fiddle of Ireland, the shakuhachi of Japan, the kulintang of The Philippines, the khim of Thailand, the dundun of Nigeria, the ntongooli of Uganda, and the songs of the Coast Salish. So it is in popular music genres, too, in which the ear is challenged to learn the nuances of the style and piece, both those parts that are fixed and certain as well as those parts that are improvised. Verbal explanations are largely unnecessary, notation systems may or may not be utilized (even when such notation is available), and "rote" imitation of those who already know the music is frequently viewed as a positive component of learning. In remarkable ways, it may be that adult student musicians may emulate children's learning strategies, finding their musical way through observation and imitation, becoming active in the kinaesthetic process of performance as a result of looking and listening (Campbell, 1991).

When learning requires the retention of skills for performance, vocalization and mnemonic devices may be critical components of the process. Orally spoken cues serve the memory well, which may be semantically meaningless and yet key to storing and later recalling passages. Japanese instruments have their own sets of syllables to designate pitches, rhythms, and the performing positions for koto, shamisen, and various drums. Drumming traditions have an elaborate mnemonic system, too, to communicate durations and drumstrokes, including a wide variety of percussion instruments in sub-Saharan Africa. Prerequisite to instrumental performance in many traditions may be the vocalization by way of the chanting and singing of syllables, including solmization. In order to play the drums of the Wolof, there is an expectation that students chant first the principal rhythmic themes. Similarly, players of Irish tunes on various traditional instruments may first have been learned by ear, and even through song. This practice extends to artistic and popular forms beyond those mentioned, as jazz musicians, for example, claim that singing must naturally precede instrumental performance, and that their ear-training is enhanced through vocalization (Berliner, 1994; Jackson, 2012).

Approaches to the study of the child as musician must encompass cross-cultural studies of their musical engagements in order to grasp the multi-splendored realities of children's interests, needs, behaviors, and values. Concurrently, considerations of music as global practice must encompass the ways in which children musically grow to express themselves, and the ways in which they are enculturated, trained, and educated. Children are a product of social organization, and they do not move through increasingly advanced stages of their biological and neurological growth without being shaped by a constellation of forces within their environments, not the least of which are the musical genres which their societies value and thus preserve. Yet also, as a perspective of children, as their own social system becomes more readily apparent through cross-disciplinary scholarship, they will need to be studied further as the young musicians they are rather than as unfinished products in motion toward adult culture. Of course, adults have much to offer children by way of musical knowledge and skills that have since the beginning of time been transmitted generationally, and yet children—their own development, their means of socialization with other children, of learning, exchanging (and even discarding) particular points of their knowledge and views—deserve support and the freedom to evolve beyond the direct influence of well-intentioned adults. With an open and receptive approach to the study of children within school, in public places such as parks and playgrounds, in their social clubs, and in their homes, they may be better understood for their musical interests and values, for how they perceive and grow their musical behaviors, so that adults can contribute in relevant ways to their musical lives.

Reflective questions

1 What is an ethnomusicology of children, and what are we learning from recent scholarship from those in pursuit of questions about children's expressive practices?

2 How is progress toward the construction of metatheories of childhood useful in developing pathways for understanding children's musical interests and needs?

3 How are cultural identities enforced through raising musical children at home and at school, and in various other venues where children gather for play and learning?

4 To what extent are aural–oral techniques present in the music transmission and learning that occurs within schools and other formal institutional settings?

5 In what ways are children active agents in discerning the music they will learn and regard as their very own? Conversely, what elements are conducive to the valuing by children of family and community music?

Key sources

Boynton, S., & Kok, R.-M. (Eds.) (2006). *Musical childhoods and the cultures of youth*. Middletown, CT: Wesleyan University Press.

Campbell, P. S., & Wiggins, T. (Eds.) (2013). *The Oxford handbook of children's musical cultures*. New York: Oxford University Press.

Lancy, D. (2008). *The anthropology of childhood: Cherubs, chattel, changelings*. Cambridge: Cambridge University Press.

Lum, C.-H., & Whiteman, P. (Eds.) (2012). *Musical childhoods of Asia and the Pacific*. New York: Information Age Publishing.

Montgomery, H. (2009). *An introduction to childhood: Anthropological perspectives on children's lives*. Malden MA: Wiley-Blackwell.

Reference list

Agawu, K. (1995). *African rhythm: A northern Ewe perspective*. Cambridge: Cambridge University Press.

Atabug, A. C. (1984). Music education in a multicultural society: The Philippine experience. *International Society of Music Education Yearbook*, **11**, 25–40.

Barz, G. (2004). *Music in East Africa*. New York: Oxford University Press.

Benthall, J. (1992). Child-focused research. *Anthropology Today*, **8**(2), 23–5.

Berliner, P. (1994). *Thinking in jazz*. Chicago: University of Chicago Press.

Bjorkvold, J. (1992). *The muse within* (W. H. Halverson, trans.). New York: Harper Collins.

Blacking, J. (1967/1995). *Venda children's song: A study in ethnomusicological analysis*. Chicago: University of Chicago.

Boynton, S., & Kok, R.-M. (Eds.) (2006). *Musical childhoods and the cultures of youth*. Middletown, CT: Wesleyan University Press.

Brailiou, C. (1984). *Problems of ethnomusiocology* (A. L. Lloyd, trans.) Cambridge, UK: Cambridge University Press. (Original work published 1954.)

Campbell, P. S. (1991). *Lessons from the world*. New York: Schirmer Books.

Campbell, P. S. (1995). The making of musicians and musical audiences in Thailand. *International Journal of Music Education*, **2**(5), 20–8.

Campbell, P. S. (1998/2010). *Songs in their heads: Music and its meaning in children's lives*. New York: Oxford University Press.

Campbell, P. S. (2001). Unsafe suppositions? Cutting across cultures on questions of music's transmission. *Music Education Research*, **3**(2), 215–26.

Campbell, P. S. (2003). Ethnomusicology and music education: Crossroads for knowing music, education, and culture. *Research Studies in Music Education*, **21**(1), 16–30.

Campbell, C. A., & Eastman, C. M. (1984). *Ngoma*: Swahili adult song performance in context. *Ethnomusicology*, **28**(3), 467–93.

Campbell, P. S., & Wiggins, T. (Eds.) (2013). *The Oxford handbook of children's musical cultures*. New York: Oxford University Press.

Castro, C.-A. (2011). *Musical renderings of the Philippine Nation*. New York: Oxford University Press.

Corsaro, W. A. (1997). *The sociology of childhood*. Thousand Oaks, CA: Pine Forge Press.

Diamond, B. (2008). *Native American music in eastern North America*. New York: Oxford University Press.

Douglas, G. (2009). *Music in Mainland Southeast Asia*. New York: Oxford University Press.

Ephrem, H. (2004). Personal communication. [See also comments by Ephrem in *Roots and Branches* (1994), P. S. Campbell, P. Shehan, E. McCullough-Brabson, & J. C. Tucker (Eds.), (pp. 8–9). Danbury, CT: World Music Press.]

Goldman, L. (1998). *Child's play: Myth, mimesis and make-believe*. Oxford: Berg.

Gottschewski, H. (1998). The development of the language of music during the introduction of European music to Japan between 1853 and 1945. *Japan Foundation Newsletter*, **25**(6), 7–9.

Gunderson, F. (1999). Music labor associations in Sukumaland, Tanzania: History and practice (Unpublished doctoral dissertation). Wesleyan University.

Hall, E. T. (1992). Improvisation as an acquired, multilevel process. *Ethnomusicology*, **36**(2), 223–45.

Hardman, C. (1973). Can there be an anthropology of children? *Journal of the Anthropological Society of Oxford*, **8**(4), 85–99.

Hargreaves, D. J., & North, A. J. (Eds.) (1997). *The social psychology of music*. New York: Oxford University Press.

Harwood, E. (1998). Go on girl! Improvisation in African-American girls' singing games. In B. Nettl & M. Russell (Eds.), *In the course of performance* (pp. 13–25). Chicago: University of Chicago Press.

Hast, D., & Scott, S. (2004). *Music in Ireland*. New York: Oxford University Press.

Herzog, G. (1950). Song. In M. Leach & J. Fried (Eds.), *Dictionary of folklore, mythology, and legend* (Vol. 2, pp. 1043–50). New York: Funk & Wagnall.

Howe, S. W. (1997). *Luther Whiting Mason: International music educator*. Warren MI: Harmonie Park Press.

Jackson, T. (2012). *Blowin' the blues away: Performance and meaning on the New York jazz scene*. Berkeley: University of California Press.

James, A., Jenks, C., & Prout, A. (1998). *Theorizing childhood*. New York: Teachers College Press.

Jorgensen, E. (1997). *In search of music education*. Urbana, IL: University of Illinois Press.

Juslin, P. N., & Sloboda, J. A. (2001). *Music and emotion: Theory and research*. New York: Oxford University Press.

Koops, L. (2013). Enjoyment and socialization in Gambian children's music making. In P. S. Campbell & T. Wiggins (Eds.), *The Oxford handbook of children's musical cultures* (pp. 266–80). New York: Oxford University Press.

Lancy, D. (2008). *The anthropology of childhood: Cherubs, chattel, changelings*. Cambridge: Cambridge University Press.

Lum, C.-H. & Whiteman, P. (Eds.) (2012). *Musical childhoods of Asia and the Pacific*. New York: Information Age Publishing.

MacDonald, R., Hargreaves, D. J., & Miell, D. (2002). *Musical identities*. New York: Oxford University Press.

Manabe, N. (2013). Songs of Japanese Schoolchildren during World War II. In P. S. Campbell & T. Wiggins (Eds.), *The Oxford Handbook of Children's Musical Cultures* (pp. 96–113). New York: Oxford University Press.

Mapana, K. (2013). Enculturational discontinuities in the musical experience of the Wagogo children of Central Tanzania. In P. S. Campbell & T. Wiggins (Eds.), *The Oxford handbook of children's musical cultures* (pp. 510–26). New York: Oxford University Press.

Marsh, K. (1997). Children's singing games: Composition in the playground? *Research Studies in Music Education*, **4**(1), 2–11.

Marsh, K. (2008). *The musical playground: Global tradition and change in children's songs and games*. New York: Oxford University Press.

Mayall, B. (2002). *Toward a sociology for childhood: Thinking from children's lives*. Buckingham, UK: Open University Press.

McAllester, D. P. (1996). David P. McAllester on Navajo music. In P. S. Campbell (Ed.), *Music in cultural context* (pp. 5–11). Reston, VA: Music Educators National Conference.

McCarthy, M. (1999). *Passing it on: The transmission of music in Irish culture*. Cork: Cork University Press.

Miller, B. S. (1999). Seeds of our ancestors. In W. Smyth & E. Ryan (Eds.), *Spirit of the first people* (pp. 25–43). Seattle: University of Washington Press.

Miller, T. E. (1992). The theory and practice of Thai musical notations. *Ethnomusicology*, **36**(2), 197–221.

Minks, A. (2002). From children's song to expressive practices: Old and new directions in the ethnomusicological study of children. *Ethnomusicology*, **46**(3), 379–408.

Montgomery, H. (2009). *An introduction to childhood: Anthropological perspectives on children's lives*. Malden MA: Wiley-Blackwell.

O'Suilleabhain, M. (2004). Personal communication.

Phaosavadi, P., & Campbell, P. S. (2003). *From Bangkok and beyond*. Danbury, CT: World Music Press.

Powers, W. K. (1980). Oglala song terminology. *Selected Reports in Ethnomusicology*, **3**(2), 23–41.

Santos, R. (1996). Beyond the song. In J. Katsumura & Y. Tokumaru (Eds.), *Report of world musics forum: Hamamatsu 1996* (pp. 96–106). Tokyo: Foundation for the Promotion of Music Education and Culture.

Schwartzman, H. B. (2001). Children and anthropology: A century of studies. *Children and anthropology: Perspectives for the 21st century*. Westport, CT: Bergin & Garvey.

Shapiro, A. D., & Talamantez, I. (1986). The Mescalero Apache girls' puberty ceremony: The role of music in structuring ritual time. *Yearbook of the International Council for Traditional Music*, **18**, 77–90.

Sijohn, C. (1999). The circle of song. In W. Smyth & E. Ryan (Eds.), *Spirit of the first people* (pp. 45–49). Seattle: University of Washington Press.

Stephens, S. (Ed.) (1995). *Children and the politics of culture*. Princeton, NJ: Princeton University Press.

Stone, R. (2004). *Music in West Africa*. New York: Oxford University Press.

Suzuki, A. (2003). The change and diversity of singing games in England and Japan: A comparative approach to their roles and construction (Unpublished doctoral dissertation). The University of Reading.

Swan, H. (1999). Makah music. In W. Smyth & E. Ryan (Eds.), *Spirit of the first people* (pp. 81–93). Seattle: University of Washington Press.

Takizawa, T. (1997). A new paradigm of world musics in Japanese music education: Japan's learning from ASEAN countries' access roads to world music. In J. Katsumura & Y. Tokumaru (Eds.), *Report of world musics forum: Hamamatsu 1996* (pp. 33–9). Tokyo: Foundation for the Promotion of Music Education and Culture.

Tang, P. (2001). *Masters of the Sabar: Wolof Griots in contemporary Senegal* (Unpublished doctoral dissertation). Harvard University.

Trimillos, R. (1989). Halau, hochschule, maystro, and ryu: Cultural approaches to music learning and teaching. *International Journal of Music Education*, **14**, 32–43.

Waterman, R. (1956). Music in Australian Aboriginal culture—some sociological and psychological implications. In E. T. Gaston (Ed.), *Music therapy 1955* (pp. 40–9). Lawrence KS: The Allen Press.

Waterman, C. (1991). *Juju music: A social history*. Chicago: University of Chicago Press.

Whiteman, P., & Campbell, P. S. (2012). "Picture it! Young children conceptualizing music." In C.-H. Lum & P. Whiteman (Eds.), *Musical childhoods of Asia and the Pacific* (pp. 161–89). Charlotte, NC: Information Age Publishing.

Wiggins, T. (2013). Whose songs in their heads? In P. S. Campbell & T. Wiggins (Eds.), *The Oxford handbook of children's musical cultures* (pp. 590–608). New York: Oxford University Press.

Wong, D. (2001). *Sounding the center: History and aesthetics in Thai Buddhist performance*. Chicago: University of Chicago Press.

Chapter 31

Transcultural childhoods

Alexandra Kertz-Welzel

Transcultural childhoods: Introduction

On a hot summer's day in 2010, while the FIFA World Cup took place in South Africa, two children in the German city of Saarbrücken started singing in the garden of their home. They constantly repeated the first phrases of the song "Waka Waka," the official song of the soccer World Cup, originally performed by the Colombian singer Shakira and the South African band Freshlyground. The German girls sang together or individually, imitating and teaching each other, trying new phrases or excerpts of other songs, and improvising. They also danced, attempting to copy the movements they knew from Shakira. After one hour, some parts of the song sounded good, while others were clearly improvised. But it did not matter to the girls. In the summer of 2010, everybody knew and loved "Waka Waka."

These two girls' musical activities raise interesting issues concerning musical childhoods in times of globalization. Children worldwide are fascinated by the global music culture and use the music they experience for creating their individual musical worlds. In fact, the scene described could have happened almost anywhere in the world. Furthermore, "Waka Waka" and the excerpts of other songs the girls used indicate that today, music of various cultures is part of children's musical worlds; they merge and mix according to their own needs. This suggests that musical childhoods today are in fact transcultural.

This chapter investigates transcultural aspects of musical childhoods in view of globalization, using a cross-cultural perspective. First, the impact globalization has on children and their musical worlds will be explored. The notion of transculturality facilitates understanding today's hybrid musical identities. Second, as an example, the musical worlds of children in Germany will be described, using the musical–ecological approach in particular and the German concept of *Musikvermittlung* as the facilitation of music. Third, selected transcultural aspects of musical childhoods worldwide will be analyzed. Finally, the perspectives that the notion of transculturality offers with regard to the musical worlds of children will be discussed.

Globalization and transculturality

There are many ways to characterize globalization, this buzzword that seems to be "overconsolidated, overhyped and under-interpreted" as Nikolas Coupland mentions (Coupland, 2010, p. 2). Scheuerman (2010) states correctly that globalization often is a synonym for economic liberalization in terms of a global marketplace, but also Westernization or Americanization with regard to the increasing dominance of specific political or cultural ideals. Furthermore, the "proliferation of new information technologies (the 'Internet Revolution'), as well as the notion that humanity stands on the threshold of realizing itself as one single unified community in which major sources of social conflict have vanished ('global integration')" (Scheuerman, 2010) are important aspects of globalization. Finally, the blurring of national borders and the increased speed of transportation have changed the world significantly.

Globalization is a dynamic force in contemporary societies, which also stands for a cluster of social changes. It has an impact on the structure of families and thereby also on childhood (Trask, 2010). Global migration and the formation of transnational families are a challenge for many children worldwide. The transformation of work in terms of the feminization of the labor force or female-headed households is the result of globalization that affects children (Trask, 2010). Furthermore, children's everyday lives are affected by global developments such as the standardization of schooling and instruction, the availability of media, and international food or clothing chains.

Even though the word *globalization* represents a controversial concept, it is not possible to abandon it completely. It clearly explains aspects of today's life that cannot be easily described otherwise. However, globalization does not match homogenization. Appadurai (1996), whose differentiation of globalization as creating distinct kinds of transcultural flows (ethnoscapes, mediascapes, technoscapes, financescapes, ideoscapes) is well known, states the following regarding globalization and homogenization:

> Most often the homogenization argument subspeciates into either an argument about Americanization or an argument about commoditization, and very often the two arguments are closely linked. What these arguments fail to consider is that at least as rapidly as forces from various metropolises are brought into new societies they tend to become indigenized in one way or another: this is true of music and housing styles as much as it is true of science and terrorism, spectacles and constitutions. (Appadurai, 1996, p. 29)

Appadurai underlines differences between globalization and homogenization: while globalization might first cause a convergence, it also has a tendency toward localization, which transforms international features according to local conventions.

The German philosopher Wolfgang Welsch (1999) tries to capture this hybridization of cultures with his concept of transculturality. While the traditional notion of single cultures based on social homogenization, ethnic consolidation, or intercultural delimination does not work anymore, Welsch suggests an understanding of cultures as "transcultural." Modern cultures transcend classical national boundaries. They are deeply interconnected and intertwined. They represent a mixture of various influences and traditions. This also concerns individuals and their way of living:

> Lifestyles no longer end at the borders of national cultures, but go beyond these, are found in the same way in other cultures. The way of life for an economist, an academic or a journalist is no longer German or French, but rather European or global in tone. The new forms of entanglement are a consequence of migratory processes, as well as worldwide material and immaterial communications systems and economic interdependencies and dependencies. (Welsch, 1999, p. 4)

For Welsch (1999), everybody is a "cultural hybrid" (p. 4). The personal and cultural identity consists of many different influences. Everybody has to negotiate between global and local elements, trying to merge these into one transcultural identity. The notion of transculturality can function as a corrective to supplement the "flaws in the globalization diagnosis" (Welsch, 1999, p. 9). While globalization seems to promote the uniform, transculturality supports diversity:

> It is able to cover both global and local, universalistic and particularistic aspects, and it does so quite naturally, from the logic of transcultural processes themselves. The globalization tendencies as well as the desire for specificity and particularity can be fulfilled within transculturality. Transcultural identities comprehend a cosmopolitan side, but also a side of local affiliation. (Welsch, 1999, p. 10)

Transculturality underlines the fact that, although globalization might aim at homogenization, localization and diversity are also a necessary part of internationalization. Using transculturality as a supplement to globalization opens up interesting perspectives on global childhoods.

Global and transcultural childhoods

While transcultural aspects of childhoods have not been at the focal point of academic studies, research on global childhoods has been a common topic in children's studies. This is surprising, because transculturality is an excellent supplement to globalization, emphasizing the meaning of diversity and local traditions for today's children. Global childhoods look different when transculturality is taken into account.

In children's studies, the term "global childhood" describes "the idea that children in different parts of the world share similar experiences of childhood" (James & James, 2012, p. 64). According to Allison and Adrian James (2012), there are various global characteristics of childhood. First, there are universal features of childhood, such as physical immaturity or dependency on adults. Second, childhood is internationally regulated and protected by laws, governments, and international organizations. The UN Convention on the Rights of the Child (The United Nations, 1989) is an example, constructing features of global childhood through the rights granted to children. Third, various aspects related to globalization shape children's lives everywhere in the world. This also concerns economics, because international market forces are interested in a "corporate construction of childhood" (Fleer, Hedegaard, & Tudge, 2009, p. 5), which creates a "global child" as consumer. Specific international ways of schooling or the impact of the media are likewise part of global childhoods. While many children might live global lives, their lives are also transcultural, shaped by local traditions and the various cultures they encounter every day. Therefore, particularity and transculturality are also important features of global childhoods.

Even though universal features in terms of global childhood exist, it is important to point out that childhood is, above all, a social construction. This insight was one of the major achievements of childhood studies, which emphasize the diversity and cultural relativity of the experience of childhood internationally (James & James, 2012). But the notion of childhood is also a Eurocentric approach, and this needs to be taken into account when talking about global childhoods. Gielen and Chumachenko (2004) emphasize that Western nations, where only a quarter of the world's child and adolescent population lives, set the norm for what childhood and appropriate development is for the other 85% of all young people. This is a challenge when trying to determine what children in various parts of the world need, what their daily lives should look like, and what kind of protection or education they should receive. Related to this issue is the notion of the "normal child," according to Western standards of appropriate development and behavior. Nsamenang (2009) notes that "the global child is Western-derived and that pathologizes all other images of childhood" (p. 24). It is crucial to take into account criticism of Eurocentric notions of childhood, because many children worldwide experience a different kind of childhood. Child labor, high mortality rates, prostitution, migration, poverty, and war shape children's lives in different ways around the globe (Gielen & Chumachenko, 2004). But even in industrialized and wealthy countries, there are completely different childhoods. This can concern children who work as caregivers for sick relatives, as Allison and Adrian James (2012) point out. While their actual number is unknown, the 2001 Census in the UK indicates that at least 114,000 children, ages 5 to 15 (53,000 boys and 61,000 girls), provided some kind of informal care at that point. Those children and young people have to balance the demands of their sick relatives, school, and friends.

They might lack the time to play, they might feel isolated, overwhelmed, and they may be without any kind of childhood at all.

When trying to determine what abilities or skills children should have and whether these are consistent across cultures, Allison and Adrian James (2012) assert that "competence is culturally relative and spans a wide range of attributes, including physical, cognitive, emotional, social and moral capacities" (p. 30). They state the following:

> As cross-cultural comparisons make abundantly clear, children cannot be viewed as a homogenous group, since their abilities and levels of functioning at any given age are far from universal. Where different assumptions about competence are made and applied, as inevitably happens in different cultures, different behaviors and practices arise. A good illustration of this is working children in the majority South, who perform many activities that, in other contexts, might be regarded as impossible for children to carry out effectively. (James & James, 2012, p. 30)

The abilities and skills children have depend on the culture they live in and the requirements and demands placed upon them. Sometimes, they have to develop quickly the skills necessary to master difficult situations in order to survive.

These aspects emphasize that the diversity of childhood experiences should be taken into account. There is no standardized childhood or child. Wells (2009) correctly remarks that "the global becomes one of several structures . . . that shape the lives of children and concepts of childhood in any specific socio-cultural setting" (p. 4). This becomes particularly obvious in the case of music.

Music and the transcultural child

When trying to apply Welsch's concept of transculturality to music and children, it can take on two different meanings. First, there is music, which can be considered transcultural in terms of merging different musical styles and traditions. "Waka Waka" is a good example of this kind of music, unifying aspects of South African and popular music. Second, children's musical identities are transcultural, being shaped by various musical cultures. Children learn to merge the different musical traditions they encounter into their own transcultural musical identities. The girls singing "Waka Waka" exemplify this. They were not only fascinated by a "transcultural" song, but also switched between this song and excerpts of other songs they liked, but they also improvised new melodies, depending on their individual needs. Their experiments with "Waka Waka" suggest that their musical world was transcultural in terms of being global as well as local.

Lum and Marsh (2012) point out, with regard to the global perspectives of children's musical development, that the effects of globalization in the areas of migration and the media are particularly significant. While migration leads to the blurring of national and cultural borders by people moving from one country to another, media connect the world electronically and turn it into a "global village." Media also offers opportunities for shaping one's musical identity in international and transcultural ways (Lum & Marsh, 2012). This means that, owing in particular to the impact of media, musical childhoods become internationally more alike. But at the same time, musical childhoods are still localized, as Welsch's concept of transculturality underlines (1999). Patricia Shehan Campbell and Trevor Wiggins (2013) are right when they state "children may act globally by virtue of their developmental passage but think locally" (p. 17). Children are experts in balancing the global and the local when it comes to their musical worlds and development. In so doing, they create transcultural musical identities.

Taking into account similar aspects and different aspects of children's musical cultures worldwide has sometimes been a challenge for research on children's musical cultures. Since John Blacking's study on the Venda children of South Africa (1967), ethnomusicology has played an important role in research on children's musical cultures internationally. It has helped to explore the ways in which children in different parts of the world make music meaningful in their lives. It has become clear that there are global and local aspects of children's musical worlds. But Campbell and Wiggins (2013) also point out that, in ethnomusicology, "the emphasis given to diversity over commonality has prevented the examination of patterns of children's practices, when in fact childhood may be best viewed for its global as well as cultural-specific entities" (p. 3). Campbell and Wiggins refer particularly to internationally similar patterns in children's songs, games, and rhythmic chanting, as shown by research investigating children's musical cultures in North America, Australia, and Europe. As Kathryn Marsh (2008) states, there are commonalities in songs and singing games internationally, both with regard to sonic properties and to the overall strophic structure in terms of repetitive or cyclical forms. But, at the same time, children's songs are influenced by the environment, their own experiences, the musical traditions and genres they encounter, and the meaning music has for them individually and in their society. This qualifies their musical worlds as transcultural, merging global and local elements. Transculturality plays a role both for children who stay in their country of birth and for immigrant children who have to adjust to a new culture. It is interesting to take a look at transcultural aspects of musical childhoods from a cross-cultural perspective.

Transcultural childhoods: Cross-cultural perspectives

Owing to globalization and its impact on children's lives, children are in touch with various musical traditions. They experience different musical cultures in their families, as well as through friends, schools, or special events. These influences shape their musical identity in terms of a transcultural identity. The musical worlds of children in Germany, as well as in other parts of the world, exemplify this.

Musical childhoods in Germany

When trying to investigate transcultural aspects of musical childhoods in Germany, it is useful first to take a look at the way children's musical worlds have been approached in German music education research. In contrast to various countries such as Australia, England, or the United States, the study of children's musical cultures in Germany is just at the beginning (Kertz-Welzel, 2013). While there are various reasons for this fact, one might be that notions of musicality and musical learning have traditionally been focused on schools as places for "making children musical." German music educator and ethnomusicologist Helmuth Segler is right when he states the following about German music education: "Luckily, teachers do not know a lot about children, because most of the time, they are interested in what children do not know" (Segler, 2003, p. 200). Music education research in Germany often searched for the best teaching approach or the right lesson content, but children's own musical culture, abilities, and skill development were often overlooked.

Childhoods and children's musical cultures in Germany vary, depending on various factors. Two important aspects having an impact on children's personal, cultural, and musical development in Germany are the so-called migration background (*Migrationshintergrund*) and the socio-economic status of parents. One-third of all German children younger than 13 years have a migration background. This means that they have been born in Germany as foreigners or have parents who immigrated to Germany (John, 2013).[1] According to the 2007 OECD (Organization for Economic Cooperation and Development) study, children from families with migration backgrounds or from families of lower social classes are less likely to go to university in Germany than in any of the other eight European states investigated (OECD Briefing Notes, 2007). The lack of support and opportunities to learn in lower social class families and in families with a migration background are problems that neither kindergarten nor school is able to compensate, particularly because the German government does not spend as much money as other European countries on education (OECD Briefing Notes, 2007). It is important to keep these social and educational issues in mind when looking at musical childhoods in Germany and the opportunities for musical engagement that children have.

A short glimpse of two different children in Germany can illustrate children's musical cultures:

> Gina, age 9, has to cope with the fact that her parents separated half a year ago. Since then, she does not live in a single family house anymore, but in a two-bedroom apartment in the city, together with her mother. Her mother is a retail saleswoman, but right now, she only works two or three times a week as maid and cleaner. Due to the emotional stress involved with the new situation, Gina's school achievement suffered so much that she might have to repeat a year. Therefore, learning for school is the most important issue right now and everything else such as biking or swimming has to stay behind. However, Gina still goes to an Aikido class once a week and meets her friends and playmates regularly. She also likes tending her pot plants and looking after her turtle. Every day after school, Gina plays on one of her three xylophones in order to take one step back and to have time to manage her emotions and to be herself. The only musical activity she does right now is being part of the instrumental ensemble of her school. (Badur, 2013, p. 143)

Gina's situation is typical for many children in Germany who are in emotional distress. Her life changed completely after her parents split up. She lives in a new apartment with her mother. Gina now has to find ways to redefine herself in this new situation. Without having the opportunity of learning an instrument in a music school, she uses her xylophones to create her own musical world, which she needs for emotional survival. Additionally, the school's instrumental ensemble plays an important role in her musical world. There, she can experience the joy of communal music-making.

For Sebastian, his musical world looks different:

> Six-year-old Sebastian lives with his parents and his little sister in an apartment building. His parents came to Germany in 1992 from the former Soviet Republic of Kazakhstan. Sebastian is growing up bilingual, speaking Russian at home and German in the kindergarten. His mother, a childcare worker, describes him as shy, but he loves to sing and tell stories. He particularly likes playing piano, which he started learning two years ago. He was already successful in the German music contest for children and young people, "Jugend Musiziert," and won a first prize in the regional competition. Sebastian starts his day at 8 with breakfast and then goes to the kindergarten, where he stays until 2. In the afternoon, he is at home and plays with his friends, practices piano, or watches TV. At around 6 or 7 in the evening, the family has dinner, and at 8, Sebastian goes to bed. (Kittel, 2008, p. 6)

Sebastian, although the son of immigrant parents, has the opportunity to learn piano and is quite successful at it. Growing up in a protected family, he enjoys this security and defines music as an important part of his life, his instrumental tuition being facilitated by a piano teacher. For Sebastian, there seems to be no problem in being part of different musical cultures, the world of classical music in his piano lessons, and the popular music world that he enjoys with his friends and on TV.

These two examples of children's musical worlds in Germany suggest that German children use music in the way they need to. It does not matter if they engage in self-initiated or teacher-facilitated activities, inside their own rooms or in schools. They also merge different musical cultures into a musical world that fits their needs. Music is a significant part of their lives, and many children worldwide would agree with this fact (Campbell, 2010).

In order to get a more precise idea of what is going on in children's musical lives, German music education scholar Renate Beckers (2004) developed the musical–ecological (*musikökologisch*) approach, which allows a very specific view of children's musical worlds, abilities, and development. It also helps to understand how children merge the different aspects of their musical experiences into a transcultural musical identity. For her model, Beckers utilizes Urie Bronfenbrenner's (1981) sociocultural perspective on children's development, positioning them in five different environmental systems which influence children, but are also influenced by children. Beckers argues that precisely this reciprocal correlation between children and environment, when children are not just passive participants, but also shape their worlds, should be at the core of studies about children's musical cultures. Using this approach, Beckers investigates the musical worlds of 4- to 10-year-old children in Germany. The five different environments range from the innermost system (microsystem) with close relatives, playmates, or teachers, up to the broadest part of children's environment, the macrosystem. The musical-ecological approach offers an excellent opportunity to monitor children's musical activities and border crossing between the different systems, thus shaping their own musical cultures and environments according to their own needs.

The musical–ecological center (*musikökologisches Zentrum*) is the starting point for all musical experiences and is at the core of children's musical lives. Listening to the mother's lullabies, communal singing at home, clapping or dancing to recordings, all these and many more musical activities take place here. According to Beckers, personal relationships, as well as material aspects, are important for the shaping of the musical–ecological center of children's musical worlds. A grandfather who plays trumpet in a Bavarian brass band, or a piano standing in a living room, will certainly have a deep impact on children. Playing or dancing with friends, inventing songs or rhythmic games, or imitating a YouTube video featuring a famous singer can also be important activities. The musical–ecological center is also the place where the work on transcultural musical identity starts. A boy from a Turkish immigrant family living in Germany, 10-year-old Bilal, explains that music is a very important part of their family life (Badur, 2013). He and his father learned to play keyboard autodidactically, performing Turkish and international hits such as "My heart will go on." They listened to the song for as long as it took to learn the melody and the harmonies. Then they played it while Bilal's mother and sister sang. They also have some sound equipment, such as loudspeakers and microphones, because they sometimes perform at Turkish celebrations and parties. For Bilal, music is an important part of his life. His musical activities are a good example of the meaning of music in the musical–ecological center and the shaping of a transcultural identity. He has been introduced to different musical traditions that became part of his musical world. He has learned to play various musical genres at home, through self-initiated activities and supported by his father. Apart from the music itself, the music equipment also motivates Bilal to perform. It helps him to feel more like a professional musician.

In general, the music and media equipment play an important role in Beckers' musical–ecological model. This is true of every section of her model, but particularly the musical–ecological center. According to the KIM Study in 2012 (Medienpädagogischer Forschungsverbund Südwest, 2013), investigating children aged 6 to 13 in Germany and their use of media, 58% of German children have a CD player in their rooms, 49% have their own mobile phone, 45% have their own MP3 player, and 36% have their personal TV. Regarding computers, in the age group of 6- to 13-year-old children in Germany, only 21% of all children have their own computer and just 15% have web access. Access to media allows children to manage their musical lives more independently;

it also facilitates access to different musical traditions and offers opportunities for developing transcultural musical identities.

Another important aspect of the musical–ecological center (and also other sections) for Beckers is the meaning music has for children's lives (*subjektive musikbezogene Deutungsmuster*). This concerns children's understanding of music and the way they make music meaningful in their lives. For many children, as a study of 5,000 German children aged 6 to 15 proves (Kleinen & Schmitt, 1991), music is meaningful in many different ways. Young people's drawings which Kleinen and his team analyzed showed that children like various musical activities, such as making music or dancing, but also picture themselves on stage or use music for mood management. For example, 11-year-old Arend drew a picture of himself playing piano, with his parents watching and supporting him (Kleinen & Schmitt, 1991). In a more recent study (Kertz-Welzel, 2013), 11-year-old Shirin made a drawing with the title "Music is the world," picturing a girl at the center, surrounded by various real and imagined musical instruments. In the background, there is a plane, sunrise, and clouds, symbolizing the world. Another drawing by 12-year-old Johanna shows the meaning of music in various situations: somebody playing a saxophone, she herself lying on a bed and listening to music, people dancing and performing, everything exemplifying the different meanings music can have. This suggests that children are often experts in how to use music for mood management; for example, 13-year-old Katharina remarks that music helps her feel better, particularly in situations when nobody understands her (Kertz-Welzel, 2013). Learning how to make music meaningful is an important part of a successful musical socialization, and also of the musical–ecological center the way Beckers describes it. Many children worldwide know how to accomplish this.

The space that Beckers calls *musikökologische Nahräume* is the closer social and musical circle or environment. Playgrounds, the gardens of neighbors, youth centers, and many more places are the realms in which children gather important musical experience, and also shape these spaces through their musical engagement. They learn how others act musically, but without somebody expecting them to already do things correctly. The closer musical circle is a realm of exploration and experiments, which can, for instance, concern the meaning of different kinds or traditions of music, their functions, and children's behavior. Dancing while singing a chorale in a small village church near Hamburg, or while attending a performance of Beethoven's first symphony in the *Gasteig* concert hall in Munich, Germany, would certainly not be appropriate behavior. But at a public festival or a party near Lake Constance, it would be all right to dance. Watching adults or adolescents perform in a Bavarian brass band and joining in by playing a simple percussion instrument during rehearsals can also be an inspiring experience for children. Being in a peer group, playing in a garage band, or just jamming with friends is likewise part of the closer circle of children's musical lives. Media play an important role in this musical–ecological space, too. Through videos and websites, children can find information about their favorite singer and establish him or her as their role model. The German girls described at the beginning of this chapter who tried to perform "Waka Waka" were acting within their closer musical circle, using what they saw on TV for their self-initiated musical activities. Media can foster children's musical development, helping them to shape their musical worlds according to their own needs. The access to information they offer also fosters the development of their transcultural musical identity. When examining German children's (age 6 to 13) favored leisure time activities, 44% listen to music every day, while 38% listen to music one or more times a week (KIM study, 2012, in Medienpädagogischer Forschungsverbund Südwest, 2013). Only 6% of all children make music every day, while 16% claim to play one or more times a week. However, this study does not reveal whether children participate in self-initiated or teacher-facilitated musical activities. According to

German music education scholar Imke Badur (2007), German third- and fourth-graders participate in much more self-initiated musical activity and learning (58%) than in activities guided by teachers. One-fifth of children's self-initiated musical activities were so-called *Rahmenaktivitäten* (framework activities), such as obtaining musical information, musical material, or looking for musical situations (Badur, 2007). German children are, as are many children worldwide, interested in the newest music trends and styles, have their favorite musicians and bands, and want to learn more about them. This is an important part of children's musical development. Badur also states that German children's musical experiences are often related to role-playing, games, TV shows, or books (Badur, 2007). While self-initiated musical activities can occur in all musical–ecological areas, whether singing in the schoolyard during recess or playing clapping games while waiting for a movie to start, they are most likely to appear within the closer musical circle.

According to Beckers' (2004) musical–ecological model, the next space in children's musical worlds is the different musical–ecological sections or areas (*musikökologische Ausschnitte*). These sections concern institutions such as schools, kindergartens, or community music schools, where a certain musical behavior is expected and where clear goals are given. There are roles, both musical and non-musical, with which children have to comply. They are supposed to learn music theory or how to play an instrument, usually facilitated by teachers. In the different musical–ecological areas, it is important for children to learn how to balance different roles in their musical lives, such as being a member in a youth brass band, having music lessons in public or community music schools, or jamming with friends. They also have to balance different musical cultures. In Germany, many children go to community music schools, some of them starting very early. In 2012, 184,703 (18%) of all age groups going to community music schools were under the age of 6, while 306,299 (30%) were between the ages of 6 and 9; 312,271 (31%) of young people aged 10 to 14 attended such schools in 2012, and 116,283 (11.5%) of all students were aged 15 to 18 (Deutscher Musikrat, 2013). This indicates that many German children go to community music schools, suggesting that making music is an important part of their lives.

The last section of Beckers' (2004) model is the musical–ecological periphery (*musikökologische Peripherie*). This encompasses events that do not take place often. Children are exposed to the music of different cultures, e.g., when they are on vacation with their parents in Spain, or they go to certain events such as recitals in a concert hall, or encounter Russian street musicians in a pedestrian area in Berlin. The musical–ecological peripheries can be crucial in making first impressions on children, very possibly changing the way they perceive music. It is important for children's musical development to include opportunities for various musical activities, no matter whether these are offered by the cultural management departments of city councils, by schools, by ensembles, or by individual musicians. This helps children to shape their musical identity in a more global and transcultural way.

The musical–ecological approach, as presented by Beckers (2004), offers interesting insights into the different levels of children's musical worlds and development. If used cross-culturally, it can help us to understand transcultural aspects of musical childhoods worldwide. Various aspects are important for the different areas, such as personal relationships that influence the meaning of music in children's lives, convenient opportunities of learning an instrument, or being able to play music with friends. Most naturally, they change from one musical tradition or style to another, merging them without any problems into their own musical and transcultural identities. Furthermore, the musical–ecological approach does not apply exclusively to a certain age group, but rather to any age in childhood, because the various sections of the musical worlds of children are often meaningful to them until they become adults. Young people permanently cross the borders between different musical areas and transform them when they grow up, according to their own needs. They also cross the borders between different musical genres and cultures, merging them into the transcultural musical worlds they live in. The shape of these transcultural music worlds depends on children's needs, but also on the opportunities for musical engagement and development which children encounter in the different musical–ecological areas.

Varying opportunities for musical experiences are important for the development of the transcultural aspects of children's musical worlds. Looking at the musical life of a specific city offers interesting insights into the possibilities for musical engagement that children have in Germany. This is particularly important in view of the fact that children of families from lower social classes or families with migrational backgrounds do not usually have easy access to music instruction in Germany, apart from public schools. The city of Augsburg, located in the state of Bavaria and famous for being the birthplace of Mozart's father, Leopold Mozart, is a well-documented example. When trying to explain the musical life of a city, the German word *Musikvermittlung* is the most appropriate term. While its literal translation is "mediation" or "facilitation" of music, it also describes a great variety of musical events, cultures, and opportunities for musical engagement. These activities can take place in public schools or community music schools, youth centers, or centers for children or elderly people, recitals or private music lessons, educational programs of theatres, or orchestras. They may be one-time opportunities or special programs. What might be unusual about the term *Musikvermittlung* is that it suggests that facilitators are always needed for valuable and viable musical engagement. The term *Musikvermittlung* illustrates the German tendency to believe in the power of teachers, mediators, or facilitators who make musical experiences meaningful or people "musical." What is also interesting about the term *Musikvermittlung* is that many musical projects carried out in Augsburg would internationally be considered community music. However, the term "community music" is very little known in Germany.

In Augsburg, there are many opportunities for children and adolescents to engage musically. In Augsburg schools, special events try to complement the usual general music education approach, either by offering a one-time opportunity or a program that children can join. During specific project days dedicated, for example, to exploring Mozart's life (*Auf den Spuren von Mozart*), children in the Augsburg primary school of Langenneufnach were able to discover more about Mozart's life and music (Eberhard & Kraemer, 2013). In 2006, in celebration of Mozart's 250th birthday, children dressed as Wolfgang and his sister Nannerl listened to performances of Mozart's music and to stories about his life, and danced to and played music of Mozart's time. The younger students also crafted wigs and other things important during Mozart's lifetime, while the older students tested their knowledge of Mozart in a special game based on the popular television show "Who wants to be a millionaire?." This project helped students to get in touch with a specific musical culture in a student- and action-orientated way, thereby offering opportunities for the enrichment of their transcultural musical identities.

While many projects like this take place in schools and are part of the musical–ecological area of music education, there are also projects outside of schools that shape children's musical lives and development in Augsburg. Projects can be part of a specific musical area, but also of the musical periphery, depending on the role they play for children. These activities include community theatre, orchestras, choirs, intercultural musical activities, and festivals, but also early childhood and traditional folk music ensembles or music therapy (Eberhard & Kraemer, 2013). Because Augsburg is a city with many immigrant children, with up to 75% (average: 51%) of pupils being of immigrant origins in elementary schools (Eberhard & Kraemer, 2013), there are many opportunities for intercultural musical activities. There are African drumming ensembles, Russian choirs, Turkish saz ensembles, and a Macedonian Roma band (Eberhard & Kraemer, 2013). There are societies such as the Turkish Parents' Society (*Türkischer Elternverein*), offering private lessons in saz and guitar. Interreligious workshops, such as "Music and Sacred Space" (*Musik und sakraler Raum*), offer children opportunities to experience sounds in three different rooms of worship in Augsburg: a Catholic church, a synagogue, and a mosque (Eberhard & Kraemer, 2013). For many immigrant parents, it is important that their children get to know their original culture's musical heritage. Children also have the chance to find private music teachers from their parents' home country, no matter whether it is Russian piano teachers, an instructor for Angolan drumming, or a teacher of saz who is needed (Eberhard & Kraemer, 2013). Cultural societies, as in many other cities worldwide, offer opportunities for an introduction to, or the transmission of, various cultural traditions. As concerns local Bavarian music and dance traditions, there are folk dance groups, brass bands, and zither or string ensembles celebrating and transmitting Bavarian culture (Eberhard & Kraemer, 2013). Through having opportunities to become acquainted with different musical cultures and traditions, children are able to shape their own transcultural musical identities, merging the different musical influences they encounter and that they consider important for themselves.

These and many more musical projects are part of different musical–ecological areas of children's musical worlds in Augsburg. They shape children's musical lives and are shaped by children's involvement, ideas, and creativity. They facilitate the development of children's transcultural musical identities through the musical opportunities offered. However, worldwide, children develop different kinds of transcultural identities in different circumstances.

International perspectives

For many children worldwide, music offers them a world of sounds and activities they like. It can be a sanctuary and a realm of their own. Music facilitates children's personal and cultural development and helps them to find out who they are and who they could be. When a German boy, Jan, age 12, explains that music means a lot to him and that he could not imagine a life without music (Kertz-Welzel, 2013), this is a statement that could be made almost anywhere in the world. The significance of music is one characteristic of global childhoods. But transcultural aspects of childhoods also play an important role for children worldwide, particularly in view of migration and the culturally diverse identities of nations. Merging global and local elements into their own musical worlds helps children to find out who they are.

In finding their own personal and cultural identity, indigenous music plays a significant role for children in many countries. For children growing up in the Yakama reservation in the American Pacific Northwest, music is important for getting to know their Native American culture. As Robert Pitzer states, "music in Native American culture has historically served as primary medium for informing new generations about their heritage" (Pitzer, 2013, p. 48). Therefore, traditional songs and dances have always been a target when the attempt was made to destroy Native American culture or to "deculturalize indigenous people" (Pitzer, 2013, p. 48). Saving traditional music culture serves as a kind of resistance against the oppressors and a safeguard for one's own identity. The *Yakama Nation Tribal School*, founded in 1980, tries to accomplish the task of transmitting traditional music and culture through the various practices of Native American music. Native American drum or flute music, as well as singing, are part of the curriculum. While helping students to become members of their Native American culture through making music, it also fosters the ability for self-expression. It helps students at risk to be part of a community and gives them opportunities for self-affirmation. Ryan, an eleventh-grader who participates in both drum and flute classes, emphasizes that, as far as his work as a mentor for younger students is concerned, he always makes sure that they not only develop their musical skills, but also experience "music's transformative power and self-affirming possibilities" (Pitzer, 2013, p. 57). This power also has much to do with the cultural and transcultural musical identity. In the *Yakama Nation Tribal School*, Native American music seems to be a valuable means of cultural transmission and personal growth. It adds one important cultural component to children's musical identities, shaping them in a transcultural way. If children are able to reconcile different musical traditions in their own transcultural musical identities, this can also support the reconciliation of their cultural and personal identities in general.

A similar significance of indigenous music can be observed in Mexico, particularly with regard to personal growth and the development of a transcultural musical identity. Janet Sturman describes the powerful performance of a girl at *Ollin Yoliztli School* in Mexico City, playing Mexican music:

> Nine-year-old Teresa strides to the front of the room, untucks her violin from beneath her arm and raises it to her chin. Standing proudly before her classmates, she glances to her teacher, Maestro Felipe, and they begin playing. Teresa bows a rapid Huastecan melody while her instructor strums the rhythmic accompaniment on the jarana. Her rhythms are perfect and her phrasing commanding. With equal confidence she stops her bow and in her clear bell-like voice sings the verses of the son de Carnaval. (Sturman, 2013, p. 179)

Teresa is confident and seems to find her personal voice in playing and singing Mexican music. The school helps her to find a musical culture which fits her, supplementing the popular music culture she has been growing up in. Sturman (2013) points out that music helps the Mexican children she observed to find their own identities. It is a way of reconciling the contrasting worlds they experience in their everyday lives. This particularly concerns balancing the various musical cultures they encounter. Special music programs, such as the *Ollin Yoliztli School*, allow children like Teresa to find ways of being Mexican today, by knowing both traditional Mexican and American popular music styles (Sturman, 2013). In her personal musical world, she is able to reconcile and merge the different traditions, thereby shaping her musical identity as transcultural.

The examples mentioned not only illustrate music's meaning with a view to personal growth through indigenous music, but also the significance of bimusicality and transculturality in a global world. It is most common to be part of several musical worlds at once, for instance the traditional and the popular music worlds. However, facilitating the development of bimusical or transcultural identities can be challenging for the institutions where children's musical learning takes place, particularly in bicultural countries. At a center for the education and care of young children in Aotearoa, New Zealand, early childhood education aims at both bicultural (New Zealanders of European and Maori descent) and multicultural education, because of the many Asian immigrants (Bodkin-Allen, 2013). Sally Bodkin-Allen states with regard to Aotearoa that "children are educated within a society that is officially bicultural and, in reality, often multicultural" (Bodkin-Allen, 2013, p. 388). Facilitating the bicultural identity of New Zealand is a political intention and has to be implemented by the people working in the care centers. This aim becomes clear when one views the different early childhood institutions in Aotearoa. While kindergartens and child-care centers are more related to the British heritage, the *Kohanga Reo* as places for Maori early childhood education, first established in 1982, are connected to indigenous traditions (Bodkin-Allen, 2013). But Maori culture and language are also part of the early childhood curriculum in different educational centers in New Zealand. Through singing traditional Maori, but also international, British, Anglo-American, or Asian songs, children experience a diversity of cultures. The "interweaving threads of music" in Aotearoa, as Bodkin-Allen (2013, p. 387) calls them, can be a way to successfully develop a transcultural musical identity. But in view of Welsch's (1999) concept of transculturality, it is important to point out that transculturality goes beyond the notions of interculturality and multiculturality. These two concepts still rely on the old notions of the homogeneity and delimitation of single cultures, no matter whether the different cultures are located in one country or in different ones (Welsch, 1999). In a global world, cultures are intertwined and linked; they no longer end at the borders of countries or specific communities. Transculturality tries to capture this kind of hybrid understanding of culture. With regard to the institutions in Aotearoa, the notion of transculturality as a goal of education might help to overcome the hidden hierarchies of cultures. It emphasizes that acknowledging diversity in terms of transculturality is an important part of globalization and helps to balance different cultural traditions.

In general, children are regularly confronted with different cultural and musical traditions that they have to balance. Often, they do this quite naturally, shaping the different musical–ecological spaces in a transcultural way, according to their own needs and the expectations of others. Hong Kong is an excellent example of this, being a place where more than one cultural and musical tradition is significant. Children in Hong Kong have to come to terms with change and tradition, as Lily Chen-Hafteck (2013) states. Living in a basically Chinese culture, traditional Chinese beliefs are important. This concerns such issues as a concept of personality which values a harmonious connectedness and a fitting-in, a notion of learning that emphasizes high achievements, competition, hard work, and the role of demanding parents (Chen-Hafteck, 2013). At the same time, the impact of Western and particularly English culture, owing to Hong Kong's past as a British colony from 1842 until 1997, has an impact on children's lives and musical development. Children learn both Chinese and English, sing songs in both languages, and celebrate Chinese and English holidays (Chen-Hafteck, 2013). For children in Hong Kong, music is a much-needed means of helping them to balance two cultures by creating their own musical and transcultural worlds, while also developing specific musical skills. Learning traditional Cantonese children's songs, but also pop songs, as well as being familiar with the Western European Art Music tradition gives children vast opportunities to shape their own musical worlds in the direction of transculturality. Music can also function as a sanctuary to which children can retreat, important in view of an educational world where competition and success are highly valued (Chen-Hafteck, 2013). It can represent their own transcultural realm where no hierarchies of cultures or pressure to favor one particular culture exist.

Music often can, in fact, be an important means to help children find their own identity in an environment that does not acknowledge them in an appropriate way. Kathryn Marsh (2013) argues that, for refugee children in Australia, music plays a significant role in "developing forms of communication, a sense of belonging and empowerment, and a contribution to cultural maintenance, identity construction, emotional release, and integration" (p. 491). Music helps them to balance their different cultural identities, while exploring new roles musically, in a safe place. They learn how to come to terms with different cultures through music and developing their transcultural identity. First, they might create a transcultural musical identity, reconciling their "old" and "new" cultures. Then, they might be able to accomplish this in other parts of their lives. For immigrant children, as Marsh states (2013), music often facilitates their personal journey from being an alien in a country with a foreign language and culture, to becoming familiar with a new environment. Music can be a safe and familiar place, but at the same time also facilitate the necessary transition through developing a transcultural identity.

While music can be a sanctuary for children, it can also be related to issues of power and oppression. This concerns particularly Western European Art Music, which is, in some parts of the world, still associated with colonial powers. The Chinese–Malaysian scholar Roe-Min Kok (2011) describes her own childhood instrumental music instruction as a "colonizing force" (p. 80), where she was supposed to submit to a colonial and authoritarian teaching style and its values. The only thing that mattered was to pass the test of the British Associated Board of The Royal Schools of Music (ABRSM). Although in Kok's childhood Malaysia had already been independent from Great Britain for more than a decade, British teaching approaches still dominated Malaysian instrumental music instruction. Kok summarizes her experiences in private music instruction as follows:

> My early music education was a process that did not much foster intellectual curiosity and musical activity, but one which I was taught to think in terms of cultural, national, ethnic, and economic hierarchies. It is the story of a colonial "violence" wrought on young minds and psyches. The violence was wrought with a cultural tool—Western European Art Music (. . .) Motivated by different reasons, all of us—the ABRSM, my parents, my piano teacher, and myself—participated willingly if unwillingly in an ideological process that ultimately reinforced the colonizers' cultural subjugation of the colonized. (Kok, 2011, p. 83)

In this description, Western European Art Music symbolizes the power of colonial forces. It was the highest value, and everything else was supposed to be subordinated to it. Finding children's own voices, paying attention to their individual needs, or any child-centered approach were not considered worthwhile. Neither Malaysian culture nor bimusicality or transculturality played any role at all. But the most frightening matter in this Malaysian experience is the fact that children internalized colonial values, even after Malaysia was no longer a British colony. Western European Art Music symbolizes this power of the oppressors, being present in the musical lives of many children who take instrumental lessons. This suggests that music is not always automatically a safe haven for children, but sometimes also a place of bad memories and musical trauma. Issues of power, oppression, and colonial ideas demand a heightened sensitivity toward the musical worlds of children globally, and toward the impact that music education has on different levels. Even if the influence of colonial forces might not be as dominant as described in Kok's memory, there are still places where Western European Art Music might play an ambivalent role, for instance in the former British colony India (Clausen & Chatterjee, 2012). According to Welsch (1999), transculturality does not imply any kind of hierarchy of cultures. Rather, according to individual needs, the meaning of different cultures can change at different times.

The discussion of global and transcultural childhoods from a cross-cultural perspective underlines various issues. The meaning of music for children worldwide is significant. They need music for their personal development, whether through indigenous music, or popular or Western European Art Music. Children are part of different musical cultures. This helps them to shape their own transcultural world of music that meets their own needs. For children in difficult situations, music can become a sanctuary to which they can retreat and where they can find the comfort the real world does not offer them. But music can also be used, as demonstrated in the case of Western European Art Music in Malaysia, as a means of power and oppression. This issue needs to be taken seriously, particularly with regard to the meaning of Western European Art Music in colonial contexts. In general, children are able to create transcultural musical identities, merging global and local aspects. Children in New Zealand or Hong Kong learn quite naturally how to navigate between different musical cultures and how to design their musical worlds. They create transcultural musical identities, using the opportunities which globalization offers in a way that meets their individual musical needs.

Global childhoods and transculturality

The notion of transcultural childhoods indicates that, despite all global commonalities, there is a diversity of childhoods. Although globalization has a huge impact on children's lives and musical worlds, the respective culture and society they live in and the musical experiences they have shape their musical identity significantly. Beckers' musical–ecological approach and the notion of *Musikvermittlung* illustrate this issue in the case of children in Germany. For many young people worldwide, it is most common to balance global and local aspects, merging them into their individual transcultural identity.

Often, children's abilities to merge various cultures, particularly the global and the local, are far more evolved than the respective skills which adults have. This ability to create hybrid or transcultural identities could be an example for a much-needed skill to overcome the problems of globalization. Regarding the need for transculturality, Wolfgang Welsch states:

> Wherever an individual is cast by differing cultural interests, the linking of such transcultural components with one another becomes a specific task in identity-forming. Work on one's identity is becoming more and more work on the integration of components of differing cultural origin. And only the ability to transculturally cross over will guarantee us identity and competence in the long run. (Welsch, 1999, p. 5)

This suggests that, in a global world, transculturality is, in fact, a necessity. While it could be taught or discussed in schools, it is also something that many children worldwide acquire in their daily lives, through self-initiated or externally facilitated musical activities. Music education can foster this development through offering opportunities for various musical experiences. But, in the end, children themselves shape their transcultural musical identities the way they like and need to. It seems that children are able to learn and practice what transculturality means in a most natural way. Transcultural musical childhoods, then, are excellent examples of successfully balancing the challenges and opportunities globalization poses.

Reflective questions

1 What does the term "global childhood" describe?
2 Explain and discuss the concept of transculturality. What could it mean in your personal and professional life?
3 Apply the musical-ecological model to your own musical experiences. What did the different spaces look like for you?
4 Describe the musical life of a city you know, according to the notion of *Musikvermittlung*.
5 How could music education support the development of transcultural musical identities?

Note

1 For more information see <https://www.destatis.de/EN/FactsFigures/SocietyState/Population/MigrationIntegration/PersonsMigrationBackground/Current.html>.

Key sources

Beckers, R. (2004). *Die musikalische Lebenswelt 4- bis 10-jähriger Kinder. Eine musikökologische Erkundung.* Münster: LIT.

Campbell, P. S., & Wiggins, T. (2013). *The Oxford handbook on children's musical cultures.* New York: Oxford University Press.

Eberhard, D. M., & Kraemer, R.-D. (2013). *Augsburger Projekte und Initiativen zur Musikvermittlung. Versuch einer gründlichen Dokumentation.* Augsburg: Wißner.

Fleer, M., Hedegaard, M., & Tudge, J. (2009). *Childhood studies and the impact of globalization: Policies and practices at the global and local levels* (World Yearbook of Education 2009). London: Routledge.

James, A., & James, A. (2012). *Key concepts in childhood studies*. London: Sage.

Reference list

Appadurai, A. (1996). *Modernity at large: Cultural dimensions of globalization*. Minneapolis, MN: University of Minnesota Press.

Badur, I.-M. (2007). Selbstinitiierte musikbezogene Aktivitäten von Kindern im Grundschulalter. In W. Auhagen, C. Bullerjahn, & H. Höge (Eds.), *Musikalische Sozialisation im Kindes- und Jugendalter* (pp. 54–70). Göttingen: Hogrefe.

Badur, I.-M. (2013). *Musikbezogene Aktivitäten von Kindern im Grundschulalter* (Unpublished doctoral dissertation). Justus-Liebig-Universität, Gießen.

Beckers, R. (2004). *Die musikalische Lebenswelt 4- bis 10-jähriger Kinder. Eine musikökologische Erkundung.* Münster: LIT.

Blacking J. (1967). *Venda children's songs: A study in ethnomusicological analysis*. Johannesburg: Wiwatersrand University Press.

Bodkin-Allen, S. (2013). Interweaving threads of music in the whariki of early childhood musical activities in Aotearoa/New Zealand. In P. S. Campbell & T. Wiggins (Eds.), *The Oxford handbook on children's musical cultures* (pp. 387–401). New York: Oxford University Press.

Bronfenbrenner, U. (1981). *Die Ökologie der menschlichen Entwicklung*. Stuttgart: Klett-Cotta.

Campbell, P. S. (2010). *Songs in their heads. Music and its meaning in children's lives* (2nd ed.). New York: Oxford University Press.

Campbell, P. S., & Wiggins, T. (2013). Giving voice to children. In P. S. Campbell & T. Wiggins (Eds.), *The Oxford handbook on children's musical cultures* (pp. 1–24). New York: Oxford University Press.

Chen-Hafteck, L. (2013). Tradition and change in the musical lives of children in Hong Kong. In P. S. Campbell & T. Wiggins (Eds.), *The Oxford handbook on children's musical cultures* (pp. 402–18). New York: Oxford University Press.

Clausen, B., & Chatterjee, S. (2012). Dealing with "Western classical music" in Indian music schools. A case study in Kolkata, Bangalore, Goa and Mumbai. In J. Knigge & A. Niessen (Eds.), *Musikpädagogisches Handeln. Begriffe, Erscheinungsformen, politische Dimensionen* (pp. 112–31). Essen: Blaue Eule.

Coupland, N. (2010). Introduction. In N. Coupland (Ed.), *The handbook of language and globalization* (pp. 1–27). Molden: Wiley-Blackwell.

Deutscher Musikrat. (2013). *Schülerzahlen und Altersverteilung an Musikschulen im VdM (Verband der Musikschulen)*. Retrieved from <http://www.miz.org/intern/uploads/statistik5.pdf>.

Eberhard, D. M., & Kraemer, R.-D. (2013). *Augsburger Projekte und Initiativen zur Musikvermittlung*. Augsburg: Wißner.

Fleer, M., Hedegaard, M., & Tudge, J. (2009). *Childhood studies and the impact of globalization: Policies and practices at the global and local levels* (World Yearbook of Education 2009). London: Routledge.

Gielen, U. P., & Chumachenko, O. (2004). All the world's children: The impact of global demographic trends and economic disparities. In U. P. Gielen & J. Roopnarine (Eds.), *Childhood and adolescence. Cross-cultural perspectives and applications* (pp. 81–109). Westport: Praeger.

James, A., & James, A. (2012). *Key concepts in childhood studies*. London: Sage.

John, S. (2013). *Kinder mit Migrationshintergrund und ihre Lebenslagen*. Retrieved from <http://www.kitaundco.de/component/themensammlung/item/45-themensammlung/paedagogische-querschnitts-aufgaben/inklusion-und-diversity/387-kinder-mit-migrationshintergrund-und-ihre-lebenslagen>.

Kertz-Welzel, A. (2013). Children's and adolescents' musical needs and music education in Germany. In P. S. Campbell & T. Wiggins (Eds.), *The Oxford handbook on children's musical cultures* (pp. 371–86). New York: Oxford University Press.

Kittel, C. (2008). Aufwachsen in Medienwelten. Die Rolle der Familie in der Mediensozialisation von Vorschulkindern. *Ludwigsburger Beiträge zur Medienpädagogik*, **11**, 1–13. Retrieved from <http://www.ph-ludwigsburg.de/fileadmin/subsites/1b-mpxx-t-01/user_files/Online-Magazin/Ausgabe11/Kittel11.pdf>.

Kleinen, G., & Schmitt, R. (1991). *Musik verbindet: Musikalische Lebenswelten auf Schülerbildern*. Essen: Blaue Eule.

Kok, R.-M. (2011). Music for a postcolonial child: Theorizing Malaysian memories. In L. Green (Ed.), *Learning, teaching and musical identity* (pp. 73–90). Bloomington, IN: Indiana University Press.

Lum, C.-H., & Marsh, K. (2012). Multiple worlds of childhood: Culture and the classroom. In G. E. McPherson & G. F. Welch (Eds.), *The Oxford handbook of music education* (Vol. 1, pp. 381–98). New York: Oxford University Press.

Marsh, K. (2008). *The musical playground: Global tradition and change in children's songs and games*. Oxford: Oxford University Press.

Marsh, K. (2013). Music in the lives of refugee and newly arrived immigrant children in Sydney, Australia. In P. S. Campbell & T. Wiggins (Eds.), *The Oxford handbook on children's musical cultures* (pp. 492–509). New York: Oxford University Press.

Medienpädagogischer Forschungsverbund Südwest. (2013). *KIM-Studie 2012: Kinder + Medien, Computer + Internet. Basisuntersuchung zum Medienumgang 6- bis 13 jähriger in Deutschland*. Retrieved from <http://www.mpfs.de/fileadmin/KIM-pdf12/KIM_2012.pdf>.

Nsamenang, A. B. (2009). Cultures in early childhood care and education. In M. Fleer, M. Hedegaard, & J. Tudge (Eds.), *Childhood studies and the impact of globalization: Policies and practices at the global and local levels* (pp. 23–45). London: Routledge.

OECD Briefing Notes für Deutschland. (2007). Retrieved from <http://www.oecd.org/edu/39317467.pdf> (last accessed February 3, 2014).

Pitzer, R. (2013). Youth music at the Yakama Nation Tribal School. In P. S. Campbell & T. Wiggins (Eds.), *The Oxford handbook on children's musical cultures* (pp. 46–60). New York: Oxford University Press.

Scheuerman, W. (2010). Globalization. In E. N. Zalta (Ed.), *The Stanford Encyclopedia of Philosophy*, Summer 2010 Edition. Retrieved from <http://plato.stanford.edu/archives/sum2010/entries/globalization>.

Segler, H. (2003). Kritik an einer Pädagogik des Kindgemäßen. In G. Kleinen (Ed.), *Musik und Kind* (pp. 197–208). Kassel: Laaber.

Sturman, J. (2013). Integration in Mexican children's musical worlds. In P. S. Campbell & T. Wiggins (Eds.), *The Oxford handbook on children's musical cultures* (pp. 179–97). New York: Oxford University Press.

Trask, B. S. (2010). *Globalization and families*. New York: Springer.

The United Nations. (1989). *Convention on the rights of the child*. Retrieved from <http://www.unicef.org/crc>.

Wells, K. (2009). *Childhood in a global perspective*. Cambridge: Polity.

Welsch, W. (1999). Transculturality—the puzzling form of cultures today. In M. Featherstone & S. Lash (Eds.), *Spaces of culture: City, nation, world* (pp. 194–213). London: Sage. Retrieved from <http://www2.uni-jena.de/welsch/Papers/transcultSociety.html>.

Chapter 32

My voice is important too: Non-formal music experiences and young people

Lee Higgins

My voice is important too: Introduction

Until recently, formal music education has dominated the research agenda of our discipline (Veblen, 2012). Over the last decade this pattern has begun to change, with informal music teaching and learning becoming a fertile ground for discussion, debate, and research.[1] Following Lucy Green (2014), formal music education refers to both types of institution and types of practice. Broadly reflecting a top-down curriculum formation involving explicit teaching and assessment strategies, Western classical music has been historically linked to formal music education, although there is now a much larger range of musical styles on offer within schools, universities, and conservatoires that would fall under this banner including jazz, popular, and musics from traditions across the world. Informal education might be understood as the other end of a continuum and thus associated with conversational forms of engagement with learning practices rooted in the passing-on of musical knowledge and skills associated with music from a particular context, culture, or society (Busch, 2005; Jeffs & Smith, 1990, 2005). If we consider formal music education and informal musical learning as part of a continuum, then it is perhaps reasonable to locate non-formal music education as siting somewhere between the two, thus reflecting a bottom-up or negotiated curriculum formation that involves a music leader, or facilitator, in continuous dialogue with the young people with whom they work.

The discourse concerning non-formal music experiences has not been a significant feature within music education scholarship. Those who have explored its efficacy mine the following themes: person-centered and peer learning, inclusivity, facilitation as a strategic approach to teaching, valuing learners' personal musical interests, the recognition that music-making can contribute to young people's overall social, educational, and personal development, the interconnections between in-school and out-of-school musical interests and experiences, and the contribution that non-formal education has to a lifelong musical journey. Examples of such enquiry can be found in the work of Abigail D'Amore (2009) and her analysis of approaches employed by musicians working in the Musical Futures project, Nina Kors (2007) and Peter Mak (2007) through their research with Rineke Smilde (2008), and the Lifelong Learning Lectorate in The Netherlands, On Nei Annie Mok (2011), who recognizes the lack of discussion surrounding the term non-formal and attempts to bridge the gap by introducing the concept by providing examples from both Japanese and Chinese musical transmission, Jo Saunders and Graham Welch's (2012) investigation into Youth Music Action Zones in England, and Kari Veblen (2012) in her discussion surrounding different types of learning under the umbrella of lifelong learning. The purpose of this chapter is to explore what non-formal music experiences are and what opportunities they can offer a young person engaged in making music.

Non-formal education

Initially an "alternative" approach to formal education within developing countries, interest in non-formal education emerged from those who felt that formal education systems alone could not respond to the challenges of modern society. These included changes in the cultural, social, economic, and political landscape such as ideas connected to globalization, government decentralization, and a growing democratization. Coming to prominence around the late 1960s, with the work of Philip Coombs (1968), non-formal education continued its growth through the 1970s within the context of development, "the idea that deliberate action can be undertaken to change society in chosen directions considered desirable" (Rogers, 2004, p. 13). Although the term non-formal education had been used prior to the 1970s, it was Coombs who claimed the first systematic study of it by laying down a number of definitional frameworks, the most refined of which states that non-formal education is "simply any organized activity with educational purposes carried on outside the highly structured framework of formal education systems as they exist today" (Coombs & Ahmed, 1974, p. 233).

As part of the lifelong learning discourse, those working in non-formal education searched for terminology which would cover alternative educational programs, especially for marginalized, excluded, and/or subordinated populations (Otero, McCoshan, & Junge, 2005). This emphasis on non-formal learning is reflected at the turn of the millennium in the Council of Europe's recommendation that non-formal education should be recognized as an essential aspect in both lifelong learning processes and youth policy (Europe, 2011). In tune with technological advances, the Council of Europe has now extended its discussion to include e-learning environments for young people within non-formal contexts (Lopez, 2012). In short, if formal education is categorized as curriculum based and leading toward some sort of certification and placed within education and training institutions, non-formal education can be understood as an alternative, born out of insufficiencies within and criticism of the formal educational system (Torres, 2001). As an educational activity, non-formal education often takes place outside the established formal education system and is highly contextualized, intending to serve identifiable learning goals, and is based on a series of learning opportunities that are tailor-made and adapted to the needs of the learner group. Schemes of work are flexible and as such signify that the structure is non-linear and thus resists top-down curriculum. Consequently, non-formal education can be characterized as "learning by doing," depending strongly on reflection ("in" and "on" action) and fostered by a leader in the field who acts as a mentor, facilitating to transform experience into knowledge, skills, attitudes, values, and convictions (Colardyn, 2001; Rogers, 2004).[2] Resonant to key educational thinkers of the time, non-formal educators place emphasis on a "bottom-up" rather than a "top-down" approach to teaching, a stress on inclusivity and participation, encouragement of a personalized learning experience, and an understanding that the work can have an impact beyond the content area itself. In order to understand non-formal music education in practice, the following section offers illustrative examples of five projects in an attempt to respond to the question: How can we describe the musical experiences of young people engaged in non-formal music education?

Music-making in a youth club

Consider the work of Caroline, a musician working within an inner-city youth service in Liverpool, UK. As a local musician known to youth workers in the area, Caroline was invited into one of its youth centers to discuss the possibility of supporting some of its young people in their musical development. This request came about through discussion between the youth workers and those who attend and use the center. It was of particular interest for a group of young males who were trying to form a cohesive rock band but were struggling to organize themselves. There were many reasons why creating an active music-making ensemble was important for the youth in the group. Many of their reasons went beyond those of a musical nature, as those in the ensemble wanted reprieve from instability at home, getting in trouble with the police, difficulty in forming healthy relationships, and lack of confidence brought about through low self-esteem.

The club that the boys attended was an after-school facility that stayed open until around 10 p.m. Young people from 12 to 19 years met at the center, where there are spaces to simply sit and chat, and regular opportunities to become involved in a range of trips, sport, and art activities. During the opening times adult youth-workers are on hand to give advice and offer instruction at the young people's request. Working in ways that might be described as "informal," the youth-workers know the local context and are well aware of the issues and pressures that surround the young people.[3] As with most youth, there has always been a great interest in music amongst both the girls and the boys. Background recorded music is always playing, predominantly the current popular sounds but also classic rock and heavy metal. A number of those who attend the center own guitars, drums, and keyboards, and play them with varying levels of expertise. In order to harness this interest, and in consultation with the young people, the youth-workers hired Caroline, a skilled and experienced local musician who regularly worked as a music facilitator in and around the city. With the help of a seeding grant, the center purchased a basic backline, a drum kit, a couple of guitar amps and guitars, a small P.A., microphones, and a keyboard. This money also enabled them to employ Caroline to facilitate their twice-weekly music club. During this time Caroline guided the young people in their musical performing by helping with instrumental technique, arrangements, and constructive criticism both on the groups' original material and on the cover numbers they had chosen to perform. Her role is not passive but rather highly engaged, and Caroline was constantly aware of the shifting group dynamics through regular conversation with youth-workers and heeding their advice.

The music club has been popular over and beyond the initial request and the center is now beginning to see an overspill of its activities into the other weekday evenings. An independent network of peer mentoring is now taking place between those with instrumental skills and those who wish to learn. Almost every night you can witness peer teaching, a young musician teaching someone else a new lick, chord sequence, or vocal line.[4] Although there is growing confidence amongst the young people, Caroline's weekly presence is still treasured and appreciated. She is seen as an important and stable influence both in terms of facilitating non-formal musical learning and as someone who knows aspects of the young people's lives. From my observations of Caroline and other community musicians that work in these ways, participants look to the facilitator for reassurance, clarity, direction, encouragement, guidance, or help in shaping their music material. In this sense there is a constant negotiation of power that the skilled educator reflects upon both within and outside their music sessions. Music facilitators who are tuned into the effects of this are often able to find a comfortable balance between being a "friend" and also taking responsibility for what comes with working with young people, such as being asked advice on a diverse range of topics which might include sexual health, bullying, careers, and parents.[5] The ability to find comfort between being prepared and being able to let go bleeds into approaches to music-making that have an emphasis on enabling the group or individuals to discover the journey of musical invention. To better understand the experiences of the young people that engage in non-formal musical projects, the next section briefly describes the key features of this approach.

Facilitating musical learning

As an approach to participatory music-making, non-formal music education provides opportunities to develop skills such as trust, respect, empathy, and creativity whilst intentionally intertwining social and personal aspects with music-making. Those who work within this domain often refer to themselves as music facilitators rather than teachers. From this perspective, facilitation is concerned with encouraging open dialogue among different individuals with differing perspectives (Benson, 2010; Hogan, 2002, 2003). As a self-reflective "teacher" who has a variety of technical skills and knowledge, together with a wide range of experiences to assist groups of people to journey together to reach their goals, non-formal music educators act as conduits who enables participants' creative energy to flow, develop, and grow through pathways specific to individuals and the groups in which they are active.

A facilitator does not mean that the musician surrenders responsibility for music leadership, but rather their sense of control in the musical learning is relinquished. In other words, the musical facilitators purposefully enable the learners to co-construct their learning, and through this indirect approach, deeper learning happens. Within any group setting, there is a fine line between leading and controlling, but the two processes are very different and therefore provide contrasting results to the group experience. For example, in controlling the group journey, there is a strong sense of the beginning, middle, and end, and the expectations and needs to be met. In facilitating the group experience, however, there may certainly be a starting point, but the rest remains uncertain. Non-formal music educators offer routes toward suggested destinations and are ready to assist if the group journey becomes lost or confused, but they are always open to the possibility of the unexpected that comes from individuals in their interactivity with the group. These possibilities cannot be predicted, and that is the excitement of facilitated music that grows from the group, be they a class of young children or members of a youth rock band. Anything can happen when musical events are proposed and facilitated but not directed in the manner of the top-down conductors/directors tradition.

Good facilitators move in and out of roles as the group dictates necessitating trust in the ability of others as well as submission to the inventiveness of others. Non-formal music educators can develop this trust as they learn to listen to others whilst maintaining the skill to enable the participants to work together. By establishing a secure but flexible framework from the outset, non-formal music educators often give over the control to the group and trust in the direction it takes. In giving up control, the possibilities emerge for musical outcomes that are unpredictable; music becomes an invention personal to the participants, owned by and meaningful, with the potential to generate an experience that can shape, create, and have an impact on identity formation (Green, 2011).

Findings from studies into effective parent–child communication provide a useful analogy to that of the facilitator–group relationship (Karofsky, Zeng, & Kosorok, 2000; Rogers, 1995; Steinberg, 2001). A young child needs clear instruction and boundaries to feel safe and secure; this is the premise that enhances the child's growth and development. As he or she becomes older, the parent needs to step back a little. The child must face some milestones alone, but is always able to return to the security of the caring parent who is ready, waiting, and expecting to offer comfort, support, guidance, and perhaps redirection. As the child moves into adolescence, so the parent needs to release the reigns further, enabling the young adult to overcome challenges, encounter new discoveries, and develop self-assurance. With the aim of enabling the development of autonomy, the diligent parent will carefully consider when to sensitively step in with offers of support, guidance, advice, or comfort.

School of Rock

Non-formal musical approaches are then predominantly rooted in group-based activities that focus on performing, listening, composing, and improvising. Learners are encouraged to have significant input in the learning and this means that the material is often co-constructed. Another good example of this, a project that serves to highlight young people's musical needs within a particular community, is the School of Rock, a twice-yearly project that is run by a village youth project on the Wirral, UK. Under the strap-line "Labels are for jars, not young people,"[6] its mission has been to support and enable young people to achieve their full and unique potential, emotionally, socially, morally, and spiritually.[7] Amongst its offerings includes a drop-in center open four days a week and providing a wide range of facilities including a café, IT suite, pool, table tennis, and a video games area, outdoor residential weeks, a shop selling a variety of clothes and gifts, plus a range of clubs including canoeing, Christian study groups, dance, and drama. As an after-school program, the School of Rock has three components. First, the young people have individual lessons on instruments of their choice from a range of guitar, bass, drums, keyboards, or vocals. The instrumental tutors are a mixture of professional and trainee facilitators drawn from a local pool of working musicians and recipients of past projects. The situation is complex, as the tutors have to deal with a range of skills from beginners upward and teach in rooms spread across the youth center and church hall. Instrumental instruction is more akin to facilitation and non-formal strategies rather than formal one-to-one instrumental teaching. Second, and after six weeks of engagement in instrumental learning, everybody is placed in an ensemble and has a further six weeks to rehearse two or three songs. Finally, and with the guidance of the music facilitators, the groups perform a number of gigs for an audience. In some instances the venues can be quite prestigious and include a full sound rig, lights, and access-all-areas passes!

As well as providing a fun and engaging learning experience for those young people who desired to "have a go," the project has created opportunities for others to explore their music further. 23 Fake Street is one such group that has benefited from the project. Starting out as a group of mates, their involvement with the Bank has helped consolidate their friendship and their musical ambition. Now an established band on the local scene, the group plays regular gigs and makes recordings of their original music. They continue to support the School of Rock project through the music development program, a training initiative that educates participants to become peer mentors and eventually music tutors.

Rock 'n' Roll for Girls After-School Music Club

In a similar vein to the School of Rock but with an overt emphasis on addressing the under-representation of female songwriters in British music, singer–songwriter and BRIT[8] award winner Kate Nash started her Rock 'n' Roll for Girls After-School Music Club.[9] Through collaboration with a number of schools across the UK, Nash and her band began running songwriting workshops in 2011. The motivation to begin the enterprise was the shocking statistic that only 14% of the 75,000 members of the Performing Rights Society, which collects and pays songwriting royalties in Britain, is female. In Nash's own words, "A lot of women in pop aren't writing their own songs and there is this preconception that women are meant mainly as performers" (Sharp, 2011). Employing non-formal music education strategies the workshops are designed to support female songwriters in finding confidence in their identity as musicians.

Fig. 32.1 Esme, a participant in Kate Nash's Rock 'n' Roll for Girls After-School Music Club, performs her own work

Photo courtesy of Deborah Krikun.

Esme, known in her school as a singer/songwriter, was invited to be involved in Nash's project (see Figure 32.1). She was asked what she played and how she would like to work with the professional musicians from Nash's band. Choosing to work with the drummer, Esme discussed with her how the music should sound. Conversation between the two of them revolved around the types of artists that were currently influential on Esme's compositions and the musical possibilities for the songs she had written. Esme recalls that "the project was about not going with the crowd, to feel self-confident about what you do, to know that everyone is different and special." Esme felt that the project was in contradiction to her school's formal music education: "Music in school was never about self-expression, it's too structured." The impact of the project has helped Esme move forward as a performer, playing in local venues around the city and continuing her music education at a community college where non-formal strategies are being used within a formal setting. From Esme's perspective, non-formal approaches to music-making have "allowed" her to make the music she wants and to express the person she is.

Connect project

Operating in a non-formal context, the Connect project, as reported by Peter Renshaw (2005), offers rich opportunities for the "voices" of its young musicians to be heard and acknowledged.

In an effort to demonstrate ways through which quality music-making can be achieved through collaborative forms of composition and performance, the connect project has made efforts to identify the leadership skills necessary for engaging in creative workshop practice. These include:

◆ Knowing how to work musically in a group that incorporates any instrument brought to an ensemble by the young musicians;

◆ Knowing how to work effectively in mixed groups varying in size, age, technical ability, and musical experience;

◆ Knowing how to make music in a genre-free ensemble, where its musical material reflects the shared interests of the leaders and participants;

◆ Knowing how to engage in music-making virtually without notation;

◆ Knowing how to create music collaboratively.

Like these examples, musicians work collaboratively with young people to create, shape, and perform new music. Underlying the teaching strategy is knowing how to incorporate a range of people, their instruments, and their musical styles into an ensemble situation. Because the ethos of the project promotes inclusion, having the facilitatory skill-set to work effectively in mixed groups becomes a vital attribute. As skilled facilitators, the musicians work with processes and strategies that enable participants to embrace their music potential while connecting it to the world in which they live. When I spoke to participants during a Connect project in Essex, UK, those that I spoke to emphasized the collaborative nature of the work. For example, Jim who played the trumpet said, "I really like the creative tasks [the facilitators] have been very helpful [. . .] you get along with them [and] that is what makes it different." Shawn and Jane reinforced this by saying, "Yeah, the [Connect] people are really helpful [. . .] they [the facilitators] like the ideas you come up with [and] encourage you." A group of five 11-year-olds told me during their lunch break that the approaches employed by the facilitators had enabled their ideas to be heard and that they felt that the "teachers" were always listening to them: "We like it" they said, "as it is a challenge."

Through a relational structure both the facilitator and the participant work alongside each other negotiating the educative journey. There is an emphasis on engaging in a "quality" learning experience rather than a focus toward making just "good" music. Context is all-important for those working with young people in non-formal music education and therefore activities must be judged fairly by the appropriateness of their learning goals and the way they make meaningful connections to the specific environment they find themselves operating in: "the criteria used for evaluating a creative project in a non-formal setting are determined as much by the workshop/performance context (e.g. school classroom, hospital ward, prison, youth club, shopping mall) as by the shared values and expectations of the participants and their leader" (Renshaw, 2005, p. 21).

Samba at the Frederick Douglass Academy

My final example is the extraordinary music program taking place at the Frederick Douglass Academy (FDA) in Harlem, New York. In this is a school where over 200 students play samba every week on instruments imported from Brazil. Students learn traditional Rio-style samba, with singing entirely in Portuguese. In 2002, prior to the Brazilian music program, music classes at the FDA were not popular. The band program had been in steady decline and in order to re-establish it the school administration hired trumpeter Dana Monteiro as its new music educator. After trying for four years to revitalize the band program, Monteiro felt that he had made little progress: numbers were still low, the young people did not seem interested, and there were significant decreases in class sizes and a growing transient student population. Whilst on vacation in Brazil, Monteiro met some Pagode musicians who encouraged him to visit a local escolar de samba. It was at this event that Monteiro witnessed young people engaged in non-formal musical experiences and thought that this approach to making music might resonate with his students back in Harlem.

An after-school club was started with an initial purchase of ten drums. It did not take long for the club to grow, as the demand for both samba drumming and the style of musical learning ignited an interest with the students. In an example of how young people can play an important role in determining their learning, what started as a non-formal after-school music club eventually superseded the entire "formal" music program. With the help of a grant to buy a larger collection of drums, Monteiro took a leap of faith and put his trust in employing non-formal strategies in his classroom teaching. Learning by doing became paramount and the needs of the learner were respected by giving them a voice through which the content was co-constructed through the creation of an open environment where active musical participation and dialogue was encouraged.

Described as a "dynasty" by senior students, samba at the FDA encourages peer mentoring and community cohesion. Students are enthusiastic toward the teamwork involved and note that being in the bands demands that you help each other out rather than being in unhealthy competition. This is a testament to how the music program has been organized, a place where creative music-making opportunities, enjoyment, and celebration become available to those that wish to participate through teaching strategies that empower students to take ownership of the music they make. As one student told me, "He [the teacher] takes the time to make sure things are a certain way [. . .] you come in and you might not know the instruments [. . .] you learn from everybody else around you [. . .] through the examples of others." This collaborative spirit is reflected in the day-to-day running of the classes, where students take leadership roles and feel ownership of the classes and their learning as two young boys told me when I asked them if they like playing: "Yes, I'm leading the repinique section [small tenor drum] and he [pointing to his mate] is the leader for the caixa section [snare drum]. I'm pretty much the music director."

As a consequence of this co-constructed learning, after graduating, the youth in the school return each year to play with the FDA performance band Harlem Samba, a group that has now performed at the Lincoln Center, the Museum of Modern Art, the Brooklyn Academy of Music, World Café Live in Philadelphia, and the Broward County Performing Arts Center in Fort Lauderdale. The samba program has also been featured in the documentary film "Beyond Ipanema: Brazilian Waves in Global Music" (Barra & Dranoff, 2009) and was the winner of the 2012 Brazilian International Press Award in the category of Best Institution for the Promotion of Brazilian Culture in the United States. Beginning as an after-school club, the FDA samba program has developed to include almost every member of the school community, resulting in just about every ninth- to twelfth-grader in the building knowing how to play and partake in ensemble music-making.

Conclusion

When young people work with musicians in non-formal musical contexts they are typically in groups co-constructing the types of music to be created, and identifying specific tasks and goals together with an emphasis on learning within the participants' life context. Inclusivity is at the heart of pedagogical methodology, with musicians working alongside the young people to actively identify their learning needs. Because context is a vital component to the agency of non-formal music education, those working as facilitators are skilled in responding to the differing demands and needs of individuals and groups. In these contexts, young people have the opportunity to be exposed to a musical interaction that is co-authored and meaningful to their lives.[10]

The examples I have used can provide an illustration to some of the benefits of non-formal music education. From a big picture perspective, the interaction of formal, non-formal, and informal learning contexts and processes is vital in the promotion of lifetime music learning. If we consider musical learning as a dynamic interaction of a multi-phased process that changes emphasis from 1) independent learning in informal settings during early childhood to 2) formalized learning during the school years followed later by 3) non-formalized interactions occurring in community settings, then recognition that teachers might (and often do) move in and between both formal and non-formal approaches may benefit the development of young people's music-making in their childhood, their adolescence, and their adulthood. From the adolescents' perspective, when they play a significant role in the development of their learning goals, active and meaningful participation increases. Those that I interviewed emphasized this by highlighting the relationship between themselves and the facilitator, and by affirming that their "voice" was more often heard.

Through strong facilitator–participant (teacher–student) relationships built through openness, trust, and empathy, young musicians engaged in non-formal music education can grow in confidence about their self-image and their musicianship. The teacher as facilitator is well placed to encourage environments where peer teaching flourishes, empowering the students through a sense of owning both the process and the product. The young people engaged in making music in the Music Club, School of Rock, the Rock 'n' Roll for Girls After-School Music Club, the Connect music projects, and the Samba program at the FDA all valued the fact that their input mattered. Although there were learning goals, they were not constructed outside of the context of each particular situation. Co-authorship ensured that the projects were owned by those whom they were meant to benefit. The very fact that the young people's ideas were listened to came as a welcome surprise for them. I believe we should be working toward a situation where young musicians expect their voices to be heard. If we create environments of trust, then responsibility will flourish and musical learning will deepen.

Research suggests that there may be a lack of mutual understanding between potential partners in formal and non-formal musical settings (Saunders & Welch, 2012). There are distinctive strengths in the different approaches, but as I have suggested, music learning contexts need to make every effort to break down silos and recognize that in order to genuinely advocate for a lifetime of active music-making, value must be given to both formal and non-formal music education. In order to strengthen partnerships it will be essential that those working within a formal education system and those who operate within the non-formal sector understand, respect, and celebrate each other's approaches. If this type of collaborative understanding can be accomplished, then young musicians will benefit in ways that enrich their active music-making both now and well into the future.

Reflective questions

1 How might you introduce non-formal musical approaches into your classrooms?
2 Is there someone in your class who appears disconnected from the music curriculum you are working with? How might an approach akin to non-formal education help?
3 Map your musical journey on a continuum. Does it reflect the schema put forwarded in the conclusion: 1) independent learning; 2) formalized learning; 3) non-formalized learning? How have you negotiated these transitions?
4 How can music educators encourage lifelong musical learning?
5 Why might non-formal music education be effective with young people?

Notes

1 See Folkestad, 2005, 2006; Green, 2008; Jaffurs, 2004, 2006; Jenkins, 2011; O'Flynn, 2006; Rodriguez, 2009; Smith, 2013; Soderman and Folkestad, 2004; Westerlund, 2006; Wright and Kanellopoulos, 2010.

2 See also The Encyclopedia of Informal Education (<http://www.infed.org>).

3 For a discussion on informal education of this nature see Jeffs and Smith, 2005.

4 For discussions on peer mentoring and music education see Baker and Krout (2012), Goodrich (2007), Green (2008), and Lebler (2008).

5 For further exploration on the idea of friendship within non-formal encounters see Higgins (2012).

6 Labels R4 Jars, Not Young People is a phrase that emulated from a piece of research carried out in an effort to warn the media of the dangers of negative labelling of young people (Wiles, Curtin, & Brown, 2007).

7 See the website: <http://thebank.org.uk/>.

8 The BRIT Awards are the British Phonographic Industry's annual pop music awards and can be likened to the American Grammy Awards. On February 20, 2008, Kate Nash received a BRIT Award for Best Female Artist.

9 See <http://www.youtube.com/watch?v=4-RLVciwbaA>.

10 Contextualization could be a possible paradigm to be used as a tool for analysis and as a tool to plan educational encounters (Rogers, 2004).

Key sources

<http://infed.org/mobi/what-is-informal-education/>.
<http://www.youthmusic.org.uk/>.
Benson, J. F. (2010). *Working more creatively with groups* (3rd ed.). London: Routledge.

Reference list

Baker, F., & Krout, R. (2012). Turning experience into learning: Educational contributions of collaborative peer songwriting during music therapy training. *International Journal of Music Education*, **30**(2), 133–47.

Barra, G., & Dranoff, B. (2009). Beyond Ipanema: Brazilian waves in global music. Brazil/USA (Documentary film).

Busch, M. R. (2005). Predictors of lifelong learning in music: A survey of individuals participating in performing ensembles at community colleges in Illinois (Doctoral dissertation). University of Illinois at Urbana-Champaign, United States, Illinois. Retrieved from <http://proxy.lib.uiowa.edu/login?url=http://proquest.umi.com/pqdweb?did=954014171&Fmt=7&clientId=29945&RQT=309&VName=PQD>.

Colardyn, D. (Ed.) (2001). *Lifelong learning: Which ways forward?* Utrecht: Lemma.

Coombs, P. (1968). *The world educational crisis.* New York: Oxford University Press.

Coombs, P. H., & Ahmed, M. (1974). *Attacking rural poverty: How nonformal education can help.* Baltimore: John Hopkins University Press.

D'Amore, A. (2009). Musical futures: An approach to teaching and learning. Retrieved from <http://www.musicalfutures.org.uk>.

Europe, C. O. (2011). Pathway 2.0 towards recognition of non-formal learning/education and of youth work in Europe. Strasbourg and Brussels: European Commission and the Council of Europe in the Field of Youth.

Folkestad, G. (2005). The local and the global in musical learning: Considering the interaction between formal and informal settings. In P. S. Campbell, J. Drummond, P. Dunbar-Hall, K. Howard, H. Schippers,

& T. Wiggins (Eds.), *Cultural diversity in music education: Directions and challenges for the 21st century* (pp. 23–8). Brisbane: Australian Academic Press.

Folkestad, G. (2006). Formal and informal learning situations or practices vs formal and informal ways of learning. *British Journal of Music Education*, **23**(2), 135–45.

Goodrich, A. (2007). Peer mentoring in a high school jazz ensemble. *Journal of Research in Music Education*, **55**(2), 94.

Green, L. (2008). *Music, informal learning and the school: A new classroom pedagogy*. Aldershot: Ashgate.

Green, L. (Ed.) (2011). *Learning, teaching, and musical identity: Voices across cultures*. Bloomington: Indiana University Press.

Green, L. (2014). *Hear, listen, play!: How to free your students' aural, improvisation, and performance skills*. Oxford: Oxford University Press.

Higgins, L. (2012). One-to-one encounters: Facilitators, participants, and friendship. *Theory into Practice*, **51**(3), 159–66.

Hogan, C. (2002). *Understanding facilitation: Theory and principles*. London: Kogan Page.

Hogan, C. (2003). *Practical facilitation: A toolkit of techniques*. London: Kogan Page.

Jaffurs, S. E. (2004). The impact of informal music learning practices in the classroom, or how I learned how to teach from a garage band. *International Journal of Music Education*, 22(3), 189–200.

Jaffurs, S. E. (2006). The intersection of informal and formal music learning practices. *International Journal of Community Music*, Vol. D. Retrieved from <http://www.intellectbooks.co.uk/MediaManager/Archive/IJCM/Volume%20D/04%20Jaffurs.pdf>.

Jeffs, T., & Smith, M. K. (1990). *Using informal education: An alternative to casework, teaching and control?* Milton Keynes: Open University Press.

Jeffs, T., & Smith, M. K. (2005). *Informal education: Conversation, democracy and learning*. Nottingham: Educational Heretics Press.

Jenkins, P. (2011). Formal and informal music educational practices. *Philosophy of Music Education Review*, **19**(2), 179–97.

Karofsky, P., Zeng, L., & Kosorok, M. R. (2000). Relationship between adolescent–parental communication and initiation of first intercourse by adolescents. *Journal of Adolescent Health*, **28**(1), 41–5.

Kors, N. (2007). *Case studies of non-formal music education and informal learning in non-formal contexts*. The Hague: Prince Claus Conservatoire, Groningen & Royal Conservatoire, Lectorate Lifelong Learning in Music.

Lebler, D. (2008). Popular music pedagogy: Peer learning in practice. *Music Education Research*, **10**(2), 193–213.

Lopez, M. A. G. (2012). *Using e-learning in intercultural non-formal education activities*. Strasbourg: Council of Europe.

Mak, P. (2007). Learning music in formal, non-formal and informal contexts. Retrieved from <http://www.emc-imc.org/fileadmin/EFMET/article_Mak.pdf>.

Mok, O. N. A. (2011). Non-formal learning: Clarification of the concept and its application in music learning. *Australian Journal of Music Education*, **1**(1), 11–15.

O'Flynn, J. (2006). Vernacular music-making and education. *International Journal of Music Education*, **24**(2), 140–7.

Otero, M. S., McCoshan, A., & Junge, K. (2005). *European inventory on validation of non-formal and informal learning: A final report to DG Education & Culture of the European Commission*. Birmingham, UK: ECOTEC Research and Consulting Ltd.

Renshaw, P. (2005). *Simply connect: "Next practice" in group music making and musical leadership*. London: The Paul Hamlyn Foundation.

Rodriguez, C. X. (2009). Informal learning in music: Emerging roles of teachers and students. *Action, Criticism, and Theory for Music Education*, **8**(2), 35–45.

Rogers, A. (2004). *Non-formal education: Flexible schooling or participatory education?* Hong Kong: Comparative Education Research Centre, University of Hong Kong.

Rogers, C. R. (1995). The implications of client-centered therapy for family life. In C. R. Rogers, *On becoming a person: A therapist's view of psychotherapy* (pp. 314–28). Boston: Houghton Mifflin.

Saunders, J., & Welch, G. (2012). *Communities of education: A pilot study.* London: International Music Education Research Centre.

Sharp, R. (2011). Kate Nash launches scheme to get girls into songwriting. *The Independent.* Retrieved from <http://www.independent.co.uk/arts-entertainment/music/news/kate-nash-launches-scheme-to-get-girls-into-songwriting-2246422.html> (accessed 19 March).

Smilde, R. (2008). Lifelong learners in music; research into musicians' biographical learning. *International Journal of Community Music, 1*(2), 243–52.

Smith, G. D. (2013). *I drum, therefore I am: Being and becoming a drummer.* Farnham: Ashgate.

Soderman, J., & Folkestad, G. (2004). How hip-hop musicians learn: Strategies in informal creative music making. *Music Education Research, 6*(3), 313–26.

Steinberg, L. (2001). We know some things: Parent–adolescent relationships in retrospect and prospect. *Journal of Research on Adolescence, 11*(1), 1–19.

Torres, R.-M. (2001). *What works in education?: Facing the new century.* Baltimore, Maryland: International Youth Foundation.

Veblen, K. (2012). Adult music learning in formal, nonformal, and informal contexts. In G. E. McPherson & G. F. Welch (Eds.), *The Oxford handbook of music education* (Vol. 2, pp. 243–56). New York: Oxford University Press.

Westerlund, H. (2006). Garage rock bands: A future model for developing musical expertise? *International Journal of Music Education, 24*(2), 119–25.

Wiles, D., Curtin, D., & Brown, J. B. (2007). *Labels R4 jars, not for young people.* London: Frontier Youth Trust, Impact, and Churches Together in England.

Wright, R., & Kanellopoulos, P. (2010). Informal music learning, improvisation and teacher education. *British Journal of Educational Studies, 27*(1), 71–87.

Chapter 33

Transformative music engagement and musical flourishing

Susan A. O'Neill

Transformative music engagement and musical flourishing: Introduction

Nearly a decade has passed since I explored *positive youth music engagement* in the first edition of *The child as musician* (O'Neill, 2006). I argued for the need to embrace an emerging vision that recognizes all young people as having the capacity for positive engagement in music. Young people's musical capacities were seen as potentials to be actualized through engagement in music activities embedded within contexts and developmental systems that leverage the affordances of *generativity* and *diversity*. The concept of generativity (Erikson, 1968; McAdams & de St. Aubin, 1992) was introduced to emphasize the social psychological effects of learner-centered processes that seek to establish and guide the next generation through introspection, service, and actions that benefit oneself and others. These relational processes of transformation are capable of bringing about positive change when music engagement emphasizes the development of strengths, capacities, and potential (O'Neill, 2006).

The concept of diversity was presented as a social practice (Beckham, 2002) to highlight the need for more equitable and empowered forms of music engagement involving shared and diverse music-learning experiences that deepen and enhance *positive youth development*—a perspective that "emphasizes the manifest potentialities rather than the incapacities of young people" (Damon, 2004, p. 15). Perhaps more specifically, I highlighted the need to explore the importance of providing more expansive and meaningful music-learning opportunities to young people across all levels of skills and interests, and "to map the multiple pathways that can lead to generative musical development within diverse contexts and cultures" (O'Neill, 2006, p. 472).

The first edition of this chapter also drew attention to the basic premise that all young people are *musical resources* that function best when engaged in learning opportunities that enable them to experience "meaningful roles and responsibilities that will foster their own sense of development, growth, transformation, and excellence" (O'Neill, 2006, p. 471). The idea was to expand beyond the "talent" or "expertise" model that permeates many music education practices. The talent model has a tendency to perpetuate a "banking concept of education" (Freire, 1970, p. 58) and an over-concern with problem prevention or interventions that might "fix" problems with the sole aim of increasing performance achievement within confined or predetermined forms of musical expression.

Instead, within a positive youth music engagement perspective, the focus is on understanding, educating, and engaging young people across all levels of skills and interests in discovering their own musical potential or *achievable aspirations* in ways that are capable of enriching their lives. This *youth-as-musical resources* approach also recognizes how fundamentally limiting it is to view music learners in terms of their problems (or lack thereof) instead of their potential and what they might pursue for their own sake. The concept of youth-as-musical resources also focuses attention on how young people *make sense* of their own music learning in ways that they find meaningful and enriching. Even if we recognize music learners as problem-free in terms of their motivation and musical achievement, this does not tell us about who they are and what benefits they derive from their music engagement. And perhaps more importantly, it does not help young people negotiate and find a *sense of place* within the unique configurations, contexts, and situations that constitute their musical lives in today's digital age.

The digital age has created an unprecedented amount of autonomy in young people's lives; more young people than ever before are shaping their music and their musical selves "in ways that are their own" (Gardner & Davis, 2013, p. 197). Identity and agency have become more intertwined (Holland et al., 1998) and learning environments more participatory in "youth-only" spaces (Goldman, Booker, & McDermott, 2008). This *meshwork* or "entanglement of lines" (Ingold, 2007, p. 81) of young people's musical lives increasingly involves blurred and fluid boundaries between physical and virtual life spaces (O'Neill, in press–a). Youth-as-musical resources approaches are focused on how young people navigate and negotiate their musical lives and how educators might best support them in these endeavors.

These ideas resonate with the growing momentum in research focused on developmental systems theories and strength-based approaches within positive psychology as the study of "ordinary human strengths" of the "average person" (Sheldon & King, 2001, p. 216) and "the conditions and processes that contribute to the flourishing or optimal functioning of people, groups, and institutions" (Gable & Haidt, 2005, p. 105). These ideas also resonate with innovations within the transformative paradigm, which emphasize the relational processes of bringing about deep and enduring change (Fisher-Yoshida, Geller, & Schapiro, 2009).

In the intervening years since the first edition of this volume, I have been working on establishing a "sense of coherence" (Evans, Marsh, & Weigel, 2010) or interconnected interplay of elements that encompass not only youth engagement in music, but also the *transformative paradigm* in general as they both relate to broad notions of *musical flourishing*. I have come to regard this sense of coherence as *transformative music engagement* (TME) (O'Neill, 2012a, 2014). TME is the fundamental substantive significance of optimizing the potential of music learners. TME both cultivates and is experienced by young people who are deeply, purposefully, and meaningfully engaged in music. As a perspective, TME comprises defining assumptions about what is needed for young musicians to become deeply engaged in the process of music learning with the aim of optimizing their full potential. To understand the notion of cultivating young people's musical flourishing in relation to transformative contexts, we need to examine young people's music engagement within dynamic learning ecologies of person-context relations that change over time, and explore how young people come to find a sense of place, or what Benson (2001) refers to as "spaces of the possible" (p. 240). The transformative paradigm represents a worldview "for addressing inequality and injustice in society" (Mertens, 2007, p. 212), which in education research and practice involves the empowerment of learners to take an active role in bringing about positive change in matters that are of importance to them and that have an impact on their lives. It also provides an overarching framework for thinking about the various change processes that take place in learning and education contexts. Understanding diverse music-learning ecologies, particularly through young people's own accounts of their experiences, provides insights into how researchers and practitioners might best encourage and enhance expansive, positive, and transformative music engagement. Through this lens, music learning can be viewed as a *transformative journey*—a concept that may be especially important for understanding music learning and social innovation in the twenty-first century.

This chapter introduces and explores some of the defining assumptions of TME for both understanding and transforming young people's music engagement in purposeful and meaningful ways. Within the TME perspective, research and practice inform and support each other and are united through theoretical frameworks focusing on 1) fostering agentive learning ecologies or personal learning environments, 2) integrating actions or dialogical encounters within multiple learning spaces and places, and 3) leveraging affordances for musical flourishing by aligning learner-centered and youth empowerment approaches to enhance young musicians' strengths and potential for music engagement. As an orientation to research, TME contributes to our understanding of young people's perspectives on what initiates their motivation to learn and sustains their meaningful involvement in music-learning activities. It does this through methods based on epistemological assumptions that recognize the need for establishing partnerships and interactive links between researchers, practitioners, educators, and learners. As a learner-centered practice, TME seeks to foster expansive learning opportunities that deepen and enhance young people's music engagement and contribute to positive youth development. In other words, TME necessitates the interrelated complexity of research and practice in music education as a *bricolage* (Kincheloe, 2005) or a critical, multifaceted approach to inquiry (Kincheloe & Berry, 2004) that is infused with a sense of coherence for cultivating musical flourishing across diverse learners and music-learning contexts.

Engaging music learners

What makes music learning engaging? The factors most often referred to in the wider student engagement literature focus on learning activities that are goal-oriented, contextual, interesting, challenging, relevant (or related to real-world experiences), and social or interactive (Christenson, Reschly, & Wylie, 2012). Others focus on the contexts in which learning activities take place and the need for these contexts to promote learner autonomy or choice, agency or voice, and personalized instruction (Toshalis & Nakkula, 2012). Contemporary research into student engagement or engaged learning builds on ideas from William James (1890) and John Dewey (1913), who emphasized the need for immediate interest and spontaneous participation to be accompanied by a reflective process that enables learners to step back and assess their aims. James and Dewey believed that there is a necessary rhythm for sustaining intrinsic motivation or interest and engagement in an activity. This rhythm involves a dialectic, or the alternation of immediate (playful/spontaneous) experience (such as improvising music or "playing by ear") with an active-voluntary (work-like) mode (such as capacity building and making connections) that helps to organize the activity and focus attention on novel or previously "hidden" characteristics. Dewey (1933) referred to this as "undivided interest," and argued that the optimal state for learning involved being "playful and serious at the same time" (p. 286).

As early as the 1960s, Csikszentmihalyi (1990) began thinking about engagement in arts activities when he was studying the creative process. He wondered why an artist would persist with a painting when it was going well "single-mindedly, disregarding hunger, fatigue, and discomfort" (Nakamura & Csikszentmihalyi, 2002, p. 89), and yet, once it was completed the artist seemed to lose interest quickly in the artistic creation. It was this phenomenon of intrinsically motivated activity that interested Csikszentmihalyi, and he conceptualized it as "flow" experience or *engagement* in a challenging activity whereby the quality of our skills precisely matches our perceived level of challenge. At the beginning of the new millennium, Larson (2000), working within a positive youth development framework, argued that focused concentration and self-directed attention on challenging tasks are key features of young people's engagement in arts activities (Csikszentmihalyi, Rathunde, & Whalen, 1993; Larson & Kleiber, 1993). He related this to Dewey's (1913) notion of "voluntary attention" and argued that young people's self-directed attention during arts activities resembles the "flow" experiences described by Csikszentmihalyi (1975, 1990).

More recently, student engagement has been described as a concept that focuses on motivation and *meaningful participation* in a learning activity from which students derive a sense of relevance, purpose, and fulfillment (Martin, 2009; Murphy & Alexander, 2000; Pintrich, 2003). This suggests that for music learning to be truly engaging, learning activities and teacher–learner relationships need to attend holistically to the cultural and political contexts in which music-making is rendered *meaningful*. Instead of trying to teach in a vacuum by shutting out influences from the world outside, educators can breathe life into lessons by inviting in real-world inquiry through reflection and dialogue, and by taking actions to bring about positive change and social transformations. According to the critical theorist Paulo Freire (1998), "our relationship with the learners demands that we respect them and demands equally that we be aware of the concrete conditions of their world, the conditions that shape them" (p. 58). Freire goes on to say, "without this, we have no access to the way they think, so only with great difficulty can we perceive what and how they know" (p. 58).

Music learners are not passive recipients, but rather active constructors not only of knowledge, meanings, and identities, but also the values that live within and among the musical communities they inhabit (Pitts, 2005). And yet, the meaning of music, the central role it plays in the emotional lives of music learners, and informal learning strategies are often at odds with many formal or school music education agendas (Green, 2001). Different socio-political agendas embedded in specific music-learning contexts and practices obfuscate music learners' worldviews and challenge them in personal and compelling ways (O'Neill & Senyshyn, 2012). We need a better understanding of the multiple pathways through which youth are actively engaged in music learning in ways that foster meaningful, positive, and enduring transformations if we are to challenge narrow conceptions and optimize music learning in generalized education (Jorgensen, 1996, 2003) to benefit the most students both now and in the future.

Engaging music students in music learning has long been recognized as a central concern for music educators. For example, in Buck's (1944) classic text *Psychology for musicians*, he noted that "possibly the single most important fact" that psychology has to offer music educators is that the mind is always attending to something. Thus, if a teacher discovers that students are not engaged, the teacher should not "lay the blame on [students]," but rather "commune with your own soul and try to discover why and where you lost hold over them" (p. 54). In other words, successful teaching requires educators to figure out how to engage learners, and this might be best facilitated by seeking to understand what their learners are attending to (whether musical or non-musical) in order to establish meaningful connections. What remains a persistent puzzle, however, is why some learners but not others are engaged in music activities in ways that promote "flow" or meaningful and deep learning experiences. There are certainly different levels of quality, intensity, and purpose among young people engaged in music. Engagement in music-making, for example, may refer to a group of children repeatedly banging on drums for the pure pleasure of making a loud noise. Some learners may merely "show up" to participate in a music activity, often because it is expected of them or they want to be with their friends. They may have little understanding of the value and importance of particular activities beyond any immediate or obvious benefit they might see. Others may take on leadership roles and/or become advocates for the value of the activity.

They may introduce others to music activities and gain a sense of empowerment and personal fulfillment by doing so (O'Neill, 2005, 2006). It is this wide interpretation of what constitutes music engagement that allows for a number of possibilities for learners "to become engaged and to achieve a first level of social inclusion" (Karkou & Glasman, 2004, p. 61). A key point here, which I will discuss further in a moment, is that educators should be cognizant of their learners' levels of engagement and mindful of ways to connect with each level of engagement and foster the conditions that empower their learners to deepen their "praxis," or what Arendt (1958) refers to as the most important level of the active [or engaged] life.

Unpacking the factors and conditions that impact on young people's engagement in music learning has tended to focus on models that create a potentially false dichotomy or continuum of polarized positions (engaged or not engaged) that fail to recognize the potential opportunities that other approaches and models might provide. It is likely that for many music learners, there is an ebb and flow to their music engagement that might oscillate along a continuum or move through cycles of different levels of engagement over time. And, perhaps even more compelling is the possibility that music engagement might resemble what Ingold (2007) refers to as "a meshwork of interwoven trails rather than a network of intersecting routes" (p. 81). Within a meshwork perspective, we might view music engagement as "trails *along* which life is lived" (original emphasis, p. 81). As individuals participate in creating their meshwork of music engagement "trails," they contribute to "its weave and texture" (p. 81) along their musical journey.

This view of music engagement acknowledges that for music learners, their learning environment may not constitute what Ingold (2007) describes as a "bounded place" (p. 103); rather, it is more likely to be perceived as "a zone in which their several pathways are thoroughly entangled" (p. 103). According to Ingold, in a zone of entanglement, "there are no insides or outsides, only openings and ways through" (p. 103). Helping music learners discover these *openings and ways through* is the fundamental substantive significance of TME aimed at optimizing the potential of music learners and cultivating musical flourishing. TME recognizes that tensions, contradictions, negotiated meanings, identities, and multiple pathways resemble a "meshwork of interwoven lines" as described in general terms by Ingold (p. 103). What this means for music education researchers and practitioners is that music engagement is no longer found within individuals or even within the relations between music learners and their external environments—it consists instead of relations along "enmeshed ways of life" (p. 103). The TME perspective involves finding ways of engaging music learners in active music learning by helping them navigate and negotiate the inevitable affordances as well as the challenges, tensions, and contradictions they will encounter as part of their learning journey. It also involves engaging music learners in seeking out new and expansive learning opportunities. We might therefore conceive of TME as a process that occurs when learners reflect critically on their values and make conscious efforts to plan and implement actions that bring about new "trails" or "entanglements" that are capable of transforming themselves, others, and their community in relation to the diverse music activities and music-learning experiences they encounter.

Exploring youth transformative music engagement (TME)

In a recent interview study with 95 young people (aged 10–18 years) attending both elementary and secondary schools in Canada, we used an integrated psychological–philosophical approach involving phenomenological interpretative analysis (Smith, Flowers, & Larkin, 2009) to explore the nuanced and contextualized meaning making in young people's accounts of the initiators, sustainers, and impacts of their everyday music activity involvement (O'Neill & Senyshyn, 2012). Our theoretical approach to exploring youth music engagement draws on a theoretical braiding from multidisciplinary perspectives to explain the cultural ecology and variations in music engagement patterns, as well as the personal, social, and educational experiences of young people from across diverse music activity experiences. One way of characterizing these interrelationships is through the metaphor of a "ripple effect" or "spheres of activity," which are found in ecological systems theories (Bronfenbrenner, 1986, 2001; Spencer, 1999).

The idea of the ecological learner "speaks of interconnectedness and of the interplay of elements of a system for the system's total wellbeing" (Barnett, 2012, pp. 16–17). This conceptualization captures the embeddedness of young people within systems that are ultimately fragile—elements of agency, responsibility, meaning, and creativity are interconnected and yet fluid and changeable. At any given time, young people's musical lives are embedded in particular musical worlds, within learning ecologies, which are located within wider societal, cultural, and global systems. However, for music learners, the boundaries around their particular musical worlds may not be perceived as bounded, but rather surrounded by a zone of entangled or interwoven pathways. Although it is impossible to disentangle these pathways and the sociocultural structures and practices that initiate and sustain them, efforts to understand young people's musical engagement processes better by gaining deeper insights into the multiple settings and relationships that comprise their learning ecologies is likely to help identify questions that will advance our theoretical understanding and inform future research.

Young people's musical lives are always constructed and maintained in relation to other music activities, to other non-music activities, and to other people who may or may not be considered part of a person's musical life. The recognition of complex learning ecologies helps us move into "relational thinking and the rejection of Cartesian splits" (Silbereisen & Lerner, 2007, p. 4) and view "all levels or organization within the ecology of human development" (pp. 4–5). We adopted this approach to emphasize how different contexts and social interactions can affect situations that are not directly related to the initial situation or interaction. Using an integrated psychological–philosophical approach involving factor analysis and phenomenological interpretative analysis, my aim was to explore the nuanced and contextualized meaning making from both young people's ratings on a music engagement scale and their detailed accounts of the initiators, sustainers, and impacts of music activity involvement through in-depth phenomenological interviews. We also used data integration analysis strategies involving cyclical, recursive, and interactional processes (Johnson & Onwuegbuzie, 2004) to help us move understanding beyond the confines of a single method, address a broad range of predetermined and emergent research questions, and demonstrate the significance and impact of the findings through convergence and corroboration across diverse data sources (McGrath, Martin, & Kulka, 1982).

A key finding from this research indicated that young people's positive emotional expressions, such as "I feel happier when I am expressing myself," were central features of meaning making associated with positive and transformative music engagement at both the elementary and secondary levels. The findings also showed an apparent inherent complexity and fluidity in their music engagement and a progression of intricate meshworks of music, media, and social contexts involving meaning making and interconnections to other people, cultures, and perspective transformations, as captured in one young person's words: "[Music] helps me to connect and think differently about things." The findings indicate that many young people no longer perceive their music engagement as a discrete activity or as part of a single music-learning context. Rather, they are increasingly involved in multimodal and multi-arts forms of communication and expression, as found in new media convergence and online participatory cultures (Jenkins, 2009). Youth are "remaking" and developing their own unique and multifaceted roles and personal meanings associated with music and media with increasingly fluid interconnections, and their music-learning ecologies show a progression of transformative engagement processes that need further in-depth investigation and more progressive pedagogical approaches.

In an earlier detailed analysis of the same dataset, we used a mapping procedure to describe the key characteristics within particular contexts to provide a useful reference and guide to understanding the changes and processes that bring about transformations in a given landscape. More specifically, we mapped the music-learning ecologies within particular contexts that rendered the young people's musical experiences meaningful within their life spaces and places of home, school, local community, online community, and (through the Internet) the wider world. The mapping exercise resulted in three portraits of young people's music learning ecologies, which I refer to as *segmented, situated*, and *agentive* (O'Neill, in press–a). There was a sense of connectedness and an evolving and transformative *engaged agency* or active engagement in both situated and agentive forms of music learning that appeared to be largely absent in segmented music learning. In the case of agentive music learning, this was particularly associated with the integration of digital media technology, which appears to empower young musicians to navigate their musical lives in ways that matter to them, and helps them negotiate affordances and music-learning opportunities that foster positive development and musical flourishing.

The following case study of "David" provides an example of transformative music engagement processes associated with agentive music learning. David is an 18-year-old male who describes his first music activity as composing music, followed by his participation in a school musical, playing the guitar and drums, and playing in a youth-led band outside of school. David describes music as something he has "always been into," stating, "I've always been inclined to do music. So when [my mom] brought home the instrument, that was kind of like a stepping-stone, I could really apply it." He views music as "a creative outlet" and as something that "enriches my life [. . .] no matter what, [music] is really important to me." For David, the significance of his music activity is in the connectedness and engaged agency that are both intentional and meaningful. He describes learning to play the guitar as "a way to express myself [. . .] it's fun to get up there and play in front of people." His connectedness to other people is in relation to his music making, "because if I'm doing music, other musicians are going to be around me [. . .] I'm around musicians all day, so I guess that helps me grow." He also describes how music provides a medium for him to express part of his identity, "Um I have a quiet side to myself, and I have this other side to me, where I like to really get out there and express myself. So . . . Maybe that's my outlet for that."

David describes his musical goal as "I would like to compose" and a key challenge that would prevent him from achieving his goal as follows: "if I didn't have access to information. So, I guess the Internet is a big help." He also states that he gets his inspiration to compose music from watching films: "sometimes if I watch something emotional, like a film or something, it will give me inspiration to write [music]." He talks about his use of digital media technology as a tool ("I write most of my music on a computer program [. . .] I transcribe it into the program [. . .] I usually improvise and something will come"), a resource ("If I'm watching a commercial, I'll hear the music and dissect it"), and a form of expression for his music activity by playing the music video game "Guitar Hero" and recording and sharing his music compositions. He describes composing as "always in the foreground of my mind," and says that although he is around other young people with similar interests, he does not believe that this impacts on his relationships with other people in general because, "I wouldn't be there if it wasn't for the music."

Conceptualizing the transformative paradigm

There are multiple pathways and processes that bring about change or transformations in learning (Tynjälä, Stenström, & Saarnivaara, 2012). Indeed, the very notion of learning is about *change*; without change, we could say that no learning has taken place. And yet, as Huebner (1975) reminds us, the concept of "learning" is a "trivial way of speaking" of the way learners, working on their own transformative journey, engage in a "struggle with spirit, the otherness beyond them" (p. 8). In a similar vein, attempting to capture what is "transformative" within contexts of music learning is likely to appear trivial no matter how multifaceted and multidimensional the conceptualization might be. McCracken (2008) argues that we have become preoccupied in today's world with the concept of transformation or what he refers to as "expansionary individualism," which leads us to claim the right of "self-authorship" as a result of many motives, "some free and some forced" (p. 306). For a growing number of young people today, their artistry or creative expression, which is intimately tied to digital media technology, is an integral part of constructing their own meaningful life project as an artist or a musician—a sense of self-identity that is *assumed, packaged*, and *shared*, rather than achieved or bestowed as it was in past generations (Kress, 2010). What this might mean for engaging learners in deep, meaningful, and transformative music learning experiences has yet to be investigated.

In considering innovations in transformative education, Fisher-Yoshida, Geller, and Schapiro (2009) bring together the concepts of *space* (i.e., creating space for transformative learning), *culture* (i.e., looking through the lens of culture, difference, and diversity), and *the arts* (i.e., animating awareness through the expressive and performative arts). They remind us that throughout history there has existed "the intentional use of educational experiences to bring about deep transformations in human consciousness and behavior" (p. 3). They note, however, that the varied use of the terms transformation and transformative make it challenging to develop an inclusive and integrating perspective. For example, the term *transformational learning* is often used "to refer at once to three different but related ideas" (p. 6) as follows: 1) a transformational outcome; 2) a process of learning that is experienced by a learner; and 3) an educational program or event designed to foster learning experiences that result in or catalyze a transformational outcome. Fisher-Yoshida and colleagues attempt some clarification in terminology and argue that there is some consensus with the concept of *transformation* tending to focus on the outcome of a process that brings about deep and enduring change or what some might refer to as a "developmental shift" or a "change in worldview" (p. 6).

According to Taylor (2007), most conceptualizations of transformation, transformative learning, and transformative education share a common emphasis on *experience, critical reflection*, and *dialogue* in the learning process. I have discussed these three processes elsewhere within the perspective I propose for transformative music engagement (O'Neill, 2012a). My use of the term transformative (rather than transformational) is intentional to emphasize the notion of young music learners having the *power to transform* or bring about positive personal and social change. This emphasis inextricably links the transformative paradigm with the goal of furthering youth empowerment and social transformations. Depending on the assumptions that underpin a particular field or theoretical framework, what constitutes change or transformations in educational contexts may look vastly different. For example, in questioning assumptions about the practice of teaching, Jackson (1986) argued that there are "two distinguishably different ways of thinking about education" (p. 116): the first is "mimetic" or learning by imitation, where the teacher is perceived to be an artist or creator; the second is "transformative," which involves changing how the learner feels and perceives, and is often associated with "unintended consequences" (p. 128).

These "unintended consequences" or what might also be thought of as *transformative experiences* create new spaces for acknowledging difference and diversity. In transformative education, the teacher is perceived as both influencing the student and being influenced through a dynamic and complex interconnectedness of factors. Giroux (2009) went on to describe these teachers as "transformative intellectuals" who recognize that "schooling represents both a struggle for meaning and a struggle over power relations" (p. 439). Transformative teachers "treat students as critical agents, question how knowledge is produced and distributed, utilize dialogue, and make knowledge meaningful, critical, and ultimately emancipatory" (p. 439).

Pinar et al. (2008) point out that the "mediation and transformations that characterize educational experience" (p. 853) require us to move beyond linear thinking and take a "leap" or shift into "porous borders" and the kinds of "hybridization" that we are beginning to see in the breakdown of boundaries in many facets of society today, including educational institutions. It is also necessary to consider a critical poststructural form of problematizing or troubling the concept to move beyond naïve pragmatism or the failure to question the assumptions and theories in which any complex phenomenon is "grounded" (Skrtic, 1995, p. 69). Poststructuralist deconstruction also recognizes that "no experience is unmediated" (McLaren, 1991, p. 10), which although destabilizing, creates an ethical stance that provides for theory and practice to be developed in relation to each other with the purpose of bettering learners' lives and educational experiences. As McLaren argues, having the means to understand the ideological dimensions of "experiences, deep memories, psychological blockages, and passionate investments in everyday life" (p. 10) and to be able to relate these to wider societal issues of power and oppression is the task of critical and transformative education. Only then can we hope to encourage young people to gain the self-knowledge necessary to *see things differently* and in doing so provide them with the potential for bringing about personal and social transformation. Although space limitations preclude a detailed critical treatment here, I urge others to take up the challenge, and continue efforts to demythologize existing structures and potential blind spots in our thinking about transformative music education.

Transformative music engagement (TME) and youth empowerment

There is no single recipe or formula for bringing about TME. It is easy to understand why this is the case if you begin to think about the unique features of different local communities, each with its own historical, economic, political, social, cultural, and environmental factors that contribute to unique ecologies, geographies, and relationships. And yet, the theoretical foundations of TME reveal a number of conditions for encouraging and fostering transformative engagement experiences. As with any innovative pedagogical approach, creating the conditions for fostering TME draws on a number of strategies that redefine the parameters of what constitutes traditional forms of knowledge and the content of what is taught (Bresler, 2009). This process begins by implementing learner-centered activities involving choice, self-expression, and self-determination, and encouraging youth empowerment (O'Neill, in press–b). I will focus on the final dimension, which is perhaps the most difficult to achieve in practice—*youth empowerment.*

TME is capable of fostering youth empowerment through expansive learning opportunities that facilitate meaningful connections, relationships, and deep engagement for bringing about personal and social change. It does this through a process of experiential, learner-centered, emergent and lived curricula, and transformative pedagogies that empower young people to undertake their own engaged praxis through a process of reflection, dialogue, inquiry, and action (O'Neill,

2012a). An overarching aim is to provide young people with the kinds of learning opportunities that will help them recognize, question, challenge, and transform unjust practices and generate greater social justice. At the same time, we offer youth opportunities to recognize, understand, and overcome constraints within their own musical and personal lives, and realize the power of their own efforts to explore untapped potential and create new possibilities.

Realizing the potential of youth empowerment through TME requires a continual process of conceptualizing how we might create expansive music-learning opportunities within a social justice orientation that will help guide youth toward developing their distinctive voice and the capacity to express and redefine what matters to them "as actions in pursuit of social justice" (Cammarota & Fine, 2008, p. 6). According to Turley (1994), "listening to the voices of students validates them as partners in the education process" (p. 4). However, as Schwarzer, Bloom, and Shono (2006) point out, we "cannot directly empower others," but we can provide opportunities for fostering "self-empowerment" or "social empowerment" by "freeing individuals from directives and inviting them to take control" (p. xxviii). As youth are increasingly braiding, blending, and blurring learning spaces, modes, structures, and practices, they are transforming their music engagement in ways that are increasingly autonomous and self-directed. TME encourages music learners to make meaningful connections and build relationships that facilitate youth empowerment and deepen engagement, and to take actions that will bring about personal and social change.

In a recent exploratory study with young people, educators, and researchers, we used youth-led participatory action research (YPAR) frameworks (Cahill, 2007; Ozer, Ritterman, & Wanis, 2010) to engage music learners in deep explorations about why music matters to them and their school community (Erickson, O'Neill, & Senyshyn, 2012, 2013). We were interested in how young people might make vital contributions to understanding the ways that youth value music learning in a school environment and how this might both empower music learners and foster transformative music engagement. YPAR involves asking learners to identify a problem or burning question, devise and research the problem or question, and propose a solution and/or a way of representing their new understanding. The YPAR process also increases young people's capacity for critical reflection and analysis, which are crucial for participating in social change. It provides them with the opportunity to explore issues in ways that incorporate their own lived experiences/geographies (Cahill, 2007). It also involves a braiding of traditional and innovative methods that speak to local conditions (Cammarota & Fine, 2008). YPAR has become an increasing part of school curricula designed to promote sustainable school and community improvements (Barton, 2001; Hughes, 2003; McIntyre, 2000).

Our research involved an interrelated program and study component with 12 middle-school learners during weekly 90-minute sessions over a 12-week period. The learners engaged in reflections, inquiry, and actions related to why they valued participation in music. Four youth-led inquiry projects were worked on collaboratively with each other, a teacher, and two researchers. We asked our young participants to *think* about their musical world and all the music activities they are involved in, what matters to them and why, what got them started and keeps them interested, what benefits they get out of being involved in music, and their struggles and passions. They were asked to *identify* and choose one thing to focus on that interested them, such as an issue, a problem, or a question that might help music learners feel one or more of the following: connected, valued, better prepared, successful, motivated, inspired, and treated equally. In the second stage, the learners were asked to *research* their focus area by locating, selecting, and gathering information and evidence. In the third stage, the learners processed the information and evidence through analysis, evaluation, testing, sorting, and synthesizing. And in the last stage, they were asked to revise, present, reflect, and transfer their findings to others by disseminating their new understandings. And ultimately, they were asked to *advocate* their main findings by selecting a key message and devising and executing a plan for getting the message out to those they felt needed to hear it if they were to promote positive change.

We videotaped each session and examined the processes the learners engaged in over the course of each project. Each project was unique and is briefly summarized here (see also Erickson, 2012). *Project A*: This group decided to deliver a motivational/inspirational message to other music students at their school by performing and creating their own original choreography to the song "Don't stop believing." *Project B*: This group consisted of soundtrack recording musicians who performed and recorded the title soundtrack for the mini documentary the full group of participants later produced. *Project C*: This group designed questions and interviewed members of a local rock band about how these musicians were inspired to write music and how they managed to keep their band working together. *Project D*: This group recorded the responses of teachers, staff, and students at the school to the question: "Why does music matter to you?."

The final result from these four projects was the creation of a music advocacy video. Drawing on the video material the researchers had collected throughout the program, the learners collaborated in the creation of a mini documentary. This short film led to an unexpected and dramatic outcome. Shortly after the study had been concluded, the authorities at this school decided to close down the popular music program, which was a favorite music program among many of our young participants. As is frequently the case, the administration was trying to save money and did not consider the impact that this decision would have on students at the school. The music teacher told us that some of the learners were traumatized by this unforeseen and highly regrettable incident. On their very own initiative, our young participants decided to post an edited version of their mini documentary on YouTube, which they called "Music matters." This video was watched by a number of people from the local community who were aware and outraged by the decision of school officials to close down the popular music program. Eventually, our participants' youth-led music advocacy drew local media attention. As a result, the administrators involved in closing down the program invited the young participants in our research to visit the local school district office and present their case for keeping the popular music program, which was soon after reinstated.

The impact these projects had on the young people involved is revealed in one student's reflection at the end of the program: "Thank you for giving me the chance to make a difference." Erickson (2012), the teacher–researcher on this project, summed up the students' experiences as follows:

> The sense of empowerment conveyed by this "gift of chance" is the kind of "problem-posing" education to which Paolo Freire (1970) refers, "responding to the essence of consciousness—*intentionality*" (p. 79). By this student "being *conscious of*" her actions as making a difference in her own life and in the lives of others, this serves as a gently understated example of Freire's goal of "liberating education" and how both teacher and student "become jointly responsible for a process in which all grow" (p. 80).

In a follow-up study of the learners in this program a year later, they identified the following features as important for helping them gain deep, meaningful, and transformative experiences from their engagement in the program: 1) consistency of the program over time; 2) being given time to reflect on what mattered to them; 3) being interviewed about something they loved to do; 4) having older, experienced musical mentors responding to their interests; and 5) meeting others that were new and different from themselves, from both inside and outside the school community, who were united by a common interest in the music. This exploratory research was based on youth-as-musical resources approaches designed to engage students in a youth-led, emergent creative process involving reflection, analysis, and actions focused on music-related areas that mattered to them and their community (see also O'Neill, 2011). According to their teacher–researcher,

> the project succeeded partly because it was able to engage students whose musical identities did not reside solely in "school music," yet these "outside" passions somehow found a way "inside." The students' positive perceptions of their engagement in the project emphasizes the notion that music programs designed to "engage the individual interests of our students, while finding ways to connect these "selves" to a greater community that helps them become who they are, should be a presiding goal for music education. In this way, music can truly *matter* (Erickson, 2012, p. 148).

Youth empowerment is based on the assumption that youth should have a voice on issues that matter to them and concern them, and they should be part of the decisions that affect them. The affordances of TME inform and support each other and are united through a theoretical orientation that focuses on youth-as-musical resources approaches and agentive learning ecologies or personal learning environments and integrated actions or dialogical encounters within multiple learning spaces and places, with the aim of enhancing musical flourishing by aligning the strengths or potentials for positive change of individuals and contexts.

Nurturing musical flourishing through TME

Flourishing or thriving is a key theme in positive psychology, which is also referred to as optimal human functioning and subjective well-being (Hart & Sasso, 2011). Keyes (2003) defines flourishing as "a state in which an individual feels positive emotion toward life and is functioning well psychologically and socially" (p. 294). Fredrickson and Losada (2005) consider flourishing to be comprised of four parts: goodness, generativity, growth, and resilience (see also a critique of their nonlinear dynamic model by Brown, Sokal, & Friedman, 2013). Seligman (2011) identifies five features of human flourishing, which he refers to as PERMA: positive emotion, engagement, good relationships, meaning and purpose in life, and accomplishment. He argues for the transformative benefits of an increased focus on these endeavors in any area of an individual's life.

Although definitions of flourishing vary, researchers working within positive youth development perspectives argue that the relative plasticity of human development, which "may both facilitate and constrain opportunities for change" (Silbereisen & Lerner, 2007, p. 5), necessitates and legitimizes "an optimistic and proactive search for characteristics of individuals and of their ecologies" (p. 6). However, as Gable and Haidt (2005) warn, although positive psychology research fills a gap by focusing on understudied phenomena, "the meaning of what is positive or good is complex and multidimensional" and a one-size-fits-all model does not work (see also Norem & Chang, 2002). If we are to achieve "a balanced, empirically grounded, and theoretically rich view of human experience," we need to focus on "frailties" as well as strengths and "how the two are linked" (p. 109). My sense is that positive youth development researchers recognize inherent tensions in complex systems as necessary catalysts for growth and change. Yet, they also view the application of developmental science (or applied research) as planned attempts to "enhance" through policies and programs "the character of humans' developmental trajectories" (Silbereisen & Lerner, 2007, pp. 5–6). In other words, because human development involves plasticity as well as complex integrated actions and individual–context relations, the practice of searching for proactive and positive affordances for "positive human development" (p. 5) is a legitimate practice for "aligning the strengths" (p. 6) or potentials for positive change among individuals.

For some, the concept of human flourishing and transformative music engagement might appear to be a utopian vision. However, my understanding is informed by Kincheloe's (2003) *critical ontology* as a necessary stance for helping us "move beyond our present state of being" and "gain new understandings and insights as to who we can become" (p. 48), which might lead to "unanticipated modes of learning and new concepts" (p. 64). A critical ontological vision blurs the boundaries between different forms of knowledge and asks questions about "ethics, morality, politics, emotion, and gut feelings" to provide a "framework of principles with which we can negotiate" (p. 48). A critical ontological vision also helps us overcome naïve pragmatism, which Skritc (1995) describes as the failure to question "the assumptions, theories, and metatheories" (p. 69) that ground our approaches to research and attempts to analyze the "nature and effects" (p. 69) of enterprises such as music education.

In the 1980s researchers studying organizational generativity as a way of understanding and enhancing innovation developed a paradigm-shifting approach called *appreciative inquiry*, with the aim of transforming the capacity of individuals to enact positive change "by deliberating focusing on positive experiences and hopeful futures" (Gergen, Gergen, & Barrett, 2004, p. 54–5). The goal was to encourage people to "develop an appreciative eye" (p. 55) and to recognize that no matter how dysfunctional or conflictual a human environment or system might be, it will have elements of beauty, goodness, and value that can become "alive with infinite capacity" (Cooperrider & Whitney, 2000, p. 3). Tapping into this generative and positive energy "is limited only by the human ability to see beyond the horizon of accepted assumptions-in-practice" (Bright et al., 2013, p. 155). As such, appreciative inquiry has been described as a "highly effective transformative practice" (Gergen et al., 2004, p. 54) that leads to deep engagement in personal and social transformations, as individuals strive to ask questions and deliberately focus on factors that contribute to the co-creation of new enhanced worlds or to "designing new futures" (p. 56).

In the 1990s O'Sullivan (1999) articulated a transformative vision of education to address "the crisis we are now facing" (p. 7) because our "conventional educational institutions are defunct and bereft of understanding in responding to our present planetary crisis" (p. 7). As such, there is "no creativity" in our current educational ventures "because there is no viewpoint or consciousness which sees the need for new directions" (p. 7). O'Sullivan argues that his use of the term "transformation" is "not Utopian or new age" (p. 6) but rather "rigorous" and "complex," and that these changes might bring with them many new possibilities as well as "their own unique problems, and whether we like it or not, their own brutal limitations" (p. 6). This reminder of the potential for change to bring about negative and unanticipated outcomes drives the momentum for a shift away from a focus on deficit-based theories and models toward a deliberate and critically reflective effort to support positive processes and outcomes. Further, if we accept the notion that "human systems" grow in the direction of what people study, we will recognize the need to search for "the best of "what is" to develop "logically, caringly, and passionately into a theoretical hypothesis of an envisioned future" (Cooperrider & Srivastva, 1987, p. 166).

In recent years, the shift to a more positive and transformative vision of youth musical potential has driven changes in research on motivation and music learning (O'Neill, 2012a, in press–a, in press–b; O'Neill & Senyshyn, 2012). Concepts such as motivation and engagement have become more interrelated despite their different paradigmatic origins and assumptions. In the wider realm of learning, Toshalis and Nakkula (2012) argue motivation, engagement, and student voice should be considered both "artifacts" of the other phenomena and "as a means of promoting" each phenomenon (p. 2). They also call for more thinking about the contributions that motivation, engagement, and student voice make "to the experience of human agency" if education is to "help students effectively act upon their strongest interests and deepest desires" (p. 2). They suggest the need for educators to develop an understanding of the connections between motivation, engagement, and student voice if they are to rise above the current "movement to raise standards" and recognize the "importance of cultivating the immeasurables—such as a love for learning, a passion for inquiry, and a zeal for creative expression" (p. 2). Understanding these connections with music learners requires a consideration of the entire situated person "connected to music learning through an evolving and transformative 'engaged agency'" (O'Neill, 2012b, p. 1), where the "ethical can be most fully integrated into the very foundations of becoming a music learner" (p. 6).

As youth are increasingly braiding, blending, and blurring learning spaces, modes, structures, and practices, they are transforming their music engagement in ways that are increasingly autonomous and self-directed (O'Neill, in press–b). We enable, encourage, and empower music learners to thrive "by nurturing their reflexive capacity to reflect inwardly about connections between self, music, and their sociocultural surroundings" (p. 6). The cultivation of this broad notion of musical thriving becomes a basis for positive musical growth and change. Ansdell and DeNora (2012) refer to this notion of musical thriving as *musical flourishing*, drawing on philosopher Carel's (2008) notion of human flourishing as an "invisible context enabling us to pursue possibilities and engage in projects. It is the condition of possibility that enables us to follow through with our aims and goals, to act on our dreams, to become who we are" (p. 53). DeNora (2013) also argues for the need to "consider the ways in which musical activity generates many types of affordances for well-being and sociability" (p. 11).

Young people's pathways through their musical worlds or music-learning ecologies are sometimes found, sometimes forged, and sometimes forced through what might seem to be ordinary educational practices (O'Neill, in press–b). Constraints on positive music engagement include controlling and manipulative educational environments, which have been found to have a negative impact on young people's motivation to learn and engagement during learning (Boggiano & Katz, 1991; Stipek, 2002). Frequent experiences of alienation and marginalization at school often result in disconnection and lack of engagement in learning and achievement (Sefa Dei, 2003; Zyngier, 2003). And despite the common-sense belief that music learners thrive in competitive "high stakes" performance environments, there is "shockingly little data" on the impact this has on motivation and student engagement (Nichols & Dawson, 2012, p. 468). The few studies that have explored learners' perceptions of the value of high stakes performance outcomes in non-musical domains suggest an increasing "disillusionment" as young people grow older about the value and validity of such performance indicators (Paris et al., 1991). By the eighth grade, learners in the United States reported "increasing cynicism" about performance achievement tests, which also seemed to undermine their views of teachers who were "preoccupied" with high stakes performance outcomes (Paris, Roth, & Turner, 2000) or who "exaggerated the importance of the test in students' lives" (Nichols & Dawson, 2012, p. 468). According to Paris (2000), high stakes testing "promotes low-level thinking, misdirects students motivation, tilts the educational playing field against minority and poor students, and narrows the instructional focus in the classroom" (p. 1). In other words, an over-focus on high stakes performance outcomes has negative implications for how the majority of young people think and feel about themselves as learners, how they perceive their capacity to learn, and how much energy they have for learning (Harlen & Deakin Crick, 2003). And, longer-term "subtle and pernicious effects" (Paris, 2000, p. 1) of implicit and explicit messages about the importance of high stakes performance outcomes (Nichols & Berliner, 2007; Perlstein, 2010) have been described as having the potential to "seriously erode students' motivation over time" (Nichols & Dawson, 2012, p. 469) and "depreciate their educational opportunities and experiences" (Paris, 2000, p. 1). These negative indicators serve as reminders that all music programs, including those focused on achieving high-quality performance outcomes, would benefit from adopting youth-as-musical resources approaches that are mindful of appreciating and cultivating young people as valued resources through the creation of expansive learning opportunities aimed at enhancing personal and musical flourishing.

Damon (2004) argues that the concept of flourishing is related to research on youth resiliency, but without the "defensive connotations" that the term resiliency implies as a "response to unfavorable circumstances" such as a "background of danger, stress, and deficit in young people's lives" (p. 16). As such, we might also consider musical flourishing as a normal adaptation to the challenges of music learning with the assumption that many (and possibly most) music-learning experiences will be enjoyable, welcome, and appreciated. However, what seems to be needed is a critical understanding of transformative processes and conditions that foster musical flourishing. And, we need to study not only positive subjective experiences and individual characteristics, but also the positive programs, communities, and institutions that increase and sustain *flourishing music education* as well as flourishing music learners.

Knowing what youth are interested and actively involved in, as well as how they think and feel about their involvement, seems an important basis for furthering our understanding of how young people navigate and negotiate their musical lives (O'Neill, in press–a). Educators need to understand their learners well enough to know what it is that they are trying to accomplish. Noddings (2002) reminds us "we cannot just pull a motive out of thin air" (p. 21). To identify a motive that resonates with a learner's sense of reality "requires knowledge of that reality" so that the learner can recognize it as his or her own: "That *is* what I was trying to do!" (original emphasis, p. 21). It is this recognition that begins the process of TME. Although we can never guarantee that the conditions we establish will facilitate TME, we can only begin to engage in the process by first recognizing the need and responsibility of educators and learners to work together continually to develop and maintain a learning environment that recognizes and fosters youth-as-musical resources approaches in which it is possible for young people's musical lives to flourish.

Reflective questions

1 How would you describe the music-learning contexts or ecologies you experienced at different ages in your musical development and what impact did they have on your music engagement?

2 What transformations have taken place through digital technology in young people's music engagement in terms of the affordances and constraints of different learning ecologies or personal learning environments?

3 Why does the author differentiate between musical flourishing and musical achievement, and what are some of the research and/or practice implications of this distinction?

4 What is meant by youth-as-musical resources approaches and what are the main features of the transformative paradigm for music education researchers and educators?

5 How might transformative music contexts foster meaningful and purposeful music engagement among music learners in today's globalized and digital age?

Key sources

O'Neill, S. A. (2012). Becoming a music learner: Towards a theory of transformative music engagement. In G. E. McPherson & G. Welch (Eds.), *The Oxford handbook of music education* (Vol. 1, pp. 163–86). New York: Oxford University Press.

O'Neill, S. A. (in press–a). Young people's musical lives: Learning ecologies, identities and connectedness. In R. A. R. MacDonald, D. J. Hargreaves, & D. Meill (Eds.), *Oxford handbook of musical identities*. New York: Oxford University Press.

O'Neill, S. A. (in press–b). Youth empowerment and transformative music engagement. In C. Benedict, P. Schmidt, G. Spruce, & P. Woodford (Eds.), *Oxford handbook of social justice and music education*. New York: Oxford University Press.

Toshalis, E., & Nakkula, M. J. (2012). *Motivation, engagement, and student voice: The students at the center series*. Boston, MA: Jobs for the Future.

Tynjälä, P., Stenström, M.-L., & Saarnivaara, M. (2012). *Transitions and transformations in learning and education*. New York: Springer.

Reference list

Ansdell, G., & DeNora, T. (2012). Musical flourishing: Community music therapy, controversy, and the cultivation of wellbeing. In R. A. R. MacDonald, G. Kreutz, & L. Mitchell (Eds.), *Music, health, and wellbeing* (pp. 97–112). Oxford: Oxford University Press.

Arendt, H. (1958). *The human condition* (2nd ed.). Chicago, IL: University of Chicago Press.

Barnett, R. (2012). The coming of the ecological learner. In P. Tynjälä, M.-L. Stenström, & M. Saarnivaara (Eds.), *Transitions and transformations in learning and education* (pp. 9–20). New York: Springer, doi: 10.1007/978–994–007–2312–2_2.

Barton, A. C. (2001). Science education in urban settings: Seeking new ways of praxis through critical ethnography. *Journal of Research in Science Teaching*, **38**(8), 899–917.

Beckham, E. F. (2002). *Diversity at the crossroads: Mapping our work in the years*. Paper presented at AAC&U's Diversity and Learning: Education for a World Lived in Common conference. Retrieved from <https://www.hampshire.edu/sites/default/files/files/BeckDive.pdf>.

Benson, C. (2001). *The cultural psychology of self: Place, morality and art in human worlds*. New York: Routledge.

Boggiano, A. K., & Katz, P. (1991). Maladaptive achievement patterns in students: The role of teachers' controlling strategies. *Journal of Social Issues*, **47**(4), 35–51.

Bresler, L. (2009). Research education shaped by musical sensibilities. *British Journal of Music Education*, **26**(1), 7–25.

Bright, D. S., Powley, E. H., Fry, R. E., & Barrett, F. (2013). The generative potential of cynical conversations. In D. L. Cooperrider, D. P. Zandee, L. N. Godwin, M. Avital, & B. Boland (Eds.), *Advances in appreciative inquiry (Vol. 4), Organizational generativity: The appreciative inquiry summit and a scholarship of transformation* (pp. 135–58). Bingley, UK: Emerald Group.

Bronfenbrenner, U. (1986). Ecology of the family as a context for human development: Research perspectives. *Developmental Psychology*, **22**(6), 723–42.

Bronfenbrenner, U. (2001). Bioecological theory of human development. In N. J. Smelser & P. B. Baltes (Eds.), *International encyclopaedia of the social and behavioural sciences* (pp. 6963–70). Oxford: Elsevier.

Brown, N. J. L., Sokal, A. D., & Friedman, H. L. (2013). The complex dynamics of wishful thinking: The critical positivity ratio. *American Psychologist*, **68**(9), 801–13, doi: 10.1037/a0032850.

Buck, P. (1944). *Psychology for musicians*. Oxford: Oxford University Press.

Cahill, C. (2007). Doing research with young people: Participatory research and the rituals of collective work. *Children's Geographies*, **5**(3), 297–312.

Cammarota, J., & Fine, M. (2008). *Revolutionizing education: Youth participatory action research in motion*. New York: Routledge.

Carel, H. (2008). *Illness*. Stocksfield: Acumen.

Christenson, S. L., Reschly, A. L., & Wylie, C. (2012). *Handbook of research on student engagement*. New York: Springer.

Cooperrider, D. L., & Srivastva, S. (1987). Appreciative inquiry in organizational life. *Research in Organizational Change and Development*, **1**, 129–69.

Cooperrider, D. L., & Whitney, D. (2000). A positive revolution in change: Appreciative inquiry. In D. L. Cooperrider, P. F. Sorensen, D. Whitney, & F. F. Yaeger (Eds.), *Appreciative inquiry: Rethinking human organization toward a positive theory of change* (pp. 3–28). Champaign, IL: Stipes Publishing.

Csikszentmihalyi, M. (1975). *Beyond boredom and anxiety: The experience of play in work and games.* San Francisco, CA: Jossey-Bass.

Csikszentmihalyi, M. (1990). *Flow: The psychology of optimal experience.* New York: Harper-Collins.

Csikszentmihalyi, M., Rathunde, K., & Whalen, S. (1993). *Talented teenagers: The roots of success and failure.* Cambridge: Cambridge University Press.

Damon, W. (2004). What is positive youth development? *Annals of the American Academy, 591*, 13–24. doi: 10.1177/0002716203260092.

DeNora, T. (2013). "Time after time": A quali-T method for assessing music's impact on well-being. *International Journal of Qualitative Studies in Health and Well-being, 8.* doi: doi.org/10.3402/qhw. v8i0.20611. Retrieved from <http://www.ijqhw.net/index.php/qhw/article/view/20611>.

Dewey, J. (1913). *Interest and effort in education.* Boston: Houghton Mifflin.

Dewey, J. (1933). *How we think: A restatement of the relation of reflective thinking to the educative process.* Boston, MA: Houghton-Mifflin.

Erickson, D. (2012). Music that matters: Reconceptualizing curriculum for the enhancement of self and others through personalized learning and youth participatory action research. In S. A. O'Neill (Series Ed. & Vol. Ed.), *Research to Practice: Vol. 5. Personhood and music learning: Connecting perspectives and narratives* (pp. 135–52). Waterloo, ON: Canadian Music Educators Association.

Erickson, D., O'Neill, S. A., & Senyshyn, Y. (2012). *Youth-led participatory action research: Building purpose through personalized music learning.* Paper presented to the Conference on Music Learning: Benefits for the 21st Century Learner, Laval University, Québec, Canada.

Erickson, D., O'Neill, S. A., & Senyshyn, Y. (2013). *Beyond Music Matters: A follow-up study of secondary school students' experiences of transformative music learning during middle school.* Poster presented at the Annual Conference of the Canadian Society for the Study of Education (CSSE), University of Victoria, Victoria, British Columbia, Canada.

Erikson, E. H. (1968). *Identity: Youth and crises.* New York: Norton.

Evans, W. P., Marsh, S. C., & Weigel, D. (2010). Promoting adolescent sense of coherence: Testing models of risk, protection, and resiliency. *Journal of Community and Applied Social Psychology, 20*(1), 30–43.

Fisher-Yoshida, B., Geller, K. D., & Shapiro, S. A. (2009). *Innovations in transformative learning: Space, culture and the arts.* New York: Peter Lang.

Fredrickson, B. L., & Losada, M. F. (2005). Positive affect and the complex dynamics of human flourishing. *American Psychologist, 60*(7), 678–86.

Freire, P. (1970). *Pedagogy of the oppressed.* New York: Continuum.

Freire, P. (1998). *Pedagogy of the heart.* New York: Continuum.

Gable, S. L., & Haidt, J. (2005). What (and why) is positive psychology? *Review of General Psychology, 9*(2), 103–10. doi: 10.1037/1089–2680.9.2.103.

Gardner, H., & Davis, K. (2013). *The app generation: How today's youth navigate identity, intimacy, and imagination in a digital world.* New Haven, CT: Yale University Press.

Gergen, K. J., Gergen, M. M., & Barrett, F. J. (2004). Dialogue: Life and death of the organization. In D. Grant, C. Hardy, C. Oswick, & L. Putnam (Eds.), *The Sage handbook of organizational discourse* (pp. 39–60). London: Sage.

Giroux, H. (2009). Teacher education and democratic schooling. In A. Darder, M. P. Baltodano, & R. D. Torres (Eds.), *The critical pedagogy reader* (2nd ed., pp. 438–59). New York: Routledge.

Goldman, S., Booker, S., & McDermott, M. (2008). Mixing the digital, social, and cultural: Learning, identity, and agency in youth participation. In D. Buckingham (Ed.), *Youth, identity, and digital media* (pp. 185–206). Cambridge, MA: MIT Press. doi: 10.1162/dmal.9780262524834.185.

Green, L. (2001). *How popular musicians learn: A way ahead for music education.* London and New York: Ashgate Press.

Harlen, W., & Deakin Crick, R. (2003). Testing and motivation for learning. *Assessment in Education*, **10**(2), 169–208.

Hart, K. E., & Sasso, T. (2011). Mapping the contours of contemporary positive psychology. *Canadian Psychology*, **52**(2), 82–92.

Holland, D., Lachicotte, W., Skinner, D., & Cain, C. (1998). *Identity and agency in cultural worlds.* Cambridge, MA: Harvard University Press.

Huebner, D. (1975). Curricular language and classroom meanings. In W. Pinar (Ed.), *Curriculum theorizing: The reconceptualists* (pp. 217–37). Berkeley, CA: McCutchan.

Hughes, J. N. (2003). Commentary: Participatory action research leads to sustainable school and community improvement. *School Psychology Review*, **32**(1), 38–43.

Ingold, T. (2007). *Lines: A brief history.* New York: Routledge.

Jackson, P. (1986). *The practice of teaching.* New York: Teacher College Press.

James, W. (1890). *The principles of psychology* (Vol. 1). New York: Henry Holt and Company.

Jenkins, H. (2009). *Confronting the challenges of a participatory culture: Media education for the 21st century.* Cambridge: MIT Press.

Johnson, R. B., & Onwuegbuzie, A. J. (2004). Mixed methods research: A research paradigm whose time has come. *Educational Researcher*, **33**(7), 14–26.

Jorgensen, E. R. (1996). Justifying music in general education: Belief in search of reason. In F. Margonis (Ed.), *Philosophy of education* (pp. 228–36). Urbana, IL: Philosophy of Education Society.

Jorgensen, E. R. (2003). *Transforming music education.* Bloomington, IN: Indiana University Press.

Karkou, V., & Glasman, J. (2004). Arts, education and society: The role of the arts in promoting the emotional wellbeing and social inclusion of young people. *Support for Learning*, **19**(2), 57–65.

Keyes, C. L. M. (2003). Complete mental health: An agenda for the 21st century. In C. L. M. Keyes & J. Haidt (Eds.), *Flourishing: Positive psychology and the life well-lived* (pp. 293–312). Washington, DC: American Psychological Association.

Kincheloe, J. L. (2003). Critical ontology: Visions of selfhood and curriculum. *JCT: Journal of Curriculum Theorizing*, **19**(1), 47–64.

Kincheloe, J. L. (2005). On to the next level: Continuing the conceptualization of the bricolage. *Qualitative Inquiry*, **11**(3), 323–50.

Kincheloe, J. L. & Berry, K. S. (Eds.) (2004). *Rigour and complexity in educational research: Conceptualizing the bricolage.* Maidenhead: Open University Press.

Kress, G. (2010). *Multimodality: A social semiotic approach to contemporary communication.* London: Routledge.

Larson, R. (2000). Toward a psychology of positive youth development. *American Psychologist*, **55**(1), 170–83.

Larson, R. W., & Kleiber, D. (1993). Daily experience of adolescents. In P. Tolan & B. Cohler (Eds.), *Handbook of clinical research and practice with adolescents* (pp. 125–45). New York: Wiley.

Martin, A. J. (2009). Motivation and engagement across the academic life span: A developmental construct validity study of elementary, high school, and university/college students. *Educational and Psychological Measurement*, **69**(5), 794–824.

McAdams, D. P., & de St. Aubin, E. (1992). A theory of generativity and its assessment through self-report, behavioral acts, and narrative themes in autobiography. *Journal of Personality and Social Psychology*, **62**(6), 1003–15.

McCracken, G. (2008). *Transformations: Identity construction in contemporary culture.* Bloomington, IN: Indiana University Press.

McGrath, J. E., Martin, J., & Kulka, R. A. (1982). *Judgment calls in research.* Beverly Hills, CA: Sage.

McIntyre, A. (2000). Constructing meaning about violence, school, and community: Participatory action research with Urban Youth. *Urban Review, 32*(2), 123–54.

McLaren, P. (1991). Critical pedagogy: Constructing an arch of social dreaming and a doorway to hope. *Journal of Education, 173*(1), 9–34.

Mertens, D. M. (2007). Transformative paradigm: Mixed methods and social justice. *Journal of Mixed Methods Research, 1*(3), 212–25.

Murphy, P. K., & Alexander, P. A. (2000). A motivated exploration of motivation terminology. *Contemporary Educational Psychology, 25*(1), 3–53.

Nakamura, J., & Csikszentmihalyi, M. (2002). The concept of flow. In C. R. Snyder & S. J. Lopez (Eds.), *Handbook of positive psychology* (pp. 89–105). New York: Oxford University Press.

Nichols, S. L., & Berliner, D. C. (2007). *Collateral damage: How high-stakes testing corrupts America's schools.* Cambridge, MA: Harvard Education Books.

Nichols, S. L., & Dawson, H. S. (2012). Assessment as a context for student engagement. In S. L. Christenson, A. L. Reschly, & C. Wylie (Eds.), *Handbook of research on student engagement* (pp. 457–77). New York: Springer.

Noddings, N. (2002). *Educating moral people: A caring alternative to character education.* New York: Teachers College Press.

Norem, J. K., & Chang, E. C. (2002). The positive psychology of negative thinking. *Journal of Clinical Psychology, 58*(9), 993–1001. doi: 10.1002/jclp.10094.

O'Neill, S. A. (2005). Youth music engagement in diverse contexts. In J. L. Mahoney, R. Larson, & J. S. Eccles (Eds.), *Organized activities as contexts of development: Extracurricular activities, after school and community programs* (pp. 255–73). Mahwah, NY: Lawrence Erlbaum Associates.

O'Neill, S. A. (2006). Positive youth musical engagement. In G. E. McPherson (Ed.), *The child as musician: A handbook of musical development* (pp. 461–74). New York: Oxford University Press.

O'Neill, S. A. (2011). Learning in and through music performance: Understanding cultural diversity via inquiry and dialogue. In M. S. Barrett (Ed.), *A cultural psychology of music education* (pp. 179–200). New York: Oxford University Press.

O'Neill, S. A. (2012a). Becoming a music learner: Towards a theory of transformative music engagement. In G. E. McPherson & G. Welch (Eds.), *The Oxford handbook of music education* (Vol. 1, pp. 163–86). New York: Oxford University Press.

O'Neill, S. A. (2012b). Personhood and music learning: An introduction. In S. A. O'Neill (Series Ed. & Vol. Ed.), *Research to practice: Vol. 5. Personhood and music learning: Connecting perspectives and narratives* (pp. 1–15). Waterloo, ON: Canadian Music Educators Association.

O'Neill, S. A. (2014). Mind the gap: Transforming music engagement through learner-centred informal music learning. *The Recorder: Journal of the Ontario Music Educators' Association, 56*(2), 18–22.

O'Neill, S. A. (in press–a). Young people's musical lives: Learning ecologies, identities and connectedness. In R. A. R. MacDonald, D. J. Hargreaves, & D. Meill (Eds.), *Oxford handbook of musical identities.* New York: Oxford University Press.

O'Neill, S. A. (in press–b). Youth empowerment and transformative music engagement. In C. Benedict, P. Schmidt, G. Spruce, & P. Woodford (Eds.), *Oxford handbook of social justice and music education.* New York: Oxford University Press.

O'Neill, S. A., & Senyshyn, Y. (2012). On meaning making and student music engagement. *Proceedings of the 24th International Seminar on Research in Music Education,* University of Macedonia, Thessaloniki, Greece. Retrieved from <http://issuu.com/official_isme/docs/2012_research_proceedings>.

O'Sullivan, E. (1999). *Transformative learning. Educational vision for the 21st century.* Toronto: University of Toronto Press.

Ozer, E. J., Ritterman, M. L., & Wanis, M. G. (2010). Participatory action research (PAR) in middle school: Opportunities, constraints, and key processes. *American Journal of Community Psychology, 46*(1–2), 152–66. doi: 10.1007/s10464–10010–9335–9338.

Paris, S. G. (2000). Trojan horse in the schoolyard: The hidden threats in high-stakes testing. *Issues in Education*, **6**(1, 2) 1–16.

Paris, S. G., Lawton, T. A., Turner, J. C., & Roth J. L. (1991). A developmental perspective on standardized achievement testing. *Educational Researcher*, **20**(5), 12–20.

Paris, S. G., Roth, J., & Turner, J. C. (2000). Developing disillusionment: Students' perceptions of academic achievement tests. *Issues in Education*, **6**(1–2), 17–45.

Perlstein, L. (2010). Unintended consequences: High stakes can result in low standards. *American Educator*, **34**(2), 6–9.

Pinar, W., Reynolds, W. M., Slattery, P., & Taubman, P. M. (2008). *Understanding curriculum*. New York: Peter Lang.

Pintrich, P. R. (2003). A motivational science perspective on the role of student motivation in learning and teaching contexts. *Journal of Educational Psychology*, **95**(4), 667–86.

Pitts, S. (2005). *Valuing musical participation*. Hants, UK: Ashgate.

Schwarzer, D., Bloom, M., & Shono, S. (2006). *Research as a tool for empowerment: Theory informing practice*. Charlotte, NC: Information Age Publishing.

Sefa Dei, G. J. (2003). Schooling and the dilemma of youth disengagement. *McGill Journal of Education*, **38**(2), 241–56.

Seligman, M. E. P. (2011). *Flourish: A visionary new understanding of happiness and well-being*. New York: Free Press.

Sheldon, K. M., & King, L. K. (2001). Why positive psychology is necessary. *American Psychologist*, **56**(3), 216–17.

Silbereisen, R. K., & Lerner, R. M. (Eds.) (2007). *Approaches to positive youth development*. Thousand Oaks, CA: Sage.

Skrtic, T. M. (1995). *Disability and democracy: Reconstructing [special] education for postmodernity*. New York: Teachers College Press.

Smith, J. A., Flowers, P., & Larkin, M. (2009). *Interpretative phenomenological analysis: Theory, method and research*. Thousand Oaks, CA: Sage.

Spencer, M. B. (1999). Social and cultural influences on school adjustment: The application of an identity-focused cultural ecological perspective. *Educational Psychologist*, **34**(1), 43–57.

Stipek, D. (2002). Good instruction is motivating. In A. Wigfield & J. Eccles (Eds.), *Development of achievement motivation* (pp. 309–32). San Diego: Academic Press.

Taylor, E. W. (2007). An update of transformative learning theory: A critical review of the empirical research (1999–2005). *International Journal of Lifelong Education*, **26**(2), 173–91.

Toshalis, E., & Nakkula, M. J. (2012). *Motivation, engagement, and student voice: The students at the center series*. Boston, MA: Jobs for the Future.

Turley, S. (1994). *"The way teachers teach is, like, totally whacked": The student voice on classroom practice*. Paper presented at the Annual Meeting of the American Educational Research Association, New Orleans, LA.

Tynjälä, P., Stenström, M.-L., & Saarnivaara, M. (2012). *Transitions and transformations in learning and education*. New York: Springer.

Zyngier, D. (2003). Connectedness—isn't it time that education came out from behind the classroom door and rediscovered social justice? *Social Alternatives*, **22**(3), 41–9.

Chapter 34

The transition from adolescent to adult music learner

Jane W. Davidson and Robert Faulkner

The transition from adolescent to adult music learner: Introduction

The creative and performing arts can be produced to near-mastery skills by the adolescent, since many of the cognitive and physical prerequisites required to learn and play an instrument with technical skill and musical understanding are developed by the teenage years. Indeed, the current volume has dedicated several chapters to demonstrating the ways in which young music learners invest in hours of accumulated practice to achieve some remarkable outcomes. But, it has only been in the last decade that the deeper social psychological aspects of how and why some individuals do or do not make the transition from adolescent to adult musician have been examined in research. The current chapter examines this transition and, in particular, the critical events that mark successful or unsuccessful navigation of self and various material, personal, and social alignments. Inevitably, it intersects with the chapter on motivation by Paul Evans (Chapter 17), who has at various times worked with Gary McPherson and both of the current authors on some of the research discussed across several chapters that appear in this book.

Identity formation

One of the foundational theoretical frameworks to assist in understanding identity formation can be found in Erikson's (1950) work on the confluence of psychosocial demands placed on the adolescent that are described as inevitably leading to tension between identity and role, resulting in confusion. Erikson theorized that the lifespan falls into eight distinct stages, with each comprising a specific task that must be achieved before progression from one state to another can occur. Adolescence features as the fifth stage, in which the crucial task is to establish a firm sense of social, sexual, and occupational identity. Clearly, moving to this stage from earlier life stages that were focused around family and peers, adolescence is a significant challenge.

As Evans and McPherson (Evans, Chapter 17; Evans & McPherson, 2015, in press) mention, Marcia's (1966) refinement of Erikson's original approach identifies two extra and critical activities in the process of adolescent identity formation: *exploration* (where the teenager explores different kinds of identity associated with activities); and *commitment* (which captures the extent to which decisions regarding personal identity have been made). Where there is an absence of either exploration or commitment, *diffusion* occurs. Where roles, activities, images, and behaviors have been investigated but no definitive identity has emerged, there is *moratorium. Foreclosure* is where the adolescent has made an early commitment to an identity without exploring the range of options available to them. Finally, *achievement* is when the adolescent has successfully experimented with personal and social identities to arrive at a conscious and coherent identity choice that then shapes their future. *Achievement* is obviously dependent on many social and personal factors, and it is vital to understanding positive identity formation.

Further refinement of Marcia's work (Luyckx et al., 2006; Luyckx et al., 2008) adds *breadth* and *depth* aspects to *exploration* to encapsulate the adolescent's search for different identity alternatives associated with goals and values and how these fit with others around them. For negative outcome, *ruminative exploration* captures indecisiveness or poor decision-making. *Commitment* is also elaborated, with the dimension relabeled *commitment making* to refer to identity choices having been made, and the dimension *identification with commitment* used to embrace the degree to which adolescents identify with the choices. These expansions to the identity model reveal that adolescents need not only experiment with these identities, but also reflect on their personal interests and values and consider the longer-term investment and potential outcomes. In the context of this book, the musical identity under construction is that of the musician, and in the case of music, of course, there are many potential identity options that vary from listener to performer, from classical through to pop music styles, and from professional to leisure engagement.

Examples of musical identity trialing have been captured in reports by a number of researchers. Looking across such studies, it seems that the students begin experimenting with friends and through associations like school music ensembles or regional groups that are often led by charismatic role models. The adolescents then seem to become hooked into the musical, social, and emotional aspects of the music-making, which in turn helps them to develop a sense of themselves based on these specific outlets in their lives (see Davidson, Howe, & Sloboda, 1997; McPherson, Davidson, & Faulkner, 2012). Thus, *exploration depth* and *identification with commitment* are achieved through positive musical opportunity, social encounter, and support.

A different but nonetheless useful theoretical account of identity development is found in Ibarra's notion of a *provisional self* (Ibarra, 1999). Again related to Erikson's ideas, in this account of identity formation individuals work to develop strategies around their identity that will enable them to progress in a certain field. This can happen either when a single role model is adopted, or when characteristics from a number of different individuals are adopted. These *provisional identities* are endorsed or rejected through social contact. Burland and Davidson (2004) were able to account for the successful transitions of young musicians through adolescence in their own study by identifying the provisional selves adopted by their participants. Studying highly successful young adult musicians, they discovered that many had negotiated adolescence drawing on "role models within touching distance" to develop their musical behaviors and personal selves, emulating the values of these individuals.

As indicated in Erikson's seminal work on identity formation, the self is multi-dimensional, and being such, the adolescent who is trialing his or her musical identity can generate highly negative as well as positive constructions. Music researchers Davidson, Howe and Sloboda (1997) reported adolescents who had committed to playing an instrument for several years yet ended up ceasing engagement, and left with very negative views of their experiences. Evans and McPherson relate results of these types to learners not having managed to project a long-term musical identity for themselves; in other words, there needed to be an *identification with commitment* for a realistic musical identity formation to develop and then be sustained (Evans, Chapter 17; Evans & McPherson, 2015, and in press).

Self-determination theory (Deci & Ryan, 2000) has offered a key framework to account for positive and committed musical identity formation through its focus on the engenderment of feelings of *competence* (effectiveness in one's efforts), *relatedness* (integration into a social group), and *autonomy* (being self-governed). According to a range of investigative and theoretical work, these psychological needs must be satisfied for self-determination to occur. Closely reflecting aspects of self-determination theory, the tripartite model of experience and beliefs for ongoing learning and success in musicians was proposed by Burland and Davidson (2004), and this offers a useful insight into the emergent identities of musicians who developed strong adolescent identifications with music which in turn led through into young adulthood.

The tripartite model emerged from detailed thematic analyses of interview transcript data, with the terminology taken from the interviewees themselves. One element of the tripartite model is referred to as "positive experience with others," which clearly parallels the concept of *relatedness*, while *autonomy* is captured in Burland and Davidson's element of "music as a determinant of self-concept." Although *competence* as such is not identified, the third element of the model is "methods of coping." This refers to the ability to cope with many of the challenges raised by the demands of the lifestyle, such as regular practice. This, therefore, seems to encompass Deci and Ryan's idea of how competency and autonomy interact so as to engage with music engaging a whole spectrum of external to intrinsic factors.

In an overview of the tripartite model, Davidson and Burland (2006) presented a case study of one of their participants arguing that he had *not* developed appropriate methods of coping. The result of this lack of coping strategy in musical performance resulted in him giving up performance in adulthood, even though he had been an extraordinarily successful adolescent. Looking at these data in retrospect, it is possible to interpret them by applying Deci and Ryan's theory and by considering the interaction between the student's description of his autonomy, competency, and his differing levels of motivation across the period of learning. The student, Carl, had a very strong initial *introjected motivation* to learn a musical instrument, sparked when his teachers humiliated him in front of his class for having failed a music test. Carl's motivation to start learning an instrument was explicitly driven by a desire to show the teacher he could achieve in music. Once lessons began, Carl seemed to find playing music very easy, and when he took up his pre-professional musical education in a leading international conservatoire, he felt that none of his teachers could play to his standard, even commenting that two of his teachers seemed resentful of his "easy" ability. The perceived lack of appropriate support Carl felt, perhaps coupled with a wavering motivation, could have led him to remain dependent on *introjected* rather than fully *intrinsically* motivated engagement. Evidently, this motivation had a profoundly negative impact on Carl's desire to continue as an instrumentalist and became inherently bound up with Carl's emergent sense of self. He gave up, as he seemed to see less value in playing than when he began, and other people did not seem to support him in ways he found motivating.

Looking at the range of theories and evidence presented thus far, it seems there are several accounts that deal with similar ideas about how the self is developed through music engagement. These are associated with *competency* and *autonomy* and their relationship to motivation and social connection—both "provisional selves" and *relatedness* being powerful constructs. At this stage, however, it is necessary to highlight an assumption that underlies the theories discussed to this point. The belief is that once the *adult* identity is found, it becomes more stable. In recent times, however, the career of the musician has been deconstructed to reveal that musicians need to develop a range of very flexible skills to undertake the wide range of jobs that permit them to make a living, and thus feeding into the increasing diversification of the music profession (see Bennett, 2008). This flexibility, invention, and re-invention impact on the self that constantly requires change and has been productively captured by Weber (2000), who demonstrates how individual choice and cultural context interact to provide a useful explanation of a self that can both expand and contract at any life stage, according to personal, material, and social concerns.

The created self

William James's classic model of self (1890) argued three principal components: the *material self*, related to the body and the physical world; the *social self*, concerned with social relationships, and the *spiritual self*, relating to belief or experience of a religious or spiritual nature. In Weber's (2000) adaptation of James's work, the material component is labeled *body*, the social is regarded as *persona*, and the spiritual is regarded as *spirit*, and all three elements are bound together by a singular self, which continually operates in an interplay of individual choices and cultural contexts, so the self is perceived to be in a state of expansion and/or contraction depending on the interplay of factors affecting it. Weber labels the outcome "The *Created Self*." The appeal of this model in the current context is that it captures the dynamic nature of the self. Also, it emphasizes the physicality of musical engagement, the place within which musical experience is developed, with different presentations of self or personae being varied according to context, number of collaborators, and even the kinds of music being explored. Finally, when applied to music, spiritual aspects are satisfied. As Faulkner (2013) points out, there is good evidence that music can bring "order, harmony and predictability to conscious life," which in turn can have positive impact on the self. This idea has further resonances in Csikszentmihalyi's (1994) ideas on spiritual skills that involve the capacity to harmonize thoughts, emotions, and will. Csikszentmihalyi believes that artists are one group of people capable of achieving these outcomes, with musicians having the advantage of music supporting consonant experience and feeling.

Returning briefly to the case of Carl, it is worth noting that although he abandoned playing as he transitioned out of adolescence, he nonetheless had a musical identity as he went on to work in music production, and was especially interested in nightclub music culture and its power to generate powerful and positive group experiences. So, in terms of the created self, it seems that the young musician adapts and develops, with fulfillment of the spiritual self being crucial to motivation, engagement, and "well-being."

In an auto-ethnographic piece, Faulkner (2013) explores his own musical transition from child to adult musician, noting how his sense of self was shaped by experiences such as attending a performance of Mahler's *Eighth Symphony* in Canterbury Cathedral, where he felt himself "levitated" by the power and spiritual impact of the music on him. Working with an Icelandic male community choir, Faulkner (2013) also found similar shared experiences between the male choristers, where they reported both religious and personal "transformation" through musical engagement, which often functioned as a crucial factor in shaping their social lives (see Faulkner, 2013 for more details).

Scripts and self

Borthwick and Davidson (2002) investigated a family that had strong "scripts" associated with the physical, temperamental, and ability resemblances between their children, parents, and grandparents. These "family scripts" (Byng-Hall, 1995) have been shown to have powerful influences over the ways in which selves develop and how individuals within families progress. In Borthwick and Davidson's study, one child was strongly identified within the family as occupying the persona of his professional musician father—same physique, like-temperament, and similar facility to make music. The other child occupied a different space, determined in large degree by the family script. Said to resemble the maternal grandmother in terms of appearance and character, the script worked negatively against the second child for music, since "it just was not in his make-up," and so the externally imposed persona seemed to be synthesized and adopted as part of the developing self. Music learning was relinquished for activities in art, which were regarded by the family as being more suitable to the individual's character. Of course physical resemblance, personality, gender, and temperament all contribute powerfully to these constructs, but for this particular adolescent, it seems that his self was contracted away from a musician identity to that of a fine artist. Indeed, in adulthood, this person went on to work as an art curator.

While these various approaches explored so far in this chapter offer interesting insights, it is necessary to find an overarching account for the development of the learner from child to adult musician. There have been a variety of explanations ranging from investigations of how environmental catalysts seem to interact (Davidson et al., 1997) through to more deterministic accounts of how natural abilities emerge (Gagné, 2009; McPherson & Williamon, Chapter 18).

Syzygies and self

Resonating with the created self, self-determination theory and the tripartite model of musical success and failure for the individual, and the theory of family scripts, the concept of "syzygies"— alignments of key physical, social, and psychological conditions that produce a strong force toward specific development and advancement of skill in a domain—operates as a gravitational system to pull individuals toward motivated and positive achievement (see Davidson & Faulkner, 2013; Faulkner & Davidson, in press). Referring to the biographies of significant musical achievers, Faulkner and Davidson (in press) have demonstrated alignments of many factors that help musicians to acquire amazing skills, but often at considerable cost and difficulty when trialing identities and creating selves. In order to consider the concept in detail, we now investigate examples that focus on the transition between child and adult musician. We look for the syzygistic alignments that shift the self in one direction, and then observe as other alignments lead to a shift in another, quite unexpected direction.

Anthony

In our study of students from Australia who were traced from 7 to 21 years of age, we were able to take frequent snapshots of their lives, allowing us to investigate their transitions in relation to their developing sense of self and music and how these interacted for positive and negative outcomes. One student we have frequently referred to in our publications is Anthony. His case is particularly intriguing and useful when exploring syzygies because when he was first tested on musical achievements prior to starting the trombone, his rhythmic abilities were poor on the measures of musical "aptitude." Even with two years of piano lessons behind him, his aural musicianship was average. This is a useful point to make, for there are cases when students are given access to musical instrument learning by being able to perform well in diagnostic tests. We are not, of course, criticizing the diagnostic tests per se, but rather observing that Anthony, who turns out to be an exceptionally able teenage musician, would have been overlooked in terms of musical test results alone.

Looking to Anthony's family circumstance, the niche for musical engagement and support was favorable: his mother was a piano teacher, and her musical and parenting skills certainly supported her son's progression in music. Initially, Anthony's mother provided him with tuition, offering the grounding for music in his life. Though he did not pursue the piano, which she had taught him for two years between 6 and 8 years of age, it did offer a context for music-making when he began to learn the trombone.

As he progressed with his trombone, Anthony's mother was always there to accompany him, offering support without pressure. Indeed, she and her husband actively decided not to monitor practice, but rather to listen when invited by their son. Supervising practice has been more generally reported as a positive approach to achieving appropriate support for the young learner (see Davidson et al., 1997). Here it is clear that the supportive but non-interventionist approach by Anthony's parents facilitated the boy's musical autonomy and so his musician identity was able to grow. His musical self emerged in the context of a supportive and musical mother. This point is worth expanding, as it highlights the thoroughly personalized nature of syzygies and how they are assimilated in the individual. It could have been that a more structured and routine-based approach to practice by the parents would have alienated Anthony. Furthermore, and particular to Anthony's story, he received highly positive extrinsic motivation in his very first explorations on the trombone with his first teacher, who was thrilled that Anthony could already read music. Somewhat surprisingly, given that there was a clear advantage of former experience on the piano, the trombone teacher took the capacity of reading music as a natural ability and a signal of a special disposition in terms of skills, personality, and physique for music.

Despite Anthony's early weakness relating to music aural skills, his teacher offered him high praise, providing positive feedback. Looking at the scripts we collected from Anthony and his family, the teacher's belief had a double benefit in that the praise was also picked up by Anthony's mother, who was then encouraged by her son's apparent "talent" and so her increased motivation fed into the boy's own approach to learning. Thus, both mother and son began to believe that any progress made was "special" and worthy of the effort involved. These alignments could have been otherwise, but they coalesced, moving Anthony along with his motivation to learn and developing his notion of self in relation to being a trombonist.

From the start, it is important to note that Anthony had a highly individualized specific love of his trombone: the construction of the trombone, its sound, its strength and the physicality of it as he played it, and the power of the sound in and through his body. His instrument offered him a special musical encounter and a unique musical identity within his family and more broadly in school. Indeed, Anthony emphasized that the trombone was "his instrument"—an autonomous belief about his relationship with the trombone and music. His attitudes reflect a personal buoyancy, referred to by both his mother and teacher as being open and motivated; "extremely keen to do his best . . . highly literate, articulate and numerate and has an insatiable appetite for work which is always of a high standard"—his classroom teacher's report of his character. The positive experiences and perception of them work to filter out negative thoughts and experiences during Anthony's early learning.

But in addition to all of this, and consonant with the other major theories outlined earlier, we see that Anthony's case follows several crucial stages for successful learning that resonate with another theory of skills development relevant in this chapter, namely Abbott and Collins' (2004) work on skill development in sports education. This specifies that it is necessary to find a route to "get there and then stay there" (see further, McPherson et al., 2012). That is, moving through the required threshold of external support from parent and teachers to work with peers, all to achieve the number of hours of amassed practice necessary for skill acquisition, and working on to achieve highly reflective and well-maintained work as a top performer. The stages the researchers define can be easily applied to Anthony's case: first, a *sampling stage*, where Anthony initially tries the trombone and enjoys positive experiences; second, a *specialization stage*, where he begins to work with colleagues and acquires technical and artistic skills; third, an *investment stage* in which high-level decisions are made about the degree of work required, with the family working around this to accommodate the effort and intensive skills training necessary, in his specific case, extra-curricular music activities, and competitions; and finally, a *maintenance stage*, where effective strategies are drawn to optimize performance and control factors that may impact negatively on skills, such as performance anxiety. For each stage to occur, a *macro transition* is required, which increasingly solidifies an identity as a musician and so the connection with music-making.

All of Abbott and Collins' theory is couched in terms of personality and motivation and how these interact, again bringing us to the power of the syzygy to explain these alignments. Indeed for Anthony, though the developmental stages were not consciously understood at the time they occurred, and given opportunity to reflect on the alignment of circumstances and Anthony's own personality, it becomes clear how the alignments he experienced facilitated further motivation. For example, in the first lessons with his trombone teacher, Anthony managed to play a B flat scale, ending successfully on the high B flat. At the time, he was pleased he could do it, but it was only on reflection in later adolescence that the impact of the action was fully realized:

> I remember my very first lesson on trombone—I learnt the B flat major scale, and my teacher said he'd never done that with anyone before, so I think that excited me a bit, made me want to play a lot. Looking back, I had no idea what that meant on the first day. Teaching students now, I realize that it might take half a year for some to be able to play the high B flat (McPherson et al., 2012, p. 102).

This successful action—whether achieved by chance or otherwise—developed the teacher's expectation that Anthony had lots of potential. For Anthony, the fact that he could achieve immediately, without much effort, and be praised for his trombone playing, offered motivation to go from the sampling stage through to specializing further.

In addition to the teacher, Anthony developed a particularly close friendship with another boy who was learning in the same school band and together they developed friendships with other students also learning in the instrumental program. This was a strongly promotive environment that enabled Anthony to form positive alignments that motivated him toward specialization and so major investment in practice and performance. Unique amongst the schools we studied, Anthony's school proactively used music grade examinations to motivate students, with some seven of the 20 students we studied from Anthony's primary cohort being encouraged and then being successful in achieving Grade 3 external music examination results within three years of starting their band instruments. In other contexts, such "pressures" may have had negative consequences, but within the milieu of the school and its support mechanisms, this worked favorably for Anthony.

Anthony's story continues in such a manner through an intensive period of investment, whereby he refines his musical experiences relative to the trombone, specializing and maintaining his skills and desires for involvement through extensive performance experiences. Eventually, at the age of 20 years, with an amazing balance of autonomy, relatedness, and high competence, Anthony wins the Australian national trombone championships, thus reaching the pinnacle of achievement, his progress though adolescence building in momentum and focus on his musical performance activities.

With all these positive alignments, Anthony's is a model case of self (*material* and *spiritual self* connected through music) and social regulation with "other" (friends and family with whom and through whom he makes music) that interact in dynamic ways to impact development. This idea of balancing elements is encapsulated in Sameroff's (2009) theory of Transactional Regulation. These transactions create those positive alignments we are calling syzygies and are created when transactions align biological, social, and psychological experience, present abilities, needs, and dispositions, ambition, and aspiration with present provision and resources. In late adolescence, this positivity of feeling and focus on the trombone begin to diminish, despite Anthony's amazing successes, and a change of focus occurs in later adolescence when he decides to study graphic design rather than music at university.

So, Anthony's is not a straightforward story of positive syzygistic alignments for music, for as he becomes highly expert in the trombone, he carefully begins to refocus the entire process of investment and maintenance in music, his trombone playing being increasingly placed in a specific niche in his life, a niche that separates off from an emergent additional identity as a graphic designer. During his university career, he is adamant that he does not want to follow his mother and become a music teacher, perceiving it as a challenging occupation with little financial reward. For Anthony as an adult, graphic design satisfies rather different personal needs of autonomy and creativity than those of music. A different aspect of his self is being forefronted.

Ironically, during his university studies, Anthony funded his graphic design course with casual work in a leading national orchestra. Of course, for many, achieving the status of playing with a prestigious orchestra would be the pinnacle of achievement, but for Anthony, playing the trombone becomes a means to an end. He loves playing, seeing his skills as a musician as a vital part of self-identity but he also recognized pitfalls in the profession. The commitment needed to maintain high performance levels across his entire lifespan is also something he cannot contemplate, and as he has a changing lifestyle the competing interests become increasingly important to him, making him all the more determined not only to focus on music.

Relational transactions offer a framework for understanding this shift in Anthony's developmental trajectory, proposing that experience is not only filtered by intrapersonal catalysts, but also that environmental experience is blended with the intrapersonal. And as such, personality characteristics remain present and may even dominate responses to experience, but personal and malleable adaptations make various changes possible, too. These adaptations are clearly influenced in turn by the experiences that blend and through subconscious and conscious responses that are made to them. We can see this in Anthony's successful musical career, and then his shifting interest and emphasis toward graphic design.

Caroline and Christina

We have encountered a number of established musicians who have come through periods of adolescence when alignments were drawn and re-framed. The vignettes offered now show examples of different but nonetheless equally strong family dynamics that shaped identity development in the transition to adult musician status.

Caroline has a professional musician mother and along with her two siblings had learned piano, but she also has her own special niche woodwind instrument. Like many others described earlier in this chapter, she was well supported in her early learning across a range of subjects, but music in particular, with lessons at school and home. As she approached adolescence, her father increasingly emphasized subjects other than music for study. After expressing the enjoyment she experienced in her music practice and performance, especially the social aspects of youth orchestra, she sustained the orchestral playing, but focused on a heavy academic loading. Aiming to please her father and compete with considerable inter-sibling rivalry, she recounts the period between 15 and 18 years of age as a stressful time, trying to please both her parents, and work hard at school, as well as keep up her love of music.

> Pressure seemed to be on me from every angle: Dad wanting me to go to the best possible university; Mum wanting me to follow through with music as she saw the love I had for it; my sister and

brother both being very studious and I felt a pressure to keep up with them. When my sister (who is older than me) got high marks for her final school exams, well then the spotlight fell on me. I wanted to please Dad and Mum, and I guess that I also wanted to show my sister I could do as well as her. Anyway, in the end, I did the exams, got the place, and then used my time at university to do as much music as possible, even though it wasn't my course of study. I became a choral singer, and through those choirs and lots of extra-curricular activities with fellow students, I was able to keep my music ticking along. It was after I'd got my degree, I then took on an office job for three years and paid for extra music lessons and worked until I could achieve entry to the conservatoire and then I started all over again. Looking back, I became a professional musician both because of and in spite of my family.

Of course we recognize the crucial role of parenting from previous examples. Caroline's compliance is something common amongst students, with most wishing to follow through on their parents' suggestions (see Hallam, 2002). But, in Caroline's case at least, personal resilience and strategic thinking go into her career, planning for life after the undergraduate degree when she is able to choose her own course of study. The alignments of extra-curricular musical activities are still sufficient to direct her toward her personal goal in music.

For Christina, both the family dynamic and the pressures of adolescence were very different to those experienced by Caroline.

Mum and Dad wanted us to be well rounded. They basically taxied us around and paid the bills. We had to do the practice and homework. Besides school subjects, we learned music and sport and had the family routine of going to church every Sunday. My brother was the scientist and sportsman, and in his adolescence became religious. I got swept along with it as it meant that I could hang out with my older brother and his friends. I went with him; a main attraction was the music. In that spiritual context, the music bowled me over. I'd never experienced anything like it: transcendent and highly emotionally charged. Anyway, we both got right into it: prayer meetings, music group, the whole thing. He then went off to university and continued with science and the church. I stayed at home and continued with sport, music and the church. I was quite good, so I sort of drifted into the music, but it could have been sport.

No one pushed us, but the activities that were valued by Mum and Dad were the ones we took on, each one of us having a slightly different focus. I sing, often in churches, worshipping the wonderful sounds and emotions music can evoke. So mine was a non-crisis teenage, really.

Here for the first time we meet in a very explicit way the spiritual self Weber speaks of, forefronted by Christina's religious and musical experiences. Her story reveals a rather more casual approach to learning and opportunity and how she and her brother took a priority learning area from the family options.

A further and more complex case of such alignments and realignments in the search for a consistent and satisfying identity can be found in the case of Bejun Mehta.

Bejun Mehta

As a 15-year-old boy, Bejun recorded a remarkable solo album, *Bejun—Arias and Songs*, that received extraordinary worldwide critical acclaim from musicians and critics alike. Bejun undoubtedly possessed an exceptional vocal instrument, and through an early childhood filled with music he also developed exceptional musicianship capacities, learning the cello alongside voice. His treble career was particularly interesting, for Bejun entered puberty considerably later than average, allowing the development of vocal skills over a far longer period than most other treble voices, so he was able to learn technically demanding repertoire by Handel, Britten, Schubert, and Brahms and sustain a treble solo across most of his adolescence. But, this also meant that he was under an extended period of extremely monitored parental control.

The young musician's biography reveals some interesting syzygies, beginning with a home environment and external motivations that provided every positive alignment for musical development. In fact, Bejun came from a strong musical family, his cousin being the world famous conductor Zubin Mehta, his father being a pianist, and his mother a fine singer. His older sibling was also a keen and supportive musician role model, and thus the entire family was feeding into Bejun's musical development. Indeed, it was his mother who gave Bejun his first singing lessons, and it was Bejun's father who was the main support behind his son's emerging strength as a musician. These important relationships are reflected in Bejun's own piece on the process of prodigy (see Kenneson, 2003). Significantly, Bejun is able to describe in great reflective detail his understanding of the spiritually uplifting effect music could have on him, to transport him to tension and resolution of harmony, and how his father patiently drew attention to the voicing in Bach keyboard pieces:

> He showed me very specific things about the piece in hand, he also showed me how much he loved the music, and by sharing these things how much he loved me. (Kenneson, 2003, p. 337)

While Bejun clearly benefited strongly from this environment and support through musical sampling and investment periods, building competency and relational elements of his psychological needs as specified in self-determination theory, this positivity was not to last. It seems that autonomy was severely undermined, and the feeling of being loved by his father, along with Bejun's own sense of himself as a young musician, became negatively entangled. Bejun perceived his father's comments on his music-making as negative criticisms. In a retrospective reconstruction of his feelings, he comments that once his treble singing was going very well, he identified a change in his father's approach and an increasing over-investment and concern with:

> the manifestations of my talent, including voice, cello and scholarship, and less with the simple maintenance of a reflecting atmosphere. The new atmosphere was marked by criticism; criticism of phrasing, comparative critiques of performances and work and caustic, at times even violent rejection of my musical and intellectual expression. (Kenneson, 2003, p. 343)

This reporting of the parental style clearly leaves Bejun struggling with an undermined sense of self and his source of love, his father and the original support, shifting to hurtful and undermining criticism:

> With every new criticism I felt increasingly pulled from the world of my imagination, less trusted and more and more alone. Being struck occasionally only cemented those feelings in place. (Kenneson, 2003, p. 343)

Here we see a case of where over-investment from the parents, the father in particular, stifles efforts for the young boy to become "self-determined" in his individual learning and also in his sense of who he is. It seems like he reached a bleak impasse. Indeed, shortly after his voice broke, Bejun left home against the wishes of his parents. He was determined to break away and find his own niche. It is of course a complex story, for he did not rebel totally from his educational background as some teenagers do, but rather he broke away from parental monitoring to pursue his own self-regulated interests in music and other subjects he had enjoyed at school. In fact, Bejun describes the period in his life as a painful psychological crisis, a time when his efforts were focused around finding a personal identity.

During these years, Bejun's direction was unclear, but the desire for opportunity and experience was voracious, as he trialed his provisional selves. Indeed, during this period, alignments were such that he was able to profit from many experiences and revealed himself able to move toward several possible career directions. The next years found him trying his hand at record production, alongside the study of German literature at Yale University and work as orchestral cellist and conductor. The appetite for educational experiences eventually brought Bejun full circle and back to his singing, now in a re-invention as a countertenor. Today Bejun plays leading roles in all of the world's greatest opera houses. But, in this astonishing life Bejun continues to direct ensembles, play his cello, and generally lead a fully charged multi-skilled existence. Amazingly rich as his life seems, it makes sense if we regard it as a series of alignments with prior musical, psychological, and social experiences that configured his childhood, for positive and negative outcomes on a complex journey that eventually enables him to balance several elements in his most recent manifestation of his "created self."

These examples reveal the complexity of syzygistic alignments, with changes in focus often being precipitated by an internal shift in sense of focus and questioning of self and career direction. For Anthony, the move was more based around career opportunity and the determination not to follow in a family tradition. For Bejun, it was not to reject music, but rather find a way of succeeding on his own terms.

Conclusions

This chapter has offered some insights into the forces in operation as the adolescent musician negotiates a route from the support mechanisms that assisted early development in childhood, through to a self-directed adult future. The case studies presented show the myriad of syzygies in operation, and reveal that these people retained interest in music as their adult self-identities were formed, but even then, the identity was dynamic, always open to adjustment and change, to realignment and re-creation. In the cases considered, there was some sense of moving away or on from some earlier experiences. Anthony's movement into graphic design was smooth and did not involve any break from his trombone playing. Bejun experienced a rapid movement through his advanced studies, revealing a search for an adult musical identity that was satisfying. Ironically, it was a route away from treble singing through different forms of music-making (cello and conducting) and other disciplines of study such as German literature that enabled Bejun to come full circle, passing over an unsuccessful attempt at singing baritone, through to finding a countertenor voice. In contrast, Caroline and Christina both complied with family norms and expectations.

From the sources explored in this chapter, we find that the construction and maintenance of material and social selves are very much accounted for, in part through the physicality of musical engagement and the satisfaction found by the performers through this means of expression, but also through the different social experiences encountered in music with a new and commonly focused group of friends. The spiritual self is also shown to be crucial to engaging interest and accessing strongly aligned and affective experiences that bring order and harmony to often turbulent conscious lives. Overall, the work explored reveals that the transition from early musical engagement (perhaps started at school or in private music lessons) through to adulthood through the highs and lows of adolescence can be negotiated, often very successfully. Music identity and engagement outcomes will depend upon a series of major transactions that are the product of crucial syzygistic alignments.

Reflective questions

1 Which of the various theoretical propositions presented in this chapter resonates most strongly with you?

2 Which issues discussed in this chapter reflect your own adolescent experiences as a musician?

3 Which of the case studies is the most intriguing and why?

4 What have you learned that you could use to encourage adolescents in their music-making?

5 What recommendations might you make to education providers on the basis of having read this chapter?

Key sources

Kaufmann, S. B. (Ed.) (2013). *Beyond "talent or practice?": The multiple determinants of greatness.* Oxford: Oxford University Press.

McPherson, G. E., Davidson, J. W., & Faulkner, R. (2012). *Music in our lives: Re-thinking musical ability, development and identity.* Oxford, UK: Oxford University Press.

Reference list

Abbott, A., & Collins, D. (2004). Eliminating the dichotomy between theory and practice in talent identification and development: Considering the role of psychology. *Journal of Sports Science,* **22**(5), 395–408.

Bennett, D. E. (2008). *Understanding the classical music profession: The past, the present and strategies for the future.* Aldershot: Ashgate.

Borthwick, S. J., & Davidson, J. W. (2002). Personal identity and music: A family perspective. In R. MacDonald, D. Miell, & D. J. Hargreaves (Eds.), *Musical identities* (pp.60–78). Oxford: Oxford University Press.

Burland, K., & Davidson, J. (2004). Tracing a musical life transition. In J. W. Davidson (Ed.), *The music practitioner: Exploring practices and research in the development of the expert music performer, teacher and listener.* Aldershot: Ashgate.

Byng-Hall, J. (1995). *Re-thinking family scripts: Improvisation and systems change.* New York: Oxford University Press.

Csikszentmihalyi, M. (1994). *The evolving self.* New York: Harper Perennial.

Davidson, J. W. & Burland, K. (2006). Musician identity formation. In G. E. McPherson (Ed.), *The child as musician: A handbook of musical development* (pp. 475–90). Oxford: Oxford University Press.

Davidson, J. W., & Faulkner, R. (2013). Music in our lives. In S. B. Kaufmann (Ed.), *Beyond "talent or practice?": The multiple determinants of greatness* (pp. 367–90). Oxford: Oxford University Press.

Davidson, J., Howe, M., & Sloboda, J. (1997). Environmental factors in the development of musical performance skill in the first twenty years of life. In D. H. A. Hargreaves & A. J. North (Eds.), *The social psychology of music* (pp. 188–203). Oxford: Oxford University.

Deci, E. L., & Ryan, R. M. (2000). The "what" and "why" of goal pursuits: Human needs and the self-determination of behavior. *Psychological Inquiry,* **11**(4), 227–68.

Erikson, E. H. (1950). *Childhood and society.* New York: W. W. Norton & Co.

Evans, P., & McPherson, G. E. (2015). Identity and practice: The consequences of a long-term musical identity. *Psychology of Music,* **43**(3), 407–22.

Evans, P., & McPherson, G. E. (in press). Processes of musical identity consolidation during adolescence. In D. Hargreaves, R. A. R. Macdonald, & D. Miell (Eds.), *Oxford handbook of musical identities.* Oxford, England: Oxford University Press.

Faulkner, R. (2013). *Icelandic men and me: Sagas of singing, self and everyday life.* Farnham: Ashgate.

Faulkner, R., & Davidson, J. W. (in press). Syzygies, social worlds and exceptional achievement in music. In G. E. McPherson (Ed.), *Musical prodigies.* Oxford: Oxford University Press.

Gagné, F. (2009). Building gifts into talents: Detailed overview of the DMGT 2.0. In B. MacFarlane & T. Stambaugh (Eds.), *Leading change in gifted education: The festschrift of Dr. Joyce Van Tassel-Baska* (pp. 61–80). Waco, Texas: Prufrock Press.

Hallam, S. (2002). Musical motivation: Towards a model synthesising the research. *Music Education Research*, **4**(2), 225–44.

Ibarra, H. (1999). Provisional selves: Experimenting with image and identity in professional adaptation. *Administrative Science Quarterly*, **44**(4), 764–91.

James, W. (1890). *The principles of psychology* (2 vols). New York: Henry Holt & Co.

Kenneson, C. (2003). *Musical prodigies—perilous journeys, remarkable lives*. Portland: Amadeus Press.

Luyckx, K., Goossens, L., Soenens, B., & Beyers, W. (2006). Unpacking commitment and exploration: Validation of an integrative model of adolescent identity formation. *Journal of Adolescence*, **29**(3), 361–78.

Luyckx, K., Schwartz, S. J., Berzonsky, M. D., Soenens, B., Vansteenkiste, M., Smits, I., & Goossens, L. (2008). Capturing ruminative exploration: Extending the four-dimensional model of identity formation in late adolescence. *Journal of Research in Personality*, **42**(1), 58–62.

Marcia, J. E. (1966). Development and validation of ego-identity status. *Journal of Personality and Social Psychology*, **3**(5), 551–8.

McPherson, G. E., Davidson, J. W., & Faulkner, R. (2012). *Music in our lives: Re-thinking musical ability, development and identity*. Oxford, UK: Oxford University Press.

Sameroff, A. (2009). The transactional model. In A. Sameroff (Ed.), *The transactional model of development: How children and contexts shape each other* (pp. 3–21). Washington, DC: American Psychological Association.

Weber, R. J. (2000). *The created self: Reinventing body, persona and spirit*. New York: W. W. Norton & Company.

Chapter 35

Fostering lifelong engagement in music

Stephanie E. Pitts

Fostering lifelong engagement in music: Introduction

Research in the developmental psychology of music has historically been very good at two things (among others): predicting the basic level of musical development that might be expected of all children, and highlighting the exceptional development of the few who attain professional standards of instrumental performing skill. Much less well documented has been the large, messy area in between—the slightly unpredictable transformation of normative musical acquisition into varying levels and types of musical skill, interest, and enthusiasm amongst the general population. Relatively little is known, for instance, about the effects of parental encouragement and attitudes on long-term musical engagement, though we have increasing insight on the value of parental support for instrumental practice (Creech & Hallam, 2009; McPherson, 2009) as well as interviews and autobiographical accounts from high-achieving musicians (Haddon, 2005). Likewise, instrumental and classroom music teachers pursue mainly short- or medium-term goals, coaching their pupils through the next exam or concert, and hearing in later years of any exceptional success stories, but less often of the day-to-day uses of music among the hundreds of students that any one teacher might influence during a career in music education.

The immediate effects of musical learning are easier to measure empirically than the lasting transformations that might occur through exposure to the musical opportunities of school years, and it is perhaps for this reason that assessment practices, school inspections, and research alike have taken a short-term approach to evaluating the usefulness of musical education. Few headteachers, school governors, or indeed parents would be persuaded that the benefits of learning in school will reach fruition many years later: the emphasis as young people leave school is on assessing what they can do now, not on the more challenging questions of how their formative years might shape them as adults. A few notable researchers in music education have argued that this approach misses the point, asserting that the values ascribed to a liberal arts education are not automatically achieved, much less carried forward into adulthood (Myers, 2007), and that self-efficacy—"the self-awareness that one could make satisfying music independently and share it with others" (p. 55)—should be the primary goal of music education. Myers points to Turton and Durrant's (2002) study of English adults recalling their experiences of singing in school as one example of how school music was felt to have been inadequate in equipping students with the skills for lifelong musical engagement, while suggesting that US band programs are similarly lacking in their vision for the future music-making of their students. Taking the argument one step further, Mantie (2013) urges music educators to reclaim the value of music as leisure, rather than only as learning, so bringing music in schools into greater alignment with music in most adult lives (and incidentally recalling some of the early twentieth-century justifications for music in the curriculum; see Pitts, 2000).

I will argue in this chapter that lifelong uses of music deserve more attention in our thinking about children as musicians. I will draw on my recent study of over a hundred written life history accounts from British and Italian respondents to provide illustrations of how the musical events and experiences of childhood have a lasting effect on the musical engagement and attitudes of each generation (see Pitts, 2012 for full details of methods; respondents are coded UK1–81 and I1–25 in the discussion that follows). In these accounts, piano lessons in childhood, for example, are shown to lead not only to musical proficiency that can be the source of enjoyable participation and performance in adulthood (see Pitts, 2005), but also to a cultural awareness that can help to shape society. Childhood experience of musical participation can lead to a realization that musical learning takes effort, not genius (Sloboda, Davidson, & Howe, 1994), and that its encouragement in young people is worthwhile; that live music is a distinct experience from recorded music listening; and that tastes and proficiencies in music are individually cultivated and a central part of both social and personal identity (MacDonald, Hargreaves, & Miell, 2002). Where formative experiences are negative or discouraging, however, their lifelong effect could be more damaging, closing down musical opportunities, and leading to a belief that it is too late to learn as an adult (despite evidence to the contrary). Paying greater attention to the potential musical futures of adolescents, I will argue, could transform music education and its relevance for the majority of the population, rather than the selected few who attain exam successes or performance glories during their school years.

The chapter will address three key questions:

+ What are the characteristics and lasting effects of a musically supportive home?

+ What are the characteristics and lasting effects of a musically supportive education?

+ How can parents, teachers, and others best equip children for lifelong engagement in music?

Before embarking on these discussions, however, we begin with the broader context of how the long-term effects of music in childhood can be investigated, and why this is valuable for music education research.

Ways of understanding formative musical experiences

Adults who engage in musical participation have been shown in previous studies to be articulate and passionate about their reasons for doing so (Pitts, 2005), and in some cases to report a sense of inevitability about their involvement: supportive parents, music playing in the home, and inspiring teachers are anecdotally cited as setting receptive children on a path to lifelong engagement. John Holt, educational psychologist and amateur musician, suggests that "musical people are particularly prone to talk this way" (Holt, 1978, p. 4), and theories of autobiographical memory would confirm that the exchange of childhood musical stories amongst like-minded people reinforces personal and collective musical identity, contributing to a life narrative which has music at its center (McAdams, 2001). Conversely, those adults who absorbed the message in childhood that music was "not for them" might carry this unquestioningly into adulthood, failing to engage with—or even to notice—musical opportunities unless a new external trigger, such as the interests of their own children or adult friends, brings them back into contact with music-making in some way.

The path from childhood experiences into adult engagement is not, however, a straightforward or universal one. If we knew that a certain number of instrumental lessons was sufficient to guarantee lasting commitment to playing, governments could decide whether this was a priority for educational funding—likewise, parents could be advised to expose their children to particular repertoire by the age of, say, 11 in order to shape their musical tastes for life. While there have been some attempts to track such data longitudinally (e.g. McPherson, Davidson, & Faulkner, 2012), such studies reveal more than anything the great variety and unpredictability of individual encounters with music and their long-term effects on motivation and engagement. A participant in Helen Gavin's study of adult recollections of formative musical experiences sums this up most vividly: "[My parents] bought me a flute when I asked, so I suppose that set me off to where I am today, but they also bought me a bike, and I'm not in the Tour de France" (Gavin, 2001, p. 57). Strong, repeated, positive experiences of music in childhood undoubtedly help to provide a secure foundation for lifelong engagement—but these can take many forms, and their specific effects will vary as they intersect with individuals' personalities, circumstances, and priorities throughout their lives.

Another limitation on previous debate around formative musical experiences arises in relation to the focus or purpose of musical learning for the long term. The emphasis on the musical life stories of professional musicians—such as evidence that these performers have typically practiced for 10,000 hours by the age of 21 (Ericsson, Krampe, & Tesch-Römer, 1993)—can give a distorted picture of the range of potential outcomes from childhood musical experiences and make "success" seem very narrowly defined and unattainable for the majority of children. This has been balanced in recent years by a new focus on the "transferable skills" benefits of musical learning (Hallam, 2010), with greater acknowledgement being made of the concentration, self-esteem, school engagement, and other qualities that might be developed through learning a musical instrument or belonging to an ensemble. In childhood, as in adulthood, making music has a wide range of benefits, from the musical skills and cultural awareness that are unique to that discipline, through to the social cohesion, personal development, and sense of purpose that will be attained in other ways by those with non-musical interests, but in which music has a valuable role to play for many individuals. Musical provision in childhood and education can be enhanced by taking this broader view of its lifelong contribution: not all children will become professional performers, but all those who have access to music will gain a greater understanding of how music is made, and many will discover qualities in themselves, as well as in music, that will shape and enhance their lives.

It is worth pausing at this point to note the life-enhancing and overwhelmingly positive qualities attributed to music in discussions of lifelong engagement—to which I am admittedly adding in this chapter. This bias in the debate is shaped by the narratives that are available to support it: the teachers whose motivation to teach comes from their valuing of music in their own lives (Cox, 1999), and the adults whose accounts of participation in middle- or older age are rich with evidence of social and personal development acquired through musical activity (Pitts, 2005; Southcott, 2009). Evidence for the damaging or negative effects of music education has been less conscientiously collected, partly because it provides a distraction from the arguments supporting an already marginalized subject in the curriculum, but also because research with non-participants in an activity is notoriously challenging, since they do not conveniently gather in one place to engage in their non-participation (Lamont, 2011). Nonetheless, it is self-evident that while music is almost certainly present in the lives of the majority of the world's population, its meaning and importance will vary according to temperament, inclination, and opportunity—and indeed for some people, music will be a matter of irrelevance, indifference, or outright irritation. Embracing the power of music to manipulate, intimidate, and divide populations—as well as to unite, encourage, and uplift them—might bring music education closer to the multiple meanings of music in the wider world (Philpott, 2012, p. 60).

Gaining understanding of how formative musical experience contributes to adult attitudes and engagement, positively or negatively, is a challenge for researchers, with both longitudinal and retrospective approaches having inevitable limitations. Rineke Smilde's (2009) "learning biographies" of 32 professional musicians trace the relationship between higher education and careers in music, with her interviewees challenging some of the "'myths' about musicians" (p. 126) by revealing an emergent path into adult musicianship, rather than having clear musical goals from early childhood. This observation shows how life history research, or autobiographical reflection, can help to illuminate the long-term impact of formative musical experiences. While this may not be compatible with the short-term, measurable goals typically used to evaluate education, the recognition that the impact of school music may be felt many decades later is an important one, which teachers will already recognize anecdotally, but which curriculum design and assessment practices rarely work to support. Tom Barone's (2001) study of art teacher Donald Forrister and his students offers a rare exploration of the life-changing impact of arts education: Forrister's charismatic teaching is credited with improving job prospects and broadening artistic horizons for many of the students he worked with, even while the apparent favoritism shown through this encouragement left other students feeling isolated. As Forrister reflects with anxiety on how his sharing of limited resources and energy amongst the varied needs of his students has affected their arts engagement and wider learning in the years after school, Barone calls for such questions to be at the heart of educational debate: "then what often is—narrow and shortsighted notions of educational outcomes—will indeed have become closer to what should be—teachers and schools dedicated to the endurance of the cognitive, the ethical, the aesthetic, and the useful, within lives that stretch out far beyond graduation day" (Barone, 2001, p. 180).

The telling of musical life histories, whether through interview or autobiographical writing, offers one route to understanding not only past musical experiences, but also how these have been interpreted and used to shape current musical identity, attitudes, and engagement. As in previous studies, the narratives used to frame the discussion in the remainder of this chapter offer few clear pathways to musical "success" (however broadly defined), not least because of the constantly shifting context of educational and societal change that lies behind the even greater variety of individual experience. These stories of musically active adults and their formative experiences do, however, highlight some key characteristics of supportive musical homes and schools, which will be explored in the sections that follow and their implications considered for the development of children as musicians.

The characteristics of musically supportive homes

The life history accounts in the *Chances and choices* study (Pitts, 2012) indicated that the key factors in providing musical support—in both home and school—were resources, attitudes, and opportunities. However, the implication that home environments therefore needed to be wealthy, with musically active parents, was contradicted by many accounts of parents struggling financially to provide lessons, indicating that a musical education was a priority for many of these parents, and one appreciated (though sometimes only in retrospect) by their children. One older respondent paints a vivid portrait of his family that highlights the precarious nature of musical involvement for many children:

> My parents: father, tone deaf (!); mother played piano (popular classical), had scarce resources with six children to care for, but chose wisely—and sacrificially—to engage two of us in music lessons from a highly qualified teacher. My sister "fell by the wayside" but I was "hooked," and was forever on the piano at home. (I learnt sight reading simply through hours and hours at my music.) [UK39, aged 81]

Amongst the cultural assumptions in this account is the normality of having a piano in the home—something shared by many of the older respondents; those in middle age recall the acquisition of an instrument more vividly, showing a societal shift in access to this once commonplace means of making music in the home. A parent who plays or sings is also a more prominent feature in earlier accounts, replaced for later generations by shared enthusiasms for listening to recorded music, and more recently still by the discussion of separately acquired listening tastes—the piano giving way first to the shared family gramophone, and then to increasingly portable means of individual music listening. The "highly qualified teacher" gains automatic respect for this respondent and his family, and while the impact and style of teachers remains important throughout the generations, younger respondents also report greater instances of self-directed learning—though this too is evident in the hours of sight-reading described by our octogenarian pianist. Most striking in this account, however, is the unpredictability of childhood lessons: in the same family, with the same resources, attitudes, and opportunities, two children begin piano lessons, and while one embarks on a lifetime of music-making, the other "falls by the wayside," perhaps overshadowed by her brother's developing skill, perhaps simply finding other interests and priorities.

The "sacrificial" provision of piano lessons indicates an awareness of the potential value of music-making for long-term development and enjoyment: the "tone deaf" father might regret his own lack of musical opportunity, while the pianist mother wants to replicate her pleasure in playing. Redressing and replicating parents' experiences are common motivations for supporting children in a musical education (Borthwick & Davidson, 2002) and indicate the lasting effects of musical learning in shaping the attitudes of future generations of parents and teachers. Where musical engagement is not part of a family's history, the routines of practice, lessons, performance, and assessment that shape instrumental learning can seem remote and unfamiliar, as described by a younger respondent from another large family:

> My eldest sister learnt the clarinet at secondary school and I remember her practising in the living room with her music balanced on the fire guard while we were in the room too. I would have been about 4 or 5 at the time. I remember thinking it was an odd thing to do and asking her what it was and what she was doing; she explained that she was learning it so that she could be in the school band with her friends and travel to other places to play. [UK5, aged 37]

In this account, the sibling effects are notably different from that of the older pianist; here the "odd thing" of learning to play an instrument is brought into the family living room, making this younger sister aware of the possibilities of making music, and so perhaps more receptive to the "inspiring" teaching that she reports having subsequently experienced in school. Her sister's motivation for playing is intriguing too: the acquisition of musical skill is explained as a means to an end, facilitating participation in an enjoyable social activity, strengthening friendships and broadening horizons through travel. The goals are immediate, concerned with short-term involvement rather than lifelong ambitions, and likely to lead to a pleasurable experience of music within school years, while making no provision for continuation into adulthood (indeed this respondent has later confirmed that this was the case for her sister, who ceased playing after her school years).

This clarinet-playing sister's reported experience is consistent with Gary McPherson's (2005) analysis that intentions for playing an instrument can be self-fulfilling: those children in a large-scale Australian study who predicted that they would give up their instrument when they transferred to high school did exactly that, while those who anticipated longer-term involvement prepared for this through greater practice in the early stages, and so progressed faster and gained more satisfaction from their playing. Extrinsic reasons for playing, such as joining a band with friends, were lower predictors of long-term engagement than the intrinsically musical reasons also highlighted in other studies of high-achieving young musicians (e.g. Sloboda, 1991). Parents and teachers both therefore have a powerful role to play in making children aware of the potential held within their first attempts to get a sound out of their instrument. But whereas research—and implicitly educational practice, with its focus on graded exams—has traditionally viewed linear progression toward technically impressive performance as the main goal of instrumental learning, the life histories illustrate that there are many other viable outcomes, which if articulated more clearly could capture the breadth of musical accomplishment in the general population. Respondents who recalled even "failed" attempts at learning were able to recognize retrospectively the value of knowing music from the inside, so enriching their appreciation as listeners, and the openness of their attitudes toward the arts as adult consumers and participants. The musically supportive home, therefore, is one in which all these possibilities are held open, and opportunities are provided for children to find their own musical direction.

Life history respondents reported varying experiences of the role of parents in supporting musical development, and in particular, the vexed question of how—and how much—to encourage and supervise practice. While the research literature is clear on the important role that parents can play in providing appropriate structure and rewards for practice (Hallam & Creech, 2010; McPherson, 2009), respondents measured their own experiences against the imagined horror of the "pushy" parent, with the ideal environment appearing to be one in which "it was always up to me whether I practised or not, but they were really encouraging" [UK12, aged 24]. However, this generally positive experience was set against the widely reported regret at having not done sufficient practice as a child, and several respondents made the connection, feeling that their progress had been hampered by "a parental wish not to struggle against my natural laziness" [UK6, aged 65]. The lack of clear goal-setting in instrumental learning might be at the heart of this dilemma: for young people whose main interest is in joining the school band and having fun, some general parental encouragement is sufficient, but those who aspire to a higher level of proficiency might require some more focused support. Parents who have experienced instrumental learning themselves are again at an advantage, able to compare their own practice regime and its consequences with that of their offspring—though translating this into well-meant advice could bring its own dangers, and there were some resentful recollections of parents who "would always notice and comment upon any wrong notes or mistakes when I played the piano" [UK38, aged 42]. While the life history respondents understandably said relatively little about the communication between their instrumental teachers and their parents, such coordination of aims and approaches has been shown in other studies to be beneficial (Davidson & Scutt, 1999; Macmillan, 2004), and its usefulness in clarifying expectations of instrumental learning is implicitly evident here.

Of course, instrumental learning was not the only way in which parents supported their children musically: a great deal of modeling and sharing of musical enthusiasms also took place through listening, and many life history respondents had specific recollections of the repertoire preferences of the adults in their lives:

> . . . we started with one LP [long-playing record] of Rimsky Korsakov's *Scheherezade*. It was some time before we added to that one disc, so we got to know that piece pretty well! But as constant radio listeners we enjoyed the "usual" classics—Dvorak's *New World*, Rachmaninov's Piano Concertos etc. I would say without question that my early home life contributed to my strong if passive love of music. [UK70, aged 67]

The expense of acquiring records for the family gramophone was remarked upon by many of the older respondents, and clearly contributed to the reinforcement of shared tastes through repeated listening to the small repertoire available in the home. A decade or so later, respondents were saving up to buy their own music collections—"with pocket money and second-hand shops" [UK22, aged 60]—so beginning the trend toward individualized listening, which continued through cheaper access to tapes and then CDs for the younger respondents, and onward to the downloading of music as an everyday commodity for today's adolescent listeners. This increasing independence led in some cases to the sharing of new musical discoveries across generations, but more typically to the development of individual listening preferences which remained significant— even if not constantly liked—throughout the lifespan (North, Hargreaves, & O'Neill, 2000). While today's teenagers will take it for granted that listening to music is part of everyday life, for the older respondents, their parents' attentive listening had been another indication of the time and resources invested in music in the home; perhaps all the more powerful for being rooted in parents' own enjoyment rather than an instructional attempt to provide music for their children.

Live music listening was also an area in which parents' musical habits and tastes were shared with their children, and recollections of concert-going in childhood were linked in some cases to decisions to play musical instruments, and more often to lifelong habits of concert attendance. Exposure to live music ranged from "a weekly orchestra stalls reservation at the Palace, a number one touring theatre with a first class orchestra of twenty players" [UK16, aged 60] to "home-grown concerts . . . in the small Methodist chapel which was the focal point of the village" [UK55, aged 70]. Through their commitment to local music-making, whether professional or amateur, parents once again demonstrated the value of music in their lives in ways that made a lasting impression on their children.

> I was taken, from a young age, to hear oratorios at other local chapels. It seemed at the time that every chapel had a large choir. Every November the Temple Street Methodist Chapel gave "The Messiah" and for the evening performance people had to queue for up to two hours to be sure of getting a seat—I can remember queuing in all weathers and not minding having to do so. Not only did we have to queue but we did not have a car and there were no buses from the village so we also had a long walk to get to the chapel. [UK55, aged 70]

In this extract the "normality" of musical engagement for families of this generation and means is again apparent: large choirs are an assumed feature of church worship, annual concerts are part of the fabric of the local community, and considerable practical effort is expended to ensure a seat at an obviously popular event. Some respondents also reported being taken to concerts with their school, and these experiences too had been a vivid introduction to live music; however, the embedding of concert-going in family life appeared to be a stronger factor in providing opportunities not only to hear music, but also to build relationships based on shared enthusiasm. Those few respondents who had not discovered live music until adult life talked of the overwhelming impression of a "real" orchestra after hearing only recordings, but despite this strong recollection felt that an earlier introduction to concert-going was a vital part of childhood experience: "I think we need children to be exposed to such live events; do not tell them what they must expect; just expose them to the music—it will work on them" [UK23, aged 66]. These informal introductions to music are perhaps best situated in the family context, where live music is part of everyday life rather than an overtly educational expedition. Certainly, the respondents appear to remember their childhood concert-going as an adult activity into which they were being inducted, rather than something that was done specifically for their benefit: joining a self-motivated audience of all ages, they were provided with another example of music as a valued leisure activity, enriching their parents' lives in ways that would later be replicated in their own.

Even within the few life history examples considered in this section, the many variables within a musically supportive home are apparent: sibling interactions, parental attitudes, parents' own music-making and listening, resources within the home, children's motivation to learn, and opportunities for musical learning, exploration, and practice. Also evident from the wider sample (see Pitts, 2012) is the porous nature of musical learning environments, with musical development being shaped not only in the home, but also by school experiences, instrumental teachers, parents' musical communities and connections, and the attitudes of friends and wider family. While a supportive musical home was highly valued by those fortunate enough to have experienced one, the interaction between home and school music-making was also a powerful one, serving either to reinforce compatible musical contexts, or to highlight their incongruities. We therefore turn next to identify the characteristics of a musically supportive education.

The characteristics of a musically supportive education

In schools, as in homes, the three influences of resources, attitudes, and opportunities were experienced in variable proportions and to different effects across the generations of life history respondents. Those educated in the 1940s and 1950s commented frequently on the limitations of educational and musical resources in the post-war years in Britain, but still had vivid recollections of their early exposure to music:

> My memories of school music are that there was only one period per week. War time restricted all sorts of activities. However, the music master was a vocalist and so we all sang. Later, he retired and the Master appointed was [an organist]. Bliss. I remember going into the dedicated music room and whilst he waited for us all to settle, he just casually played Chopin's black key study. That I still remember tells you that it influenced me. [UK36, aged 81]

School music education was slow to catch up with the innovations in art and creative writing that flourished in more forward-looking schools of this time (Finney, 2011; Pitts, 2000), and older respondents gave accounts of quite traditional lessons focused on listening and singing. Even as creative music-making in the classroom became more widespread in the 1970s and 1980s (Paynter, 1982), the life history accounts reveal a patchiness of provision across the UK, with some respondents very grateful for their inspiring teachers and varied opportunities, while others were conscious that their musical experiences were somewhat lacking:

> I was fortunate enough to attend a grammar school with a very strong musical ethos and took part in a wide range of musical activities, including choirs, orchestras and other ensembles, with regular concerts and music festivals as well as a dedicated Saturday morning music school. [UK3, aged 52]

> The school orchestra was very poor, but I had to go, otherwise I wouldn't have been allowed to do A Level music. It was conducted by the visiting viola teacher, who was very boring, and would rehearse exactly one piece per term, over and over again, for the end of term concert. The school choir was similar, and had no appeal for the few of us who were seriously interested in music. [UK35, aged 52]

These two extracts from respondents of the same age illustrate how the provision of resources and opportunities is not in itself sufficient to give a school the "strong musical ethos" [UK3] that the first respondent describes. How strikingly different are the abundant enthusiasm of the first school's activities and the slow progress of the ensembles in the second: the personalities of teachers and their ambitions for their students here make the difference between a thriving musical school and one that deadened the passions of all involved. Opportunities to sustain musical engagement are clearly important, but need to be driven by the enjoyment of collective music-making and performing, not by dutiful provision or limited musical ambitions.

Just as teacher personality was a factor in successful extra-curricular music-making, so it featured prominently in respondents' accounts of their classroom music experience. From the eccentric music master who put miscreant boys in the choir rather than in detention [UK70, aged 67] to the "archetypical inspirational teacher, totally devoted to her subject and her pupils" [UK29, aged 54], the character of the music teacher was closely bound with the musical ethos of the school and its accessibility (or otherwise) to students. Some respondents had benefited from the attention and support of their teacher, even while noting that this was not extended throughout their peer group: one teacher was described as being "close to retirement and a pretty strict disciplinarian, which put off people who were not interested, but he had such a profound love and enthusiasm for music that this rubbed off on those who were already inclined in that direction" [UK64, aged 55]. The challenge of identifying the "musically inclined" while providing a meaningful musical experience for all abilities is a familiar one in UK classrooms, where the diverse musical backgrounds and prior learning of students demand agile teaching and differentiated opportunities. Providing encouragement in the right way and at the right moment is perhaps one of the teacher's hardest tasks, and there were many instances of disappointment in this respect: "the head of music seemed only interested in children who learnt instruments in school and I was never allowed to play in assembly like them" [UK17, aged 65]. Moments of invitation and recognition—to join the orchestra, to play an instrument, to consider pursuing music at university—were vividly recalled decades later, showing how the incidental exchanges of the classroom can be more lasting and powerful than the hours of well-planned lessons and extra-curricular opportunities into which teachers understandably put most of their energy. When Estelle Jorgensen (2008, p. 55) encourages tact and compassion in music teachers, she captures the essence of human interaction that lies at the heart of the wide range of experiences reported in these musical life histories.

With the challenges of mixed-ability music teaching evident in the UK responses, the specialist music conservatoires experienced by the Italian respondents might be assumed to offer a solution. Under this system, typical of Continental Europe, generalist music education in schools is minimal, and students opt instead to attend instrumental lessons at a nearby conservatoire outside school hours. However, the responses suggest that a more segregated system of music education only reinforces the belief that music is for some children but not for all: those who had been through the conservatoire system had often found it "too rigid with little attention to our interests" [I5, aged 27], while experiences outside the conservatoire were dismissed as being inconsequential, as for the respondent who "played the recorder for three years, but not out of passion, it was part of the music education curriculum" [I12, aged 24]. The decision to pursue lessons at the conservatoire was often strongly attributed to parents, such as the respondent whose "father, who had been a violin player and had studied at the music school for a few years, insisted (too much) that I carried on with the instrument, sending me to the music school" [I24, aged 23]. The Italian sample is small, and these questions need more extensive exploration before any firm conclusions can be drawn, but it does seem as though, as with the UK respondents, the attitudes of teachers and provision of opportunities are strong influences on students' perceptions of themselves as musicians. Access to music is highly valued in both contexts, and its absence—or restriction to the few "talented" students—noted as a limiting factor in school music experience.

If the accounts of music in schools seem to prioritize personality and enthusiasm for music, it must be emphasized that this was closely linked in many of the UK responses to particular musical passions and the pursuit of high standards of performance. Just as parents shared their specific listening preferences with their offspring, so teachers who had a focused musical interest were remembered, sometimes teasingly, for their "obsess[ion] with John Cage" [UK2, aged 19] or the "disciplines of choral singing" [UK42, aged 62]. Enthusiasm in itself, therefore, was not enough, but needed to be underpinned by clear musical goals and the appropriate skills to achieve them. While research with primary-school teachers often portrays these requirements as a source of anxiety (e.g. Hennessy, 2000), the life history respondents illustrate that learning alongside students was warmly recalled and later interpreted as valuable role modeling: one teacher had introduced her pupils to the treble recorder, and a respondent remembered that this "was a new thing for her as well and I remember she learnt with us" [UK51, aged 29]. Although teachers were therefore respected for their musical knowledge, it was their open-mindedness to musical learning that made a more lasting impression, along with their willingness to identify and nurture the enthusiasms of their students. A musically supportive education, therefore, is shown in these accounts to be one that is adaptable to the needs of its students, providing rich opportunities for engagement, along with the encouragement needed for all children to experience music as an accessible and worthwhile part of their school lives.

Bridging the gap: The privileged role of the instrumental tutor

In the home and school settings described in the previous section, the life history accounts make clear that while access and opportunity were important to all respondents, the individual recognition and affirmation of musical potential were vital ingredients in ensuring that these opportunities were embraced to the full. Parents and teachers provided guidance and encouragement (or otherwise) as much through their musical priorities and choices as through the deliberate provision of teaching and resources. Through their own demonstration of skills, commitment, and enthusiasm, they acted as role models for musical engagement, in ways that were sometimes only retrospectively noted by the children that they influenced. Bridging the gap between home and school, instrumental tutors were often best placed to understand and nurture the musical interests and ambitions of their students, and recollections of these lessons were a prominent feature of the life histories:

> My first piano teacher, who was a wonderful performer herself, was extremely patient with me as a pupil and when I was a teenager she became a friend and we used to talk about all sorts of things after the lessons were over. Many years later she said she had always thought I would do well with my music although she never said that at the time. [UK17, aged 65]

In this account, the teacher's personality, performing skill, and educational style are intertwined in her pupil's recollections of her lessons: this accomplished pianist has apparently imparted confidence through her patience and attention, rather than by overtly voicing her belief in the pupil's potential, which has nonetheless been fulfilled as she anticipated. The role of confidante and mentor to a teenage student is a privileged one for the instrumental tutor, and other respondents recalled being made to "feel special" [UK26, aged 52] by their teacher, sometimes described as "the only adult, it felt to me, who was remotely interested in me" [UK38, aged 42]. While this brings great responsibility for the teacher to avoid the "rather unhealthy dependent relationship" [UK59, aged 33] reported by one respondent, at its best this sustained individual connection can be very valuable in supporting young musicians' emerging musical identity. The anonymity or lack of recognition reported in some classroom contexts is less likely to occur in the instrumental lesson; meanwhile, tutors can also provide some of the guidance and goal-setting that was observed to be beyond the musical expertise of some parents.

The influence of instrumental tutors was directly acknowledged in many of the life histories, as respondents attributed the development of musical skills and ambitions to the one-to-one tuition they had received during their formative years. The stories were not all positive, with the most extreme featuring "a really nasty teacher, the sort we hope doesn't exist any more, [who] used to rap me over the knuckles with a ruler" [UK37, aged 42], and a few others reporting stories of frustrating limitations on choice of repertoire, or personality clashes where a pupil "didn't like the teacher or lessons much so I packed it in" [UK12, aged 24]. Even the kindest teachers were later evaluated for their judgment in directing practice and the development of technique, with several respondents feeling that they could have progressed further with better guidance, while others were fortunate enough to have made this switch in time: "I had a new piano teacher when I was 17 and this changed my practice habits drastically—I was very self-motivated because I felt I was learning much more about technique and interpretation" [UK60, aged 24]. These observations highlight the need for a balance of encouragement and challenge in instrumental teaching, broadly consistent with Howe and Sloboda's (1991) study of high-achieving young musicians, which demonstrated the benefits of a nurturing first teacher followed by a more demanding professional role model. The first of these teachers might help to connect the musical worlds of home and school, so strengthening a child's sense of musical identity and building a support network of parents and teachers; the second bridges the greater gap between the musical worlds of childhood and adulthood, guiding musical ambitions toward further study, careers, or lifelong amateur engagement. For some of these respondents, all of these qualities had been present in one teacher, affectionately remembered as a substantial influence "not just due to skills she taught, but also to her passion for music" [UK4, aged 30]. Others had returned to lessons in adulthood to remedy the perceived shortcomings of their adolescent teaching, showing that if nothing else they had gained an awareness of the work needed to progress as an instrumentalist, and a willingness to engage with this later in life.

Of course, provision of instrumental lessons is dependent on parental priorities, both financial and educational: some UK respondents in their forties and fifties were aware of their good fortune in having grown up at the time when instrumental lessons were "available free of charge, from a county peripatetic teacher" [UK54, aged 54], but with this no longer the case, uncomfortable questions need to be asked about whether the instrumental teacher is essential for secure foundations for lifelong musical engagement—and if so, how access can be more widely guaranteed. Addressing first of all the alternative forms of instrumental learning, those respondents who identified themselves as pop musicians were the most likely to have engaged in deliberate, self-directed learning, though there were examples also of self-taught pianists, whose explorations of the piano in the home often instigated the provision of lessons at a later stage: "When my voice broke in my mid teens, and I started reading bass clef in the school choir, I would often sit down at the piano and play through classical pieces very slowly, chord by chord, enjoying the harmony, despite having virtually no technical facility on the instrument" [UK72, aged 45]. For the pop musicians, self-teaching was sometimes a rebellion against lessons that had already been provided, one example being the reluctant trumpet pupil who saved up his pocket money to buy a drum kit until "by the time I was 16 or so it was clear that I was not going to stop, and my dad offered to pay for some lessons" [UK73, aged 48]. For others, learning with peers had been the most obvious way to master their instrument, though sometimes left perceived deficiencies in particular skills, as for the student who felt that "no choirs [. . .] will have me because I cannot sight read" [UK79, aged 20].

Lucy Green (2002) has documented the self-directed learning strategies of popular musicians, and suggested that the motivation to play in bands with their peers reduces the risk that playing will cease once young people leave the teacher-directed musical environment of their school. Nonetheless, the popular musicians in the life-history study had appreciated their teachers' recognition of their skills, perhaps showing a generational shift as pop music practices have become more widespread and therefore raised the expectation that school music will connect with these in some way: "My music teacher at school was amazing—she really embraced my passion and musical ability and would encourage and empower me for in and out of class activities" [UK74, aged 18]. Where an instrumental teacher is not present to provide the guidance and affirmation that had benefited many of the more conventionally trained respondents, the responsibilities of the classroom teacher to recognize the musical needs of his or her students are once again heightened. One-to-one tuition can no longer be assumed to be the standard model of instrumental training, losing its hold both through educational policy that prioritizes whole class access (Bamford & Glinkowski, 2010) and financial constraints that leave schools and parents struggling to invest in costly lessons. With the life-history responses illustrating the lasting impact of instrumental tutors, this gradual decline in access is a source of real concern, and even while young people themselves take up the challenge of acquiring musical skills through self-directed and peer learning, the responsibility for encouraging and modeling lifelong musical participation must be taken up again by teachers, parents, and the growing numbers of adult musicians who have themselves followed these new, more independent routes to musical engagement.

Conclusions: Pathways from childhood to lifelong engagement

In some ways, the lack of predictability in the musical life histories examined here is a source of encouragement: there are plenty of stories of adults who have overcome the limitations or omissions of their musical education to pursue their ambitions later in life. It would be fair to say, however, that these tales are reported with an evident sense of disappointment, or even anger, that the path to musical fulfillment had not been smoother:

> My parents had the best of intentions, and would have done just about anything for me, but had no idea how talented I was and also had no idea that music colleges had junior departments. I now know I could have gone. The school knew though, and didn't do anything about it, and I feel slightly resentful about that. [UK37, aged 42]

These "redemption" stories (Pillemer, 2001) have in common an awareness that something was missing: adults recall being alienated in a school where the emphasis was on "rugby and results" [UK72, aged 45] or being aware that "the music staff had about as much kudos as the RE [religious education] staff" [UK7, aged 63]. Conversely, the recollection of a "very strong musical ethos" [UK3, aged 52] framed more positive recollections of school music for many respondents, serving as a shorthand for the presence of an inspiring teacher and varied opportunities to make and learn music. The life-history accounts therefore illustrate—sometimes explicitly, but more often by implication—what would be lost if music were not included in the school curriculum: for those young people who already had an interest in music, any lack of provision in school was keenly felt, while for the many others who were not already primed for musical engagement, an apparently chance encounter in the classroom or the school choir had been the foundation for lifelong involvement and enjoyment.

The unpredictability of the musical life histories also presents a challenge in defining the purpose of school music education. The most satisfied of the respondents were those who charted a very coherent musical story, rooted in a supportive family, with opportunities at school that had provided skills to be used throughout the lifespan in musical participation and appreciation. Compatibility between home and school musical lives had been important to many respondents, leading to a sense of inevitability in musical involvement: "the combination of encouragement at home and at school more or less determined that I would do music in some form or another later on" [UK53, aged 69]. However, the greatest coherence of this kind was achieved in the older generations, where a similar repertoire of light classical music had been heard in the home and classroom, and the "lusty unison singing" [UK19, aged 74] of school music lessons had awakened an interest in joining one of the many adult amateur choirs that were flourishing at that time. For younger generations, exposure to a much wider range of music in home, school, and later life meant that such a clear linear progression was no longer possible or desirable. Satisfied musicians in their fifties and under were more likely to be receptive to learning new instruments as adults, and to enjoy teaching, composing, and conducting, particularly where these activities allowed them to support and nurture the next generation of musicians. These respondents had made sense of their sometimes patchy formative musical experiences and acquired a capacity for pursuing musical goals that would serve them well in a wide variety of settings. However, even amongst the self-selecting sample represented here, there was evidence that this transition to independent musical learning was not always successful—as would be even more the case in the wider population.

One reason for the only partial effectiveness of school music as a foundation for lifelong learning and participation is that this is rarely articulated as a deliberate goal for music education. The UK education system presents obstacles to continued involvement even within the school years, as music becomes optional at the age of 14 (or even earlier, in some combined arts programs), and the exams available at ages 16 and 18 rely increasingly on skills gained through private instrumental tuition (Lamont & Maton, 2008). Earlier segregation in the Italian system and other European countries creates even stronger division between those who engage with music and those who do not, while in America and similar "band programs" elsewhere, the continuation of playing after school is rare, and becoming a source of concern to researchers (Mantie & Tucker, 2008). The small number of students who pursue music to the end of school, compared with the much larger number of adults who find meaningful leisure engagement as listeners and amateur performers, suggests that current ways of evaluating the impact of music education are inadequate, and the arguments for funding and supporting music in the curriculum need to take greater account of its lifelong benefits.

The one hundred or so life histories analyzed in this study are of course only a tiny fraction of the musical childhoods experienced in the UK and Italy (for a much wider global remit, see Boynton & Kok, 2006, and Green, 2011), but they do offer some clear insights on how strongly the environments of home and school influence lifelong musical engagement. The provision of resources and opportunities are undoubtedly important, and concerns about their uneven distribution and privileged access need to remain at the forefront of debate and policy in music education. I would argue, however, that it is the attitudes absorbed in the formative musical years that have the strongest impact, positively or negatively, on young people's future musical ambitions and inclinations. What sociologists would call the "habitus" (Froehlich, 2007) and education researchers the "hidden curriculum" (Pitts, 2003) are prominent in the life-history accounts, as respondents reflect not just on what they were able to do as young musicians, but also on how the adults around them communicated their own enthusiasm (or otherwise) for music, and provided invitations or barriers to join that musical world. Supporting children as musicians, therefore, combines the structured imparting of skills and goals that is a feature of the best teaching, along with the modeling of valued leisure activities and open-minded cultural awareness that are features of good parenting. Even more than this, the life histories suggest that these two influences need to be coherent and compatible if they are to achieve their greatest effect. This is a lot to ask of parents and teachers, but articulating the aim is the first step in realizing it, and in valuing formative musical experiences for their lifelong benefits to individuals and societies. If the next steps are sometimes a little muddled or misplaced, the routes to musical fulfillment can nonetheless remain open throughout the lifespan—musical development does not stop when children leave their school and family, but the evidence is compelling for it being vital that it should be started and supported there.

Reflective questions

1 How has your own musical life history shaped your development as a musician, an educator, a parent, a concert-goer . . . ?
2 Is lifelong engagement in music necessarily a desirable outcome for music education?
3 How could home and school experiences of music be made more coherent for young people—and whose responsibility is this?
4 How might current education policies be shaping the musical attitudes and ambitions of the next generation?
5 What are the inhibiting factors in making lifelong learning a stronger focus for school music education—and how could these be overcome?

You can upload your own musical life history and read others at the online forum for the *Chances and choices* project: <http://www.chancesandchoices.group.shef.ac.uk/>.

Key sources

Barone, T. (2001). *Touching eternity: The enduring outcomes of teaching*. New York: Teachers College Press.

Gavin, H. (2001). Reconstructed musical memories and adult expertise. *Music Education Research*, 3(1), 51–61.

McPherson, G. E., Davidson, J. W., & Faulkner, R. (2012). *Music in our lives: Rethinking musical ability, development and identity*. New York: Oxford University Press.

Pitts, S. E. (2012). *Chances and choices: Exploring the impact of music education*. New York: Oxford University Press.

Smilde, R. (2009). *Musicians as lifelong learners: Discovery through biography*. Delft: Eburon.

Reference list

Bamford, A., & Glinkowski, P. (2010). *"Wow, it's music next": Impact evaluation of Wider Opportunities programme in music at Key Stage two*. Leeds: The Federation of Music Services.

Barone, T. (2001). *Touching eternity: The enduring outcomes of teaching*. New York: Teachers College Press.

Borthwick, S. J., & Davidson, J. W. (2002). Developing a child's identity as a musician: A family "script" perspective. In R. A. R. MacDonald, D. J. Hargreaves, & D. Miell (Eds.), *Musical identities* (pp. 60–78). Oxford: Oxford University Press.

Boynton, S., & Kok, R. (2006). *Musical childhoods and the cultures of youth*. Middletown, CT: Wesleyan University Press.

Cox, G. (1999). Secondary school music teachers talking. *Music Education Research*, 1(1), 37–46.

Creech, A., & Hallam, S. (2009). Interaction in instrumental learning: The influence of interpersonal dynamics on parents. *International Journal of Music Education*, 27(2), 94–106.

Davidson, J. W., & Scutt, S. (1999). Instrumental learning with exams in mind: A case study investigating teacher, student and parent interactions before, during and after a music examination. *British Journal of Music Education*, 16(1), 79–95.

Ericsson, K. A., Krampe, R., & Tesch-Römer, C. (1993). The role of deliberate practice in the acquisition of expert performance. *Psychological Review*, 100(3), 363–406.

Finney, J. (2011). *Music education in England, 1950–2010: The child-centred progressive tradition*. Farnham: Ashgate.

Froehlich, H. C. (2007). *Sociology for music teachers: Perspectives for practice*. Upper Saddle River, NJ: Pearson Prentice Hall.

Gavin, H. (2001). Reconstructed musical memories and adult expertise. *Music Education Research*, 3(1), 51–61.

Green, L. (2002). *How popular musicians learn.* Aldershot: Ashgate.

Green, L. (Ed.) (2011). *Learning, teaching, and musical identity: Voices across cultures.* Bloomington, IN: Indiana University Press.

Haddon, E. (2005). *Making music in Britain: Interviews with those behind the notes.* Aldershot: Ashgate.

Hallam, S. (2010). The power of music: Its impact on the intellectual, personal and social development of children and young people. In S. Hallam & A. Creech (Eds.), *Music education in the 21st century in the United Kingdom: Achievements, analysis and aspirations* (pp. 2–17). London: Institute of Education.

Hallam, S., & Creech, A. (2010). Learning to play an instrument. In S. Hallam & A. Creech (Eds.), *Music education in the 21st century in the United Kingdom: Achievements, analysis and aspirations* (pp. 85–104). London: Institute of Education.

Hennessy, S. (2000). Overcoming the red feeling: The development of confidence to teach music in primary school amongst student teachers. *British Journal of Music Education,* **17**(2), 183–96.

Holt, J. (1978). *Never too late: My musical life story.* New York: Merloyd Lawrence.

Howe, M. J., & Sloboda, J. A. (1991). Young musicians' accounts of significant influences in their early lives: 2. Teachers, practising and performance. *British Journal of Music Education,* **8**(1), 53–63.

Jorgensen, E. R. (2008). *The art of teaching music.* Bloomington, IN: Indiana University Press.

Lamont, A. (2011). The beat goes on: Music education, identity and lifelong learning. *Music Education Research,* **13**(4), 369–88.

Lamont, A., & Maton, K. (2008). Choosing music: Exploratory studies into the low uptake of music GCSE. *British Journal of Music Education,* **25**(3), 267–82.

MacDonald, R. A. R., Hargreaves, D. J., & Miell, D. (Eds.) (2002). *Musical identities.* Oxford: Oxford University Press.

Macmillan, J. (2004). Learning the piano: A study of attitudes to parental involvement. *British Journal of Music Education,* **21**(3), 295–311.

Mantie, R. (2013). Music and/as leisure: Old wine in new bottles? *International Journal of Community Music,* **6**(2), 135–9.

Mantie, R., & Tucker, L. (2008). Closing the gap: Does music-making have to stop upon graduation? *International Journal of Community Music,* **1**(2), 217–27.

McAdams, D. P. (2001). The psychology of life stories. *Review of General Psychology,* **5**(2), 100–22.

McPherson, G. E. (2005). From child to musician: Skill development during the beginning stages of learning an instrument. *Psychology of Music,* **33**(1), 5–35.

McPherson, G. E. (2009). The role of parents in children's musical development. *Psychology of Music,* **37**(1), 91–110.

McPherson, G. E., Davidson, J. W., & Faulkner, R. (2012). *Music in our lives: Rethinking musical ability, development and identity.* New York: Oxford.

Myers, D. E. (2007). Freeing music education from schooling: Toward a lifespan perspective on music learning and teaching. *International Journal of Community Music,* **1**(1), 49–61.

North, A. C., Hargreaves, D. J., & O'Neill, S. A. (2000). The importance of music to adolescents. *British Journal of Educational Psychology,* **70**(2), 255–272.

Paynter, J. (1982). *Music in the secondary school curriculum.* Cambridge: Cambridge University Press.

Philpott, C. (2012). The justification for music in the curriculum: Music can be bad for you. In C. Philpott & G. Spruce (Eds.), *Debates in music teaching* (pp. 48–63). Routledge: London.

Pillemer, D. (2001). Momentous events and the life story. *Review of General Psychology,* **5**(2), 123–34.

Pitts, S. E. (2000). *A century of change in music education.* Aldershot: Ashgate.

Pitts, S. E. (2003). What do students learn when we teach music? An investigation of the "hidden" curriculum in a university music department. *Arts and Humanities in Higher Education,* **2**(3), 281–92.

Pitts, S. E. (2005). *Valuing musical participation.* Aldershot: Ashgate.

Pitts, S. E. (2012). *Chances and choices: Exploring the impact of music education*. New York: Oxford University Press.

Sloboda, J. A. (1991). Biographical precursors of musical excellence: An interview study. *Psychology of Music*, **19**(1), 3–21.

Sloboda, J. A., Davidson, J. W., & Howe, M. J. A. (1994). Is everyone musical? *The Psychologist*, **7**(8), 287–309.

Smilde, R. (2009). *Musicians as lifelong learners: Discovery through biography*. Delft: Eburon.

Southcott, J. E. (2009). And as I go, I love to sing: The Happy Wanderers, music and positive ageing. *International Journal of Community Music*, **2**(2 & 3), 143–56.

Turton, A., & Durrant, C. (2002). A study of adults' attitudes, perceptions, and reflections on their singing experience in secondary school: Some implications for music education. *British Journal of Music Education*, **19**(1), 31–48.

Index

Notes: Page numbers suffixed by 'f' indicate material in figure, 't' in tables.

Printed and bound by CPI Group (UK) Ltd, Croydon, CR0 4YY